Consumer Bankruptcy Law in Focus

Focus Casebook Series

Consumer Bankruptcy Law in Focus

Stephen P. Parsons

Printed in the United States of America.

1 2 3 4 5 6 7 8 9 0

ISBN 978-1-4548-6805-7

Library of Congress Cataloging-in-Publication Data

Names: Parsons, Stephen P., 1949- author.
Title: Consumer bankruptcy law in focus / Stephen P. Parsons.
Description: New York: Wolters Kluwer, 2016. | Includes bibliographical
  references and index.
Identifiers: LCCN 2015034493 | ISBN 9781454868057
Subjects: LCSH: Bankruptcy — United States. | Bankruptcy — United
  States — Cases. | LCGFT: Casebooks.
Classification: LCC KF1524 .P37 2013 | DDC 346.7307/8 — dc23
LC record available at http://lccn.loc.gov/2015034493

MIX
Paper from
responsible sources
FSC® C014174

About Wolters Kluwer Legal & Regulatory US

Wolters Kluwer Legal & Regulatory US delivers expert content and solutions in the areas of law, corporate compliance, health compliance, reimbursement, and legal education. Its practical solutions help customers successfully navigate the demands of a changing environment to drive their daily activities, enhance decision quality and inspire confident outcomes.

Serving customers worldwide, its legal and regulatory solutions portfolio includes products under the Aspen Publishers, CCH Incorporated, Kluwer Law International, ftwilliam.com and MediRegs names. They are regarded as exceptional and trusted resources for general legal and practice-specific knowledge, compliance and risk management, dynamic workflow solutions, and expert commentary.

This book is dedicated to the memory of Mr. and Mrs. William H. Parsons:

Bill and Juanita

Mom and Dad

Some debts can never be repaid

Summary of Contents

Table of Contents

Chapter Six: The Chapter 7 Consumer Bankruptcy Case: The Petition, Supporting Schedules, and Statements

The Focus Casebook Series

Help students reach their full potential with the fresh approach of the Focus Casebook Series. Instead of using the "hide the ball" approach, selected cases illustrate key developments in the law and show how courts develop and apply doctrine. The approachable manner of this series provides a comfortable experiential environment that is instrumental to student success.

Students perform best when applying concepts to real-world scenarios. With assessment features, such as Real Life Applications and Applying the Concepts, the Focus Casebook Series offers many opportunities for students to apply their knowledge.

Focus Casebook Features Include:

Case Previews and Post-Case Follow-Ups — To succeed, law students must know how to deconstruct and analyze cases. Case Previews highlight the legal concepts in a case before the student reads it. Post-Case Follow-Ups summarize the important points.

Case Preview

In re Hlavin

As the hypothetical of Mary Jones and her loaves of bread illustrates, the number of potential disputes about the kinds of debt that are or are not to be considered consumer debts is simply limitless. The lawyer has to recognize when the issue matters and can be contested. As you read In re Hlavin, a case involving the 11 U.S.C §707(b) dismissal for abuse provision, consider the following questions:

1. Why is it the debtors and not the bankruptcy trustee who are arguing that their home mortgage is not a consumer debt?
2. What does this court s[...] gage is or isn't a consu[...]

Post-Case Follow-Up

Is this opinion making a distinction between the repossessor himself disturbing the peace and his committing an act that motivates another to disturb the peace once the repossessor is gone? Would the result in this case have been different if the activities of the repossessors had awakened the debtor or the neighbor and the one awakened had shouted at them out of a window something like, "Stop, thief! I've called the police"? See Robinson v. Citicorp National Services, Inc., 921 S.W.2d 52 (Mo. Ct. App. 1996), and Chrysler Credit Corp. v. Koontz, 661 N.E.2d 1171 (1996). If the debtor's husband had raced outside with a firearm while the repossessors were pulling away from the property? If he or the neighbor had fired a firearm at the fleeing repossessors? If a sleeping child had been in the car unseen by the repossessor when the car was driven off? See Chapa v. Traciers & Associates, 267 S.W.3d 386 (Tex. App. 2008)? If the repossessor had violated a driving ordinance in the course of repos-

The Focus Casebook Series

Real Life Applications — Every case in a chapter is followed by Real Life Applications, which present a series of questions based on a scenario similar to the facts in the case. Real Life Applications challenge students to apply what they have learned in order to prepare them for real-world practice. Use Real Life Applications to spark class discussions or provide them as individual short-answer assignments.

> ### In re Hlavin: Real Life Applications
>
> 1. Would the result in *Hlavin* have been different if the loans secured by their home had originally been taken out to fund a failed business venture? What if they had been taken out for home improvement or a vacation but then actually used to fund a business venture? Would it matter if they told the bank the money was being borrowed for home improvement or vacation but intended it to be used to fund a business venture? What if the home loans had been taken out for mixed personal/business reasons?
> 2. If the debtors in *Hlavin* had 30 different consumer debts totaling $75,000 and only one business debt totaling $76,000, would that court find that they had "primarily consumer debts" under §707(b)(1)? What would be the result if a court utilized one of the alternative approaches to this question mentioned in *Hlavin*?

Applying the Concepts — These end-of-chapter exercises encourage students to synthesize the chapter material and apply relevant legal doctrine and code to real-world scenarios. Students can use these exercises for self-assessment or the professor can use them to promote class interaction.

Applying the Concepts

1. Assume you are consulted by the following potential bankruptcy clients. Which of these appear at first blush to be candidates for a consumer bankruptcy filing as opposed to a non-consumer or business filing?

   a. The individual owners of an unincorporated video rental store whose business has plummeted due to the popularity of Internet movie-streaming services.

   b. A married couple both employed but who have abused their credit card spending and now owe more than they make together in a year.

   c. A recently divorced woman with two children whose ex-husband is unemployed and not contributing child support and who is having trouble paying her monthly living expenses.

   d. A married couple, one of whom has suffered major health problems resulting in medical expenses in excess of what they can expect to earn in ten years.

Preface

Ensure student success with the Focus Casebook Series.

THE FOCUS APPROACH

In a law office, when a new associate attorney is being asked to assist a supervising attorney with a legal matter in which the associate has no prior experience, it is common for the supervising attorney to provide the associate with a recently closed case file involving the same legal issues so that the associate can see and learn from the closed file to assist more effectively with the new matter. This experiential approach is at the heart of the *Focus Casebook Series.*

In this particular casebook, the author provides two "inactive" bankruptcy case files from 2016 on the Companion Web Site. The filings in the case files are referenced throughout the casebook to illustrate the concepts being learned just as the supervising attorney might assign the associate to prepare something for a current case.

Additional hands-on features, such as Real Life Applications, Application Exercises, and Applying the Concepts provide more opportunities for critical analysis and application of concepts covered in the chapters. Professors can assign problem-solving questions as well as exercises on drafting documents and preparing appropriate filings.

CONTENT SNAPSHOT

The casebook is divided into two sections. **Part I** includes Chapters 1 through 3 and introduces the distinct concept of consumer bankruptcy along with fundamental pre-filing concerns in a consumer case. **Part II** focuses on consumer bankruptcy practice. Specific chapter coverage is as follows:

Chapters 1-3: distinguishes between secured and unsecured debt, non-consensual liens, surety and guaranty arrangements, non-judicial debt collection, Fair Debt Collection Practices Act, and judicial debt collection.

Chapter 4: acquaints the student with the bankruptcy code, rules, and official forms; structure and basic jurisdiction of bankruptcy courts.

Chapters 5-11: follows the Chapter 7 bankruptcy case in chronological detail from the filing of the petition and completion of the means test for the individual consumer debtor through final discharge.

Chapters 12-16: follows the Chapter 13 bankruptcy case in chronological detail from the filing of the petition and determination of the applicable commitment period and projected disposable income through final discharge.

Chapter 17: looks at Chapter 12 bankruptcy proceeding, which can sometimes involve consumer debtors.

Chapter 18: provides detailed analysis of the thorny jurisdictional and procedural issues that arise in a modern bankruptcy case.

RESOURCES

Companion Web Site: Web site resources include "inactive" bankruptcy case files and information for two new bankruptcy clients, and a full Teacher's Manual in addition to the classroom discussion questions in the text.

Casebook: The casebook is structured around text, cases, and application exercises. Highlighted cases are introduced with a *Case Preview,* which sets up the issue and identifies key questions. *Post-Case Followups* expand on the holding in the case. *Real Life Applications* present two to four opportunities to challenge students to apply concepts covered in the case to realistic hypothetical cases. *Application Exercises* offer a mix of problem solving and research activities to determine the law of the state where the student plans to practice. State law application exercises better prepare the student to actually handle bankruptcy cases. *Applying the Concepts* feature provides occasions for critical analysis and application of concepts covered in the chapter.

Other resources to enrich your class include: PracticePack exercises, Study Aid titles such as *Examples & Explanations: Bankruptcy and Debtor/Creditor* or *Glannon Guide To Bankruptcy: Learning Bankruptcy Through Multiple-Choice Questions and Analysis, 3e.* Ask your Wolters Kluwer sales representative or visit the wolters kluwer site to learn more about building the product package that's right for you.

Acknowledgments

Returning to first things, I would like to express heart-felt appreciation to all of my professors at the University of Tennessee College of Law for providing me with the foundation for what has turned out to be a fortunate and fulfilling career as legal practitioner, professor, and author. Special thanks to the late Professor Forrest Lacy of UT Law who first terrified then mesmerized by introducing the fascinating world of contracts, secured transactions, and payment systems to my astonished mind. I will always be grateful to partners Glenn C. Stophel and E. Stephen Jett at the former Stophel, Caldwell & Heggie firm in Chattanooga, Tennessee who proved my mentors in bankruptcy practice. It was Glenn who first handed me a closed bankruptcy file and told me to "review it to get an idea of how these bankruptcy cases work in the real world" and Steve who first took me to bankruptcy court with him. And while I'm rummaging about in the attic of my memory, let me express gratitude to the late U.S. Bankruptcy Judge Ralph H. Kelly of the Eastern District of Tennessee whose "come in here prepared or don't come in here at all" and "get to the point if you've got one" style of judging made me a much better advocate.

Many thanks to all of my law students at Appalachian School of Law over the years and to my learned colleagues there. What fun it's been. A special word of appreciation goes to my debtor/creditor law and secured transactions students at ASL who proved such willing guinea pigs for much of this material.

I am grateful to the reviewers of the first draft of these chapters whose suggestions made it better and whose candid critiques furthered the process of getting it right. Any remaining misstatements are my responsibility alone. Respect and appreciation to everyone at Wolters Kluwer who conceived this project and made it happen.

Many thanks to my wife, Marcia, for her patience and support throughout the project and to the rest of the home team—Emily Grayce, Casey, Andrew, Laura, and Grayce Kathleen—who make it all worthwhile.

Consumer Bankruptcy Law in Focus

Introduction to Consumer Bankruptcy and Pre-Bankruptcy Filing Considerations

Introduction to Consumer Bankruptcy

The beginning point for a course in consumer bankruptcy is not the Bankruptcy Code, it is the consumer. In this chapter we will consider who a consumer is, how a consumer bankruptcy case differs from a non-consumer or business bankruptcy case, consider the main reasons why consumers file for bankruptcy relief, and look at a profile of the typical consumer who files for bankruptcy relief. We will also see how and why the law has come to recognize consumer bankruptcy as an area of specialization for attorneys.

A. CONSUMER DEBT AND THE RISE OF CONSUMER BANKRUPTCY

In this study we will be concerned with consumer bankruptcy as distinguished from business bankruptcy, so we need to begin by determining who is a consumer and what we mean by consumer debt. A **consumer** is an individual who purchases or obtains (as by rental) the use of real or personal property or services primarily for personal, family, or household use. An entity (for example, a corporation, limited liability company, partnership, joint venture, trust, unincorporated association, etc.) cannot be a consumer. An entity may indeed purchase or obtain the use of real or personal property or

Key Concepts

- The Bankruptcy Code distinguishes between consumer and non-consumer debt in a number of situations
- A consumer bankruptcy case is procedurally different from a non-consumer or business bankruptcy case in several respects
- There are a small number of primary causes of consumer bankruptcy
- The profile of a typical consumer who files for bankruptcy relief can be constructed and is helpful to know

3

services but it does do not do so for its individual, family, or household use — in fact that kind of purchase makes no sense for an entity. In addition, the entity may purchase goods to be sold to consumers or it may provide services to consumers, but the entity is not a consumer under our definition.

At the same time, the term consumer is not synonymous with an individual. An individual is a consumer within our definition only if that individual is purchasing or obtaining the use of real or personal property for one of the three designated purposes: individual, family, or household use. Like an entity, an individual can be engaged in business and incur non-consumer debt, which we will call business debt. For example, if Mary Jones purchases a loaf of bread to take home to be consumed by her family, that is a consumer purchase. Mary is a consumer purchaser for that transaction. But if that same Mary Jones purchases the same loaf of bread to use in her sandwich shop, that is not a consumer purchase. Mary is not a consumer purchaser for that transaction.

Of course consumer bankruptcy would not be an issue if consumers were not driven into bankruptcy by debt. There is an astounding amount of consumer debt among individual Americans, and year after year the vast majority of bankruptcy filings are by consumers overwhelmed in some way by consumer debt. The United States Bankruptcy Code (hereinafter, "the Code") which is Title 11 of the United States Code (hereinafter "U.S.C."), defines **consumer debt** as follows:

> The term "consumer debt" means debt incurred by an individual primarily for a personal, family, or household purpose. 11 U.S.C. §101(8).

Consider the broad scope of consumer debt by considering your own finances or those of a family member or friend. Do you own a home for which you are paying? The mortgage on that home is consumer debt. Do you rent a home or apartment? The rental obligation is consumer debt. Do you own a car that you are paying for in installments? That car payment is consumer debt. Do you have any school loans? Those loans represent consumer debt. Do you use a credit card? The charges on that card are consumer debt. Have you received services from a doctor or hospital recently? Those healthcare bills are consumer debt. Have you had to call a plumber, electrician, painter, carpenter, landscaper, etc., to do some work around the house or apartment? Consumer debt. Had to have repairs done on the car? Consumer debt. Have you borrowed money for a vacation, a computer or TV purchase, a boat or motorcycle, etc.? Consumer debt. And those monthly bills you probably pay — electric, gas, water, sewer, cell phone, cable, etc. Guess what? Consumer debt.

Of course, if you entered into the same transactions on behalf of a business venture rather than for a personal, family, or household purpose, or if an entity incurred those same obligations, we would not consider it consumer debt within the Code definition.

Note that the Code definition of consumer debt uses the word "primarily" to qualify the purpose of incurring the debt, so there can be disputes over the proper characterization of debt incurred by an individual. Assume that Mary Jones purchases 200 loaves of bread from a supplier on credit. She purchases them intending to use them all in her sandwich shop business, a sole proprietorship. The next day she decides to use 50 of the loaves to make food for a family reunion. Then, not yet having paid the supplier what she owes, Mary files a petition in bankruptcy. Is that debt to the supplier consumer or business debt? What arguments would you make either way based on what you know at this point? (Either way, of course, because you might be retained by a party on either side of the issue and must be prepared to argue . . . either way.)

Why does it matter in a bankruptcy case whether an individual debtor's obligation is a consumer or business debt? In fact, it matters for two reasons. First, it matters because in a bankruptcy case, the Code treats certain (not all) consumer debts differently than it does non-consumer debts. We will see examples of this in later chapters as we walk through how a consumer bankruptcy case actually works, but if you just can't wait, take a peek at 11 U.S.C §523(a)(2)(C), which makes certain consumer debts non-dischargeable in a bankruptcy case. Don't try to figure out how that section works now — we'll come to it later — just note that some consumer debts are treated differently in the Code than other debts.

Second, the difference between consumer and business debt matters because the Code also contains certain rules for debtors holding "primarily consumer debts" as opposed to debts that are not primarily consumer debts. Again, we will see examples of this in later chapters, but if you still can't wait, go ahead and look at 11 U.S.C. §707(b), which authorizes a bankruptcy judge to dismiss or convert a Chapter 7 case filed by "an individual debtor . . . whose debts are primarily consumer debts" if there is a finding of abuse. There is much to learn regarding this notion of abuse and we will consider it in depth beginning in Chapter Five, but for now, simply note that it applies only to cases where the debtor is an individual (not an entity) and has primarily consumer debts. Do you see now why there might be a dispute over the bread bill in Mary Jones' case if she files for relief under Chapter 7 of the Code?

Case Preview

In re Hlavin

As the hypothetical of Mary Jones and her loaves of bread illustrates, the number of potential disputes about the kinds of debt that are or are not to be considered consumer debts is simply limitless. The lawyer has to recognize when the issue matters and can be contested. As you read In re Hlavin, a case involving the 11 U.S.C §707(b) dismissal for abuse provision, consider the following questions:

1. Why is it the debtors and not the bankruptcy trustee who are arguing that their home mortgage is not a consumer debt?
2. What does this court say determines whether a debt secured by a home mortgage is or isn't a consumer debt for purposes of 11 U.S.C. §101(8)?

3. What was the basis of debtors' argument that a debt secured by a mortgage in real property cannot be a consumer debt?
4. What are the different approaches taken by courts to determine whether a debtor's debts are "primarily consumer debts" within the meaning of §707(b)(1)?
5. Which approach does this court take and why?

In re Hlavin
394 B.R. 441 (Bankr. S.D. Ohio 2008)

[The Debtors accumulated debt from general expenses and pursuing unsuccessful business ventures. They also purchased a home and obtained a loan secured by a first mortgage. They later obtained a second loan secured with a second mortgage on the home. As of the petition date, the aggregate amount owed on the home loans combined with other consumer debts would constitute 59 percent of the Debtors' liabilities if the home loans were classified as consumer debts. The number of their non-consumer debts exceeds the number of their consumer debts regardless of how the loans are classified. After the Debtors' petition in Chapter 7 bankruptcy was filed, the United States Trustees (UST) requested dismissal of their bankruptcy case for abuse under 11 U.S.C. §707(b)(1), which applies only if the Debtors have "primarily consumer debts." The Debtors responded with a motion for partial summary judgment raising two issues: whether a debt secured by a mortgage in a debtor's real property is a consumer debt within the meaning of §101(8) and what standard should be applied to determine whether the debts are primarily consumer debts.]

HOFFMAN, JR., Bankruptcy Judge. . . .

The Debtors . . . argue that the Home Loans — which they concede were incurred primarily for a Consumer Purpose — are non-consumer debts because they are secured by the Home Mortgages. The UST's response is that a debt incurred primarily for a Consumer Purpose is a consumer debt even though it is secured by a debtor's real property.

Second, the Debtors argue that they have primarily non-consumer debts because their business-related debts outnumber their consumer debts and were the primary cause of their filing for bankruptcy. For its part, the UST contends that numerosity should not be outcome determinative. Rather, the UST argues, an individual's liabilities should be found to be primarily consumer debts if the dollar amount of consumer debt exceeds 50% of the total debt. . . .

Under §707(b)(1), the Court "may dismiss a case filed by an individual debtor under [Chapter 7] whose debts are primarily consumer debts . . . if it finds that the granting of relief would be an abuse of the provisions of [Chapter 7]." 11 U.S.C. §707(b)(1). To determine whether the Debtors' liabilities are primarily consumer debts, the Court must first decide the threshold issue of whether a loan incurred primarily for a Consumer Purpose is a consumer debt if it is secured by a debtor's real property.

The Bankruptcy Code defines consumer debt as "debt incurred by an individual primarily for a personal, family, or household purpose." 11 U.S.C. §101(8). Nothing in §101(8) suggests that a debt meeting this definition nonetheless mutates into a non-consumer debt merely because it is secured by real property. Rather, under the plain language of §101(8), a debt incurred by an individual primarily for a Consumer Purpose is a consumer debt regardless of whether it is secured or unsecured. And the Court must follow the plain statutory language. Indeed, the majority of courts have held that a debt secured by a debtor's real property is a consumer debt if it is incurred primarily for a Consumer Purpose. . . .

The Debtors do not argue that the Home Loans were incurred for a business purpose or for any purpose other than a Consumer Purpose. Nor do they argue that the language of §101(8) is ambiguous. Rather, their argument rests on statements made by two members of Congress that "[a] consumer debt does not include a debt to any extent the debt is secured by real property." 124 Cong. Rec. H11,089 (daily ed. Sept. 28, 1978) (statement of Rep. Edwards); 124 Cong. Rec. S17,406 (daily ed. Oct. 6, 1978) (statement of Sen. DeConcini). The Debtors also rely on several older decisions in which courts, following this legislative history, have held that a debt secured by the debtor's real property is never a consumer debt. *See In re Restea,* 76 B.R. 728, 734 (Bankr. D.S.D. 1987); *In re Stein,* 18 B.R. 768, 769 (Bankr. S.D. Ohio 1982). . . . Legislative history, however, does not override the plain language of a statute. *See, e.g.,* U.S. v. Ron Pair Enters., Inc., 489 U.S. 235, 241 (1989) ("The language before us expresses Congress' intent . . . with sufficient precision so that reference to legislative history . . . is hardly necessary."). . . .

In light of the plain language of §101(8) — and the Supreme Court pronouncements regarding the application of clear statutory language — the Court concludes that loans incurred primarily for a Consumer Purpose are consumer debts even though they are secured by mortgages on a debtor's real estate. Thus, the Court finds that the Home Loans are consumer debts.

Anticipating the Court's ruling that the Home Loans constitute consumer obligations, the Debtors contend that they nonetheless have primarily non-consumer debts because the number of such debts exceeds the number of their consumer liabilities. Taking the contrary position, the UST argues that the Debtors have primarily consumer debts because the aggregate dollar amount of their consumer debt exceeds 50% of their total liabilities.

Courts have interpreted the phrase "primarily consumer debts" in several different ways. The majority view is that a debtor's liabilities are primarily consumer debts if the aggregate dollar amount of such debts exceeds 50% of the debtor's total liabilities. . . .

There are a number of minority approaches. Some courts consider the relative dollar amount of consumer and non-consumer debt and, if those amounts are "approximately equal," the number of consumer and non-consumer debts as well. *See In re Bell,* 65 B.R. 575, 577-78 (Bankr. E.D. Mich. 1986). . . . Other courts hold that a debtor has primarily consumer debts only if the dollar amount of such debts exceeds 50% of the debtor's total liabilities and . . . the consumer debts outnumber the non-consumer debts. *See In re Vianese,* 192 B.R. 61, 68 (Bankr. N.D.N.Y. 1996).

Still other courts hold that a debtor has primarily consumer debts only if the amount of consumer debt actually being discharged and not reaffirmed exceeds 50% of the debtor's total liabilities. *See Restea,* 76 B.R. at 734.

[The court concludes it cannot find that the meaning of the phrase "primarily consumer debts" as used in §707(b)(1) is unambiguous and must look to legislative history, policy rationales, and the context in which the statute was passed.]

In summarizing the context in which §707(b)(1) was passed, and the policy rationale motivating its enactment, the Sixth Circuit has explained:

> Section 707(b) was among the consumer credit amendments to the Bankruptcy Code enacted in 1984. These amendments were passed in response to an increasing number of Chapter 7 bankruptcies filed each year by non-needy debtors. Under prior practice, aside from potential §523(a) exceptions, §707(a) dismissals, and §727(a) objections to discharge, debtors enjoyed an unfettered right to a "fresh start" under Chapter 7, in exchange for liquidating their nonexempt assets for the benefit of their creditors. Section 707(b) introduces an additional restraint upon a debtor's ability to attain Chapter 7 relief. . . . Bankruptcy judges now have discretion to dismiss a consumer case when the filing is abusive.
>
> In essence, §707(b) allows a bankruptcy court to deal equitably with the unusual situation where an unscrupulous debtor seeks to enlist the court's assistance in a scheme to take unfair advantage of his creditors; it serves notice upon those tempted by unprincipled accumulation of consumer debt that they will be held to at least a rudimentary standard of fair play and honorable dealing.

In re Krohn, 886 F.2d 123, 125-26 (6th Cir. 1989). In short, §707(b)(1) was passed in part to protect creditors against abusive Chapter 7 filings. . . .

Based on the context in which §707(b)(1) was passed and the policy concerns it was intended to address, the Court adopts the majority view and concludes that a debtor has "primarily consumer debts" if the aggregate amount of his or her consumer debt exceeds 50% of the total debt. To hold otherwise and determine the primary nature of debts based on the relative number of consumer versus non-consumer obligations could lend itself to pre-bankruptcy manipulation. For example, a debtor with total consumer debts of $ 50,000 owed on five credit cards could attempt to avoid §707(b)(1)'s abuse analysis by consolidating the $50,000 of debt onto one credit card, leaving the debtor with only one consumer debt to weigh against a larger number, but lesser amount, of non-consumer debts. If this same debtor owes several small tax debts to multiple taxing authorities — which the Sixth Circuit has held is non-consumer debt, . . . then the debtor would have a greater number of non-consumer debts than consumer debts. If a bankruptcy court were to determine the nature of the debts based on numerosity, then the debtor would not be subject to scrutiny under §707(b)(1) — contrary, it would seem, to Congress's aim of addressing the perceived abuse of Chapter 7. By contrast, if the primary nature of a debtor's liabilities is measured by the relative amount of debt, then a prospective debtor planning ahead to avoid a Chapter 7 dismissal might do so by paying down consumer debt, consistent with the policies behind §707(b)(1).

For these reasons, the Court concludes that the appropriate method for ascertaining §707(b)(1)'s applicability is to determine whether the aggregate amount of a debtor's consumer debt exceeds 50% of his/her total liabilities. If so, then §707(b)(1) applies. Application of this methodology here leads to the inescapable conclusion that the Debtors' obligations are primarily consumer debts.

For the foregoing reasons, the Court holds that a loan incurred primarily for a Consumer Purpose is a consumer debt even if it is secured by a mortgage on a debtor's real property. The Court also concludes that a debtor has "primarily consumer debts" if the aggregate amount of consumer debt exceeds 50% of the total debt. The Court accordingly finds that the Debtors are not entitled to judgment in their favor as a matter of law. . . .

Post-Case Follow-Up

Determine whether the federal district or circuit where you plan to practice has ruled on whether a debt secured by a home mortgage can be considered a consumer debt for purposes of §101(8). If so, does it follow the majority rule announced in *Hlavin*? Has your district or circuit ruled on the question of how to determine whether a debtor's debts are "primarily consumer debts" within the meaning of §707(b)(1)? If so, does it follow the approach utilized in *Hlavin*, one of the alternative approaches mentioned in that case, or some other approach?

In re Hlavin: Real Life Applications

1. Would the result in *Hlavin* have been different if the loans secured by their home had originally been taken out to fund a failed business venture? What if they had been taken out for home improvement or a vacation but then actually used to fund a business venture? Would it matter if they told the bank the money was being borrowed for home improvement or vacation but intended it to be used to fund a business venture? What if the home loans had been taken out for mixed personal/business reasons?

2. If the debtors in *Hlavin* had 30 different consumer debts totaling $75,000 and only one business debt totaling $76,000, would that court find that they had "primarily consumer debts" under §707(b)(1)? What would be the result if a court utilized one of the alternative approaches to this question mentioned in *Hlavin*?

American Board of Certification

The American Board of Certification (ABC) (www.abcworld.org/), which through sponsorship of the American Bankruptcy Institute (www.abiworld.org/) and the Commercial Law League of America (www.clla.org/) provides the most widely recognized and respected specialization certification for attorneys and judges in the bankruptcy field, now offers certification in three separate categories: Consumer Bankruptcy, Business Bankruptcy, and Creditor's Rights. To date almost 1,000 judges and lawyers across the country have achieved board certification from ABC. A number of state bar organizations also recognize the distinction between consumer bankruptcy and business bankruptcy specialists, and allow attorneys to advertise their services based on those certifications (e.g., North Carolina: www.nclawspecialists.gov/search.asp).

It is in part because of the Code's different treatment of consumer debt and business debt and its different rules for individual debtors having primarily consumer debt than for other debtors that consumer bankruptcy has become a recognized area of specialty within the broader field of bankruptcy for purposes of both law practice and law school study. Many lawyers who represent debtors in bankruptcy handle consumer bankruptcy cases exclusively, taking no business cases. Others specialize in business bankruptcy cases.

Application Exercise 1

Go to the ABC website at www.abcworld.org/ and determine the requirements of that organization for certification as a consumer bankruptcy specialist. Determine if your state offers attorney certification in bankruptcy law and, if so, whether it distinguishes between consumer and business bankruptcy certification. If your state recognizes certification for attorneys in bankruptcy law, what are the requirements to achieve state certification? Using the search feature on the ABC website, see if you can locate one or more attorneys in the city where you plan to practice law who hold ABC certification as consumer bankruptcy specialists. Check online or print advertising of attorneys in the city where you plan to practice law to see if you can locate one or more attorneys advertising for consumer bankruptcy clients only.

The Code's differing treatment of consumer debt and its different rules for individual debtors with primarily consumer debt is only part of the reason that consumer bankruptcy has become an area for specialized practice and study. The other part of the story is the staggering amount of consumer debt that exists in the United States, and the number of individual debtors who find it necessary to file for bankruptcy relief in any given year because they cannot manage their consumer debt. According to the Federal Reserve Bank of New York's Household Debt and Credit Report, in mid-2014 Americans collectively owed $7.8 trillion to creditors on home mortgages and another half trillion dollars in home equity lines of credit. Approximately 176 million of us carried credit cards on which we collectively owed about $858 billion, an average of more than $7,000 in credit card debt per American household. Forty-seven percent of households carry a credit card balance over from month to month instead of paying off the balance each month, usually incurring an annualized double-digit interest rate charge on the balance for doing so. For those households that carry over credit card balances from month to month, the average card balance owed at any one time is over $15,000. And in 2012 came the startling news that total student loan debt owed by Americans exceeds our total credit card debt for the first time. By 2014 total student debt topped $1 trillion and the delinquency rate was 11.5 percent.

Application Exercise 2

Do your own research to update the consumer debt figures provided here. What are the consumer debt statistics for the state where you plan to practice and how do they compare to the national numbers? A good place to start is the latest quarterly Household Debt and Credit Report from the Federal Reserve Bank of New York (www.newyorkfed.org/). You would also do well to familiarize yourself with the history of the explosion in consumer spending and consumer debt in this country during the twentieth century via eased monetary policy to make more money available to financial lenders, expanded mortgage lending, installment purchasing, credit cards, subprime lending, the relaxation of usury rules, etc. Two good sources include *Debtor Nation*, by Louis Hyman (Princeton, N.J.: Princeton U. Press, 2011), and *Financing the American Dream: A Cultural History of Consumer Credit*, by Lendol Calder (Princeton, N.J.: Princeton U. Press, 1999).

It is this tremendous surge in consumer spending and resultant consumer debt that spurred the dramatic increase in bankruptcy filings in the modern era. In 1980 there were approximately 300,000 total bankruptcy filings in the United States. But the rise in consumer debt caused that number to swell to more than 1 million per year by 1996. In 2005 filings exceeded 2 million for the first time ever, although that number was inflated by filings intended to beat the October 17, 2005 effective date of the Bankruptcy Abuse Prevention and Consumer Protection Act of 2005 (BAPCPA) (pronounced "bap-SEE-pah"), which placed new restrictions on Chapter 7 filings by individual debtors with primarily consumer debts. (The numerous significant features of BAPCPA will be discussed in upcoming chapters.) After BAPCPA went into effect, filings for 2006 fell sharply to a little over 600,000, then climbed back to 850,000 in 2007 as debtors' lawyers became acquainted with the BAPCPA changes. With the bursting of the real estate bubble in 2007, the consequent mortgage foreclosure crisis, and the onset of what is now generally referred to as the Great Recession, filings surged to 1.1 million for calendar year 2008, 1.47 million for 2009, and approximately 1.6 million for 2010 before drifting lower in the years since. By 2014 annual filings had fallen below a million. Exhibit 1.1 charts the total number of bankruptcy filings for the period from 1980 to 2015.

EXHIBIT 1.1   **Total Bankruptcy Filings from 1980 to 2015**

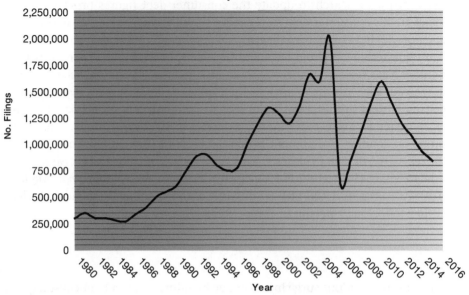

The vast majority of bankruptcy filings since 1980 that you see charted in Exhibit 1.1 are consumer bankruptcy cases, i.e., they are cases filed by individuals with primarily consumer debt. Government agencies like the Administrative Office of the Federal Courts (www.uscourts.gov) and private organizations like the American Bankruptcy Institute (www.abiworld.org) compile statistics regarding bankruptcy filings that distinguish between consumer and business bankruptcy filings. This information originates with bankruptcy court clerks who designate each case filed in their courts as a business or consumer bankruptcy. According to statistics compiled by the Administrative Office of the Federal Courts (www.uscourts.gov/report-name/bankruptcy-filings), in calendar year 2015 there were 844,495 total bankruptcy cases filed, of which only 24,735 or about 3 percent were categorized by bankruptcy court clerks as business bankruptcies. All other filings (97%) were categorized as consumer bankruptcies (see Exhibit 1.2).

In viewing the Administrative Office website cited in the above paragraph, you will see that the majority of consumer bankruptcy cases were filed under either Chapter 7 (a liquidation proceeding) or Chapter 13 (a debt adjustment proceeding for individuals with regular income) of the Code, whereas the majority of business bankruptcy cases were filed under either Chapter 7 or Chapter 11 (a reorganization proceeding used mostly by businesses) of the Code. We will consider all the different kinds of bankruptcy proceedings authorized by the Code in Chapter Four, but for now simply recognize that the vast majority of consumer cases are filed under Chapter 7 or Chapter 13 of the Code.

EXHIBIT 1.2   **Consumer vs. Business Bankruptcy Filings in 2015**

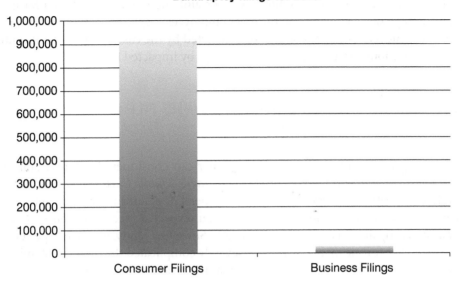

Bankruptcy filings for 2015

Application Exercise 3

From the Administrative Office website at www.uscourts.gov/ or some other authoritative source, locate the national bankruptcy filing statistics through the most recent quarter: What percentage were business filings? What percentage consumer filings? What percentage of the consumer case filings were Chapter 7s? What percentage were Chapter 13s? Check the filings for the particular state where you plan to practice law for the same period: How do the percentages of business versus consumer case filings in your state compare to the national percentages? Is the ratio of Chapter 7s to Chapter 13s among consumer case filings similar to the nationwide ratio?

A word of caution: Don't conclude that the tremendous disparity between the number of consumer and business bankruptcy filings means that consumer bankruptcies are somehow more important than business bankruptcies. Business bankruptcies commonly involve more debt, more assets, more creditors, more disputes, and more issues generally than do consumer bankruptcy cases. In addition, the vast majority of Chapter 11 filings are business bankruptcies, and the rules and procedures governing Chapter 11 cases are in many ways more detailed and complex than those governing Chapter 7 and 13 cases. Moreover, a business bankruptcy is likely to have significant consequences for a wider range of people than a consumer bankruptcy—like the difference between the ripple caused by throwing a brick versus that caused by throwing a pebble in a pond. In a consumer bankruptcy, the debtor, his family, and his creditors will certainly be impacted, but in a business bankruptcy you may also have business employees, suppliers reliant on the business, and indeed an entire community impacted by the case. Business bankruptcy filings commonly precipitate consumer filings by impacted individuals.

B. BRIEF PROFILE OF CONSUMERS WHO FILE FOR BANKRUPTCY RELIEF

According to the now classic study of American consumers by Teresa Sullivan, Elizabeth Warren, and Jay Westbrook, *The Fragile Middle Class: Americans in Debt* (Yale University Press, 2001), more than 90 percent of consumer bankruptcies are triggered by sudden job loss or downsizing, unexpected medical expenses, or loss of a spouse by divorce, separation, or death. Since that study, we have experienced the mortgage foreclosure crisis, which severely complicated the finances of millions of middle-class homeowners, and the Great Recession, which dramatically exacerbated sudden job loss as a bankruptcy trigger.

People with children at home are nearly three times as likely to file bankruptcy as people with no children. A single woman raising a child alone is more than four times as likely to file bankruptcy as a single woman with no children. Divorced fathers also file with much greater frequency than men with no children. Unmanageable prescription drug expenses and other medical costs are a primary reason that older Americans file for relief. More than one-half of Chapter 7 cases filed by Americans of all ages involve excessive medical bills (see Exhibit 1.3).

EXHIBIT 1.3   **Profile of Consumers Filing for Bankruptcy Relief**

Average age	38
Median income	$20,172
Total median assets	$37,000
Homeowners	50%
Median value of homes owned by debtors who are homeowners	$90,000
Median non-home assets	$9,657
Median total debt-to-income ratio	3.04 (the median debtor owes 3.04 times more total debt than his annual income)
Median non-mortgage debt-to-income ratio	1.48 (the median debtor owes 1.48 times more non-mortgage debt than his annual income)
Percentage of median non-mortgage debt represented by credit card debt	50%

EXHIBIT 1.3   **(Continued)**

Percentage of debtors who owe more than a year's income in credit card debt	21.8%
Percentage of debtors who owe more than $10,000 in credit card debt on date of filing	56.2%
Percentage of debtors who owe more than $20,000 in credit card debt on date of filing	34.6%
Married couples	44%
Single women	30%
Single men	26%
Slightly better educated than the general population	----
Sustained job loss or downsizing that contributed to filing	66%
Have not experienced a contributing medical problem, job loss, or divorce	<9%

The easy availability of credit cards, the popularity of payday loans, and the failure of some debtors to constrain or manage the resulting debt, even without individual or family emergencies, are significant factors in bankruptcy filings as well. The substantial role of credit card debt in bankruptcy filings can be seen in the following list, which sets forth a comprehensive profile of consumers filing for bankruptcy relief:

In the past 30 years, approximately one in seven American households has filed for some type of bankruptcy relief. Exhibit 1.4 lists the five states with the highest per capita rate of bankruptcy filings in 2015.

EXHIBIT 1.4   **States with the Highest Bankruptcy Filings per Capita (per 1,000 Residents) in 2015**

1.	Tennessee	5.73
2.	Alabama	5.36
3.	Georgia	5.02
4.	Illinois	4.34
5.	Utah	4.28

In the remaining two chapters of Part I of the text we will examine consumer debt and consumer debtors in more detail by considering the most common kinds of debt that consumers incur, the legal consequences of their defaulting on that debt, and the debt collection process utilized by creditors that is often the last pre-cipitating cause of the bankruptcy filing. Examining these pre-filing aspects of consumer debt is by no means a purely academic exercise. Not only will you find yourself representing the consumer debtor or the creditor in disputes that never reach the bankruptcy courts, when a bankruptcy case is filed, the nature of the debts and the pre-filing actions by the parties can be determinative of how a debt obligation is treated in the bankruptcy process. Thus consideration of the various pre-filing issues we will examine is not only helpful, it is an essential corner of the foundation for a successful consumer bankruptcy practice.

Chapter Summary

- The U.S. Bankruptcy Code defines consumer debt as debt incurred by an individual primarily for a personal, family, or household purpose. A consumer bankruptcy case brought under the Code involves individual debtors who have primarily consumer debt. A majority of courts hold that a debtor's liabilities are "primarily consumer debts" if the aggregate dollar amount of such debts exceeds 50 percent of the debtor's total liabilities. Other courts weigh the number of consumer debts versus business debts as well as the dollar amounts.
- The dramatic rise in consumer spending in the modern era accompanied by an equally dramatic increase in consumer debt fueled an explosion in consumer bankruptcy filings since 1980. Though still historically high, filings nationwide have been drifting steadily lower since 2010.
- Approximately 97 percent of bankruptcy cases filed each year are classified as consumer bankruptcy cases. A 2001 study found that 90 percent of consumer bankruptcies are triggered by sudden job loss or downsizing, unexpected medical expenses, or loss of a spouse by divorce, separation, or death.
- Almost all consumer bankruptcy cases are filed under either Chapter 7 (covering a liquidation proceeding) or Chapter 13 (covering a debt adjustment proceeding) of the Code. The Code has a number of special rules and procedures for consumer bankruptcy debtors and treats consumer debt differently in many respects than it does business debt. This is particularly true since enactment by Congress of the Bankruptcy Abuse Prevention and Consumer Protection Act of 2005.
- Both the Administrative Office of the U.S. Courts and private organizations concerned with bankruptcy matters such as the American Bankruptcy Institute collect and publish statistics for consumer and business bankruptcies.

Applying the Concepts

1. Assume you are consulted by the following potential bankruptcy clients. Which of these appear at first blush to be candidates for a consumer bankruptcy filing as opposed to a non-consumer or business filing?

   a. The individual owners of an unincorporated video rental store whose business has plummeted due to the popularity of Internet movie-streaming services.

   b. A married couple both employed but who have abused their credit card spending and now owe more than they make together in a year.

   c. A recently divorced woman with two children whose ex-husband is unemployed and not contributing child support and who is having trouble paying her monthly living expenses.

   d. A married couple, one of whom has suffered major health problems resulting in medical expenses in excess of what they can expect to earn in ten years.

   e. Two lawyers whose general partnership law practice employing ten other individuals is failing due to lack of business and unable to meet its payroll or other debt obligations.

   f. A young man just out of college and gainfully employed for the first time who caused a car accident and has had a $500,000 civil judgment entered against him as a result, an amount that is $250,000 in excess of his liability insurance coverage.

   g. A plumbing contractor limited liability company whose finances have been crippled due to theft by a trusted bookkeeper employee.

2. For each potential client in Question 1 that you identified as a likely candidate for a non-consumer business case, can you think of individuals who might be negatively impacted by a business bankruptcy filing and who as a result might file a consumer bankruptcy case?

3. For each potential client in Question 1 that you identified as a candidate for a likely consumer case filing, can you think of other facts or circumstances that, if known, might make them a candidate for a non-consumer business filing?

4. Review Assignment Memorandum #1 in the case of Abelard Mendoza in Appendix C together with the Summary of Assets, Liabilities, Current Income, and Expenses attached to it. For now, ignore the assignment given to the associate attorney in that memorandum but do determine whether Mr. Mendoza would qualify for a consumer bankruptcy filing or a business bankruptcy filing given his current state of affairs. Had he come to the lawyer three years ago, might your answer have been different?

5. Review Assignment Memorandum #1 in the case of Nicholas and Pearl Murphy in Appendix D together with the Summary of Assets, Liabilities, Current Income, and Expenses following it. For now, ignore the assignment given to the associate attorney in that memorandum but do determine whether Mr. and Mrs. Murphy would qualify for a consumer bankruptcy filing or a business bankruptcy filing given their current state of affairs.

Secured and Unsecured Consumer Debt

按揭与租金.

Consider the various kinds of debt carried by the typical American consumer. There is debt directly related to housing — a monthly lease or mortgage payment. There is debt related to transportation — a monthly car payment or two. There is debt related to normal living expenses — food and clothing for the family, educational expenses for the kids, childcare expenses for the youngest, gas for the cars, utility bills, cell phone, cable or direct streaming TV, and internet service provider. There is probably credit card debt. There may be debt for insurance premiums — life insurance, health insurance, renters or homeowners insurance. There is debt for income and property taxes. If there has been a legal separation or divorce there may be debt for child support or alimony. A long-term debt obligation may have been undertaken with an educational loan, a loan related to a business venture, or even a loan to fund that once-in-a-lifetime vacation. There may be debt owed primarily by another but for which the consumer is liable as well by reason of having signed or co-signed a promissory note. There may be debt associated with supporting an aging relative or a struggling adult child. At any given time, there may be unexpected debt — medical bills, car and

Key Concepts

- The creation and perfection of consensual security interests in personal property owned by a debtor is controlled by Article 9 of the Uniform Commercial Code
- The perfection of a consensual mortgage interest in a debtor's real property is controlled by the applicable state recording statute
- A consensual suretyship or guaranty arrangement is a form of security for the creditor
- States recognize a number of non-consensual liens that may attach to a debtor's property by statute or common law
- Predatory lending in the form of payday loans and car title loans is a significant contributor to consumer debt

home repair bills, adverse court judgments for tortious conduct, involuntary liens placed on real or personal property — that place the consumer on or over the edge of default as to other obligations. Any of this sound familiar?

These are the kinds of debts we are dealing with in this study of consumer bankruptcy. But before we begin looking at the Bankruptcy Code itself to learn the nuts and bolts of how a consumer bankruptcy case works, we want to examine in this chapter the critical distinction between secured and unsecured consumer debt. That distinction is critical to understanding the rights of a creditor seeking to collect debt that is in arrears outside of bankruptcy. And it is equally critical to understanding the rights of a creditor when the debtor files for bankruptcy relief. Thus the distinction between secured and unsecured debt is an essential part of the foundation for the practice of consumer bankruptcy law.

A. CONSENSUAL SECURITY INTERESTS IN THE DEBTOR'S PROPERTY

Most consumer debts are unsecured. The unsecured creditor has only the bare promise of the debtor to pay the amount owed. If the debtor defaults on the obligation, the remedy of the creditor will be to file a collection lawsuit in the appropriate court, obtain a final judgment against the debtor, then utilize authorized methods of executing on the final judgment in order to seize the assets of the debtor and liquidate (sell) them in order to satisfy the final judgment. Judicial debt collection is a topic we will examine in the next chapter.

On the other hand, many consumer debts are consensually secured. The debtor has voluntarily granted the creditor an interest in the debtor's real property (e.g., the debtor's home) or personal property (e.g., the debtor's car) that authorizes the creditor to take possession of and sell the designated property in the event of default and apply the proceeds to the balance owed. Generally, if the designated property is realty, the creditor has a mortgage in the real property; the debtor is the mortgagor and the creditor is the mortgagee. If the designated property is personal property, the creditor holds a security interest in the personal property. In either event we may say that there is a lien on the property in favor of the creditor. The property, real or personal, on which the lien is granted is properly referred to as the collateral.

Assuming the collateral has value, the secured creditor is in a much more favorable position than the unsecured creditor when default occurs. The secured creditor can reach and liquidate that property more quickly and inexpensively than the unsecured creditor can. And if the secured creditor has properly perfected his security interest in the collateral he enjoys a priority position as to it that prevents any unsecured creditor or any other secured creditor with a junior position in the collateral from taking it before him. Perfection of a security interest and priority disputes are discussed in more detail below. As we will see, the favorable position enjoyed by the properly perfected secured creditor continues into a bankruptcy case filed by the debtor.

1. Consensual Security Interests in Personal Property of the Debtor

Issues regarding the creation, attachment, and perfection of security interests in personal property in consumer cases are governed by Article 9 of the Uniform Commercial Code (UCC). Since Secured Transactions is a separate and often required course in the law school curriculum, only a quick summary of that statutory scheme is offered here.

Creation and attachment of a security interest in personal property is governed in the first instance by UCC §9-203, which in general requires that the debtor have rights in the property named as collateral (the **nominated property** or the **collateralized property**) and the power to transfer those rights (i.e., you can't grant a security interest in property you have no ownership interest in), that the creditor must give value in exchange for the granting of the interest in the property named as collateral, and that the debtor must sign or otherwise authenticate a security agreement containing an adequate description of the collateral. The debtor need not actually sign or otherwise authenticate the security agreement (though there must still be such agreement) where the collateral is in the possession of the creditor (e.g., jewelry given as collateral left with creditor).

The secured creditor can then **perfect** its interest in the collateral, most commonly in consumer transactions, by filing a **financing statement** (also known as a UCC-1) that complies with UCC §9-502 and with the local (county) or state office designated in UCC §9-501, thus giving public notice (and constructive notice to the world) of its interest in the collateral or by taking physical possession of the collateral (in which case we say that the property has been **pledged** to the creditor) pursuant to UCC §9-313. If the collateral is property for which the state issues a **certificate of title** (e.g., automobiles, watercraft, motor homes) perfection of the security interest is achieved by noting the creditor's interest on the certificate of title itself rather than by filing a financing statement. See UCC §§9-303(b) and 311(a).

It is difficult to understate the significance of the determination of whether a creditor is secured and perfected in collateral, and in many states the date of perfection relates back to the date the application for certificate of title was applied for and fees paid rather than the date the certificate is actually issued. If the creditor's security interest in the collateral has been created and attached that means, as between the creditor and the debtor, the creditor can exercise its rights against the collateral in the event of default. Whether the creditor's security interest is also perfected does not matter at all in such a dispute. But perfection does matter when there is another party pursuing the collateral — an unsecured creditor now holding a final judgment and seeking to execute on the property or a second secured creditor consensually granted a security interest in the same collateral as the first. Generally, a perfected security interest will have priority over all later claims to the collateral. And as we will see, a security interest properly perfected pre–bankruptcy petition is generally granted the same priority in the bankruptcy case prevailing over later claims to the collateral by both creditors and the bankruptcy trustee.

For example, assume a debtor has purchased a car on credit and granted the seller a security interest in the car purchased to secure payment of the amount owed.

Once the security interest in the creditor has been created and attached, if the debtor defaults the secured creditor can exercise its rights to repossess and sell the car and apply the proceeds to the amount owed. And this is true even if the creditor does not perfect by noting its security interest on the title to the car. But if the debtor files bankruptcy before the creditor repossesses the car the secured but unperfected creditor will lose in a priority struggle for the car versus the bankruptcy trustee.

A particular issue that often arises in consumer bankruptcy cases is the **purchase money security interest** (PMSI) in consumer goods. Per UCC §9-103 a purchase money security interest arises in favor of a *vendor* who sells goods to a buyer on credit and retains a security interest in the goods to secure payment of the purchase price or a *lender* who loans a debtor money to enable purchase of goods and takes a security interest in the goods purchased with the loan.

For example, if Nick and Pearl Murphy (a married couple and debtors whose circumstances are summarized in Appendix D and for whom we will later consider filing a Chapter 13 bankruptcy case) purchase living room furniture from Shears Department Store on credit and Shears has them execute a security agreement granting Shears a security interest in the furniture to secure payment of the purchase price, Shears has a PMSI in the couch. On the other hand, if Nick and Pearl already own the furniture but grant a security interest in it to Bank in exchange for a loan, Bank does not have a PMSI in the furniture.

UCC §9-309(1) provides that a PMSI in consumer goods is **automatically perfected** upon attachment without the filing of a financing statement by the secured creditor. Thus in the last example, Shears is automatically perfected in the living room furniture as soon as the Murphys purchase the furniture and sign the security agreement. This is true because Shears as a vendor is being granted a security interest in property it sold to the Murphys on credit and because the property sold is consumer property. Bank, however, is not automatically perfected when the Murphys sign a security agreement with Bank because Bank does not have a PMSI. Bank will have to file an appropriate financing statement in the right public office to perfect.

Application Exercise 1

In the last example, assume the Murphys borrow money from Bank in order to purchase the furniture from Shears and sign a security agreement with Bank granting Bank a security interest in the furniture to secure payment of the amount borrowed. The Murphys have now purchased the furniture from Shears using the money borrowed from Bank. Does Bank have a PMSI per UCC §9-103? Is Bank automatically perfected per UCC §9-309(1) or will it need to file a financing statement?

UCC Article 9 grants other priority advantages to creditors whose security interest in collateral qualifies as a PMSI. Under UCC §9-324(a), a creditor who holds a PMSI in goods "other than inventory or livestock" is granted priority over an earlier perfected security interest if the PMSI is perfected when the debtor takes possession of the collateral "or within 20 days thereafter." The 20-day relation back period for perfection gives the creditor holding a PMSI in most kinds of personal property a decided advantage in achieving priority.

For example, assume Sarah owns a business and purchases a laptop computer on credit to use exclusively in the business. Sarah grants the seller a security interest in the laptop to secure payment of the purchase price. Since seller is financing the purchase of the laptop, it holds a PMSI in it. But the laptop is not consumer goods in the hands of Sarah since it was purchased for business use only so there is no automatic perfection under UCC §9-309(1). Assume Sarah takes possession of the laptop the day of the purchase. Under state law the security interest in the laptop is perfected by filing a financing statement, but this is not done by seller until five days after the sale. Meanwhile, Sarah procures a short term loan from a lender and grants lender a security interest in some of her business assets including the laptop that is perfected by leaving the assets in possession of lender. Who has priority? Since seller's financing statement was filed within 20 days of when Sarah took possession, seller will prevail over lender under UCC §9-324(a). Seller's perfected status relates back to the date Sarah took possession and constitutes a superior lien to that of the lender. [This example assumes that the state would not treat the laptop as inventory under §9-102(a)(48)(D).]

UCC §9-317(e) contains a similar provision with regard to a PMSI that can be perfected by filing a financing statement where the secured creditor perfects by filing a financing statement within 20 days after the debtor receives delivery of the collateral. The perfected PMSI will relate back to the time the security interest attached and defeat the claim of any intervening buyer, lessee, or lien creditor of the collateral.

For example, assume Dave owns a car repair shop. On October 1 he purchases a set of tools from Hand Tool Supply (HTS) to use in his business. Dave buys them from HTS on credit, grants HTS a security interest in the tools that same day and takes them to his workshop. Since HTS sold the tools to Dave on credit it has PMSI in the tools but since they are not consumer goods in the hands of Dave, HTS's interest in them is not automatically perfected under §9-309(1). Assume HTS does not file a financing statement covering the tools until October 10. In the meantime, a judgment creditor of Dave's executes on its judgment by seizing the tools. Under state law the judgment creditor is now a lien creditor in the tools. In this priority struggle, HTS will prevail under UCC §9-317(e). Its filing of the financing statement on October 10 was within the 20 window and relates back to the date its security interest in the tools attached, October 1. The lien of the judgment creditor did not attach until later.

Unlike UCC 9-324(a), UCC 9-317(e) does not grant the holder of the PMSI priority over the claim of a prior consensual lien holder in the collateral, only over the claims of intervening buyers, lessees, or lien creditors.

Upon default in the underlying debt obligation, the security agreement between the debtor and the secured creditor will typically authorize the creditor not already in possession of the collateral to declare default and repossess the collateral as is allowed by UCC §9-609(a). No judicial action is required; the creditor is entitled to use **self-help repossession** so long as it can be accomplished with no breach of the peace. If a breach of the peace is threatened or actual during attempted repossession, the creditor must resort to judicial action in which event repossession will be accomplished by court order executed by a designated public officer, usually the sheriff of the county where the property is located. See UCC §9-609(b). A creditor who engages in self-help repossession despite a threatened or actual breach of the peace may be liable for **conversion** of the property as well as other civil or criminal liability.

Case Preview

Giles v. First Virginia Credit Services, Inc.

Self-help repossessions can be very noisy, confused, and messy when the debtor does not know the repossessor is coming. Sorting out exactly what happened after the fact can be challenging for the court and deciding the perimeters of what constitutes a threatened breach of the peace during the repossession event can be tricky. As you read Giles v. First Virginia Credit Services, Inc., consider the following questions:

1. Can there be a breach of the peace if there is no literal confrontation between the debtor and the repossessor? Can shouting constitute a breach of the peace? Can activity that causes turmoil and unrest among neighbors of the debtor constitute a breach of the peace? Can activity that is likely to incite violence but does not do so constitute a breach of the peace?
2. What are the factors this court utilizes to determine whether a breach of the peace occurred during the repossession?
3. Why does the court reject debtor's argument that a subjective standard should be used?
4. Is the question of whether a breach of the peace was threatened or occurred ever a question of law or is it always a question of fact?

Giles v. First Virginia Credit Services, Inc.
149 N.C. App. 89, 560 S.E.2d 557 (2002)

[Joann Giles entered into an installment sale contract on or about January 18, 1997, for the purchase of an automobile. The contract was assigned to First Virginia, which obtained a senior perfected purchase money security interest in the automobile. The terms of the contract required Giles to make sixty regular monthly payments to First Virginia, stipulated that Giles' failure to make any payment due under the contract within ten days after its due date would be a default, and contained a consent to self-help repossession in the event of default.

Giles became delinquent in her payments to First Virginia. At approximately 4 A.M. on June 17, 1999, Professional Auto Recovery, at the request of First Virginia, repossessed the locked automobile from Giles' front driveway by breaking into it, hotwiring it, and driving it away noisily and in great haste. A neighbor, Mr. Mosteller, heard and saw the repossessors' noisy diesel truck pull up to the debtor's house and saw the repossessing agent run up the debtor's driveway toward the debtor's parked car. Moments later he saw the car "flying out back down the driveway making a loud noise and [] screeching off." The repossessors' truck also gunned its engine and fled in a hurry. Mosteller phoned the debtor and her husband to report that their car was being stolen. The debtor and her husband, believing the car had been stolen, became agitated, and the police were called. The debtor's husband and the neighbor shouted back and forth from the front yards of their homes about what had happened and the entire neighborhood was awakened. At least two police cars arrived at the scene to investigate.

Debtor sued First Virginia and Professional Auto Recovery for wrongful repossession and conversion of the vehicle. The trial court dismissed on motion for summary judgment finding that there had been no breach of the peace during the repossession. Debtor appeals.]

MCGEE, Judge.

Our Courts have long recognized the right of secured parties to repossess collateral from a defaulting debtor without resort to judicial process, so long as the repossession is effected peaceably [citation omitted] . . . Our General Assembly codified procedures for self-help repossessions, including this common law restriction, in the North Carolina Uniform Commercial Code (UCC). N.C. Gen. Stat. §25-9-503 (1999), in effect at the time of the repossession in this case, reads in part,

> Unless otherwise agreed a secured party has on default the right to take possession of the collateral. In taking possession a secured party may proceed without judicial process if this can be done without breach of the peace or may proceed by action.

The General Assembly did not define breach of the peace but instead left this task to our Courts, and . . . none have clarified what actions constitute a breach of the peace. . . .

In a pre-UCC case, Rea v. Credit Corp., 127 S.E.2d 225 (1962), a defaulting debtor left his locked automobile on his front lawn. An agent of the mortgagee went to the debtor's home to repossess the automobile, saw the automobile parked on the lawn, found no one at home, and asked a neighbor where the debtor was. The agent was told no one was at home and he thereafter opened the automobile door with a coat hanger and removed the automobile on a wrecker. Our Supreme Court found that this evidence could not warrant a finding by a jury that the mortgagee's agent wrongfully took possession of the automobile because no breach of the peace occurred. In Rea, although our Supreme Court did not define breach of the peace, it reiterated the common law rule that the right of self-help repossession "must be exercised without provoking a breach of the peace[.]" Id. at 127 S.E.2d at 227. Our Supreme Court thought the law "well stated" by the South Carolina Supreme Court in the case of *Willis v. Whittle*, that

> "if the mortgagee finds that he cannot get possession without committing a breach of the peace, he must stay his hand, and resort to the law, for the preservation of the public peace is of more importance to society than the right of the owner of a chattel to get possession of it." *Rea*, 127 S.E.2d at 227.

In Everett v. U.S. Life Credit Corp., 327 S.E.2d 269, 269 (1985) our Court stated that repossession can be accomplished under the statute without prior notice so long as the repossession is peaceable. Without specifically defining breach of the peace, our Court explained that "[o]f course, if there is confrontation at the time of the attempted repossession, the secured party must cease the attempted repossession and proceed by court action in order to avoid a 'breach of the peace.'" Id. at 270. This indicates, as argued by First Virginia, that confrontation is at least an element of a breach of the peace analysis.

In that breach of the peace has not heretofore been clarified by our appellate courts, but instead only vaguely referred to, we must construe this term as the drafters intended. . . .

In a criminal case, our Supreme Court defined breach of the peace as "a disturbance of public order and tranquility by act or conduct not merely amounting to unlawfulness but tending also to create public tumult and incite others to break the peace." State v. Mobley, 83 S.E.2d 100, 104 (1954). . . .

We must also consider the nature and purpose of Chapter 25 of the North Carolina General Statutes, the UCC, which is to be "liberally construed and applied to promote its underlying purposes and policies." N.C. Gen. Stat. §25-1-102 (1999). . . .

In carrying out the policy of uniformity with other jurisdictions, we consider their treatment of the term of breach of the peace. While cases from other jurisdictions are not binding on our courts, they provide insight into how this term has been analyzed by other courts and therefore are instructive.

The courts in many states have examined whether a breach of the peace in the context of the UCC has occurred. Courts have found a breach of the peace when actions by a creditor incite violence or are likely to incite violence. Birrell v. Indiana Auto Sales & Repair, 698 N.E.2d 6, 8 (Ind. App. 1998) (a creditor cannot use threats, enter a residence without debtor's consent and cannot seize property over a debtor's objections); Wade v. Ford Motor Credit Co., 668 P.2d 183, 189 (1983) (a breach of the peace may be caused by an act likely to produce violence); Morris v. First National Bank & Trust Co. of Ravenna, 254 N.E.2d 683, 686-87 (1970) (a physical confrontation coupled with an oral protest constitutes a breach of the peace).

Other courts have expanded the phrase breach of the peace beyond the criminal law context to include occurrences where a debtor or his family protest the repossession. Fulton v. Anchor Sav. Bank, FSB, 452 S.E.2d 208, 213 (1994) (a breach of the peace can be created by an unequivocal oral protest); Census Federal Credit Union v. Wann, 403 N.E.2d 348, 352 (Ind. App. 1980) ("if a repossession is . . . contested at the actual time . . . of the attempted repossession by the defaulting party or other person in control of the chattel, the secured party must desist and pursue his remedy in court"); Hollibush v. Ford Motor Credit Co., 508 N.W.2d 449, 453–55 (Wis. App. 1993) (in the face of an oral protest the repossessing creditor must desist). Some courts, however, have determined that a mere oral protest is not sufficient to constitute a breach of the peace. Clarin v. Minnesota Repossessors, Inc., 198 F.3d 661, 664 (8th Cir. 1999) (oral protest, followed by pleading with repossessors in public parking lot does not rise to level of breach of the peace); Chrysler Credit Corp. v. Koontz, 661 N.E.2d 1171, 1173-74 (1996) (yelling "Don't take it" is insufficient).

If a creditor removes collateral by an unauthorized breaking and entering of a debtor's dwelling, courts generally hold this conduct to be a breach of the peace. Davenport v. Chrysler Credit Corp., 818 S.W.2d 23, 29 (Tenn. App. 1991) and General Elec. Credit Corp. v. Timbrook, 291 S.E.2d 383, 385 (1982) (both cases stating that breaking and entering, despite the absence of violence or physical confrontation, is a breach of the peace). Removal of collateral from a private driveway, without more however, has been found not to constitute a breach of the peace. Hester v. Bandy, 627 So. 2d 833, 840 (Miss. 1993). Additionally, noise alone has been determined to not rise to the level of a breach of the peace. Ragde v. Peoples Bank, 767 P.2d 949, 951 (1989) (unwilling to hold that making noise is an act likely to breach the peace).

Many courts have used a balancing test to determine if a repossession was undertaken at a reasonable time and in a reasonable manner, and to balance the interests of debtors and creditors. See e.g., Clarin v. Minnesota Repossessors, Inc., 198 F.3d 661, 664 (8th Cir. 1999); Davenport v. Chrysler Credit Corp., 818 S.W.2d 23, 29 (Tenn. App. 1991). Five relevant factors considered in this balancing test are: "(1) where the repossession took place, (2) the debtor's express or constructive consent, (3) the reactions of third parties, (4) the type of premises entered, and (5) the creditor's use of deception." Davenport, 818 S.W.2d at 29. . . .

Relying on the language of our Supreme Court in Rea, plaintiffs argue that the "guiding star" in determining whether a breach of the peace occurred should be whether or not the public peace was preserved during the repossession. Rea, 127 S.E.2d at 228. Plaintiffs contend "the elements as to what constitutes a breach of the peace should be liberally construed" and urge our Court to adopt a subjective standard considering the totality of the circumstances as to whether a breach of the peace occurred.

Plaintiffs claim that adopting a subjective standard for N.C. Gen. Stat. §25-9-503 cases will protect unwitting consumers from the "widespread use of no notice repossessions, clandestine and after midnight repossessions" and will protect "our State's commitment to law and order and opposition to vigilante policies, opposition to violence and acts from which violence could reasonably flow[.]" If a lender is not held to such a high subjective standard, plaintiffs contend that self-help repossessions should be disallowed altogether.

First Virginia, in contrast, argues that a breach of the peace did not occur in this case, as a matter of law, because there was no confrontation between the parties. Therefore, because the facts in this case are undisputed concerning the events during the actual repossession of the automobile, the trial court did not err in its partial grant of summary judgment.

First Virginia disputes plaintiffs' contention that a determination of whether a breach of the peace occurred should be a wholly subjective standard, because if such a standard is adopted, every determination of whether a breach of the peace occurred would hereafter be a jury question and "would run directly contrary to the fundamental purpose of the Uniform Commercial Code, which is to provide some degree of certainty to the parties engaging in various commercial transactions." Further, First Virginia argues that applying a subjective standard to a breach of the peace analysis could be detrimental to borrowers, with lenders likely increasing the price of credit to borrowers to cover the costs of having to resort to the courts in every instance to recover their collateral upon default. The standard advocated by plaintiffs would "eviscerate" the self-help rights granted to lenders by the General Assembly, leaving lenders "with no safe choice except to simply abandon their 'self help' rights altogether, since every repossession case could [result] in the time and expense of a jury trial on the issue of 'breach of the peace[.]' " Finally, First Virginia argues that a subjective standard would be detrimental to the judicial system as a whole because "[w]ith a case-by-case, wholly subjective standard . . . the number of lawsuits being filed over property repossessions could increase dramatically[.]"

. . . [W]e find that a breach of the peace, when used in the context of N.C. Gen. Stat. §25-9-503, is broader than the criminal law definition. A confrontation is not always required, but we do not agree with plaintiffs that every repossession should be analyzed subjectively, thus bringing every repossession into the purview of the jury so as to eviscerate the self-help rights duly given to creditors by the General Assembly. Rather, a breach of the peace analysis should be based upon the reasonableness of the time and manner of the repossession. We therefore adopt a balancing test using the five factors discussed above to determine whether a breach of the peace occurs when there is no confrontation.

In applying these factors to the undisputed evidence in the case before us, we affirm the trial court's determination that there was no breach of the peace, as a matter of law. Professional Auto Recovery went onto plaintiffs' driveway in the early morning hours, when presumably no one would be outside, thus decreasing the possibility of confrontation. Professional Auto Recovery did not enter into plaintiffs' home or any enclosed area. Consent to repossession was expressly given in the contract with First Virginia signed by Joann Giles. Although a third party, Mr. Mosteller, was awakened by the noise of Professional Auto Recovery's truck, Mr. Mosteller did not speak with anyone from Professional Auto Recovery, nor did he go outside until Professional Auto Recovery had departed with the Giles' automobile. Further, neither of the plaintiffs were awakened by the noise of the truck, and there was no confrontation between either of them with any representative of Professional Auto Recovery. By the time Mr. Mosteller and plaintiffs went outside, the automobile was gone. Finally, there is no evidence, nor did plaintiffs allege, that First Virginia or Professional Auto Recovery employed any type of deception when repossessing the automobile.

There is no factual dispute as to what happened during the repossession in this case, and the trial court did not err in granting summary judgment to First Virginia on this issue.

Post-Case Follow-Up

Is this opinion making a distinction between the repossessor himself disturbing the peace and his committing an act that motivates another to disturb the peace once the repossessor is gone? Would the result in this case have been different if the activities of the repossessors had awakened the debtor or the neighbor and the one awakened had shouted at them out of a window something like, "Stop, thief! I've called the police"? See Robinson v. Citicorp National Services, Inc., 921 S.W.2d 52 (Mo. Ct. App. 1996), and Chrysler Credit Corp. v. Koontz, 661 N.E.2d 1171 (1996). If the debtor's husband had raced outside with a firearm while the repossessors were pulling away from the property? If he or the neighbor had fired a firearm at the fleeing repossessors? If a sleeping child had been in the car unseen by the repossessor when the car was driven off? See Chapa v. Traciers & Associates, 267 S.W.3d 386 (Tex. App. 2008)? If the repossessor had violated a driving ordinance in the course of repossession? See Wallace v. Chrysler Credit, Corp., 743 F. Supp. 1228 (W.D. Va. 1990). The vehicle in *Giles* was sitting in the debtor's driveway when it was repossessed. Would the result have been different if the car had been sitting in a garage with the garage door up? With the garage door down but unlocked? With the garage door down and locked? See Pantoja-Cahue v. Ford Motor Credit, Co., 872 N.E.2d 1039 (Ill. 2007). Note that the debtor's lawsuit alleging the tort of conversion was brought against the creditor as well as its repossessing agent, Professional Auto Recovery. Though normally there is no vicarious liability of a principal for the torts of an independent contractor, there is a well-recognized exception in the self-help repossession context, where the duty on the creditor to preserve public safety during the repossession is deemed non-delegable to the independent contractor. See General Finance Corp., v. Smith, 506 So. 2d 1045 (Ala. 1987).

Giles v. First Virginia Credit Services, Inc.: *Real Life Applications*

1. You represent a local financial institution that makes consumer loans. A vice-president of your client awakens you with a 4 A.M. phone call with an urgent question. The client sent agents out to a debtor's home at 2 A.M. to effect a self-help repossession of a boat in which client held a security interest to secure a loan that is seriously in default. The repossessors backed away when the debtor heard them hitching up the boat and began shouting at them to stop and threatening to "blow them away" if they wouldn't. However, the agents have now reported that the debtor just drove away from his property leaving the boat where it was. The client wants to know if it's okay to send the agents back to the debtor's home before daylight to complete the repossession. See Wade v. Ford Motor Credit, Co., 668 P.2d 183 (Kan. 1983).

2. Your client from Question 1 calls again a week later. Given the problems they've been having recently with debtor's objecting to their attempted self-help

repossessions, they would like to hire off-duty sheriff's deputies to accompany their repossessing agents. The client feels the presence of the uniformed deputies will help quell objections and decrease the likelihood of any breach of the peace occurring during repossession. The client wants you to sign off on the idea before it is implemented. Is this a good idea? See First & Farmers Bank v. Henderson, 763 S.W.2d 137 (Ky. App. 1988), Stone Mach. Co. v. Kessler, 463 P.2d 651 (Wash. App. 1970), and Wright v. Nat'l Bank of Stamford, 600 F. Supp. 1289 (N.D.N.Y.), aff'd without opinion, 767 F.2d 909 (2d Cir. 1985).

3. Your client from Question 1 comes up with another idea. They would like to use harmless subterfuge to effect self-help repossession. The idea is to have an employee contact a the debtor who is in default by phone to advise that the manufacturer of the collateralized property is offering a free cleaning or servicing of the product for promotional purposes. Owners only have to bring the item to a designated place at a designated time to receive the free cleaning or servicing. Of course once the owner turns the property over to the agents of client, they will be told it is now repossessed. Will you sign off on this idea? Compare Ford Motor Credit, Co v. Byrd, 351 So. 2d 557 (Ala. 1974), and Cox v. Galigher Motor Sales Co., 213 S.E.2d 475 (W. Va. 1975).

4. Your client from Question 1 again awakens you with an early morning phone call. In a panicked voice, the VP explains that a company the client recently contracted with to do repossessions successfully repossessed a car earlier in the night. However, it seems a ten-year-old child of the debtor was asleep in the back seat of the car when it was towed away from debtor's home. The repossessing agents did not see the child. The car was towed to an enclosed storage area patrolled by a German Shepherd guard dog, which bit the child when the child emerged sleepily from the car sometime later. Since the company hired by client was an independent contractor, client wants to know whether client can be held liable for any tortious conduct the contractor may have committed and, if so, what tortious conduct might be alleged on these facts. See Sanchez v. MBank of El Paso, 792 S.W.2d 530 (Tex. App. 1990), aff'd, 836 S.W.2d 151 (Tex. 1992).

Following default and repossession, the creditor will normally sell (by public or private sale) or otherwise dispose of the property and apply the proceeds to the indebtedness owed. The disposition of the property must be accomplished in a **commercially reasonable manner** per UCC §9-610 and appropriate notices given to the debtor, co-obligors, and secondary (junior) secured parties or lien holders as required by UCC §§9-611 to 614.

Alternatively to sale or other disposition of the collateral, UCC §9-620 authorizes the secured creditor to retain the collateral in full or partial satisfaction of the obligation (called a **strict foreclosure**) where the security agreement does not require the creditor to sell the collateral and where the proposal and consent provisions of that section are complied with. There are limits however on the creditor's right to retain collateral that is consumer goods. UCC §§9-620(e) and (f) require sale or other disposition of consumer goods collateral where 60 percent of the cash price has been paid and the security interest is a PMSI or where 60 percent of the obligation has been paid and the security interest is a non-PMSI. Moreover, UCC §9-620(g) prohibits retention of the collateral in a consumer transaction in only partial (as opposed to full) satisfaction of the obligation.

Per UCC §9-601(a) the secured creditor need not rely on repossession of the collateral at all to satisfy the underlying obligation but may choose instead to institute legal action to obtain a final judgment for the amount owed enabling the creditor to execute on other property of the debtor as would an unsecured creditor. A secured creditor may choose this option where the collateral has no value or cannot be located. For example, if Shears is secured in the living room furniture of the Murphys but, upon default, it concludes that furniture has little or no value, it may choose not to repossess at all and sue for the entire balance owed instead.

Where the collateral has been repossessed and disposed of UCC §9-615 controls the order in which the proceeds are applied. The expenses of repossession and disposition are paid first. Then the proceeds are applied to the balance owed the repossessing creditor and then to any subordinate or junior secured creditors or lien holders in the collateral. Any remaining proceeds are paid to the debtor.

If it is a junior secured creditor who declares default and repossesses the collateral, none of the proceeds need be paid to the senior secured creditor but that senior creditor will retain its security interest in the collateral notwithstanding the sale or other disposition per UCC §§9-617(3) and 622(a)(3)(4).

Where the collateral has been repossessed and disposed of and a deficiency balance remains owing the secured creditor may institute legal action against the debtor to obtain a judgment for the deficiency balance owing. For example, if Shears repossesses and sells the living room furniture of the Murphys following default but the foreclosure sale only produces half of what is owed, Shears may sue the Murphys seeking a judgment for the balance owed.

Not unusually in deficiency lawsuits the debtor raises defenses alleging that the secured creditor did not comply with the requirements of Article 9 in the repossession process (e.g., the creditor did not give proper notice under UCC §9-611 or did not dispose of the property in a commercially reasonable manner per UCC §9-610). In many courts, where the debtor is able to show non-compliance by the secured creditor in a consumer transaction, the creditor is absolutely barred from recovering on the deficiency. In effect there is a non-rebuttable presumption that had the secured creditor complied with the requirements no deficiency would have resulted. See, e.g., Coxall v. Clover Commercial Corp., 781 N.Y.S.2d 567 (N.Y. Cty. Civ. Ct. 2004). In other courts, the established non-compliance by the consumer debtor only raises a rebuttable presumption that the deficiency would not have resulted had the creditor complied. See, e.g., Central National Bank v. Butler, 294 A.D.2d 881, 882, 741 N.Y.S.2d 643 (4th Dept. 2002). And see UCC 9-626(b). In non-consumer transactions, the finding of non-compliance by the creditor only raises the rebuttable presumption per UCC §9-626(a).

Application Exercise 2
....

Determine how the courts of the state where you plan to practice apply UCC §9-626(b) in a consumer transaction. Is the presumption in that case treated as rebuttable or non-rebuttable?

UCC §9-625 authorizes a court to enjoin a secured creditor's non-compliance with the statutory procedures for repossession. It also authorizes the debtor or secondary obligor (such as a guarantor) or other secured party or lien holder to recover actual damages for the secured creditor's non-compliance with those procedures and statutory damages for the creditor's non-compliance with certain provisions. Per UCC §9-625(b) a debtor or secondary obligor whose liability for a deficiency is eliminated or reduced under UCC §9-626 cannot also recover actual damages. Statutory damages can still be awarded to the debtor or a consumer secondary obligor under UCC §9-625(e) notwithstanding reduction or elimination of the deficiency under UCC §9-626.

2. Consensual Security Interests in Real Property of the Debtor

Consumer debtors often own an interest in real property, usually a family home, when they file for bankruptcy relief and in the vast majority of cases have at least one and sometimes multiple mortgages on that property at the time of filing. The law concerning the creation, attachment, and perfection of mortgages in real property is governed by the laws of the state where the property lies. For our purposes, what follows is a brief summary of how those laws work.

The legal document by which a mortgage in real property is created is called a **mortgage** or **mortgage deed** or, in some states, **a deed of trust** or **security deed**. The security interest in the real property that the owner/mortgagor conveys to the creditor/mortgagee is called a **right of foreclosure** or **power of sale** and authorizes the mortgagee to take possession of the property upon default and to then sell it, applying the proceeds to the debt owed. In most states it is understood that the mortgagor maintains legal title to the property, while the mortgagee holds equitable title to it — that is, the right to take possession of and sell the property in the event of default.

In the most common situation, consumers purchase a home, borrow a portion of the purchase price from a lender, sign a promissory note evidencing the obligation to repay the amount borrowed (often called a **mortgage note**), and convey a mortgage interest in the property purchased to the lender to secure repayment of the note. Sometimes there is no lender involved in the transaction. Instead the owner of a home or other real property will **self-finance** or **owner finance** the buyer by conveying title to the buyer, allowing the buyer to take immediate possession, and agreeing to accept payment of all or a portion of the purchase price over some agreed period of time. In a self-financing transaction, the buyer will execute a promissory note in favor of the seller for the balance owed and grant the seller a mortgage in the property to secure the future payments. This type of mortgage is usually called a **purchase money mortgage**.

Usually, when a consumer first purchases a home there is little or no owner's equity in it since the amount borrowed and still owed on the mortgage is equal or close to the actual value of the house. **Owner's equity** is the market value of property in excess of the balance owed on it. Over time, as the balance due on the note underlying the mortgage is paid down, the owner's equity in the property should increase. Changes in the market value of the property can also impact on the amount of equity that exists in property.

For example, assume a husband and wife purchase a home for $300,000, its appraised value, and borrow $280,000 from Bank to finance the purchase. They provide the remaining $20,000 of the purchase price from savings. The buyers execute a promissory note payable to Bank promising to repay the money borrowed over 30 years in equal monthly installments at a stated rate of interest. They buyers also execute a mortgage deed in favor of Bank granting Bank a mortgage interest in the home purchased. At the time the transaction closes, the buyers have only $20,000 of owner's equity in the property. However, if after five years the owners have made payments on the underlying obligation reducing the balance owed to $225,000, they will have $75,000 of owner's equity in the home. And if during the same five years the value of the house has risen to $350,000 they will have $125,000 of equity in the home.

Not uncommonly in consumer transactions, homeowners who have built up sufficient equity in their home may obtain a second loan equal to all or some percentage of the equity and grant a mortgage interest in the property to the second lender even though the property is subject to the first mortgage and payments on that first mortgage are still being made to the first lender. A secured loan based on the owner's equity in a home is called a **home equity loan**.

For example, if the consumers in our last example have built up owner's equity of $125,000 in their home after five years, they may choose to borrow against that equity by taking out a home equity loan even though the original loan is still being paid down and the first mortgage is still in place. The second lender is unlikely to loan an amount equal to the entire owner's equity, however. That would be far too risky since property values can fall as well as rise. Instead, the lender will have the property appraised and confirm the balance owed on the first mortgage in order to ensure that there will be sufficient equity remaining in the property after it makes the home equity loan. So on confirmed equity of $125,000 the second lender might make a loan of half that amount. State or federal regulations governing the lender may also control how much of the existing equity can be loaned.

Another variation increasingly common in consumer transactions is the **reverse mortgage**, in which a homeowner aged 62 or older borrows against the **equity** built up in the residence and receives that equity from the lender in either a lump sum or in installment payments. The loan is repaid when the homeowner dies or no longer lives in the home and the home is sold.

As the discussion of the home equity loan suggests, it is not unusual for real property owned by consumers to be subject to more than one mortgage simultaneously. The first mortgage on the property is called just that, the first mortgage. That first mortgage may prohibit the property owner from using the property as security for any other debt and if the owner does so it may constitute an act of default under the first mortgage. But if it does not prohibit subsequent mortgaging of the property, or if the mortgagee consents to a subsequent mortgage notwithstanding the prohibition, the owner may mortgage the property as security for a second or even third debt, thus creating a second mortgage or a third mortgage on the property. Often the first mortgage is referred to as the **senior mortgage**, or **senior lien**, and the subsequent ones as a **junior mortgage**, or a **junior lien**.

The security interest of a creditor in real property conveyed in a mortgage instrument is created and attaches when (1) the mortgagor obtains an interest in the real property that can be conveyed as security; (2) value is given by the mortgagee in exchange for the security interest; and (3) the appropriate mortgage document is properly executed. At that point, as between the owner and the secured creditor, the creditor has the right of sale or the power of foreclosure in the event of default. But when the dispute is between multiple creditors and the question is which competing claim has priority over the others, we are again faced with the question of who was first to perfect its mortgage interest.

Priority between plural mortgages is determined by which kind of **recording statute** is in effect in the state where the property lies. Most states have **race-notice statutes**, whereby priority is created by being the first to record a mortgage in the public office responsible for maintaining land records (in different jurisdictions that may be the office of the Registrar of Deeds, Register of Deeds, Recorder, or the city or county clerk) while having no actual notice of any prior unrecorded claim to the property. The recording of the mortgage serves as constructive notice to the world of the recording mortgagee's claim.

A few states have **pure notice statutes**, which give priority to a prior unrecorded mortgage so long as subsequent mortgagees have actual notice of the prior unrecorded mortgage. A very few states have **race statutes**, which give priority to the first mortgage recorded regardless of actual notice.

With this recording system to establish priority among mortgages in mind, reconsider the nomenclature of senior and junior mortgages discussed above. That phraseology can refer to which mortgage interest was created and attached first, or it can refer to which mortgage interest has priority under the applicable recording statute.

The main idea behind a mortgage is that if the mortgagor defaults on the underlying debt evidenced by a promissory note, the mortgagee can take possession of the mortgaged property, sell it, and apply the proceeds to the satisfaction of the debt. This process is called **foreclosure**. Almost universally, the promissory note secured by the mortgage will contain an **acceleration of indebtedness clause** authorizing the mortgagee to declare all amounts due from the mortgagor immediately due and payable. Thus, the foreclosure can proceed in order to produce funds sufficient to pay off the entire indebtedness and other charges and expenses authorized by the note and mortgage. Exhibit 2.1 sets out a typical default clause in a mortgage note containing acceleration of indebtedness language.

EXHIBIT 2.1 ### Default Clause from Mortgage Note with Acceleration of Indebtedness Language

If Lender fails to receive payment from Makers of any monthly payments called for in Paragraph ___ by the _____ day of any month in which a payment is due, or if default is made in the payment of the indebtedness hereunder at maturity, or in the event of default in or breach of any of the terms, provisions or conditions of this Promissory Note or any instrument evidencing or securing the indebtedness evidenced hereby, or any other instrument evidencing indebtedness from Makers, or either of them, to Lender, Makers will then be in DEFAULT. In that event, at the option of the Lender, the entire amount of the indebtedness will become immediately due and payable. Further in that event, the whole of the unpaid principal and any accrued interest shall, to the extent permitted by law, bear interest at the highest lawful rate then in effect pursuant to applicable law, or at the rate provided herein in the event no highest applicable rate is then in effect. Furthermore in that event, Lender shall be entitled to pursue all remedies available to it at law and/or equity to collect all amounts due under this Promissory Note and Makers shall pay all costs and expenses of collection, including court costs and a reasonable attorneys' fee, incurred by or on behalf of Lender in collecting the amounts due under this Promissory Note to the extent not prohibited by applicable law. Lender's failure to declare a default due to Makers' failure to make any monthly payment as called for in this Promissory Note shall not waive or otherwise prejudice Lender's right to declare a default in connection with Makers' failure to make any other monthly payment as called for in this Promissory Note.

As we will see, many a consumer bankruptcy is triggered by a foreclosure begun on the consumer's home. Various states have authorized two different procedures for foreclosure: **power of sale foreclosure** and **judicial foreclosure**. A handy summary of the foreclosure laws of all 50 states is accessible at www.biggerpockets.com/foreclosurelaw/index.html. Almost all states that authorize a power of sale foreclosure permit judicial foreclosure as an alternative. But almost half the states mandate judicial foreclosure and permit no alternative.

Power of Sale Foreclosure

A slight majority of the states allow mortgage instruments to convey a power of sale to the mortgagee. States allowing a power of sale use either a deed of trust or a security deed form of mortgage.

Upon default of an instrument granting a power of sale, the mortgagee (or a trustee for the mortgagee named in the mortgage instrument or a substitute trustee appointed after default) may institute foreclosure proceedings without first having to obtain any judicial or administrative approval. The mortgagee must be careful to comply with statutes governing the power of sale foreclosure. These statutes typically require the trustee to prepare a **notice of sale**, containing details of the intended public sale of the property (e.g., description of the property, time and place of the sale) and to provide the notice of sale to the mortgagor, any junior mortgage holders, and any other parties known to have an interest in the property (e.g., guarantors of the underlying debt). In addition to sending the notice of sale to designated interested parties, the trustee is typically required either to post the notice in a public place for some designated period of time before the sale (usually four to six weeks) or to run for a designated number weeks prior to sale an advertisement in the classified section of a newspaper of general circulation in the county where the land to be sold lies.

For example, First Bank of Capital City holds the first mortgage on the home of Nick and Pearl Murphy from Appendix D. If the Murphys had conveyed a power of sale to FBCC and then defaulted on their payments, FBCC or a trustee acting for it may have initiated a power of sale foreclosure using the notice of foreclosure sale set forth in Exhibit 2.2.

EXHIBIT 2.2   Notice of Foreclosure Sale

WHEREAS, Nicholas W. Murphy and wife, Pearl E. Murphy, by Deed of Trust (the "Deed of Trust") dated January 12, YR-10, of record in Mortgage Book 99, Page 077 in the Register's Office of Capital County, Yourstate, conveyed to Howard J. Sands, Trustee, the hereinafter described real property to secure the payment of a certain Promissory Note (the "Note") described in the Deed of Trust, which Note was payable to First Bank of Capital City;

WHEREAS, default has been made in the payment of the Note; and

WHEREAS, the owner and holder of the Note has demanded that the hereinafter described real property be advertised and sold in satisfaction of indebtedness and costs of foreclosure in accordance with the terms and provisions of the Note and Deed of Trust.

NOW, THEREFORE, notice is hereby given that Trustee, pursuant to the power, duty and authority vested in and conferred upon me, by the Deed of Trust, will on May 1, YR00 at 9 A.M. at the front door of the Capital County Courthouse in Capital City, Yourstate, offer for sale to the highest bidder for cash, and free from all legal, equitable and statutory rights of redemption, exemptions of homestead, rights by virtue of marriage, and all other exemptions of every kind, all of which have been waived in the Deed of Trust, certain real property located in Capital County, Yourstate, described as follows: [property description deleted from illustration]. . . . Being the same property conveyed to Nicholas W. Murphy and wife, Pearl E. Murphy, by deed from Francis H. Harmon, of record in Deed Book 813, Page 908 in the Register's Office for Capital County, Yourstate and further conveyed by the Deed of Trust to the Trustee, of record in Mortgage Book 99, Page 077 in the Register's Office for said County.

The address of the above-described property is 3521 West Cherry Street, Capital City, Yourstate.

DATED this February 1, YR00.

_____

Francis H. Harmon, Trustee

Following the foreclosure sale in a power of sale foreclosure, title to the property is conveyed to the new owner through a **trustee's deed**. Proceeds of the sale will be applied first to satisfy the costs of the sale (e.g., advertising, site preparation, and auctioneer's fee), second to pay any taxes or special assessments still owed on the property, and third to pay the balance owed senior and other mortgage holders. Finally, any balance left goes to the borrower. The minimum bid set at a foreclosure sale is normally equal to the amount owed to the foreclosing mortgagee. If no third-party bid on the property at the foreclosure sale exceeds that minimum amount, the foreclosing mortgagee is entitled to (and in some states required to) enter a bid on the property itself in an amount equal to the amount owed, a common practice known as **bidding in** or **credit-bidding**, which means the creditor takes absolute title to the property in exchange for extinguishment of the indebtedness and for no additional payment. If there is equity in the property then the purchasing mortgagee captures the equity.

Distributing Proceeds of a Foreclosure Sale

There is quite a bit of variation among the states regarding how proceeds of a foreclosure sale are to be distributed. In some states, after the balance owed to the foreclosing mortgagee has been paid, excess proceeds must go to other creditors of the mortgagor/debtor before any are paid to him. Some states allow the mortgagee to credit-bid at an amount less than the total amount owed on the property, although this may raise questions of good faith or unconscionability if the mortgagee is allowed to (see discussion of arrearages, below) and does then pursue the debtor for any balance remaining on the account. Many states authorize a special court proceeding wherein disputes over distribution of sales proceeds can be resolved within some designated time period following the sale (e.g., six months or one year).

Application Exercise 3

Research the statutes or regulations of the state where you plan to practice to determine how that state regulates the distribution of proceeds from foreclosure sales.

Until the foreclosure sale occurs, all states recognize an **equity of redemption** right in the mortgagor. That is, the right of the mortgagor to redeem the property from foreclosure by paying all amounts due to the mortgagee. On the designated day and time, if the mortgagor has not exercised his equity of redemption, the trustee or a public official (e.g., the county sheriff) will conduct the foreclosure sale. The property will be sold to the highest bidder. The mortgagee is allowed to bid in the amount of the debt owed to it as the purchase price.

If holders of junior mortgages were given proper notice of the foreclosure sale, their mortgage interests in the real property are extinguished by the foreclosure sale under the laws of most states such that the purchaser at foreclosure will take title free and clear of those claims even if the proceeds of sale are insufficient to pay off both the foreclosing and junior mortgages. If the proceeds of the sale produced an excess (there was more than enough money made on the sale to pay all the debts and expenses owed to the foreclosing mortgagee), that excess will go to the junior interests or to the mortgagor. The foreclosing mortgagee holding excess funds often initiates a civil lawsuit called an **impleader action**, naming the junior interest holders and the mortgagor as parties, pays the excess funds into the clerk of the court where the impleader action is filed, and requests the court to determine who is entitled to what share of those excess funds. The foreclosure of a junior mortgage will have no effect on a senior mortgage.

For example, let's say Bank #1 holds a senior mortgage in a debtor's home. Bank #2 holds a second mortgage in the home to secure a home equity line of credit. Bank #3 holds a third mortgage in the home to secure payment of a small construction loan the owners have taken out. Owners are in default to Bank #2, which forecloses giving proper notice to Bank #3. Latisha purchases the home at the foreclosure sale, which did not raise enough to satisfy the balance owed to Bank #2 so Bank #3 received nothing. Latisha will take title to the home subject only to the mortgage of Bank #1. As senior mortgagee, the foreclosure by a junior mortgagee cannot disturb the interest of Bank #1. On the other hand, the mortgages of both Bank #2 and Bank #3 were eliminated by the foreclosure. The foreclosure by Bank #2 eliminates both its own and all junior mortgage interests so long as statutory notice was given to the junior mortgagees. The fact that the foreclosure sale brought insufficient funds to pay off either the foreclosing mortgagee or a more junior mortgagee does not affect this result. (This example is based on a bar examination question appearing on the Virginia bar exam in July 2014.)

In addition to the mortgagor's equity of redemption right, already discussed, some states provide the mortgagor with a **statutory right of redemption**. Such statutes authorize the mortgagor, for a period of time after the foreclosure sale (six to twelve months is typical), to buy back the property for the foreclosure sale price. Some of the states that recognize the right of statutory redemption permit the mortgagor to waive that right in the mortgage document.

Judicial Foreclosure

Judicial foreclosure is initiated by the mortgagee filing a lawsuit alleging default in a debt properly secured by the mortgage and the right to foreclose and asking the court to issue an order that the property be sold to pay the indebtedness secured. Judicial foreclosure is mandated in states that do not recognize a power of sale foreclosure and is an option available to the mortgagee in states that do.

The mortgagee initiating the judicial foreclosure will name the mortgagor, junior mortgage holders, and others with an interest in the property as parties so that all alleged claims and defenses can be fully litigated in the action. If the court finds for the mortgagee and orders the property sold, required notice will be given, the property levied on or seized by the sheriff or other public official, and the sale conducted publicly by auction (a **sheriff's sale** or **referee's sale**). Title to the new owner is then conveyed by a **sheriff's deed** or **referee's deed**. Distribution of proceeds from a judicial sale will be strictly governed by statute, but generally follows the scheme discussed in connection with power of sale foreclosure.

Application Exercise 4

Locate the judicial foreclosure statute or regulation in the state where you plan to practice. What is the mandated order of distribution of proceeds of a foreclosure sale? If your state allows power of sale foreclosure, are there any differences in how proceeds of sale are distributed in judicial and power of sales foreclosures?

Many attorneys prefer the judicial foreclosure over the power of sale foreclosure, even in states authorizing the latter, because of the finality of the court decision. In a non-judicial power of sale foreclosure, there is always the possibility the mortgagor will file suit contesting the right of the mortgagee to proceed or contesting the propriety of a foreclosure sale already conducted. All those issues should be resolved by the court in the judicial foreclosure prior to the sale. The rights and priorities of junior mortgage holders will be resolved there, too, negating the need for a subsequent impleader action.

Another consideration in choosing between a judicial foreclosure and a power of sale foreclosure is the possibility that the property sold at foreclosure may not bring enough to satisfy the full amount owed — there is a **deficiency balance**. In a judicial foreclosure, the court in most instances can enter a judgment against the mortgagor for the deficiency (a **deficiency judgment**) without a separate lawsuit being filed. In a power of sale foreclosure, however, the mortgagee must file a lawsuit following the foreclosure sale in order to obtain a deficiency judgment. Some states recognize an **election of remedies** doctrine, prohibiting the mortgagee from obtaining a deficiency judgment following a power of sale foreclosure. The mortgagee is held to have elected its sole remedy by proceeding with the foreclosure and cannot bring a deficiency action if the price received on foreclosure did not fully satisfy the debt.

Another source of controversy over a deficiency balance can arise when the foreclosing mortgagee enters a credit bid on the property at the foreclosure sale for less than the total amount owed and then seeks a judgment against the debtor for the deficiency balance in jurisdictions where that is allowed. In many states a mortgagee who enters a credit bid on the property cannot then sue for a deficiency. Where a credit-bidding mortgagee is allowed to sue for a deficiency, there is often an issue as to whether the value of the property exceeded the amount of the credit bid entered by the mortgagee.

Application Exercise 5

Determine if the foreclosure procedures of the state where you plan to practice allow the foreclosing mortgagee who enters a credit bid on the property to then seek a deficiency balance. If so, and the debtor sued for the deficiency contends the value of the property exceeded the amount of the credit bid entered by the mortgagee, who has the burden of proof on the value issue?

The Servicemembers Civil Relief Act (SCRA)

The SCRA, found at U.S.C.A. App. §§501 et seq., as revised in 2003, restricts foreclosure of properties owned by active duty members of the military. Check the Web site of the U.S. Department of Housing and Urban Development for a summary of the protections from foreclosure provided to our active duty servicepeople: http://portal.hud.gov/hudportal/HUD?src=/program_offices/housing/sfh/nsc/qasscra1.

Of course, if the underlying promissory note or mortgage instrument is **nonrecourse** the creditor cannot pursue a deficiency judgment against the mortgagor since a nonrecourse clause limits the creditor's remedy to the collateral and bars any further action against the debtor for a deficiency judgment regardless of whether a judicial or power of sale foreclosure was authorized. Nonrecourse clauses are rare in consumer transactions. A further consideration in electing between a judicial foreclosure and a power of sale foreclosure is that purchasers of the property at the foreclosure sale often have more confidence in the title they receive to the property by foreclosure deed when the sale is the result of a court order. On the other hand, a downside to judicial foreclosure is the delay in the mortgagee being able to move ahead with a foreclosure sale by reason having to file the lawsuit, effect service of process on the mortgagee, and await a hearing date.

Alternatives to Foreclosure

Foreclosure is not a happy solution for anyone, including the foreclosing creditor. Unless the real estate market is hot, the foreclosed property may sit empty for months or years with the attendant risks of deterioration in value and vandalism. Taxes still have to be paid and insurance maintained on the property. There are always costs associated with the foreclosure sale, reducing the take of the creditor and increasing the potential liability of the debtor. Foreclosure is often devastating to the credit rating of the debtor. For these and other reasons, the debtor and creditor may agree to any of several alternatives to foreclosure:

- **Temporary Forbearance**: The creditor agrees to temporarily lower or suspend mortgage payments without declaring default and foreclosing.
- **Mortgage Modification**: The creditor agrees to permanently modify the mortgage terms by extending the term of repayment and thus reducing the amount of the periodic payments or by reducing the interest rate, or even by forgiving a portion of the principal.
- **Short Sale**: The creditor allows the homeowner time to sell the property and agrees to accept the net proceeds of the sale in full satisfaction of the indebtedness even though the sale may not bring enough to cover the entire indebtedness and even if the underlying note is not nonrecourse.
- **Deed in Lieu of Foreclosure**: The debtor agrees voluntarily to transfer title to the property to the creditor in exchange for cancelling the mortgage loan. The creditor may also agree to forgive any deficiency balance remaining when the property is finally resold.

B. CONSENSUAL SURETYSHIP AND GUARANTY ARRANGEMENTS AS A FORM OF SECURITY

A **surety agreement** is one in which a person makes himself liable for the promised performance of another (e.g., to pay a money obligation or to perform a service). The surety is sometimes referred to as an **accommodation party**. A surprising number of consumer bankruptcies involve a consumer having co-signed a promissory note as an accommodation to another; a form of suretyship. Parents often co-sign promissory notes on loans made to children and siblings sometimes co-sign for each other, even friends co-sign for each other. For example, a Report on Private Student Loans prepared for Congress by the Consumer Financial Protection Bureau (CFPB) and Department of Education in 2012 (available online at http://files.consumerfinance.gov/f/201207_cfpb_Reports_Private-Student-Loans.pdf) reported the surprising finding that in 2011, 90 percent of private student loans were co-signed. Correspondingly, a September 2014 report by the U.S. Government Accountability Office (available online at www.gao.gov/products/GAO-14-866T) found that liability for student loan debt carried by Americans aged 65 to 74 increased from $2.8 billion in 2005 to $18.2 billion in 2013.

For example, assume David Hayes, 20 years old, wants to borrow $10,000 from a bank to finance the purchase of a car. If David is deemed too great a credit risk by the bank, it may require David to provide a creditworthy co-signer on the note. John and Mary Hayes, David's parents, co-sign the promissory note payable to the bank and the loan is made to David. Although the loan was made for the benefit of David, his parents have agreed to make themselves **primarily liable**, along with David, on the note. David is the principal debtor on the note, while John and Mary are sureties. Both David and his parents are primarily liable on the note.

To say that the co-signer is primarily liable on a debt along with the principal debtor means that the creditor can look to the co-signer for payment of the debt whether or not the principal debtor is able to pay and whether or not the creditor first seeks to collect the debt from the principal debtor. If the co-signer were only **secondarily liable** on the debt, the creditor would have to seek collection first from the principal debtor and only then could the creditor seek collection from the co-signer. But the co-maker of a promissory note makes himself primarily liable on the debt along with the principal debtor. Thus in our example, if David fails to repay the note as it comes due, the bank or subsequent holder of the note is not required to pursue collection from David before pursuing collection from John and Mary even though David is the principal debtor on the note. It is no defense to the holder's collection action against John and Mary that David is able to pay but didn't. Nor is it a defense that the holder did not pursue David at all on the obligation before commencing collection against the co-signers.

Co-signing a note is only one way to create a surety arrangement on a debt. Another way is for the accommodation party to execute a separate surety agreement, or surety bond, promising to be responsible for the debt either primarily or secondarily. Surety agreements and bonds are far more common in business transactions than in consumer transactions.

Another type of surety arrangement in which a party makes herself liable for the debt of another is the **guaranty agreement**. By executing a guaranty agreement, the guarantor makes herself secondarily liable for the debt of the principal debtor. Typically in a guaranty arrangement, the guarantor is only secondarily liable, not primarily liable.

Assume David Hayes fails to repay the note that his parents guaranteed but did not co-sign. If the guaranty makes the parents only secondarily liable, the holder of the note is required to pursue collection from David as the principal debtor before pursuing collection from John and Mary, who only promised to pay the guaranteed debt in the event that David defaulted on it. The holder of the note must prove the default by David as a condition precedent to collecting from the parents as guarantors.

Issues often arise in actions brought against an accommodation party as to whether those defendants can raise the same defenses to liability that the principal debtor could have raised.

Generally, an accommodation party can raise any defense to liability that the principal debtor could raise, including failure of consideration, fraud, duress, breach of contract, breach of warranty, and so on. However, the surety or guarantor cannot raise personal defenses available to the principal debtor. A **personal defense** is a defense unique to the circumstances of the principal debtor that does not go to the merits of the underlying transaction. Personal defenses would include discharge in bankruptcy or lack of capacity to contract due to age or disability, and the like.

For example, assume that John and Mary Hayes have guaranteed the promissory note signed by their son, David. Later David files a bankruptcy case and discharges any legal obligation he might have for the note, but had he been sued by the lender he was prepared to show by way of defense that he never received the funds from the lender. As you know from your study of contract law, we would call that defense a failure of consideration. When the bank sues John and Mary Hayes on their guaranty, they can raise the failure of consideration defense just as David could have but they cannot raise David's discharge of the note obligation in bankruptcy as a defense to their liability on the guaranty. That is a personal defense. Likewise if David were only 17 years old when he signed the note and could raise incapacity due to age if sued on it, John and Mary as guarantors could not raise that defense; it is personal to David.

Another important principle of surety/guaranty law is that if the creditor and principal debtor agree to make any material change in the terms of the original obligation for which the accommodation party is potentially liable, and do so without obtaining the prior consent of the accommodation party to that material change, the obligation of the accommodation party will be discharged by operation of law. That is because the material change alters the risk that the accommodation party agreed to assume.

Assume the note that John and Mary Hayes have guaranteed is due but David cannot pay. David and the lender agree that David will have six months more time to pay than the note allows but will pay a 0.25 percent higher rate of interest in exchange for the extension. No one advises John and Mary of this alteration in the obligation or obtains their consent. David defaults on the obligation even with the extension, and the lender seeks collection from John and Mary. On these facts, John and Mary are likely discharged from any liability on his guaranty due to the material change.

Some states make a distinction between an accommodation surety and a compensated surety in applying this doctrine of discharge by material change. An **accommodation surety** is one who receives no compensation for serving as surety; he does so gratuitously. A **compensated surety** is one that receives a fee or other compensation for agreeing to serve as surety or guarantor.

John and Mary co-signing David's note and signing the guaranty for another are examples of an accommodation surety. They did this to help their son, not for any compensation from the lender or the principal.

In those states that make this distinction, an accommodation surety will be relieved from its obligation whether the material change in the obligation puts it at greater risk or not, but a compensated surety will be relieved only if the material change causes it harm or puts it at demonstrably greater risk.

For example, assume the lender on the note guaranteed by John and Mary agrees to give David an additional year to pay it but does not increase the amount of the principal or the interest rate payable on the note. We can argue over whether this material change puts the guarantors at greater risk or not, but here it doesn't matter; as accommodation sureties, John and Mary will be relieved of their obligation as guarantors.

Application Exercise 6

If John and Mary had agreed to sign the guaranty of David's note in exchange for his promise to paint their house, would that make them compensated sureties? If so, does the bank giving David an additional year to pay the note but not increasing the principal amount due or altering the interest rate due on the note put them at demonstrably greater risk such that the loan obligation should be discharged as to them? What are the arguments either way on this question? Is it an easier case for them if the bank agrees to the one-year extension in exchange for an increase of 1 percent on the interest rate payable on the note? Is it a harder case for them if the extension agreed to by the bank is only for a week? Is that even a material change that might cause a surety to be discharged on the obligation?

C. NON-CONSENSUAL LIENS IN THE DEBTOR'S PROPERTY

To be distinguished from consensual security interests granted by a consumer in his personal or real property are a variety of **non-consensual liens** recognized in every state by statute or common law. Where created by statute they may be referred to generally as **statutory liens**. Whether the non-consensual lien that attaches to the consumer's property will be recognized as valid when the consumer files for bankruptcy relief and what priority it will be given relative to other claims to the same property are both questions that commonly arise in consumer bankruptcy cases. In this section, we briefly note the most commonly recognized non-consensual liens.

1. Possessory Liens on Personal Property

The Artisan's Lien

The **artisan's lien** (sometimes called an **artificer's lien** or a **workman's lien**) applies to personal property, not real property. Originally a common law lien, most states now regulate it by statute (though in some states it may be both statutory and common law, a significant fact as we will see when we discuss the priority question below). The artisan's lien is a type of possessory lien in that it only works in favor of one lawfully in possession of tangible personal property, to secure payment of reasonable charges for services rendered and materials supplied. A typical artisan's lien statute defines artisans to include "Persons with whom are left goods or products to be repaired, developed, processed, or improved." And such persons are declared to have a lien on goods that have been left with them for repair or improvement to the extent of the artisan's charges related to the goods. There are any number of businesses that may be entitled to assert an artisan's lien, including:
vehicle/small engine mechanics

jewelers	computer repair	cotton ginners
cobblers	technicians	veterinarians
tailors	aircraft maintenance	
picture framers	technicians	
dry cleaners	upholsterers	
printers and bookbinders	appliance repairers	
pet groomers	metal fabricators	

Some states cover all such businesses under a single artisan's lien statute, whereas others have a variety of business-specific lien statutes (e.g., a vehicle repair lien and a separate launderer's lien).

Application Exercise 7

Locate the artisan's lien statute in the state where you plan to practice. Does your state have a single artisan's lien statute or separate ones for the kinds of businesses in the preceding list? Are other types of "artisans" covered under statutes in your state?

Normally, the artisan retains possession of the property hoping the owner will pay the bill owed or negotiate a settlement of it. But if that does not happen, the artisan, after some statutory period of time (e.g., 90 days or six months) can enforce the lien by selling the property in satisfaction of the debt. To enforce the lien, the artisan must give written notice to the owner and anyone else she determines claims an interest in the property (e.g., if she knows of a co-owner or a secured party in the property). The purpose of the notice is to enable the owner, or other person having an interest, to pay the debt and recover the property prior to sale.

The notice typically must describe the property, itemize the services performed by the artisan, state the amount owed, and demand payment by a stated date from the date of the notice. Assume Nick and Pearl Murphy take a couch to an upholsterer for recovering. A dispute arises over the upholsterer's work or the amount of his bill and he refuses to return the couch to them and they refuse to pay. Exhibit 2.3 shows the artisan's lien notice the upholsterer might send to the Murphys regarding the couch.

EXHIBIT 2.3   **Notice of Artisan Lienor's Intent to Sell**

NOTICE OF ARTISAN LIENOR'S INTENT TO SELL

TO: Nick and Pearl Murphy [Address]

For the past three months I have retained possession of your Shears 10' living room couch (the property) as I am empowered to do under Yourstate Statutory Code §66-11-205 (the statute) to secure my charges, amounting to $350, due as a reasonable, customary, and usual compensation for the recovering service that I provided in connection with the couch.

You are hereby notified to come forward and pay these charges. On your failure to do so within ten (10) days after this notice has been given to you, I shall sell the property at public sale and apply the proceeds to the payment of such charges, paying over the balance, if any, to you or to the person entitled to it, or holding you liable for any deficiency.

Dated: June 1, YR-1

Martha's Fabric Services, Lienor

By:_____

Martha S. Fillers, Owner

In some states, the artisan must also advertise, for some statutory number of times (e.g., twice for two consecutive weeks), the intended sale of the item in a newspaper of general circulation in the county where the sale is to be held. In most states, the sale can be public or private. In some states, judicial foreclosure action is required to authorize the sale, and, in others, self-help foreclosure and sale is allowed if the statutory notice requirements have been satisfied. The proceeds of sale are applied first to cover the costs of the notice and any advertisement, then the claim of any other lien holder in the property over which the artisan's lien does not have priority, and then to the amount owed the artisan. Any surplus proceeds are returned to the owner.

The artisan's lien, like any possessory lien, remains perfected so long as the claimant maintains possession of the property subject to it. If the holder of the artisan's lien relinquishes possession of the property, the lien is extinguished.

The Landlord's Lien

The landlord's lien operates on property of the tenant located on the leased premises if the tenant has defaulted in his obligations to pay the landlord. Absent proof of abandonment, most states require express and conspicuous consent to the lien in the lease agreement or the granting of an Article 9 security interest to the landlord before the landlord can seize a tenant's property for nonpayment of rent. Certain property of the debtor is usually exempted from seizure by the landlord and the landlord must leave written notice of entry and provide an itemized list of items taken. The landlord can sell the seized property by giving statutory notice so many days before the sale (e.g., 30 days) and the property may be redeemed by the tenant prior to sale by paying all amounts owed for rent and expenses. If no landlord's lien was reserved in the lease agreement the landlord must rely on abandonment of the premises by the tenant and take judicial action. On proof of abandonment the court will issue what is often called a **warrant of distress** (from the old common law action for distress or distraint), authorizing the removal of the tenant's property from the premises, but in most states it cannot be sold by the landlord.

Application Exercise 8

Locate the landlord's lien statute in the state where you plan to practice and determine how it works procedurally. What property is made exempt from the lien? If the lien is not created but the tenant abandons the premises, what can be done with tenant's property?

The Warehouseman's Lien

The **warehouseman's lien** recognizes the right of a party who has transported or stored a commodity (e.g., oil or corn), an animal, or other personal property that belongs to another to declare a lien on such commodity or goods still in the warehouse's possession to secure payment for unpaid transportation or warehousing charges.

For example, in the commercial context, an oil refinery in Texas may purchase oil from an international seller. The oil is shipped and delivered to a storage facility that takes possession of and then stores the oil until the buyer can pick it up. In the consumer context, a garage keeper may agree to let the owner of a vehicle store his vehicle in the garage keeper's facility. Or, a self-service storage business may lease storage units to consumers and other customers in which to store their property. Or, a pet hotel may keep an owner's pet while the owner is on vacation. Or, a shipping company transports goods on behalf of a seller. In any of these situations, whether commercial or consumer, if the agreed fee for transport or storage is not paid when due, then the party transporting or storing the other's property may refuse to turn over the property to the party demanding possession, assert the lien in the property, and retain it until payment is made.

The warehouseman's lien existed at common law and the common law lien is still recognized in many states. However, it has been made statutory in UCC §7-209. And UCC §7-210 controls the procedure for enforcing the lien and requires notice to all parties having an interest in the goods.

Application Exercise 9

Locate the version of UCC §7-210 adopted in the state where you plan to practice. What information is the required notice to contain? How long must the warehouse wait after notice is given before the goods can be sold? Can the sale be executed by either public (auction) or private sale? Must the goods be sold by the warehouse at their absolute best price or is a commercially reasonable price good enough?

In states that still recognize the warehouseman's lien at common law, it may apply only to those that store goods and not to those that transport them. But those states will likely recognize a separate lien for those that transport goods, usually called a **carrier's lien**, and it will work the same way as the warehouseman's lien.

The Article 2 Buyer's Lien

UCC §2-711(3) creates a non-consensual possessory lien in favor of a buyer in a transaction for the sale of goods. It arises wherein a buyer of goods who receives shipment of the goods from the seller and who then properly rejects the goods or properly revokes his acceptance of the goods is authorized to declare a non-consensual security interest in goods in his possession until the seller reimburses him for any down payment made to seller for the goods and any expenses incurred in inspection, transportation, care, and custody of the goods. This buyer can refuse to return the goods to the seller until those obligations are paid, and if the seller refuses to pay, then the buyer can sell the goods to recover the costs.

For example, assume Henrietta orders a new computer from Bell Computers. She pays for it in advance. The computer is delivered to Henrietta but she quickly discovers that it doesn't work. She notifies Bell Computers that she is rejecting the computer and demands a refund of her money. Bell demands that she return the computer to Bell before it will refund her money. Henrietta may be able to refuse that demand, declare a UCC §2-711(3) lien in the computer, and sell it to recoup her costs if refund is not forthcoming.

Application Exercise 10

Locate the version of UCC §2-711(3) in effect in the state where you plan to practice. What is the procedure for a buyer to follow in this situation when he wants to sell the goods in which the lien is asserted?

The Attorney or Accountant's Retaining Lien

Many states recognize an attorney's or accountant's retaining lien (or a lien benefiting other licensed professionals) authorizing the professional to retain possession of a client's books, papers, securities, money, or other property (but not to dispose of as by sale, because it is a "passive" or "retention" lien only (see, e.g., Brauer v. Hotel Associates, Inc., 192 A.2d 831, 833-834 (N.J. 1963)) until the client pays his bill or posts adequate security to cover it. Similarly, a banker's lien may authorize a bank or other financial institution to assert the lien in a customer's property in the bank's possession (e.g., cash on deposit or certificates of deposit) and to take it to satisfy debts owed the bank.

The Vendor's Lien

Many states recognize a vendor's lien in favor of a party that sells personal property but retains possession of it until the full purchase price is paid (sometimes called a layaway or layby arrangement), usually enforceable as if an Article 9 consensual security interest had been granted by the buyer to the seller in the goods.

Other Possessory Liens

There are any number of other possessory liens recognized by various states. For example, a banker's lien may authorize a bank or other financial institution to assert the lien in a customer's property in the bank's possession (e.g., cash on deposit in checking or savings accounts or certificates of deposit) and to take it to satisfy obligations owed to the bank by the debtor (e.g., an unpaid loan, an overdrawn checking account, etc.). Or the state may recognize a hotel operator's lien imposed on a guest's personal property stored on the hotel premises, including automobiles and baggage, to secure reasonable room rents.

Priority of Possessory Liens

Interestingly, UCC §9-333 gives possessory liens priority over prior security interests in the property subject to the lien whether the prior security interest is perfected or not. That section provides that "a possessory lien on goods has priority over a security interest in the goods unless the lien is created by a statute that expressly provides otherwise." Note the important caveat at the end: the possessory lien has priority *unless* the statute creating the possessory lien says it doesn't.

For example, look at the warehouseman's lien created in UCC §7-209. Subsection (c) contains a "provides otherwise" clause of the type referenced in UCC §9-333 that prevents the warehouseman's lien created by §7-209 from achieving priority over a prior, properly perfected security interest unless the holder of that security interest expressly or impliedly approved the debtor's submitting the goods to another's lien claim as by shipment or storage of the goods. The possessory lien will, however, defeat a prior unperfected security interest in the property.

In fact, most statutory possessory liens will provide expressly that the lien will not attain priority over preexisting and properly perfected mortgages, security interests, or other liens on the property unless notice is given to the creditors holding such preexisting claims and they consent in writing. For example, a typical artisan's lien statute may read, "A lien under this section shall be subject to all prior liens of record, unless notice is given to all lien holders of record and written consent is obtained from all lien holders of record to the making, repairing, improving, or enhancing the value of any personal property and in this event the lien created under this section shall be prior to liens of record."

Application Exercise 11

Assume that the Murphys purchased the couch recovered by Martha's from Shears Department Store on credit and Shears retained a purchase money security interest (PMSI) in it. Between Martha's Fabric Service, asserting an artisan's lien in the couch, and Shears Department Store, asserting a consensual security interest in the couch, who has the priority position under the statutory language in the preceding example? Might the result turn on whether the security interest of Shears is a lien "of record"? If Shears filed a financing statement to perfect its security interest in the couch, it is of record. But if Shears did not file a financing statement and is depending on perfection by way of a purchase money security interest in consumer goods, Martha's artisan's lien may be deemed senior. Locate the artisan's lien statute in effect in the state where you plan to practice. Does it expressly provide that prior perfected security interests have priority over it? How would the dispute between Shears and Martha's Fabric Service be decided under that statute?

Case Preview

Charter One Auto Finance v. Inkas Coffee Distributors Realty

Note that UCC §9-333 says that a possessory lien will have priority "unless the lien is created by a statute that expressly provides otherwise. . . ." Many states still recognize one or more common law possessory liens, leaving the question of whether the priority scheme mandated by UCC §9-333 applies to those common law liens. As you read Charter One Auto Finance v. Inkas Coffee Distributors Realty, consider the following questions:

1. What is the difference between a common law lien and a statutory lien?
2. Once a common law lien is recognized in a jurisdiction, how might it be abolished?
3. What is Charter One's argument that the common law possessory lien at issue did not apply on the facts of the case?

Charter One Auto Finance v. Inkas Coffee Distributors Realty
57 UCC Rep. Serv. 2d 672, 39 Conn. L. Rptr. 110 (Conn. Super. Ct. 2005)

SHAPIRO, Judge. . . .

Plaintiff Charter One Auto Finance (Charter) was assigned a retail installment contract (contract) in which the defendant, Inkas Coffee Distribution Realty and Equipment LLC (Inkas) purchased a 2001 Ford F250 (the motor vehicle) for $36,340.00, which was to be paid in 60 monthly installments. Charter was granted a security interest in the motor vehicle on or about September 20, 2000 which lien was duly noted on the certificate of title of the motor vehicle. Inkas is currently in default under the contract for failure to make payments due for July 4, 2001 to the present. Inkas' debt to Charter, exclusive of legal fees and costs was $33,391.57. The reasonable value of the motor vehicle was $24,350.00.

Connecticut International Parking, LLC (Connecticut International) is engaged in the business of storing motor vehicles at its open air parking lot located in East Granby, Connecticut. On or about May 10, 2001, Inkas delivered the motor vehicle to Connecticut International pursuant to an oral agreement to store it. Pursuant to that agreement, Inkas agreed to pay Connecticut International its standard rate of $9.25 per day for storage.

Pursuant to the oral agreement, Connecticut International took and maintained lawful possession of the motor vehicle from May 10, 2001 through May 16, 2004, and incurred $9,851.00 for storage fees during that period. Also, while the motor vehicle was in its possession, Connecticut International maintained and cared for it by regularly checking it. Connecticut International started and moved the motor vehicle on at least a monthly basis to ensure that its engine, mechanical system, and tires would remain in operating condition. Connecticut International did not send any notices to Charter during the period in which the motor vehicle was in Connecticut International's possession.

On or about April 16, 2004, Charter, claiming that it had lien rights in the motor vehicle, demanded that Connecticut International deliver it to Charter. Connecticut International offered to deliver the motor vehicle to Charter upon proof of Charter's rights, but demanded that Connecticut International be paid for the storage charges owed to it. Charter refused the demand and obtained an order of replevin for the motor vehicle pursuant to which a bond was posted.

Connecticut International believes it is entitled to recover the sum of $9,851.00, plus interest. By virtue of its prior perfected security interest in the motor vehicle, Charter believes that it is not obligated to pay Connecticut International. Inkas filed for bankruptcy, which case was dismissed in December 2001. Charter and Connecticut International stipulated also, upon information and belief that Inkas is unable to pay either of them.

In its complaint, Charter One seeks replevin, which, as noted above, already has occurred, and other relief, including money damages and attorney's fees. Connecticut International filed a two-count counterclaim seeking a determination of the rights of the parties, and various other forms of relief. . . .

Charter One's recorded security interest of September 20, 2000 pre-dated the date, May 10, 2001, when Connecticut International took and maintained lawful possession of the motor vehicle and when storage fees began to be incurred. The pivotal legal issue in this matter is whether or not a common-law possessory lien has priority over a previously recorded security interest.

Connecticut law long has recognized a common-law possessory lien. In Leavy v. Kinsella, 39 Conn. 50, 53 (1872), concerning the keeping of two pigs, our Supreme Court stated that "in general all bailees for hire have a lien on the thing bailed for the amount of their compensation, and common carriers and innkeepers have peculiar claims to their liens, because they cannot refuse to incur the expense cast upon them by their customers. And here the defendant may ground his right to a lien upon similar principles of justice and equity."

Subsequently, in a matter involving the keeping and feeding of a horse, the Supreme Court reiterated, "A lien is the right which a creditor has of detaining in his possession the goods of his debtor until the debt is paid. To the common-law idea of a lien it is necessary that the creditor should have the actual possession of the goods over which the lien is claimed, and that the debt should have been incurred in respect to the very goods detained." Fishell v. Morris, 57 Conn. 547, 551, 18 A. 717 (1889). The court noted also that such a common law lien is distinct from that created by a statute. See id., at 552. "In all cases where statutes have created any right of security on the property of a debtor in the nature of a lien, not depending on possession, they have provided carefully for a registration of the transaction." Id. See State v. Marsala, 59 Conn. App. 755 A.2d 965, cert. denied, 762 A.2d 902 (2000).

In addition to the common law underpinnings of the possessory lien, General Statute §49-61(a), concerning an artificer's lien, provides a mechanism by which a personal property owner may apply to the Superior Court to dissolve a bailee for hire's lien upon substitution of bond. Subsequent subsections of General Statute

49-61 provide for a procedure by which, as to a motor vehicle, a bailee for hire may give notice of his lien and for a sale of the property. See General Statute §49-61(b)-(e). [I]n view of the court's finding as to Connecticut International's priority status as a common-law possessory lienholder, it need not determine whether Connecticut International has any lien rights under §49-61.

The similarity between a possessory lien for the keeping of a horse and one for storing and maintaining a motor vehicle is obvious. While the passage of time and the development of the automobile may now have made the latter a more common occurrence than the former, the legal principles underlying such a possessory lien remain intact.

In seeking summary judgment, Charter One . . . argues that the decisional law on the common law possessory lien . . . is unavailing "since [those cases] simply did not involve prior lienholders." See Charter One's memorandum of law, p. 7.

The court concludes that Connecticut's [UCC] provides that such a possessory lien has priority over a previously recorded security interest. [O]ur legislature revised Article 9 of the Uniform Commercial Code, effective on October 1, 2001. General Statute §42a-9-709 provides, "Public Act 01-132 . . . determines the priority of conflicting claims to collateral. However, if the relative priorities of the claims were established before October 1, 2001, sections 42a-9-101 to 42a-9-507, inclusive, of the general statutes, revision of 1958, revised to January 1, 2001, determine priority."

Since the relative priorities here were established prior to October 1, 2001, the court looks to the prior version of the Uniform Commercial Code. Former Section 42a-9-310 provides, "When a person in the ordinary course of his business furnishes services or materials with respect to goods subject to a security interest, a lien upon goods in the possession of such person given by statute or rule of law for such materials or services takes priority over a perfected security interest unless the lien is statutory and the statute expressly provides otherwise." In discussing former Section 9-310, White & Summers notes that, "State statutory and common-law liens are excluded from the scope of Article 9, with the exception of the section 9-310 priority rule." J. White & R. Summers, Uniform Commercial Code (4th Ed. 1995) §30-12, p. 93. . . .

Applying §9-310's priority rule, it is undisputed here that, in the ordinary course of its business, Connecticut International furnished services with respect to the motor vehicle. Until the motor vehicle was replevied by Charter One, Connecticut International was lawfully in possession of the motor vehicle. By operation of the common law, it was entitled to a possessory lien. This possessory lien is not premised on a statute; accordingly, the "unless" part of §9-310s rule is inapplicable. Also, the court is unaware of a statute which expressly provides that a perfected security interest has priority over such a common law possessory lien and Charter One has not cited any. Pursuant to former §42a-9-310, Connecticut International's possessory lien has priority over Charter One's perfected security interest. . . .

In view of the court's conclusion as to the priority status of Connecticut International's common-law possessory lien, the court need not determine the applicability of any statutory lien rights which Connecticut International may have had. See General Statutes §49-61 (artificer's lien), discussed above, and General Statute §42a-7-209 (warehouseman's lien).

Accordingly, judgment as to liability may enter for Connecticut International as to its claim on the replevin bond and for unjust enrichment.

Post-Case Follow-Up

Note that Charter One, the properly perfected secured creditor in the vehicle, had obtained an order of replevin as to the vehicle and the resulting claims of Connecticut International, the possessory lien holder, were for wrongful replevin and unjust enrichment. Replevin is a remedy available not only to a secured creditor where the collateral is in the possession of a third party with an inferior claim to it, but one available to a creditor holding a final judgment seeking to execute on the collateral in the hands of the third party. Replevin is an extraordinary remedy requiring the posting of a bond by the party seeking it. Thus one theory of Connecticut International was wrongful replevin and it sought to recover damages based on the replevin bond posted by Charter One. It also sought to recover for unjust enrichment. Could an action in conversion have also sounded on these facts?

Charter One Auto Finance v. Inkas Coffee Distributors Realty: Real Life Applications

1. Because of the dates on which the transactions in this case occurred, it was decided based on the version of Article 9 in effect in Connecticut prior to the 2001 revisions to Article 9; thus the reference in the opinion to Connecticut General Statute Annotated (C.G.S.A.) §42a-9-310. The 2001 revision to Article 9 adopted in Connecticut that same year (and now in all states) revised and renumbered C.G.S.A. §42a-9-310 as C.G.S.A. §42a-9-333. Locate the current wording of the revised statute. Would the case likely be decided the same way under the revised statute? How would it likely be decided under the wording of UCC §9-333 now in effect in the state where you plan to practice?

2. Assume you represent Bank in each of the following scenarios. Identify the possessory lien, *if any*, that the other party might assert to gain priority over Bank and advise your client as to how a court will likely rule. If necessary, identify what additional information you will need to make that determination.

   a. Debtor has given Bank a security interest in her car and Bank has perfected by noting its security interest on the title. Debtor is in default and Bank wishes to repossess but debtor's son has possession of the car at his college in Canada.

   b. Same situation as in Scenario "a" except that debtor has left the car at Mike's Repair Shop for maintenance and has not yet paid Mike.

   c. Same situation as in Scenario "a" except that debtor left the car with neighbor for safekeeping for a month while debtor travels. Neighbor agreed to keep the car as a favor. Would the result be different if debtor promised to pay neighbor $10 a day?

d. Debtor lives in a resort area that attracts tourists and makes and sells hand carved items from local hardwoods that are sold in arts and crafts stores in the area. Debtor has a loan from Bank properly secured and perfected in part by the carvings debtor makes and sells. Debtor enters a contract to sell 100 carvings to Craft Store and delivered the carvings to Craft Store last week. However, the carvings delivered to Craft Store were defective and Craft Store rejected the carvings but retained possession of them until debtor refunds the purchase price which was paid in advance. Debtor is in default to Bank and Bank wishes to repossess all the collateralized property of debtor including the rejected carvings. See UCC §2-711(3).

These priority disputes between holders of consensual and non-consensual liens in the property of a debtor are not just questions to be resolved outside of bankruptcy. As we will see, if any of the interested parties files for bankruptcy relief, the questions regarding the validity of the asserted liens and their priority will be very much alive in the bankruptcy case.

Application Exercise 12

Determine the various kinds of possessory liens recognized by statute or common law in the state where you plan to practice. See if your state follows the reasoning of *Charter One Auto Finance* as to the distinction between priority given to common law and statutory possessory liens.

2. The Attorney's Charging Lien

In contrast to the attorney's retaining lien mentioned in the previous section, which authorizes an attorney to retain possession of, but not sell, a client's books, papers, or other properties until the attorney is paid, most states recognize a separate lien, called the attorney's charging lien either by statute, common law, or both (for a good discussion of the distinction between the two liens, see Starks v. Browning, 20 S.W.3d 645, 650 (Tenn. Ct. App. 1999)). The charging lien is a nonpossessory lien imposed on any judgment rendered in the client's favor or on settlement proceeds due to the client in which the attorney has an interest (e.g., an undistributed contingency fee). To enforce the lien in most states, the attorney must give written notice of the lien, record a notice of lien in the designated public records office, and file suit against the client to enforce the lien. Often the attorney's retainer agreement with the client will include a notice of the lien, using language similar to that in Exhibit 2.4.

EXHIBIT 2.4   **Notice of Attorney's Charging Lien in Retainer Agreement**

The parties agree that the attorney hereby claims a lien on any and all property of the client that is or may come into the possession of the attorney in connection with this representation and on any judgment or settlement amount that is or may become payable to the client as a result of this representation.

3. The Healthcare Services Lien

Most states authorize a **healthcare services lien** to be asserted by a wide range of licensed healthcare professionals (e.g., physicians, dentists, optometrists, therapists) and providers (e.g., hospitals, clinics, EMS services, rehabilitation services) against any claim or cause of action that the patient may have against a third party who may be liable to the patient for injuries related to the healthcare service provided. The lien goes by various names in different states: medical lien, hospital lien, or personal injury lien, to name a few. The lien is satisfied out of the proceeds of any judgment, award (as by arbitration), or settlement that the patient receives from the third party. Typically, a limit is imposed on the percentage of the patient's recovery that the lienholders as a class can take (e.g., 40 percent). Though the procedures for enforcing the healthcare services lien vary considerably among the states, the claimant is typically required to file or record a verified (sworn) statement setting forth the name and address of the patient; the name and address of the operator of the claimant; the dates of the patient's treatment or admission and discharge; the amount claimed to be due for the healthcare or hospital care provided; and to the best of the claimant's knowledge, the names and addresses of those claimed by such patient to be liable for damages arising from the patient's illness or injuries. The statement must be filed or recorded in a designated public office (e.g., the county recorder's office or the county trustee's office for the county in which the services were provided) within a designated period of time (e.g., no later than 30 days after the services were provided).

Notice of the lien must then be given to each person believed to be liable on account of the illness or injury, and to the patient or the patient's attorney, usually by providing them with a copy of the sworn statement asserting the lien. Such notice can be mailed by certified or registered mail or hand delivered. At this point, the lien has been properly created and perfected. Thereafter, no settlement, judgment, or award resulting from the patient's claim against the responsible third party is free of the lien unless the lien holder joins in the settlement or executes a release of the lien.

If the healthcare professional or provider fails to file the lien in a timely manner or otherwise fails to follow the prescribed procedures to create and perfect it, that entity will be deemed to have waived the rights to the lien for the amounts it/he could have asserted in it (but not for charges for future services). Of course, a healthcare services lien can be granted by the patient by contract at any time, in which case a waiver will not be an issue.

For example, assume a person is involved in a car accident and receives medical services from the local hospital at a total cost of $10,000. The patient plans to file suit against the other driver. If the hospital for some reason fails to file and perfect its lien in a timely manner, it has waived the statutory or common law lien. However, the hospital may include the lien in the contract that the patient signs as part of the patient services rendered. Or, after waiver has occurred, the hospital may negotiate a contractual lien with the patient. The patient may do this to keep the hospital from filing suit against him to collect the amount owed while the suit against the other driver is still pending.

If the patient accepts any payment on the claim against the third party without obtaining a release or satisfaction of the healthcare services lien, the lien holder is entitled to enforce the lien by judicial action. In most states, that suit may be against the patient, the patient's attorney, or any other creditor of the patient who received proceeds impressed with the lien.

4. Mechanics' and Materialman's Liens on Real Property

A **mechanics' and materialman's lien** (sometimes called a **construction lien** or **supplier's lien**) is a nonpossessory lien that can be placed on real property to secure payment to one who has performed labor on the property (the mechanic) or supplied materials (the materialman) to it. For convenience, we will refer to it as the mechanics' lien. The mechanics' lien is typically asserted by contractors (including both general contractors and subcontractors), laborers, and suppliers of materials for the job. In some states, surveyors, architects, and engineers who have worked on the project may also be entitled to lien protection.

For example, assume that Santiago's Concrete Service (SCS) enters a contract with Adams Construction Company (ACC) to pour concrete slabs for a house that ACC is building for Sofia Rodriguez. SCS supplies the concrete, pours the slabs, and sends ACC an invoice for its work. However, a dispute has arisen between ACC and Sofia and ACC tells SCS it does not have the money to pay SCS until that dispute is cleared up. To protect itself, SCS files a mechanics' lien on Sofia's lot where the concrete was poured.

State law varies in the procedures for creating a mechanics' lien. In most states, the contractor or supplier wishing to assert the lien must send a written notice of nonpayment to the owner of the property and the general contractor within some specified time frame. Let's assume the law of the state where Sofia's property is located requires the formal notice of nonpayment to be sent "within 90 days of the last day of the month when the goods or services were supplied," which is a typical provision. The notice of nonpayment that SCS sends to Sofia might look like what you see in Exhibit 2.5.

EXHIBIT 2.5   **Notice of Nonpayment**

NOTICE OF NONPAYMENT

TO: Sofia Rodriguez, Owner
   Address

   Adams Construction Company, General Contractor
   Address

FROM: Santiago's Concrete Service, Claimant
      Address

Pursuant to Yourstate Statutory Code §66-11-101, et seq., claimant hereby gives notice that it provided labor and materials for the improvement of real property located at 2100 Cactus Lane, Capital City, Yourstate as described in the instrument of record in Book 897, Page 455, Register's Office for Capital County, Yourstate and more particularly described as follows:

[Property description]

The labor and material provided were as described in the subcontract between claimant and Adams Construction Company dated January 30, YR-1, and consisted of the delivery of concrete to the construction site located on the property and the construction of 2 concrete pads on the property. The claim of claimant for the labor and material provided totals $15,000. The claim of claimant for the labor and material provided remains unpaid.

The last day that claimant performed labor or provided materials was February 25, YR-1.

Dated this _____ day of April, YR-1

Santiago's Concrete Service

By:_____

Raymond Santiago, Owner

Next, the contractor or supplier must file (the statute may say "record" or "register") his notice of lien or abstract of lien in a designated public records office (often the office where land records are recorded or filed) and send a copy of it (usually by registered or certified mail) to the owner, general contractor, and any other claimant of record (e.g., a bank holding a mortgage on the property). A typical state statute provides that the notice of lien or abstract of lien must be filed "within 90 days after work on the project has been substantially completed or the contract terminated." The notice of lien filed or recorded by SCS might look like Exhibit 2.6.

EXHIBIT 2.6   **Notice of Lien**

NOTICE OF LIEN

Santiago's Concrete Service ("SCS"), a sole proprietorship owned by Raymond Santiago of Capital City, Yourstate, having furnished labor and materials to improve the real property described herein pursuant to a contract with Adams Construction Company ("ACC"), for the purpose of giving notice of and/or perfecting a lien on real property and improvements to secure the amount of its claim pursuant to Yourstate Statutory Code §66-11-101, et seq., through its duly authorized officer or representative, states:

That SCS claims a lien upon all interests to which it is entitled under law in the following property situated in Capital County, Yourstate to-wit:

[Property description]
This property is also known as 2100 Cactus Lane, Capital City, Columbiana and is described in the instrument of record in Book 897, Page 455, Register's Office for Capital County, Yourstate.

That, based on information and belief, the owner of the above-described property is Sofia Rodriguez.

That, to the extent allowable under law, a lien is hereby claimed to secure an indebtedness of $15,000 for labor and materials furnished relative to the above-described real property and improvements thereon and/or owed under SCS's contract with ACC. This amount includes amounts owed under the original subcontract between SCS and ACC. This lien is also claimed to secure any other allowable interest or service charges, as well as expenses relating to the recording of this Notice in the Register's Office for Capital County, Yourstate. The last day which RCS supplied labor or materials under its contract with ACC relative to this property was February 25, YR-1.

RCS reserves the right to amend this notice of lien.

Filed this 10th day of September, YR-1

SANTIAGO'S CONCRETE SERVICE

By:_____

Raymond Santiago, Owner

[Notarization]

Once the notice of lien has been duly filed, it is only good for a certain number of days. In many states, a mechanics' lien created by a subcontractor is good for only 90 days. The same lien created by a general contractor may be good for a longer period, up to a year. What that means is that the party who has created the lien must file suit to enforce the lien before it expires. And the suit to enforce the lien, like the judicial foreclosure on a consensual mortgage, asks the court for an order directing the sale of the property and distribution of proceeds in order of priority to the various creditors. It is not unusual for multiple mechanics' liens to be filed on a parcel where several subcontractors have not been paid. The question of priority among multiple holders of such a lien is a question of who was first to perfect their mechanics' lien.

As with consensual security interests in personal property and mortgages on real property, a mechanics' lien must be created and attach before it can be perfected. There is wide variation among the states as to when the mechanics' lien attaches to the improved realty. In some states, the lien comes into existence and attaches as soon as the contract for services or materials is executed. In other states, it comes into existence the moment services are actually provided or materials delivered to the real property. In some other states, the lien comes into existence only when the contractor or supplier asserting the lien gives the owner and contractor (if it is a subcontractor asserting the lien) formal notice of nonpayment. And in still other states, the lien does not arise until the contractor or supplier files (registers or records) the required notice of lien in the county or city land records office (or other designated local or state office) where the improved property is located and gives formal notice to the owner and other appropriate parties of the filing. There is also considerable variation among the states as to how a mechanics' lien is perfected. In most states, the lien is deemed perfected when the notice of lien is properly filed (recorded or registered) in the proper county or city office of land records and served on the owner and other appropriate parties. However, if the holder of the lien does not thereafter file suit to enforce the lien within the statutorily allowed time after filing (e.g., 90 days for a subcontractor or supplier, one year for a general contractor), the lien will have no priority at all and will be unenforceable for any purpose. Both the creation and perfection are forfeited. In a minority of states, the holder of the lien must actually file the lawsuit to enforce the lien in order for it to be deemed perfected.

Application Exercise 13

Determine how a mechanics' lien is created and enforced under the laws of the state where you plan to practice. When is it deemed to exist? How is it perfected?

A serious question arises regarding what priority a properly created and perfected mechanics' lien has against an existing and properly perfected consensual mortgage on the liened property. Assume that Sofia had borrowed money from Bank on March 1, YR-1, and granted Bank a mortgage in the property that was properly recorded in the land records office that same day, perfecting it. When SCS files its notice of lien at any time after March 1, YR-1, and files suit to enforce it within the statutory time allowed, common sense might suggest that its lien on the property will be junior to the previously created and perfected mortgage in favor of Bank. But that is not necessarily the outcome here. It depends on the language of the controlling statute.

Mechanics' lien statutes commonly provide that such a lien, once created, "relates back to the date when the services or materials were first supplied." If that is the case, then the mechanics' lien of SCS in the preceding example will be treated as having attached and been perfected not when the notice of lien was filed or on the date the lawsuit to enforce the lien was filed, but on February 25, YR-1, prior to the creation of the Bank's mortgage. This **relation back** feature of a mechanics' lien is not recognized in all states, and where it is not, the mechanics' lien will only have priority from the date it is perfected. In other states the relation back feature is present but cannot attain priority over a previously perfected construction loan.

In other states, the relation back feature is present and goes all the way back, not to the date the contractor first performed work on the site, but to "the effective date of the lienor's contract" or "to the visible commencement of [any] operations" on the site. But usually these generous relation back features are available only for general contractors or architects, not subcontractors or suppliers. In any state, whatever date the mechanics' lien is deemed to be effective and perfected, it will defeat a prior unperfected mortgage or other unsecured claim to the property. In any event, the relation back feature of statutory liens can create some dramatic priority clashes.

Application Exercise 14

Determine if the mechanics' lien statute of the state where you plan to practice contains a relation back feature.

Real property owned by the federal, state, or local government is normally not subject to attachment by mechanics' lien — a sovereign immunity concept. And state statutory liens cannot be asserted in federally funded construction projects. To protect subcontractors and suppliers on federal projects, where the contract price exceeds $100,000, the Miller Act, 40 U.S.C. §3131, requires general contractors performing public works projects to provide a performance bond (sometimes called a performance and payment bond) guaranteeing the faithful performance of the job and payment of all labor and materials obligations to subcontractors and suppliers on the project. Many state and municipal governments similarly require contractors on public works projects to be bonded.

In some states, mechanics' liens may be available to those who have contributed labor or materials to the improvement of personal property.

5. Lien Lis Pendens

A **lien lis pendens** (lien pending the suit) is a statutory lien that may be created in favor of one having a claim against a particular parcel of real property. The purpose of the lien is to put potential purchasers of the property and creditors on formal notice of the lien holder's claim against the property until such time as a lawsuit regarding that claim can be litigated in court. This lien is not available against personal property.

In most states, to create a lien lis pendens, the claimant must file an abstract (or notice) of lien lis pendens in the designated public office (usually the county office where land records are filed or recorded). The abstract typically must contain the names of the parties to the suit, a description of the real estate affected, its ownership, and a brief statement of the nature of the claim and the amount of the lien sought to be fixed. The lawsuit regarding the claim is normally filed simultaneously with the abstract so that the abstract can reference the pending suit. Some states require the lawsuit to be filed before the abstract; others require the suit to be filed within a stated number of days after the abstract is filed (e.g., five days).

The filing or recording of the abstract or notice puts the world on constructive notice of the lien holder's claim to the property and has the practical effect of creating a cloud on the title to the property, preventing its sale or further encumbrance, until a lawsuit to enforce the lien can be filed and litigated.

A lien lis pendens can only be filed when the lien holder has a claim to an interest in the property encumbered with the lien. It cannot be filed against any real property owned by the person with whom the lien holder has a dispute just because there is a dispute, and it cannot be used to secure property in a contract or tort action in which the property is not in dispute.

Assertion of a constructive trust in real property as a result of theft or fraud is a common basis for filing a lien lis pendens. A **constructive trust** is an involuntary trust declared by a court to exist in (real or personal) property owned or controlled by one person who must then hold it for the benefit of another in order to prevent an injustice. Other common grounds for assertion of a lien lis pendens are a genuine dispute over ownership, fraudulent conveyance, and enforcement of an equitable vendor's lien.

Assume Abelard Mendoza is owner of Mendoza Construction. His bookkeeper, Hilda Montgomery, embezzles funds from the company over a period of years before being discovered and fired. Mendoza files suit against Montgomery to recover. He learns in discovery that Montgomery used the embezzled funds to purchase a parcel of real property and Mendoza amends his complaint to allege that Montgomery holds title to the parcel in a constructive trust for his benefit. Mendoza's lawyer may simultaneously file an abstract of lien lis pendens as seen in Exhibit 2.7.

EXHIBIT 2.7	**Abstract of Lien Lis Pendens**

IN THE CAPITAL COUNTY YOURSTATE CIRCUIT COURT

ABELARD MENDOZA, d/b/a   )
MENDOZA CONSTRUCTION   )
    Plaintiff   )
    v.   )   DOCKET NO. 15-98777
HILDA MONTGOMERY   )
    Defendant   )

ABSTRACT OF LIEN LIS PENDENS

Pursuant to Yourstate Statutory Code §66-10-212, notice is hereby given of a suit filed in the Circuit Court for Capital County, Yourstate bearing Case No.15-98777, where Abelard Mendoza, d/b/a Mendoza Construction is the Plaintiff, and Hilda Montgomery is the Defendant (the "Lawsuit"). A certified copy of the complaint in the Lawsuit is attached to this Abstract.

The Lawsuit is a complaint on behalf of Plaintiff alleging embezzlement and theft of funds which Plaintiff alleges were wrongfully used by Defendant to purchase the real property described below entitling Plaintiff to have a constructive trust declared in that real property for the amount of his funds used to purchase it.

The real property that is the subject of the Lawsuit is located at 765 Western Heights Blvd. in Capital City, Yourstate and is more particularly described as follows:

[Legal description of property]

Plaintiff is asserting a lien lis pendens upon the property in the amount of its claim against Defendant totaling $100,000 plus any prejudgment interest that may be awarded in the Lawsuit.

Respectfully submitted,

_____

Carlton W. Fisk,
Attorney for Plaintiff

The holder of a lien lis pendens has no right per se to foreclose on the lien. The claimant's rights in the property will be litigated in the lawsuit filed and are subject to the court's ruling. The owner of the property may sell or encumber the property after the lien lis pendens is created and before the lawsuit is over, unless the court issues a restraining order or a prejudgment attachment, freezing title to the property pending the suit. However, any purchaser or mortgagee will take title subject to the senior claim of the lien holder in the property.

6. Tax Liens

A **tax lien** is one imposed by law on the property of the delinquent taxpayer in favor of the governmental taxing authority to secure payment of the taxes owed as well as interest and penalties assessed on the delinquent tax. Tax liens operate in favor of the federal, state, and local governments.

The Federal Tax Lien

A **federal tax lien** can be imposed for nonpayment of income, estate, gift, excise, or other taxes owed to the federal government. The Federal Tax Lien Statute is found at 26 U.S.C. §§6321–6323. Section 6321 states:

> If any person liable to pay any tax neglects or refuses to pay the same after demand, the amount (including any interest, additional amount, addition to tax, or assessable penalty, together with any costs that may accrue in addition thereto) shall be a lien in favor of the United States upon all property and rights to property, whether real or personal, belonging to such person.

The tax lien does not arise until an assessment is made by the IRS (§6201), sometimes following an audit of the taxpayer's tax return. Once the tax liability has been assessed, the IRS sends the taxpayer a Notice and Demand for Payment, essentially a formal bill telling the taxpayer how much tax is owed. The notice will advise the taxpayer that he has ten days within which to pay the assessment. If the taxpayer fails to pay within the ten-day period, the tax lien attaches automatically to all real and personal property owned by the taxpayer and to all the taxpayer's "rights to property" (e.g., accounts receivables, or salary). The date of attachment is retroactive to the date of the assessment. Internal Revenue Code section 6322 (26 U.S.C. §6322) provides:

> Unless another date is specifically fixed by law, the lien imposed by section 6321 shall arise at the time the assessment is made and shall continue until the liability for the amount so assessed (or a judgment against the taxpayer arising out of such liability) is satisfied or becomes unenforceable by reason of lapse of time.

The U.S. Supreme Court, in Glass City Bank v. United States, 326 U.S. 265 (1945), held that the federal tax lien applies not only to property owned by the taxpayer at the time of the assessment, but to all property acquired by the taxpayer during the life of the lien. This is the important after-acquired property scope of a federal tax lien. A federal tax lien has an effective term of ten years and can be renewed for another ten-year term during a period of up to 30 days following expiration of the original term (26 U.S.C. §6323).

As between the federal government and the taxpayer, the lien is effective as of the date of attachment. However, to perfect the tax lien and thus attain priority status over other subsequent claimants to the taxpayer's property, the federal government must properly file a Notice of Federal Tax Lien (NFTL). 26 U.S.C. §6323 allows states to designate the public office where the NFTL is to be filed, and many states have adopted the Revised Uniform Federal Tax Lien Registration Act or the more recent Uniform Federal Lien Registration Act, which make such designations (e.g., NFTLs on personal property of corporations, partnerships, and trusts to be filed in the Office of the Secretary of State; NFTLs on real property to be filed in the public office for filing land records for the county in which the property is located). Absent designation by the state of a specific public office for filing a NFTL, it is to be filed with the U.S. District Court for the federal district in which the property is located.

It is important to understand that although the effective date of attachment of a federal tax lien is retroactive to the date of the assessment, the effective date of perfection of the lien will be the date the notice of lien is properly filed, not the date of assessment.

If the taxpayer wishes to sell property subject to a federal tax lien, he can apply to the IRS for a discharge of tax lien on that property so the buyer can take free and clear of the lien. Obviously the IRS is not going to agree to that unless the taxpayer/seller agrees that the IRS will receive all or some agreed part of the proceeds of sale. A discharge certificate is also issued when the taxpayer pays off the indebtedness (26 U.S.C. §6325). The IRS can also agree to withdraw a lien from property if the taxpayer consents to pay the indebtedness in agreed-upon installments. The IRS can also agree to subordinate its tax lien in certain property to another creditor.

The federal government may **levy** (execute) on its tax lien without court action by issuing a notice of intent to levy to the taxpayer. The notice of intent to levy must be provided to the taxpayer at least 30 days before the levy occurs (26 U.S.C. §6331). The federal tax levy can also include a garnishment or wage attachment.

The IRS maintains a helpful Web site explaining how the federal tax lien works at www.irs.gov/Businesses/Small-Businesses-&-Self-Employed/Understanding-a-Federal-Tax-Lien.

State and Local Tax Liens

State and local governments may also assert tax liens on property of a taxpayer for the failure to pay state income taxes or state or local property taxes on real or personal property. Probably the most common scenario giving rise to a state or local tax lien is a property owner's failure to pay the property tax on real estate. In most states the procedure for creating and perfecting the lien is similar to that used in federal tax liens. The government entity asserting the lien must give notice to the taxpayer of the delinquency, identify the property in question, state the amount owed, provide a due date, and state the intent to subject the real property in question to a tax lien. The notice must also go to any mortgage holder of record in the property since its interest may be affected by a foreclosure on the tax lien. If the debt is not paid by the due date, the government must then file a notice of lien with the appropriate public office, perfecting the lien.

In many states, the state tax lien is given superpriority status over not just subsequent claims against the property but also over preexisting, perfected security interests, whether consensual or non-consensual. And 26 U.S.C. §6323(b) allows states to assert priority of a state or local tax lien over a previously existing federal tax lien. In states electing to exercise that priority, a statute such as the one shown in Exhibit 2.8 is common.

EXHIBIT 2.8	**Typical State Statute Claiming Superpriority Status for Tax Lien**

The taxes assessed by the state of Yourstate, a county, or municipality, taxing district, or other local governmental entity, upon any property of whatever kind, and all penalties, interest, and costs accruing thereon, shall become and remain a first lien upon such property from January 1 of the year for which such taxes are assessed.

If payment is not made after the required notice has been given to the debtor and the notice of tax lien filed, the state or local government may foreclose or execute on its lien. In some states, the government entity is permitted to proceed with non-judicial self-help foreclosure or seizure of the burdened property. In others, a judicial foreclosure is required, which, we have learned, means the government must file a lawsuit and obtain a court order allowing sale. There usually is a statutory right of redemption in favor of the taxpayer either up until the time of sale or, in some states, for a designated period after the sale (e.g., one year).

7. The Lien for Unpaid Child Support

As part of the Personal Responsibility and Work Opportunity Reconciliation Act of 1996 (PRWORA), Congress required the states, as a condition to receiving federal funding for job training and other programs intended to reform public assistance programs in this country, to establish new procedures for enforcing child support orders. The statute, 42 U.S.C. §666(a)(4), now requires all states to have laws or procedures pursuant to which child support arrearages become liens, by operation of law, against all real and personal property owned by an obligor who either resides or owns property in that state.

8. The Judicial Lien

In the next chapter we will consider pre-bankruptcy collection efforts a creditor can take against a debtor against whom he obtains a final money judgment. As part of that study we will examine the various ways that the judgment creditor can execute on the property of the debtor in order to satisfy the judgment focusing on the writ of execution, writ of garnishment, and judgment lien on real property. With variations in state law, we will see that at some point in the execution process the judgment creditor is recognized as having a **judicial lien**, essentially a non-consensual security interest in the debtor's property on which he is executing.

Case Preview

Muggli Dental Studio v. Taylor

Significantly, UCC §9-317(a)(2) gives the judicial lien creditor priority status over any creditor holding a prior but unperfected security interest in the property executed on. As you read Muggli Dental Studio v. Taylor, consider the following questions.

1. Who was the judgment creditor in this case and what property of the debtor was executed on?
2. Who held the competing consensual security interest in the same property and why was it not perfected?
3. What was the basis of the argument of the holder of the consensual security interest in the property that the execution on the property by the judgment creditor was insufficient to create a judicial lien on it?

Muggli Dental Studio v. Taylor
142 Wis. 2d 696, 419 N.W.2d 322 (Ct. App. 1987)

NETTESHEIM, Judge.

Following a court trial, a judgment was entered in favor of the Muggli Dental Studio (the studio) against Dr. Ted Taylor. An execution was then issued against Dr. Taylor's personal property and the Manitowoc County Sheriff's Department levied against such property. This appeal relates to the sufficiency of the levy by the sheriff and whether the levy operated to create a priority lien in favor of the studio. The trial court ruled against Dr. Taylor on these questions. Dr. Taylor appeals pro se. We reject Dr. Taylor's arguments and affirm the trial court's post-judgment order.

Dr. Taylor first contends that the levy was ineffective to accomplish a seizure of his property. He cites sec. 815.19, Stats., which provides in part that "[p]ersonal property shall be bound from the time it is seized." In Brown v. Pratt, 4 Wis. 513 (1855), the supreme court held that a levy upon personal property is not valid unless the officer has the property in his view and under his control. Id. at 519. However, the effectiveness of a levy will not be defeated by failing to remove the property from the site of the execution. See Johnson v. Iron Belt Mining Co., 78 Wis. 159, 162-63, 47 N.W. 363, 364 (1890).

Testimony at the post-judgment proceeding established that sheriff's deputy Edward Stuhr went through a checklist to assure himself that the items to be levied upon were, in fact, present. Officer Stuhr then informed Dr. Taylor that the items should be considered as tagged and seized and were not to be disposed of in any manner. The trial court determined that the officer's actions sufficiently exerted control over the property such that a seizure occurred.

We conclude that a determination of whether a levy is legally effective to bind the property presents this court with a mixed question of fact and law. We separate the factual findings of a trial court from the conclusions of law and apply the appropriate standard to each. Geis v. City of Fond du Lac, 140 Wis. 2d 205, 209, 409 N.W.2d 148, 150 (Ct. App. 1987). A trial court's findings of fact will not be disturbed on appeal unless they are clearly erroneous. Laribee v. Laribee, 138 Wis. 2d 46, 54, 405 N.W.2d 679, 683 (Ct. App. 1987). However, an appellate court must decide questions of law without deference to the trial court's decision. Cobb State Bank v. Nelson, 141 Wis. 2d 1, 5, 413 N.W.2d 644, 645-46 (Ct. App. 1987).

The testimony established that Deputy Stuhr had Dr. Taylor's property in his view and under his control at the time of the alleged levy. The testimony also established that the officer informed Dr. Taylor that the property was considered seized and not subject to disposition. These findings are not clearly erroneous. See sec. 805.17(2), Stats.

We also conclude that these facts sufficiently establish an effective levy for purposes of sec. 815.19, Stats. Removal of the seized property from the situs of the execution is not necessary. See *Johnson*, 78 Wis. at 162-63, 47 N.W. at 364.

Dr. Taylor next alleges that the lien created in favor of Muggli by the levy does not have priority over a security interest held by Dr. Taylor's father (Taylor, Sr.). In 1982, the Citizens Lakeshore Bank obtained a security interest in Dr. Taylor's property by virtue of a financing statement filed at that time. Prior to the levy in this case, Taylor, Sr. paid this debt for Dr. Taylor. However, Taylor, Sr.'s financing statement was not filed until January 2, 1987. The levy in this case occurred on December 9, 1986.

When it is the intention of the parties to create a security interest, the case is governed by ch. 409, Stats. Clark Oil and Refining Co. v. Liddicoat, 65 Wis. 2d 612, 620, 223 N.W.2d 530, 534-35 (1974); sec. 409.102(1)(a), Stats. Chapter 409 sets out rules of priority. A lien creditor has priority over a person holding an unperfected security interest. Sec. 409.301(1)(b), Stats. To perfect a security interest in the property in question, a financing statement must be filed or the collateral must be in the possession of the secured party. Sec. 409.302, Stats.

Here, because Taylor, Sr.'s financing statement was not filed until after the levy of execution by the studio and also because Taylor, Sr. did not have the collateral in his possession, Muggli, the lien creditor, has priority over the holder of the unperfected security interest. *Clark Oil*, 65 Wis. 2d at 621, 223 N.W.2d at 535; sec. 409.301(1)(b), Stats. Taylor, Sr.'s subsequent perfection has no impact on these priority rules. . . .

Accordingly, we affirm the order of the trial court.

Post-Case Follow-Up

This case raises the question of whether the officer serving the writ of execution has exercised sufficient dominion and control over the property for there to have been an effective levy on the property at all. In most cases the executing officer will take actual physical possession of the property and remove it to a secure place for storage until sale. For items too large or heavy to move, stickers or tags will be placed on the property declaring the levy and seizure. But when items that are removable are left in place by the executing officer, the issue of whether such constructive possession results in an effective levy is raised. Some jurisdictions agree with *Muggli Dental Studio* that actual removal of the property is not essential to levy and that constructive possession can be recognized. See, e.g., U.S. Leather, Inc. v. Mitchell Mfg. Group, Inc., 276 F.3d 782 (6th Cir. 2002) (constructive possession of physical assets of business by obtaining consent of debtor's attorney that property would be left in place subject to later sale by executing officer); Harbour Towne Marina Ass'n v. Geile (In re Fees of Court Officer), 564 N.W.2d 509 (Mich. App. 1997) (constructive possession of boat left in dock where executing officer attached a writ of execution to the boat, gave a copy to the marina manager, seized the ship's log, and prepared a notice of sale); and Credit Bureau of Broken Bow v. Moninger, 284 N.W.2d 855 (Neb. 1979) (officer serving writ placing hand on truck and announcing in the presence of debtor, "I execute on the pickup for the County of Custer" held sufficient levy). Other jurisdictions require the officer to either take actual possession or to retain a custodian on site to ensure the property is not removed. See, e.g., New York City Marshal's Handbook, Chapter II, Section 4-2.

Muggli Dental Studio v. Taylor: Real Life Applications

1. The court in *Muggli* says that a determination of whether a levy is legally effective to bind the property presents this court with a mixed question of fact and law. What are the questions of fact subject to review in *Muggli*? What is the question(s) of law to be decided?
2. What would be the result in this case if the debtor's father, Taylor Sr., had the collateral in his possession when the writ of execution was served?
3. The debtor's father in this case, Taylor Sr., apparently paid the secured indebtedness his son owed to Citizens' Lakeshore Bank (CLB), the original creditor, then took a security interest in the same collateral to secure his son's new indebtedness to him. If Taylor Sr. had not paid off that secured debt to CLB, would Muggli's judicial lien have been deemed superior to the security interest of CLB in the collateral? Why do you think the father paid off the indebtedness to CLB? If the father and son had come to you the day after the final judgment in favor of Muggli against the debtor had been entered and they had advised you of the security interest of CLB in the collateral, the newly entered final judgment, and

the debtor's need to retain possession and use of his collateral, what would you have advised? Would it matter whether the debtor was current in his payments to CLB or in default on that obligation and in danger of repossession by CLB?

4. Assume that a week after the deputy served the writ of execution on the debtor, Dr. Taylor, and informed him that "the items should be considered as tagged and seized and were not to be disposed of in any manner," Dr. Taylor is happily continuing to use the collateral in his dental practice. Your client, a new dentist, visits Dr. Taylor's practice that day and, with no knowledge of the levy, purchases all the collateral for use in starting up her own dental practice. When a priority dispute over the collateral arises between Muggli Dental, claiming to be a judicial lien creditor, and your client, who will prevail? See UCC §9-320(a). If your client loses, what are your client's causes of action against Dr. Taylor?

When a debtor files for bankruptcy relief and a bankruptcy trustee is appointed, §544 of the Bankruptcy Code grants that trustee the status of a judicial lien creditor in all the property of the debtor. Called the "strong-arm clause" of the Bankruptcy Code, this section means the bankruptcy trustee will take property of the debtor for the benefit of the bankruptcy estate over the claim of any creditor asserting a prior security interest in the same property if that creditor's security interest in the property was not perfected prior to filing of the bankruptcy petition. We'll look at the strong-arm clause in much more detail later.

Another judicial lien question that arises in a bankruptcy case is whether such a lien, even though valid under state law, can be set aside under any circumstances. We will deal with these questions when we begin our study of how a consumer bankruptcy case proceeds, but you cannot make an argument for your client in the bankruptcy case unless you understand what judicial liens are and when they attach under the relevant state law.

9. The Vendor's Lien on Real Property

A **vendor's lien** (also called a **mortgage lien**), a lien recognized in some states by statute or common law or both, is afforded to sellers of real property on the real property sold in the event the buyer fails to make payment when due. It is referred to as an equitable lien or special lien and is not dependent on the seller retaining possession of the property.

This lien scenario arises most commonly where the seller of land self-financed the sale by agreeing to accept direct payment(s) from the buyer rather than requiring the buyer to obtain financing to pay the seller in full at closing, but failed to have the buyer convey a consensual mortgage in the property to the seller to secure payment (a purchase money mortgage). It might also arise where an owner of land agreed to convey a mortgage in the land to a creditor and then refused to cooperate in finalizing the mortgage. Or it might arise when one in possession of property and believing herself to be the owner makes permanent improvements to property, enhancing its value, and then is dispossessed by the true owner.

Where it is recognized, this lien authorizes the holder to pursue recovery of the real property in the hands not only of the buyer but also of anyone who has purchased the property from the buyer with actual or constructive notice that the purchase price to the seller has not been paid. The lien is typically created by recording the contract of sale or other documentation establishing the transaction and obligation in the county office where land records are to be filed.

Assume you have an owner of real property very eager to sell it. The owner has found a buyer, but the buyer is unable to qualify for a traditional mortgage loan from any lender, owing to poor credit or questions about whether the buyer's projected income flow is sufficient. The owner decides to assume the risk that the lenders will not and agrees to self-finance this purchase by the buyer. However, the owner fails to require the buyer to grant the owner a purchase money mortgage. If the buyer defaults, then the owner may be able to assert the equitable vendor's lien to retake possession of the property notwithstanding the absence of a mortgage. If the buyer has not only defaulted but also transferred an interest in the property to someone else (e.g., has resold it or granted a security interest in it to a third party), the owner may be able nonetheless to assert the lien against the property in the hands of that third party if the owner can show that the third party knew or should have known that a balance was still owed to the owner on the initial sale at the time it received an interest in the property.

In the personal property context, equitable liens are essentially identical to constructive trusts and arise under the same circumstances.

D. PREDATORY LENDING TO CONSUMER DEBTORS

The **payday loan** — also called variously a **cash advance, check advance, postdated check loan, deferred deposit check loan,** or **deferred presentment loan** — has become a major source of debt, primarily for low-income consumers who have little or no savings and cannot qualify for a traditional bank loan. The payday loan

Payday loans have become a major source of debt. *dcwcreations / Shutterstock.com*

is a short-term loan for a small amount under terms that charge the borrower an astronomically high interest rate, sometimes camouflaged as a transaction fee or finance charge and that grants the lender access to the borrower's checking account to obtain payment.

Assume Marta needs $100 cash right now but her checking account is empty and she doesn't get paid again until the end of the month, 14 days away. She goes to a check-cashing business and writes a check payable to the company for $115 and receives a cash loan of $100. Marta is told to postdate the check to the last day of the month and the company promises to hold and not cash the $115 check until that date, when her next paycheck will be deposited. Fourteen days later the company cashes the $115 check. The check pays them back the $100 they loaned Marta plus $15, which they receive as "interest" or "fees" or "finance charges."

Marta just paid $15 to borrow $100 for 14 days. That's a full 15 percent charge for using someone else's money for only two weeks. Annualized, Marta is paying 391 percent per annum interest for that loan. And, if Marta extends or rolls over her loan for another 10- or 14-day term, the same charge is imposed a second time. If Marta asks for another 14 days to pay back the $100 she borrowed, the charge will be an additional $15 for a total of $30 paid in interest and fees to borrow $100 for 28 days. That's a full 30 percent charge to use someone else's money for less than a month. If she rolls over the loan a second time (four out of five payday loans are rolled over at least once), for an additional 14 days, the finance charge goes to 45 percent of the amount borrowed, and so on. The loan shark in the alley could do no better.

Closely related to the payday loan is the **car title loan**, where the consumer conveys a security interest in his or her vehicle to the lender in exchange for a short-term loan at a triple-digit rate of annualized interest. A study released by the CFPB in May 2016 found that one in three car title loans are defaulted on and one in five result in repossession of the collateralized vehicle.

In the mid-1990s there were only a few hundred payday and car title loan companies scattered around the country. Today there are thousands of storefront operations and online sites as well. Most commonly, store locations are in or near low-income neighborhoods and, until recently, around military bases. In the 2007 Defense Authorization Act, Congress capped rates on such loans made to military personnel at 36 percent per annum, resulting in a migration of payday and title loan companies away from military bases. In addition, the Servicemembers Civil Relief Act (SCRA), U.S.C.A. App. §§501 et seq., authorizes military personnel going on active duty to reduce interest due on pre–active duty monetary obligations to 6 percent per annum if active duty would materially affect their ability to pay a higher interest rate.

As payday loan businesses proliferated, legislation was passed in many states specifically exempting such businesses from state usury statutes, which would otherwise control small loans and limit them to the lower double-digit range (e.g., 25 percent per annum). These statutory or regulatory exemptions are called **safe harbor provisions** for the benefit of the financial services companies operating these businesses. Approximately a dozen states have enacted legislation regulating payday and car title loan companies to some extent, capping the interest rate that can be charged and/or limiting the number of rollovers per customer per year.

Application Exercise 15

Take a look at Virginia's Payday Loan Reform Act (well summarized at www.scc.virginia.gov/bfi/files/pay_guide.pdf). The bill caps interest rates lenders may charge at 36 percent per annum. Lenders must give borrowers two pay periods to repay a loan. Lenders are limited to making one loan at a time to borrowers, who must wait one day after repaying a loan to take out another. Borrowers who take out at least five loans in a six-month period must either wait 45 days before getting another loan or extend the payment term on the fifth loan to two months or more. Anyone taking a two-month extension option has to wait another two months before getting a new loan. An extended payment plan is available once a year, followed by a three-month cooling-off period. Lenders that falsely threaten criminal prosecution for failure to make good on the check used to obtain the loan are subject to a fine three times the cost of the loan. Determine if your state has adopted any statutory or regulatory rules limiting the interest rate or fees these companies can charge or otherwise regulating their behavior.

After releasing its formal research report on payday lending in March 2014 (available online at http://files.consumerfinance.gov/f/201403_cfpb_report_payday-lending.pdf) and its research report on car title loans in May 2016 (available online at http://files.consumerfinance.gov/f/documents/201605_cfpb_single-payment-vehicle-title-lending.pdf), the CFPB in June 2016 released its first proposed formal regulations of these loans. The proposed regulations, to be found at 12 CFR part 1041 when finalized, which were issued subject to public comment and later finalization would require that a lender reasonably determine that the consumer has the ability to repay the loan before making it, limit the number of times a loan can be renewed (three times in most cases) and the number of months in a year the debtor can owe the lender for the loan (nine months in most cases), restrict the making of new loans to a consumer who has or recently had other outstanding loans, require lenders to provide advance notice to the consumer before attempting to withdraw payment from the consumer's account, and prohibit the lender from attempting to withdraw payment from a consumer's account after two consecutive attempts have failed unless the consumer specifically consents to further attempts.

Who Uses Payday Loans?

Though the median income for payday/car title borrowers is less than $25,000 per year, a 2010 investigation by National Public Radio's Planet Money ("Inside a Payday Loan Shop" at www.npr.org/sections/money/2010/05/the_tuesday_podcast_payday_len.html) revealed that a significant number of regular users of payday loan shops are solidly middle class. Payday and car title loans are often justified by the financial services industry as providing a quick, convenient, short-term loan source. However, 80 percent of payday and car title loan customers renew or roll over their loan once or more. In fact, the average payday/car title loan customer takes out a loan nine times per year, a debt trap that keeps such debtors perpetually in debt and quickly paying more in interest and fees than was borrowed.

Application Exercise 16

Do you think the proposed FRCB regulations of payday and car title loans go far enough? Too far? Go to the CFPB web site at www.consumerfinance. gov/ and see if the agency's proposed regulations have been finalized at this time and, if so, how the final language compares to the summary provided in the text.

Payday and car title loans are the best known examples of predatory consumer lending, but there are many others. In a **pawn shop loan**, somewhat similar to the car title loan, the consumer takes out a short-term loan (usually 30 days) and puts up some kind of personal property (e.g., jewelry, gun, computer, appliance, antique) as security for repayment of the loan. The property so collateralized is left in the physical possession of the pawn shop lender (thus it is "pledged"). The loan is made in an amount equal to a reduced value of the property pledged (usually 30 to 50 percent). If the borrower does not repay the loan by the due date, the pawn shop can sell the property for its full value and keep it. If the loan plus accrued interest and other charges (e.g., storage and transaction fees) is paid, the borrower can recover possession of the property pledged. Like other short-term consumer loans, pawn shop loans are often renewed or extended indefinitely with payment of accrued interest.

Buy Here Pay Here used car transactions are often subject to predatory credit terms and questionable business practices. Catering to low-income Americans who cannot qualify for a conventional car loan, these used car dealers offer the convenience of financing a car purchase through the dealer. This may seem like a good deal, except that the interest rate charged is often a multiple of the current rates of conventional loans, often 30 percent per annum or more.

Same as Cash financing offers, seen often in ads for the purchase of furniture, appliances, and other consumer goods, may contain hidden dangers for unsophisticated buyers. Seeming to offer an extended term for payment of the purchase price with no interest charged ("No interest for 24 months! Same as cash!"), the transaction may actually be a deferred interest trap containing a nasty surprise for the consumer. Typically in these transactions, if full payment is not made within the free term, then an interest rate much higher than conventional rates (40 percent per annum is not unusual) is assessed on the entire purchase price (even though a portion of the price has been paid) and the interest due is calculated over the entire period since purchase, including what the consumer thought was the interest-free period. These deals are often criticized as well for not making it clear what the length of the free term actually is and for not disclosing in advance the interest rate to be charged.

Delayed title transactions such as **rent-to-own** (RTO) contracts can pose risks for consumers. In such transactions the contract will provide that title to the property remains with seller until the buyer makes the final lease payment. The obvious risk to the consumer buyer in such a situation is that he is acquiring no equity or ownership interest in the property as he makes the payments. If he defaults at any point during the payment term, the contract is terminated and he receives no refund of payments made. The buyer builds up no equity to which he is entitled upon default as he would be if title was conveyed at the beginning of the transaction and seller retained only a security interest in the property. Consumer advocates argue that RTO transactions should be treated as sales on credit and in the absence of legislation at the federal or state level courts in a few states have so held. See, e.g., Perez v. Rent-A-Center, Inc., 186 N.J. 188, 892 A.2d 1255 (2006).

Chapter Summary

- Most consumer debt is unsecured but consumers do commonly grant creditors consensual security interests in personal or real property to secure debt. The creation and perfection of consensual security interests in personal property are governed by Article 9 of the UCC. Most security interests in personal property are perfected by the filing of financing statement in the appropriate public office. A security interest in personal property that constitutes consumer goods granted to one who sells the goods on credit or who finances the purchase of the goods is a purchase money security interest and is automatically perfected upon attachment.

- Most security agreements authorize the creditor to repossess the collateralized property upon default by the debtor. Repossession may be by self-help so long as it can be accomplished without a threatened or actual breach of the peace. Otherwise the repossession constitutes a conversion of the debtor's property by the creditor and its agents. Repossessed property may be sold by the creditor and the proceeds credited to the expenses of repossession and amounts owed so long as the sale is conducted in a commercially reasonable manner.

- A consensual security interest granted in the debtor's real property is called a mortgage and is created by the execution of a deed of trust or mortgage instrument that must be recorded in the appropriate land records office to perfect the creditor's interest. Priority among competing mortgage holders is controlled by the kind of recording statute in effect in the state where the land lies.

- The mortgage document conveys to the creditor a right of foreclosure or power of sale in the event of default. Some states allow a self-help power of sale foreclosure that requires a notice of foreclosure procedure followed by foreclosure sale and delivery of a trustee's deed to the purchaser. Other states require a judicial foreclosure where the property is sold on court order and delivery of a sheriff's deed. All states recognize an equity of redemption right in the mortgagor that must be exercised before the foreclosure sale. Some states have created a statutory right of redemption in the mortgagor that can be exercised for some stated period following the foreclosure sale. In some states the mortgagee can sue for the deficiency balance following foreclosure while in others the mortgagee must elect to foreclose or sue.

▣ Many consumers enter into consensual surety agreements making themselves primarily liable for the debt of another as by co-signing a promissory note. Others make themselves secondarily liable by signing a guaranty agreement. Some states distinguish between a compensated surety and an accommodation surety for purposes of the availability of the material change in obligation defense.

▣ Non-consensual security interests in the debtor's personal or real property can be created by statutory or common law liens. Most states recognize a number of non-consensual possessory liens in personal property in favor of designated artisans, landlords, warehousemen, buyers of rejected goods who have prepaid, and professionals such as attorneys and accountants. Article 9 grants possessory liens priority over existing consensual liens in the property unless the possessory lien is created by statute that expressly says otherwise.

▣ Non-consensual non-possessory liens recognized in most states include the attorney's charging lien on any judgment rendered in the client's favor or on settlement proceeds due to the client in which the attorney has an interest; a healthcare services lien in favor of healthcare providers on proceeds of any judgment, award, or settlement that the patient receives from a third party; a mechanics' and materialman's lien on real property in favor of those who provide services or materials for the improvement of the realty; and a lien lis pendens in favor of one claim an interest in a particular parcel of real property.

▣ The federal and state governments can impose a non-consensual tax lien on real and personal property of the taxpayer for unpaid taxes. All states recognize the non-consensual child support lien on real and personal property of obligor within the state. One who takes a final judgment against another in a judicial action and properly executes on that judgment against property of the judgment debtor takes a non-consensual judicial lien in the property executed on.

▣ Payday loans, which are short-term loans for a small amount that charge the borrower an astronomically high interest rate, cash advances, car title loans, pawn shop loans, same as cash financing, and rent-to-own transactions have become major sources of consumer debt, particularly for low-income, financially unsophisticated individuals. Most states have imposed very little regulation on payday lenders or the interest and fees they can charge, making the industry a prime example of predatory lending.

Applying the Concepts

1. A friend from college contacts you and advises that he wants to start a repossession business to be named Reliable Property Recovery (RPR). In addition to asking you to set up his new business and advise him on the law controlling repossession, the client asks you to draft a brief set of instructions he can provide to his employees who will actually do the repossessions regarding what they can/should do or not do in certain repossession scenarios. Draft a single page double spaced set of instructions your client can provide his employees.

Your draft should cover giving advance notice to the debtor of the repo; repossessing property left out in the open versus property in a garage or other storage unit versus property located inside a home; entering through open, closed, or locked doors without consent; who can give consent; use of subterfuge, false promises, threats, physical force, or other violence; reacting to questions, objections, or threats from the debtor, family, or neighbors during the repo; and generally when to safely discontinue a repo effort to avoid liability.

2. Gloria Sabatz has been a coin collector all of her life. She now has a coin collection that has been valued at $20,000.

   a. Assume that last year Gloria borrowed $10,000 from Bank and granted Bank a security interest in the coin collection that Bank properly perfected by taking possession of the coin collection. No financing statement was filed. Last month Gloria obtained permission from Bank to exhibit the coin collection at a collector's convention in Atlantic City. While in Atlantic City with the coin collection Gloria decided to borrow $25,000 to purchase an interest in a condo and arranged a loan from Atlantic City Finance (ACF) for such loan which was secured in part by the coin collection. ACF did not take possession of it but did properly file a financing statement reciting its security interest in the coin collection the same day the loan was made. The next day Gloria returned the coin collection to Bank. If Gloria now defaults on both loans, which creditor has the senior claim to the coin collection? See UCC §9-313(a)(c)(d).

   b. Would your answer to Question 2.a change if ACF had filed no financing statement before the coin collection was returned to Bank? Why?

   c. Assume ACF does not file a financing statement and that Gloria never returns the coin collection to Bank. When she defaults on both loans, which creditor has the senior claim to the coin collection? See UCC §9-322(a)(3).

   d. Assume that Bank did not take possession of the coin collection but did properly file a financing statement last year when its loan was made. ACF also filed a financing statement to secure the loan it made last month. Gloria is now in default on the loan from ACF but not on the loan from Bank. Can ACF repossess the coin collection? If ACF does repossess and sell the coin collection is the security interest of Bank in the coin collection extinguished?

   e. Assume that neither Bank nor ACF filed a proper financing statement covering the coin collection or have possession of the coin collection. However, when Gloria defaults on her obligation to ACF, it immediately files a lawsuit and obtains a final judgment by default for the amount owed. It then causes a writ of execution to issue on the final judgment and the sheriff executing the writ seizes the coin collection. As between Bank and ACF, which has the senior claim to it? See UCC §9-322(a)(1).

3. Sally is off to college. With the help of her parents, she arranges for a school loan of $30,000 from Bank to cover her tuition, books, and living expenses for the first year. Monthly payments are to begin five years from the date of the note

and to be completed in five years from the date of the first payment. Bank has Sally sign the promissory note as "Maker" and each of her parents sign as "Co-Maker." Neither Sally nor her parents grant Bank a security interest in any real or personal property in connection with the loan.

    a. Who is properly referred to as the principal debtor on this obligation? Who is properly referred to as a surety on this obligation? Which debtors are primarily liable on the debt?

    b. Assume the first payment on the note is not made as promised. May Bank sue only Sally's parents for the note obligation or must they sue Sally as well?

    c. Assume that, unknown to Sally's parents, Sally contacts Bank shortly before the first payment is due, advises that she will be unable to pay it, and works out an agreement with Bank to extend the payment period on the note from five to ten years. Sally never makes a payment on the note and Bank makes demand on Sally's parents for payment. They are sitting in your office now asking if there is any defense to their obligation to pay this note. What do you tell them?

    d. Assume Sally did not negotiate an extension of the term of the note but did file a Chapter 7 bankruptcy case and discharge her obligation under the note just before the first payment was due. Is Sally's discharge of the obligation in bankruptcy a defense her parents can use? Why or why not?

4. Assume that you represent Sofia Rodriguez, whose home is subject to a mechanics' lien in favor of SCS as discussed in Section C. Assume further that the state notice of lien statute requires filing and notice to others "within 90 days after the project has been substantially completed or the contract terminated," a common requirement. SCS files its notice of lien on September 10, YR-1 as seen in Exhibit 2.6. What issues might arise regarding whether it was timely filed? What information do you need to determine whether SCS timely filed its notice of lien? What if the contractor has filed a notice of completion stating that the project was completed on June 1, YR-1? What if the contractor has filed no notice of completion but has filed a notice of cessation of work stating that all work on the project ceased as of July 1, YR-1?

5. Jack has rented a self-storage unit from Local Storage, Inc. (LSI) and pays $100 per month for the unit. He has a number of possessions stored in his unit including a riding lawn mower he purchased on credit a year ago from City Appliances Company (CAC). CAC took a purchase money security interest in the riding mower and is still owed $1,000. No financing statement was filed by CAC. Four months ago Jack lost his job and is now in arrears to LSI for $400. CAC has properly declared a possessory lien in the mower for all amounts owed to it and still has possession of it. Assume the state's possessory lien statute is based on UCC §7-209. As between LSI and CAC, which creditor has the priority claim to the mower? See UCC §§7-209(c) and 9-309(1).

6. Locate and read Assignment Memorandum #4 and attachments in Appendix D regarding Mid-State Grading. If your instructor so directs, draft the notice of mechanics' lien and letter to the client assigned in that memorandum in conformity with the mechanics' lien laws of the state where you plan to practice.

Collection of Consumer Debt Prior to Bankruptcy

In this chapter we consider methods by which creditors seek to collect consumer debt before a bankruptcy petition is filed by the consumer debtor. Creditors commonly engage in informal pre-judicial debt collection efforts before turning to the judicial system by filing a collection lawsuit. Pre-judicial collection efforts today are more regulated by federal and state laws than in the past and pose certain liability risks for the debt collector, as well as the attorneys engaged in debt collection for clients.

When creditors turn to the judicial system by filing a collection lawsuit, the rules of civil procedure for the applicable jurisdiction will control the timing and procedure of the case. When a final judgment is obtained, execution on the property of the debtor may begin to satisfy the judgment. Every state declares certain property of the debtor to be exempt from execution and the manner in which the debtor owns an interest in non-exempt property may affect the ability of the executing creditor to seize it.

Key Concepts

- Most pre-bankruptcy debt collection activities targeted at consumer debtors are regulated by the Fair Debt Collection Practices Act and analogous state legislation
- Overly aggressive debt collection practices can give rise to various tort causes of action on behalf of the debtor as well as to criminal charges against the debt collector
- The ability of a creditor who obtains a final judgment in a debt collection lawsuit to have the judgment satisfied is impacted by applicable exempt property statutes, rules regarding concurrent ownership of property, and various trust arrangements
- There are a number of different methods for executing on a final judgment, all of which can have ramifications in a later bankruptcy case filed by the judgment debtor
- Every state recognizes a creditor's right to seek the recovery of property of the debtor fraudulently transferred to defeat the creditor's rights in it

Every state recognizes various methods by which non-exempt property of the debtor may be executed on and in this chapter we will examine the most common methods as well as the creditor's right to have prejudgment interest included in the judgment and to collect postjudgment interest. How judgments rendered in one state are enforced in other states where the debtor has assets well be considered as well. Finally, we will examine fraudulent transfer law as it affects debt collection.

A. NON-JUDICIAL DEBT COLLECTION

According to the Consumer Financial Protection Bureau (CFPB), in the aftermath of the housing crisis and Great Recession, approximately 30 million Americans (about 1 in 10) are being pursued by a debt collector on any given day for debt that averages $1,500 per debtor. Debt collection is a big business in America today.

Debt collection practices have historically been subject to a great deal of abuse. Before such practices were prohibited, it was common for creditors or their representatives to harass, embarrass, and humiliate debtors until a bill was paid. Insulting letters were common. Threats were made to sue, to commit violence, to get the debtor fired, to pursue the debtor for the rest of his life. Profanity, browbeating, insults, and name calling (deadbeat, bum, cheat, thief, liar, etc.) were common both in correspondence and conversations. Telephone calls could be made as frequently as the debt collector wished and at any time, night or day. Personal visits to the debtor's house or workplace to demand payment could be made at any time, night or day. Relatives, neighbors, friends, employers, and coworkers of the debtor could be contacted and told of the debt, embarrassing the debtor and putting pressure on the debtor to pay. Creditors could undertake these debt collection efforts themselves or hire a business that specialized in debt collection. Or they could hire an attorney to do it for them.

1. The Fair Debt Collection Practices Act

In 1977, because of the growing amount of debt in our consumer society and the growing awareness of excessive debt collection practices by creditors and the debt collection industry, Congress passed the **Fair Debt Collection Practices Act** (FDCPA), 15 U.S.C. §§1601 et seq. What follows is a summary of how the FDCPA works.

Whom the FDCPA Regulates

The FDCPA regulates those defined by the statute (§803(6)) as **debt collectors**. Persons acting for businesses, "the principal purpose of which" is to collect debts owed to another, are included, as is any individual who "regularly collects or attempts to collect" debts owed to another. This can include **third-party collection agencies** retained by the creditor to collect debt owed to the creditor by the debtor. It can also include **debt buyers** (also called **asset buyers**), who purchase delinquent credit card, auto loan, and other accounts from creditors for a fraction of the face value of the debt and then seek to collect it themselves. According to the Federal Trade Commission, between 2006 and 2009 the top nine debt buyers purchased 90 million consumer accounts valued at about $143 billion. Though a perfectly legal industry in itself, controversy continues to swirl around collection tactics used by some debt buyers including the fabrication of missing documentation on debts purchased in bulk and the filing of time-barred claims in collection lawsuits unlikely to be defended and in the bankruptcy proceedings of the debtors (see Crawford v. LVNV Funding LLC, highlighted later in this section).

The statute excludes creditors themselves from the definition of debt collector since the creditor would be attempting to collect his own debt and not debt owed to another. However, the creditor himself can qualify as a debt collector under the statute if he "uses any name other than his own which would indicate that a third person is collecting or attempting to collect such debts" (§803(6)). And even where a creditor may not be regulated by the FDCPA, the creditor must be aware of potential tort liability arising from its collection activities as discussed later in this chapter.

History of the Debt Buying Industry

The history of the debt buying industry is interesting. There has always been some market for debts that a creditor has given up on and is considering writing off as uncollectible. But the industry boomed as a result of the Savings and Loan Crisis of the 1980s (read the history at www.fdic.gov/bank/historical/history/167_188.pdf) when 118 state and federally insured savings and loan (S&L) institutions holding $43 billion in assets failed over a two-year period. The Federal Deposit Insurance Corporation (FDIC), which insured deposits in those institutions, took over those failing S&Ls and made good all amounts on deposit at the expense of the taxpayers. The Resolution Trust Corporation (RTC) was then formed by the FDIC and began to actively seek buyers willing to purchase the assets of closed S&Ls, including both current and delinquent accounts. Auctions were held around the country at which performing and nonperforming accounts were bundled and sold to the highest bidder with no opportunity by the bidder to evaluate the specific accounts in the bundle purchased. Thus was birthed the modern debt or asset buying industry.

Case Preview

Heintz v. Jenkins

What about attorneys who are hired by a client to engage in pre-litigation debt collection efforts? Are they debt collectors for purposes of the statute's regulation? The statute does not expressly include attorneys hired by creditors in the definition of debt collectors and for years after it was passed no one thought attorneys were regulated by the statute. Then came Heintz v. Jenkins.

As you read Heintz v. Jenkins, look for the following:

1. What is the significance of the language Congress used or didn't use in the original and amended FDCPA in the court's determination of congressional intent?
2. What aspects of the legislative history of the Act does attorney Heintz rely on in support of his argument?
3. What is the "harmful anomalous result" that Heintz warns might occur if a collection lawyer who is deemed subject to FDCPA regulation then files a collection lawsuit against a consumer debtor but loses that lawsuit?

Heintz v. Jenkins
514 U.S. 291 (1995)

Justice Stephen Breyer wrote the majority opinion for *Heintz. Collection of the Supreme Court of the United States, Photographer: Steve Petteway*

[Plaintiff, Darlene Jenkins, took out a loan from Gainer Bank to buy a car and later defaulted on the loan. The bank sued Jenkins in state court to recover the balance due. Heintz, one of the bank's lawyers, wrote Jenkins a letter that listed the amount shown owed under the loan and included a $4,173 debt for insurance bought by the bank because she did not keep the car insured as she had promised to do. Jenkins then brought this Fair Debt Collection Practices Act suit against Heintz and his firm claiming that the letter violated the Act's prohibitions against trying to collect an amount not "authorized by the agreement creating the debt," §1692f(1), and against making a "false representation of . . . the . . . amount . . . of any debt," §1692e(2)(A). The District Court dismissed Jenkins' Fair Debt Collection lawsuit for failure to state a claim and held that the Act does not apply to lawyers engaging in litigation. The Court of Appeals for the Seventh Circuit reversed the District Court's judgment, interpreting the Act to apply to litigating lawyers. The Seventh Circuit's view in this respect conflicts with that of the Sixth Circuit. See Green v. Hocking, 9 F.3d 18 (1993). The Court granted certiorari to resolve the conflict.]

BREYER, Justice:
    There are two rather strong reasons for believing that the Act applies to the litigating activities of lawyers. *First,* the Act defines the "debt collector[s]" to whom

it applies as including those who "regularly collect or attempt to collect, directly or indirectly, [consumer] debts owed or due or asserted to be owed or due another." §1692a(6). In ordinary English, a lawyer who regularly tries to obtain payment of consumer debts through legal proceedings is a lawyer who regularly "attempts" to "collect" those consumer debts. . . .

Second, in 1977, Congress enacted an earlier version of this statute, which contained an express exemption for lawyers. That exemption said that the term "debt collector" did not include "any attorney-at-law collecting a debt as an attorney on behalf of and in the name of a client." In 1986, however, Congress repealed this exemption in its entirety, without creating a narrower, litigation-related, exemption to fill the void. Without more, then, one would think that Congress intended that lawyers be subject to the Act whenever they meet the general "debt collector" definition. . . .

Heintz argues that many of the Act's requirements, if applied directly to litigating activities, will create harmfully anomalous results that Congress simply could not have intended. . . . Many of Heintz's "anomalies" are not particularly anomalous. For example, the Sixth Circuit pointed to §1692e(5), which forbids a "debt collector" to make any "threat to take action that cannot legally be taken." The court reasoned that, were the Act to apply to litigating activities, this provision automatically would make liable any litigating lawyer who brought, and then lost, a claim against a debtor. . . . [T]he Act says explicitly that a "debt collector" may not be held liable if he "shows by a preponderance of evidence that the violation was not intentional and resulted from a bona fide error notwithstanding the maintenance of procedures reasonably adapted to avoid any such error." §1692k(c). Thus, even if we were to assume that the suggested reading of §1692e(5) is correct, we would not find the result so absurd as to warrant implying an exemption for litigating lawyers. In any event, the assumption would seem unnecessary, for we do not see how the fact that a lawsuit turns out ultimately to be unsuccessful could, by itself, make the bringing of it an "action that cannot legally be taken."

The remaining significant "anomalies" similarly depend for their persuasive force upon readings that courts seem unlikely to endorse. For example, Heintz's strongest "anomaly" argument focuses upon the Act's provisions governing "communication in connection with debt collection." §1692c. One of those provisions requires a "debt collector" not to "communicate further" with a consumer who "notifies" the "debt collector" that he or she "refuses to pay" or wishes the debt collector to "cease further communication." §1692c(c). In light of this provision, asks Heintz, how can an attorney file a lawsuit against (and thereby communicate with) a nonconsenting consumer or file a motion for summary judgment against that consumer? . . .

[I]t would be odd if the Act empowered a debt-owing consumer to stop the "communications" inherent in an ordinary lawsuit and thereby cause an ordinary debt-collecting lawsuit to grind to a halt. But, it is not necessary to read §1692c(c) in that way . . . because that provision has exceptions that permit communications "to notify the consumer that the debt collector or creditor may invoke" or "intends to invoke" a "specified remedy." . . . Courts can read these exceptions, plausibly, to imply that they authorize the actual invocation of the remedy that the collector "intends to invoke." The language permits such a reading, for an ordinary court-related document does, in fact, "notify" its recipient that the creditor may "invoke" a judicial remedy. Moreover, the interpretation is consistent with the statute's apparent objective of preserving creditors' judicial remedies. We need not authoritatively interpret the Act's conduct-regulating provisions. . . . [W]e rest our conclusions upon the fact that it is easier to read §1692c(c) as containing some such additional, implicit, exception than to believe that Congress intended, silently and implicitly, to create a far broader exception, for all litigating attorneys, from the Act itself.

Heintz points to a statement of Congressman Frank Annunzio, one of the sponsors of the 1986 amendment that removed from the Act the language creating a blanket exemption for lawyers. Representative Annunzio stated that, despite the exemption's removal, the Act still would not apply to lawyers' litigating activities. Representative Annunzio said that the Act

> "regulates debt collection, not the practice of law. Congress repealed the attorney exemption to the act, not because of attorney[s'] conduct in the courtroom, but because of their conduct in the backroom. Only collection activities, not legal activities, are covered by the act. . . . The act applies to attorneys when they are collecting debts, not when they are performing tasks of a legal nature. . . . The act only regulates the conduct of debt collectors, it does not prevent creditors, through their attorneys, from pursuing any legal remedies available to them."

132 Cong. Rec. 30842 (1986). This statement, however, does not persuade us.

For one thing, the plain language of the Act itself says nothing about retaining the exemption in respect to litigation. The line the statement seeks to draw between "legal" activities and "debt collection" activities was not necessarily apparent to those who debated the legislation, for litigating, at first blush, seems simply one way of collecting a debt. . . . Congressman Annunzio made his statement not during the legislative process, but *after* the statute became law. It therefore is not a statement upon which other legislators might have relied in voting for or against the Act, but it simply represents the views of one informed person on an issue about which others may (or may not) have thought differently.

Finally, Heintz points to a "Commentary" on the Act by the FTC's staff. It says: "Attorneys or law firms that engage in traditional debt collection activities (sending dunning letters, making collection calls to consumers) are covered by the [Act], but those whose practice is limited to legal activities are not covered." We cannot give conclusive weight to this statement. The Commentary of which this statement is a part says that it "is not binding on the Commission or the public." . . . [W]e find nothing either in the Act or elsewhere indicating that Congress intended to authorize the FTC to create this exception from the Act's coverage — an exception that, for the reasons we have set forth above, falls outside the range of reasonable interpretations of the Act's express language. . . .

For these reasons, we agree with the Seventh Circuit that the Act applies to attorneys who "regularly" engage in consumer-debt-collection activity, even when that activity consists of litigation. Its judgment is therefore *Affirmed.*

Post-Case Follow-Up

Heintz holds that attorneys who "regularly" engage in debt collection for clients are regulated debt collectors under the FDCPA. But how frequently does an attorney have to undertake collection work before she is considered one who "regularly" attempts to obtain payment for clients? The Supreme Court didn't make it clear in *Heintz*. The few decisions out there seem to interpret "regularly" as debt collection that amounts to a substantial percentage of a lawyer's total business or that is a substantial amount of work in and of itself. See, e.g., Garrett v. Derbes, 110 F.3d 317, 318 (5th Cir. 1997) ("[I]f the volume of a person's debt collection activity is great enough, it is irrelevant that these services only amount to a small fraction of his total business activity; the person still renders them 'regularly.'"); Fox v. Citicorp Credit Servs., Inc., 15 F.3d 1507, 1513 n.5 (9th Cir. 1994) (attorney liable as a debt collector where at least 80 percent of his legal fees came from the collection of debts); Camara v. Fleury, 285 F. Supp. 2d 90, 95 (D. Mass. 2003) (attorney and law firm not debt collectors where only 4.57 percent of the firm's business involved debt collection activities); Ditty v. CheckRite, Ltd., Inc., 973 F. Supp. 1320, 1336 (D. Utah 1997) (attorney a debt collector where collection represented one-third to one-half of the firm's income). See if the federal courts of your federal district or circuit have adopted one of these tests or some other.

Heintz v. Jenkins: Real Life Applications

1. Your law practice is six months old. You handled one small collection matter during that time but made no effort to comply with the FDCPA. Now a second small collection matter has been referred to you, this one for a different client. Is it time for you to begin complying with the FDCPA?

2. Would your answer to Question 1 change if the collection matter you handled in your first six months of practice was a large one and accounted for half of your income for the period?

3. Would your answer to Question 1 change if you had handled five collection matters in your first six months of practice but all of them were pro bono?

Activities Regulated by the FDCPA

The FDCPA regulates attempts to collect debt from "any natural person obligated or allegedly obligated to pay any debt" (§803(3)). Thus, the FDCPA does not regulate attempts to collect debt from a debtor who is not a natural person, such as a corporate debtor. It only regulates attempts to collect debts from natural persons who are called consumers under the statute. There are five categories of collection activity regulated by the FDCPA:

▪ Locating the consumer debtor
▪ Communicating with the consumer debtor

- Harassing or abusing the consumer debtor
- Making false or misleading representations
- Using unfair or unconscionable means

Locating the Consumer Debtor

Pursuant to §804 of the FDCPA, a debt collector contacting someone other than the consumer himself in order to locate the consumer must properly identify himself but avoid stating that he works for a debt collection company unless specifically asked. The debt collector must state that he is looking for information to help him locate the consumer but cannot mention that the consumer owes a debt. The debt collector must not contact the same person more than once unless that person invites a subsequent contact or unless the debt collector reasonably believes the person previously contacted now has more correct information. Communications from the debt collector seeking contact information for the debtor that are placed in writing must not be by postcard (where anyone handling the card can read the message) and nothing on the envelope or in the contents of the message can disclose that the sender is a debt collector or that the debtor owes a debt.

Application Exercise 1

What is the policy at work behind the limitations on locating the consumer debtor outlined in §804 of the FDCPA? Are these limitations fair to the debt collector? Should there be more stringent prohibitions on the debt collector making location contacts?

Communicating with the Consumer Debtor

Pursuant to §805 of the FDCPA, the debt collector cannot make contact with the consumer at any unusual time or place or at any time and place the creditor knows or should know would be inconvenient to the consumer. Absent information to the contrary, the debt collector is to assume that a convenient time for contacting the consumer is between 8 A.M. and 9 P.M. in the consumer's time zone.

If the debt collector knows that the consumer is represented by an attorney, contact must be with that attorney unless the consumer's attorney will not respond or consents to direct contact with the consumer. Contacting a consumer at work is prohibited if the debt collector knows the employer disallows such contacts.

Contacting third persons regarding the consumer's obligation is strictly limited. The debt collector is allowed to contact only the consumer himself, the consumer's attorney, the creditor, the creditor's attorney, the debt collector's attorney, or credit reporting agencies. Note carefully the definition of consumer in §805(d), however. For purposes of restrictions on contacting the consumer himself, consumer is defined to include not just the individual who owes the debt, but his spouse, parent (if he is a minor), guardian, executor, or administrator.

Finally, if the consumer advises the debt collector verbally or in writing that he refuses to pay the debt or does not want to be contacted any further, the contact must stop, other than the limited right of the debt collector to confirm that contact will cease or that other remedies may be or are going to be pursued.

Harassing or Abusing the Consumer

Pursuant to §806 of the statute, the debt collector cannot use or threaten to use violence or other criminal means to harm the person, reputation, or property of the consumer or anyone else. The debt collector cannot use profanity or obscene language, cannot include the consumer's name on any published list of persons who haven't paid their debts, cannot disclose the debt by publicly advertising its sale or assignment, and cannot make anonymous phone calls or continuous phone calls intended to harass.

Making False or Misleading Representations

Pursuant to §807 of the FDCPA, a debt collector cannot use "any false, deceptive, or misleading representation or means" in collecting a debt. The statute gives a number of nonexclusive examples of such prohibited acts, including

- the use of any language, clothing, or symbols that would suggest that the debt collector is affiliated with a governmental entity or a credit reporting agency, or that he is an attorney when he is not;
- saying anything false about the debt or the amount owed;
- suggesting that nonpayment of the debt is a crime or that it will result in the debtor or a codebtor being arrested or imprisoned;
- suggesting that nonpayment will result in the debtor's property being taken other than as the law allows; or
- using any false name or false paperwork.

Using Unfair or Unconscionable Means

Pursuant to §808 of the FDCPA, the debt collector "may not use unfair or unconscionable means" to collect a debt. The statute gives a number of nonexclusive examples of such practices, including

- collecting any amount not actually owed, or communicating with the consumer by postcard;
- using an envelope for communication with the consumer that identifies the sender as a debt collector;
- accepting a postdated check and then depositing or threatening to deposit it early; or
- soliciting a postdated check for the very purpose of attempting to cash it before funds are available in order to allege a criminal act by the consumer.

| **Case Preview** | ***Crawford v. LVNV Funding LLC*** |

Courts have expanded the scope of what is unfair or unconscionable under §808. For example, in Phillips v. Asset Acceptance, LLC, 736 F.3d 1076 (7th Cir. 2013), the court held that a debt collector governed by the FDCP who threatens to sue or actually sues on a time-barred claim violates the Act. But what if the debtor files a case in bankruptcy and the debt collector files a formal claim in the bankruptcy case based on a time-barred debt? Every bankruptcy practitioner knows that this is a very common practice by debt buyers, those companies that purchase charged-off debts (mostly credit card debt) at a steep discount from major banks and then aggressively pursue the debtors into litigation usually with little or no effort at negotiation or compromise. Often such aggressive litigation tactics prove the proverbial last straw compelling the debtor to file for bankruptcy protection. The debt buyers have routinely filed formal claims in the bankruptcy case notwithstanding the claim being time-barred. Finally, a court has spoken regarding whether this tactic is a violation of the FDCPA.

As you read Crawford v. LVNV Funding LLC, look for the following:

1. Did it seem to matter to the court's decision whether LVNV knew the claim was time-barred when it filed its proof of claim in the debtor's bankruptcy case?
2. What reason did the court suggest as to why a debt buyer would want to file a time-barred claim in the debtor's Chapter 13 bankruptcy case?
3. What were LVNV's arguments that filing a time-barred proof of claim in the debtor's bankruptcy case should not be deemed a violation of FDCPA?
4. What provision of the FDCPA did the court find that LVNV had violated by filing a proof of claim on the time-barred obligation?

Crawford v. LVNV Funding LLC
758 F.3d 1254 (11th Cir. 2014)

[Crawford owed $2,037.99 to the Heilig-Meyers furniture company. Heilig-Meyers charged off the debt in 1999, and in 2001, LVNV Funding, LLC, acquired the debt. The last transaction on the account occurred October 26, 2001, and the debt became unenforceable under the three-year Alabama statute of limitations in October 2004. Crawford filed for Chapter 13 bankruptcy in February 2008. LVNV filed a proof of claim to collect the debt even though the limitations period had expired. Crawford filed a counterclaim against LVNV via an adversary proceeding pursuant to Bankruptcy Rule 3007(b) alleging that LVNV's attempting to claim Crawford's time-barred debt violated the FDCPA. The Bankruptcy Judge dismissed Crawford's counterclaim and the decision was affirmed on appeal by the district court. Crawford appeals.]

GOLDBERG, Circuit Judge.

A deluge has swept through U.S. bankruptcy courts of late. Consumer debt buyers — armed with hundreds of delinquent accounts purchased from creditors — are filing proofs of claim on debts deemed unenforceable under state statutes of limitations. This appeal considers whether a proof of claim to collect a stale debt in Chapter 13 bankruptcy violates the Fair Debt Collection Practices Act. . . .

The FDCPA is a consumer protection statute that "imposes open-ended prohibitions on, inter alia, false, deceptive, or unfair" debt-collection practices. . . . Finding "abundant evidence" of such practices, Congress passed the FDCPA in 1977 to stop "the use of abusive, deceptive, and unfair debt collection practices by many debt collectors." 15 U.S.C. §1692(a). Congress determined that "[e]xisting laws and procedures" were "inadequate" to protect consumer debtors. Id. at 1692(b). . . .

[T]he FDCPA regulates the conduct of debt-collectors, which the statute defines as any person who . . . "regularly collects . . . debts owed or due or asserted to be owed or due another." 15 U.S.C. §1692a(6). Undisputedly, LVNV and its surrogates are debt collectors and thus subject to the FDCPA.

To enforce the FDCPA's prohibitions, Congress equipped consumer debtors with a private right of action, rendering "debt collectors who violate the Act liable for actual damages, statutory damages up to $1,000, and reasonable attorney's fees and costs." Owen v. I.C. Sys., Inc., 629 F.3d 1263, 1270 (11th Cir. 2011) (citing 15 U.S.C. §1692k(a)). . . . To determine whether LVNV's conduct, as alleged in Crawford's complaint, is prohibited by the FDCPA, we begin "where all such inquiries must begin: with the language of the statute itself." [Citation omitted.]

Section 1692e of the FDCPA provides that "[a] debt collector may not use any false, deceptive, or misleading representation or means in connection with the collection of any debt." 15 U.S.C. §1692e. Section 1692f states that "[a] debt collector may not use unfair or unconscionable means to collect or attempt to collect any debt."

Because Congress did not provide a definition for the terms "unfair" or "unconscionable," this Court has looked to the dictionary for help. "The plain meaning of 'unfair' is 'marked by injustice, partiality, or deception.'" LeBlanc v. Unifund CCR Partners, 601 F.3d 1185, 1200 (11th Cir. 2010) (quoting Merriam-Webster Online Dictionary (2010)). Further, "an act or practice is deceptive or unfair if it has the tendency or capacity to deceive." Id. . . . We also explained that "[t]he term 'unconscionable' means 'having no conscience'; 'unscrupulous'; 'showing no regard for conscience'; 'affronting the sense of justice, decency, or reasonableness.'" Id. (quoting Black's Law Dictionary 1526 (7th ed. 1999)). We have also noted that "[t]he phrase 'unfair or unconscionable' is as vague as they come." Id. . . .

Given this ambiguity, we have adopted a "least-sophisticated consumer" standard to evaluate whether a debt collector's conduct is "deceptive," "misleading," "unconscionable," or "unfair" under the statute. . . . The inquiry is not whether the particular plaintiff-consumer was deceived or misled; instead, the question is "whether the 'least sophisticated consumer' would have been deceived" by the debt collector's conduct. . . . The "least-sophisticated consumer" standard takes into account that consumer-protection laws are "not made for the protection of experts, but for the public—that vast multitude which includes the ignorant, the unthinking, and the credulous." . . . "However, the test has an objective component in that while protecting naive consumers, the standard also prevents liability for bizarre or idiosyncratic interpretations of collection notices by preserving a quotient of reasonableness." *LeBlanc*, 601 F.3d at 1194. . . .

Given our precedent, we must examine whether LVNV's conduct—filing and trying to enforce in court a claim known to be time-barred—would be unfair, unconscionable, deceiving, or misleading towards the least-sophisticated consumer. See id. at 1193-94. . . .

The reason behind LVNV's practice of filing time-barred proofs of claim in bankruptcy court is simple. Absent an objection from either the . . . debtor or the trustee, the time-barred claim is automatically allowed against the debtor pursuant to 11 U.S.C. §502(a)-(b) and Bankruptcy Rule 3001(f). As a result, the debtor must then pay the debt from his future wages as part of the Chapter 13 repayment plan, notwithstanding that the debt is time-barred and unenforceable in court.

That is what happened in this case. LVNV filed the time-barred proof of claim in May of 2008, shortly after debtor Crawford petitioned for Chapter 13 protection. But neither the bankruptcy trustee nor Crawford objected to the claim during the bankruptcy proceeding; instead, the trustee actually paid monies from the . . . estate to LVNV. . . . It wasn't until four years later, in May 2012, that debtor Crawford . . . objected to LVNV's claim as unenforceable.

LVNV acknowledges, as it must, that its conduct would likely subject it to FDCPA liability had it filed a lawsuit to collect this time-barred debt in state court. Federal circuit and district courts have uniformly held that a debt collector's threatening to sue on a time-barred debt and/or filing a time-barred suit in state court to recover that debt violates §§1692e and 1692f. . . .

As an example, the Seventh Circuit has reasoned that the FDCPA outlaws "stale suits to collect consumer debts" as unfair because (1) "few unsophisticated consumers would be aware that a statute of limitations could be used to defend against lawsuits based on stale debts" and would therefore "unwittingly acquiesce to such lawsuits"; (2) "the passage of time . . . dulls the consumer's memory of the circumstances and validity of the debt"; and (3) the delay in suing after the limitations period "heightens the probability that [the debtor] will no longer have personal records" about the debt. Phillips v. Asset Assistance, 736 F.3d 1077, 1079 (7th Cir. 2013). . . .

These observations reflect the purpose behind statutes of limitations. . . . Statutes of limitations "protect defendants and the courts from having to deal with cases in which the search for truth may be seriously impaired by the loss of evidence, whether by death or disappearance of witnesses, fading memories, disappearance of documents, or otherwise." United States v. Kubrick, 444 U.S. 111, 117 (1979). . . .

The same is true in the bankruptcy context. In bankruptcy, the limitations period provides a bright line for debt collectors and consumer debtors, signifying a time when the debtor's right to be free of stale claims comes to prevail over a creditor's right to legally enforce the debt. A . . . debtor's memory of a stale debt may have faded and personal records documenting the debt may have vanished, making it difficult for a consumer debtor to defend against the time-barred claim.

Similar to the filing of a stale lawsuit, a debt collector's filing of a time-barred proof of claim creates the misleading impression to the debtor that the debt collector can legally enforce the debt. The "least sophisticated" Chapter 13 debtor may be unaware that a claim is time barred and unenforceable and thus fail to object to such a claim. Given the Bankruptcy Code's automatic allowance provision, the otherwise unenforceable time-barred debt will be paid from the debtor's future wages as part of his Chapter 13 repayment plan. Such a distribution of funds to debt collectors with time-barred claims then necessarily reduces the payments to other legitimate creditors with enforceable claims. Furthermore, filing objections to time-barred claims consumes energy and resources in a debtor's bankruptcy case, just as filing a limitations defense does in state court. For all of these reasons, under the "least-sophisticated consumer standard" in our binding precedent, LVNV's filing of a time-barred proof of claim against Crawford in bankruptcy was "unfair," "unconscionable," "deceptive," and "misleading" within the broad scope of §1692e and §1692f. . . .

[W]e disagree with the contention that LVNV's proof of claim was not a "collection activity" aimed at Crawford and, therefore, not "the sort of debt-collection activity that the FDCPA regulates." As noted earlier, the broad prohibitions of §1692e apply to a debt collector's "false, deceptive, or misleading representation or means" used "in connection with the collection of any debt." 15 U.S.C. §1692e. . . . [L]VNV's filing of the proof of claim fell well within the ambit of a "representation" or "means" used in "connection with the collection of any debt." It was an effort "to obtain payment" of Crawford's debt "by legal proceeding." In fact, payments to LVNV were made from Crawford's wages as a result of LVNV's claim. . . .

LVNV also argues that considering the filing of a proof of claim as a "means" used "in connection with the collection of debt" for purposes §§1692e and 1692f of the FDCPA would be at odds with the automatic stay provision of the Bankruptcy Code, 11 U.S.C. §362(a)(6). We disagree. The automatic stay prohibits debt-collection activity outside the bankruptcy proceeding, such as lawsuits in state court. . . . It does not prohibit the filing of a proof of claim to collect a debt within the bankruptcy process. Filing a proof of claim is the first step in collecting a debt in bankruptcy and is, at the very least, an "indirect" means of collecting a debt.

Just as LVNV would have violated the FDCPA by filing a lawsuit on stale claims in state court, LVNV violated the FDCPA by filing a stale claim in bankruptcy court.

Because we hold that LVNV's conduct violated the FDCPA's plain language, we vacate the district court's dismissal of Crawford's complaint and remand for further proceedings.

Post-Case Follow-Up

Crawford highlights a significant problem being experienced with debt buyers. According to the Office of the Comptroller of the Currency, the five banks that issue the great majority of credit cards used by Americans sell more than 80 percent of their charged-off credit card debt to fewer than 20 national debt buyers. During 2013, debt buyers filed between 10 million and 15 million debt collection lawsuits against consumers rather than attempting work outs. A 2014 study conducted by the Center for Consumer Recovery, A Study of the Causes of Consumer Bankruptcy, available online at www.centerforconsumerrecovery.org/ResourceCenter/CenterForConsumerRecovery-2013BankruptcyStudySummary.pdf, found that many consumers, while in arrears and struggling, are not hopelessly in debt and could ultimately manage their past due debt with the cooperation of their creditors but decide to file for bankruptcy relief out of collection fatigue: exhaustion from the constant bombardment of debt collection activities, especially debt collection litigation, aimed at them by debt buyers.

The study suggested that 78 percent of consumers who filed for bankruptcy relief in 2013 did so as result of collection litigation instigated against them by a debt buyer. Worse, debt buyers are notorious for filing collection lawsuits and proofs of claim in consumer bankruptcy cases where there is a known defense to the debtor's obligation, such as a statute of limitations having run. But if the civil collection suit is decided by default, the defense is never raised and the judgment becomes final. And in a Chapter 13 bankruptcy case, as we will see, a proof of claim filed by a creditor is automatically allowed unless specifically objected to by the debtor or the Chapter 13 trustee within a certain time frame. As Judge Goldberg said in *Crawford*, the filing of such stale claims in Chapter 13s by debt buyers has become a "deluge." Thus for the 11th Circuit to find that the FDCPA applies to proofs of claim filed in a bankruptcy case is huge. And to find that a proof of claim containing any information that could be construed as untrue (like not mentioning that the statute of limitations has run for pursuing payment via litigation) makes it "unfair," "unconscionable," "deceptive," and "misleading" under §1692(e) and §1692(f) is ground-moving. Debt buyers may never be able to operate the same way again. Not all courts are likely to be convinced by the reasoning of *Crawford* and may see an important

Least Sophisticated Consumer or Reasonable Consumer?

Though the statute does not expressly require it, a number of federal circuits, including the 11th Circuit as mentioned in *Crawford*, have determined that §§804-808 of the FDCPA are to be applied using the **least sophisticated consumer standard** rather than a **reasonable consumer standard**. See, e.g., Smith v. Consumer Credit, Inc., 167 F.3d 1052, 1054 (6th Cir. 1999), Swanson v. Southern Oregon Credit Service, Inc., 869 F.2d 1222, 1225 (9th Cir. 1988), and Jeter v. Credit Bureau, Inc., 760 F.2d 1168, 1179 (11th Cir. 1985). The least sophisticated standard is intended to protect even naïve or overly trusting consumers from deceptive debt collection practices. However, even the least sophisticated standard is applied objectively to protect debt collectors from liability for bizarre or idiosyncratic allegations from debtors. See Arteaga v. Asset Acceptance, LLC, 733 F. Supp. 2d 1218, 1230 (E.D. Cal. 2010).

distinction between the filing of a collection suit by the creditor based on the time-barred debt and the filing of a proof of claim on that time-barred debt in a bankruptcy case instituted by the debtor. The former seems clearly to be an attempt to collect debt from the debtor while the latter can be characterized as a response to the debtor's action on the debt and at most an effort to collect from the estate of the debtor, not the debtor himself. See, e.g., In re LeGrone, 525 B.R. 419 (Bankr. N.D. Ill. 2015) (proof of claim is filed against the estate not the debtor and Code provides adequate remedy since bankruptcy trustee can object to time-barred claim). Determine if the courts of the federal district or circuit where you plan to practice have addressed the issue raised in *Crawford* and, if so, how they have ruled.

Crawford v. LVNV Funding LLC: Real Life Applications

1. How certain does a defense to a debt obligation have to be for it to constitute a violation of the FDCPA if the debt collector files suit to collect or files a claim in the debtor's bankruptcy? For example, if the debtor had advised the debt collector that it would defend any lawsuit based on unconscionability or capacity or mutual mistake, etc., must the debt collector not pursue the claim? What's the difference between these defenses and the statute of limitation defense?
2. If there was a genuine dispute over whether the statute of limitations had run could the debt collector file suit to collect or file a claim in the bankruptcy proceeding? What kinds of issues can arise in an argument over what statute of limitations controls, or when it began to run, or whether it has been stayed for some length of time?
3. Debt buyers are controversial, but does that mean it would be unethical for you to represent them in their debt collection activities? What if any ethical considerations should go through an attorney's mind when approached to represent an aggressive debt buyer who is known to file time-barred claims and hope for default in a civil suit or absence of objection to a bankruptcy claim?

Application Exercise 2

Determine if the federal district or circuit where you plan to practice has adopted the least sophisticated consumer standard for interpreting the abuse provisions of the FDCPA. If not, does your district or circuit follow the reasonable consumer standard or some other standard that it has articulated? If your state regulates debt collection practices, what standard have your state courts adopted for applying the state act?

The "Initial Communication" and Section 809 Demand Letter

Section 809(a) of the FDCPA provides that within five days following the initial communication between the debt collector and the debtor, the debt collector must send to the debtor a written communication that contains the following

- the amount of the debt [§809(a)(1)]
- the name of the creditor owed [§809(a)(2)]
- a statement that the debt will be assumed valid unless the debtor disputes the debt within 30 days of receipt of the written communication [§809(a)(3)]
- a statement that if the debtor, within the 30-day period, notifies the debt collector in writing that the debt is disputed in whole or in part, the debt collector will then obtain verification of the debt (including a copy of any judgment upon which the debt is based) and mail it to the debtor [§809(a)(4)]
- a statement that if the debtor, within the 30-day period, requests in writing the name of the original creditor, the debt collector will provide that name if it is different from the current creditor [§809(a)(5)]

Section 809(b) provides that if the debtor does, in a timely writing, either dispute the debt or request the name of the original creditor in writing, debt collection activities must cease until verification of the debt and/or name of the original creditor has been mailed to the debtor. Section 809(c) provides that the failure of a debtor to dispute a debt cannot be used against him as an admission of liability for the debt in a subsequent collection lawsuit.

The scheme contemplated by §809 is that the initial communication between the debtor and the debt collector will be verbal (e.g., by phone call). Then within five days of that verbal communication, the §809 letter must be sent.

For example, Pearl Murphy, from Appendix D, owed Capital City Medical Equipment Co (CCME) $2,247.70 for medical supplies provided during her illness as described in Assignment Memorandum #1 in that appendix. If that debt was turned over to a debt collector and the initial communication between the debt collector and Pearl Murphy is a phone call, the debt collector must send the §809 letter within five days of the phone call.

Section 809 permits the initial communication with the debtor to be in writing so long as that writing complies with the requirements of that section. If the initial communication is in writing and complies with §809, no additional written communication within five days is required. In many law offices doing collection work and at some debt collection agencies, the initial communication is indeed in writing and lawyers typically refer to that first writing as the demand letter. Consequently, it is important that the demand letter comply with the requirements of §809. Exhibit 3.1 shows a demand letter from an attorney for CCME to Pearl Murphy seeking to collect the $1,200 debt she owes CCME.

EXHIBIT 3.1 **Demand Letter**

ROYAL AND ASSOCIATES
Attorneys and Counselors at Law
115 Commerce Street
Capital City, Yourstate
(555) 961-9087
July 1, YR-1

Ms. Pearl E. Murphy
3521 West Cherry Street
Capital City, Yourstate

In re: Indebtedness of $1,200 to Capital City Medical Equipment

Dear Ms. Murphy:

Your name has been brought to our attention to collect from you the entire balance of a debt you owed Capital City Medical Equipment (CCME) in the amount of $1,200 under the terms of that certain Medical Equipment Rental Agreement (the Agreement) that you executed on February 1, YR-1. A bill for the $1,200 that you owe CCME under the terms of the Agreement was sent to you on May 15, YR-1, and CCME advises us that you have failed and refused to pay any portion of that amount within 30 days of receipt of the bill as you are obligated to do under the terms of the Agreement.

If you want to resolve this matter without a lawsuit, you must, within 30 days of the date of this letter, either pay the entire amount owed or call the undersigned at the number shown above and work out arrangements for payment with us. If you do neither of these things, we have been authorized to file suit on behalf of CCME for the collection of this debt.

Federal law gives you thirty (30) days after you receive this letter to dispute the validity of the debt or any part of it. If you do not dispute it within that period, we will assume that it is valid. If you do dispute it by notifying us in writing to that effect we will, as required by the law, obtain and mail to you proof of the debt. And if, within the same period, you request in writing the name and address of your original creditor, if the original creditor is different from the current creditor CCME, we will furnish you that information also. The law does not require us to wait until the end of the 30-day period before suing you to collect this debt. If, however, you request proof of the debt or the name and address of the original creditor within the 30-day period that begins with your receipt of this letter, the law requires us to suspend our efforts until we have mailed information to you.

Please make arrangements immediately to pay this debt. I trust you will give this matter priority attention.

Sincerely,

_____

Edmond T. Royal, Attorney at Law

Section 809 is primarily concerned with giving the debtor the opportunity to validate or dispute the debt, and its provisions can be a bit tricky. Note that §809(a)(3) advises the debtor that the debt will be assumed valid unless the debtor disputes it within 30 days, but it does not expressly require the debtor to dispute the debt in writing to avoid that assumption. On the other hand, §809(a)(4), referred to as the **validation notice**, provides that if the debtor does dispute the debt in writing within 30 days, the debt collector will obtain verification of the debt and provide it to the debtor. And 809(b) requires that collection efforts stop until the verification has been mailed to the debtor.

The reference to a writing in the §809(a)(4) validation notice requirement but its absence in the §809(a)(3) right to dispute provision has led to confusion among the courts. If the debtor wishes to dispute the debt, must he put his dispute in writing or is that only an option? Even if the debtor is not required to state his dispute of the debt in writing, can a §809 letter require him to do so in order to avoid the assumption that the debt is valid? There is a split of authority among the federal circuits as to whether a §809 demand letter does requires or can require the debtor to dispute the debt in writing to avoid the assumption of validity. Compare Graziano v. Harrison, 950 F.2d 107, 112 (3d Cir. 1991) (debtor must dispute debt in writing), with Camacho v. Bridgeport Financial, Inc., 430 F.3d 1078, 1080-1082 (9th Cir. 2005) (§809 does not impose a writing requirement on debtors).

Regardless of whether §809(a)(3) requires or can be used to require the debtor to provide written dispute of the debt, it is clear that the obligation of the debt collector to provide the debtor with verification of the debt under §809(a)(4) is triggered only by receiving written notice from the debtor sent within the 30-day window that the debt is disputed in whole or part. Neither verbal notice nor dispute nor untimely notice of dispute will trigger that obligation.

Section 809(a)(5) requires inclusion of a statement in the demand letter that, upon the debtor's written request within the 30-day period, the debt collector will provide the debtor with the name and address of the original creditor, if different from the current creditor. Remember, as you learned in your Contracts course, contracts creating a debt obligation are often assigned by one creditor to another. Therefore, the creditor identified in the demand letter may not be the original creditor. Section 809(a)(5) provides the debtor with a means of contacting the original creditor.

Assume that Pearl Murphy has made a number of small payments to CCME on the debt she owes. She receives a demand letter written by a debt collector on behalf of AAA Finance Company (AAA) advising that AAA is now the creditor to whom the debt is owed and that she should pay the balance of $950 to AAA to satisfy the claim. Pearl thinks she only owes $800 on the bill and attempts to contact CCME, only to find that it has changed its phone number and apparently its name, too, because she can't find it in the phone book. Pearl may want to exercise her rights under §809(a)(5) to learn how to contact CCME if it is still in business.

Notwithstanding the language required to be included in a demand letter, nothing in the FDCPA requires a creditor to wait 30 days after sending the demand letter to file suit to collect the debt. Theoretically, the creditor could cause the demand letter to be sent today and file suit tomorrow without violating the FDCPA. One exception to that is §809(b). Under that provision, if the debtor does exercise his right under §809(a)(4) to timely notify the debt collector in writing that the debt is disputed in whole or part, or under §809(a)(5) to request the name and address of the original creditor, collection efforts must stop . . . but only until the information requested by the debtor has been mailed to him. Then collection efforts, including the filing of a lawsuit, can resume.

Assume that AAA causes the demand letter to be sent to Pearl. Pearl receives the letter today. A week later, AAA decides to file suit and authorizes its attorney to do so. The next day, however, Pearl's letter requesting the name and address of the original creditor arrives. Filing the suit or any other collection action must be delayed until Pearl's request is complied with. Once it is, the suit may then be filed. What if the attorney for AAA filed the lawsuit the day before Pearl's letter arrived? In that case, there is no violation of the FDCPA by filing the suit because the attorney did not know Pearl's letter was coming. However, the collection lawsuit must not move forward until the response is in the mail.

What if a debt-collecting attorney makes no contact with the debtor before filing the collection lawsuit? Could the filing of the lawsuit via service of a complaint and summons be the §809(a) initial communication triggering inclusion of the validation notice and other requirements of that section and constituting an FDCPA violation if not included? Prior to 2006 there was a split on this issue but in 2006 §809 was amended to specifically provide that "a communication in the form of a formal pleading in a civil action shall not be treated as an initial communication for purposes of subsection (a) of this section."

Application Exercise 3

Assume Department Store is owed $1,000 by Consumer, who files for bankruptcy relief. Department Store has not undertaken any debt collection efforts against Consumer other than sending his monthly bill. (Recall that creditors seeking to collect their own debt are not debt collectors under FDCPA.) However, now that Consumer is in bankruptcy, Department Store has its outside counsel file a routine proof of claim for it in the bankruptcy case. After *In re Crawford*, supra, could filing that proof of claim without including the validation notice or other statements required by §809(a) be a violation of the FDCPA? Would filing that proof of claim under circumstances where Department Store knows the claim is inaccurate or unjustified be a violation?

Penalties for Violating the FDCPA

The FDCPA authorizes a **private right of action** on behalf of the consumer debtor for any violations of its provisions. Pursuant to §813 of the FDCPA, a debt collector found to have violated these provisions may be civilly liable to the consumer/debtor for the debtor's actual damages, plus a statutory penalty of up to $1,000 per violation, plus the attorney's fee incurred by the debtor, plus court costs. The debtor has one year from the date of the alleged violation to initiate the civil lawsuit in state or federal court to recover such private damages.

It is a defense to the debt collector in the debtor's suit under the FDCPA if the debt collector can show by a preponderance of the evidence (more likely than not) that the violation "was not intentional and resulted from a bona fide error notwith-standing the maintenance of procedures reasonably adapted to avoid any such error" (§813(c)). In Jerman v. Carlisle, McNellie, Rini, Kramer & Ulrich, LPA, 559 U.S. 573 (2010), the U.S. Supreme Court held that this **bona fide error defense** of the FDCPA does not include mistakes of law regarding the requirements of the statute. The defendant law firm in *Jerman*, seeking to collect a debt for a client, demanded that the debtor dispute the validity of the debt in writing. When the debtor sued, the trial court, affirmed by the Sixth Circuit, chose to follow the view expressed in Camacho v. Bridgeport Financial, Inc., supra, that §809(a)(3) does not impose a writing requirement on debtors and ruled that the defendant's demand that he dispute the validity of the debt in writing was a violation of the FDCPA. The defendant law firm asserted the bona fide error defense on the grounds that it had mistakenly but in good faith construed §809 to require that the debtor dispute the debt in writing. Although the Supreme Court rejected defendant's mistake of law as being within the bona fide error defense of §813(c), it did not resolve the lingering question of whether §809(a)(3) should be interpreted to require a debtor to put his dispute of the debt in writing since that precise issue was not raised in the appeal. See *Jerman*, supra, at 1610.

The FDCPA is administered in the first instance by the Federal Trade Commission (FTC), and any violation can be deemed by the FTC to be an unfair or deceptive act or practice by the debt collector under the Federal Trade Commission Act (FTCA). Such a finding authorizes the FTC to enforce compliance with the FDCPA on debt collectors and to assess fines and penalties for noncompliance. In an extreme case, the FTC could order a debt collector to stop doing business. The FTC maintains a helpful information site regarding the FDCPA at www.ftc.gov/bcp/edu/pubs/consumer/credit/cre18.shtm.

When it was created in 2010 by the Dodd-Frank Wall Street Reform and Consumer Protection Act of 2010, the CFPB was granted supervisory and enforcement authority over large collectors of consumer debt, those with receipts of more than $10 million per year in debt collection activities. That includes about 175 debt collection companies, which collectively account for more than 60 percent of the consumer debt collection business. In October 2012 the CFPB issued its Debt Collection Examination Procedures Manual (http://files.consumerfinance.gov/f/201210_cfpb_debt-collection-examination-procedures.pdf) to alert debt collectors to the procedures and standards that the CFPB will use to determine if regulated debt collectors are following the law.

Application Exercise 4

Look at the Background section of the CFPB Manual (pages 1-3) mentioned in the text (http://files.consumerfinance.gov/f/201210_cfpb_debt-collection-examination-procedures.pdf). What federal statutes other than the FDCPA impact the activities of debt collectors? Look at Module 7 of the manual. What kinds of abusive litigation practices does the CFPB seem to be concerned about? What kinds of abusive repossession practices? What concerns does it seem to have about collecting time-barred debt?

2. State Statutory Regulation of Debt Collection Practices

A number of states have passed their own debt collection practices regulations, usually enforced by a state agency charged with consumer protection or by the state attorney general (www.naag.org/). In other states, there is no specific debt collection regulation but relief may be had by debtors under the state's generic consumer protection act, which provides remedies for any unfair or deceptive trade practice directed at a consumer. Most states enacting specific debt collection regulation closely track the federal law concerning what constitutes a violation and remedies. In a few such states, however, the regulation of debt collection activity is even more stringent than the federal FDCPA, or state law imposes more substantial penalties than the FDCPA.

For example, California's Fair Debt Collection Practices Act (California Civil Code §§1788 et seq.), known generally as the Rosenthal Act, regulates creditors collecting their own debt, which the FDCPA does not. The California act also places more limitations than the FDCPA does on a debt collector contacting the debtor's employer. Many states also require debt collectors to be licensed or registered by the state, a level of regulation not imposed by the FDCPA.

Application Exercise 5

The Privacy Rights Clearinghouse maintains a Web site with links to state debt collection laws at www.privacyrights.org/fs/fs27plus.htm. Is your state listed there? If so, what agency or government department enforces your state law? Is there a private right of action allowed for violation of your state law? Must debt collectors be licensed in your state? Does your statute appear to impose more stringent limitations on debt collectors than those in the FDCPA, summarized below? If your state attorney general's office enforces your state debt collection law, locate that office using the Web site of the National Association of Attorneys General (www.naag.org/). Does your attorney general's Web site mention abusive debt collection practices? Does it provide a convenient way to file a complaint regarding such practices?

3. Tort, Criminal, and Ethical Considerations in Debt Collection

Attorneys engaging in debt collection work, debt collection companies, and creditors themselves (even if not regulated by the FDCPA), must also beware of several tort theories that debtors may assert against them in order to recover damages for wrongful conduct arising out of collection practices. Some behavior that is tortious may also be considered criminal. Such tort liability or criminal exposure can exist whether or not the collection practice complained of violates the FDCPA and without regard to whether the debtor actually owes the debt or not.

For example, a debt collector who publishes a false statement concerning the debtor to third persons may be sued for defamation. A debt collector who resorts

:al attack on the debtor may prosecuted for assault and battery or sued in
\at behavior. A debt collector who threatens criminal prosecution or other
he debtor or someone close to the debtor unless a debt is paid may face
minal allegations of extortion or blackmail. Other causes of action that
\an arise in non-judicial debt collection include

- Intentional infliction of emotional distress (outrageous conduct). See, e.g., Moorhead v. J.C. Penney, 555 S.W.2d 713 (Tenn. 1977) (decided before enactment of the FDCPA), and Perk v. Worden, 475 F. Supp. 2d 565 (E.D. Va. 2007).
- Invasion of privacy. See, e.g., Kuhn v. Account Control Technology, 865 F. Supp. 1443 (D. Nev. 1994), and Sofka v. Thal, 662 S.W.2d 502 (Mo. 1983).
- Malicious harassment, civil or criminal. See, e.g., Sams v. State, 271 Ga. App. 617, 610 S.E.2d 592 (2005).
- Conversion or theft. See, e.g., Darcars Motors of Silver Springs, Inc. v. Borzym, 379 Md. 249, 841 A.2d 828 (2004).

Debt collection activities found to be in violation of the FDCPA or culpable under state tort or criminal law may also be grounds for disciplinary action against the attorney involved since they will likely constitute a violation of legal ethics. For example, Rule 4.4 of the American Bar Association Rules of Professional Conduct prohibits an attorney from threatening criminal prosecution in order to induce payment to a client. Such conduct could therefore not only be construed as civil or criminal extortion or blackmail as discussed in the last section, but could result in disciplinary action against the attorney. Rule 4.4 states:

In representing a client, a lawyer shall not:

. . .

(b) threaten to present a criminal charge, or to offer or to agree to refrain from filing such a charge, for the purpose of obtaining an advantage in a civil matter.

After considering so many abuses of debt collection activity, it is good to remind ourselves that debt collection is an honest way to make a living—a necessary and honorable trade. As always, it is the bad apples that give the barrel that sour smell. There are a number of organizations made up of members of the debt collection community who are all dedicated to the ethical and professional practice of their trade. Exhibit 3.2 lists a number of the more prominent ones.

EXHIBIT 3.2 **Prominent Debt Collectors Organizations**

- ACA International, the Association of Credit and Collection Professionals (http://www.acainternational.org/)
- Commercial Collection Agency Association (CCAA) (http://commercialcollectionagenciesofamerica.com/)
- International Association of Commercial Collectors, Inc. (IACC) (www.commercialcollector.com/iacc/main/)
- The Equipment Leasing and Finance Association (ELFA) (www.elfaonline.org/)
- The Finance, Credit and International Business Association (FCIB) (www.fcibglobal.com/)

4. The Debt Settlement Industry

One consequence of American consumers having taken on such great amounts of debt in the last generation has been the explosion of the **debt settlement industry** in the guise of **credit counseling agencies** (CCAs) (sometimes called debt management, debt relief, debt settlement, debt negotiation, or credit repair companies). These companies offer to assist debt-strapped individuals to avoid bankruptcy by negotiating a **debt management plan** (DMP) with the client's creditors. Ideally the DMP will lower the client's required payments by extending the time for repayment, eliminate or reduce late fees and interest rates, and, in rare cases, even reduce the principal amount owed. The CCAs also provide clients financial literacy and budget counseling.

At the end of the twentieth century, there were approximately 200 CCAs around the country, most of which were legitimate businesses assisting consumers and small businesses on a not-for-profit basis and charging minimal fees. A decade later, with the effects of the Great Recession still lingering, more than a thousand CCAs exist, many of which are for-profit. Approximately nine million Americans seek credit counseling each year. Though most CCAs are perfectly legitimate, the industry is now rife with complaints of false and deceptive promises regarding results to be obtained, charging excessive fees (often in advance and regardless of results obtained), charging undisclosed fees, and simply failing to provide promised services.

Since 2003, the Federal Trade Commission (FTC) has instituted at least six administrative actions against CCAs, including one of the largest, AmeriDebt, Inc., under the auspices of the Telemarketing and Consumer Fraud and Abuse Prevention Act of 1994 (15 U.S.C. §§6101 et seq.) for various violations of that Act. (CCAs often market their services via telephone solicitation.) The FTC's Telemarketing Sales Rule (TSR), 16 CFR Part 310, was recently amended to add new restrictions aimed at curbing CCA abuse (see, e.g., the FTC's news release at www.ftc. gov/opa/2012/11/robocalls.shtml announcing the filing of complaints against A+ Financial Center, LLC, and four other companies allegedly using deceptive "This is Rachel from cardholder services" robocalls falsely promising to reduce the consumer's credit card debt).

The attorneys general in a number of states have brought suit against CCAs using their state consumer protection acts and antifraud laws. A number of states have legislated licensing and/or disclosure requirements on CCAs or prohibitions on up-front fees, and four states (Connecticut, Louisiana, Wyoming, and North Dakota) prohibit for-profit CCAs entirely. In 2003 the IRS began to crack down on for-profit CCAs masquerading as not-for-profit and in 2006 Congress amended the Internal Revenue Code (IRC) to add what is now 26 U.S.C. §501(q) imposing a number of requirements on CCAs wishing to receive tax-exempt status as nonprofit businesses, including a dictate that fees be reasonable and prohibiting fees based on a percentage of a client's debt or DMP payments unless state law expressly permits.

United States Organizations for Bankruptcy Alternatives

One of the leading trade associations for CCAs is the United States Organizations for Bankruptcy Alternatives (www.usoba.org/). Visit the USOBA site and see if you can determine the association's general position on industry regulation. What are the requirements for CCA membership in their association?

When a CCA succeeds at working out a DMP for a consumer client, it is a form of what has historically been known as a composition and extension agreement. A **composition agreement** is nothing more than a private, voluntary arrangement between a debtor and her creditors, pursuant to which the creditors agree to take a stated partial payment in full satisfaction of their claims. The composition agreement is often accompanied by an **extension agreement**, whereby the creditors agree to give the debtor additional time to make the agreed payments. The DMP or composition and extension agreement, whatever it is called, might be preferable to bankruptcy in terms of cost and time, but it is contingent on the cooperation of creditors. The agreement will typically stipulate that if the debtor defaults on any promised payment, the original debt will be revived in full.

Application Exercise 6

Determine if the state where you plan to practice has enacted any regulation of CCAs.

B. THE JUDICIAL COLLECTION PROCESS AND EXECUTION ON A FINAL JUDGMENT

When pre-judicial debt collection efforts fail, the creditor may choose to file a civil lawsuit to collect the amount owed or to liquidate the claim as in a tort action. Upon obtaining a **final judgment** in the civil lawsuit, the creditor can then utilize the various methods available for execution on that judgment.

The decision to file a collection lawsuit is not always automatic for the unpaid creditor. There are often considerations, such as weighing the likely costs of suing relative to the size of the claim; the time and expense required to pursue a judicial remedy; the likelihood of the debtor raising valid defenses to the debt or claim; whether there might be questions of personal jurisdiction over the defendant in the court where the debtor could most conveniently and economically file the suit; and whether the debtor may in fact have no assets on which to execute if and when a final judgment is obtained. Such a debtor is referred to by practitioners as being **judgment proof**.

Not every creditor needs to utilize the judicial collection process to collect what is owed. Creditors who are secured in property of the debtor may rely instead on self-help repossession of personal property collateral under Article 9 of the UCC or self-help foreclosure on mortgaged real property where state law allows. But even secured creditors who foreclose or repossess may be left with a deficiency balance owing to them after the collateral is sold and may choose a collection action in order to obtain a final judgment on that deficiency, which can then be satisfied by execution on non-collateralized assets of the debtor. Moreover, where binding arbitration is mandated by contract or statute or is agreed to post-dispute, judicial review on behalf of the losing party is limited to an attack on the validity of the arbitration process itself. But judicial collection action is available to the prevailing party in the arbitration proceeding in order to enforce an unpaid award.

It is beyond the scope of our study to review the rules of civil procedure regarding pleadings, service of process, pretrial discovery, pretrial motion practice, trial process, entry of final judgment, as well as the related topics of subject matter and personal jurisdiction of the courts. Needless to say, the practitioner must be thoroughly versed in the applicable civil rules and procedures. We will observe here that very frequently in debt collection actions involving contracts where the amount owed is liquidated, the final judgment is obtained fairly quickly by **default judgment** (under Rule 55 of the Federal Rules of Civil Procedure in federal lawsuits and analogous state rules of procedure in state court actions) since the debtor does not dispute the underlying debt or the amount — he simply cannot pay it. But where the underlying contractual obligation or the amount of it is contested or in tort claims where liability is denied, civil litigation may be hotly contested, expensive, and time consuming.

Many a consumer bankruptcy filing is triggered by a final judgment entered against the consumer in a civil lawsuit in favor of a preexisting creditor or a plaintiff who has brought an unliquidated claim against the consumer in tort or other theory. Because the prevailing plaintiff, now a **judgment creditor**, has the right to execute on his final judgment against the consumer defendant, now the **judgment debtor**, the assets of the consumer are in peril. In this section we will consider how the judgment creditor goes about enforcing the final judgment in his favor.

1. Postjudgment Motions or Right to Appeal as Delaying Execution on a Final Judgment

In the normal case, execution on a final judgment cannot begin immediately upon its entry by the court. Both the federal and state rules recognize a brief grace period following entry of final judgment during which execution is suspended as the judgment debtor decides whether to appeal or makes arrangements to pay the judgment. In some states, when judgment is entered by default in state court there is no grace period and execution can begin immediately.

Postjudgment motions may be filed, which also delay execution until the trial court has ruled.

Application Exercise 7

1. Review Rules 50, 52, 59, 62, and 69 of the Federal Rules of Civil Procedure and Rule 4(a)(1) and (4) of the Federal Rules of Appellate Procedure regarding postverdict or postjudgment motions that a losing party may file in a jury or bench trial and reacquaint yourself with how they may impact the timing of the judgment creditor's right to begin execution on the judgment and the right of the judgment debtor to appeal the final judgment. Then locate the analogous rules that control a civil lawsuit in the courts of the state where you plan to practice. Be sure you understand how the procedure works in both federal and state court.

2. Review Rule 62(a)(b) and (d) of the Federal Rules of Civil Procedure and Rule 8 of the Federal Rules of Appellate Procedure regarding the right of a judgment debtor to stay execution on a final judgment pending appeal and the requirement of a supersedeas bond. Then locate the analogous rules that control a civil lawsuit in the courts of the state where you plan to practice. Be sure you understand how the procedure works in both federal and state court.

2. Discovery in Aid of Execution (Postjudgment Asset Discovery)

Once a final judgment is entered, the judgment creditor seeking to execute on the judgment can utilize some or all of the formal discovery methods recognized in the rules of civil procedure to locate assets of the judgment debtor that may be available for execution in satisfaction of the final judgment. This is called discovery in aid of execution or postjudgment asset discovery. Federal Rule of Civil Procedure 69(a)(2) authorizes the judgment creditor to obtain postjudgment discovery in aid of execution from the debtor or any other person using discovery procedures authorized by either the federal rules or the rules of the state where the court is located.

The right to engage in postjudgment discovery in aid of execution is automatic under the federal rules and under the rules of most states. In some states, however, the judgment creditor must first attempt execution (by one of the methods discussed later in this section) and then seek court permission to engage in postjudgment discovery. In a very few states the creditor must first attempt execution and then initiate a second lawsuit by filing a creditor's bill alleging the failure of execution to locate sufficient assets to pay the judgment.

The most common discovery methods used in postjudgment asset discovery are interrogatories, document requests, and depositions. Such discovery may be used to obtain information from third persons, as well as from the judgment debtor, and subpoena power is available to compel attendance of such third parties at depositions, as well as to compel the production of documents and things that might be in their possession.

3. Property Exempt from Execution

Every state declares some property of the judgment debtor exempt from execution. The judgment creditor can only execute on non-exempt property. The federal government also mandates that various types of federal government benefits are exempt from execution on final judgments entered in either federal or state court. A summary of those exempt federal benefits is set out in Exhibit 3.3. There are exceptions. The federal benefits listed in Exhibit 3.3 may be seized to pay delinquent federal taxes or student loans or to satisfy state child support or spousal support obligations (see 42 U.S.C. §407 and 20 CFR 404.970).

EXHIBIT 3.3 **Federal Government Benefits Exempt from Execution**

- Social Security benefits
- Supplemental Security Income (SSI) benefits
- Veterans' benefits
- Civil service and federal retirement and disability benefits
- Service members' pay
- Military annuities and survivors' benefits
- Student assistance
- Railroad retirement benefits
- Merchant seamen's wages
- Longshoremen's and harbor workers' death and disability benefits
- Foreign service retirement and disability benefits
- Compensation for injury, death, or detention of employees of U.S. contractors outside the United States
- Federal Emergency Management Agency federal disaster assistance

---

In addition to mandated exemption of these federal benefits, §206(d) of the Employee Retirement Income Security Act of 1974 (ERISA) mandates that states exempt qualified pension, profit-sharing, SEP, and 401(k) plans with exceptions for Qualified Domestic Relations Orders, tax levies, and payment of criminal fines and penalties. (IRAs and private annuities do not receive such federal protection, though states may choose to exempt them.) Section 525 of the Internal Revenue Code mandates the exemption of proceeds in college savings plans up to a maximum of $25,000.

Subject to these federal mandates, state property exemption laws apply generally to executions undertaken to enforce both state and most federal court final judgments. For example, assume that a creditor in New York files suit against a Florida resident in a U.S. District Court in New York based on diversity of citizenship and takes a final judgment against that defendant. When the judgment creditor seeks to execute on property owned by the judgment debtor in New York, it will be New York state law that controls the property exemption issue. However, where you are dealing with enforcement of a federal tax lien or other lien created by federal law (e.g., to collect unpaid federal or federally guaranteed student loans) state exemption laws will not protect a debtor's property from the reach of such federal liens; state exemption laws are preempted by federal law authorizing the lien (see United States v. Bess, 357 U.S. 51 (1958), and Commissioner v. Stern, 357 U.S. 39 (1958)). You must look to federal exemption law in such situations (see, e.g., property exempted from federal tax lien by 26 U.S.C. §6334).

When a final judgment is entered in one state and the debtor owns property in another state, the law of the state where the property is located will control the exemption issue. For example, if a judgment creditor holding a final judgment issued by a New York state court (or U.S. District Court in New York) seeks to execute on property owned by the judgment debtor in Florida, the Florida exemption laws, not New York exemption laws, will control the disposition of that Florida property.

The Homestead Exemption

Forty-six of the 50 states currently recognize a homestead exemption, allowing the debtor to retain some or all owner's equity in the family home or domicile (the primary home or domicile when the debtor owns more than one). There is, however, tremendous variation among the states in the dollar amount of the allowed exemption. In Texas, for example, the constitutional homestead exemption is unlimited in dollar amount, though subject to certain acreage limits, while in Tennessee, by statute, the homestead exemption is limited to owner's equity of $5,000 for an individual owner and $7,500 (total) for a married couple unless the owner has a minor child, in which case the exemption is $25,000. Minnesota, on the other hand, falls somewhere in the middle of those extremes, allowing a $200,000 statutory homestead exemption for urban property and $500,000 for rural property, subject to acreage limits and subject to adjustment for inflation every other year. Quite a difference.

Application Exercise 8

Assume that Nick and Pearl Murphy had filed a medical malpractice suit against Dr. Samuel Craft for botching Pearl's appendectomy procedure and that they obtain a final judgment against Dr. Craft for $500,000. Dr. Craft is single and owns his home. He purchased the home on one acre five years ago for $1.2 million and has a mortgage on it in favor of Capital City Bank (CCB), with a current balance owed of $900,000. The home is appraised today at $1.5 million. How much equity in the home can Dr. Craft exempt from execution by the Murphys if the homestead exemption rules of the state of Washington apply (see Wash. Rev. Code §6.13.030)? South Dakota (see S.D. Cod. Laws §43-45-3)? Tennessee (Tenn. Code Ann. §26-2-301)? Rhode Island (see R.I. Gen. Laws §9-26-4.1)?

If a debtor's equity in the homestead exceeds the applicable homestead exemption, the executing creditor can force the property to be sold, pay the debtor the homestead amount and apply the rest of the proceeds to the debt. For example, assume Dr. Craft's home is in a state that allows a $50,000 homestead exemption. When the Murphys execute on their judgment and the property is sold for $1.5 million, the first $900,000 will go to pay off the existing mortgage to CCB, assuming it is properly perfected giving it senior status and the first right to proceeds of the collateralized property. The next $50,000 will go to Dr. Craft as his homestead exemption amount. The Murphys can then apply the balance of $650,000, minus the costs of sale, to satisfy the judgment owed them.

As the preceding example illustrates, an executing judgment creditor will not have a claim to the debtor's property that is superior to a previously secured and perfected interest (the CCB mortgage in the Murphy/Craft example). That example also illustrates that exemptions do not apply to a creditor to whom the debtor has granted a security interest in the property.

Assume that Dr. Craft owes CCB $1.5 million and the entire indebtedness is secured by a mortgage on his home. If Craft defaults on his obligation to CCB and the bank forecloses on the home and sells it for $1.5 million, all of the proceeds of sale will go to retire the indebtedness owed to CCB. What about Dr. Craft's $50,000 homestead exemption? It doesn't apply between him and the bank since he voluntarily mortgaged the property in which he would have had the exemption. Creditors consensually secured in property that the debtor could otherwise claim as exempt are not bound by those exemptions.

In many states, the homestead exemption is declared inapplicable to mechanics' and materialman's liens filed against the property claimed as homestead, to family support obligations, and to tax obligations.

Personal Property/Income Source Exemptions

States also exempt various types and dollar amounts of personal property or income sources from execution. The variation of personal property/income exemptions among the states is significant. We have already seen in Exhibit 3.3 and the text following that federal law mandates that states exempt some categories of personal property and income sources. Exhibit 3.4 sets out other commonly recognized personal property/income source exemptions adopted by the states.

EXHIBIT 3.4   **Common State Personal Property and Income Source Exemptions**

▪ Household furniture, up to a designated dollar amount of current value or equity (e.g., $5,000)
▪ Vehicles, up to a designated dollar amount of current value or equity
▪ Equipment or tools used by the debtor in a trade or business
▪ Necessary and proper clothing and personal possessions, such as the family Bible or Koran, family photographs/portraits, pets, school books

EXHIBIT 3.4 **(Continued)**

- Livestock, up to a designated dollar amount of current value or equity
- Any personal property, up to a designated dollar amount of current value or equity (e.g., $10,000 of value and the debtor can choose the property to be exempted)
- IRAs (including Roths) and private annuities
- State or local government employee retirement funds (often including teachers, police officers, firefighters, etc.)
- Disability or unemployment payments
- Child support or alimony payments
- Life insurance policies covering the life of the debtor on which the debtor's spouse or children are the sole beneficiaries
- Proceeds of a disability policy or annuity constituting compensation of debtor for his personal injury or the personal injury or death of one upon whom the debtor was dependent

As we saw with the homestead exemption in real property, no exemption can be claimed by the debtor in personal property in which a security interest has been granted when it is the secured creditor seeking to repossess and sell that property. For example, if a department store sought to repossess living room furniture in which it was granted a security interest by a consumer buyer to secure the debt the consumer owed to the department store, the consumer could not claim an exemption in the furniture to block the repossession. However, if a creditor not holding a security interest in the furniture obtained a final judgment against consumer and sought to execute on the furniture, the consumer could likely assert an exemption in it for household furniture up to the allowed dollar amount of such exemption.

Applicability of Property Exemptions to Government Claims

As previously noted, the federal government enforcing a federal tax lien or other obligation to the federal government (e.g., federal student loan, farm, or small business loan) is not subject to any state property exemption law affecting real or personal property due to the Supremacy Clause of the U.S. Constitution (Article VI, Paragraph 2). However, in 26 U.S.C. §6334, Congress has created specific exemptions applicable to execution on a federal tax lien, which include:

- Worker's compensation benefits
- Unemployment benefits
- Necessary clothing and school books
- Furniture and personal effects up to a total value of $6,250
- Necessary books and tools of the trade up to a total value of $3,125
- Income or wages equal to the applicable standard deduction allowed the debtor for federal income tax purposes

Though 26 U.S.C. §6334 appears to also exempt social security benefits from execution on a federal tax lien, subsequent legislative enactments suggest otherwise, and the IRS has taken the position that such benefits are subject to levy (see 20 CFR 404.970).

The federal government may also offset (deduct) amounts owed to any federal agency from social security payments or income tax refunds due the debtor. For example, assume an individual defaults on a federal student loan administered by the U.S. Department of Treasury or on a small business loan administered by the U.S. Small Business Administration. Either of those federal agencies could have amounts withheld from the individual's social security check (including SSI payments) or tax refund to satisfy the obligation.

The homestead exemption will not defeat a state or local tax lien arising out of unpaid property taxes on the homestead property.

Exempt property issues arise in consumer bankruptcy cases as well. Individual consumer debtors are allowed to exempt certain property from their creditors in those cases. And as we will learn, the state and federal exemption laws summarized in this section are by no means irrelevant in the context of a bankruptcy case.

Application Exercise 9

Now might be a good time to locate the exemption statutes of the state where you plan to practice. What is the homestead exemption there? Are there any exceptions to the applicability of that exemption? What personal property exemptions are recognized?

4. The Effect of Concurrent Ownership of Property on Creditor Execution Efforts

Concurrent ownership raises questions regarding the right of the judgment creditor of only one of the concurrent owners to execute on the ownership interest of that owner of the property.

For example, assume Nick and Pearl Murphy concurrently own their home and there is equity in the home. Assume CCME has taken a final judgment against Pearl. CCME is now a judgment creditor of Pearl, but not Nick. Issues will be whether the judgment creditor can execute on both Pearl and Nick's interest in the property and maybe whether it can even execute on Pearl's interest in it. Assume that Pearl and her brother Paul concurrently own a valuable antique vase. CCME has a judgment against Pearl but not Paul. The issue raised is whether CCME can execute on Pearl's ownership interest in the vase.

Of course, if the final judgment is entered against all the concurrent owners of property, the judgment creditor can execute on the property. In our example, if CCME has a final judgment against both Nick and Pearl, it could clearly execute on the equity in the home despite the concurrent ownership. If CCME has a final judgment against both Pearl and her brother Paul, it could execute on the vase despite the concurrent ownership.

But whether the judgment creditor holding a final judgment against only one concurrent owner of property can execute on the interest of that one owner of the property depends on what type of concurrent ownership it is. There are several.

Property Owned by a Married Couple

In many states, married couples can choose to own property together as **tenants by the entireties**, a form of concurrent ownership in which each spouse has only a **right of survivorship** in the property. On the death of one spouse, the survivor takes the entire ownership interest as a matter of law. So long as both spouses are alive, neither can transfer their individual interest in the property (which is only the right of survivorship) either consensually (as by selling, granting a securing interest in, or gifting it to another) or non-consensually as in judgment execution. States recognizing the tenancy by the entireties limit it to property owned only by the married couple (no third party can be on the title — but see the joint tenancy below) and most such states presume the entireties arrangement when only the spouses are on the title to the property. However, spouses in these states can choose to own property together as tenants in common (discussed below) if they choose.

For example, assume that CCME executes on the final judgment in its favor against Pearl Murphy. If Pearl and Nick own their home as tenants by the entireties, CCME, as the judgment creditor of Pearl only, may be unable to force the homestead to be sold as part of the execution. In other words, it cannot reach either Nick or Pearl's equity in the home because all either has is the right of survivorship. If Nick should die before Pearl then her right of survivorship would result in her having sole ownership of the homestead and CCME could execute on it subject to her right to claim the state exemption.

Note however, that in some states that recognize the tenancy by the entireties between a married couple, some debts may be considered jointly owed even though incurred by only one spouse. For example, the state where Nick and Pearl live may declare medical bills incurred by one spouse to be the obligation of both so the tenancy by the entireties will no bar to CCME executing on the judgment against the home. Of course, the Murphys will still be able to assert the state homestead exemption.

Ten states (Arizona, California, Idaho, Louisiana, Nevada, New Mexico, Texas, Washington, Wisconsin, and optionally by election of the spouses in Alaska) along with Puerto Rico are **community property** jurisdictions. In those states and territory there is a presumption that all property acquired by either spouse during the marriage is wholly owned by both spouses (regardless of how it is titled) so that all such property can be executed on to satisfy a judgment against either spouse. The presumption also results in debts incurred by only one spouse being deemed the obligation of both. The presumption of ownership does not apply to property owned by either spouse prior to marriage or to property inherited by only one spouse during marriage. And some community property states limit the presumption of joint debt in some instances. For example, Texas prohibits judgment liens from attaching to community property that is titled only in the non-debtor's name. Furthermore, the presumption of community ownership of property can be rebutted by proof that the spouses agreed in good faith and with no intent to defraud that certain property is in fact separately owned.

Tenancy in Common

A **tenancy in common** is a form of concurrent ownership in which each owner has an undivided interest in the property owned. If the judgment debtor owns property concurrently with a spouse or anyone else as tenants in common, the undivided interest of the judgment debtor in the property can be partitioned or sold as part of the execution process.

Assume that Pearl and her brother Paul own a one-acre parcel of unimproved land as tenants in common with Pearl having an undivided, one-third interest in the property and Paul an undivided two-thirds interest. CCME, as the judgment creditor of Pearl, can execute on Pearl's undivided one-third interest in the property, ask a court to partition it from Paul's two-thirds interest, and then sell her partitioned portion of the land and apply the proceeds in satisfaction of the judgment. If the parcel cannot be partitioned (perhaps the parcel only has value as a whole), the entire parcel will be sold and Pearl's share of the proceeds (one-third in this example) paid to the executing creditor. If Pearl and Paul also own the antique vase as tenants in common, it cannot be partitioned as realty can, so it will be sold and Pearl's share of the proceeds paid over to the executing creditor.

Joint Tenancy

In a **joint tenancy**, the concurrent owners each own an equal, undivided interest in the property and there is a right of survivorship as in a tenancy by the entireties. That means that when one joint tenant dies, the surviving joint tenants will take the decedent's interest in the property rather than it passing through her will or to her heirs by intestate succession. The joint tenancy is different from the tenancy by the entireties, however, in that, prior to death, a joint tenant may transfer her interest in the property to another by sale, pledge, or gift. The transferee of the joint tenant's interest does not become a joint tenant in the property but a tenant in common only. The joint tenancy is broken by the transfer. Significantly for our purposes, judgment creditors of a single joint tenant, like creditors of a single tenant in common, can execute on the joint tenant's interest in the property jointly owned. For example, assume Pearl and her two brothers, Paul and Peter, concurrently own the antique vase as joint tenants. CCME, as the judgment creditor of Pearl only, can execute on Pearl's undivided interest in the vase, force it to be sold and her one-third of the proceeds paid over to it.

Application Exercise 10

Determine if the state where you plan to practice recognizes the tenancy by the entireties or is a community property state as to property owned by spouses. How would your state decide the issues of concurrent ownership arising when CCME executes on the final judgment it has against Pearl Murphy only, assuming (1) Pearl and her husband Nick own an undeveloped acre of land worth $100,000, title to which is in both names? (2) Pearl owns the undeveloped acre together with her brother and title is in both names? (3) Pearl owns the undeveloped acre together with her husband and her brother and title is in all three names? (4) Pearl inherited cash from a deceased relative three years ago and has always kept it in a certificate of deposit in her name only?

5. Trust Arrangements that May Defeat Creditor Execution Efforts

A trust is an arrangement whereby the owner of property (called variously the grantor, trustor, or settlor) conveys title in the property to a designated trustee to be held by the trustee for the benefit of another party, called the trust beneficiary. The property placed in trust is called the trust principal or the trust property or the trust res. There are many different kinds of trusts, but we will focus only on two that have special consequences for efforts to execute on a final judgment.

Spendthrift Trust

A **spendthrift trust** is a trust established to provide certain benefits to a designated beneficiary from time to time that prohibits the beneficiary from selling or pledging as security any of the trust principal or any future distributions to be received from the trust. The idea behind the spendthrift trust is to protect the beneficiary from his own poor judgment by limiting his access to trust principal or interest. In most states, the spendthrift trust has the added benefit to the beneficiary of preventing his creditors from executing on assets of the trust unless and until they are distributed to the beneficiary. For example, assume Pearl Murphy's parents had created a spendthrift trust containing a one-acre parcel and naming her as the sole beneficiary. Assume further that the land is income-producing because coal is mined from beneath it. Under the spendthrift provisions of the trust, Pearl could not sell or mortgage her interest in the land or the income from it while either is held in trust for her, nor could her creditor, CCME, seize the land or income still held in the trust to satisfy its judgment against Pearl. If and when payments of interest were made to Pearl by the trustee of the trust or if the land itself was conveyed to her at the conclusion of the trust, then those payments or the land could be seized.

The reason that qualified retirement plans are exempt from execution is that Section 206(d)(1) of ERISA requires that in order to be qualified, a retirement plan must include an anti-assignment clause and prohibit alienation of plan assets by the beneficiary. This section is known as the **federal spendthrift clause** and has been construed to defeat both the claims of creditors of the beneficiary and the beneficiary's own worst instincts to spend the assets on anything other than retirement.

Domestic Asset Protection Trust

A **domestic asset protection trust** (DAPT) (sometimes called a **self-settled trust**) is an arrangement whereby the settlor can convey his own property into trust, name himself the beneficiary to receive distributions of principal or interest as proscribed in the trust document, and yet prevent his creditors from seizing trust assets not yet distributed. Previously available only as questionable **foreign asset protection trusts** or **offshore trusts** under the laws of other nations (typically a Caribbean island), approximately fourteen states have authorized DAPT by statute. To obtain the protection of the trust assets from creditors of the settlor/beneficiary, the conveyance of the property into trust must be irrevocable (i.e., the settlor cannot ever withdraw the assets from the trust; he can only receive the distributions from the trust as a named beneficiary); and the settlor cannot also serve as trustee of the trust (although most states allow the settlor to remove a trustee and appoint someone else to serve).

Like any trust arrangement, a DAPT is subject to legal attack if the creation of the trust itself can be demonstrated to be a fraudulent transfer as to creditors. However, in order to protect known creditors at the time the trust is created, states that recognize DAPT have a built-in statutory period that delays the effective date of protection of the trust res from execution (e.g., 2-3 years). The states will also except some creditors from the ban on execution, like child support or alimony claimants, divorcing spouses, and, in some states, preexisting tort claimants.

Application Exercise 11

Determine if the state where you plan to practice recognizes the spendthrift trust or the domestic asset protection trust. If Pearl Murphy was the beneficiary of a spendthrift trust holding real property, at what point could her creditors seize either income generated by the property or the real property itself? If your state recognizes the DAPT and Pearl creates such a trust for the real property naming herself as sole beneficiary, can she also serve as trustee? Can she replace a named trustee? Must the trust be irrevocable? Can she receive income distributions from the trust during her life? How much time must elapse following creation of the trust until it is exempt from creditors? Are there some creditors who are not barred from reaching the principal of the trust in execution?

---

6. Methods of Executing on a Final Judgment

In this section we will consider the three most common methods of executing on a final judgment under state law. Recognize, however, that there is tremendous variation among the states regarding the specific methods of execution allowed, the procedures that must be followed, and the relevant nomenclature used for the execution process. Consequently, the material presented here is necessarily generalized and not state specific.

The Judgment Lien

The judgment creditor can create an involuntary lien on any real property owned by the judgment debtor by filing a **judgment lien**. Commonly the judgment lien is created by obtaining a certified copy of the final judgment from the clerk of the court that issued the judgment and then recording, filing, or registering that certified copy in the designated public office for the filing of land records. Exhibit 3.5 sets out a typical statute dealing with the procedure for creating a judgment lien.

EXHIBIT 3.5	**Typical Statute Regarding Procedure for Creating a Judgment Lien**

> Judgments and decrees in any court of record and judgments in excess of five hundred dollars ($500) in any court not of record in this state shall be liens upon the debtor's land from the time a certified copy of the judgment or decree shall be registered in the lien book in the register's office of the county where the land is located. Such lien shall be valid against any person having, or later acquiring, an interest in such property who is not a party to the action wherein such judgment is issued.

In some states the judgment lien is created by recording a writ of execution (discussed in the next section) along with a notice of levy. Such states may also require that the writ of execution be served first on the personal property of the debtor and returned before being recorded as a lien on the real property of the debtor. However it is affected, the judgment lien becomes a cloud on the title to any real property owned by the debtor in the county where the judgment is recorded, just as a consensual mortgage would.

For example, assume that Nick and Pearl Murphy obtain a certified copy of their final judgment against Dr. Samuel Craft and properly record it in the county where Craft's home is located. Assume also that Dr. Craft is single and owns a home in Capital County, which he purchased five years ago for $1.2 million and on which he has an existing mortgage in favor of Capital City Bank (CCB) with a current balance owed of $900,000. As of the moment of recording their judgment, the Murphys have a lien against Dr. Craft's home in Capital County in the amount of the final judgment plus the postjudgment interest, which is continuing to accumulate. It is just as if Dr. Craft had conveyed a second mortgage to the Murphys in that amount. Of course, if CCB has properly perfected its first mortgage, the judgment lien in favor of the Murphys will be second, or junior, to that first mortgage. But if Dr. Craft now seeks to sell his home, both the CCB mortgage and the Murphys' judgment lien are of public record, and any buyer must either pay them off or take title to the property subject to those two liens. (See the last sentence of the statute in Exhibit 3.5.)

Not only does a judgment lien create a cloud on title to the debtor's real property, effectively preventing its sale, but the judgment creditor holding the judgment lien can also foreclose on the lien, sell the real property subject to it, and apply the proceeds to the judgment amount owed. Since no consensual power of sale has been conveyed by the debtor to the judgment creditor, the lien holder must seek a judicial foreclosure either by applying to the court for an order of sale or by having the sheriff seize the property by writ of attachment or writ of execution (discussed below in this section) and then conducting a sheriff's sale. Exhibit 3.6 sets forth a typical state statute authorizing this procedure.

EXHIBIT 3.6	**Typical Statute Authorizing Foreclosure on a Judgment Lien**

As long as a judgment lien is effective, no levy is necessary; the judgment creditor may move for an order of sale. Otherwise a levy occurs when the sheriff exercises control over the judgment debtor's realty.

When the real property is sold, the proceeds will be applied first to the expenses incurred in the sale and then to the amount of the judgment, including accrued post-judgment interest. Of course, if there are other liens on the property senior to the judgment lien or if there are any exemptions, those must be satisfied in full before any proceeds are applied to the judgment amount. For example, if the Murphys create a judgment lien on Dr. Craft's home in Capital County and then obtain an order of sale, proceeds of the sale will be applied first to the expenses of the sale, then to pay off the balance in full of the mortgage held by CCB, and only then to the Murphys. This is so because the CCB mortgage on the property is senior to the Murphys' judgment lien.

In most states, a judgment lien will attach to any real property the judgment debtor acquires after the judgment lien has been created so long as it is still in effect. Assume that the Murphys create their judgment lien in Capital County today. Six months from now, Dr. Craft purchases an interest in an empty lot in a residential area of the county. The Murphys will have an automatic lien against Dr. Craft's interest in that lot without having to re-record their judgment. The judgment lien created today will attach to the property acquired in six months if it has not been satisfied in the interim. The preceding example raises the question of how long a judgment lien is valid. States differ, but a common term of validity is ten years from the date the lien was created. The judgment lien holder typically has the option to revive the judgment lien before the end of that term either by re-recording the original judgment or by obtaining an order from the court granting an extension of the judgment and then recording (registering or filing) that order of extension. Exhibit 3.7 sets out a typical statute regarding this procedure.

EXHIBIT 3.7	**Typical Statute Regarding Term of Judgment Lien and Revival of Lien**

Once a judgment lien is created by registration, it will last for the time remaining in a ten-year period from the date of final judgment entry in the court clerk's office and for any extension granted by the court. For the extension of the lien to be enforceable, the judgment creditor must register the court's order extending the judgment lien.

If a judgment debtor pays off the indebtedness owed to the judgment creditor after a judgment lien has been created on the debtor's property (or after a lien lis pendens has been created on it), the now-satisfied judgment creditor will record (register or file) a release of lien or termination statement. Exhibit 3.8 sets out a typical state statute regarding this procedure.

EXHIBIT 3.8   ## Typical Statute Regarding Terminating an Involuntary Lien on Property Following Satisfaction of Indebtedness

Upon satisfaction of the judgment, the judgment debtor may demand that the judgment creditor record in the register's office a termination statement to supersede any lien lis pendens or judgment lien of record. If the judgment creditor fails to register a termination statement within ten days after demand, the judgment creditor shall be liable to the judgment debtor for $100 and for any loss caused to the judgment debtor by failure to register.

Similarly, if the judgment creditor has created a judgment lien on the debtor's property and the debtor thereafter obtains a stay of execution pending appeal, the trial court may order the judgment creditor to remove the lien pending the outcome of the appeal.

In some states, the judgment lien is deemed to attach to the judgment debtor's personal property when the lien has been properly filed (or recorded or registered) in the public office responsible for UCC filings.

Application Exercise 12

Locate the statutes of the state where you plan to practice regarding how a judgment lien is created, authorizing foreclosure on a judgment lien, regarding effective term of a judgment lien and its revival, and termination of the lien on satisfaction of the underlying judgment.

Case Preview

Currier v. First Resolution Investment Corp.

These methods of executing on a final judgment are a type of debt collection of course and may trigger issues involving the FDCPA when undertaken by a debt collector against a consumer. As you read Currier v. First Resolution Investment Corp. consider the following questions:

1. What action did the debt collector, First Resolution, take that violated Kentucky state law and was determined to be a violation of the FDCPA?
2. What provision of the FDCPA did the court find that First Resolution had violated by the action?
3. Does every violation of state law by a debt collector executing on a judgment against a consumer amount to a violation of the FDCPA?

Currier v. First Resolution Investment Corp.
762 F. 3d 529 (6th Cir. 2014)

[In May 2012, First Resolution brought an action against Currier to collect charged-off credit card debt of $1,000.51 plus interest. A default judgment was entered by the court after Currier's counsel failed to appear at an October 1, 2012, hearing. Currier filed a motion to vacate the default judgment and asked for an extension of time to file an answer. As of that date, the judgment against Currier was not final under Kentucky law. After obtaining the default judgment, First Resolution filed a judgment lien against Currier's home. Under Kentucky law, a judgment lien can only arise from a final judgment so the lien was invalid. On October 29, 2012, a judge granted Currier's motion to vacate the default judgment. Even though First Resolution knew the judgment would be vacated, it did not release the lien until November 5. Currier sued First Resolution in federal court, alleging that the invalid lien violated various provisions of the FDCPA. Finding that a violation of state law is not a per se violation of the FDCPA and that the invalid lien was not a threat, the district court dismissed the claims. Currier appealed.]

STRANCH, Circuit Judge.

Congress passed the FDCPA to address the widespread and serious national problem of debt collection abuse by unscrupulous debt collectors. . . . The Act prohibits a wide array of specific conduct, but it also prohibits, in general terms, any harassing, unfair, or deceptive debt collection practice, which enables "the courts, where appropriate, to proscribe other improper conduct which is not specifically addressed." . . . [S]ee generally 15 U.S.C. §§1692d-1692f. . . . [T]he Act is "extraordinarily broad." Barany-Snyder v. Weiner, 539 F.3d 327, 333 (6th Cir. 2008). . . . To determine whether conduct fits within the broad scope of the FDCPA, the conduct is viewed through the eyes of the "least sophisticated consumer." Id. This standard recognizes that the FDCPA protects the gullible and the shrewd alike while simultaneously presuming a basic level of reasonableness and understanding on the part of the debtor, thus preventing liability for bizarre or idiosyncratic interpretations of debt collection notices. Id.

Currier alleges that filing and failing to release the invalid lien against her home violated multiple provisions of the FDCPA, "including, but not limited to": 15 U.S.C. §1692f, which prohibits using "unfair or unconscionable means . . . to collect any debt"; §1692f(1), which prohibits the "collection of any amount . . . unless such amount is expressly authorized by the agreement creating the debt or permitted by law"; and §1692e(5), which prohibits "threat[ening] to take any action that cannot legally be taken or that is not intended to be taken." First Resolution admits . . . that Currier has alleged that: she is a "consumer" within the meaning of the Act; the debt arose for personal, family, or household purposes; and First Resolution is a "debt collector." See 15 U.S.C. §§1692(e), 1692a(3), 1692a(5)-(6). We conclude that Currier sufficiently alleged conduct that falls within the broad scope of practices prohibited by the FDCPA. . . .

First Resolution raises a defense to the FDCPA claims — that the invalid lien was not a violation of the FDCPA because a violation of state law is not a per se violation of the FDCPA. Our sister circuits have indeed concluded — usually in the context of licensing violations — that not every technical violation of state debt collection law rises to the level of unfair or otherwise prohibited conduct under the FDCPA. See, e.g., LeBlanc v. Unifund CCR Partners, 601 F.3d 1185, 1192 (11th Cir. 2010) (holding that debt collector's failure to have a proper license, a violation of state law, is not a per se violation of the FDCPA but that it may support a violation of the FDCPA); Carlson v. First Revenue Assurance, 359 F.3d 1015, 1018 (8th Cir. 2004) (holding that a debt collector's failure to have the proper license was not the kind of "false or misleading" practice barred [16] by §1692e); Wade v. Reg'l Credit Ass'n, 87 F.3d 1098, 1100-01 (9th Cir. 1996) (holding that sending a debtor correct notice of debt and risks to her credit was not a violation of the FDCPA even though debt collector was not licensed in debtor's state). A sister circuit has also rejected the contention that using the proper state procedure to freeze a debtor's bank account after receiving a valid final judgment was unfair under §1692f where the debt collector unknowingly froze an account that contained exempt funds. Beler v. Blatt, Hasenmiller, Leibsker & Moore, LLC, 480 F.3d 470, 472, 473-74 (7th Cir. 2007). There, the court said that the FDCPA is not an enforcement mechanism for state laws and it declined to create a hearing requirement in the state system. Id. at 473-74.

We agree that Congress did not turn every violation of state law into a violation of the FDCPA. But that does not mean that a violation of state law can never also be a violation of the FDCPA. The proper question in the context of an FDCPA claim is whether the plaintiff alleged an action that falls within the broad range of conduct prohibited by the Act. The legality of the action taken under state law may be relevant, as it is in this case. See LeBlanc, 601 F.3d at 1192 (considering the state law violation relevant to the FDCPA analysis). If the judgment lien had been valid under state law for the month that First Resolution held it, we could not say that it was an unfair debt collection practice even though it was coercive in nature. But the same action becomes unfair when accomplished by using a state mechanism that does not authorize it.

First Resolution also argues that it cannot be held liable under the FDCPA because it did not have reason to know that the lien was invalid at the time it mailed the notice of judgment lien. According to this version of events, the normal rule that a successful plaintiff in Kentucky court must wait 10 days to execute on a judgment did not apply here because the default judgment stated that "[t]his is a final judgment" and "execution may issue forthwith." See Ky. Rev. Stat. Ann. §426.030 (setting a waiting period "unless ordered by the court"). Although the motion to vacate unquestionably rendered the judgment non-final, First Resolution contends that it did not know about the motion until the end of the day on October 8, 2012, after it had already mailed the notice of judgment lien. See Pers. Bd. v. Heck, 725 S.W.2d 13, 18 (Ky. Ct. App. 1986) ("A motion [to vacate a judgment] converts a final judgment to an interlocutory judgment.").

This argument fails for two reasons. First, whether or not First Resolution had reason to believe that the lien was valid when filed is an issue of fact that is not relevant at the motion to dismiss stage. Second, even if First Resolution's version of the facts were construed to be part of a bona fide error defense, we note that it would not establish all the elements of such defense. See 15 U.S.C. §1692k(c). . . . To qualify for this defense, a debt collector must prove by a preponderance of the evidence that the violation was unintentional, that it was the result of a bona fide error, and that the debt collector maintained procedures to avoid the error. Hartman v. Great Seneca Fin. Corp., 569 F.3d 606, 614 (6th Cir. 2009). Although First Resolution alleges that the invalid lien began as an unintentional bona fide error, it admits that it learned of Currier's motion to vacate the judgment on the same day it filed the judgment lien and nonetheless failed to release the lien for a month. And it has alleged nothing to show that it maintains a procedure to avoid the error. In Kentucky, a losing party has only 10 days after entry of the final judgment to file a motion to vacate the judgment. Ky. R. Civ. P. 59.05. The error at issue could have been avoided if First Resolution had established a practice of waiting to file a judgment lien until 10 days after obtaining a judgment or of checking the docket before filing a lien. It could also have maintained a procedure for immediate correction of error. But First Resolution admits that it had implemented none of these procedures. First Resolution is not entitled to the bona fide error defense. . . .

Post-Case Follow-Up

Currier also illustrates a debt collector asserting the bona fide error defense discussed earlier. What is the three-part test for that defense used in the Sixth Circuit according to the Hartman v. Great Seneca case cited in *Currier*? Between the debtor and the debt collector, which party has the burden of proof when the bona fide error defense is raised? What part(s) of the test did First Resolution fail to establish? Look at the discussion of the Jerman v. Carlisle, McNellie, Rini, Kramer & Ulrich, L.P.A. decision earlier in this chapter and determine whether the courts of your federal circuit allow assertion of the bona fide error defense for genuine mistakes regarding the legal requirements of the FDCPA.

Currier v. First Resolution Investment Corp.: Real Life Applications

1. Assume a debt collector obtains a final judgment in a collection lawsuit against a consumer named John Alex Smith and causes a judgment lien to be issued

attaching property of Smith. One day later, the debt collector learns that service of process of the complaint on Smith at the beginning of the lawsuit was defective because the summons served contained a clerical typo misspelling the name of the defendant as John Alec Smith. Under state law this makes the final judgment later obtained in the lawsuit invalid. The debt collector calls you for advice. What should the debt collector do to avoid potential liability under the FDCPA?

2. Regardless of what advice you give the debt collector client as to what to do next, what questions do you want to ask to evaluate whether the bona fide error defense might be available in the event of a FDCPA claim?

3. What kind of "procedures to avoid the error" might a debt collector be advised to have in place to avoid the kind of clerical error described in No. 1?

The Writ of Execution

The method of execution most commonly used to seize non-exempt personal property of the debtor is the **writ of execution**, sometimes called a **writ of fieri facias**. The writ is typically applied for from the clerk of the court that rendered the final judgment. Exhibit 3.9 sets forth an application for writ of attachment that CCME might file once its judgment against Pearl Murphy becomes final and executable.

EXHIBIT 3.9   **Application for Writ of Execution**

The Plaintiff hereby makes application to the Clerk of the Circuit Court to issue a writ of execution in the above styled case to satisfy a judgment against the defendant Pearl E. Murphy in the amount of $2,247.70 entered on September 20, YR-1. The balance of the judgment that remains unsatisfied after the defendant is credited with payments made on said judgment is $2,247.70 plus postjudgment interest accruing on said amount from September 20, YR-1, through the date of payment.

This 1st day of November, YR-1

Attorney's signature

The clerk issues the writ, which is then delivered to the sheriff (or other government officer charged with executing it), and directs the sheriff to seize property of the debtor to satisfy the indebtedness. What the writ of execution issued on behalf of CCME against Pearl Murphy might look like is shown in Exhibit 3.10.

EXHIBIT 3.10 **Writ of Execution**

To the Sheriff of Capital County, Yourstate:

On September 20, YR-1, a judgment was entered in the docket of this court in favor of Capital City Medical Equipment Company as judgment creditor and against Pearl E. Murphy as judgment debtor, for $2,247.70 the full amount of which is due on the judgment as entered together with interest on the judgment amount at 10% per annum, or $.62 per day, from the date of entry of the judgment to the date of issuance of this writ, to which must be added court costs of $255 and the commissions and costs of the officer executing this writ.

You are hereby commanded to satisfy the judgment with interest, commissions, and costs as provided by law, out of the personal property of the debtor. If sufficient personal property cannot be found, then this judgment may be satisfied out of the debtor's real property or if the judgment is already a lien on real property, then out of the debtor's real property. You are to make return of this writ within not less than 10 days nor more than 60 days after satisfaction of this judgment, with what you have done endorsed on this writ.

Dated: November 1, YR-1

_____
[Clerk]

By:

_____
[Deputy Clerk]

Rule 69 of the Federal Rules of Civil Procedure provides that in executing on a final judgment entered in the U.S. District Court, the practice and procedure of the state in which the district court is held may be utilized. Thus, writs of execution issued by the U.S. District Court Clerk can be directed to the U.S. Marshal or to the county sheriff. In some states, a writ of execution can only authorize the seizure of a debtor's personal property. As noted earlier, in other states it can authorize the seizure of either the debtor's personal or real property. And in those latter states, there may be an order of priority in which the debtor's property can be seized. A typical mandated order of priority is that the sheriff must first attempt to satisfy the execution out of the debtor's personal property, and only if that property is insufficient can

Consumer Protection Laws and Bankruptcy Practice

Attorneys involved in consumer bankruptcy cases, whether on behalf of the debtor, a creditor, or the bankruptcy trustee, will routinely encounter issues involving a wide range of consumer protection laws. In this chapter we have examined one of those, the FDCPA, in some detail because of its central role in prepetition consumer debt collection. But the FDCPA and numerous others can come into play in the administration of a bankruptcy case.

In the most common scenarios the debtor may challenge the validity of a creditor's claim due to an alleged violation by the creditor of a consumer protection law. Or, since many federal and state consumer protection laws recognize a private right of action in the consumer against the offending creditor (as with the FDCPA), the debtor may list such a claim against the offending creditor as an asset of the estate.

Significant federal consumer protection laws with which the consumer bankruptcy lawyer may deal include the Truth in Lending Act and its Regulation Z mandating certain disclosures in consumer credit transactions; the Real Estate Settlement Procedures Act of 1974 and its Regulation X mandating certain disclosures in consumer mortgage transactions; the Federal Trade Commission Act prohibiting unfair and deceptive trade practices in consumer transactions; the Equal Credit Opportunity Act of 1974 prohibiting discrimination on certain bases in credit decisions; the Fair Credit Reporting Act of 1970 regulating the collection, maintenance and distribution of consumer credit information by credit reporting agencies; the Fair Credit Billing Act of 1974 mandating procedures for resolving disputes between credit card holders and the issuers; the Credit Card Accountability, Responsibility and Disclosure Act of 2009 imposing regulations on issuers of credit cards to consumers; the Magnuson-Moss Warranty Act of 1975 and the Consumer Leasing Act of 1976 that provide consumers protections in the purchase or lease of consumer goods; the Consumer Product Safety Act of 1972 regulating the safety of a broad range of consumer products; and the various statutory protections related to employment discrimination including

the sheriff then seize the debtor's real property. This mandatory ranking or order of priority in seizing the debtor's property is often called the **marshalling of assets**. In executing the writ, the sheriff (or U.S. Marshal in a federal case) will locate and **levy** on (take possession of) property of the debtor. This may include cash, in which case the sheriff will be careful not only to inventory the cash on the return (discussed below) but to specify how the cash was applied. When cash is taken from the cash register of a debtor, that is sometimes called a **till tap**. If personal property is seized pursuant to the writ, the sheriff will store it, and then sell it either by advertised auction (often called a **sheriff's sale**) or, in some states, by a private sale if the sheriff concludes that will bring more money.

Of course, the debtor may be able to claim some property as exempt from execution. In most instances, the sheriff takes personal property into his possession by moving it to a storage facility. But if that is not practical, the sheriff may leave the property in place, secure it with chains and locks as needed, and post a prominent notice advising anyone reading it that the property is in the possession of the sheriff and is not to be disturbed. The same will be done when real property is seized. For example, assume a writ of execution is issued on a docked boat. The sheriff might move the boat to another facility but, if that is not feasible, the sheriff might leave the boat in the dock, disable it from being operated, chain and lock it to the dock so it cannot be towed away, and place yellow tape across the entrance to it along with a posted notice of the seizure and penalties for trespassing or tampering. If the sheriff seizes a house next to the dock, a similar procedure will be followed. The house will be securely locked, yellow tape placed across all entrances, and a written notice posted. The sheriff executing the writ must make a **return of the writ** to the clerk of the court. That means physically returning the executed writ to the clerk, stating the date(s) it was executed, and itemizing the assets seized (sometimes called the **inventory**).

If the writ was executed but no assets were found, it will be returned **nulla bona** (with nothing found). The writ must be served within some number of days after it is issued by clerk (e.g., 60 days) and is deemed void if not timely returned. The lien that now exists on the seized property in favor of the judgment creditor is called **a lien of levy** in some states. Exhibit 3.11 sets out a typical state statute regarding the creation of a lien of levy.

States typically require the sheriff to conduct the sheriff's sale of the property within some designated time period following levy and to give prior public notice of the sale. Some states require specific notice of the sale to the debtor. A typical statute setting forth the procedure for notice and sale is shown in Exhibit 3.12.

Title VII of the 1964 Civil Rights Act, the Age Discrimination in Employment Act of 1967, the Americans with Disabilities Act of 1990, the Rehabilitation Act of 1973, the Equal Pay Act of 1963, the Pregnancy Discrimination Act of 1978, the Family and Medical Leave Act of 1993 and the wage and hour standards under the Fair Labor Standards Act.

States have their own laws in some of these areas that may provide broader protections or more expansive remedies for consumers. States also legislate on behalf of consumers where the federal government does not as illustrated by state fraudulent transfer acts, products liability acts, lemon laws and consumer protection acts, many of which provide broad protection to consumers from unfair or deceptive acts or practices.

EXHIBIT 3.11 State Statute Creating Lien of Levy

(1) Levy. A levy is effective when the sheriff with a writ of execution exercises control over the judgment debtor's personalty.

(2) Lien of Levy. A lien of levy in the judgment creditor's favor is effective when the sheriff levies on the judgment debtor's personalty. The first judgment creditor to deliver a writ of execution to the sheriff, as shown by record in the clerk's office, has priority over other judgment creditors as to the property levied upon. A lien of levy remains effective until the property is sold or otherwise released from the sheriff's control.

EXHIBIT 3.12 State Statute Setting Forth Procedure for Notice and Sale

The sheriff shall sell personalty by auction. At least ten days before the sale, a notice, generally describing the personalty and stating the time, place, and terms, shall be published in a newspaper of general circulation at the judgment creditor's expense, taxable as court costs. If the personalty is perishable, no notice of sale is required.

Once the judgment debtor's assets seized pursuant to the writ are sold, the proceeds will go first to pay the sheriff's administrative expenses involved in seizing, storing, and selling the property, and then to pay court costs assessed against the judgment debtor, and then to satisfy the judgment of the levying creditor (unless another creditor has a priority position in the property), and then to satisfy any other consensual or non-consensual lien existing in the property. Any excess proceeds go to the debtor.

In most states, the purchaser of property at the sheriff's sale is considered **a bona fide purchaser for value** and his title cannot be disturbed, even by a late exemption claim from the owner, who is now nothing but a prior owner as to the property.

The Writ of Garnishment

The method of execution used to obtain non-exempt personal property that belongs to the debtor or that is owed to the debtor from a third person (rather than from the debtor herself) is the **writ of garnishment**. Typical targets of a garnishment are the employer of the judgment debtor (called a **wage garnishment**), a financial institution holding funds of the judgment debtor in a checking or savings account (a **bank garnishment**), or anyone who owes the judgment debtor money (e.g., tenants of the judgment debtor who owe him rent). Like the writ of execution, the writ of garnishment is applied for by the judgment creditor to the clerk of the court that rendered the final judgment.

For example, assume that Pearl Murphy, a substitute teacher, has a paycheck due at the end of the month from the Capital City School District. Assume that CCME is ready to execute on its final judgment by default against Pearl. If the attorney for judgment creditor CCME decides to garnish that paycheck, the application for writ of garnishment might look something like what is shown in Exhibit 3.13.

EXHIBIT 3.13 **Application for Writ of Garnishment**

State of Yourstate)
County of Capital)

Capital City Medical Equipment Company, Judgment Creditor, makes oath that the Judgment Debtor's last known address is 3521 West Cherry Street, Capital City, Yourstate and the Judgment Creditor's address for mailing any notice required by Yourstate Statutory Code §26-2-204 is 413 Richardson Avenue, Capital City, Yourstate.

The Judgment Creditor hereby makes application to the Clerk of the Circuit Court to issue a writ of garnishment in the above styled case to satisfy a judgment entered against the Defendant herein on September 20, YR-1, in the amount of $2,247.70 plus interest on the judgment amount at 10% per annum, or $.62 per day, from the date of entry of the judgment to the date of issuance of this writ, plus court costs of $255.

EXHIBIT 3.13 **(Continued)**

This 1st day of November YR-1
Capital City Medical Equipment Company

By:_____
Mark Andrews, Manager

Serve the garnishment execution on: Capital City Public School System at the following
address: 1211 Post Road, Capital City, Yourstate.

The party who is served with the writ of garnishment is called the **garnishee**.
In some states the writ served on the garnishee advises that party of its duty to
turn over the property of the debtor in its possession, or to pay the wages or other
amounts owed to the debtor, to the clerk of the court that issued the writ. The clerk
will then deliver the property or pay the funds over to the judgment creditor. In
other states the writ orders the garnishee to hold any funds it has in its possession
payable to the judgment debtor and to await further order of the court before paying them over. The writ of garnishment served on the Capital City Public School
System pursuant to the application seen in Exhibit 3.13 might look something like
what is shown in Exhibit 3.14.

EXHIBIT 3.14 **Writ of Garnishment**

TO: Capital City Public School System
1211 Post Road
Capital City, Yourstate

TAKE NOTICE: The earnings of your employee, Pearl E. Murphy ("Employee"), are hereby
garnished and attached in satisfaction of a judgment rendered in favor of plaintiff, Capital
City Medical Equipment Company, against Employee in this action on September 20, YR-1,
in the amount of $2,742.70 plus interest on the judgment amount at 10% per annum, or
$.62 per day, from the date of entry of the judgment to the date of issuance of this writ,
plus court costs of $255. Capital City Medical Equipment Company, Judgment Creditor,
makes oath that the Judgment Debtor's last known address is 321 West Cherry Street,
Capital City, Yourstate and the Judgment Creditor's address for mailing any notice required
by Yourstate Statutory Code §26-2-204 is 413 Richardson Avenue, Capital City, Yourstate.

YOU ARE HEREBY COMMANDED to appear in person or by sworn affidavit before the Clerk
of the Circuit Court of Capital County, Yourstate (the "Clerk") within ten (10) days of your
receipt of this writ and to then and thereby answer this garnishment under oath as to:
(1) Whether you are or were at the time of this garnishment was issued, indebted to the
Employee; if so, how and to what amount;

EXHIBIT 3.14   **Writ of Garnishment (Continued)**

(2) Whether you have in your possession or under your control any property, debts, or effects belonging to the Employee, at the time of serving this garnishment, or have at the time of answering, or have had at any time between the date of service and the time of answering; if so, the kind and amount;

(3) Whether there are, to such garnishee's knowledge and belief, any and what property, debts, and effects in the possession or under control of any other, and what, person; and

(4) Such other questions as may be put to you by the court or the judgment creditor as may tend to elicit the information sought.

YOU ARE HEREBY FURTHER COMMANDED to calculate the portion of Employee's wages that are payable to the Clerk pursuant to this garnishment as set forth in Yourstate Statutory Code §26-2-205 and to pay said amounts to the Clerk within 30 days of the date of this writ and thereafter as they become due and payable to Employee. THE MAXIMUM PART OF THE AGGREGATE DISPOSABLE EARNINGS OF AN INDIVIDUAL FOR ANY WORK WEEK WHICH IS SUBJECTED TO GARNISHMENT MAY NOT EXCEED:

(A) Twenty-five percent (25%) of his disposable earnings for that week, minus two dollars and fifty cents ($2.50) for each of her dependent children under the age of sixteen (16) who reside in the state of Yourstate as provided in §26-2-102; or

(B) The amount by which her disposable earnings for that week exceed thirty (30) times the federal minimum hourly wage at the time the earnings for any pay period become due and payable, minus two dollars and fifty cents ($2.50) for each of his dependent children under the age of sixteen (16) who reside in the state of Yourstate, whichever is less.

"Disposable earnings" means that part of the earnings of an individual remaining after the deduction from those earnings of any amounts required by law to be withheld.

BE ADVISED that, pursuant to §26-2-207, you are liable for failure to withhold the proper garnishment amount from the Employee's wages and for failure to pay these moneys to the Clerk.

Clerk

In some states, the judgment creditor may also be obligated to provide the judgment debtor with notice of the garnishment (sometimes called notice of levy). Typically, the garnishment lien attaches to the property of the debtor held by the garnishee as soon as the garnishment is served on the garnishee.

As reflected in the language of Exhibit 3.14, the garnishee typically has a duty to respond to a writ of garnishment by making a personal appearance in the court issuing the writ or, more commonly, by filing a written answer within some designated time period (ten days under the terms of Exhibit 3.14) acknowledging that it does hold property of the judgment debtor or funds due her and describing the property or funds. Thereafter the garnishee must turn over property of the debtor or pay over the garnished funds owed to the debtor within some designated time period (30 days under the terms of Exhibit 3.14) or upon receipt of further court order. If the garnishee answers the garnishment by saying the judgment debtor is no longer employed by the garnishee or that the garnishee no longer has funds of the judgment debtor, the judgment creditor can typically engage in discovery from the garnishee (deposition, interrogatory, or document request) to obtain more information on the location of the judgment debtor or his property.

Each state regulates how much of a debtor's paycheck may be garnished (e.g., maximum of 25 percent), and that amount is typically calculated based on the debtor's **disposable income**, which is defined, generally, as after-tax income. Most states also permit the judgment debtor whose employer or other income source has been garnished to move the court for permission to pay the judgment amount in installments less than what the payments would be from the garnishment. When such a **motion to pay judgment in installments** (sometimes referred to informally as a **slow pay motion**) is filed, the burden is on the judgment debtor to demonstrate to the court that his income sources are insufficient to live on with the garnished amounts deducted. The judgment debtor will ask the court to set an alternative amount of payments in equity.

Application Exercise 13

Determine if your state allows a judgment debtor to apply to pay a judgment in installments. If so, what are the grounds for such a motion and what is the judgment debtor's burden of proof?

If the garnishee fails to respond to the writ of garnishment by answer or appearance or fails to pay over the property or funds as it is obligated to do, many states make the garnishee itself liable to the judgment creditor for either the value of the property that should have been delivered to the court clerk pursuant to the garnishment or for the entire amount of the debt. What happens procedurally is that, upon default by the garnishee, a conditional judgment against the garnishee is applied for by the attorney for the judgment creditor and issued by the court. The garnishee then has ten days to request a hearing and show cause why the conditional judgment should not be made final. Exhibit 3.15 sets out a typical statute regarding this aspect of garnishment law.

EXHIBIT 3.15   State Statute Regarding Garnishee's Liability

If the garnishee fails to timely answer or pay money into court, a conditional judgment may be entered against the garnishee and an order served requiring the garnishee to show cause why the judgment should not be made final. If the garnishee does not show sufficient cause within ten days of service of the order, the conditional judgment shall be made final and a writ of execution may issue against the garnishee for the entire judgment owed to the judgment creditor, plus costs.

Garnishments typically have an effective time limit on them (e.g., six months from date of issue) and may need to be renewed until the judgment is satisfied. As with the judgment lien and writ of execution, proper service of a writ of garnishment creates a judicial lien in favor of the executing judgment creditor.

Application Exercise 14

Locate the procedures for the judgment lien, writ of garnishment, writ of execution, or other method for executing on a judgment authorized in the state where you plan to practice. Compare the procedures set out for that state to the procedures described in the text.

The lien that the executing judgment creditor obtains through any of these methods is deemed a judicial lien since it arises from the judicial process. As we saw in Chapter Two, Section C, the judicial lien creditor is granted priority over a prior unsecured interest in the same property (see *Muggli Dental Studio v. Taylor* highlighted there).

For example, assume that on November 4 Pearl Murphy borrows money from First City Bank (FCB) and grants FCB a security interest in her jewelry to secure repayment of that loan. FCB perfects its security interest in the jewelry by filing a financing statement the same day. If the sheriff seizes the jewelry on November 5, the lien of levy in favor of CCME will be subordinate, or junior, to the consensual lien of FCB in the jewelry, and if the sheriff sells the jewelry, the proceeds will go first to repay FCB in full before they are applied to the CCME judgment. However, if FCB failed to properly perfect its lien in the jewelry before the sheriff seized it on November 5, then CCME's lien of levy will be superior to the FCB security interest in the jewelry.

7. Priority Among Competing Judicial Liens Created by Execution on the Debtor's Property

Competing claims to priority among two or more judicial lien creditors are typically given priority on a first-to-attach basis but state laws differ on when the lien created by the writ is deemed to attach. Depending on the type of execution involved it may be:

▪ Date of the actual levy — the date on which the sheriff took possession of particular property, and what constitutes possession (physical seizure or symbolic as by posting a notice) can vary depending on the state.

- Date of delivery of writ — the date on which writs of execution are delivered to the sheriff for service.
- Date of service of a writ of garnishment to the bank, employer, or other third person holding property of the judgment debtor.
- For a judgment lien, date of recordation of judgment or delivery of the judgment to the appropriate filing or recording officer.

For example, assume the writ of execution in Exhibit 3.14 is issued by the clerk and delivered to the sheriff on November 2. On November 3, before the sheriff has attempted execution on the writ delivered to him on November 2, a second writ of execution is delivered to the sheriff on behalf of a second judgment creditor of Pearl Murphy, directing the sheriff to seize her assets in satisfaction of that judgment as well. When the sheriff seizes Pearl's property, which judgment creditor gets paid first? If the statute in Exhibit 3.11 is in effect in the state, the writ delivered on November 2 will have priority and must be satisfied in full before proceeds of sale can be applied to the writ delivered on November 3.

Property that the debtor can exempt from execution and property that contains no equity for the executing creditor because it is subject to a prior perfected security interest should not be executed on. As mentioned in the earlier discussion on exempt property, states have different procedures by which a debtor can advise the court of property he claims as exempt and public records (e.g., UCC filings and vehicle title registrations records) should be consulted if possible to identify property already subject to an unchallengeable prior security interest. When such property does get inadvertently seized in execution the debtor or secured creditor can file a motion with the court from which the execution issued contesting the seizure.

Debtor's Prison

For many years debtors could be imprisoned for nonpayment of private debts. The practice was prohibited at the federal level by 1833. Most states also enacted such bans in their constitutions or by statute. Regarding incarceration for nonpayment of public debt (criminal fines and court costs), Williams v. Illinois, 399 U.S. 235 (1970), held it a violation of Equal Process for a state to subject a convicted defendant to a period of imprisonment beyond the statutory maximum solely because he is too poor to pay an accompanying fine. Tate v. Short, 401 U.S. 395 (1971), held it an Equal Protection violation for a state to convert the penalty under a fine-only statute to a jail term solely because the defendant cannot immediately pay the fine in full. And Bearden v. Georgia, 461 U.S. 660 (1983), held that a court cannot revoke a defendant's probation for failure to pay an imposed fine and restitution, absent evidence and findings that the defendant has the means to pay or was somehow responsible for the failure to pay or that alternative forms of punishment were inadequate. Notwithstanding these decisions, incarceration of indigents unable to pay fines and costs assessed against them for

A debtor's prison in Accomack County, Virginia. *Library of Congress Prints and Photographs Division Washington, D.C.*

often minor criminal infractions continues in many states. See, e.g., *Supreme Court Ruling Not Enough to Prevent Debtor's Prisons*, N.Y. Times, Mar. 27, 2015, at http://opinionator.blogs.nytimes.com/2015/03/27 and www.npr.org/2014/05/21/313118629/supreme-court-ruling-not-enough-to-prevent-debtors-prisons. Imprisonment for private debt may not really be a thing of the past either due to the employment of "pay or appear" tactics whereby the judgment creditor notices the judgment debtor to a postjudgment deposition. If the debtor fails to attend the judgment creditor asks the judge to find the debtor in contempt of court. A capias, or bench warrant, for the arrest of the defendant (informally called a body attachment), is issued by the court pursuant to which the debtor is taken into custody until there is a court hearing or the debtor posts bond (which often they cannot do). Debtor's prison redux?

Application Exercise 15

In 2012, Illinois passed the Debtors' Rights Act requiring judges to make an affirmative finding of the debtor's ability to pay out of non-exempt sources of income before using a pay or appear provision in an order and requiring proof that a debtor received actual notice of a postjudgment deposition. In 2014, Colorado began requiring its state courts to conduct on-the-record indigency hearings before incarcerating defendants for failing to pay criminal fines and costs. See Note, "Criminal Procedure — Indigency Tests," 128 Harv. L. Rev. 1312 (Feb. 2015). Also in 2014, the Ohio Supreme Court distributed a "bench card" to state trial judges reminding them that they must conduct financial status hearings before jailing defendants for non-payment of fines and costs and cannot jail defendants unable to pay (www.supremecourt.ohio.gov/Publications/JCS/FinesCourtCosts.pdf). Determine if the courts or legislature of the state where you plan to practice have addressed these problems of incarceration of indigent debtors for private or public debt.

8. Continuing Execution on a Final Judgment

Often, a final judgment cannot be immediately satisfied in full by execution. The judgment debtor may not have sufficient non-exempt income or assets that can be located and taken. But, of course, that could always change in the future: The judgment debtor could become employed or better employed, acquire non-exempt assets, or receive non-exempt assets by gift or inheritance. And that raises the question of how long the judgment creditor can continue to execute on the judgment. States differ in the term of viability granted a final judgment but, whatever the term of enforceability, it can be renewed or extended if proper procedures are followed. Exhibit 3.16 sets out a typical statutory term of viability and the procedure for extension or renewal.

EXHIBIT 3.16 **State Statute Regarding Term of Viability of a Final Judgment and the Procedure for Extension or Renewal**

Within ten years from entry of a judgment, the judgment creditor whose judgment remains unsatisfied may move the court for an order requiring the judgment debtor to show cause why the judgment should not be extended for an additional ten years. A copy of the order shall be mailed by the judgment creditor to the last known address of the judgment debtor. If sufficient cause is not shown within thirty (30) days of mailing, another order shall be entered extending the judgment for an additional ten years. The same procedure can be repeated within any additional ten-year period until the judgment is satisfied.

9. The Inclusion of Prejudgment Interest in Final Judgments and the Creditor's Entitlement to Postjudgment Interest

In some circumstances the prevailing plaintiff in a collection lawsuit is entitled to have prejudgment interest added to the principal amount owed and included in the final judgment amount. And almost always a judgment creditor is entitled to receive postjudgment interest on the judgment amount. In this section we will consider these two different but equally important aspects of interest.

Prejudgment Interest

A plaintiff suing a consumer debtor to collect a preexisting liquidated amount is normally entitled to have interest that has accrued on the debt up until the date the final judgment is entered (**prejudgment interest**) included in the judgment amount. Exhibit 3.17 shows a typical state statute establishing applicable rates of prejudgment interest.

EXHIBIT 3.17 **Typical Prejudgment Interest Statute**

Prejudgment interest, i.e., interest as an element of, or in the nature of, damages, may be awarded by courts or juries in accordance with the principles of equity at any rate not in excess of a maximum effective rate of six percent (6%) per annum. In addition, contracts may expressly provide for the imposition of the same or a different rate of interest to be paid after breach or default within the limits set by [other applicable provisions].

The statute posits two different ways of calculating the rate of prejudgment interest where a plaintiff is deemed entitled to it. Where the parties have an enforceable contract specifying a rate of postbreach interest to be applied to the amount owed, the courts will typically enforce that contractual rate. For example, if the

The Uniform Enforcement of Foreign Judgments Act

Commonly, a final judgment is entered in one state and the judgment debtor has assets in another state. Most states have adopted some version of the Uniform Enforcement of Foreign Judgments Act (UEFJA). Under the UEFJA, the judgment creditor seeking to enforce the foreign judgment must petition a court in the state where enforcement is sought for permission to register the judgment in that state for purposes of executing on it. Normally the court in which the "petition for permission to register foreign judgment" is filed or registered is a court of record in the county where the property to be executed on is located. The petition must be accompanied by an attested copy of the final judgment from the clerk of the court that issued it. Many states also require that the petition be verified by the person signing it.

The clerk of the court where the petition is filed will issue a summons to be served on the judgment debtor along with a copy of the petition and all exhibits. Typically, no execution can begin on the foreign judgment until the judgment debtor has been served with the summons and petition and has been given some time (e.g., 30 days following service) to file a response raising a defense to the validity of the foreign judgment. The judgment debtor cannot relitigate the underlying debt or liability claim because that was decided by the court that issued the final judgment. The judgment debtor may be in a position to attack the underlying validity of the final judgment, however, by arguing that the court that entered the final decree lacked subject matter jurisdiction over the case or personal jurisdiction over the debtor.

Determine if the state where you plan to practice has adopted the UEFJA.

Medical Equipment Lease Agreement between Pearl Murphy and CCME specifically provides for CCME to receive interest at a stated rate (e.g., 10 percent per annum) on late payments or in the event of a default by Pearl, the trial judge will likely order the prejudgment interest calculated at the contract rate in the final judgment. Of course if the contractual rate of interest is deemed usurious or otherwise unenforceable (e.g., due to public policy, unconscionability, absence of notice and mutuality) the court will not apply it.

Where there is no such contractual provision (or it is deemed unenforceable) but the court deems plaintiff entitled to prejudgment interest, the statutory rate is applied.

The generally recognized rule among the states for when prejudgment interest should be awarded, established either by statute or case law, is that prejudgment interest can be awarded as part of the final judgment where the loss was certain or readily ascertainable as of a particular time and can be measured with mathematical certainty by objective and admissible facts and figures.

An award of prejudgment interest is most clearly appropriate where the defendant owes the plaintiff a known, liquidated amount, an amount that is readily ascertainable and quantifiable based on a preexisting contract. For example, under the Medical Equipment Lease Agreement between CCME and Pearl Murphy, Pearl owes CCME $1,200 that should have been paid within 30 days of the billing. The amount owed is liquidated and the court will award CCME prejudgment interest on that $1,200 from the date of breach through the date of final judgment. An award of prejudgment interest in such situations is deemed necessary to fully compensate the plaintiff who has lost the use of the principal amount owed since the ascertainable date of breach.

In most states, where there is an underlying agreement from which the amount owed was readily ascertainable and quantifiable, it does not matter that liability was vigorously disputed — the priority is that the prevailing plaintiff be fully compensated for the loss including the lost use of the amount owed from the time it was owed. See, e.g., Royal Elec. Constr. Corp. v. Ohio State Univ., 652 N.E.2d 687 (Ohio 1995). In a few states, however, if liability under a preexisting agreement is contested, prejudgment interest is deemed inappropriate. See, e.g., Theobald v. Nasser, 784 So. 2d 142 (Miss. 2001) (where damages are disputed by the parties and the contract contained no liquidated damages clause, damages were not ascertainable until determined by trial court), and Lincoln Benefit Life Co. v. Edwards, 243 F.3d 457 (8th Cir. 2001) (applying Nebraska law) (interest accrues on the unpaid balance of any liquidated claim from the date the cause of action arose through the date of judgment only when no reasonable controversy exists as to either plaintiff's right to recover or as to the amount of such recovery).

Where recovery is had on a quasi-contract or unjust enrichment theory rather than express or implied contract, courts are split. Some allow prejudgment interest in such cases while others do not. Compare LTD v. American Bridge Co., 2010 WL 703077 (N.D. Ohio 2010) (allowed), with Clear One Communications, Inc. v. Chiang, 432 Fed. Appx. 770, 776 (10th Cir. 2011) (not allowed).

In tort claims involving personal injury, wrongful death, defamation, false imprisonment, malicious prosecution, assault and battery involving determination of claims for pain and suffering, loss of enjoyment of life, emotional distress, harm to reputation, etc., courts deem it inequitable to award prejudgment interest even though the claimant ultimately prevails. In such cases the damages are deemed incomplete and continuing, and uniquely within the province of the jury to assess at the time of the trial. The amount of the loss in such cases is not knowable until the finder of fact renders a decision.

For example, in Nick and Pearl Murphy's medical malpractice action against Dr. Craft, they may request that prejudgment interest be awarded on the jury verdict from the date of the negligence. But a court is very unlikely to grant such a request because neither the basis for liability nor the amount of the damages was established prior to the entry of judgment.

On the other hand, if the tort action involves harm to property, prejudgment interest is allowable in many jurisdictions even though the amount of damage is contested and not determined (liquidated) until trial. See, e.g., Harlan Sprague Dawley, Inc. v. S.E. Lab Group, Inc., 644 N.E.2d 615 (Ind. 1994) (prejudgment interest allowed on final judgment in products liability action resulting in death of lab rats even though value of rats not determinable until trial and even though value disputed at trial). And a handful of states have adopted statutes authorizing awards of prejudgment interest in any civil tort case where the party prevailing at trial made a timely offer of settlement according to terms specified in the statute. See, e.g., the Indiana Tort Prejudgment Interest Statute at I.C. §§34-51-4-1 et seq.

Prejudgment interest is normally denied to awards for lost future profits on the grounds that such awards are not provable with sufficient mathematical certainty. See, e.g., Clear One Communications, Inc. v. Chiang, supra, at 774 ("[T]he very nature of lost future profits injects an air of uncertainty and speculation into the calculation of damages, because a jury must speculate when it determines what profits would have been generated had the defendant not acted wrongfully."). To be distinguished are awards based on lost profits incurred prior to defendant's breach. See, e.g., Encon Utah, LLC v. Fluor Ames Kraemer, LLC, 210 P.3d 263, 274 (Utah 2009) (affirming award of prejudgment interest on lost profits for work that the plaintiff had performed under a fixed-price contract).

The common law rule was that prejudgment interest could not be compounded. See Restatement (Second) of Contracts §354, cmt. a (1981). Today, some states allow compounding by statute. The decision of whether to allow prejudgment interest is committed to the sound discretion of the trial judge and is reviewed for abuse of discretion. See Hughes Aircraft Co. v. United States, 86 F.3d 1566 (Fed. Cir. 1996).

Procedurally, in many states, entitlement to prejudgment interest must be demanded in the party's pleadings whereas in others the request for postjudgment interest can be made by motion following judgment.

Postjudgment Interest

In many states **postjudgment interest** begins to accrue, at a statutory rate, on money judgments as a matter of law. A typical postjudgment statute is shown in Exhibit 3.18.

EXHIBIT 3.18   **Typical Postjudgment Interest Statute**

Interest on judgments, including decrees, shall be computed at a rate equal to 1% plus the average interest rate paid at auctions of 5-year United States Treasury notes during the 6 months immediately preceding July 1 and January 1, as certified by the state treasurer, and compounded annually provided that where a judgment is based on a note, contract, or other writing fixing a rate of interest within the limits provided in [other applicable provisions] for that particular category of transaction, the judgment shall bear interest at the rate so fixed.

Because the right to postjudgment interest is statutory, a creditor does not have to ask for it in the complaint. Once the judgment is final and can be executed on, postjudgment interest can be collected, calculated at the statutory rate, from the date of the judgment until payment. Further, as the statute in Exhibit 3.18 suggests, many states allow parties to agree by contract to a rate of postjudgment interest different from the statutory rate, so long as the agreed rate does not violate the state's usury laws.

Application Exercise 16

Locate the statutes, regulations, or court rulings regarding prejudgment and postjudgment interest in the state where you plan to practice. Under what circumstances will prejudgment interest be allowed and in what amount? Will your state enforce contractual provisions for prejudgment interest and are there any legal or public policy limitations on such provisions? Are there pleading or other procedural requirements for recovering prejudgment interest? Is postjudgment interest automatically collectible following entry of a final judgment in your state? Is the rate of postjudgment interest set by law or up to the discretion of the judge?

C. FRAUDULENT TRANSFERS OF A DEBTOR'S PROPERTY

What if the judgment creditor undertaking execution on its judgment discovers that the judgment debtor has transferred ownership of non-exempt assets to a third party? Counsel for the judgment creditor will examine the asset transfer to determine if it can be set aside as a **fraudulent transfer**. Of course, a fraudulent transfer action can also form the basis of an original cause of action by a plaintiff to recover property in which he has an interest. It can also be asserted in a motion for **prejudgment attachment** in a pending civil case in state court where the plaintiff discovers prior to entry of final judgment that the defendant is disposing of assets in order to defeat anticipated execution by the plaintiff once the judgment is entered.

In any context in which it is asserted, what distinguishes a fraudulent transfer action is that title to the property has been previously transferred or conveyed to someone other than the debtor. The transferee is therefore a proper and necessary party to the action to set aside the transfer.

For example, if the Murphys are executing on their judgment against Dr. Craft and discover that he gave non-exempt assets to his brother the day after the judgment was entered, the Murphys might seek to have the gift set aside as a fraudulent transfer. Once the gift transferred is reversed and the assets retitled in Dr. Craft, they can be executed on. Because the Murphys would be asking the court to take action against property then titled in Dr. Craft's brother, the brother would have to be made a party to the fraudulent conveyance action.

In more than 40 states, fraudulent transfer law and procedure is governed by the Uniform Fraudulent Transfer Act of 1984 (UFTA). Under the UFTA, a transfer of the transferor's property may be fraudulent as to a creditor if the creditor can show either intentional fraud or constructive fraud in connection with the transfer.

1. Transfers Made with Intent to Defraud

The UFTA provides the creditor with relief if it can be shown that the transfer was made with the "intent to defraud, hinder or delay" the creditor. With regard to what constitutes a transfer of property, §1(12) of the UFTA defines transfer as "every mode, direct or indirect, absolute or conditional, voluntary or involuntary, of disposing of or parting with an asset or an interest in an asset, and includes payment of money, release, lease, and creation of a lien or other encumbrance."

Under this broad definition, a fraudulent transfer could include not just selling property for less than it is worth, but also (1) making a gift of property, (2) changing of beneficiary designation on an insurance policy, (3) renouncing an inheritance in a decedent's estate, (4) pledging the property as collateral to secure a debt to another creditor, or (5) allowing foreclosure or repossession of collateralized property.

Of course, just because a defendant in a collection or liability suit transfers property does not make the transfer fraudulent. The fraudulent intent must be proven by the plaintiff. Proving fraudulent intent is difficult. Who knows the intent of a person in his own mind and heart?

Because of the difficulty of proving fraudulent intent, the courts, beginning with the venerable Twyne's Case, 3 Coke 80, 76 Eng. Rep. 809 (1601), developed what came to be called **badges of fraud**, circumstances or indicia surrounding the transfer that were relevant and provable as tending to show the fraudulent intent. Those badges of fraud have now been incorporated into the UFTA and are set forth in Exhibit 3.19.

EXHIBIT 3.19 **The Badges of Fraud as They Now Appear in §4(b) of the UFTA**

- The transfer or obligation was to an insider.
- The transferor retained possession or control of the property transferred after the transfer.
- The transfer or obligation was disclosed or concealed.
- Before the transfer was made or obligation was incurred, the transferor had been sued or threatened with suit.
- The transfer was of substantially all the transferor's assets.
- The transferor absconded.
- The transferor removed or concealed assets.
- The value of the consideration received by the transferor was not reasonably equivalent to the value of the asset transferred or the amount of the obligation incurred.
- The transferor was insolvent or became insolvent shortly after the transfer was made or the obligation was incurred.
- The transfer occurred shortly before or shortly after a substantial debt was incurred.
- The transferor transferred the essential assets of the business to a lienor who transferred the assets to an insider of the transferor.

---

2. Transfers Made with Constructive Fraud

As an alternative to proving fraudulent intent, §4(a)(2) of the UFTA allows a court to find a fraudulent transfer has occurred if (1) the debtor transfers the property without receiving reasonably equivalent value in exchange for the transfer and (2) the debtor is insolvent at the time of the transfer or becomes insolvent as a result of the transfer or is left with unreasonably small capital to continue in business as a result of the transfer. This is **constructive fraud** (sometimes called **presumed fraud**). Unlike the intentional fraudulent transfer, no actual intent to defraud need be proven.

Note the "and" in the definition of constructive fraud under §4(a)(2) of the UFTA. There are two mandatory findings required to apply the constructive fraud theory. Whether the debtor receives reasonably equivalent value for a transfer is a question of fact based on the circumstances of the case.

Reasonably equivalent value is normally determined using the **fair market value** of the property involved as of the date of the transfer. Fair market value is generally considered to be the price at which the property would change hands between a willing buyer and a willing seller, neither being under any compulsion to buy or to sell and both having reasonable knowledge of relevant facts. See United States v. Cartwright, 411 U.S. 546, 551 (1973).

Under §2(a)(b) of the UFTA, **insolvency**, the second requirement of constructive fraud, can be established by using either the **balance sheet test** of insolvency (the sum of the debtor's debts is greater than all of the debtor's assets, at a fair valuation) or the **equity test** of insolvency (the debtor is not paying his debts as they become due).

We will revisit fraudulent transfer and the issue of what constitutes reasonably equivalent value in Parts C and D of the text in the context of a bankruptcy case in which a debtor has made a prepetition fraudulent transfer of property.

3. Remedies for Fraudulent Transfer

In a fraudulent transfer action, the most common remedy sought by the plaintiff is to have the court void or set aside the fraudulent transfer and order that title to the property be returned to the debtor. If the fraudulent transfer claim is made in a prejudgment attachment context, the plaintiff may also seek to attach the property, pending final resolution of the suit. If the fraudulent transfer claim is being made in a postjudgment context, the plaintiff/judgment creditor likely is seeking to execute on the property once it is returned to the debtor in order to satisfy the judgment.

Section 7 of the UFTA provides a number of different remedies that the court can impose once it finds a fraudulent transfer has occurred. A list of those remedies is provided in Exhibit 3.19.

EXHIBIT 3.19   **Remedies Available Under §7 of the UFTA**

- Avoid the transfer or obligation to the extent necessary to satisfy the creditor's claim.
- Attach the asset transferred or other property of the transferee.
- Obtain an injunction against further disposition by the debtor or a transferee, or both, of the asset transferred or of other property.
- Obtain the appointment of a receiver to take charge of the asset transferred or of other property of the transferee.
- Obtain any other relief the circumstances may require.
- If the creditor has already obtained a judgment against the debtor, levy execution on the asset transferred or its proceeds.

Application Exercise 17

Determine if the state where you plan to practice adopted the UFTA. If not, determine if fraudulent transfer is governed by some other statute or by case law in that state.

Chapter Summary

▪ The FDCPA regulates those who collect consumer debts owed to another. Attorneys who regularly engage in consumer debt collection are considered debt collectors subject to the FDCPA. The FDCPA regulates what the debt collector can say and do in locating and communicating with the consumer debtor. It broadly prohibits harassing or abusive conduct and language, the making of false or misleading statements to collect a debt, and using unfair or unconscionable means to do so. Suing or threatening to sue on a time-barred claim violates the FDCPA as does filing such a claim in the debtor's bankruptcy, a common practice among debt buyers who purchase charged-off debts from banks and other creditors.

▪ Within five days of the initial verbal communication with the debtor or in the first written communication with the debtor, the FDCPA requires the debt collector to disclose certain specific information to the debtor in writing. For attorneys doing collection work from consumer debtors, this means the traditional demand letter must comply with the disclosure requirements. The FDCPA is administered by the FTC and also grants debtors a private right of action. Many states provide broader debt collection regulation providing that the FDCPA and debt collectors may also be subject to tort claims or even criminal prosecution for wrongful acts.

▪ The increase in consumer debt in the modern era has given rise to an expanding debt settlement industry in the guise of credit counseling agencies that offer to negotiate debt management plans with the creditors of the debtor.

▪ Creditors unable to collect a debt through non-judicial debt collection activity may file suit and secure a final judgment against the debtor. Where there is no defense to the obligation such final judgment is likely to be taken by default. Most collection suits are brought in state court.

▪ The creditor granted a final judgment against a debtor may have to wait until the expiration of a grace period before executing on the judgment against the debtor's assets and such grace period may be extended by post-trial motions or an appeal of the judgment by the debtor during which execution is stayed. A judgment creditor seeking assets of the debtor on which to execute may engage in postjudgment discovery in aid of execution in the form of interrogatories, document requests, and depositions.

▪ Every state declares some personal property of the debtor exempt from execution by judgment creditors. Likewise, every state allows the debtor to exempt some amount of equity in the debtor's homestead. Concurrent ownership of property by the debtor with another may limit the ability of the judgment creditor to seize such property in execution. This is particularly true where the debtor owns property jointly with a spouse and the debtor's interest in marital property is indivisible or limited to a right of survivorship. Property held as tenants in common can be partitioned and the judgment debtor's interest liquidated. Assets of spendthrift trusts and, in some states, domestic asset protection trusts cannot be executed on where the judgment debtor is a beneficiary.

- States authorize various methods for a judgment creditor to execute on the judgment. A judgment lien can be created on the judgment debtor's real property normally by recording a certified copy of the final judgment in the land records where the property lies. The writ of execution issued by the court and served by the sheriff authorizes the seizure of debtor's personal property creating a lien of levy on that property, which is then sold by the sheriff and the proceeds applied to the expenses of execution and the underlying judgment. The writ of garnishment issued by the court is served on third parties who may hold money or other assets of the judgment debtor, such as employers and financial institutions, and such assets must be delivered to the court for distribution to the judgment creditor.
- A final judgment may include an award of prejudgment interest at the contract or a statutory rate where the amount owed was readily ascertainable and quantifiable as in a contract dispute. Prejudgment interest is not generally included on judgments arising from claims of tortious conduct. All states authorize the recovery of postjudgment interest at a statutory rate from the date of judgment until paid.
- Execution on final judgments may involve claims of fraudulent transfer against the debtor and transferees of property. Most states have adopted the UFTA, which allows recovery of transfers of debtor's property made either with actual intent, in which case intent can be inferred from the traditional badges of fraud, or by constructive fraud where the debtor was insolvent at the time of transfer and received less than reasonably equivalent value of the property.

Applying the Concepts

1. Assume you represent Nick and Pearl Murphy. Pearl has medical bills following an appendectomy, including one from Capital City Medical Equipment (CCME) in the amount of $1,200. Assume Nick is not liable on the debt to CCME under state law. The Murphys phoned today concerning contacts they received yesterday from a debt collector hired to collect the bill for CCME. How would you advise them in the following scenarios?

   a. The debt collector called the Murphy home at 7:30 A.M. It was 8:30 A.M. in the debt collector's time zone. Nick Murphy answered and advised the caller that his wife was not home. The debt collector proceeded to discuss the overdue bill with Nick and asked when payment could be expected. Has the debt collector violated any provisions of the FDCPA?

   b. Later that evening, at 8:30 P.M. the debt collector called again and spoke with the Murphys' 11-year-old son, Lyndon. The debt collector discussed the overdue bill with Lyndon and asked if his mother had the money to pay it. Has the debt collector violated any provisions of the FDCPA?

   c. Later that evening the debt collector called a third time at 9:15 P.M. and spoke with Lyndon. Disguising his voice, the debt collector identified himself as a police officer calling for Pearl to talk with her about a crime that had been committed about which she may have knowledge, and stating that he needed to talk with her urgently. Pearl came immediately came to the phone. Has the debt collector violated any provisions of the FDCPA?

2. Assume that CCME has obtained a final judgment against Pearl Murphy and is now seeking to collect on the judgment. Without regard to the exempt property statutes, which of the following categories of property can CCME execute on to satisfy its judgment? For each category of property, what method of execution should it use? Nick and Pearl live in a state that recognizes the tenancy by the entireties.

   a. A vehicle owned by Nick and Pearl on which there is no lien
   b. A vehicle owned by Pearl on which there is no lien
   c. A vehicle owned by Pearl on which there is a lien in excess of the vehicle's value
   d. The joint checking account of Nick and Pearl at a local bank
   e. Pearl's future paychecks from her employer
   f. An empty lot owned by Pearl and her sister as tenants in common
   g. The assets in a spendthrift trust created by Pearl's parents of which Pearl and her sister are joint beneficiaries

3. Assume you represent Nick and Pearl Murphy in their medical malpractice action against Dr. Craft. Assume that final judgment in favor of the Murphys has been entered today in federal court or in a state court in the state where you plan to practice (as your instructor may direct).

   a. Assuming Dr. Craft files no postjudgment motions and assuming he does not voluntarily pay the judgment, on what date can you initiate collection on behalf of the Murphys? ? See FRCP 62(a).
   b. Would the date be different if judgment was entered by default? See FRCP 55 and 62(a).
   c. If Dr. Craft files a motion for new trial tomorrow, when can execution begin? See FRCP 59 and 62(b).
   d. If Dr. Craft wishes to appeal the judgment against him, when is his notice of appeal due and where should he file it? See FRAP 3(a)(1) and 4(a).
   e. If Dr. Craft files a motion for new trial tomorrow when is his notice of appeal due? See FRCP 59 and FRAP 4(a)(4)(A).
   f. If Dr. Craft files a notice of appeal tomorrow when can execution on the judgment begin? See FRCP 61(d) and FRAP 8(a)(1)(2).

4. Assume Dr. Craft, against whom the Murphys have a final judgment, not only owns real property in Capital County, Yourstate, but in Silver County, Yourstate, as well. Carefully read the language of the statute in Exhibit 3.5. If the Murphys record their judgment lien in Capital County only, does that subject the Silver County property to the lien? If not, what must the Murphys do to create a

judgment lien on the Silver County property owned by Dr. Craft? Since the final judgment on which the Murphys are executing was entered by a court in Capital County, Yourstate does that mean it cannot be recorded in another county to create a judgment lien on property there? If Dr. Craft owns property in a state other than Yourstate can the Murphys execute on that property to satisfy their Yourstate final judgment?

5. Assume you are zealously seeking to execute on the assets of Dr. Craft on behalf of the Murphys. In the course of postjudgment discovery, you learn that Dr. Craft has made the following transfers. Identify which may constitute fraudulent transfers.

   a. As a gift, Dr. Craft conveyed title to all his solely owned property, real and personal, to his wife a month before final judgment was entered against him.

   b. Dr. Craft created and funded a testamentary trust for his grandchildren with a $1 million cash transfer the week after the medical malpractice action was filed against him.

   c. Dr. Craft purchased a vacation home in Barbados for $500,000 the week before trial began, putting $50,000 down in cash and borrowing $450,000 from a lender to whom he granted a mortgage in the home to secure payment. Today the condo is still worth the same $500,000 it was appraised for at the time of purchase.

   d. Eight years ago, Dr. Craft borrowed $400,000 to purchase a condominium in a resort area, granting the lender a mortgage in the condo purchased. Appraised at $425,000 at the time of purchase, today the value of the condo has dropped to about $200,000 and the balance owed the lender is $250,000. Though the lender has not asked for additional collateral, Dr. Craft granted it a security interest in personal property worth $50,000 shortly before final judgment was entered for the Murphys against him.

   e. A year ago, while the malpractice action was pending, Dr. Craft loaned his brother $100,000 as start-up money for a new business. The brother has not yet begun that business.

Consumer Bankruptcy Practice

Introduction to Consumer Bankruptcy Practice

In this chapter we will introduce the U.S. Bankruptcy Code by first examining the policy and purpose of having bankruptcy laws. We will take a brief tour of how the Code is organized and the specific types of bankruptcy proceedings it authorizes. The most recent amendment to the Code is the Bankruptcy Abuse Prevention and Consumer Protection Act of 2005 and that significant amendment is introduced here. There are a number of different sources of law that come into play in bankruptcy practice and we will take a brief look at those including the Federal Rules of Bankruptcy Practice and the Official Bankruptcy Forms. We will consider the number and location of the U.S. bankruptcy courts and review a synopsis of their subject matter jurisdiction and internal procedures. Various other key players in a bankruptcy case will be introduced and we will get an idea of what their various responsibilities are as a case moves through the

Key Concepts

- Today's Bankruptcy Code seeks to strike a balance between the notion that a debtor ought to pay what he owes and that the idea that some debtors are entitled to a fresh start
- The Bankruptcy Code is located in Title 11 of the U.S. Code and authorizes six different types of bankruptcy cases
- In addition to the Bankruptcy Code itself, there are several important sources of law that apply in a bankruptcy case
- The U.S. bankruptcy courts are located in each federal district and have referral jurisdiction over bankruptcy cases from the U.S. district courts
- Issues that arise in a bankruptcy case are decided as either contested matters or adversary proceedings
- All U.S. bankruptcy courts today utilize electronic filing
- There are a number of alternatives to bankruptcy filing for consumer debtors

bankruptcy process. We will consider modern electronic filing in bankruptcy courts. And finally, we will examine alternatives to bankruptcy that might be available to consumer debtors.

A. A BRIEF HISTORY OF DEBT RELIEF AND BANKRUPTCY LAWS

A fundamental premise underlying modern American bankruptcy law is that in certain circumstances, debtors are entitled to some form of relief from their debts and that such relief will provide them with a **fresh start**. As stated by the U.S. Supreme Court:

> [I]t gives to the honest but unfortunate debtor . . . a new opportunity in life and a clear field for future effort, unhampered by the pressure and discouragement of preexisting debt. Local Loan Co. v. Hunt, 292 U.S. 234, 244 (1934).

The basic human compassion in that premise is moderated by a second fundamental premise underlying our laws: One who incurs a debt ought to pay it. Striking the balance between these two premises has never been easy or simple. Not all human societies have even attempted to strike such a balance. Look through the timeline set out in Exhibit 4.1 to get an idea of the ebb and flow of attitudes and practices toward debt punishment/forgiveness.

EXHIBIT 4.1	Timeline of Debt Punishment/Forgiveness Attitudes and Practices

2400-1600 B.C.E. — *Clean Slate* proclamations by various kings of ancient Sumeria, Assyria, and Babylon mandate the periodic forgiveness of debt and the restoration of land given as security or persons sold for debt. E.g., Code of Hammurabi §117 (circa 1754 B.C.E.): "If any one fail to meet a claim for debt, and sell himself, his wife, his son, and daughter for money or give them away to forced labor, they shall work for three years in the house of the man who bought them and in the fourth year they shall be set free."

1400 B.C.E. — Moses' law mandates a *Sabbatical Year* every seven years, when all debts are to be forgiven. At the end of every seventh Sabbatical Year (thought to be every 50th year) a *Year of Jubilee* is declared when debts are forgiven, slaves freed, and land taken for nonpayment of debt is returned to former owners or their heirs (other than the houses of laypersons within walled cities). These practices are discontinued following the Babylonian captivity in the sixth century B.C.E.

1000 B.C.E. — By this time, credit arrangements are firmly established as basis of commerce by and among Assyria, Babylon, and Egypt.

500 B.C.E. — Ancient Greece has no bankruptcy relief laws. Debtors, their families, or servants can be reduced to serfdom or even slavery for unpaid debt (debt slavery). Crises

EXHIBIT 4.1   **(Continued)**

develop when such portion of the farming class is in jail or enslaved that there aren't enough workers to tend the crops. Crisis temporarily relieved in Athens by the Seisachtheia (burden-shaking) laws of Solon in 594 B.C.E. that cancel existing debt, mandate the return of debtor's forfeited property, and end debt slavery. Other Greek city-states limit the term of debt slavery to five years and protect them from severe abuse (*protection of life and limb*).

250 B.C.E. — In the days of the Roman Republic, debtors, or their families or servants, can be sold into slavery, imprisoned, and even killed by creditors. (It is said that in Roman times, creditors not only divided the debtor's property, but they also took him to the public plaza and bodily divided him.)

100 C.E. — Under the Caesars, the Roman Empire adopts some debt collection laws, including the appointment of a trustee to sell off a merchant debtor's assets after the merchant ceases business still owing money. The trustee is called the *curator bonorum* (caretaker) of the debtor's property for the benefit of creditors. Practice of *cession bonorum* (cessation of goods) allows debtor to surrender property to creditor to avoid imprisonment.

1285 — England's *Statute of Merchants* allows imprisonment of merchant debtors.

1400 — In Italian city-states, the defaulting merchant's trade bench or selling counter is destroyed to publicly announce his failure, literally *banca rotta* (broken bench), which may be the source of our modern word, *bankruptcy*.

1542 — The state of being bankrupt is made an official crime in England, mandating a hearing before the chancellor, and is punishable by confiscation of property and imprisonment.

1570 — Under Queen Elizabeth I of England, the first official bankruptcy law is passed by Parliament. It is exclusively a creditor's device, involuntary for the debtor. The creditor can formally declare a merchant bankrupt and seek official relief, including confiscation of property, imprisonment, and corporal punishment, the last of which could include having the debtor pilloried (a form of public humiliation that involved having hands and head locked in place by wooden stock) or having an ear cut off. In Padua, Italy, the bankrupt is required to appear nearly naked in the Palace of Justice and to slap his buttocks three times against "The Rock of Shame" while loudly proclaiming, "I declare bankruptcy!"

1705 — England's *Statute of Queen Anne* marks the first attempt at a humane reform of bankruptcy law. At the request of the debtor and with creditors' consent, debt can be discharged following liquidation of assets. The death penalty for the debtor is allowed for committing fraud in bankruptcy but is only known to have been enforced five times.

1788 — The U.S. Constitution is ratified, including Article I, §8, which authorizes Congress "[t]o establish . . . uniform laws on the subject of bankruptcies throughout the United States." In its first session, Congress considers adopting a bankruptcy law but demurs. Without federal rules, states follow their colonial practices based on English precedent, including imprisonment and pillorying.

EXHIBIT 4.1   **(Continued)**

Article I, Section 8 allows Congress to establish uniform bankruptcy laws. *Collection of the Supreme Court of the United States, Photographer: Steve Petteway*

1800—The Panic of 1797 in America leads to the imprisonment of thousands of debtors by the states, including the "Financier of the Revolution," Robert Morris. As a result, Congress passes the first federal bankruptcy law. It allows only creditors to declare a person bankrupt. Debts can be discharged after liquidation of the debtor's assets if they have been cooperative and two-thirds of their creditors consent. Repealed in 1803.

1833—Federal imprisonment for debt is abolished in the United States by act of Congress (now 28 U.S.C. §2007). Individual states begin to follow suit.

1841—The economic depression of 1837 results in Congress passing its second bankruptcy law, which for the first time permits debtors, including nonmerchants, to voluntarily file for bankruptcy relief. Due to high administrative costs, questions of constitutionality, and the discontent of creditors, the law is repealed in 1843.

1867—Following the turmoil of the Civil War, northern creditors want a system to collect from southern debtors. Congress passes a third bankruptcy law to enable them to do so, but it is repealed in 1878, again due to high administrative costs, an unwieldy bureaucracy, and little return to creditors.

1898—The economic panic of 1893 results in passage of the landmark Nelson Act, initiating the modern effort to balance debtor/creditor interests. The law, formally called the **Bankruptcy Act**, acknowledges the new credit economy, provides for a debtor-initiated discharge of debts, allows debtors to keep significant exempt property, and establishes

EXHIBIT 4.1   **(Continued)**

the **bankruptcy referee** (predecessor of the modern bankruptcy judge) as the designated officer of the U.S. district court to administer the law.

1938—The Chandler Act amends the existing Bankruptcy Act to allow reorganizations in bankruptcy for both individual and business debtors (today known as Chapter 13 and Chapter 11 bankruptcies, respectively), enabling debtors with the means to repay all or a part of their debts under court supervision as an alternative to liquidation. For the first time, bankruptcy becomes a viable option to achieve economic survival rather than the failure of liquidation.

1950—The first modern or "universal" credit card, the Diners' Club card, is introduced, accelerating the expansion of consumer debt.

1978—The **Bankruptcy Reform Act** substantially rewrites the nation's bankruptcy law. Now formally known as the **Bankruptcy Code**, the law contains the current chapter numbering (Chapter 7, Chapter 13, Chapter 11, etc.); bankruptcy judges are given expanded judicial powers to administer bankruptcy cases, Chapter 11 business reorganizations are made more feasible, and states are given the option to "opt out" of the Code's property exemptions and apply their own exemption laws instead.

1982—The U.S. Supreme Court decides Northern Pipeline Construction Co. v. Marathon Pipeline Co., 458 U.S. 50 (1982), declaring the Bankruptcy Reform Act of 1978 unconstitutional. The court rules that Congress had overstepped its bounds in granting bankruptcy judges, created under Article I of the Constitution, powers of Article III judges in administering the Code. The court grants Congress a grace period to amend the Bankruptcy Reform Act to cure the defect.

1984—The Bankruptcy Amendments and Federal Judgeship Act finally address the *Northern Pipeline* decision, reconstituting bankruptcy courts and judges as units of the U.S. district courts, with bankruptcy proceedings officially "referred" to bankruptcy courts under the standing orders of the district courts.

1986—The Code is amended to create the Chapter 12 proceeding for family farmers with regular income on a test basis and to make permanent the U.S. Trustee system to help administer bankruptcy cases, a system that had been tested on a pilot basis since 1978.

1994—The **Bankruptcy Reform Act of 1994** further amends the Code to clarify when bankruptcy courts can conduct jury trials, to expedite bankruptcy proceedings, to encourage individual debtors to use Chapter 13 to reschedule their debts rather than Chapter 7 to liquidate, and to aid creditors in recovering claims against bankrupt estates.

1996—For the first time ever, one million Americans file for bankruptcy in a single year.

2005—After over a decade of study and debate, Congress passes the **Bankruptcy Abuse Prevention and Consumer Protection Act (BAPCPA)**, a significant amendment to the Code, intended to reduce the number of individual consumer bankruptcies and encourage repayment by making it more difficult for individual debtors to file for Chapter 7 liquidation

EXHIBIT 4.1   **(Continued)**

relief and to force more of them to file for Chapter 13 reorganization. The Chapter 12 family farmer proceeding is made permanent and expanded to include family fishermen. The Chapter 15 proceeding is added to provide a mechanism for dealing with bankruptcy proceedings across international borders.

2011 — The U.S. Supreme Court decides Stern v. Marshall, 131 S. Ct. 2594 (2011), reviving *Northern Pipeline* concerns over constitutional power of Article I bankruptcy courts to decide core proceedings.

B. AN OVERVIEW OF THE BANKRUPTCY CODE AND THE TYPES OF AUTHORIZED BANKRUPTCY FILINGS

As noted in the timeline set out in Exhibit 4.1, the current bankruptcy law in this country is the United States Bankruptcy Code adopted by Congress in the Bankruptcy Reform Act of 1978 and located in Title 11 of the United States Code. We will refer to it as the **Bankruptcy Code** or just the **Code** (e.g., "§547 of the Code" instead of "11 U.S.C. §547"). The Code was enacted pursuant to Article I, §8, of the U.S. Constitution, which states that "Congress shall have the power to establish uniform laws on the subject of bankruptcies throughout the United States."

The Bankruptcy Code should be seen as a formal system of compulsory debt adjustment that seeks to balance the interests of both the debtor and his creditors. The interests of the debtor seeking bankruptcy relief are (1) to stop or at least delay debt collection efforts of creditors and then (2) to obtain some form of long-term, court-sanctioned debt relief, which may take the form of either the permanent discharge of some or all the debt or the reorganization of the debt obligations to make them more manageable for the debtor. When a debtor files for bankruptcy relief, the primary concern of creditors is to obtain payment of as much of the debt as possible as quickly as possible. The Code then is best understood as a statutory scheme created by Congress to regulate and balance these competing interests and, ideally, to produce a workable result that is palatable (if only barely sometimes) to both debtors and creditors.

Exhibit 4.2 lists and identifies the subject matter of each chapter of the Code. Three of these chapters contain definitional, administrative, and procedural types of rules (Chapters 1, 3, and 5), while six of them set forth specific types of bankruptcy cases that qualifying debtors can file (Chapters 7, 9, 11, 12, 13, and 15). We use the Code's chapter designation to identify and describe the type of bankruptcy case that a debtor files (e.g., "John and Carol Jones have filed a Chapter 7 case" or "ABC, Inc. is in Chapter 11").

EXHIBIT 4.2   **The Chapters of the Bankruptcy Code**

Chapter   1 — General Provisions
Chapter   3 — Case Administration
Chapter   5 — Creditors, the Debtor, and the Estate
Chapter   7 — Liquidation
Chapter   9 — Adjustment of Debts of a Municipality
Chapter   11 — Reorganization
Chapter   12 — Adjustment of Debts of a Family Farmer or Fisherman with Regular
                      Annual Income
Chapter   13 — Adjustment of Debts of an Individual with Regular Income
Chapter   15 — Ancillary and Other Cross-Border Cases

Exhibit 4.3 sets forth a brief summary of each of the six different types of bankruptcy proceedings authorized by the Code.

As discussed in more detail later, the vast majority of bankruptcy cases filed today are Chapter 7 liquidations or Chapter 13 adjustments of debts for individuals with regular income. Next in frequency come Chapter 11 business reorganization proceedings, followed by Chapter 12 family farmer/fisherman proceedings. Chapter 15 cross-border cases are still rare in most jurisdictions but are increasing in number. Chapter 9 municipality filings are fortunately rare though there have been several in the wake of the Great Recession that have received noticeable publicity including Jefferson County, Alabama, in 2011, Stockton, California, in 2012, and the city of Detroit in 2013.

EXHIBIT 4.3   **Brief Summary of the Six Types of Bankruptcy Proceedings**

A **Chapter 7 bankruptcy** is a **liquidation proceeding**. All of the debtor's non-exempt property is turned over to a *bankruptcy trustee* appointed by the **bankruptcy court** administering the case. The bankruptcy trustee will sell that property (thus the "liquidation") and distribute the proceeds to the various creditors of the Chapter 7 debtor based on claims they have filed with the court that the trustee will have reviewed and verified. The debtor thus loses all his or her property that is non-exempt in the liquidation proceeding, but in exchange gets a permanent **discharge** from future liability for most but not all of the debts that remain unpaid. Chapter 7 is the classic **fresh start**, or **clean slate**, bankruptcy.

A **Chapter 11 bankruptcy** is not a liquidation proceeding like a Chapter 7. Instead it is a **reorganization proceeding** designed for a business or business person. In a Chapter 11, the debtor (or its creditors) will propose a **plan of reorganization** pursuant to which, if it is approved by the bankruptcy court, the debtor will restructure the debts and sometimes the assets of its business and repay some or all of its debts out of future income. Some debt may be liquidated as part of the reorganization.

A **Chapter 13 bankruptcy** is also a reorganization-type proceeding, but Chapter 13 is designed not for a business, like Chapter 11, but for an "individual with regular

EXHIBIT 4.3   **(Continued)**

income" and thus is more accurately referred to as a debt adjustment proceeding. The individual debtor will propose a debt adjustment plan of no more than five years duration for court approval. If the plan is approved, the debtor will use income received during the plan to pay off all or part of his or her debts. Some debt may be discharged as part of the adjustment.

A **Chapter 9 bankruptcy** is designed specifically for "municipalities," which are defined in §101(40) of the Code to include political subdivisions of a state such as cities, counties, towns, villages, and public agencies or instrumentalities of a state such as taxing districts, municipal districts, school districts, or public utilities. This is a highly specialized type of bankruptcy and, fortunately, one that very rarely occurs.

A **Chapter 12 bankruptcy** proceeding is a reorganization-type proceeding designed for debtors who qualify as **family farmers** or **family fishermen**. It is very similar to a Chapter 13 debt adjustment proceeding but not as frequently used.

A **Chapter 15 bankruptcy** proceeding is an **ancillary proceeding** filed in a bankruptcy court in the United States after the primary proceeding has been commenced in a foreign country. It provides mechanisms for dealing with insolvency cases involving debtors, assets, and creditors in more than one country (**cross-border cases**) and allows adjudication of those interests located in the United States.

The vast majority of consumer bankruptcies as we have defined them in Chapter One involve either Chapter 7 or Chapter 13 cases and it is those that we will focus on for the remainder of this study. Since the infrequently filed Chapter 12 bankruptcy can involve individual debtors who qualify as family farmers or family fishermen and whose debts are primarily consumer debts, we will take a brief look at it at the conclusion of our detailed study of Chapter 7 and Chapter 13 bankruptcies.

Exhibit 4.4 contains a brief summary of the definitional, administrative, and procedural chapters of the Code. In general, the provisions in these chapters apply to all six types of bankruptcy proceedings summarized in Exhibit 4.3.

EXHIBIT 4.4   **Summary of the Definitional, Administrative, and Procedural Chapters of the Code**

- Chapter 1 of the Code contains general provisions, definitions, and rules of construction that govern the bankruptcy case.
- Chapter 3 of the Code sets out the procedures for commencing the bankruptcy case and administering it.
- Chapter 5 of the Code contains specific provisions pertaining to the rights and responsibilities of the debtor and creditors in the bankruptcy case, as well as indicating what property is to be included in the bankruptcy estate.

Application Exercise 1

To become more familiar with the chapters of the Code dealing with definitional, administrative, and procedural matters, consult the Code and find the answers to the following questions. (If you're not using a paper copy of the Code you can access it online from Cornell Law School's Legal Information Institute at www.law.cornell.edu/uscode/text/11.) Find these answers and indicate the specific Code provision (e.g., §101(2)) that provides the answer. The table of contents at the beginning of each Code chapter might be a good place to start to locate the answers quickly.

■ Locate the section in Chapter 1 of the Code controlling who can be a debtor in a Chapter 7 case to determine if a railroad can file for bankruptcy relief under Chapter 7 or Chapter 11 of the Code.
■ Locate the section in Chapter 3 of the Code that tells you under which chapters of the Code an involuntary bankruptcy case may be commenced and what document has to be filed to commence an involuntary bankruptcy case.
■ Locate the section in Chapter 5 of the Code authorizing a bankruptcy trustee to avoid a prepetition fraudulent transfer of property by the debtor and designating the prepetition time period during which transfers are subject to such an avoidance claim by the trustee.

C. THE BANKRUPTCY ABUSE PREVENTION AND CONSUMER PROTECTION ACT OF 2005

Go back and look at Exhibit 1.1 tracing the dramatic rise in bankruptcy filings in this country from 1980 forward. From about 300,000 a year in 1980, filings soared to over a million by 1996 and climbed steadily toward the two million mark in the decade following. In response to the dramatic rise in bankruptcy filings and concerns, warranted or not, that the bankruptcy process was being abused by some number of unscrupulous debtors, Congress in 2005 passed the **Bankruptcy Abuse Prevention and Consumer Protection Act** (BAPCPA) (pronounced "bap-SEE-pah").

BAPCPA made sweeping changes in the Code for both consumer and business cases. Its most dramatic effect was to impose new restrictions on consumers seeking to file Chapter 7 liquidation cases, with the intended effect of forcing more of them to file Chapter 13 reorganization cases instead. A decade later, it does not appear that BAPCPA achieved that intended effect to any significant degree (early studies suggest that very few debtors wishing to file for Chapter 7 relief are forced into a Chapter 13 instead because of the BAPCPA requirements), but it has certainly made consumer bankruptcy more complicated and expensive for debtors.

We will refer to the numerous new Code requirements introduced by BAPCA as we proceed. But it is worth noting that the new law is not without continuing controversy. Consumer advocates and others continue to urge Congress to revisit provisions of the law that are considered onerous to consumer debtors and unfairly biased toward creditors, and to enact additional consumer protection legislation to curtail perceived abusive lending practices that cause or contribute to consumer financial problems that eventually leave those consumers no choice but to seek bankruptcy protection.

D. IMPORTANT SOURCES OF LAW FOR BANKRUPTCY PRACTICE

In addition to the Code itself, there are a number of legal sources that play a critical role in bankruptcy practice, and the legal professional working in the bankruptcy field must be familiar with them.

1. The Federal Rules of Bankruptcy Procedure

In addition to the Code itself, Congress has adopted the **Federal Rules of Bankruptcy Procedure (FRBP)**. We will refer to the FRBP frequently, as they comprise the procedural rules that provide guidance and detail regarding how to comply with the Code requirements in all six types of bankruptcy cases.

Application Exercise 2
....

To become more familiar with the FRBP, consult those rules and find the answers to the following questions. (If you're not using a paper copy of the FRBP you can access them online from the Federal Judiciary Web site at www. uscourts.gov/rules-policies/current-rules-practice-procedure) Find these answers and indicate the specific FRBP (e.g., FRBP 1007) that provides the answer. The table of contents at the beginning of each part of the FRBP would be a good place to start to locate the answers quickly.

- Locate the rule in Part I of the FRBP specifying to whom the filing fee is paid when a bankruptcy case is commenced.
- Locate the rule in Part V of the FRBP dealing with what days the bankruptcy courts and bankruptcy court clerk's offices are open.
- Consult the definitions in Part IX of the FRBP to determine whether the Federal Rules of Evidence apply in cases under the Code.

---

2. The Official Bankruptcy Forms

In addition to the Code and the FRBP, Congress has adopted **Official Bankruptcy Forms**. The Official Forms are drafted by the Administrative Office of the U.S. Courts (the AO) (www.uscourts.gov/) and that office frequently revises the forms to comply with changes in the Code or the FRBP, new court decisions, or recommendations from judges and practitioners. FRBP 9009 provides that the official forms "shall be observed and used."

Application Exercise 3

To become more familiar with the Official Forms locate the particular form requested in the list below. (If you don't have a paper copy of the Official Forms you can access them online from the Federal Judiciary Web site at www.uscourts.gov/forms/bankruptcy-forms.) Indicate the specific official form requested by its number and name (e.g., Official Form 105: Involuntary Petition Against Individual).

1. Voluntary Petition for an individual debtor
2. Schedule A/B for an individual debtor
3. Statement of Financial Affairs for an individual debtor
4. Proof of Claim for a creditor
5. Reaffirmation Agreement

---

3. The Federal Rules of Civil Procedure

The **Federal Rules of Civil Procedure (FRCP)** control the procedure in all types of civil proceedings in bankruptcy courts. As we will see, some disputes that arise in a bankruptcy case that must be resolved by the bankruptcy judge are treated by the Code and the FRBP as mini-lawsuits, which we will learn to call **adversary proceedings**. The FRCP govern the procedure in adversary proceedings in bankruptcy court, just as they would in any civil trial before a federal judge. If you are not using a paper copy of the FRCP you can access them online at www.uscourts.gov/rules-policies/current-rules-practice-procedure or www.law.cornell.edu/rules/frcp/.

4. The Federal Rules of Evidence

The **Federal Rules of Evidence (FRE)** govern the admissibility of evidence at hearings conducted in all federal courts, including the U.S. Bankruptcy Courts. Whenever the bankruptcy judge conducts a hearing where evidence is presented (called an **evidentiary hearing**), the FRE will control the presentation of that evidence. See FRE 1101(a). If you are not using a paper copy of the FRE you can access them online at www.uscourts.gov/rules-policies/current-rules-practice-procedure or www.law.cornell.edu/rules/fre/.

5. Local Court Rules

FRBP 9029(a)(1) provides in pertinent part as follows:

> Each district court acting by a majority of its district judges may make and amend rules governing practice and procedure in all cases and proceedings within the district court's bankruptcy jurisdiction which are consistent with — but not duplicative of — Acts of Congress and these rules and which do not prohibit or limit the use of the Official Forms. . . . A district court may authorize the bankruptcy judges of the district . . . to make and amend rules of practice and procedure which are consistent with — but not duplicative of — Acts of Congress and these rules and which do not prohibit or limit the use of the Official Forms.

Pursuant to the authority granted by FRBP 9029(a)(1), bankruptcy courts around the country have adopted their own **local court rules**. These local rules are important and will control the way that the particular court processes bankruptcy cases in accordance with the Code and FRBP.

For example, in some bankruptcy courts, by local rule, the party filing a motion for the judge to decide is required to arrange a date for the motion to be heard and to notify the other interested parties. In other bankruptcy courts, by local rule, the party need only file the motion and the clerk of the court will arrange the date for the motion to be heard.

Or, for example, when a creditor files a proof of claim in a debtor's bankruptcy case in accordance with the Code and FRBP, some bankruptcy courts require by local rule that a copy of the filing be sent directly to the bankruptcy trustee by the creditor. Others require by local rule that the bankruptcy court clerk send a copy of the proof of claim to the bankruptcy trustee after it has been filed with the clerk by the creditor.

Application Exercise 4

Locate the local rules for the U.S. bankruptcy court located in the federal district where you plan to practice. See if you can locate a rule there dealing with:

- The allowed attorney's fee for an attorney representing a debtor in a Chapter 13 case
- The availability of electronic filing of documents with the court
- The procedure for conversion of a case from a Chapter 13 to a Chapter 7
- The procedure for amendment of a Chapter 13 plan
- The approved manner for payment of filing and other fees (e.g., by credit card, personal check, etc.)

---

6. Miscellaneous Provisions of the U.S. Code

Although, as we have noted, the Bankruptcy Code is found in Title 11 of the U.S. Code, other provisions of the U.S. Code come into play in bankruptcy cases. Most notably, Title 28 of the U.S. Code contains provisions identifying the various federal districts where bankruptcy courts are located (§152), the procedures for the appointment of bankruptcy judges (§152), procedures for the referral of bankruptcy cases from the district court to the bankruptcy court (§159), and other details concerning their duties. Title 28 also sets out the extent of bankruptcy jurisdiction (§1334) and venue (§§1408-1412). And it contains provisions creating and regulating the U.S. Trustee system (§§581-589), discussed in the next chapter.

Title 18 of the U.S. Code contains provisions regarding the offenses of bankruptcy fraud (§157), embezzlement against a bankruptcy estate (§153), false oaths and claims (§152), and other federal crimes that may arise in bankruptcy cases.

7. State Law

Though the bankruptcy code is a federal statute, state law plays a major role in the administration of a bankruptcy case. Two Supreme Court cases make this clear. In Vanston Bondholders Protective Committee v. Green, 329 U.S. 156 (1946), decided under the old Bankruptcy Act that preceded the modern Code adopted in 1978 and amended in 1994 and 2005, Inland Gas Company was placed in a state-court-supervised receivership in Kentucky and later forced into bankruptcy by its creditors. It was uncontested in the case that creditors of the debtor who held corporate bonds were entitled under the terms of the bond instruments to receive interest on the unpaid interest obligations due on the bonds; i.e., they were entitled to interest on unpaid interest. However, an issue arose regarding whether that interest on interest contractual obligation had to be given priority in the bankruptcy distribution where to do so would mean other classes of creditors would receive less. The Supreme Court held that although the issue of whether the bond instruments themselves in fact entitled the bondholders to interest on unpaid interest was a question of state law ("What claims of creditors are valid and subsisting obligations against the bankrupt at the time a petition in bankruptcy is filed is a question which, in the absence of overruling federal law, is to be determined by reference to state law" 329 U.S. at 161), the question of what priority such claims were to be given in the bankruptcy case as against the claims of other creditors was a question of federal bankruptcy law, not state law ("[B]ankruptcy courts must administer and enforce the Bankruptcy Act as interpreted by this Court in accordance with authority granted by Congress to determine how and what claims shall be allowed under equitable principles" 329 U.S. at 162-63).

Case Preview

Butner v. United States

The distinction first noted in *Vanston* between determining the nature and extent of a creditor's claim and the treatment of that claim in a bankruptcy case was brought into sharper focus in Butner v. United States, where the very nature of a creditor's property interest is at issue and the court has to instruct as to how such interest is to be determined when the debtor's case is pending in a federal bankruptcy court. As you read *Butner*, consider the following questions:

1. What was the difference between the majority and minority views that had been adopted among the circuits and that the Supreme Court resolved to clarify?
2. Could Congress, as part of the bankruptcy statute, have dictated what the interests of a mortgagee would be in rents and profits from real property when that property was part of a bankrupt estate?
3. Why does the Supreme Court conclude that the minority view that it rejects produces an inequity?
4. Once it has decided that state law will control the nature of the creditor's interest in property in a bankruptcy case, the Supreme Court does not take up the question of whether the lower courts correctly interpreted North Carolina property law. Why not?

Butner v. United States
440 U.S. 48 (1979)

Justice John Paul Stevens wrote the majority opinion for *Butner. Collection of the Supreme Court of the United States, Photographer: Steve Petteway*

[Butner held a second mortgage in certain real property located in North Carolina that was owned by Golden Enterprises, Inc., a company undergoing reorganization in bankruptcy. An issue arose concerning the whether Butner's security interest extended to the rents and profits derived from the property or whether Butner was unsecured as to those rents and profits. The bankruptcy court ruled that Butner's security interest did not extend to the rents and profits. The U.S. district court reversed, citing North Carolina property law. On appeal, the Fourth Circuit agreed that North Carolina property law controlled the issue but interpreted that law differently from the district court to reach a different result. The Supreme Court accepted cert, not in order to clarify North Carolina property law, but to decide the larger question that was dividing the circuits of whether state law or federal law determined the nature and extent of a creditor's property interests in a bankruptcy case.]

STEVENS, Justice:

We did not grant certiorari to decide whether the Court of Appeals correctly applied North Carolina law. Our concern is with the proper interpretation of the federal statutes governing the administration of bankrupt estates. Specifically, it is our purpose to resolve a conflict between the Third and Seventh Circuits on the one hand, and the Second, Fourth, Sixth, Eighth, and Ninth Circuits on the other, concerning the proper approach to a dispute of this kind.

The courts in the latter group regard the question whether a security interest in property extends to rents and profits derived from the property as one that should be resolved by reference to state law. In a few States, sometimes referred to as "title States," the mortgagee is automatically entitled to possession of the property, and to a secured interest in the rents. In most States, the mortgagee's right to rents is dependent upon his taking actual or constructive possession of the property by means of a foreclosure, the appointment of a receiver for his benefit, or some similar legal proceeding. Because the applicable law varies from State to State, the results in federal bankruptcy proceedings will also vary under the approach taken by most of the Circuits.

The Third and Seventh Circuits have adopted a federal rule of equity that affords the mortgagee a secured interest in the rents even if state law would not recognize any such interest until after foreclosure. Those courts reason that since the bankruptcy court has the power to deprive the mortgagee of his state-law remedy, equity requires that the right to rents not be dependent on state-court action that may be precluded by federal law. Under this approach, no affirmative steps are required by the mortgagee — in state or federal court — to acquire or maintain a right to the rents.

We agree with the majority view.

The constitutional authority of Congress to establish "uniform Laws on the subject of Bankruptcies throughout the United States" would clearly encompass a federal statute defining the mortgagee's interest in the rents and profits earned by property in a bankrupt estate. But Congress has not chosen to exercise its power to fashion any such rule. The Bankruptcy Act does include provisions invalidating certain security interests as fraudulent, or as improper preferences over general creditors. Apart from these provisions, however, Congress has generally left the determination of property rights in the assets of a bankrupt's estate to state law.

Property interests are created and defined by state law. Unless some federal interest requires a different result, there is no reason why such interests should be analyzed differently simply because an interested party is involved in a bankruptcy proceeding. Uniform treatment of property interests by both state and federal courts within a State serves to reduce uncertainty, to discourage forum shopping, and to prevent a party from receiving "a windfall merely by reason of the happenstance of bankruptcy." [Citation omitted.] The justifications for application of state law are not limited to ownership interests; they apply with equal force to security interests, including the interest of a mortgagee in rents earned by mortgaged property.

The minority of courts which have rejected state law have not done so because of any congressional command, or because their approach serves any identifiable federal interest. Rather, they have adopted a uniform federal approach to the question of the mortgagee's interest in rents and profits because of their perception of the demands of equity. The equity powers of the bankruptcy court play an important part in the administration of bankrupt estates in countless situations in which the judge is required to deal with particular, individualized problems. But undefined considerations of equity provide no basis for adoption of a uniform federal rule affording mortgagees an automatic interest in the rents as soon as the mortgagor is declared bankrupt.

In support of their rule, the Third and Seventh Circuits have emphasized that while the mortgagee may pursue various state-law remedies prior to bankruptcy, the adjudication leaves the mortgagee "only such remedies as may be found in a court of bankruptcy in the equitable administration of the bankrupt's assets." [Citation omitted.] It does not follow, however, that "equitable administration" requires that all mortgagees be afforded an automatic security interest in rents and profits when state law would deny such an automatic benefit and require the mortgagee to take some affirmative action before his rights are recognized. What does follow is that the federal bankruptcy court should take whatever steps are necessary to ensure that the mortgagee is afforded in federal bankruptcy court the same protection he would have under state law if no bankruptcy had ensued. This is the majority view, which we adopt today.

The rule of the Third and Seventh Circuits, at least in some circumstances, affords the mortgagee rights that are not his as a matter of state law. The rule we adopt avoids this inequity because it looks to state law to define the security interest of the mortgagee. At the same time, our decision avoids the opposite inequity of depriving a mortgagee of his state-law security interest when bankruptcy intervenes. For while it is argued that bankruptcy may impair or delay the mortgagee's exercise of his right to foreclosure, and thus his acquisition of a security interest in rents according to the law of many States, a bankruptcy judge familiar with local practice should be able to avoid this potential loss by sequestering rents or authorizing immediate state-law foreclosures. Even though a federal judge may temporarily delay entry of such an order, the loss of rents to the mortgagee normally should be no greater than if he had been proceeding in a state court: for if there is a reason that persuades a federal judge to delay, presumably the same reason would also persuade a state judge to withhold foreclosure temporarily. The essential point is that in a properly administered scheme in which the basic federal rule is that state law governs, the primary reason why any holder of a mortgage may fail to collect rent immediately after default must stem from state law. . . .

In this Court the parties have argued the state-law question at great length, each stressing different aspects of the record. We decline to review the state-law question. The federal judges who deal regularly with questions of state law in their respective districts and circuits are in a better position than we to determine how local courts would dispose of comparable issues.

The judgment is affirmed.

Post-Case Follow-Up

The significance of *Butner* to bankruptcy law practice is profound. Bankruptcy judges routinely have to determine the nature and extent of a debtor or creditor's interest in property and this case tells us that unless some federal interest requires a different result, state law is to determine those issues. That means a federal bankruptcy judge sitting in Ohio and applying a federal statute to administer a bankruptcy case may have to determine and apply the state law of Ohio to determine a party's interest in contested property. Or the state law of Illinois, or Indiana, or Florida, or Texas if one of those is the state where the property at issue is located or the state having sufficiently close connections with the property or the underlying transaction in which the party acquired an interest in the property that its laws should determine the ownership interest. You can see from that last sentence that conflict of law issues (which state law should control the determination of the ownership interest where several states have interests served by that determination) arise routinely in bankruptcy cases because of *Butner.*

Butner v. United States: Real Life Applications

1. The minority rule that the Supreme Court rejected in *Butner* certainly had one thing going for it — it would have produced uniform results across the country regarding property interests adjudicated in a bankruptcy case. And that uniformity would have likely produced greater predictability, which is generally perceived as a good thing. Assume you are retained to represent a financial services company in the state where you plan to practice. Your client routinely makes loans to consumers and takes a security interest in their autos and other personal property. When a consumer defaults on a loan the law of your state permits the client, as a secured party, to either repossess and sell the collateral or, upon written notice given after default, to repossess and keep the collateral in satisfaction of the debt (a practice known as strict foreclosure where allowed). So if a consumer grants a security interest in a car worth $5,000 to secure a $3,000 loan, upon default the client may be able to repossess and keep the car, thus capturing the equity. In many states this practice is not permissible in consumer loans, but let's assume it is in yours. And let's assume further that when consumers file for bankruptcy relief the bankruptcy courts located in your state have routinely upheld that state law. But now your client plans to expand its business to a neighboring state whose laws do not permit strict foreclosure in consumer transactions. What do you need to explain to your client regarding whether they can depend on this strict foreclosure practice being given effect in bankruptcy proceedings in those neighboring states? Might you consider a way to structure the transactions your client enters into with consumers living in those neighboring states to ensure that the law of your state will control the secured party's interests and rights even though the debtor and the collateral are in a different state?

2. Do not overlook that qualifying language in *Butner,* "Unless some federal interest requires a different result. . . ." We will see instances where the Code does in fact state a hard and fast rule that changes ownership interests under state property law. A striking example is §522(f)(1)(A) of the Code, which allows an individual bankruptcy debtor to avoid a judicial lien in his property to the extent it impairs an exemption the debtor can claim in his bankruptcy case.

We will look at that section closely later but you can see here that it represents a specific federal interest that dramatically changes the interest the judgment creditor would have in that property under state law. Here's another example of that qualifying language. Assume the law of the state where you plan to practice allows married couples a 25 percent reduction in property taxes when one or both of the spouses turn 65 years of age. However, assume further that the consanguinity provision in the state's marriage and family code does not permit marriages between persons who are related to each other as first cousins and the state supreme court recently decided a case in which it refused on the grounds of public policy to extend the property tax reduction to a first-cousin couple lawfully recognized as married in another state. You represent a first-cousin couple, one of whom is 67 years of age, legally married in a sister state. Your clients have filed for bankruptcy relief and the state has filed a creditor's proof of claim in the case claiming to be owed for 100 percent of last year's unpaid property taxes due under state law. Can you think of a "federal interest" that might be asserted on behalf of your clients to contend that the state's claim should be reduced by 25 percent notwithstanding state law? See Obergefell v. Hodges, 135 S. Ct. 1039 (2015).

Per *Butner*, in a bankruptcy case, whether a debt created by contract is valid and collectible will normally be determined by state law. Whether a creditor is properly secured and perfected in personal property of the bankrupt debtor will be determined by the state's version of Article 9 of the UCC. Whether a creditor holds a mortgage in the debtor's real property will be determined by state law. Whether a creditor holds a valid non-consensual lien in property of the bankrupt will be determined by state law. Even the question of where the debtor resides for purposes of deciding the proper bankruptcy court in which to file his case is a question of state law. Bankruptcy law practitioners are constantly dealing with various aspects of state law. On the other hand, per *Vanston* and *Butner*, the Bankruptcy Code contains its own procedures for administering a case and its own rules for recognizing, prioritizing, and paying creditor claims and for gathering, liquidating (selling), and distributing the property of the debtor and the practitioner must constantly deal with those specialized bankruptcy procedures and rules.

Application Exercise 5

Recall from Chapter One the Code's definition of what constitutes a consumer debt in 11 U.S.C. §101(8). Recall too the example we used of Mary Jones who purchases 200 loaves of bread to use in her sandwich shop but who then takes 50 of them home to use in preparing food for a family reunion. Mary has now filed a Chapter 7 bankruptcy case and there is a motion to dismiss her case under 11 U.S.C. §707(b) for abuse by an individual filing a case with primarily consumer debt. If a question arises concerning whether Mary owes this particular debt to the supplier who sold her the loaves of bread, what law will control: state contract law or §707(b) of the Code? If there is a question of whether her debts, including this one, are primarily consumer debts for purposes of §707(b), what law will control: state contract law or the Code provision? Would it change your answer to the second question if state law also defined what is or is not a consumer debt?

E. NUMBER AND LOCATION OF THE U.S. BANKRUTPCY COURTS

Congress has divided the United States geographically into 94 different **federal districts**. Each of those federal districts, in turn, lies within a larger **federal circuit**, over which sits one of the 13 **U.S. circuit courts of appeal**. In each of the 94 federal districts, there are one or more **district judges** presiding over a **U.S. district court**. And in each of those 94 federal districts, there are also one or more **bankruptcy judges** presiding over a **U.S. bankruptcy court**.

Application Exercise 6

Go to the Court Links Web site of the Administrative Office of the Federal Courts (www.uscourts.gov/about-federal-courts/federal-courts-public/court-website-links) and locate the bankruptcy court in the federal district and division where you plan to practice. On your computer, bookmark this Web site for further use.

F. SYNOPSIS OF JURISDICTIONAL ISSUES, APPELLATE PROCESS, AND DECISION-MAKING PROCEDURES IN BANKRUPTCY COURT

1. Subject Matter Jurisdiction of the Bankruptcy Courts

The subject matter jurisdiction of the U.S. bankruptcy courts is a complex and multi-layered subject. It is challenging even for experienced practitioners to grasp. Moreover, it is still evolving, as the Supreme Court continues to sort out significant constitutional and statutory interpretation issues that have a dramatic and practical impact on the scope of that jurisdiction. Your ability to grasp this challenging topic will be enhanced by first learning the mechanics of how consumer bankruptcy cases work. This is so because the statutes, rules, and court rulings regarding

When Bankruptcy Judges Were Only Referees

The position of "bankruptcy judge" has only been around since the Bankruptcy Reform Act of 1978. For the preceding 80 years they were known as "bankruptcy referees," a position created by the Bankruptcy Act of 1898. Bankruptcy referees were appointed by the U.S. district judges in many but not all federal districts to aid in administering bankruptcy cases. Congress slowly expanded the duties of the referees as their expertise in this specialized area became more widely appreciated and in 1973 the Supreme Court issued rules that, for the first time, referred to the referees as judges. It was not until the Reform Act of 1978 that the title of bankruptcy judge was formalized and the bankruptcy courts established in every federal district. The Reform Act of 1978 also created the U.S. Trustee position as a pilot program later made permanent in order to relieve bankruptcy judges of many of the routine administrative tasks associated with a bankruptcy case. The Federal Judgeship Act of 1984 established the current system whereby bankruptcy judges are appointed by the federal circuit courts to serve 14-year terms. In 1997 the National Bankruptcy Review Commission recommended that Congress declare bankruptcy courts to be Article III courts, which would require those judges to be nominated by the president and confirmed by the Senate and would provide them with the lifetime tenure granted Article III judges. Congress has never acted on that proposal.

bankruptcy jurisdiction are encountered in the context of those mechanics and can be even more challenging if the student is not already grounded in bankruptcy vocabulary and procedures. For all these reasons, our detailed study of bankruptcy subject matter jurisdiction is reserved for Chapter Eighteen, following our study of how Chapter 7 and 13 consumer cases work.

Having said that, in true chicken or egg fashion, it will enhance your study of the mechanics of the consumer bankruptcy case to have some rudimentary understanding of bankruptcy jurisdiction as you begin. The following synopsis of subject matter jurisdiction is intended to serve that purpose. Remember as you read this synopsis that the "why" question (as in, "Why in the world does it work that way?") will be answered in Chapter Eighteen. For now be content to have the "how" explained to you briefly.

28 U.S.C. §1334(a) grants the U.S. district courts (not the U.S. bankruptcy courts) "original and exclusive" jurisdiction over cases under Title 11 (the Bankruptcy Code). 28 U.S.C. §1334(b) then grants the district courts "original but not exclusive jurisdiction over civil proceedings, arising under title 11, or arising in or related to cases under title 11." Proceedings that are "arising in or related to" cases under Title 11 are generally understood to include any issues that could conceivably have an impact on the property of the estate to be administered in the bankruptcy case. See In re Wood, 825 F.2d 90 (5th Cir. 1987). So the U.S. district courts are given "original and exclusive" jurisdiction over all bankruptcy cases filed under Title 11 but "original but not exclusive" jurisdiction over issues that arise in or are related to bankruptcy cases filed under Title 11.

This "original but not exclusive" jurisdiction allows a district court to delegate the authority to handle proceedings arising in or related to bankruptcy cases to a lower court that answers to it while retaining "original and exclusive" jurisdiction over the bankruptcy cases themselves. 28 U.S.C. §151 provides: "In each judicial district, the bankruptcy judges in regular active service shall constitute a unit of the district court to be known as the bankruptcy court of that district." Thus bankruptcy courts in each federal district across the country serve as units or adjuncts of the district courts in those districts.

It is 28 U.S.C. §157(a) that specifically authorizes the district courts to refer bankruptcy cases to the bankruptcy courts in their districts. Consequently, the bankruptcy courts, as adjuncts or units of the district courts per 28 U.S.C. §151, obtain jurisdiction over bankruptcy cases only by referral from the district courts. Bankruptcy courts have **referral jurisdiction** from the district courts over bankruptcy cases. And the district court that has referred jurisdiction to a bankruptcy court (usually done routinely and automatically by standing court order of the district) has the discretion to **revoke the reference** at any time on its own motion or upon the motion of any party in interest for cause shown per 28 U.S.C. §157(d).

Remember that we will consider the "why" question regarding this odd jurisdictional arrangement in Chapter Eighteen, but for now do understand that this scheme is made necessary by the historical fact that while the district courts are deemed Article III courts (established under Article III of the U.S. Constitution), bankruptcy courts are deemed only Article I courts (created by Congress for a narrow legislative purpose under Article I of the Constitution). As Article I courts, the bankruptcy courts cannot enter binding final judgments in all of the proceedings that are referred to them by the district courts. The proceedings in a bankruptcy case referred to the bankruptcy court in which it has the power, as an Article I court, to enter a binding final judgment are called **core proceedings**. Proceedings that arise in a bankruptcy case referred to the bankruptcy court in which the court may not enter a binding final judgment are called **non-core proceedings**.

28 U.S.C. §157(b)(1) provides that the bankruptcy court may enter a final judgment or dispositive order in a core proceeding but §157(c)(2) provides that the court may *not* do so in a non-core proceeding *unless* all the parties consent. When the matter before the bankruptcy court is non-core, §157(c)(1) limits the power of that court to making proposed findings of fact and conclusions of law for review de novo by the district court.

So what is a core proceeding in a bankruptcy case and what isn't? 28 U.S.C. §157(b)(2) designates a number of specific matters that arise in a bankruptcy case as core proceedings. In deciding disputes involving any of those enumerated matters, the bankruptcy court can enter a final order or judgment per the statutory scheme. Exhibit 4.5 lists the proceedings designated as core by Congress.

EXHIBIT 4.5	**Types of Proceedings Arising in a Bankruptcy Case Designated as Core Proceedings (Based on 28 U.S.C. §157(b)(2))**

- Matters concerning the administration of the estate
- Allowance or disallowance of claims against the estate
- Counterclaims by the estate against persons filing claims against the estate
- Exemptions of property from the estate
- Orders in respect to obtaining credit

EXHIBIT 4.5   **(Continued)**

- Orders to turn over property of the estate
- Proceedings to determine, avoid, or recover preferential transfers
- Motions to stay, annul, or modify the automatic stay
- Proceedings to determine, avoid, or recover fraudulent transfers
- Determinations as to the dischargeability of particular debts
- Objections to discharge
- Determinations as to the validity, extent, or priority of liens
- Confirmation of plans
- Orders approving the use or lease of property, including the use of cash collateral
- Orders approving the sale of property (other than property resulting from claims brought by the estate against persons who have not filed claims against the estate)
- Other proceedings affecting the liquidation of assets of the estate or the adjustment of the debtor/creditor relationship or the equity security holder relationship
- Recognition of foreign proceedings and other matters under Chapter 15 of the Code

The matters listed in §157(b)(2) do not constitute an exclusive list of core proceedings ("Core proceedings include, but are not limited to . . .") and as we will see when we return to this issue in Chapter Eighteen, courts continue to struggle and in some cases disagree over whether a particular matter excluded from the list is to be treated as core or non-core. When a matter is determined to be non-core and the parties will not consent to the bankruptcy court entering a final order on the matter, one of two things can happen. First, the bankruptcy court can go ahead and hear the matter as non-core, which means it can only enter proposed findings and conclusions for the district court's review or, second, one of the parties can move to revoke the reference to the bankruptcy court as to that non-core matter and the district court will then hear and decide it. Remember, district courts retain overall jurisdiction over bankruptcy cases filed in their district and may revoke the jurisdiction they referred to the bankruptcy courts at any time per 28 U.S.C. §157(d).

Pursuant to 28 U.S.C. §157(b)(5), bankruptcy courts may not conduct trials involving personal injury or wrongful death regardless of whether they qualify as core proceedings and may not even make proposed findings in them as in a non-core proceeding. The U.S. district court is to hear and decide such claims.

It is imperative to recognize that there is much more to say and learn on the topic of bankruptcy subject matter jurisdiction. These are bare basics. But for the reasons indicated, we will wait until Chapter Eighteen to consider questions such as how to determine whether a matter arising in a bankruptcy case that is not listed in §157(b)(2) is a core or non-core proceeding, how a party consents to the entry of a final judgment by a bankruptcy court in a non-core matter, and the current hot topic in bankruptcy law — whether and to what extent the core/non-core distinction created by Congress is even constitutional.

2. Appellate Process in a Bankruptcy Case

As with subject matter jurisdiction, we will reserve a detailed discussion of the topic of the appellate process in bankruptcy to Chapter Eighteen. But again, it will help you to understand the bare basics as we begin our study of how consumer bankruptcy cases work.

Where the bankruptcy court exercising its referral jurisdiction enters a final judgment, the appeal lies to the district court that referred jurisdiction pursuant to 28 U.S.C. §158(a). The standard of review utilized by the district court in considering whether to reverse a final judgment entered by the bankruptcy court is de novo as to questions of law but clearly erroneous as to findings of fact and due regard is given to the opportunity of the bankruptcy court to judge the credibility of the witnesses. See, e.g., In re Nosek, 544 F.3d 34, 43 (1st Cir. 2008). A party unhappy with the decision of the district court may then appeal that ruling to the appropriate U.S. circuit court pursuant to 28 U.S.C. §158(d) where the same standard of review will prevail. A party unhappy with the decision of the circuit court of appeals may file an application for writ of certiorari to the U.S. Supreme Court.

In five federal circuits (the 1st, 6th, 8th, 9th, and 10th), appeals of final judgments entered by bankruptcy courts may go to a special panel of bankruptcy judges selected from the entire federal circuit instead of to the district court *if* all parties consent. These are **Bankruptcy Appellate Panels** (BAPs) authorized by 28 U.S.C. §158(b). Decisions of the BAP are appealable directly to the circuit court per 28 U.S.C. §158(d), effectively bypassing the district court.

There is more to be said concerning the appellate process in bankruptcy and that will be accomplished in Chapter Eighteen. There we will consider the rules governing the time frame and procedures for filing an appeal to the district court or BAP, the judicial doctrine of finality in bankruptcy appellate procedure, and the availability of discretionary appeal in a bankruptcy case.

3. Decision-Making Procedures in Bankruptcy Court

While not nearly as complex as bankruptcy subject matter jurisdiction, the particular procedures authorized by the Code and the FRBP for decision making in a bankruptcy case are unusual and challenging to master. As with the other topics in this session, rather than trying to cover the decision-making procedures in detail here, we will only provide a synopsis and reserve the detailed discussion for Chapter Eighteen.

As you will soon discover, in bankruptcy practice there are myriad issues that a bankruptcy judge may have to decide in a given case. The Code and the FRBP recognize two broadly different procedures for deciding those issues: Some are decided as **contested matters** and others are decided as **adversary proceedings**.

Most issues that arise in a bankruptcy case are considered contested matters and that procedure is governed by FRBP 9014. A contested matter is the simpler and quicker process for deciding an issue that arises in a case. It requires a hearing before the bankruptcy judge but not a full-blown trial as does an adversary proceeding. At the hearing on the contested matter, the bankruptcy judge may consider written briefs filed by the contesting parties and the oral arguments of counsel. If necessary, the court may also listen to the sworn testimony of witnesses. But contested matter procedure can become confusing because the Code and FRBP provide that some contested matters are initiated by filing a **motion**, some by filing an **objection**, and some by filing what is called a **notice of intended action** that is then followed by an objection to that intended action.

Briefly, a motion in bankruptcy procedure is essentially the same as you learned it in Civil Procedure: it is a written request made to a court seeking an order granting the moving party affirmative relief regarding the subject of the request (e.g., a motion to lift automatic stay or a motion for additional time to file bankruptcy schedules that accompany a petition). An objection is very similar. It is a written request to a court seeking an order denying another party some relief or adjusting the rights of the other party in some way in connection with the subject of the request (e.g., an objection to a debtor's claimed property exemption). FRBP 9013 governs the required content of motions and objections as well as who is to be served with copies.

The oddest of the three methods of initiating a contested matter is the notice of intended action. In some situations the Code and FRBP allow a party to simply give notice that it intends to take some action rather than filing a motion to obtain court permission to do it (e.g., the intent of a bankruptcy trustee to abandon property of the estate as having no value to the estate as authorized by §554 of the Code and FRBP 6007(a)). If a notice of intended action is given and no objection to it is made within the time allowed, the action can be taken with no formal order of the court. No hearing will be scheduled or conducted. Only if a timely objection to the intended action is made will a hearing be scheduled and held and an order entered allowing or disallowing the intended action (e.g., FRBP 6007(a) requires that an objection to a notice of intent to abandon property be filed and served within 14 days).

Issues that arise in a bankruptcy case that are not designated as contested matters will be resolved instead as adversary proceedings. An adversary proceeding is essentially a formal civil lawsuit initiated within the bankruptcy case and decided there. Part VII of the FRBP (Rules 7001 through 7087) apply in adversary proceedings and those rules incorporate most of the formal Federal Rules of Civil Procedure (FRCP) to such actions. Thus they must be commenced by filing a complaint and accomplishing service of process. Motions under FRCP 12 or 56 may be made; counterclaims, cross claims, and third-party complaints filed; formal discovery had; and formal trials conducted.

One rule of civil procedure that is not incorporated into Part VII of the FRBP governing adversary proceedings is FRCP 38, regarding the demand for a jury trial. That is because per 28 U.S.C. §157(e) a bankruptcy court is authorized to conduct a jury trial when demanded *only* when all parties consent and the district court specifically designates the bankruptcy court to conduct that trial. Generally, when a party to a bankruptcy dispute desires a jury trial, the reference will be revoked either at request of a party or by the district court acting *sua sponte* and the case tried to a jury by the district court.

FRBP 7001 lists the types of disputes that must be treated as adversary proceedings, and they are summarized in Exhibit 4.6.

EXHIBIT 4.6 **Disputes That Must Be Resolved as Adversary Proceedings**

- A proceeding to bar the debtor from receiving a discharge in bankruptcy or to revoke a discharge previously granted
- A proceeding to declare a particular debt non-dischargeable
- A proceeding to determine the validity, extent, or priority of a lien on property of the debtor
- A proceeding to recover money or property from a third party
- A proceeding to obtain an injunction or other equitable relief
- A proceeding to obtain approval to sell property in which both the debtor and a non-debtor have an interest
- A proceeding to subordinate a creditor's claim or interest to other claims
- A proceeding to revoke an order confirming a plan in a Chapter 11, 12, or 13 case

---

As we have noted in connection with the other topics in this section, there is more to be said on the question of how the bankruptcy court makes decisions, but that more detailed discussion will await Chapter Eighteen. This synopsis provides bare basics, sufficient to allow you to begin learning how a consumer bankruptcy case is filed and administered.

G. OTHER IMPORTANT PLAYERS IN A BANKRUPTCY CASE

Needless to say, the bankruptcy judge is a key player in the administration of a bankruptcy case. But let's briefly consider the other key actors in the drama.

The party that files the bankruptcy proceeding is of course the debtor. In the forms that the debtor files in connection with his bankruptcy case he will identify his creditors and will state whether each creditor is secured or unsecured and so forth. Beginning with the petition in bankruptcy the debtor files to begin the case, all documents in a bankruptcy case are filed with the bankruptcy court clerk's office in most federal districts, though a few require filing with the district court clerk. The court clerk is the administrative officer for the court in which the case is pending. The clerk's office will maintain all records regarding the case and is responsible for sending out various notices regarding actions taken or to be taken in the case (e.g., notice to listed creditors of the filing of the case, notice of the first meeting of creditors, notice of upcoming hearings on disputed matters).

Most debtors hire attorneys to help them prepare and file the necessary papers and to represent them throughout the bankruptcy proceeding. These attorneys are known as debtor's attorneys. Creditors also often retain attorneys to assist them in processing their claim through the bankruptcy proceeding. These attorneys are known as creditor's attorneys.

In most bankruptcy cases (and always in Chapter 7 and 13 cases), as soon as the petition is filed, beginning the case, the bankruptcy court will appoint a bankruptcy trustee to administer the case. As we shall see later, the bankruptcy trustee is given broad powers under the Code and is responsible to the court and to the creditors of the estate for his actions. Sometimes the bankruptcy trustee finds it appropriate to hire an attorney to represent him in some proceeding in the case, like an adversary proceeding. The attorney the trustee hires is known as the bankruptcy trustee's attorney.

In most but not all federal districts, there is another government official involved in bankruptcy cases: the U.S. Trustee (never to be confused with the bankruptcy trustee). The U.S. Trustee is given responsibilities under §586 of the Code and various FRBP to perform duties such as:

- to determine who is eligible to serve as a bankruptcy trustee;
- to oversee and monitor the work of the bankruptcy trustees;
- to monitor pending cases; and
- to make recommendations to the bankruptcy judge on contested issues that arise before the bankruptcy judge.

The U.S. Trustee program is administered and overseen by the U.S. Department of Justice (www.usdoj.gov/ust). In North Carolina and Alabama, there are no U.S. Trustees, but bankruptcy administrators perform the same tasks in those states, overseen by the Administrative Office of the U.S. Courts (www.uscourts. gov).

In the course of administering a bankruptcy case, the services of a number of different professionals and businesspeople may be utilized by the bankruptcy trustee, the debtor, or creditors. Those may include *auctioneers, realtors, appraisers, insurance agents, bankers, economists, accountants*, and *repossession* and *storage services*.

A number of Code provisions refer to the right of a party in interest to take some action in a bankruptcy case. For example, §502(a) authorizes a party in interest to object to the claim filed in a case by a creditor of the debtor (discussed in Chapter Eight, Section C). FRBP 4003(b) authorizes a party in interest to object to a debtor's claim of exempt property (discussed in Chapter Six, Section B). Curiously, neither the Code nor the FRBP define who is a party in interest, leaving courts to make that determination based on the particular right to act being granted by the Code. But, generally speaking, a **party in interest** is a person or entity who is deemed to have standing to be heard by the court on a matter to be decided in the bankruptcy case. For most matters, the debtor, the bankruptcy trustee, the U.S. trustee or bankruptcy administrator, and creditors or other third parties (e.g., persons who are not in bankruptcy but who are jointly liable with the bankruptcy debtor on certain obligations or nondebtor owners of an entity in bankruptcy) who may be affected by the action taken will be deemed parties in interest.

H. ELECTRONIC FILING IN BANKRUPTCY COURT

Every bankruptcy court in the country now employs electronic case filing instead of paper filing for all or most documents. A few courts still require the petition itself to be filed in paper, but most have gone completely paperless. Using **electronic case filing** for filings by the various parties in interest to the bankruptcy case (the petition, supporting schedules, statements and lists, motions, objections, reports, applications, etc.) are submitted electronically, the court's orders are entered electronically, and all notices and other communications from the court to case participants are distributed electronically. Needless to say, lawyers and those assisting them in the bankruptcy field must become familiar with the e-filing system utilized in bankruptcy courts.

The electronic system used in all bankruptcy courts is known as **Case Management/Electronic Case Files** (CM/ECF). The way the system works is that documents created in a lawyer's office by word processing software are saved in a portable document format (PDF). The attorney then logs in by computer to the local court's CM/ECF system using a log-in name and password provided by the court clerk, identifies the case in which the document is to be submitted, attaches the PDF file containing the document to be filed in the case, and presses a "submit" button. In the clerk's office, the CM/CEF immediately sends the lawyer's office by e-mail an **electronic receipt** confirming receipt of the document filed. The receipt can be saved or printed by the lawyer's office. The CM/ECF system allows 24-hour, 7-day-a-week filing for case participants. Once a party has made an appearance in a pending case, they then receive electronic notification of case activity (other filings, entry of orders, etc.) by means of a **Notice of Electronic Filing** (NEF), which allows the recipient a one-time look at the document filed and the opportunity to copy or save it. The system also allows the payment of filing fees by credit card.

In order to be able to view all documents in a case (any case) at any time and as frequently as desired (rather than the one-free-look allowed by CM/ECF), lawyers must subscribe to **Public Access to Court Electronic Records** (PACER). Members of the public may also subscribe to PACER. To avoid having to pay for access to electronic records, lawyers or members of the public may also go physically to the office of the bankruptcy court clerk and view files on screens made available there. A charge will be made, however, for documents copied.

Notices from the bankruptcy court to case participants is also done electronically through **Electronic Bankruptcy Noticing** (EBN), which allows attorneys and others to receive notices from the bankruptcy court by e-mail link, e-mail with PDF attachment, or fax.

Application Exercise 7

Go to www.pacer.gov/ and choose one or more of the video tutorials available there explaining how the CM/ECF, PACER, and EBN systems work.

If a party in interest is entitled to notice or service of a motion or other document filed in the case but does not participate in CM/CMF, notice or service on that party must then be accomplished by sending a paper copy by first class mail or hand delivery. Typically, a party filing a motion or other document will utilize electronic filing and then examine the electronic receipt to make sure all parties entitled to notice received it by the electronic filing. If any party did not receive it electronically, they are then served with paper copy by hand delivery or first class mail. The certificate of service included on the document filed will advise that service was accomplished electronically or by hand delivery or mailing.

I. BANKRUPTCY SOFTWARE

Attorneys who represent bankruptcy debtors utilize **bankruptcy software** programs to expedite the preparation of the numerous schedules and statements required in every case. A good software program can save time for the debtor's attorney and assist legal professionals by automatically filling in repetitive information, performing calculations, and formatting the documents in a way that complies with electronic filing requirements. Some programs allow for unlimited use and some are limited to one-time use. A number of bankruptcy software providers and their Web sites are listed in Exhibit 4.7. A number of the Web sites provide a free online demonstration and/or permit the free download of forms that can be used for demonstration purposes.

EXHIBIT 4.7	A Sampling of Bankruptcy Software Providers

- BestCase (www.bestcase.com)
- TopForm (www.fastcase.com/topform/)
- BankruptcyPRO (www.bankruptcy-pro.com/)
- Bankruptcy Case Software (www.nationallawforms.com/bankruptcy/software-bankruptcy.htm)
- NextChapter (www.nextchapter.com/)
- New Hope (www.bankruptcysoftware.com)
- Blumberg Blankrupter (www.blumberg.com/)
- Standard Legal (www.standardlegal.com)

Application Exercise 8

Visit some or all of the Web sites listed in Exhibit 4.7 and try the online demonstrations or download and compare the free forms. Which provider seems to offer the software that is the easiest to use? Which seems to provide the most comprehensive services? Which allow unlimited use and which only one-time use? Why would an attorney choose a one-time use software package?

J. WEB-BASED RESOURCES FOR LEARNING ABOUT BANKRUPTCY

There are a number of excellent Web sites providing free access to current news and information of interest to bankruptcy professionals, as well as bankruptcy-specific legal research. Exhibit 4.8 lists a number of these.

EXHIBIT 4.8 **Useful Bankruptcy Information Sites**

The Bankruptcy Code, Rules, Forms, and General Information:

- Title 11 of the U.S. Code (//uscode.house.gov/download/download.shtml or www.law.cornell.edu/uscode/text/11)
- Rules of Bankruptcy Procedure (www.uscourts.gov/rules-policies/current-rules-practice-procedure))
- Official Bankruptcy Forms (www.uscourts.gov/forms/bankruptcy-forms)
- Administrative Office of the Federal Courts' Federal Judiciary Home Page (www.uscourts.gov)
- United States Trustees Program (administered by the U.S. Department of Justice) (www.usdoj.gov/ust)
- Electronic Bankruptcy Noticing Center (www.ebnuscourts.com)
- AO Bankruptcy Basics (www.uscourts.gov/services-forms/bankruptcy/bankruptcy-basics)
- Cornell University Law School's Legal Information Institute's Bankruptcy Information Page (www.law.cornell.edu/wex/index.php/Bankruptcy)
- The Internet Bankruptcy Library (http://bankrupt.com)
- FindLaw's Internet Guide to Bankruptcy Law (http://library.findlaw.com/1999/Mar/1/128347.html)
- Bernstein's Dictionary of Bankruptcy Terminology (www.bernsteinlaw.com/publications/bankdict.htm)
- NOLO Bankruptcy in Your State (http://www.thebankruptcysite.org/topics/bankruptcy-your-state)

Organizations Concerned with Bankruptcy Practice:

- American Bankruptcy Institute (www.abiworld.org)
- National Bankruptcy Conference (www.nationalbankruptcyconference.org)
- The American College of Bankruptcy (www.amercol.org)
- National Association of Bankruptcy Trustees (www.nabt.com/faq.cfm)
- National Association of Chapter 13 Bankruptcy Trustees (www.nactt.com)
- National Association of Consumer Bankruptcy Attorneys (www.nacba.org)
- National Consumer Law Center (www.nclc.org)
- The Commercial Law League of America (www.clla.org)

Bankruptcy Blogs and Other News and Information Sites:

- ABA Journal Blawg Directory (www.abajournal.com/blawgs/topic/bankruptcy+law)
- ABI Blog Exchange (http://blogs.abi.org/)

EXHIBIT 4.8   **(Continued)**

- Bankruptcy Attorneys on the Web (www.bestcase.com/bkattys.htm)
- Bankruptcy Law Network (www.bankruptcylawnetwork.com)
- Bankruptcy Lawyers Blog (http://blog.startfreshtoday.com)
- Bankruptcy Litigation Blog (http://www.bankruptcylitigationblog.com/)
- LAW 360: Bankruptcy (www.law360.com/bankruptcy)
- Bankruptcy Preference Digest (http://www.burbageweddell.com/blog/)
- Becker & Posner Blog (http://www.becker-posner-blog.com/)
- BKBlog (http://www.thebklawyer.com/thebkblog/)
- Credit Slips Blog on Credit, Finance, and Bankruptcy (www.creditslips.org/creditslips)
- Daily Bankruptcy News (http://bkinformation.com/news/dailynews.htm)
- Finance and Bankruptcy Blog (http://www.bankruptcylawblog.com/)
- In the Red Business Bankruptcy Blog (http://bankruptcy.cooley.com/)
- New Generation Research (NGR) (www.turnarounds.com)
- Wall Street Journal Bankruptcy Beat Blog (http://blogs.wsj.com/bankruptcy/)
- Weil Bankruptcy Blog (http://business-finance-restructuring.weil.com/)

K. INTRODUCTION TO THE BANKRUPTCY CASE STUDIES

To learn how Chapter 7 and Chapter 13 consumer bankruptcy cases work we will reference two fictitious but realistic case studies: the Chapter 7 case of Marta Rinaldi Carlson filed in 2016 in a U.S. bankruptcy court in Minnesota and the Chapter 13 case of Roger and Susan Matthews filed in 2016 in a U.S. bankruptcy court in Pennsylvania. (Minnesota and Pennsylvania were selected for use in these case studies primarily because neither state has opted out of the federal exemptions for individual filers as will be discussed in Chapter Six.)

In Appendix A you will find the original assignment memorandum prepared by a supervising attorney directing an associate attorney to assist in filing the Chapter 7 case for Marta Carlson and the case file index illustrating the various filings that were subsequently made in the course of Ms. Carlson's Chapter 7 case. On the companion Web site to this text (aspenlawschool.com/books/parsons_consumer bankruptcy) you will find all the documents listed in the Carlson case file index.

In Appendix B you will find the original assignment memorandum prepared by a supervising attorney directing an associate attorney to assist in filing a Chapter 13 case for the Matthews, the initial prepetition budget for the Matthews, and the case file index illustrating the various filings that were made in the course of the Matthews' Chapter 13 case. On the companion Web site you will find all the documents listed in the Matthews case file index. You should bookmark that site.

As we work our way through the upcoming material on Chapter 7 and Chapter 13 bankruptcies, we will reference the Carlson and Matthews files frequently as a practical way of illustrating the points being made — much as a supervising attorney training you in an area of the law might show you a closed case file to learn from. Some of the Carlson and Matthews filings are reproduced in the text itself for more intense scrutiny, but all of the filings in both cases are available to you on the companion Web site.

As part of this study of consumer bankruptcy, your instructor may want you to apply what you are learning by preparing the petition, schedules, etc., in new hypothetical Chapter 7 and 13 cases. With that possibility in mind, Appendix C contains assignment memoranda and other information for a potential Chapter 7 client, Abelard Mendoza. Similarly, Appendix D contains assignment memoranda and other information for potential Chapter 13 clients, Nicholas and Pearl Murphy. You will see references to optional writing assignments for Mendoza and the Murphys in the Applying the Concepts sections of upcoming chapters. Your instructor may have you prepare the petition, schedules, etc., for filing in either or both the Mendoza and Murphy cases on the assumption those cases would be filed in the state where you are studying law or in the state where you plan to practice.

L. ALTERNATIVES TO BANKRUPTCY FOR THE CONSUMER DEBTOR

Debt problems do not drive all consumer debtors into bankruptcy. Where a creditor's right to receive payment or the amount of its claim is disputed the parties may negotiate a private settlement that relieves the crisis for the debtor. Some debtors are able to negotiate such a settlement themselves while others are represented by attorneys or credit counselors (discussed in Chapter Three, Section A) who negotiate on behalf of the debtor. Technically, the negotiation and compromise of a disputed claim is called an **accord and satisfaction**. The agreement as to how much will be paid is the accord and the payment of the agreed amount in lump sum or over an agreed period is the satisfaction. Typically, if the disputing parties reach an accord but the debtor party does not pay the satisfaction as promised, the creditor party retains the right to pursue the judicial collection process for the entire indebtedness or claim.

Privately negotiated settlements involving accord and satisfaction can be worked out even after a judicial collection action (or mandatory arbitration) has been commenced. The litigating parties may agree to **mediation** of the dispute utilizing a trained neutral mediator or experienced jurist other than the presiding judge (in which case the procedure may be called a **judicial settlement conference**). In a mediation, the mediator conducts discussions among the disputing parties designed to enable them to reach a mutually acceptable agreement among themselves on all or any part of the issues in dispute. Litigating parties may also opt for other forms of **alternative dispute resolution** (ADR) including **mini-trial** (an abbreviated summary of each side's case presented to persons authorized to settle and presided over by a neutral), **summary jury trial** (an abbreviated trial with a jury in which litigants present their evidence in an expedited fashion; presided over by a neutral), or **non-binding arbitration**.

In many states, statutes or court rules authorize trial courts to require the parties to engage in good faith mediation or other ADR in most civil suits before the case can proceed to trial.

Application Exercise 9

Determine if the statutes or rules of the supreme court of the state where you plan to practice authorize trial courts to order mediation or other ADR in civil cases.

Of course, many consumer debtors do not dispute creditor claims; they simply cannot pay them. And a consumer who lacks the means to pay one undisputed debt is likely to be in arrears on a number of them such that there is a plurality of creditors, secured and unsecured, simultaneously demanding immediate payment. Consumer debtors in that situation may be able to negotiate with the various creditors to delay payments, allow payments over time, reduce the amount of installment payments due and extend the number of such payments, or even to reduce the total amount of indebtedness in exchange for immediate payment of a percentage of it. What is being described is a **composition agreement**, which is nothing more than a private, voluntary arrangement between a debtor and her creditors, pursuant to which the creditors agree to some adjustment of the debtor's obligation to make immediate payment in full. Where the creditor agrees to give the debtor additional time to make agreed payments it may also be called an **extension agreement**. The benefit of such an agreement to the creditor is that if the debtor files for bankruptcy relief their debt, if unsecured, might be completely discharged or reduced to much less than the debtor is offering to pay. The secured creditor has the safety net of the collateral and bankruptcy is not perceived as such a threat to such creditor. Having said that, most secured creditors would rather a debtor retain possession of the collateral and make a good faith effort to pay the debt than default completely. With many types of collateral, repossession or foreclosure by the creditor is expensive and quick resale for a reasonable amount is hardly guaranteed.

The composition and extension agreement might be preferable to bankruptcy in terms of cost and time, but it is of course contingent on the cooperation of some number of disgruntled creditors who may be angry at the debtor. For that reason, and because of the possible complexity of these agreements, consumer debtors are well advised to utilize an attorney or competent credit counselor to negotiate such agreements. Like the accord and satisfaction, the composition and extension agreement will typically stipulate that if the debtor defaults on any promised payment, the balance of the original debt will be immediately payable in full.

Another alternative to bankruptcy for consumers is the **assignment for the benefit of creditors** (commonly called an ABC). In an ABC, the debtor conveys his or her non-exempt property to an assignee, often a lawyer or accountant, who will liquidate the property and then distribute the proceeds pro rata to the claimants. The property of the debtor is immune from attachment or execution while the ABC is in effect. The ABC does not discharge the balance remaining on any indebtedness, as a bankruptcy proceeding might, and so its usefulness is limited. But if the debtor has reason to believe that creditors will not file suit to collect the deficiencies, the ABC may be a cheaper, quicker route than bankruptcy.

In some states, ABCs are regulated by statute and, in others, by common law decision. Once the property has been assigned by the debtor to the assignee as part of an ABC, the property is exempt from execution by individual creditors (other than those previously secured and perfected in the property). And, typically, the assignee of the ABC takes title to the property as a lien creditor with a superior claim to any prior unsecured claim to the property (see UCC Article 9, §§309(12) and 317). Some states allow the ABC to prefer some creditors over others in the distribution, while others forbid any such preference.

Alternatively, a consumer in distress might file a **receivership** action; effectively a civil lawsuit in which the court is asked to appoint a receiver to take legal control of the debtor's property, along with the power to manage that property. In most states, receivership actions are controlled by statute, and there are also some federal receivership laws, notably for railroads and securities businesses. Receiverships can be chosen voluntarily by a qualifying debtor without consent of his creditors, but creditors can also seek the receivership for dissenting debtors. This is an important aspect of receivership law for creditors of certain debtors like churches, political committees, or other nonprofit organizations, which cannot be forced into involuntary bankruptcy.

Like an ABC, once the assets of the debtor are place in receivership, they are immune from attachment or execution by individual creditors. The receiver will act on behalf of all the creditors to liquidate the assets and distribute the proceeds pro rata to creditors. Disputes among creditors as to the validity of their claims will be resolved by the court that ordered the receivership.

The scope of our study is limited to consumer debt. Individual debtors who own a business normally do not qualify as consumer debtors because most of their debts are business related rather than consumer debts. Having said that, we will take brief note here of a couple of other alternatives to bankruptcy that might be available to an individual debtor who owns a business as a sole proprietor or with others as a general partnership or who operates the business as a closely held corporation or limited liability company.

A handful of states have adopted Article 6 of the Uniform Commercial Code (UCC), which is known as the **Bulk Sale Transfer Act (BSTA)**. The BSTA requires a business that be selling "all or substantially all" of its assets "outside of the ordinary course of business" to give prior written notice of the sale to its creditors. A sale outside the ordinary course of business is usually defined as the sale of more than one-half of a business's assets at one time or to one buyer. In a typical BSTA statute, the notice given to creditors must advise of the assets being sold, the price, the identity of the buyer, the expected payout (i.e., "pro rata" or "share and share alike"), and must be given at least 45 days before the sale. The creditors of the seller then have six months following the date of the sale to submit claims to the buyer of the business assets. The buyer is then required to pay the creditors of the seller on some fair basis.

The BSTA became popular at the beginning of the 20th century as a means to avoid a businessperson selling all of his assets and disappearing without paying his business creditors. With the popularity of the Uniform Enforcement of Foreign Judgment Act, which we considered in Chapter Three, the need for the BSTA has diminished and today only very few states still have it.

The BSTA applies primarily to the payment of unsecured creditors. Creditors secured in property of the debtor/seller will typically have the right to repossess the collateralized property in the event of default so it is not available to be sold in the bulk sale.

Every state has laws under which a business entity such as a corporation, limited liability company, or partnership may simply dissolve and go out of business as an alternative to bankruptcy. Such laws contain detailed procedures for the entity to elect dissolution, give notice to the state and to creditors, wind up its business, and distribute its assets in an orderly fashion and according to a strict priority (e.g., creditors of a business entity being dissolved under state law are to be paid in full before any distribution of assets to owners). Creditors of a business entity may have standing to compel an involuntary dissolution on certain grounds such as insolvency of the entity, failure to pay its debts as they come due, or fraud by management. The state may also have authority to compel dissolution for failure of the entity to pay taxes and assessments or other grounds.

Chapter Summary

■ The U.S. Bankruptcy Code, which is Title 11 of the U.S. Code, authorizes six different types of bankruptcy proceedings for qualifying debtors and contains definitions and provisions for case administration and procedure. The last significant amendment to the Code was the Bankruptcy Abuse Prevention and Consumer Protection Act of 2005.

■ The Federal Rules of Bankruptcy Procedure (FRBP) supplement the Code and provide detailed guidance on numerous procedural aspects of a bankruptcy case. Congress has also approved Official Bankruptcy Forms for use in bankruptcy cases across the country. Each bankruptcy court has its own local rules that further supplement the Code, the FRBP, and the Official Forms.

■ The Federal Rules of Civil Procedure are followed in adversary proceedings in bankruptcy cases and the Federal Rules of Evidence apply in evidentiary hearings before a bankruptcy judge.

■ In a bankruptcy case, state law controls the validity and amount of a creditor's claim as well as the validity of various property rights dealt with in the case, while bankruptcy procedure and rules will govern the treatment of such claims in the bankruptcy case, the makeup and disposition of property of the estate, and the payment of creditor claims.

■ U.S. district courts have original and exclusive subject matter jurisdiction over bankruptcy cases but are authorized to refer issues that arise in or are related to bankruptcy cases to the bankruptcy courts. Thus U.S. bankruptcy courts have referral jurisdiction over bankruptcy cases from the district court. Bankruptcy courts exercising that referral jurisdiction are empowered to enter final orders and judgments in certain core proceedings. In non-core proceedings the bankruptcy court can only enter proposed findings and conclusions for the district court to consider unless all parties consent to the bankruptcy court entering a final order or judgment in the matter. Bankruptcy courts may not hear or decide matters involving personal injury or wrongful death.

■ An appeal from a final order or judgment entered by a bankruptcy court lies to the U.S. district court in that federal district. Five federal circuits have created Bankruptcy Appellate Panels and in those circuits the appeal may be taken to the BAP rather than the district court but only if all parties consent.

■ Issues that arise in a bankruptcy case are decided as either contested matters raised by motion or objection or as adversary proceedings that involve a formal civil trial process and the bankruptcy rules incorporate most of the Federal Rules of Civil Procedure in connection with such proceedings.

■ All bankruptcy courts utilize electronic filing via the Case Management/Electronic Case Files system.

Applying the Concepts

1. Using the Court Web site Links feature at the Administrative Office of the Federal Courts Web site at www.uscourts.gov/about-federal-courts/federal-courts-public/court-website-links or other information you can find, answer the following questions:

   a. How many different divisional offices does the bankruptcy court maintain in your federal district?

   b. Where is the main office located?

   c. What are the names of the U.S. bankruptcy judges who hold court at each office?

   d. Who is the chief bankruptcy judge in your federal district?

   e. Who is the clerk of the bankruptcy court in your federal district?

   f. Does the Web site provide a link to the local rules of the bankruptcy courts in your federal district?

   g. Does the Web site provide a link to recent decisions of the bankruptcy courts in your federal districts?

   h. Does the Web site provide a link to the Code, the FRBP, or the Official Forms?

2. Assume you are consulted by the following potential clients. Using the brief summary of the various types of bankruptcies authorized by the Code as summarized in Exhibit 4.3, determine which kind of case would be suitable for each client.

   a. Local Realty Partners is a general partnership engaged in managing rental properties in the area. The business is failing and unable to meet its financial obligations. The owners feel that the business can survive but only if it can have the time to dispose of some of its least productive properties. The business needs relief from threatening creditors until it can do so.

   b. Juan and Sofia Calderon are a married couple who own a home. Juan is employed with a local contractor as a carpenter and Sofia is a nurse employed by a local hospital. Last year Sofia was diagnosed with cancer and is still undergoing treatment though she is able to work part-time. The medical bills not covered by Sofia's health insurance (Juan has no such coverage) have exceeded their capacity to pay and still make payments on their home (they have made some late payments on the mortgage recently but the bank holding the home mortgage has been working with them) and support themselves and their three children. The hospital where Sofia has received treatments and various doctors who treated her are threatening legal action if they are not paid and two have already filed lawsuits and obtained default judgments. Sofia hopes to return to full-time employment in the next few months and the couple feels that they can pay most if not all of the debt they owe if they had a reasonable amount of time to do so.

c. Abhay Patel is a 35-year-old architect. Until recently he was a partner in an architectural firm. That firm has recently ceased doing business and Abhay is currently unemployed though he is interviewing with other firms and hopes to have a job soon. Four years ago, when things were going well for his firm, the firm contracted to purchase an office building for $3 million. A local bank loaned the firm the money for the purchase. All of the partners, including Abhay, were required to sign personal guarantees for the firm's indebtedness. Six months ago, as the firm was failing, it went into default on the bank loan and the bank has now demanded that Abhay pay the entire balance outstanding, $2,750,000, based on his personal guaranty. Abhay has only $10,000 in cash savings, a 401(k) plan with a value of $75,000, a vehicle on which he is current with payments, and various other personal property with a total value of perhaps $20,000.

3. Assume you represent Gilda Thorpe, a Chapter 7 debtor who resides in the state where you plan to practice. When Gilda filed her bankruptcy petition she was in dispute with a local car dealership from whom she purchased a used automobile a year ago. She purchased the vehicle from the dealer on credit, promising to make payments for the purchase price over five years. Shortly after the purchase she experienced multiple problems with the vehicle and tried to return it to the dealer but the dealer refused and filed suit to collect the amount owed when she stopped making payments. Gilda contends that the dealer lied to her about the condition of the vehicle when she purchased it, that there was an express warranty made to her by the salesman for the dealer that was breached by the poor condition of the vehicle, and that she should be able to cancel the purchase contract and return the vehicle. The dealer has filed a claim as a creditor in Gilda's bankruptcy case. The dealer denies that any false or fraudulent statements were made to Gilda concerning the condition of the vehicle or that there was any express warranty made to her concerning its condition. The dealer has further asserted that Gilda should not be able to discharge this debt in her Chapter 7 case because she lied about her income on the loan application. The dealer is relying on §523(a)(2) of the Code for its non-dischargeability argument. What law will control whether this loan is a valid and enforceable contract? What law will control whether Gilda is able to discharge the debt in her bankruptcy case?

The Chapter 7 Consumer Bankruptcy Case: The Means Test and Other Qualifications to File

Approximately 70 to 75 percent of all bankruptcy filings nationwide are Chapter 7 liquidation cases and about 98 percent of those are consumer bankruptcies filed by individuals with primarily nonbusiness debt (see Exhibit 1.2). Chapter 7 is a liquidation proceeding in which a bankruptcy trustee is authorized to locate and take possession of the non-exempt assets of the debtor, **liquidate** (sell) those assets, and distribute the proceeds to creditors of the estate per a distribution formula established by the Code. Either an individual or an entity may be a Chapter 7 debtor but, as we will see, that is not to say that *any* individual or entity can file for the Chapter 7 fresh start.

Most debts remaining unpaid after the distribution and not formally reaffirmed by the debtor in the bankruptcy proceeding will be permanently **discharged** by order of the bankruptcy court. Thus, the basic idea in a Chapter 7 is that the debtor makes all of her non-exempt assets available to her creditors in exchange for a discharge of most of her unpaid debts. We will learn, however, that some debts cannot be discharged in a Chapter 7 and some Chapter 7 cases do not result in any discharge at all.

Key Concepts

- The basic qualifications to file a Chapter 7 case are set out in §109 of the Code
- A person cannot file a Chapter 7 case who has received a discharge in Chapter 7 within eight years or a discharge under Chapter 13 within six years
- An individual with primarily consumer debts cannot file a Chapter 7 case unless they satisfy the means test
- An individual filing a Chapter 7 case must receive prepetition credit counseling

For our study of Chapter 7 in this and the next six chapters, we will focus on the case of Marta Rinaldi Carlson, an individual who in many ways fits the profile of the typical debtor whom you saw described in Exhibit 1.3. As you already know, Appendix A of the text contains the initial assignment memorandum prepared in June 2016 by a supervising attorney for an associate attorney regarding her planned Chapter 7 case as well as the case file index listing all filings in her subsequent case. On the companion Web site to this text at aspenlawschool.com/books/parsons_consumerbankruptcy you will find all the documents listed in the case file index. Be prepared to consult it frequently.

A. THE BASIC §109 QUALIFICATIONS

Section 109(a) of the Code provides that, "only a person that resides or has a domicile, a place of business, or property in the United States, or a municipality" can file as a debtor under any of the six chapters of the Code. Regarding who can file for Chapter 7 relief, §109(b) says any "person" can, and "person" is defined by §101(41) to include both individuals (natural persons) and business entities, such as corporations (including limited liability companies) and partnerships, but not governmental units. However, §109(b) specifically prohibits railroads, insurance companies, commercial banks chartered by federal or state governments, savings banks, savings and loan associations, credit unions, and some other financial institutions from filing for Chapter 7 liquidation relief. Such entities are liquidated under state law or specialized federal regulation, and railroads may file for Chapter 11 reorganization. Those types of bankruptcy proceedings are not within the scope of our study.

For example, if Abelard Mendoza from Appendix C decides to file for Chapter 7 relief, he will qualify under §109 because he is an individual. If Mendoza owed money to City Plumbing, LLC and that company decided to file under Chapter 7 it would qualify to do so as a limited liability company. But if Security Trust Bank, which holds the mortgage on Abe Mendoza's home, decides to file for Chapter 7 relief it will not qualify and will have to seek relief under separate statutory authority involving both state and federal law. If the municipality of Capital City itself decides to file for Chapter 7 relief, it will not qualify and will have to seek relief under Chapter 9 of the Code.

B. THE §727(a) PRIOR DISCHARGE LIMITATIONS

Pursuant to §727(a), a debtor qualified to file a Chapter 7 case under §109 cannot receive a discharge in Chapter 7 if he previously received a discharge in a Chapter 7 or Chapter 11 case within *eight years* preceding the filing of the petition or in a Chapter 13 or Chapter 12 case within *six years*.

For example, if Marta Carlson had received a discharge in Chapter 13 in YR-4 she could not now file under Chapter 7. As we will see when we study Chapter 13 bankruptcy, she might be able to file another Chapter 13 but not a Chapter 7 because of the six-year prohibition.

C. THE §707(b) MEANS TEST AND PRESUMPTION OF ABUSE LIMITATION FOR INDIVIDUAL CONSUMER DEBTORS

1. Introduction to the Means Test and the Presumption of Abuse

Recall that in Chapter One, we distinguished between non-consumer or business bankruptcy cases and consumer bankruptcy cases, defining the latter as the case of an individual with primarily consumer debts. And recall that §101(8) of the Code defines consumer debt as "debt incurred by an individual primarily for a personal, family or household purpose."

Section 707(b)(1) authorizes the court to dismiss a Chapter 7 case filed by a consumer debtor if it finds that the granting of relief would be an "abuse of the provisions of this chapter." Section 707(b)(2)(A)(i), as amended by BAPCPA, raises a **presumption of abuse** if the debtor fails a **means test** created by that section. The means test essentially compares the debtor's average monthly income to the median income of a family the size of the debtor's in the state where the debtor resides. If the debtor's income is equal to or less than the state median income figure, the debtor can file for Chapter 7 relief. If the debtor's income (calculated with the debtor's spouse if the spouse is not filing) exceeds the state median income figure, the presumption of abuse arises and the debtor cannot file for Chapter 7 relief. Debtor's income from the following sources is included in the calculation:

- Wages, salary, tips, bonuses, overtime, and commissions
- Gross income from a business, profession, or a farm
- Interest, dividends, and royalties
- Rental and real property income
- Regular child support or spousal support
- Unemployment compensation
- Pension and retirement income
- Workers' compensation
- Annuity payments
- State disability insurance

Debtor's income from the following sources is excluded from the calculation:

- Tax refunds
- Social Security retirement benefits
- Social Security Disability Insurance
- Supplemental Security Income
- Temporary Assistance for Needy Families

The object of the means test is to identify what practitioners call "**can-pay debtors**" and to funnel them into Chapter 13 filings, where the excess disposable income is made available to pay all or a portion of the debtor's unsecured debts.

Entity debtors and individual debtors whose debts are primarily business rather than consumer debts are not subject to the means test. Veterans suffering from a 30 percent or higher permanent disability and whose indebtedness arose primarily during active duty or while performing a homeland defense activity are expressly exempted from the means test, as are certain members of the National Guard and armed forces reserves who were called to duty for at least 90 days following September 11, 2001, pursuant to the **National Guard Reservists Debt Relief Act of 2008**.

For example, the vast majority of Marta Carlson's debt, as described in the Assignment Memorandum in Appendix A, will qualify as consumer debt. One exception might be the indebtedness to Dreams Come True Finance Company, which was incurred to fund a business venture for her ex-husband. Since Marta is an individual consumer debtor, she will have to satisfy the means test of §707(b) in order to maintain a Chapter 7 filing.

What happens if a debtor files a petition in Chapter 13 (which as we will see requires a calculation of disposable income for purposes of a Chapter 13 plan but does not involve a means test) and then converts the case to one in Chapter 7? Will that debtor have to satisfy the means test in order to proceed in Chapter 7? There is actually a split on this question with a majority of courts following what is called the "common sense" view that the means test must still be satisfied because Congress intended all Chapter 7 debtors to satisfy it (see, e.g., In re Kellett, 379 B.R. 332 (Bankr. D. Ore. 2007)), but a strong minority follow the "plain language" view, saying that the debtor converting a Chapter 13 case over need not satisfy the means test because, literally read, §707(b) only requires the test in consumer cases "filed" under Chapter 7 and a converted Chapter 13 case was not filed under Chapter 7 (see, e.g., In re Layton, 480 B.R. 392 (Bankr. M.D. Fla. 2012)).

Application Exercise 1

Determine how the bankruptcy or district courts of the federal district or circuit where you plan to practice have decided this issue.

The means test is completed using Official Bankruptcy Form 122A-1, **Chapter 7 Statement of Your Current Monthly Income** (all official bankruptcy forms are available at www.uscourts.gov/forms/bankruptcy-forms and you should bookmark that site if you have not done so already)*. If the debtor claims exemption from having to satisfy the presumption of abuse because his or her debts are not primarily consumer debts or because of qualifying military service, the debtor must still complete Form 122A-1 but will attach Statement of Exemption from Presumption of Abuse Under § 707(b)(2) (Form 122A-1Supp) to the form.

*__Note:__ The official forms used in this discussion and in the accompanying banktuptcy case studies are those in use in 2016 when the fictitious Chapter 7 case of Marta Carlson was filed. The bankruptcy forms are frequently amended, however, and consequently the ones used here may not be what is currently when you read this.

If Form 122A-1 demonstrates that the non-exempt consumer debtor's current monthly income is below the applicable median income, that debtor's filing does not raise the presumption of abuse; that debtor can proceed in Chapter 7. However, if the debtor's Form 122A-1 demonstrates that the debtor's current monthly

EXHIBIT 5.1   **Marta Carlson's Form 122A-1**

Fill in this information to identify your case:

Debtor 1   **Marta**   **Rinaldi**   **Carlson**
First Name   Middle Name   Last Name

Debtor 2
(Spouse, if filing) First Name   Middle Name   Last Name

United States Bankruptcy Court for the: District of Minnesota

Case number   **16-7-XXXX**
(If known)

Check one box only as directed in this form and in Form 122A-1Supp:

☑ 1. There is no presumption of abuse.

☐ 2. The calculation to determine if a presumption of abuse applies will be made under *Chapter 7 Means Test Calculation* (Official Form 122A–2).

☐ 3. The Means Test does not apply now because of qualified military service but it could apply later.

☐ Check if this is an amended filing

Official Form 122A–1

Chapter 7 Statement of Your Current Monthly Income   12/15

Be as complete and accurate as possible. If two married people are filing together, both are equally responsible for being accurate. If more space is needed, attach a separate sheet to this form. Include the line number to which the additional information applies. On the top of any additional pages, write your name and case number (if known). If you believe that you are exempted from a presumption of abuse because you do not have primarily consumer debts or because of qualifying military service, complete and file *Statement of Exemption from Presumption of Abuse Under § 707(b)(2)* (Official Form 122A-1Supp) with this form.

Part 1:	Calculate Your Current Monthly Income

1. **What is your marital and filing status?** Check one only.

☑ **Not married.** Fill out Column A, lines 2-11.
☐ **Married and your spouse is filing with you.** Fill out both Columns A and B, lines 2-11.

☐ **Married and your spouse is NOT filing with you.** You and your spouse are:

☐ **Living in the same household and are not legally separated.** Fill out both Columns A and B, lines 2-11.

☐ **Living separately or are legally separated.** Fill out Column A, lines 2-11; do not fill out Column B. By checking this box, you declare under penalty of perjury that you and your spouse are legally separated under nonbankruptcy law that applies or that you and your spouse are living apart for reasons that do not include evading the Means Test requirements. 11 U.S.C. § 707(b)(7)(B).

Fill in the average monthly income that you received from all sources, derived during the 6 full months before you file this bankruptcy case. 11 U.S.C. § 101(10A). For example, if you are filing on September 15, the 6-month period would be March 1 through August 31. If the amount of your monthly income varied during the 6 months, add the income for all 6 months and divide the total by 6. Fill in the result. Do not include any income amount more than once. For example, if both spouses own the same rental property, put the income from that property in one column only. If you have nothing to report for any line, write $0 in the space.

	Column A Debtor 1	Column B Debtor 2 or non-filing spouse
2. **Your gross wages, salary, tips, bonuses, overtime, and commissions** (before all payroll deductions).	$ 3,888.88	$
3. **Alimony and maintenance payments.** Do not include payments from a spouse if Column B is filled in.	$ 0.00	$
4. **All amounts from any source which are regularly paid for household expenses of you or your dependents, including child support.** Include regular contributions from an unmarried partner, members of your household, your dependents, parents, and roommates. Include regular contributions from a spouse only if Column B is not filled in. Do not include payments you listed on line 3.	$ 0.00	$

5. **Net income from operating a business, profession, or farm**

	Debtor 1	Debtor 2			
Gross receipts (before all deductions)	$	$			
Ordinary and necessary operating expenses	– $	– $			
Net monthly income from a business, profession, or farm	$ 0.00	$	Copy here ➡	$ 0.00	$

6. **Net income from rental and other real property**

	Debtor 1	Debtor 2			
Gross receipts (before all deductions)	$	$			
Ordinary and necessary operating expenses	– $	– $			
Net monthly income from rental or other real property	$ 0.00	$	Copy here ➡	$ 0.00	$

7. **Interest, dividends, and royalties**	$ 0.00	$

EXHIBIT 5.1 **(Continued)**

Debtor 1   Marta   Rinaldi   Carlsor
    First Name   Middle Name   Last Name

Case number *(if known)* 16-7-XXXX

	Column A Debtor 1	Column B Debtor 2 or non-filing spouse
8. **Unemployment compensation**	$ 0.00	$
Do not enter the amount if you contend that the amount received was a benefit under the Social Security Act. Instead, list it here: ⬇		
For you .... $		
For your spouse.. $		
9. **Pension or retirement income.** Do not include any amount received that was a benefit under the Social Security Act.	$ 0.00	$
10. **Income from all other sources not listed above.** Specify the source and amount. Do not include any benefits received under the Social Security Act or payments received as a victim of a war crime, a crime against humanity, or international or domestic terrorism. If necessary, list other sources on a separate page and put the total below.		
_____	$ 0.00	$
_____	$ 0.00	$
Total amounts from separate pages, if any.	+ $ 0.00	+ $
11. **Calculate your total current monthly income.** Add lines 2 through 10 for each column. Then add the total for Column A to the total for Column B.	$ 3,888.88	+ $ = $ 3,888.88

Total current monthly income

Part 2:   **Determine Whether the Means Test Applies to You**

12. **Calculate your current monthly income for the year.** Follow these steps:

   12a.   Copy your total current monthly income from line 11. .... Copy line 11 here ➡ $ 3,888.88

        Multiply by 12 (the number of months in a year).   **x 12**

   12b.   The result is your annual income for this part of the form.   12b. $ 46,666.56

13. **Calculate the median family income that applies to you.** Follow these steps:

   Fill in the state in which you live.   MN

   Fill in the number of people in your household.   3

   Fill in the median family income for your state and size of household. .... 13. $ 80,900.00

   To find a list of applicable median income amounts, go online using the link specified in the separate instructions for this form. This list may also be available at the bankruptcy clerk's office.

14. **How do the lines compare?**

   14a. ■   Line 12b is less than or equal to line 13. On the top of page 1, check box 1, *There is no presumption of abuse.* Go to Part 3.

   14b. ❑   Line 12b is more than line 13. On the top of page 1, check box 2, *The presumption of abuse is determined by Form 122A–2.* Go to Part 3 and fill out Form 122A–2.

Part 3:   **Sign Below**

By signing here, I declare under penalty of perjury that the information on this statement and in any attachments is true and correct.

✗ /s/ Marta Rinaldi Carlson   **✗** _____

Signature of Debtor 1   Signature of Debtor 2

Date 06/17/2016   Date _____
     MM / DD / YYYY   MM / DD / YYYY

If you checked line 14a, do NOT fill out or file Form 122A–2.

If you checked line 14b, fill out Form 122A–2 and file it with this form.

income is higher than the applicable median income figure then that debtor must also complete Form 122A-2, **Chapter 7 Means Test Calculation** to determine if the presumption of abuse arises. This one or two step process for running the presumption of abuse gauntlet is illustrated in the following sections of this chapter.

The means test and the forms used to complete it are new with BAPCPA and many questions concerning how it works remain unanswered. As we work through Form 122A-1 (and later Form 122A-2) using Marta Carlson's case, we will look at a number of recent cases beginning to interpret the test. Additionally, the U.S. Trustee Program has issued its own Statement on Legal Issues Arising under the Chapter 7 Means Test that can be accessed at www.justice.gov/sites/default/files/ust/legacy/2015/03/03/ch7_line_by_line.pdf and can be consulted with profit as we venture through Form 122A-2.

2. Comparing the Debtor's Current Monthly Income to the State Median Family Income Using Official Form 122A-1

As already stated, the means test for determining whether the presumption of abuse arises in a consumer debtor's case is a one- or two-step process. As a first step the debtor completes Form 122A-1 to compare the debtor's annualized **current monthly income** (CMI) to the annualized **median family income** for a similar size household in the debtor's state of residence. Section 707(b)(7) provides that if the debtor's current monthly income is equal to or less than the applicable median family income, no presumption of abuse arises and the means test is satisfied for that debtor. Marta Carlson's Form 122A-1 is set out in Exhibit 5.1 and can also be seen as Document 19 in her case file available on the companion Web site at aspenlawschool.com/books/parsons_consumer bankruptcy.

The **median family income** numbers are published by the U.S. Census Bureau by state and family size and are updated annually**. The Web site of the U.S. Trustee Program (at www.justice.gov/ust/means-testing) sets forth the Census Bureau's current tables for median family income and you should bookmark this site.

Note: Since the median income figures from the Census Bureau are adjusted annually, Marta's form uses the correct median income figure for Minnesota as of June 2016, but that figure may be different when you read this.

Application Exercise 2

Our fictitious Chapter 7 client, Marta Carlson, resided in Minnesota and filed her bankruptcy case there. There are three persons in Marta's family and her bankruptcy case was filed in June 2016. Go to the U.S. Trustees Web site and locate the Census Bureau's current tables for median family income for a family of three in the state of Minnesota as of June 2016. This is the median family income figure that will be used on her Form 122A-1 to compare with her annual income to determine if she passed the means test. The median income figures from the Census Bureau are adjusted annually and Marta's case was filed using the correct median income figure for Minnesota as of June 2016. If Marta's case was being filed in Minnesota today, what would the relevant median income figure be for a family of three? If Marta was a resident of the state where you plan to practice what would the relevant median income figure be today?

To determine the debtor's annual income that will be compared with the relevant median family income figure, we first calculate the debtor's **current monthly income (CMI)**, defined in §101(10A) to include the average monthly income from all sources that the debtor has received during the six months preceding the filing of the petition (known to practitioners as the "**look back period**"), regardless of whether such income is taxable, as well as any amounts paid by a third party for the household expenses of the debtor. The sixth month to be included in the look back period is the month immediately preceding the date the case is filed.

For example, if a Chapter 7 petition is filed on September 15, the applicable look back period for calculating the debtor's CMI will be income from all sources received from March through August of that year. Income from those six months will be averaged to arrive at the current monthly income figure. So if the debtor had income totaling $26,400 during the look back period, the applicable CMI will be $4,400 ($26,400 divided by six).

Marta Carlson's Chapter 7 petition was filed on June 4, 2016, so the look back period for calculating her CMI ran from December 2015 through May 2016. In 2015, her annual salary at TTI was $40,000 so in December 2015 she made $3,333.33. Beginning in January 2016, she received a raise to an annual salary of $48,000 so her average monthly income for January through May 2016 was $4,000. Her average monthly income during the look back period from June 1, 2016 is therefore $3,888.88 ($23,333.33 ÷ 6 = $3,888.88).

The debtor's CMI is calculated in Part 1 of Form 122A-1 (see Exhibit 5.1). Determining Marta's current monthly income is a simple calculation since she is the sole debtor and currently has only one source of income, her salary from TTI. On Line 1 of Part 1 of Form 122A-1 she will check the "Not married" box and report only her own income in Column A in Lines 2-11. But it's not always so simple. If a husband and wife file a joint petition, then the "Married and your spouse is filing with you" box must be checked on Line 1 and the income of both spouses must be reported in Columns A and B respectively in Lines 2-11 of Part 1 of the form. If a married debtor files, but a spouse from whom the debtor is either living separately or is legally separated does not, the debtor must the appropriate box on Line 1 of the form and the income of the nonfiling spouse need not be reported. But if a married debtor files and a spouse living in the same household and from whom the debtor is not legally separated does not file, the debtor must check the appropriate box on Line 1 of the form and include the non-filing spouse's income in column B of Part 1 of the form. There is a presumption in the latter circumstance, but not the former, that the income of the non-filing spouse is available to support the debtor's household. If in fact any of the reported income of the nonfiling spouse is not available on a regular basis to help with household expenses of the debtor or the debtor's dependents, that will be reported if necessary on Form 122A-2.

If Marta were receiving child support she would report that income on Line 3. She would also include alimony or separate maintenance payments here unless she had remarried and was including her new spouse's income in Column B of the form. If Marta was receiving child support payments from her ex-husband or if her parents had been helping her out with occasional payments during the look back period, those payments would be reported on Line 4. If she owned and operated a business, she would include net income from that business on Line 5. If she was leasing a house or apartment and had rental income, she would include net income from that rental on Line 6. If she had received interest income on a savings or checking account or other source, she would include that income on Line 7. If she had lost her job but received unemployment compensation, she would report that on Line 8. If she had received pension or retirement income during the relevant six-month period, she would report that on Line 9. If she was receiving income from any other source those would be reported on Line 10. Note that Social Security payments do not have to be reported on the form. Once the CMI itemized in Part 1 of the form has been totaled on Line 11, we then take that total to Part 2 of the form. On Line 12 the CMI from Line 11 is annualized by being multiplied by 12 (CMI × 12). For Marta, her total CMI from the past six months is $3,888.88 based on her salary from TTI, and we annualize that to get $46,666.56 for her annual income for purposes of the means test.

On Line 13 the debtor lists the state of residence and the size of debtor's household. Using that information the debtor determines the median family income figure for the debtor's state and household size from the Census Bureau's tables posted on the U.S. Trustee Program's Web site mentioned above and enters that number on Line 13 of the form.

Next we compare the debtor's annualized monthly income number with the median family income number. If the debtor's annual income is *equal to* or *less than* the applicable median family income for his state, he is what practitioners call a "below median debtor" and the presumption of abuse does not arise in his case. The below median debtor has passed the means test and need do nothing further to satisfy the means test. Instead, he or she will merely complete the verification in Part 3 of Form 122A-1 and indicate in the box at the top right of the first page of the form that the presumption of abuse does not arise in the case.

As can be seen in Exhibit 5.1 (or Document 19 in her case file available on the companion Web site), Marta's annualized monthly income is $46,666.56. The median family income for a family of three living in Minnesota as of June 2016 was $80,900. Since her annualized monthly income is less than the state median income for her size family, the presumption does not arise. She is a below median debtor and has passed the means test. She has indicated on the box at the top right of the first page of the form that the presumption does not arise in her case. She has signed and dated the form in Part 3. (Remember that the median income figures from the Census Bureau are adjusted annually and numbers for the current year may be different from the illustration and document in the case file when you read this. She filed in June 2016 and the figures for that month and year were used in her case.)

You may initially find it perplexing that the annualized CMI figure used on Marta's Form 122A-1 ($46,666.56) is less than her actual annual income ($48,000) at the time she files her petition. But the CMI figure calculated using the look back period is the "snapshot" view of the debtor's income Congress has chosen to use for the means test. It is easy to imagine a resulting potential misuse of the system (e.g., what if Marta had found a new job as of June 1, 2016 paying $100,000 per year), but the 707(b)(2) presumption of abuse that gives rise to the means test is actually only the first tier of a two-tiered inquiry under §707(b) to determine if the Chapter 7 filing is abusive.

In Chapter Eleven, Section C, we will take a close look at the second tier of the test, which is found in 707(b)(3) and allows a court to dismiss the case of a debtor who passes the means test if the debtor filed the petition in bad faith or if "the total-ity of the circumstances of the debtor's financial situation demonstrates abuse." An actual annual income demonstrably higher than that calculated using the look back period might constitute just such a circumstance to warrant the court dismissing the case for abuse, though not for the 707(b)(2) "presumption" of abuse. And as we will see in the next chapter, the debtor must also file a Schedule I showing their current income as of the date of filing which includes a disclosure of anticipated changes to debtor's income in the twelve months following the date of filing. This enables the bankruptcy trustee or any curious creditor to get a truer picture of the debtor's actual income than Form 122A-1 provides.

Remember too, as you get a handle on the means test, that calculation of the debtor's CMI using the look back formula could distort the debtor's income in a way that makes it look greater than it actually is when the petition is filed. For example, if Marta had been laid off by TTI on June 1 and was unemployed when she filed her petition on June 4, she would still have to calculate her CMI as she did even though her actual income at the time of filing was nil. That won't matter if the debtor satisfies the means test notwithstanding the distortion, but it could cause that debtor to trigger the presumption of abuse under 707(b)(2). Again, the debtor's Schedule I will provide clarity on the debtor's actual income situation as of the date of filing and we will see as we go along in this chapter how the Code resolves the situation where a true picture of either the income or expenses of the debtor is not provided by the means test forms.

Case Preview

In re Herbert

The Code itself provides little guidance in determining who should be included in a debtor's "household" for use on Line 13 of Form 122A-1 in calculating the median family income from the Census Bureau's tables as part of the means test. Should individuals living in the debtor's home but who are unrelated to the debtor be included? Should individuals who are not dependents of the debtor be included? As you read In re Herbert, consider the following questions:

1. How many people living in the debtor's home were related to him by blood or marriage? How many of them did he include in his household number to use in calculating his median family income?
2. What difference did the determination of debtor's household size make to debtor's right to proceed in Chapter 7?
3. What is the "heads on bed" or Census Bureau approach to determining household size for purposes of the means test? The Internal Revenue Manual approach? The "dependency on the debtor" approach?

   *Note: In re Herbert refers to Form 22A, which at the time performed the same function as today's Form 122A-1.

In re Herbert
405 B.R. 165 (Bankr. W.D.N.C. 2008)

HODGES, Bankruptcy Judge.

This matter is before the court on the Motion to Dismiss filed by the Bankruptcy Administrator ("BA"). The sole issue presented by the BA's motion is the definition of the phrase "household size" as it is used on Form B22A. Having considered the pleadings and the arguments of counsel, the court denies the BA's Motion to Dismiss and finds that the debtor may claim a household size of 11 on Form B22A.

BACKGROUND

The debtor filed a Chapter 7 petition on March 28, 2008. He lives with his girlfriend and nine children. One of the children is the debtor's biological daughter with his girlfriend, and the remaining eight children are the girlfriend's children from a previous relationship.

The debtor, his girlfriend, their child, and the girlfriend's eight children have lived together for several years, and the debtor has supported the girlfriend and her children during that time because their biological father is incarcerated. The debtor has claimed all of the children as dependents on his tax returns and he has attempted to adopt the eight children, but their father will not consent to the adoption.

With respect to his bankruptcy schedules, the debtor claims all nine children as dependents on Schedule I. Specifically, he lists one as his daughter and the other eight as stepchildren. [A]lthough the debtor lists the 8 children as his stepchildren, they do not legally fall within that category because he and his girlfriend are not married. See Black's Law Dictionary 255 (8th ed. 2004) (defining stepchild as the "child of one's spouse by a previous marriage.").

In addition, the debtor claims a household size of 11 on line 14(b) of Form B22A and an applicable median family income of $111,469.00. The household size of 11 includes the debtor, his girlfriend, and the nine children living in the house.

The debtor listed Current Monthly Income for §707(b)(7) of $9,125.00, which includes $1,600.00 his girlfriend receives for food stamps each month. Therefore, his Annualized Current Monthly Income on line 13 of Form B22A is $109,500.00, which is less than the applicable median family income of $111,469.00 for a household size of 11 in North Carolina. Therefore, the debtor was not required to complete the remaining portions of Form B22A.

The BA moved to dismiss the debtor's case on the basis that the debtor is entitled to claim only a household size of 2, which includes himself and his daughter. Therefore, the BA argues that the debtor's applicable median family income should be $49,259.00, which is the applicable median family income for a household size of 2 in North Carolina. And if the debtor's applicable median family income is $49,259.00, it would appear he has sufficient disposable income to pay unsecured creditors some portion of their claims over 60 months. For that reason, the BA moved to dismiss the case pursuant to 11 U.S.C. §707(b) as an abuse of Chapter 7.

DISCUSSION

The facts in this case are not in dispute. Thus, the sole issue to be determined by the court is what number the debtor should use for household size when completing Form B22A. Unfortunately, the phrase is not defined in either the Bankruptcy Code or on Form B22A.

. . .

One of the leading cases to have considered the definition of "household size" is In re Ellringer, 370 B.R. 905 (Bankr. D. Minn. 2007). In *Ellringer*, the court held that the Census Bureau's definition of household is the most appropriate one because §101(39A)(A) defines median family income as "the median family income both calculated and reported by the Bureau of the Census." *See Ellringer* at 910. The Census Bureau defines "household" as "'all of the people, related and unrelated, who occupy a housing unit.'" *See Ellringer* at 911 (quoting the U.S. Census Bureau, Current Population Survey (2004), http://www.census.gov/population/www/cps/cpsdef.html). The *Ellringer* court concluded that using the Census Bureau's definition "ensures that a household in the means test will have the same number of members as the calculation of median family income." *See id.* at 910-911. This approach has been referred to as the "heads on beds" approach, and it does not take into consideration financial contributions of the household member, dependency, or the relationship of the household member to the debtor.

[T]he *Ellringer* court found that Congress meant two different things by family size and household size on Form B22A. In addition, the court noted that Congress elected to use the broader term "household size" on line 14(b) of Form B22A in recognition of the fact that there may be instances in which two unrelated, non-dependent individuals should be treated as a household for purposes of the means test. *See id.* at 911. Using the "heads on beds" approach, the court concluded that the debtor resided in a household size of 2. Included in that number was the debtor's roommate of several years with whom she owned her home as joint tenants; was jointly liable for the mortgage; had a joint bank account; and jointly owned a 2002 Ford Focus. *See id.* at 910.

Another leading case to interpret the phrase household size is In re Jewell, 365 B.R. 796 (Bankr. S.D. Ohio 2007). In *Jewell*, at the time the debtors[] filed their case, they lived with their two dependent children, an adult daughter, Crystal, her three minor children, and an adult son, Chris. Crystal and her children had lived with the debtors for approximately six months at the time the debtors filed their petition. Crystal did not help pay any of the household expenses, and the debtors provided Crystal and her children funds for medical care, gas, and other needs. *See Jewell* at 798.

The other adult child, Chris, never left home, but he attended college and had a full-time job. He neither contributed to the household expenses nor accepted financial assistance from the debtors. Finally, the two dependent children were both employed, but they did not contribute financially to the household expenses. *See id.*

In their second amended Form B22A, the debtors claimed a household size of 8, which resulted in their Annualized Current Monthly Income being less than the applicable median family income in Ohio. As a result, they were not required to calculate the monthly disposable income on Form B22A. The United States Trustee moved to dismiss the case for abuse pursuant to 11 U.S.C. §707(b)(2)(A) on the basis that the debtors were claiming a household size larger than that to which they were entitled. *See id.*

The United States Trustee argued that the court should look to the Internal Revenue Manual (the "IRM") as guidance for determining the definition of household size. *See id.* at 800. The IRM in turn states that the number of household members allowed for purposes of determining the applicable National Standards should generally be the same as the number of household members allowed as dependents on a tax return. *See id.* The *Jewell* court rejected this approach as being too narrow because it fails to recognize those instances when a debtor may be actually providing support for a household member. *See id.* at 801. In that regard, the court noted that even the IRS acknowledges that there may be reasonable exceptions to the general rule stated above. *See id.*

The Jewell court also rejected the Census Bureau definition of household or the "heads on beds" approach argued by the debtors because the court found that it is inconsistent with the purpose of Form B22A, which is a "means test" designed to determine disposable income. *See Jewell* at 800. Specifically the court found that:

> Such a definition is inconsistent with the methodology and purpose of Official Form 22A for calculating a debtor['s] disposable income in that it does not include the element of a debtor's support of the person who puts the head on the bed. If a person lives in the home with the debtor but the debtor does not support that person, then inclusion of that person for purposes of calculating the applicable median family income and disposable income would give rise to a faulty calculation and would result in an inaccurate figure for both.

See id. The court also noted that the purpose for which the Census Bureau determines household size is "radically different" than the purpose of Form B22A. *See id.*

The *Jewell* court ultimately held that the debtors could claim a household size of 8, which included the debtors, the two dependent children, Crystal, and her three children. *See id.* at 802. The court concluded that Crystal and her three children should be counted as part of the household because they had been dependent on the debtors for support during the six months prior to the filing of the case. *See id.* at 801. On the other hand, the court did not include the debtors' adult son, Chris, who it considered to be "merely a head on a bed." *See id.* Although the debtors occasionally provided Chris funds, the court emphasized that he did not regularly receive financial assistance from the debtors, and they did not provide him support in the form of food and clothing. Neither did the debtors claim Chris as a dependent on their tax returns. *See id.*

This court is persuaded to follow the reasoning in *Jewell* because it seems the most consistent with the purpose of Form 22A, which, as the *Jewell* court noted, is a means test designed to determine a debtor's disposable income. While this court agrees with the *Ellringer* court to the extent it recognizes that there will be instances in which unrelated, non-dependent individuals should be treated as part of a household, the "heads on bed" approach adopted by that court is too broad because it includes anybody who may be residing under the debtor's roof without regard to their financial contributions to the household or the monetary support they may be receiving from the debtor. Neither does it take into consideration their dependency or relationship to the debtor. On the other hand, the court declines to adopt the standards of the Internal Revenue Manual for purposes of determining household size because they do not account for the situation in which a debtor may be supporting an individual without declaring that person as a dependent on his tax return.

And although the *Jewell* court did not delineate hard and fast guidelines for calculating household size, it looked primarily to the debtors' financial support of their household members to determine whether those individuals should be included within the household size for purposes of Form B22A. This approach recognizes that debtors have a variety of different living arrangements that defy being pigeonholed into a neat formula for purposes of defining household size. In that regard, this court notes that it will consider the issue of household size on a case by case basis with key considerations being the debtor's history of support of a household member as well as the debtor's good faith.

Applying that analysis to this case, the court finds that the debtor has a household size of eleven. The reality of this debtor's situation is that he is — and has been for several years — supporting his girlfriend, their daughter, and her eight children. That support, while voluntary, has been consistent and of long standing. It is not contrived or concocted for the purpose of this bankruptcy filing. But, rather, appears to be simply the fact of this debtor's life.

The court is satisfied that the debtor's applicable median family income should be calculated based upon that reality rather than on some artificial construct. Consequently, the court concludes that this debtor's "household size" is determined by the actual number of people supported by the debtor; and that his applicable median family income should be calculated based on a "household size" of 11.

It is therefore ORDERED that the BA's Motion to Dismiss is DENIED.

Post-Case Follow-Up

Note that the motion to dismiss the debtor's case in In re Herbert was brought by a bankruptcy administrator, not the U.S. Trustee. Do you recognize why that is? If not, go back and read the discussion of the U.S. Trustee position in Chapter Four, Section G. Read In re Ellringer, 370 B.R. 905 (Bankr. D. Minn. 2007), for a reasonable defense of the head on beds approach to determining household size. Which approach do you find most appropriate given the language of the Code and Form 122A-1 itself and the purposes to be accomplished by the means test?

In re Herbert: Real Life Applications

1. Which of the three methods of determining household size did the court adopt in In re Herbert (Census Bureau or heads on beds method, the dependency on the debtor method, or the Internal Revenue Manual method)? What was debtor's household size determined to be based on the method adopted? What would it have been under each of the other two methods mentioned?

2. Assume you are filing a Chapter 7 case for Roscoe Millan, a recently divorced man of 45 years of age. Roscoe has three children who live with his ex-wife but who stay with him on weekends. He pays child support to his ex-wife faithfully though under the divorce decree she claims the children as dependents on her tax return. Roscoe's brother lives with him and since the brother only works part-time, Roscoe provides all the food in the apartment and only occasionally charges the brother rent. The brother's 14-year-old stepson has been living with them for three months as well since he had an argument with his mother, who has custody of him. He could move back in with his mom any day. What household size will you claim for Roscoe on his Schedule I and Form 122A-1 using the heads on beds method of calculating it? The dependency on the debtor method? The Internal Revenue Manual method?

3. Note that Schedule J: Your Expenses uses a mixed approach, asking about dependents on Line 2 and about expenses for others on Lines 3 and 19. How would you complete those lines of Schedule J for Roscoe Millan?

4. Note that Form 122A-2: Chapter 7 Means Test Calculation (to be discussed in detail in the next section) does not use the number in household approach for calculating expenses of the above median debtor to be deducted from current monthly income. Line 5 of that form asks for the number of people the debtor can claim as exemptions for purposes of federal income tax (the Internal Revenue Manual method) plus the number of additional dependents supported. What number would you enter for Roscoe Millan on Line 5 of Form 122A-2?

---

3. The Means Test for the Above Median Debtor: Determining that Debtor's Disposable Monthly Income to Determine the Feasibility of Funding a Chapter 13 Plan Using Official Form 122A-2

If the debtor's annualized CMI as calculated on Form 122A-1 is greater than the applicable median family income figure, the debtor is an **"above median debtor"** and must go to Step 2 of the means test by completing Official Form 122A-2, Chapter 7 Means Test Calculation. The purpose of Form 122A-2 is to determine if the debtor will have sufficient disposable monthly income to fund a Chapter 13 reorganization plan. Specifically, we calculate the debtor's disposable income by deducting from his current monthly income a mix of actual and standardized expenses based on the **National Standards for Allowable Living Expenses** and **Local Standards for Transportation and Housing and Utilities Expenses** published by

EXHIBIT 5.2   Marta Carlson's Form 122A-1 Assuming Annual Income of $84,000

Fill in this information to identify your case:

Debtor 1   <u>Marta</u>   <u>Rinaldi</u>   <u>Carlson</u>
            First Name   Middle Name   Last Name

Debtor 2
(Spouse, if filing) First Name   Middle Name   Last Name

United States Bankruptcy Court for the: District of Minnesota

Case number   <u>16-7-XXXX</u>
(If known)

Check one box only as directed in this form and in Form 122A-1Supp:

❑ 1. There is no presumption of abuse.

☑ 2. The calculation to determine if a presumption of abuse applies will be made under *Chapter 7 Means Test Calculation* (Official Form 122A–2).

❑ 3. The Means Test does not apply now because of qualified military service but it could apply later.

❑ Check if this is an amended filing

Official Form 122A–1

Chapter 7 Statement of Your Current Monthly Income   12/15

Be as complete and accurate as possible. If two married people are filing together, both are equally responsible for being accurate. If more space is needed, attach a separate sheet to this form. Include the line number to which the additional information applies. On the top of any additional pages, write your name and case number (if known). If you believe that you are exempted from a presumption of abuse because you do not have primarily consumer debts or because of qualifying military service, complete and file *Statement of Exemption from Presumption of Abuse Under § 707(b)(2)* (Official Form 122A-1Supp) with this form.

Part 1:   Calculate Your Current Monthly Income

1. **What is your marital and filing status?** Check one only.

   ☑ **Not married.** Fill out Column A, lines 2-11.

   ❑ **Married and your spouse is filing with you.** Fill out both Columns A and B, lines 2-11.

   ❑ **Married and your spouse is NOT filing with you.** You and your spouse are:

      ❑ **Living in the same household and are not legally separated.** Fill out both Columns A and B, lines 2-11.

      ❑ **Living separately or are legally separated.** Fill out Column A, lines 2-11; do not fill out Column B. By checking this box, you declare under penalty of perjury that you and your spouse are legally separated under nonbankruptcy law that applies or that you and your spouse are living apart for reasons that do not include evading the Means Test requirements. 11 U.S.C. § 707(b)(7)(B).

   Fill in the average monthly income that you received from all sources, derived during the 6 full months before you file this bankruptcy case. 11 U.S.C. § 101(10A). For example, if you are filing on September 15, the 6-month period would be March 1 through August 31. If the amount of your monthly income varied during the 6 months, add the income for all 6 months and divide the total by 6. Fill in the result. Do not include any income amount more than once. For example, if both spouses own the same rental property, put the income from that property in one column only. If you have nothing to report for any line, write $0 in the space.

	Column A Debtor 1	Column B Debtor 2 or non-filing spouse
2. **Your gross wages, salary, tips, bonuses, overtime, and commissions** (before all payroll deductions).	$ 7,000.00	$_____
3. **Alimony and maintenance payments.** Do not include payments from a spouse if Column B is filled in.	$ 0.00	$_____
4. **All amounts from any source which are regularly paid for household expenses of you or your dependents, including child support.** Include regular contributions from an unmarried partner, members of your household, your dependents, parents, and roommates. Include regular contributions from a spouse only if Column B is not filled in. Do not include payments you listed on line 3.	$ 0.00	$_____

5. **Net income from operating a business, profession, or farm**

	Debtor 1	Debtor 2			
Gross receipts (before all deductions)	$_____	$_____			
Ordinary and necessary operating expenses	– $_____	– $_____			
Net monthly income from a business, profession, or farm	$ 0.00	$_____	Copy here ➔	$ 0.00	$_____

6. **Net income from rental and other real property**

	Debtor 1	Debtor 2			
Gross receipts (before all deductions)	$_____	$_____			
Ordinary and necessary operating expenses	– $_____	– $_____			
Net monthly income from rental or other real property	$ 0.00	$_____	Copy here ➔	$ 0.00	$_____

7. **Interest, dividends, and royalties**	$ 0.00	$_____

EXHIBIT 5.2 (Continued)

Debtor 1   Marta   Rinaldi   Carlsor   Case number (if known) 16-7-XXXX
         First Name   Middle Name   Last Name

	Column A Debtor 1	Column B Debtor 2 or non-filing spouse
8. **Unemployment compensation**	$ 0.00	$
Do not enter the amount if you contend that the amount received was a benefit under the Social Security Act. Instead, list it here: .... ↓		
For you .... $		
For your spouse.. $		
9. **Pension or retirement income.** Do not include any amount received that was a benefit under the Social Security Act.	$ 0.00	$
10. **Income from all other sources not listed above.** Specify the source and amount. Do not include any benefits received under the Social Security Act or payments received as a victim of a war crime, a crime against humanity, or international or domestic terrorism. If necessary, list other sources on a separate page and put the total below.		
_____	$ 0.00	$
_____	$ 0.00	$
Total amounts from separate pages, if any.	+ $ 0.00	+ $

11. **Calculate your total current monthly income.** Add lines 2 through 10 for each column. Then add the total for Column A to the total for Column B.

$ 7,000.00 + $ _____ = $ 7,000.00

Total current monthly income

Part 2: **Determine Whether the Means Test Applies to You**

12. **Calculate your current monthly income for the year.** Follow these steps:

12a.   Copy your total current monthly income from line 11. .... Copy line 11 here➜ $ 7,000.00

Multiply by 12 (the number of months in a year).   **x 12**

12b.   The result is your annual income for this part of the form.   12b. $ 84,000.00

13. **Calculate the median family income that applies to you.** Follow these steps:

Fill in the state in which you live.   MN

Fill in the number of people in your household.   3

Fill in the median family income for your state and size of household. ....   13. $ 80,900.00

To find a list of applicable median income amounts, go online using the link specified in the separate instructions for this form. This list may also be available at the bankruptcy clerk's office.

14. **How do the lines compare?**

14a.   ☐   Line 12b is less than or equal to line 13. On the top of page 1, check box 1, *There is no presumption of abuse.* Go to Part 3.

14b.   ☑   Line 12b is more than line 13. On the top of page 1, check box 2, *The presumption of abuse is determined by Form 122A-2.* Go to Part 3 and fill out Form 122A–2.

Part 3: **Sign Below**

By signing here, I declare under penalty of perjury that the information on this statement and in any attachments is true and correct.

✗ /s/ Marta Rinaldi Carlson   **✗** _____

Signature of Debtor 1   Signature of Debtor 2

Date 06/17/2016   Date _____
   MM / DD / YYYY   MM / DD / YYYY

If you checked line 14a, do NOT fill out or file Form 122A–2.

If you checked line 14b, fill out Form 122A–2 and file it with this form.

the Internal Revenue Service and available at www.justice.gov/ust/means-testing. Section 707(b)(2)(A)(i) of the Code provides that if the debtor has sufficient disposable income to pay $12,850 over five years, or as little as $214 a month to creditors, the presumption of abuse arises and the case *must* be dismissed or converted (with the debtor's consent) to a Chapter 13 case. If the debtor does not have more than the stated minimal amount of disposable income then the means test is satisfied (the §707(b) presumption of abuse does not arise).

*****Note:** The disposable income figure of $12,850 found in §707(b)(2)(A)(i) is as of April 2016. The dollar amounts will be adjusted again in April 2019 per Code §104.

To see how this calculation for the above median debtor works, let's assume that Marta Carlson's salary at TTI at the time she filed was $84,000 a year and had been during the entire look back period. In that case, she would have been an above median debtor since her CMI calculated at that rate would have exceeded the median income figure for a family of three in Minnesota in 2016 when she filed ($80,900). Thus she would not satisfy the means test under Step 1 utilizing only Form 122A-1. As an above median debtor, she would have had to complete Form 122A-2 to see if the presumption of abuse arose in her case. Marta's alternative Form 122A-2 based on the assumption of higher income is set out in Exhibit 5.2 (and is also included as Extra Material in her case file and can be seen on the companion Web site).

Observe that in Lines 12 and 13 of Part 2 of Marta's alternative Form 122A-1 her annualized current monthly income exceeds the median family income figure for her family of three. Accordingly, in the box at the top right of page one of the form she has checked the box indicating that the calculation to determine if the presumption of abuse arises in her case is to be made under Form 122A-2.

Before we look at what Marta Carlson's Form 122A-2 would look like (on the assumption she had annual income of $84,000), note that while some of the living expense standards published by the IRS and utilized in Form 122A-2 are national (food, clothing, and healthcare) others (housing, utilities, and transportation) are local. Thus to illustrate how Form 122A-2 works, we have located our fictional Marta Carlson in Roseville, Ramsey County, Minnesota.

In addition, though many of the expenses we will see used in that form come from the IRS living expense standards, others do not. Some of the deductions allowed in Form 122A-2 are unique to the individual debtor. So some of the expenses we will see on Marta's Form 122A-2 are based on her actual expenses as described in the Assignment Memo in Appendix A to the text.

Now we're ready to consider what her Form 122A-2 as would look like had she had annual income of $84,000 and been required to file that form. You can see her hypothetical Form 122A-2 in Exhibit 5.3 (it is also included as Extra Material in her case file and can be seen on the companion Web site).

Part 1 of Form 122A-2: The Marital Adjustment

Marta does not utilize the marital adjustment seen on Lines 2-3 of the form because she is not married. But recall from our earlier discussion that a married debtor who does include the income of a non-filing spouse on Form 122A-1 can adjust his or her annualized monthly income figure from that form by deducting in Part 1 of Form 122A-2 as much of the nonfiling spouse's income as is not actually made available for household expenses. The reason that the nonfiling spouse's income is not available for household expenses must be stated on Line 3 by explaining the non-household support use that was made of that income. The most common reason is that the nonfiling spouse is required to pay taxes or spousal or child support from an earlier marriage.

Part 2 of Form 122A-2: Deductions from the Debtor's Annualized Monthly Income

Part 2 of the form allows the debtor to deduct a variety of expenses from his or her annualized monthly income computed in Form 122A-1. On Line 5 the debtor enters the number of persons used to calculate the expenses to be deducted in Part 2. Why doesn't Line 5 of Form 122A-2 simply ask for the debtor's household size again? Because §707(b)(2)(A)(ii)(I) provides that the debtor's monthly expenses calculated using this combination of actual and standardized expenses shall include such expenses "for the debtor, the dependents of the debtor, and the spouse of the debtor in a joint case, if the spouse is not otherwise a dependent." So the expense number in the form may be calculated for the debtor and debtor's dependents who make up debtor's household but also for dependents of the debtor who reside elsewhere (e.g., a dependent aging parent who still lives on her own). A dependent on Form 122A-2 is the same as a dependent on the debtor's Schedule J, Your Expenses (to be discussed in the next chapter), though the expenses listed on Schedule J are all actual expenses and are not derived from the IRS standards. Generally, the debtor must provide at least 50 percent of the support for a person for that person to be considered a dependent of the debtor.

On Line 6 the debtor enters a deduction for food, clothing, housekeeping supplies, personal care products, and related services calculated, not from his or her actual expenses, but from the IRS national standards for such expenses accessible at the Web site of the U.S. Trustee Program. (Remember when comparing the current IRS national and local standard amounts that they are adjusted annually. Exhibit 5.3 reflects the applicable amounts as of June 2016.)

On Line 7, the debtor again accesses the IRS national standards to deduct an amount for projected out-of-pocket healthcare costs including medical services, prescription drugs, and medical supplies for each member of his family.

On Line 8 the debtor utilizes the IRS local standards for projected housing operation expenses such as homeowner's or renters insurance and utilities (gas, electric, water, etc.). Due to the wide variation in such expenses around the country, the IRS local standards are organized by state and county as well as by family size. On Exhibit 5.3, since Marta resides in Ramsey County, Minnesota, we use the Ramsey County figure on Line 8.

Be careful here. The IRS local housing and utility expense standards can be confusing to the first-time user. Note that for each family size identified in the standards there are two categories of costs: non-mortgage expenses and mortgage/rent expenses. The non-mortgage expense number is what is entered on Line 8.

The mortgage/rent number is then entered on Line 9a. If the debtor actually owns a home and has one or more mortgages against it, the projected monthly average amount of such mortgage payments over the 60 months following the filing of the bankruptcy petition is calculated and entered on Line 9b. (The reason the form utilizes a forward-looking 60-month average for projected mortgage payments has to do with the overall purpose of the means test and the 122A forms — to see if the debtor has enough income to fund a Chapter 13 plan of up to 60 months in duration. Determining the income the debtor would need to meet mortgage obligations in a Chapter 13 is part of that calculation. This will become clearer when we study the Chapter 13 bankruptcy proceeding.)

Note that the mortgage expense from the local standards entered on Line 9a must be reduced by the amount of the debtor's actual monthly mortgage payment as calculated on 9b and the result entered on Line 9c. That may seem unfair, but the debtor will be able to receive a deduction for his future mortgage payments on Line 33. The applicable IRS local standard for non-mortgage housing and utility expenses in Ramsey County, Minnesota, where Marta Carlson resides is $526 (as of June 2016) so she enters that amount on Line 8. The local standard for mortgage/rental expense is $1,420 so she enters that amount on Line 9a. But the two mortgages on her residence will require her to pay an average of $1,442 per month over the next 60 months (see the Assignment Memo in Appendix A) so she must enter that projected actual payment amount on Line 9b and deduct it from the amount on Line 9a. Since the amount of her actual projected monthly payments ($1,442) exceeds the local standard for mortgage/rent ($1,420 as of June 2016), she enters zero on Line 9c. But on Line 33 she will enter and receive a deduction for her actual mortgage payments.

If the debtor contends that the IRS local standards do not accurately reflect actual expense for housing and utility expenses (e.g., a debtor lives in a remote location and pays a premium for utility service) debtor can enter an adjustment to be made to such deduction (i.e., increase it) on Line 10. The bankruptcy trustee will question that entry closely so the debtor will need to document this contention.

On Line 11 the debtor indicates the number of vehicles owned or operated and then utilizes the IRS regional transportation expense standards to deduct an amount for the expense of operating up to two vehicles or, if the debtor does not pay operating expenses on a vehicle, for public transportation. Note that these transportation expense standards are arranged by region of the country or large metropolitan area and broken down into operating costs and ownership costs for owners of vehicles and public transportation costs for non-owners of vehicles. The vehicle operating cost figure is entered in Line 12.

Marta Carlson operates one vehicle and so indicates on Line 12 of her Form 122A-2. Note that Line 12 instructs the debtor to enter the operating costs that "apply for your Census region or metropolitan statistical area." Roseville, as part of Ramsey County, Minnesota, is part of the Midwest Census Region for purposes of the IRS local standards. But since Ramsey County is also part of the greater Minneapolis-St. Paul metropolitan area, on Line 12 Marta enters the single vehicle operating cost figure ($217 as of June 2016) provided for that metro area rather than for the wider census region ($212). If she did not have a motor vehicle, she could enter $185 for public transportation costs

EXHIBIT 5.3	**Marta Carlson's Form 122A-2 Assuming Annual Income of $84,000**

Fill in this information to identify your case:

Debtor 1   Marta   Rinaldi   Carlson
           First Name   Middle Name   Last Name

Debtor 2
(Spouse, if filing) First Name   Middle Name   Last Name

United States Bankruptcy Court for the: District of Minnesota

Case number 16-7-XXXX
(If known)

Check the appropriate box as directed in lines 40 or 42:

According to the calculations required by this Statement:

☑ 1. There is no presumption of abuse.

☐ 2. There is a presumption of abuse.

☐ Check if this is an amended filing

Official Form 122A–2

Chapter 7 Means Test Calculation

04/16

To fill out this form, you will need your completed copy of *Chapter 7 Statement of Your Current Monthly Income* (Official Form 122A-1).

Be as complete and accurate as possible. If two married people are filing together, both are equally responsible for being accurate. If more space is needed, attach a separate sheet to this form. Include the line number to which the additional information applies. On the top of any additional pages, write your name and case number (if known).

Part 1:   Determine Your Adjusted Income

1. **Copy your total current monthly income.** .... Copy line 11 from Official Form 122A-1 here ➔ .... $ 7,000.00

2. **Did you fill out Column B in Part 1 of Form 122A–1?**

   ☑ No. Fill in $0 for the total on line 3.

   ☐ Yes. Is your spouse filing with you?

      ☐ No. Go to line 3.

      ☐ Yes. Fill in $0 for the total on line 3.

3. **Adjust your current monthly income by subtracting any part of your spouse's income not used to pay for the household expenses of you or your dependents.** Follow these steps:

   On line 11, Column B of Form 122A–1, was any amount of the income you reported for your spouse NOT regularly used for the household expenses of you or your dependents?

   ☐ No. Fill in 0 for the total on line 3.

   ☐ Yes. Fill in the information below:

State each purpose for which the income was used For example, the income is used to pay your spouse's tax debt or to support people other than you or your dependents	**Fill in the amount you are subtracting from your spouse's income**
_____	$_____
_____	$_____
_____	+ $_____
Total.	$ 0.00 Copy total here ➔ – $ 0.00

4. **Adjust your current monthly income.** Subtract the total on line 3 from line 1. $ 7,000.00

EXHIBIT 5.3   **(Continued)**

Debtor 1	Marta	Rinaldi	Carlson	Case number (if known) 16-7-XXXX
	First Name	Middle Name	Last Name	

Part 2:   Calculate Your Deductions from Your Income

The Internal Revenue Service (IRS) issues National and Local Standards for certain expense amounts. Use these amounts to answer the questions in lines 6-15. To find the IRS standards, go online using the link specified in the separate instructions for this form. This information may also be available at the bankruptcy clerk's office.

Deduct the expense amounts set out in lines 6-15 regardless of your actual expense. In later parts of the form, you will use some of your actual expenses if they are higher than the standards. Do not deduct any amounts that you subtracted from your spouse's income in line 3 and do not deduct any operating expenses that you subtracted from income in lines 5 and 6 of Form 122A-1.

If your expenses differ from month to month, enter the average expense.

Whenever this part of the form refers to *you*, it means both you and your spouse if Column B of Form 122A-1 is filled in.

5. **The number of people used in determining your deductions from income**

    Fill in the number of people who could be claimed as exemptions on your federal income tax return, plus the number of any additional dependents whom you support. This number may be different from the number of people in your household. | 3 |

National Standards   You must use the IRS National Standards to answer the questions in lines 6-7.

6. **Food, clothing, and other items:** Using the number of people you entered in line 5 and the IRS National Standards, fill in the dollar amount for food, clothing, and other items. $ 1,249.00

7. **Out-of-pocket health care allowance:** Using the number of people you entered in line 5 and the IRS National Standards, fill in the dollar amount for out-of-pocket health care. The number of people is split into two categories—people who are under 65 and people who are 65 or older—because older people have a higher IRS allowance for health care costs. If your actual expenses are higher than this IRS amount, you may deduct the additional amount on line 22.

    People who are under 65 years of age

    7a. Out-of-pocket health care allowance per person $ 60.00

    7b. Number of people who are under 65   x 3

    7c. **Subtotal.** Multiply line 7a by line 7b. $ 180.00   Copy here ➔ $ 180.00

    People who are 65 years of age or older

    7d. Out-of-pocket health care allowance per person $ _____

    7e. Number of people who are 65 or older   x _____

    7f. **Subtotal.** Multiply line 7d by line 7e. $ 0.00   Copy here ➔   + $ 0.00

    7g. **Total.** Add lines 7c and 7f.. $ 180.00   Copy total here ➔ $ 180.00

EXHIBIT 5.3 **(Continued)**

Debtor 1 ___Marta___ ___Rinaldi___ ___Carlson___   Case number (if known) 16-7-XXXX
        First Name   Middle Name   Last Name

Local Standards   You must use the IRS Local Standards to answer the questions in lines 8-15.

Based on information from the IRS, the U.S. Trustee Program has divided the IRS Local Standard for housing for bankruptcy purposes into two parts:

■ **Housing and utilities – Insurance and operating expenses**
■ **Housing and utilities – Mortgage or rent expenses**

To answer the questions in lines 8-9, use the U.S. Trustee Program chart.

To find the chart, go online using the link specified in the separate instructions for this form. This chart may also be available at the bankruptcy clerk's office.

8. **Housing and utilities – Insurance and operating expenses:** Using the number of people you entered in line 5, fill in the dollar amount listed for your county for insurance and operating expenses. .... $____526.00

9. **Housing and utilities – Mortgage or rent expenses:**

   9a. Using the number of people you entered in line 5, fill in the dollar amount listed for your county for mortgage or rent expenses.. $__1,420.00

   9b. Total average monthly payment for all mortgages and other debts secured by your home.

   To calculate the total average monthly payment, add all amounts that are contractually due to each secured creditor in the 60 months after you file for bankruptcy. Then divide by 60.

Name of the creditor	Average monthly payment
Capital Savings Bank	$____965.00
Dreams Come True Financing Company	$____477.00
_____	+ $_____
Total average monthly payment	$__1,442.00

   Copy here ➜   – $___1,442.00   Repeat this amount on line 33a.

   9c. Net mortgage or rent expense.
   Subtract line 9b (*total average monthly payment*) from line 9a (*mortgage or rent expense*). If this amount is less than $0, enter $0. .... $____0.00   Copy here ➜ $____0.00

10. **If you claim that the U.S. Trustee Program's division of the IRS Local Standard for housing is incorrect and affects the calculation of your monthly expenses, fill in any additional amount you claim.** $_____

    Explain why: _____
    _____

11. **Local transportation expenses:** Check the number of vehicles for which you claim an ownership or operating expense.

    ☐ 0. Go to line 14.
    ☑ 1. Go to line 12.
    ☐ 2 or more. Go to line 12.

12. **Vehicle operation expense:** Using the IRS Local Standards and the number of vehicles for which you claim the operating expenses, fill in the *Operating Costs* that apply for your Census region or metropolitan statistical area. $____217.00

EXHIBIT 5.3   **(Continued)**

Debtor 1   Marta   Rinaldi   Carlson   Case number *(if known)* 16-7-XXXX

         First Name   Middle Name   Last Name

13. **Vehicle ownership or lease expense:** Using the IRS Local Standards, calculate the net ownership or lease expense for each vehicle below. You may not claim the expense if you do not make any loan or lease payments on the vehicle. In addition, you may not claim the expense for more than two vehicles.

    Vehicle 1   **Describe Vehicle 1:**   YR-4 Toyota Camry

    13a.   Ownership or leasing costs using IRS Local Standard. .... $_____517.00

    13b.   Average monthly payment for all debts secured by Vehicle 1.

        Do not include costs for leased vehicles.

        To calculate the average monthly payment here and on line 13e, add all amounts that are contractually due to each secured creditor in the 60 months after you filed for bankruptcy. Then divide by 60.

Name of each creditor for Vehicle 1	Average monthly payment
Automotive Financing, Inc.	$_____210.00
	+ $_____
Total average monthly payment	$_____210.00

        Copy here ➜   − $_____210.00   Repeat this amount on line 33b.

    13c.   Net Vehicle 1 ownership or lease expense

        Subtract line 13b from line 13a. If this amount is less than $0, enter $0. .... $_____307.00   Copy net Vehicle 1 expense here ..... ➜ $_____307.00

    Vehicle 2   **Describe Vehicle 2:**   _____

    13d.   Ownership or leasing costs using IRS Local Standard. .... $_____

    13e.   Average monthly payment for all debts secured by Vehicle 2.

        Do not include costs for leased vehicles.

Name of each creditor for Vehicle 2	Average monthly payment
	$_____
	+ $_____
Total average monthly payment	$_____

        Copy here ➜   − $_____   Repeat this amount on line 33c.

    13f.   Net Vehicle 2 ownership or lease expense

        Subtract line 13e from 13d. If this amount is less than $0, enter $0. .... $_____0.00   Copy net Vehicle 2 expense here ... ➜ $_____0.00

14. **Public transportation expense:** If you claimed 0 vehicles in line 11, using the IRS Local Standards, fill in the *Public Transportation* expense allowance regardless of whether you use public transportation. $_____0.00

15. **Additional public transportation expense:** If you claimed 1 or more vehicles in line 11 and if you claim that you may also deduct a public transportation expense, you may fill in what you believe is the appropriate expense, but you may not claim more than the IRS Local Standard for *Public Transportation*. $_____0.00

EXHIBIT 5.3 (Continued)

Debtor 1 _____Marta_____Rinaldi_____Carlson_____   Case number *(if known)* 16-7-XXXX _____
                First Name   Middle Name   Last Name

Other Necessary Expenses   In addition to the expense deductions listed above, you are allowed your monthly expenses for the following IRS categories.

16. **Taxes:** The total monthly amount that you will actually owe for federal, state and local taxes, such as income taxes, self-employment taxes, Social Security taxes, and Medicare taxes. You may include the monthly amount withheld from your pay for these taxes. However, if you expect to receive a tax refund, you must divide the expected refund by 12 and subtract that number from the total monthly amount that is withheld to pay for taxes. $ 1,583.00

Do not include real estate, sales, or use taxes.

17. **Involuntary deductions:** The total monthly payroll deductions that your job requires, such as retirement contributions, union dues, and uniform costs.

Do not include amounts that are not required by your job, such as voluntary 401(k) contributions or payroll savings. $_____0.00

18. **Life insurance:** The total monthly premiums that you pay for your own term life insurance. If two married people are filing together, include payments that you make for your spouse's term life insurance. Do not include premiums for life insurance on your dependents, for a non-filing spouse's life insurance, or for any form of life insurance other than term. $_____0.00

19. **Court-ordered payments:** The total monthly amount that you pay as required by the order of a court or administrative agency, such as spousal or child support payments.

Do not include payments on past due obligations for spousal or child support. You will list these obligations in line 35. $_____0.00

20. **Education:** The total monthly amount that you pay for education that is either required:
   ■ as a condition for your job, or
   ■ for your physically or mentally challenged dependent child if no public education is available for similar services. $_____0.00

21. **Childcare:** The total monthly amount that you pay for childcare, such as babysitting, daycare, nursery, and preschool.

Do not include payments for any elementary or secondary school education. $ 100.00

22. **Additional health care expenses, excluding insurance costs:** The monthly amount that you pay for health care that is required for the health and welfare of you or your dependents and that is not reimbursed by insurance or paid by a health savings account. Include only the amount that is more than the total entered in line 7.
Payments for health insurance or health savings accounts should be listed only in line 25. $ 720.00

23. **Optional telephones and telephone services:** The total monthly amount that you pay for telecommunication services for you and your dependents, such as pagers, call waiting, caller identification, special long distance, or business cell phone service, to the extent necessary for your health and welfare or that of your dependents or for the production of income, if it is not reimbursed by your employer.   + $_____0.00

Do not include payments for basic home telephone, internet and cell phone service. Do not include self-employment expenses, such as those reported on line 5 of Official Form 122A-1, or any amount you previously deducted.

24. **Add all of the expenses allowed under the IRS expense allowances.**
Add lines 6 through 23. $ 4,882.00

EXHIBIT 5.3   (Continued)

Debtor 1   Marta _____ Rinaldi _____ Carlson _____   Case number (if known) 16-7-XXXX _____
        First Name   Middle Name   Last Name

Additional Expense Deductions   These are additional deductions allowed by the Means Test.
                                        Note: Do not include any expense allowances listed in lines 6-24.

25. **Health insurance, disability insurance, and health savings account expenses.** The monthly expenses for health
    insurance, disability insurance, and health savings accounts that are reasonably necessary for yourself, your spouse, or your
    dependents.

    Health insurance $_____ 85.00

    Disability insurance $_____ 0.00

    Health savings account   + $_____ 0.00

    Total $_____ 85.00   Copy total here➜ .... $_____ 85.00

    Do you actually spend this total amount?

    ☐ No. How much do you actually spend? $_____

    ☑ Yes

26. **Continuing contributions to the care of household or family members.** The actual monthly expenses that you will
    continue to pay for the reasonable and necessary care and support of an elderly, chronically ill, or disabled member of
    your household or member of your immediate family who is unable to pay for such expenses. These expenses may
    include contributions to an account of a qualified ABLE program. 26 U.S.C. § 529A(b). $_____ 0.00

27. **Protection against family violence.** The reasonably necessary monthly expenses that you incur to maintain the safety
    of you and your family under the Family Violence Prevention and Services Act or other federal laws that apply. $_____ 0.00

    By law, the court must keep the nature of these expenses confidential.

28. **Additional home energy costs.** Your home energy costs are included in your insurance and operating expenses on line 8.

    If you believe that you have home energy costs that are more than the home energy costs included in expenses on line
    8, then fill in the excess amount of home energy costs. $_____ 0.00

    You must give your case trustee documentation of your actual expenses, and you must show that the additional amount
    claimed is reasonable and necessary.

29. **Education expenses for dependent children who are younger than 18.** The monthly expenses (not more than $160.42*
    per child) that you pay for your dependent children who are younger than 18 years old to attend a private or public
    elementary or secondary school. $_____ 150.00

    You must give your case trustee documentation of your actual expenses, and you must explain why the amount claimed is
    reasonable and necessary and not already accounted for in lines 6-23.

    * Subject to adjustment on 4/01/19, and every 3 years after that for cases begun on or after the date of adjustment.

30. **Additional food and clothing expense.** The monthly amount by which your actual food and clothing expenses are
    higher than the combined food and clothing allowances in the IRS National Standards. That amount cannot be more than
    5% of the food and clothing allowances in the IRS National Standards. $_____ 0.00

    To find a chart showing the maximum additional allowance, go online using the link specified in the separate instructions for
    this form. This chart may also be available at the bankruptcy clerk's office.

    You must show that the additional amount claimed is reasonable and necessary.

31. **Continuing charitable contributions.** The amount that you will continue to contribute in the form of cash or financial
    instruments to a religious or charitable organization. 26 U.S.C. § 170(c)(1)-(2).   + $_____ 0.00

32. **Add all of the additional expense deductions.**
    Add lines 25 through 31. $_____ 235.00

EXHIBIT 5.3   **(Continued)**

Debtor 1   Marta _____ Rinaldi _____ Carlson _____   Case number *(if known)* 16-7-XXXX _____
              First Name   Middle Name   Last Name

Deductions for Debt Payment

33. For debts that are secured by an interest in property that you own, including home mortgages, vehicle loans, and other secured debt, fill in lines 33a through 33e.

    To calculate the total average monthly payment, add all amounts that are contractually due to each secured creditor in the 60 months after you file for bankruptcy. Then divide by 60.

		Average monthly payment
Mortgages on your home:		
33a. Copy line 9b here .... →		$_____1,442.00
Loans on your first two vehicles:		
33b. Copy line 13b here. .... →		$_____210.00
33c. Copy line 13e here. .... →		$_____

    33d. List other secured debts:

Name of each creditor for other secured debt	Identify property that secures the debt	Does payment include taxes or insurance?	
_____	_____	☐ No ☐ Yes	$_____
_____	_____	☐ No ☐ Yes	$_____
_____	_____	☐ No ☐ Yes	+ $_____

	Copy total
33e. Total average monthly payment. Add lines 33a through 33d.............. $_____1,652.00	here → $____1,652.00

34. Are any debts that you listed in line 33 secured by your primary residence, a vehicle, or other property necessary for your support or the support of your dependents?

    ☐ No. Go to line 35.
    ☑ Yes. State any amount that you must pay to a creditor, in addition to the payments listed in line 33, to keep possession of your property (called the *cure amount*). Next, divide by 60 and fill in the information below.

Name of the creditor	Identify property that secures the debt	Total cure amount		Monthly cure amount
Capital Savings B.	Residence	$ 1,930.00	÷ 60 =	$_____32.16
Dreams Come Tru	Residence	$ 1,431.00	÷ 60 =	$_____23.85
Automotive Fin.	YR-4 Toyota	$ 420.00	÷ 60 =	+ $_____7.00
			Total	$_____63.01

    Copy total here → $_____63.01

35. Do you owe any priority claims such as a priority tax, child support, or alimony — that are past due as of the filing date of your bankruptcy case? 11 U.S.C. § 507.

    ☑ No. Go to line 36.
    ☐ Yes. Fill in the total amount of all of these priority claims. Do not include current or ongoing priority claims, such as those you listed in line 19.

    Total amount of all past-due priority claims .... $_____0.00 ÷ 60 = $_____0.00

EXHIBIT 5.3   (Continued)

Debtor 1	Marta	Rinaldi	Carlson	Case number (if known) 16-7-XXXX
	First Name	Middle Name	Last Name	

36. **Are you eligible to file a case under Chapter 13?** 11 U.S.C. § 109(e).
    For more information, go online using the link for *Bankruptcy Basics* specified in the separate
    instructions for this form. *Bankruptcy Basics* may also be available at the bankruptcy clerk's office.

    ☐ No. Go to line 37.

    ☑ Yes. Fill in the following information.

    Projected monthly plan payment if you were filing under Chapter 13 $_____1,700

    Current multiplier for your district as stated on the list issued by the
    Administrative Office of the United States Courts (for districts in Alabama and
    North Carolina) or by the Executive Office for United States Trustees (for all
    other districts).   x   0.07

    To find a list of district multipliers that includes your district, go online using the
    link specified in the separate instructions for this form. This list may also be
    available at the bankruptcy clerk's office.

    Average monthly administrative expense if you were filing under Chapter 13 $_____122.40 | Copy total here➡ | $_____122.40

37. **Add all of the deductions for debt payment.**
    Add lines 33e through 36. .... $1,837.40

Total Deductions from Income

38. **Add all of the allowed deductions.**

    Copy line 24, *All of the expenses allowed under IRS
    expense allowances* .... $_____4,882.00

    Copy line 32, *All of the additional expense deductions*......... $_____235.00

    Copy line 37, *All of the deductions for debt payment*............. + $_____1,837.41

    Total deductions $_____6,954.41   Copy total here .... ➡ $_____6,954.41

Part 3:   Determine Whether There Is a Presumption of Abuse

39. **Calculate monthly disposable income for 60 months**

    39a. Copy line 4, *adjusted current monthly income* ..... $_____7,000.00

    39b. Copy line 38, *Total deductions*.......... – $_____6,954.41

    39c. Monthly disposable income. 11 U.S.C. § 707(b)(2).
          Subtract line 39b from line 39a. $_____45.59 | Copy here➡ | $_____45.59

          For the next 60 months (5 years)..   x 60

    39d. **Total**. Multiply line 39c by 60. .... $ 2,735.40 | Copy here➡ | $ 2,735.40

40. **Find out whether there is a presumption of abuse.** Check the box that applies:

    ☑ **The line 39d is less than $7,700***. On the top of page 1 of this form, check box 1, *There is no presumption of abuse.* Go
      to Part 5.

    ☐ **The line 39d is more than $12,850***. On the top of page 1 of this form, check box 2, *There is a presumption of abuse.* You
      may fill out Part 4 if you claim special circumstances. Then go to Part 5.

    ☐ **The line 39d is at least $7,700*, but not more than $12,850***. Go to line 41.

       * Subject to adjustment on 4/01/19, and every 3 years after that for cases filed on or after the date of adjustment.

EXHIBIT 5.3   (Continued)

Debtor 1   Marta _____ Rinaldi _____ Carlson _____   Case number (if known) 16-7-XXXX _____
         First Name   Middle Name   Last Name

---

41. 41a. **Fill in the amount of your total nonpriority unsecured debt.** If you filled out *A Summary of Your Assets and Liabilities and Certain Statistical Information Schedules* (Official Form 106Sum), you may refer to line 3b on that form.. $_____

                                                                                          x .25

    41b. **25% of your total nonpriority unsecured debt.** 11 U.S.C. § 707(b)(2)(A)(i)(I).
         Multiply line 41a by 0.25. .... $_____   Copy here → $_____

42. **Determine whether the income you have left over after subtracting all allowed deductions is enough to pay 25% of your unsecured, nonpriority debt.**
    Check the box that applies:

    ☐ **Line 39d is less than line 41b.** On the top of page 1 of this form, check box 1, *There is no presumption of abuse.* Go to Part 5.

    ☐ **Line 39d is equal to or more than line 41b.** On the top of page 1 of this form, check box 2, *There is a presumption of abuse.* You may fill out Part 4 if you claim special circumstances. Then go to Part 5.

Part 4:   Give Details About Special Circumstances

43. **Do you have any special circumstances that justify additional expenses or adjustments of current monthly income for which there is no reasonable alternative?** 11 U.S.C. § 707(b)(2)(B).

    ☐ No. Go to Part 5.

    ☐ Yes. Fill in the following information. All figures should reflect your average monthly expense or income adjustment for each item. You may include expenses you listed in line 25.

        You must give a detailed explanation of the special circumstances that make the expenses or income adjustments necessary and reasonable. You must also give your case trustee documentation of your actual expenses or income adjustments.

Give a detailed explanation of the special circumstances	Average monthly expense or income adjustment
_____	$_____
_____	$_____
_____	$_____
_____	$_____

Part 5:   Sign Below

By signing here, I declare under penalty of perjury that the information on this statement and in any attachments is true and correct.

✗ /s/ Marta Rinaldi Carlson _____   ✗ _____
Signature of Debtor 1   Signature of Debtor 2

Date 06/17/2016 _____   Date _____
    MM / DD / YYYY   MM / DD / YYYY

The Ownership Expense Deduction

May a debtor take the expense deduction for vehicle ownership allowed in Line 13a if the vehicle is paid for and is subject to neither a lease nor a secured debt? That issue has arisen under BAPCPA and Form 122A-2 (as well as Form 122C-2, used in Chapter 13 cases, as we will see later). Lower courts were badly split on this issue until the Supreme Court held in Ransom v. FIA Card Services, N.A., 131 S. Ct. 716 (2011), that a debtor cannot use the IRS Local Standards Transportation Ownership Costs for a car that is owned free of debt or lease obligations. Although *Ransom* involved a Chapter 13 debtor and Form 122C-2, the decision is controlling in Chapter 7 cases involving what is now Form 122A-2 as well.

on Line 14 instead, but note, interestingly, that that is a national not a regional figure. If she had both operating costs for a vehicle and also used public transportation she could enter the operating costs figure on Line 12 and the public transportation figure on Line 15. Again, a bankruptcy trustee may well challenge such deductions, and the debtor should be prepared to corroborate both categories of expense.

On Line 13a the debtor enters the figure for vehicle ownership/lease costs for up to two vehicles from the IRS regional transportation expense standards. However, as with the mortgage expense standard entered on Line 9, the local standard amount for vehicle ownership/lease expense must be reduced by the projected average monthly payment the debtor will make over the 60 months following the filing of the petition to any creditor holding a security interest in the vehicle. That projected average monthly payment is calculated on Line 13b and subtracted from the figure on 13a with the result entered on Line 13c. Again, that initially seems unfair, but the debtor will be able to enter and deduct future payments on the secured vehicle on Line 33.

For example, Marta Carlson only has one vehicle and so indicates on Line 11. On Line 12 she enters her vehicle operation expense number from the IRS standards, which was $217 for the Minneapolis-St. Paul metro area in June 2016. On Line 13a she then enters the ownership expense figure for one vehicle from the IRS standards, which was $517 as of June 2016. But since she makes monthly payments totaling $210 on her car to a secured creditor, Automotive Financing, Inc. (AFI) (see the Assignment Memo in Appendix A), she shows that amount on Line 13b and deducts it from the IRS standard ownership expense figure, leaving a balance of $307 entered on Line 13c. However, on Line 33, discussed below, she will enter and deduct the amount of her monthly payment to AFI. Lines 13d-f are left blank on Marta's Form 122A-2 because she does not own a second car.

On Lines 16-23 the debtor is allowed to enter and deduct his or her average monthly payments made on categories of expenses not expressly covered by the IRS standards so the figures are derived from the debtor's actual expenses including taxes (other than real estate, sales, and use taxes) (Line 16), payroll deductions for items such as retirement contributions, union dues, and uniform costs (Line 17), term life insurance for policies covering the debtor's life only (Line 18), court-ordered payments such as child support or alimony (in their full amount, not averaged) (Line 19), education expenses for the debtor that are a condition of employment or for a physically or mentally challenged dependent child for whom no such public education service is available (Line 20), child care (Line 21), unreimbursed healthcare expenses in excess of the amount entered on Line 7 and not including health insurance premiums (Line 22), and telecommunication expenses in excess of home phone and cell phone service but only to the extent necessary to the health and welfare of the debtor or his dependents (Line 23). These expense amounts are totaled on Line 24.

For example, Marta Carlson's average monthly expense for income, Social Security, and Medicare taxes is $1,583, and she enters that amount on Line 16. She does not include real estate taxes because those are included in her mortgage payments that she will deduct on Line 33. Sales taxes are excluded too since they are part of the calculation of the IRS's standards for food and clothing, etc., deducted on Line 6. She has not deducted any of her educational expenses on Line 20, concluding that they are not a "condition" of her continued employment at TTI. She is currently incurring $100 per month in child care expense and enters that amount on Line 21. She has incurred additional healthcare expenses for her daughter (see the Assignment Memo in Appendix A) and in recent months has been paying an average of $900 a month on those obligations, even though she is in arrears on her mortgages and car payment. But she does not enter the full $900 on Line 22 because that line instructs that only the total in excess of the amount appearing on Line 7 is to be entered on Line 22. On Line 7 Marta entered $180 for her standard out-of-pocket health care expense. So on Line 22 she deducts that $180 and enters the excess of $720. She can expect to be challenged on such a large deduction for this item and should have documentation ready to support it.

On Line 24 of the form the debtor totals all of the expense allowances from Lines 6 through 23.

Lines 25-31 of Form 122A-2 allow the debtor to list additional expense deductions based on actual expenses.

Line 25 allows the debtor to deduct actual premiums paid monthly for health and disability insurance or payments into a health savings account, items that were excluded from Line 22.

For example, on Line 22 Marta Carlson entered an amount equal to the average payment she has been making on unreimbursed healthcare expenses for herself and the two children, but health insurance premiums she pays for the TTI group coverage were not included there. The monthly premium for that group coverage is included on Line 25.

Line 26 allows the debtor to enter and deduct extraordinary expenses incurred for the care and support of a member of the debtor's household or a member of the debtor's immediate family who is elderly, chronically ill, or disabled.

For example, if Marta Carlson's elderly mother was still living and was a member of her household, Marta might be able to deduct any extra expenses incurred for her mother's upkeep here (e.g., having someone stay with her during the day). Or if her chronically ill daughter was incurring expenses other than medical costs Marta has deducted on Line 22 (e.g., expensive foods for a special diet) those could be deducted here. This is again the kind of unusual deduction a bankruptcy trustee will examine closely and the debtor must have supporting documentation.

On Line 27 a debtor who has been the victim of domestic violence or stalking and who qualifies for protection under the **Family Violence Prevention and**

Who Can Deduct a Charitable Contribution Expense and in What Amount?

The issue of limiting a debtor's deductions for charitable contributions to a religious organization raises First Amendment Free Exercise Clause issues that have never been completely resolved. In the Religious Liberty and Charitable Donation Clarification Act of 2006 Congress made clear its intent in the Religious Liberty and Charitable Contribution Protection Act of 1998 that debtors in bankruptcy be allowed to claim charitable contribution expenses as part of their adjustment of income as part of the means test. Such contributions cannot be disallowed as being not reasonably necessary to the support of the debtor and his dependents as part of the Chapter 7 means test (or as we will see later, as part of the determination of a Chapter 13 debtor's disposable income). Notwithstanding that, per the "continue to contribute" language of the form, listed contributions must be continuing. A debtor who has rarely if ever made charitable contributions may not enter an amount here on the grounds that he or she intends to begin making those contributions without drawing a challenge. Moreover, trustees will generally limit the amount claimed to 10 to 15 percent of the debtor's gross income (and §1325(b)(2)(A)(ii) specifically limits this deduction to 15 percent of the debtor's gross income for purposes of determining a Chapter 13 debtor's disposable income). Though there is no such statutory limitation on the charitable contribution deduction in the Chapter 7 means test, the U.S. Trustee Program has taken the position that such contributions by a Chapter

Services Act may deduct expenses related to keeping the family safe (e.g., home security system).

If the average monthly amount the debtor actually expends on utilities exceeds the IRS local standard for that item used on Line 8, the debtor may deduct the excess on Line 28 but will need to provide documentation if challenged.

On Line 29 the debtor with minor children may deduct average monthly school costs actually incurred in connection with their attendance at a public or private elementary or secondary school up to a current maximum of $160.42 per child (that amount will be next adjusted in April 2019 per §104 of the Code).

For example, Marta Carlson has calculated that she spends an average of $75 a month on each of her two children for special equipment or supplies or field trips. Thus, she has deducted a total of $150 here. Such expenses must be documented and must be beyond routine costs of sending children to school (e.g., normal school clothes and supplies).

If the average monthly amount the debtor *actually* spends on food and clothing and other items exceeds the amount allowed by the IRS local standard for such items that was entered on Line 6, a debtor may deduct the excess on Line 30 up to a maximum of 5 percent of the IRS standard but will need to provide documentation if challenged.

On Line 31 the debtor may enter and deduct charitable contributions the debtor plans to "continue" making. This wording suggests that the debtor must have a legitimate and provable history of making such contributions to justify this deduction from annualized monthly income and the amount must be reasonable.

Section 707(b)(1) says that in making the determination of whether to dismiss a Chapter 7 case for abuse, "the court may not take into consideration whether a debtor has made, or continues to make, charitable contributions. . . ." That language could be construed to mean that the form's limitation of this deduction to continuing contributions is inappropriate and that a bankruptcy judge may not limit the amount of such deductions if they are bona fide. A form, even an official form, cannot vary the terms of a bankruptcy rule or the Code itself. FRBP 9009 states, "The forms shall be construed to be consistent with these rules and the Code." See In re Meyer, 355 B.R. 837, 843 n.6 (Bankr. D.N.M. 2006) ("[O]ne looks to the statute to determine what the law is, and then interprets the form in light of the statute's dictate.") There is little case law interpreting §707(b)(2) or the apparent inconsistency of the form language, probably since statistics suggest that few Chapter 7 debtors claim the charitable deduction and only about 2 percent claim a charitable deduction of more than 5 percent of their gross income.

The additional expense deductions allowed in Lines 25-31 are totaled on Line 32.

Lines 33-36 of Form 122A-2 allow the deduction of various debt payments owed by the debtor.

On Line 33 the debtor may enter and deduct scheduled monthly payments on debt secured by the debtor's home, vehicles, or other property. Only secured obligations can be entered here. (This entry was referenced in connection with the discussion of Lines 9 and 13 above.) The average monthly payment on all of the debtor's secured debt is totaled and entered on Line 33e.

7 debtor should not be allowed in excess of 15 percent of gross income (see Statement of U.S. Trustee at www.justice.gov/sites/default/files/ust/legacy/2015/03/03/ch7_line_by_line.pdf). A debtor who decides to begin making a charitable contribution (and claims the expense deduction for it) when he has no provable history of making such contributions or who decides to increase a charitable contribution (and claim the expense deduction for the increase) runs the risk of having their Chapter 7 case dismissed on a finding of bad faith (as discussed in Chapter Eleven, Section C) (a Chapter 13 debtor runs the same risk — his Chapter 13 plan will not be confirmed unless the court finds it was proposed in good faith as discussed in Chapter Sixteen, Section B).

For example, on Line 33a and b of her Form 122A-2, Marta Carlson enters her scheduled monthly payments for both mortgages and the payment to AFI secured by her automobile. If she had debts secured by other collateral those would be listed on Line 33d.

Commonly in a Chapter 13 case, the debtor will propose a plan to continue paying the mortgage debt on his or her home and the secure debt on at least one car in order to keep those items of property, and those continued payments are what is contemplated here. Remember, the purpose of Step 2 of the means test for the over median debtor is to see if that debtor might have enough remaining disposable income after making such payments to fund a Chapter 13 plan. We will consider all that later when we take up Chapter 13.

Case Preview

In re Rivers and In re Fredman

An issue has arisen under the new means test regarding whether a debtor may deduct secured payments for her mortgaged home or secured vehicles on Line 33 of Form 122A-2 where the debtor intends to surrender such property to the secured party rather than keep it (as Marta Carlson plans to do per her Debtor's Statement of Intent, which is Document 18 in the Carlson case file). We will consider the surrender of property in more detail later, but it essentially means that the debtor intends to stop paying for the property and relinquish possession of it to the secured creditor. But the debtor has not yet surrendered the property when completing Form 122A-2. Some courts have held that the debtor who intends to surrender secured property may deduct those payments on Line 33 as part of the means test determination, while other courts have held that he may not. As you read In re Rivers and In re Fredman, consider the following questions:

1. What kind of secured debt were the respective debtors in these cases taking the expense deduction for on their Form 22A notwithstanding their plans to surrender the property securing the debt?
2. What difference would it have made to each of these respective debtors if the expense deduction was disallowed on their Form 22A?
3. Why do these courts reach different decisions on the same issue?

    *Note: These cases refer to Form 22A, which at the time performed the same function as today's Form 122A-1 and 122A-2.

In re Rivers
466 B.R. 558 (Bankr. M.D. Fla. 2012)

[The Debtor is married and has six dependent children. She is employed and earns more than $11,000.00 per month. Before moving to Florida in 2010, the Debtor and her family previously lived in Stafford, Virginia. She owned a home in Virginia with a scheduled value of $289,300.00, and a scheduled mortgage in the amount of $462,120.00. On April 4, 2011, the Debtor filed a petition under Chapter 7 of the Bankruptcy Code. The petition was accompanied by the Debtor's Statement of Intention, in which she indicated that the Virginia home was not claimed as exempt and would be surrendered.

    On Amended Form 22A (the Means Test Calculation), the Debtor listed her gross income combined with her husband's as $11,839.54 per month. The amount of their annualized income exceeded the applicable median income for a family of eight in Florida, and the Debtor therefore completed Amended Form 22A by entering certain "deductions from income" in the total amount of $11,685.36. After subtracting the total deductions (and certain paycheck adjustments) from the total monthly income, the Debtor listed the amount of $102.73 on the Form as her "monthly disposable income." The deductions from income entered on the Form include $2,778.00 as the mortgage payment to Wells Fargo Home Mortgage on the Virginia residence. The UST filed a Motion to Dismiss the Debtor's case as an abuse of the provisions of Chapter 7.]

GLENN, Bankruptcy Judge. . . .
    In this case, the UST asserts that the case should be dismissed "under §707(b) (1) based on the presumption of abuse that arises under §707(b)(2)." According to the UST, the mortgage payment for the Virginia residence was not properly deducted from the Debtor's monthly income in her Means Test calculation, because the Debtor is surrendering the property. If the deduction is not allowed, the UST asserts that the

Debtor's disposable income would equal the approximate sum of $2,594.58 per month, and the presumption of abuse would arise under §707(b)(2) of the Bankruptcy Code.

The starting point for determining whether a case is presumptively abusive under §707(b)(2) is the debtor's "current monthly income." The term "current monthly income" is defined in §101(10A) of the Bankruptcy Code as the debtor's average monthly income during the 6-month period immediately preceding the filing of the bankruptcy case. 11 U.S.C. §101(10A). Section 707(b)(2) then provides that the debtor's "current monthly income" is "reduced by the amounts determined under clauses (ii), (iii), and (iv)" of subsection (b)(2) to calculate whether the debtor's income exceeds the threshold levels set forth in the section.

The reduction taken by the Debtor in this case is found in clause (iii) of §707(b)(2)(A). Clause (iii) provides a deduction for the debtor's "average monthly payments on account of secured debts," and provides that the average monthly payments "*shall be* calculated as . . . the total of all *amounts* scheduled as *contractually due* to secured creditors in each month of the 60 months following the date of the filing of the petition." 11 U.S.C. §707(b)(2)(A)(iii) (emphasis supplied).

The issue is whether the Debtor can deduct the mortgage payments for the Virginia residence from her income under §707(b)(2), even though she is surrendering the property.

A. Majority Position Before Supreme Court Decisions

Prior to 2010, the "vast majority of courts to consider this issue have concluded that the plain language of the statute permits a Chapter 7 debtor to deduct payments on secured debt even when the debtor plans to surrender post-petition the collateral underlying the debt." In re Perelman, 419 B.R. 168, 173 (Bankr. E.D.N.Y. 2009) (other citations omitted). . . .

B. The Supreme Court Decisions

On June 7, 2010, the United States Supreme Court decided the case of Hamilton v. Lanning, 130 S. Ct. 2464 (2010). The decision arises under §1325(b) of the Bankruptcy Code. If an objection to a Chapter 13 plan is filed, §1325(b) requires a Chapter 13 debtor either to pay his unsecured creditors in full, or to submit all of his "projected disposable income" to the plan. 11 U.S.C. §1325(b).

In *Lanning*, a debtor had received a one-time payment from her former employer within the six-month period before she filed her Chapter 13 petition. Consequently, the one-time payment was factored into the calculation of her "current monthly income" under §101(10A), and affected the amount of her "projected disposable income" under §1325(b) of the Bankruptcy Code.

The term "projected disposable income" is not defined in the Bankruptcy Code. Under §1325(b), however, a debtor's "disposable income" is his current monthly income, less expenses that are "reasonably necessary to be expended" for maintenance and support. 11 U.S.C. §1325(b)(2). The section implicates the Means Test under §707(b) because §1325(b)(3) provides that expenses "shall be determined in accordance with subparagraphs (A) and (B) of section 707(b)(2)" if the Chapter 13 debtor's "current monthly income" exceeds the state median.

Since the debtor's current income in *Lanning* was skewed by the one-time prepetition payment, the issue for the Supreme Court was "how a bankruptcy court should calculate a debtor's 'projected disposable income'" under §1325(b). . . .

The Supreme Court concluded that "when a bankruptcy court calculates a debtor's projected disposable income, the court may account for changes in the debtor's income or expenses that are known or virtually certain at the time of confirmation." Id. at 2478. . . .

Approximately seven months after *Lanning*, on June 11, 2011, the Supreme Court decided the case of Ransom v. FIA Card Services, N.A., 131 S. Ct. 716 (2011). Whereas *Lanning* involved the income side of the "disposable income" equation, *Ransom* involved the expense side of the equation in a Chapter 13 case. As the Court explained:

> To determine how much income the debtor is capable of paying, Chapter 13 uses a statutory formula known as the "means test." §§707(b)(2) (2006 ed. and Supp. III), 1325(b)(3)(A) (2006 ed.). The means test instructs a debtor to deduct specified expenses from his current monthly income. The result is his "disposable income" — the amount he has available to reimburse creditors. §1325(b)(2).

Ransom v. FIA Card Services, 131 S. Ct. at 721. The issue was "whether a debtor who does not make loan or lease payments on his car may claim the deduction for vehicle-ownership costs." Id. at 723.

In order to advance the statute's core purpose, the Court found that a debtor's Means Test calculations should only include expenses that he actually incurs. "Because Congress intended the means test to approximate the debtor's reasonable expenditures on essential items, a debtor should be required to qualify for a deduction by actually incurring an expense in the relevant category. If a debtor will not have a particular kind of expense during his plan, an allowance to cover that cost is not 'reasonably necessary' within the meaning of the statute." Id. at 725.

In *Ransom*, therefore, the Court concluded that the debtor was not permitted to claim a car ownership cost as a deduction on his Means Test calculation, because he did not actually have a loan or lease expense. Id. at 730.

C. Means Test After The Supreme Court Decisions

Clearly, *Lanning* and *Ransom* both arise in the context of Chapter 13 cases, and both involve a determination of projected disposable income and the question of how much the debtors were required to submit to their Chapter 13 plans for payment to creditors. . . .

[The opinion notes that after *Lanning* and *Ransom* a disagreement remains among the courts as to whether the cases mandate that a Chapter 7 debtor can claim expenses that they will not actually pay post-petition.]

D. Application . . .

1. "A screening mechanism to determine whether a Chapter 7 proceeding is appropriate"

The Supreme Court recognized that the purpose of the Means Test in Chapter 13 cases differs significantly from its purpose in Chapter 7 cases. In Chapter 13 cases, the Means Test is the calculation by which above-median debtors deduct the expenses specified in §707(b)(2) from their current monthly income in order to determine "amounts reasonably necessary to be expended" for the purpose of determining their "disposable income." The goal is to determine whether the debtor is submitting all of his "projected disposable income" to his Chapter 13 plan. . . . "In Chapter 13 proceedings, the means test provides a formula to calculate a debtor's disposable income, which the debtor must devote to reimbursing creditors under a court-approved plan generally lasting from three to five years." *Ransom*, 131 S. Ct. at 721.

The purpose of the Means Test in Chapter 7 cases, on the other hand, is to determine whether the granting of relief would be an abuse of the provisions of Chapter 7. 11 U.S.C. §707(b). This purpose of the Chapter 7 Means Test is highlighted in footnote 1 of *Ransom*:

> *Chapter 13 borrows the means test from Chapter 7, where it is used as a screening mechanism to determine whether a Chapter 7 proceeding is appropriate. Individuals who file for bankruptcy relief under Chapter 7 liquidate their nonexempt assets, rather than dedicate their future income, to repay creditors.* See 11 U.S.C. §§704(a)(1), 726. If the debtor's Chapter 7 petition discloses that his disposable income as calculated by the means test exceeds a certain threshold, the petition is presumptively abusive. §707(b)(2)(A)(i).

Ransom, 131 S. Ct. at 722 n.1 (Emphasis supplied). In this passage, the Supreme Court recognizes that the Means Test functions in Chapter 7 cases "as a screening mechanism" to determine whether it is appropriate to permit a debtor to proceed in a liquidating case.

The determination should be made as of the petition date.

It is a fundamental principle of bankruptcy law that the petition date is a key date for the determination of both debtors' and creditors' rights. Under §301 of the Bankruptcy Code, the filing of a voluntary petition "constitutes an order for relief" under the chapter designated in the petition.

> The date on which the bankruptcy petition is filed and the order for relief is entered is the watershed date of a bankruptcy proceeding. As of this date, creditors' rights are fixed (as much as possible), the bankruptcy estate is created, and the value of the debtor's exemptions is determined.

In re Johnson, 165 B.R. 524, 528 (S.D. Ga. 1994). . . .

The determination of whether to permit a Chapter 7 debtor to proceed in a liquidating case should be made as of the petition date. Since the eligibility determination is made as of the petition date, and since the Chapter 7 Means Test is a "screening mechanism to determine whether a Chapter 7 proceeding is appropriate," the Court finds that the Chapter 7 Means Test should be applied as of the petition date. Accordingly, a Chapter 7 debtor's deductions from income on his Means Test calculation should also be determined as of the petition date, and a Chapter 7 debtor may deduct a mortgage payment from income even if he intends to surrender the underlying property. . . .

CONCLUSION

The UST filed a Motion to dismiss this case pursuant to § 707(b) of the Bankruptcy Code. The Motion should be denied.

In re Fredman
471 B.R. 540 (Bankr. S.D. Ill. 2012)

[Above median Chapter 7 debtors owned a home in Colorado that was subject to two mortgages. Debtors indicated on their statement of intent that they would surrender the home to the mortgagees. Nonetheless debtors listed both mortgage payments on line 42 of the B22A form, entitled "Future payments on secured claims." Inclusion of the phantom Colorado mortgage payments resulted in the debtors' determination that the presumption of abuse did not arise in their case. The bankruptcy trustee has challenged that determination by filing a motion to dismiss the case as presumptively abusive under §707(b)(2) and (3).]

GRANDY, Bankruptcy Judge. . . .

[T]he Supreme Court rejected a mechanical approach while evaluating the debtor's income in the case of Hamilton v. Lanning, 130 S. Ct. 2464 (2010). In *Lanning*, the Supreme Court determined that, in calculating a chapter 13 debtor's projected disposable income, bankruptcy courts may use a forward looking approach to "account for changes in the debtor's income or expenses that are known or virtually certain at the time of confirmation." Id. at 2478. . . .

This Court agrees with those decisions that interpret the phrase "scheduled as" to be a term of art in bankruptcy parlance that refers to a debtor placing information on the bankruptcy schedules. . . . For a debt to be "scheduled as contractually due to secured creditors in each month of the 60 months following the date of the filing of the petition," a debtor's schedules must show a secured payment arising out of a contractual relationship that is due and being paid post-petition. . . .

In addition, this Court follows that line of reasoning that adopts a realistic approach when property is slated for surrender. When considering a motion to dismiss for abuse under 11 U.S.C. §§707(b)(1) and (2), if a debtor's decision to surrender secured property is "known or virtually certain," *Lanning*, 130 S. Ct. at 2478, that information should be taken into account. . . .

[A]lthough the instant case does not involve a calculation of "projected disposable income," the tenets articulated in *Lanning* are applicable here. They lead to the conclusion that "foreseeable changes in a debtor's income or expenses" should not be ignored in favor of "rigid adherence to [a] mechanical approach" that disregards known facts. 130 S. Ct. at 2477. Here, on the petition date, the record was unequivocal that the debtors were not paying, and it was a virtual certainty that they would never again pay, the mortgages on the Colorado real estate. To allow them to deduct a fictitious monthly payment of $1,973.23 would be senseless and contrary to the intent of Congress to steer debtors who are able to fund a chapter 13 plan into that chapter. . . . .

In [*Ransom*], the Supreme Court discussed the anomaly of allowing a phantom vehicle ownership expense to above-median income chapter 13 debtors while those with incomes below the median, who must justify each expense as reasonably necessary on a case-by-case basis, cannot claim a deduction for a fictitious expense. *Ransom*, 131 S. Ct. at 725 n.5. In disallowing such "preferential treatment," the Court concluded that "[i]f a below-median-income debtor cannot take a deduction for a nonexistent expense, we doubt Congress meant to provide such an allowance to an above-median-income debtor — the very kind of debtor whose perceived abuse of the bankruptcy system inspired Congress to enact the means test." Id. In much the same way, the instant debtors' reading of §707(b)(2)(A)(iii) affords "preferential treatment" to those debtors who opted for larger mortgages initially. Allowing nonexistent mortgage payments to be deducted in the amount "contractually due" bestows a disproportionate benefit upon debtors surrendering property encumbered by larger mortgages. This is an absurd result considering that all debtors who have ceased payment on their surrendered real property, regardless of the contractual payment amount, are now paying the same amount on their mortgages — nothing. . . .

Based on the above analysis, this Court holds that to harmonize the language of §707(b)(2)(A)(iii) with the intent of the drafters, and to avoid a senseless result, the Fredmans may not deduct the $1,973.23 phantom monthly mortgage payments at line 42 of form B22A.

Post-Case Follow-Up

The majority view (at least prior to *Lanning* and *Ransom*) that a Chapter 7 debtor can deduct secured payments on Form 122A-2 notwithstanding his intent to surrender the collateral and terminate the payments is called the "snapshot" or "mechanical" approach seen in *Rivers*. The minority view that the debtor cannot deduct such payments, adopted in *Fredman*, is called the "realistic" or "forward looking" approach. The disagreement is sharp, as evidenced by the dismissive tone of the *Fredman* opinion. Do you agree with the judge in *Fredman* that the mechanical approach is "senseless" and "leads to an absurd result" in light of the purpose of the Chapter 7 means test? Is the mechanical approach too legalistic in focusing on the date the petition is filed as the exclusive date to determine the debtor's rights? Obviously, either Congress needs to clarify its intent here or the Supreme Court needs to clarify the statutory language we have. Determine if the courts of the federal district or circuit where you plan to practice have taken a position on this issue.

In re Rivers and In re Fredman: Real Life Applications

1. Assume you are preparing a Chapter 7 filing for an above median consumer debtor who owns two cars. Your federal district follows *Fredman*. Car #1 is paid off. A balance is owed on Car #2 to a creditor that holds a security interest in it. The debtor can exempt (to be discussed in Chapter Eight) and plans to keep Car #1. In completing Form 122A-2 for the debtor, can you deduct the ownership costs for Car #1 on Line 13a using the IRS local standards? The debtor is undecided about whether to try to exempt and keep Car #2 or just surrender it to the secured creditor. Should you go ahead and enter a deduction for the monthly payment for Car #2 on Line 33?

2. Answer the same questions posed in Question 1 assuming your federal district follows *Rivers*.

3. Look at Marta Carlson's Statement of Intent, which is Document 18 in her case file. What is her intent with regard to her vehicle, which is collateral for the loan from Automotive Financing, Inc.? What is her intent with regard to her residence, which is subject to a first mortgage in favor of Capital Savings Bank and a second mortgage in favor of Dreams Come True Financing? Since she is claiming the expenses associated with those secured obligations on her Form 122A-2, Line 33, does the jurisdiction appear to follow *Rivers* or *Fredman*?

We will learn in our study of a Chapter 13 bankruptcy that a debtor may propose a plan to keep secured property during the term of his plan and continue to make the monthly payments on such debt as were identified on Line 33 of Form 122A-2. But often the Chapter 13 debtor is in arrears on some or all of his secured debt so in addition to proposing in his plan to make those payments in the future he must propose a way to cure the arrearages on that secured debt as well. Most Chapter 13 plans run five years or 60 months, so the proposal to cure the arrearage may include payments made over 60 months. Line 34 of Form 122A-2 first asks the debtor to indicate whether any of the secured debts listed on Line 33 are necessary for the support of the debtor or debtor's dependents. If the answer is no that is an indication that the debtor would not seek to keep any secured property if he or she were to file a Chapter 13 case so there is no need to address arrearages in that secured debt. But if the answer is yes then Line 34 further asks about those arrearages. Specifically, Line 34 has the debtor calculate the average monthly amount needed over the 60-month term of a Chapter 13 plan (and that would presumably be proposed in such plan) to cure the arrearages in the secured property the debtor would want to keep in a Chapter 13 case.

For example, at the time she files her petition, Marta Carlson is two payments in arrears on the mortgage held by Capital Savings Bank for a total of $1,930. If she wanted to keep her home and not lose it in a Chapter 13 case she would have to not only make the future mortgage payments due, she would have to cure those arrearages as part of her Chapter 13 plan. She calculates that to cure that arrearage to Capital Savings Bank over 60 months she would need to pay $32.16 a month for that purpose. She is three payments in arrears on the mortgage held by Dreams Come True Finance Company for a total of $1,431. Over a 60-month plan she would need to pay $23.85 to cure that arrearage. She is two payments behind to AFI on her secured car debt for a total of $420 and would need to make 60 payments of $7 per month to cure that arrearage. Those are the cure amounts she lists on Line 34 even though she is filing under Chapter 7 not Chapter 13.

In the next chapter, we will learn that there are some creditors who hold claims that enjoy a priority over others in a bankruptcy case when it comes to distributing proceeds in a Chapter 7 or making payments under a Chapter 13 plan. If the debtor is in arrears on such priority claims at the time a Chapter 13 petition is filed, those priority claims must be paid in full in the debtor's plan. On Line 35 the debtor enters the monthly payments that he would propose in a Chapter 13 plan to bring those priority claims current over the term of a 60-month plan. Marta Carlson has no priority claims.

On Line 36 the debtor indicates whether he or she qualifies as a Chapter 13 debtor under §109 of the Code. If the answer is no and the presumption of abuse arises in the debtor's Chapter 7 case, the Chapter 7 case will be dismissed and no Chapter 13 case will be filed because the debtor is ineligible. If, however, the answer is yes then if the presumption of abuse arises in the debtor's Chapter 7 case, the debtor will have the alternative to convert the case to one under Chapter 13 in lieu of having his Chapter 7 case dismissed.

In a Chapter 13 case, once a proposed plan is approved, the debtor will make payments, usually monthly, to a Chapter 13 trustee who will then distribute the payments among the creditors of the debtor as called for in the plan. The trustee will receive a fee for doing so that is a percentage of the payments distributed. That fee is an administrative expense of the Chapter 13 case. We will learn more about this later when we study Chapter 13 in earnest, but, for now, on Line 36 of Form 122A-2 the Chapter 7 debtor who answer yes to whether he or she is eligible to file for Chapter 13 relief is required to state a projected monthly payment he or she would make into a Chapter 13 plan that is then multiplied by the then-current monthly administrative expense established for the debtor's federal district.

For example, Marta Carlson projects that the best she could do in funding a Chapter 13 plan would be to pay in $1,700 per month (which as we will see when we study the Chapter 13 bankruptcy would include payments on debtor's secured debt such as mortgage and car payments and would by no means all go to satisfy unsecured claims of debtor's creditors). Based on an applicable current multiplier (7.2 percent or .072 in effect in her federal district in June 2016), this results in a projected monthly administrative expense on such a plan of $122.40.

All the debt payment deductions from Lines 33-36 are totaled on Line 37. On Line 38 the debtor then totals all deductions from current monthly income that were allowed in Part 2 of the form.

Part 3 of Form 122A-2: Determination of the Presumption

On Line 39 the debtor enters the current monthly income from Line 4 of the form (the monthly income figure from Form 122A-1 as modified by the marital adjustment) and subtracts from it the total allowed deductions from Part 2 of the form to come up with a monthly disposable income figure that is entered on Line 39c. The **monthly disposable income** figure is the amount the debtor would have available to fund a Chapter 13 plan over the next five years after all projected expenses were deducted as was done in Part 2 of the form. On Line 39d we then multiply that number by 60, again because the typical Chapter 13 plan would run 60 months.

For example, subtracting Marta Carlson's total deductions from Part 2 of Form 122A-2 from her monthly income of $7,000 leaves her a monthly disposable income of only $45.59 and this is the amount she enters on Line 39c. Multiplied times 60, the amount she would have available during a five-year Chapter 13 plan is only $2,735.40 and this is the amount she enters on Line 39d. The presumption of abuse does not arise in her case even with the higher income so as instructed by

Line 40 she checks Box 1 on the top right side of the first page of her Form 122A-2, and completes the verification portion of the form in Part 5. She is done with the form.

Recall that the means test for the above median debtor is controlled by §707(b)(2)(A)(i), which provides that if the debtor has *more than* $12,850 (the current figure, to be adjusted again in 2019) in disposable income after payment of living expenses which can be applied to pay unsecured claims over the course of a 5-year plan under Chapter 13 ($214 a month) the presumption of abuse arises and that debtor may not continue in Chapter 7. That debtor will check the second box on Line 40 of the form, note in the box at the top right hand side of page 1 that the presumption of abuse does arise and can expect the U.S. Trustee to seek dismissal of the Chapter 7 case. (In the next section we will discuss the debtor's right to challenge that presumption of abuse in the face of a motion to dismiss.)

If the debtor's disposable income totaled on Line 39d is less than $7,700 (the current figure, to be adjusted again in April 2019) the presumption of abuse does not arise. That debtor will check the first box in Line 40, note in the box at the top right hand side of page 1 that the presumption does not arise, complete the verification in Part 5 of the form and can expect to proceed in Chapter 7.

However, if the debtor has *less than* $12,850 but *more than* $7,700 in disposable income, we have to ask one more question before we can conclude that the presumption does not arise: Is the debtor's total disposable income over the projected 60 months of the plan also *less than* 25 percent of the debtor's nonpriority unsecured debts. The above median debtor whose total disposable income falls in this range will check the third box on Line 40 and must complete Lines 41-42 of the form to determine if his or her disposable income is less than 25 percent of the nonpriority unsecured debts.

We mentioned earlier that some creditor claims enjoy a priority in a bankruptcy case. Unpaid taxes and past due child support are frequent examples in consumer bankruptcy cases. We will consider priority and nonpriority claims in more detail in Chapter Ten, Section B. But understand now that if the total disposable income of above median debtor completing Form 122A-2 is more than $7,700 but less than $12,850, that disposable income figure must also be compared in Line 41 to the debtor's nonpriority claims if any. If the disposable income figure is also less than 25% of such nonpriority claims, the presumption does not arise. That debtor will check the first box on Line 42 of the form, note on page 1 of the form that the presumption does not arise, complete the verification in Part 5 of the form, and can expect to proceed in Chapter 7. But if that debtor's disposable income figure exceeds 25% of his or her nonpriority claims as calculated on Line 41, the presumption of abuse will arise. That debtor must check the second box on Line 42 of the form, and note on page 1 of the form that the presumption does arise in the case. Like the debtor whose disposable income figure was in excess of $12,850, a motion to dismiss filed by the U.S. Trustee can be expected.

For example, Marta Carlson calculates having only $2,735.40 in disposable income over the projected five years of a Chapter 13 plan as noted on Line 39d of her form. Since that is less than $7,700, the presumption does not arise in her case. She has checked the first box on Line 40 of her Form 122A-2, noted on page 1 that the presumption does not arise in her case, and completed the verification in Part

5 of the form. She is ready to proceed in Chapter 7, assuming there is no challenge by the trustee to her income stated in Form 122A-1 or her deductions taken in Part 2 of Form 122A-2.

But let's assume for the moment that she had $10,000 in projected disposable income on her Line 39d. That is more than $7,700 but not more than $12,850. To complete her calculation of whether the presumption of abuse arises, she would check the third box on Line 40 and go to Line 41. First she would enter on Line 41a her total non-priority unsecured debt. That figure is available on her Form 106Sum, Summary of Your Assets and Liabilities and Certain Statistical Information Schedules (Document 15 in her case file), which will be discussed in the next chapter. The figure from Line 3b of Marta's Form 106Sum is $199,312. That is her total non-priority unsecured debt. Line 41b then has the debtor multiply that number by .25, which would produce for Marta a figure of $49,828. Since her projected disposable income of $10,000 under this hypothetical would be less than that 25 percent of her non-priority unsecured debt she still would not raise the presumption of abuse and could proceed in Chapter 7.

For the debtor for whom the presumption of abuse arises using Forms 122A-1 and 122A-2, there is one last hope to keep their Chapter 7 case alive.

4. The Right to Challenge the Presumption of Abuse by Showing Special Circumstances

The presumption of abuse is just that — a presumption. That means that if the debtor cannot satisfy the means test using Form 122A-1 for the below median debtor or Form 122A-2 for the above median debtor, the debtor may still challenge the presumption by filing a motion with the bankruptcy court and presenting proof of special circumstances sufficient to rebut the presumption of abuse. Section 707(b)(2)(B) defines **special circumstances** sufficient to rebut the presumption of abuse as those that "justify either additional expenses or adjustments of current monthly income for which there is no reasonable alternative" and gives examples such as a serious medical condition of the debtor or a dependent or a call to active duty in the military that is likely to impact future income or future expenses in a way not disclosed on either form.

Line 43 in Part 4 of Form 122A-2 is where the debtor for whom the presumption of abuse is raised may indicate the special circumstances that should result in a reconsideration of either the income debtor as reported on Form 122A-1 or expenses deducted on Form 122A-2. But note that the debtor is not allowed to adjust the results of the raising of the presumption using Form 122A-2 based on the circumstances entered on Line 43. The presumption is still raised and the debtor will have to ask the bankruptcy court pursuant to §707(b)(2)(B) to reverse the presumption of abuse based on those special circumstances so that the debtor can proceed in Chapter 7. An evidentiary hearing will be required for the court to consider the motion.

In connection with a debtor's claim of special circumstances under §707(b)(2)(B), Line 13 of debtor's Schedule I: Your Income, to be discussed in the next chapter, provides debtor the opportunity to identify changes to income the debtor is expecting in the year following the filing of the petition. Similarly, Line 24 of debtor's Schedule J: Your Expenses provides debtor the opportunity to identify changes to expenses the debtor is expecting in the next year. Certainly, any debtor planning to rely on the §707(B)(2)(B) special circumstances exception to the presumption of abuse should reference the circumstances in those schedules. In fact, the U.S. Trustee or any other party in interest examining the consumer debtor's Forms 122A-1 and 122A-2 will compare the income and expense information set out on those forms with the same or similar information provided on that debtor's Schedules I and J. The one assisting the debtor in preparing those various forms and schedules must be sure they are consistent.

Application Exercise 3

The BAPCPA changes are still new enough that we do not know what other circumstances may or may not satisfy the special circumstances test of §707(b)(2)(B). For example, if the debtor shows she is facing the possibility of a layoff that will dramatically reduce the income reported on Form 122A-1, will that suffice or would the court expect the debtor to file a Chapter 13 and then convert the case to a Chapter 7 if the layoff actually occurred and no substitute employment could be found? Or if the debtor is in the process of adopting a child that will result in a dramatic increase in expenses not reported on Form 122A-2?

Determine whether the courts of the federal district or circuit where you plan to practice have decided any special circumstances cases and, if so, how they have interpreted that exception including the grounds constituting special circumstances and what Congress meant by the "no reasonable alternative" criteria.

---

5. Claiming Exemption from the Presumption of Abuse: Official Form 122A-1Supp

The individual debtor who does not have primarily consumer debts does not have to satisfy the means test. However, beginning in December 2014, individual debtors claiming exemption from the means test for that reason are required to file Official Form 122A-1Supp stating affirmatively that their debts are not primarily consumer debts. And they have to file Form 122A-1 as well, though they do not have to complete either Part 1 or 2 of that form. They merely have to check Box 1 "There is no presumption of abuse" on the top of page 1 of Form 122A-1 and sign Part 3.

Certain individuals must also now claim the exemption by filing Form 122A-1Supp and Form 122A-1 with Box 1 on page 1 checked and Part 3 signed: veterans suffering from a 30 percent or higher permanent disability, reservists, and certain members of the National Guard claiming the exemption from the means test provided by the National Guard Reservists Debt Relief Act of 2008 if their indebtedness arose primarily during active duty or while performing a homeland defense activity.

6. The U.S. Trustees Duty to Report on the Presumption of Abuse and the Right to Challenge the Debtor's Conclusion that the Presumption of Abuse Does Not Arise

Code §704(b)(1)(A) requires the U.S. Trustee, in all Chapter 7 cases involving individual debtors, to file a statement with the court within 10 days following the first meeting of creditors advising as to whether the presumption of abuse arises under §707(b). The UST's statement is sent to creditors by the clerk of the court within seven days thereafter per §704(b)(1)(B).

Within 30 days of filing the notice with the court the UST must file a motion to dismiss (or convert to Chapter 13 with the debtor's consent) based on the presumption of abuse or explain to the court why it does not consider such motion appropriate. If the UST's motion to dismiss is not filed within the 30-day window, it is thereafter barred.

Even if a debtor concludes that the presumption of abuse does not arise in the case using Form 122A-1 or Form 122A-2, that conclusion is not binding on the court. The bankruptcy trustee, the U.S. Trustee, any party in interest (e.g., a creditor), or the bankruptcy court acting *sua sponte* may challenge the debtor's numbers and seek dismissal of the case under §707(b)(1). The same challenge can be made to an individual's claim to be exempt from the means test on Form 122A-1 Supp.

If the bankruptcy court finds that the presumption of abuse arises in a Chapter 7 case filed by an individual debtor, the case will be dismissed under §707(b)(1). Alternatively, that section allows the case to be converted to a Chapter 13 case with the debtor's consent.

7. The Right to Seek Dismissal of a Chapter 7 Case for Abuse Arising from Bad Faith Filing or Evident from the Totality of the Circumstances of the Debtor's Financial Situation

As mentioned earlier in the chapter, even a debtor in whose case the presumption of abuse does not arise using the 122A forms may face a motion to dismiss under §707(b)(3) for a filing found to be abusive because it was filed in bad faith or where the "totality of the circumstances of the debtor's financial situation" demonstrates abuse. These two bases to dismiss a Chapter 7 case are distinct from the means test and presumption of abuse that have concerned us in this chapter, so we will postpone a detailed consideration of them until Chapter Eleven, Section C. But certainly in the situation posited earlier where a debtor satisfies the means test by reason of an anomaly arising from the look back period utilized by Form 122A-1 (e.g., if Marta Carlson were to file on June 6 using her lower income during the look back period to meet the means test when in fact she will enjoy a substantially higher income from new employment found in early June), both abuse from bad faith filing or from totality of the debtor's financial circumstances might be asserted by a UST seeking dismissal of the Chapter 7.

8. Final Thoughts on the BAPCPA Means Test

A primary purpose of BAPCPA was to push more debtors away from Chapter 7 liquidation and toward Chapter 13 repayment plans. Its primary tool to accomplish that goal was the presumption of abuse. Has it worked? Studies to date suggest no. One study suggested that no more than 1 percent of Chapter 7 debtors failed the means test and triggered the BAPCPA presumption of abuse. See Clifford J. White III, Making Bankruptcy Reform Work: A Progress Report in Year 2, 26 Am. Bankr. Inst. J. 16 (June 2007), reporting that only 7.9 percent of Chapter 7 debtors who have above median incomes triggered Step 2 of the test, and of those, only 9.5 percent triggered the presumption of abuse. An empirical study reported in Robert M. Lawless, Angela K. Littwin, Katherine M. Porter, John A.E. Pottow, Deborah K. Thorne & Elizabeth Warren, Did Bankruptcy Reform Fail? An Empirical Study of Consumer Debtors, 82 Am. Bankr. L.J. 349, 361 (2008) demonstrates that between 2001 (pre-BAPCPA) and 2007 (post-BAPCPA) the inflation-adjusted median income of Chapter 7 and Chapter 13 filers did not change. These studies are consistent with reports of many practitioners who say that not only do the vast majority of above-median debtors using Step 2 of the test not trigger the presumption, the few that do are clients they would have steered toward a Chapter 13 filing even without the BAPCPA changes.

If the means test of BAPCPA has not accomplished its purpose of curing abuse by directing more debtors into Chapter 13, it has certainly increased the complications and expense of filing Chapter 7 cases for debtors and of administration of those cases by the courts. See the 2008 Report of the U.S. Government Accountability Office on Dollar Costs Associated with BAPCPA at www.gao.gov/new.items/d08697.pdf, reporting an increase in the average cost to a debtor for filing Chapter 7 from $921 to $1,477 attributable to BAPCPA.

The 2011 Consumer Bankruptcy Fee Study Final Report funded by the American Bankruptcy Institute and the National Conference of Bankruptcy Judges (available online at https://bapcpastudy.wordpress.com/2011/12/09/the-consumer-bankruptcy-fee-study-final-report/) concluded that BAPCPA has made the bankruptcy system more time-consuming and costlier for debtors. That study found a significant increase in post-BAPCPA total direct access costs (TDAC) for consumers in both Chapter 7 and Chapter 13 cases.

While the 2011 report found the difference in actual returns to unsecured creditors in consumer cases before and after BAPCPA to be "statistically insignificant," the 2013 Consumer Bankruptcy Creditor Distribution Study sponsored by those same organizations (available online at http://abi-org.s3.amazonaws.com/Endowment/ Research_Grants/Creditor_Distributions_ABI_Final.pdf) determined that under BAPCPA unsecured creditors are actually receiving less than they did under the pre-BAPCPA regime ("BAPCPA does not appear to have achieved the primary objective of its proponents as unsecured distributions as a percentage of unsecured claims declined nationally by a statistically significant 3.2 percentage points in the post-BAPCPA time period. Moreover, unsecured distributions as a percentage of total distributions declined by 2.5 percentage points, a result that was also statistically significant.").

D. THE PREPETITION CREDIT COUNSELING REQUIREMENT FOR ALL INDIVIDUAL DEBTORS

Section 109(h)(1) of the Code, also added by BAPCPA, provides that no individual (either individual consumer or individual business debtors, but not entities) may be a debtor under any chapter of the Code unless, within 180 days before filing the petition, the individual receives "an individual or group briefing" (which can be by phone or Internet) from "an approved nonprofit budget and credit counseling agency" that outlines "the opportunities for available credit counseling" and assists the individual "in performing a related budget analysis." The court may grant an exemption to the prepetition credit counseling requirement based on the debtor's sworn statement that he needed emergency relief and did not have time to complete it prepetition, but the exemption expires 30 days *after* the petition is filed, and so the counseling must be completed by that time. The briefing is not required if the court determines that the debtor is incapacitated (mentally), disabled (physically), active military in a combat zone, or where the U.S. Trustee determines that there are insufficient approved agencies to provide the required counseling. Debtors themselves must pay any costs associated with this required counseling but the cost is not prohibitive and the counseling can often be accomplished by phone or Internet.

Fortunately, not just any credit counseling agency (**CCA**) can provide these required services (see the discussion of CCAs and the current problems with some of them in Chapter Four, Section D). CCAs desiring to provide these services to debtors sufficient to satisfy the §109(h)(1) requirement must be *non-profit* and certified by the U.S. Trustee, and to become and remain certified they must successfully complete in-depth preliminary and subsequent examinations by the office of the U.S. Trustee. The current list of CCAs certified by the U.S. Trustee to provide these services can be seen at www.usdoj.gov/ust/eo/bapcpa/ccde/cc_approved. htm. The bankruptcy court clerks are also required by §111 of the Code to maintain a list of approved CCAs.

The individual debtor's compliance with the prepetition credit counseling requirement is addressed on Line 15 of the voluntary petition. (See Document 2 in the Carlson case file.)

Chapter Summary

- Chapter 7 is a liquidation proceeding in which a bankruptcy trustee appointed by the court locates and takes possession of the non-exempt assets of the debtor, liquidates those assets, and distributes the proceeds to creditors of the estate per a distribution formula established by the Code. In Chapter 7 most debts left unpaid by an individual debtor are permanently discharged and the debtor receives a fresh start. The vast majority of bankruptcy cases filed each year are Chapter 7 cases, and the very great majority of those are consumer bankruptcy cases.

- An individual debtor may not proceed in Chapter 7 if he received a discharge in a Chapter 7 or Chapter 11 case within eight years preceding the filing of the petition or in a Chapter 13 or Chapter 12 case within six years of filing the petition.

- Individual consumer debtors must also satisfy the means test introduced by BAP-CPA in 2005 in order to proceed in Chapter 7. Utilizing Official Form 122A-1, the means test compares the debtor's annualized monthly income to the median family income for a similar size household in the debtor's state of residence. If the debtor's income is equal to or less than the applicable median income, no presumption of abuse arises in the case and he may proceed in Chapter 7. The size of a debtor's household for purposes of 122A-1 is determined in different ways with some courts using a heads on beds approach, others a dependency on the debtor approach, and others an IRS dependent approach.

- If the debtor's income exceeds the applicable median income the debtor must complete Official Form 122A-2, which is a detailed itemization of expenses to determine if he has sufficient projected disposable income over the next 60 months to fund a Chapter 13 plan of reorganization. Some of the expenses listed on Form 122A-2 are the debtor's actual expenses but others are standardized expenses based on national or local figures published by the IRS. If the above median income debtor does not have sufficient projected disposable income to fund a Chapter 13 plan, the presumption of abuse still does not arise and he may proceed in Chapter 7. If, however, the debtor's income exceeds the applicable median income and the debtor does have sufficient projected income to fund a Chapter 13 plan of reorganization, the presumption of abuse arises and the case must be either converted to a Chapter 13 or dismissed, unless the debtor can show special circumstances justifying the case continuing in Chapter 7.

- The individual debtor's determination that the presumption of abuse does not arise in his case can be challenged by the bankruptcy trustee or the court *sua sponte*. Alternatively, even where the presumption of abuse does not arise, the trustee can seek dismissal of the Chapter 7 case where abuse is shown by a petition filed in bad faith or is evident from the totality of the circumstances of the debtor's financial situation.

- Within ten days following the first meeting of creditors the U.S. Trustee must file a statement with the court regarding whether the presumption of abuse arises and must file any motion to dismiss on that basis within 30 days of filing that statement. Where the presumption of abuse arises and is not rebutted the Chapter 7 case will be dismissed or, on request of the debtor, be converted to Chapter 13.

Applying the Concepts

1. You have been retained by Denzel and Tashika Martin, a married couple you think may be candidates for a Chapter 7 bankruptcy due to enormous debts they have accrued due to unexpected health bills compounded by irresponsible credit card spending. Tashika works as the receptionist in a dentist's office and makes $28,000 a year. She receives $1,200 per month in child support from the father of her three-year-old child. Tashika also operates a web-based business as a sole proprietor selling hand-made Christmas ornaments. Last year her business took in $12,000 and on the tax return for that year she reported taxable profits of $8,400 against expenses of $3,600. Denzel works as manager of a local fast food restaurant and makes $50,000 a year. He also receives $300 per month as a beneficiary of a family trust. Assuming Denzel and Tashika plan to file a joint petition in Chapter 7, prepare a Form 122A-1 for them and determine if they satisfy the means test as below median debtors assuming that they reside in the state where you plan to practice.

2. Assume Denzel and Tashika want to include the following persons in their household on Line 13 of Form 122A-1 for purposes of calculating the median family income from the Census Bureau's tables as part of the means test. The jurisdiction follows In re Herbert, 405 B.R. 165 (Bankr. W.D.N.C. 2008). Which of the following can be included in their household on Line 13?

   a. Tashika's three-year-old child, who lives with them
   b. Denzel's 85-year-old father, who lives in a nearby nursing home
   c. Denzel's 20-year-old son and his wife, who live in the basement of Denzel and Tashika's house and pay monthly rent
   d. Tashika's 25-year-old sister, who has been staying with them for six months since she separated from her husband and who is still looking for her own place to live

3. Assume Marta Carlson's ex-husband had been paying her $2,000 per month in child support for the six months preceding her filing. Assume also that she was making $84,000 per year at TTI. Would the presumption of abuse arise in her case using Form 122A-2? What if her jurisdiction disallowed the deduction from income of her mortgage payments on the house and her car payments on the YR-04 Toyota Camry on Line 33 of her Form 122A-2 since she plans to

surrender the house and car to the creditors secured in those assets (see *Fredman*, supra)? Would the presumption of abuse then arise in her case, requiring her to file under Chapter 13 or not at all? You may want to consult Marta Carlson's Alternative Form 122A-1 and her Form 122A-2 (assuming the higher income) set out in Exhibits 5.2 and 5.3.

6

The Chapter 7 Consumer Bankruptcy Case: The Petition, Supporting Schedules, and Statements

In this chapter we consider the bankruptcy petition that initiates a bankruptcy case and sets in motion all the unique procedural mechanisms of the Code. We will also examine in detail the numerous schedules and statements that must be filed with the petition. Throughout we will stress the responsibility of the attorney for the debtor to ensure that the information provided to the court on the petition and supporting schedules and statements is complete and accurate.

A. THE PETITION COMMENCING THE CASE

1. The Voluntary Petition

A bankruptcy case under any chapter is commenced by the filing of the bankruptcy **petition** per §301(a) of the Code and Federal Rules of Bankruptcy Procedure (FRBP) 1002. The voluntary petition for individual debtors is Official Form 101. Per §301(b), the filing of the petition constitutes an **order for relief** under the Code, a term used often in the Code as we will see.

Key Concepts

- A bankruptcy case begins with the filing of a petition in bankruptcy
- The petition is accompanied by a number of schedules, statements, and lists that require the attorney for the debtor to obtain substantial financial and other information from the debtor
- By signing the petition for a debtor client, the attorney certifies to the court that after reasonable inquiry he has no knowledge that any information on the petition, schedules, and statements is incorrect
- Attorneys for debtors in bankruptcy are considered Debt Relief Agencies and must comply with the Code's requirements for DRAs concerning advertising and mandatory disclosures to clients

---

Application Exercise 1

Go to www.uscourts.gov/forms/bankruptcy-forms and view the voluntary bankruptcy petition for individuals, Official Form 101. Scroll down through the voluntary petition form and note the kinds of information that have to be provided there. Just some of the information to be provided includes:

- Not just the debtor's full name, but all other names used in the preceding eight years
- The address where the debtor's principal assets are located
- The type of debtor (individual, corporation, partnership, etc.)
- The chapter of the Code the filing is under (7, 11, 13, etc.)
- The nature of the debts (primarily consumer or business)
- How the filing fee will be paid
- Estimates regarding number of creditors and dollar amount of assets and debts
- Whether a prior case has been filed within eight years
- Whether any other case is pending

At this point, you should understand the reasons why much of the information on the petition is sought. For example, you should see immediately why questions are asked about the type of debtor, which chapter of the Code the case is filed under, the nature of the debts as consumer or business, and prior cases within eight years. As we continue you will come to realize the reasons for the other questions on the petition.

2. The Joint Petition, Consolidation, and Joint Administration

A married couple may file a **joint petition** (see §302 of the Code), in which case they will identify themselves as debtor and joint debtor (with the Supreme Court having stricken down the Defense of Marriage Act in United States v. Windsor, 133 S. Ct. 2675 (2013), this should now include same-sex couples legally married under the laws of a state recognizing same-sex marriage). When a married couple files a joint petition, only one set of schedules is required. Other closely related debtors cannot file a joint petition, but the court may order the joint administration of related cases, pursuant to FRBP 1015(b). **Joint administration** is where two or more related bankruptcy cases are ordered to be administered by the same trustee to save administrative costs. And if two or more petitions are pending in the same court involving the same debtor, the court may order those cases **consolidated** pursuant to FRBP 1015(a).

For example, assume a brother and sister are partners in a business. They both decide to file for bankruptcy relief. Even though the two debtors are closely related and share the same income sources and debts they cannot file a joint petition.

However, once both of them have filed individual petitions, the court may order the joint administration of their cases. If the business partnership files a separate petition, its case may be ordered jointly administered with those of the two partners. If a corporation is in bankruptcy and one of its subsidiaries files a separate petition in the same court, the court might order joint administration if the assets and obligations of the two corporations are intertwined and creditors will not be prejudiced. If a debtor files a voluntary petition and his creditors then file an involuntary petition (discussed below) against him in the same court, the court might consolidate the two cases into one.

Marta Carlson is a divorced, single woman. Her individual voluntary petition for Chapter 7 relief is shown in Document 2 in the Carlson case file.

3. Proper Venue for Filing the Petition

Lines 5 and 6 of Part 1 of the voluntary petition form deal with venue. In a bankruptcy case, **venue** has to do with which bankruptcy court the case should be filed in or, more specifically, which federal district the case should be filed in. The general venue rule in bankruptcy cases is that the petition should be filed in the bankruptcy court in the district where the debtor has resided or had its principal place of business for the 180 days preceding filing (see 28 U.S.C. §1408). If the debtor has resided or had his primary place of business in more than one district during that time frame, then venue is proper in whichever district the debtor has had such contacts for the longer part of the past 180 days.

Notwithstanding proper venue, pursuant to 28 U.S.C. §1412, a court can transfer an entire case or any particular proceeding within a case (e.g., the trial of a preference action) to another federal district "in the interest of justice and for the convenience of the parties." Factors considered by the courts on a motion to transfer venue focus on the economic and efficient administration of the case including the location of the debtor and creditors, the location of assets of the estate, and the likely impact of the transfer decision on administrative expenses. Where change of venue is sought for only a particular proceeding in a case, most courts recognize a "strong presumption" in favor of maintaining venue where the bankruptcy case is pending. See, e.g., In re Onco Invest. Co., 320 B.R. 577 (Bankr. D. Del. 2005), but compare Brown v. C.D. Smith Drug Co., 1999 WL 709992 (D. Del. 1999).

Motions for change of venue are uncommon in consumer bankruptcy cases.

4. Signatures on the Petition

The Debtor's Signature

Pursuant to FRBP 1008, the debtor(s) must sign the voluntary petition **under oath** (see Part 7 at the bottom of page 6 of the voluntary petition), which means the debtor is subject to penalties of **perjury** for a deliberate misstatement or omission on the petition and supporting schedules. If the debtor is filing the petition without the assistance of an attorney (**pro se**), the debtor must also answer the questions asked on page 8 in Part 7 of the form and sign there as well. The questions on page 8 of the form are not answered by the pro se debtor under oath but are sobering nonetheless in their import since they alert the debtor to the complexity of the bankruptcy process and the dangers of proceeding pro se (the reference in this section of the form to the debtor having received non-attorney assistance is discussed below).

The Signature and Certification of the Attorney for the Debtor

The attorney for the debtor will sign the voluntary petition as well (see Part 7 at the top of page 7 of the voluntary petition). Pursuant to FRBP 9011, the attorney's signature on the petition or any other document filed with the court constitutes a certification to the court that "to the best of the attorney's knowledge, information and belief formed after an inquiry reasonable under the circumstances,"

- The filing is not done for any improper purpose (e.g., to harass or delay),
- The factual allegations or denial of an opponent's factual contentions have or likely will have evidentiary support,
- And all legal contentions are warranted by existing law or a nonfrivolous argument for what the law should be.

BAPCPA, however, added a new dimension to the attorney's signature on the petition. New §707(b)(4)(D) of the Code provides as follows:

> The signature of an attorney on the petition shall constitute a certification that the attorney has no knowledge after an inquiry that the information in the schedules filed with such petition is incorrect.

Note that this certification by the attorney extends not just to the information on the petition itself but to information contained on the debtor's many schedules filed with the petition. What exactly is the "inquiry" required of debtor's attorneys regarding the information his client provides to him? Is the attorney being asked to guarantee the accuracy of his client's information? Is the attorney responsible if the client misstates or falsifies information that appears in the petition and schedules? Can an attorney not simply rely on the veracity and accuracy of the information his client gives him? What exactly are the penalties to be imposed on the debtor's attorney if he is deemed by the court to have breached the certification? Neither the Code nor the Bankruptcy Rules answer these questions and case law is still threshing it out. One oft-cited decision construed the new inquiry requirement to mean that the attorney's inquiry need only be "a reasonable one" to "be tested objectively" and stressed that the debtor's attorney "is not a guarantor of the accuracy of any information contained in bankruptcy documents prepared . . . with information provided by that debtor." See In re Withrow, 391 B.R. 217, 227 (Bankr. D. Mass. 2008).

Accordingly, it seems to this Court that the answers to at least the following questions are germane to a Rule 9011 and §707(b)(4)(C) analysis: (1) did the attorney impress upon the debtor the critical importance of accuracy in the preparation of documents to be presented to the Court; (2) did the attorney seek from the debtor, and then review, whatever documents were within the debtor's possession, custody or control in order to verify the information provided by the debtor; (3) did the attorney employ such external verification tools as were available and not time or cost prohibitive (e.g., on-line real estate title compilations, on-line lien search, tax "scripts"); (4) was any of the information provided by the debtor and then set forth in the debtor's court filings internally inconsistent — that is, was there anything which should have obviously alerted the attorney that the information provided by the debtor could not be accurate; and (5) did the attorney act promptly to correct any information presented to the Court which turned out, notwithstanding the attorney's best efforts, to be inaccurate. These questions can be further simplified and reduced to one question, their common denominator: Did the attorney do his or her level best to get it right?

In re Withrow, 391 B.R. at 228.

Case Preview

In re Dean

Notwithstanding the attempts of the court to describe and quantify the inquiry duty imposed on the debtor's attorney by FRBP 9011 and new §707(b)(4)(D), these cases are still very fact sensitive. As you read In re Dean consider the following questions:

1. What exactly was the conduct of the attorney alleged to have violated the inquiry duty? What were his arguments that he had not violated that duty?
2. What party in the case made the allegation against the attorney and what motion was before the court involving the allegation?
3. What test does the court use to determine the scope of the duty for inquiry and whether the attorney breached it?
4. What sanctions were imposed on the attorney for the breach of that duty?

In re Dean

401 B.R. 917 (Bankr. D. Idaho 2008)

[Debtors Michael and Peni Dean ("Debtors") sought relief under Chapter 7 by filing a voluntary petition on February 11, 2008. Beeman, Debtors' attorney, had practiced bankruptcy law for 25 years. In December 2007, Debtors retained Beeman to analyze their financial situation. One of the Debtors' principal assets was a motorhome that Debtors purchased from Peni's mother, Diane Gladman ("Gladman"). Debtors acknowledged that Gladman had been given a security interest in the motorhome, but they were unable to produce any documents that evidenced a security interest.

Beeman became concerned about a potential conflict of interest if, in representing Debtors, he also helped one of their creditors perfect a lien. Beeman advised Debtors to seek independent counsel to assist them in perfecting Gladman's lien on the motorhome before any bankruptcy petition was filed. The Debtors did not retain another attorney and unsuccessfully attempted to perfect Gladman's lien on their own home.

The Debtors then contacted Beeman about filing the bankruptcy petition, and told him the lien on the motorhome was perfected. Based on the assurances that the motorhome lien was no longer an issue, Beeman filed Debtors' bankruptcy petition on February 11, 2008. In the bankruptcy schedules prepared by Beeman, the motorhome was listed as an asset in Debtors' Schedule B, and Gladman was listed as a secured creditor in Schedule D. Beeman did not conduct an investigation to verify that Gladman was properly listed as a lienholder on the title to the motorhome. On February 23, 2008, the Trustee sent an e-mail to Beeman indicating that there were no liens on the motorhome. On March 7, 2008, Debtors took the steps required to perfect Gladman's lien. On March 14, 2008, the Trustee initiated an adversary proceeding against Debtors and Gladman to recover the possession of the motorhome. Eventually, Gladman agreed to release her lien on the motorhome, and Debtors turned the vehicle over to Trustee; it was later sold at auction for $8,000.]

PAPPAS, Bankruptcy Judge. . . .

Though Debtors ultimately received a discharge of their debts, in his §329(b) motion, Trustee argues that Debtors did not receive adequate representation from Beeman, or as he put it at the hearing, "they got short changed" for the fees they paid Beeman. . . . Trustee therefore asks the Court to order Beeman to disgorge the fees Debtors paid to him.

It seems clear that, at the time Beeman filed Debtors' bankruptcy petition, that based upon Beeman's advice, Debtors anticipated they would be able to retain the motorhome and that Gladman's claim was secured. As noted above, it was important that this occur. Debtors used the motorhome as Michael Dean's residence while at his job site in Nevada. Moreover, because she was Peni Dean's mother, Debtors were especially concerned that Gladman could be repaid in preference to their unsecured creditors. Unfortunately, as things turned out, Debtors' intentions were frustrated by their bankruptcy filing. In the end, Gladman's lien was unenforceable in bankruptcy, and Debtors were compelled to surrender the motorhome to Trustee.

Trustee argues that, had Beeman been more vigilant in his role as their attorney prior to filing Debtors' petition, they would not have lost this important asset. To partially assuage this bad result, Trustee requests that Beeman be ordered to disgorge some of the fees Debtors paid to him. . . .

Section 329(b) allows the Court to examine the reasonableness of the fees paid by a debtor to an attorney in connection with a bankruptcy case. Hale v. U.S. Trustee, 509 F.3d 1139, 1147 (9th Cir. 2007). If the Court determines that an attorney's compensation is excessive, it may reduce or deny compensation, and order any excess returned. *Id.* . . .

[O]ne of the important purposes of §329 is to ensure that attorneys provide competent representation to debtors. *See* In re Grant, 14 B.R. 567, 569 (Bankr. S.D.N.Y.

1981) (explaining that "[i]n reviewing an attorney's fee to determine whether it is reasonable under the circumstances the Court must consider the nature of the services and the competence of the performance."). If a bankruptcy court finds that an attorney fails to competently perform his or her duties, an order requiring the attorney to disgorge fees pursuant to §329(b) is proper. *See* In re Wilson, 11 B.R. 986, 991 (Bankr. S.D.N.Y. 1981) (finding that an attorney's representation of the debtor was neither competently performed or zealously provided, it ordered that all fees paid to the attorney be remitted to the debtor). In other words, in considering the "value" of the services provided to a debtor by an attorney, the Court must consider the quality, not just the quantity, of those services . . .

The Court concludes that, because he did not make an adequate inquiry into the status of the Gladman lien prior to filing Debtors' bankruptcy case, Beeman did not competently represent them.

If Gladman's loan balance was properly secured by an unavoidable lien on the motorhome, Trustee would have had no motivation to seize and sell it in Debtors' bankruptcy case. At the hearing, Beeman explained, quite adamantly, that he felt he could not properly assist Debtors in their efforts to protect Gladman or to help perfect her purported lien on the motorhome because of what he perceived to be a conflict of interest. Rather than abandon Debtors to their own devices, or advise them they should not seek bankruptcy relief, Beeman referred them to someone he felt could competently assist them in perfecting Gladman's security interest. Beeman should not be faulted, nor should his fees be jeopardized, for deferring to appropriate ethical concerns.

That said, however, Beeman's performance was lacking in this case when Debtors returned and told him the Gladman problem had been resolved. Prior to placing the motorhome within the grasp of a diligent bankruptcy trustee, Beeman should have exercised more care and initiative in determining that the Gladman lien had now been perfected, and that Debtors would not be prejudiced by a bankruptcy filing.

Amendments to the Code occasioned by passage of the Bankruptcy Abuse Prevention and Consumer Protection Act of 2005 ("BAPCPA") significantly augmented an attorney's duties concerning the accuracy of information included in bankruptcy filings. For example, new §707(b)(4)(D) provides that:

> The signature of an attorney on the petition shall constitute a certification that the attorney has no knowledge *after an inquiry* that the information in the schedules filed with the petition is incorrect.

11 U.S.C. §707(b)(4)(D) (emphasis added). Only a handful of bankruptcy courts have examined this provision since it became effective. One explained that the language of this provision and the history surrounding Rule 9011 suggests that the "inquiry" referred to in the statute "need only be a 'reasonable' one." In re Withrow, 391 B.R. 217, 227 (Bankr. D. Mass. 2008). That decision cautioned courts to exercise care in not imposing burdens on debtors' counsel which are impractical to satisfy under the real-life circumstances implicated in bankruptcy cases. *Id.* However, commenting upon the debtor's attorneys' new heightened duty of verification, another court explained:

[the] general drift [of BAPCPA's amendments] is clear: debtors' counsel are to exercise significant care as to the completeness and accuracy of all recitations on their clients' schedules, after they have made a factual investigation and legal evaluation that conforms to the standards applicable to any attorney filing a pleading, motion, or other document in a federal court.

In re Robertson, 370 B.R. 804, 809 n. 8 (Bankr. D. Minn. 2007).

In his affidavit, Beeman explained that he assumed the Gladman lien was enforceable in bankruptcy because Peni Dean told him so and because Debtors later initialed the schedules indicating that they were accurate. . . . He argues this assumption was reasonable because he had previously referred Debtors to another attorney and he had no reason to believe that the lawyer had not assisted them in perfecting the lien. . . . The Court disagrees that Beeman's inquiry was adequate under these circumstances.

Several of the questions framed by the Court in *In re Withrow* for determining whether a debtor's attorney had satisfied his statutory duties are helpful in analyzing Beeman's position here:

(1) did the attorney impress upon the debtor the critical importance of accuracy in the preparation of documents to be presented to the Court; (2) did the attorney seek from the debtor, and then review, whatever documents were within the debtor's possession, custody or control in order to verify the information provided by the debtor; (3) did the attorney employ such external verification tools as were available and not time or cost prohibitive (e.g., on-line real estate title compilations, on-line lien search, tax "scripts") . . . .

In re Withrow, 391 B.R. at 228.

Although Beeman's practice of asking his clients to initial each page of the petition and schedules to verify their accuracy arguably allows him to answer the first question posed above in the affirmative, the facts show Beeman's performance fell short under the latter two standards. Beeman recognized there was a problem with the Gladman lien to the extent that he advised Debtors to seek other counsel to address the issue. But he concedes that, when they returned to him, he never obtained or reviewed Debtors' contract with Gladman, or documents evidencing the notation of the lien on the certificate title to the motorhome. He also never accessed the Idaho Transportation Department's website to review the title information on the motorhome. Moreover, Beeman never attempted to contact the other attorney, although a simple phone call could have alerted him to the fact that Debtors had decided to forgo the other attorney's help and to adopt a "do-it-yourself" approach to resolving the lien issues. Simply put, having previously identified that a problem may exist with the Gladman lien, Beeman could not reasonably rely upon his clients' statements that it was resolved to satisfy his responsibility to present accurate schedules and to protect Debtors' interests in the bankruptcy case. Following up on the validity of the Gladman lien was not an impractical burden that could not be easily accomplished by Beeman under these circumstances.

Apart from any special duty imposed upon him by the Code as Debtors' lawyer in a bankruptcy case, all attorneys appearing in bankruptcy cases in this District must adhere to the standards of professional responsibility applicable to all licensed

Idaho lawyers. *See* LBR 9010.1(g) (providing that "[t]he members of the bar of this court shall adhere to the Rules of Professional Conduct promulgated and adopted by the Supreme Court of the State of Idaho. These provisions, however, shall not be interpreted to be exhaustive of the standards of professional conduct and responsibility."). In Idaho, lawyers have a duty to zealously represent their clients' interests and to provide competent representation. *See* IDAHO RULES OF PROF'L CONDUCT R. 1.1 (2003). . . .

In this case, as an experienced bankruptcy lawyer and former chapter 7 trustee, Beeman appreciated that any lien on Debtors' motorhome would be carefully scrutinized by Trustee. Moreover, even apart from the fact that the purported secured creditor in this case was Debtors' close relative, in an earlier hearing in this case, Michael Dean testified that he was unable to locate an apartment or other living arrangements in Elko, Nevada, where he was working. He further testified that the motorhome was going to be his permanent residence in Nevada. Given Beeman's familiarity with the potential for avoidance of liens in bankruptcy cases, and the importance of this asset to Debtors, the Idaho Rules of Professional Conduct required that Beeman make an effective investigation of the validity of Gladman's lien in order to protect Debtors' continued possession and ownership of the motorhome. Beeman's "assumption" that the lien had been properly perfected, based solely upon his clients' statements to him, was inadequate. . . .

Conclusion . . .

Under these circumstances, the Court concludes that the fee Beeman collected from Debtors exceeds the reasonable value of his services, and a reduction pursuant to §329(b) is warranted. A separate order will be entered requiring Beeman to disgorge one-half, or $937.50, of the fee he received from Debtors. Under §329(b), the Court may order the disgorged fees returned to the bankruptcy estate "or" to "the entity that made such payment." Exercising the discretion granted by this statute, the Court in this case determines it appropriate that the fees be refunded to Debtors, since it was their rights, not the bankruptcy estate's, that were most prejudiced by Beeman's lack of diligence.

Post-Case Follow-Up

Note that the actions of the attorney in this case were found to constitute an ethical violation as well as a failure to comply with the requirements of §707(b)(4)(D). The only sanction imposed by the court on the attorney was disgorgement of one-half the fee he had received from his clients. In many states a finding by a court of an ethical violation by the attorney is routinely reported to the state authority responsible for enforcing attorney ethical standards and sanctioning attorneys for violation. What, if any, sanction should be imposed on this lawyer for the ethical violation found? A private letter or reprimand? A public reprimand? License suspension? What does the opinion suggest in that regard? Does this case stand for the proposition that the debtor's attorney cannot assume his client is telling the truth or that all information provided by the client must be independently verified by the attorney? This attorney had 25 years of experience in bankruptcy practice including experience as a Chapter 7 trustee himself. Does that explain this result? Would an attorney with less experience have been held to the same duty of inquiry?

In re Dean: Real Life Applications

1. *Dean* was one of the very first cases construing the duty of inquiry imposed by the new §707(b)(4)(D). Determine if the courts of your federal district or circuit have decided cases involving that section. If so, would they likely have made the same finding as the judge in *Dean*?

2. Assume you represent a Chapter 7 debtor who provides you with the following information unsupported by any records or other documentary evidence. For which of the following would you deem it reasonable and appropriate to make further inquiry ("external verification") and for those what further inquiry would you make?

   a. Her name is Sheila Marie Jones and she is 47 years of age.

   b. She has lived in her current residence for seven years and six months.

   c. She bought the home she lives in seven years and six months ago, borrowed $250,000 from Bank for the purchase, and still owes Bank $175,000.

   d. Bank has the sole mortgage on the home.

   e. She owns one vehicle and there is no lien on it. The vehicle is worth $5,000.

   f. She was divorced from David Jones 13 months ago and he quitclaimed his interest in the home to her at that time.

   g. She is employed by Baker Industries as an administrative assistant and makes $33,000 per year.

   h. All of the furnishings in her home are paid for and worth a total of $12,000.

The Signature of a Debt Relief Agency (DRA) Providing Assistance in a Consumer Debtor Case: The Debtor's Attorney as a DRA

BAPCPA introduced the concept of a **debt relief agency** (DRA) to the Code. Section §101(12A) defines a DRA in part as one "who provides any bankruptcy assistance to an assisted person in return for the payment of money or other valuable consideration...." An **assisted person** is defined in §101(3) as an individual debtor with primarily consumer debts. Sections 526-528 of the Code impose a number of restrictions on DRAs and authorize a number of sanctions on them for violation of those restrictions including forfeiture of fees and other charges to assisted persons, liability to such persons for actual damages, and attorney's fees.

Of course there are numerous private, non-attorney businesses that are engaged in providing financial advice to consumers for a fee to which this definition applies. We have met them before in the guise of **credit counseling agencies** discussed in Chapter Three, Section A. But an immediate issue arose after BAPCPA became law as to whether Congress intended that debtor's attorneys be considered DRAs and thus be required to comply with the requirements imposed on DRAs by the BAPCPA amendments.

Case Preview

Milavetz, Gallop & Milavetz v. United States

New §526(a)(4) of the Code prohibits a DRA from advising an assisted person to incur more debt in contemplation of bankruptcy (e.g., to refinance debt at a lower rate, pay certain bills, or purchase a reliable car), something attorneys routinely do. Thus critical free speech and attorney client privilege issues were implicated by the question of whether attorneys are DRAs. New §528 of the Code requires that DRAs identify themselves as such in any advertising and make certain disclosures in advertising about their services that attorneys do not normally make. Thus the question of whether lawyers representing debtors in bankruptcy are DRAs under these Code sections was a serious one with significant consequences. As you read *Milavetz, Gallop & Milavetz*, consider the following questions:

1. What was the statutory construction issue in the case and what were the constitutional issues in the case?
2. What was the basis for the Court's conclusion that Congress did intend debtor's attorneys to be considered DRAs?
3. How narrowly did the court construe the scope of §526(a)(4) to avoid the free speech constitutional issue?
4. What problem did the court find that §528 was intended to combat?

Milavetz, Gallop & Milavetz v. United States
559 U.S. 229 (2010)

[The plaintiffs in this litigation, the law firm Milavetz, Gallop & Milavetz, P. A. ("Milavetz"), filed a pre-enforcement suit in federal district court seeking declaratory relief with respect to the Bankruptcy Abuse Prevention and Consumer Protection Act of 2005 ("BAPCPA" or "Act") debt-relief-agency provisions. Milavetz asked the Court to hold that it is not bound by these provisions and thus may freely advise clients to incur additional debt and need not identify itself as a debt relief agency in its advertisements.

Milavetz argued that attorneys are not "debt relief agenc[ies]" as that term is used in the BAPCPA. In the alternative, Milavetz sought a judgment that §§526(a)(4) and 528(a)(4) and (b)(2) are unconstitutional as applied to attorneys. The district court agreed with Milavetz that the term "debt relief agency" does not include attorneys, but only after finding that §§526 and 528 — provisions expressly applicable only to debt relief agencies — are unconstitutional as applied to this class of professionals. The Court of Appeals for the

Justice Sonia Sotomayor wrote the majority opinion for *Milavetz. Collection of the Supreme Court of the United States, Photographer: Steve Petteway*

Eighth Circuit unanimously rejected the district court's conclusion that attorneys are not "debt relief agenc[ies]" within the meaning of the Act. The court of appeals also disagreed with the district court concerning the constitutionality of §528. Concluding that the disclosures are intended to prevent consumer deception and are "reasonably related" to that interest, the court upheld the application of §528's disclosure requirements to attorneys.

A majority of the Eighth Circuit panel, however, agreed with the district court that §526(a)(4) is invalid. Determining that §526(a)(4) broadly prohibits a debt relief agency from advising an assisted person . . . to incur *any* additional debt when the assisted person is contemplating bankruptcy, even when that advice constitutes prudent pre-bankruptcy planning not intended to abuse the bankruptcy laws, the majority held that §526(a)(4) could not withstand either strict or intermediate scrutiny. In light of a conflict among the courts of appeals, the Supreme Court granted certiorari to resolve the question of §526(a)(4)'s scope. The Court also agreed to consider the threshold question whether attorneys who provide bankruptcy assistance to assisted persons are debt relief agencies within the meaning of §101(12A) and the related question whether §528's disclosure requirements are constitutional.]

SOTOMAYOR, Justice.

. . .

We first consider whether the term "debt relief agency" includes attorneys. If it does not, we need not reach the other questions presented, as §§526 and 528 govern only the conduct of debt relief agencies, and Milavetz challenges the validity of those provisions based on their application to attorneys. The Government contends that "debt relief agency" plainly includes attorneys. . . . We conclude that the Government has the better view.

. . . [A] debt relief agency is "any person who provides any bankruptcy assistance to an assisted person" in return for payment. §101(12A). By definition, "bankruptcy assistance" includes several services commonly performed by attorneys. Indeed, some forms of bankruptcy assistance, including the "provi[sion of] legal representation with respect to a case or proceeding," §101(4A), may be provided only by attorneys. See §110(e)(2) (prohibiting bankruptcy petition preparers from providing legal advice). Moreover, in enumerating specific exceptions to the definition of debt relief agency, Congress gave no indication that it intended to exclude attorneys. See §§101(12A)(A)-(E). Thus, as the Government contends, the statutory text clearly indicates that attorneys are debt relief agencies when they provide qualifying services to assisted persons.

In advocating a narrower understanding of that term, Milavetz relies heavily on the fact that §101(12A) does not expressly include attorneys. That omission stands in contrast, it argues, to the provision's explicit inclusion of "bankruptcy petition preparer[s]" — a category of professionals that excludes attorneys and their staff, see §110(a)(1). But Milavetz does not contend, nor could it credibly, that only professionals expressly included in the definition are debt relief agencies. On that reading, no professional other than a bankruptcy petition preparer would qualify — an implausible reading given that the statute defines "debt relief agency" as "any person who provides any bankruptcy assistance to an assisted person . . . *or* who is a bankruptcy petition preparer." §101(12A) (emphasis added). The provision's silence regarding attorneys thus avails Milavetz little. Cf. Heintz v. Jenkins, 514 U.S. 291, 294 (1995) (holding that "debt collector" as used in the Fair Debt Collection Practices Act, 15 U.S.C. §1692a(6), includes attorneys notwithstanding the definition's lack of an express reference to lawyers or litigation).

Milavetz next argues that §101(12A)'s exception for any "officer, director, employee, or agent of a person who provides" bankruptcy assistance is revealing for its failure to include "partners." §101(12A)(A). In light of that omission, it contends, treating attorneys as debt relief agencies will obligate entire law firms to comply with §§526, 527, and 528 based on the conduct of a single partner, while the agents and employees of debt relief agencies not typically organized as partnerships are shielded from those requirements. Given that the partnership structure is not unique to law firms, however, it is unclear why the exclusion would be revealing of Congress' intent only with respect to attorneys. In any event, partnerships are themselves "person[s]" under the BAPCPA, see §101(41), and can qualify as "debt relief agenc[ies]" when they meet the criteria set forth in §101(12A). Moreover, a partnership's employees and agents are exempted from §101(12A) in the same way as the employees and agents of other organizations. To the extent that partners may be subject to the debt-relief-agency provisions by association, that result is consistent with the joint responsibilities that typically flow from the partnership structure. . . . Accordingly, we decline to attribute the significance Milavetz suggests to §101(12A)(A)'s failure to include partners among the exempted actors.

All else failing, Milavetz urges that the canon of constitutional avoidance requires us to read "debt relief agency" to exclude attorneys in order to forestall serious doubts as to the validity of §§526 and 528. The avoidance canon, however, "is a tool for choosing between competing plausible interpretations of a statutory text." . . . In applying that tool, we will consider only those constructions of a statute that are "'fairly possible.'" . . . For the reasons already discussed, the text and statutory context of §101(12A) foreclose a reading of "debt relief agency" that excludes attorneys. Accordingly, we hold that attorneys who provide bankruptcy assistance to assisted persons are debt relief agencies within the meaning of the BAPCPA.

. . .

Having concluded that attorneys are debt relief agencies when they provide qualifying services, we next address the scope and validity of §526(a)(4). Characterizing the statute as a broad, content-based restriction on attorney-client communications that is not adequately tailored to constrain only speech the Government has a substantial interest in restricting, the Eighth Circuit found the rule substantially overbroad. . . . For the reasons that follow, we reject that conclusion.

Section 526(a)(4) prohibits a debt relief agency from "advis[ing] an assisted person" either "to incur more debt in contemplation of" filing for bankruptcy "or to pay an attorney or bankruptcy petition preparer fee or charge for services" performed in preparation for filing. Only the first of these prohibitions is at issue. In debating the correctness of the Court of Appeals' decision, the parties first dispute the provision's scope. The Court of Appeals concluded that "§526(a)(4) broadly prohibits a debt relief agency from advising an assisted person . . . to incur *any* additional debt when the assisted person is contemplating bankruptcy." . . . Under that reading, an attorney is prohibited from providing all manner of "beneficial advice — even if the advice could help the assisted person avoid filing for bankruptcy altogether." *Ibid.*

Milavetz contends that §526(a)(4) prohibits a debt relief agency from advising a client to incur any new debt while considering whether to file for bankruptcy. Construing the provision more broadly still, Milavetz contends that §526(a)(4) forbids not only affirmative advice but also any discussion of the advantages, disadvantages, or legality of incurring more debt. . . . Milavetz's reading rests primarily on its view that the ordinary meaning of the phrase "in contemplation of" bankruptcy encompasses any advice given to a debtor with the awareness that he might soon file for bankruptcy, even if the advice seeks to obviate the need to file. Milavetz also maintains that if §526(a)(4) were construed more narrowly, . . . it would be so vague as to inevitably chill some protected speech.

The Government continues to advocate a narrower construction of the statute. The Government contends that §526(a)(4)'s restriction on advice to incur more debt "in contemplation of" bankruptcy is most naturally read to forbid only advice to undertake actions to abuse the bankruptcy system. Focusing first on the provision's text, the Government points to sources indicating that the phrase "in contemplation of" bankruptcy has long been, and continues to be, associated with abusive conduct. For instance, Black's Law Dictionary 336 (8th ed. 2004) (hereinafter Black's) defines "contemplation of bankruptcy" as "[t]he thought of declaring bankruptcy because of the inability to continue current financial operations, often coupled with action designed to thwart the distribution of assets in a bankruptcy proceeding." . . . The Government also points to early American and English judicial decisions to corroborate its contention that "in contemplation of" bankruptcy signifies abusive conduct. . . .

[T]he Government relies on §526(a)(4)'s immediate context. According to the Government, the other three subsections of §526(a) are designed to protect debtors from abusive practices by debt relief agencies: Section 526(a)(1) requires debt relief agencies to perform all promised services; §526(a)(2) prohibits them from making or advising debtors to make false or misleading statements in bankruptcy; and §526(a)(3) prohibits them from misleading debtors regarding the costs or benefits of bankruptcy. When §526(a)(4) is read in context of these debtor-protective provisions, the Government argues, construing it to prevent debt relief agencies from giving advice that is beneficial to both debtors and their creditors seems particularly nonsensical. . . .

After reviewing these competing claims, we are persuaded that a narrower reading of §526(a)(4) is sounder, although we do not adopt precisely the view the Government advocates. The Government's sources show that the phrase "in contemplation of" bankruptcy has so commonly been associated with abusive conduct that it may readily be understood to prefigure abuse. As used in §526(a)(4), however, we think the phrase refers to a specific type of misconduct designed to manipulate the protections of the bankruptcy system. . . . [W]e conclude that §526(a)(4) prohibits a debt relief agency only from advising a debtor to incur more debt because the debtor is filing for bankruptcy, rather than for a valid purpose. . . .

. . . [A]dvice to incur more debt because of bankruptcy, as prohibited by §526(a)(4), will generally consist of advice to "load up" on debt with the expectation of obtaining its discharge — *i.e.*, conduct that is abusive *per se*. . . .

The Government's contextual arguments provide additional support for the view that §526(a)(4) was meant to prevent this type of conduct. The companion rules of professional conduct in §§526(a)(1)-(3) and the remedies for their violation in §526(c) indicate that Congress was concerned with actions that threaten to harm debtors or creditors. Unlike the reasonable financial advice the Eighth Circuit's broad reading would proscribe, advice to incur more debt because of bankruptcy presents a substantial risk of injury to both debtors and creditors. . . . Specifically, the incurrence of such debt stands to harm a debtor if his prepetition conduct leads a court to hold his debts nondischargable, see §523(a)(2), convert his case to another chapter, or dismiss it altogether, . . . thereby defeating his effort to obtain bankruptcy relief. If a debt, although manipulatively incurred, is not timely identified as abusive and therefore is discharged, creditors will suffer harm as a result of the discharge and the consequent dilution of the bankruptcy estate. By contrast, the prudent advice that the Eighth Circuit's view of the statute forbids would likely benefit both debtors and creditors and at the very least should cause no harm. . . . For all of these reasons, we conclude that §526(a)(4) prohibits a debt relief agency only from advising an assisted person to incur more debt when the impelling reason for the advice is the anticipation of bankruptcy.

. . .

Finally, we address the validity of §528's challenged disclosure requirements . . . [C]ounsel for Milavetz insisted at oral argument that this is "not a facial challenge; it's an as-applied challenge." . . . We will approach the question consistent with Milavetz's characterization.

We next consider the standard of scrutiny applicable to §528's disclosure requirements. The parties agree, as do we, that the challenged provisions regulate only commercial speech. Milavetz contends that our decision in Central Hudson Gas & Elec. Corp. v. Public Serv. Comm'n of N. Y., 447 U.S. 557 (1980), supplies the proper standard for reviewing these requirements. The Court in that case held that restrictions on nonmisleading commercial speech regarding lawful activity must withstand intermediate scrutiny — that is, they must "directly advanc[e]" a substantial governmental interest and be "n[o] more extensive than is necessary to serve that interest." *Id.*, at 566. Contesting Milavetz's premise, the Government maintains that §528 is directed at *misleading* commercial speech. For that reason, and because the challenged provisions impose a disclosure requirement rather than an affirmative limitation on speech, the Government contends that the less exacting scrutiny described in Zauderer v. Office of Disciplinary Counsel of Supreme Court of Ohio, 471 U.S. 626 (1985) governs our review. We agree.

Zauderer addressed the validity of a rule of professional conduct that required attorneys who advertised contingency-fee services to disclose in their advertisements that a losing client might still be responsible for certain litigation fees and costs. Noting that First Amendment protection for commercial speech is justified in large part by the information's value to consumers, the Court concluded that an attorney's constitutionally protected interest in *not* providing the required factual information is "minimal." 471 U.S., at 651. . . . Unjustified or unduly burdensome disclosure requirements offend the First Amendment by chilling protected speech, but "an advertiser's rights are adequately protected as long as disclosure requirements are reasonably related to the State's interest in preventing deception of consumers." *Ibid.*

The challenged provisions of §528 share the essential features of the rule at issue in *Zauderer.* As in that case, §528's required disclosures are intended to combat the problem of inherently misleading commercial advertisements — specifically, the promise of debt relief without any reference to the possibility of filing for bankruptcy, which has inherent costs. Additionally, the disclosures entail only an accurate statement identifying the advertiser's legal status and the character of the assistance provided, and they do not prevent debt relief agencies like Milavetz from conveying any additional information . . .

Milavetz makes much of the fact that the Government in these consolidated cases has adduced no evidence that its advertisements are misleading. *Zauderer* forecloses that argument: "When the possibility of deception is as self-evident as it is in this case, we need not require the State to 'conduct a survey of the . . . public before it [may] determine that the [advertisement] had a tendency to mislead.' " 471 U.S., at 652-653. . . . Evidence in the congressional record demonstrating a pattern of advertisements that hold out the promise of debt relief without alerting consumers to its potential cost, . . . is adequate to establish that the likelihood of deception in this case "is hardly a speculative one," 471 U.S., at 652. . . .

Milavetz alternatively argues that the term "debt relief agency" is confusing and misleading and that requiring its inclusion in advertisements cannot be "reasonably related" to the Government's interest in preventing consumer deception, as *Zauderer* requires. *Id.,* at 651. This contention amounts to little more than a preference on Milavetz's part for referring to itself as something other than a "debt relief agency" — *e.g.,* an attorney or a law firm. For several reasons, we conclude that this preference lacks any constitutional basis. First, Milavetz offers no evidence to support its claim that the label is confusing. Because §528 by its terms applies only to debt relief agencies, the disclosures are necessarily accurate to that extent: Only debt relief agencies must identify themselves as such in their advertisements. This statement provides interested observers with pertinent information about the advertiser's services and client obligations.

Other information that Milavetz must or may include in its advertisements for bankruptcy-assistance services provides additional assurance that consumers will not misunderstand the term. The required statement that the advertiser " 'help[s] people file for bankruptcy relief' " gives meaningful context to the term "debt relief agency." And Milavetz may further identify itself as a law firm or attorney. Section 528 also gives Milavetz flexibility to tailor the disclosures to its individual circumstances, as long as the resulting statements are "substantially similar" to the statutory examples. §§528(a)(4) and (b)(2)(B).

Finally, we reject Milavetz's argument that §528 is not reasonably related to any governmental interest because it applies equally to attorneys who represent creditors, as Milavetz sometimes does. The required disclosures, Milavetz contends, would be counterfactual and misleading in that context. This claim is premised on an untenable reading of the statute. We think it evident from the definition of "assisted person" — which is stated in terms of the person's debts, see §101(3) — and from the text and structure of the debt-relief-agency provisions in §§526, 527, and 528 that those provisions, including §528's disclosure requirements, govern only professionals who offer bankruptcy-related services to consumer debtors. Section 528 is itself expressly concerned with advertisements pertaining to "bankruptcy assistance services," "the benefits of bankruptcy," "excessive debt, debt collection pressure, or inability to pay any consumer debt," §§528(a)(3) and (b)(2). Moreover, like the other debt-relief-agency provisions, that section is codified in a subchapter of the Bankruptcy Code entitled "DEBTOR'S DUTIES AND BENEFITS." 11 U.S.C., ch. 5, subch. II. In context, reading §528 to govern advertisements aimed at creditors would be as anomalous as the result of which Milavetz complains. Once again, we decline Milavetz's invitation to adopt a view of the statute that is contrary to its plain meaning and would produce an absurd result.

Because §528's requirements that Milavetz identify itself as a debt relief agency and include certain information about its bankruptcy-assistance and related services are "reasonably related to the [Government's] interest in preventing deception of consumers," *Zauderer*, 471 U.S., at 651, we uphold those provisions as applied to Milavetz.

Post-Case Follow-Up   This case began as a declaratory judgment action instituted by the law firm seeking to have the court declare that it was not a DRA. Was that the responsible professional thing for a firm doing debtor's work to do or might it have been better strategy to wait until there was an accusation made by an aggrieved person that they were a DRA? What risks would be associated with adopting the latter strategy? Many debtor's lawyers comply with the DRA disclosure requirements of §527 in their fee agreement with the client while others do so in a separate writing and others still do it in both. Review the fee agreement between Marta Carlson and her attorney (Document 1 in the Carlson case file) to see an example of the §527 disclosures made there.

Milavetz, Gallop & Milavetz: Real Life Applications

1. Assume you have decided to expand your law practice to represent consumer debtors in bankruptcy. Review §§526-528 as well as §§101(3) and (12A) and answer the following questions:
   a. Do you have to utilize a written contract of representation with each client?
   b. In advertisements to the public do you have to mention that you provide bankruptcy services or can you merely say you provide debt management assistance?
   c. If your contract with the client does not comply with the requirements imposed by these sections, can the bankruptcy court in which you have filed a case refuse to enforce it?
   d. If you do not comply with the restrictions imposed on DRAs by §526, can state authorities enjoin such violation or take other action against you?
   e. For how long do you have to keep copies of required notices provided to debtors under §527(a)?

2. If you plan to represent only business debtors filing for Chapter 11 relief do you have to comply with the DRA requirements? Why or why not?
3. Remember that there are many non-lawyer DRAs out there and these provisions apply to them with equal force. Determine if the federal courts of the federal district or circuit where you plan to practice have decided a DRA sanctions case against a lawyer or non-lawyer DRA. If so, what were the specific violations alleged and, if liability was found, what damages were awarded or other sanctions imposed?

The Supreme Court in *Milavetz* pretty much let lawyers off the hook with regards to the restriction of §526(a)(4), construing it to prohibit only advice to a client to load up on debt because they plan to file for bankruptcy, advice that would likely be unethical and possibly fraudulent anyway. But since the court upheld the §528 DRA advertising disclosures as applicable to attorneys, debtor's attorneys, most of whom do significant advertising, must be careful to identify themselves in their advertising as DRAs and make the other required disclosures in that advertising.

Code §527(a)(1) requires DRAs to comply with the requirements of §342(b) by providing consumer debtors with written notice explaining all the options for filing bankruptcy (usually Chapters 7, 11, 12, and 13 for the individual debtor) and the differences between the respective types of filing. The written notice that must be provided to consumer debtors to comply with §342(b) is included in the fee agreement between Marta Carlson and her attorney (Document 1 in the Carlson case file). Attorneys for individual debtors must also certify that they have complied with their §527(a)(1) obligations as DRAs by their signature on page 7 of the voluntary petition.

Section 342(b) seems to literally place the requirement of providing debtors with written notice of their filing options and the differences between the various bankruptcy filings on the clerk of the bankruptcy court, not the DRA/debtor's attorney. So, pursuant to §527(a)(1), do both the attorney *and* the clerk have to give the debtor this notice? No. The clerk will typically provide the notice only if the debtor has no attorney (such a debtor is filing *pro se*) or if the debtor's attorney fails to sign the petition.

The Signature of the Non-Attorney Petition Preparer

Section 110 of the Code authorizes non-attorneys to assist debtors in preparing the petition and supporting schedules and to receive a fee for doing so. However, the **non-attorney bankruptcy petition preparer** (NABPP) is subject to numerous limitations and requirements. The NABPP is strictly prohibited from providing the client with any legal advice, including advice concerning the petition or what chapter of bankruptcy to file under, and the NABPP must disclose those limitations in writing to the client per Official Form 119. The pro se debtor who utilizes the assistance of a NABPP in preparation of the bankruptcy petition or supporting schedules must disclose that in response to the question asked in Part 7, page 8 of the petition and the completed Form 119 must then be attached to the petition. The debtor must sign Part 1 of Form 119 acknowledging receipt of a copy of the form which contains the required disclosures.

The NABPP must sign Form 119 under oath subject to penalties of perjury. The NABPP is also subject to the forfeiture of any fee deemed excessive or the entire fee collected for failure to comply with the requirements imposed on the NABPP, plus an additional $500 penalty for failure to comply with a turnover order (the court order to disgorge and refund fees received from the debtor), and possible criminal prosecution under 18 U.S.C. §156 for the knowing disregard of a bankruptcy law or rule.

NABPPs are also considered DRAs per the definition of Code §101(12A) and must comply with those provisions as well. See, e.g., Jonak v. McDermott, 511 B.R. 586 (D. Minn. 2014) (non-attorney principal of company that claimed to provide only lawyer referral and scrivener services to potential bankruptcy debtors found to be a NABPP and a DRA and to be practicing law without a license where, for a fee, principal explained to customers how different chapters of the Bankruptcy Code worked, explained how exemptions work, recommended and encouraged certain choices regarding filing, and advertised in a way that suggested he was an attorney).

As one court put it, "So what does §110 tacitly permit? The answer in a nutshell is 'not much.'" In re Grissett, 2008 WL 4553083, at *4 (Bankr. E.D. Mich. Oct. 8, 2008). Section 110 "proscribes virtually all conduct falling into the category of guidance or advice, effectively restricting 'petition preparers' to rendering only 'scrivening/typing' services." *Id.* Moreover, the case law makes it "abundantly clear that providing anything more than typing services is prohibited under §110." *Id.*

5. The Filing Fee

Per FRBP 1006, the filing fee is normally paid to the clerk of the bankruptcy court at the time the petition is filed, although the Code does permit a debtor to pay the fee in installments. In that event, the debtor must file Official Form 103A, Application to Pay Filing Fee in Installments, along with the petition. (See Document 3 in the Carlson case file.) The number of installments is limited to four, and the debtor must make the final installment no later than 120 days after filing the petition. However, that time limit can be extended to 180 days on motion and for cause shown. In Chapter 7 cases only, the debtor may request waiver of the fee entirely by filing Form 103B with the petition, but as you can see by reading that form, that remedy is only available to the very poor.

6. The Involuntary Petition

The vast majority of bankruptcy cases are filed voluntarily, meaning the debtor makes the decision to file for relief. But §303 of the Code does permit a debtor to be forced into a Chapter 7 (or Chapter 11 business reorganization) bankruptcy by creditors filing an **involuntary petition**. Three creditors with undisputed, noncontingent, unsecured claims totaling at least $15,775 (the current figure, subject to change in April 2019 per §104) may join in the petition. If the debtor has fewer than 12 unsecured creditors, then a single creditor with a claim of at least $15,775 can initiate the involuntary petition. The debtor must of course be otherwise qualified to be a debtor in Chapter 7. Involuntary petitions are unusual in consumer bankruptcy cases.

FRBP 1010 through 1013 provide that when an involuntary petition is filed it must be served on the debtor along with a summons, just as would happen in a civil lawsuit under the Federal Rules of Civil Procedure. Once the debtor is served with the petition and summons, he must file an answer to the petition within 21 days raising any defenses or objections to the petition. If debtor fails to do so, the court will enter an order for relief on the involuntary petition by default and the case will proceed. FRBP 1011(a) allows a non-petitioning partner to contest an involuntary petition against the partnership but does not allow a non-petitioning creditor or other party in interest to contest an involuntary petition.

Application Exercise 2

Look at §101 of the Code and FRBP 9001. Is "party in interest" defined in either place? Generally, a party in interest is the debtor and any other person or entity sufficiently affected by the bankruptcy case that it is reasonable to grant him standing to be heard on a matter. What argument would you make that each of the following should or should not be considered a party in interest: the U.S. Trustee, the bankruptcy trustee appointed to administer the case, the creditors of the debtor or any committees of creditors, business associates of the debtor, the debtor's parents or other family members who are not creditors or business associates of the debtor, the local media, the debtor's non-creditor nosey neighbor, the debtor's employer, co-workers?

If the involuntary petition is properly answered and contested, the court will then conduct an evidentiary hearing where live testimony is given and relevant exhibits introduced, all subject to the Federal Rules of Evidence. At the hearing, the court must decide whether to enter an order for relief allowing the involuntary case to proceed or to dismiss the petition. The creditors filing the involuntary petition have the burden of proof at the hearing to demonstrate that sufficient grounds exist to justify proceeding with the bankruptcy case over the debtor's objection. To satisfy their burden, the creditors must demonstrate that one or both of the following grounds are present:

- the debtor is not generally paying bona fide debts as they come due; or
- within 120 days preceding the filing of the involuntary petition, a receiver, assignee, or custodian has taken possession of all or substantially all of the debtor's property.

The first ground, that the debtor is not paying his debts as they come due, is the ground most frequently asserted in an involuntary case. Consider why creditors force a debtor into bankruptcy: Because the creditors are unsecured or undersecured in specific property of the debtor, they are not being paid, and they cannot gain access to the debtor's assets without suing him and obtaining a judgment, which could take months or years. And those creditors fear that the debtor will have dissipated his assets by then, so there will be no property to execute on to satisfy the judgment when it is finally rendered. Forcing the debtor into a liquidation bankruptcy is seen as the quickest and surest way to stop the debtor from further dissipating his assets and to force a distribution of the remaining assets for the benefit of all the creditors.

Creditors must proceed with caution in filing an involuntary petition. If the petition is contested and dismissed then §303(i) of the Code permits the bankruptcy court to award court costs and attorney fees to the debtor for contesting the petition. And if the judge finds that the petition was filed in bad faith then the court may award the debtor consequential damages (e.g., lost profits to the business caused by the filing) and even punitive damages.

B. SCHEDULES, STATEMENTS, AND OTHER DOCUMENTS THAT ACCOMPANY THE PETITION

As required by §521 of the Code and FRBP 1007, the debtor must file a number of schedules, statements, and other documents in addition to the voluntary petition and its exhibits. Section 521, as amended by BAPCPA, is dense, poorly structured, and not well worded. However, the BAPCPA changes have now been in effect long enough for bankruptcy practitioners and judges to figure out with some confidence what is required.

This section will summarize the schedules, statements, and other documents that must be prepared and filed in support of the consumer debtor's Chapter 7 petition. Where there is an official form for the required schedules, statements, and the like, that form is referenced in the summary. Remember that the official forms can be accessed and viewed at www.uscourts.gov/forms/bankruptcy-forms if you do not have them in paper form.

The schedules, statements and other documents filed by Marta Carlson in connection with her Chapter 7 case are set forth in the Carlson case file on the companion Web site. As you read the description of each schedule below, compare that description to the Carlson filings in her case file. Keep in mind as you review these schedules, statements, and other documents that if you are working as a debtor's attorney, these are the forms you will be responsible for preparing with information provided by your client. If you are the bankruptcy trustee or U.S. trustee, or are representing a creditor or the U.S. trustee, you will be reviewing these to verify the accuracy of the information.

1. The List of Creditors

Section 521(a)(1) of the Code and Bankruptcy Rule 1007(a)(1) require that the debtor file a list of creditors. (See Document 4 in the Carlson case file.) There is no official form for this list, but most bankruptcy courts provide practitioners with a matrix form accessible from the court's Web site. The list will serve as a mailing matrix for the clerk's office to provide creditors notice of the bankruptcy filing and of other proceedings in the case.

2. Schedule A/B: Property (Official Form 106A/B)

On this form the debtor must list, by description and location, all real and personal property in which the debtor owns an interest. In Part 1 of the form the debtor lists each parcel of real property by street address, describes the property (e.g., unimproved land, single family home, timeshare, etc.), states whether others have an interest in the property, identifies the interest held (fee simple, life estate, leasehold, etc.), states the estimated value of the entire property and the value of the debtor's interest in it.

On this form the debtor must also list, describe, and place a value on personal property owned by the debtor including vehicles (Part 2), personal and household items (Part 3), financial assets (Part 4), non-realty business related property (Part 5), and farm of fishing-operation property (Part 6). There is a comprehensive "other" category in Part 7 of the form for property not listed elsewhere in it. See Document 7 in the Carlson case file.

3. Schedule C: The Property You Claim As Exempt (Official Form 106C)

How Exemptions Work

In Chapter Three, Section B, we considered exempt property in the context of a judgment creditor executing on a judgment. Similarly, the Code allows an individual bankruptcy debtor to claim certain property as exempt. Exemptions are not available to Chapter 7 entity debtors (corporations and partnerships) since such debtors go out of business at the end of the liquidation and do not retain assets. Individual debtors are required to set forth the property they claim as exempt on Schedule C. Exhibit 6.1 shows Marta Carlson's Schedule C (it is also Document 8 in the Carlson case file).

The Chapter 7 bankruptcy trustee cannot seize the property that is fully exempt and sell it for the benefit of the creditors. Instead the debtor will retain possession of the fully exempt property.

For example, in her Schedule C Marta Carlson has claimed her jewelry to be fully exempt under §522(d)(4). It is worth $1,350 and as of April 2016 that Code section allows her to exempt such property up to $1,550. If her valuation of the jewelry is correct, she has fully exempted it and the trustee cannot seize it.

EXHIBIT 6.1	**Marta Carlson's Schedule C — Property Claimed as Exempt**

Fill in this information to identify your case:

Debtor 1	Marta	Rinaldi	Carlson
	First Name	Middle Name	Last Name

Debtor 2			
(Spouse, if filing) First Name		Middle Name	Last Name

United States Bankruptcy Court for the: District of Minnesota

Case number   16-7-XXXX
(If known)

☐ Check if this is an amended filing

Official Form 106C

Schedule C: The Property You Claim as Exempt   04/16

Be as complete and accurate as possible. If two married people are filing together, both are equally responsible for supplying correct information. Using the property you listed on *Schedule A/B: Property* (Official Form 106A/B) as your source, list the property that you claim as exempt. If more space is needed, fill out and attach to this page as many copies of *Part 2: Additional Page* as necessary. On the top of any additional pages, write your name and case number (if known).

For each item of property you claim as exempt, you must specify the amount of the exemption you claim. One way of doing so is to state a specific dollar amount as exempt. Alternatively, you may claim the full fair market value of the property being exempted up to the amount of any applicable statutory limit. Some exemptions—such as those for health aids, rights to receive certain benefits, and tax-exempt retirement funds—may be unlimited in dollar amount. However, if you claim an exemption of 100% of fair market value under a law that limits the exemption to a particular dollar amount and the value of the property is determined to exceed that amount, your exemption would be limited to the applicable statutory amount.

Part 1:	**Identify the Property You Claim as Exempt**

1. **Which set of exemptions are you claiming?** *Check one only, even if your spouse is filing with you.*

   ☐ You are claiming state and federal nonbankruptcy exemptions. 11 U.S.C. § 522(b)(3)

   ☑ You are claiming federal exemptions. 11 U.S.C. § 522(b)(2)

2. **For any property you list on** *Schedule A/B* **that you claim as exempt, fill in the information below.**

Brief description of the property and line on *Schedule A/B* that lists this property	Current value of the portion you own Copy the value from *Schedule A/B*	Amount of the exemption you claim *Check only one box for each exemption.*	Specific laws that allow exemption
Brief description: Residence Line from *Schedule A/B*: 1.1	$255,000.00	☑ $ 11,825.00 ☐ 100% of fair market value, up to any applicable statutory limit	11 U.S.C. § 522(d)(1)
Brief description: YR-4 Toyota Camry Line from *Schedule A/B*: 3.1	$8,500.00	☑ $ 5,025.00 ☐ 100% of fair market value, up to any applicable statutory limit	11 U.S.C. § 522(d)(2) and (d)(5)
Brief description: Washing machine Line from *Schedule A/B*: 6	$350.00	☑ $ 350.00 ☐ 100% of fair market value, up to any applicable statutory limit	11 U.S.C. § 522(d)(3)

3. **Are you claiming a homestead exemption of more than $160,375?**

   (Subject to adjustment on 4/01/19 and every 3 years after that for cases filed on or after the date of adjustment.)

   ☑ No

   ☐ Yes. Did you acquire the property covered by the exemption within 1,215 days before you filed this case?

       ☐ No

       ☐ Yes

EXHIBIT 6.1   (Continued)

Debtor 1	Marta	Rinaldi	Carlson		Case number *(if known)* 16-7-XXXX
	First Name	Middle Name	Last Name		

Part 2:   Additional Page

Brief description of the property and line on *Schedule A/B* that lists this property	Current value of the portion you own	Amount of the exemption you claim	Specific laws that allow exemption
	Copy the value from *Schedule A/B*	*Check only one box for each exemption*	
Brief description: Clothes dryer Line from *Schedule A/B*: 6	$ 250.00	☑ $ 250.00 ☐ 100% of fair market value, up to any applicable statutory limit	11 U.S.C. § 522(d)(3)
Brief description: Other furnishings Line from *Schedule A/B*: 6	$ 6,500.00	☑ $ 6,500.00 ☐ 100% of fair market value, up to any applicable statutory limit	11 U.S.C. § 522(d)(3)
Brief description: Electronics Line from *Schedule A/B*: 7	$ 900.00	☑ $ 900.00 ☐ 100% of fair market value, up to any applicable statutory limit	11 U.S.C. § 522(d)(3)
Brief description: Clothes Line from *Schedule A/B*: 11	$ 1,000.00	☑ $ 1,000.00 ☐ 100% of fair market value, up to any applicable statutory limit	11 U.S.C. § 522(d)(3)
Brief description: Doll collection Line from *Schedule A/B*: 8	$ 15,125.00	☑ $ 15,125.00 ☐ 100% of fair market value, up to any applicable statutory limit	11 U.S.C. § 522(d)(3) & $11500 of unused exemption from 11 U.S.C. § 522(d)(1)
Brief description: Retriever dog (Max) Line from *Schedule A/B*: 13	$ 50.00	☑ $ 50.00 ☐ 100% of fair market value, up to any applicable statutory limit	$50 of unused exemption from 11 U.S.C. § 522(d)(1)
Brief description: Cash Line from *Schedule A/B*: 16	$ 50.00	☑ $ 50.00 ☐ 100% of fair market value, up to any applicable statutory limit	$50 of unused exemption from 11 U.S.C. § 522(d)(1)
Brief description: Deposits Line from *Schedule A/B*: 17	$ 250.00	☑ $ 250.00 ☐ 100% of fair market value, up to any applicable statutory limit	$250 of unused exemption from 11 U.S.C. § 522(d)(1)
Brief description: TTI 401(k) Line from *Schedule A/B*: 21	$ 7,600.00	☑ $ 7,600.00 ☐ 100% of fair market value, up to any applicable statutory limit	11 U.S.C. § 522(d)(10)(E)
Brief description: Support arrearage Line from *Schedule A/B*: 29	$ 15,000.00	☑ $ 15,000.00 ☐ 100% of fair market value, up to any applicable statutory limit	11 U.S.C. § 522(d)(10)(D)
Brief description: Jewelry Line from *Schedule A/B*: 12	$ 1,350.00	☑ $ 1,350.00 ☐ 100% of fair market value, up to any applicable statutory limit	11 U.S.C. § 522(d)(4)
Brief description: Line from *Schedule A/B*:	$	☐ $ ☐ 100% of fair market value, up to any applicable statutory limit	

If the debtor is unable to fully exempt property, the trustee may seize it and sell it in order to realize the equity in the property for the benefit of the estate. But the debtor is entitled to receive the exempted value following the sale.

For example, in her Schedule C Marta Carlson has claimed exemptions totaling $5,025 in her YR-4 Toyota Camry. But the vehicle is worth $8,500 so she is unable to fully exempt it. Once the trustee determines there is equity for the estate in that property, he will seize the car and sell it. But Marta will have to be paid her exempt amount of $5,025 from the proceeds of the sale.

If a creditor is properly secured and perfected in the property claimed as exempt, the debtor's claimed exemption normally cannot defeat that secured claim (subject to an exception for judicial liens discussed later in this section) and there is no equity for the estate in the property to the extent of the secured claim.

For example, Automotive Finance, Inc. (AFI) has a claim in the amount of $1,750 secured by the YR-4 Toyota Camry in which Marta also claims an exemption of $5,025. If the trustee seizes and sells the vehicle, AFI's secured claim must be paid in full first from the proceeds, then Marta's exemption claim. Only after those two superior claims are satisfied can the trustee take the balance of the proceeds of the sale into the estate for the benefit of creditors.

Application Exercise 3

On her Schedule C, Marta Carlson has claimed an exemption in her home of $11,825. As you can see on her Schedule D (Document 9 in the Carlson case file), she has two mortgages on the property and those two secured claims together total $180,000. The home is valued by Marta on her Schedules A and D at $255,000. Assume her bankruptcy trustee seizes the home and sells it for that price and incurs no sales commission in doing so. Using the last example, in what order will the proceeds of sale be distributed? If the trustee incurs a 6 percent realtor's commission on the sale of the home, that expense will come out of his share of the proceeds. We will learn later that the realtor's postpetition commission will be treated as a priority administrative claim in the bankruptcy case.

The Federal Exemptions and Right of States to Opt Out

The Code contains a uniform set of federal exemptions for individual debtors set out in §522(d). In a case where husband and wife are joint debtors, §522(m) provides that each debtor may claim the stated exemption separately, a process practitioners call **doubling** or **stacking**. As mandated by §104, the dollar value of the federal exemptions is adjusted in April of every third year. The last adjustment was on April 1, 2016, and the next will be on April 1, 2019.

For example, as of April 1, 2016, the federal homestead exemption allowed under §522(d)(1) is $23,675. If a husband and wife both own the homestead and they are joint bankruptcy debtors, they may each claim the full exemption amount and, together, exempt $47,350 of equity in their home.

Exhibit 6.2 summarizes the federal exemptions.

EXHIBIT 6.2   Summary of §522 Federal Exemptions (All Dollar Values Stated Are as of April 1, 2013)

- $23,675 of equity in the residence of the debtor and used by the debtor or a dependent (§522(d)(1))
- $3,775 of equity in one vehicle (§522(d)(2))
- $12,625 of equity (not to exceed $600 per item) in household goods and furnishings, appliances, wearing apparel, books, animals, crops, or musical instruments held for personal, family, or household use by the debtor or a dependent (§502(d)(3))
- $1,600 of equity in jewelry used by the debtor or a dependent (§502(d)(4))
- $1,250, plus up to $11,850 of any unused balance of the homestead exemption of §522(d)(1) (§522(d)(5)) (known as the **wild card exemption**)
- $2,375 of equity in implements or tools of the trade or professional books of the debtor or a dependent (§522(d)(6))
- An unlimited amount in unmatured life insurance policies owned by the debtor, excluding credit life contracts (§522(d)(7))
- $12,625 in cash value of an insurance policy (e.g., a whole life policy) (§522(d)(8))
- An unlimited amount in prescription health aids for the debtor or a dependent (§522(d)(9))
- An unlimited amount in Social Security, welfare, disability, unemployment, or veteran's benefits and in alimony, child support, or separate maintenance, to the extent reasonably necessary to support the debtor or a dependent, and in qualified pension and profit sharing plans (§522(d)(10))
- An unlimited amount as crime victim's reparation benefits and wrongful death recovery or life insurance benefits if the debtor was a dependent of the deceased, to the extent reasonably necessary for the support of the debtor or a dependent, and up to $23,675 in recovery on a personal injury claim involving the debtor or a dependent, and compensation for lost future earnings of the debtor or one of whom the debtor was a dependent, to the extent reasonably necessary for the support of the debtor or a dependent (§522(d)(11))
- An unlimited amount in any retirement fund exempted from taxation by the IRS (e.g., 401(k) and 403(b) plans) (§522(b)(3)(C) and (d)(12)) (excluding inherited retirement accounts per Clark v. Rameker, 134 S. Ct. 2242 (2014))

Section 522(b) allows states, acting through their legislatures, to opt out of using the federal exemptions set out in §522(d) and to use state exemption laws instead. More than 30 states have opted out of the federal exemptions. In those opt-out states, bankruptcy filers must use the state exemption laws that control in executions on final judgments. In states that have not opted out of the federal exemptions, §522(b) permits the individual bankruptcy filer to choose between the federal exemptions and the applicable state exemptions. The filer in those states cannot pick and choose among the federal and state exemption provisions, however and must use only the federal exemptions or only the state exemptions. And a husband and wife filing a joint petition in those states must both use the federal exemptions or both use the state exemptions.

Application Exercise 4

Minnesota has not opted out of the federal exemptions and Marta Carlson's Schedule C utilizes the federal exemptions of §522(d) rather than the Minnesota state exemptions. If hers was an actual case, the debtor's attorney might have used the state exemptions had the attorney concluded they were more favorable to Marta. Go through each exemption she has claimed and be sure you understand why she is claiming each exemption listed. Has she cited the proper subsection of §522(d) in connection with each claimed exemption?

Application Exercise 5

Locate the exempt property statutes or regulations of the state where you plan to practice and compare them to the federal exemptions set forth in §522(d) of the Code. Which appear to be more generous to the debtor? Determine if the state whose property exemptions you have located has opted out of the federal exemptions. Whether or not it has, assume Marta was filing in a bankruptcy court in your state and prepare her Schedule C using the applicable state exemptions and the information concerning her property found on the Schedule C in her case file and in Appendix A.

The right of individual states to opt out of the federal exemption scheme and apply their own exemptions in bankruptcy cases filed in the federal courts within those states is a striking example of the variation allowed in the application of what was intended to be a uniform national bankruptcy process imposed by federal law. As was discussed in more detail in Chapter Three, Section B, there is tremendous variation in property exemptions allowed among the states. Thus the exemptions a debtor in a federal bankruptcy proceeding in one state might enjoy can be quite different from those a debtor in an identical bankruptcy proceeding in another state may have to settle for.

Application Exercise 6

Is this right in a moral/ethical sense? Does it encourage forum shopping, in the sense that a financially challenged debtor might change his state of residence in advance of a foreseeable bankruptcy filing? Is it ethical for an attorney to advise a client to do that?

Are After-Tax Funded IRA Accounts Exempted Under §522(d)(10)(E)?

Section 522(d)(10)(E) exempts a debtor's right to receive payment under a pension, profit-sharing, annuity, or similar plan or on contract "on account of age." Does that include after-tax funded IRA accounts since they can be accessed prior to age 59½ subject to statutory penalty? In Rousey v. Jacoway, 544 U.S. 320 (2005), the Court held that assets in Individual Retirement Accounts (IRAs) are protected under §522(d)(10)(E) as payments "on account of age" notwithstanding that they can be accessed prior to age 59½ and are thus exempt. This decision has broad implications for the baby-boomer generation (those born between 1946 and 1964, now 26 percent of the American population), providing millions of Americans nearing retirement with increased protection of their life savings. According to the Pew Research report on baby boomers at www.pewresearch.org/daily-number/baby-boomers-retire/, 10,000 baby boomers are turning 65 each day and that will continue to be the case until the year 2029.

Another consideration in determining what exemptions apply in a particular case is §522(b)(3)(A), which provides that it is the law of the debtor's **domicile** (place of a debtor's primary residence) that will determine what exemptions apply in his case but only if he has been domiciled there 730 days (two years) prior to the date the petition is filed. If he or she has not been domiciled in any one state for the requisite 730 days, then the law of the state where debtor was domiciled for the 180 days preceding the 730-day period will determine the exemptions.

For example, assume a debtor files for bankruptcy relief in a U.S. bankruptcy court in California. The debtor moved to California from Texas six months ago. He had lived in Texas five years before moving to California. Though California is now the debtor's domicile, he has not lived there 730 days preceding the filing of the petition, and so California exemption laws will not control his Schedule C exemptions. Because he lived in Texas for the requisite 180 days preceding the 730-day period, Texas exemption laws will control his Schedule C exemptions.

Applicable exemptions will control property of the debtor wherever it is located. For example, assume the debtor from the previous example owns real property in Ohio. Texas exemption laws will control his right to exempt any such property on his Schedule C, not Ohio law. Of course, if there was a dispute over the nature or extent of the debtor's ownership interest in the Ohio property, Ohio law is likely to control those issues, but not the exemption question in debtor's bankruptcy case.

Limitations on the Homestead Exemption: The 1,215-Day Rule

There is an important limitation on the right of a debtor in bankruptcy to claim the homestead exemption (for the principal residence) in a state that has opted out of the federal exemptions. As we considered in Chapter Three when studying state exemption laws in the context of a judgment debtor executing on a final judgment, some states have very generous homestead exemptions, far more generous than the federal homestead exemption, which is limited to $23,675 for a sole individual debtor or $47,350 for a husband and wife filing as joint debtors (per §522(d)(1) as of April 1, 2016, subject to adjustment in 2019 per §104).

For example, a bankruptcy debtor residing in a state that allows an unlimited homestead exemption and that has opted out of the federal exemptions could theoretically exempt all the equity in his principal residence just as he could exempt it from executing judgment creditors. Thus, that bankruptcy debtor could emerge from a Chapter 7 liquidation with his debts discharged and not lose his home.

However, §522(p)(1), added by BAPCPA, provides that if the bankruptcy debtor has not owned the principal residence for more than 1,215 days preceding the filing of the petition debtor cannot exempt more than $160,375 of equity in it (as of April 1, 2016, subject to adjustment in 2019) regardless of the applicable homestead exemption. This is the **1,215-day rule**.

For example, assume the debtor in the previous example bought his home 24 months before filing for bankruptcy relief and has a total of $250,000 of equity in the home. He has owned the home only 730 days. So even though the state where he resides allows him an unlimited homestead exemption, and even though that state has opted out of the federal exemptions for bankruptcy cases, he will be limited to a homestead exemption of no more than $160,375.

Section 522(p)(2)(B) does say that the limitation of §522(p)(1) does not apply to any equity the debtor has in a current principal residence that was transferred from a prior principal residence so long as the prior residence was acquired outside of the 1,215-day limit and was in the same state.

The Bankruptcy Code and the Use of State Exemption Laws

The Bankruptcy Act of 1898 did not set out any federal exemptions and applied state exemption laws exclusively. The constitutionality of the Act was challenged on that basis since Article I §8, cl. 4 of the U.S. Constitution empowers Congress to "establish uniform Laws on the subject of Bankruptcies" and thus arguably prohibits the use of non-uniform state exemption laws. In Hanover Nat'l Bank v. Moyses, 186 U.S. 181, 189-90 (1902), the Supreme Court upheld the use of state exemptions in the Act. The Court reasoned that uniformity was satisfied since the contractual obligations of any bankrupt debtor wherever located were made with reference to existing state exemption laws and no unsecured creditor wherever located could recover more from his debtor in bankruptcy than the unexempted part of his assets as anticipated under those laws when the contract was made. ("This is not unjust, as every debt is contracted with reference to the rights of the parties thereto under existing exemption laws, and no creditor can reasonably complain if he gets his full share of all that the law, for the time being, places at the disposal of creditors. One of the effects of a bankrupt law is that of a general execution issued in favor of all the creditors of the bankrupt, reaching all his property subject to levy, and applying it to the payment of all his debts according to their respective priorities. It is quite proper, therefore, to confine its operation to such property as other legal process could reach. A rule which operates to this effect throughout the United States is uniform within the meaning of that term, as used in the Constitution. We . . . hold that the system is, in the constitutional sense, uniform throughout the United States, when the trustee takes in each state whatever would have been available to the creditor if the bankrupt law had not been passed.") When the 1978 Bankruptcy Act created the current Bankruptcy Code, which included uniform federal exemptions but authorized states to "opt out" and require the use of state exemptions, the constitutionality of that scheme was also challenged but upheld under the reasoning of *Moyses*. See In re Sullivan, 680 F.2d 1131 (7th Cir. 1982), cert. denied, 459 U.S. 992 (1983).

For example, assume the debtor in our previous example bought his first home six years (2,190 days) before filing for bankruptcy relief. Then 24 months ago he sold that first residence and used $225,000 of the equity he realized from that sale to purchase his current home. At the time he files his petition in bankruptcy, he has a total of $250,000 equity in his home. That debtor can exempt all of the $225,000 equity he transferred from his first home to his second but not the additional $25,000 of equity he has accumulated since the purchase of the second home less than 1,215 days before filing. But note that if the first home of the debtor had been located in a different state from the second home, he would not get the benefit of this exception to the 1,215-day rule.

Valuing Property Claimed as Exempt

Schedule C requires the debtor to state the as exempt and the dollar amount of the claimed exemption. That can be confusing.

As you can see on her Schedule C, Marta Carlson claims an exemption in her four-year old Toyota Camry. She is the sole owner of the vehicle and it is valued at $8,500 so that is the value of the portion she owns and she so indicates on the form. The Camry is collateral for the debt owed to Automotive Financing, Inc., which has a balance of $1,750 owed at the time the petition is filed so there is a total of $6,750 of equity in the car ($8,500-$1750=$6,750). However, Marta decides to exempt only $5,025 of that equity and that is the dollar amount of the exemption for the Camry that she enters on the schedule. To reach that exemption amount she combined the $3,775 exemption for motor vehicles authorized by §522(d)(2) with the $1,250 wildcard exemption of §522(d)(5) (both values as of April 1, 2016). If Marta's claimed exemptions in the vehicle are approved, it will be sold and the proceeds applied first to pay off the claim of AFI, totaling $1,750, which is secured by the vehicle, and second to pay Marta $5,025 as her total exemption in the vehicle. The balance will then be used by the bankruptcy trustee for estate administration costs or distribution to creditors.

Application Exercise 7

Marta has a total of $6,750 of equity in the YR-4 Toyota Camry ($8,500 value minus the $1,750 owed to AFI). She could have exempted all of that equity using §522(d)(2), the wildcard exemption of §522(d)(5), plus a portion of her homestead exemption under §522(d)(1) as is allowed by §522(d)(5). If she had chosen to do that, what would be the maximum homestead exemption she could have claimed under §522(d)(1)? Note also that Marta has claimed only $11,825 of the §522(d)(1) homestead exemption in connection with her residence even though there is $75,000 owner's equity in the home ($255,000 value minus $180,000 balance owed on two mortgages). But note from her Schedule C that she uses a portion of her §522(d)(1) homestead exemption to exempt her cash ($50), her bank account balance ($250), her pet dog ($50), and her doll collection ($11,500). That borrowing of the unused portion of the §522(d)(1) homestead exemption is expressly authorized by the wild card exemption of §522(d)(5). But Marta's use of those amounts leaves only $11,825 available for her homestead exemption. What does that use of the homestead and wild card exemptions by Marta tell you about the priority she places on that doll collection?

Section 522(a)(2) and Schedule C require the debtor to list the fair market value of property claimed as exempt, "as of the date of the filing of the petition." Undefined in the Code, **fair market value** has been construed to mean the estimated price that a willing buyer would pay to a willing seller for the item, neither being under a compulsion to sell or buy and both having reasonable knowledge of the underlying facts (see United States v. Cartwright, 411 U.S. 546 (1973)). So property claimed as exempt must be valued by the debtor at what it would sell for in a normal, non-emergency situation, not what it would sell for or be bought for out of desperation.

The Right to Object to a Claimed Exemption

The bankruptcy trustee appointed to administer the Chapter 7 case does not have to accept the debtor's Schedule C exemptions. FRBP 4003 authorizes the trustee or other party in interest to object to the debtor's claimed exemptions if the objection is filed within 30 days of the first meeting of creditors or within 30 days of an amendment to the Schedule C. The court can extend the time for objection on motion filed before the deadline. The objection may contend that the debtor is not entitled to exempt a particular item of property listed on Schedule C or that the value assigned by the debtor to an item of property claimed as exempt is too low. Challenges to a debtor's claimed exemptions are common and we will consider them further in Chapter Nine, Section B, where we consider the various actions that a bankruptcy trustee may take to identify and take possession of property of the estate for the benefit of creditors. Procedurally, an objection to debtor's claimed exemption is treated as a contested matter.

For example, in her Schedule C, Marta claims her jewelry as exempt, assigning it a value of $1,350, which is $250 below the maximum exemption amount for jewelry allowed by §522(d)(4) ($1,600 as of April 2016 subject to adjustment in 2019). If that valuation is correct, she will be able to keep the jewelry because it has no value in excess of the allowed exemption. But if the bankruptcy trustee can prove that the jewelry is actually worth $5,000, he will object to Marta's valuation in that exemption and if he prevails on his objection, will take possession of it as property of the estate, sell it, pay Marta the $1,350 she claimed as exempt in the property (see *Schwab v. Reilly* discussed below) then take the balance for the estate. The trustee has objected to Marta's valuation of the doll collection (see Document 32 in the case file).

What happens if a debtor claims as exempt the full value of property having an actual value in excess of the maximum dollar amount of the exemption applicable to that property but no timely objection is filed? The U.S. Supreme Court has held that, absent a timely objection, the property claimed as exempt will be excluded from the estate and retained by the debtor even if the exemption's actual value exceeds what the Code permits. See *Taylor v. Freeland & Kronz*, 503 U.S. 638, 642-643 (1992) (Debtor who listed expected proceeds of pending employment discrimination lawsuit as exempt on Schedule C entitled to keep all those proceeds even though the dollar amount of recovery exceeded all allowable exemption amounts where trustee failed to file timely objection to claimed exemption.).

On the other hand, what happens if a debtor assigns a specific dollar amount to property claimed as exempt thinking that is its full value but the property turns out to have a higher value than that claimed? In *Schwab v. Reilly*, 560 U.S. 770 (2010) the Supreme Court held that a debtor is only entitled to the dollar amount of the exemption actually claimed on Schedule C, not the full value of the exempted property where that value turns out to be more than the claimed exempted amount even though the debtor intended to and could have exempted the full value of the property and was merely mistaken as to its true value. Moreover, the court held that in such situations the failure of the trustee to file a timely objection to the exemption on the basis of the incorrect value is no bar to the trustee treating the dollar value of the property in excess of the claimed exemption amount as **property of the estate** (a concept to be considered in depth in Chapter Nine, Section A).

Application Exercise 8

Some of you reading this will serve someday as counsel for creditors in bankruptcy cases or as bankruptcy trustees. What is the practical lesson of *Taylor* for an attorney for a creditor or a bankruptcy trustee examining a debtor's Schedule C? What does the result in *Schwab* mean for the attorney assisting the debtor client in filling out the debtor's Schedule C? In light of Schwab, should Marta's attorney consider amending her Schedule C to claim the full §522(d)(4) exemption in the jewelry? To value the doll collection differently given the trustee's objection to the original valuation? (See Document 32 in the case file.) Should the attorney have checked the "100% of fair market value, up to any applicable statutory limit" box on Schedule C to begin with?

The Right to Avoid a Judicial Lien in Property Claimed as Exempt

As noted earlier in this section, if a debtor has granted a consensual security interest in property he could exempt in bankruptcy, the secured creditor's claim to the property will be superior to the debtor's claimed exemption in the property.

For example, if the debtor in our series of homestead exemption examples has obtained a home equity loan for an amount equal to all his equity in the principal residence and granted the lender a mortgage interest in the residence to secure repayment, the debtor will have no equity in the home to exempt when he files a petition in bankruptcy. His right of homestead exemption will not defeat the mortgagee's secured position in the home.

The same is true as to statutory liens in the debtor's property (see Chapter Two, Section C). They are superior to a claimed exemption in the property that is subject to the statutory lien.

For example, if the debtor in our series of homestead exemption examples enters into a contract to sell his principal residence but that contract subsequently falls through, the frustrated buyer who believes the debtor has breached the contract of sale may file a lien lis pendens on the property and file suit to enforce it. The lien lis pendens is a statutory lien. If the debtor then files a petition in bankruptcy, his right of homestead exemption will not defeat the claim of the holder of the lien lis pendens.

Interestingly though, §522(f)(1)(A) empowers the debtor to avoid a judicial lien on his property to the extent that the lien impairs an exemption the debtor would otherwise have in the property. **Judicial liens** are defined by §101(36) as liens obtained by judgment, levy sequestration, or other legal or equitable process and include those postjudgment execution remedies we considered in Chapter Three. FRBP 4003(d) provides that a proceeding to avoid a judicial lien to preserve an exemption is to be initiated by motion, not adversary proceeding.

For example, if the debtor in our series of homestead exemption examples has a judgment entered against him for $100,000 and the judgment creditor has created a judgment lien on the debtor's principal residence by recording the judgment, when the debtor files his bankruptcy petition he may avoid that judgment lien under §522(f)(1)(A) to the extent it impairs his exemption. So if the debtor has $250,000 of equity in his home, all of which state law allows him to exempt as homestead, and debtor has owned it more than 1,215 days so that the 1,215-day rule does not limit his right to claim all his equity as exempt, he can avoid the creditor's judgment lien on the property entirely and claim his full exemption.

Section 522(f)(1)(A) does provide, however, that a judicial lien resulting from a **domestic support obligation** (child support, alimony, or maintenance recoverable by a spouse, former spouse, or child of the debtor) cannot be avoided by the debtor.

For example, if the creditor holding the judgment lien in the previous example is the ex-spouse of the debtor and the judgment is for unpaid child support, the debtor will be unable to avoid that lien on his principal residence.

Section 522(f)(1)(B) also authorizes the individual debtor to avoid a nonpossessory, nonpurchase money security interest in certain household items and tools of the trade to the extent the lien impairs an exemption. We will illustrate that section later in connection with the Chapter 13 case (see Chapter Fourteen, Section B).

In Chapter Nine we will consider various powers granted to the bankruptcy trustee to compel the turnover of debtor's property by third parties having custody or control of such property and to avoid (cancel or set aside) certain prepetition transfers of property from the debtor to third parties and to set off creditor claims against certain obligations of the creditor to the debtor in order to recover the property involved for the estate. The debtor may claim an exemption in property returned to the estate as a result of the trustee's turnover or avoidance actions. Moreover, §§522(g), (h), and (i) authorize the Chapter 7 debtor to initiate such turnover, avoidance, or setoff actions if the trustee refuses to do so in order to assert an exemption in property recovered.

4. Schedule D, Creditors Holding Claims Secured by Property (Official Form 106D)

The debtor must list on Schedule D every creditor who claims a security position in the debtor's property, along with detailed information about any codebtors, the value of the property, the amount of the claim, whether the claim is contingent, unliquidated, or disputed, and whether there is any portion of the claim that is not secured. (See Document 9 in the Carlson case file.)

5. Schedule E/F, Creditors Holding Unsecured Priority and Non-Priority Claims (Official Form 106E/F)

When it is time for the bankruptcy trustee to distribute proceeds of the estate to the various creditors of the estate, some creditors get paid in full before others are paid anything, pursuant to §726 of the Code. We will examine the distribution process and order of priority in detail in Chapter Ten, Section B. But note here that, certain unsecured creditor claims are designated as priority claims by §507 of the Code and, as such, enjoy a high priority in the distribution process under §726. The debtor is required to list §507 priority claims in Part 1 of Schedule E/F.

There are a number of claims designated as priority claims in §507. In consumer bankruptcy cases, the ones most commonly present are

- Domestic support obligations of the debtor, per §507(a)(1)(A)
- Prepetition deposits of money for the lease or purchase of real property or consumer services up to $2,850 per claimant, per §507(a)(7)
- Various tax claims including income and property taxes assessed at varying times before the petition was filed, per §507(a)(8)
- Personal injury or wrongful death claims arising out of DUI, per §507(a)(10)

Marta Carlson's Schedule E/F is Document 10 in her case file. She lists no priority claims. Recall from the Assignment Memorandum in Appendix A and Line 29 of her Schedule A/B that Marta's ex-husband, Eugene, is $15,000 in arrears on his child support obligation to Marta. Were Eugene to file a bankruptcy case he would list that obligation on his Schedule E/F as an unsecured priority claim. He would also list that claim on his list of creditors naming Marta as the creditor.

In Part 2 of Schedule E/F the debtor lists all creditors who have unsecured claims that have no priority over other general creditors under §507 of the Code. The debtor must also state whether each claim is disputed or undisputed, contingent or not, and whether it is liquidated or unliquidated. It is important to note that a debtor must list a claim even if the debtor disputes all or part of it. (See Document 12 in the Carlson case file.)

For example, in Part 1 of her Schedule E/F (Document 10 in the Carlson case file) Marta lists the claim of Pine Ridge Nursing Home against her in the amount of $45,290 but designates it as disputed and contingent on the outcome of the lawsuit Pine Ridge has filed against her. The claim is also listed as unliquidated. Although that claim is liquidated in the sense that Pine Ridge is seeking a sum certain against Marta, she lists it as unliquidated because the exact amount that she might ultimately owe, if anything, might be less than the full amount sought. (See the Assignment Memorandum in Appendix A.)

6. Schedule G, Executory Contracts and Unexpired Leases (Official Form 106G)

An **executory contract** is one that is ongoing and on which both parties still owe some performance. Executory contracts and unexpired leases may give rise to additional claims by the other party to the contract if the debtor intends to discharge continuing obligations under the contract in a Chapter 7. Marta Carlson's Schedule G lists executory contracts common to consumer debtors. (See Document 11 in the Carlson case file.) She is not a party to any leases.

7. Schedule H, Codebtors (Official Form 106H)

What happens if the bankruptcy debtor wants to discharge a debt on which someone else is also liable as a codebtor? Of course the codebtor may have also filed bankruptcy and, if the codebtor is a spouse of the debtor, the codebtor may be a joint petitioner in the same bankruptcy case. But if the codebtor has not also filed for bankruptcy relief is that codebtor still liable for the debt even though this debtor has filed for bankruptcy relief? Yes. A Chapter 7 discharge releases only the debtor from the discharged debts. The liability of a codebtor to a creditor is not affected by that discharge.

In Chapter Seven, Section F, we will see that the filing of the bankruptcy petition triggers an automatic stay, prohibiting creditors of the debtor from continuing to pursue collection of the debts owed to them. In a Chapter 7 case, a codebtor does not benefit from the automatic stay and collection efforts can continue against him unless he is also a joint petitioner or has filed his own bankruptcy case. In Chapter Twelve, Section C, we will learn that in a Chapter 13 case under the Code the codebtor does enjoy the benefit of the automatic stay.

For example, in her Schedule H (Document 12 in the Carlson case file) Marta identifies her ex-husband, Eugene, as a codebtor on obligations that originated during the marriage. Those obligations on which Eugene is a codebtor were also listed on her Schedule D if secured and on her Schedule E/F if unsecured (Documents

9 and 10 in the Carlson case file) and a codebtor noted. But since this is a case under Chapter 7 and not Chapter 13, Eugene does not receive the protection of the automatic stay, and so those creditors can continue collection efforts against him. And though Marta may receive a discharge from those obligations, Eugene will not unless he files his own bankruptcy case.

8. Schedule I, Your Income (Official Form 106I)

All individual debtors (not entities) must complete this form whether their debts are primarily consumer or business. (See Document 13 in the Carlson case file.)

Schedule I is not primarily intended to be used to determine whether the individual Chapter 7 debtor satisfies the means test (and indeed has been required since well before there even was a means test) but it certainly can be used for that purpose. Routinely, a bankruptcy trustee or other party in interest suspicious of a debtor's determination on Form 122A-1 and A-2 that the presumption of abuse does not arise in the case, may compare the information provided on Schedule I with that provided on the means test forms to see if there are discrepancies.

Of course, Schedule I, captures the income picture of the debtor as of the date the petition in bankruptcy is filed. You will recall from our discussion of Form 122A-1 that it determines the debtor's current monthly income (CMI), defined in §101(10A) to include the average monthly income from all sources that the debtor has received during the six months preceding the filing of the petition. So, technically, Schedule I is measuring debtor's income at a different period of time than is Form 122A-1.

For example, a debtor who is unemployed when he or she files the bankruptcy petition will report no income on Schedule I. But if debtor was employed during the six months preceding the filing that income will be used in determining debtor's CMI on Form 122A-1. Though it does not look backward, the latest version of Schedule I does look forward in that Line 13 of the schedule now includes the debtor's statement disclosing reasonably anticipated increase or decrease in income over the 12-month period following the date of filing the petition as required by Code §521(a)(1)(B)(vi).

9. Schedule J, Your Expenses (Official Form 106J)

Schedule J is a companion form to Schedule I, requiring individual debtors to list their average monthly expenses. (See Document 14 in the Carlson case file.)

As with Schedule I, though Schedule J is not primarily intended to be used to determine whether the individual Chapter 7 debtor satisfies the means test (and indeed it too has been required since well before there even was a means test), it certainly can be used for those purposes. That suspicious bankruptcy trustee may well examine the debtor's Schedule J and compare the expense information set out on it with the expense information set on the above median debtor's Form 122A-2. Line 24 of Schedule J now includes the debtor's statement disclosing reasonably anticipated increase or decrease in expenditures over the 12-month period follow-ing the date of filing the petition required by Code §521(a)(1)(B)(vi). If husband and wife have filed a joint petition but maintain separate households they must use Schedule J-2 to report the living expenses separately.

10. Summary of Assets and Liabilities and Certain Statistical Information (Official Form 106-Summary)

This form requires the debtor to enter the totals from Schedules A/B through J and to summarize them. Individual consumer debtors (not individual business debtors or entity debtors) must provide additional information as well. (See Document 15 in the Carlson case file.)

11. Declaration Concerning Debtor's Schedules (Official Form 106-Declaration)

On this form, the individual debtor will sign, declaring under penalty of perjury that the information contained on the various schedules is true and correct to the best of the debtor's knowledge, information, and belief. If the petition and sched-ules were prepared by a non-attorney bankruptcy petition preparer (NABPP), that person must also sign under oath, not affirming that the information is true, but that the preparer has complied with all his obligations under the Code. (See Docu-ment 16 in the Carlson case file.)

The attorney assisting the debtor in gathering and entering all the information contained in the various schedules has a large responsibility in making sure the debtor's declaration is true not only because the attorney by signing the petition is making his or her own certifications per FRBP 9011 and §707(b)(4)(D) regard-ing the information on these schedules as discussed in Part A of this chapter, but because the client, the debtor, is signing under penalty of perjury.

12. Statement of Financial Affairs for Individuals Filing for Bankruptcy (Official Form 107)

This is a comprehensive form that the debtor must complete and file along with the schedules and which is due, like the schedules, within 14 days of filing the petition, per FRBP 1007(b) and (c). This form requires disclosure of different types of finan-cial information than was disclosed in the schedules.

For example, the form asks about payments to creditors in the 90-day and one-year period prior to filing the petition, lawsuits to which the debtor has been a party, as well as any garnishments, repossessions, or seizures of the debtor's prop-erty within one year preceding the filing, and gifts made within one year of filing. We will see in Chapter Nine, Section D, that this information relates to powers given the bankruptcy trustee to cancel certain transfers of the debtor's property made within a certain number of months of the bankruptcy filing and to bring the transferred property back into the bankrupt estate. (See Document 17 in the Carlson case file.)

The statement of financial affairs also has items regarding safety deposit boxes, closed financial accounts, current and former businesses, former spouses, the location of financial records, and so on. The bankruptcy trustee is entitled to know where all the debtor's property is or may be located and is empowered to search thoroughly for undisclosed assets of the debtor that may be in someone else's possession. As part of that task, the trustee may want to obtain and review the debtor's financial records to make sure all property and income is accounted for. We consider the Chapter 7 bankruptcy trustee's duties in more detail in Chapter Seven, Section B.

13. Statement of Intention for Individuals Filing Under Chapter 7 (Official Form 108)

If an individual Chapter 7 debtor has listed property in which a creditor has a security interest, §521(a)(2) of the Code requires the debtor to state in this form whether he or she intends to surrender the property to the secured creditor or try to retain it in one of the ways permitted by the Code. If the debtor states the intent to surrender collateralized property, the debtor is giving notice that debtor will voluntarily relinquish possession of that property to the creditor.

However, as we will see, a Chapter 7 debtor's statement of intent to abandon is not the end of the matter, since the bankruptcy trustee may assert an interest in it for the benefit of the estate if the property has value in excess of the amount owed together with any exemption of the debtor, or if the trustee can avoid the lien (to be considered in Chapter Nine, Section D). We will also learn that the creditor to whom the property is going to be abandoned must also make sure the automatic stay of §362 (to be considered in Chapter Seven, Section F) has been lifted before proceeding to repossess the property notwithstanding the debtor's statement of intent. All of this in due time.

If the individual Chapter 7 debtor intends to retain collateralized property by avoiding the lien because it impairs an exemption as discussed above in connection with Schedule C or by reaffirming the underlying debt and continuing to make payments or by redeeming the property, topics to be considered in Chapter Ten, Section C, the debtor must indicate that intent on the statement of intent form. The debtor's statement of intent must be filed within 30 days after the petition is filed or before the first meeting of creditors, whichever is earliest.

In her Statement of Intent (Document 18 in the Carlson case file), Marta Carlson indicates that she intends to surrender both her home and her YR-4 Toyota Camry. She apparently has made other arrangements regarding where to live (maybe she will rent a place she can afford or move in with a friend or relative) and how to get around (maybe someone is going to give or loan her a car or she's planning to buy something more affordable). But note that in her Schedule C she still claims an exemption in that property she is surrendering. So once the home and vehicle are sold by either the creditors secured in those items or the bankruptcy trustee (who may want to sell them since there is equity for the estate in both the home and the vehicle) and the secured claims satisfied out of the proceeds, the amount of her exemption amounts will have to be paid to her before they go to the benefit of the estate. If the individual debtor is a party to an unexpired lease, debtor must state the intent on this form to either discharge debtor's obligation under the lease or to reassume that obligation.

14. Statement About Your Social Security Numbers (Official Form 121)

This form is required of all individual debtors (both consumer and business). (See Document 20 in the Carlson case file.) To protect the privacy of the debtors, it is filed with the bankruptcy court clerk separately from the petition, schedules, and statements and is withheld by the clerk from the publicly accessible case file.

15. Disclosure of Compensation of Attorney for the Debtor (Official Form 2030)

This disclosure form is required of all debtors whether individuals or entities pursuant to Code §329(a). (See Document 21 in the Carlson case file.) This is not the same as requiring the fee agreement itself to be in writing. However, since the attorney for a consumer debtor is a DRA (see discussion of *Milavetz* in Section A, supra), §528(a)(1) effectively requires that the attorney/client fee agreement in consumer debtor cases be in writing. Otherwise the Code does not require fee agreements between debtors and attorneys to be in writing, but state professional rules governing attorneys may so require. Whether required or not, having the fee agreement in writing is always a good idea for both the attorney and the client.

Furthermore, although Form 2030 requires the disclosure of attorney's fees in a Chapter 7 case, such fees need not be approved by the bankruptcy court, as we will learn is required in a Chapter 13 case. Thus, the fee that debtor's attorneys charge their Chapter 7 clients is determined for the most part by the marketplace. However, §329(b) of the Code gives the bankruptcy court authority in any case filed under title 11, in the event a debtor or other party in interest objects to the attorney's fee, to cancel the fee agreement or to order the attorney to disgorge (refund) as much of a fee already paid that it finds excessive. The test in such a case is whether the fee charged by the attorney "exceeds the reasonable value of any such service." And as we saw illustrated in the *Dean* case cited in Section A, supra, the court can order a disgorgement of fees by an attorney for misconduct or failure to comply with requirements of the Code.

Attorneys representing debtors in Chapter 7 cases typically get their full fee in advance to eliminate the risk that their claim as a creditor for the unpaid portion of the fee will be discharged.

The fee agreement between Marta Carlson and her attorney is Document 1 in her case file and can be seen on the companion Web site.

16. Copies of All Payment Advices or Other Evidence of Payment Received from Any Employer Within 60 Days Before the Filing of the Petition

This is required of all individual debtors (both consumer and business). (See Document 22 in the Carlson case file.)

17. Copy of the Debtor's Last Federal Income Tax Return

This is required of all individual debtors by §521(e)(2)(A)(i) and is to be provided to the bankruptcy trustee (not filed with the clerk with the petition) no later than seven days before the first meeting of creditors (to be discussed in Chapter Seven, Section E). In addition, a copy of all tax returns filed during the case, including tax returns for prior years that had not been filed when the case began, must be supplied. Section 521(e)(2)(B) calls for mandatory dismissal of the case if the debtor fails to comply with this requirement and cannot show that failure to comply was beyond debtor's control.

18. Other Required Filings Mandated by Local Court Rules

The **local court rules** of particular bankruptcy courts may mandate other filings and should always be consulted. In addition, local court rules may mandate use of a designated form for providing some of the information mandated by §521 and FRBP 1007 but that does not have a corresponding official form.

C. THE TIME FRAME FOR FILING THE SUPPORTING SCHEDULES, STATEMENTS, AND LISTS AND FRBP 9006 FOR COMPUTING TIME DEADLINES

The list of creditors must be filed with the petition. The required schedules and statements usually are filed then as well, but §521(a) and FRBP 1007(c) allow the schedules, statement of affairs, and most other documents to be filed within 14 days after the petition without penalty, and the statement of intent by an individual debtor may be filed within 30 days after the petition. In addition, those grace periods may be extended by motion filed with the bankruptcy court and cause shown per FRBP 1007(c). (See Documents 5 and 6 in the Carlson case file.)

There is a limit to the time extension the court can grant a debtor to comply with his obligation to file the various schedules, however. Section 521(i)(1) of the

Code provides that if the debtor fails to file the required schedules within 45 days following the date the petition is filed, the petition is to be "automatically dismissed effective on the 46th day after the date of the filing of the petition." This section could be read to mean that bankruptcy judges have no discretion to grant extensions beyond 45 days and that the failure to comply with the 45-day filing requirement cannot be forgiven or cured. To date, however, two circuits have found an ambiguity between the apparent mandate of §521(i)(1) and the arguably conflicting language of §521(a)(1)(B) directing the debtor to file the various schedules and statements "unless the court orders otherwise" and have construed the sections to mean that bankruptcy courts retain discretion to waive or excuse the failure to file the required information within the 45-day window notwithstanding the automatic dismissal language (see In re Acosta-Rivera, 557 F.3d 8 (1st Cir. 2009), and In re Warren, 568 F.3d 1113 (9th Cir. 2009)).

Application Exercise 9

See if the bankruptcy, district, or circuit courts of the state where you plan to practice have addressed this issue.

FRBP 9006 is the primary source for guidelines governing the computation of time periods for all actions mandated or allowed under the Code.

Application Exercise 10

Using FRBP 9006 answer the following questions: What happens if the last day to file something falls on a weekend or legal holiday? Which legal holidays are recognized for purposes of extending a deadline? Does the *last day* to file something end at midnight that day or when the clerk's office closes for that day? What happens if the clerk's office is unexpectedly closed for weather or other eventuality on the day something is due and it cannot be filed electronically?

D. THE IMPORTANCE OF REPORTING ACCURATE AND COMPLETE INFORMATION AND OF EMPLOYING WELL-QUALIFIED ASSISTANTS

It is critical to both the debtor and his or her attorney that all information reported in the petition, schedules, statements, and other documents filed in connection with a bankruptcy case be accurate and complete. In addition to the reasons discussed in this chapter, we will learn in Chapter Eleven that failing to list a creditor in Schedule D, E, or F can result in that creditor's claim not being discharged. Moreover, providing inaccurate or incomplete information can result in denial of any discharge or even revocation of a discharge already granted. And if the debtor is found to have acted intentionally with regard to the withheld, incomplete, or inaccurate information, there can be state or federal criminal charges brought against the debtor and anyone who knowingly assisted, including charges of bankruptcy fraud or making false oaths and claims under 18 U.S.C. §§157 or 152.

Lawyers who routinely represent debtors in consumer bankruptcy cases often have large caseloads. The attorney's fee earned on a single Chapter 7 or Chapter 13 case is usually quite modest. Because they have many clients at any point in time and because debtor's representation involves the gathering and reporting of so much information for each client, most of these attorneys rely on non-lawyer assistants, usually designated as paralegals or legal assistants. Typically, the non-lawyer assistants will gather from the client or other sources the information necessary to complete the petition and supporting schedules and then draft those documents for the lawyers review prior to filing. Similarly, lawyers representing creditors make significant use of non-lawyer assistants to obtain information from clients or from public records and to draft various documents that impact the debt obligation and the creditor's claim.

Two things are absolutely essential for the debtor or creditor's lawyer employing such assistants. First, the lawyer must employ only trained, competent assistants. The law treats those assisting the lawyer as the agents of the lawyer so any mistake made by the assistants will be attributable to the lawyer both for purposes of a legal malpractice claim by the client and for purposes of an alleged ethical violation that could threaten the lawyer's license to practice. Only employ competent, well-trained assistants.

Second, the lawyer must never rely so completely on the assistants that the lawyer fails to fulfill his or her own obligations to the client and to the court before which the lawyer is admitted to practice. That can happen when the lawyer fails to have in place procedures to ensure to the extent reasonable under the circumstances that the information filed with the court on behalf of a client is complete and accurate. And it can happen when the lawyer fails to actually review documents prepared by an assistant before they are delivered to clients for signature or filed with the court or in another public office. See, e.g., In re Motors Liquidation, 777 F.3d 100 (2d Cir. 2015) (UCC-3 statements prepared by debtor's law firm to release security interest of creditor in debtor's property securing a $300 million obligation that was being paid off inadvertently included the security interest of creditor in debtor's property securing a separate $1.5 billion obligation. Partner in law firm preparing the UCC-3 had assigned associate to prepare the UCC-3 and associate in turn had assigned paralegal unfamiliar with the underlying transaction or debt structure of debtor to list the secured debts to be released in the UCC-3s. No one with debtor, debtor's law firm, creditor, or creditor's law firm caught the error prior to filing of the UCC-3s. In later bankruptcy of debtor, creditor's security interest in property securing $1.5 billion obligation deemed terminated despite inadvertence of error.).

Application Exercise 11

Assume you have just been hired as an associate in the office of a practitioner in your community with an active debtor's practice, specializing in Chapter 7 and 13 consumer bankruptcy cases. Her practice averages 75 new clients per month and the volume of data and paperwork that her office processes is enormous. She employs two paralegals who conduct the initial meeting with potential clients, explain how bankruptcy works, make the fee arrangements, obtain the information from them necessary for completion of the petition and schedules, and then make a recommendation to the attorney regarding what chapter the potential client should file under. If she agrees to take a case, the paralegals then advise the clients of the representation, draft the appropriate petition, supporting schedules, and plan in the Chapter 13 cases; the paralegals then have the clients review and sign them, obtain the necessary fee payments, and forward the file to the attorney for final review and signature. The attorney normally does not actually meet or speak with any client until the day before or morning of the first meeting of creditors in the client's case. This arrangement minimizes the time the attorney has to spend with clients and frees her to concentrate on hearings on matters that arise in her many pending cases that require her attendance in court. The two paralegals are experienced and, in the attorney's opinion, trustworthy, so she gives the documents they draft for her only a cursory review before signing and giving them back for filing. When she is out of town she authorizes the senior paralegal to do the final review and sign her name to the petitions that need to be filed while she is gone. She tells you that she's been doing this for several years now and there's never been a problem.

a. Do you see any potential ethical violations in the procedures used by this attorney?
b. Assume the attorney turns the new client aspects of her bankruptcy practice over to you. What changes will you make in these procedures?

Chapter Summary

▪ A Chapter 7 case is commenced by filing a voluntary petition with a bankruptcy court having proper venue. Married couples may file a joint petition. The bankruptcy court may order two or more cases involving debtors with related assets and debt obligations to be jointly administered and two or more cases involving the same debtor to be consolidated. In certain circumstances, creditors of a debtor may force him into bankruptcy by filing an involuntary petition for the debtor. Venue for an individual bankruptcy case is proper in the district where the debtor has resided for the 180 days preceding filing.

▓ The individual debtor must file a number of supporting schedules showing assets, liabilities, and claimed exemptions as well as a list of creditors, a statement of affairs, and a number of other documents either with the petition or within 14 days after the petition is filed unless that time is extended by the bankruptcy court. The individual debtor must also file a statement of intent with the petition or within 30 days thereafter indicating whether the debtor intends to surrender collateralized property to the creditor, redeem the property by paying the creditor all that is owed, or reaffirm the debt and continue paying per the contract in order to retain possession.

▓ The attorney for the debtor must conduct a reasonable inquiry to ensure the accuracy of the information contained in a bankruptcy petition and supporting schedules and the attorney's signature on the petition certifies to the court that he has done so. Attorneys representing individual debtors are also considered to be "debt relief agencies" under a BAPCPA provision and that provision requires those attorneys to include certain statements in their advertising and to provide certain written disclosures to their clients. Though the BAPCPA DRA provision prohibits a DRA from advising an assisted person to incur more debt in contemplation of bankruptcy, the Supreme Court has interpreted that phrase to prohibit only advising a debtor to incur more debt in order to manipulate the bankruptcy system rather than for a valid purpose.

▓ The individual Chapter 7 debtor is entitled to claim certain property as exempt using federal exemptions set forth in the Code or the exemption laws of his state of residence unless his state has elected to opt out of the federal exemptions in which case the debtor must use the state exemptions. In states that have opted out of the federal exemptions, a BAPCPA amendment limits the homestead exemption to no more than $160,375 if the debtor has not owned the residence for more than 1,215 days preceding the filing of the petition.

▓ Exempt property is to be valued at its fair market value, which is the estimated price that a willing buyer would pay to a willing seller for the property, neither being under a compulsion to sell or buy and both having reasonable knowledge of the underlying facts. The trustee or other party in interest can object to an exemption or its valuation within 30 days following the first meeting of creditors. An individual debtor can avoid a judicial lien on property to the extent the debtor can claim that property as exempt.

Applying the Concepts

1. Assume Gerald and Maryann, a married couple, have retained you to file a Chapter 7 bankruptcy for them. If possible, they would like to exempt the following property and keep the bankruptcy trustee from taking it in the bankruptcy proceeding. Using the federal exemptions, prepare a proposed Schedule C for Gerald and Maryann.

   a. A certificate of deposit with a current value of $53,000
   b. Savings account with a balance of $1,250

    c. A YR-2 Silverado truck that is paid for and worth $13,500

    d. A YR-3 Toyota Camry on which $8,500 is still owed to a creditor secured in it but that is worth $15,000

    e. Maryann's diamond necklace appraised for $7,500

    f. Household furniture, appliances, and furnishings valued at $15,000

    g. A whole life insurance policy with built up cash value of $14,000

    h. Balance in Maryann's 401(k) plan of $75,000

    i. Home worth $300,000 on which there is a mortgage in favor of Bank with a current balance of $195,000

2. Prepare an alternative Schedule C for Gerald and Maryann from Question 2 using the state exemptions for the state where you plan to practice. Which set of exemptions is more generous to these debtors, state or federal?

3. Assume Buster and Kathy, a married couple, own a home on which they owe a balance of $250,000 to Bank and Bank holds a mortgage in the home to secure payment. But the home is valued at $325,000, which means Buster and Kathy have some owner's equity in the home. However, there is a mechanics' lien on the home as well in the amount of $5,000 in favor of a subcontractor who did some work on the house a few months ago and didn't get paid by the general contractor. In addition, last month an unsecured creditor obtained a $10,000 final judgment against Buster and Kathy and has caused a judicial lien to be filed on the home in that amount. Buster and Kathy have come to you to discuss filing a Chapter 7 bankruptcy. They cannot afford the mortgage payments on the home and are prepared to lose it in the bankruptcy. However, they very much want to exempt all the equity they can in the home. Which if any of the following liens can Buster and Kathy avoid in order to claim a homestead exemption in bankruptcy?

    a. The $250,000 mortgage held by Bank

    b. The $5,000 mechanics' lien

    c. The $10,000 judicial lien

Using the federal exemptions, can Buster and Kathy exempt all of their owner's equity in the home?

4. Read Jonak v. McDermott, 511 B.R. 586 (D. Minn. 2014), cited in the discussion of NABPPs in Section A of this chapter, then assume the following: You have built up a successful consumer debtor's bankruptcy practice. One day one of your most experienced non-lawyer paralegals comes to you and advises that she has decided to set up a professional limited liability corporation (PLLC) that will provide debt management advice to customers that will include assisting them in the preparation of bankruptcy filings. She is leaving your employment but asks you to represent her in setting up her new business. Here are some questions she asks you — how will you answer?

    a. Hasn't she already been functioning as a §110 non-attorney petition preparer while working for you?

    b. Will doing business through the PLLC protect her from personal liability as a NABPP or a DRA?

    c. As an NABPP can she at least advise customers whether to file under Chapter 7 or Chapter 13 or some other chapter of the Code?

    d. Will it be okay if her PLLC advertises for business under the name, "Non-Lawyer Legal Debt Consulting Services"?

    e. How can her new company become an approved §109(h) Credit Counseling Company for individual debtors? See §111.

5. Locate and read Assignment Memorandum #1 in Appendix C. If your instructor so directs, prepare the designated Chapter 7 filing documents for Abelard Mendoza assuming that Mendoza resides and will file in the state and community where you plan to practice.

The Chapter 7 Consumer Bankruptcy Case: The Order for Relief, Bankruptcy Trustee, First Meeting of Creditors, and Automatic Stay

Once the bankruptcy petition is filed, the case is deemed commenced and important consequences flow from that fact for both the debtor and his creditors. From the very moment the case is filed the provisions of the Code and the Rules of Bankruptcy Procedure are set in motion. Filing a bankruptcy petition is somewhat like turning the ignition switch in a car. The machine roars to life as numerous systems inside begin to operate — warming up, lighting up, lubricating, rotating, inspecting themselves, preparing to perform. In this chapter, we will see how the various systems that make up the great machine of bankruptcy procedure roar to life with the filing of the Chapter 7 petition and then methodically grind forward to administer the case.

A. THE ORDER FOR RELIEF

The Chapter 7 case is commenced by the filing of the bankruptcy petition per

Key Concepts

- Immediately upon the filing of a Chapter 7 petition, the bankruptcy court will appoint a bankruptcy trustee to administer the case
- Most Chapter 7 consumer cases are no-asset cases in which there are no non-exempt assets to be liquidated and no distribution to unsecured creditors
- Upon filing of the petition an automatic stay goes into effect causing most collection-type activities against the debtor to stop
- A creditor may ask the court to lift the automatic stay if one of the statutory grounds for lifting is present
- Actual and punitive damages can be awarded against a creditor who willfully violates the automatic stay
- A first meeting of creditors is to be held within 21-40 days of the order for relief

§301(a) of the Code and Federal Rules of Bankruptcy Procedure (FRBP) 1002. Per §301(b), the filing of the petition constitutes an **order for relief** under the Code, a term used often in the Code as we will see. The Code and a number of the Official Bankruptcy Forms refer to the order for relief as if it were something separate from the petition. For example, §341(a) says, "Within a reasonable time after the order for relief in a case under this title, the United States trustee shall convene and preside over a meeting of creditors." Some courts do enter a formal order for relief after the petition is filed but in most districts the petition itself is treated as the order for relief and no separate order is entered.

When an involuntary petition is filed and granted, a separate order for relief will be entered (see Official Forms 105 and 205). In this chapter, we refer interchangeably to the filing of the petition, the commencement of the case, and the order for relief.

B. THE CHAPTER 7 BANKRUPTCY TRUSTEE

Section 701 of the Code provides that, "promptly after the order for relief under this chapter" (i.e., Chapter 7), the U.S. Trustee is to appoint a person to serve as **bankruptcy trustee** in the Chapter 7 case. Section 586(a)(1) of Title 28 directs the U.S. Trustee in each federal district to, "establish, maintain, and supervise a panel of private trustees that are eligible and available to serve as trustees in cases under Chapter 7." It is from this **trustee panel** that the U.S. Trustee will select the bankruptcy trustee for each Chapter 7 case. Persons selected to serve on the panel of trustees may be lawyers, accountants, retired bankers, and other businesspeople.

Though it is rare for creditors to *not* accept the initial choice of trustee made by the U.S. Trustee, §702 authorizes them to elect someone else to serve as trustee at the first meeting of creditors (discussed in Section F). Thus, the trustee appointed by the U.S. Trustee serves only in an interim capacity until after that meeting. Section 324 of the Code authorizes the court to remove a trustee for cause. Though cause for removal is not defined in the Code and is, fortunately, a rare event, cause for removal can be anything from dishonesty to dilatoriness to inability to work with the debtor.

The creditors may form a **creditors committee** to work closely with the trustee and to represent the creditors before the court (see §705). Creditors' committees (common in Chapter 7 business liquidations and Chapter 11 business reorganizations) are unusual in a Chapter 7 consumer bankruptcy case.

Bankruptcy trustees must be bonded because they are handling the property of the estate. They are responsible not only to the debtors, the creditors of the estate, and the U.S. Trustee who selects and supervises them, but also to the bankruptcy judge before whom they will appear as the representative of the estate (see §323(a)). In the notice to creditors of the filing of the case (discussed in more detail in Section D), parties are advised of the identity of the person appointed to serve as trustee. (See Document 23 in the Carlson case file.)

Application Exercise 1

Locate the bankruptcy trustee panel for the federal district where you plan to practice. This information might be available on the Web sites of the bankruptcy courts in the district. The U.S. Trustee Web site has a Private Trustee Locator page that will assist you as well at www.justice.gov/ust/chapter-7-12-13-private-trustee-locator.

1. Duties of the Bankruptcy Trustee

The duties of the Chapter 7 trustee are set out in §701 of the Code. Exhibit 7.1 summarizes those duties. We will examine many of these duties in detail as we move work through the administration of the case.

Once a Chapter 7 case is filed, the bankruptcy trustee becomes the primary actor in the case. FRBP 2015 requires the trustee to file a complete inventory of the property of the estate within 30 days following his appointment, to keep detailed records of the receipt and disposition of property of the estate, and to provide interim reports (often quarterly) regarding affairs of the estate. Section 345 of the Code requires the trustee to invest cash belonging to the estate in government-insured accounts or certificates unless the court otherwise orders. All records of the trustee's handling of estate property are open to examination by the debtor, creditors, the U.S. Trustee, and the court.

EXHIBIT 7.1   **Duties of the Bankruptcy Trustee in a Chapter 7 Case**

- To investigate the financial affairs of the debtor
- To locate and take possession of all non-exempt property of the debtor (called **property of the estate** under the Code)
- To preserve the property of the estate and then liquidate it (in a Chapter 7) for the benefit of the creditors of the estate, or abandon it if it has no value to the estate
- To examine the exempt property claims of the debtor and challenge them if there are disputes as to the legitimacy of the claimed exemption or the value claimed by the debtor
- To examine the claims of creditors in an asset case, to allow those that appear properly supported, and to challenge and disallow those that are not
- To raise objections to discharge of the debtor if grounds for such objection are present
- To distribute property of the estate in the order of priority dictated by the Code
- To prepare and file reports with the U.S. Trustee and the court, fully disclosing actions taken with regard to the debtor and the property of the estate (see FRBP 2015)

It is generally understood that the bankruptcy trustee owes a fiduciary duty to the estate, its beneficiaries, and its creditors. The trustee enjoys a quasi-judicial immunity from personal liability for actions taken pursuant to his authority as trustee or according to court order. See Lonneker Farms, Inc. v. Klobucher, 804 F.2d 1096, 1097 (9th Cir. 1986) (bankruptcy trustee receives "derived judicial immunity" because he performs "integral part of the judicial process"). Even with regard to third persons unconnected to the bankruptcy estate the bankruptcy trustee enjoys absolute immunity for actions taken with the scope of the position. See, e.g., In re Bryan, 308 B.R. 583, 587 (Bankr. N.D. Ga. 2004) (Chapter 7 trustee sued by individual concerning whom trustee had initiated an unlicensed practice of law inquiry with state bar had absolute immunity from allegations of slander and libel since trustee acted in his capacity as trustee and in accordance with his statutory duty to protect assets of the estate from dissipation via frivolous pleading drafted with plaintiff's assistance), and In re Heinsohn, 247 B.R. 237, 244 (E.D. Tenn. 2000) (trustee sued for malicious prosecution and defamation by a non-debtor prosecuted and acquitted of bankruptcy fraud upon referral of charges by the trustee had absolute immunity from suit).

2. Compensation of the Bankruptcy Trustee

Sections 326 and 330 of the Code govern the trustee's fees. In general, the trustee is entitled to reasonable compensation based on the nature of the services rendered to the estate, their market value, and the time spent. A minimum payment is allowed a trustee under §330(b), which comes in part from the filing fee. In a no-asset case (discussed in the next section), that may be the only compensation the trustee receives. Where there are assets in the estate to be distributed to creditors, the trustee also receives as compensation a percentage of the value distributed, within certain limits established by §326. The trustee's fee is considered an administrative expense and is given a significant priority in the distribution of the estate, as discussed in Chapter Ten, Section B.

3. Hiring Professional Persons to Assist the Bankruptcy Trustee

Section 327 of the Code and FRBP 2014 authorize the bankruptcy trustee to hire professional persons such as attorneys, accountants, appraisers, auctioneers, real estate agents, or other professionals to assist the trustee with administering the estate.

For example, if the trustee is going to initiate an adversary proceeding, he will usually hire an attorney to represent him in that litigation. When the time comes to liquidate property of the estate the trustee may conduct a public auction and need to retain the services of an auctioneer for that purpose. If the trustee encounters complicated financial dealings by the debtor or other party that he lacks the sophistication to understand, he may need an accountant or other financial professional to assist him. If he has a question regarding the value of realty, he may need an appraiser to tell him the likely value and, later, a real estate agent to help sell it.

Professionals can only be hired with the approval of the bankruptcy court. So the trustee will file a motion with the court seeking authorization to do so and obtain a court order approving the hiring.

For example, in the Marta Carlson case, the bankruptcy trustee has decided that Marta's home needs to be appraised to determine its potential value to the estate. He has filed a motion for authorization to hire a real estate appraiser, which is shown in Document 29 in the Carlson case file. The order granting that authorization is shown in Document 30.

FRBP 6003 provides that, absent a showing of immediate and irreparable harm, the court cannot grant an application for permission to hire a professional person during the first 21 days following the filing of the petition.

Section 327(a) requires that any professional hired by the trustee be a **disinterested person** and not hold or represent an **adverse interest** to the estate. The term disinterested is defined in 11 U.S.C. §101(14) as pertaining to a person who (1) "is not a creditor, an equity security holder, or an insider"; (2) "is not and was not, within 2 years before the date of the filing of the petition, a director, officer, or employee of the debtor"; and (3) "does not have an interest materially adverse to the interest of the estate or of any class of creditors or equity security holders, by reason of any direct or indirect relationship to, connection with, or interest in, the debtor, or for any other reason." Professionals have an adverse interest to the estate if they "(1) possess or assert any economic interest that would tend to lessen the value of the bankruptcy estate or that would create either an actual or potential dispute in which the estate is a rival claimant; or (2) possess a predisposition under circumstances that render such a bias against the estate." In re AroChem Corp., 176 F.3d 610, 623 (2d Cir. 1999). For example, the trustee in Marta Carlson's case could not hire an appraiser who was also a creditor of Marta unless the appraiser agreed to waive its claim against the estate. (See the affidavit of the appraiser that is part of Document 29 in the case file.) The trustee could not hire as an attorney a lawyer who also represents Pine Ridge Nursing Home which has a lawsuit pending against her at the time she files. That lawyer represents an adverse interest to Marta's estate.

The compensation of professionals is governed by §328 and OBR 2016. Under §328, the trustee is authorized to employ professionals on any reasonable terms, including retainer, hourly rate, fixed fee, or contingency. In order to be paid, however, Rule 2016 requires the professional seeking payment to file a **fee application** containing a description of services performed, payments to date, and any fee sharing agreements. Most bankruptcy courts have local rules and customized forms governing fee applications. In practice, bankruptcy courts want to see a sufficiently detailed description of all services performed, dates, attorney names, the amount of time spent, and other relevant information so that the court can be satisfied that payment of estate funds to the professionals is commensurate with the value received by the estate.

To the extent the court finds the fee application excessive in light of the benefit to the estate, the court has authority under §328(a) to modify or deny the compensation requested. If the court finds that the professional seeking compensation was not a disinterested person or held or represented an interest adverse to the estate, compensaton may be denied under §328(c).

Per §331, professionals may apply to the court for compensation on an interim basis, but not more than once every 120 days. While this is better than waiting until the end of a case, for many professionals waiting four months to be paid can be a serious burden. Accordingly, many courts will enter orders allowing professionals to file interim fee applications on a monthly basis, such as a final fee order at the end of the case. Interim fee orders commonly include a **holdback provision** of 5 to 20 percent of the requested fee until the final order.

C. THE NO-ASSET CASE

The first thing the newly appointed trustee will do in a Chapter 7 case is review the petition and supporting schedules to make an initial determination as to whether the case is an **asset case** or a **no-asset case**. A no-asset case is one in which all of the debtor's assets are either properly exempted (which means the debtor can keep the property, despite the bankruptcy proceeding) or subject to validly perfected prepetition security interests or liens that give the secured creditors a priority claim to the collateralized property over the claim of the bankruptcy trustee. (See discussion of the trustee's lien avoidance powers in Chapter Nine, Section D.) Approximately 90 percent of all Chapter 7 cases nationwide are no-asset cases.

A review of Marta Rinaldi Carlson's schedules in the Carlson case file will quickly disclose that hers is an asset case and, in that sense, her Chapter 7 case is atypical. But we use a Chapter 7 asset case study in order to illustrate various aspects of case administration that would not arise in a no-asset case. Working through a no-asset case will not teach you how to handle an asset case. Working through an asset case will teach you how to handle both.

Since bankruptcy trustees are compensated out of the filing fee paid by the debtor and a percentage of property located and sold for the benefit of creditors in the case, the trustee's compensation can be dramatically impacted by whether a case is an asset case or a no-asset case.

Before finally concluding that the case is a no-asset one, the bankruptcy trustee will question the debtor at the first meeting of creditors and do any further investigation he deems appropriate. As suggested in the list of the trustee's duties in Exhibit 7.1, that may include a close review of the debtor's claimed exemptions and the values asserted by the debtor and a close review of the claims of listed secured creditors. If the trustee concludes that the case is a no-asset one, he will file a **no-asset report** with the bankruptcy court and a discharge in bankruptcy will be issued promptly and the case closed.

D. NOTICE TO CREDITORS OF FILING OF THE CASE

Pursuant to §342 of the Code, upon the filing of the petition, the bankruptcy court clerk will issue a **Notice of Chapter 7 Bankruptcy Case** (sometimes called a **notice of commencement**) to the creditors and the U.S. Trustee. Section 342(d) provides that if the case is filed by a consumer debtor, the notice is to be given no later than ten days after the petition is filed. This notice is Official Form 309 and there are separate notice forms for cases filed under Chapter 7, 11, 12, or 13. (Remember that all official bankruptcy forms are available at www.uscourts. gov/forms/bankruptcy-forms.) There are also different notice of commencement forms for Chapter 7 cases, depending on whether the debtor is an individual or an entity and on whether the case is an asset case or a no-asset case.

Marta Carlson's Chapter 7 case is by an individual with assets so the clerk has used Form 309B (see Document 23 in the Carlson case file). Observe that the first page of the notice provides the creditor with the name, address, and phone number of the bankruptcy trustee appointed in the case. As we move through the other aspects of case administration, refer back to the notice to see how it advises creditors of the various aspects of case administration that apply to them.

E. THE FIRST MEETING OF CREDITORS

Pursuant to §341 of the Code and FRBP 2003, the U.S. Trustee is required to call a meeting of creditors within 21 to 40 days following the order for relief in a Chapter 7 case. This **first meeting of creditors** is required in a case filed under any chapter of the Code, but the timing of the meeting varies (e.g., 21 to 40 days after the order for relief in Chapter 7s and 11s; 21 to 35 days in a Chapter 12; and 21 to 50 days in a Chapter 13). Practitioners often refer to the first meeting of creditors as the **341 meeting**.

The notice of filing of the case advises creditors of the date and time set for the 341 meeting.

The 341 meeting is conducted by the bankruptcy trustee. This is not a court hearing and the bankruptcy judge is not present. The debtor is put under oath and must answer questions regarding his assets and financial affairs. Frequently non-exempt property of the debtor is turned over to the bankruptcy trustee at this meeting: keys to cars, houses, lockboxes, and the like. There are often questions about assets or liabilities the debtor has or hasn't listed in his schedules, or issues discussed regarding the valuation of property claimed as exempt. All these matters may be inquired into at the 341. Since the debtor is under oath, it is important that he answer truthfully and candidly.

Section 341(d) requires that the bankruptcy trustee examine a Chapter 7 debtor on several matters at the 341 meeting. Those required topics are set forth in Exhibit 7.2.

EXHIBIT 7.2	**Questions the Bankruptcy Trustee Is Required to Ask the Chapter 7 Debtor at the First Meeting of Creditors**

- Debtor's awareness of the consequences of receiving a discharge in bankruptcy, including the effect on credit history
- Debtor's ability to file for relief under another chapter of the Code
- Debtor's awareness of the effect of a discharge of debt under Chapter 7
- Debtor's awareness of the effect of reaffirming debt rather than discharging it

Application Exercise 2

Research the court rulings of the federal district or circuit (including ethical rules of the applicable state) where you plan to practice to determine the prevailing rule there, or check the local rules of your bankruptcy court to see if that issue is addressed there.

May a Non-Attorney Agent of a Creditor Ask Questions at the 341 Meeting?

One question that has arisen historically in 341 meetings is whether a non-attorney employee of a creditor can attend and ask questions of the debtor on behalf of the creditor. Some courts have allowed that and some have not on the grounds that asking questions on behalf of another at the 341 hearing is the practice of law. Under that view, an individual creditor could appear and ask questions himself at the hearing, but if he sends an agent to speak for him, that agent must be an attorney. Since corporations are not natural persons like the individual creditor and must always be represented by an agent, the practical effect of this view is to require entity creditors such as corporations to

Within ten days following the 341 meeting, the U.S. Trustee is required by §704(b)(1) to file a report with the bankruptcy court advising whether any presumption of abuse should arise in the case because of the means test of §704(b). The clerk then provides a copy of that statement to creditors within five days. If the U.S. Trustee concludes that the presumption of abuse is still present, he is required to file a motion to dismiss the case or convert it to a Chapter 13 within 30 days of filing the §704(b)(1) report. The §704(b)(1) report filed by the U.S. Trustee in Marta Carlson's case can be seen in Document 26 in the Carlson case file.

The 341 meeting is not the only time that a debtor can be examined under oath in a case. If at any time there is a dispute about the debtor's 341 meeting testimony or if any new issue arises in the case requiring sworn testimony of the debtor or anyone else, FRBP 2004 authorizes any party in interest to file a motion with the courts asking permission to conduct a sworn examination of the debtor or any other witness. This is called a **Rule 2004 examination**.

For example, assume that the bankruptcy trustee in Marta Carlson's case is considering an objection to the claim of Pine Ridge Nursing Home based on the debtor's dispute of that debt. The trustee may want to examine Marta further on this dispute and he may want to examine one or more persons from Pine Ridge as well. To accomplish those examinations, the trustee may utilize Rule 2004.

F. THE AUTOMATIC STAY

The **automatic stay** is one of the most important events in a bankruptcy case. Section 362(a) of the Code provides that the filing of a bankruptcy petition automatically stays (stops) any action by a creditor to enforce a claim or to collect an indebtedness owed to him by the debtor or any action by the creditor to improve his position vis-à-vis other creditors (e.g., by obtaining a postpetition security interest in the debtor's property). The stay mandates the following:

- All informal collection efforts against the debtor must stop.
- All pending collection lawsuits must stop.
- All efforts to collect on a final judgment previously entered must stop.
- All efforts to obtain a security interest in debtor's property must stop.
- All efforts to repossess or foreclose on the debtor's property pursuant to a consensual or non-consensual lien must stop.
- Debtor's right to the possession and use of property must not be interfered with (e.g., property repossessed but not yet sold must be returned to debtor)

always be represented by counsel at the 341 meeting, adding to the expense of the proceeding for that creditor. BAPCPA revised §341(c) to provide that a creditor holding a consumer debt (one related to personal or household goods) may be represented at the meeting by an employee or agent of the creditor who need not be an attorney.

A closely related question is whether a paralegal or legal assistant for the attorney representing a creditor can attend and ask questions of the debtor in lieu of the attorney herself. In some districts that has been prohibited as constituting the practice of law.

Automatic Stay = STOP

FMStox/Shutterstock.com

For example, as indicated in the Assignment Memorandum in Appendix A, Pine Ridge Nursing Home has filed suit against Marta Carlson to collect on amounts allegedly owed on the personal guaranty she signed. If that case is scheduled to go to trial the day after her petition in bankruptcy is filed, the trial must be continued to avoid violating the automatic stay. If her petition is filed in the morning and motions are scheduled to be heard in that case later in the afternoon, the motions will have to be postponed. If the judge has just entered a judgment in favor of Pine Ridge Nursing Home, it must take no action to collect on the judgment lest it be found in violation of the automatic stay. According to the Assignment Memorandum in Appendix A, the Dreams Come True Financing Company has declared the loan to Marta to be in default and is preparing to foreclose on her home. With the filing of the bankruptcy petition, that foreclosure proceeding must stop.

The rationale behind the automatic stay provision is that once the debtor has filed the petition seeking bankruptcy relief, he is immediately entitled to the protections afforded by the Code, and his property is also immediately subject to the procedures outlined in the Code. Consequently, the automatic stay serves to freeze actions against the debtor's property at the commencement of the case so that the bankruptcy procedure can control what happens to the debtor and his property from that point on.

1. Exceptions to the Automatic Stay

Section 362(b) of the Code sets out a number of exceptions to the automatic stay — collection activities that are not stayed by the bankruptcy filing and can continue. A number of these are actions involving domestic disputes. Exhibit 7.3 lists various domestic disputes that, per §362(b), are not automatically stayed by the filing of a bankruptcy petition.

Per §362(b)(10), a landlord's eviction action against a debtor involving a nonresidential lease is not stayed where the eviction is based on expiration of the agreed lease term either before or after the bankruptcy petition is filed. The stay will apply to such eviction action if it is based on some other ground (e.g., nonpayment of rent). Per §§362(b)(22) and (23), a landlord's eviction action against a debtor involving a residential lease is not stayed where:

- The landlord has obtained a prepetition judgment of eviction;
- The landlord certifies that the basis of the eviction action is the debtor's endangerment of the property; or
- The landlord certifies that the basis of the eviction action is the debtor's illegal use of controlled substances on the property.

EXHIBIT 7.3   **Domestic Actions Not Subject to the §362 Automatic Stay**

- To establish paternity
- To establish or modify an order for domestic support obligations
- Concerning child custody or visitation
- To dissolve a marriage, except to the extent that such proceeding seeks to determine the division of property that is property of the estate
- Regarding domestic violence
- To collect a domestic support obligation from property that is not property of the estate
- To withhold income of the debtor or intercept a tax refund due the debtor in order to satisfy a domestic support obligation under state law
- To withhold or restrict a driver's license or a professional, occupational, or recreational license for nonpayment of domestic obligations under state law
- To report nonpayment of a domestic obligation to a credit reporting agency

Per §362(b)(1), neither state nor federal criminal actions against a debtor are stayed by the filing of a petition. Per §362(b)(4), regulatory actions against a debtor by any governmental unit that involves protecting public health and safety (e.g., a state department of health acting to shut down debtor's business for violations of state fire code or state food handling regulations) are not stayed.

Though §362(a)(8) provides that tax disputes pending in U.S. Tax Court when the petition is filed are stayed, §362(b)(9) provides that state or federal government actions to audit a debtor for tax liability, to issue tax deficiency notices, to demand tax returns, or to issue a past-due tax assessment and demand payment are not stayed. Other actions to collect a tax from the debtor will be stayed, as will any other action to create, perfect, or enforce a tax lien. Section §362(b)(18) does exempt from the stay an action by a governmental unit to create or perfect a statutory tax lien arising from a property tax or special assessment on debtor's real property, but only where such tax or assessment becomes due after the petition if filed.

Though most foreclosure actions are subject to the stay, §362(b)(8) does except from the stay foreclosure actions initiated by the U.S. Department of Housing and Urban Development (HUD) on properties consisting of five or more living units.

And sometimes federal statutes outside the Bankruptcy Code override the stay provision. See, e.g., In re Robinson, 764 F. 3d 554, 559-60 (6th Cir. 2014) (debtor who was convicted of mail and wire fraud and ordered to make restitution filed for Chapter 13 relief and government sought enforcement of restitution against property of the estate; though §361(b)(1) only excepted criminal action against "the debtor" from automatic stay, 18 U.S.C. §3613(a) authorizes enforcement of a judgment imposing a fine against all property or rights to property of the person fined "notwithstanding any other Federal law" so that government not stayed against proceeding against property of the estate).

Recall from Chapter Two, Section C, our consideration of non-consensual statutory liens, how they are created and perfected, and how the date on which such a lien is deemed to exist or deemed to be perfected may be impacted by the relation back feature of the state statutes regulating those liens. What does that have to do with the automatic stay? Actions by a creditor to create, perfect, or renew a security interest in the debtor's property are subject to the automatic stay of §362(a), with an important exception. Section 362(b)(3) excepts from the operation of the automatic stay the creation or perfection of a security interest where applicable state law authorizes a grace period (such as the relation back feature of non-consensual statutory liens) for determining the effective date or date of perfection of a prepetition security interest.

For example, assume a state's mechanics' lien statute provides that such a lien is created and perfected by filing of a notice of lien and giving the owner of the real property written notice of the filing. The statute also provides that the lien, once created, "relates back to the date when the services or materials were first supplied." Now suppose a subcontractor provides services for the improvement of the owner's real property on March 1. Payment is not made when due, and on June 10 the subcontractor's lawyer is preparing to file the required notice of lien and to give the owner notice of the filing when she learns that the owner filed a bankruptcy petition on June 9. Does the automatic stay prevent filing and service of the notice of lien? No. Because the statute contains the relation back feature and will deem the lien created and perfected on March 1 (prepetition), §362(b)(3) allows the attorney to file and serve the notice of lien postpetition without violating the stay.

For another example of how §362(b)(3) works, recall from Chapter Two, Section A, how consensual security interests in personal property are perfected under the Article 9 of the Uniform Commercial Code (UCC). For most kinds of collateral, perfection is accomplished by filing a financing statement (UCC-1) in the designated state or local government office. Per UCC §9-515, once filed, a financing statement is valid for only a stated number of years (typically five years), but can be renewed under state law by filing a continuation statement within six months of the expiration of the original five-year term. What if a creditor filed a financing statement properly perfecting a security interest in personal property of the debtor four years and five months ago and is now preparing to file a continuation statement when debtor files a bankruptcy petition? Does the automatic stay bar the creditor from filing the continuation statement? No. This is because the security interest existed prepetition and filing the continuation statement during the six-month grace period created by state law merely continues (relates back to) the security interest that was created prepetition. Section 362(b)(3) allows the creditor to file the continuation statement postpetition without violating the stay.

In addition to recognizing state law grace periods or relation back periods impacting when a security interest is created or perfected, §362(b)(3) creates its own relation back period for perfecting a security interest postpetition without violating the stay. By referencing §547(e)(2)(A) (a section of the Code that we will look at in more detail in Chapter Nine, Section D), §362(b)(3) allows a security interest to be perfected postpetition in a consensual prepetition transfer of property to the debtor so long as the perfection is completed within 30 days of the transfer.

For example, assume a borrower purchases a house on June 1 and borrows money from Bank to make the purchase. At the closing on June 1, the borrower provides Bank with a mortgage on the house to secure repayment of the amount borrowed. Bank does not record the mortgage (an act required to perfect its secured position in the property) until June 3. Meanwhile, the borrower files a bankruptcy petition on June 2. Has Bank violated the automatic stay by recording the mortgage instrument on June 3? No. Per §362(b)(3), the bank has the 30 days following transfer of the property to the debtor on June 1 allowed by §547(e)(2)(A) to perfect its secured position in the property without running afoul of the automatic stay provision.

2. Enforcing the Automatic Stay and Sanctions for Violation

As the name implies, the automatic stay is truly automatic; the debtor does not have to ask for it. It goes into effect as a matter of law upon the filing of the petition.

In most bankruptcy courts, the procedure for obtaining damages or other relief for violation of the automatic stay is for the debtor to file a motion in his bankruptcy case alleging the violation and seeking appropriate sanctions. A motion creates a contested matter in the bankruptcy case that the bankruptcy judge will hear and decide. In a minority of federal districts, allegations of violation of the automatic stay must be brought as formal adversary proceedings, essentially mini-lawsuits within the bankruptcy case. (You may want to review the distinctions in these procedures discussed in Chapter Four, Section F.)

Application Exercise 3

Determine which procedure (contested matter or adversary proceeding) the bankruptcy courts of federal district where you plan to practice require a debtor to use to allege violation of the automatic stay.

The typical remedies sought against a creditor accused of violating the automatic stay are for the court to enjoin any continuing violation by the creditor, to declare any actions taken by the creditor in violation of the stay void and of no effect (e.g., to cancel the repossession of a vehicle and order the vehicle returned to debtor), and, if the violation of the stay was undertaken with knowledge that a bankruptcy case was pending, to declare the creditor in contempt of the bankruptcy court since the automatic stay is a court order that has been violated by the creditor.

For example, the first page of the notice of filing of the case sent to creditors specifically references the danger of proceeding with postpetition collection activities (see Document 23 in the Carlson case file).

For any "willful violation" of the stay, §362(k)(1) provides that the individual debtor "shall recover actual damages, including costs and attorneys' fees, and, in appropriate circumstances, may recover punitive damages."

For example, Pine Ridge Nursing Home filed a motion for summary judgment in its collection lawsuit after receiving notice of Marta Carlson's bankruptcy filing. Marta's attorney responded with a motion for order of contempt for violation of the automatic stay (see Document 24 in the Carlson case file). Following the hearing on the motion, the court found Pine Ridge Nursing Home in contempt, ordered it to pay Marta's attorney fee incurred in making the motion, and enjoined any further violation of the stay (see Document 25 in the Carlson case file).

Case Preview

In re Butz

Not surprisingly, there is considerable dispute over what constitutes a "willful violation" of the stay under §362(k)(1). As you read In re Butz, consider the following questions:

1. Did the creditor in this case intend to violate the automatic stay?
2. What was the "willful" act that the defendant committed?
3. Would the result in this case have been different if the statement sent to debtor had been sent by mistake?

In re Butz
444 B.R. 301 (Bankr. M.D. Pa. 2011)

[Freda Butz, an individual bankruptcy debtor, received a computer-generated print-out from one of her creditors, People First Federal Credit Union, five weeks after filing a joint petition with her husband and four weeks after Credit Union had received notice of the filing. The statement identified the balance owed and included language saying, "Your account is 10 or more days past due. Please remit the amount due immediately. If you feel an error has been made please contact us." The debtor filed a complaint with the bankruptcy court alleging that Credit Union had committed a willful violation of the automatic stay under §362(k) and sought actual damages. The debtor then filed a motion for summary judgment on the complaint. Credit Union defended the motion on the grounds that the statement was not an effort to collect a prepetition debt and was instead informational only and did nothing more than advise the debtor of the status of her account, which the Credit Union had properly marked internally as a not-for-collection account. The Credit Union also defended on the grounds that the statement was not a willful violation of the automatic stay since it was an automatically computer-generated statement routinely sent to all Credit Union customers.]

OPEL, Bankruptcy Judge:

. . .

Generally, to prove a violation of the automatic stay, a debtor/plaintiff must show both that the defendant (1) knew of the automatic stay, and (2) acted willfully to violate the stay. A "willful" violation is a condition precedent to receiving damages under §362(k). "It is a willful violation of the automatic stay when a creditor violates the stay with knowledge that the bankruptcy petition has been filed." In re Lansdale Family Restaurants, Inc., 977 F.2d 826, 829 (3d Cir. 1992). . . . Courts in the Third Circuit have consistently recognized that "willfulness" under §362(k) does not require a finding of a creditor's specific intent to violate the stay. In re Nixon, 419 B.R. 281, 288 (Bankr. E.D. Pa. 2009). . . .

The Defendant admits receiving notice of the bankruptcy filing when it received the Notice of 341 Meeting of Creditors on May 5, 2010. The Defendant also admits that it sent the Statement to the Plaintiff on June 14, 2010. With these admissions, I find that there are no genuine issues of material fact in this case. I find that the Defendant had notice of the bankruptcy filing when it mailed the Statement to the Plaintiff on or about June 14, 2010.

Since the Defendant admits it had notice of the bankruptcy when it sent the Statement, the question I must now decide is whether sending the Statement was a willful violation of the automatic stay. The Defendant has explained that it sent the Statement to the Plaintiff because she continues to conduct post-petition business with the Credit Union and has both a savings account and a line of credit. Mr. Kurtz, the Defendant's Asset Recovery Supervisor, stated in his Affidavit that monthly, the Defendant mails what it calls a "combined statement" to the Plaintiff, and its other customers. The combined statement outlines the activity and balances of the line of credit and the savings account. Paragraph 6 of the Affidavit states "Defendant is unable to segregate loans from savings or checking accounts for purposes of mailing [s]tatements to Plaintiff or any other members of the Credit Union." Kurtz Aff. 6. Finally, Mr. Kurtz verified that the Statement was only sent when the Plaintiff's line of credit became past due, and clarified that the Defendant's system is programmed to forward one notice only, regardless of whether or not payment is tendered.

To further substantiate its position, the Defendant contends that it took several actions which demonstrate that it complied with the requirements of the automatic stay. Upon receipt of the Notice of the 341 meeting, the Defendant states that the Plaintiff's line of credit was immediately marked as "no collection activity." The Defendant also reported the line of credit to the three major credit bureaus as included in a Chapter 13 bankruptcy. Finally, through the Defendant's internal procedures, the line of credit was charged off in July 2010.

In determining whether or not sending the Statement was a violation of the stay, the Defendant's other acts, which appear to be harmonious with the stay, are irrelevant to the analysis. Sending the Statement itself was either a violation of the stay, or it was not. The Statement is addressed to the Plaintiff and includes her member number; it is a preprinted form with several blank boxes for the computer to fill with the appropriate member specific information. The Statement indicates that payments are due monthly and it is dated "6/14/10." It states, "Your account is 10 or more days past due. Please remit the amount due immediately. If you feel an error has been made please contact us." It further states a loan balance of "4809.76," that the last payment was made on "4/19/10," the loan paid through date is "5/25/10" and an amount due of "125.00." Finally, there is a line to indicate the "amount paid" and the form is perforated such that a Credit Union member may separate a portion of the statement to presumably return with a payment.

Tasked to evaluate the Statement, I conclude that it is, in part, an invoice demanding payment on the account. The Defendant's arguments that the Statement is a simple notice to keep the Plaintiff informed of the status of her account is unpersuasive. If the Statement were only an informative notice, it would not use the language, "Your account is 10 or more days past due. Please remit the amount due immediately." nor would it state "125.00" in the amount due box. Finally, if the Statement was only informative, and not for collection purposes, the computer would not have been triggered to send it only after when the Plaintiff's line of credit became past due as explained by Mr. Kurtz. I find that by sending the Statement to the Plaintiff, the Defendant violated the automatic stay under §362(a).

Similarly, the Defendant's position that it was necessary for the computer to send such statements to the Plaintiff, as it does all other customers, is unpersuasive. When considering the willfulness of acts which violate the stay, courts have rejected the so called "computer did it" defense. See In re Wingard, 382 B.R. 892, 902 (Bankr. W.D. Pa. 2008). . . . Where there is actual notice of the bankruptcy, the defendant has the burden of proving that it took steps to prevent violations of the stay. See In re Rijos, 263 B.R. 382, 392 (1st Cir. BAP 2001). The computer did it defense has been characterized as a non-starter "since intelligent beings still control the computer and could have altered the programming appropriately." In re McCormack, 203 B.R. 521, 524 (Bankr. D.N.H. 1996).

The supposed necessity in this case is of the Defendant's own creation; it arises because of the Credit Union's own internal policies and procedures. The Defendant has an obligation to shape its policies and procedures such that they are harmonious with the legal requirements placed upon it by the Bankruptcy Code and otherwise. "Sophisticated commercial enterprises have a clear obligation to adjust their programming and procedures and their instruction to employees to handle complex matters correctly." McCormack, 203 B.R. at 525.

I find that the Defendant's act of sending the Statement to the Plaintiff was a willful violation as described in §362(k). Therefore, the Plaintiff is entitled to judgment as a matter of law on the issue of violation of the automatic stay. A hearing must still be held to determine if the Plaintiff is entitled to recover any damages.

Post-Case Follow-Up

Butz illustrates the widely accepted view that in order to prove a willful violation of the automatic stay under §362(k), the debtor is not required to show that the creditor acted with the specific intent to violate the stay. "The willfulness requirement refers to the deliberateness of the conduct and the knowledge of the bankruptcy filing, not to a specific intent to violate a court order." In re Wagner, 74 B.R. 898, 903 (Bankr. E.D. Pa. 1987). "The question is not whether the creditor intended to violate the stay, but whether the creditor intended the act." In re Kinsey, 349 B.R. 48, 52 (Bankr. D. Idaho 2006). Of course, the willful action taken by the creditor must be an attempt to collect a debt in a way forbidden by §362(a). For example, if a creditor does send a postpetition notice to a debtor regarding a prepetition debt for genuinely informational or account status purposes only, there is no violation even though sending the notice was willful and done with knowledge of the filing. See, e.g., In re Schatz, 452 B.R. 544, 549-50 (Bankr. M.D. Pa. 2011).

In re Butz: Real Life Applications

1. Assume you are counsel for the Credit Union in the *Butz* case. Since the court rejected the "computer made me do it" defense and stressed that creditors have an obligation to shape their policies and procedures to make them harmonious with legal requirements such as the automatic stay, what recommendations will you make to your client regarding changes it needs to make (1) to its

computerized records system and (2) instructions to its employees regarding an alternative system for identifying accounts subject to the automatic stay and preventing even routine billing of such accounts?

2. Even where a creditor has policies and procedures in place designed to avoid violating the stay, inadvertent violations can occur, giving rise to the issue of whether the creditor should be deemed to have acted willfully. Should "oops" be a defense in the following scenarios?

   a. ABC Collection Company purchases charged-off consumer debt and quickly files suit to obtain judgment, usually by default. ABC uses Quick Serve, Inc., to achieve service of process on defendants in its collection lawsuits. ABC has in place a policy and procedures to pull unserved process for debtors upon receipt of notice of their filing for bankruptcy so that process is not delivered to Quick Serve for service on those debtors. Where process has already been delivered to Quick Serve when notice of bankruptcy filing is received the procedure is to immediately contact Quick Serve by phone and e-mail to prevent service of process that would violate the automatic stay. Today, ABC receives notice that Martha Jones has filed a case in Chapter 7. The procedures are followed but her process papers cannot be located in the office. On the assumption the process papers have already been forwarded to Quick Serve, ABC contacts Quick Serve, notifies it of the bankruptcy filing and instructs it to not serve Martha. Quick Serve acknowledges receipt of the information but thereafter has Martha served with process. Has ABC violated the stay? See In re Kinsey, 349 B.R. 48, 52 (Bankr. D. Idaho 2006).

   b. Fast Collect Corp. has purchased a debt owed by "Mike P. Campion" and has filed suit against him to collect it. While the collection suit is pending, Fast Collect receives notice that "Michael P. Campion" has filed a petition in Chapter 7. Using its recently updated software system, it notes the Michael P. Campion bankruptcy filing in its Mike P. Campion file and the collection lawsuit is stayed. Three months later Fast Collect purchases another debt owed by "Michael P. Campion." When the new account is entered into Fast Collect's computer system, it does not find a match with the Mike P. Campion file because the software searches only for similarities between last names and the first three letters of the first name. Not recognizing that Michael P. Campion is the same person as Mike P. Campion and is in a Chapter 7 case, Fast Collect files suit against Campion. Has Fast Collect violated the stay? See In re Campion, 294 B.R. 313 (B.A.P. 9th Cir. 2003).

3. The *Butz* court says that a violation of the automatic stay occurs only where the creditor commits the willful act with "knowledge of the automatic stay." The creditor in *Butz* admitted to having actual knowledge of the bankruptcy filing prior to the statement being sent and as a commercial lender clearly knew that such filing triggered the automatic stay. But there can be disputes regarding whether a creditor has the requisite knowledge to substantiate a finding of violation.

a. Is it a defense if the creditor knows that a bankruptcy petition has been filed but is not familiar with the automatic stay? See In re Wagner, 74 B.R. 898 (Bankr. E.D. Pa. 1987).

b. Is it a defense if a creditor hears through the grapevine that a debtor has or may have filed for bankruptcy relief but the creditor has not received any official notice from the debtor or the bankruptcy court? See In re Rhyne, 59 B.R. 276 (Bankr. E.D. Pa. 1986)and In re Flack, 239 B.R. 155, 163 (Bankr. S.D. Ohio 1999).

c. Is it a defense if a creditor learns of a debtor's bankruptcy filing but continues collection efforts after an attorney tells him (mistakenly) that the automatic stay does not go into effect until formal notice is received from the court? See In re Ashby, 36 B.R. 976 (Bankr. D. Utah 1984).

d. Is it a defense if a creditor continues collection efforts after learning of a debtor's bankruptcy filing but does so believing in good faith that his debt is not one subject to the automatic stay and in fact the law is sharply divided on the point? See United States v. Norton, 717 F.2d 767 (3d Cir. 1983), and In re Wilson, 19 B.R. 45 (Bankr. E.D. Pa. 1982).

e. Is it a defense if the debt that is owed the creditor is a non-dischargeable debt such as a student loan? See In re Walker, 336 B.R. 534 (Bankr. M.D. Fla. 2005), but compare In re Billingsley, 276 B.R. 48, 53 (Bankr. D.N.J. 2002).

f. Is it a defense if the creditor itself has no knowledge of the bankruptcy filing but an agent or affiliate of the creditor does when the willful act occurs? See Green Tree Servicing, LLC v. Taylor, 369 B.R. 282 (Bankr. S.D. W. Va. 2007) (attorney of creditor given notice), and Haile v. New York State Higher Educ. Servs. Corp., 90 B.R. 51, 55 (W.D.N.Y. 1988) (collection agency retained by creditor given notice).

A Safe Harbor for Creditors Violating the Automatic Stay?

Section 342(g)(1), added by BAP-CPA, provides that if the creditor designates a person or organizational subdivision to receive bankruptcy notices and has a reasonable procedure to deliver notices to such person or subdivision, then a notice has not been "brought to the attention" of the creditor until the designated person or subdivision receives the notice. Early indications are that this very pro-creditor provision is not being well received by bankruptcy courts, which generally take violations of the automatic stay very seriously. Several decisions interpreting §342(g)(1) have held that even where the creditor has designated someone to receive notice for them, if the creditor otherwise had actual notice of the bankruptcy filing (as opposed to constructive or imputed knowledge) the creditor cannot rely on that safe harbor provision. See In re Murray, 2013 WL 6800881 (Bankr. N.D. Cal. 2013); In re Davis, 498 B.R. 64, 69 (Bankr. D.S.C. 2013); and Opinion on Motion to Dismiss entered on October 3, 2014 in Adversary Proceeding No. 5-14-ap-00016-JJT in In re Walsh, Bankruptcy Case No. 5-13-bk-05293-JJT (Bankr. M.D. Pa.), available online at www.gpo.gov/fdsys/pkg/USCOURTS-pamb-5_14-ap-00016/pdf/USCOURTS-pamb-5_14-ap-00016-0.pdf.

If a creditor continues with collection efforts after the filing of the petition but does not have any actual or constructive notice of the filing of a bankruptcy case by the debtor, much less the automatic stay itself, the court will not hold the creditor in contempt and award damages but will likely set aside any actions taken by the creditor after the filing of the petition. Here, there has been a "technical" but not a "willful" violation of the stay (see discussion of the difference in In re Taylor, 369 B.R. 282, 286-87 (S.D. W. Va. 2007).

For example, if Pine Ridge Nursing Home had filed its motion for summary judgment after Marta's petition was filed but before receiving notice, the judge likely would not have imposed sanctions on Pine Ridge but instead would have ordered the motion stricken until the stay is lifted, as discussed below.

In many federal districts, the debtor must prove willfulness only by a preponderance of the evidence. See, e.g., In re Johnson, 501 F.3d 1163 (10th Cir. 2007). Others hold the debtor to a clear and convincing standard. See, e.g., In re Bennett, 135 B.R. 72 (Bankr. S.D. Ohio 1992).

Application Exercise 4

Determine what standard of proof is required to establish a willful violation of the automatic stay in the federal district or circuit where you plan to practice.

Upon a showing of willful violation of the stay, the debtor is entitled to recover actual damages but has the burden of proving such damages apart from the proof of willful violation. Note that in *Butz* the court, having found a willful violation, reserved the question of whether the debtor could prove actual damages for a later hearing. Actual damages sought by debtors for violation of the automatic stay are typically economic loss that can be shown to be causally related to the stay violation (e.g., lost income, lost future profits, lost use of property wrongfully withheld from debtor, lost value of property wrongfully seized and not returned).

For example, a debtor who has to miss work in order to attend a court hearing made necessary by the stay violation may ask for her lost income; a debtor who has to lease a rental car because the creditor seized or kept his in violation of the stay may seek that rental expense; a debtor whose vehicle is wrongfully repossessed in violation of the stay but sold to a good faith purchaser for value may seek the value of the lost vehicle; a debtor who is a house painter and who lost job opportunities due to his vehicle or trade tools being seized or kept in violation of the stay may seek lost profits from those jobs.

It is generally understood that since §362(k)(1) uses the phrase "*shall* recover actual damages" (italics supplied), that the bankruptcy court has no discretion and must award such damages to the debtor so long as the debtor has proven both a willful violation and the actual damages themselves. See, e.g., In re Gene-Sys, Inc., 273 B.R. 290, 295 (Bankr. D.D.C. 2001) ("[The court] has no discretion to withhold an award of compensatory damages for violation of the automatic stay.").

Though §362(k)(1) literally says that upon the finding of a willful violation the debtor can recover "actual damages including . . . attorney's fees," there is a split of authority over whether that includes attorney's fees incurred by the debtor in prosecuting the stay violation itself as opposed to attorney's fees incurred by the debtor in avoiding the consequences of the stay violation itself (e.g., seeking dismissal of a collection lawsuit filed in state court postpetition in violation of the stay). Compare Sternberg v. Johnston, 595 F.3d 937 (9th Cir. 2010), cert. denied, 131 S. Ct. 102 (2010) (Congress legislates against the backdrop of the "American Rule" pursuant to which each party is responsible for its own attorney's fees; once the stay violation has ended, any fees the debtor incurs after that point in pursuit of a damage award would not be to compensate for "actual damages" under §362(k)(1)) and In re Durby, 451 B.R. 664 (B.A.P. 1st Cir. 2011) (since most decisions pre-BAPCPA held attorney's fees for prosecuting the stay violation recoverable under old §362(h), Congress's failure to change the language of the provision indicates an intent that they be recoverable and policy supports that construction; what good is it to be entitled to damages and attorney's fees for a violation of the automatic stay if it costs a debtor much more in unrecoverable fees to recover such damages and recoverable attorney's fees).

Application Exercise 5

Determine if the decisions in the federal district or circuit where you plan to practice allow the debtor to recover attorney's fees under §362(k)(1) for prosecuting the stay violation. Based on the order entered on Marta Carlson's motion for order of contempt for violation of the automatic stay against Pine Ridge Nursing Home (Documents 24 and 25 in the Carlson case file), which view does that court follow?

Another question that has divided the courts is whether actual damages recoverable for a willful violation under §362(k)(1) include only economic loss to the debtor or can include emotional distress damage as well. As you learned when studying torts, claims for emotional distress are often suspect due to their subjective nature. Compare Fleet Mortg. Group, Inc. v. Kaneb, 196 F.3d 265, 269 (1st Cir. 1999) (emotional distress recoverable under §362(k) if supported by "specific information" rather than "generalized assertions"), with Aiello v. Providian Fin. Corp., 239 F.3d 876, 880 (7th Cir. 2001) (emotional distress compensable under 362(k) only if accompanied by economic loss), and U.S. v. Harchar, 331 B.R. 720 (N.D. Ohio 2005) (when §362(h) was enacted in 1984, Congress was concerned not with providing debtors compensation for emotional harms, but with providing explicit statutory authorization for contempt, the only previously available remedy for a stay violation, and awarding damages for emotional harm was never commonplace under the bankruptcy court's traditional contempt procedures; the problems of proof, assessment, and appropriate compensation attendant to awarding damages for emotional distress are troublesome enough in the ordinary tort case, and should not be imported into civil contempt proceedings).

Application Exercise 6

Determine if the courts of the federal district or circuit where you plan to practice have ruled on whether damages for emotional distress are recoverable for a willful violation of the automatic stay under §362(k)(1) and, if so, what proof is required for their recovery.

Section 362(k)(1) also provides that the debtor who demonstrates a willful violation of the stay can recover punitive damages "in appropriate circumstances." This phrase is universally understood by the courts to require proof of something more than a willful violation of the stay by the offending creditor, although the something more that is required is stated variously by different courts. In re Taylor, 369 B.R. 282 (S.D. W. Va. 2007) involved a willful violation of the automatic stay and an award of actual damages to an individual debtor where a creditor who had been awarded a prepetition writ of possession to the debtor's mobile home and whose lawyer had been given notice of the bankruptcy filing thereafter entered the mobile home twice, once to post a "for sale" sign and a second time to verbally instruct debtor to leave the home. The debtor in *Taylor* also sought punitive damages. In the course of deciding what standard to apply to determine the punitive damage claim, the *Taylor* court provided a good summary of the various standards utilized:

> The relevant statute provides for punitive damages "in appropriate circumstances." 11 U.S.C. §362(k). There is a lack of uniform guidance on what is meant by "appropriate circumstances." Several standards have been adopted by the various courts that have considered the question. (Taylor Br. at 17–19).
>
> One group uses "**maliciousness or bad faith**" as the guide. See Crysen/Montenay Energy Co. v. Esselen Associates, 902 F.2d 1098, 1104–05 (2d Cir. 1990); Atlantic Business and Community Corp., 901 F.2d 325, 329 (3d Cir. 1990); In re Rutherford, 329 B.R. 886, 898 (Bankr. N.D. Ga. 2005); In re Calvin, 329 B.R. 589, 604 (Bankr. S.D. Tex. 2005); In re Harris, 310 B.R. 395, 400 (Bankr. E.D. Wis. 2004); In re Bivens, 324 B.R. 39, 42 (Bankr. N.D. Ohio 2004). Another group of cases uses "**arrogant defiance of federal law**" as the touchstone. See In re Curtis, 322 B.R. 470, 486 (Bankr. D. Mass. 2005); In re Bishop, 296 B.R. 890, 898 (Bankr. S.D. Ga. 2003); In the Matter of Mullarkey, 81 B.R. 280, 284 (Bankr. D.N.J. 1987).
>
> Other courts have used **egregious, vindictive or intentional misconduct** as the standard. Lovett v. Honeywell, 930 F.2d 625, 628 (8th Cir. 1991); In re McHenry, 179

Can an Entity Debtor Recover for Willful Violation of the Automatic Stay?

Most courts limit the recovery of §362(k)(1) willful violation damages to individual debtors and disallow them to entity debtors (corporations, partnerships, etc.) since the section references "an individual injured. . . ." (See, e.g., In re Spookyworld, Inc., 346 F.3d 1, 6 (1st Cir. 2003).) However, a minority construe "individual" to include entity debtor (see, e.g., Budget Service Co. v. Better Homes of Virginia, Inc., 804 F.2d 289, 292 (4th Cir. 1986)), finding it difficult to accept that Congress meant to give remedy for intentional violation to individual debtors only and emphasizing the important role of §362(k) in repairing and deterring willful violations.

B.R. 165, 168 (B.A.P. 9th Cir. 1995); Davis v. IRS, 136 B.R. 414, 423, n. 20 (E.D. Va. 1992); In re Hampton, 319 B.R. 163, 174 (Bankr. E.D. Ark. 2005); In re Cullen, 329 B.R. 52, 57–58 (Bankr. N.D. Iowa 2005). Still other courts have used a **multi-factor approach** and considered the following four factors: (1) the nature of the defendant's conduct; (2) the defendant's ability to pay; (3) the motives of the defendant; and (4) any provocation by the debtor. Heghmann v. Indorf (In re Heghmann), 316 B.R. 395, 405 (B.A.P. 1st Cir. 2004); In re B. Cohen & Sons Caterers, Inc., 108 B.R. 482, 487–88 (E.D. Pa. 1989).

One point that seems clear from the different standards articulated is that "punitive damages usually require more than mere willful violation of the automatic stay." *Heghmann*, 316 B.R. at 405. It is elsewhere suggested that "the Bankruptcy Code does not attempt to delineate what 'appropriate circumstances' means, leaving it to the sound discretion of the bankruptcy court." Id.; In re Smith, 296 B.R. 46, 56 (Bankr. M.D. Ala. 2003).

In re Taylor, 369 B.R. at 289 (emphasis supplied).

Application Exercise 7

Read In re Taylor. Which standard for determining punitive damages did that court adopt? Did that court award punitive damages? Why or why not? Determine what standard for the award of punitive damages under §362(k) is utilized by the courts of the federal district or circuit where you plan to practice.

Section 362(k)(2) provides a creditor accused of willfully violating the automatic stay with a defense wherein the action taken by the creditor involved collateralized property and the creditor can show that it believed in good faith that debtor had failed to file a timely §521(a)(2) statement of intent (Form 108, discussed in Chapter Six, Section B) with regard to such property (see Document 18 in the Carlson case file).

Case Preview

Eskanos & Adler, P.C. v. Leetien

It is not just the offending creditor who may be tagged with damages and costs in a proceeding alleging willful violation of the stay. Attorneys who represent the creditor are at risk as well. But do attorneys for creditors have a duty to take affirmative action to stay pending collection efforts upon learning of the bankruptcy filing or is it sufficient that they simply maintain the status quo of the collection efforts and undertake no further actions to collect? As you read Eskanos & Adler, P.C. v. Leetien, consider the following questions:

1. When did the Eskanos law firm learn of the bankruptcy filing by Leetien? What actions had it taken on behalf of its client prior to learning of the filing? How long after learning of the filing did the Eskanos law firm finally take affirmative action to stay the collection action?
2. What was the Eskanos law firm's argument concerning what "continuation" means as it is used in §362(a)(1)? How did the Ninth Circuit disagree with that interpretation?
3. What was the basis for the court's finding that the client of the Eskanos law firm had violated the automatic stay as well?

Note: Section 362(h) referred to in the case is now 362(k).

Eskanos & Adler, P.C. v. Leetien
309 F. 3d 1210 (9th Cir. 2002)

Hug, Circuit Judge.

Somkiat Leetien ("Leetien") filed for bankruptcy. Shortly thereafter, her creditor, First Select, Inc. ("First Select"), through its legal counsel and collection agent, Eskanos & Adler ("Eskanos"), filed in state court a collection action against Leetien. The bankruptcy judge jointly sanctioned Eskanos and First Select $1,000 for willfully violating the automatic stay protection in federal bankruptcy law by failing to timely dismiss or stay the state collection action. The district court affirmed.

Eskanos appeals, claiming that federal bankruptcy law imposes no affirmative duty to discontinue post-petition state collection actions. Eskanos also contends that no willful violation occurred, and that Leetien did not sustain actual damages. We disagree with Eskanos and AFFIRM.

On August 18, 2000, Leetien voluntarily filed a Chapter 7 bankruptcy petition. This filing engages the automatic stay protection pursuant to 11 U.S.C. §362(a) of the Bankruptcy Code. First Select, listed as an unsecured creditor from Leetien's schedules, was notified via first class mail on August 23, 2000. On August 28, 2000, Eskanos filed a collection action on behalf of First Select in California state court against Leetien. Leetien received a summons for this action on September 5, 2000.

On September 6, 2000, counsel for Leetien, Michael Doan ("Doan"), made several attempts to speak by telephone with an attorney at Eskanos, but no lawyer at the firm would speak with him. Ultimately Doan managed to leave a message of Leetien's pending bankruptcy petition with a legal assistant. He also notified Eskanos on this date through two faxes. Doan requested that the state action be either dismissed or placed on the state's stay calendar by September 20, 2000. On September 26, failing to receive communication from Eskanos, Doan contacted the state court, which confirmed the collection action remained active.

Eskanos did not dismiss its state collection action until September 29, 2000, and made no attempt to explain its delay to Leetien. Moreover, Eskanos did not contact Leetien until October 3, 2000, the date Leetien filed its automatic stay violation motion against First Select and Eskanos in federal bankruptcy court.

Bankruptcy Judge Louise Adler ruled that Eskanos willfully violated the automatic stay. She concluded that sanctions were appropriate under 11 U.S.C. §362(h) because Eskanos knew of the bankruptcy filing on September 6, 2000, and unjustifiably delayed in dismissing the state action until September 29, 2000. She rejected Eskanos's proffered excuses that delay resulted from problems with its process server, and misplacing the case number to the state collection action. Judge Adler found that Leetien sustained actual damages defending against a potential default judgment from the active state collection action.

Judge Adler additionally ruled that First Select received notice of Leetien's bankruptcy on August 23, 2000, in time to notify Eskanos before it served Leetien with the state action summons on September 5, 2000. She expressly rejected First Select's defense that due to its large size and the many thousand collection accounts it monitors, it did not have knowledge of the August 23 notice until it registered the notice into its computer system on September 12, 2000. . . .

Here, we must decide for the first time whether a party has an affirmative duty under §362(a) to discontinue post-petition collection actions in non-bankruptcy fora against a debtor.

Whether a party has willfully violated the automatic stay is a question of fact reviewed for clear error. Fed. R. Bankr. P. 8013. . . . The amount of sanctions imposed for a willful violation of the stay is reviewed for an abuse of discretion. . . .

The plain language of §362(a)(1) prohibits the continuation of judicial actions. Section 362(h) permits a person injured by any willful violation to recover actual and punitive damages. The continuation against judicial actions includes the maintenance of collection actions filed in state court. It contradicts the plain meaning of the statute to suggest that the §362(a)(1) stay against the continuation of judicial actions does not prohibit the maintenance of an active collection action or the unjustified delay in the dismissal of such. A party violating the automatic stay, through continuing a collection action in a non-bankruptcy forum, must automatically dismiss or stay such proceeding or risk possible sanctions for willful violations pursuant to §362(h).

It would be inconsistent with the statutory scheme to countenance post-petition collection actions filed in state court. In providing the automatic stay, Congress intended all claims against a debtor be brought in a single forum, the bankruptcy court. . . . The scope of protections embodied in the automatic stay is quite broad, and serves as one of the most important protections in bankruptcy law. . . . Collection actions maintained in state court threaten the proper execution of bankruptcy proceedings by exposing the debtor's estate to multiple collection actions, undermining the debtor's ability to reorganize her financial affairs, and jeopardizing the creditors as a class with the possibility that one creditor will obtain payment to the detriment of all others. For these reasons we have held that the automatic stay requires an immediate freeze of the status quo by precluding and nullifying post-petition actions.

Eskanos contends that §362(a)(1)'s prohibition against "continuation" should be interpreted narrowly to require conduct beyond maintaining an active claim. It suggests additional efforts in prosecuting the claim should be required. Eskanos cites a Western District of Pennsylvania bankruptcy court decision supporting the proposition that: "continuation in the context of §362(a) means to carry forward or persist." Taylor v. Slick (In re Taylor), 207 B.R. 995, 999-1000 (Bankr. W.D. Pa. 1997) (*citing Webster's II New Riverside University Dictionary* 305 (1984)). Eskanos asserts that it did not carry forward or persist in its collection action, but rather merely calendared the action for future determination.

This proposition does little to advance Eskanos's argument. Maintenance of an active collection action in state court does nothing if not carry forward or persist against a debtor. A debtor enjoys little satisfaction from a creditor's honest words that it files a collection action in state court but refrains from persisting in the collection action until bankruptcy proceedings sort itself out. Active state filings exist as more than placeholders — the risk of default judgment looms over the debtor throughout. Counsel must be engaged to defend against a default judgment. Additionally, state collection actions are not to be used as leverage in negotiating collection over the debtor's estate already in bankruptcy.

Alternatively, Eskanos cites two Ninth Circuit cases holding the postponement of foreclosure sales by creditors does not violate an automatic stay. In re Roach, 660 F.2d 1316, 1318 (9th Cir. 1981); In re Peters, 101 f.3d 618, 620 (9th Cir. 1996).

Both *Roach* and *Peters* are inapposite. In each the legal holding addressed postponements of actions to collect debts where the creditor notified the debtor of the postponement and maintained the bankruptcy proceeding's status quo. *Roach,* 660 F.2d at 1317; *Peters,* 101 F.3d at 619. The postponement acted as an immediate freeze of non-bankruptcy proceedings. Maintenance of an active collection action against a debtor, on the other hand, neither postpones collection nor maintains the status quo.

Consequently, we reject Eskanos's interpretation that "continuation" requires additional efforts beyond sustaining an active claim. The maintenance of an active collection action alone adequately satisfies the statutory prohibition against "continuation" of judicial actions. Consistent with the plain and unambiguous meaning of the statute, and consonant with Congressional intent, we hold that §362(a)(1) imposes an affirmative duty to discontinue post-petition collection actions. . . .

15 Section 362(h) permits sanctions for willful violations of §362(a). . . . [E]vidence in the record supports the bankruptcy court's finding that Eskanos willfully violated the automatic stay. The bankruptcy court found that: Eskanos was promptly notified of Leetien's filing on September 6, 2000; lawyers at Eskanos refused to take Leetien's counsel's telephone calls; Leetien's counsel left a message with a legal assistant and

faxed to Eskanos a request to stay its state action by September 20, 2000; Eskanos did not dismiss its state collection action until September 29, 2000; lawyers at Eskanos made no attempt to explain its delay to Leetien's counsel prior to then; and Eskanos demonstrated no indication that it was attempting to move expeditiously to cure the automatic stay violation. The bankruptcy court also ruled that Eskanos's problem with its process server and missing case number lacked merit, noting that Eskanos was able to serve Leetien on September 5 with a summons and complaint containing a case number.

Eskanos concedes that it received notice on September 6 and did not dismiss the state collection action until September 29. It offers no evidence to the contrary that it refused to answer Leetien's counsel's calls or failed to receive the faxed requests. Nor does it offer any evidence that once it received notice of the bankruptcy filing, that it moved expeditiously to cure the automatic stay violation or attempt to contact Leetien informing her that it halted and discontinued its collection activity.

Eskanos continues to assert that sanctions are inappropriate because any delay in dismissal was due to problems with its process server. We disagree. Eskanos's internal disorder does not excuse it from complying with the automatic stay. Eskanos had knowledge of the bankruptcy filing. We find no clear error in the bankruptcy judge's finding that Eskanos willfully violated the automatic stay. . . .

Section 362(h) allows for actual and punitive damages, including costs and attorneys' fees, as sanctions for willful violations. Leetien sustained actual damages in defending against a continuing stay violation and preventing a default judgment. We find no abuse of discretion from the bankruptcy court's joint award of $1,000 against Eskanos and First Select for its willful violation of §362(a). . . .

We conclude that §362(a) imposes an affirmative duty to discontinue post-petition collection actions. Sanctions are appropriate pursuant to §362(h) because Eskanos willfully violated the automatic stay by maintaining the active collection action and unjustifiably delaying its dismissal after receiving notice of the bankruptcy petition. Leetien sustained actual damages defending against the state action.

Post-Case Follow-Up

Does *Eskanos* stand for the proposition that pending lawsuits against the debtor must be actually dismissed once notice of the bankruptcy filing is received? After all, the lawsuit might involve the claim of a secured creditor who will be able to obtain a lifting of the automatic stay in short order. Or the debtor's bankruptcy case might be dismissed, negating the stay. In many jurisdictions the common practice once a bankruptcy petition is filed is to file a "Suggestion of Bankruptcy" with the trial or appellate court in which the action against the debtor is pending. The suggestion will advise the forum court of the bankruptcy court where the petition was filed and the bankruptcy case number. The suggestion may be filed by any party to the action. Many courts have local rules that address the procedure and effect of filing a suggestion. Typically, upon filing of the suggestion, the matter will be stayed in the forum court for some stated period of time and later dismissed without prejudice if the stay is not lifted as to the claim. The court in *Eskanos* awarded Leetien actual damages of $1,000 against the law firm and its client jointly under §362(k) for their willful violation of the automatic stay. What did those actual damages appear to be? Using the standard for awarding punitive damages discussed earlier, could this have been "an appropriate case" for the award of punitive damages as well?

Eskanos & Adler, P.C. v. Leetien: Real Life Applications

1. In its defense, the Eskanos law firm cited In re Roach and In re Peters, which held that mere postponement of a scheduled foreclosure sale did not amount to a violation of the automatic stay. If you were representing Leetien before the bankruptcy court when her motion for violation of the stay was argued there, how would you distinguish those creditor actions from the actions of the Eskanos law firm?

2. Assume you represent the creditor in each of the following situations when notice of the bankruptcy filing of the debtor is received. In light of *Eskanos*, what is the appropriate action to take and in what time frame?
   a. Trial of tort claim against the debtor is scheduled to begin tomorrow.
   b. Demand letter to debtor was signed by you an hour ago and your secretary has delivered it to the office runner to take to the post office with the other outgoing mail.
   c. You obtained a writ of execution on a final judgment for the client yesterday and the sheriff's office promised to act on it as soon as possible.
   d. The uncollected account receivable involving the debtor was assigned to a debt collection agency two days ago.
   e. A vehicle repossessed from the debtor by your client last week is in storage awaiting a repossession sale not yet scheduled.

3. Assume you represent an individual debtor who files a petition in Chapter 7 on May 1. On May 24 a creditor to whom debtor had provided a personal guaranty and who has no constructive or actual notice of the bankruptcy filing sends a letter to your client demanding payment on the guaranty. Your client does not show you the letter and does not respond to it. On June 27 the creditor, still having no notice of the bankruptcy filing, files a lawsuit against the principal obligor and your client (on the guaranty) in state court. Your client advises you of the lawsuit and on June 28 you write a letter on behalf of debtor to the attorney for the creditor advising of the bankruptcy filing. That letter is received by creditor's counsel on June 29. On that same day, counsel for creditor writes you and promises to take no further action against your client in the lawsuit; she also asks that you file a suggestion of bankruptcy with the state court. You receive that letter on June 30 and immediately file a suggestion of bankruptcy with the state court. You also write another letter to counsel for creditor that day demanding that the state court action against your client be dismissed by the end of the week. On July 15, lawsuit against your client having not been dismissed, you file a motion with the bankruptcy court asking for creditor to

be found in contempt of the automatic stay and seeking actual and punitive damages. After your motion is filed but before it is heard by the court, creditor files a motion for default judgment in the state court action against the principal obligor but not against your client. The motion for default against the principal obligor is granted by the state court in August and creditor dismisses the state court action against your client. Did creditor violate the automatic stay by filing the state court lawsuit against debtor and, if so, was it a willful violation? Did creditor violate the automatic stay by failing to dismiss the state court lawsuit earlier and, if so, was it a willful violation? Assuming there has been a willful violation of the stay, is this an appropriate case for imposition of punitive damages? See Alley Cassetty Companies, Inc. v. Wren, 502 B.R. 609 (N.D. Ga. 2013).

There are some special rules added by BAPCPA pertaining to the automatic stay for the individual debtor (not the entity debtor) who has previously filed a case under Chapter 7, 11, or 13 and had it dismissed within one year preceding the filing of the current case. If an individual debtor filing today has filed a different bankruptcy case within one year preceding this filing and had the preceding filing dismissed, then the automatic stay goes into effect, but only for 30 days, pursuant to §362(c). To extend the stay, that debtor must file a motion for extension of stay with the court. A hearing will be conducted and the court will decide whether to extend the stay or not. The burden in such a hearing is placed on the debtor to show by clear and convincing evidence that this bankruptcy case has been filed in good faith and that the debtor is entitled to the stay per §362(c)(3).

If the individual debtor has filed two bankruptcy cases within the year preceding the filing of this one, whether Chapter 7, 11, or 13, and both have been dismissed, there is no automatic stay at all upon the filing of the third petition. In such case, the debtor must file his motion for automatic stay immediately upon filing his petition and carry his burden of showing a good faith filing by clear and convincing evidence per §362(c)(4).

Application Exercise 8

Remember, one purpose of BAPCPA was to stop debtor abuse of the Code. Do you see why repeated bankruptcy filings by a debtor triggering the automatic stay provision might be a tactic to unfairly delay or complicate a creditor's efforts to collect on a legitimate debt? Do you think these BAPCPA provisions are fair and reasonable? What ethical implications might there be for an attorney who cooperates with a debtor client to make repeated filings for the primary purpose of delaying collection efforts by triggering the automatic stay with no real intent to see the bankruptcy case through?

3. Lifting the Automatic Stay

The automatic stay created by §362(a) does not necessarily last for the duration of the case as against secured creditors of the debtor in a Chapter 7 liquidation. A creditor who is properly secured and perfected in property of the debtor will typically have a superior claim to it over that of the bankruptcy trustee unless the value of the secured property exceeds the amount of the creditor's claim.

For example, recall from the Assignment Memorandum in Appendix A that Marta Carlson has two mortgages on her home, one in favor of Capital City Savings Bank (CCSB) with a balance of $142,500, and one in favor of Dreams Come True Finance Company (DCT) with a balance of $37,500. Marta is in default on the debt owed to DCT and, prior to the bankruptcy, it declared foreclosure and initiated foreclosure proceedings. But DCT's plan to foreclose is delayed by Marta's filing of the Chapter 7 petition, triggering the automatic stay. If DCT files a motion to lift the stay, the bankruptcy trustee will object. Do you see why? Assuming the property is worth $255,000, as the realtor has estimated to Marta, if it sells for that amount, the first $142,500 would go to CCSB, holder of the first mortgage. The next $37,500 would go to DCT, holder of the second mortgage. Per §522(d)(1) of the Code, Marta would take the next $11,825 as her federal homestead exemption in the home claimed on her Schedule C (Document 8 in the case file). But that leaves $63,175, to which the bankruptcy trustee will be entitled, subject to expenses of sale, and the bankruptcy judge will not lift the stay and allow repossession. Instead, it will order the stay kept in place and allow the bankruptcy trustee to liquidate the property and distribute the proceeds as indicated.

If the value of the secured property is less than the amount of the debt, however, and the security interest of the creditor is properly perfected and superior to any claim the bankruptcy trustee can make to the property, then the trustee will not object to the lifting of the stay.

For example, as indicated in Marta's Schedule D (Document 9 in the Carlson case file), she owes $900 to Shears Department Store for a washer and dryer she purchased nine months ago. Shears is perfected in the washer and dryer for the entire amount of the indebtedness and the washer and dryer together are valued at only $600. Thus, if Marta is in default on her obligation to Shears and it seeks the lifting of the stay to repossess the washer and dryer, the bankruptcy trustee will not object. He will, of course, review the claim of Shears closely and the paperwork offered in support of its perfected security interest before conceding the superiority of Shears' claim to the property.

Section §362(d) sets out the procedure available to a creditor for lifting the automatic stay so that it can proceed against the property of the debtor. In most circumstances the creditor will file a motion to lift stay, per FRBP 4001. If the motion is contested, the bankruptcy judge will conduct a hearing on the motion at which the creditor has the burden of showing that one of the grounds set forth in §362(d) for lifting the stay is present. (Motion procedure is discussed in more detail in Section G, below.)

Grounds for Lifting the Automatic Stay for Cause: Debtor in Default to Secured Creditor

The most common scenario for a motion to lift stay in a consumer bankruptcy case is where a secured creditor moves to lift the stay so that it can repossess or fore-close on the property securing the debt. The secured creditor will allege as "cause" to satisfy §362(d)(1) that the debtor is in default and that the contract between the parties entitles the creditor to repossess or foreclose on the collateral upon default. Often such motions to lift stay are routinely granted by the court on adequate proof of perfection and default. But not always. As we will learn in Chapter Ten, Section C, several options may be available to the Chapter 7 debtor to retain the collateral notwithstanding the bankruptcy. We've already seen one of those options in Chapter Six, Section B, where we considered the debtor's right under §522(f)(1)(A) to avoid a judicial lien on his property to the extent that the lien impairs an exemption the debtor would otherwise have in the property.

For example, assume a debtor owns a home worth $200,000. Bank holds a mortgage on the home and is owed $100,000 leaving Debtor with $100,000 in own-er's equity. Debtor files a Chapter 7 case but Bank does not move to lift the auto-matic stay and foreclose because Debtor is current on his payments to Bank. Bank will be happy for debtor to reaffirm his debt to Bank secured by the home and for the obligation to ride through the bankruptcy case undisturbed (we will consider the reaffirmation and ride-through options in Chapter Eleven). Assume the appli-cable state homestead exemption enables Debtor to exempt all of his $100,000 own-er's equity in the home so the bankruptcy trustee appointed in his Chapter 7 case cannot reach it.

However, assume further that another creditor of Debtor has filed suit prep-etition, obtained a final judgment, and caused a judicial lien to attach to Debtor's home in the amount of $50,000. The judicial lien creditor now files a motion to lift the automatic stay so it can foreclose on its judicial lien, sell the home, and distrib-ute the proceeds first to the Bank which has a priority position, then to itself, then any remaining proceeds to Debtor. If Debtor acts to avoid the judicial lien on the grounds that it impairs his right to exempt all of his equity in the home, the bank-ruptcy court will likely deny the motion to lift stay.

In the example, note that the judicial lien creditor winds up being treated effec-tively as an unsecured creditor. Of course, an unsecured creditor could file a motion to lift stay and ask the court to allow it to proceed with its collection efforts but it will not be granted absent exceptional circumstances (e.g., the debt is a contingent unliquidated claim pending in a state court action where it can be conveniently decided). And certainly if the unsecured debt is one that is going to be discharged in the bankruptcy there is no reason to let collection efforts proceed. Having said that, as we have seen, there are a number of domestic or other collection activities against a debtor involving unsecured debt as well as criminal or governmental reg-ulatory actions against a debtor that are not subject to the automatic stay at all (see Exhibit 9.2).

Grounds for Lifting the Automatic Stay for Cause: Lack of Adequate Protection

Another ground for lifting the stay in §362(d)(1) frequently asserted in consumer bankruptcy cases is that the secured creditor's interest collateral is not being adequately protected. That means the collateral securing the obligation to the creditor or its value is at risk for some reason. Maybe it is at risk because the debtor does not have it insured so that if it is damaged or stolen the creditor effectively loses its security for the debt. Maybe it is a risk because the debtor is misusing it or not properly protecting it. Maybe the debtor is now current on his payment obligations but the creditor has reason to believe he will not remain so (due to job loss, etc.) Maybe it is at risk due to rapid depreciation of the collateral (e.g., the creditor is secured by the debtor's inventory of iPhone 2017s but the new iPhone 2019 is due out next month, which will dramatically reduce the value of the 2017 model).

For example, recall from the Assignment Memorandum in Appendix A that Marta Carlson owns a Toyota Camry with a book value of $8,500 and that she owes a balance on it of $1,750 to Automotive Financing, Inc. (AFI), which holds a security interest in the car. If Marta had let her insurance policy on the Toyota lapse because she could not afford the premiums, AFI would consider itself at risk (e.g., Marta could total the car leaving AFI with no security). The bankruptcy trustee will consider the interests of the estate at risk as well since there is $1,725 of equity in the car for the estate (the value of the car minus the amount owed to AFI and Marta's $522(d)(2) exemption of $5,025). Either of these parties in interest would have standing to ask that the stay be lifted so that the car could be taken into custody and protected from risk of loss until it could be sold.

Of course if the debtor can satisfy the court that the creditor is adequately protected (insurance is obtained; the misuse has ended; the debtor gives proof of ability to pay) the motion will be denied.

Ground for Lifting the Automatic Stay: No Equity and Collateral Not Needed in a Reorganization

Section 362(d)(2) provides another basis for a secured creditor to move to lift stay to enable repossession or foreclosure. The stay can be lifted under §362(d)(2) where:

- the debtor has no equity in the property (more is owed on it than it is worth), and
- the debtor does not need it for an effective reorganization.

Since Chapter 7 is a liquidation proceeding and not a reorganization as in Chapters 11, 13, and 12, the second criterion, that the debtor does not need it for an effective reorganization, is obviously satisfied. But the creditor seeking to lift the stay on this second ground must also show that there is no equity in the property.

For example, assume Marta Carlson owed AFI $10,000 on the Toyota Camry that is worth only $8,500. She is not in a reorganization proceeding and has no equity in the vehicle. Even if she is not currently in default to AFI, that creditor may be in a position to ask that the stay be lifted under §362(d)(2). But is the creditor likely to do so long as it is being paid?

Where the undervalue of the collateral is the basis for the motion to lift stay, the debtor may be able to cure the problem by applying payments to bring the amount owed in line with the current value of the collateral. But for a debtor in such distress that a bankruptcy filing has been deemed necessary, that option may not be realistic.

Hearings on motions to lift stay are often hotly contested on the critical valuation/equity issues raised by these provisions and experts often are called to testify for the competing parties. Where the valuation issue is complex or particularly close, the contesting parties may choose to settle the issue rather than risk a hearing before the bankruptcy judge. But often there is simply no practical basis on which to settle and the dispute goes to the judge on a win-lose basis. If the stay is lifted as to the secured creditor, it will be allowed to take the property just as it would have if the debtor had not filed for bankruptcy relief.

4. Expiration of the Automatic Stay for Secured Personal Property of the Individual Chapter 7 Debtor

BAPCPA created a creditor-friendly automatic expiration of stay on personal property only, in Chapter 7 cases only, and involving individual debtors only. The procedure, set out in §521(a)(6), provides that the automatic stay in personal property of the individual Chapter 7 debtor automatically expires 45 days after the first meeting of creditors unless the debtor enters into a reaffirmation agreement with the creditor or redeems the property from the security interest. (We consider reaffirmation agreements and the redemption option in Chapter Ten, Section C.)

The effect of §521(a)(6) is to save the secured creditor the trouble and expense of having to file a motion to lift stay and of having to establish one of the grounds of §362(d) in order to prevail on such motion. It effectively shifts the burden to the debtor to file a motion seeking to extend the stay and to show the court why the stay should not be automatically lifted. It also forces the debtor to take the initiative to file that motion within 45 days after the first meeting of creditors. Likewise, if the bankruptcy trustee believes there is equity for the Chapter 7 estate in the collateralized property, he must file a motion with the court to retain the property in the estate before that deadline runs.

For example, since Marta Carlson is an individual debtor in a Chapter 7, §521(a)(6) applies in her case. So if Shears wishes to repossess the washer and dryer (personal property in which it is secured), instead of filing its own motion under §362(d) seeking an order lifting the stay, it can simply wait until the §521(a)(6) deadline expires and then repossess the property. The stay will have expired automatically. The Code is unclear as to whether the bankruptcy court must enter a formal order lifting the stay upon the expiration of the 45 days; in practice, some do and some don't. The attorney must check the local rules of the court or learn the informal local practice.

5. Effect of Individual Debtor's Surrender of Collateralized Property on the Automatic Stay

In Chapter Six, Section B, we learned that one of the statements that an individual Chapter 7 debtor must file with their petition is a statement of intent with regard to collateralized property, indicating whether the debtor will surrender that property to the secured creditor or seek to retain it. If the debtor indicates an intent to surrender that property, the secured creditor must still take appropriate action to have the automatic stay lifted or await the automatic lifting of the stay before taking possession of the property. And, of course, the creditor must await the decision of the bankruptcy trustee regarding whether to abandon the collateralized property to the creditor as being of no interest to the estate (to be considered in Chapter Ten, Section A) or to assert an interest in the property for the benefit of the estate by avoiding the lien (to be considered in Chapter Nine, Section D) or by contending that there is equity in the property for the estate (i.e., it is worth more than is owed the creditor).

However, if an individual debtor fails to file the required statement of intent with regard to collateralized *personal* property, §362(h)(1) provides that the automatic stay is lifted as to such personal property and it is no longer to be considered property of the estate. We have already seen that §362(k)(2) provides a creditor accused of willfully violating the automatic stay as to such property with a good faith defense.

6. The Automatic Stay and Utility Service

An issue that can arise in any bankruptcy case, but that is most common in consumer cases, involves a debtor who is in arrears to a public utility (water, gas, electric, etc.) at the time the petition is filed. Section 366(a) prohibits the utility from discontinuing service to the debtor postpetition, notwithstanding the arrearage. The utility may, however, demand a reasonable deposit or security as adequate assurance of future performance and may discontinue service after 20 days following the filing of the petition if the deposit or security is not provided per §366(b). Disputes over what is a "reasonable" deposit are resolved by the court.

Chapter Summary

- The filing of the Chapter 7 petition in bankruptcy constitutes an order for relief under the Code. The clerk of the bankruptcy court will immediately issue a notice of filing of the case to the U.S. Trustee and to creditors listed on debtor's schedules.
- Upon receiving notice of the filing the U.S. Trustee will promptly appoint a bankruptcy trustee to administer the case from a panel of trustees overseen by

the U.S. Trustee. The bankruptcy trustee's duties include locating and taking possession of the non-exempt property of the debtor to be liquidated, liquidating that property, and distributing the proceeds to creditors in the order of priority mandated by the Code. Approximately 90 percent of all Chapter 7 cases are no-asset cases.

■ Within 21 to 40 days following the entry of the order for relief the U.S. Trustee calls a first meeting of creditors or 341 meeting, where the debtor must answer case-relevant questions under oath. The meeting is presided over by the bankruptcy trustee. Within ten days following the 341 meeting, the U.S. Trustee is required to file a report with the court advising whether any presumption of abuse should arise in the case because of the means test.

■ Upon filing of the petition an automatic stay goes into effect prohibiting most formal and informal debt collection efforts against the debtor from proceeding. Excepted from the operation of the automatic stay are certain landlord eviction actions against debtors involving residential leases, certain actions involving domestic disputes, criminal prosecutions, and some administrative enforcement actions against the debtor.

■ If the stay is violated even inadvertently the debtor may seek to have the violation enjoined. If the stay is violated knowingly the creditor may be held in contempt of the bankruptcy court. If the violation was willful the debtor may recover actual and punitive damages from the creditor. Most courts define willful in this context as a deliberate act taken with knowledge of the bankruptcy filing and do not require proof of specific intent to violate the stay. Courts use varying standards for the award of punitive damages in willful violation cases and there is a split over whether the debtor can recover his attorney's fee incurred in prosecuting the stay violation.

■ The automatic stay can be lifted by order of the bankruptcy court on motion by a creditor properly secured in property of the debtor where the debtor is in default and the creditor is entitled to repossess or foreclose, or where the secured creditor can show that its interest in collateral is not being adequately protected, or where the estate has no equity in the collateral and it is not needed for a reorganization.

■ In Chapter 7 cases involving individual debtors, the automatic stay against personal property expires automatically 45 days following the first meeting of creditors unless the debt has been reaffirmed or the collateral redeemed by the debtor. If an individual debtor fails to file the required statement of intent with regard to collateralized personal property the automatic stay is lifted as to such personal property and it is no longer to be considered property of the estate.

■ Public utilities are subject to the automatic stay and may not terminate service after the petition is filed even if the customer is in arrears. The utility may however, demand a reasonable deposit or security as adequate assurance of future performance and discontinue service after 20 days following the filing of the petition if the deposit or security is not provided.

Applying the Concepts

1. Assume you represent Mark Brewster and have just filed a Chapter 7 bankruptcy petition for him. Brewster is married but separated from his wife, who has filed a divorce action against him in state court. Which of following proceedings are subject to the automatic stay in his case?

   a. A child custody hearing scheduled week after next in his divorce case.
   b. A hearing on property settlement scheduled for next week in his divorce case.
   c. A trial scheduled for next month in his landlord's eviction action seeking to evict Mark from the apartment he has been living in since his separation on the basis of nonpayment of rent.
   d. A deposition scheduled next month in a personal injury negligence lawsuit brought against Mark in state court arising out of a car accident last year.
   e. An administrative hearing scheduled next month in a proceeding by the state to suspend Mark's professional surveyor's license due to nonpayment of child support.
   f. An office audit scheduled for next month at the local IRS office as part of the IRS's audit of Mark's tax returns for the past three years.
   g. An ongoing garnishment of Mark's wages served on his employer six months ago arising from a final judgment entered against him in a contract dispute last year.

2. Which of the following creditors in Mark's case is likely to convince the court to lift the automatic stay if they file a motion to lift stay? On what grounds will they argue for lifting the stay? Are they likely to succeed?

   a. Bank that was preparing to repossess Mark's automobile due to his being three payments behind on the note secured by the auto.
   b. Bank holding the note secured by Mark's boat that has learned Mark has allowed the insurance policy on his boat to lapse. Mark is up to date on his payments on the note.
   c. Credit card company that has cancelled Mark's credit card for nonpayment and is anxious to file suit and obtain a judgment against him for the balance owed before other unsecured creditors do the same.
   d. Credit Union holding note secured by Mark's Harley-Davidson motorcycle upon learning that Mark crashed the motorcycle and doesn't plan to have it repaired because of the high deductible on his insurance policy covering it. He now owes far more on the note than the Harley is worth.

3. Assume you represent the local office of Quick Finance Inc., a national financial services company specializing in consumer and business loans in the area. Quick Finance has recently foreclosed on a home owned by Frank and Frannie Smith, who are in default on the note secured by the home and who were given all proper notices of default and intended foreclosure. The national office of

Quick Finance, located in Kansas City, has utilized the safe harbor provision of §342(g)(1) of the Code by designating the company's general counsel in the Kansas City office as its agent to receive bankruptcy notices. The foreclosure sale of the Smith's home is scheduled to occur in one hour and you are handling it. The manager of the local office is anxious to get this done and you are anxious to keep her pleased because the manager can use whatever local counsel she wishes. Just as you are leaving the office to go to the sale, you receive a panicked phone call from Frannie Smith advising that she and her husband are filing a case in bankruptcy and begging you to hold off on the foreclosure sale. You ask if she has counsel representing her and she says she and her husband are at the bankruptcy clerk's office now trying to figure out how to file without a lawyer. You ask if she notified the general counsel in Kansas City but she says she has to go and hangs up. Should you proceed with the foreclosure sale? What are the risks in doing so? If you decide not to go forward with the foreclosure sale, how will you explain your decision to the the local manager of Quick Finance?

4. Locate and read Assignment Memorandum #2 in Appendix C. If your instructor so directs, prepare the motion to lift stay, etc., on behalf of Automotive Financing, Inc., assuming the Chapter 7 case of Abelard Mendoza is pending in the U.S. bankruptcy court of your federal district.

8

The Chapter 7 Consumer Bankruptcy Case: Creditor Claims

In this chapter we will study the Code procedures for administering the claims of creditors in a Chapter 7 case including the creditor's responsibility to file a proof of claim in order to participate in a distribution in the case. We will examine the unique way that the Code bifurcates undersecured claims, the procedures and best practices for filing a claim in a Chapter 7 case, when and how interest is calculated on a creditor's claim, the procedure for objecting to a creditor's claim, and how the doctrine of setoff works in the bankruptcy context.

A. DISTINGUISHING BETWEEN SECURED AND UNSECURED CLAIMS IN BANKRUPTCY: BIFURCATION OF THE UNDERSECURED CLAIM

When a creditor files a claim against a debtor in a bankruptcy case, the claim will be treated as an **unsecured claim** if the creditor is unsecured and as a **secured claim** to the extent the creditor holds a consensual or non-consensual security interest or lien in any of the debtor's property.

To understand how the Code treats secured claims, you must keep in mind that a creditor may be **fully secured** (the dollar value of the collateral is at least as much as the dollar amount of the claim), **oversecured** (the dollar value of the

Key Concepts

- Unsecured creditors must file a proof of claim in order to participate in any distribution to creditors in a Chapter 7
- The failure of a secured creditor to file a timely proof of claim does not impair its secured position in the property of the debtor
- Undersecured claims are bifurcated into the secured and unsecured parts and a proof of claim must be filed for the unsecured portion to participate in distribution
- A creditor's claim is deemed allowed unless a timely objection is made
- The right to setoff is recognized as between the debtor and creditors in the bankruptcy case
- Generally, postpetition interest is not payable on creditor claims

collateral exceeds the dollar amount of the claim), or **undersecured** (sometimes called **partially secured**) (the dollar value of the collateral is less than the dollar amount of the claim).

For example, assume creditor #1 has a prepetition secured claim against the debtor in the amount of $100,000 and the property in which he is secured has a value of $100,000. That creditor is fully secured. Creditor #2 has a prepetition secured claim against the debtor in the amount of $100,000 and the property in which he is secured has a value of $125,000. That creditor is oversecured. Creditor #3 has a prepetition secured claim against the debtor in the amount of $100,000 and the property in which he is secured has a value of $75,000. That creditor is undersecured, or only partially secured.

Section 506(a)(1) of the Code provides that a secured claim in bankruptcy is only secured up to the value of the collateral at the time the petition is filed. For the wholly secured and oversecured creditor that presents no problem — their secured claim will be valued at the full amount of the indebtedness. But for the undersecured creditor that means his secured claim will be allowed only up to the value of the collateral and as to the balance of what he is owed over the value of the collateral, his claim will be treated as unsecured. Thus, §506(a) effectively bifurcates the undersecured claim into its secured and unsecured portions. Practitioners sometimes refer to this mandated bifurcation as a **strip down** or **write down** of an undersecured claim to the value of the collateral. Note that the undersecured creditor does not forfeit the unsecured portion of his claim, but he can only pursue that claim through the bankruptcy process as an unsecured claim.

There are numerous other consequences of this bifurcation of an undersecured claim in a bankruptcy case, including how the collateral securing the claim is to be valued. We will consider each consequence and valuation issue as we come to it in our study of Chapters 7 and 13.

B. THE PROOF OF CLAIM

The notice of commencement of a Chapter 7 case advises the creditors whether to file a written **proof of claim** and, if so, the deadline (called the **claims bar date**) by which such claim must be filed. If a case is a no-asset one, creditors will be advised not to file a proof of claim since no distribution (payout) to creditors is anticipated. Since the Marta Rinaldi Carlson case is an asset case, the notice of the filing of the case does advise creditors of a filing deadline for proofs of claim (see Document 23 in the Carlson case file).

Section 501(a) of the Code authorizes the filing of the proof of claim. Official Form 410 is the proof of claim form. In some districts, the court clerk will attach a copy of the form to the notice of commencement. In other districts, the creditor must download the form from the clerk's Web site or obtain one from the clerk's office. Pursuant to FRBP 3001 and 3002, the proof of claim form must be completed by the creditor, signed, and mailed or delivered to the bankruptcy court clerk or the bankruptcy trustee or both, as the form directs. Per FRBP 3002(c), the proof of claim in a Chapter 7, Chapter 13, or Chapter 12 case must be filed not later than 90 days after the first date set for the meeting of creditors (the 341 meeting) unless one of six enumerated exceptions applies. The exceptions pertain to claims of governmental units, infants and incompetent persons, recipients of avoided transfers, parties to executory contracts or unexpired leases, foreign creditors, and claims in Chapter 7 cases that began as no-asset cases. A governmental unit, however, has 180 days to file a claim from the "date of the order for relief" which is normally the date the petition was filed.

A timely filed proof of claim can be amended freely "where the purpose is to cure a defect in the claim as originally filed, to describe the claim with greater particularity or to plead a new theory of recovery on the facts set forth in the original claim." In re South Atlantic Financial Corp., 767 F.2d 814, 819 (11th Cir. 1985). However, an amendment sought after the claims bar date will not be allowed where it attempts to add a new claim that could have been filed timely. See, e.g., In re Chavis, 160 B.R. 804, aff'd, 47 F.3d 818 (6th Cir. 1995) (IRS amendment to add new tax years was untimely and disallowed).

FRBP 3001 requires that if the claim is based on a writing (e.g., promissory note, written contract, security agreement, mortgage), a copy of the writing must be attached to the proof of claim.

The proof of claim filed by Pine Ridge Nursing Home in Marta Carlson's Chapter 7 case (Document 27 in the Carlson case file) is set out in Exhibit 8.1. Note that the guaranty she executed, which forms the basis of the claim, is attached.

If the creditor asserts a security interest in any property of the debtor, proof of perfection of that interest must accompany the claim form (e.g., copy of title to collateralized vehicle with security interest noted thereon, copy of security agreement and financing statement with date of filing, affidavit that collateral perfected by possession of the creditor is in fact in creditor's possession, etc.)

FRBP 3001 and Official Form 410 require creditors to provide more specific information where claims are filed in cases of individual debtors, including:

- An itemized statement of interest, fees, expenses, or other charges sought in addition to the principal indebtedness
- If a security interest is asserted in debtor's property, the amount of any arrearage (amount needed to cure any default) as of the date of the petition
- If a mortgage is asserted in debtor's principal residence, an attachment (Form 410) must accompany the proof of claim, providing details of the outstanding loan as of the date the petition is filed
- If the claim is based on a revolving or open-end consumer credit account (like a credit card or department store account), a statement containing details of the last transaction, payment, and posting on the account

It is important that creditors in a Chapter 7 who wish to participate in any distribution from the estate file the proof of claim and file it within the time allowed. If an unsecured creditor fails to file a proof of claim the bankruptcy trustee will

EXHIBIT 8.1	Pine Ridge Nursing Home Proof of Claim

Fill in this information to identify the case:

Debtor 1   Marta Rinaldi Carlson

Debtor 2
(Spouse, if filing)

United States Bankruptcy Court for the: District of Minnesota

Case number 16-7-XXXX

Official Form 410

Proof of Claim

04/16

Read the instructions before filling out this form. This form is for making a claim for payment in a bankruptcy case. Do not use this form to make a request for payment of an administrative expense. Make such a request according to 11 U.S.C. § 503.

Filers must leave out or redact information that is entitled to privacy on this form or on any attached documents. Attach redacted copies of any documents that support the claim, such as promissory notes, purchase orders, invoices, itemized statements of running accounts, contracts, judgments, mortgages, and security agreements. Do not send original documents; they may be destroyed after scanning. If the documents are not available, explain in an attachment.

A person who files a fraudulent claim could be fined up to $500,000, imprisoned for up to 5 years, or both. 18 U.S.C. §§ 152, 157, and 3571.

Fill in all the information about the claim as of the date the case was filed. That date is on the notice of bankruptcy (Form 309) that you received.

Part 1:	Identify the Claim

1. Who is the current creditor?

Marta Rinaldi Carlson
Name of the current creditor (the person or entity to be paid for this claim)

Other names the creditor used with the debtor

2. Has this claim been acquired from someone else?

☑ No
☐ Yes. From whom? _____

3. Where should notices and payments to the creditor be sent?

Federal Rule of Bankruptcy Procedure (FRBP) 2002(g)

Where should notices to the creditor be sent?

Pine Ridge Nursing Home
Name

4203 Mulberry Drive
Number   Street

St. Paul   MN   55113
City   State   ZIP Code

Contact phone (651) 555-2290

Contact email PineRidgeNH@quicknet.com

Where should payments to the creditor be sent? (if different)

Name

Number   Street

City   State   ZIP Code

Contact phone

Contact email

Uniform claim identifier for electronic payments in chapter 13 (if you use one):

__ __

4. Does this claim amend one already filed?

☑ No
☐ Yes. Claim number on court claims registry (if known) _____   Filed on _____
                                            MM / DD / YYYY

5. Do you know if anyone else has filed a proof of claim for this claim?

☑ No
☐ Yes. Who made the earlier filing? _____

EXHIBIT 8.1   (Continued)

Part 2:   **Give Information About the Claim as of the Date the Case Was Filed**

6. **Do you have any number you use to identify the debtor?**

   ☐ No

   ☑ Yes. Last 4 digits of the debtor's account or any number you use to identify the debtor: _8_ _8_ _4_ _5_

7. **How much is the claim?** $_____ 45,290.00 . **Does this amount include interest or other charges?**

   ☑ No

   ☐ Yes. Attach statement itemizing interest, fees, expenses, or other charges required by Bankruptcy Rule 3001(c)(2)(A).

8. **What is the basis of the claim?**

   Examples: Goods sold, money loaned, lease, services performed, personal injury or wrongful death, or credit card.

   Attach redacted copies of any documents supporting the claim required by Bankruptcy Rule 3001(c).

   Limit disclosing information that is entitled to privacy, such as health care information.

   Personal guaranty _____

9. **Is all or part of the claim secured?**

   ☑ No

   ☐ Yes.   The claim is secured by a lien on property.

   Nature of property:

   ☐ Real estate. If the claim is secured by the debtor's principal residence, file a *Mortgage Proof of Claim Attachment* (Official Form 410-A) with this *Proof of Claim.*

   ☐ Motor vehicle

   ☐ Other. Describe: _____

   Basis for perfection: _____

   Attach redacted copies of documents, if any, that show evidence of perfection of a security interest (for example, a mortgage, lien, certificate of title, financing statement, or other document that shows the lien has been filed or recorded.)

   Value of property: $_____

   Amount of the claim that is secured: $_____

   Amount of the claim that is unsecured: $_____ (The sum of the secured and unsecured amounts should match the amount in line 7.)

   Amount necessary to cure any default as of the date of the petition: $_____

   Annual Interest Rate (when case was filed)_____%

   ☐ Fixed

   ☐ Variable

10. **Is this claim based on a lease?**

    ☑ No

    ☐ Yes. **Amount necessary to cure any default as of the date of the petition.** $_____

11. **Is this claim subject to a right of setoff?**

    ☑ No

    ☐ Yes. Identify the property: _____

Official Form 410   **Proof of Claim**   page 2

EXHIBIT 8.1 **(Continued)**

12. **Is all or part of the claim entitled to priority under 11 U.S.C. § 507(a)?**

A claim may be partly priority and partly nonpriority. For example, in some categories, the law limits the amount entitled to priority.

☑ No

☐ Yes. *Check one:*

	Amount entitled to priority
☐ Domestic support obligations (including alimony and child support) under 11 U.S.C. § 507(a)(1)(A) or (a)(1)(B).	$_____
☐ Up to $2,850* of deposits toward purchase, lease, or rental of property or services for personal, family, or household use. 11 U.S.C. § 507(a)(7).	$_____
☐ Wages, salaries, or commissions (up to $12,850*) earned within 180 days before the bankruptcy petition is filed or the debtor's business ends, whichever is earlier. 11 U.S.C. § 507(a)(4).	$_____
☐ Taxes or penalties owed to governmental units. 11 U.S.C. § 507(a)(8).	$_____
☐ Contributions to an employee benefit plan. 11 U.S.C. § 507(a)(5).	$_____
☐ Other. Specify subsection of 11 U.S.C. § 507(a)(__) that applies.	$_____

* Amounts are subject to adjustment on 4/01/19 and every 3 years after that for cases begun on or after the date of adjustment.

Part 3: **Sign Below**

The person completing this proof of claim must sign and date it. FRBP 9011(b).

If you file this claim electronically, FRBP 5005(a)(2) authorizes courts to establish local rules specifying what a signature is.

A person who files a fraudulent claim could be fined up to $500,000, imprisoned for up to 5 years, or both. 18 U.S.C. §§ 152, 157, and 3571.

Check the appropriate box:

☐ I am the creditor.

☑ I am the creditor's attorney or authorized agent.

☐ I am the trustee, or the debtor, or their authorized agent. Bankruptcy Rule 3004.

☐ I am a guarantor, surety, endorser, or other codebtor. Bankruptcy Rule 3005.

I understand that an authorized signature on this *Proof of Claim* serves as an acknowledgment that when calculating the amount of the claim, the creditor gave the debtor credit for any payments received toward the debt.

I have examined the information in this *Proof of Claim* and have a reasonable belief that the information is true and correct.

I declare under penalty of perjury that the foregoing is true and correct.

Executed on date   07/20/2016_____
                    MM / DD / YYYY

/s/ Carol W. Evans_____
Signature

Print the name of the person who is completing and signing this claim:

Name	Carol	W.	Evans
	First name	Middle name	Last name

Title   Administrator

Company   Pine Ridge Nursing Home
           Identify the corporate servicer as the company if the authorized agent is a servicer.

Address   4203 Mulberry Drive
           Number   Street

           St. Paul   MN   55113
           City   State   ZIP Code

Contact phone   (651) 555-2290   Email PineRideNH@quicknet.com

GUARANTY AGREEMENT

THIS GUARANTY, is made this October 1, 2013, by Marta Rinaldi Carlson of 301 Pugh Street, Roseville, Minnesota ("Guarantor"), in favor of Pine Ridge Nursing Home, 4203 Evergreen, St. Paul, Minnesota ("Nursing Home").

Guarantor is the daughter of Estell Rinaldi, a resident in the Nursing Home ("Resident"). In consideration of the care and services to be provided to Resident by the Nursing Home, Guarantor hereby promises to pay Nursing Home all obligations owed to Nursing Home on the account of Resident not otherwise paid or satisfied within ninety (90) days of the obligation being incurred.

/s/ Marta R. Carlson

Marta Rinaldi Carlson, Guarantor

not include that creditor in a distribution. If the proof of claim is filed late (after the claims bar date), the trustee may object to it on that basis under §502(b)(9) or seek to have it subordinated (made inferior or junior in status) to other claims of equal rank, pursuant to the **equitable subordination** doctrine of §510 (discussed in more detail in Chapter Ten, Section B).

Pursuant to §726(a)(1), **priority claims** (also discussed in Chapter Ten, Section B) are to be allowed if filed on or before ten days after the date the trustee mails a summary of his final report to creditors or the date on which final distribution in the case is commenced, whichever is earlier. And §726(a)(2)(C) provides that any late-filed unsecured claim will be allowed if the filing was late due to the creditor's lack of notice or actual knowledge of the case filing and the claim is filed in time to permit payment. If the initial notice to creditors did not require that a proof of claim be filed but a later notice is given to that effect, the proof of claim must be filed within 90 days of the later notice.

The failure of a secured creditor to file a timely proof of claim does not impair its secured position in the property of the debtor per §506(d)(2). So, technically, the secured creditor need not file a proof of claim to preserve its secured status in the debtor's property. The lien on the property if properly perfected will pass through the bankruptcy case unmolested and the creditor can continue to look to its collateral for satisfaction of the underlying obligation (as by, in the event of default, asking for lifting of the stay so that it can foreclose or repossess). (As we will see in Chapter Twelve, Section E, however, in a Chapter 13 case, the secured creditor must file a proof of claim in order to receive payments under a confirmed plan. But all that in due time.)

Case Preview

In re Nowak

What about the creditor who is secured but undersecured in the collateral, i.e., the debtor owes the creditor more than the collateral securing the debt is worth? Remember that the Code is going to bifurcate that claim pursuant to §506(a)(1) and treat the claim as unsecured to the extent it exceeds the value of the collateral. Does that mean the secured creditor must file a proof of claim as to the unsecured portion of its claim? As you read *Nowak*, consider the following questions:

1. What are the two situations in which a secured creditor must file a proof of claim?
2. What is the informal proof of claim doctrine and what is the policy behind it?
3. Why do you think that the Sixth Circuit BAP reversed the bankruptcy judge's ruling that the various filings of the creditor failed to rise to the level of an informal proof of claim?
4. What was the significance of the creditor being a sophisticated financial services company represented by counsel throughout on the court's weighing of the equities in this case?

In re Nowak
586 F.3d 450 (6th Cir. 2009)

GILMAN, Circuit Judge. . . .

On March 6, 1998, the Nowaks executed a $470,900 mortgage on their . . . residence in favor of PCFS. Three years later, the Nowaks jointly filed for Chapter 7 bankruptcy relief. Spragin was appointed as trustee for the Nowaks' estate and issued notices to the Nowaks' creditors to file proofs of claim. The bar date for filing such claims was July 24, 2001. At the time these notices were issued, PCFS was considered a secured creditor and therefore was not required to file a proof of claim. See Fed. R. Bankr. P. 3002(a) (requiring only unsecured creditors to file proofs of claim against non-corporate bankruptcy estates). The Nowaks received a discharge from the bankruptcy court in August 2001.

On the day after all proofs of claim were due, Spragin moved to employ an attorney for the purpose of voiding the lien of PCFS on the Nowaks' residence pursuant to 11 U.S.C. §544(a). The bankruptcy court granted this motion and, in October 2001, Spragin filed a separate adversary proceeding to void PCFS's lien. Spragin contended that PCFS's mortgage was invalid under Ohio law because the execution of the mortgage had not been witnessed by two people.

Meanwhile . . . Spragin filed a notice of intent to sell the residence. She proposed the sale because PCFS's lien on the residence was the subject of a "bona fide dispute." PCFS objected, arguing that there was no bona fide dispute and that the proposed sale price would not satisfy the lien, but instead would create a deficiency. In addition, PCFS filed a motion for relief from the automatic stay . . . and for the abandonment of the Nowaks' residence by the bankruptcy estate. The bankruptcy court overruled PCFS's objection to the sale of the residence, and PCFS subsequently withdrew its motion for relief from the automatic stay. . . .

[T]he bankruptcy court agreed with Spragin that PCFS's mortgage was not executed with the proper formalities. Accordingly, the court entered an order voiding PCFS's lien on June 9, 2003, causing PCFS to become an unsecured creditor. PCFS appealed that decision to the BAP.

While PCFS's appeal was pending . . . Spragin filed an amended notice of intent to sell the Nowaks' residence in the underlying bankruptcy case. PCFS did not file an objection to the notice. The residence was sold in the spring of 2003 for $300,000. In September 2005, the BAP affirmed the decision of the bankruptcy court in the adversary proceeding, and PCFS did not appeal.

No documents were filed by the parties in the bankruptcy case during 2006. In January 2007, Spragin filed a final report and accounting. She recommended the distribution of funds to all unsecured creditors who had filed allowed claims. Because PCFS had not filed a proof of claim, however, Spragin did not include PCFS as a creditor in the proposed distribution.

PCFS objected to Spragin's final report and moved the bankruptcy court to allow an informal proof of claim. The motion stated that "[t]he filings made to the court, including the motion for relief from stay and documents filed within the adversary proceeding, and the debtors['] testimony" collectively qualified as an informal proof of claim. Spragin responded by arguing that PCFS's claim should not be allowed because PCFS had ample opportunity to file a formal proof of claim but failed to do so.

The bankruptcy court ruled in favor of Spragin. First, the court determined that PCFS's various filings did not constitute an informal proof of claim because they did not contain a demand on the Nowaks' estate and did not express an intent to hold the Nowaks liable for the debt. In the alternative, the court concluded that the equities weighed in favor of disallowing PCFS's informal proof of claim. The court reasoned that PCFS had not filed anything prior to the claims-bar deadline, that PCFS had not explained its failure to file a formal proof of claim, and that the allowance of PCFS's claim would reduce the recovery of the other creditors from 100 percent to 29 percent. Accordingly, the court overruled the objection of PCFS and denied PCFS's motion to allow an informal proof of claim.

PCFS appealed the bankruptcy court's decision to the BAP. The BAP majority concluded that PCFS's filings in the bankruptcy court did in fact qualify as an informal proof of claim, but nevertheless deferred to the court's discretion regarding the disallowance of the claim based on a weighing of the equities. In contrast, the BAP dissent opined that the bankruptcy court's decision to disallow PCFS's claim lacked reasonable justification. PCFS appeals the decision of the BAP, arguing that the BAP erred in upholding the bankruptcy court's conclusion that the equities weighed against allowing PCFS's claim.

If an unsecured creditor wishes to participate in the distribution of the assets of a bankruptcy estate, the creditor must file a timely proof of claim with the bankruptcy court. Fed. R. Bankr. P. 3002(a). A proof of claim "executed and filed in accordance with [Rule 3001] shall constitute prima facie evidence of the validity and amount of the claim." Fed. R. Bankr. P. 3001(f). Where a creditor has failed to file a formal proof of claim prior to the claims-bar date, the creditor may nevertheless seek allowance of its untimely claim through the common law doctrine of an informal proof of claim. In re M.J. Waterman & Assocs., Inc., 227 F.3d at 608-09. This doctrine is intended to "alleviate problems with form over substance" where a creditor has "failed to adhere to the strict formalities of the Bankruptcy Code," but has made filings that "put[] all parties on sufficient notice that a claim is asserted by a particular creditor." Id.

The doctrine "permits a bankruptcy court to treat the pre-bar date filings of a creditor as an informal proof of claim which can be amended after the bar date so that it is in conformity with the requirements of [Rule 3001]." Id. at 608. Pre-bar date filings must meet four elements to constitute an informal proof of claim: "(1) The proof of claim must be in writing; (2) The writing must contain a demand by the creditor on the debtor's estate; (3) The writing must express an intent to hold the debtor liable for the debt; and (4) The proof of claim must be filed with the bankruptcy court." Id. at 609 (citation omitted). If all four of these conditions are met, "the court may examine a fifth factor — whether it would be equitable to allow the amendment of the informal proof." Id.

The fifth factor of the informal-proof-of-claim doctrine is an equitable determination . . . is within the sound discretion of the bankruptcy court. Id. at 607. As this court has explained:

> Creditors who ignore the formalistic requirements of the Code do so at their own peril, however, as they run the risk of being denied use of the informal proof of claims doctrine if their pre-bar date actions do not meet the standards imposed in their jurisdiction. These standards are designed to protect the interests of the debtor as well as the other creditors who saw fit to follow the Code's rules and whose interests may be directly affected by the delinquent creditor's failure to file in a timely fashion. It is a delicate balance. On the one hand we do not wish to enact too heavy-handed a measure to punish a creditor who may not have strictly adhered to the formalities of the filing requirements, but whose actions were sufficient to put the court and the debtor on notice of his or her intention to seek to hold the debtor liable. On the other hand, we must protect the rights and interests of the parties at interest whose diligence entitles them to a timely distribution of the estate.

Id. at 609. This fifth factor does not lend itself to bright-line rules. Rather, the bankruptcy court is charged with balancing the interests of the parties to determine whether the equities favor the allowance of the informal proof of claim.

A secured creditor is usually not required to file a proof of claim to maintain its interest in the collateral to which its security interest attaches. See 11 U.S.C. §506(d) & note (Subsection (d)); Fed. R. Bankr. P. 3002(a); Talbert v. City Mortgage Servs. (In re Talbert), 344 F.3d 555, 561 (6th Cir. 2003) (recognizing the traditional rule that "real property liens emerge from bankruptcy unaffected"). But there are two situations in which a secured creditor does have to file a proof of claim to preserve its interests in the assets of the bankruptcy estate. First, where a creditor's lien on the collateral exceeds the value of the property, that creditor has a partially unsecured claim and must file a proof of claim with the bankruptcy court if it wishes to receive any distribution from the estate to compensate for this deficiency. See 11 U.S.C. §506(a)(1); Fed. R. Bankr. P. 3002(a).

The second situation is where the trustee of a bankruptcy estate successfully voids a creditor's lien in an adversary proceeding brought under 11 U.S.C. §544(a). If this occurs, the creditor loses its secured status and has 30 days from the judgment that voids its security interest to file proof of an unsecured claim. Fed. R. Bankr. P. 3002(c)(3) & advisory committee note (Subsection (c)). And if the creditor does not file a timely proof of its now-unsecured claim, the bankruptcy court may refuse to allow the claim. 11 U.S.C. §502(b)(9). . . .

[T]he sole issue on appeal is whether the bankruptcy court abused its discretion in not allowing PCFS's informal proof of claim. The court relied on three factors in denying the claim: (1) the length of PCFS's delay in pursuing an unsecured claim in light of the notice to PCFS that it might lose its secured status, (2) the lack of any explanation from PCFS for this delay or for the failure to file any formal proof of claim, and (3) the significantly reduced distribution available to the other creditors if PCFS's claim were allowed. After a thorough review of the record, we conclude that the bankruptcy court's determination was not unreasonable for the reasons set forth below.

1. Notice to PCFS of the need to file a claim . . .

PCFS had ample notice of the likelihood that it would lose its status as a secured creditor, necessitating the filing of a proof of claim. By mid–2001, PCFS and its counsel knew that Spragin was planning to challenge PCFS's lien on the Nowaks' residence. Spragin initiated the adversary proceeding in October 2001 to litigate this very issue. Indeed, another creditor that was a party to the adversary proceeding and claimed a second mortgage on the residence — Key Bank N.A. — recognized the likelihood of losing its secured status and agreed to surrender its lien on the property. A stipulated order provided that Key Bank would "take in proportion with the unsecured creditors in [the] action," and Key Bank was given 30 days to file its proof of claim pursuant to Rule 3002(c)(3) of the Federal Rules of Bankruptcy Procedure. The record of the adversary proceeding thus provided PCFS with clear notice of the consequences of losing its security interest in the Nowaks' residence.

Moreover, even if PCFS had maintained its secured-creditor status, the sale of the Nowaks' residence created an unsecured deficiency for which PCFS would have had to file a claim to receive a distribution from the estate. PCFS recognized the existence of the deficiency at the time it objected to Spragin's proposed sale of the residence in September 2002. Yet when the bankruptcy court overruled PCFS's objection in February 2003, PCFS still did not file a claim for the unsecured deficiency. PCFS thus failed to protect its interests despite repeated notice of the need to file a proof of claim. As the United States Court of Appeals for the Tenth Circuit has stated, "the equities do not favor protecting a financial organization that had numerous opportunities to protect itself." In re Reliance Equities, Inc., 966 F.2d 1338, 1345 (10th Cir. 1992).

PCFS attempts to rebut the negative implications of its failure to act by arguing that the other creditors would not be unfairly surprised by the allowance of PCFS's claim because they had clear and repeated notice of its existence. According to PCFS, the other creditors had to be aware that any distribution of assets from the bankruptcy estate would come almost entirely from PCFS's collateral and that PCFS had by far the largest claim against the estate. PCFS argues that its failure to file a formal proof of claim, when viewed in light of the notice to the other creditors of PCFS's interest in the estate, does not weigh against allowing an informal proof of claim.

We find this argument unpersuasive because it fails to take into account the conduct of PCFS in the bankruptcy proceedings, which suggested that PCFS was no longer pursuing its claim against the estate. First, PCFS withdrew one of the key filings that it relies on as evidence of its informal proof of claim—the motion for relief from the automatic stay filed in January 2003. It withdrew this motion only two months later, in March 2003.

Another example of PCFS's inaction is its failure to object to Spragin's November 2003 amended notice of intent to sell the residence. And even after the BAP affirmed the bankruptcy court's decision to void PCFS's lien in September 2005, PCFS did not pursue an appeal to this court. Finally, PCFS did not make any filings whatsoever with the bankruptcy court for the entirety of 2006.

The creditors could have concluded from this conduct that PCFS had abandoned its claims against the bankruptcy estate. Spragin herself believed this to be the case when she filed her final report and accounting in January 2007. Thus, PCFS's argument about the lack of unfair surprise to the other creditors is questionable and does not show that the bankruptcy court abused its discretion.

2. PCFS's unexplained failure to file a timely claim . . .

PCFS failed to file any formal proof of claim and did not explain its delay in filing the motion to allow an informal proof of claim. PCFS contends that this factor should not weigh against it because "[i]n all cases where an informal proof of claim is at issue the time for filing a timely proof of claim must have passed, otherwise, there would be no need to have an informal proof of claim." Although . . . there is always untimeliness when a party seeks allowance of an informal proof of claim, the issue here is the lack of any explanation for PCFS's conduct in this case. Only when Spragin filed her final report in January 2007 did PCFS seek recognition of an unsecured claim against the estate. PCFS did not offer any explanation to the bankruptcy court for PCFS's failure to timely file a formal proof of claim or for its delay in moving for the allowance of an informal proof. At oral argument before us, the only explanation offered by PCFS's counsel for the error was that it was "an oversight."

The bankruptcy court determined that PCFS's unexplained conduct weighed against recognizing its informal proof of claim. This conclusion is supported by the Seventh Circuit . . . which . . . reasoned:

> Perhaps most importantly, [the creditor] has not offered any convincing justification or explanation for its untimely filing. Despite having actual knowledge of the Bar Date and being represented by counsel at all relevant times, [the creditor] failed to timely file its proof of claim. As noted by the district court, [the creditor's] problem is a "self-inflicted wound," and it has no one to blame but itself for this predicament. This is not the case of an unsophisticated claimant confused by complex terms in a bankruptcy notice.

In re Outboard Marine Corp., 386 F.3d 824, 828 (7th Cir. 2004). Similarly . . . PCFS is a sophisticated lender that has been represented by counsel throughout the proceedings. Its failure to file a timely claim is therefore a "self-inflicted wound," and the bankruptcy court did not abuse its discretion in determining that the unexplained delay weighed against allowing PCFS's informal proof of claim.

3. Distribution available to other creditors

The third factor on which the bankruptcy court based its decision was the substantial dilution in the distribution to the other creditors that would occur if the court allowed PCFS's claim. As the court explained, the percentage distribution "to holders of allowed unsecured claims would drop from 100% plus interest to approximately 29%." The court concluded that such a large dilution in the distribution, coupled with the lack of explanation for PCFS's untimeliness, "would work too large an inequity for an 'informal' proof of claim by PCFS Financial to be allowed." . . .

PCFS argues that the bankruptcy court abused its discretion in making this determination by failing to adequately consider that (1) a dilution in the distribution to the other creditors is always a necessary consequence of allowing an informal proof of claim, and is therefore not remarkable, (2) the estate consists almost entirely of PCFS's security interest, (3) PCFS's claim is not disputed, (4) the percentage distribution that would be paid to the other creditors if PCFS's claim were allowed is reasonable and well above the national average for Chapter 7 cases, (5) equity favors inclusion of all creditors, and (6) the purpose of the Bankruptcy Code is to provide pro rata distribution to all unsecured creditors. Although PCFS's arguments are not without force, it has failed to demonstrate that the bankruptcy court's decision to the contrary was so unreasonable as to constitute an abuse of discretion. See In re M.J. Waterman & Assocs., Inc., 227 F.3d 604, 612 (6th Cir. 2000) (explaining that an abuse of discretion should be found only where "the bankruptcy court's conclusion . . . was so unreasonable as to be unsupportable or to leave us with a definite and firm conviction that the bankruptcy court committed a clear error of judgment").

The bankruptcy court determined that the significant reduction in percentage distribution to the other creditors that would result from allowing PCFS's informal proof of claim weighed against PCFS. At least one other bankruptcy court applied the same reasoning in similar circumstances, stating that, among other things, the reduction of a dividend from 33 percent to "a fraction" of that percentage "is prejudicial to the creditors and cannot be allowed." In re Wigoda, 234 B.R. 413, 417 (Bankr. N.D. Ill. 1999); see also In re Outboard Marine Corp., 386 F.3d at 829 (recognizing the effect "on the payout to the creditors with timely-filed claims" as an equitable factor militating against permitting an untimely claim). Although we view the degree of dilution as a questionable factor to take into account, the above-cited cases indicate that other reasonable jurists would agree with the bankruptcy court's determination that the large dilution in the present case was an appropriate consideration weighing against allowing PCFS's claim.

4. The balancing of the equities

This is not a case in which an unsophisticated lender complied with the substance of the bankruptcy rules but unknowingly failed to file the appropriate form. Rather, the lender in this case, a financial institution represented by counsel from the beginning of the bankruptcy proceedings, failed to timely file a proof of claim despite repeated opportunities to do so. . . .

For all of the reasons set forth above, we AFFIRM the judgment of both the BAP and the bankruptcy court.

Post-Case Follow-Up

The informal proof of claim doctrine is not recognized in all federal circuits. See, e.g., In re Brooks, 370 B.R. 194, 201 (Bankr. C.D. Ill. 2007), interpreting Matter of Greenig, 152 F.3d 631 (7th Cir. 1998), to have effectively "gutted" the doctrine in the Seventh Circuit, limiting the bankruptcy court's power to allow a late-filed proof of claim to the six exceptions enumerated in FRPB 3002(c). This case illustrates one of the great unwritten laws of legal practice: when advising a client, adopt the better safe than sorry approach. It will rarely fail you and often save you.

In re Nowak: Real Life Applications

1. Had the creditor in *Nowak* contacted you after receiving notice of the bankruptcy filing and you had determined that it was secured and perfected in the debtors' home but undersecured as to the balance owed, what would be your advice regarding filing a proof of claim? Would that advice be the same if the client was well oversecured in the collateral?

2. Assume you are contacted by a creditor who advises that he has just learned today that a debtor who owes him an unsecured obligation of $20,000 filed a petition in Chapter 7 three months ago. This creditor was also told that the trustee in the Chapter 7 case has located assets and is going to be making a distribution to unsecured creditors of approximately thirty cents on the dollar. You check the bankruptcy file and see that the creditor was listed in debtor's schedules, the creditor has not filed any proof of claim, and the claims bar date has passed. None of the exceptions for an untimely filed claim set forth in FRBP 3002(c) apply. However, creditor insists he did not receive any notice of the bankruptcy filing, formal or informal. Should you file a proof of claim for this creditor and, if you do, will it be allowed? See In re Adams, 502 B.R. 645 (Bankr. N.D. Ga. 2013).

3. Assume that you are contacted by a creditor secured in the home of a debtor who has filed a petition in Chapter 7. At the time the petition was filed, creditor was owed a balance of $175,000 and assumed that the home securing the debt had a value in excess of the balance owed. Creditor filed a timely proof of claim for the amount owed designating its claim as secured by a mortgage in the home. The proof of claim did not indicate any unsecured claim, nor did it indicate any intention to amend or supplement the claim to include an unsecured deficiency claim at a later time in the event the home sold for an insufficient amount to pay the claim in full. Creditor then filed a motion to lift the automatic stay on the home and sold it. Unfortunately, the sale produced proceeds of only $160,000 to apply to the indebtedness leaving the creditor with an unsecured claim of $15,000. The claims bar date has now passed. If you now file an amended proof of claim for this creditor as to the unsecured $15,000 balance, will it be allowed by the bankruptcy court if the trustee objects on the grounds of timeliness? Compare In re Winters, 380 B.R. 855, 860 (Bankr. M.D. Fla. 2007), with In re Jackson, 482 B.R. 659, 665-666 (Bankr. S.D. Fla. 2012), and In re Spurling, 391 B.R. 783, 786-787 (Bankr. E.D. Tenn. 2007)

4. Assume that Marta Carlson owes Automotive Financing, Inc. (AFI) $10,000 on the Toyota Camry that the debtor estimates is worth only about $8,500. She is going to surrender the vehicle to AFI. When the automatic stay is lifted, AFI will repossess and sell the vehicle. But if the value of the vehicle is indeed less than the amount owed to AFI, there will be an unsecured balance owing after the sale. Pursuant to §506(a), AFI's claim is secured only up to the value of the collateral and is unsecured as to the balance owed in excess of that value. Per §506(a) its claim will be bifurcated into its secured and unsecured portions. Consequently, any balance owed to AFI over the value of its collateral will be treated as a general unsecured claim in Marta's bankruptcy case. Assume the claims bar date in Carlson's Chapter 7 case is coming up next week. Based on what you learned in *Nowak*, advise AFI regarding whether to file a proof of claim at all, whether to file it as secured or unsecured, and in what amount under each of the following scenarios:
   a. The stay has been lifted and the vehicle sold for $7,800.
   b. The stay has been lifted and the vehicle sold for $10,000 plus expenses.
   c. The stay has not yet been lifted and the projected value of the vehicle once sold is $7,500 to $9,000. It will not be possible to sell it until after the claims bar date.
   d. The stay has not yet been lifted and the projected value of the vehicle once sold is $11,500. It will not be possible to sell it until after the claims bar date.
5. Determine if the informal proof of claim doctrine is recognized by the courts of the federal district or circuit where you plan to practice. If so, how would a court there likely decide *Nowak*? Determine if those courts permit a late-filed proof of claim where the creditor received no timely notice of the bankruptcy filing.

C. OBJECTIONS TO CLAIMS

As claims are filed, they will be entered on a **claims docket** (or claims register) by the clerk of the court. One of the duties of the bankruptcy trustee is to examine the proofs of claim filed by creditors to determine if they are valid (see Exhibit 7.1). Section 502(a) provides that unless an objection to claim by the trustee or other party in interest is filed, the claim will be **deemed allowed**.

Sections 502(b)(d)(e) and (k) set forth several grounds for objecting to a claim. The most general of these grounds is §502(b)(1), which authorizes an objection if the claim is unenforceable against the debtor under the terms of the underlying agreement or due to controlling law. Thus, the trustee's (or other party in interest's) examination will include a determination of whether the claim is valid at all, whether it is made in the correct amount, whether the creditor is secured in property of the estate, or whether the debtor has any counterclaim or other offset (discussed in Section D, below) to the claim. In addition, a creditor who is in possession of the debtor's property or who is the transferee of a voidable transfer from the debtor (to be considered in Chapter Nine, Sections C and D) and who refuses to turn the property over or pay the amount of the voidable transfer upon proper demand by the trustee may have its claim disallowed pursuant to §502(d).

If a claim is filed as a secured one, the trustee will examine the claim not only to make sure the claim is in fact secured but to determine if the security interest is properly perfected. As we will see in the next chapter, if the security interest of the creditor is not properly perfected prior to the filing of the bankruptcy petition, §544 of the Code, informally called the "strong-arm provision," empowers the trustee to avoid the creditor's security interest or lien in the collateral and take the property for the benefit of the estate.

If the bankruptcy trustee concludes that any claim, secured or unsecured, is invalid in whole or in part, FRBP 3007 requires that he file a written objection to the claim.

For example, the bankruptcy trustee in Marta Carlson's Chapter 7 filed an objection to the claim of Pine Ridge Nursing Home that is set out in Exhibit 8.2 (also Document 28 in the Carlson case file).

Pursuant to §502(b) and FRBP 3007, the creditor whose claim is objected to must receive a 30-day notice of the objection and of the proposed hearing date. Thus the notice of hearing on the objection that appears in Exhibit 8.2 is given to Pine Ridge on August 3 notifying that the hearing is set on September 17.

Since most objections to claims are controlled by the "after notice and a hearing" procedure, the objection will be treated as a disputed matter (rather than an adversary proceeding, see distinction discussed in Chapter Four, Section F) and an evidentiary hearing conducted only if the creditor contests the objection. If the creditor does not contest the objection, it will be sustained without a hearing. If the objection to the creditor's claim involves an attack on the validity or sufficiency of the creditor's claimed security interest in property of the debtor, however, the trustee must initiate an adversary proceeding to set aside that security interest as required by FRBP 7001 (see Exhibit 4.6).

Though it is most often the bankruptcy trustee who initiates an objection to a creditor's claim, note that §502(a) authorizes any party in interest to do so. If a trustee refuses to file such an objection, then another creditor who could be benefited by the disallowance of the contested claim may do so. In some situations, the Chapter 7 debtor himself may file an objection to a claim.

Interestingly, the Code does not set out a time frame in which an objection to a creditor's claim must be made. Normally such objections will be made prior to distribution of the estate to creditors, but there is no time bar to a trustee who, having made a distribution to a creditor, seeks to recover it based on information learned after the distribution. Even after a case has been closed, a trustee may move to reopen it in order to object to a creditor's claim, recover the distribution to that creditor, and redistribute to others. Of course, attempts by a trustee to object to a claim after distribution may be met with defenses such as waiver (the voluntary relinquishment of a known right), promissory estoppel (the preclusion of one from acting now because he earlier made promises on which others reasonably relied, to their detriment), equitable estoppel (the preclusion of one from acting now because his earlier wrongful or dishonest actions or inactions worked to the detriment of others), or laches (the neglect of a claim or right for an inordinate period of time under the circumstances).

EXHIBIT 8.2   **Trustee's Objection to the Claim of Pine Ridge Nursing Home**

UNITED STATES BANKRUPTCY COURT

DISTRICT OF MINNESOTA

In re: Marta Rinaldi Carlson,	)	
Debtor	)	
	)	Case No. 16-7-XXXX
	)	
	)	Chapter 7
	)	

OBJECTION TO CLAIM

The Trustee, Jacob W. Braham, pursuant to 11 USC §502 and Bankruptcy Rule 3007, hereby objects to the claim of Pine Ridge Nursing Home, Claim No. NP-UNSEC-3 in this case.

In support of this objection, the Trustee will show that this creditor's right to recover is barred by novation, waiver, promissory estoppel and/or fraud committed on the debtor, Marta Rinaldi Carlson.

The Trustee asks that the court schedule a date for a hearing on this objection and that claimant be required to respond in writing.

August 3, 2016

/s/ Jacob W. Braham

Jacob W. Braham
Bankruptcy Trustee Suite 200
Metro Building 55101
St. Paul, MN
(555) 555-8842

CERTIFICATE OF SERVICE

I certify that the foregoing Objection to Claim was served upon [names and addresses of each person or entity served omitted from illustration] by first class United States mail, hand-delivery, or electronic mail on August 3, 2016.

/s/ Jacob W. Braham

Jacob W. Braham
Bankruptcy Trustee Suite 200
Metro Building 55101
St. Paul, MN
(555) 555-8842

EXHIBIT 8.2   **(Continued)**

UNITED STATES BANKRUPTCY COURT

DISTRICT OF MINNESOTA

In re: Marta Rinaldi Carlson,   )
      Debtor   )
)
)   Case No. 16-7-XXXX
)
)   Chapter 7
)

NOTICE OF OBJECTION AND HEARING ON OBJECTION

NOTICE is hereby given that the Chapter 7 trustee, Jacob W. Braham, has filed an Objection to Claim regarding the claim of Pine Ridge Nursing Home. A copy of the objection is attached.

If a response is filed to the objection on or before September 15, 2016, the court will conduct a hearing on said objection and the response at 9 a.m. on the 17th day of September, 2016 at the United States Bankruptcy Court, Room 301 of the Federal Building in St. Paul, Minnesota.

This notice is being provided by electronic filing or by United States mail, first class to all parties in interest this 3rd day of August, 2016.

Clerk of the United States
Bankruptcy Court for the
District of Minnesota

The validity and enforceability of most contracts as well as questions regarding attachment and perfection of security interests that arise in objections to claims are, as we now know, controlled by state law.

D. CREDITORS' CLAIMS AND THE RIGHT TO SETOFF

The doctrine of **setoff** is recognized in most states by common law or by statute. The idea behind the doctrine is a simple one: If two persons are indebted to each other, the debt of either is offset by the amount of the debt of the other.

For example, assume that Pete borrows $2,000 from Sally. Later, Pete does $1,000 worth of work for Sally. If Sally ever sues Pete for the $2,000 he owes her, the debt will be offset by what Sally owes Pete, so Sally will obtain a judgment for only $1,000. And if the value of Pete's services to Sally is $2,000, the debts mutually offset, so neither owes the other anything. If the value of Pete's work is $2,200, the debt he owes Sally for the loan is completely offset and Sally owes Pete $200.

Or, assume Pete has a loan from Bank and also has a savings account at Bank. That savings account is in the nature of a loan by Pete to Bank. If Pete misses a payment on the loan obligation he owes to Bank, the Bank can set off what Pete owes it against what it owes Pete by transferring the amount of the missed payment from Pete's savings account.

Section 553 of the Code provides that the right to setoff recognized under non-bankruptcy law (common law or statute) is alive and well in the bankruptcy context subject to some limitations, most of which rarely arise in consumer bankruptcy cases. For example, assume Pete in our last example files a petition in Chapter 7 listing his savings account at Bank as an asset he can exempt and listing the loan obligation he owes Bank as an unsecured debt. If the Code did not honor the right to setoff in bankruptcy, Bank could find itself in the position of having its claim against Pete for the loan completely discharged while Pete is able to take the money in his savings account at Bank. But not only does §553 provide that the right to setoff will be recognized in the bankruptcy case, §506(a) mandates that a setoff claim that can be asserted against property of the estate under non-bankruptcy law be treated as a secured claim. The right to setoff is not an actual type of security interest in real or personal property, but the Code mandates that it be treated as such in this context.

In Pete's Chapter 7 case, Bank will be treated as being secured in his savings account at Bank up to the amount of the setoff claim and his attempt to exempt the cash in that savings account will not trump that secured status awarded Bank by §506(a). Other unsecured creditors may see their claims against Pete discharged in the bankruptcy case but Bank, though an unsecured creditor, will see its setoff claim honored against the funds in the savings account.

Notwithstanding the Code's recognition of a creditor's right to setoff against debtor's property in a bankruptcy case, the automatic stay still goes into effect against the setoff creditor. Thus Bank, exercising its setoff rights against Pete's savings account, could not transfer funds out of it once the petition is filed without violating the stay. See Citizens Bank of Maryland v. Stumpf, 516 U.S. 16 (1995). *Stumpf* did hold, however, that a creditor in the position of Bank in our example could freeze or place an administrative hold on the account after the petition is filed without violating the stay.

What about Sally from our first example in this section? When Pete files his bankruptcy petition he will list the $2,000 debt he owes her as an unsecured debt. He will also list the claim he has against her for services rendered as an asset. There is not particular property of the estate against which Sally can assert her right to setoff so §506(a) is inapplicable to her situation, but her right to setoff is still recognized by §553. Thus if the bankruptcy trustee chooses to pursue Pete's claim against Sally for the $1,000 in services, she can defend with her offset claim, which, since it exceeds the $1,000 claim, will completely offset it. But since Sally, unlike Bank, has no particular property against which she can assert her offset claim against Pete, her remaining claim is subject to being treated as any other unsecured obligation and may be discharged.

E. INTEREST ON CLAIMS IN CHAPTER 7 CASES

1. Interest on Unsecured and Undersecured Claims

Section 502(b)(2) disallows claims made for **unmatured interest**. That phrase refers to interest that is not yet due and owing to the creditor at the time the petition is filed and is sometimes called **postpetition interest**. Unsecured claims may include charges for **prepetition interest** that were due and owing on the date the petition was filed but are not entitled to receive postpetition interest.

For example, Marta owed an unsecured debt to Capital City Bank (CCB) on her Visa credit card in the amount of $8,200 at the time her petition and Schedule E/F were filed (Document 10 in the Carlson case file). A portion of that $8,200 may include prepetition interest charges by CCB for a carryover balance or for late payments on the account. If the underlying card agreement permits CCB to make such interest charges, it can include them in its claim. But if CCB files a proof of claim stating a claim for not just the $8,200 balance owed at the time of the petition filing but adding a claim for interest that has accrued since the petition was filed, the trustee will object to that portion of the claim, pursuant to §502(b)(2). If Marta had not filed her petition, the interest would have continued to accrue, but once she has filed her petition, the unsecured creditor cannot seek to recover it on a claim made in her bankruptcy case.

A secured creditor who is undersecured in the property of the debtor securing the claim is in the same situation as the unsecured creditor, like CCB in the previous example as to interest.

For example, assume that Marta owes AFI $10,000 on the Toyota Camry that is worth only $8,500. Assume that the automatic stay is lifted, and AFI repossesses and sells the car for $8,500. Pursuant to §506(a)(1), AFI now has a bifurcated, general unsecured claim for the $1,500 balance but *may not* include postpetition interest in that claim per §502(b)(2). The fact that AFI was a secured creditor as to part of its claim does not change its treatment under §502(b)(2) for the unsecured portion of its claim.

In the very rare case, there may be sufficient assets in a Chapter 7 case to pay all expenses of administration and all the claims of creditors in full and still have cash left over. In that case, §726(a)(5) allows the trustee to pay postpetition interest on unsecured creditors' claims (see Exhibit 10.1).

2. Interest, Fees, and Other Charges on Oversecured Claims

If a creditor is not just fully secured but oversecured in the collateral at the time the petition is filed (i.e., the value of the collateral not only equals but exceeds the amount of the claim), then §506(b) allows the creditor to include in its claim post-petition interest up to the value of the collateral, as well as other fees, costs, and charges but only if those fees, costs, and charges are authorized by the underlying agreement or by state law and only up to the value of the collateral.

For example, Capital Savings Bank (CSB) holds the first mortgage on Marta's residence. The principal amount of its claim at the time the petition is filed is $142,500 and the residence securing the debt is valued at $255,000. CSB is fully secured in the residence because its value exceeds the principal amount of the debt. Section 506(b) allows CSB to file a claim in Marta's Chapter 7 case for the principal amount owed ($142,500) plus (if the underlying mortgage agreement allows) unpaid postpetition interest, fees, and charges up to the value of the collateral ($225,000). And CSB's right to do this would not be affected by the fact that another creditor, Dreams Come True Finance Company, is also secured in the residence. CSB has a first position in the property and its claim will take priority up to the full amount allowed by the Code.

As previously noted, the failure of a secured creditor to file a timely proof of claim does not impair its secured position in the property of the debtor per §506(d)(2). It can still seek to lift the stay on the collateral and sell it in full satisfaction of its claim or, if there is equity for the estate in the property in excess of the creditor's claim, simply wait for the trustee to sell the property, at which time its full claim plus postpetition interest, fees, and charges will be paid to it, per §506(d)(2). For this reason, many bankruptcy courts do not require fully secured creditors to file formal proofs of claim and instead require only that the creditor informally make available to the trustee the documentation demonstrating that the creditor holds a perfected security interest in the property.

For example, the local rules of the bankruptcy court handling Marta's Chapter 7 case might not require Capital Savings Bank to file a formal proof of claim but, instead, to provide the trustee with a copy of the mortgage or deed of trust establishing its secured, perfected position in the residence.

Chapter Summary

- In a Chapter 7 asset case, creditors must file a proof of claim by the claims bar date in order to participate in any distribution from the estate. The claims bar date is generally 90 days after the first date set for the meeting of creditors. Late-filed claims are permitted prior to distribution if the creditor had no notice or actual knowledge of the filing. Priority claims may be filed on or before ten days after the date the trustee sends a summary of his final report to creditors or the date on which final distribution in the case is commenced, whichever is earlier.
- The failure of a secured creditor to file a timely proof of claim does not impair its secured position in the property of the debtor. However, since the Code treats claims as secured only up to the value of the collateral at the time the petition is filed, an undersecured creditor must file a proof of claim in order to participate in any distribution as to the unsecured portion of its claim.

- The bankruptcy trustee reviews submitted claims and may object to their allowance, raising a contested matter. Claims are deemed allowed if no objection is filed by the trustee or other party in interest. There is no time bar for the filing of objections to claims.
- The right to setoff is recognized in bankruptcy cases where the debtor and creditors have claims against each other. A creditor may include matured prepetition interest in his claim. Generally, unsecured and undersecured creditors are not entitled to receive postpetition interest on their claims. Fully secured creditors any include postpetition interest in their claims as well as postpetition fees, costs, and charges if the underlying agreement allows, up to the value of the collateral.

Applying the Concepts

1. Mark and Freda Jackson borrowed $300,000 from Bank three years ago to finance the purchase of their home. Bank holds a properly perfected first mortgage in the Jacksons' home to secure repayment. The Jacksons have fallen several payments behind on their house payments to Bank and today they filed a petition in Chapter 7. The balance owed by the Jacksons to Bank is $273,522, which includes the full accelerated principal balance owed plus accrued interest on the overdue payments since the underlying loan agreement allows Bank to charge and recover interest at 10 percent per annum on overdue payments. The home is currently appraised at $310,000. You represent Bank. Answer the following questions asked by your client:

   a. Does Bank need to file a proof of claim in order to preserve its secured status in the Jackson's home?
   b. Can Bank recover postpetition interest on the overdue payments?
   c. As a secured creditor, is Bank subject to the automatic stay or can it move to foreclose?
   d. If so, can Bank file a motion to lift stay even though it has not filed a formal proof of claim?

2. If Bank were owed $350,000 by the Jacksons at the time the Chapter 7 petition was filed, does that change any of your answers to the questions in Question 1?

3. Mark and Freda Jackson borrowed $25,000 from Credit Union two years ago to finance their daughter's wedding. The Jacksons are several payments behind to Credit Union on this loan. The loan is unsecured and the balance owed on the date the Jacksons file their Chapter 7 petition is $17,498, which includes the full accelerated principal balance owed plus accrued interest on the overdue payments since the underlying loan agreement allows Credit Union to charge and recover interest at 10 percent per annum on overdue payments. The Jacksons also have a savings account at Credit Union with a balance of $750 on the

day they file their petition. You represent Credit Union. Answer the following questions asked by your client:

   a. Does Credit Union need to file a proof of claim in order to participate in any distribution in the Jackson's Chapter 7?
   b. Can Credit Union include postpetition interest on the overdue payments in its claim?
   c. Can Credit Union go ahead and seize the funds in the Jackson's savings account to offset what the Jacksons owe Credit Union? Can the Credit Union at least freeze those funds?

4. Could you properly represent both Bank and Credit Union in the Jackson's Chapter 7 case?

5. Locate and read Assignment Memorandum #2 in Appendix C. If your instructor so directs, prepare a proof of claim on behalf of Automotive Financing, Inc. in the Chapter 7 case of Abelard Mendoza assuming that case is pending in the U.S. bankruptcy court for the federal district where you plan to practice.

9

The Chapter 7 Consumer Bankruptcy Case: Property of the Estate

In this chapter we examine the all-important concept of what constitutes property of the estate. We will see the dramatic powers the Code grants the bankruptcy trustee to compel turnover of that property from the debtor or others and to avoid a number of prepetition transfers of the debtor's property in order to capture that property for the estate and the ultimate benefit of unsecured creditors.

A. PROPERTY OF THE ESTATE DEFINED

What constitutes the **property of the estate** is one of the most important concepts in bankruptcy law. Section 541(a) of the Code provides that the commencement of a case under any chapter of the Code creates such estate and that it consists of all property in which the debtor holds a legal or equitable interest at the time of commencement. Section 541(b) contains some minor exceptions to this very broad definition of what constitutes property of the estate. What property makes up the bankruptcy estate is critical because it is from this pool of assets that the claims of the creditors will be satisfied. What constitutes property of the estate under §541 is ultimately a federal question governed by that statute though the underlying question of whether the debtor has a legal or equitable interest in

Key Concepts

- Property of the estate includes all property in which the debtor has a legal or equitable interest at the time the petition is filed
- The bankruptcy trustee may challenge a debtor's claimed exemptions in order to increase the property of the estate
- The Code provides the bankruptcy trustee with the power to compel turnover of property of the estate in the hands of the debtor, custodians, or other third persons
- The Code provides the bankruptcy trustee with a wide range of powers to avoid prepetition transfers of the debtor's property

certain property at the beginning of the case will normally be governed by applicable state law. See In re Yonikus, 996 F.2d 866, 869 (7th Cir. 1993).

For example, recall the discussion in Chapter Three, Section B, of property owned by a married couple. If the spouses own property as tenants by the entireties and only one of them files for bankruptcy relief, both spouses have only a right of survivorship in marital property while alive so that the interest of the non-filing spouse in such property which will not then become property of the estate and the tenancy cannot be severed by the bankruptcy trustee in hopes of reaching a greater interest in the property than the filing spouse has—the right of survivorship. On the other hand, if the same spouses own property in a community property state, all the community property may be deemed property of the estate even though only on spouse files sine each spouse is deemed to own it entirely. (Note that Form A/B (Official Form 106A/B) specifically asks who has an ownership interest in the property listed and whether it is community property.) Unless the filing spouse can exempt that property, the bankruptcy trustee will take and sell it. If the filing spouse cannot exempt marital property in a community property state, it's best if the two spouses file jointly so they can stack their exemptions and protect as much marital property as possible. You may want to review the discussion of concurrently owned property as well as property held in trust. The same challenges presented to the prepetition judgment creditor seeking to seize debtor's property to satisfy the judgment at least initially confront the bankruptcy trustee seeking property to liquidate for the benefit of all unsecured creditors of the estate.

Generally, property acquired by the debtor after the commencement of the Chapter 7 case does not belong to the estate because that will be the property available for debtor's fresh start. But §541(a)(5) includes within the definition of "property of the estate" property the debtor inherits up to 180 days after the petition is filed, insurance proceeds received by the debtor within 180 days of filing, and property received from a spouse as a result of a property settlement agreement or divorce decree within 180 days of filing.

The concept of property of the estate focuses on the interest the debtor has at the time the petition is filed. Thus, if the debtor is the beneficiary of a trust, the trust property to which the debtor is entitled (but which has not yet been distributed to him) now belongs to the estate unless the trust was set up as a spendthrift trust. If the debtor has earned a paycheck or commission at the time he files the petition, that property belongs to the estate even though it is not paid until after the petition is filed. Stocks or bonds held for the debtor by a brokerage house belong to the estate. Any debts owed to the debtor by another when the case is filed become the property of the estate. If the debtor has the right to file a lawsuit at the time the petition is filed, the claim underlying the lawsuit now becomes the property of the estate and the bankruptcy trustee has standing to pursue the lawsuit in the place of the debtor. If the debtor holds a mortgage on the property of another, the mortgage and all the rights under it, including the right to foreclose in the event of default, become the property of the estate. If the debtor buys a lottery ticket before filing the petition and wins after filing the petition, the proceeds belong to the estate since the ticket became property of the estate upon filing. If stock owned by the debtor at the time the petition is filed splits after the filing, the estate gets the benefit of the stock split.

Property held in trust by the debtor as trustee (as opposed to property held in trust for the debtor as beneficiary) raises some difficult questions since the debtor as trustee does have legal title to such property under trust law but not equitable title. However, §541(d) makes it clear that such property interest becomes property of the estate "only to the extent of the debtor's legal title to such property, but not to the extent of any equitable interest in such property the debtor does not hold." Since the beneficiaries of the trust have the equitable interest in the trust res and that equitable interest is not subject to the claims of the debtor's creditors, no equitable interest in the res becomes property of the estate when the trustee files. "Where the debtor holds bare legal title without an equitable interest, the estate acquires bare legal title without any equitable interest." In re N.S. Garrott & Sons, 772 F.2d 462, 466 (8th Cir. 1985).

For example, assume Chris establishes an express trust and names his children as beneficiaries. He names his sister Alexia as trustee. If Alexia files a petition in bankruptcy the property in the trust does not become property of the estate and subject to being liquidated by the bankruptcy trustee for the benefit of Alexia's creditors. Alexia had only the bare legal title to the property subject to the trust and that is all that passes to the estate upon the filing of the petition.

Where the debtor has both legal and equitable title to property at the time of filing but such property is subject to a claim by another that debtor holds such property in a constructive trust for the benefit of the other, the courts are split. Some courts treat property subject to a constructive trust claim just like express trust property under §541(d) and exclude the equitable interest in that property from the estate. See, e.g., Connecticut Gen. Life Ins. Co., v. Universal Ins. Co., 838 F.2d 612, 618 (1st Cir. 1988) (when a debtor is in possession of property impressed by constructive trust, the estate holds the property subject to the outstanding interest of the beneficiaries where claimant can prove the existence and legal source of a trust relationship and identify the trust fund or property). Other courts emphasize that a constructive trust is a remedy for unjust enrichment, not a property interest, and refuse to recognize the equitable interest of the one claiming beneficiary status unless a court has already declared the constructive trust on specific property prepetition. See, e.g., In re Foos, 183 B.R. 149 (Bankr. N.D. Ill. 1995) (creditor asserting that it was beneficiary of constructive trust imposed over funds transferred during Chapter 7 debtor's Ponzi scheme did not have equitable interest in funds because no judicial determination had been made to that effect prepetition; funds are property of the estate and creditor can file an unsecured claim).

Of course, some of the property of the estate will be claimed as exempt by the debtor and retained by him. And creditors holding a perfected security interest in property of the estate may have a priority claim to it over the trustee (see the next section). Additionally, the bankruptcy trustee may consider some of the property of the estate to have no value to the estate and abandon it pursuant to §554 (see discussion in Chapter Ten, Section A). But otherwise the property of the estate comes under the control of the bankruptcy trustee at the time the case is commenced and will be liquidated by the trustee for the benefit of all creditors of the estate. As we have seen, however, the trustee may contest the validity of a secured creditor's claim to certain property of the debtor as collateral, hoping to defeat the allegedly perfected security interest and seize that collateral as property of the estate. With the same goal in mind, the trustee may challenge exemptions claimed by the individual debtor, as we consider in the next section. Property in which the debtor has a legal or equitable interest may not be in the debtor's possession when the case is commenced. It may be held by another. That does not prevent it becoming property of the estate. The definition in §541(a) specifically says that qualifying property belongs to the estate, "wherever located and by whomever held."

For example, salary the debtor has earned as of the filing of the petition may be held by the employer. A car the debtor owns may be loaned to a family member or friend. Funds of the debtor in checking and savings accounts will be held by the financial institution.

Contingent, disputed, and unliquidated claims that the debtor has against third parties are property of the estate, and the trustee has standing, pursuant to §704(a)(1), to pursue those claims to judgment for the benefit of the estate. Normally, that will be done by filing an adversary proceeding against the third party (see Exhibit 4.6). Whether the bankruptcy court can hear and enter a final order in an adversary proceeding brought to collect a claim of the estate will depend in the first instance on whether it is a core or noncore proceeding under 28 U.S.C. §157(b), as discussed in Chapter Four, Section F (see Exhibit 4.5). And regardless of whether or not it qualifies as a core proceeding, if the claim is one for wrongful death or personal injury it *cannot* be tried in the bankruptcy court. Instead, it must be tried in the district court pursuant to 28 U.S.C. §157(b)(5) or a state court having jurisdiction pursuant to 28 U.S.C. §1334(c).

For example, recall that Nick and Pearl Murphy from Appendix D have a professional malpractice claim for Pearl and a loss of consortium claim for Nick against the doctor who performed her botched appendectomy and the hospital where the surgery was performed. If the couple files a joint petition in Chapter 7 before those claims are resolved, the claims themselves are assets that they must list on their Schedule A/B and assign a value to. At that point the claims are contingent on Nick and Pearl prevailing, disputed because the doctor and hospital are not admitting liability, and unliquidated because we do not yet know the dollar amount, if any, of any settlement or verdict to be rendered on the claims. But the claims are assets that become property of the estate unless properly exempted and the lawsuit to liquidate those claims likely qualifies as a core proceeding under 28 U.S.C. §157(b)(2)(O). However, since these claims are in the nature of a personal injury action, 28 U.S.C. §157(d) mandates that the claims be tried in the U.S. district court rather than in a bankruptcy court adversary action. United States district courts have subject matter jurisdiction to hear such cases even without diversity of citizenship between the parties under 28 U.S.C §1334. As a practical matter, however, personal injury and wrongful death cases that arise in a bankruptcy case are normally tried in the state court having jurisdiction as authorized by 28 U.S.C. §334(c). Thus in the Murphys' bankruptcy case, the trustee is likely to ask for and receive permission from the court to pursue the Murphys' malpractice claim in state court. Since the claim is property of the estate, only the trustee now has the right to file suit on it. The Murphys will be nominal (in name only) plaintiffs in that lawsuit, and proceeds from any judgment or settlement of the claim will become property of the estate.

B. CHALLENGING THE DEBTOR'S CLAIMED EXEMPTIONS IN ORDER TO INCREASE THE PROPERTY OF THE ESTATE

In Chapter Six, Section B, we learned that per §522(a)(2) of the Code, the individual Chapter 7 debtor sets out his claimed exemptions on Schedule C at their fair market value as that phrase has been interpreted by the U.S. Supreme Court in U.S. v. Cartwright, 411 U.S. 546 (1973). We also observed there that the bankruptcy trustee will not automatically accept the debtor's claimed exemptions or their valuation but instead will carefully examine the exemptions on Schedule C, to see if a challenge can be made to either (1) the property claimed as exempt, or (2) the valuation of the exempt property by the debtor. You may want to review that section at this time.

For example, assume a Chapter 7 debtor owns a house and lot. He owes a secured creditor $200,000 on the house, lists its fair market value on Schedule C as $220,000, and claims the $20,000 of equity in the house as exempt as a homestead under Code §522(d)(1). If the trustee in his case discovers that this is actually a rental house owned by the debtor and not a residence for the debtor or a dependent, the trustee may object to the claimed exemption on the grounds that the equity in that house and lot cannot be exempted at all under §522(d)(1). On the other hand, if the house and lot are used as a residence by the debtor, but the trustee discovers the fair market value is $250,000, the trustee may object, not to the exemption itself, but to the low valuation of the exempted property by the debtor. After all, if that house and lot are worth $250,000 that means the debtor has $50,000 of equity in it — not just $20,000. And since, under §522(d)(1), the debtor may currently exempt only $23,675 (as of April 2016) of that equity, the trustee wants to claim the balance of the equity as property of the estate. The bankruptcy trustee in Marta Carlson's case is challenging her valuation of the doll collection she claims as exempt. See Document 32 in the Carlson case file.

FRBP 4003(b) authorizes not just the bankruptcy trustee but any other party in interest to object to a debtor's claimed exemption or its value, but most commonly it is the trustee who files the objection, creating a contested matter. FRBP 4003(b)(1) requires that any objection to a debtor's claimed exemptions be made within 30 days following the first meeting of creditors or within 30 days following any amendment to Schedule C, although that time period can be extended by motion and for cause shown. FRBP 4003(b)(2) allows a year beyond the date the case is closed to object to an exemption fraudulently claimed. Section 522(*l*) of the Code provides that if no timely objection to a claimed exemption is made, the exemption is **deemed allowed**.

Due to this "deemed allowed" feature of §522(*l*), bankruptcy trustees and creditors must examine a debtor's claimed exemptions closely and timely move the court to extend the time for objecting if there is any question at all about the nature of property claimed as exempt or the value attached to it by debtor. Taylor v. Freeland & Kronz, 503 U.S. 638 (1992), illustrates the need for diligence.

In *Taylor*, the debtor filed a petition in Chapter 7 while an employment discrimination claim she was pursuing in state court was still pending. On her Schedule C, debtor claimed the proceeds from the lawsuit as exempt and for value stated, "$ unknown." The bankruptcy trustee asked about the lawsuit in debtor's 341 meeting and heard estimates that the suit might have a value of $90,000 or more. The trustee concluded however that the lawsuit likely had no value and neither filed an objection to the claimed exemption nor sought additional time to do so. Several years later, the lawsuit settled for $110,000 and the trustee reopened the case and sought to recover the settlement proceeds for the benefit of the estate. The Supreme Court held the trustee's objection to the exemption time barred by §522(*l*) and FRBP 4003(b), rejecting the trustee's argument that a claimed exemption can be objected to after expiration of the 30-day period if the debtor did not have a good-faith or reasonably disputable basis for claiming it and that failing to impose such good-faith requirement will create an improper incentive for debtors to engage in "exemption by declaration" — claiming improper exemptions in hopes no one timely objects.

Case Preview

Schwab v. Reilly

The Supreme Court's narrow interpretation and strict application of §522(*l*) and FRBP 4003(b) in *Taylor* was taken to heart by lower courts, many of which proceeded to apply the ruling not only in cases where claimed exemptions were still contingent and of unknown value but also in cases involving the not-uncommon scenario in which the debtor understates the value of exempt property on their Schedule C and a higher non-exemptable value is discovered only after the time for objection has expired. Finally, in 2010, the Supreme Court accepted cert in such a case and addressed whether *Taylor* was in fact controlling. As you read Schwab v. Reilly, consider the following questions:

1. How is *Schwab* factually different from *Taylor*?
2. How do you explain the differing results in these two cases? Why is the trustee in *Schwab* allowed to retain for the benefit of the estate the value of the property in excess of the allowed exemption even though no timely objection to the claimed exemption was filed while the trustee in *Taylor* was barred from doing so?
3. What is the remaining scope of the ruling in *Taylor* after *Schwab*?

Schwab v. Reilly
560 U.S. 770 (2010)

[Nadejda Reilly filed for Chapter 7 bankruptcy when her catering business failed. On her Schedule B, on which the Bankruptcy Rules require debtors to list their assets, Reilly listed an itemized list of cooking equipment that she described as "business equipment" with an estimated value of $10,718. On her Schedule C Reilly claimed a "tools of the trade" exemption of $1,850 in the equipment under §522(d)(6), and a miscellaneous exemption of $8,868 in the equipment under §522(d)(5) that permitted a debtor to take an exemption equal to the debtor's interest in any property not to exceed $10,255 in value. The trustee, William Schwab, did not object to Reilly's claimed exemptions because Reilly's assigned dollar amounts for the equipment fell within the limits of §§522(d)(5) and (6). After an appraisal revealed the equipment could be worth $17,200, Schwab moved the Bankruptcy Court for permission to auction the equipment so Reilly could receive the $10,718 she claimed as exempt with the excess going to creditors. Reilly opposed Schwab's motion by saying that the failure to object to the claimed exemptions within the requisite time period forfeited any claim Schwab had to an excess in value. The Bankruptcy Court denied Schwab's motion and the District Court affirmed. The court of appeals also affirmed and held that Schwab's failure to object to Reilly's claimed exemptions entitled Reilly to the equivalent of an in-kind interest in her business equipment, even though the value of that equipment exceeded the value that Reilly declared on Schedule C and the amount that the Code allowed her to withdraw from the bankruptcy estate. The Court granted certiorari to resolve conflict among the circuits about what constitutes a claim of exemption to which an interested party must object under §522(*l*).]

THOMAS, Justice. . . .

II

The starting point for our analysis is the proper interpretation of Reilly's Schedule C. If we read the Schedule Reilly's way, she claimed exemptions in her business equipment that could exceed statutory limits, and thus claimed exemptions to which Schwab should have objected if he wished to enforce those limits for the benefit of the estate. If we read Schedule C Schwab's way, Reilly claimed valid exemptions to which Schwab had no duty to object. The Court of Appeals construed Schedule C Reilly's way and interpreted her claimed exemptions as improper, and therefore objectionable, even though their declared value was facially within the applicable Code limits. . . . [T]he Court of Appeals held that trustees evaluating the validity of exemptions in cases like this cannot take a debtor's claim at face value, and specifically cannot rely on the fact that the amount the debtor declares as the "value of [the] claimed exemption" is within statutory limits. Instead, the trustee's duty to object turns on whether the interplay of various schedule entries supports an inference that the debtor "intended" to exempt a dollar value different than the one she wrote on the form. . . . This complicated view of the trustee's statutory obligation, and the strained reading of Schedule C on which it rests, is inconsistent with the Code. . . .

[T]his case is governed by §522(*l*), which states that a Chapter 7 debtor must "file a list of property that the debtor claims as exempt under subsection (b) of this section," and further states that "[u]nless a party in interest objects, the property claimed as exempt on such list is exempt." The parties further agree that the "list" to which §522(*l*) refers is the "list of property . . . claim[ed] as exempt" currently known as "Schedule C." . . . The parties, like the Courts of Appeals, disagree about what information on Schedule C defines the "property claimed as exempt" for purposes of evaluating an exemption's propriety under §522(*l*). Reilly asserts that the "property claimed as exempt" is defined by reference to all the information on Schedule C, including the estimated market value of each asset in which the debtor claims an exempt interest. Schwab and the United States as *amicus* argues that the Code specifically defines the "property claimed as exempt" as an interest, the value of which may not exceed a certain dollar amount, in a particular asset, *not* as the asset itself. Accordingly, they argue that the value of the property claimed exempt, *i.e.*, the value of the debtor's exempt interest in the asset, should be judged on the value the debtor assigns the interest, *not* on the value the debtor assigns the asset. The point of disagreement is best illustrated by the relevant portion of Reilly's Schedule C:

Schedule C-Property Claimed as Exempt

Description of Property	Specify Law Providing Each Exemption	Value of Claimed Exemption	Current Market Value of Property Without Deduction Exemptions
Schedule B Personal Property			
. . . . .	. . . . .	. . . . .	. . . . .
See attached list of business equipment.	11 U.S.C. §522(d)(6) 11 U.S.C. §522(d)(5).	1,850 8,868	10,718

According to Reilly, Schwab was required to treat the estimate of market value she entered in column 4 as part of her claimed exemption in identifying the "property claimed as exempt" under §522(*l*). . . . Relying on this premise, Reilly argues that where, as here, a debtor equates the total value of her claimed exemptions in a certain asset (column 3) with her estimate of the asset's market value (column 4), she establishes the "property claimed as exempt" as the full value of the asset, whatever that turns out to be. . . . Accordingly, Reilly argues that her Schedule C clearly put Schwab on notice that she "intended" to claim an exemption for the full value of her business equipment, and that Schwab's failure to oppose the exemption in a timely manner placed the full value of the equipment outside the estate's reach.

Schwab does not dispute that columns 3 and 4 apprised him that Reilly equated the total value of her claimed exemptions in the equipment ($1,850 plus $8,868) with the equipment's market value ($10,718). He simply disagrees with Reilly that this "identical listing put [him] on notice that Reilly intended to exempt the property fully," regardless of whether its value exceeded the exemption limits the Code prescribes. . . . Schwab and *amicus* United States instead contend that the Code defines the "property" Reilly claimed as exempt under §522(*l*) as an "interest" whose value cannot exceed a certain dollar amount. . . . Construing Reilly's Schedule C in light of this statutory definition, they contend that Reilly's claimed exemption was facially unobjectionable because the "property claimed as exempt" (*i.e.*, two interests in her business equipment worth $8,868 and $1,850, respectively) is property Reilly was clearly entitled to exclude from her estate under the Code provisions she referenced in column 2. . . . Accordingly, Schwab and the United States conclude that Schwab had no obligation to object to the exemption in order to preserve for the estate any value in Reilly's business equipment beyond the total amount ($10,718) Reilly properly claimed as exempt.

We agree. The portion of §522(*l*) that resolves this case is not, as Reilly asserts, the provision stating that the "property claimed as exempt on [Schedule C] is exempt" unless an interested party objects. Rather, it is the portion of §522(*l*) that defines the target of the objection, namely, the portion that says Schwab has a duty to object to the "list of property that the debtor claims as exempt *under subsection (b)*." (Emphasis added.) That subsection, §522(b), does *not* define the "property claimed as exempt" by reference to the estimated market value on which Reilly and the Court of Appeals rely. . . . Section 522(b) refers only to property defined in §522(d), which in turn lists 12 categories of property that a debtor may claim as exempt. As we have recognized, most of these categories (and all of the categories applicable to Reilly's exemptions) define the "property" a debtor may "clai[m] as exempt" as the debtor's "interest" — up to a specified dollar amount — in the assets described in the category, *not* as the assets themselves. §§522(d)(5)-(6). . . . Viewing Reilly's form entries in light of this definition, we agree with Schwab and the United States that Schwab had no duty to object to the property Reilly claimed as exempt (two interests in her business equipment worth $1,850 and $8,868) because the stated value of each interest, and thus of the "property claimed as exempt," was within the limits the Code allows.

Reilly's contrary view of Schwab's obligations under §522(*l*) does not withstand scrutiny because it defines the target of a trustee's objection — the "property claimed as exempt" — based on language in Schedule C and dictionary definitions of "property," . . . that the definition in the Code itself overrides . . . [T]he Code's definition of the "property claimed as exempt" in this case is clear. As noted above, §§522(d)(5) and (6) define the "property claimed as exempt" as an "interest" in Reilly's business equipment, *not* as the equipment *per se*. Sections 522(d)(5) and (6) further and plainly state that claims to exempt such interests are statutorily permissible, and thus unobjectionable, if the value of the claimed interest is below a particular dollar amount. That is the case here, and Schwab was entitled to rely upon these provisions in evaluating whether Reilly's exemptions were objectionable under the Code. . . .

For all of these reasons, we conclude that Schwab was entitled to evaluate the propriety of the claimed exemptions based on three, and only three, entries on Reilly's

Schedule C: the description of the business equipment in which Reilly claimed the exempt interests; the Code provisions governing the claimed exemptions; and the amounts Reilly listed in the column titled "value of claimed exemption." In reaching this conclusion, we do not render the market value estimate on Reilly's Schedule C superfluous. We simply confine the estimate to its proper role: aiding the trustee in administering the estate by helping him identify assets that may have value beyond the dollar amount the debtor claims as exempt, or whose full value may not be available for exemption because a portion of the interest is, for example, encumbered by an unavoidable lien. . . . As noted, most assets become property of the estate upon commencement of a bankruptcy case, see 11 U.S.C. §541, and exemptions represent the debtor's attempt to reclaim those assets or, more often, certain interests in those assets, to the creditors' detriment. Accordingly, it is at least useful for a trustee to be able to compare the value of the claimed exemption (which typically represents the debtor's interest in a particular asset) with the asset's estimated market value (which belongs to the estate subject to any valid exemption) without having to consult separate schedules. . . .

III

The Court of Appeals erred in holding that our decision in *Taylor* dictates a contrary conclusion. . . . *Taylor* does not rest on what the debtor "meant" to exempt. 534 F.3d, at 178. Rather, *Taylor* applies to the face of a debtor's claimed exemption the Code provisions that compel reversal here.

The debtor in *Taylor*, like the debtor here, filed a schedule of exemptions with the Bankruptcy Court on which the debtor described the property subject to the claimed exemption, identified the Code provision supporting the exemption, and listed the dollar value of the exemption. Critically, however, the debtor in *Taylor* did *not*, like the debtor here, state the value of the claimed exemption as a specific dollar amount at or below the limits the Code allows. Instead, the debtor in *Taylor* listed the value of the exemption itself as "$ *unknown*." . . .

The interested parties in *Taylor* agreed that this entry rendered the debtor's claimed exemption objectionable on its face because the exemption concerned an asset (lawsuit proceeds) that the Code did not permit the debtor to exempt beyond a specific dollar amount. . . . Accordingly, although this case and *Taylor* both concern the consequences of a trustee's failure to object to a claimed exemption within the time specified by Rule 4003, the question arose in *Taylor* on starkly different facts. In *Taylor*, the question concerned a trustee's obligation to object to the debtor's entry of a "value claimed exempt" that was *not* plainly within the limits the Code allows. In this case, the opposite is true. The amounts Reilly listed in the Schedule C column titled "Value of Claimed Exemption" *are* facially within the limits the Code prescribes and raise no warning flags that warranted an objection. . . .

Taylor supports this conclusion. In holding otherwise, the Court of Appeals focused on what it described as *Taylor's* "'unstated premise'" that "'a debtor who exempts the entire reported value of an asset is claiming the "full amount," whatever it turns out to be.'" 534 F.3d, at 179. But *Taylor* does not rest on this premise. It establishes and applies the straightforward proposition that an interested party must object to a claimed exemption if the amount the debtor lists as the "value claimed exempt" is not within statutory limits, a test the value ($ *unknown*) in *Taylor* failed, and the values ($8,868 and $1,850) in this case pass. . . .

IV

In a final effort to defend the Court of Appeals' judgment, Reilly asserts that her approach to §522(*l*) is necessary to vindicate the Code's goal of giving debtors a fresh start, and to further its policy of discouraging trustees and creditors from sleeping on their rights. . . . We agree that "exemptions in bankruptcy cases are part and parcel of the fundamental bankruptcy concept of a 'fresh start.'" . . . We disagree that this policy required Schwab to object to a facially valid claim of exemption on pain of forfeiting his ability to preserve for the estate any value in Reilly's business equipment beyond the value of the interest she declared exempt. This approach threatens to convert a fresh start into a free pass. . . .

Reilly nonetheless contends that our approach creates perverse incentives for trustees and creditors to sleep on their rights. . . . Again, we disagree. Where a debtor intends to exempt nothing more than an interest worth a specified dollar amount in an asset that is not subject to an unlimited or in-kind exemption under the Code, our approach will ensure clear and efficient resolution of competing claims to the asset's value. If an interested party does not object to the claimed interest by the time the Rule 4003 period expires, title to the asset will remain with the estate pursuant to §541, and the debtor will be guaranteed a payment in the dollar amount of the exemption. If an interested party timely objects, the court will rule on the objection and, if it is improper, allow the debtor to make appropriate adjustments.

Where, as here, it is important to the debtor to exempt the full market value of the asset or the asset itself, our decision will encourage the debtor to declare the value of her claimed exemption in a manner that makes the scope of the exemption clear, for example, by listing the exempt value as "full fair market value (FMV)" or "100% of FMV." Such a declaration will encourage the trustee to object promptly to the exemption if he wishes to challenge it and preserve for the estate any value in the asset beyond relevant statutory limits. If the trustee fails to object, or if the trustee objects and the objection is overruled, the debtor will be entitled to exclude the full value of the asset. If the trustee objects and the objection is sustained, the debtor will be required either to forfeit the portion of the exemption that exceeds the statutory allowance, or to revise other exemptions or arrangements with her creditors to permit the exemption. See Fed. Rule Bkrtcy. Proc. 1009(a). Either result will facilitate the expeditious and final disposition of assets, and thus enable the debtor (and the debtor's creditors) to achieve a fresh start free of the finality and clouded-title concerns Reilly describes. . . .

We reverse the judgment of the Court of Appeals for the Third Circuit and remand this case for further proceedings consistent with this opinion.

It is so ordered.

Post-Case Follow-Up

It is important to distinguish *Taylor* and *Schwab*. What are the implications of the two holdings for debtor's lawyers in valuing property claimed as exempt on their client's Schedule C where the client needs to exempt the entire value of an item? What are the implications of the two holdings for bankruptcy trustees or other interested parties in deciding whether to object to a claimed exemption where the debtor places a dollar value on the property claimed as exempt? Where the debtor places no particular dollar value but claims the entire value exempt? Do you see how the trustees in both cases were trying to increase the property of their respective estates at the expense of the debtors' claimed exemptions? Focusing on *Taylor*, should the court have read an implied good faith requirement into the debtor's valuation of a claimed exemption? Is the potential for "exemption by declaration" still present after *Schwab*?

Schwab v. Reilly: Real Life Applications

1. Assume you are the bankruptcy trustee in Chapter 7 cases in which the debtors claim the following exemptions on their Schedule Cs. Decide if you should object.
   a. Debtor lists a penny stock having a value of "unknown" on his Schedule C and claims a "full exemption" in it. Your research suggests that the stock in fact has a probable maximum value of no more than $10.00. The applicable exemption statute permits the debtor to exempt $25,000 of value in such property.
   b. Debtor lists a pending lawsuit in which he is plaintiff on his Schedule C and lists the value at "between $0 and $1,000,000." He claims an exemption in all of the asset's value. Your research shows that the debtor has lost his case at trial and at the court of appeals level and that it is now pending before the state supreme court. The applicable exemption statute permits the debtor to exempt $100,000 of value in such an asset. Would your answer change if the applicable exemption statute permitted the exemption in an unlimited amount?
   c. Debtor lists a diamond ring on his Schedule C and assigns it a value of $500. He claims an exemption in all of the asset's value. An anonymous phone caller warns you that the debtor is trying to pull a fast one and that the ring is worth at least $10,000 in excess of the applicable exemption statute. Aside from the decision of whether to object to this claim, what other action might you take in the debtor's case based on this incident?
2. Assume you represent the Chapter 7 debtors in the following cases. Decide how to list the claimed exemptions in the following cases.
   a. The debtor wants to exempt a diamond ring that she has been told is valuable but she has no idea of its exact or approximate worth. The applicable exemption statute permits the debtor to exempt $10,000 of value in such an asset.

b. Debtor claims his home is worth $200,000, that he owes the bank $150,000 on it, and that he wants to exempt his $50,000 of equity in it. The applicable homestead exemption allows him to exempt up to $100,000 in equity. An appraiser tells you the real estate market is fluid and the property could be worth as little as $175,000 or as much as $300,000.

c. A debtor who has been told about the Supreme Court's decision in *Taylor* says he has a diamond ring worth $50,000 and that since he can only exempt $25,000 of value in such property he wants you to refrain from placing a dollar value on it and simply exempt it at "full value" on his Schedule C. "Maybe the trustee won't look into it," he says.

In a hearing on an objection to a debtor's exemption, FRBP 4003(c) places the burden of showing why the debtor is not entitled to the claimed exemption on the objecting party.

Under FRBP 4003(c), an objection to a claimed exemption is to be decided "after hearing on notice," which most, but not all, courts treat as after notice and a hearing. Consequently, if the debtor contests the trustee's objection to the exemption, it will be treated as a contested matter and a hearing scheduled. If the debtor does not contest the trustee's objection, the objection will be sustained and the challenged exemption disallowed.

C. THE TRUSTEE'S POWERS TO COMPEL TURNOVER OF THE PROPERTY OF THE ESTATE

The Code also grants the bankruptcy trustee broad power to locate and take possession of property of the estate from the debtor and from third parties who refuse to turn it over. There are three **turnover** provisions in the Code empowering the bankruptcy trustee to compel a person or entity holding property of the estate to deliver that property to him.

1. The Debtor's Duty to Turn Over Property to the Bankruptcy Trustee

Section 521(a)(4) of the Code imposes an obligation on the debtor to turn over to the trustee, "all property of the estate and any recorded information, including books, documents, records, and papers relating to property of the estate." If the debtor fails to comply with a turnover demand from the trustee, the trustee will file a motion to compel the turnover, which is treated as a contested matter, not an adversary proceeding. The debtor's failure to comply with this duty is also a basis for the trustee to ask the court to deny the debtor a discharge of his debts pursuant to §727 or to dismiss the case pursuant to §707 (to be discussed in detail in Chapter Eleven).

2. The Duty of Third Persons to Turn Over Property of the Estate

Section 542 of the Code empowers the trustee to compel third persons (who are not custodians within the meaning of §101(11)) holding the property of the debtor to turn it over to him or to account for its value if the property no longer exists. Since the trustee is seeking to recover money or property from a third party in such an action, it must be brought as an adversary proceeding pursuant to FRBP 7001 rather than by motion (see Exhibit 4.6).

For example, prior to filing her Chapter 7 petition Marta Carlson loaned her doll collection to her sister, Evelyn Rinaldi, as disclosed in her Schedule B (see Document 8 in the Carlson case file). Once the trustee concluded that the doll collection had value in excess of that claimed by Marta on her Schedule C and that there was equity for the estate in excess of the exemption amount claimed by Marta in the collection, the trustee demanded that Evelyn return the doll collection, not to Marta, but to the trustee. Evelyn refused and the trustee filed a complaint (Document 31 in the Carlson case file) instituting an adversary action against her, pursuant to §542 and FRBP 7001, seeking the return of the doll collection or a money judgment for its value.

Application Exercise 1

In the complaint filed against Evelyn Rinaldi to recover the doll collection in her possession or its value (Document 31 in the Carlson case file), note the allegations in Paragraph 3 of the complaint regarding the subject matter jurisdiction of the bankruptcy court over the adversary proceeding. Do you understand the source of the court's power to hear this case? If not, review the discussion of those issues in Chapter Four, Section F.

3. The Duty of Custodians to Turn Over Property of the Estate

If the property of the estate is in the hands of a custodian such as an assignee for the benefit of creditors or a trustee or receiver appointed as part of a prebankruptcy effort to work out the debtor's financial problems, §543 of the Code empowers the bankruptcy trustee to compel that custodian to deliver the held property to him or to account for its proceeds.

For example, if Marta Carlson had attempted an assignment for benefit of creditors prior to filing her petition in bankruptcy, the trustee designated to hold her property as part of that assignment would be the target of the bankruptcy trustee's §543 turnover demand.

If the custodian fails to turn over the property, the trustee can enforce the §543 turnover demand by filing an adversary proceeding. In addition, a third person or custodian who refuses to turn over property to the trustee pursuant to a §542 or 543 demand and who is also a creditor of the estate can have his claim set off per §553 or disallowed per §502(d).

D. THE TRUSTEE'S AVOIDANCE POWERS REGARDING PROPERTY OF THE ESTATE

The bankruptcy trustee not only has power to demand the turnover of property of the debtor, but to set aside certain voluntary and involuntary transfers of the debtor's property to others that occurred before the petition was filed. In Code parlance, the trustee can *avoid* these prepetition transfers. Thus, we speak of the **avoidance powers** of the trustee. There are several of them. Since all of these avoidance actions involve the trustee's effort to determine the validity, extent, or priority of a lien on the debtor's property or to recover money or property from a third party, they must be brought as adversary proceedings pursuant to FRBP 7001 and not by motion. As with the targeted party in a turnover action, if the party targeted by the trustee's avoidance action is also a creditor of the estate and fails to consent to the avoidance or pay the amount demanded by the trustee, that creditor may have its claim set off per §553 or disallowed per §502(d).

1. The Power to Avoid Unperfected Security Interests in the Debtor's Property

Section 544(a) of the Code, known as the **strong-arm clause**, provides that, as of the moment the case is commenced by the filing of the petition, the bankruptcy trustee has the status of a perfected secured creditor in all the property of the estate, whether as a judicial lien creditor (§544(a)(1)) or as a judgment creditor who has had a writ of execution issued in his favor (§544(a)(2)) or as the holder of a consensual mortgage or deed of trust in the real property of the debtor (§544(a)(3)). As judges and practitioners say, this makes the trustee a **supercreditor** of the debtor. Note that this status given the trustee is a legalized fiction: The trustee need not take any action to become a judicial lien creditor or judgment creditor or mortgagee, as we considered those concepts in Part A of the text. Instead, the Code simply declares him to have that legal status as of the date the petition is filed.

The most dramatic result of that supercreditor status is that the trustee can defeat

- the claim of any unsecured creditor to the property of the debtor or
- the claim of any secured creditor whose security interest in the property was not properly perfected prior to the filing of the petition.

For example, recall from the Assignment Memorandum in Appendix A that Marta Carlson has two mortgages on her home, one in favor of CSB with a balance of $142,500 and one in favor of DCT with a balance of $37,500. If the trustee determines that CSB failed to properly record its mortgage or deed of trust prior to the filing of the bankruptcy petition, he would initiate an adversary proceeding by filing a complaint, pursuant to §544(a) and FRBP 7001, seeking to avoid the security interest CSB claims in the home. If the trustee prevailed in avoiding CSB's lien in the home, that would mean that when the home was sold, DCT would be paid first out of the proceeds (assuming it did properly record its mortgage or deed of trust, thus perfecting its secured interest in the home). Marta would receive her homestead exemption next, and the rest of the proceeds would go to the trustee to be used for the benefit of all other creditors of the estate. CSB would still be a creditor, of course, but its claim would now be an unsecured claim, not a secured claim.

Prepetition security interests in both the personal and real property of the debtor that were not properly perfected are subject to the avoidance powers of the trustee under §544(a). However, §546(b) recognizes the right of a creditor to perfect its security interest in property of the estate postpetition so long as, under applicable law (usually the law of the state where the debtor or the property is located), the creditor's interest relates back to a date prior to the commencement of the case.

For example, recall the discussion of UCC §9-324 in Chapter Two, Section A regarding a creditor who holds a purchase money security interest in goods other than inventory or livestock being granted priority over an earlier perfected security interest if the PMSI is perfected when the debtor takes possession of the collateral or within 20 days thereafter. And recall the discussion of UCC §9-317(e) providing that a PMSI that can be perfected by filing a financing statement where the secured creditor perfects by filing a financing statement is deemed perfected as of the date the security interest attaches to the goods so long as the financing statement is filed within 20 days of delivery of the goods to the debtor. At this time you may want to review the examples of these UCC sections that were provided in Chapter Two, Section A. Where applicable, these provisions will work to the benefit of the secured creditor against the bankruptcy trustee when the debtor files for relief.

Section 546(c) recognizes the superiority of the rights of a seller of goods to reclaim such goods from possession of a debtor/buyer who has taken possession of the goods within 45 days of the commencement of the case and at a time when the debtor was insolvent (compare the right of reclamation outside of bankruptcy given a seller of goods for buyer's insolvency under UCC §2-702). To exercise this reclamation right in the goods, the seller must give the trustee a written demand for reclamation of the goods within 20 days following commencement of the case. This right of reclamation is deemed superior to the trustee's strong-arm power under §544(a) as to those goods even though the seller is not perfected in them.

2. The Power to Avoid Statutory Liens in Property of the Estate

Recall the discussion of non-consensual statutory liens in Chapter Two: the mechanics' lien, artisan's lien, landlord's lien, and so on. Section 545 of the Code grants the bankruptcy trustee a very limited power to avoid prepetition statutory liens asserted against the property of the debtor. Most statutory liens are not subject to this particular avoidance power of the trustee. The ones that are subject to avoidance are listed in Exhibit 9.1.

EXHIBIT 9.1 **Prepetition Statutory Liens Subject to Avoidance Under §545**

- A statutory lien that only goes into effect upon the debtor's insolvency or financial distress, or upon the bankruptcy filing or the commencement of a non-bankruptcy insolvency proceeding against the debtor (§545(1))
- A statutory lien that would not be enforceable under applicable state law against a bona fide purchaser of the property for value as of the date the case was commenced (§545(2))
- Landlord liens (§545(3))

For example, assume that the state had a statute providing that car repair businesses having an unpaid bill for car repair have a lien on any car repaired for the amount owed if the owner of the car filed for bankruptcy relief before paying the debt in full. If Marta owed a repairperson for work on her car when she filed the petition, the trustee could avoid that statutory lien on Marta's car under §545(1).

Or, assume that the state had a statute providing that car repair businesses having an unpaid bill for car repair have an automatic lien on any car repaired for the amount owed if the debt is not paid within 30 days of the repair but only if the business gives notice of its lien by certified mail. If, under state law, a bona fide purchaser of the car from Marta could take the car free from that lien by purchasing it before the 30 days ran out or before the statutory notice was given, the bankruptcy trustee could likewise defeat the lien under §545(2) if Marta filed her petition before the 30 days ran out or before the statutory notice was given.

Or assume Marta rented her home instead of owning it and that, pursuant to state law, her landlord was asserting a lien against her personal property in the home for the amount of the unpaid rent. The bankruptcy trustee may avoid that landlord's lien pursuant to §545(3).

Actions brought by the trustee to avoid a statutory lien in the debtor's property pursuant to §545 are adversary proceedings.

3. The Power to Avoid a Fraudulent Transfer of Property of the Estate

Code §548 authorizes the trustee to set aside a fraudulent transfer of debtor's property made within two years (or longer per §544(b)(1) if state fraudulent transfer law permits) preceding the petition. Such property transfers are fraudulent against creditors since they deplete debtor's estate having been made for less than equivalent value.

Like the Uniform Fraudulent Transfer Act (UFTA), considered in Chapter Three, Section C, §548 defines a fraudulent transfer to include not just a transfer made with actual intent to "hinder, delay or defraud" a creditor per §548(a)(1)(A) but also constructive fraud. The constructive fraud concept is governed by §548(a)(1)(B) and requires a showing that the transfer was made for less than the "reasonably equivalent value" and one or more of the following:

- Was made at a time when the debtor was insolvent (see §101(32))
- Caused the debtor to become insolvent
- Left the debtor undercapitalized for current or planned business transactions
- Was made at a time the debtor had or planned to incur other debts beyond its ability to pay or
- Was to or for the benefit of an insider (see §101(31) and further discussion in the next section) not in the ordinary course of business.

For example, assume that Marta Carlson, instead of loaning her doll collection to her sister, Evelyn Rinaldi, had made a gift of it to the sister after deciding to file for bankruptcy but before the actual petition was filed. This gift would be disclosed in Marta's Statement of Financial Affairs (Document 17 in the Carlson case file) because it was made within one year of filing. The circumstances of this "gift" would look very suspicious to the trustee searching for property of the estate, and the purported gift might well be attacked as a fraudulent transfer both because it was made when Marta was insolvent and it was arguably made with actual intent to defraud.

The phrase "reasonably equivalent value" is not defined in the Code. It is normally determined using the fair market value of the property involved as of the date of the transfer. Fair market value has been defined by the Supreme Court to be the price at which the property would change hands between a willing buyer and a willing seller, neither being under any compulsion to buy or to sell and both having reasonable knowledge of relevant facts (United States v. Cartwright, 411 U. S. 546, 551 (1973)).

Applying a strict fair market value standard to determine reasonable equivalence does not always work, however, particularly where the benefit received by the transferee is indirect or intangible. See, e.g., Mellon Bank N.A. v. Metro Commc'ns, Inc., 945 F.2d 635, 644-645 (3d Cir. 1991) (value of transfer was the intangible benefit of improving debtor's ability to borrow capital); In re Jumer's Castle Lodge, Inc., 338 B.R. 344 (C.D. Ill. 2006) (debtor received more in value than it transferred, since transfer made it more attractive to investors and financiers); and In re Tousa, Inc., 680 F.3d 1298 (11th Cir. 2012) (refused to decide whether a transfer intended in part to reduce the likelihood of the transferor having to file for bankruptcy relief could constitute value because even if it did it was not equivalent value). The most that can be said about reasonable equivalence, then, is that it "should depend on all the facts of each case an important element of which is market value. Such a rule requires case-by-case adjudication with fair market value of the property transferred as a starting point" (In re Morris Commc'ns, Inc., 914 F.2d 458, 466-467 (4th Cir. 1990)).

Actions brought by the trustee to avoid alleged fraudulent transfers of the debtor's property pursuant to §548 are adversary proceedings.

4. The Power to Avoid Preferential Transfers of Property of the Estate

Perhaps the most breathtaking example of avoidance powers given the bankruptcy trustee is the preferential transfer provision of §547. This section allows the trustee to set aside any transfer of the debtor's property made within 90 days preceding the filing of the petition if the following additional elements are present:

- The transfer was "to or for the benefit of a creditor"
- The transfer was made for or on account of an antecedent (preexisting) debt
- The debtor was insolvent at the time of the transfer
- The transfer would enable the creditor to receive more than it would have received if the transfer had not been made

For example, one of Marta's unsecured debts is to Crisis Counseling Center (CCC) for the counseling services rendered to her son, Chris (see the Assignment Memorandum in Appendix A and Line 4.7 in her Schedule E/F, Document 10 in the Carlson case file). The total amount owed to CCC was $1,250 and let's say it was due and payable on February 1, 2016. Assume that Marta did finally make a payment of $700 to CCC on May 15 before filing her Chapter 7 petition on June 6. The bankruptcy trustee will demand that CCC return that $700 payment as a preferential transfer. It was a payment made by the debtor within 90 days of the date the petition was filed, was a payment to a creditor on account of a preexisting debt and paid at a time when Marta was insolvent, and that payment would enable CCC to receive more than it would have had the payment not been made. If CCC refuses to return the money to the trustee, he will institute an adversary proceeding, pursuant to §547 and FRBP 7001, to recover it as a preferential transfer.

Consider why allowing CCC to keep the $700 payment in the previous example would enable it to receive more than it would have had the payment not been made. If the payment had not been made, CCC would file a proof of claim in the bankruptcy case as an unsecured creditor for the full amount owed, $1,250. When the time comes for a distribution to unsecured creditors, it is very unlikely that they will all receive 100 cents on each dollar owed. Instead they will probably receive some percentage of what they are owed. But if CCC is allowed to keep the $700 payment, it is getting 100 cents on the dollar from the debtor for that portion of the debt, more than it would receive had the payment not been made.

Application Exercise 2

When Marta filed her bankruptcy petition in June 2016, she was seriously in arrears in her payments to DCT, holder of the second mortgage on her home. She had failed to make the payments due on March 1, April 1, and May 1, 2016. However, on May 15, 2016, she did pay DCT $954 to cover the missed payments that were due March 1 and April 1. This May 15 payment is disclosed in Section 3a of Marta's Statement of Financial Affairs (Document

17 in the Carlson case file). Will the bankruptcy trustee demand that DCT return the $954 payment it received from Marta on May 15 to the trustee as a preferential transfer? It was a payment made by the debtor within 90 days of the date of the petition, to a creditor on account of a preexisting debt, at a time when Marta was insolvent. But the last element is missing. Based on the estimated value of the real property securing the debt owed to DCT, it is going to receive the full amount Marta owes it from the proceeds of the sale of the property even though it is a junior lien holder in the property. Thus, her May 15 payment does not satisfy the last element of the preferential transfer definition because the payment does not enable the creditor to receive more from the estate than it would have had the payment not been made. But assume Marta made a late mortgage payment on May 15 to CSB. If the trustee succeeds in avoiding CSB's secured position in the home using the strong arm clause, will the trustee also be able to recoup the May 15 payment to this creditor as preferential?

Application Exercise 3

Assume that the May 15 payment is made to DCT as described above, but assume further that the real property securing that DCT debt is not worth as much as what DCT is owed. Will the May 15 payment to DCT now be deemed preferential?

To be preferential, the payment also has to have been made on account of an antecedent debt. An antecedent debt is a preexisting one.

For example, if Marta made a car payment to AFI on May 15 but it was an installment payment that was only then due from her, that payment cannot be considered preferential. It was a payment for a current debt, not an antecedent one.

To be preferential, the payment must also have been made while the debtor was insolvent. Recall from Chapter Three, Section C, that under the UFTA, there are two definitions of insolvency, the **balance sheet test** (the sum of the debtor's debts is greater than all of the debtor's assets, at a fair valuation) and the **equity test** (the debtor is not paying his debts as they become due). Section 101(32) of the Code defines insolvency using only the balance sheet test. Thus, when insolvency is at issue in a bankruptcy case, as it often is in a preference action, valuation of the assets of the debtor as part of the balance sheet test of insolvency is often vigorously contested.

Significantly, §547(f) aids the trustee asserting preferential transfer by creating a rebuttable **presumption of insolvency** as to the debtor during the 90 days immediately preceding the filing of the petition — the preferential transfer period. Pursuant to Rule 301 of the Federal Rules of Evidence, which controls presumptions that arise in federal courts, the effect of the presumption of insolvency is to effectively shift the burden of coming forward with evidence of solvency to the creditor being sued. Though the burden of proof regarding insolvency always remains on the trustee alleging the preferential transfer, the presumption will be sufficient to satisfy that element for the trustee unless the transferee presents sufficient evidence to rebut the presumption. If the presumption is effectively rebutted by the transferee then the burden of persuasion is on the trustee to present other evidence of insolvency. For a good discussion of how the presumption works, see In re Koubourlis, 869 F.2d 1319, 1321-1322 (9th Cir. 1989).

Forcing a creditor to return a payment received from a debtor within 90 days of the petition being filed may not seem fair to the creditor. After all, the creditor receiving the payment may not even have known the debtor was insolvent when the payment was made. The creditor was legitimately owed the money and did nothing illegal or unethical to collect the payment. But the policy behind the preferential transfer avoidance power given the bankruptcy trustee is that it is not fair to all creditors for one to be "preferred" by receiving a payment or other transfer of the debtor's property so close to the date of filing bankruptcy when the debtor was already insolvent. So every transfer of property by the debtor within the 90-day window is immediately suspect and will be closely examined by the trustee to see if the elements of a preference are present. The trustee's duty is to all the creditors of the estate, so he will aggressively pursue each preferential transfer.

When payments from the debtor must be returned to the trustee as preferential, the creditor's only remedy is to file a proof of claim for the amount of the preferential transfer returned and stand in line with other general unsecured creditors hoping that there is eventually a distribution from the estate. Of course, how much the general unsecured creditors ultimately receive will depend on the total assets located by the trustee, and they may ultimately get only pennies on each dollar owed. We will consider the distribution to creditors in Chapter Ten, Section B.

A preferential transfer need not involve the payment of money by the debtor to a creditor during the preference period. 11 U.S.C. §101(54) defines "transfer" as follows:

> The term "transfer" means —
>   (A) the creation of a lien;
>   (B) the retention of title as a security interest;
>   (C) the foreclosure of a debtor's equity of redemption; or
>   (D) each mode, direct or indirect, absolute or conditional, voluntary or involuntary, of disposing of or parting with —
>   (i) property; or
>   (ii) an interest in property.

Using this broad definition, the transfer of any property interest of the debtor within 90 days of filing may trigger a preference claim if the other elements of §547 are satisfied.

For example, assume that Marta transferred title to her doll collection to her sister a month before the petition was filed but did so in payment of an old debt she owed her sister. The transfer of the doll collection is a transfer of the debtor's property within 90 days of filing to a creditor in payment of an antecedent debt and made when the debtor was insolvent. It is a preferential transfer within the meaning of §547 and the doll collection will have to be returned to the estate. If Evelyn no longer has the doll collection (e.g., it was stolen, sold, or lost) she will have to return its dollar value to the trustee. Evelyn can file a claim with the estate for the debt owed her by Marta.

Or assume that to keep the CCC from suing her for the amount she owes, Marta had agreed on May 15 to give CCC a security interest in all her personal property. And assume she signed a proper security agreement to create that security interest and that CCC filed a proper financing statement to perfect its secured position in that property. When she files her petition on June 6, the trustee will seek to avoid the security interest Marta granted CCC on the grounds that it was preferential. What "property" did the debtor convey to CCC on May 15? The security interest in her personal property is a type of property interest and is subject to avoidance as preferential.

In addition to the standard 90-day preferential transfer provision, §547 allows the bankruptcy trustee to avoid preferential transfers to **insiders** of the debtor made within one year preceding the date the petition was filed. 11 U.S.C. §101(31) contains an extensive definition of who is an insider but essentially an insider is a person in close relationship with a debtor such that he may be assumed to have superior access to information and be subject to special treatment.

Application Exercise 4

Assume that Marta transfers title to her doll collection to her sister, Evelyn, six months before the bankruptcy petition is filed in payment of an old debt. The transfer occurred more than 90 days prior to the filing of the petition, but using the definition in §101(31), can the trustee avoid the transfer of the doll collection to Evelyn on the basis that she was an insider as to the debtor? What if the debtor is a partnership and the questioned transfer was made to a partner six months before the partnership files its bankruptcy case? To a receptionist who works for the partnership as an employee only? To the wife of a partner? What if the debtor is a corporation and the transfer was to a shareholder? An officer? A director? To an attorney who does legal work for the corporation?

The §547(c)(1) Equivalent Value Exception to the Trustee's Right to Avoid Preferential Transfers

Section 547(c)(1) recognizes an important exception to the trustee's right to avoid and recover preferential transfers where the transfer was intended as and in fact was a contemporaneous exchange for equivalent value.

Assume that Marta Carlson had ordered a new car on January 2, 2016, from AAA Chevrolet. The purchase price was $15,000 and was to be paid on delivery. The car is delivered on April, 2016, and Marta pays AAA cash for it. She is insolvent at the time she does so. When she files her bankruptcy petition on June 6, 2016, the trustee will look at the April 1 payment and see a transfer of the debtor's property made within the 90-day preference window to a creditor in payment of a preexisting debt made at a time when the debtor was insolvent, all of which enables the creditor to receive more than it would have had the payment not been made. Looks like a preferential payment all right. But if the car purchased was in fact worth $15,000, it is not preferential because the transfer of cash was in exchange for something of "equivalent value," the $15,000 car, which is now property of the estate. So this transfer would not be preferential under the Code and the trustee could not set it aside.

Or assume that the car Marta purchases from AAA for $15,000 is actually worth only $12,000. That's not equivalent value. On those facts, the trustee would likely succeed in his preference claim against AAA to recover the full $15,000 for the estate. Could AAA get the car back under those circumstances? Not unless it retained a perfected security interest in the car, which it would not do if it received cash in full payment. That car is property of the estate. File your proof of claim, AAA, and get in line with the other unsecured creditors.

The §547(c)(2) Ordinary Course of Business Exception to the Trustee's Right to Avoid Preferential Transfers

Section 547(c)(2) recognizes a second important exception to the trustee's right to avoid and recover preferential transfers where the transfer was in payment of a debt incurred in the ordinary course of business or financial affairs of the debtor and transferee and the transfer itself was made either (and note this alternative for the transfer) in the ordinary course of business or financial affairs of the debtor and transferee or was made according to ordinary business terms. Thus the debt at issue must have been incurred in the ordinary course of business or financial affairs of the both the debtor and the transferee and the transfer must be made in the ordinary course of business or financial affairs of both the debtor and the transferee (§547(c)(2)(A)), or according to ordinary business terms (§547(c)(2)(B)).

Assume that the bankruptcy debtor is in the grocery business. Sixty days before filing his bankruptcy petition the debtor orders inventory for his store, which is delivered five days later, together with an invoice stating that payment is due within ten days of receipt of the goods. The debtor pays the invoice from his supplier within the ten days even though he is insolvent at the time. Then he files a case in bankruptcy. That payment to the supplier is immediately suspect because it was made within the 90-day preferential window. But there is nothing extraordinary about the payment because the debtor only paid what was owed and he paid it on time. The debt was created in the ordinary course of the debtor's business as well as the supplier's business (note that to qualify for the exception the debt must be created in the ordinary course of business of both the debtor and the transferee) and it was paid (that's the transfer) in the ordinary course of both the debtor's and the transferee's business (note that to qualify for the exception under §547(c)(2)(A) the transfer must be made in the ordinary course of business or financial affairs of both the debtor and the transferee). This transfer is probably not preferential and the supplier can keep the money.

It has long been understood that whether a debt is created or a transfer made in the ordinary course of the debtor's and transferee's business is a subjective inquiry focusing on what is "ordinary" for those particular parties. See, e.g., In re Fred Hawes Organization, Inc., 957 F.2d 239 (6th Cir. 1992).

For example, assume that our bankruptcy debtor who is in the grocery business pays the invoice 12 days after the goods are delivered, two days late under the terms of the invoice. That payment is now likely to be found preferential and the trustee will recover it for the estate. Do you see why? Because payments made late will not be considered "ordinary" unless the debtor and transferee have an established course of dealing whereby past payments have been made late and accepted by the transferee without complaint. If that course of dealing exists, then the late payment may be in the ordinary course of business as between the debtor and transferee.

Even the slightest deviation from normal business behavior or practice of a debtor and transferee may render a payment extraordinary and thus unqualified for the ordinary course of dealing exception to the preferential transfer statute.

For example, assume that our bankruptcy debtor who is in the grocery business pays the invoice on time, within ten days. However, the supplier has heard rumors that the debtor may be in financial trouble and so he demands payment of this invoice by cashier's check. Previously the supplier has always allowed payment by personal check. Even if the debtor makes the payment on time, if he does so by cashier's check, that's not the usual practice and the transfer will be deemed preferential and recoverable by the trustee when the debtor files his petition.

But note that per §549(c)(2)(B) the transfer part of the challenged transaction can qualify for the exception either by having been made in the ordinary course of business or financial affairs of the debtor and the transferee, or by having been made according to "ordinary business terms." Unlike "ordinary course of business," "ordinary business terms" is understood to involve an objective inquiry focusing not on ordinary business terms between the debtor and the transferee, but on ordinary business terms in the relevant business or industry. See, e.g., In re Nowlen, 452 B.R. 619, 621-622 (Bankr. E.D. Mich. 2011).

For example, assume that our bankruptcy debtor who is in the grocery business cannot pay the invoice within the ten days of delivery when it is due although he has always paid this supplier on time in the past. This time debtor calls the supplier and asks for five additional days to pay even though he knows he will be late in doing so. Debtor makes the payment on the fifteenth day after delivery, paying by check as he always has, and then files bankruptcy. Must the transferee supplier disgorge the payment to the trustee as preferential? This payment was not in the ordinary course of business of the debtor and supplier since they had no course of dealing allowing debtor to pay late. But supplier may be able to successfully defend against the preference action if he can show that payment by check is a standard method of payment in the industry and that there is an industry custom of allowing customers such as debtor to occasionally make a payment slightly late. By making such argument, supplier transferee is arguing that the payment he received from debtor was according to ordinary business terms in the industry.

The §547(c)(3) Enabling Loan Exception to the Trustee's Right to Avoid Preferential Transfers

Under §547(c)(3), the bankruptcy trustee cannot avoid a transfer that creates a security interest in property to secure payment of the loan or credit that enabled the debtor to purchase the property and the security interest "is perfected on or before 30 days after the debtor receives possession of such property." This exception is asserted frequently in consumer bankruptcy cases where the consumer debtor purchases a vehicle (or other consumer item) shortly before filing the bankruptcy petition and grants the seller or lender a security interest in the vehicle.

For example, Joe and Alice, husband and wife, purchase a used car from Carla's Used Cars on March 1. They purchase the car on credit and sign a purchase and security agreement requiring them to pay in installments over 36 months. The agreement grants Carla's a security interest in the car to secure payment of the debt. Joe and Alice drive home in their new car and apply the next day for new title, which is issued by the state on March 21 with the security interest of Carla's properly noted thereon; Carla's security interest in the car is now perfected under state law. Joe and Alice then file for Chapter 7 bankruptcy on April 10 and are able to claim as exempt all of their property not subject to security interests so it appears to be a no-asset case. The bankruptcy trustee will examine this transaction to see if there might be a basis to set aside the transfer of the security interest in the car from Joe and Alice to Carla's as a preference. The granting of the security interest to Carla's is a transfer within §101(54). Carla's was a creditor of the debtors when the transfer was made. The transfer occurred within the 90-day preference period. The trustee can rely on the presumption of insolvency per §547(f). Carla's is in a position to receive more than it would have received had the security interest not been granted since even if the trustee were able to sell the car for the benefit of unsecured creditors, none of them, including Carla's, is going to get anything near 100 percent of what is owed. But as a secured creditor, Carla's can expect to get most or all of what is owed. Finally the transfer is made on account of an antecedent debt since application for the title was made on March 2 and the title issued on March 21 making March 2 the

BAPCPA'S Revision of the Ordinary Course of Business Exception to the Preference Action

Prior to BAPCPA in 2005 a transferee defending against a preferential transfer allegation on the basis of the ordinary course of business exception was required to establish both the ordinary course of business and the ordinary business terms prongs of §547(c)(2). BAPCPA changed the "and" to "or," separating those concepts in §547(c)(2)(A) and (B) and thus created two alternative ways to establish the ordinary course of business defense as to the transfer itself, one objective and one subjective. Note that In re Fred Hawes, supra, was decided prior to BAPCPA while In re Nolen, supra, was decided afterward. If you are not aware of the change made in this statute by BAPCPA, trying to read both decisions will likely confuse you. This illustrates how essential it is that attorneys stay abreast of changes in areas of the law in which they work.

earliest date the security interest was perfected under UCC 9-303(b) for this debt created March 1.

It appears that all the elements of a preferential transfer are present in the last example, but now look at the §547(c)(3) exception. The security interest in the car was given to Carla's to secure new credit ("new value"); the credit was given to debtors on March 1 at the time the security agreement describing the vehicle was executed; the credit was given to enable the debtors to acquire the vehicle; and they did in fact obtain title to the vehicle using the credit given. All the elements of §547(c)(3)(A) are satisfied but subsection (B) must be satisfied as well, and on the facts of our example it is — the new title noting Carla's security interest was issued by the state on March 21, fewer than 30 days after Joe and Alice took possession of the car on March 1. Since Carla's security interest in the vehicle was perfected within 30 days of debtors taking possession the enabling loan exception will defeat trustee's preference claim. (BAPCPA amended the §547(c)(3) exception in a way that favors secured creditors over the bankruptcy trustees by changing the permissible time window for perfection from 20 to 30 days.)

Application Exercise 5

What is the result in the last example if the new title noting Carla's security interest in the vehicle is not issued by the state until April 5? Or if Joe and Alice grant a security interest in the vehicle on March 2 to Joe's mother to secure a loan Joe's mother made to them two years ago that was originally unsecured?

Case Preview	*In re Carpenter*

Note the use of the word "and" connecting all the subsections of §547(c)(3). That means all of the elements set out in those subsections must be satisfied for the enabling loan exception to the preferential transfer to apply. And the exception is in the nature of an affirmative defense so the transferee has the burden of proving them just as the trustee initially has the burden of proving all the elements of the preferential transfer. As you read In re Carpenter, consider the following questions:

1. When did the security interest of the seller/creditor attach to the truck? When was it perfected under Idaho law?
2. What facts convinced the court that the debtor had "received possession" of the truck on December 11?

In re Carpenter

378 B.R. 274 (Bankr. D. Idaho 2007)

PAPPAS, Bankruptcy Judge:

On July 27, 2006, Debtor filed for relief under chapter 7 of the Bankruptcy Code. Several months prior to filing his bankruptcy petition, Debtor had purchased a 2003 Chevrolet Silverado Duramax pickup truck from Defendant. Debtor and Defendant agreed Defendant would retain a security interest in the truck to secure Debtor's payment of the purchase price to Defendant at a later date.

Debtor and Defendant negotiated the purchase and sale of the Silverado in December of 2005. After settling the various terms of their arrangement, the parties decided that Debtor would draft a simple written purchase agreement, and travel from his home in Preston to Defendant's residence in Blackfoot on December 11, 2005 to sign the contract and finalize the sale.

The simple written agreement Debtor prepared was executed by the parties at Defendant's house that day. It called for Debtor to pay Defendant a total purchase price for the Silverado of $22,000, but the spaces in the agreement providing for an initial down payment and for subsequent monthly payments were left blank. The agreement provided that Debtor was to take delivery of the pickup on the date it was executed, December 11, 2005. The contract required Debtor to secure insurance coverage on the truck by December 12, 2005.

The day before the parties were to meet to sign the deal, Debtor telephoned his insurance agent to inquire about insuring the Silverado. Debtor discovered that it would be too expensive to carry insurance on both his current Ford pickup and the Silverado. Debtor therefore decided it would be best not to take delivery of pickup from Defendant, nor to insure it, until he could sell the Ford. Despite this decision, on December 11, 2005, Debtor traveled to Blackfoot with his spouse, met with Defendant, and signed the agreement as originally planned, making no changes to the contract's terms regarding the delivery date or his obligation to insure the Silverado by December 12, 2005. Debtor did not take delivery of pickup at that time, and instead returned to Preston, leaving the Silverado in Defendant's garage in Blackfoot. This arrangement was satisfactory to Defendant, and she continued her insurance coverage on the Silverado.

A few days later, Debtor found a buyer for the Ford. On December 17, 2005, after being informed of this development by Debtor, Defendant cancelled her insurance coverage on the Silverado. On December 18, 2005, Debtor closed the sale on the Ford. On December 19, 2005, Debtor called his insurance agent, cancelled the coverage on the Ford pickup, and added the Silverado to his policy.

Debtor testified at trial that, having sold the Ford and obtained insurance on the Silverado, he had hoped to return to Blackfoot to retrieve the Silverado. However, this plan proved inconvenient. With the rapidly approaching holiday season, Debtor and his wife decided it would be best to wait until after Christmas to get the Silverado. Then, on December 27, 2005, Debtor's wife broke her wrist and underwent surgery; the following week Debtor's son required dental surgery. Because of these complications, it was not until January 4, 2006, that Debtor was able to return to Blackfoot. He took the Silverado from Defendant's garage and returned home with it.

Debtor then attempted to obtain a certificate of title to the Silverado. However, the county assessor's office informed him that to do so he needed the existing title certificate. Debtor contacted Defendant and asked her to sign off and send him the certificate. On January 27, 2006, Debtor received the title certificate from Defendant. Debtor returned to the county assessor's office with the title and other necessary paperwork, and on January 31, 2006, the Idaho Department of Motor Vehicles issued a new certificate of title for the Silverado showing Debtor as owner and noting that Defendant held a lien on the pickup.

CONCLUSIONS OF LAW AND ANALYSIS

Given these facts, two legal issues require analysis by the Court. First, was the Defendant's retention of a security interest in the Silverado a preference under §547(b)? And second, if Defendant's retention of a security interest is a preference, is the transfer insulated from avoidance by §547(c)(3)?

A. The Transfer of the Security Interest in the Silverado Was an Avoidable Preference

[The court finds that the trustee/plaintiff has satisfied his burden of proving all the elements of a §547(b) preferential transfer.]

B. The Enabling Loan Exception to Preference Avoidance Does Not Apply

Plaintiff may avoid the Debtor's transfer of the security interest to Defendant unless one of the statutory safe harbors to avoidance is shown to apply to the transaction. As affirmative defenses, it is Defendant's burden to prove she is protected by one or more of the preference exceptions under §547(c). . . . 11 U.S.C. §547(g). . . .

Defendant acknowledges that the only provision of §547(c) that is arguably applicable is the so-called "enabling loan" exception under §547(c)(3). . . . Under this exception, a trustee may not avoid a transfer that creates a security interest in property to secure payment of the purchase price "that is perfected on or before 30 days after the debtor receives possession of such property." 11 U.S.C. §547(c)(3)(B). Here, whether this provision shields Defendant from avoidance of her security interest depends upon when Debtor "received possession" of the Silverado.

Plaintiff argues that upon execution of the agreement by the parties, Debtor was given "constructive" possession of the pickup, and thus the 30-day time limit for perfection of Defendant's security interest began to run on December 11, 2005. Since Defendant's security interest was not perfected by noting her lien on the certificate of title to the Silverado until January 31, 2006, Plaintiff contends the enabling loan exception does Defendant no good.*5

Defendant, on the other hand, argues that the 30–day perfection period did not commence until Debtor received actual, physical possession of the Silverado on January 4, 2006. If Defendant's construction of §547(c)(3)(B) is correct, her security interest may not be avoided by Plaintiff.

The Bankruptcy Code contains no definition of the term "possession." However, this Court has interpreted the meaning of possession in the context of §547(c)(3)(B) to refer to "physical control or custody of the collateral, as opposed to the acquisition of a right of ownership." See In re Tuttle, 2003 WL 22221330 (Bankr. D. Idaho 2003). See also, In re B & B Utilities, Inc., 208 B.R. 417, 424 (Bankr. E.D. Tenn. 1997) (quoting In re Trott, 91 B.R. 808, 811 (Bankr. S.D. Ohio 1988)). In *Trott*, the bankruptcy court concluded that there was "simply no reason . . . to depart from the definition of the word possession which has gained acceptance throughout the law[.]" In re Trott, 91 B.R. at 811. The court explained that possession, as generally understood in legal matters, meant "[t]he detention and control, or the manual or ideal custody [of something] . . . either held personally or by another who exercises it in one's place and name." Id. (citing Black's Law Dictionary 1047 (5th ed. 1979). In *Tuttle*, this Court agreed with *Trott*, noting that "to add gloss to the concept of possession [is] inconsistent with the plain language of the Code." In re Tuttle, 2003 WL 22221330. The Court further observed that the language of §547(c)(3)(B) "contains no qualification or condition on the nature of a debtor's possession."

In this case, from and after December 11, 2005, the date the parties executed the agreement by which Debtor purchased the Silverado and Defendant retained a security interest in it, the pickup, while still parked in Defendant's garage, was under Debtor's control. Defendant did not require that the Silverado be left with her after December 11. Instead, the arrangement was merely a convenience to Debtor. Importantly, both Defendant and Debtor testified that Debtor could have taken the Silverado at any time thereafter. Defendant never denied Debtor access to the pickup, nor did she charge Debtor to store the Silverado at her home. Moreover, during the time the Silverado remained in Defendant's garage, Defendant cancelled her insurance, and Debtor added the pickup to his insurance policy. This is consistent with the notion that, after December 11, Debtor was in control of the truck. Furthermore, as Defendant's counsel conceded during argument at trial, after the purchase agreement was executed, Defendant had the original certificate of title to the Silverado, and nothing prevented her from immediately taking the necessary steps to transfer

---

*5 Under §547(e)(1)(B) and (2), the transfer of a security interest in a debtor's personal property is deemed to occur for preference purposes at the time such transfer is perfected under applicable law as against third parties, where that perfection occurs after 30 days from the date "such transfer takes effect between the transferor and the transferee . . . ." Defendant does not dispute Plaintiff's position that the transfer of the security interest in the Silverado from Debtor to Defendant was effective between the parties when they signed the purchase agreement on December 11, 2005. Therefore, since Defendant's security was not perfected under Idaho law until the application for certificate of title was filed on January 31, 2006, see Idaho Code §49–510, for preference purposes, the transfer is deemed to have occurred on that date.

title and perfect her security interest in the Silverado, as opposed to waiting for Debtor to have the title transfer completed.

Under these facts, the Court finds that Debtor had actual control of the Silverado as of December 11, 2005, and that from and after that date, Defendant held the pickup merely as Debtor's agent for purposes of storing it until it was convenient for Debtor to retrieve it. "If a debtor has actual physical control over the property before or at the time of an agreement granting a purchase money security interest therein, the [thirty] day window for the creditor's perfection of that interest under §547(c)(3)(B) begins to close from the date of the agreement." In re Tuttle, 2003 WL 22221330.

CONCLUSION

Plaintiff has shown by a preponderance of the evidence that Defendant's retention of a security interest in the Silverado was a preferential transfer for the purpose of §547(b). Because Debtor had "possession" of the pickup by virtue of his right to control it from and after December 11, 2005, even though it remained stored at Defendant's premises, and because Defendant did not perfect her security interest until January 31, 2006, the exception to avoidance in §547(c)(3) does not protect Defendant. Plaintiff is therefore entitled to avoid Defendant's security interest.

Post-Case Follow-Up

Not all courts might have reached the same result on the possession issue as in *Carpenter*. Though the concept of constructive possession or right of possession to property not literally in a debtor's hands is generally recognized, the debtor's decision to delay taking actual possession until the Ford truck was sold and his delay in securing insurance to cover the Silverado truck could have persuaded a court that debtor was willfully postponing taking physical control. See, e.g., In re Ashworth, 227 B.R. 801 (Bankr. S.D. Ohio 1998) (debtor's delay in making first payment and acquiring insurance for mobile home defeated claim to have taken possession). *Carpenter* provides a reminder of the critical role that state law plays in bankruptcy practice, a principle established by the Supreme Court in Butner v. United States, highlighted in Chapter Four. Though the preferential transfer statute is federal, what constitutes perfection of a security interest in contested property under §547(c)(3)(B) will be governed by applicable state law. For a dramatic example of the difference this can make, read In re Conklin, 511 B.R. 688 (Bankr. D. Idaho 2014), another enabling loan exception case involving a vehicle, decided by the same bankruptcy judge who authored *Carpenter* and also controlled by Idaho law regarding registration of vehicles. In *Conklin* the certificate of title evidencing the creditor's security interest was not issued until 34 days after debtor took possession, but the creditor's security interest was deemed perfected on the thirtieth day following possession when the application for title was received by the state. A 2007 change in the Idaho vehicle registration statute was decisive.

In re Carpenter: Real Life Applications

1. Locate the vehicle registration statute in the state where you plan to practice. How would *Carpenter* have been decided under that statute?
2. Assume that each of the following transfers has been found to be preferential. What issues might arise if the creditor/transferee asserts the enabling loan exception of §547(c)(3) as a defense?
   a. Debtor leased a vehicle three years ago and the lease contained an option to purchase for $5,000 at the conclusion of the lease on June 1. On May 25, debtor borrowed $5,000 from Bank to exercise the option to purchase and granted Bank a security interest in the vehicle. On June 1, debtor paid the $5,000 to lessor, kept the vehicle, and an application for title in debtor's name was initiated the same day. Bank's security interest was perfected by being noted on title issued to debtor on June 30. Debtor filed a Chapter 7 petition on September 1. See In re Moon, 262 B.R. 97 (Bankr. D. Or. 2001).
   b. Debtor purchased a used vehicle from coworker on credit on June 1 by promising to pay for the car in twelve monthly installments beginning July 1. Coworker signed title over to debtor on June 1 and gave him possession that day as well. Debtor made the first promised payment on July 1 but missed the August payment. Coworker then demanded a security interest in the vehicle to secure future payments. Debtor agreed and the security interest of the coworker was noted on the title on August 3, perfecting it under state law. Debtor filed a Chapter 7 petition on August 30.
   c. Debtor borrowed $20,000 from Bank on June 1 to purchase a mobile home. The June 1 agreement granted Bank a security interest in the mobile home to secure repayment of the loan. On the same day, the loan proceeds were paid to the mobile home dealer/seller and debtor received the keys to the mobile home. An application for title was initiated that day as well. Due to some unforeseen delays the mobile home was not delivered to debtor's property by dealer until July 30. The certificate of title noting Bank's security interest in the mobile home was issued by the state on July 3, properly perfecting Bank's interest under state law. After delivery of the mobile home to debtor's property, debtor had to have the mobile home leveled and tied down, the tires removed, steps and skirting installed, and utilities connected; because of this, debtor did not move in until August 10. Debtor filed a Chapter 7 petition on August 20. See In re Winnett, 102 B.R. 635 (Bankr. S.D. Ohio 1989).

Section 547(c) contains a number of other exceptions to the preferential transfer, some of which are pertinent to the consumer bankruptcy debtor. Transfers that constitute the fixing of a statutory lien that is avoidable under §545 are not preferential per 547(c)(6). To the extent a transfer during the preference period was for a bona fide domestic support obligation (e.g., child support or alimony) it is not considered preferential per §547(c)(7). In cases involving consumer debtors, transfers having an aggregate value of less than $600 are not preferential per §547(c)(9).

5. Avoidance of Postpetition Transfers

Section 549 grants the trustee the power to avoid unauthorized transfers of property of the estate made after commencement of the case. An exception is the postpetition transfer of real property to a good faith purchaser without knowledge of the filing who pays a fair equivalent value, unless a copy of the petition or notice of the bankruptcy filing was previously filed or recorded where the deed of transfer would be recorded. The trustee's action under §549 must be commenced within two years after the date of the transfer or before the case is closed or dismissed, whichever is earlier.

6. Recovery of Avoided Transfer from the Party for Whose Benefit It Was Made

Section 550(a)(1) of the Code provides that if a transfer is avoided under one of these avoidance powers, the trustee can recover the property itself or the value of such property from either the initial transferee or the entity for whose benefit the transfer was made.

For example, assume that Marta Carlson's May 15 payment was not made to DCT but instead was made to her parents who held the mortgage on her sister's house to satisfy a past-due mortgage payment owed by the sister to her parents. Assuming all the requirements for constructive fraudulent transfer under §548(a)(1) are present (made while the debtor was insolvent and for less than reasonably equivalent value), the trustee could pursue the parents as transferees of the payment under §548 or, if the transfer is avoided, may pursue recovery from the sister under §550. He might well do this if the parents are unable to pay. The sister is "the entity for whose benefit such transfer was made." Don't be thrown off by the use of the word "entity" in §550(a)(1). Section 1101(15) of the Code defines entity to include "person" and §1101(41) defines person to include an individual as well as non-governmental entities. Section 550(a)(2) also allows the trustee to recover the property or its value from a transferee other than the initial transferee (called an immediate or mediate transferee of the initial transferee) unless per §550(b)(1) that subsequent transferee gave value for the transfer in good faith and without actual or constructive knowledge of the voidability of the transfer.

For example, assume that Marta Carlson's parents, after receiving the May 15 preferential payment from Marta, transfer the funds to their son, Marta's brother, as a gift. The son is an immediate transferee under §550(a)(2) who likely took without knowledge of the voidability of the original transfer but did not do so for value. The son may be a target of the trustee if neither the parents nor the sister can pay.

Application Exercise 6

If Marta Carlson's parents, sister, and brother are all potentially liable to the trustee under §§548 and 550, does that mean the trustee can recover the full amount of the avoided transfer from each of them? See §550(d). If the brother, upon receipt of the funds from his parents and before having any knowledge that the transfers are voidable, transfers the funds to his girlfriend as a gift, may the trustee pursue recovery from the girlfriend in the event neither the parents, sister, or brother can pay? See §550(b)(2).

7. Time Limitations on the Trustee's Right to Bring an Avoidance Action

Section 546(a) establishes a time limitation on the right to bring an avoidance action under any of the provisions we have just considered other than §549. Under all the other avoidance sections the suit must be commenced within two years from the order of relief or one year from the date a trustee is first appointed, whichever is later. And, in any event, it must be filed before the case is closed, which could occur earlier than either of those two events.

Chapter Summary

- Property of the bankruptcy estate includes all property in which the debtor has a legal or equitable interest at the time the case is commenced wherever located and by whoever held at the time. Some property the debtor becomes entitled to within 180 days of filing the petition is considered property of the estate, including inherited property, insurance proceeds, and property received as the result of a domestic property settlement agreement. If debtor is trustee of a trust, only debtor's legal interest in the trust res becomes property of the estate, not the equitable interest of beneficiaries in the res.
- The bankruptcy trustee may challenge debtor's claimed exemptions by objection to increase the property of the estate and objection must normally be filed within 30 days following the first meeting of creditors. Where the value of a claimed exemption is listed on Schedule C as contingent or unknown timely objection must be made or the estate forfeits any later-determined value of the property in excess of the exemption allowance. A debtor who understates the value of an exemption on Schedule C is bound by that value.
- The bankruptcy trustee is empowered to compel the turnover of property of the estate by the debtor or third persons, including legal custodians of that property. Using the strong-arm clause of the Code, the trustee, as a supercreditor, can defeat the claim of any unsecured creditor to the property of the debtor or the claim of any secured creditor whose claim to the debtor's property was not perfected prior to the filing of the petition. The trustee is also empowered to set

aside certain prepetition transfers of the debtor's property, including some statutory liens, fraudulent transfers made within two years preceding the filing of the petition, and preferential transfers of debtor's property made within the 90 days preceding the filing of the petition and within one year of that date for insiders. All such actions are adversary proceedings except the turnover action against the debtor, which is initiated by motion creating a disputed matter.

▦ In a preference action the trustee must show that the transfer was made to or for the benefit of a creditor within the requisite time period for or on account of an antecedent debt while the debtor was insolvent and enabled the transferee creditor to receive more than it would have had the transfer not been made. There is a rebuttable presumption of the debtor's insolvency during the preference period to aid the trustee. Any transfer of debtor's property or an interest of debtor in that property may be preferential including the creation of a consensual or nonconsensual line on debtor's property.

▦ An exception to a preferential transfer claim is recognized for transfers for which the debtor received equivalent value. An exception is also made for transfers made in satisfaction of a debt that was incurred in the ordinary course of business or financial affairs of the debtor and transferee where the transfer itself was made either in the ordinary course of business or financial affairs of the debtor and transferee or was made according to ordinary business terms. An exception is also recognized for transfers creating a security interest in property to secure payment of an enabling loan where the security interest was perfected within 30 days after the debtor receives possession of such property.

▦ The bankruptcy trustee can also avoid an unauthorized postpetition transfer of property of the estate unless the transfer was for equivalent value and without notice. Avoidance actions by the trustee can be maintained against the transferee or other party for whose benefit the transfer was made.

Applying the Concepts

1. Carl and Carol Beatty, a married couple, have filed a joint petition in Chapter 7. Assume you have been appointed to serve as the bankruptcy trustee in their case. Answer the following questions.

   a. The Beattys own a home that has been appraised for $400,000. Bank holds the mortgage on the home and the note secured by the mortgage has a current balance of $250,000. How much of Bank's claim is secured and how much is unsecured?

   b. Assume the Beattys can and do exempt $100,000 of their equity in the home using the applicable homestead exemption. Does the bankruptcy estate have any interest in this property or will you abandon it to Bank and the Beattys?

   c. Assume Bank forgot to record the deed of trust granted to Bank by the Beattys at the time of the home loan but did record it the day after the bankruptcy petition was filed. What is the significance of this to the bankruptcy estate?

d. A week before they filed their bankruptcy petition, the Beattys loaned one of their cars to their daughter, Laura. The car is paid for and is worth $10,000. Can you recover that car for the benefit of the estate and, if so, how will you do it?

e. Carl Beatty is a beneficiary along with his brother (who is not in bankruptcy) of a non-spendthrift family trust. The total value of the trust res is currently $50,000. The trustee is a local lawyer. Is there any value to the estate in this trust and, if so, how will you recover it?

f. Carl and Carol own a YR-2 Chevrolet Impala. Bank, which loaned the Beattys the money to purchase the car, is properly secured in it and the Beattys owe Bank $15,000 on the note secured by the car. Assume that under the applicable exemption scheme, the Beattys can exempt up to $5,000 of equity in a vehicle. The Beattys' Schedule C lists the car, discloses the Bank's lien on it and the balance owed bank, states a value of $20,000 for the car and claims a $5,000 exemption in all of the owner's equity. Your information is that the car has a value of $23,500. What steps will you take to challenge the Beattys' claimed exemption in the car? How will you prove the value you contend the car has? If you succeed what is the potential gain to the estate?

2. Adol and Agata Pelanowski, a married couple, have filed a joint petition in Chapter 7. Assume you have been appointed the bankruptcy trustee in the case. Answer the following questions.

a. A year ago, the Pelanowskis borrowed $10,000 from Bank and granted Bank a security interest in various personal property including a valuable ring that Agata inherited from her grandmother. The current balance owed the bank on the loan is $7,500. The ring was appraised for $12,000 at the time of the loan. The Bank has possession of the ring pursuant to the security agreement with the Pelanowskis but has never filed a financing statement concerning it. The Pelanowskis did not list the ring on their Schedule C. Can you as trustee defeat the security interest that Bank claims in the ring? If not, does the estate have any interest in this ring?

b. The Pelanowskis also own a YR-15 Dodge Charger automobile that they have not listed on their Schedule C. The vehicle has a book value of $1,500. However, the debtors' Schedule B indicates that the vehicle is currently in the possession of Tony's Auto Repair Shop and their Schedule D indicates that Tony's is asserting a possessory artisan's lien in the vehicle for unpaid repairs in the amount of $1,600. Can you as trustee defeat the claim of Tony's Repair Shop to this vehicle?

c. The Pelanowskis' Statement of Affairs lists a transfer by them of title to an unimproved one-acre lake lot one month before filing their petition in bankruptcy. The lot, valued at $75,000, was transferred to Stan Stakowsky "in satisfaction of financial planning services." Under questioning at their 341 meeting, the Pelanowskis acknowledged that Stakowsky is Agata's brother, that he is not a certified financial planner, and that they received no bill or statement for services rendered from him before the transfer of title. Can you as trustee attack this transfer and recover this lake lot for the estate and, if so, on what basis? What other information would you like to have before proceeding?

d. Until three months ago Adol Pelanowski owned and operated an unincorporated locksmith business. You learn from the debtor's Statement of Affairs that six weeks before filing of the petition Adol paid his largest supplier, ABC Padlock, Inc., $20,000 that was 60 days in arrears. In his testimony at the 341 meeting, Adol said he had done business with ABC for ten years, that their established course of dealing was payment due within 30 days of delivery, that he usually paid them on time but had occasionally paid them late — but never 60 days late. Can you recover the $20,000 payment for the estate and, if so, how will you proceed to do so. What additional information would you like to have? Would it matter if ABC has filed a proof of claim in the bankruptcy case alleging it is owed an additional $21,000 by Adol?

3. Locate and read Assignment Memorandum #4 in Appendix C. If your instructor so directs, prepare the complaint to recover preferential transfer assuming the Chapter 7 case of Abelard Mendoza was pending in the U.S. bankruptcy court for the federal district where you plan to practice.

10

The Chapter 7 Consumer Bankruptcy Case: Liquidation, Distribution, and the Debtor's Right to Reaffirm Debt or Redeem Property

In this chapter we consider how the bankruptcy trustee liquidates the property of the estate in an asset case in order to generate a distribution of proceeds to the unsecured creditors. We will learn the order of priority in which creditors receive that distribution. There are a number of ways that Chapter 7 debtors can manage to retain possession of property in which the debtor has granted a creditor a security interest notwithstanding the bankruptcy case and we will examine those in depth.

Key Concepts

- In liquidating property of the estate the bankruptcy trustee may sell property by public or private sale, may obtain authority to sell encumbered property free and clear of liens, or may abandon property of no value to the estate
- Allowed claims against the estate are paid by the trustee in an established order of priority
- The debtor may be permitted by the court to reaffirm a debt in bankruptcy rather than discharge it or may redeem collateralized property by paying the value of the collateral to the secured creditor
- In some districts the debtor may be able to retain collateral by ride through without court approval or to strip down the balance owed on a secured claim to the collateral's then-current value

A. LIQUIDATING PROPERTY OF THE ESTATE

In a Chapter 7 asset case, the trustee will liquidate non-exempt property of the estate and distribute the proceeds in an order of priority we consider in Section B, below. First, we consider how the trustee liquidates the property of the estate. Of course, if the trustee determines the filing to be a no-asset case and

373

files a no-asset report, that means there is no non-exempt property to liquidate and the case will be closed quickly.

1. Abandonment of Property of the Estate

If a timely objection to the debtor's claimed Schedule C exemptions is not made, that property is **deemed abandoned** by the trustee and the estate has no further interest in it.

Pursuant to §554 and FRBP 6007, the trustee can abandon any other property of the estate that is

- Of inconsequential value to the estate or
- Burdensome to the estate.

Abandonment of Secured Property

The most common example of abandonment arises in connection with property in which a security interest has been granted. If the security interest is perfected and the trustee cannot avoid it as considered in the last chapter, the secured claim will be allowed under §502. And if there is no equity for the estate in the collateralized property (i.e., the amount of the allowed claim equals or exceeds the value of the collateral), that property is of no value to the estate and will be abandoned to the creditor. If the value of the collateral abandoned to the creditor is equal to the full amount of the allowed claim, the claim of the creditor is fully satisfied by that abandonment. On the other hand, if the value of the abandoned collateral is insufficient to satisfy the full amount of the allowed claim (i.e., the creditor is undersecured or partially secured), the creditor's claim is bifurcated pursuant to §506(a)(1). The trustee will abandon the collateral to the undersecured creditor in full satisfaction of the secured portion of the creditor's bifurcated claim. But the creditor still has a general unsecured claim (as opposed to a priority unsecured claim) for the balance owed in excess of the value of the collateral.

If there is equity for the estate in the collateralized property (i.e., the creditor is oversecured; the value of the property exceeds the amount owed), the trustee will usually not abandon the property to the creditor. Instead, the trustee will sell the property himself, pay the creditor the full amount of his allowed secured claim from the proceeds (which may include postpetition interest and fees per §506(b) as we saw in Chapter Eight, Section E), and will then include the excess proceeds of the sale in the property of the estate available to other creditors.

Abandonment of Other Property of the Estate

Any property of the estate may be abandoned by the trustee whether it is collateral for a security interest or not, if the trustee concludes that it is burdensome to the estate.

For example, assume the property of the estate includes a claim the debtor has made against a local clothes cleaning business alleging that the cleaner lost a shirt worth $20. The cleaner denies liability on the claim and refuses to settle. The trustee may conclude that it will cost the estate more to litigate that small claim than it is worth and abandon the claim as burdensome to the estate.

Procedure for Abandonment

Section 554 abandonment is governed by the Code's "after notice and a hearing" procedure (discussed in Chapter Four, Section F), which means the trustee must give notice to all parties in interest of his intent to abandon and a hearing is conducted only if an objection is made within 14 days following notice. A notice of intent to abandon property filed by the trustee in Marta Carlson's case is seen in Document 34 in the Carlson case file.

Recall that in Chapter Six, Section B, we learned that an individual Chapter 7 debtor must file a statement of intent with regard to property in which a security interest has been granted, indicating whether debtor will surrender that property to the secured creditor or seek to retain it. If the debtor does indicate an intent to surrender collateralized property, the secured creditor must still await the trustee's decision as to whether to abandon that property as having no benefit to the estate or to assert an interest in it for the benefit of the estate as by avoiding the creditor's security interest or lien as we considered in the last chapter or by contending that there is equity in the property for the estate (i.e., it is worth more than the amount owed the creditor). And even if the trustee does decide to abandon, the secured creditor must also take appropriate action to have the automatic stay of §362 lifted per the procedures discussed in Chapter Seven, Section F.

As a practical matter, the trustee will make the decision as to whether to abandon collateralized property or challenge the lien at or shortly after the first meeting of creditors. By then the individual Chapter 7 debtor will have filed his or her statement of intent with regard to the property so the intent to surrender the property or not will be known to all parties. Some secured creditors will await the decision of the debtor and trustee regarding surrender and abandonment before filing a motion to lift stay while others will file a motion to lift stay as soon as the petition is filed and they receive notice of the case filing.

2. The Sale of Property Free and Clear of Liens

When a creditor has a perfected security interest in some property of the estate but there is still equity (dollar value of the property in excess of the claim that it secures) for the estate in that property (i.e., the creditor is oversecured), the trustee may seek permission from the court to sell the property free and clear of liens, pursuant to §363(f) and FRBP 6004(c). The property is sold and the security interest then attaches to the proceeds of sale up to the amount of the secured claim. Permission for a sale free and clear of liens is obtained by filing a motion subject to the "after notice and a hearing" procedure.

For example, recall from the Assignment Memorandum in Appendix A that Marta Carlson has two mortgages on her home, one in favor of Capital Savings Bank (CSB) with a balance of $142,500 and one in favor of Dreams Come True

Finance Company (DCT) with a balance of $37,500. In her Schedule C (Document 8 in the Carlson case file) Marta has claimed a homestead exemption of $11,825 in the home. No objection has been filed to these secured claims or to Marta's claimed exemption amount. The home has appraised for $255,000 and the trustee has filed a motion for permission to sell the home free and clear of liens (Document 37 in the Carlson case file). If permission is granted by the court and the sale brings the full $255,000, the proceeds will be distributed as follows: the realtor's 6 percent fee ($15,300) as an administrative expense; $142,500 to pay off CSB; $37,500 to pay off DCT; $11,875 to Marta for her exemption; and the balance of $47,875 will go to the estate. But by order of the court, that sale will terminate the liens of CSB and DCT in the property, as well as Marta's exemption in it. It is a sale free and clear of liens.

Pursuant to §524(e), discharge of a debt in bankruptcy does not also discharge any non-bankruptcy party who might be liable on the debt, such as a guarantor. Thus when property of the state is sold free and clear of liens, that sale will have no effect on the remaining liability of any nonbankruptcy guarantor of the debt. See, e.g., In re Applewood Chair Co., 203 F.3d 914 (5th Cir. 2000) (sale of property pursuant to bankruptcy court's order approving sale has no effect on guarantor's liability).

For example, assume Marta's brother, who is not in bankruptcy, had guaranteed the debt Marta owed to DCT secured by her home and the guaranty agreement contained an "other indebtedness clause" covering not only the secured indebtedness on the home but the second unsecured obligation as well. Assume Marta had a second unsecured obligation to DCT at the time of her bankruptcy in the amount of $7,000. Marta will discharge that second unsecured debt to DCT in her Chapter 7 bankruptcy case but per §524(e) her brother will not be relieved of his obligation as guarantor on that debt. DCT may still pursue him on that obligation to collect. Assume further that following her discharge in bankruptcy (in which Marta will have discharged all her then existing obligations to DCT) Marta borrows $5,000 from DCT to purchase a used car. Again, per §524(e), Marta's brother will be liable as a guarantor on the $5,000. Nothing that happened in Marta's bankruptcy case, including the sale of the home that secured one of her debts to DCT that her brother had guaranteed, will discharge his obligations to DCT on the guaranty. State guaranty law may have something to say about his continuing obligation as guarantor, but bankruptcy law will not.

Section 363(k) preserves the right of a creditor secured in the property to be sold in the bankruptcy case to bid on the property at the sale and in doing so to receive credit against the purchase price for the amount of its unpaid claim, a practice known as **credit-bidding** (or **bidding in**).

For example, if Marta's trustee receives permission to sell her home free and clear of liens, either or both of the secured creditors have the right under §363(k) to bid at the sale. If CSB chose to credit-bid at the sale and the amount of its winning bid was $151,050 (an amount equal to the $142,500 balance owed to it, plus $8,550 representing the 6 percent realtor's fee), CSB would only have to pay cash in the amount of $8,550 because the amount CSB is owed is credited against the bid amount.

The Code gives a secured creditor this right as a means of assuring that the property is not sold at a price less than what is owed to the creditor. After all, the sale is going to extinguish the creditor's security interest in the property.

For example, if a third party appears at the sale and bids in at the $255,000 appraised value, then neither CSB nor DCT is likely to bid—the sale will bring enough to satisfy both their claims. But what if the high bid by a third party at the sale is only $125,000? If that bid is accepted, CSB is going to receive only a portion of what it is owed and DCT, whose lien on the property is junior to CSB's, will get nothing. So both CSB and DCT will likely be ready to credit-bid as necessary to protect their respective interests.

Application Exercise 1

What would DCT have to do to protect itself if this scenario played out? A third party bids $125,000 for the property. CSB then enters a credit-bid in the amount of $151,050 to protect its interest in the property. But that bid by CSB will not result in DCT's receiving anything and its second mortgage will be wiped out by the sale. If it wants to protect itself, then it will need to bid an amount in excess of CSB's bid, and it will only receive credit against the amount owed for the balance owed to it (i.e., it will actually have to pay enough to satisfy CSB's senior claim plus the realtor's fee). What practical considerations would go into DCT's decision to do this in order to acquire the property?

The Application Exercise and the two examples preceding it are offered to show how credit-bidding works but present unlikely scenarios in the real world. A trustee will not seek to sell property unless the trustee is confident that there is equity in the property for the estate over and above all administrative expenses of sale, all perfected liens on the property, and any exemption amount due the debtor. To assure that result, the trustee's auction sale will likely not be an absolute sale (high bid takes title regardless of amount) but will instead be conducted as a reserve sale (high bid will not be accepted unless it meets a minimum amount decided by the trustee).

3. The Sale of Other Property of the Estate

Section 363(b)(1) and FRBP 6004(a) permit the trustee to notice his intent to sell other property of the estate "after notice and a hearing." No hearing will be conducted unless an objection is filed not less than five days before the date of the proposed sale per FRBP 6004(b). If an objection is filed, it becomes a contested matter and a hearing will be conducted.

The sale of property of the estate can be accomplished by public or private sale. FRBP 2002(c) requires that the notice of a proposed sale, use, or lease of property include:

- The time and place of a public sale;
- The terms and conditions of a private sale; and
- The time fixed for filing objections.

A public sale is by auction, properly advertised and usually conducted by an auctioneer retained as a professional, pursuant to §327 and FRBP 2014. If the order authorizing the hiring of the professional person did not specifically approve the manner of his compensation, the trustee must obtain court approval for that compensation before paying the professional from the assets of the estate.

Application Exercise 2

Look at the motion for authorization to hire real estate appraiser filed by the trustee in Marta Carlson's case (Document 29 in the Carlson case file) and the order granting that motion (Document 30 in the Carlson case file). Did the trustee properly obtain permission in that motion and order to compensate the appraiser from estate funds?

Section 363 and other sections of the Code deal with other ways the bankruptcy trustee may need to utilize property of the estate, some of which include:

- Operating an ongoing business of the debtor;
- Leasing estate property; or
- Pledging property of the estate as collateral to raise cash or obtain credit.

These options can be utilized in a Chapter 7 consumer case, though it is uncommon. For example, if Marta Carlson owned a rental house that the trustee planned to liquidate but a realtor advised waiting six months until the area real estate market improved, the trustee might choose to lease the house for that six months.

Liquidating Property of the Estate via the Internet

Bankruptcy trustees are increasingly using the Internet to liquidate property of the estate. The trustee's notice of intent to sell will have to disclose that means of public sale. To learn more, go to www .marketassetsforsale.com/index. cfm and note the kinds of property being offered for sale by bankruptcy trustees around the country. See if you can find a property listing for a case pending in the federal district where you plan to practice.

4. Continuing Operation of a Business Debtor as Part of the Liquidation

When an ongoing business, or an individual debtor who owns an ongoing business, files for Chapter 7 liquidation, the bankruptcy trustee may determine that it is in the best interest of the creditors to continue operating the business for a certain period of time postpetition in order to maximize the value of the property of the estate and the ultimate payout to creditors. It is unusual for this to occur in a Chapter 7 liquidation but §721 of the Code authorizes the trustee to seek court permission to operate the business postpetition for this purpose.

When a liquidating business does continue to operate postpetition under Chapter 7, there are a number of operational motions that will need to be made to deal with matters such as using property of the estate postpetition, which could put that property at risk of deterioration or loss; using property — such as cash — postpetition in which a security interest has been given to one or more creditors; obtaining postpetition financing, thus increasing the total indebtedness of the business; and so on. These operational concerns are similar to those that routinely arise in a Chapter 11 reorganization in which the business debtor is not liquidating but continuing to operate under the postpetition protection of the Code. We will not consider these operational concerns since consumer bankruptcy is the focus of our study.

B. DISTRIBUTION OF THE ESTATE TO CREDITORS AND THEIR ORDER OF PRIORITY

Once the bankruptcy trustee has liquidated the other property of the estate, including the settlement of allowed secured claims as discussed in the last section, the proceeds will be distributed to pay administrative expenses of the case and claims of creditors in a certain order of priority. Administrative expenses are defined in §503(b)(1)(A) as "the actual, necessary costs and expenses of preserving the estate, including wages, salaries, or commissions for services rendered after the commencement of the case" and include:

- The trustee's fee;
- Fees of professionals hired by the trustee;
- Certain taxes incurred by the estate;
- "Actual and necessary" costs and expenses of preserving the estate, which can include wages, salaries, and commissions incurred after the commencement of the case; and
- "Actual and necessary" expenses incurred by creditors who file an involuntary petition in the case or who, with court permission, recover property for the estate transferred or concealed by the debtor.

Section 507 establishes an order of priority for various administrative expenses and other claims. Section 726 then mandates the particular order in which distributions on claims not secured by property of the estate are to be made by the Chapter 7 trustee. Secured claims have the highest priority to the extent of the value of the collateral per §506(a)(1). See also Hartford Underwriters Ins. Co. v. Union Planters Bank, 530 U.S. 1, 5 (2000), and United Sav. Assn. of Tex. v. Timbers of Inwood Forest Associates, Ltd., 484 U.S. 365, 378-379 (1988). Section 507 **priority claims** (see itemization of such claims in Part B of Exhibit 10.1) have the next priority followed by the claims of general unsecured creditors, and then certain miscellaneous claims. Exhibit 10.1 summarizes the order of distribution mandated by the Code.

Each class of claims listed in Exhibit 10.1 is entitled to be paid in full before the next class in priority receives anything. For example, if all property of the estate is subject to a properly perfected security interests, no other claims will be paid. If all the available uncollateralized assets are exhausted in paying $507 priority claims, general unsecured creditors will receive nothing. If all available assets are exhausted paying priority and general unsecured claims that were timely filed, general unsecured claims not timely filed will receive nothing.

EXHIBIT 10.1   **Order of Priority for Creditor Claims**

A. Secured claims
    1) Allowed fully secured or oversecured claims are satisfied entirely out of the secured property up to its value, per §§506(a) and (b)
    2) Allowed partially secured (undersecured) claims are satisfied out of the secured property up to the value of the secured property and the deficiency is treated as a general unsecured claim, per §506(a)(1)

B. Section 507 priority claims
    1) The bankruptcy trustee's fee and expenses attributable to payment of domestic support obligations of the debtor, per §507(a)(1)(C)
    2) Domestic support obligations of the debtor, per §507(a)(1)(A)
    3) Administrative expenses authorized by §503(b), per §507(a)(2)
    4) Allowed §502(f) unsecured claims arising in an involuntary case between the time the petition is filed and the time the trustee is appointed (called the **gap period**), per §507(a)(3)
    5) Claims for employee's wages, salaries, or commissions and some benefits earned within 180 days prior to the filing of the petition not to exceed $10,000 per claim, per §507(a)(4)
    6) Claims for unpaid contributions to any employee benefit plan arising from services rendered within 180 days prior to filing of the petition not to exceed $10,000 per claim, per §507(a)(5)
    7) Certain farmer and fishermen claims up to $10,000 each, per §507(a)(6)
    8) Prepetition deposits of money for the lease or purchase of real property or consumer services up to $2,225 per claimant, per §507(a)(7)
    9) Various tax claims including income and property taxes assessed at varying times before the petition was filed, per §507(a)(8)
   10) Certain claims arising out of federal depository insurance, per §507(a)(9)
   11) Personal injury or wrongful death claims arising out of DUI, per §507(a)(10)

C. General (i.e., nonpriority) unsecured claims, per §726, including deficiency claims of partially secured creditors whose collateral was insufficient to cover the entire debt per §506(a)(1)
    1) General unsecured claims timely filed, per §726(a)(2)
    2) General unsecured claims untimely filed, per §726(a)(3)

D. Claims for fines, penalties, forfeiture, or punitive damages other than compensation for actual pecuniary loss, per §726(a)(4)

E. Interest at the legal rate on priority and general unsecured claims, per §726(a)(5)

F. Remaining surplus, if any, returned to debtor, per §726(a)(6)

Within a particular class of claims not involving secured claims, the distribution will be *pro rata*. For example, assume the trustee has $10,000 available to distribute to general unsecured claimants. But there is a total of $100,000 owed to all the creditors in that classification. The distribution will be *pro rata*, with each unsecured creditor receiving ten cents on the dollar for its claim regardless of whether their claim was larger or smaller than others in the same class. The holder of a $10 claim will receive $1 and the holder of a $100 claim will receive $10.

A general unsecured debt that is not dischargeable (non-dischargeable claims are discussed in the next chapter) still participates in the distribution under §726. For example, the educational loans that Marta Carlson owes to Columbiana Federal Savings & Loan, in the amount of $5,000, and Capital City Bank (CCB), in the amount of $10,000, are unsecured nonpriority but non-dischargeable debts. Even though Marta cannot discharge those debts and will remain liable for them, those creditors will participate with other general unsecured creditors in any distribution to that class of creditors.

Section 510 provides for the **subordination** of a claim to others of equal rank under certain circumstances. Section 510(a) provides that a prepetition **subordination agreement** will be enforced in bankruptcy if it is otherwise valid under non-bankruptcy law. A subordination agreement is most commonly used where the owner of property needs to refinance property on which there is an existing mortgage. The new lender will not agree to loan funds unless the existing mortgagee agrees to take a second or junior position to the new lender, who will take a first mortgage position in the property after it makes the loan.

Why would the original mortgagee voluntarily agree to subordinate its mortgage position to the new lender? Well, if the owner/mortgagor is in arrears on its payments to the original mortgagee, the original mortgagee might have a lot to gain by allowing the refinancing even though it gives up its priority position (i.e., the deficiencies get paid off and future payments are more likely due to the refinancing). Often, to induce the original mortgagee to agree to the subordination, the pot is sweetened in some way (e.g., by increasing the interest rate on that obligation).

The court may order involuntary **equitable subordination** of all or part of a creditor's claim pursuant to §510(c). Equitable subordination is most typically exercised where the creditor has engaged in inequitable or dishonest conduct that resulted in unfair advantage to him or prejudice to other creditors.

For example, assume a creditor holding a senior security interest in property of the estate misrepresents the value of its secured claim to a creditor holding a junior secured position in the same property. If that misrepresentation causes the junior creditor to be prejudiced in some way, the court may order the senior claim equitably subordinated to the junior claim.

C. THE DEBTOR'S RIGHT TO RETAIN PROPERTY IN A CHAPTER 7 CASE: REAFFIRMATION, REDEMPTION, EXEMPTION, RIDE THROUGH, AND LIEN STRIPPING

1. The Reaffirmation Agreement

Recall from Chapter Six, Section B, that the individual Chapter 7 debtor must file Form 108, Statement of Intention by Individual Chapter 7 Debtor, indicating debtor's intent with regard to his or her secured property. One option is to surrender the collateral to the secured creditor and discharge the balance of the debt.

Another option, provided by §524(c) of the Code, permits a Chapter 7 debtor to agree with the creditor to retain the collateral and reaffirm the secured debt. The typical example of a debt that the debtor is eager to reaffirm rather than to discharge is one that is secured by property that the debtor needs to keep, such as a home or car in which there is no equity or in which debtor can exempt the equity on Schedule C.

For example, assume that a Chapter 7 debtor owns a car that is worth $6,000 and on which he owes $6,500 to the creditor who holds a security interest in it. There is no equity in the car for the debtor to exempt and no equity for the estate either since the creditor's secured claim against the car exceeds its value. The trustee will abandon this property for the estate. The debtor could allow the creditor to repossess the car and discharge the $6,500 debt he owes the creditor. But the debtor needs a car, and would like to keep this one. The debtor may therefore enter into a reaffirmation agreement with the creditor in which debtor agrees to remain legally liable for the debt following the discharge in bankruptcy.

Application Exercise 3

Do you see the risk to the debtor in reaffirming a debt that he could discharge in the Chapter 7? If debtor reaffirms this debt and then receives a discharge in bankruptcy, how long will it be before debtor can file another Chapter 7 proceeding? If, following the reaffirmation and the discharge, the debtor defaults on payments to the still-secured creditor, what rights does the creditor have against the debtor?

Debtors may choose to reaffirm a dischargeable debt in the full amount owed and according to the original terms of the obligation. Or they may negotiate with the creditor to reaffirm only a portion of the balance owed or on more favorable terms (e.g., lower monthly payments, longer amortization, or lower interest rate). You can understand why unsecured creditors facing the possibility of a full discharge of the obligation owed to them would be amenable to such compromise in order to obtain a reaffirmation.

It is important that the individual debtor seeking to reaffirm a secured debt indicate his or her intention to retain the property by reaffirming on the statement of intent. If the debtor's original statement of intent indicated the intent to surrender the collateralized property and the debtor later decides to reaffirm the debt and keep the property, the statement of intent must be amended.

Section 524(c) requires that in order to reaffirm a debt the debtor and creditor must enter into a written **reaffirmation agreement**. The bankruptcy court must review the agreement and has the power to disapprove it. The reaffirmation agreement will provide that the debtor will remain liable and pay all or a portion of the money owed, even though the debt would otherwise be discharged in the bankruptcy. In return, the creditor promises that it will not repossess or take back the automobile or other property so long as the debtor continues to pay the debt.

For example, recall that Marta Carlson owes Shears Department Store $900 and the debt is secured by her washer and dryer, worth only $600 together. Marta would like to reaffirm her debt to Shears in order to keep her washer and dryer. Although Marta claimed an exemption in the washer and dryer in her Schedule C (Document 8 in the Carlson case file) under §522(d)(3), that alone will not entitle her to keep possession of that property since she has given Shears a security interest in the washer and dryer. So Marta decides to enter a reaffirmation agreement with Shears, promising to pay the entire indebtedness in exchange for Shears allowing her to keep the washer and dryer. That reaffirmation agreement is set out in Exhibit 10.2 (and Document 36 in the Carlson case file). The court still has to approve the agreement.

The procedure for obtaining the approval of a reaffirmation agreement set out in §524(c) and FRBP 4008 is quite complex. Section 524(c) says that the reaffirmation agreement must be entered into before the discharge is entered by the court in order to be valid and that the agreement must be signed by the parties and filed with the court. But FRBP 4008 supplements the time frame of the statute by requiring that the signed reaffirmation agreement be filed with the court within 60 days following the 341 meeting. Section 524(k) requires that a reaffirmation agreement contain an extensive set of disclosures. Among other things, the agreement must advise the debtor of the amount of the debt being reaffirmed and how it is calculated, and that reaffirmation means that the debtor's personal liability for that debt will not be discharged in the bankruptcy.

The disclosures also require the debtor to sign and file a statement of his or her current income and expenses that shows that the balance of income available after paying living expenses is sufficient to pay the reaffirmed debt. If the balance is not enough to pay the debt to be reaffirmed, there is a **presumption of undue hardship**, and the court may decide not to approve the reaffirmation agreement. If the court is inclined to disapprove the reaffirmation agreement because the presumption of hardship is present or for any other reason, the court must conduct a hearing and give the debtor and creditor an opportunity to overcome the presumption of undue hardship or to otherwise convince the court that the agreement is in the debtor's best interest.

EXHIBIT 10.2   **Reaffirmation Agreement between Marta Carlson and Shears Department Store**

Form 2400A (12/15)

Check one.
- ☐ **Presumption of Undue Hardship**
- ☑ **No Presumption of Undue Hardship**

See Debtor's Statement in Support of Reaffirmation, Part II below, to determine which box to check.

UNITED STATES BANKRUPTCY COURT

District of Minnesota

In re Marta Rinaldi Carlson
_____,
                    Debtor

Case No. 16-7-XXXX

Chapter 7

REAFFIRMATION DOCUMENTS

Name of Creditor: Shears Department Store _____

☐ Check this box if Creditor is a Credit Union

PART I. REAFFIRMATION AGREEMENT

Reaffirming a debt is a serious financial decision. Before entering into this Reaffirmation Agreement, you must review the important disclosures, instructions, and definitions found in Part V of this form.

A. Brief description of the original agreement being reaffirmed: Appliance purchase agreement _____

For example, auto loan

B. ***AMOUNT REAFFIRMED***: $_____ 900.00

> The Amount Reaffirmed is the entire amount that you are agreeing to pay. This may include unpaid principal, interest, and fees and costs (if any) arising on or before   07/07/2016   , which is the date of the Disclosure Statement portion of this form (Part V).

> *See the definition of "Amount Reaffirmed" in Part V, Section C below.*

C. The ***ANNUAL PERCENTAGE RATE*** applicable to the Amount Reaffirmed is   6.5000 %.

> *See definition of "Annual Percentage Rate" in Part V, Section C below.*

> This is a *(check one)* ☑ Fixed rate   ☐ Variable rate

If the loan has a variable rate, the future interest rate may increase or decrease from the Annual Percentage Rate disclosed here.

EXHIBIT 10.2 (Continued)

Form 2400A, Reaffirmation Documents   Page 2

D. Reaffirmation Agreement Repayment Terms *(check and complete one)*:

☑ $ __45.00__ per month for ___20___ months starting on __08/01/2016__ .

☐   Describe repayment terms, including whether future payment amount(s) may be different from the initial payment amount.

E. Describe the collateral, if any, securing the debt:

> Description: Shears washer and dryer
> Current Market Value $_____ 600.00

F. Did the debt that is being reaffirmed arise from the purchase of the collateral described above?

☑ Yes. What was the purchase price for the collateral? $_____ 1,200.00

☐ No. What was the amount of the original loan? $_____

G. Specify the changes made by this Reaffirmation Agreement to the most recent credit terms on the reaffirmed debt and any related agreement:

	Terms as of the Date of Bankruptcy	Terms After Reaffirmation
Balance due *(including fees and costs)*	$ 900.00	$ 900.00
Annual Percentage Rate	6.5000 %	6.5000 %
Monthly Payment	$ 45.00	$ 45.00

H. ☐   Check this box if the creditor is agreeing to provide you with additional future credit in connection with this Reaffirmation Agreement. Describe the credit limit, the Annual Percentage Rate that applies to future credit and any other terms on future purchases and advances using such credit:

PART II.   DEBTOR'S STATEMENT IN SUPPORT OF REAFFIRMATION AGREEMENT

A. Were you represented by an attorney during the course of negotiating this agreement?

Check one. ☐ Yes   ☑ No

B. Is the creditor a credit union?

Check one. ☐ Yes   ☑ No

EXHIBIT 10.2 **(Continued)**

Form 2400A, Reaffirmation Documents   Page 3

C. If your answer to EITHER question A. or B. above is "No," complete 1. and 2. below.

1.   Your present monthly income and expenses are:

a. Monthly income from all sources after payroll deductions
(take-home pay plus any other income) $ 3,888.00

b. Monthly expenses (including all reaffirmed debts except
this one) $ 3,550.00

c. Amount available to pay this reaffirmed debt (subtract b. from a.) $ 338.00

d. Amount of monthly payment required for this reaffirmed debt $ 45.00

If the monthly payment on this reaffirmed debt (line d.) **is greater than** *the amount you have available to pay this reaffirmed debt (line c.), you must check the box at the top of page one that says "Presumption of Undue Hardship." Otherwise, you must check the box at the top of page one that says "No Presumption of Undue Hardship."*

2.   You believe that this reaffirmation agreement will not impose an undue hardship on you or your dependents because:

Check one of the two statements below, if applicable:

☑   You can afford to make the payments on the reaffirmed debt because your monthly income is greater than your monthly expenses even after you include in your expenses the monthly payments on all debts you are reaffirming, including this one.

☐   You can afford to make the payments on the reaffirmed debt even though your monthly income is less than your monthly expenses after you include in your expenses the monthly payments on all debts you are reaffirming, including this one, because:

Use an additional page if needed for a full explanation.

D. If your answers to BOTH questions A. and B. above were "Yes," check the following statement, if applicable:

☐   You believe this Reaffirmation Agreement is in your financial interest and you can afford to make the payments on the reaffirmed debt.

Also, check the box at the top of page one that says "No Presumption of Undue Hardship."

EXHIBIT 10.2 **(Continued)**

Form 2400A, Reaffirmation Documents   Page 4

PART III. CERTIFICATION BY DEBTOR(S) AND SIGNATURES OF PARTIES

I hereby certify that:

(1)   I agree to reaffirm the debt described above.

(2)   Before signing this Reaffirmation Agreement, I read the terms disclosed in this Reaffirmation Agreement (Part I) and the Disclosure Statement, Instructions and Definitions included in Part V below;

(3)   The Debtor's Statement in Support of Reaffirmation Agreement (Part II above) is true and complete;

(4)   I am entering into this agreement voluntarily and am fully informed of my rights and responsibilities; and

(5)   I have received a copy of this completed and signed Reaffirmation Documents form.

SIGNATURE(S) (If this is a joint Reaffirmation Agreement, both debtors must sign.):

Date ___07/07/2016___   Signature _/s/ Marta Rinaldi Carlson_____
                                                                Debtor
Date _____   Signature _____
                                                          Joint Debtor, if any

Reaffirmation Agreement Terms Accepted by Creditor:

Creditor _Shears Department Store_____   _411 Woodlands Place, Roseville, MN. 55113___
                          Print Name   *Address*

Martha Adkins, Regional Credit Mgr.   _/s/ Martha Adkins_____   _07/07/2016____
        Print Name of Representative   *Signature*   *Date*

PART IV. CERTIFICATION BY DEBTOR'S ATTORNEY (IF ANY)

To be filed only if the attorney represented the debtor during the course of negotiating this agreement.

I hereby certify that: (1) this agreement represents a fully informed and voluntary agreement by the debtor; (2) this agreement does not impose an undue hardship on the debtor or any dependent of the debtor; and (3) I have fully advised the debtor of the legal effect and consequences of this agreement and any default under this agreement.

☐ A presumption of undue hardship has been established with respect to this agreement. In my opinion, however, the debtor is able to make the required payment.

Check box, if the presumption of undue hardship box is checked on page 1 and the creditor is not a Credit Union.

Date _____   Signature of Debtor's Attorney_____

                         Print Name of Debtor's Attorney _____

As curious as it may sound, it is not unusual for the debtor's attorney to abstain from representing the debtor in connection with a reaffirmation agreement. This is so because if the attorney chooses to represent her client in connection with the agreement, the attorney must certify in writing that she advised the debtor of the legal effect and consequences of the agreement, including a default under the agreement. The attorney must also certify that the debtor was fully informed and voluntarily entered into the agreement and that reaffirmation of the debt will not create an undue hardship for the debtor or the debtor's dependents. It is no small thing for a debtor with a history of severe financial problems to reaffirm a debt that he could discharge in bankruptcy. There may be disagreements between the debtor and the attorney regarding whether it is in the best interests of the debtor to reaffirm. Even if it appears to be at the time, it may not turn out well if the debtor reaffirms, then defaults later and can no longer discharge the debt. The attorney who has certified that reaffirmation will not create an undue hardship for the debtor could face malpractice charges if it does.

If the debtor who enters the reaffirmation agreement and files it with the court is not represented by counsel in connection with the agreement, a hearing on the proposed reaffirmation agreement will be held, and the bankruptcy judge will decide whether to approve the agreement. However, in many districts, if the debtor is represented by an attorney in connection with the reaffirmation agreement, and the presumption of undue hardship is not present, the reaffirmation agreement may become effective without court approval. Even if the debtor is represented by counsel, if the presumption of hardship arises in connection with the proposed reaffirmation agreement, a hearing will be held and the judge will decide whether the reaffirmation is in the best interests of the debtor.

Application Exercise 4

Look at Marta Carlson's reaffirmation agreement with Shears again. Did the presumption of hardship arise in connection with that agreement? Check the local rules of the bankruptcy court in the district where you plan to practice. If Marta was a debtor in that court, would a hearing be needed on her reaffirmation agreement?

Some bankruptcy judges are reluctant to allow debtors to reaffirm debts absent a showing of real need. For example, if a debtor wanted to reaffirm debts on three different vehicles when he needed only one or two for personal and business purposes, many judges would limit the debtor to the one or two vehicles needed. And reaffirming a debt on that recreational Jet Ski or bass boat? The debtor and the lawyer recommending reaffirmation of such debts should be prepared to be lectured by these judges on the inadvisability of coming out of bankruptcy with such debts.

Sometimes debtors see reaffirmation as a way to salvage their credit history or their relationship with a particular creditor, even though it is not essential to do so and the obligation is unsecured by any property of the debtor.

For example, a debtor may have a long-standing credit account with a local or national department store where the debtor likes to shop. Even though the balance owed the department store is unsecured and the debtor could discharge it, the debtor chooses to reaffirm the debt just to keep the credit account with the department store in good standing.

Of course, a debtor who has received a discharge may repay any debt voluntarily whether or not a reaffirmation agreement exists and this does sometimes occur.

For example, a debtor may formally discharge a debt arising from a family loan but still feel a moral obligation to pay the debt. The creditor whose debt has been discharged will not be able to sue or otherwise take action to collect that debt; it has been discharged.

2. The Right to Redeem Personal Property

Another option available to the Chapter 7 debtor to retain secured property arises from §722, which allows an individual consumer debtor in Chapter 7 the right to redeem tangible personal property (not realty) intended primarily for personal, family, or household use (consumer property) from a lien securing such property where the property has been claimed as exempt by the debtor under §522 or has been abandoned by the trustee under §554.

This **right of redemption** is exercised by the debtor paying the amount of the allowed secured claim to the creditor. Recall that §506(a)(1) provides that a secured creditor's claim is only a secured claim up to the value of the collateral. The creditor's claim is unsecured (and probably dischargeable) as to all amounts owed over that value. The value of personal property securing a claim for purposes of determining the secured portion of the claim is defined in §506(a)(2), added by BAP-CPA, as the replacement value of the goods on the date the petition is filed without deduction for sale or marketing costs. For goods acquired for personal, family, or household purposes (consumer goods), such as those subject to §722 redemption, replacement value means *the price a retail merchant would charge for property of that kind, given its age and condition.*

For example, Marta Carlson owes Shears Department Store $900 and the debt is secured by her washer and dryer, which she values at only $600 together. In her Schedule C (Document 8 in the Carlson file), she has exempted the total $600 value of the washer and dryer from any claim of the trustee. The trustee has abandoned this property for the estate because there is no equity in it since both Shears' lien and Marta's claimed exemption in the property are superior to trustee's claim (see Document 34 in the Carlson case file). It is tangible consumer property within the meaning of §722 since it is property used for personal, family, or household purposes. As an alternative to reaffirming her debt to Shears, Marta could seek to redeem this property from the lien by paying the debtor the full amount of the allowed secured claim.

Before There Was BAPCPA There Was *Rash*

Prior to BAPCPA's addition of the new §506(a)(2), the Supreme Court had adopted the replacement value rule in Associates Commercial Corp. v. Rash, 520 U.S. 953 (1997). *Rash* rejected the debtor's argument that the present value of the collateral under §506(a)(1) should be the liquidation or foreclosure value of the property, which is essentially what the property would sell for in a rushed, even emergency, situation, likely to produce far less than its retail value. So the replacement value of the washer and dryer that Marta Carlson might like to redeem from the lien of Shears would be not what a consumer would sell it for in a garage sale, and not what a consumer who needed quick cash would sell it for to a neighbor or friend, and not what it would be sold for wholesale, but instead what a retail merchant would ask for it given its present age and condition. Do you see how the latter value is likely to be higher than the others? Those interested in the history of bankruptcy practice might want to read *Rash* to understand why BAPCPA did what it did on this issue and to understand that the debtor's argument in *Rash* was by no means unreasonable.

In actual practice, the codification of the *Rash* replacement value rule in §506(a)(2) is highly beneficial to the secured creditor and has made it more difficult for Chapter 7 consumer debtors to utilize the §722 right of redemption in consumer property. Some debtors can exempt enough cash to redeem an automobile of modest value. Some are able to borrow from relatives or friends. And

But Shears may not agree that Marta's valuation of the washer and dryer at $600 is accurate. Shears may contend that the value she has placed on the washer and dryer is the liquidation value of the property but not the replacement value, which is the required valuation under §506(a)(2). The court may have to decide the valuation dispute. If the court does find the replacement value of the washer and dryer to be less than the full amount of the debt ($900) and Marta can exempt that value in her Schedule C, then Marta can redeem the property by paying Shears that replacement value. The balance owed to Shears becomes an unsecured claim that can be discharged if there are insufficient non-exempt assets in the estate available to pay it. Of course, Marta will have to come up with the $600 or other dollar amount determined to be the replacement value of the collateral to pay Shears and that may be difficult for someone already in bankruptcy.

As with the intent to reaffirm a debt, the individual debtor's intent to redeem collateralized property must be noted on debtor's statement of intent.

3. Debtor's Right to Avoid Liens Impairing an Exemption

In Chapter Six, Section B, we learned that an individual debtor can exempt certain real and personal property from the bankruptcy trustee. In most situations, however, an exemption cannot prevail over a perfected security interest of a creditor in the property sought to be exempted. Thus exemptions are mostly claimed in unsecured property. However, §522(f)(1)(A) of the Code empowers the individual debtor to avoid a judicial lien on his property to the extent that the lien impairs an exemption the debtor would otherwise have in the property. Judicial liens are defined by §101(36) as liens obtained by judgment, levy sequestration, or other legal or equitable process and include prejudgment remedies such as prejudgment attachment as well as the postjudgment execution remedies we considered in Chapter Three.

For example, assume that an individual Chapter 7 debtor owns a residence worth $200,000 that is encumbered by a mortgage in favor of the bank in the amount of $150,000. If the jurisdiction allows the debtor a $30,000 homestead exemption, then there would be only $20,000 in non-exempt equity in the residence. If another creditor of the debtor had taken a prepetition final judgment against the debtor in the amount of $40,000 and filed a judgment lien against the debtor's residence in that amount, once the debtor files in Chapter 7 he can avoid $20,000 of that judgment lien on the residence, the amount by which the judgment lien impairs his exemption based on the value of the property.

Section 522(f)(1)(A) prohibits a judicial lien resulting from a domestic support obligation (child support, alimony, or maintenance recoverable by a spouse, former spouse, or child of the debtor) from being avoided by the debtor.

Section 522(f)(1)(B) also authorizes the debtor to avoid a nonpossessory, nonpurchase money security interest in certain household items and tools of the trade to the extent the lien impairs an exemption (to be illustrated later in connection with the Chapter 13 case in Chapter Fourteen, Section B). Moreover, §§522(g), (h), and (i) authorize the Chapter 7 debtor to initiate turnover, avoidance, or setoff actions if the trustee refuses to do so in order to assert an exemption in property recovered.

there are lenders who specialize in making bankruptcy redemption loans, particularly for vehicles. See, e.g., www.globeloans.com/en/redemption_loan_program/ and www.722redemption.com/ and http://rightsizefunding.com/. Such companies typically offer redemption loans for periods of two to six years at high interest rates commensurate with the high risk of lending to a borrower whose credit rating is wrecked. Of course, those lenders will take a security interest in the redeemed vehicle safe in the knowledge that the debtor who just received a discharge in Chapter 7 has severely limited options for seeking further bankruptcy relief during the term of the redemption loan. But all things considered, it is now the rare case in which a right to redeem is exercised by the debtor. Instead, debtors will opt if possible for a debt reaffirmation for property they would like to keep.

As with the intent to reaffirm a debt and the right to redeem, the individual debtor's intent to avoid one of these liens in order to claim an exemption must be noted on debtor's statement of intent. Per FRBP 4003(d), the proceeding to avoid judicial lien impairing an exemption is brought by motion, not adversarial proceeding. FRBP 4003(d) also recognizes the creditor's right to object to such a motion by challenging the exemption claimed by the debtor.

4. The Ride-Through Option

Before BAPCPA, many federal circuits recognized an additional option for a Chapter 7 debtor to retain secured property following discharge. A typical scenario was this: The debtor owns a car worth $10,000 and owes $10,500 on it to the creditor holding a security interest in the car to secure payment of the debt. The bankruptcy trustee has abandoned the car since there is no equity in it for the estate. The debtor is not in default on the payments to the creditor and the creditor has not repossessed and does not want to. The debtor needs the

The Rationale for the Ride Through Pre-BAPCPA

The rationale for the ride-through option was that §521(a)(2), the Code provision requiring the individual debtor to file his statement of intent regarding property, was not limited by that section to the options of surrender, exemption, redemption, or reaffirmation. Though the ride-through option was not expressly granted in the Code, it was a long-recognized practice and, because it was not prohibited by §521(a)(2), was allowed in these circuits for debts secured by both personal property (e.g., vehicles) and real property (e.g., home mortgages). Although debtors often sought reaffirmation before choosing the ride-through option, doing so was not a necessary prerequisite to ride through. Read In re Waller, 394 B.R. 111 (S.D.C. 2008), highlighted below, for a discussion of the pre-BAPCPA ride through practice and a list of the federal circuits that recognized it.

car but is unable to redeem it. So the debtor asks the court for permission to reaffirm the debt. The court refuses the application to reaffirm, finding that it is not in the best interests of the debtor (perhaps he has another car and the judge concludes that all he needs is one car, or perhaps he is reaffirming other debts that the court believes will put him at high risk of default on the car note if it is reaffirmed as well so the presumption of hardship is not overcome). What happens now? The debtor is in no position to redeem the vehicle. Must the debtor surrender the car he would like to keep, is paying for, and that the creditor would like him to keep and continue paying for?

Prior to 2005, five federal circuits recognized that a debtor had an additional option. With the acquiescence (rather than formal agreement, as in a reaffirmation) of the creditor, he could allow the debt to the secured creditor to be formally discharged but keep the car and continue making the payments. This option was called a **ride through** (or a **pay through** or, if the collateral was a vehicle, a **pay and ride**) by practitioners because the debtor's possession of the collateral was riding through and beyond the bankruptcy case. This arrangement was quite favorable to the debtor because the underlying debt to the creditor was discharged. If at any time before the debtor completed the payments due the creditor he no longer wanted the car (or if it were wrecked), he could simply surrender it back to the creditor and have no further liability on the debt — it had been discharged. Of course, the lien on the property survived the bankruptcy case even if the underlying debt did not; if there were a postdischarge default by the debtor, the creditor could repossess. However, with ride through, that was the creditor's sole remedy upon default.

In 2005 BAPCPA added §362(h)(1), stating that, in an individual bankruptcy case, the automatic stay terminates with respect to personal property securing an obligation of the debtor and such property is no longer deemed property of the estate if the debtor does not file a statement of intention in a timely manner or does not perform the stated intention (surrender, redemption, or reaffirmation) by the statutory deadline — 30 days after the petition is filed or before the first meeting of creditors, whichever is earliest per §521(a)(2).

Case Preview

In re Waller

Section §362(h)(1) has been interpreted as eliminating the ride through option concerning personal property in which a creditor holds a security interest leaving the debtor the options of reaffirming the debt or redeeming the property if possible under §722 in order to retain possession. See, e.g., In re Jones, 591 F.3d 308, 311-312 (4th Cir. 2010). But what about debts secured by the debtor's real property? As you read In re Waller, consider the following questions:

1. Why does the court decide that reaffirmation of debtors' mortgage obligations on their home is not in their best interests?
2. What is the court's rationale for holding that §362(h)(1) did not eliminate the ride-through option on debts secured by real property?
3. When Congress enacts legislation, is it presumed to know both the existing law and the court interpretations of that law?

In re Waller
394 B.R. 111 (Bankr. D.S.C. 2008)

Duncan, Bankruptcy Judge.

THIS MATTER is before the Court on two Reaffirmation Agreements between Steven Alan Waller, Monique Tonia Waller ("Debtors"), and South Carolina State Housing Finance and Development Authority ("Creditor"), which were filed by Creditor on August 21, 2008. The Court has jurisdiction over this matter under 28 U.S.C. §§157(b) and 1334(a) and (b). Pursuant to Fed. R. Civ. P. 52 made applicable to this proceeding by Fed. R. Bankr. P. 7052, the Court makes the following Findings of Fact and Conclusions of Law:

FINDINGS OF FACT

1. On May 21, 2008, Debtors jointly filed a voluntary petition under chapter 7 of the United States Bankruptcy Code.

2. Debtors owe Creditor on two notes secured by a first and second mortgage on their residence located at 630 Greenwich Drive, Aiken, South Carolina.

3. Debtors' Schedule I, Current Income of Individual Debtors, reflected that Mr. Waller is employed while Mrs. Waller is unemployed, with the potential for seasonal employment. According to Schedule I, Debtors' monthly take home pay is $2,163.00. Debtors' Schedule J, Current Expenditures of Individual Debtors, lists their average monthly expenses as $3,382.00. Together Schedules I and J demonstrate a deficit in the Debtors' monthly net income of $1,219.00.

4. Creditor, through counsel, filed two reaffirmation agreements between Debtors and Creditor on August 21, 2008. The first agreement sought to reaffirm

Debtor's first mortgage in the amount of $105,372.93. The second agreement sought to reaffirm Debtors' second mortgage in the amount of $2,009.99. Both agreements were filed on an outdated form requiring a hearing for proper determination of the whether the reaffirmation agreements created a presumption of undue hardship on the Debtors. The matter was set for a hearing on September 16, 2008.

5. Debtors, through counsel, filed two amended reaffirmation agreements using the current official form on September 11, 2008. The amended reaffirmation agreements indicated a presumption of undue hardship. The amended reaffirmation agreements differed from Debtors' schedules I and J indicating that Mrs. Waller is now employed.

6. A hearing was held on September 16, 2008. Debtors' stated at the hearing that they were current on their payments with Creditor on both mortgages and were current at the time of filing for chapter 7 relief. Creditor did not appear at the hearing.

7. Additionally, Debtors indicated that Mrs. Waller was now working part-time in the golf shop at Woodside Plantation Country Club and occasionally serves as a substitute teacher in the local school district.

8. Debtors' income from teaching is sporadic, unreliable, and insufficient to rebut the presumption of undue hardship.

9. Reaffirmation of debts secured by real estate, when the debtors are current with the payments, is not in Debtors' best interest.

CONCLUSIONS OF LAW

An individual chapter 7 debtor receives a discharge from all debts save those specified in 11 U.S.C. §727(a), those within the scope of §523(a), and those subject to an agreement for reaffirmation pursuant to §524(c). The discharge of debt is the foundation for a debtor's fresh start. Exceptions to discharge are narrowly construed. . . . The Bankruptcy Abuse Prevention and Consumer Protection Act of 2005 ("2005 Amendments") amended the Bankruptcy Code and extensively revised those provisions relating to reaffirmation of a debt. The Bankruptcy Code has always permitted only those reaffirmation agreements that do not impose an undue hardship on the debtor or a dependant of the debtor. A separate provision of the 2005 Amendments deals with a debtor's options for property used as collateral for debts.

Debtors who are current with payments on debts secured by real property are not limited to the options of surrender, reaffirmation, or redemption found in §521(a)(2), but may also choose to continue with the payments and retain possession of the property. This option, commonly known as "ride-through," was embraced by a number of federal judicial circuits, prior to the enactment of the 2005 Amendments and applied to both real property and personal property. . . .

This Court recently confirmed the viability of the "ride-through" option for debts secured by real property. *In re Wilson,* 372 B.R. 816, 820 (Bankr. D.S.C. 2007). In *Wilson,* the Court noted the changes made to the Bankruptcy Code by the 2005 Amendments and stated that the changes apply only to debts secured by personal property. *Id.* at 818. The relevant language of §521(a)(2)(C) provides that "nothing in subparagraphs (A) and (B) of this paragraph shall alter the debtor's or the trustee's rights with regard to such property under this title, except as provided in section

362(h)." 11 U.S.C. §521(a)(2)(C). Section 362(h) employs limiting language that terminates the automatic stay as to *personal property* when the debtor fails to state an intention to surrender, reaffirm, redeem, or does not perform the stated intention within a prescribed period. *Wilson* at 818, *citing* 11 U.S.C. §362(h). The plain language of §§521(a)(2)(C) and 362(h) "limits their application to a debtor's rights with regard to personal property." *Id.*

It is presumed that Congress enacts legislation "with knowledge of the law, including knowledge of the interpretation that courts have given to an existing statute." . . . For this reason, the right of debtors to continue current payments on debts secured by real property and retain the collateral established in *Belanger* remains intact. *Id. See also, Wilson* at 819. Congress curtailed the ride-through option for debts secured by personal property but not with regard to debts secured by real property. . . . "Limiting a debtor to the three choices of surrender, redeem, or reaffirm for real property would impair the debtor's ability to obtain a fresh start, which is one of the primary purposes of bankruptcy law." . . .

In this case, the Reaffirmation Agreements are not in Debtors' best interest because Debtors can retain the real property without reaffirming the debt. For this reason, approval of the Reaffirmation Agreements is denied.

Post-Case Follow-Up

Be sure you understand why formal reaffirmation of debt in bankruptcy favors the creditor: the debtor is contractually back on the hook for a debt it could have discharged and may not meet the qualifications for filing a second bankruptcy case for some time. Reaffirmation poses real risks for debtors. On the other hand, ride through, where it is still an option for debts secured by real property, favors the debtor. The underlying debt is discharged in the bankruptcy case and only the creditor's security interest in the property and the debtor's obligation to remain current in her payments and comply with any other contractual obligations related to the collateralized property, such as maintaining insurance on it, remain. Ride through poses real risks for the creditor and the creditor's consent to it is not required. Of course, a creditor unhappy with the ride through will watch for any post-discharge breach by the debtor in order to foreclose on the property. See, e.g., In re Wilson, 372 B.R. 816 (Bankr. D.S.C. 2007). Not all courts agree that ride through is permitted on debt secured by realty post-BAPCPA. Those courts rejecting the idea are typically those that rejected ride through as an option for both personal and real property pre-BAPCPA. See, e.g., In re Linderman, 435 B.R. 715 (Bankr. M.D. Fla. 2009) (pre-BAPCPA, the Eleventh Circuit construed the language of §521(a)(2)(A) to prohibit ride through regardless of the property involved, personal or real; BAPCPA merely confirms that ride through is not available for debts secured by personal property, it does not impliedly make it available for debts secured by real property. In the Eleventh Circuit, a Chapter 7 debtor must either redeem or reaffirm a debt if the debtor wants to keep the collateral.)

In re Waller: Real Life Applications

1. You represent debtors in Chapter 7 cases who have the following debts. Which of those debts might qualify for ride-through treatment?
   a. Debtor owns a boat in which Bank holds a security interest to secure a loan with balance of $5,000. Debtor is current on the payments to Bank.
   b. Debtor owns a boat in which Bank holds a security interest to secure a loan with balance of $5,000. Debtor is not current on the payments to Bank.
   c. Debtor owns a home that is mortgaged to Bank to secure a loan with balance of $50,000. Debtor is current on the payments to Bank.
   d. Debtor owns a home that is mortgaged to Bank to secure a loan with balance of $50,000. Debtor is not current on the payments to Bank.
2. For each of the debts listed in Question 1 that do not qualify for ride-through treatment, what would you recommend to your debtor client to enable them to keep the collateral through the bankruptcy case?

Application Exercise 5

Determine if the courts of the federal district or circuit where you plan to practice are allowing post-BAPCPA ride throughs for debts secured by mortgages on the debtor's real property.

But has BAPCPA totally eliminated the ride-through option for debts secured by personal property? Maybe not. Some courts are construing §521(a)(2) and new §362(h) together to mean that what the debtor must do is ask the court to reaffirm the debt secured by personal property. If a timely notice of intent to reaffirm is filed and a timely application to reaffirm the debt is sought but not approved, those courts are saying the requirements of §362(h) are complied with and the debtor may still choose ride through with the acquiescence of the creditor. Called a **back door ride through** by practitioners, the procedure is being recognized in those federal districts where pre-BAPCPA ride through was recognized. See, e.g., In re Chim, 381 B.R. 191 (Bankr. D. Md. 2008), and In re Moustafi, 371 B.R. 434 (Bankr. D. Ariz. 2007).

Once the bankruptcy case is closed, the postdischarge legal rights as between the ride through debtor and the secured creditor will be governed by state law. The lien on the personal property (or the mortgage in the case of real property) survives the end of the bankruptcy case and the creditor will have the right to repossess (or foreclose) upon default. But regarding what constitutes default, state law (e.g., some state consumer protection laws prohibiting repossession of a vehicle or other personalty when there is no default on payments), not bankruptcy law, will control. See, e.g., In re Dumont, 383 B.R. 481 (B.A.P. 9th Cir. 2008), and In re Steinhaus, 349 B.R. 694 (Bankr. D. Idaho 2006).

In bankruptcy courts where ride through is still deemed an option, debtors will often state their intent to pursue that option on their statement of intent even though the official form (Form 108) does not contain that option. And in many bankruptcy courts where the controlling law says ride through is not a viable option, it has been and still is done informally between debtor and acquiescing creditor. After all, who is to complain if the creditor does not? The trustee has abandoned the property as having no value to the estate. For the same reason no other creditor will care, having no interest in the collateral. The debtor is delighted to keep the property and the creditor is delighted to keep receiving payments. All's well that ends well?

Application Exercise 6

Determine if the courts of the federal district or circuit where you plan to practice recognize the back door ride through for personal property post-BAPCPA. For a good discussion of this interesting post-BAPCPA development, read Christopher M. Hogan, "Will the Ride-Through Ride Again?" 108 Colum. L. Rev. 882 (2008).

Application Exercise 7

Determine if the state where you plan to practice enforces *ipso facto* clauses in consumer contracts.

---

5. The Lien Stripping Option

Recall the bifurcation of an undersecured claim mandated by §506(a) pursuant to which the value of a secured claim is stripped down to the value of the collateral and bifurcated between its secured and unsecured portion. Section 506(d) provides that a lien is void "[t]o the extent that [it] secures a claim against the debtor that is not an allowed secured claim." How do those two provisions work in the following scenario? The creditor is owed $250,000 and the debt is secured by a perfected mortgage on the debtor's residence. The residence is valued at only $200,000, so the creditor is undersecured. The Chapter 7 trustee decides there is no equity in the residence for the estate and abandons it to the debtor.

Can debtor use §§506(a) and (d) to ask the court to reduce the lien of the creditor on the residence to

Ipso Facto Clauses in Bankruptcy

An *ipso facto* (Latin for "by the act itself") clause in a contract is one that makes the act of one party becoming insolvent, acknowledging insolvency, filing a bankruptcy case or state law receivership proceeding (or having one filed involuntarily for them), or making an assignment for the benefit of creditors an act of default by that party. Many states disallow *ipso facto* clauses in consumer contracts. Section 365(e) of the Code together with §541(c) effectively make *ipso facto* clauses in executory contracts ineffective postpetition. However, BAPCPA added §521(d) which makes *ipso facto* clauses in contracts enforceable when

- an individual debtor fails to comply with §362(h)(1)(A) by filing the required statement of intent as to a debt secured by personal property within the time allowed by §521(a)(2) or
- an individual debtor in Chapter 7 fails to reaffirm or redeem a debt secured by personal property within 45 days following the 341 meeting as required by §521(a)(6).

In other words, even if the debtor is not otherwise in default under the contract with the secured creditor, if the debtor fails to reference the debt on his statement of intent and then to reaffirm or redeem in a timely manner and if the contract contains an *ipso facto* clause, these sections authorize the creditor to utilize that clause to declare the debtor in default, have the automatic stay lifted (it is automatically terminated by §362(h)(1) for failure to file the timely statement of intent regarding debts secured by personal property), and repossess the collateral. The continuing post-petition effect of an *ipso facto* clause in a contract where the debtor rides through on a debt secured by personal property is unclear. See, e.g., In re Wilson, 372 B.R. 816 (Bankr. D.S.C. 2007) (creditor unhappy with proposed ride through on debt secured by real property could not declare default by debtor by reason of *ipso facto* clause in mortgage since §521(d) allowing enforcement of such clauses refers to them in agreements covered by §521(a)(6) and §362(h), which address only personal property liens. Section 521(d) only preserves the enforceability of *ipso facto* clauses in personal property loans).

the $200,000 value? Note that the debtor is not simply asking for what §506(a) already does — bifurcate the bankruptcy claim of this undersecured creditor into a secured claim for $200,000 and an unsecured claim for $50,000. The debtor is asking that the secured position of creditor in the residence be limited to the $200,000 present value and the mortgage declared void for all amounts above $200,000. The creditor is left with an unsecured claim for the amounts owed in excess of the value of the property. This is an effort to **strip down** or **write down** the lien not just for purposes of treating the creditor's claim in a distribution but to actually void the balance of the secured debt.

For example, assume a Chapter 7 debtor owns a home secured by a mortgage having a balance of $200,000 but the home is only valued at $180,000 when the petition is filed. We know that this creditor is undersecured and that pursuant to §506(a) its claim is bifurcated: Its claim is secured in the amount of $180,000 and unsecured in the amount of $20,000. If the debtor can succeed in having the court void the mortgage on the $20,000, consider the consequences. The trustee may abandon the residence as having no equity for the estate. The creditor may then effectively redeem the property by paying the secured creditor only the $180,000 secured value and discharge the unsecured $20,000 balance even though §722 limits the right of redemption to certain personal property. Or the debtor may remain current on the payments to the creditor and retain possession via a pay through, paying only the $180,000 secured balance as it comes due. If at any time property values go back up, say to $220,000, debtor could then sell the residence for the increased value, pay off the $180,000 secured balance, and retain the balance of the proceeds. In other words, any increase in equity after the mortgage is stripped down accrues to the debtor.

Sections 506(a) and (d) could certainly be read as allowing if not intending the kind of strip down illustrated in the last example. But in Dewsnup v. Timm, 502 U.S. 410 (1997), the Supreme Court, while recognizing some ambiguity in the meaning of the provisions, held it was not allowable. The reasoning is that Congress intended the two sections to be read independently of each other and that the claim bifurcation feature of §506(a) does not mandate or authorize an otherwise legitimate security interest to be otherwise stripped down or voided under §506(d), regardless of the value of the collateral. To read §§506(a) and (d) to allow stripping of the lien down to the value of the collateral would run afoul of the basic notion imbedded in §502 that properly perfected liens pass through bankruptcy unaffected. The court adopted the view that:

> [T]he words "allowed secured claim" in §506(d) need not be read as an indivisible term of art defined by reference to §506(a), which by its terms is not a definitional provision. Rather, the words should be read term-by-term to refer to any claim that is, first, allowed, and, second, secured. Because there is no question that the claim at issue here has been "allowed" pursuant to §502 of the Code and is secured by a lien with recourse to the underlying collateral, it does not come within the scope of §506(d), which voids only liens corresponding to claims that have not been allowed and secured. This reading of §506(d) . . . gives the provision the simple and sensible function of voiding a lien whenever a claim secured by the lien itself has not been allowed.

502 U.S. at 515-516.

The court was bothered by the idea that the debtor would benefit by any post–strip down increase in the value of the collateral and decided to preserve the pre-Code rule reflected in §502 that liens on real property should pass through bankruptcy unaffected unless a Code provision expressly said otherwise.

Notwithstanding the decision in *Dewsnup*, some courts continued to allow a strip off under §§506(a) and (d) in the following scenario: Creditor #1 is owed $250,000 and the debt is secured by a mortgage on debtor's residence. The residence is valued at only $240,000, meaning that Creditor #1 is undersecured. *Dewsnup* says that the lien of Creditor #1 cannot be stripped down to the value of the collateral. However, Creditor #2 is owed $30,000 by our debtor and that debt is secured by a second mortgage on the debtor's residence, junior to the mortgage held by Creditor #1. Both mortgages are properly perfected but if the residence is sold, all the proceeds of sale will go to Creditor #1 and none to Creditor #2. Creditor #2 is not just undersecured, it is wholly undersecured — there is no equity in the collateral for Creditor #2.

In that scenario, some courts said *Dewsnup* did not apply to protect Creditor #2 and that the debtor could not just strip down, but **strip off** the second mortgage since the secured claim of Creditor #2 was valueless. The rationale was that under §506(a) the junior lien was completely unsecured and could thus be stripped off under §506(d). *Dewsnup* was distinguishable because, unlike the undersecured creditor in *Dewsnup* (and Creditor #1 in our example), Creditor #2 arguably had no allowed secured claim at all. Thus the lien-preserving imperative of §502 the Supreme Court held preeminent in *Dewsnup* was irrelevant as to Creditor #2. (Compare In re McNeal, 477 Fed. Appx. 562, 564 (11th Cir. 2012, unpublished)

("A wholly unsecured lien is voidable under the plain language of 506(d) and the Supreme Court — noting the ambiguities in the bankruptcy code and the 'the difficulty of interpreting the statute in a single opinion that would apply to all possible fact situations' — limited its *Dewsnup* decision expressly to the precise issue raised by the facts of the case"), and In re Lavelle, 2009 WL 4043089, at *4-5 (Bankr. E.D.N.Y. 2009) ("the wholly unsecured lien cannot qualify as an 'allowed secured claim' under §506(a), and is void under §506(d)"), with Talbert v. City Mortgage Service, 344 F.3d 555, 560 (6th Cir. 2003) ("The Supreme Court's reasoning for not permitting 'strip downs' in the Chapter 7 context applies with equal validity to a debtor's attempt to effectuate a Chapter 7 'strip off.'"), and In re Webster, 287 B.R. 703, 708 (Bankr. N.D. Ohio 2002 ("The analysis does not change depending on the available equity in the collateral to which the lien attaches.").

Case Preview

Bank of America, N.A. v. Caulkett

As the dispute over the scope of *Dewsnup* might suggest, it is a controversial decision that has gendered a fair share of criticism beginning with the dissent of Justice Scalia in the case itself ("the Court replaces what Congress said with what it thinks Congress ought to have said — and in the process disregards, and hence impairs for future use, well-established principles of statutory construction"). 502 U.S. at 780. In 2015, the Supreme Court finally revisited *Dewsnup* in a case that raised the question of whether it applied to wholly undersecured liens. As you read Bank of America, N.A. v. Caulkett consider the following questions:

1. What is the difference between the "strip down" and the "strip off" of a lien?
2. What is the basis of the court's conclusion that allowing the strip down of a wholly unsecured mortgage would lead to "arbitrary results" in light of *Dewsnup*?
3. Does the court appear wholly satisfied with its construction of §§506(a) and (d) in *Dewsnup*?
4. Is the result here fair to debtors seeking a fresh start? Would a contrary decision have been fair to secured creditors?

Bank of America, N.A. v. Caulkett
135 S. Ct. 1995 (2015)

[Order was entered by the United States Bankruptcy Court allowing Chapter 7 debtor to "strip off" junior mortgagee's wholly underwater lien. Junior mortgagee appealed.

The District Court and Eleventh Circuit affirmed. To resolve a conflict between the circuits, certiorari was granted.]

THOMAS, Justice. . . .

Section 506(d) provides, "To the extent that a lien secures a claim against the debtor that is not an allowed secured claim, such lien is void." Accordingly, §506(d) permits the debtors here to strip off the Bank's junior mortgages only if the Bank's "claim" — generally, its right to repayment from the debtors, §101(5) — is "not an allowed secured claim." Subject to some exceptions not relevant here, a claim filed by a creditor is deemed "allowed" under §502 if no interested party objects or if, in the case of an objection, the Bankruptcy Court determines that the claim should be allowed under the Code. §§502(a)-(b). The parties agree that the Bank's claims meet this requirement. They disagree, however, over whether the Bank's claims are "secured" within the meaning of §506(d).

The Code suggests that the Bank's claims are not secured. Section 506(a)(1) provides that "[a]n

Justice Clarence Thomas wrote the majority opinion for Bank of America, N.A. v. Caulkett. *Collection of the Supreme Court of the United States, Photographer: Steve Petteway*

allowed claim of a creditor secured by a lien on property . . . is a secured claim to the extent of the value of such creditor's interest in . . . such property," and "an unsecured claim to the extent that the value of such creditor's interest . . . is less than the amount of such allowed claim." In other words, if the value of a creditor's interest in the property is zero — as is the case here — his claim cannot be a "secured claim" within the meaning of §506(a). And given that these identical words are later used in the same section of the same Act — §506(d) — one would think this "presents a classic case for application of the normal rule of statutory construction that identical words used in different parts of the same act are intended to have the same meaning." Desert Palace, Inc. v. Costa, 539 U.S. 90, 101 (2003). Under that straightforward reading of the statute, the debtors would be able to void the Bank's claims.

Unfortunately for the debtors, this Court has already adopted a construction of the term "secured claim" in §506(d) that forecloses this textual analysis. See Dewsnup v. Timm, 502 U.S. 410 (1992). In *Dewsnup*, the Court confronted a situation in which a Chapter 7 debtor wanted to "'strip down'" — or reduce — a partially underwater lien under §506(d) to the value of the collateral. Id., at 412-413. Specifically, she sought, under §506(d), to reduce her debt of approximately $120,000 to the value of the collateral securing her debt at that time ($39,000). Id., at 413. Relying on the statutory definition of "'allowed secured claim'" in §506(a), she contended that her creditors' claim was "secured only to the extent of the judicially determined value of the real property on which the lien [wa]s fixed." Id., at 414.

The Court rejected her argument. Rather than apply the statutory definition of "secured claim" in §506(a), the Court reasoned that the term "secured" in §506(d) contained an ambiguity because the self-interested parties before it disagreed over the term's meaning. Id., at 416, 420. Relying on policy considerations and its understanding of pre-Code practice, the Court concluded that if a claim "has been 'allowed' pursuant to §502 of the Code and is secured by a lien with recourse to the underlying collateral, it does not come within the scope of §506(d)." Id., at 415; see id., at 417-420. It therefore held that the debtor could not strip down the creditors' lien to the value of the property under §506(d) "because [the creditors'] claim [wa]s secured by a lien and ha[d] been fully allowed pursuant to §502." Id., at 417. In other words, *Dewsnup* defined the term "secured claim" in §506(d) to mean a claim supported by a security interest in property, regardless of whether the value of that property would be sufficient to cover the claim. Under this definition, §506(d)'s function is reduced to "voiding a lien whenever a claim secured by the lien itself has not been allowed." Id., at 416.

Dewsnup's construction of "secured claim" resolves the question presented here. *Dewsnup* construed the term "secured claim" in §506(d) to include any claim "secured by a lien and . . . fully allowed pursuant to §502." Id., at 417. Because the Bank's claims here are both secured by liens and allowed under §502, they cannot be voided under the definition given to the term "allowed secured claim" by *Dewsnup*.

The debtors do not ask us to overrule *Dewsnup*,[†] but instead request that we limit that decision to partially — as opposed to wholly — underwater liens. We decline to adopt this distinction. The debtors offer several reasons why we should cabin *Dewsnup* in this manner, but none of them is compelling. . . . .

[T]he debtors rely on language in *Dewsnup* stating that the Court was not addressing "all possible fact situations," but was instead "allow[ing] other facts to await their legal resolution on another day." Id., at 416-417. But this disclaimer provides an insufficient foundation for the debtors' proposed distinction. *Dewsnup* considered several possible definitions of the term "secured claim" in §506(d). See id., at 414-416. The definition it settled on — that a claim is "secured" if it is "secured by a lien" and "has been fully allowed pursuant to §502," id., at 417 — does not depend on whether a lien is partially or wholly underwater. Whatever the Court's hedging language meant, it does not provide a reason to limit *Dewsnup* in the manner the debtors propose.

The debtors next contend that the term "secured claim" in §506(d) could be redefined as any claim that is backed by collateral with some value. Embracing this

---

† From its inception, *Dewsnup* . . . has been the target of criticism. See, e.g., id., at 420–436 (SCALIA, J., dissenting); In re Woolsey, 696 F.3d 1266, 1273–1274, 1278 (C.A.10 2012); In re Dever, 164 B.R. 132, 138, 145 (Bkrtcy. Ct. C.D. Cal. 1994); Carlson, Bifurcation of Undersecured Claims in Bankruptcy, 70 Am. Bankr. L. J. 1, 12–20 (1996); Ponoroff & Knippenberg, The Immovable Object Versus the Irresistible Force: Rethinking the Relationship Between Secured Credit and Bankruptcy Policy, 95 Mich. L. Rev. 2234, 2305–2307 (1997); see also Bank of America Nat. Trust and Sav. Assn. v. 203 North LaSalle Street Partnership, 526 U.S. 434, 463, and n. 3 (1999) (THOMAS, J., concurring in judgment) (collecting cases and observing that "[t]he methodological confusion created by *Dewsnup* has enshrouded both the Courts of Appeals and . . . Bankruptcy Courts"). Despite this criticism, the debtors have repeatedly insisted that they are not asking us to overrule *Dewsnup*.

reading of §506(d), however, would give the term "allowed secured claim" in §506(d) a different meaning than its statutory definition in §506(a). We refuse to adopt this artificial definition. . . .

The debtors alternatively urge us to limit *Dewsnup*'s definition to the facts of that case because the historical and policy concerns that motivated the Court do not apply in the context of wholly underwater liens. Whether or not that proposition is true, it is an insufficient justification for giving the term "secured claim" in §506(d) a different definition depending on the value of the collateral. We are generally reluctant to give the "same words a different meaning" when construing statutes, Pasquantino v. United States, 544 U.S. 349, 358 (2005), and we decline to do so here based on policy arguments.

Ultimately, embracing the debtors' distinction would not vindicate §506(d)'s original meaning, and it would leave an odd statutory framework in its place. Under the debtors' approach, if a court valued the collateral at one dollar more than the amount of a senior lien, the debtor could not strip down a junior lien under *Dewsnup*, but if it valued the property at one dollar less, the debtor could strip off the entire junior lien. Given the constantly shifting value of real property, this reading could lead to arbitrary results. To be sure, the Code engages in line-drawing elsewhere, and sometimes a dollar's difference will have a significant impact on bankruptcy proceedings. See, e.g., §707(b)(2)(A)(i) (presumption of abuse of provisions of Chapter 7 triggered if debtor's projected disposable income over the next five years is $12,475). But these lines were set by Congress, not this Court. There is scant support for the view that §506(d) applies differently depending on whether a lien was partially or wholly underwater. Even if *Dewsnup* were deemed not to reflect the correct meaning of §506(d), the debtors' solution would not either.

The reasoning of *Dewsnup* dictates that a debtor in a Chapter 7 bankruptcy proceeding may not void a junior mortgage lien under §506(d) when the debt owed on a senior mortgage lien exceeds the current value of the collateral. The debtors here have not asked us to overrule *Dewsnup*, and we decline to adopt the artificial distinction they propose instead. We therefore reverse the judgments of the Court of Appeals and remand the cases for further proceedings consistent with this opinion.

It is so ordered.

Post-Case Follow-Up

Should the debtors here have asked the court to reverse *Dewsnup*? After all, the opinion observes that "The Code suggests that the Bank's claims are not secured" before relying on its interpretation of a secured claim in *Dewsnup*. And look at the footnote to the case where Justice Thomas documents the significant criticism *Dewsnup* has engendered before noting again that debtors did not ask that it be reversed. Did attorneys for the debtors here miss an opportunity by failing to be bolder? Is it possible that the final word has yet to be written on this issue?

Bank of America, N.A., v. Caulkett: Real Life Applications

1. Assume you represent a Chapter 7 debtor who owns a home that has been valued at $200,000. Bank #1 holds the first mortgage on the home and the balance owed Bank #1 is $210,000. Bank #2 holds the second mortgage on the home and the balance owed Bank #2 is $25,000. Your client is current on the loan from Bank #1 but three payments behind on the loan from Bank #2. Only the lack of equity in the home prevented Bank #2 from instituting a prepetition foreclosure action. Nonetheless, your client is desperate to retain possession of the home if possible.
   a. Will the fact that your client can claim a homestead exemption of $100,000 be of any use in this case?
   b. What will the bankruptcy trustee probably do with the home as far as the bankruptcy estate is concerned?
   c. After *Dewsnup* and *Caulkett*, what options does your client have to retain possession of his home post-discharge?
2. If a search of the public records revealed that Bank #1 in the above scenario did not properly perfect its mortgage interest in the home prepetition, how does that change your analysis?
   a. Does the homestead exemption matter now?
   b. What is the bankruptcy trustee likely to do now?
   c. Have the options your client has to retain possession post-discharge changed?

Chapter Summary

■ The bankruptcy trustee can abandon property of the estate that is of inconsequential value or burdensome to the estate on notice and a hearing. Property that is burdened by a perfected security interest but in which there is equity for the estate may be sold by the trustee free and clear of all liens with prior permission of the court. The trustee will liquidate other property of the estate by selling it at public or private sale approved using the notice and a hearing procedure.

■ Assets of the estate are distributed by the trustee to satisfy administrative expenses of the case and creditor claims in a mandated order of priority. Allowed secured claims have the highest priority as to their respective collateralized property of the estate up to the value of such collateral. Section 507 priority claims such as trustee's fees, domestic support obligations, and administrative expenses enjoy the next priority followed by general unsecured claims. Each priority class of claims is entitled to be fully satisfied before a lower class receives anything. Within a particular priority classification, distribution is *pro rata* among unsecured creditors in the class. A court may order equitable subordination of a creditor's claim upon a finding of inequitable or dishonest conduct that resulted in unfair advantage to the creditor or prejudice to other creditors.

■ A Chapter 7 debtor may attempt to retain property pledged as collateral that the trustee has abandoned on behalf of the estate either by consensual reaffirmation of the debt. Reaffirmation agreements must be approved by the bankruptcy judge. If an attorney advises the debtor in connection with negotiation of a reaffirmation agreement, the attorney must certify that the debtor was fully informed and voluntarily entered into the agreement and that reaffirmation will not create an undue hardship for the debtor or the debtor's dependents.

■ A Chapter 7 debtor may also redeem consumer personal property that pledged as collateral where the debtor could otherwise exempt or the estate has abandoned by paying the creditor the full amount of its secured claim with the collateral valued at its replacement value. The debtor may also avoid judicial liens on property to the extent they impair an exemption in such property.

■ In some districts the debtor may have a ride through option regarding debt secured by realty. In some districts there may also be a back-door-ride-through option for debts secured by personalty where a reaffirmation of such debt is proposed but refused by the court. In many districts, informal ride throughs are practiced by debtors and creditors without formal court sanction, enabling debtors to maintain possession of collateral.

■ The practice of stripping down an undersecured claim to the value of the collateral securing it or stripping off a fully undersecured claim is no longer available in a Chapter 7 case.

Applying the Concepts

1. Assume you are the bankruptcy trustee in a case where the following expenses and allowed claims are present. You have funds in the estate to pay most but not all of these. Arrange the list of expenses and claims in the order of priority mandated by §726:

   a. debtor's unpaid federal income taxes for the past two tax years
   b. unpaid unsecured bills from the debtor's suppliers
   c. debtor's unpaid child support to an ex-spouse
   d. unpaid Social Security withholdings on the debtor's employees
   e. an unpaid student loan
   f. your travel expenses in the case as bankruptcy trustee.

2. As trustee in various bankruptcy cases, you are contemplating taking the following actions. For each, identify the proper procedure to be followed (e.g, motion, objection, notice and a hearing, adversary proceeding):

   a. objecting to the debtor's claimed exemption in her home on the grounds she is undervaluing the property in order to exempt and keep it when there is actually equity for the estate in excess of the allowable homestead exemption

    b. abandoning for the estate unexempted furniture in such bad shape it has no salable value

    c. challenging the claim of a creditor to be secured on the grounds that the creditor did not perfect its security interest prepetion

    d. action to recover a preferential transfer to a creditor

    e. objecting to the debtor receiving a discharge in Chapter 7 because he attempted to hide property (gold bars) from you by burying it in his backyard and not disclosing it on his bankruptcy schedules.

3. Assume the total administrative expenses for Marta Carlson's estate, excluding the realtor's fee associated with selling the residence on Spruce Street, and other §507 priority claims total $3,000. All of Marta's claimed exemptions are allowed. The residence is sold free and clear of liens, netting the estate $38,075. The doll collection is purchased from the estate for $4,000 after expenses of sale. The Toyota Camry is sold, netting the estate $1,725 after the claim of AFI in the amount of $1,750 secured by the vehicle is satisfied and Marta's $5,025 exemption in the car is paid. The Shears washer and dryer are not sold but instead are retained by Marta pursuant to a court-approved reaffirmation agreement between Marta and Shears. Finally, assume that the trustee's objection to the claim of Pine Ridge Nursing Home is upheld so that creditor receives nothing. All other unsecured claims are allowed.

    a. Determine how much cash the estate will have available to distribute to general unsecured creditors.

    b. Based on the total amount of general unsecured debt owed on the allowed unsecured claims, what percentage of the total unsecured debt will be paid?

4. Locate and read Assignment Memorandum #3 in Appendix C. If your instructor so directs, draft the notice of intent to abandon property and agreed order lifting stay assuming the Chapter 7 case of Abelard Mendoza is pending in the U.S. bankruptcy court for the federal district where you plan to practice.

5. Locate and read Assignment Memorandum #5 in Appendix C. If your instructor so directs, draft the reaffirmation agreement between Mendoza and Friendly Finance assuming the Chapter 7 case of Abelard Mendoza is pending in the U.S. bankruptcy court for the federal district where you plan to practice.

The Chapter 7 Consumer Bankruptcy Case: Non-Dischargeable Debts, Objections to Discharge, Dismissal or Conversion, and the Final Discharge

Not all debts that a Chapter 7 debtor has can be discharged in a bankruptcy case and in this chapter we will identify those non-dischargeable debts. The Code also sets out grounds to deny a Chapter 7 debtor any discharge at all or to involuntarily dismiss the case; we will cover those important topics in this chapter too. A Chapter 7 debtor whose case is dismissed or who has a debt declared non-dischargeable may choose to convert her case to one under Chapter 13 and we will consider that option here. Finally, we will examine the procedures for winding up a Chapter 7 case, including the trustee's final accounting to the court and the entry of discharge.

A. NON-DISCHARGEABLE DEBTS

The primary purpose of filing a Chapter 7 petition from the individual debtor's standpoint is to receive a discharge of his debts. Once discharged, the debtor can never again be held legally responsible for the discharged debts. This is part of

Key Concepts

- A number of debts are non-dischargeable in a Chapter 7 bankruptcy
- A number of grounds exist to deny a Chapter 7 debtor any discharge at all or to involuntarily dismiss the case
- A debtor who originally filed under Chapter 7 can convert the case to one under Chapter 11, 12, or 13 if she qualifies as a debtor under the alternative chapter
- The final discharge granted an individual Chapter 7 debtor forever protects debtor from liability for discharged debts and includes a prohibition on discrimination

the fresh start public policy behind Chapter 7. The concept of a discharge is irrelevant to an entity debtor like a corporation or partnership since the effect of liquidation for such a debtor is that it will simply cease doing business. However, not all debts can be discharged in bankruptcy by the individual debtor. Section 523(a) identifies debts that cannot be discharged in bankruptcy and the primary ones are summarized in Exhibit 11.1.

FRBP 4007 provides that any creditor can file a complaint objecting to the discharge of a particular debt or the debtor himself can file a complaint to determine the dischargeability of a particular debt. Any such action is an adversary proceeding, not just a contested matter (see Exhibit 4.6). Rule 4007 also provides that any complaint contesting the dischargeability of a debt must be filed within 60 days following the first meeting of creditors though the time can be extended by motion. Rule 2002(f) requires the bankruptcy court clerk, or some other person as the court may direct, to provide notice by mail of the time fixed for filing a complaint objecting to discharge of a particular debt.

EXHIBIT 11.1   **Debts That Cannot Be Discharged in a Chapter 7 Bankruptcy**

- Taxes entitled to priority payment and tax obligations related to a fraudulent return, failure to file a return, or a late return filed within two years preceding the petition and withholding taxes that should have been collected from third parties [§523(a)(1)]
- Debts for money, property, services, or an extension of credit obtained by fraudulent pretenses or by the use of a false financial statement [§523(a)(2)(A)(B)]
- Last-minute consumer cash advances or spending for luxury goods or services [§523(a)(2)(C)]
- Debts that were not listed on the debtor's schedules so that the creditor could not file a timely proof of claim [§523(a)(3)]
- Debts arising from the debtor's fraud or defalcation while he was acting in a fiduciary capacity [§523(a)(4)]
- Debts arising from embezzlement or larceny [§523(a)(4)]
- Domestic support obligations such as alimony and child support [§523(a)(5)]
- Debts or claims arising out of the willful or malicious injury to another or the property of another [§523(a)(6)]
- Student loans, unless the debtor can convince the court that not discharging this obligation will work an undue hardship on the debtor or his dependents [§523(a)(8)]
- Certain fines and penalties imposed by the government [§523(a)(7)]
- Claims arising from the wrongful death or personal injury caused by the debtor's driving under the influence of drugs or alcohol [§523(a)(9)]
- Claims not properly listed or scheduled [§523(a)(3)]

---

1. Taxes [§523(a)(1)]

Generally speaking, income taxes (whether federal, state, or local) for which the tax return was due during the three tax years preceding the filing of the petition cannot be discharged, nor can property taxes coming due during the year preceding the petition. Regardless of the tax year in question, a debtor filing a false tax return, or filing with willful intent to evade taxes, cannot discharge those obligations. Even for tax obligations that are dischargeable, properly recorded tax liens that attached to debtor's property prior to filing the petition survive the bankruptcy. Employer debtors who failed to withhold payroll "trust fund" taxes including FICA, Social Security (employee's share), or Medicare premiums from employee paychecks as required by law also cannot discharge those obligations.

2. Debts Obtained by False Pretenses, False Representation, False Financial Statement, or Actual Fraud [§523(a)(2)(A)(B)]

Debts created by fraudulent means are non-dischargeable.

For example, assume that a person obtains a loan from a bank to buy a car. Debtor borrows $10,000 from the bank but has a kickback deal with the seller of the car to get $2,000 of the purchase price back after the deal is done. When the buyer of the car files for bankruptcy the bank can argue that the debt to it should be declared non-dischargeable under §523(a) due to the fraudulent pretenses used to obtain the loan. Or assume that a real estate developer obtains a million dollar loan from a bank to develop a subdivision. Developer presents a personal financial statement to the bank as part of the loan application but materially exaggerates the value of his assets in order to qualify for the loan. If he files bankruptcy the entire debt may be declared non-dischargeable due to the fraudulent financial statement if the lender reasonably relied on the false statement.

Case Preview

Husky Int'l Electronics, Inc. v. Ritz

Does the statutory "obtained by...actual fraud" language of §523(a)(2)(A) mean that the debt had to be originally obtained by fraud in order to be declared nondischargeable? Can that language be fairly applied to a debt involving no fraud in its inception but subject later to a fraudulent scheme to avoid repayment? As you read *Husky Int'l Electronics*, consider the following questions:

1. What was the debt alleged to be nondischargeable in this case?
2. Was there any contention that the debt was originally obtained by actual fraud of the debtor?
3. Who participated in the alleged fraudulent conveyance scheme in this case?
4. What transfer does the court say satisfied the "obtained by" requirement of the statute?

Husky Int'l Electronics, Inc. v. Ritz
136 S. Ct. 445 (2016)

[Chrysalis incurred a debt of $164,000 to Husky. Ritz, Chrysalis' director and then-part-owner, drained Chrysalis of assets available to pay the debt by transferring large sums to other entities Ritz controlled. Husky sued Ritz, who then filed for Chapter 7 bankruptcy. Husky filed a complaint in Ritz' bankruptcy case, asserting "actual fraud" under the Code's discharge exceptions, 11 U.S.C. 523(a)(2)(A). The district court held that Ritz was personally liable under state law but that the debt was not "obtained by . . . actual fraud" and could be discharged. The Fifth Circuit affirmed.]

OPINION by Justice SOTOMAYOR:

The Bankruptcy Code prohibits debtors from discharging debts "obtained by . . . false pretenses, a false representation, or actual fraud." 11 U. S. C. §523(a)(2) (A). The Fifth Circuit held that a debt is "obtained by . . . actual fraud" only if the debtor's fraud involves a false representation to a creditor. That ruling deepened an existing split among the Circuits over whether "actual fraud" requires a false representation or whether it encompasses other traditional forms of fraud that can be accomplished without a false representation, such as a fraudulent conveyance of property made to evade payment to creditors. We granted certiorari to resolve that split and now reverse. . . . The term "actual fraud" in §523(a)(2)(A) encompasses forms of fraud, like fraudulent conveyance schemes, that can be effected without a false representation.

Before 1978, the Bankruptcy Code prohibited debtors from discharging debts obtained by "false pretenses or false representations." §35(a)(2) (1976 ed.). In the Bankruptcy Reform Act of 1978, Congress added "actual fraud" to that list. The prohibition now reads: "A discharge under [Chapters 7, 11, 12, or 13] of this title does not discharge an individual debtor from any debt . . . for money, property, services, or an extension, renewal, or refinancing of credit, to the extent obtained by . . . false pretenses, a false representation, or actual fraud." §523(a)(2)(A).

When "'Congress acts to amend a statute, we presume it intends its amendment to have real and substantial effect.'" *United States* v. *Quality Stores, Inc.*, 572 U. S. ___, ___ (2014) (slip op., at 7). It is therefore sensible to start with the presumption that Congress did not intend "actual fraud" to mean the same thing as "a false representation," as the Fifth Circuit's holding suggests. But the historical meaning of "actual fraud" provides even stronger evidence that the phrase has long encompassed the kind of conduct alleged to have occurred here: a transfer scheme designed to hinder the collection of debt.

[F]rom the beginning of English bankruptcy practice, courts and legislatures have used the term "fraud" to describe a debtor's transfer of assets that, like Ritz' scheme, impairs a creditor's ability to collect the debt.

One of the first bankruptcy acts, the Statute of 13 Elizabeth, has long been relied upon as a restatement of the law of so-called fraudulent conveyances (also known as"fraudulent transfers" or "fraudulent alienations"). See generally G. Glenn, The Law of Fraudulent Conveyances 89–92 (1931). That statute, also called the Fraudulent Conveyances Act of 1571, identified as fraud "feigned covenous and fraudulent

Feoffmentes Gyftes Grauntes Alienations [and] Conveyaunces" made with "Intent to delaye hynder or defraude Creditors." 13 Eliz. ch. 5. In modern terms, Parliament made it fraudulent to hide assets from creditors by giving them to one's family, friends, or associates. The principles of the Statute of 13 Elizabeth — and even some of its language — continue to be in wide use today. See *BFP* v. *Resolution Trust Corporation*, 511 U. S. 531, 540 (1994) ("The modern law of fraudulent transfers had its origin in the Statute of 13 Elizabeth"); *id.*, at 541 ("Every American bankruptcy law has incorporated a fraudulent transfer provision"); Story §353, at 393 ("[T]he statute of 13 Elizabeth . . . has been universally adopted in America, as the basis of our jurisprudence on the same subject"); *Boston Trading Group, Inc.* v. *Burnazos*, 835 F. 2d 1504, 1505-1506 (CA1 1987) (Breyer, J.) ("Mass. Gen. Laws ch. 109A, §§1-13 . . . is a uniform state law that codifies both common and statutory law stretching back at least to 1571 and the Statute of Elizabeth"). The degree to which this statute remains embedded in laws related to fraud today clarifies that the common-law term "actual fraud" is broad enough to incorporate a fraudulent conveyance.

Equally important, the common law also indicates that fraudulent conveyances, although a "fraud," do not require a misrepresentation from a debtor to a creditor. As a basic point, fraudulent conveyances are not an inducement based fraud. Fraudulent conveyances typically involve "a transfer to a close relative, a secret transfer, a transfer of title without transfer of possession, or grossly inadequate consideration." BFP, 511 U. S., at 540-541 (citing Twyne's Case, 3 Co. Rep. 80b, 76 Eng. Rep. 809 (K. B. 1601)); O. Bump, Fraudulent Conveyances: A Treatise Upon Conveyances Made by Debtors To Defraud Creditors 31-60 (3d ed. 1882)). In such cases, the fraudulent conduct is not in dishonestly inducing a creditor to extend a debt. It is in the acts of concealment and hindrance. In the fraudulent-conveyance context, therefore, the opportunities for a false representation from the debtor to the creditor are limited. The debtor may have the opportunity to put forward a false representation if the creditor inquires into the where abouts of the debtor's assets, but that could hardly be considered a defining feature of this kind of fraud.

Relatedly, under the Statute of 13 Elizabeth and the laws that followed, both the debtor and the recipient of the conveyed assets were liable for fraud even though the recipient of a fraudulent conveyance of course made no representation, true or false, to the debtor's creditor. The famous Twyne's Case, which this Court relied upon in BFP, illustrates this point. See Twyne's Case, 76 Eng.Rep., at 823 (convicting Twyne of fraud under the Statute of 13 Elizabeth, even though he was the recipient of a debtor's conveyance). That principle underlies the now-common understanding a "conveyance which hinders, delays or defrauds creditors shall be void as against [the recipient] unless . . . th[at] party . . . received it in good faith and for consideration." Glenn, Law of Fraudulent Conveyances §233, at 312. That principle also underscores the point that a false representation has never been a required element of "actual fraud," and we decline to adopt it as one today. . . .

It is of course true that the transferor does not "obtai[n]"debts in a fraudulent conveyance. But the recipient of the transfer — who, with the requisite intent, also commits fraud — can "obtai[n]" assets "by" his or her participation in the fraud. See, *e.g., McClellan* v. *Cantrell*, 217 F. 3d 890 (CA 7 2000); see also *supra*, at 6. If that recipient later files for bankruptcy, any debts "traceable to" the fraudulent conveyance, see

Field, 516 U. S., at 61; *post,* at 3, will be nondischargable under §523(a)(2)(A). Thus, at least sometimes a debt "obtained by" a fraudulent conveyance scheme could be nondischargeable under §523(a)(2)(A). Such circumstances may be rare because a person who receives fraudulently conveyed assets is not necessarily (or even likely to be) a debtor on the verge of bankruptcy, but they make clear that fraudulent conveyances are not wholly incompatible with the "obtained by" requirement. . .

We therefore reverse the judgment of the Fifth Circuit and remand the case for further proceedings consistent with this opinion.

Post-Case Follow-Up

In his dissent to this 7-1 majority decision, Justice Thomas challenges the majority's conclusion that a debt can be "obtained by" actual fraud where there was no fraud in the creation of the debt itself but where there was a subsequent fraudulent conveyance by the debtor in which the recipient of the transfer participates because if that transferee later files for bankruptcy relief, the debt transferee owes as a fraudulent schemer might be nondischargeable under §523(a)(2)(A). Thomas responds, "But §523(a)(2)(A) does not exempt from discharge any debts 'traceable to the fraudulent conveyance.' Instead, §523(a)(2)(A) exempts from discharge 'any debt for' goods that are 'obtained by' actual fraud." Who do you think gets this interpretation of the statute right? In briefs filed with the Supreme Court in this case, Husky and its supporters urged the court to adopt this expansion of the actual fraud exception of §523(a)(2)(A) to include a post-debt creation fraudulent transfer for an important policy reason: it would prohibit debtors using the Bankruptcy Code as an "engine of fraud." On the other hand, a group of consumer bankruptcy attorneys urged the court to not adopt this expansion of actual fraud nondischargeability because it would render debtors who are self-employed or owners of small businesses and who often transfer funds informally between personal and business accounts more vulnerable to §523(a)(2)(A) challenges arising from alleged post-debt creation fraudulent transfers. Which policy argument do you find more persuasive? Husky does not stand for the proposition that any post-debt creation transfer of assets by the debtor will make the debt non-dischargeable—fraudulent transfer must still be proven. But the case does represent a fascinating expansion of the actual fraud concept of §523(a)(2)(A) that may motivate more unsecured creditors to look for questionable asset transfers by the debtor and to contest dischargeability of their claim on that basis.

Husky Int'l Electronics, Inc. v. Ritz: Real Life Applications

1. Terry borrows money from Alice. There is no fraud involved in the transaction. Before Terry repays Alice, Terry conveys his property available to pay Alice to Frank for less than its ordinary value in order to deprive Alice of payment. Terry then files for bankruptcy under Chapter 7 and seeks to discharge

the obligation to Alice. Alice contends the debt owed to her by Terry is non-dischargeable under §523(a)(2)(A). Under the rule of Husky, did Terry obtain the loan from Alice using actual fraud within the meaning of §523(a)(2)(A)? If Alice makes a claim against Frank for liability to her for fraudulent transfer and Frank responds by filing under Chapter 7, is Alice's claim against Frank dischargeable?

2. Assume the same facts as in #1 except that Frank is unaware actually or constructively that the property Terry conveys to him is undervalued and has no idea that Terry is conveying the property to him in order to defraud Alice. Under the rule of Husky, is the debt that Terry owes to Alice nondischargeable in Terry's bankruptcy per §523(a)(2)(A)?

3. Presumption of Fraud in "Last-Minute" Consumer Purchases of Luxury Goods or Services [§523(a)(2)(C)]

Section 523(a)(2)(C) creates a rebuttable presumption that consumer debts aggregating more than $500 owed to a single creditor for luxury goods or services purchased within 90 days preceding the petition are fraudulent and non-dischargeable. The phrase "luxury goods or services" is not defined but expressly does not include goods or services reasonably necessary for the maintenance or support of the debtor or a dependent.

The same section also makes cash advances aggregating more than $750 obtained within 70 days preceding the petition on an open end credit plan non-dischargeable. The policy behind these consumer provisions is to punish last-minute spending sprees by unethical debtors. But the presumption of fraud is rebuttable by the debtor.

For example, assume that in the 90 days preceding the filing of her bankruptcy petition Marta Carlson charged almost $1,000 on her Capital City Bank Visa card for an iPod, several video games, and tuition to a 3-week science camp for her son, Chris. In her bankruptcy case, CCB may seek to have these charges declared non-dischargeable under 523(a)(2)(C) as luxury goods and services. At the trial, Marta testifies that each of those purchases was necessitated by the emotional problems suffered by her son and all represented efforts on her part to provide him with healthy diversions and positive experiences to improve his emotional state. If the court concludes that these charges were reasonably necessary for the maintenance or support of Chris, she may be allowed to discharge them. How do you think the court will rule on that?

4. Debts Arising from Fraud or Defalcation in a Fiduciary Capacity [§523(a)(4)]

A fiduciary capacity arises when the debtor occupies a position of trust and confidence as to another person who relies on the debtor to exercise competence, honesty, and loyalty. Generally speaking, some courts construe this "fraud or defalcation in a fiduciary capacity" language narrowly and hold it only applies to express or implied trusts (see, e.g., In re Burress, 245 B.R. 871 (Bankr. D. Colo. 2000)). Other courts construe the language more broadly to apply to any person entrusted with the property or confidential affairs of others raising an expectation of loyalty and care (e.g., attorneys, trustees, brokers, bankers) (see, e.g., In re McDade, 282 B.R. 650 (N.D. Ill. 2002)). If an obligation arises out of fraud or defalcation (dishonesty) by the debtor acting in such capacity, that obligation may not be dischargeable in bankruptcy.

For example, assume an accountant (or lawyer or trustee) is sued for lying to the client regarding the investment of the client's money entrusted to her for safe investment, and a prepetition judgment is entered against her for fraud. If the accountant files in Chapter 7 to discharge that judgment, it may be deemed nondischargeable since it arose out of the accountant's fraud in a fiduciary capacity, depending on whether the bankruptcy court follows *Burress* or *McDade* in interpreting the scope of §523(a)(4).

There has also been a question regarding the degree of culpability that should be required to bar the fiduciary from discharging an obligation arising from defalcation of his obligation. Should a knowing, intentional violation of the fiduciary duty be required in order to block discharge, or is a negligent or technical but innocent violation of duty that results in loss to the beneficiary enough? The lower courts were split on this issue until the Supreme Court decision in Bullock v. BankChampaign N.A., 133 S. Ct. 1754 (2013) holding that defalcation does require a culpable state of mind beyond mere negligence, which can consist of knowledge of, or gross recklessness in respect to, the improper nature of the relevant fiduciary behavior.

5. Debts Arising from Embezzlement or Larceny [§523(a)(4)]

Regardless of whether a fiduciary capacity is involved, any obligation arising out of embezzlement or larceny cannot be discharged in bankruptcy.

For example, assume a bookkeeper employee steals from her employer. The employer files a civil suit based on the embezzlement and obtains a final judgment. The final judgment obligation arising from that embezzlement will be non-dischargeable if the employee files for Chapter 7 relief.

6. Domestic Support Obligations [§523(a)(5)]

Section 101(14A) of the Code defines **domestic support obligations** generally as debts for "alimony, maintenance or support" of a spouse, former spouse, or child of the debtor. Generally these obligations must arise from a court decree of divorce or separation or from a property settlement agreement. Both domestic support obligations and other debts to a former spouse or child of the debtor arising in the course of a divorce or separation are exempted from discharge by §523(a)(5)(15).

7. Debts Arising from Willful or Malicious Injury to the Person or Property of Another [§523(a)(6)]

In Kawaauhau v. Geiger, 523 U.S. 57, 61-62 (1998), the Supreme Court made it clear that a judgment of liability arising out of mere negligent or even reckless conduct does not fall within the exception to discharge. Nor do judgments based on intentional torts where all that is proven (or required) is an intent to perform the intentional act. What is required is that the debtor intended the harm or injury itself. As the courts have interpreted *Kawaauhau*: "A debtor is responsible for a 'willful' injury when he or she commits an intentional act the purpose of which is to cause injury or which is substantially certain to cause injury." In re Jennings, 670 F.3d 1329, 1334 (11th Cir. 2012). The debtor need not have held any personal animosity against the creditor, but must have intended the consequences of his act.

Application Exercise 1

The courts disagree regarding whether the "substantially certain" aspect of the debtor's intent for purposes of §523(a)(6) is to be measured subjectively or objectively. Compare In re Ormsby, 591 F.3d 1199, 1206 (9th Cir. 2010) (requiring creditor to show that "debtor believes that injury is substantially certain to result from his own conduct"), with In re Shcolnik, 670 F.3d 624, 630 (5th Cir. 2012) (finding willfulness where creditor showed an "objective substantial certainty of harm"). Most courts also interpret *Kawaauhau* to require that the debtor have committed an intentional tort recognized under state law. See, e.g., Lockerby v. Sierra, 535 F.3d 1038 (9th Cir. 2008)(a debt arising from a willful breach of contract by debtor is not nondischargeable under §523(a)(6) unless accompanied by conduct that would give rise to a tort action under state law). Determine how the courts of the federal district or circuit where you plan to practice measure substantial certainty for purposes of §523(a)(6) and whether they follow Lockerby as to whether a claim arising from a breach of contract must also be tortious under state law.

8. Student Loans [§523(a)(8)]

At one time, student loan debt could be discharged in bankruptcy as easily as an auto loan or credit card debt. Congress implemented the prohibition on discharge of student loans in 1976 after widespread reports of new college and professional school graduates (including doctors and lawyers) filing Chapter 7 cases to discharge their considerable (and often taxpayer-guaranteed) student loan debt before undertaking successful and even lucrative careers.

Until BAPCPA in 2005, the prohibition on discharge only applied to a federal student loan meaning an educational loan made, subsidized, or guaranteed by the government or made under a program funded by either a governmental unit or a non-profit institution. In one of its more controversial provisions, BAPCPA expanded the non-dischargeability provision to include private student loans

Stephanie Zieber/Shutterstock.com

(meaning loans made by for-profit lenders, not subsidized or guaranteed by the government and thus not subject to government regulation on amount, interest rate, or fees) as well. Thus today, neither a public nor a private student loan can be discharged absent a showing of undue hardship.

The only exception to the prohibition on discharge of student loans is a showing by debtor that disallowing discharge of the student loan obligation will cause **undue hardship** to the debtor and his dependents. Undue hardship is an undefined term in the Code but has always been construed by the courts as a demanding standard. In the oft-cited case of In re Briscoe, 16 B.R. 128, 131 (Bankr. S.D.N.Y. 1981), the court said, "Dischargeability of student loans should be based upon the certainty of hopelessness, not simply present inability to fulfill financial commitment." That "certainty of hopelessness" test was cited with approval in the leading case of Brunner v. New York State Higher Edu. Serv. Corp., 831 F.2d 395, 396 (2d Cir. 1987), which held that in order to establish undue hardship the debtor must show:

■ That the debtor cannot maintain, based on current income and expenses, a "minimal" standard of living for herself and her dependents if forced to repay the loan;

■ That additional circumstances exist indicating that this state of affairs is likely to persist for a significant portion of the repayment period of the student loan; and

■ That the debtor has made good faith efforts to repay the loan.

In *Brunner* the Second Circuit said of Congress' decision to exempt student loan debt from discharge in bankruptcy: "In return for giving aid to individuals who represent poor credit risks, it strips these individuals of the refuge of bankruptcy in all but extreme circumstances." It was "a conscious Congressional choice to override the normal 'fresh start' goal of bankruptcy."

Application Exercise 2

Determine if the courts of the federal district or circuit where you plan to practice follow *Brunner* and the certainty-of-hopelessness test in applying the undue hardship standard for discharge of student loan debt. If not, what standard do they apply? Marta Carlson has two educational loans (see the Assignment Memorandum in Appendix A and her Schedule E/F, Document 10 in the Carlson case file), one to Columbiana Federal Savings & Loan in the amount of $5,000 and one to Capital City Bank in the amount of $10,000.

Looking at Marta's overall financial situation and that of her two children, can you construct a plausible argument under the standard used in your federal circuit that excepting these two loans from discharge would work an undue hardship on her or her dependents?

The second prong of the *Brunner* formula, requiring the debtor seeking to discharge student debt to show "additional circumstances" indicating that the debtor's inability to maintain a minimal standard of living will continue for all or a significant portion of the loan payback period, has proved to be the most difficult for debtors to meet. As summarized in In re Nys, 308 B.R. 436 (B.A.P. 9th Cir. 2004), such circumstances may include:

- Serious mental or physical disability of the debtor or the debtor's dependents that prevents employment or advancement
- The debtor's obligations to care for dependents
- Lack of, or severely limited, education
- Poor quality of education
- Lack of usable or marketable job skills
- Underemployment, maximized income potential in the chosen educational field, and no other, more lucrative job skills
- Limited number of years remaining in the debtor's work life to allow payment of the loan
- Age or other factors that prevent retraining or relocation as a means for payment of the loan
- Lack of assets, whether or not exempt, which could be used to pay the loan
- Potentially increasing expenses that outweigh any potential appreciation in the value of the debtor's assets and/or likely increases in the debtor's income
- Lack of better financial options elsewhere.

How Hard Is the Hardship Test, Really?

Maybe the undue hardship test is not as intimidating in the application as it sounds in theory. A 2012 study found that 4 out of 10 debtors who sought partial or total discharge of student debt in bankruptcy were successful notwithstanding the undue hardship test. Remarkably, the study found that only one-tenth of 1 percent of bankruptcy debtors with student loan debt even attempted to discharge it. See Jason Iuliano, *An Empirical Assessment of Student Loan Discharges and the Undue Hardship Standard*, 86 Am. Bankr. L.J., 495 (Sept. 25, 2012). If this is a subject that interests you, read the study and determine the common characteristics of the debtors whose student debt was discharged in whole or part.

The U.S. Department of Education has instituted a new **Income Based Repayment (IBR) Plan** that caps the required monthly payment on a federal student loan obligation at an amount calculated based on the former student's income and family size. The qualifying former student is given 25 years to repay the loan rather than the standard 10 years and any amounts still owing after 25 years will be forgiven under the plan. The DOE also offers a **Public Service Loan Forgiveness (PSLF) Plan**, pursuant to which graduates who choose to work as public school teachers or in other government positions or for non-profit organizations can repay their student loans at reduced amounts and receive forgiveness of the balance after only ten years. You can read up on these DOE repayment options at http://studentaid.ed.gov/.

Case Preview

In re Barrett

The decision of a debtor in bankruptcy to participate or not in one of these DOE programs could have a bearing on whether the debtor can satisfy the third prong of the *Brunner* formula for determining undue hardship — whether the debtor has made a good faith effort to repay the loan. As you read In re Barrett, consider the following questions:

1. What government program could the debtor have applied for to manage his student loans that he did not?
2. Which prong of the Brunner test for undue hardship does ECMC contend the debtor failed to satisfy due to his not enrolling in the program?
3. Why does the court reject the argument of ECMC that the debtor's failure to apply for the government program does not prevent him from satisfying the undue hardship test under §523(a)(8)?
4. When a debtor relies on health problems to satisfy the undue hardship test, must he present expert medical testimony to establish such problems?

In re Barrett
487 F.3d 353 (6th Cir. 2007)

[Plaintiff-debtor Thomas Barrett incurred student loan debt totaling $94,751 while earning masters degrees from Saint Louis University in 1999. Barrett has a long history of medical problems. After receiving his graduate degrees, Barrett was diagnosed with Hodgkin's disease in the summer of 2000 and had to undergo nine months of chemotherapy treatment. While recovering from the treatment, Barrett's student loans became due, but he received an economic hardship deferment for his loans. Due to the inability to work and accumulated medical bills, Barrett filed for Chapter 7 bankruptcy on December 28, 2001. In October 2002, Barrett was diagnosed with avascular necrosis, a condition that causes the patient's bones to die due to lack of blood supply. This diagnosis required an increase in pain medication and medical procedures.

Barrett testified that he was unable to find full-time employment because of his medical condition. He also testified that since his Chapter 7 petition was filed, he has incurred an additional $20,000 in medical bills. Barrett's schedule J lists his projected monthly income as $868 with his monthly expenses totaling $3,575. On November 23, 2004, the bankruptcy court conducted an adversary proceeding and issued a memorandum opinion on December 14, 2004. The memorandum opinion stated that the bankruptcy court found Barrett's testimony to be credible and concluded that Barrett had demonstrated it would be an undue hardship if his student loans were excepted from his Chapter 7 discharge. On appeal, the Sixth Circuit Bankruptcy Appellate Panel ("BAP") unanimously affirmed the bankruptcy court's determination. Defendant Educational Credit Management Corporation ("ECMC") now appeals.]

GRIFFIN, Circuit Judge. . . .

III.

The Bankruptcy Code limits the discharge of student loans only to those circumstances where repayment "will impose an undue hardship on the debtor and the debtor's dependents." 11 U.S.C. §523(a)(8). As "undue hardship" is not defined in the Bankruptcy Code, we have joined most of our sister circuits in adopting the three-part *Brunner* test, named for the case in which it originated. Oyler v. Educ. Credit Mgmt. Corp., 397 F.3d 382, 385 (6th Cir. 2005). The *Brunner* test requires the debtor to prove, by the preponderance of the evidence:

> (1) that the debtor cannot maintain, based on current income and expenses, a "minimal" standard of living for [himself] and [his] dependents if forced to repay the loans; (2) that additional circumstances exist indicating that this state of affairs is likely to persist for a significant portion of the repayment period of the student loans; and (3) that the debtor has made good faith efforts to repay the loans.

Id. (quoting Brunner v. New York State Higher Educ. Serv. Corp., 831 F.2d 395, 396 (2d Cir. 1987)). . . .

On appeal, ECMC does not challenge the bankruptcy court's finding that Barrett satisfied the first prong of the Brunner test: that Barrett cannot maintain, based on current income and expenses, a "minimal" standard of living if forced to repay the loans. Rather, ECMC argues that Barrett was required, and failed, to provide expert corroborating evidence to carry his burden of proof in satisfying the second prong. In particular, ECMC contends that Barrett could not competently testify to his prognosis or future health, and that expert medical evidence was necessary to competently project Barrett's future ability to repay his student loans.

In our prior interpretations of "undue hardship" under 11 U.S.C. §523(a)(8), we have not declared that expert medical evidence is necessary to corroborate a claim of "additional circumstances" premised on the debtor's health. In re Tirch, 409 F.3d 677, the most recent Sixth Circuit case to apply the Brunner test to §523(a)(8), held that a debtor's student loans are nondischargeable where the debtor fails to demonstrate how her physical condition prevented her from working. Id. at 682. Despite ECMC's argument to the contrary, we did not hold that the debtor's claim was foreclosed by the lack of corroborating expert medical evidence. Rather, we emphasized repeatedly that the debtor's testimony by itself failed to meet the "undue hardship" standard. See id. at 681. In fact, we explicitly declined to consider whether expert corroboration was necessary to satisfy the second Brunner prong: "We have no occasion to delve into the BAP's holding that the bankruptcy court's assessment of the debtor's testimony regarding her mental and emotional health is sufficiently reliable to support the bankruptcy court's findings in that regard, without the necessity of expert corroboration, because the bankruptcy court made no such assessment." Id. at 681. Under *Tirch*, to satisfy Brunner's second prong, Barrett must "precisely identify [his] problems and explain how [his] condition would impair [his] ability to work in the future." Id. at 681. *Tirch*, however, does not require Barrett to offer corroborating expert testimony to meet this burden. . . .

We decline to adopt here ECMC's position that Barrett was required to produce an expert witness to corroborate his health status, and instead concur with the BAP that "a requirement of corroborating evidence 'when Plaintiff is unable to afford expert testimony or documentation imposes an unnecessary and undue burden on Plaintiff in establishing his burden of proof,' if corroborating evidence is understood to be limited to expert medical testimony." Even where some corroborating evidence of the debtor's claimed illness is required, the notion that only expert medical testimony would suffice has been rejected. See, e.g., In re Burton, 339 B.R. 856, 879 (Bankr. E.D. Va. 2006) ("This Court, in light of . . . the fact that other credible evidence often exists, does not suggest expert testimony is the only method of corroboration available to debtors."); In re Swinney, 266 B.R. 800, 805 (Bankr. N.D. Ohio 2001) ("Although such [corroborating] evidence does not have to necessarily consist of extensive expert testimony, such evidence should consist of more than simply bare allegations; that is, whenever a debtor's health, whether mental or physical, is directly put at issue some corroborating evidence must be given supporting the proponent's position. . . . For example, if properly authenticated, letters from a treating physician could be utilized.").

We also find unpersuasive Barrett's position that, because of the expense involved with obtaining corroborating medical evidence, requiring such evidence creates a significant and unnecessary bar to debtors seeking discharge of student debt. At the adversary proceeding, Barrett argued that he was unable to submit his medical records or to obtain expert medical testimony because the cost to procure such evidence was prohibitive. ECMC disputes Barrett's contention, pointing to Ohio Rev. Code §3701.741, which limits a patient's copying costs for his medical records. Ohio Rev.Code §3701.741(B)(1) (limiting copying costs to two dollars and fifty cents per page for the first ten pages, fifty-one cents per page for pages eleven through fifty, and twenty cents per page for pages fifty-one and higher); see also 45 C.F.R. §164.524(c)(4) (requiring health care providers to impose "reasonable" copying costs in response to patient's request for medical records). We agree with ECMC that the copying costs of medical records are reasonable costs that a debtor may bear in order to substantiate his claim of undue hardship. In any event, we note that other forms of corroborating evidence may suffice — and, in this case, do suffice — to corroborate a debtor's claim of undue hardship based on illness. Medical bills, letters from treating physicians, and other indicia of medical treatment aside from medical records or expert medical testimony may corroborate a debtor's claim of undue hardship based on the debtor's health.

We hold that the evidence in the record is sufficient to support the bankruptcy court's finding that additional circumstances exist indicating that Barrett's current financial state is likely to persist for a significant portion of the repayment period. . . .

IV.

ECMC . . . argues that Barrett failed to satisfy the third prong of the *Brunner* test — that is, Barrett failed to show that he has made a good faith effort to repay his student loans — because he did not enroll in the Income Contingent Repayment Program ("ICRP"). ECMC contends that "Barrett's refusal to apply for the ICRP payment option was without factual and legal justification" and that this refusal demonstrates a lack of good faith under *Brunner*. We find ECMC's position unpersuasive.

As described by the bankruptcy court in In re Korhonen, 296 B.R. 492, 496 (Bankr. D. Minn. 2003), the ICRP:

> permits a student loan debtor to pay twenty percent of the difference between his adjusted gross income and the poverty level for his family size, or the amount the debtor would pay if the debt were repaid in twelve years, whichever is less. Under the program, the borrower's monthly repayment amount is adjusted each year to reflect any changes in these factors. The borrower's repayments may also be adjusted during the year based on special circumstances. *See* 34 C.F.R. §685.209(c)(3). At the end of the twenty five year payment period, any remaining loan balance would be cancelled by the Secretary of Education. However, the amount discharged would be considered taxable income.

. . . Although ECMC doesn't state so explicitly, its position would create a per se rule requiring enrollment in the ICRP to satisfy the third *Brunner* prong and thus would, in effect, eliminate the discharge of student loans for undue hardship from the Bankruptcy Code.

We have already rejected ECMC's per se position. *See Tirch*, 409 F.3d at 682 (noting that a debtor's decision not to enroll in ICRP is "not a *per se* indication of a lack of good faith"). Moreover, Congress recently enacted "the most sweeping reform of bankruptcy law since the enactment of the Bankruptcy Code in 1978." . . . Yet Congress left §523(a)(8)'s "undue hardship" language intact. Had Congress intended participation in the ICRP — implemented in 1994 — to effectively repeal discharge under §523(a)(8), it could have done so. In addition, requiring enrollment in the ICRP runs counter to the Bankruptcy Code's aim in providing debtors a "fresh start." The debtor is encumbered with the debt for an additional twenty-five years, regardless of the length of the student loans. If, at the end of the twenty-five years, the debtor has been unable to repay all the student loans, the remaining debt is canceled and that discharge of indebtedness is treated as taxable income. . . . The result, as the bankruptcy court noted, would be that Barrett would "be trading one nondischargeable debt for another."

Although Barrett's decision to forgo the ICRP is not a per se indication of a lack of good faith, his decision "is probative of [his] intent to repay [his] loans." . . . Nevertheless, we conclude that Barrett has demonstrated sufficient good faith to satisfy the third *Brunner* prong. Barrett testified that he looked into the ICRP, but declined to enroll in the program because the tax consequences would be too burdensome. . . .

The bankruptcy court credited Barrett's testimony, concluding that Barrett "has used his best efforts to maximize financial potential; recognizing that his health has not permitted him to work full time, he still works part time to the best of his ability." In light of the significant tax consequences of enrolling in the ICRP due to his present and future inability to pay his student debt, Barrett's decision to forgo the ICRP was reasonable and is not grounds for finding bad faith.

Although Barrett has made no payments on his student loans, no loan payments have come due; Barrett has received economic hardship deferments for each year since graduation due to his health. Even had payments become due, his inability to repay the loans was unlikely to evidence bad faith, as his monthly expenses exceed by double his monthly income. Despite his health problems that have prevented him from working full-time since graduation, Barrett has made repeated efforts to work as his health and opportunities have allowed, even as his physical capability has been limited to moving a computer mouse. Further, Barrett testified that but for the medical bills, he would not have filed his Chapter 7 petition.

In sum, we concur with the BAP's analysis of the third prong of the *Brunner* test:

> The Debtor in this case has reasonable expenses, yet continues to accrue debt for medical care. He has made efforts to increase his income within his ability. He has cooperated in providing information to his student loan creditors on an annual basis to obtain deferments. He has never had the ability to repay his student loans as evidenced by the deferments granted to him as the result of economic hardship. . . . Utilization of the ICRP would likely result in a substantial increase in his student loan debts over the repayment period. The Debtor has amply demonstrated his good faith.

V.

The BAP's judgment affirming the bankruptcy court's December 14, 2004, order discharging Barrett's student loan obligation to defendant ECMC is therefore affirmed.

Post-Case Follow-Up

Barrett does not stand for the proposition that the debtor's decision to participate in a government program for management of student loan debt is irrelevant on the issue of whether debtor has made a good-faith effort to pay the debt. The court merely held that the debtor's failure to participate is not a basis to find lack of good faith, per se. In fact, courts appear to give varying weight to the debtor's decision to not participate in a government student loan management program. Compare In re Gibson, 428 B.R. 385, 391-392 (Bankr. W.D. Mich. 2010) (debtor who declined to participate in DOE IBR plan did not use good faith efforts to repay her loans), with In re Bene, 474 B.R. 56, 71-72 (Bankr. W.D.N.Y. 2012) (debtor's decision not to participate outweighed by other circumstances and no bar to finding of good faith). Determine if the courts of the federal district or circuit where you plan to practice have decided a case involving a debtor seeking to discharge student debt who did or did not choose to participate in one of the government programs and, if so, what weight they gave to it.

In re Barrett: Real Life Applications

1. You represent Charles, a Chapter 7 debtor who has more than $100,000 in student loans from spending 8 years obtaining his B.A. degree during which time

he attended four different universities and changed his major six times. He's been looking for a job in his degree field (journalism, finally) for nine months since graduation without success. The fast food job he has pays minimum wage and leaves him unable to make any payment on the student loan balance. Charles calls today and asks about the possibility of discharging the student loan obligation. What will you tell him?

2. You represent Carey, a Chapter 7 debtor who has more than $100,000 in student loans from undergraduate and graduate work. Her masters and PhD degrees are in history and she was planning on a university level academic career but has had no success in landing even an instructor's position at that level in the two years since she received her PhD. She's had to settle for part-time teaching at the local high school while she lives with her parents. She considered the ICRP program mentioned in *Barrett* but like the debtor there was scared away by the potential long-term tax consequences of the program. She's been making very small payments on her student loan debt, usually about one-fourth of what is owed in each installment. It is all she can afford. Carey calls today and asks about the possibility of discharging the student loan obligation. What will you tell her?

3. You represent Clay, a Chapter 7 debtor who has more than $100,000 in student loans from undergraduate and graduate work. He received his master's degree in economics eighteen months ago and had a really good job offer from a national company but had to refuse it when he became ill with a rare virus he picked up on a post-graduation trip to Fiji. He came close to death several times and needed a number of blood transfusions while suffering from the virus. His medical bills from the ordeal exceed $250,000. The prognosis is finally somewhat positive: he will have mostly a full recovery but will always have breathing problems if placed under too much stress; he has a greatly enhanced chance of suffering cardiovascular problems compared to other men his age; and he faces 25 percent chance of a relapse in the next ten years and the odds for it grow as he ages. With that prognosis, Clay expects to be back in the job market within nine months. However, the gap in his employment history resulting from the health problems together with permanent health problems and the significant risk of a relapse are likely to make it harder for him to find a position like the one he had to pass up and to permanently handicap his ability to go as far in his field as he could have both in terms of position and income. Clay's parents made payments on his student loan debt for several months following his graduation but had to stop for financial reasons. Clay has participated in every federal and state program he can qualify for to defer payment on and otherwise manage his student debt obligation. Clay calls today and asks about the possibility of discharging the student loan obligation. What will you tell him?

4. You represent Clarissa, a Chapter 7 debtor who has more than $100,000 in student loans from undergraduate and graduate work. She received her master's degree in early childhood education three years ago. A month before that she was diagnosed with Hodgkin's lymphoma and has been in the fight of her life since. She has undergone three rounds of radiation and chemotherapy that, together with the powerful medications she must take, have left her unable to

handle any employment for the present. She lost her home and her vehicle and lives with and depends on her sister. Currently the disease does not seem to be worsening and it is still possible that she might be declared cancer free at some point but doctors will not do that until it has been at least five years since the last chemotherapy. Even in the best-case scenario she will have lost a decade in her career that she cannot recover. She has not made any payments on her student loan obligation and has not participated in any government programs to defer or manage such debt. Clarissa calls today and asks about the possibility of discharging the student loan obligation. What will you tell her?

Another issue raised by these DOE programs for student loan repayment is the potential tax liability for debtors who are ultimately able to write off all or a portion of the student loan debt as a result of participating in such a program (cancellation of debt income or COD). Should a debtor who chooses not to participate because of the potential for tax liability years down the road when the balance of a loan is written off nonetheless be held to have failed the good faith prong of the *Brunner* test? The courts are split. Compare In re Gibson, 428 B.R. 385 (Bankr. W.D. Mich. 2010) ("the court is not persuaded that a debtor's long-term tax strategy or concerns should foreclose the possibility of at least some debt repayment over the next twenty-five years, particularly in the case of a bright, well-educated, healthy debtor"), with In re Nixon, 453 B.R. 311, 335, 392-393 (Bankr. S.D. Ohio 2007) ("At the end of the 25-year repayment period, if the debt is cancelled, there are tax consequences for the Debtor. The Debtor would be 81 years old at the end of the 25-year repayment period, and likely still on a fixed income. The tax consequences for someone in that position could be devastating.").

Application Exercise 3

Determine if the courts of the federal district or circuit where you plan to practice have addressed this aspect of the dischargeable student loan issue. In the last generation the cost of a college education has accelerated far faster than inflation. At the same time, most states have reduced aid to public institutions, placing more of the increasing cost on the student and her family. In 2012 the total student loan debt in the United States, for the first time, actually exceeded total consumer credit card debt, second only to total indebtedness for home loans. As of 2016 student loan debt in the U.S. exceeds $1.3 trillion, approximately 11 percent of which is delinquent or in default. Forty million Americans carry student loan debt, including a number of seniors who either returned to school late in life or co-signed for a child or grandchild's loan. Is it time to revisit the undue hardship standard for discharge of student loan debt and give bankruptcy judges more flexibility to modify such obligations in particular cases? Should BAPCPA's expansion of the discharge restriction to private student loans made by for-profit lenders be reconsidered? Can you think of other approaches to this vexing problem that ought to be considered?

9. Fines, Penalties, and Forfeitures Owed to the Government [§523(a)(7)]

Governmental fines and penalties imposed to punish the debtor for wrongdoing are non-dischargeable if not more than three years old when the petition is filed. Examples include speeding tickets, penalties on unpaid taxes, and liability for bail bond forfeiture.

10. Personal Injury and Wrongful Death Claims Arising from DUI [§523(a)(9)]

Judgments and pending claims arising out of simple or even gross negligence are generally dischargeable in bankruptcy, but if the wrongful death or personal injury claim against the debtor arises out of the debtor's driving while intoxicated by alcohol or drugs, it will not be a dischargeable debt.

11. Unlisted Debts [§523(a)(3)]

When preparing their schedules and lists to accompany the bankruptcy petition, debtors must be very careful to list every single debt they owe, whether contingent or fixed, disputed or undisputed. Any debt not listed may not be discharged whether the error was intentional or accidental. For reasons we have discussed, attorneys must take reasonable steps to ensure debtor's schedules are complete and accurate.

Section 523(a)(3) makes claims omitted from the debtor's lists and schedules non-dischargeable, with the result that the creditor fails to file a timely proof of claim *unless* the creditor in question had other notice or actual knowledge of the bankruptcy filing. Certain claims are given protection on the same grounds for failure of the creditor to file a timely objection to discharge.

When a debtor's lawyer belatedly discovers that a claim was omitted from the debtor's lists and schedules, the thing to do is to promptly file an amended list or schedule including the claim. FRBP 1009 provides that a voluntary petition, list, statement or schedule can be amended by the debtor at any time before the case is closed. If the case has been closed when the omission of a creditor from the schedules is discovered, the case may be reopened by motion pursuant to §350(b) and FRBP 5010, and the schedules then amended. However, the debtor will be required to pay a new filing fee for reopening the case as well as the additional attorney fee involved.

B. OBJECTIONS TO DISCHARGE

An individual Chapter 7 debtor can be denied any discharge at all (i.e., no relief from any debts) if one of the grounds set forth in §727(a) of the Code and summarized in Exhibit 11.2 is established.

EXHIBIT 11.2	Grounds for Denying a Discharge to an Individual Chapter 7 Debtor

- The debtor has transferred, removed, destroyed, or concealed property with the intent to hinder, delay, or defraud a creditor or the trustee within either a year preceding the filing of the petition or after the petition was filed [§727(a)(2)]
- The debtor has concealed, destroyed, falsified, or failed to keep books and records from which debtor's financial condition or business transactions may be ascertained unless there is justification [§727(a)(3) & 4(D)]
- The debtor has knowingly made a false oath or account, or presented or used a false claim in connection with the bankruptcy case [§727(a)(4)]
- The debtor has failed to satisfactorily explain any loss of assets or deficiency of assets to meet his liabilities [§727(a)(5)]
- The debtor has failed to obey a lawful order of the bankruptcy court [§727(a)(6)]
- The debtor has been previously granted a discharge in a Chapter 7 or 11 within eight years prior to filing the petition in the current case or a discharge in a Chapter 13 within six years prior to filing the petition in the current case [§727(a)(8)(9)]
- The debtor has failed to complete an instructional course concerning financial management [§727(a)(11)]

The bankruptcy trustee, U.S. Trustee, or any creditor is given standing to object to the debtor's discharge by filing a complaint and instituting an adversary proceeding. FRBP 4004 requires that a complaint to deny discharge be initiated within 60 days following the first meeting of creditors subject to extension by motion and, as with complaints objecting to discharge of a particular debt, FRBP 2002(f) requires the bankruptcy court clerk, or some other person as the court may direct, to provide notice by mail of the time fixed for filing a complaint objecting to discharge.

1. Dealing with Property for the Purpose of Hindering, Delaying, or Defrauding a Creditor [§727(a)(2)]

Debtors must be very careful not to play games with the bankruptcy process by hiding assets, putting them into the name of a third person prior to filing, or similar gambits. The trustee will aggressively look for that type of thing and most bankruptcy judges will have little sympathy for debtors engaged in such behaviors when a denial of discharge is requested.

2. Concealing, Destroying, Falsifying, or Not Keeping Books and Records [§727(a)(3) & (4)(D)]

Debtors must be very careful not to destroy, alter, or hide their financial records as part of an attempt to hide assets or deceive as to their value. Bankruptcy trustees know the kinds of records consumer and business debtors should have and will aggressively pursue any situation that looks suspicious. Note that it is not just concealing, destroying, or falsifying books and records that is punishable, but the failure to keep adequate records.

3. Making a False Oath or Account or Using a False Claim [§727(a)(4)]

The petition and supporting schedules and lists filed by the debtor are signed under penalty of perjury and the debtor must be sure before signing that they are accurate and complete. The failure to do so can be construed as a false oath and a discharge denied. In addition, the debtor is examined under oath at the first meeting of creditors (the 341 meeting) and must be careful to give truthful answers there.

4. Lack of Satisfactory Explanation of Loss of or Inadequate Assets [§727(a)(5)]

At the 341 meeting and at informal meetings with the bankruptcy trustee the debtor may be questioned closely regarding assets he once had but now does not. Where did those assets go? If the debtor seemed to have adequate income flow to pay his obligations but did not pay them, where did that income go? If the debtor cannot give a plausible explanation, deception may be suspected and the unsatisfactory explanation will form the basis of this objection to discharge.

5. Failure to Obey a Lawful Court Order or to Answer When Asked [§727(a)(6)]

Assume a debtor fails to come to the 341 meeting as required by §521 and the court orders debtor to be present for the rescheduled date. Assume a debtor refuses to turn over property to the trustee as required by §521 and the court orders the turnover. Assume the trustee requests a Rule 2004 examination of a debtor, the debtor fails to attend, and the court orders debtor's attendance. The debtor must obey the court's orders. Failure to obey even one lawful order forms the basis for this objection to discharge. A pattern of refusal to obey practically guarantees the motion being granted.

The debtor must also respond to material questions posed by the court and to testify when asked to do so whether at the 341 meeting or at a Rule 2004 examination (discussed in Chapter Seven, Section E), at any other evidentiary hearing, or in connection with discovery undertaken in an adversary proceeding. A claim by the debtor of the Fifth Amendment privilege against self-incrimination will not prevent denial of discharge on this basis if the judge has granted the debtor immunity in connection with the testimony.

6. A Prior Discharge [§727(a)(8)(9)]

Section 727(a)(8) stipulates that a bankruptcy court is to deny a Chapter 7 discharge if the debtor previously received a discharge in a Chapter 7 or 11 case within eight years preceding the filing of the petition.

The court will also deny a Chapter 7 discharge if the debtor previously received a discharge in a Chapter 13 or Chapter 12 case within six years preceding the petition under §727(a)(9) unless:

- The debtor paid all allowed unsecured claims in the earlier case in full, or
- The debtor made payments under the plan in the earlier case totaling at least 70 percent of the allowed unsecured claims and the debtor's plan was proposed in good faith and the payments represented the debtor's best effort.

7. Failure to Complete the Postpetition Financial Management Course [§727(a)(11)]

In addition to the prepetition credit counseling requirement imposed on individual debtors considered in Chapter Five, Section D, §727(a)(11), added by BAPCPA, requires those debtors to complete a postpetition financial management instructional course before the discharge will be granted. The individual debtor must also file a Certification About a Financial Management Course (Official Form 423) unless the provider of the course notifies the court that the debtor has completed the course. See Document 33 in the Carlson case file. As with the prepetition credit counseling, the postpetition and predischarge financial management instructional course must be conducted by a non-profit budget and credit counseling agency approved by the U.S. Trustee.

C. INVOLUNTARY DISMISSAL OF A CHAPTER 7 CASE

Related to the topic of the §727 objection to discharge is the possibility that a Chapter 7 case may simply be dismissed by the bankruptcy judge making the subject of discharge irrelevant. This can happen for a number of different reasons.

1. "For Cause" Dismissal for Unreasonable Delay, Nonpayment of Fees, or Failure to File Schedules

Section §707(a) provides that the court may dismiss a Chapter 7 case after notice and a hearing "for cause" including:

- Unreasonable delay by the debtor that is prejudicial to creditors;
- Nonpayment of any required fees or charges; or
- Failure to timely file the required schedules supporting the debtor's petition.

Most of the motions seeking dismissal for cause under this section involve the latter two grounds, which are fairly objective. The first though, unreasonable delay prejudicial to creditors, is a little trickier. It seems clear that the unreasonable delay must arise from postpetition actions of the debtor, not prepetition actions that may have hindered or frustrated the creditor. See, e.g., In re Jackson, 258 B.R. 272, 277 (Bankr. M.D. Fla. 2000) ("[A]ny successful motion to dismiss for delay as 'cause' must be grounded on allegations of post-petition hindrance by a debtor, rather than on prepetition avoidance of service or prepetition avoidance of repossession."). And while courts make it clear that the "for cause" grounds set out in §707(a) are not exclusive, the fact that the debtor has the means to pay a creditor's claim in whole or part is not itself cause to dismiss under that provision. See, e.g., In re Bushyhead, 525 B.R. 136, 142, 152 (Bankr. N.D. Okla. 2015) ("The Bushyheads have sought Chapter 7 relief to discharge several debts. . . . The only remarkable aspect of this case is the Bushyheads' income. If they did not earn a lot of money, we would not be here. On that issue, Congress has spoken. The ability to pay is not cause for dismissal under §707(a).").

Courts in the Second, Third, and Sixth federal Circuits have construed dismissal for cause under §707(a) to include a bad faith filing (or lack of good faith in filing) by the Chapter 7 debtor. See In re Zick, 931 F.2d 1124 (6th Cir. 1991); In re Tamecki, 229 F.3d 205 (3d Cir. 2000); and In re Aiello, 428 B.R. 296, 301-302 (Bankr. E.D.N.Y. 2010). To justify the drastic remedy of dismissing the case, the bad faith alleged and proven against the debtor must involve egregious conduct.

> Dismissal based on lack of good faith must be undertaken on an ad hoc basis. It should be confined carefully and is generally utilized only in those egregious cases that entail concealed or misrepresented assets and/or sources of income, and excessive and continued expenditures, lavish life-style, and intention to avoid a large single debt based on conduct akin to fraud, misconduct, or gross negligence.

Zick, 931 F.2d at 1129. See also In re Lombardo, 370 B.R. 506, 511-512 (Bankr. E.D.N.Y. 2007) identifying fourteen factors to be considered in a for cause bad faith allegation under §707(a)(1).

Application Exercise 4

The Eighth and Ninth Circuits held that bad faith should generally not be a basis for dismissal under §707(a). See In re Huckfeldt, 39 F.3d 829, 832 (8th Cir. 1994) ("framing the issue in terms of bad faith may tend to misdirect the inquiry away from the fundamental principles and purposes of Chapter 7" and concluding that dismissal under §707(a) for bad faith should be limited to extreme misconduct that was not worthy of bankruptcy protection, such as using bankruptcy "as a 'scorched earth' tactic against a diligent creditor, or using bankruptcy as a refuge from another court's jurisdiction"), and In re

Padilla, 222 F.3d 1184, 1191 (9th Cir. 2000) ("bad faith as a general proposition does not provide 'cause' to dismiss a Chapter 7 petition under §707(a)"). Determine whether the federal circuit or district where you plan to practice recognizes bad faith as a basis for dismissal for cause under §707(a) and, if so, what factors or tests those courts utilize in determining bad faith.

2. Dismissal for Abuse by Reason of Bad-Faith Filing or as Evident from the Totality of the Debtor's Financial Circumstances

Dismissal for cause under §707(a) is applicable to all Chapter 7 filings. In contrast §707(b) dismissal for "abuse of the provisions of this chapter" applies only to a Chapter 7 case filed by a consumer debtor. We learned in Section C of Chapter Five that §707(b)(2) raises a presumption of abuse if the consumer debtor fails the means test that can only be overcome by the debtor showing special circumstances involving extraordinary expenses or adjustments to income. But "abuse" under §707(b) is a broader concept than the means test and its presumption of abuse.

Sections 707(b)(1) and (3) allow the court in all Chapter 7 cases to consider whether (1) the debtor filed the petition in bad faith or (2) "the totality of the circumstances of the debtor's financial situation" demonstrates that it would be an abuse of the system to allow the debtor a Chapter 7 discharge. The court can look at any relevant factors in making the decision except that §707(b)(1) specifically says the court may not consider charitable contributions by the debtor.

For example, assume a debtor files a Chapter 7 to stop foreclosure on his home. He fights the lifting of the stay on the creditor's foreclosure on his home then dismisses that case without receiving a discharge. A year and a day later (to avoid the application of the 30-day automatic stay of §362(c) discussed in Chapter Seven, Section F) he files another Chapter 7 case to prevent foreclosure and again fights the lifting of the stay for a while and dismisses this case too. Now, another year and a day later (again to avoid the application of §362(c)), he files yet another Chapter 7 to delay the latest foreclosure actions against him. Regardless of other circumstances, the bankruptcy court could conclude that this third filing is in bad faith and that the debtor is abusing the system by manipulating it only to stop foreclosures using the automatic stay while never intending to allow the case to proceed against his non-exempt assets for the benefit of his creditors. A case like that might well be dismissed under §707(b)(3).

Or assume a physician just finishing her residency and carrying a substantial amount of debt from her medical education and training signs a personal services contract agreeing to provide medical services for a physician's group for three years. The physician begins performance on the agreement but is immediately sorry she entered into it. Unhappy with where she is living and working, the physician breaches the agreement after six months and moves to another location to practice.

When the physician's group with which she contracted files suit, the physician files a Chapter 7 case to discharge the claims arising from the agreement. In examining the totality of the physician's financial circumstances the court may conclude that although the debtor can avoid the presumption of abuse based on the educational loan debt she is still carrying, her projected income in the near future will quickly enable her to pay off that debt at which point she will not be able to rebut the presumption of abuse from the means test. Based on the totality of circumstances the court may dismiss this case.

Or consider a debtor who files for Chapter 7 relief where it is learned that the debtor is unable to pay his creditors because he gave almost everything he owned away to charities. Per §707(b)(1) this arguably cannot be a ground for dismissal based on either bad faith or abuse evident from the totality of the circumstances.

In applying the bad faith filing test of §707(b)(3)(A), courts consider similar factors to those we considered in connection with bad faith as cause under §707(b)(1). See, e.g., In re Guiterrez, 528 B.R. 1, 26-27 (Bankr. D. Vt. 2014) (abuse by bad faith filing applicable only in Chapter 7 consumer bankruptcy case but finding of no bad faith to justify for cause dismissal under §707(a) conclusive on abuse by bad faith filing issue).

Case Preview

Calhoun v. U.S. Trustee

Prior to BAPCPA it was generally recognized that a bankruptcy case could be dismissed only upon a showing of "substantial abuse" and there was a presumption in favor of granting the debtor relief. (For a good case illustrating how the substantial abuse test with the pro-debtor presumption worked, see In re Shaw, 311 B.R. 180 (Bankr. M.D.N.C. 2003).) BAPCPA lowered the standard for dismissal to simply "abuse," eliminated the pro-debtor presumption, and in individual Chapter 7 cases replaced it with the presumption of abuse and means test that we studied in Chapter Five. But the dual grounds of bad-faith filing and abuse of the system evident from totality of the debtor's financial circumstances from §707(b)(3) are clearly intended to be something different. As you read Calhoun v. U.S. Trustee consider the following questions.

1. Why isn't the means test of §707(b)(2) conclusive as to an individual Chapter 7 debtor's good faith in filing?
2. Why isn't the means test of §707(b)(2) conclusive as to the debtor's ability to pay his debts?
3. Did the Fourth Circuit affirm the bankruptcy court's conclusion that it can dismiss an individual Chapter 7 case under §707(b)(3) solely on the basis of a finding that the debtor can pay his debts even though the petition was filed in good faith?

Calhoun v. U.S. Trustee
650 F.3d 338 (4th Cir. 2011)

[John and Glenda Calhoun filed a voluntary Chapter 7 bankruptcy petition on February 27, 2008, seeking to discharge $106,707 in unsecured debt. Mr. Calhoun's monthly income totaled $8,722. The Calhouns had attempted to sell their house in 2000 and after being unsuccessful, they spent $130,000 renovating the home with the intention of staying. Mr. Calhoun's IRAs were significantly reduced during the economic downturn. After accumulating debt on a second mortgage and five credit cards, the Calhouns entered into a payment plan with a credit management company whereby they reduced their monthly expenses and paid their creditors a total of $2,638 per month. The payment plan continued for twenty-two months until the Calhouns' became discouraged at the small amount of money that was left for expenses after fulfilling their payment plan obligations. The bankruptcy court dismissed the Calhoun's Chapter 7 case on grounds of §707(b)(3) abuse, concluding "This Court now holds that, while the totality of all of the debtor's financial circumstances must be examined, the ability to pay a significant dividend to creditors and the failure to do so standing alone can be an abuse of chapter 7, absent mitigating factors." 396 B.R. at 275-276. The district court affirmed and the Calhouns appeal.]

BERGER, District Judge, sitting by designation. . . .

III.

Congress enacted the Bankruptcy Abuse Prevention and Consumer Protection Act of 2005 ("BAPCPA") and amended Section 707(b) of the Bankruptcy Code with the intent of relaxing the standard for dismissing a petition brought under Chapter 7 and characterized as abusive. . . . Specifically, the standard for dismissal under section 707(b) was changed from "substantial abuse" to simply "abuse." 11 U.S.C. §707(b)(1). The amendment also eliminated a presumption in favor of granting a debtor's discharge. As amended by the BAPCPA, §707(b) permits the court's dismissal of "a case filed by an individual debtor under this chapter whose debts are primarily consumer debts . . . if it finds that the granting of relief would be an abuse of the provisions of this chapter." 11 U.S.C. §707(b)(1).

An essential element to the BAPCPA is the "means test," a formula that screens a debtor's income and expenses to determine whether the debtor is able to repay his debt. 11 U.S.C. §707(b)(1), (2). . . . When the debtor's income exceeds the "highest median family income of the applicable State for a family of the same number or fewer individuals," the means test is applied to create a rebuttable presumption of abuse. 11 U.S.C. §707(b)(2), (6), (7).

The means test takes into account the debtor's monthly income and certain deductible expenses such as the cost of housing, utilities, taxes, health insurance and an allowance for food and clothing. 11 U.S.C. §707(b)(2)(A). Some of these expenses may be calculated by using national or local standards. 11 U.S.C. §707(b)(2)(A). The debtor's monthly disposable income is determined by subtracting these allowable expenses from his monthly income, and if that number is greater than a statutory benchmark then the presumption of abuse arises.

In cases where the presumption does not arise or is rebutted, the court still must determine whether granting a debtor relief would be an abuse of the provisions of Chapter 7 by considering "whether the debtor filed his petition in bad faith" and/or by considering "the totality of the circumstances . . . of the debtor's financial situation." 11 U.S.C. §707(b)(3).

IV.

The Calhouns' fixed income, excluding Mr. Calhoun's Social Security benefits, is $7,313 per month or $87,756 per year — well above the $46,521 median income for a household of two in South Carolina. Including the Social Security benefits, their average monthly income is $8,772. The means test splits the Calhouns' monthly expenses into three categories: (A) expenses allowed under IRS standards, (B) additional expense deductions under §707(b), and (C) deductions for debt payment.

The Calhouns list $3,917.83 in monthly expenses allowed under IRS standards, including $925 for food, clothing, household supplies, personal care, and miscellaneous; $426 for housing and utilities, non-mortgage expenses; $1,318 for transportation and expenses for their two vehicles; $556.83 for taxes; $439 for two life insurance policies; $76 for health care and $69 for telecommunication services. In additional expense deductions under §707(b), they claim $286 for health insurance and $884 for charitable contributions. Their total deductions for debt payment include a $2,151 mortgage payment and $91.36 for payments on priority claims. The total of all of the Calhouns' monthly deductions allowed under the means test is $7,330.19. The Calhouns' expenses, when subtracted from their income, left a monthly net income that was insufficient to trigger a presumption of abuse under §707(b)(2).

However, the bankruptcy court proceeded under §707(b)(3) and concluded that the totality of the Calhouns' financial situation evidenced an abuse of Chapter 7. In so concluding, the court found the factors set forth in In re Green, 934 F.2d 568, 571-572 (4th Cir. 1991) [a debtor's ability to pay cannot alone establish substantial abuse under chapter 7 and the court must consider the totality of the debtor's circumstances including whether the petition was filed because of sudden illness, calamity, disability or unemployment; whether the debtor incurred cash advances and made consumer purchases far in excess of his ability to repay; whether the debtor's proposed family budget is excessive or unreasonable; whether the debtor's schedules and statement of current income and expenses reasonably and accurately reflect the true financial condition; and whether the petition was filed in good faith] to be instructive, while recognizing that "the underpinnings of *Green* have been removed" with the amendment of §707(b). The court concluded that there was no illness, calamity, disability or unemployment that precipitated the Calhouns' filing for bankruptcy, and that they had the ability to repay their debt.

The Calhouns object to the court's dismissal based on their ability to pay, and assert that *Green* prohibits a dismissal on that ground alone. They further assert that Mr. Calhoun's Social Security benefits should be excluded from the analysis of their ability to pay. Finally, the Calhouns posit that the means test is conclusive of eligibility for Chapter 7 relief.

We can readily dispense with the last argument. The means test provides a formula by which a court can presume abuse on the part of above-income debtors and dismiss their case on that basis. The means test is not conclusive, the presumption is rebuttable, and a court may still find abuse even if there is no presumption. *See* In re Crink, 402 B.R. 159, 168 (Bankr. M.D.N.C. 2009). Indeed, §707(b)(3) describes precisely that situation and provides considerations for determining abuse when the presumption does not arise or is rebutted.

With respect to the Calhouns' other objections, we need not make a determination as to the enduring applicability of the holding in *Green* or the inclusion of Social Security benefits in an analysis of the totality of financial circumstances. The bankruptcy court found a multitude of factors weighing in favor of abuse, and we discern no error in those findings.

The bankruptcy court ultimately found that the Calhouns were able to pay their creditors based on the totality of the circumstances of their financial situation, including the following evidence:

— The Calhouns made payments in the amount of $2,638 a month to their unsecured creditors for twenty-two (22) months before filing for Chapter 7 relief;

— Testimony demonstrated that the Calhouns did not file for bankruptcy as a result of sudden illness, calamity, disability, or unemployment;

— The Calhouns' monthly expenses "border on the extravagant" and their budget leaves "ample room for reduction";

— The Calhouns paid $439 per month on two life insurance policies, including one that would provide for Mrs. Calhoun after Mr. Calhoun's death, even though Mrs. Calhoun will receive 75% of Mr. Calhoun's monthly income from his retirement account;

— The Calhouns claim to spend $930 per month on food and have expenses for cable and internet, laundry and dry cleaning; and

— The Calhouns did not justify their excessive transportation expenses.

This evidence amply supports the bankruptcy court's finding that granting the Calhouns' Chapter 7 relief would be an abuse of the provisions of that chapter. This conclusion holds firm even without considering Mr. Calhoun's Social Security benefits. A finding of abuse based on the above-stated evidence of the Calhouns' excessive budget and unjustifiable expenses does not depend on the additional $1,459 in Social Security benefits they receive each month.

AFFIRMED.

Post-Case Follow-Up

It is currently unclear whether a court can base a finding of §707(b)(3) abuse solely on a finding of the debtor's ability to pay his debts where the debtor has passed the means test. Compare In re Walker, 381 B.R. 620, 624 (Bankr. M.D. Pa. 2008) ("inclusion of the income and expenses calculation in §707(b)(2) precludes reconsideration of income and expenses in §707(b)(3) pursuant to the canon of negative implication"), with In re Sonntag, 2012 WL 1065482, *4 (Bankr. N.D. W. Va. 2012) (while declining to hold that ability to pay alone is sufficient to find abuse, the court concludes that ability to pay may weigh significantly in the court's determination of abuse under §707(b)(3)(B)), and In re Lipford, 397 B.R. 320 (Bankr. M.D.N.C. 2008) (Chapter 7 debtor is entitled to a fresh start but not a head start; in determining §707(b)(3) abuse claim the court must determine whether debtors are misusing the bankruptcy process to achieve some illicit purpose). Determine if the courts of the federal district or circuit where you plan to practice have ruled on this issue and how those courts interpret the §707(b)(3) abuse test generally.

Calhoun v. U.S. Trustee: Real Life Applications

1. Roy and Matilda Gladden are Chapter 7 debtors. For several years, Roy was in business with his brother who, it turned out, systematically stole money from their partnership. The stolen funds are gone and cannot be recovered and the whereabouts of the brother are unknown. Because of these thefts, the business failed and Roy, as a general partner, has been found personally liable for the partnership debts, which are considerable and which the Gladdens are unable to pay. They have filed Chapter 7 in order to discharge the partnership debts so they can move on with their lives. At the time of their filing, the §707(b)(2) abuse of presumption was rebutted as Roy and Matilda are below median debtors. However, the week before the case was filed, Roy's aunt died and now, a month after the filing, Roy has learned that she left him a cash inheritance barely sufficient to pay the partnership debts. Roy and Matilda are desperate to rid themselves of the partnership debts that have destroyed their credit rating and would like to use the inheritance to start a new business and to adopt two or more children since they themselves are childless. If you are the bankruptcy trustee in their case, what arguments will you make that their case should be dismissed under §707(b)(3)? If you are counsel for the Gladdens, what arguments will you make that their case should not be dismissed under §707(b)(3)?

2. Lawrence Gilbert has owned and operated an auto repair business for 15 years. He has filed a Chapter 7 case and identified his debts as primarily consumer debts. At the time of the filing, the §707(b)(2) abuse of presumption was rebutted in his case even though he is an above median debtor. A number of the unsecured non-priority claims listed on his Schedule F are pending lawsuits

and demands for refunds from customers of his business alleging poor workmanship and the use of used parts while charging for new parts. Lawrence filed a Chapter 7 case two years ago that was dismissed for abuse based on a finding that it had been filed only to delay a scheduled foreclosure on his home and that when the stay was lifted to allow the foreclosure to move forward, he trashed the interior of the house. Six months before this second filing, Lawrence's wife, Gloria, purchased a $750,000 home that is titled in her own name. A substantial down payment was made on the purchase using funds from joint accounts with her husband. Gloria is not a debtor in the bankruptcy case. Many of Lawrence's expenses listed in his schedules are related to the new home even though Lawrence is not on the title. She does have substantial assets of her own, however, including several parcels of real estate that, if liquidated, would provide more than enough funds to pay all of her husband's liabilities. Gloria herself filed in Chapter 7 three years ago to discharge a seven figure judgment against her for damages caused in a car accident. The trustee believes, but cannot prove, that Lawrence and Gloria have considerable cash and gold assets stashed away somewhere, none of which were disclosed on Lawrence's schedules. If you are the bankruptcy trustee in Lawrence's case, what arguments will you make that his case should be dismissed under §707(b)(3)? If you are counsel for the Lawrence, what arguments will you make that his case should not be dismissed under §707 (b)(3)?

Frankly, where a court is convinced that a debtor has the ability to pay creditors notwithstanding the debtor's having technically satisfied the means test so that no presumption of abuse applies under §707(b)(2), it often isn't difficult for the court to find other circumstances suggesting §707(b)(3) abuse from a review of the totality of the debtor's circumstances and to dismiss the case on that basis as is seen in Calhoun. But not always. Recall In re Rivers, highlighted in Chapter Five, Section C. *Rivers* held that the above median debtor's mortgage payment on her former home in Virginia, which she planned to abandon, could nonetheless be deducted from her income on her Form 122A-2 as part of the means test calculation. Without being able to deduct that mortgage payment, the presumption of abuse could not have been rebutted in her case. With the deduction allowed, however, the presumption was rebutted. The U.S. Trustee made an alternative argument that this debtor's case should be dismissed under §707(b)(3) as abuse evident from the totality of the financial circumstances because she had a substantial monthly income with which to pay her debts notwithstanding the results of the means test. Below is the court's analysis of the §707(b)(3) argument.

> In this case . . . the presumption of abuse arising here hinges entirely on the validity of the Debtor's claimed mortgage deductions on the Virginia Property. Since the deduction should be determined as of the petition date, the Debtor's deduction for her former residence should be allowed, and the presumption of abuse does not arise. . . .

However, in cases where the presumption does not arise or is rebutted, §707(b)(3) provides that the Court shall consider the "totality of the circumstances . . . of the debtor's financial situation" to determine whether the granting of relief would be an abuse of the provisions of Chapter 7.

It is generally accepted that a debtor's ability to repay his creditors is the primary factor to consider under the "totality of the circumstances" analysis of §707(b)(3). It is also accepted that the debtor's ability to pay is not the conclusive factor, and that other factors must be taken into account to the extent that they are helpful in determining whether the case is abusive. In re Lavin, 424 B.R. 558, 563 (Bankr. M.D. Fla. 2010); In re Norwood-Hill, 403 B.R. at 912.

The Court has considered the totality of the Debtor's circumstances in this case, and finds that the granting of relief would not be an abuse of the provisions of Chapter 7.

The Debtor in this case earns a substantial income. . . . [S]he listed gross income in the amount of $11,376.65 per month, and joint annualized income with her husband in the amount of $142,074.48.

Despite the Debtor's income, however, her total circumstances do not indicate that this case is an abuse of the provisions of Chapter 7. Specifically, the Debtor's family situation and conduct show that Chapter 7 relief is appropriate in this case.

The Debtor has six dependent children. At the time that the petition was filed, two of the children were eight years old, and three of the children were teenagers. The Debtor's husband does not have stable employment, and the Debtor is the primary source of financial support for the children.

At trial, the Debtor testified that she had surgery in September of 2010 for endometriosis and other medical conditions, and that she was scheduled for additional surgery the week following the trial. She also testified that two of her children have severe allergies that require restricted diets and medication, and that one child suffers from a severe form of eczema that also requires a special diet and medication. The Debtor's Schedule F reflects a number of medical bills among her unsecured debts. The general unsecured debts scheduled by the Debtor total $18,760.00.

Additionally, the events that precipitated the bankruptcy filing do not evidence any improper purpose or conduct. Rather, the Debtor's marital and family difficulties were primary factors that led to the Chapter 7 petition. The Debtor testified that she and her husband were anticipating a divorce in 2010, and those difficulties led to her family's relocation from Virginia to Florida.

Finally, the UST does not assert that the Debtor has acted in bad faith, and the record does not indicate that the Debtor engaged in any unusual financial transactions or incurred any extraordinary debts in the period leading up to the bankruptcy petition. Although the UST contends that certain of the Debtor's expenses are excessive and that the Debtor should "tighten her belt," it does not appear that either the Debtor or her family enjoys an extravagant lifestyle. The Debtor rents a home for the family for $1,800.00 per month, and the two vehicles listed on the Debtor's schedules are a 1997 Hyundai and a 2002 Chevrolet. The Debtor drives the Chevrolet, which is in need of repair, and makes a vehicle payment for the Chevrolet in the amount of $467.00 per month.

Based on the record and the totality of the circumstances, the Court finds that granting relief in this case would not be an abuse of the provisions of Chapter 7.

Rivers, 466 B.R. at 569-571.

Application Exercise 5

What additional or different facts could have changed the result on the §707(b)(3) abuse issue in *Rivers*? What if there had been some hint of bad faith in debtor's filing? What if the bankruptcy judge had been more sympathetic to the UST's suggestion that some of debtor's expenses were excessive or her lifestyle extravagant? What if she had run up some unnecessary or unusual debts in the months prior to filing her petition? What if there were no marital problems between debtor and her husband? What if she had two or three dependent children instead of six? Or what if her case had simply drawn a less sympathetic judge?

Remember that the abuse by bad faith filing or abuse evident from the totality of debtor's financial circumstances grounds for dismissal under §707(b)(3), though they apply only in a consumer debtor case, constitute distinct grounds for dismissal from the presumption of abuse and may be raised later in the case. The presumption of abuse and means test calculation of §707(b)(2) must be dealt with at the beginning of an individual consumer Chapter 7 case. The U.S. Trustee, pursuant to §704(b)(1)(A), must file a statement with the court as to whether the presumption of abuse arises under §707(b) and must then file a motion to dismiss on that basis within 30 days thereafter or be barred from doing so thereafter. The notice requirement of §704(b)(1) does not apply to a motion to dismiss on one of the §707(b)(3) grounds (note carefully that §704(b)(1) references only the presumption of abuse). See, e.g., In re Reed, 422 B.R. 214 (C.D. Cal. 2009) (the ten-day statement under §704(b)(1) is superfluous to a filing under §707(b)(3); if a UST fails to file a statement as required under §704(b)(1) she still may proceed under §707(b)(3)).

Motions to dismiss under §707(b)(3) are governed by FRBP 1017(e), which provides that they must be filed within 60 days following the first date set for the meeting of creditors unless the time is extended on timely motion for cause.

D. DEBTOR'S RIGHT TO CONVERT A CHAPTER 7 CASE

So long as the case was originally filed as a Chapter 7 (and not converted to a Chapter 7 from another chapter of the Code), §§706(a) and (d) permit the debtor, on motion, to convert the case to a case under Chapter 11, 12, or 13 so long as the debtor qualifies as a debtor under the chapter of the Code to which he converts the case.

On motion, a party in interest may request the conversion of a Chapter 7 case to one under Chapter 11 and such motion is decided using the "after notice and a hearing" procedure per §706(b). But a Chapter 7 case cannot be converted to one under Chapter 12 or 13 without the debtor's request or consent per §706(c).

A case that has been or is likely to be converted from one chapter of the Code to another is commonly referred to by practitioners as one that has or is likely to go "downstream." For example, if a debtor files a shaky Chapter 13 case that is likely to be converted later to a Chapter 7 liquidation, a practitioner might say, "That is a downstream liquidation if I ever saw one."

Consider the circumstances under which a Chapter 7 consumer debtor might seek conversion of his case to one under Chapter 13. If the court is going to involuntarily dismiss the Chapter 7 case for one of the reasons we've considered, the debtor may want to covert in order to prevent the automatic stay from expiring, leaving him at the mercy of his creditors. Or if the court has ruled a particular debt non-dischargeable, the debtor may want to convert to Chapter 13 in order to manage that non-dischargeable debt in the confines of a three- to five-year plan, as we will discuss beginning in the next chapter.

Although the Code itself does not impose any test of good faith on the debtor's right to voluntarily convert a case from Chapter 7 to Chapter 13 or another chapter under the Code, the Supreme Court has held that debtors who have not engaged in good faith conduct do not have an unqualified right to convert a Chapter 7 case to one under Chapter 13 and that the bankruptcy court may deny the motion to convert if the court finds that the case would likely be dismissed under Chapter 13 on the basis of bad faith, a topic to be discussed in Chapter Sixteen, Section F. See Marrama v. Citizens Bank of Massachusetts, 549 U.S. 365 (2007).

E. THE FINAL DISCHARGE, CLOSING THE CASE, AND PROHIBITION ON DISCRIMINATION

The individual Chapter 7 debtor receives a final **discharge in bankruptcy** from the court under §727 of the Code (see Official Form 318 Order of Discharge). The Order of Discharge entered in Marta Carlson's case is Document 37 in the Carlson case file. In a no-asset case the discharge may be entered in as little as 30 to 60 days following filing of the petition. In asset cases it takes approximately four months. Some cases get bogged down with disputes and go on significantly longer.

The procedure for handling the final discharge varies among federal districts. In most districts the entry of the discharge is done automatically without any hearing being held. In the past bankruptcy judges routinely conducted a discharge hearing where they would endeavor to make sure the debtor understood the significance of the discharge but most judges now do not. In some districts the court requires the debtor's attorney to file a certification or affidavit stating that the attorney has reviewed the significance of the discharge with the debtor before the discharge will be granted. The local rules of the bankruptcy court will typically address how the judge handles the discharge.

Application Exercise 6

Determine the discharge procedure used in the bankruptcy court in the federal district where you plan to practice. Does the judge conduct a formal discharge hearing? Is the debtor's attorney required to make any certifications or to file an affidavit concerning discussions with his client? Check the local rules of your court or discuss this issue with the U.S. Trustee, a trustee panel member, or a bankruptcy practitioner.

The discharge releases the debtor from any further personal liability for dischargeable debts. The debtor is no longer legally required to pay those debts and the discharge operates as a permanent injunction prohibiting creditors from ever undertaking any form of collection action on the discharged debts.

For example, look at the explanation of a Chapter 7 discharge included in Form 318B, Discharge of Debtor, and note the various warnings and other information set out there concerning the effect of the discharge.

If a creditor does violate the permanent injunction against attempting to collect a discharged debt the debtor can file a motion with the bankruptcy court asking that the offending creditor be enjoined for continuing to violate the discharge order and found in contempt of the court's discharge order. An injunction and a monetary fine for civil contempt is the usual result. If the case has been closed when the creditor violates the order of discharge, the debtor must move to reopen the case pursuant to §350(b) and FRBP 5010 in order to seek relief from the court. The filing fee is waived when a case is reopened for this purpose.

As has been mentioned, only an individual debtor actually receives a discharge. An entity debtor simply goes out of business.

A discharge, once granted, can be revoked. Section 727(d) sets forth the reasons why a **revocation of discharge** can be entered by the bankruptcy court upon request of the bankruptcy trustee, U.S. Trustee, or a creditor and those are summarized in Exhibit 11.3.

A request to revoke the debtor's discharge on the first ground listed in Exhibit 11.3 must be filed within one year of the date the discharge was granted. For the other grounds the request must be filed within a year of the date the discharge was granted or the date that the case is closed, whichever is later. If the case has been closed when the creditor seeks to revoke the discharge it must move pursuant to §350(b) and FRBP 5010 to reopen the case.

The granting of the discharge does not mean that the case itself is closed. Following discharge, the bankruptcy trustee may still have property of the estate to seize or liquidate and proceeds to distribute. When that process is completed and if there are no other matters pending, the trustee will file the final report and accounting required by §704(a)(9) and the case will be closed pursuant to §350(a).

Application Exercise 7

Let's look at Marta Carlson's fresh start following her discharge in Chapter 7. What property was she able to exempt and keep for use in her fresh start? What debts does she remain liable for postdischarge? She lost her house in the liquidation so will now need a new place to live with her children. She lost her car in the liquidation and so will need a new one. She needs to make wise financial decisions now. How long will it be before she can file another Chapter 7 case?

Section 525 of the Code contains a broad prohibition on discrimination against a debtor because he has been through bankruptcy. Though §525 applies to any debtor invoking any chapter of bankruptcy relief, it is the Chapter 7 debtor who is most likely to suffer discrimination as a result of the stigma of having filed. Section 525(a) prohibits any governmental entity from denying, revoking, conditioning, or refusing to renew any license, permit, charter, or employment solely because the person or entity has been a bankruptcy debtor. Section 525(b) prohibits private employers from discriminating in employment solely because the person or someone associated with the person has been a bankruptcy debtor. And §525(c) prohibits both public and private makers of student loans from discriminating in making such a loan on that basis.

EXHIBIT 11.3   Grounds Supporting a Revocation of Discharge

- The debtor obtained the discharge fraudulently
- The debtor failed to disclose the fact that he or she acquired or became entitled to acquire property that would constitute property of the bankruptcy estate
- The debtor has refused to obey any lawful order of the court
- The debtor has failed to explain misstatements discovered in an audit of the case
- The debtor has failed to provide documents or information requested in an audit of the case

Chapter Summary

- Some debts cannot be discharged in a Chapter 7 case, including certain tax obligations, fines, and penalties owed to the government; domestic support obligations; student loans; consumer debts aggregating more than $500 owed to a single creditor for luxury goods or services purchased within 90 days preceding the petition unless the debtor can overcome the presumption of fraud; debts created by means of fraudulent pretenses or use of a fraudulent financial statement;

debts arising from fraud or defalcation in a fiduciary capacity or from embezzlement or larceny; debts arising from willful or malicious injury to person or property; wrongful death or personal injury claims arising out of operation of a vehicle while intoxicated; and unscheduled claims. An action to determine dischargeability of a debt is an adversary proceeding.

- For purposes of the willful or malicious injury to person or property ground for denying discharge of a debt, an intentional breach of contract does not qualify unless accompanied by tortious conduct. Student loans may be discharged if the debtor can satisfy the "undue hardship" test interpreted in most districts to involve a certainty of hopelessness standard met by showing that debtor cannot currently maintain even a minimal standard of living for himself and dependents if required to repay the loan, that such circumstances are likely to continue for all or a substantial portion of the payback period, and the debtor has made a good faith effort to repay the loan.

- A number of grounds exist for the denial of any discharge to an individual Chapter 7 debtor including hiding or concealing property to hinder, delay, or defraud a creditor; concealing, destroying, or altering books and records without adequate explanation; unexplained loss of an asset; making a false oath or using a false claim; failure to obey a court order or to answer when asked; prior discharge in a Chapter 7 or 11 within eight years or in a Chapter 12 or 13 within six years; or failure to complete the postpetition financial course. An objection to discharge must be pursued as an adversary proceeding.

- A Chapter 7 case can be involuntarily dismissed for cause for nonpayment of fees or costs or failure to timely file schedules or unreasonable postpetition delay by the debtor that prejudices creditors. It can also be dismissed upon a finding that the petition was filed in bad faith or that the filing is abusive considering the totality of debtor's financial circumstances notwithstanding that no presumption of abuse arose from the means test. In totality of the circumstances cases, most districts say the court can consider the debtor's ability to pay his creditors notwithstanding having passed the means test but cannot rely on that factor alone to find abuse and instead must examine all of the debtor's financial circumstances.

- A Chapter 7 debtor can voluntarily converted his case to one under Chapter 13, 12, or 11 so long as the debtor qualifies for relief under the chapter converted to. Debtor may seek such conversion if the presumption of abuse arises in his case and cannot be rebutted or if the court involuntarily dismisses the Chapter 7 or denies discharge in the case or of a particular debt. If a case is dismissed because the petition was filed in bad faith, conversion may be denied.

- The individual Chapter 7 debtor receives a discharge from the bankruptcy court, which operates as a permanent injunction prohibiting creditors from ever undertaking any form of collection action on the discharged debts. For a year following the discharge it can be revoked upon the showing that it was obtained by fraud and other limited grounds for revoking a discharge also exist.

Applying the Concepts

1. You are the Chapter 7 trustee in cases involving the following scenarios. Identify action you can take and, for any action you decide to take, state all the grounds supporting the action and the procedure for taking the action.

   a. Following the first meeting of creditors, a relative of debtors contacts you and says that debtors purchased $100,000 worth of gold coins six months before filing their petition, paying cash for the coins. No mention is made of the purchase or the coins in their schedules or statement of affairs. You have conducted a Rule 2004 examination [discussed in Chapter Seven, Section E] of debtors where they denied under oath purchasing the coins, having any gold coins, or ever having the cash to purchase such coins. Now the relative has put you in touch with a niece of the debtors who says debtors gave her 10 gold coins as a graduation present three months before their petition was filed.

   b. At his first meeting of creditors, debtor acknowledges having inherited several valuable paintings worth half a million dollars from an aunt who died three years before the petition was filed. However, debtor testifies that the paintings were destroyed two years ago when he was traveling with them in a covered trailer when the trailer and its contents caught fire and burned. Debtor is unable to produce any police report concerning the incident or any insurance claim made in connection with the loss. In fact, debtor denies ever having them insured. As a result of an investigation you determine that debtor did in fact have an insurance policy covering the paintings and that it is still in effect and premiums are current.

   c. Debtor, a former recording artist, acknowledges having owned and operated an unincorporated voice training business for aspiring new artists out of his home for five years. He says the business never made any money and he closed it down nine months ago. You request records of the business and tax returns reflecting profits and losses from the business but he is unable to produce any such records. His explanation is that he didn't maintain any records while the cash only business was operating and did not make any profits from it so didn't file tax returns regarding it.

   d. Debtor filed a Chapter 13 case two years before filing his Chapter 7 petition but his proposed Chapter 13 plan was never confirmed and the case was dismissed without any discharge being granted.

   e. Debtor was seriously in arrears on his home mortgage on which he owes $200,000. Bank was preparing to foreclose when debtor filed his Chapter 7 petition. His notice of intent stated that he would surrender the home to Bank. At his first meeting of creditors, debtor testifies that he has now vacated the home. However, Bank advises that when it took possession of the home from debtor it found the premises severely damaged. Built-in appliances had been destroyed, walls defaced, water left to run on floors and through ceilings, pipes broken, and walls cracked and broken, and there was some evidence of fire damage. Bank appraiser estimates that the value of the home has been reduced from $190,000 to $75,000.

   f. Debtor received a discharge in Chapter 7 six months ago. More than $100,000 in unsecured debt was discharged. Now it comes to your attention that debtor had $75,000 of U.S. savings bonds that he owned under a fictitious name that were never disclosed in the bankruptcy case.

2. You represent the creditor in each of the following Chapter 7 scenarios. What action will you recommend on behalf of your client and what is the proper procedure in the event your client authorizes such action?

   a. Debtor borrowed $300,000 from Bank two years before the petition was filed and loan is secured by a first mortgage on the debtor's home. The balance owed is $275,000 but the home is appraised at only $250,000. Debtor's schedules indicate that debtor makes $90,000 per year at a job he has held for five years. However, the loan application that debtor provided Bank states his income to be $150,000 per year.

   b. Debtor, who is a used car salesman with non-filing spouse and three dependent children, acquired a credit card from Bank 18 months before the petition was filed. At the time of filing, balance owed is $15,500 including the following charges:

   • $2,000 to Luxury Caribbean Cruise Lines 60 days before the petition was filed

   • $1,500 to Rick's Sporting Goods 91 days before the petition was filed

   • $50 to local movie theatre the day before the petition was filed

   • $120 to local grocery store two weeks before petition was filed

   • $500 to local liquor store a week before petition was filed

   • $5,000 to state university for "tuition" 75 days before petition was filed

   c. Debtor accepted position at Employer as bookkeeper and treasurer 18 months ago. Debtor signed an employment agreement that included a non-compete provision pursuant to which if debtor voluntarily left the employ of Employer within two years she would (1) not work for a competitor in the area for twelve months and (2) reimburse Employer for amounts expended by Employer for training and continuing education. During her nine months with Employer, debtor was sent to two educational seminars at a total cost to Employer of $4,400 and she received software training at a cost to Employer of $500. Nine months ago debtor unexpectedly resigned from her position with Employer and moved out of the area. Employer wrote her letters demanding reimbursement of those costs but all were returned undeliverable and unforwardable. Employer has just learned that debtor filed her Chapter 7 petition in a bankruptcy court in a neighboring state three months ago.

Employer was not listed as a creditor and the time for filing a proof of claim in that proceeding has expired.

3. Ted Starnes files for Chapter 7 bankruptcy and seeks discharge of three student loans based on undue hardship. Student loan #1 was taken from Bank #1 eight years ago and has a balance of $20,000. Student loan #2 was taken from Bank #2 five years ago and has a balance of $15,000. Student loan #3 was taken from Bank #3 three years ago and has a balance of $10,000. The bankruptcy court concludes that Starnes has satisfied the *Brunner* test for undue hardship but not as to the entire student loan balance of $45,000. Instead the court concludes that Starnes should have sufficient income to repay $10,000 of student loan debt without undue hardship. May the court discharge some but not all of Starnes' student loan debt under the undue hardship test of §523(a)(8)? If so, how should the court determine which loan or which parts of the three loans are to be discharged? Compare In re Saxman, 325 F.3d 1168 (9th Cir. 2003), and In re Hornsby, 144 F.3d 433 (6th Cir. 1998), with In re Skaggs, 196 B.R. 865 (Bankr. W.D. Okla. 1996).

The Chapter 13 Case: Debt Adjustment for an Individual with Regular Income — Filing the Case

In this chapter we begin our examination of the Chapter 13 bankruptcy case. We will take note of the key differences between a Chapter 7 liquidation proceeding and the Chapter 13 debt adjustment for an individual. The individual in a Chapter 13 must demonstrate a regular source of income to fund his plan and we will consider what income qualifies. We will review the petition and other documents that a debtor must file in connection with a Chapter 13 and meet the Chapter 13 standing trustee who is appointed to administer the case. The automatic stay and property of the estate concepts as well as the proof of claim requirements work slightly differently in a Chapter 13 than in a Chapter 7 and we will consider those distinctions.

Key Concepts

- Chapter 13 is a debt adjustment proceeding for an individual with regular income
- Any legal source of income that is sufficiently regular and stable to enable the debtor to fund his plan will qualify
- A Chapter 13 case is commenced by the filing of a petition and the debtor is required to provide the same schedules and statements as a Chapter 7 debtor
- The debtor is to file a Chapter 13 plan with the petition or within 14 days thereafter
- Each federal district has one or more standing Chapter 13 trustees who will be appointed to administer the case
- In a Chapter 13 case, non-filing codebtors on consumer debt enjoy the benefit of the automatic stay along with the debtor in bankruptcy
- Property of the estate in a Chapter 13 case includes non-exempt postpetition property acquired by the debtor

A. INTRODUCTION TO THE CHAPTER 13 CASE

1. The Purpose of Chapter 13

Chapter 13 bankruptcy is a creature of the 1978 Code, adopted in response to exploding consumer debt and corresponding widespread default on that debt. It provides a flexible, court-supervised, debt repayment scheme for can-pay debtors. It does not require full repayment of unsecured debt if the debtor is unable to fully repay it, it eliminates the requirement of creditor approval, and it provides debtors with powerful tools to cure arrearages on secured debt in order to retain possession of the collateral notwithstanding the bankruptcy. Chapter 13 has proved a rousing success and filings under that chapter of the Code have swelled from about 15 percent of all consumer filings in 1978 to about one-third today.

A Chapter 13 bankruptcy case is not a liquidation proceeding like a Chapter 7 case. It is a reorganization or debt adjustment proceeding designed for an **individual with regular income** (see §109(e)). In a Chapter 13 case the debtor proposes a plan that requires the debtor to use future income to pay all or some of his or her unsecured debts in exchange for which the debtor will be able to keep all or most of debtor's non-exempt assets.

The plan may call for the modification of debt obligations to enable the debtor to repay what is owed on more favorable terms. For example, assume a debtor borrows money and signs a promissory note calling for repayment to the creditor over five years at $100 per month. Assume the debtor files for Chapter 13 relief when he still owes 24 more payments at $100 per month, or $2,400. The debtor's Chapter 13 plan may call for the balance of the debt to be paid over 60 additional months at $40 per month. If the plan is approved by the court, the creditor must accept the extended plan payments.

The plan may also call for all or a portion of some debts to be discharged. For example, regarding the debt described in the preceding example, the plan may call for 60 payments of $20 each to the creditor, for a total of $1,200, and for the remaining $1,200 balance to then be discharged. If the plan is approved, the 60 monthly payments of $20 each will be the only payments to which the creditor is entitled and the balance will be discharged.

Of course, the debtor cannot arbitrarily alter the repayment schedule or reduce the payments due a creditor. In Chapters Fourteen and Fifteen we will learn what kinds of debt modification Chapter 13 allows. And in Chapter Sixteen we will consider the requirements for approval of a Chapter 13 plan by the bankruptcy court.

Pursuant to §1325(b)(4) a Chapter 13 plan must run between three to five years under the close supervision of a named trustee. Because the Chapter 13 debtor is using future income to fund the plan, the plan itself is sometimes referred to informally as a **wage earner plan**, though, as we will see, the Chapter 13 debtor need not necessarily be a wage earner. Many judges and practitioners prefer to call it a **debt adjustment plan** or just a Chapter 13 plan.

After BAPCPA and the new means test that we considered in Chapter Five, the Code now contains a clear bias in favor of an individual debtor filing a Chapter 13 rather than a Chapter 7. The idea is that if the debtor is in a position to pay off even some of his or her debt, debtor should do that rather than liquidating under a Chapter 7. Thus, if the debtor filing for Chapter 7 relief triggers the presumption of abuse under that chapter and cannot rebut it, the case will be dismissed unless debtor voluntarily converts it to a Chapter 13. The means test and the presumption of abuse are the Code's way of not so gently pushing individual debtors toward a Chapter 13 and away from a Chapter 7.

2. Eligibility to File a Chapter 13 Case

Chapter 13 is limited to debtors with relatively small amounts of debt. Section 109(e) places strict dollar limits on how much debt a prospective Chapter 13 debtor can have. The dollar limits are subject to adjustment every third year, as mandated by §104. As of April 1, 2016, an individual filing for Chapter 13 relief can have no more than $394,725 in unsecured debt and $1,184,200 in secured debt. These amounts will be adjusted in April 2019 pursuant to §104. Individuals with debt in excess of either the secured or unsecured debt limits can reorganize under Chapter 11, though a Chapter 11 case contains many more technicalities and is much more expensive. In order to file for Chapter 13 relief, the individual must have "**regular income**," which will be used to fund the reorganization plan. Section 101(30) defines the phrase, "an individual with regular income" to mean an "individual whose income is sufficiently stable and regular to enable such individual to make payments under a plan under Chapter 13. . . ."

What is or is not "regular income" has been left largely to the courts to determine, and the courts have identified a congressional intent that the phrase be interpreted broadly. As stated in In re Baird, 228 B.R. 324, 327-328 (Bankr. M.D. Fla. 1999):

> The legislative history of §101(30) is unusually clear and indicates that Congress intended to expand and broadly define "individual with regular income" to include funding from diverse and nontraditional sources.

Where the debtor is employed and has a regular wage or salary, there is rarely a problem, even if that wage or salary varies from period to period.

For example, assume the debtor is a used car salesperson whose monthly income depends on commissions from sales. Though his income may vary depending on how well he does from month to month, he will qualify as an individual with regular income. The same is true for a debtor who works in construction and whose income may be both seasonal and weather-dependent.

If a debtor is retired or disabled and living on a fixed income (e.g., pension, disability, or Social Security benefits), he will qualify for a Chapter 13 so long as those payments are regular and stable. A debtor who is unemployed at the time the petition is filed but who has good prospects for employment in the immediate future will also qualify.

Although the Code does not specifically prohibit illegal sources of income from being used to meet the stable and regular requirement of §109(30), disclosing such sources in a bankruptcy filing could of course subject the debtor to criminal prosecution, and, as we will learn in Chapter Sixteen, Section B, §1325(a)(3) requires that, to be confirmed, a Chapter 13 plan must have been "proposed in good faith and not by any means forbidden by law." Thus a Chapter 13 filing where income to fund the plan will be derived from illegal sources is likely to be dismissed as a bad faith filing under §1307(c) (to be discussed in Chapter Sixteen, Section F). See, e.g., In re Arenas, 514 B.R. 887 (Bankr. D. Colo. 2014) (motion to convert Chapter 7 case to Chapter 13 denied where any plan would be funded primarily from the cultivation and sale of marijuana under license granted by the State of Colorado but still in violation of federal law; cause existed to dismiss Chapter 13 case under §1307(c) and therefore debtor did not qualify to be debtor under Chapter 13).

Case Preview

In re Murphy

What about a debtor who has no income himself but has received the support or promise of support from another? As you read In re Murphy consider the following questions:

1. What is this Chapter 13 debtor's source of "stable and regular" income to fund her plan?
2. Why does the court reject the argument that a Chapter 13 debtor must have a "legal right" to the funding source or that the source have a "legal duty" to make payments to the debtor?
3. What other examples of nontraditional income sources does the court mention?
4. Should the law distinguish between a family and non-family sponsor in this context?

In re Murphy
226 B.R. 601 (Bankr. M.D. Tenn. 1998)

[The Debtor shared a household with Sam Hambrick for 11 years prior to filing her Chapter 13 case. The home is owned by Hambrick and his mother. Hambrick's twin daughters also live in the house and have been raised by the Debtor. One of the twins has asthma and needs special medical attention. Hambrick nets $3,800 per month from his business. At times the Debtor worked at a market owned by Hambrick over the last 11 years until the market closed. The Debtor has not worked outside the home since then. Throughout their relationship, Hambrick deposited $800 a month into the Debtor's account. The Debtor owns a 1994 Cadillac with a scheduled value of $14,750. In July of 1998, Constance Morris took a default judgment against the

Debtor for $15,000. Ms. Morris executed on this judgment during the first week of August 1998 and the sheriff seized the Debtor's 1994 Cadillac. This Chapter 13 case was filed on August 12, 1998, after seizure but before sale of the car to satisfy the judgment. The statements and schedules show current the current income and expenses of the Debtor's household with Hambrick. Attached to the schedules is an affidavit of Hambrick where he agrees to make the proposed Chapter 13 payments on the Debtor's behalf. The Debtor filed a motion to partially avoid the Morris lien and a motion for turnover of the 1994 Cadillac. Ms. Morris objected arguing that the Debtor is not eligible for Chapter 13 because the Debtor does not have "regular income" as required by 11 U.S.C. §§109(e) and 101(30).]

LUNDIN, Bankruptcy Judge. . . .

II.

Bankruptcy Code §109(e) provides, "only an individual with *regular income* . . . may be a debtor under Chapter 13 of this title." 11 U.S.C. §109(e) (emphasis added). Section 101(30) of the Code further defines "individual with regular income" to mean "individual whose income is sufficiently stable and regular to enable such individual to make payments under a plan under chapter 13 of this title." 11 U.S.C. §101(30). The Bankruptcy Code does not define the word "income" within §101(30).

That §101(30) defines individual with regular income by reference to stability and regularity suggests that the existence of regular income is predominantly a fact question answered by examining the flow of money available to the debtor. Put another way, the Bankruptcy Code does not specifically exclude any *source* of funding from the regular income calculus; the Code does require that whatever source of income is claimed by a debtor, it must be regular and stable enough to fund a plan. The stable and regular focus of §101(30) has led several courts to state that "the test for 'regular income' is not the type or source of income, but rather its regularity and stability." [Citations omitted]. . . .

If the monthly contribution of money committed by Mr. Hambrick to the Debtor is income, the facts overwhelmingly support the finding that this Debtor's income is sufficiently regular and stable to fund a Chapter 13 plan. For 11 years Mr. Hambrick has maintained unbroken financial support to the Debtor. The Debtor has raised Mr. Hambrick's twin daughters and taken care of Mr. Hambrick's elderly parent while maintaining a home for herself, Mr. Hambrick, and Mr. Hambrick's children. Mr. Hambrick's income is substantial and regular and for many years has produced at least the amount he has committed to funding this plan. The expenses in the budget for the Debtor and Mr. Hambrick are comprehensive, modest and appropriate. Mr. Hambrick has signed an unconditional written commitment to provide the Debtor with money sufficient to fund the proposed Chapter 13 plan. Mr. Hambrick was forthright and honest in his testimony. Both Mr. Hambrick and the Debtor presented undisputed and convincing evidence of their commitment to each other and to their collective family and of their intent and ability to fund a Chapter 13 plan.

If Congress intended the word "income" in §101(30) to excluded [*sic*] the money Mr. Hambrick will pay to the Debtor, that less inclusive definition is not apparent in the Bankruptcy Code or its legislative history. The Code easily could but does not restrict the notion of income to wages, salary, return on investment or any of the other restrictions suggested in reported cases. *See, e.g.,* In re Hanlin, 211 B.R. 147, 149 (Bankr. W.D.N.Y. 1997) (citing dictionary definitions of income). The legislative history of what is now 11 U.S.C. §101(30) is unusually clear that Congress intended to expand and broadly define "individual with regular income" to include funding from diverse and nontraditional sources. As explained in the Senate Report:

> Paragraph [(30)] defines "individual with regular income." The effect of this definition, and of its use in section 109(e), is to expand substantially the kinds of individuals that are eligible for relief under chapter 13, Adjustment of Debts of an Individual with Regular Income. Chapter XIII is now available only for wage earners. The definition encompasses all individuals with incomes that are sufficiently stable and regular to enable them to make payments under a chapter 13 plan. Thus, individuals on welfare, social security, fixed pension incomes, or who live on investment incomes, will be able to work out repayment plans with their creditors rather than being forced into straight bankruptcy. Also, self-employed individuals will be eligible to use chapter 13 if they have regular incomes.

S. REP. NO. 95-989, at 24 (1978). *See also* H. REP. NO. 95-595, at 311-12 (1977).

The examples in the legislative reports demonstrate congressional intent that regular income need not have as its source employment or the provision by the debtor of services or property to another. Income includes entitlements and benefits that can be freely given and freely taken away by governments. The legislative history of §101(30) supports the view that the touchstone for an individual with regular income is not the source of the income, but its regularity and stability.

Many reported decisions recognize that nontraditional sources of money can generate income for §101(30) purposes. Social security benefits can be regular income. In re Cornelius, 195 B.R. 831 (Bankr. N.D.N.Y. 1995); [other citations omitted]. Disability benefits can be regular income. In re Tucker, 34 B.R. 257 (Bankr. W.D. Okla. 1983); [other citations omitted]. Unemployment compensation can be regular income. In re McMonagle, 30 B.R. 899 (Bankr. D.S.D. 1983); [other citation omitted]. Aid to Families with Dependent Children can be regular income. Bibb County Dep't of Family & Children's Servs. v. Hope (In re Hammonds), 729 F.2d 1391 (11th Cir. 1984); [other citation omitted]. A debtor who was employed, but then became unemployed may have regular income. McMonagle, 30 B.R. at 902-03. A self-employed debtor who essentially determines his or her own income can have regular income. See In re Monaco, 36 B.R. 882 (Bankr. M.D. Fla. 1983); [other citations omitted]. Odd jobs can produce regular income. In re Cole, 3 B.R. 346 (Bankr. S.D. W. Va. 1980). Several courts have held that a nonfiling spouse's income can be regular income for §101(30) purpose. See In re Sigfrid, 161 B.R. 220 (Bankr. D. Minn. 1993); [other citations omitted]. . . . .

[The court finds that the word "income" elsewhere in Chapter 13 supports a broad definition of the term for eligibility purposes under §101(3).]

Some courts have narrowed the definition of income for §101(30) purposes by requiring that the debtor have a "legal right" to the funding or that the source have a "legal duty" to make payments to the debtor. In cases involving contributions by a significant other of the debtor, some decisions use the absence of a "legal duty of support" as the basis for finding the debtor ineligible. See *Hanlin*, 211 B.R. at 148 (parents); [other citations omitted].

What does legal duty or legal right mean in this context? By statute or common law spouses, for example, have a mutual duty or right of support. See, e.g., In re Antoine, 208 B.R. 17, 20 (Bankr. E.D.N.Y. 1997) (spouse's "legal duty to provide spousal support" provides income to unemployed debtor for eligibility purposes). But the absence of similar law with respect to the support obligations of unmarried couples hardly proves the absence of income for §101(30) purposes. In states like Tennessee, in the absence of a contrary contract or overriding public interest, an employer has the right to fire an employee at will and without cause. . . . There is no "legal right" in Tennessee to continued employment — it depends on the pleasure of the employer, the quality of a debtor's work, the success of the employer's business, the weather, the economy in Asia — conditions to a debtor's right to wages that are in many ways less within a debtor's control than this Debtor's relationship to Mr. Hambrick. Yet, no one would seriously contend that the money a debtor expects to receive from employment is not income for §101(30) purposes just because the debtor has no legal right to continued employment. A definition of income for Chapter 13 eligibility purposes cannot be bottomed alone on the presence or absence of statutory or common law support obligations.

Maybe these courts mean that there is income only if a debtor has a remedy through the courts if payments stop. This notion is also too narrow for §101(30) purposes. Entitlements such as welfare and social security are income for eligibility purposes in a Chapter 13 case yet such benefit programs can be limited or abolished at the will of the legislature. And once (constitutionally) altered by the legislature, there is no recourse through the courts to force the payment of benefits.

Mr. Hambrick could employ the Debtor to take care of his twin teenagers and that employment would most likely be found to produce income for §101(30) purposes. *See* In re Ellenburg, 89 B.R. 258, 260 (Bankr. N.D. Ga. 1988) ($ 500 per month for "bookkeeping services for her husband" constitutes regular income). In Tennessee, Mr. Hambrick could also fire the Debtor from that employment at any time, with or without cause. Mr. Hambrick's written promise to fund this Chapter 13 plan coupled with Mr. Hambrick's convincing testimonial commitments is at least as formal and concrete as legislative largess in a welfare program or as an employer's promises of work in the typical Chapter 13 case.

Mr. Hambrick's promise to fund this plan together with continued performance by this Debtor may generate rights and obligations that are every bit as enforceable as an employment contract. Reported decisions from many jurisdictions confirm that on theories of unjust enrichment, quantum meruit, restitution and express or implied contract, unmarried individuals sharing a household have successfully enforced financial commitments by their significant others.[5] These cases are not based on marital support obligations found in statutes. Rather, recoveries typically are allowed on contract theories. If there is an amorphous requirement of legal rights or legal duties as predicate to a finding of income for §101(30) purposes, such rights and duties are found in the promises and performance by unmarried couples like this Debtor and Mr. Hambrick. . . .

. . . IT IS ORDERED, ADJUDGED and DECREED that this Debtor is an individual with regular income eligible for Chapter 13 relief.

Post-Case Follow-Up

Most but not all bankruptcy courts interpret the "regular income" requirement broadly, as illustrated in *Murphy*. But given the fact that, nationwide, only one out of three Chapter 13 cases succeeds (see sidebar titled How Many Chapter 13 Cases Succeed? at the end of Chapter Sixteen, Section F) is there reason to be more demanding regarding the stability and reliability of the income source for Chapter 13 debtors? After all, a Chapter 13 plan is going to run from three to five years and approving an income source for that duration from a source with whom the debtor is in a casual or informal relationship seems risky. On the other hand, as the judge in Murphy noted, what employment status isn't inherently risky and possibly temporary? What do you think were the main factors in the court's approval of debtor's income source in this case? If the boyfriend had not made a "written promise" to fund debtor's plan, would the court have approved it? If the couple had been together six months (rather than eleven years) would the court have approved

---

5. A cross section of such cases might include: Marvin v. Marvin, 557 P.2d 106 (1976) (allegation that woman gave up career to become companion, cook and housekeeper in exchange for man's promise of financial support stated a cause of action based on an express contract); Levar v. Elkins, 604 P.2d 602 (Alaska 1980) (jury verdict on express or implied contractual theory where 20 years of cohabitation included promise to provide financial support in exchange for services as a homemaker and caretaker of children); Burns v. Koellmer, 527 A.2d 1210 (Conn. App. 1987) (quantum meruit and unjust enrichment may support recovery between unmarried couple); Bright v. Kuehl, 650 N.E.2d 311, 315 (Ind. Ct. App. 1995) ("a party who cohabits with another without subsequent marriage is entitled to relief upon a showing of an express contract or available equitable theory such as an implied contract or unjust enrichment."); Wilcox v. Trautz, 693 N.E.2d 141 (Mass. 1998) (contractual agreement between unmarried cohabitates is enforceable so long as it conforms with ordinary rules of contract law); Hudson v. DeLonjay, 732 S.W.2d 922 (Mo. Ct. App. 1987) (implied contract to share assets between parties living together); Kinkenon v. Hue, 301 N.W.2d 77 (Neb. 1981) (express oral contract regarding disposition of personal property between cohabitants); Dominguez v. Cruz, 617 P.2d 1322 (N.M. App. 1980) ("It is well-established that this state does not recognize 'common law marriage.' . . . The presence or absence of the marital state is not relevant in this action. . . . If an agreement such as an oral contract can exist between business associates, one can exist between cohabiting adults who are not married if the essential elements of the contractual relationship are present.") (internal citations omitted); Crowe v. De Gioia, 495 A.2d 889 (N.J. App. Div. 1985) (court should enforce contracts between unmarried parties so long as not based only on a promise to marry); Suggs v. Norris, 364 S.E.2d 159 (N.C. 1988) (agreements regarding finances and property of unmarried cohabiting couple whether express or implied are enforceable as long as sexual services or promises thereof do not provide the consideration); McHenry v. Smith, 609 P.2d 855 (Or. 1980) (enforcing oral agreements with respect to pooling income, providing companionship, cooking and homemaking); Knauer v. Knauer, 470 A.2d 553 (Pa. Super. 1983) (agreements between nonmarried cohabitors are enforceable in an action for breach of contract); Brooks v. Steffes, 290 N.W.2d 697 (Wis. 1980) (implied contract between housekeeper and former partner for personal services).

it? The court seemed to think that the boyfriend's written and verbal promises of funding as well as his performance in doing so "may generate rights and obligations that are every bit as enforceable as an employment contract" and cites contract cases like Marvin v. Marvin in footnote 5. Of course, even today, not all jurisdictions allow recovery on such theories as between unmarried cohabiting couples. Are there policy reasons to bring more uniformity and definiteness to the "regular income" requirement?

In re Murphy: Real Life Applications

1. You represent Elliot Bernard, aged 52, who was divorced last year and is struggling financially. He plans to file a Chapter 13 case but is fired from his job the day before the petition is to be filed. Elliot calls and tells you that and says his 30-year old son who is employed will make the plan payments for him "as long as he can." Should you go ahead and file? If a challenge is made to your client having sufficient regular income to fund his plan, can you prevail? See In re Baird, 228 B.R. 324, 327-328 (Bankr. M.D. Fla. 1999).

2. You represent Nicole Watson, aged 49, who lost her IT job during the Great Recession. While she was living exclusively on unemployment compensation, you filed a Chapter 13 case for Nicole that has now been operating successfully two years. However, she called today and advised that her eligibility for unemployment compensation has expired and she is still unemployed. The good news is she's found a boyfriend who she's been living with for the past year and he provides her with support "as needed." If a challenge is made to your client having sufficient regular income to fund her plan, can you prevail? See In re Loomis, 487 B.R. 296 (Bankr. N.D. Okla. 2013).

3. After Nicole Watson from Question 2 lost her eligibility for unemployment compensation and became dependent on her boyfriend for support he did make the plan payments for her. You notified the standing trustee of the change in your client's source of income and, fortunately, no objection was made. However, after the boyfriend has made plan payments for Nicole for six months they break up and he stops making the payments. The standing trustee in the case is threatening to file a motion to dismiss Nicole's case if the missed payments are not made up immediately and regular timely payments resumed. Nicole is distraught at the thought of her Chapter 13 case being dismissed and her creditors descending on her and taking judgments against her. She keeps saying, "He promised, he promised. I thought I was going to be okay." Is Nicole in a position to compel her ex-boyfriend to resume plan payments or to sue him for damages if he fails to do so? After reading Murphy, what theories might you assert against the ex-boyfriend on behalf of Nicole?

    Married couples can be joint debtors in a Chapter 13 case, under §§109(e) and 302(a), and commonly are because they share joint liability for debts and joint ownership of property. However, the combined debts of the joint debtors cannot exceed the monetary debt limits set by §109(e), discussed above. Only one of the spouses needs to have regular income to fund the plan in a joint case.

The most obvious requirement for Chapter 13 eligibility is that the debtor must be an individual. Thus, Chapter 13 is not available to an entity. (Entities can reorganize under Chapter 11, as can individuals.) Pursuant to §1304, an individual who owns a business as a sole proprietor can file Chapter 13 since the law does not consider the owner to be a separate legal person from his business. Such a debtor is permitted by §1304 to maintain control of his business and to operate it post-petition. The standing trustee in the case is required by §1302(c) to monitor the business and to provide reports on its operation to the court and creditors.

Case Preview

In re Brown

Pursuant to §109(g), an individual cannot file under Chapter 13 or any other chapter if, during the preceding 180 days, a prior bankruptcy petition was either (1) involuntarily dismissed due to the debtor's willful failure to appear before the court or comply with orders of the court, or (2) voluntarily dismissed by the debtor after creditors sought relief from the automatic stay to recover property of the debtor upon which they hold liens. As you read In re Brown, consider the following questions:

1. Why was the first Chapter 13 case filed by these debtors dismissed? Was it dismissed voluntarily or involuntarily?
2. What was the basis of the debtors' argument that the foreclosure by Shackleton on their real property violated the automatic stay?
3. Why does the court find that the automatic stay did not prevent Shackleton's foreclosure on the real property during debtor's second Chapter 13 case?

In re Brown
2013 WL 2318414 (Bankr. E.D. Va. May. 28, 2013)

[The Debtors owned real property located in Richmond, Virginia (the "Property"). In July of 2011, the Debtors filed a Chapter 13 Case (the "Prior Case"), which immediately preceded this case. In the Prior Case, Aspen Shackleton III, LLC ("Shackleton") obtained a lifting of stay to foreclose on the Debtors' property. After the Debtors filed a Motion to Reconsider, the parties agreed to a Consent Order that vacated the first order and modified the automatic stay. The Debtors did not perform their obligations in accordance with the Consent Order and Shackleton filed a Notice of Default. The Debtors did not cure the default and a Supplemental Order Granting Relief from Stay was entered on July 12, 2012. The Debtors filed a Motion to Voluntarily Dismiss their case in accordance with 11 U.S.C. §1307(b). The motion for voluntary dismissal was granted and the Debtors' Prior Case was dismissed on August 15, 2012.

The very next day, the Debtors filed the instant case under Chapter 13 of the Bankruptcy Code. On August 23, 2012, the Debtors filed a Motion to Extend the Automatic Stay Pursuant to 11 U.S.C. §362(c)(3)(B) (the "Motion to Extend Stay"). The Court granted the Motion to Extend Stay as to all creditors except Shackleton. An Order extending the stay on these conditions was entered on October 5, 2012 (the "October 5 Order Extending Stay"). On March 14, 2013, the Debtors filed the present Motion to Set Aside Foreclosure Sale. The Debtors allege that Shackleton conducted a foreclosure sale of their Property on February 8, 2013, in contravention of the Debtors' plan, which was confirmed on November 20, 2012. The Debtors allege that Shackleton was stayed from foreclosing the Property pursuant to 11 U.S.C. §§362(a), 1325, and 1327. Shackleton responded to the Debtors' motion by filing a Motion for Relief from Automatic Stay Subsequent to Foreclosure Sale in which it maintained that, consistent with the exception for which the Court's October 5 Order Extending Stay provided, the automatic stay never became effective as to Shackleton. Furthermore, plan confirmation did not re-impose an automatic stay to prevent Shackleton's enforcement of the Deed of Trust.]

HUENNEKENS, Bankruptcy Judge.

The filing of a petition under the Bankruptcy Code imposes an automatic stay of a wide range of actions that a creditor may take against the debtor, 11 U.S.C. §362(a)(1), (2), (6), (7), against property of the debtor, *id.* §362(a)(5), and against property of the estate, *id.* §362(a)(2), (3), (4). Section 362(c)(3) provides that where an individual has been a debtor in a previous bankruptcy case that was dismissed within one year of the filing of a new bankruptcy case, the automatic stay terminates as to the debtor on the thirtieth day following the new filing unless within those thirty days the debtor seeks and the courts grants an extension of the stay. *Id.* §362(c)(3). In order to obtain an extension of the stay, the debtor must prove that the filing of the new case was in good faith as to the creditors that would be affected by the stay. *Id.*

The Debtors assert that, while the Court did except Shackleton from the provisions of its October 5 Order Extending Stay, it nevertheless "is abundantly clear from the plain language of 11 U.S.C. §362(c)(3)(A) that the stay that [terminated was] not the stay that protects property of the estate." . . . Debtors argue that the Court's October 5 Order Extending Stay pertained only to the stay provided under 11 U.S.C. §362(a)(1), (2), (6), and (7) that protects against actions "with respect to the debtor." The Debtors contend that the stay against property of the estate provided under 11 U.S.C. §362(a)(2), (3), and (4) remained in effect notwithstanding the prior bankruptcy filing and was not otherwise implicated by the Court's October 5 Order Extending Stay. As Shackleton's attempted foreclosure was an action against property of the estate to which the stay remained applicable, the sale was invalid and should be set aside.

The filing of a petition, however, does not stay all actions against property of the estate. Section 362(b)(21) provides an exception. The filing of a petition does not operate as a stay under any provision of subsection (a) of section 362 of "any act to enforce any lien against or security interest in real property" "if the debtor is ineligible under section 109(g) to be a debtor" in a bankruptcy case. 11 U.S.C. §362(b)(21)(A). Section 109(g) of the Bankruptcy Code provides that "no individual . . . may be a debtor under this title who has been a debtor in a case pending under this title at any time in the preceding 180 days if" "the debtor requested and obtained the voluntary dismissal of the case following the filing of a request for relief from the automatic stay provided by section 362 of this title." 11 U.S.C. §109(g)(2).

Shackleton did file a Motion for Relief from Stay in the prior case. The Debtors requested and obtained the voluntary dismissal of their Prior Case shortly after Shackleton had been granted relief from stay. Shackleton argues that this rendered the Debtors ineligible under the provisions of §109(g). The Debtors' ineligibility made the exception to the automatic stay set forth in §362(b)(21)(A) of the Bankruptcy Code applicable. Shackleton contends, therefore, that the automatic stay did not operate to prevent enforcement of its Deed of Trust lien against the Debtors' Property.

The Court agrees that the Debtors were ineligible to be debtors under §109(g). The filing of the petition in the present case did not impose a stay against actions by Shackleton to enforce its Deed of Trust. 11 U.S.C. §362(b)(21)(A). Consistent with these statutory provisions, the Court's October 5 Order Extending Stay specifically excepted Shackleton from its provisions. The Court concludes that the foreclosure sale conducted by Shackleton did not violate the automatic stay. Therefore, Debtors' Motion to Set Aside Sale will be denied.

Post-Case Follow-Up

If you had been advising Shackleton in this case, would you have filed a motion to lift stay in the second Chapter 13 case filed by these debtors? Was its failure to do so an oversight or was it confident that it was within the exception eventually recognized by the court? Note that after debtors filed their motion to set aside the foreclosure sale, Shackleton did not simply sit on its hind legs and await the hearing. Instead it was proactive in filing its own motion for relief from automatic stay *after foreclosure sale* (emphasis supplied). Why do you think Shackleton filed that motion rather than simply arguing its position in response to the debtors' motion? Was that good lawyering or frightened lawyering? Did the court rule on Shackleton's motion in its opinion?

In re Brown: Real Life Applications

1. Assume that each of the following debtors filed their Chapter 13 petition today. Which of them is in danger of having the case involuntarily dismissed on the grounds that they are not eligible to be debtors under Chapter 13?
   a. Debtor who filed another Chapter 13 case four months ago and had it involuntarily dismissed three months ago for bad faith filing.
   b. Debtor with $400,000 in credit card debt.
   c. Debtor who filed another Chapter 13 case four months ago and had it involuntarily dismissed for failure to appear and testify at his first meeting of creditors even after being explicitly ordered to do so by the bankruptcy judge.

2. Assume you are consulted by Vickie Long who is experiencing problems paying her debts as they come due and who asks you to represent her in a Chapter 13 bankruptcy. You learn that she went through a Chapter 13 more than a decade ago, when she completed a five-year plan and received a discharge. She also filed a second Chapter 13 case about twelve months ago, had a plan confirmed, and was making payments under the plan including payments to Bank that holds the mortgage on her house. But when she missed some payments to Bank two months ago, Bank filed a motion with the bankruptcy court to lift the automatic stay and foreclose. She decided then to just voluntarily dismiss her case and let Bank have the house and that's what happened. Now she rents but is still in financial trouble. Is Vickie eligible to file a third Chapter 13 case? Would it matter if Bank had threatened to file a motion to lift stay in the second case but had not done so before Vickie voluntarily dismissed that case? Would it matter if the motion to lift stay had been filed in the second case and that case was voluntarily dismissed nine months ago instead of two months ago?

You may hear a bankruptcy practitioner speak of a **Chapter 20 case**. There is no Chapter 20 in the Code, of course, but that phrase is used to describe the not uncommon practice of a debtor obtaining a discharge in a Chapter 7 case and then filing a Chapter 13 case shortly thereafter (7 + 13 = 20). Section 1328(f) provides that a Chapter 13 debtor cannot receive a discharge in his Chapter 13 case if he has received a discharge under Chapter 7, 11, or 12 during the four years preceding his filing of the Chapter 13 petition (we will consider discharge in a Chapter 13 case in detail in Chapter Sixteen). However, a Chapter 13 case can be filed and a plan approved even though no discharge is granted in the case (e.g., the debtor proposes a 100 percent plan involving no discharge of debt).

Why would a debtor who has received a discharge in Chapter 7 file a Chapter 13 less than four years later? Sometimes it is planned, a calculated strategy. A debtor goes through a Chapter 7 to discharge all the debt he can and then immediately files a Chapter 13 and proposes a plan that will enable him to make payments on his remaining debt on a more flexible schedule than his creditors would allow otherwise. Or he proposes a plan to take advantage of the more generous lien-stripping options that Chapter 13 allows, as we will learn in Chapter Fourteen. Often the Chapter 13 filing so soon after the Chapter 7 discharge is unplanned but necessary because the debtor has fallen behind on payment schedules and needs a Chapter 13 plan to cure arrearages and perhaps even to obtain court assistance to control his own spending.

Since the Chapter 13 filer is by definition an individual, he or she must comply with the prepetition credit counseling requirement of §109(h)(1), imposed on all individuals filing under any chapter of the Code. (See discussion of this requirement in Chapter Five, Section D.)

For our detailed study of how a Chapter 13 proceeding works, we will focus on a married couple that in many ways fits the profile of typical Chapter 13 debtors. Let's meet Roger and Susan Matthews. Go to Appendix B at this time and read the Assignment Memorandum.

Application Exercise 1

Based on the budget for Roger and Susan Matthews shown in the Assign-ment Memorandum in Appendix B, how much money do the Matthews have available each month to apply to the bills not being paid? How financially vulnerable are they to unexpected expenses in excess of those budgeted or to job loss? Does it appear likely at this point that the Matthews will be able to propose a plan that will pay 100 percent of their secured and unsecured debts over a three- to five-year period?

B. FILING A CHAPTER 13 CASE

1. The Petition, Schedules, and Other Documents

A Chapter 13 case is commenced in the same way as a Chapter 7, by filing Official Form 101, Voluntary Petition for Individuals Filing for Bankruptcy (see the Matthews' Chapter 13 petition, Document 1 in the Matthews case file on the companion Web site at aspenlawschool.com/books/parsons_consumerbankruptcy) in a bankruptcy court of proper venue (see discussion of venue in Chapter Six, Section A). Per FRBP 1007(b), the Chapter 13 debtor, like the Chapter 7 individual debtor, must also file a list of creditors (see Document 2 in the Matthews case file), along with the various sched-ules of assets and liabilities, a statement of financial affairs, and the other statements and documents discussed in Chapter Six, Section B (see Documents 3 through 13 and 15 through 17 in the Matthews case file), except for the Statement of Intent. Section 521(a)(2) requires the filing of a Statement of Intent only of an individual Chapter 7 debtor. The Chapter 13 debtor's proposed plan will indicate how debtor intends to deal with property that is subject to a security interest. Pursuant to FRBP 3015(b), the debtor's Chapter 13 plan is to be filed with the petition or within 14 days thereafter.

Application Exercise 2

Review the exemptions claimed by the Matthews on their Schedule C (Docu-ment 4 in the Matthews case file). Do all of those claimed exemptions appear to comply with §522? Note that Roger Matthews is reporting a priority claim on Schedule E/F in favor of the IRS for $1,000 in back taxes he has not paid. You may want to review the discussion of priority claims in Chapter Ten, Sec-tion B, and the treatment such claims receive in a Chapter 7 liquidation. In Chapter Fourteen we will see how they are treated in a Chapter 13. Go ahead and look at the Matthews' Chapter 13 plan (Exhibit 15.2). The plan indicates that they are going to surrender one of their vehicles to the secured creditor. Since the Chapter 13 plan states the debtor's intent with regard to secured property, no statement of intent is required.

The Chapter 13 filer is not required to complete either Form 122A as the Chapter 7 consumer debtor filer is. Instead, the Chapter 13 debtor must file Form 122C-1, **Chapter 13 Statement of Your Current Monthly Income and Calculation of Commitment Period.** The above median Chapter 13 debtor must also file Form 122C-2, **Chapter 13 Calculation of Your Disposable Income**, used to determine the **applicable commitment period** of the debtor's plan and the amount of **disposable income** the debtor is expected to have available during the plan term to pay to creditors. We will consider these forms in detail in the next chapter.

The signatures on a Chapter 13 petition involve the same considerations as those on a Chapter 7 petition. This might be a good time to review that discussion in Chapter Six, Section A.

A Chapter 13 case can only be commenced voluntarily. The Code does not authorize an involuntary Chapter 13 filing.

2. Attorney's Fees in a Chapter 13 Case

As previously noted, in all bankruptcy cases the attorney fee agreement between the debtor and debtor's attorney must be in writing, per §528(a)(1). FRBP 2016 requires the debtor to file Official Form 2030 **Disclosure of Compensation of Attorney for Debtor**. (See Document 16 in the Matthews case file.) However, attorney's fees work differently in a reorganization case than in a Chapter 7 liquidation (discussed in Chapter Six, Section B). In a Chapter 13 case, the fees charged by the debtor's attorney must not only be disclosed, they must also be approved by the court. And they can be paid by the debtor through the plan. If the fees are disclosed and payment is provided in the plan, the **order confirming the plan** (see Chapter Sixteen, Section B) is a sufficient court approval of the fees. Some federal districts may require a formal application for payment of attorney's fees separate from the plan.

For example, the Disclosure of Compensation of Attorney for Debtor filed by the Matthews' attorney (Document 16 in the Matthews case file) discloses that $2,000 of the $3,000 fee was paid prior to filing of the petition. The balance of $1,000 will be paid through the plan (Document 18 in the Matthews case file) and the order confirming the plan (Document 21 in the Matthews case file) is sufficient court approval.

Sometimes attorneys for the Chapter 13 debtor are called upon to provide legal assistance not contemplated by the initial fee paid prepetition or through the plan. In that event, the attorney will be required to file an **application for additional compensation** and obtain court approval of the proposed fee.

For example, assume that the attorney for the Matthews discloses his initial fee agreement with the clients and a plan is confirmed that calls for that fee to be paid through the plan. A year later, the Matthews need to modify the plan due to changed circumstances (modification is discussed in Chapter Sixteen, Section D) and call on the attorney again. The original fee did not contemplate this additional work, and so the attorney will file an application for additional compensation and obtain court approval for the additional fee. FRBP 2016 will apply, requiring the attorney to submit a detailed, itemized statement of services rendered and expenses incurred.

Fees allowed to debtor's attorneys for Chapter 13 work vary considerably among bankruptcy courts across the country.

3. The Standing Chapter 13 Trustee

In most federal districts, the trustee in a Chapter 13 case is not appointed from the trustee panel, as are trustees in Chapter 7 cases (see discussion in Chapter Seven, Section B). Instead, there is one individual designated by the U.S. Trustee to serve as the Chapter 13 **standing trustee** pursuant to 28 U.S.C. 586(b). The standing trustee will automatically serve as trustee in all Chapter 13 cases filed in that district. In districts with heavier Chapter 13 filings, there may be more than one standing trustee. In most districts the standing trustee also handles Chapter 12 cases.

Section 1302(b) assigns the Chapter 13 standing trustee many of the same duties as those of the Chapter 7 trustee (see Exhibit 7.1), with the important exception that the Chapter 13 standing trustee's duties do not include the Chapter 7 trustee's duty under §704(a)(1) to "collect and reduce to money" the property of the estate. Thus the Chapter 13 trustee will not seize non-exempt assets, liquidate them, and distribute the proceeds to creditors. In fact, per §1327(b), upon confirmation of the Chapter 13 plan all property of the estate (to be discussed in Section D) vests in the debtor, not the standing trustee, unless the plan or court order directs otherwise. Remember, Chapter 13 is an individual reorganization or adjustment of debts proceeding, not a liquidation. But §1302(b) imposes unique duties on the Chapter 13 standing trustee, and those duties are summarized in Exhibit 12.1.

EXHIBIT 12.1 Unique Duties of the Chapter 13 Standing Trustee

- To evaluate the case to make sure it is filed in good faith and in compliance with all Code requirements
- To ensure that the debtor begins making payments under the plan as required by the Code (which often occurs before plan confirmation, as discussed later)
- To review the debtor's proposed plan for feasibility and good faith and to be heard in support or opposition to its confirmation
- To review any proposed modifications of the debtor's plan after confirmation or to propose such modification and to be heard in support or opposition to any proposed modification
- Upon approval of the plan, to collect the payments made by the debtor under the plan and to distribute those payments to pursuant to the plan
- To advise the debtor on other than legal matters and to assist the debtor in performance of the plan
- If any claim for a domestic support obligation is made in the case, to advise the holder of the claim of their rights including the right to utilize the state child support enforcement agency to collect the amount owed

We will have more to say about the duties of the Chapter 13 standing trustee as we consider other aspects of administering a Chapter 13 case.

C. THE ORDER FOR RELIEF, NOTICE TO CREDITORS, AND AUTOMATIC STAY UNDER CHAPTER 13

As was discussed in Chapter Seven, Section A, most bankruptcy courts treat the filing of the petition as the entry of an order for relief in the case, while some enter a formal order to that effect. Pursuant to §342, the clerk of the bankruptcy court will give immediate notice to all creditors and other parties in interest of the filing of the case using Official Form 309I. (See Document 19 in the Matthews case file.)

Filing the petition under Chapter 13 triggers the **automatic stay** provision of §362. As we have learned, the stay arises by operation of law, with the exception of the BAPCPA limitations imposed on debtors who have filed once (stay limited to 30 days unless debtor moves for extension) or twice (no stay at all) in the year preceding the current filing. (See discussion in Chapter Seven, Section F.) As long as the stay is in effect, creditors may not initiate or continue collection demands, lawsuits, or execution on judgments. The notice of commencement to creditors advises creditors of the stay and the danger of penalties if they continue collection efforts.

Section 1301(a) of the Code provides that unless the bankruptcy court authorizes otherwise, a creditor may not seek to collect a consumer debt from any individual who is liable along with the debtor. This is the **codebtor stay** of Chapter 13. It does not apply in Chapter 7 or 11 cases. It does not apply to codebtors on non-consumer debts in Chapter 13. As we have learned, consumer debts are those incurred by an individual primarily for personal, family, or household purposes (see §101(8)).

For example, a married person may file a Chapter 13 and the debtor's spouse, who does not file, will be protected by the stay from being pursued on any consumer debts she owes with her debtor/husband. Of course, if the spouse files as a joint debtor, they both have the benefit of the automatic stay.

The rationale behind the codebtor stay of Chapter 13 is that persons who do not themselves receive the actual consideration for a consumer debt often volunteer to become liable for such a debt and it would be unfair to stay collection against the person who did receive the actual consideration while collection proceeded against the person who didn't.

For example, assume Susan Matthews' parents co-signed the promissory note when Roger and Susan borrowed money to purchase furniture for their house. When Roger and Susan file for Chapter 13 relief, the automatic stay goes into effect on their behalf. But what about the parents? They are not in a bankruptcy proceeding. Without the codebtor stay, the creditor could proceed with collection efforts against the parents even though they received no actual consideration (furniture) for the debt.

Sections 1301(a)(1) and (2) provide that the codebtor stay is automatically lifted when the Chapter 13 debtor receives a discharge and the case is closed or when the case is dismissed or converted to a Chapter 7. Per §§1301(c)(2) and (d), the codebtor stay is to be lifted on motion of the creditor and after notice and a hearing *to the extent that* the plan does not provide for paying the creditor. Twenty days after the filing of a motion to lift stay under §1301(c)(2), the stay is automatically terminated per the mandate of §1301(d) unless the debtor or codebtor files a written objection in which a hearing will be conducted.

For example, assume a married person files a Chapter 13 case but the spouse does not. The spouse initially gets the benefit of the codebtor stay as to consumer debts. But if the debtor files a plan that calls for paying only half of that debt and the plan is confirmed, the creditor may file a motion to have the codebtor stay lifted as to the half of the debt not to be paid under the plan. The codebtor stay will automatically terminate 20 days after the motion is filed unless the debtor or codebtor files a written objection. If an objection is filed a hearing will be conducted at which the burden will be on the party filing the objection to show cause why the stay should be continued as to the codebtor.

Per §1301(c), the codebtor stay can also be lifted by motion of the creditor and after notice and a hearing if the creditor can show that either

- The creditor will be irreparably harmed if the stay is not lifted or
- Between the debtor and the codebtor, the codebtor received the actual consideration for the claim.

For example, assume a married person files a Chapter 13 but the spouse does not. The spouse gets the benefit of the codebtor stay as to joint consumer debts, but if the creditor can show that the consumer item purchased was for the exclusive benefit of the spouse and not the debtor, the stay may be lifted. Or, if the creditor can show that the codebtor is disposing of assets and will be judgment proof when the case is over, that may constitute irreparable harm to the creditor.

D. PROPERTY OF THE ESTATE IN A CHAPTER 13 CASE

Just as in a Chapter 7, all of the Chapter 13 debtor's non-exempt property becomes **property of the estate** upon filing of the petition and, as such, is subject to the control of the court, per §§1306(a) and 541(a). However, as noted earlier, the standing trustee will not take possession of and sell the property of the estate unless the debtor's plan contemplates a surrender and sale of property in which the estate has equity. Instead the debtor will retain possession of the property, subject to the terms of debtor's plan per §1306(b).

The standing trustee in a Chapter 13 case has the same powers as a Chapter 7 trustee to challenge a debtor's claimed exemptions (Chapter Nine, Section B) and to pursue disputed, contingent, or unliquidated claims of the debtor against third parties (see Chapter Nine, Section A). If the debtor has already filed suit to collect on those claims when the petition is filed, the standing trustee may simply authorize the debtor to continue that suit. The standing trustee also has the same power to compel turnover of the debtor's property from third persons and custodians holding it (see Chapter Nine, Section C) and to avoid other prepetition transfers of the debtor's property (see Chapter Nine, Section D) as a Chapter 7 trustee.

Having said all that, Chapter 13 standing trustees rarely pursue prepetition claims on behalf of the debtor even though they might increase the property of the estate. And Chapter 13 trustees only rarely exercise their turnover and avoidance powers on behalf of the estate. Instead the trustee will normally leave such actions to the debtor. Remember the statutory duties of the standing trustee in a Chapter 13 do not include liquidating the estate as in a Chapter 7. Instead, the trustee's functions are to examine the debtor at the 341 hearing and review the petition, supporting schedules, and the debtor's proposed plan to determine if the case is properly filed and plan confirmation is feasible and otherwise appropriate. Following plan confirmation the trustee will receive and disburse payments to creditors and follow up on the administration of cases as needed.

The debtor may be handicapped in accomplishing that task since, other than the limited power to avoid a lien to protect an exemption (discussed in Chapter Fourteen, Section B) and the power granted the debtor in §522(h) to avoid a transfer of property or recover a setoff in order to protect an exemption (discussed in more detail below) the Code does not specifically grant the Chapter 13 debtor the power to compel turnover or to avoid prepetition transfers. The standing trustee's reluctance to utilize the turnover or avoidance powers (or as we will see in the next section, to object to claims despite having standing to do so) is often a point of contention in light of the trustee's duty under §1302(b) (see Exhibit 12.1) to assist the debtor in performance under the plan. But, where challenged, the courts grant the standing trustee discretion in the performance of that duty and recognize that "the Trustee must balance this duty with his other duties." In re Mallory, 444 B.R. 553, 561-562 (S.D. Texas 2011).

The common reluctance of a Chapter 13 standing trustee to exercise turnover or avoidance powers on behalf of the estate has also led to Chapter 13 debtors attempting to use those powers themselves and courts are split on whether the debtor has standing to do so. The narrow view of the debtor's powers reasons that since §323 designates the trustee as the representative of the estate and grants him capacity to sue and be sued; since §1303, enumerating the powers of the trustee that the debtor has, does not reference the turnover or avoidance sections; and since the various turnover and avoidance sections of the Code expressly confer those powers on "the trustee"; the Chapter 13 debtor does not have standing to act under such provisions without the trustee joining in. See, e.g., In re Mitrano, 468 B.R. 795 (E.D. Va. 2012) (only Chapter 13 trustee has standing to bring §548 fraudulent transfer action), and In re Gardner, 218 B.R. 338 (Bankr. E.D. Pa. 1998), and cases cited therein.

The competing view notes that under §1306(b) property of the estate is retained by the Chapter 13 debtor and since the various turnover and avoidance powers are intended to capture the property of the estate as defined in §541 the debtor should have power to utilize those powers for that purpose, at least where the standing trustee refuses to do so. See, e.g., In re Freeman, 72 B.R. 850, 854-855 (Bankr. E.D. Va. 1987) ("Although there is a substantial split of authority among the courts which have considered this issue, this Court is satisfied that in cases such as this one, where the trustee does not act, the debtor himself may exercise the trustee's 'strong arm' powers under §544(a)."), and In re Willis, 48 B.R. 295, 302-303 (S.D. Tex. 1985) (the "realities of bankruptcy practice" require allowing Chapter 13 debtors to pursue avoidance power actions).

In those districts following the narrow view that denies debtor standing to exercise the turnover and avoidance powers on his own, the debtor may be able to convince the trustee to agree to a provision in the plan providing that the trustee will pursue the action. Sometimes debtors convince the trustee to bring the action jointly with the debtor and to retain debtor's attorney as special counsel under §327(e) so that a single attorney represent both. In some of those districts the courts allow the plan to delegate the standing of the trustee to bring an avoidance or turnover action to the debtor and consider this "derivative standing" of the debtor sufficient. In some districts this derivative standing is accomplished separate from the plan by a post-confirmation court order. See In re Cohen, 305 B.R. 886, 891 n.5 (B.A.P. 9th Cir. 2004) (even if Chapter 13 debtor lacked concurrent statutory standing with trustee to maintain avoidance action, the court has authority in a Chapter 13 case to permit a party other than trustee to bring a trustee avoidance action with explicit court approval).

Where the debtor is allowed to maintain a turnover or avoidance action, either in the plan or a post-confirmation court order, the plan or order will typically require the debtor to pay such amounts recovered to the standing trustee per §1325(c) for distribution to creditors under the plan.

Application Exercise 3

Determine if the courts of the federal district or circuit where you plan to practice have decided the question of whether a Chapter 13 debtor may utilize the turnover and avoidance powers of the Code. If so, is the right to do so limited to situations where the standing trustee is requested to bring the action but refuses, or is standing treated as completely concurrent?

Ironically, the debtor's inability to bring property transferred prepetition back into the estate to be made available to creditors through the plan may cause the standing trustee to object to the plan on the basis that it doesn't provide unsecured creditors as much as they would receive in a Chapter 7 liquidation (a requirement for plan confirmation discussed in Chapter Sixteen, Section B) since the Chapter 7 trustee would exercise the avoidance and turnover powers for the benefit of these creditors. This can be a real catch-22 for Chapter 13 debtors.

There are two exceptions to this controversy over the debtor's standing to commence an avoidance or turnover action without the trustee. Section 522(h) specifically authorizes a debtor to institute an action to avoid a transfer of property or recover a setoff to the extent that the transfer would be avoidable if brought by a trustee and the debtor can claim an exemption in the property effected. And, as discussed in Chapter Ten, Section C, an individual debtor has power to institute an action to avoid a judicial lien and some other liens that impair an exemption as authorized by §522(f)(1)(A).

For example, even in a district that did not allow a Chapter 13 debtor to file a §547 preferential transfer action on his own in order to increase the property of the estate and increase the payout to unsecured creditors, that debtor, pursuant to 522(h), could maintain that action but only to the extent the debtor could and intended to exempt the property to be recovered in the action. Let's say a debtor being hard pressed by a creditor on an overdue debt agrees to transfer title to his car to the creditor in partial satisfaction of the obligation. Two months later debtor files a Chapter 13 case. The transfer of the vehicle occurred during the 90-day preference period and if debtor could recover it he could exempt it in his bankruptcy case. A §547 preference action might be just the ticket and if the standing trustee won't bring that action, the debtor can under §522(h).

Application Exercise 4

In contrast to the silence of the Code regarding a Chapter 13 debtor having the turnover and avoidance powers of the trustee, §1203 does specifically grant those powers to a Chapter 12 debtor (as discussed in Chapter Seventeen, Section E) and §1107(a) grants those powers to a Chapter 11 debtor. Technically, the reason for that distinction is that a bankruptcy trustee is not initially appointed in a Chapter 11 case and the debtor continues to operate his business as a debtor in possession. Although there is a standing trustee in a Chapter 12 case, that debtor, too, is considered a debtor in possession and given some of the powers of a trustee. Is this an oversight in the Code's treatment of a Chapter 13 debtor? Should the standing trustee in a Chapter 13 be required to pursue turnover and avoidance actions that appear to have merit? Is the fact that most such prepetition transfers by the Chapter 13 debtor were voluntary a sufficient reason to deny him the right to exercise such powers if the standing trustee declines?

Closely related to the Chapter 13 debtor's standing to commence a turnover or avoidance action in lieu of the standing trustee doing so is debtor's right to pursue a prepetition cause of action in contract, tort, or statutory relief (e.g., employment discrimination) when the standing trustee will not do so. Such claims are choses in action and constitute property of the estate under §541. In Chapter 7 cases trustees routinely pursue such claims if they have validity to enhance the property of the estate, but for the reasons we have discussed, standing Chapter 13 trustees will rarely do so. That leaves the question of whether the debtor may pursue such prepetition claims when the standing trustee abstains.

Cable v. Ivy Tech State College

It is clear that in a Chapter 7 liquidation, only the bankruptcy trustee has standing to maintain a prepetition cause of action belonging to the debtor on behalf of the estate. See, e.g., Bauer v. Commerce Union Bank, 859 F.2d 438, 441 (6th Cir. 1988), where the Sixth Circuit explained that upon filing the petition in a Chapter 7 case such claims became the property of the estate and that, absent abandonment of the claim by the trustee, only the trustee could file suit to liquidate them: "[T]he trustee in bankruptcy acts as representative of the estate. It is the trustee who has capacity to sue and be sued. It is well settled that the right to pursue causes of action formerly belonging to the debtor — a form of property under the Bankruptcy Code — vests in the trustee for the benefit of the estate. The debtor has no standing to pursue such causes of action." In the absence of any specific provision in Chapter 13 dealing with the procedure for maintaining an action based on a non-bankruptcy prepetition claim of the debtor, some courts have extended the rule of Bauer to deny Chapter 13 debtors standing to maintain such an action where the trustee refuses to pursue it. See, e.g., Smith v. Cumulus Broadcasting, LLC, 2011 WL 3489820 (D.S.C. 2011), and In re Gardner, 218 B.R. 338 (Bankr. E.D. Pa. 1998). Not all courts agree, however. As you read Cable v. Ivy Tech State College, consider the following questions:

1. What kind of action is the Chapter 13 debtor attempting to bring in his own name and what is the status of that action?
2. What is the significance for this court of the distinction between a Chapter 7 liquidation case and a Chapter 13 adjustment of debts case?
3. What is the distinction between an action brought for the benefit of the estate and one brought for the benefit of the debtor?
4. What is the significance of FRBP 6009 for this court on the issue before it?

Cable v. Ivy Tech State College
200 F.3d 467 (7th Cir. 1999)

[Bruce Cable, a former instructor at Ivy Tech State College ("Ivy Tech") filed a Chapter 7 case. Later he filed a lawsuit in the U.S. district court against Ivy Tech for discrimination and retaliation under the Americans with Disabilities Act ("ADA"). The Chapter 7 trustee was substituted as plaintiff in the ADA suit and proposed a settlement. Cable, unhappy with the proposed settlement, voluntarily converted his case to one under Chapter 13. Thereafter the district court granted summary judgment to Ivy Tech in ADA action even though the Chapter 13 trustee, Brothers, had never been substituted as party plaintiff. Brothers was later substituted as plaintiff in the ADA action but would not appeal the grant of summary judgment for the estate so

Cable appealed it himself. Ivy Tech moves to dismiss the appeal on the grounds that the Chapter 13 debtor lacks standing to maintain the appeal himself.]

KANNE, Circuit Judge. . . .

II. ANALYSIS

We first address the issue of whether a debtor has standing to appeal an adverse judgment in a claim for relief owned by the bankrupt estate. . . .

A. Debtor Standing

Both parties marshal some support for the question of whether a Chapter 13 debtor can bring a claim on behalf of the estate. Admittedly, the decisions of the lower courts are not uniform. Brothers [the Chapter 13 trustee] contends that Chapter 13 establishes the debtor-in-possession as a proper party to bring legal claims, which facilitates the prompt and efficient payment of creditors. Ivy Tech uses the decisions of some bankruptcy courts to argue that the trustee must act as the sole legal representative of the estate who alone can sue and be sued over its debts.

Ivy Tech mistakes a fundamental difference between Chapter 7 and Chapter 13. Chapter 7 establishes a much more radical solution to indebtedness, requiring the liquidation of the debtor's property, to which end Congress granted the trustee broad powers without interference from the debtor. The trustee has sole authority to dispose of property, including managing litigation related to the estate. See 11 U.S.C. §§541(a)(1), 704(1). Chapter 13, on the other hand, encourages the debtor to pay his debts over time by establishing a court-approved payment plan but leaving the debtor in possession of the estate. See 11 U.S.C. §1303 (debtor-in-possession has substantially same powers as the trustee in other chapters); §1306(b) (debtor retains possession of estate except as limited by plan). The trustee acts as an adviser and administrator to facilitate the repayment of debts according to the plan. *See id.* §1302.

In liquidation proceedings, *only* the trustee has standing to prosecute or defend a claim belonging to the estate. *See In re New Era, Inc.,* 135 F.3d 1206, 1209 (7th Cir. 1998) (holding that Chapter 7 trustee has exclusive right to represent debtor in court). . . . The same cannot be said for trustees under the reorganization chapters. In those regimes, the debtor has express authority to sue and be sued. Bankruptcy Rule 6009, which applies to Chapters 7, 11 and 13, directs that "with or without court approval, the *trustee or debtor in possession* may prosecute or may enter an appearance and defend any pending action or proceeding by or against the debtor, or commence and prosecute any action or proceeding in behalf of the estate before any tribunal." Fed. R. Bankr. P. 6009 (emphasis added); *see also* Chapman v. Currie Motors, Inc., 65 F.3d 78, 81 (7th Cir. 1995) (holding that federal courts have jurisdiction to hear state law claims brought by Chapter 13 debtor-in-possession); In re Kutner, 3 B.R. 422, 426 (Bankr. N.D. Tex. 1980) (stating that Chapter 13 debtor has standing to sue and be sued). Furthermore, the Chapter 13 debtor has been considered analogous to Chapter 11, see e.g., *Chapman,* 65 F.3d at 79, which grants the debtor full authority as representative of the estate typical of a trustee. . . .

Chapter 13 grants the debtor possession of the estate's property, 11 U.S.C. §1306(b), which is defined by §541 to include "all legal or equitable interests of the debtor in property as of the commencement of the case." 11 U.S.C. §541(a)(1). The phrase "legal or equitable interests . . . in property" includes choses in action and other legal claims that could be prosecuted for benefit of the estate. *See* In re Smith, 640 F.2d 888 (7th Cir. 1981) ("All causes of action become property of the estate under §541."). . . . The chose in action, here a discrimination case, belongs to the estate and was being prosecuted for the benefit of its creditors. It would frustrate the essential purpose of §1306 to grant the debtor possession of the chose in action yet prohibit him from pursuing it for the benefit the estate. Significantly, the Second and Third Circuits have agreed that Chapter 13 debtors can bring claims in their own name. *See* Olick v. Parker & Parsley Petroleum Co., 145 F.3d 513, 515 (2d Cir. 1998); Maritime Elec. Co. v. United Jersey Bank, 959 F.2d 1194, 1209 n. 2 (3d Cir. 1992); *see also* Donato v. Metropolitan Life Insurance Co., 230 B.R. 418, 425 (N.D. Cal. 1999); In re Wirmel, 134 B.R. 258, 260 (Bankr. S.D. Ohio 1991).

Ivy Tech misreads In re Heath, 115 F.3d 521 (7th Cir. 1997), for the proposition that only a trustee can assert claims on behalf of the estate. Rather, Heath holds that the trustee may bring actions *only for the benefit* of the estate, rather than for the benefit of the debtor. *Id.* at 523-24. In *Heath*, the estate and its creditors would not have benefitted at all if the trustee succeeded in its claim because the creditors were already receiving full satisfaction under the plan. The potential recovery would have benefitted only the debtor. Here, the plan specifically directs that the potential proceeds from Cable's . . . claim benefit the estate and its creditors.

Heath stands for the second proposition that §323 vests the trustee in bankruptcy, as the representative of the estate, with exclusive authority to sue and be sued. *Id.* at 523 and cases cited therein; 11 U.S.C. §323(a)-(b). We do not question that principle, but only note that *Heath* and the cases cited therein do not concern the authority of debtors-in-possession under Chapter 11 or 13. The several cases cited in *Heath* concern the exclusive right of trustees to bring suits under Chapter 7, which, in contrast to Chapters 11 and 13, does not recognize the legal entity debtor-in-possession. . . . Therefore, those cases cannot mean that a debtor-in-possession under Chapter 13 does not have the power to sue on behalf of the estate.

Heath itself deals with Chapter 13, but not specifically with a debtor-in-possession. While this Court stated that the trustee exercises exclusive authority to sue and be sued, *see Heath*, 115 F.3d at 523, we did not address the situation presented when a debtor-in-possession acts, pursuant to its statutory command, in the role of trustee. Under the reorganization chapters, the debtor-in-possession steps into the role of trustee and exercises concurrent authority to sue and be sued on behalf of the estate. *See* Fed. R. Bankr. P. 6009. To say that the trustee has "exclusive authority" does not mean that the debtor-in-possession cannot act as a trustee and therefore enjoy that same authority. Ruling otherwise would conflict with the explicit language of Rule 6009 that the "trustee or debtor in possession may . . . prosecute any action or proceeding in behalf of the estate before any tribunal." *Id.*

Similarly, Richardson v. United Parcel Service, 195 B.R. 737 (E.D. Mo. 1996), concerned whether a debtor could bring a claim, not as debtor-in-possession for the benefit of creditors, but in his own name and apparently for his separate benefit. The court held that because the chose in action remained estate property and had not been abandoned pursuant to §554, it had to be pursued for the benefit of the estate. *See id.* at 739. *Richardson* did not discuss whether the district court thought a debt-or-in-possession could bring the action for the benefit of the estate. *See id.*

Finally, defendant cited In re Gardner, 218 B.R. 338 (Bankr. E.D. Pa. 1998), but that case concerns the trustee's avoidance power under §548(a) of the Bankruptcy Code. Section 548 unequivocally limits the avoidance power to the trustee, and for good reason: Its aim is to prevent the debtor from transferring property with the intent to "hinder, delay, or defraud" creditors. *Id.* It would invite abuse to allow debtors to avoid transfers that the debtor knew at the time of transfer would work to the detriment of the creditors. Such is not the case here where the debtor is attempting to recover damages in a suit that, under §541, should benefit creditors.

. . .

III. CONCLUSION

Because a Chapter 13 debtor-in-possession has standing to sue on behalf of the estate, we hold that Cable can appeal the denial of summary judgment in his own name. . . . The district court's grant of summary judgment on behalf of Ivy Tech is AFFIRMED.

Post-Case Follow-Up

Be sure you understand the distinction between the issue we considered earlier regarding whether a Chapter 13 debtor can exercise the trustee's avoidance and turnover powers and the distinct issue presented here of whether that debtor himself can institute a postpetition action based on a prepetition common law or statutory cause of action in order to enhance the property of the estate (note the Cable court's distinction of In re Gardner on this difference). Would the Seventh Circuit, based on what you read in *Cable*, allow a Chapter 13 debtor to bring a §548 fraudulent transfer action without the trustee? Any other avoidance or turnover action under the Code without the trustee? Would *Cable* allow a Chapter 13 debtor to pursue a prepetition claim for reasons other than to benefit the estate? On this point see In re Heath, 115 F.3d 521, 523-524 (7th Cir. 1997). Does this court correctly construe FRBP 6009 to include a Chapter 13 debtor as a debtor in possession? The view expressed in *Cable* is the majority view on this question of debtor's standing. One decision has even gone so far as to hold that *only* the Chapter 13 debtor has standing to maintain an action based on a non-bankruptcy prepetition action. See In re Bowker, 245 B.R. 192 (Bankr. D.N.J. 2000). In districts that do not grant the debtor standing to pursue these prepetition causes of action, the debtor may be able to negotiate with the standing trustee to include a provision in the plan calling for joint prosecution of the action or delegation of the standing to the debtor or to obtain a post-confirmation court order authorizing the same as discussed above in connection with the trustee's avoidance and turnover powers.

Cable v. Ivy Tech State College: Real Life Applications

1. Assume you practice in a federal district that follows *Cable*. Which of the following actions might a bankruptcy debtor have standing to initiate on his own if the trustee refuses to do so?
   a. Chapter 13 debtor with confirmed 100 percent plan wants to bring prepetition breach of contract action in his bankruptcy case in order to obtain funds for his children's college education.
   b. Chapter 13 debtor with confirmed 50 percent plan wants to bring prepetition tort action in his bankruptcy case in order to increase payout to creditors.
   c. Chapter 7 debtor wants to bring questionable prepetition breach of contract action in order to enhance property of the estate for creditors.
2. Assume you practice in a federal district that follows *Cable*. Which of the following actions might a Chapter 13 debtor have standing to initiate on his own if the standing trustee refuses to do so?
   a. A fraudulent transfer action under §448 in order to enhance the property of the estate and increase the payout to creditors.
   b. An action to avoid a lien on property of the estate in order to protect an exemption in the collateral.
   c. An action to avoid a preferential transfer under §547 in order to exercise an exemption in the transferred property.
   d. An action to avoid a preferential transfer under §547 in order to enhance the property of the estate and increase the payout to creditors.

The definition of property of the estate is actually broader in a Chapter 13 than in a Chapter 7. Per §1306(a), what becomes property of the estate in a Chapter 13 includes postpetition property: all non-exempt property acquired by the debtor *after* the petition is filed and while the plan is in effect, including postpetition earnings and other income received by the debtor. The reason for including postpetition property, including income and earnings in the Chapter 13 estate, is that the plan is going to be funded from the postpetition income of the debtor, and that income and any other property the debtor acquires during the term of the plan must be subject to court supervision.

For example, assume a Chapter 13 debtor's petition was filed one month ago and the proposed plan was confirmed today and will last for 48 months. The property of the estate will include: all non-exempt property owned by the debtor as of the date the petition was filed; all income received by the debtor between the date the petition was filed and the date of confirmation; all income received by the debtor during the 48 months that the plan will run; and all non-exempt property acquired by the debtor by purchase, gift, inheritance, or otherwise during the 48 months of the plan's duration.

The rights of creditors secured in the property of the debtor when a Chapter 13 petition is filed are governed in the first instance by §506, which provides that such claim is secured up to the value of the property securing the claim. We will consider the options of a Chapter 13 debtor in dealing with secured claims in Chapter Fourteen, Section B.

E. THE FIRST MEETING OF CREDITORS AND FILING PROOFS OF CLAIM IN A CHAPTER 13 CASE

Pursuant to §341 and FRBP 2007(a), between 21 and 50 days after the debtor files the Chapter 13 petition the first meeting of creditors (the 341 meeting) is held. The Notice of Chapter 13 Case, Official Form 309I, will advise the creditors of the time and place of the meeting. (See Document 19 in the Matthews case file.) As in a Chapter 7 case, the Chapter 13 debtor is placed under oath at the meeting and will answer questions asked by the standing trustee and creditors. Significantly, the debt adjustment plan proposed by the debtor will be available to the trustee and creditors at the meeting because per FRBP 3015(b) it must be filed by the debtor with the petition or within 14 days thereafter. Most of the questions at the 341 meeting will typically relate to the plan.

As discussed in Chapter Eight, Section B, the proof of claim in a Chapter 7, Chapter 13, or Chapter 12 case must be filed not later than 90 days after the first date set for the meeting of creditors per FRBP 3002(c). A governmental unit, however, has 180 days from the date the case is filed to file its claim.

The failure of a secured creditor to file a timely proof of claim does not impair its secured position in the property of the debtor per §506(d)(2). So, technically, the secured creditor need not file a proof of claim to preserve its secured status in the debtor's property. The lien on the property if properly perfected will pass through the bankruptcy case unmolested and the creditor can continue to look to its collateral for satisfaction of the underlying obligation (as by, in the event of default, asking for lifting of the stay so that it can foreclose or repossess). However, §1326(c) requires the standing trustee in a Chapter 13 to make plan distributions to creditors under the confirmed plan and the standing trustee can only make those distributions on account of allowed claims. Fed. R. Bankr. P. 3021 ("after a plan is confirmed, distribution shall be made to creditors whose clams have been allowed . . ."). Consequently, most courts read §506 and §1326 together to mean that although the secured creditor's lien on the collateral continues without the filing of a proof of claim, that secured creditor cannot receive payments under the Chapter 13 plan unless a timely proof of claim is filed. See, e.g., In re Dumain, 492 B.R. 140 (Bankr. S.D.N.Y. 2013). Thus the secured creditor in a Chapter 13 case should, as a practical matter, always file a proof of claim and attach proof of its security interest in the debtor's property and the perfected status of that interest.

The timing rule for filing proofs of claim in a Chapter 13, set forth in FRBP 3002(c), illustrates how tricky such deadlines can become and the importance of the attorney knowing the deadlines that apply and of having a system in place to make sure those deadlines are met. For example, assume a Chapter 13 case is filed and the 341 meeting is scheduled for September 1. Then, the meeting is rescheduled for September 15. The proofs of claim are due in that case 90 days from September 1, not 90 days from September 15. If you are responsible for preparing the proof of claim for a client or if you are representing the standing trustee or the debtor, it is imperative that you know the applicable deadline.

Any party in interest may object to a claim filed by a creditor in a Chapter 13 case pursuant to §502, just as can be done in a Chapter 7 (see Chapter Eight, Section C). That objecting party is most likely to be the debtor himself. As with the exercise of avoidance powers discussed in the last section, the standing trustee in many districts leaves it to the debtor to object to creditor claims.

Chapter Summary

- A Chapter 13 bankruptcy case is a debt adjustment proceeding in which an individual with regular income formulates a plan to use future income to pay some or all of his debts over the following three to five years. Husbands and wives may be joint debtors in Chapter 13. Most courts utilize a broad definition of the regular income eligibility requirement and include both earned and unearned income of the debtor and even dependable support from a third person.

- An individual cannot file under Chapter 13 if, during the preceding 180 days, a prior bankruptcy petition was either involuntarily dismissed due to the debtor's willful failure to appear before the court or comply with orders of the court, or voluntarily dismissed by the debtor after creditors sought relief from the automatic stay to recover property of the debtor upon which they hold liens. A Chapter 13 debtor cannot receive a discharge in his Chapter 13 case if he has received a discharge in under Chapter 7, 11, or 12 during the four years preceding his filing of the Chapter 13 petition. A Chapter 13 may be filed less than four years following a Chapter 7 discharge if the Chapter 13 does not involve any discharge.

- A Chapter 13 is commenced by filing a petition with supporting schedules. The proposed plan of reorganization must be filed by the debtor with the petition or within 14 days thereafter. Attorney's fees in a Chapter 13 must be disclosed and approved by the court.

- An order for relief is entered or deemed entered with the filing of the petition, and the automatic stay goes into effect. In a Chapter 13, the automatic stay includes a stay against proceeding against non-filing codebtors on consumer debts. The codebtor stay can be lifted on motion if the creditor can show it will otherwise be irreparably harmed or that the codebtor received the actual consideration.

- A Chapter 13 standing trustee will administer the case under the supervision of the U.S. Trustee. The standing trustee will ensure that the plan of reorganization is proposed in good faith and is feasible and will then collect debtor's plan payments and distribute funds to creditors pursuant to the plan.

■ Property of the estate in a Chapter 13 includes both prepetition and postpetition property of the debtor for the duration of the plan. However, in a Chapter 13, the standing trustee does not take possession of, abandon, or sell property of the estate unless the plan calls for it; the debtor retains possession of his property. The Chapter 13 standing trustee may, but rarely does, pursue contested claims on behalf of the estate or exercise his turnover or avoidance powers, leaving it to the debtor to pursue such matters as state law allows. Courts are divided over whether the Chapter 13 debtor himself has standing under the Code to maintain an avoidance or turnover action other than an action to avoid a judicial lien to preserve an exemption and an action to avoid a transfer avoidable by the trustee under one of those powers and which would preserve an exemption in the debtor. Most courts hold that a Chapter 13 debtor can also institute a postpetition action based on a prepetition common law or statutory cause of action on his own in order to enhance the property of the estate.

■ A first meeting of creditors is conducted at which questions about the plan or objections to it are often resolved. In order to participate in distributions under the plan, both secured and unsecured creditors must file proofs of claim within 90 days following the meeting of creditors. A governmental creditor, however, has 180 days from the date the petition is filed to file its proof of claim.

Applying the Concepts

1. Use §109(e) and the other information on eligibility supplied in this chapter to decide which of the following debtors qualifies to file a petition for Chapter 13 relief:

   a. A corporation, owned by husband and wife, that operates a small deli and has only $100,000 in unsecured debt and $225,000 in secured debt

   b. An unemployed, single woman who has a job set to begin the first of next month

   c. A man who is sole owner of an unincorporated real estate brokerage and has $300,000 in unsecured debt and $750,000 in secured debt

   d. A retired couple living on a small pension and Social Security benefits

   e. A woman who owns stock in the company she works for

   f. A man who filed a Chapter 7 case six months ago and dismissed it voluntarily three months ago when the company holding the mortgage on his home sought to lift the automatic stay

   g. A man who owns an unincorporated car repair shop and his wife, who is a homemaker

   h. A lawyer who has her own unincorporated solo law practice and who has $400,000 in unsecured debt and $500,000 in secured debt

2. Assume the federal district in which you have filed a Chapter 13 case for husband and wife debtors follows the holding in Cable v. Ivy Tech State College. The Chapter 13 standing trustee refuses to pursue any of the following actions on behalf of the estate. Which of these do your clients have standing to pursue?

   a. A preference action to recover the late payment of a $500 medical bill three weeks before the petition was filed

   b. A turnover action to recover a valuable coin collection belonging to the husband from his brother, who refuses to return it

   c. An employment discrimination claim against the wife's former employer arising from alleged prepetition gender discrimination

   d. A breach of contract and fraud claim against a former partner of the husband arising from prepetition transactions

3. Which of the following can claim the benefit of the co-debtor stay in a Chapter 13 case?

   a. A corporate officer who signed a personal guaranty for his corporate employer when the employer files for Chapter 7 liquidation

   b. A wife who co-signed the promissory note with her husband when they bought their house after the husband files a Chapter 7 case

   c. A wife who co-signed the promissory note with her husband when they bought their house after the husband files a Chapter 13 case

   d. A one-shareholder corporation that signed a guaranty for the promissory note executed by the shareholder's son to enable the son to purchase a car when the son files a Chapter 13 case

   e. A husband and wife who file a joint petition in Chapter 13

4. Locate and read Assignment Memorandum #1 and the accompanying Summary of Assets and Liabilities, Current Income, and Expenses in Appendix D. If your instructor so directs, prepare the petition, schedules and statements designated in that memorandum assuming Nick and Pearl Murphy were filing a case under Chapter 13 in the U.S. bankruptcy court for your federal district.

The Chapter 13 Case: Determining the Applicable Commitment Period and Debtor's Disposable Income

The idea behind a Chapter 13 plan is that for the term of the plan, three to five years (the **commitment period** required by §1325(b)(4)), the debtor retains enough monthly income to pay his basic living expenses, either surrenders secured property to the secured creditors or makes arrangements to pay the full value of secured debt on some allowed terms (to be considered in the next chapter), and then turns over the excess income, called his **disposable income**, to the trustee, who will disperse that amount to unsecured creditors as called for in the plan. Thus, the first step in calculating a Chapter 13 plan is to determine the **applicable commitment period** for the debtor's plan. The second step is to determine the debtor's **projected disposable income** during the plan period. We will consider these two important steps in this chapter. In the next chapter we will look at the various ways that a Chapter 13 debtor can propose to deal with secured and unsecured debts in his plan.

Key Concepts

- A Chapter 13 plan must run from 36 to 60 months, and the debtor must complete Form 122C-1 to determine the applicable commitment period for the debtor's plan
- If the current monthly income of the Chapter 13 debtor as calculated on Form 122C-1 is below the applicable median income for debtor's state and household size, the applicable commitment period is 36 months and the debtor's disposable income is determined primarily from Schedules I and J
- If the current monthly income of the Chapter 13 debtor as calculated on Form 122C-1 is above the applicable media income for debtor's state and household size, the applicable commitment period is 60 months and the debtor's disposable income is calculated on Form 122C-2

A. DETERMINING THE APPLICABLE COMMITMENT PERIOD FOR A CHAPTER 13 PLAN

Looming over the questions of applicable commitment period and projected disposable income is §1325(b)(1), which provides that if the trustee or an unsecured creditor objects to a proposed plan, the court may not confirm the plan unless it either (1) provides for the payment in full of all unsecured claims (called a **100 percent plan**), or (2) provides that all of the debtor's projected disposable income to be received in the applicable commitment period is paid to unsecured creditors.

The form used to calculate the debtor's applicable commitment period is Official Form 122C-1, **Chapter 13 Statement of Your Current Monthly Income and Calculation of Commitment Period**. Every Chapter 13 debtor must complete Form 122C-1. In this section we will work through Roger and Susan Matthews' Form 122C-1 set out in Exhibit 13.1 (and in Document 14 in the Matthews case file) to learn how the applicable commitment period is determined. In the next section we will use it to learn how the debtor's projected disposable income is calculated. As set out in the assignment memorandum in Appendix B, our fictitious Chapter 13 debtors, Roger and Susan Matthews, reside in Harrisburg, Dauphin County, Pennsylvania.

Whether a debtor's commitment period can run as little as three years per §1325(b)(4)(A)(i) or must run for the maximum of five years per §1325(b)(4)(A)(ii) is determined by whether the debtor's **current monthly income** is less than the median family income for the debtor's state and size of household. Every year the U.S. Census Bureau publishes median family income figures for households of a certain size in all 50 states. Briefly, the determination of the Chapter 13 debtor's applicable commitment period works like this: Part 1 of Form 122C-1 calculates the debtor's average current monthly income. In Part 2 of the form that income figure is annualized and compared to the applicable median family income figure for the debtor's state and household size. If the debtor is a **below median debtor** (the debtor's annualized current average monthly income is less than the applicable median family income) the commitment period is three years and that is shown in Part 3 of the form. If the debtor is an **above median debtor** (the debtor's annualized current monthly income is more than the applicable median family income figure) the commitment period is five years and that is shown in Part 3 of the form. (The determination of how a debtor's projected disposable income is to be calculated is also made in Part 2 of Form 122C-1. We will consider the disposable income calculations in the next section.)

Current monthly income (CMI) is defined in §101(10A) to include the **average monthly income from all sources** that the debtor has received during the six months preceding the filing of the petition (known as the **look back period**) regardless of whether such income is taxable, as well as any amounts paid by a third party for the household expenses of the debtor. The sixth month to be included in the look back period is the month immediately preceding the date the case is filed.

For example, if a Chapter 13 petition is filed on September 15, the applicable look back period for calculating the debtor's CMI March through August of that year. Income from all sources received during those six months will be averaged to arrive at the current monthly income figure. So if the debtor had income totaling $26,400 during the look back period, the applicable CMI will be $4,400 ($26,400 divided by 6).

EXHIBIT 13.1   **Official Form 122C-1 for Roger and Susan Matthews**

Fill in this information to identify your case:

Debtor 1	Roger	H.	Matthews
	First Name	Middle Name	Last Name
Debtor 2	Susan	J.	Matthews
(Spouse, if filing)	First Name	Middle Name	Last Name

United States Bankruptcy Court for the: Middle District of Pennsylvania

Case number _____
(if known)

Check as directed in lines 17 and 21:

According to the calculations required by this Statement:

☑ 1. Disposable income is not determined under 11 U.S.C. § 1325(b)(3).

☐ 2. Disposable income is determined under 11 U.S.C. § 1325(b)(3).

☑ 3. The commitment period is 3 years.

☐ 4. The commitment period is 5 years.

☐ Check if this is an amended filing

Official Form 122C-1

Chapter 13 Statement of Your Current Monthly Income and Calculation of Commitment Period

12/15

Be as complete and accurate as possible. If two married people are filing together, both are equally responsible for being accurate. If more space is needed, attach a separate sheet to this form. Include the line number to which the additional information applies. On the top of any additional pages, write your name and case number (if known).

Part 1:   Calculate Your Average Monthly Income

1. **What is your marital and filing status?** Check one only.

☐ **Not married.** Fill out Column A, lines 2-11.

☑ **Married.** Fill out both Columns A and B, lines 2-11.

Fill in the average monthly income that you received from all sources, derived during the 6 full months before you file this bankruptcy case. 11 U.S.C. § 101(10A). For example, if you are filing on September 15, the 6-month period would be March 1 through August 31. If the amount of your monthly income varied during the 6 months, add the income for all 6 months and divide the total by 6. Fill in the result. Do not include any income amount more than once. For example, if both spouses own the same rental property, put the income from that property in one column only. If you have nothing to report for any line, write $0 in the space.

	Column A Debtor 1	Column B Debtor 2 or non-filing spouse
2. **Your gross wages, salary, tips, bonuses, overtime, and commissions** (before all payroll deductions).	$ 3,000.00	$ 2,167.00
3. **Alimony and maintenance payments.** Do not include payments from a spouse.	$ 0.00	$ 0.00
4. **All amounts from any source which are regularly paid for household expenses of you or your dependents, including child support.** Include regular contributions from an unmarried partner, members of your household, your dependents, parents, and roommates. Do not include payments from a spouse. Do not include payments you listed on line 3.	$ 0.00	$ 0.00

5. **Net income from operating a business, profession, or farm**

	Debtor 1	Debtor 2		Column A	Column B
Gross receipts (before all deductions)	$_____	$_____			
Ordinary and necessary operating expenses	– $_____	– $_____			
Net monthly income from a business, profession, or farm	$ 0.00	$ 0.00	Copy here➡	$ 0.00	$ 0.00

6. **Net income from rental and other real property**

	Debtor 1	Debtor 2		Column A	Column B
Gross receipts (before all deductions)	$_____	$_____			
Ordinary and necessary operating expenses	– $_____	– $_____			
Net monthly income from rental or other real property	$ 0.00	$ 0.00	Copy here➡	$ 0.00	$ 0.00

EXHIBIT 13.1 **(Continued)**

Debtor 1   Roger   H.   Matthew   Case number *(if known)* _____

First Name   *Middle Name*   *Last Name*

	Column A Debtor 1	Column B Debtor 2 or non-filing spouse
7. **Interest, dividends, and royalties**	$ 0.00	$ 0.00
8. **Unemployment compensation**	$ 0.00	$ 0.00

Do not enter the amount if you contend that the amount received was a benefit under the Social Security Act. Instead, list it here: .... ↓

For you.. $ _____

For your spouse .... $ _____

9. **Pension or retirement income.** Do not include any amount received that was a benefit under the Social Security Act.	$ 0.00	$ 0.00

10. **Income from all other sources not listed above.** Specify the source and amount. Do not include any benefits received under the Social Security Act or payments received as a victim of a war crime, a crime against humanity, or international or domestic terrorism. If necessary, list other sources on a separate page and put the total below.

_____	$ 0.00	$ 0.00
_____	$ 0.00	$ 0.00
Total amounts from separate pages, if any.	+ $ 0.00	+ $ 0.00

11. **Calculate your total average monthly income.** Add lines 2 through 10 for each column. Then add the total for Column A to the total for Column B.

$ 3,000.00   **+** $ 2,167.00   **=** $ 5,167.00

Total average
monthly income

Part 2:   **Determine How to Measure Your Deductions from Income**

12. Copy your total average monthly income from line 11. .... $ 5,167.00

13. **Calculate the marital adjustment.** Check one:

☐ You are not married. Fill in 0 below.

☑ You are married and your spouse is filing with you. Fill in 0 below.

☐ You are married and your spouse is not filing with you.

Fill in the amount of the income listed in line 11, Column B, that was NOT regularly paid for the household expenses of you or your dependents, such as payment of the spouse's tax liability or the spouse's support of someone other than you or your dependents.

Below, specify the basis for excluding this income and the amount of income devoted to each purpose. If necessary, list additional adjustments on a separate page.

If this adjustment does not apply, enter 0 below.

_____	$ _____
_____	$ _____
_____	+ $ _____
Total..............................	$ 0.00 Copy here → **—** 0.00

14. **Your current monthly income.** Subtract the total in line 13 from line 12. $ 5,167.00

15. **Calculate your current monthly income for the year.** Follow these steps:

15a. Copy line 14 here ➡ .... $ 5,167.00

Multiply line 15a by 12 (the number of months in a year).   **x**   12

15b. The result is your current monthly income for the year for this part of the form. .... $ 62,004.00

EXHIBIT 13.1 **(Continued)**

Debtor 1	Roger	H.	Matthews	Case number *(if known)*_____
	First Name	Middle Name	Last Name	

16. **Calculate the median family income that applies to you.** Follow these steps:

16a. Fill in the state in which you live. PA

16b. Fill in the number of people in your household. 4

16c. Fill in the median family income for your state and size of household. .... $ 86,112.00

To find a list of applicable median income amounts, go online using the link specified in the separate instructions for this form. This list may also be available at the bankruptcy clerk's office.

17. **How do the lines compare?**

17a. ☑ Line 15b is less than or equal to line 16c. On the top of page 1 of this form, check box 1, *Disposable income is not determined under 11 U.S.C. § 1325(b)(3)*. **Go to Part 3.** Do NOT fill out *Calculation of Your Disposable Income* (Official Form 122C–2).

17b. ☐ Line 15b is more than line 16c. On the top of page 1 of this form, check box 2, *Disposable income is determined under 11 U.S.C. § 1325(b)(3)*. **Go to Part 3 and fill out Calculation of Your Disposable Income (Official Form 122C–2).** On line 39 of that form, copy your current monthly income from line 14 above.

Part 3: **Calculate Your Commitment Period Under 11 U.S.C. § 1325(b)(4)**

18. **Copy your total average monthly income from line 11.** .... $ 5,167.00

19. **Deduct the marital adjustment if it applies.** If you are married, your spouse is not filing with you, and you contend that calculating the commitment period under 11 U.S.C. § 1325(b)(4) allows you to deduct part of your spouse's income, copy the amount from line 13.

19a. If the marital adjustment does not apply, fill in 0 on line 19a. .... – $ 0.00

19b. **Subtract line 19a from line 18.** $ 5,167.00

20. **Calculate your current monthly income for the year.** Follow these steps:

20a. Copy line 19b. .... $ 5,167.00

Multiply by 12 (the number of months in a year). x 12

20b. The result is your current monthly income for the year for this part of the form. $ 62,004.00

20c. Copy the median family income for your state and size of household from line 16c. .... $ 86,112.00

21. **How do the lines compare?**

☑ Line 20b is less than line 20c. Unless otherwise ordered by the court, on the top of page 1 of this form, check box 3, *The commitment period is 3 years.* Go to Part 4.

☐ Line 20b is more than or equal to line 20c. Unless otherwise ordered by the court, on the top of page 1 of this form, check box 4, *The commitment period is 5 years.* Go to Part 4.

Part 4: **Sign Below**

By signing here, under penalty of perjury I declare that the information on this statement and in any attachments is true and correct.

✗ /s/ Roger H. Matthews	✗ /s/ Susan J. Matthews
Signature of Debtor 1	Signature of Debtor 2
Date 06/06/2016	Date 06/06/2016
MM / DD / YYYY	MM / DD / YYYY

If you checked 17a, do NOT fill out or file Form 122C–2.

If you checked 17b, fill out Form 122C–2 and file it with this form. On line 39 of that form, copy your current monthly income from line 14 above.

You can see the §101(10A)(A) definition of CMI reflected just above Line 2 in Part 1 of Form 122C-1. After debtor enters his or her marital status on Line 1, the remainder of Part 1 of the form then requires the debtor to report debtor's average monthly income, so defined, from a number of different categories.

Joint debtors must report their income figures separately in Columns A and B. A debtor with a non-filing spouse must still include that spouse's income in Column B. (The form includes a marital adjustment later to deduct amount of the non-filing spouse's income that is not regularly available for household expenses of the debtor and dependents. We will examine the marital adjustment later.)

On Line 2 the debtor lists gross wages, salary, and tips. That gross wages, etc., figure is to be entered *without* deductions or withholdings for tax, insurance, etc.; it is a gross income figure. On Line 3 the debtor lists alimony or maintenance payments, excluding such payments if the spouse paying them is a joint debtor. On Line 4 the debtor lists child support payments received, again excluding such payments if the spouse paying them is a joint debtor. On Line 4 the debtor also lists "regular contributions" to household expenses from other sources such as parents, dependents, an unmarried partner, etc. On Line 5 the debtor who operates a business reports his net income from that business (gross income minus ordinary and necessary business expenses). Similarly, on Line 6, the debtor who leases a house or apartment and had rental income for the preceding six months will report that net rental income. Line 7 requires the inclusion of passive income from various kinds of investments, Line 8 unemployment compensation, Line 9 retirement income, and Line 10 income from any other source excluding Social Security benefits. Remember, the amounts entered in each of the lines in Part I of the form are an average of the monthly amounts received during the applicable look back period.

For example, Mr. and Mrs. Matthews are joint debtors, so they list their income separately in Columns A and B of Part 1. The only source of income for either of them is the salaries they are paid by their respective employers, so they enter the six-month average of their respective salaries in Columns A and B of Line 2. In Lines 3 through 10 they enter zero, then show the subtotals and combined total in Line 11.

Application Exercise 1

The definition of CMI used in connection with Form 122C-1 in a Chapter 13 case is the same as that used in connection with Form 122A-1 utilized for the means test in a Chapter 7 case filed by an individual debtor with primarily consumer debts (see discussion in Chapter Five, Section C). In both forms, CMI is calculated using the same definition of that term. But the two forms are used for different purposes. This is a good time to review the reason why Form 122A-1 is used in Chapter 7 cases for individual consumer debtors. There is no means test for a Chapter 13 debtor, however. If you are ready to do so, verbalize the reasons for using the Form 122A-1 form in a Chapter 7 bankruptcy case involving a consumer debtor and the different reasons for using the Form 122C-1 form in a Chapter 13 case. What is the purpose for calculating CMI in each form? If you can't verbalize that distinction yet, you certainly should be able to do so once you've finished this chapter.

In the vast majority of cases, calculating the debtor's CMI using the six-month look back period makes perfect sense because the debtor expects his or her income during the upcoming plan period to be identical or very similar to what it has been during the look back period. But occasionally that is not the case because the debtor's income during the look back period was higher or lower than what it will be during the plan period. And since, as we will see, the CMI figure is used in calculating the debtor's projected disposable income (PDI), that PDI number may be inaccurate as well.

For example, assume the debtor receives a one-time buyout from an employer during the look back period, causing her CMI figure calculated per §101(10A)(A) to be substantially higher than what her actual monthly income will be during the period of her plan. Or a debtor gets a new job that will significantly increase her real income during the plan period in excess of the CMI calculated using income from the look back period. Or a debtor is in the process of changing jobs when the petition is filed and the new job will pay less. For each of these debtors the CMI figure will not be an accurate forecast of the debtor's income during the plan period and any PDI calculated using the CMI figure is going to be inaccurate. And that is critical since most debtors cannot satisfy the confirmation requirement of §1325(b)(1)(A) by filing a 100 percent plan and must rely on satisfying §1325(b)(1)(B) by proposing a plan that will pay all their PDI to unsecured creditors.

Case Preview

Hamilton v. Lanning

In dealing with debtors like the ones in the last example, some bankruptcy courts, after BAPCPA, utilized a strict mechanical approach to CMI calculation that focused exclusively on income/ expenses in the look back period without regard to any upcoming changes in the debtor's income or expenses. In these districts, debtors either had to delay filing until the applicable look back period encompassed the change in income or expenses (which was not always possible due to repossessions, foreclosures, or other financial emergencies) or go ahead and propose a plan based exclusively on numbers from the look back period, have it confirmed, and then file a proposed modification to the plan based on changed circumstances (to be considered in Chapter Sixteen, Section D), which would add to their attorney's fees and the administrative expenses of the case. Other courts developed a forward-looking approach that allowed/required debtors when doing their initial CMI calculation to consider the upcoming changes, notwithstanding the unequivocal language of §101(10A)(A). As you read Hamilton v. Lanning consider the following questions:

1. What were the statutory construction arguments favored by lower courts utilizing the mechanical approach to the calculation of CMI and disposable income?
2. What were the statutory construction arguments of those favoring the forward-looking approach?
3. Why does the Supreme Court choose the latter over the former?
4. Form 22C referenced in the opinion has been updated and is now Forms 122C-1 and 122C-2 as discussed in the text.

Hamilton v. Lanning
560 U.S. 505 (2010)

Justice Samuel Alito wrote the majority opinion in Hamilton v. Lanning. *Collection of the Supreme Court of the United States, Photographer: Steve Petteway*

[Debtor Stephanie Kay Lanning had $36,793.36 in unsecured debt when she filed for Chapter 13 bankruptcy protection in October 2006. In the six months before her filing, she received a buyout from her former employer, and this payment greatly inflated her gross income for April 2006 (to $11,990.03) and for May 2006 (to $15,356.42). As a result of these payments, respondent's current monthly income for the look back period on her Form 22C was $5,343.70 — a figure that exceeds the median income for a family of one in Kansas. Lanning's monthly expenses, calculated pursuant to §707(b)(2), were $4,228.71. Thus Lanning reported a monthly "disposable income" of $1,114.98 on Form 22C. However, on the form used for reporting monthly income (Schedule I), she reported gross income from her new job of only $1,922 per month — which is below the state median. On the form used for reporting monthly expenses (Schedule J), she reported actual monthly expenses of $1,772.97. Subtracting the Schedule J figure from the Schedule I figure resulted in monthly disposable income of $149.03. Lanning filed a plan that would have required her to pay $144 per month for 36 months. The Chapter 13 trustee objected to confirmation of the plan because the amount respondent proposed to pay was less than the full amount of the claims against her, and because, in petitioner's view, respondent was not committing all of her projected disposable income to the repayment of creditors.

The Bankruptcy Court endorsed respondent's proposed monthly payment of $144 but required a 60-month plan period. The court agreed with the majority view that the word "projected" in §1325(b)(1)(B) requires courts "to consider at confirmation the debtor's *actual* income as it is reported on Schedule I." Lanning appealed to the Tenth Circuit Bankruptcy Appellate Panel, which affirmed. The Tenth Circuit affirmed. This petition followed, and the Court granted certiorari to decide how a bankruptcy court should calculate a debtor's "projected disposable income."]

ALITO, Justice. . . .

I

[Section] 1325 provides that if a trustee or an unsecured creditor objects to a Chapter 13 debtor's plan, a bankruptcy court may not approve the plan unless it provides for the full repayment of unsecured claims or "provides that all of the debtor's projected disposable income to be received" over the duration of the plan "will be applied to make payments" in accordance with the terms of the plan. 11 U.S.C. §1325(b)(1). . . .

The Code did not define the term "projected disposable income," and in most cases, bankruptcy courts used a mechanical approach in calculating projected disposable income. That is, they first multiplied monthly income by the number of months in the plan and then determined what portion of the result was "excess" or "disposable." . . .

In exceptional cases, however, bankruptcy courts took into account foreseeable changes in a debtor's income or expenses. . . .

BAPCPA left the term "projected disposable income" undefined but specified in some detail how "disposable income" is to be calculated. "Disposable income" is now defined as "current monthly income received by the debtor" less "amounts reasonably necessary to be expended" for the debtor's maintenance and support, for qualifying charitable contributions, and for business expenditures. §§1325(b)(2)(A)(i) and (ii) (2006 ed.). "Current monthly income," in turn, is calculated by averaging the debtor's monthly income during what the parties refer to as the 6-month lookback period, which generally consists of the six full months preceding the filing of the bankruptcy petition. See §101(10A)(A)(i). The phrase "amounts reasonably necessary to be expended" in §1325(b)(2) is also newly defined. For a debtor whose income is below the median for his or her State, the phrase includes the full amount needed for "maintenance or support." . . .

III

A

The parties differ sharply in their interpretation of §1325's reference to "projected disposable income." Petitioner, advocating the mechanical approach, contends that "projected disposable income" means past average monthly disposable income multiplied by the number of months in a debtor's plan. Respondent, who favors the forward-looking approach, agrees that the method outlined by petitioner should be determinative in most cases, but she argues that in exceptional cases, where significant changes in a debtor's financial circumstances are known or virtually certain, a bankruptcy court has discretion to make an appropriate adjustment. Respondent has the stronger argument.

First, respondent's argument is supported by the ordinary meaning of the term "projected." "When terms used in a statute are undefined, we give them their ordinary meaning." . . . Here, the term "projected" is not defined, and in ordinary usage future occurrences are not "projected" based on the assumption that the past will necessarily repeat itself. For example, projections concerning a company's future sales or the future cash flow from a license take into account anticipated events that may change past trends. . . . On the night of an election, experts do not "project" the percentage of the votes that a candidate will receive by simply assuming that the candidate will get the same percentage as he or she won in the first few reporting precincts. And sports analysts do not project that a team's winning percentage at the end of a new season will be the same as the team's winning percentage last year or the team's winning percentage at the end of the first month of competition. While a projection takes past events into account, adjustments are often made based on other factors that may affect the final outcome. . . .

Second, the word "projected" appears in many federal statutes, yet Congress rarely has used it to mean simple multiplication. For example, the Agricultural Adjustment Act of 1938 defined "projected national yield," "projected county yield," and "projected farm yield" as entailing historical averages "adjusted for abnormal weather conditions," "trends in yields," and "any significant changes in production practices." 7 U.S.C. §§1301(b)(8)(B), (13)(J), (K).

By contrast, we need look no further than the Bankruptcy Code to see that when Congress wishes to mandate simple multiplication, it does so unambiguously — most commonly by using the term "multiplied." See, e.g., 11 U.S.C. §1325(b)(3) ("current monthly income, when multiplied by 12"); §§704(b)(2), 707(b)(6), (7)(A) (same); §707(b)(2) (A)(i), (B)(iv) ("multiplied by 60"). Accord, 2 U.S.C. §58(b)(1)(B) ("multiplied by the number of months in such year"); 5 U.S.C. §8415(a) ("multiplied by such individual's total service"); 42 U.S.C. §403(f)(3) ("multiplied by the number of months in such year").

Third, pre-BAPCPA case law points in favor of the "forward-looking" approach. Prior to BAPCPA, the general rule was that courts would multiply a debtor's current monthly income by the number of months in the commitment period as the first step in determining projected disposable income. . . . But courts also had discretion to account for known or virtually certain changes in the debtor's income. . . . This judicial discretion was well documented in contemporary bankruptcy treatises. See 8 Collier on Bankruptcy ¶ 1325.08[4][a], p. 1325-50 (rev. 15th ed. 2004) (hereinafter Collier) ("As a practical matter, *unless there are changes which can be clearly foreseen,* the court must simply multiply the debtor's current monthly income by 36 and determine whether the amount to be paid under the plan equals or exceeds that amount" (emphasis added)); . . . see also In re Greer, 388 B.R. 889, 892 (Bkrtcy. Ct. CD Ill. 2008) ("'As a practical matter, unless there are changes which can be clearly foreseen, the court must simply multiply the debtor's current monthly income by thirty-six.'" . . . Indeed, petitioner concedes that courts possessed this discretion prior to BAPCPA. . . .

Pre-BAPCPA bankruptcy practice is telling because we "'"will not read the Bankruptcy Code to erode past bankruptcy practice absent a clear indication that Congress intended such a departure."'" . . . Congress did not amend the term "projected disposable income" in 2005, and pre-BAPCPA bankruptcy practice reflected a widely acknowledged and well-documented view that courts may take into account known or virtually certain changes to debtors' income or expenses when projecting disposable income. In light of this historical practice, we would expect that, had Congress intended for "projected" to carry a specialized — and indeed, unusual — meaning in Chapter 13, Congress would have said so expressly. . . .

B

The [mechanical] approach also clashes repeatedly with the terms of 11 U.S.C. §1325.

First, §1325(b)(1)(B)'s reference to projected disposable income "to be received in the applicable commitment period" strongly favors the forward-looking approach. There is no dispute that respondent would in fact receive far less than $756 per month in disposable income during the plan period, so petitioner's projection does not accurately reflect "income to be received" during that period. . . . The mechanical approach effectively reads this phrase out of the statute when a debtor's current disposable income is substantially higher than the income that the debtor predictably will receive during the plan period. . . .

Second, §1325(b)(1) directs courts to determine projected disposable income "as of the effective date of the plan," which is the date on which the plan is confirmed and becomes binding, see §1327(a). Had Congress intended for projected disposable income to be nothing more than a multiple of disposable income in all cases, we see no reason why Congress would not have required courts to determine that value as of the *filing* date of the plan. . . . In the very next section of the Code, for example, Congress specified that a debtor shall commence payments "not later than 30 days after the *date of the filing of the plan.*" §1326(a)(1) (emphasis added). Congress' decision to require courts to measure projected disposable income "as of the *effective* date of the plan" is more consistent with the view that Congress expected courts to consider postfiling information about the debtor's financial circumstances. . . .

Third, the requirement that projected disposable income "will be applied to make payments" is most naturally read to contemplate that the debtor will actually pay creditors in the calculated monthly amounts. §1325(b)(1)(B). But when, as of the effective date of a plan, the debtor lacks the means to do so, this language is rendered a hollow command.

C

The arguments advanced in favor of the mechanical approach are unpersuasive. Noting that the Code now provides a detailed and precise definition of "disposable income," proponents of the mechanical approach maintain that any departure from this method leaves that definition "'with no apparent purpose.'" . . . This argument overlooks the important role that the statutory formula for calculating "disposable income" plays under the forward-looking approach. As the Tenth Circuit recognized in this case, a court taking the forward-looking approach should begin by calculating disposable income, and in most cases, nothing more is required. It is only in unusual cases that a court may go further and take into account other known or virtually certain information about the debtor's future income or expenses.

Petitioner faults the Tenth Circuit for referring to a rebuttable "presumption" that the figure produced by the mechanical approach accurately represents a debtor's "projected disposable income." . . . Petitioner notes that the Code makes no reference to any such presumption but that related Code provisions expressly create other rebuttable presumptions. See §§707(b)(2)(A)(i) and (B)(i). He thus suggests that the Tenth Circuit improperly supplemented the text of the Code.

The Tenth Circuit's analysis, however, simply heeds the ordinary meaning of the term "projected." As noted, a person making a projection uses past occurrences as a starting point, and that is precisely what the Tenth Circuit prescribed. . . .

Petitioner argues that only the mechanical approach is consistent with §1129(a)(15)(B), which refers to "projected disposable income of the debtor (as defined in section 1325(b)(2))." This cross-reference, petitioner argues, shows that Congress intended for the term "projected disposable income" to incorporate, presumably in all contexts, the defined term "disposable income." It is evident that §1129(a)(15)(B) refers to the defined term "disposable income," see §1325(b)(2), but that fact offers no insight into the meaning of the word "projected" in §§1129(a)(15)(B) and 1325(b)(1)(B). We fail to see how that word acquires a specialized meaning as a result of this cross-reference — particularly where both §§1129(a)(15)(B) and 1325(b)(1)(B) refer to projected disposable income "to be received" during the relevant period. . . .

Petitioner also notes that §707 allows courts to take "special circumstances" into consideration, but that §1325(b)(3) incorporates §707 only with respect to calculating expenses. . . . Thus, he argues, a "special circumstances" exception should not be inferred with respect to the debtor's income. We decline to infer from §1325's incorporation of §707 that Congress intended to eliminate, *sub silentio*, the discretion that courts previously exercised when projecting disposable income to account for known or virtually certain changes. . . .

D

In cases in which a debtor's disposable income during the 6-month look back period is either substantially lower or higher than the debtor's disposable income during the plan period, the mechanical approach would produce senseless results that we do not think Congress intended. In cases in which the debtor's disposable income is higher during the plan period, the mechanical approach would deny creditors payments that the debtor could easily make. And where, as in the present case, the debtor's disposable income during the plan period is substantially lower, the mechanical approach would deny the protection of Chapter 13 to debtors who meet the chapter's main eligibility requirements. Here, for example, respondent is an "individual whose income is sufficiently stable and regular" to allow her "to make payments under a plan," §101(30), and her debts fall below the limits set out in §109(e). But if the mechanical approach were used, she could not file a confirmable plan. Under §1325(a)(6), a plan cannot be confirmed unless "the debtor will be able to make all payments under the plan and to comply with the plan." And as petitioner concedes, respondent could not possibly make the payments that the mechanical approach prescribes.

In order to avoid or at least to mitigate the harsh results that the mechanical approach may produce for debtors, petitioner advances several possible escape strategies. He proposes no comparable strategies for creditors harmed by the mechanical approach, and in any event none of the maneuvers that he proposes for debtors is satisfactory.

IV

We find petitioner's remaining arguments unpersuasive. Consistent with the text of §1325 and pre-BAPCPA practice, we hold that when a bankruptcy court calculates a debtor's projected disposable income, the court may account for changes in the debtor's income or expenses that are known or virtually certain at the time of confirmation. We therefore affirm the decision of the Court of Appeals.

Post-Case Follow-Up

Do you think the Supreme Court got this one right in terms of statutory construction? In terms of policy? It's one thing for the court to hold that in calculating a debtor's projected disposable income, the court (and the lawyer for the debtor who is drafting the debtor's plan) may account for changes in the debtor's income or expenses that are "known or virtually certain" at the time of confirmation, but how, practically, is that done? In *Lanning* itself, debtor's lawyer, notwithstanding the inflated average monthly income numbers recorded (properly) on debtors form, used the more accurate current income numbers from debtor's Schedule I to determine debtor's projected disposable income, and that's what the Supreme Court approved where the calculation of income on Form 22C (now 122C-1) does not show debtor's true current monthly income due to the mechanical six-month averaging formula used there. Of course, even recording a debtor's true current income on Schedule I would not reflect known or expected future changes in income. And the same issue exists with debtor's current expenses recorded on Schedule J and Form 122C-2 if changes are expected in such expenses. Post-*Lanning*, the Schedule I form has been revised to allow the debtor to indicate (on Line 13) expected increases or decreases in income. The Schedule J form has been revised to allow the debtor to indicate (on Line 24) expected changes in expenses. And new Form 122C-2 allows the above median debtor to indicate (on Line 46) expected changes to income or expenses. Nonetheless, calculating the Chapter 13 debtor's projected disposable income is not an easy, mechanical process. It is accomplished using the data made available on Schedules I, J, and Forms 122C-1 and 122C-2 (for the above median debtor). The lawyer for the debtor makes the best calculation possible from these sources in proposing the plan. Questions raised by the standing trustee or creditors regarding the accuracy of the numbers used in the calculation or the veracity of debtor's claimed upcoming changes to income or expenses (or for that matter to current income or expenses) are usually argued over and worked out at the 341 meeting. If no agreement can be reached there then an objection to confirmation is filed and the judge conducts a hearing and decides the issue. When is an upcoming change in income or expense "known or virtually certain" so as to be properly reportable on the bankruptcy forms and fair game for use in calculating the debtor's disposable monthly income? Is a "likely" or "probable" change enough? A "maybe" change? Should those be included notwithstanding the phrase used by the court? See In re Connor, 463 B.R. 14 (E.D. Mich. 2012).

Hamilton v. Lanning: Real Life Applications

1. You represent a below median debtor who needs to file his Chapter 13 petition immediately to stay an imminent foreclosure on his home. He is currently employed by a local company making $2,500 per month, gross. However, he has been advised by his employer that in sixty days he will receive a promotion and a raise to $3,200 per month, which will make him an above median debtor. How will you show that anticipated change in income on the forms you are preparing for this debtor? Should you go ahead and treat him as an above median debtor and complete Form 122C-2 for him?

2. You represent a divorced debtor who is preparing to file under Chapter 13 and who has total monthly expenses for Schedule J purposes of $2,333. However, she has a sixteen-year-old son who has been living with her who plans to go to live full-time with his father in approximately three months. If that happens it will reduce her monthly expenses by about $400. On the other hand, the ex-husband has been paying her child support for the boy and that may end if and when the boy goes to live with his father although there are other children of the couple living with your client, the father has not mentioned changing child support, and your client thinks he won't file a petition with the divorce court seeking a modification. Should you report one or both of these anticipated changes on the forms you are preparing for debtor and, if so, on what forms should you report them?

3. You represent an above median debtor whose income is not expected to change in the foreseeable future. Neither are her expenses, with one exception. Her aged mother has been diagnosed with Alzheimer's and the family expects she will not be able to live by herself much longer. Your client and her siblings have discussed what they will do and have tentatively agreed that the mother will live with the debtor, probably starting some time in the next 6 to 18 months depending on how rapidly her condition deteriorates. Debtor knows her expenses will rise in that event but really has no idea by how much. Should you report this possible change on the forms you are preparing for debtor and, if so, on what forms will you report it? In drafting the debtor's proposed Chapter 13 plan, should you go ahead and reduce her projected income by some amount of anticipated expenses associated with the mother moving in or wait and amend her plan later if and when that event occurs? If you go ahead and reduce her projected monthly income available over the term of her five-year plan and propose a plan based on that projection do you think the standing trustee or a creditor might object?

Once the CMI itemized in Part 1 of Form 122C-1 has been totaled on Line 11, we then take that total to Part 2 of the form and enter it on Line 12. Chapter 13 debtors who are married but who did not file jointly and who entered the non-filing spouse's average income in Column B of Part 1 may subtract that portion of the non-filing spouse's income on Line 13 that was not paid on a regular basis to defer household expenses of the debtor or dependents of the debtor and enter the balance on Line 14. This is the **marital adjustment** of Form 122C-1. As we saw earlier, the income of a non-filing spouse must be reported in Column B of Part 1 of the form. And if the income of the non-filing spouse is regularly available for household expenses of the debtor or his dependents, it must be listed and included in the debtor's total CMI entered on Line 11. It is only where the non-filing spouse's income is not regularly available for household expenses that it can be deducted from the debtor's CMI. And the reason that the non-filing spouse's income is not available for household expenses must be stated. The most common reason is that the non-filing spouse is required to pay spousal or child support from an earlier marriage.

The marital adjustment seen on Line 13 of Form 122C-1 is similar to that seen on Line 3 in Part 1 of Form 122A-2 as part of the Chapter 7 individual consumer debtor's means test (see discussion in Chapter Five, Section C). Both the qualifying Chapter 13 debtor and the qualifying Chapter 7 consumer debtor can make this adjustment to CMI. But don't forget, we're calculating the debtor's CMI in each case for different reasons.

For example, the Matthews enter the total of their joint CMI on Line 12 of their Form 122C-1. No reduction is made for the marital adjustment since they are both debtors. Instead, a zero is entered on Line 13, and the total from Line 13 is carried forward to Line 14.

On Line 15 of the form, the CMI total from Line 14 is annualized by being multiplied by 12 (current monthly income × 12). Then on Line 16 we enter the **median family income** figure for a household the size of the debtor's household living in the debtor's state of residence (the size of a debtor's household for purposes of Line 16 of Form 122C-1 is the same as that determined for purposes of Line 13 of Form 122A-1 by the individual Chapter 7 debtor; recall the discussion of what persons make up a debtor's household in Chapter Five, Section C). The median family income figures are drawn from the Census Bureau's tables and posted on the U.S. Trustee Program's website at www.justice.gov/ust/means-testing.

Application Exercise 2

Since our fictional Chapter 13 debtors live in Harrisburg, Dauphin County, Pennsylvania, the median family numbers for Pennsylvania are used as of June 2016 when they filed. There are four persons in the Matthews family. Go to the U.S. Trustee website and locate the Census Bureau's current tables for median family income for a family of four in the state of Pennsylvania. This is the median family income figure the Matthews use on Line 16 of their Form 122C-1. (Remember that the median income figures from the Census Bureau are adjusted annually. The Matthews' form uses the correct median income figure for Pennsylvania as of June 2016 but that figure may be different when you read this.) If the Matthews lived in the state where you plan to practice and were filing their case there today, what would the applicable median income for them be?

Next we compare the debtor's annualized CMI on Line 15 with the state's median family income number on Line 16. This comparison will determine the applicable commitment period for the debtor's Chapter 13 plan. If the Chapter 13 debtor's annualized CMI is less than the applicable median family income figure, debtor is a **below median debtor** and §1325(b)(4)(A) provides that the plan may run anywhere from 36 months (three years) to 60 months (five years). It must run at least three years. However, if the debtor's annualized CMI is equal to or more than the applicable median family income figure, debtor is an **above median debtor** and §1325(b)(4)(A) requires that the plan run for a full five years. An important exception to these applicable time period is found in §1325(b)(4)(B), which provides that if the plan of a below median or above median debtor calls for unsecured creditors to be paid 100 percent of what they are owed, the plan can run for less than the applicable period calculated under §1325(b)(4)(A). After all, those unsecured creditors are going to be pleased to receive 100 percent of what they are owed and would much rather receive it in fewer than three or five years.

The formal determination of the commitment period is done in Part 3 of the form in an arguably redundant manner using the calculations made in Parts 1 and 2 of the form. First, the average monthly income number from Line 11 of Part 1 is again entered on Line 18 of Part 3. If the debtor claimed the marital deduction on Line 13 of Part 2 that amount is again entered on Line 19 of Part 3 and subtracted from the average monthly income number on Line 18. On Line 20 the average monthly income number is again multiplied by 12 to generate the debtor's current monthly income for the year, which is entered on Line 20b. The debtor's applicable median family income figure based on state and family size that was entered on Line 16 is again entered on Line 20c. The amount of the debtor's annualized current income appearing on Line 20b is then compared with the median family income appearing on Line 20c to determine if the debtor is an above or below median debtor. If the debtor is below median the first box on Line 21 is checked along with Box 3 at the top right of page one of the form indicating that the applicable commitment period of the debtor is three years. If the debtor is above median the second box on Line 21 is checked along with Box 4 at the top right of page one of the form indicating that the applicable commitment period of the debtor is five years.

For example, the Matthews' annualized CMI falls below their state's median family income figure, making them below median debtors. They check the first box on Line 21 of their Form 122C-1 and the third box on the top right of page one of the form indicating that their commitment period is three years. They can propose a plan that will call for them to pay out their disposable income to unsecured creditors for as little as three years and no more than five. Their plan must run for at least three years.

Application Exercise 3

The applicable commitment period of the Matthews is only three years but they have proposed a five-year plan (see Exhibit 15.2). Can you think of reasons why a debtor might choose to do this? Might moral attitudes regarding a perceived duty to pay as much debt as possible be involved in this decision? Might practical concerns regarding the impact on the debtor's credit rating be involved? Or the debtor's desire to do business in the future with certain creditors?

B. DETERMINING THE PROJECTED DISPOSABLE INCOME FOR A CHAPTER 13 PLAN

You may have noticed that we did not reference Line 17 in Part 2 of Form 122C-1 in the last section. Although that form determines the applicable commitment period for both the above and below median Chapter 13 debtor, it does not determine the projected disposable income that a debtor, either above or below median income, will have available to fund the Chapter 13 plan during the applicable commitment period. It does, however, indicate whether or not the debtor's disposable income is to be calculated under §1325(b)(3). To understand the significance of that determination, let's start with the Code's definition of disposable income. Disposable income is defined by §§1325(b)(2) as current monthly income (other than child support, foster care, and disability payments for a dependent child) received by the debtor, less amounts "reasonably necessary" for the maintenance or support of the debtor or dependents or to satisfy a domestic support obligation and also less charitable contributions up to 15 percent of the debtor's gross income. If the debtor operates a business, the definition of disposable income excludes those amounts that are necessary for ordinary operating expenses.

Section 1325(b)(3) then says that if the debtor is an above median debtor, what constitutes "reasonably necessary" amounts to be deducted from currently monthly income of the debtor is to be determined under §707(b)(2), the section of the Code that determines whether a Chapter 7 debtor satisfies the means test (as examined using Marta Carlson's hypothetical Form 122A-2 in Chapter Five, Section C). In a Chapter 13 case, when the debtor's disposable income is to be determined under §1325(b)(3), that debtor must complete Form 122C-2, which we will see is very similar to Form 122A-2 used in Chapter 7 cases.

Form 122C-1, in addition to determining the debtor's applicable commitment period as discussed in the last section, also determines whether or not the debtor must calculate his or her disposable income using §1325(b)(3). This is what Line 17 of Form 122C-1 accomplishes. Having calculated the debtor's annualized monthly income and compared it to the median income for the applicable state and household size, the debtor whose annualized monthly income is less than the median is instructed to check Box 17a and Box 1 on the top right of page one of the form indicating that disposable income for this debtor will not be calculated under §1325(b)(3) (we will examine how it is calculated next). If the debtor's annualized monthly income exceeds the median the debtor is instructed to check Box 17b and Box 2 on the top right of page 1 of the form indicating that disposable income for this debtor will indeed be calculated under §1325(b)(3). The above median debtor is also instructed to complete Form 122C-2 (we will consider the disposable income calculation for the above median debtor under §1325(b)(3) and using Form 122C-2 later in this chapter).

For example, on their Form 122C-1 the Matthews have determined that their annualized current monthly income is less than the applicable state median for their size family. They are below median debtors. Accordingly, they check Box 17a on their form and Box 1 on the top right of page 1 of the form indicating that their disposable income will not be calculated using §1325(b)(3).

Before we begin to look at how disposable income is calculated for the below and above median debtor, be sure you are aware of how critical that calculation is in a Chapter 13 case. Essentially, the disposable income calculation is a determination of how much money the debtor will have available on a monthly basis to pay unsecured creditors during the term of the plan. The disposable income calculation is concerned with money available for unsecured claims because the debtor is going to retain sufficient funds to support him or herself and dependents during the term of the plan and the plan will propose separate treatment of secured claims, as we will consider in the next chapter. But remember the dictate of §1325(b)(1): The Chapter 13 plan cannot be confirmed over an objection unless it proposes to pay unsecured creditors 100 percent of what they are owed or to utilize *all* of the debtor's projected disposable income to be received in the applicable commitment period to pay those unsecured creditors. That's what makes this calculation so critical.

The U.S. Trustee's office has formulated a Statement on the Trustee Program's Position on Legal Issues Arising under the Chapter 13 Disposable Income Test that is accessible online at www.justice.gov/sites/default/files/ust/legacy/2015/03/03/chapter13_analysis.pdf. This a good site to bookmark if you have not already done so.

1. Calculating Disposable Income for the Below Median Debtor

Once the below median Chapter 13 debtor has completed Form 122C-1 we know the debtor's annualized currently monthly income figure. But that is not the same as disposable income. And the below median debtor is not required to complete Form 122C-2 as the above median debtor is. So how do we determine the disposable income figure for the below median debtor?

It is §1325(b)(2) that controls the disposable income calculation unless the debtor is above median. That section provides that the debtor will deduct amounts reasonably necessary for the maintenance or support of himself and his dependents. We begin by examining the debtor's Schedule I, Your Income, and comparing it with the CMI calculation made on the debtor's 122C-1. Note that the Schedule I provides a snapshot picture of debtor's income as of the day the petition is filed while the 122C-1 provides an average income over the six months of the look back period. But comparing the data on the two forms should provide a somewhat accurate picture of the debtor's income as of the date the case is filed and any changes in income over the preceding six months. The income information from Form 122C-1 and

Schedule I is then compared with the debtor's actual expenses to determine what is reasonably necessary for his and his dependents' maintenance and support, always remembering that such actual expenses must be reasonable under §1325(b)(2). For the below median debtor, the Schedule J, Your Expenses, is the primary source of information regarding the debtor's reasonably necessary expenses.

Application Exercise 4

The Matthews' Schedules I and J are Documents 9 and 10 in their case file. For convenience their Schedule J is also set out in Exhibit 13.2. Notice how much like a budget it is. Compare the Schedule J with the informal budget drawn up by their lawyer in the Assignment Memorandum in Appendix B of the text. From the budget document, can you determine where much of the Schedule J information came from?

Although the Schedule J now in use is a useful starting point to determine the below median debtor's disposable income, the monthly net income figure calculated on Line 23c of Schedule J likely is not that debtor's actual disposable income that must be paid to unsecured creditors. It is only the *starting point* to determine it. Why do we say that?

Expenses listed on Schedule J may be modified or even eliminated in the actual Chapter 13 plan, leaving more disposable income to apply to unsecured debts that will be paid in the plan. Collateralized obligations listed on Schedule J may disappear or change when the collateral is surrendered to the secured creditor and the remaining obligation is discharged in the plan. As will see in the next chapter, if the value of the collateral securing a loan exceeds the balance owing on the loan, Chapter 13 may allow the debtor to strip down the balance owed to the creditor to the current value of the collateral and adjust payments accordingly in the plan. These are only two of several options a Chapter 13 debtor may be able to utilize to adjust his Schedule J expenses in the actual Chapter 13 plan.

For example, the Matthews currently make monthly payments totaling $720 on three vehicles. If their plan proposes to reaffirm those three debts, retain possession of all three vehicles, and continue paying the monthly obligations as they come due, that will be $720 per month that will not be available to unsecured creditors during the term of the plan. However, if the Matthews' plan proposes to surrender one or more of the vehicles or other secured property and stop paying the affected secured creditors, that decision will free up additional "disposable" dollars to go to unsecured creditors each month. That decision is not reflected on Schedule J. Thus, for this reason too, the amount of monthly net income entered on Line 23c of Schedule J is only a suggestion or a starting point for the trustee to determine if the debtor is making all of his projected disposable income available to unsecured creditors as required by §1325(b).

| **EXHIBIT 13.2** | **Roger and Susan Matthews Schedule J** |

Fill in this information to identify your case:

Debtor 1	Roger	H.	Matthews
	First Name	Middle Name	Last Name
Debtor 2	Susan	J.	Matthews
(Spouse, if filing)	First Name	Middle Name	Last Name

United States Bankruptcy Court for the: Middle District of Pennsylvania

Case number
(If known) _____

Check if this is:

☐ An amended filing

☐ A supplement showing postpetition chapter 13 expenses as of the following date:

_____
MM / DD / YYYY

Official Form 106J

Schedule J: Your Expenses

12/15

Be as complete and accurate as possible. If two married people are filing together, both are equally responsible for supplying correct information. If more space is needed, attach another sheet to this form. On the top of any additional pages, write your name and case number (if known). Answer every question.

| **Part 1:** | **Describe Your Household** |

1. **Is this a joint case?**

   ☐ No. Go to line 2.

   ☑ Yes. **Does Debtor 2 live in a separate household?**

   　　☑ No

   　　☐ Yes. Debtor 2 must file Official Form 106J-2, *Expenses for Separate Household of Debtor 2.*

2. **Do you have dependents?**   ☐ No

   Do not list Debtor 1 and   ☑ Yes. Fill out this information for
   Debtor 2.   each dependent.........................

   Do not state the dependents' names.

	Dependent's relationship to Debtor 1 or Debtor 2	Dependent's age	Does dependent live with you?
	Daughter	7 yr	☐ No ☑ Yes
	Daughter	11 mo	☐ No ☑ Yes
	_____	____	☐ No ☐ Yes
	_____	____	☐ No ☐ Yes
	_____	____	☐ No ☐ Yes

3. **Do your expenses include**   ☑ No
   expenses of people other than   ☐ Yes
   yourself and your dependents?

| **Part 2:** | **Estimate Your Ongoing Monthly Expenses** |

Estimate your expenses as of your bankruptcy filing date unless you are using this form as a supplement in a Chapter 13 case to report expenses as of a date after the bankruptcy is filed. If this is a supplemental *Schedule J*, check the box at the top of the form and fill in the applicable date.

Include expenses paid for with non-cash government assistance if you know the value of such assistance and have included it on *Schedule I: Your Income* (Official Form 106I.)

Your expenses

4. **The rental or home ownership expenses for your residence.** Include first mortgage payments and any rent for the ground or lot.　　　　4.　$_____850.00

   If not included in line 4:

   4a.　Real estate taxes　　　　　　　　　　　　　4a.　$_____0.00

   4b.　Property, homeowner's, or renter's insurance　　4b.　$_____0.00

   4c.　Home maintenance, repair, and upkeep expenses　4c.　$_____75.00

   4d.　Homeowner's association or condominium dues　　4d.　$_____0.00

EXHIBIT 13.2 **(Continued)**

Debtor 1   Roger _____ H. _____ Matthews _____   Case number *(if known)* _____
          First Name   Middle Name   Last Name

		Your expenses
5. **Additional mortgage payments for your residence**, such as home equity loans	5.	$ 700.00
6. **Utilities:**		
6a. Electricity, heat, natural gas	6a.	$ 315.00
6b. Water, sewer, garbage collection	6b.	$ 50.00
6c. Telephone, cell phone, Internet, satellite, and cable services	6c.	$ 135.00
6d. Other. Specify: _____	6d.	$ 0.00
7. **Food and housekeeping supplies**	7.	$ 475.00
8. **Childcare and children's education costs**	8.	$ 0.00
9. **Clothing, laundry, and dry cleaning**	9.	$ 200.00
10. **Personal care products and services**	10.	$ 40.00
11. **Medical and dental expenses**	11.	$ 100.00
12. **Transportation.** Include gas, maintenance, bus or train fare. Do not include car payments.	12.	$ 150.00
13. **Entertainment, clubs, recreation, newspapers, magazines, and books**	13.	$ 50.00
14. **Charitable contributions and religious donations**	14.	$ 50.00
15. **Insurance.** Do not include insurance deducted from your pay or included in lines 4 or 20.		
15a. Life insurance	15a.	$ 0.00
15b. Health insurance	15b.	$ 0.00
15c. Vehicle insurance	15c.	$ 60.00
15d. Other insurance. Specify: _____	15d.	$ 0.00
16. **Taxes.** Do not include taxes deducted from your pay or included in lines 4 or 20. Specify: _____	16.	$ 0.00
17. **Installment or lease payments:**		
17a. Car payments for Vehicle 1	17a.	$ 360.00
17b. Car payments for Vehicle 2	17b.	$ 240.00
17c. Other. Specify: Vehicle 3	17c.	$ 120.00
17d. Other. Specify: _____	17d.	$ 0.00
18. **Your payments of alimony, maintenance, and support that you did not report as deducted from your pay on line 5, *Schedule I, Your Income* (Official Form 106I).**	18.	$ 0.00
19. **Other payments you make to support others who do not live with you.** Specify: _____	19.	$ 0.00
20. **Other real property expenses not included in lines 4 or 5 of this form or on *Schedule I: Your Income*.**		
20a. Mortgages on other property	20a.	$ 0.00
20b. Real estate taxes	20b.	$ 0.00
20c. Property, homeowner's, or renter's insurance	20c.	$ 0.00
20d. Maintenance, repair, and upkeep expenses	20d.	$ 0.00
20e. Homeowner's association or condominium dues	20e.	$ 0.00

EXHIBIT 13.2 (Continued)

Debtor 1   Roger   H.   Matthews   Case number (if known)_____
        First Name   Middle Name   Last Name

21. **Other.** Specify: Miscellaneous _____   21. **+$** _____100.00

22. **Calculate your monthly expenses.**

    22a. Add lines 4 through 21.   22a. $ _____4,070.00

    22b. Copy line 22 (monthly expenses for Debtor 2), if any, from Official Form 106J-2   22b. $ _____0.00

    22c. Add line 22a and 22b. The result is your monthly expenses.   22c. $ _____4,070.00

23. **Calculate your monthly net income.**

    23a. Copy line 12 (*your combined monthly income*) from *Schedule I.*   23a. $ _____4,133.00

    23b. Copy your monthly expenses from line 22c above.   23b. **–$** _____4,070.00

    23c. Subtract your monthly expenses from your monthly income.
        The result is your *monthly net income.*   23c. $ _____63.00

24. **Do you expect an increase or decrease in your expenses within the year after you file this form?**

    For example, do you expect to finish paying for your car loan within the year or do you expect your
    mortgage payment to increase or decrease because of a modification to the terms of your mortgage?

    ☐ No.

    ☑ Yes.   Explain here: We intend to surrender vehicle #3 immediately. We anticipate having to incur monthly child
                               care expenses of $250 beginning in August 2016.

Another reason that current Schedule J does not calculate the debtor's disposable income for plan purposes is that it does not calculate certain anticipated expenses that may arise during the term of the plan.

For example, Line 24 of the Matthews' Schedule J indicates that they expect to begin incurring childcare expenses of $250 per month in the next year. That expense will obviously have an impact on their disposable income. But note that Schedule J does not allow that anticipated future expense to be added to the average monthly expense total showing on Line 23c. In Hamilton v. Lanning (highlighted above), the Supreme Court held that upcoming changes in debtor's income or expenses that are "virtually known or certain" can be considered in determining the debtor's disposable income. But Schedule J does not include that calculation in the monthly net income total.

For these reasons, Schedule J does not accurately calculate the Chapter 13 debtor's disposable income. It is nothing more than a starting point to figure it out. Thus, although Line 23c on the Matthews' Schedule J shows a *monthly net income* available to them of $63 after deducting the various expenses listed on the form, that is not their disposable income for purposes of determining debtors' projected disposable income under §1325(b)(2).

In actuality, the debtor must decide on the specific terms of the plan, including how secured claims will be treated and what likely changes there will be to debtor's income and expenses during the term of the plan before actual disposable income can be determined. In Chapter Fifteen, we will look at the decisions the Matthews have made regarding those things and the actual terms of the Chapter 13 plan they put together. Only then can we determine if the plan actually proposes paying all their disposable income to unsecured creditors over the term of the plan as required by §1325(b).

2. Calculating Disposable Income for the Above Median Debtor

Let's assume for the moment that Roger Matthews has a gross salary of $50,000 per year ($4,166.66 per month) at City Plumbing Company and Susan Matthews has a gross salary of $45,000 per year ($3,750 per month) at Heart and Soul Academy. Based on those assumptions, their CMI is $7,916.66 and their annualized CMI is $95,000, which puts them above their applicable median income level in June 2016 when they filed. They are now above median debtors and will be required to propose either a five-year plan or a shorter 100 percent plan. Exhibit 13.3 shows what the Matthews' Form 122C-1 would look like if they had the higher incomes (this form is also included in the Matthews' case file on the companion Web site as Extra Material). As above median debtors in this alternative scenario the Matthews check the second box on Line 21 of their form and Box 4 on the top right of page one of the form, indicating that their applicable commitment period is five years. They also check box 17b and Box 2 on the top right of page 1 of the form, indicating that their disposable income will be calculated using §1325(b)(3).

EXHIBIT 13.3   Alternative Official Form 122C-1 for Roger and Susan Matthews Assuming Above Median Income

Fill in this information to identify your case:		
Debtor 1	Roger First Name	H. Middle Name	Matthews Last Name
Debtor 2 (Spouse, if filing)	Susan First Name	J. Middle Name	Matthews Last Name

United States Bankruptcy Court for the: Middle District of Pennsylvania

Case number
(if known) _____

Check as directed in lines 17 and 21:

According to the calculations required by this Statement:

☐ 1. Disposable income is not determined under 11 U.S.C. § 1325(b)(3).

☑ 2. Disposable income is determined under 11 U.S.C. § 1325(b)(3).

☐ 3. The commitment period is 3 years.

☑ 4. The commitment period is 5 years.

☐ Check if this is an amended filing

Official Form 122C-1

Chapter 13 Statement of Your Current Monthly Income and Calculation of Commitment Period

12/15

Be as complete and accurate as possible. If two married people are filing together, both are equally responsible for being accurate. If more space is needed, attach a separate sheet to this form. Include the line number to which the additional information applies. On the top of any additional pages, write your name and case number (if known).

Part 1:   Calculate Your Average Monthly Income

1. **What is your marital and filing status?** Check one only.

   ☐ **Not married.** Fill out Column A, lines 2-11.

   ☑ **Married.** Fill out both Columns A and B, lines 2-11.

   Fill in the average monthly income that you received from all sources, derived during the 6 full months before you file this **bankruptcy case.** 11 U.S.C. § 101(10A). For example, if you are filing on September 15, the 6-month period would be March 1 through August 31. If the amount of your monthly income varied during the 6 months, add the income for all 6 months and divide the total by 6. Fill in the result. Do not include any income amount more than once. For example, if both spouses own the same rental property, put the income from that property in one column only. If you have nothing to report for any line, write $0 in the space.

		Column A Debtor 1	Column B Debtor 2 or non-filing spouse
2.	**Your gross wages, salary, tips, bonuses, overtime, and commissions** (before all payroll deductions).	$ 4,166.66	$ 3,750.00
3.	**Alimony and maintenance payments.** Do not include payments from a spouse.	$ 0.00	$
4.	**All amounts from any source which are regularly paid for household expenses of you or your dependents, including child support.** Include regular contributions from an unmarried partner, members of your household, your dependents, parents, and roommates. Do not include payments from a spouse. Do not include payments you listed on line 3.	$ 0.00	$ 0.00

5. **Net income from operating a business, profession, or farm**

	Debtor 1	Debtor 2			
Gross receipts (before all deductions)	$_____	$_____			
Ordinary and necessary operating expenses	– $_____	– $_____			
Net monthly income from a business, profession, or farm	$ 0.00	$ 0.00	Copy here ➔	$ 0.00	$ 0.00

6. **Net income from rental and other real property**

	Debtor 1	Debtor 2			
Gross receipts (before all deductions)	$_____	$_____			
Ordinary and necessary operating expenses	– $_____	– $_____			
Net monthly income from rental or other real property	$ 0.00	$ 0.00	Copy here ➔	$ 0.00	$ 0.00

EXHIBIT 13.3 **(Continued)**

Debtor 1   Roger   H.   Matthew   Case number *(if known)*_____
            First Name   Middle Name   Last Name

	Column A Debtor 1	Column B Debtor 2 or non-filing spouse
7. **Interest, dividends, and royalties**	$_____0.00	$_____0.00
8. **Unemployment compensation**	$_____0.00	$_____0.00

Do not enter the amount if you contend that the amount received was a benefit under the Social Security Act. Instead, list it here: ....↓

For you.. $_____

For your spouse .... $_____

9. **Pension or retirement income.** Do not include any amount received that was a benefit under the Social Security Act.

	Column A	Column B
9.	$_____0.00	$_____0.00

10. **Income from all other sources not listed above.** Specify the source and amount. Do not include any benefits received under the Social Security Act or payments received as a victim of a war crime, a crime against humanity, or international or domestic terrorism. If necessary, list other sources on a separate page and put the total below.

	Column A	Column B
_____	$_____0.00	$_____0.00
_____	$_____0.00	$_____0.00
Total amounts from separate pages, if any.	+ $_____0.00	+ $_____0.00

11. **Calculate your total average monthly income.** Add lines 2 through 10 for each column. Then add the total for Column A to the total for Column B.

$ 4,166.66 + $ 3,750.00 = $ 7,916.66

Total average
monthly income

Part 2:   **Determine How to Measure Your Deductions from Income**

12. **Copy your total average monthly income from line 11.** .... $ 7,916.66

13. **Calculate the marital adjustment.** Check one:

☐ You are not married. Fill in 0 below.

☑ You are married and your spouse is filing with you. Fill in 0 below.

☐ You are married and your spouse is not filing with you.

Fill in the amount of the income listed in line 11, Column B, that was NOT regularly paid for the household expenses of you or your dependents, such as payment of the spouse's tax liability or the spouse's support of someone other than you or your dependents.

Below, specify the basis for excluding this income and the amount of income devoted to each purpose. If necessary, list additional adjustments on a separate page.

If this adjustment does not apply, enter 0 below.

_____	$_____
_____	$_____
_____	+ $_____
Total..	$_____0.00 Copy here ➜	— _____0.00

14. **Your current monthly income.** Subtract the total in line 13 from line 12. $ 7,916.66

15. **Calculate your current monthly income for the year.** Follow these steps:

15a. Copy line 14 here ➜ .... $ 7,916.66

Multiply line 15a by 12 (the number of months in a year).   x 12

15b. The result is your current monthly income for the year for this part of the form. .... $ 94,999.92

EXHIBIT 13.3 **(Continued)**

Debtor 1	Roger	H.	Matthews	Case number (if known) _____
	First Name	Middle Name	Last Name	

---

16. **Calculate the median family income that applies to you.** Follow these steps:

   16a. Fill in the state in which you live.   PA

   16b. Fill in the number of people in your household.   4

   16c. Fill in the median family income for your state and size of household. .... $ 86,112.00

      To find a list of applicable median income amounts, go online using the link specified in the separate
      instructions for this form. This list may also be available at the bankruptcy clerk's office.

17. **How do the lines compare?**

   17a. ☐ Line 15b is less than or equal to line 16c. On the top of page 1 of this form, check box 1, *Disposable income is not determined under*
      11 U.S.C. § 1325(b)(3). **Go to Part 3.** Do NOT fill out *Calculation of Your Disposable Income* (Official Form 122C–2).

   17b. ☑ Line 15b is more than line 16c. On the top of page 1 of this form, check box 2, *Disposable income is determined under*
      11 U.S.C. § 1325(b)(3). **Go to Part 3 and fill out Calculation of Your Disposable Income (Official Form 122C–2).**
      On line 39 of that form, copy your current monthly income from line 14 above.

Part 3:   **Calculate Your Commitment Period Under 11 U.S.C. § 1325(b)(4)**

---

18. Copy your total average monthly income from line 11. .... $ 7,916.66

19. **Deduct the marital adjustment if it applies.** If you are married, your spouse is not filing with you, and you contend that
   calculating the commitment period under 11 U.S.C. § 1325(b)(4) allows you to deduct part of your spouse's income, copy
   the amount from line 13.
   19a. If the marital adjustment does not apply, fill in 0 on line 19a. .... – $ 0.00

   19b. **Subtract line 19a from line 18.** $ 7,916.66

20. **Calculate your current monthly income for the year.** Follow these steps:

   20a. Copy line 19b. .... $ 7,916.66

      Multiply by 12 (the number of months in a year).   x 12

   20b. The result is your current monthly income for the year for this part of the form. $ 94,999.92

   20c. Copy the median family income for your state and size of household from line 16c. .... $ 86,112.00

21. **How do the lines compare?**

   ☐ Line 20b is less than line 20c. Unless otherwise ordered by the court, on the top of page 1 of this form, check box 3,
     The commitment period is 3 years. Go to Part 4.

   ☑ Line 20b is more than or equal to line 20c. Unless otherwise ordered by the court, on the top of page 1 of this form,
     check box 4, *The commitment period is 5 years.* Go to Part 4.

Part 4:   **Sign Below**

     By signing here, under penalty of perjury I declare that the information on this statement and in any attachments is true and correct.

     X /s/ Roger H. Matthews   **X** /s/ Susan J. Matthews

      Signature of Debtor 1   Signature of Debtor 2

      Date 06/06/2016   Date 06/06/2016
         MM / DD / YYYY   MM / DD / YYYY

     If you checked 17a, do NOT fill out or file Form 122C–2.
     If you checked 17b, fill out Form 122C–2 and file it with this form. On line 39 of that form, copy your current monthly income from line 14 above.

Official Form 122C-1   **Chapter 13 Statement of Your Current Monthly Income and Calculation of Commitment Period**   page 3

To calculate their disposable income as above median debtors the Matthews must complete Official Form 122C-2. Before we go through that form using the higher income assumptions for the Matthews, it may be helpful for you to review the step-by-step discussion of Marcia Carlson's Form 122A-2 in Chapter Five, Section C, Exhibit 5.3, since the deductions allowed on the two forms are substantially similar and calculated in the same way. As we have noted, this is the case because §1325(b)(3) dictates that the reasonably necessary expenses of the above median Chapter 13 debtor allowed in order to determine his disposable income are to be calculated according to §707(b)(2), the same section that controls the determination of the means test for the Chapter 7 consumer debtor.

The Matthews' Form 122C-2 assuming they were above median debtors is set out in Exhibit 13.4 (this form is also included in the Matthews' case file on the companion Web site as Extra Material).

Because of the similarity between Form 122C-2 used by above median debtors in Chapter 13 cases and Form 122A-2 used in the Chapter 7 means test by above median debtors (and illustrated in detail in Chapter Five) our examination of the former here will be cursory. Thus on Line 5 of Part 1 of the form, where the debtor calculates deductions from income, the Matthews first enter the number of persons whose expenses will be considered in calculating the deductions. Like Line 5 of Form 122A-2 for the above median debtor in a Chapter 7, the persons whose expenses can be considered on Form 122C-2 potentially include more than the persons who make up his household. Section 1325(b)(2)(A)(i) provides that the debtor's monthly expenses shall include such expenses "for the debtor, the dependents of the debtor, and the spouse of the debtor in a joint case, if the spouse is not otherwise a dependent."

Using the number of persons designated on Line 5 the debtor then enters the standardized expense amounts for food and clothing (Line 6) and healthcare (Line 7) using the IRS National Standards for Allowable Living Expenses posted on the U.S. Trustee Program website at www.justice.gov/ust/means-testing for a household of that size living in Pennsylvania, the debtor's state of residence. Note that the instructions on Line 7 indicate that if the debtor's actual healthcare expenses are greater than the standard figure that can be noted on Line 22, discussed below.

The Matthews then utilize the IRS Local Standards for Transportation and Housing and Utilities Expenses to enter the standardized expenses for non-mortgage housing and utility expenses (Line 8), mortgage/rent expense (Line 9), vehicle operation expense (Lines 11 and 12), and vehicle ownership or lease expense for up to two vehicles (Line 13) in Dauphin County, Pennsylvania.

With regard to the deduction for vehicle ownership expense on Line 13 of Form 122C-2 (and Line 13 of Form 122A-2 discussed in Chapter Five), recall that there was an issue of whether that deduction is allowable where the debtor owns the vehicle outright so there is no lease or debt secured by the vehicle. The Supreme Court resolved the issue in Ransom v. FIA Card Services, N.A., 131 S. Ct. 716 (2011), holding that the deduction is not allowable for a car that is owned free of debt or lease obligations. All three vehicles owned by the Matthews are security for debt, so *Ransom* is no bar to their taking the deduction for all three vehicles. However, the ownership expense deduction can only be taken for up to two vehicles

EXHIBIT 13.4   **Official Form 122C-2 for Roger and Susan Matthews Assuming Above Median Income**

Fill in this information to identify your case:

Debtor 1	Roger	H.	Matthews
	First Name	Middle Name	Last Name
Debtor 2	Susan	J.	Matthews
(Spouse, if filing) First Name		Middle Name	Last Name

United States Bankruptcy Court for the: Middle District of Pennsylvania

Case number
(If known) _____

☐ Check if this is an amended filing

Official Form 122C-2
_____

Chapter 13 Calculation of Your Disposable Income   04/16

To fill out this form, you will need your completed copy of *Chapter 13 Statement of Your Current Monthly Income and Calculation of Commitment Period* (Official Form 122C–1).

Be as complete and accurate as possible. If two married people are filing together, both are equally responsible for being accurate. If more space is needed, attach a separate sheet to this form. Include the line number to which the additional information applies. On the top of any additional pages, write your name and case number (if known).

Part 1:   Calculate Your Deductions from Your Income

The Internal Revenue Service (IRS) issues National and Local Standards for certain expense amounts. Use these amounts to answer the questions in lines 6-15. To find the IRS standards, go online using the link specified in the separate instructions for this form. This information may also be available at the bankruptcy clerk's office.

Deduct the expense amounts set out in lines 6-15 regardless of your actual expense. In later parts of the form, you will use some of your actual expenses if they are higher than the standards. Do not include any operating expenses that you subtracted from income in lines 5 and 6 of Form 122C–1, and do not deduct any amounts that you subtracted from your spouse's income in line 13 of Form 122C–1.

If your expenses differ from month to month, enter the average expense.

Note: Line numbers 1-4 are not used in this form. These numbers apply to information required by a similar form used in chapter 7 cases.

5.   **The number of people used in determining your deductions from income**
     Fill in the number of people who could be claimed as exemptions on your federal income tax
     return, plus the number of any additional dependents whom you support. This number may
     be different from the number of people in your household. | 4.00 |

National Standards   You must use the IRS National Standards to answer the questions in lines 6-7.

6.   **Food, clothing, and other items:** Using the number of people you entered in line 5 and the IRS National
     Standards, fill in the dollar amount for food, clothing, and other items. $ 1509

7.   **Out-of-pocket health care allowance:** Using the number of people you entered in line 5 and the IRS National
     Standards, fill in the dollar amount for out-of-pocket health care. The number of people is split into two
     categories—people who are under 65 and people who are 65 or older—because older people have a higher IRS
     allowance for health care costs. If your actual expenses are higher than this IRS amount, you may deduct the
     additional amount on line 22.

EXHIBIT 13.4 **(Continued)**

Debtor 1 ___Roger_____H._____Matthew____   Case number (*if known*)_____
         First Name   Middle Name   Last Name

People who are under 65 years of age

7a. Out-of-pocket health care allowance per person $_____54.00_____

7b. Number of people who are under 65   X ___4___

7c. Subtotal. Multiply line 7a by line 7b. $_____216.00   Copy here ➡ $_____216.00

People who are 65 years of age or older

7d. Out-of-pocket health care allowance per person $_____

7e. Number of people who are 65 or older   X _____

7f. Subtotal. Multiply line 7d by line 7e. $_____0.00   Copy here ➡   + $_____0.00

7g. **Total**. Add lines 7c and 7f. .... $_____216.00   Copy here ➡ ...... $_____216.00

Local Standards   You must use the IRS Local Standards to answer the questions in lines 8-15.

Based on information from the IRS, the U.S. Trustee Program has divided the IRS Local Standard for housing for bankruptcy purposes into two parts:

■ **Housing and utilities – Insurance and operating expenses**
■ **Housing and utilities – Mortgage or rent expenses**

To answer the questions in lines 8-9, use the U.S. Trustee Program chart. To find the chart, go online using the link specified in the separate instructions for this form. This chart may also be available at the bankruptcy clerk's office.

8. **Housing and utilities – Insurance and operating expenses:** Using the number of people you entered in line 5, fill in the dollar amount listed for your county for insurance and operating expenses. $_____644.00

9. **Housing and utilities – Mortgage or rent expenses:**

9a. Using the number of people you entered in line 5, fill in the dollar amount listed for your county for mortgage or rent expenses. $___1,239.00

9b. Total average monthly payment for all mortgages and other debts secured by your home.

To calculate the total average monthly payment, add all amounts that are contractually due to each secured creditor in the 60 months after you file for bankruptcy. Next divide by 60.

Name of the creditor	Average monthly payment
First Bank of Capital City	$_____850.00
Capital Savings Bank	$_____700.00
_____	+ $_____
9b. Total average monthly payment	$___1,550.00

Copy here ➡   − $___1,550.00   Repeat this amount on line 33a.

9c. Net mortgage or rent expense.

Subtract line 9b (*total average monthly payment*) from line 9a (*mortgage or rent expense*). If this number is less than $0, enter $0. $_____0.00   Copy here ➡ ...... $_____0.00

10. **If you claim that the U.S. Trustee Program's division of the IRS Local Standard for housing is incorrect and affects the calculation of your monthly expenses, fill in any additional amount you claim.** $_____0.00

Explain why: _____

_____

EXHIBIT 13.4 (Continued)

Debtor 1 Roger _____ H. _____ Matthews _____
First Name   Middle Name   Last Name

Case number (if known)_____

11. Local transportation expenses: Check the number of vehicles for which you claim an ownership or operating expense.

☐ 0. Go to line 14.
☐ 1. Go to line 12.
☐ 2 or more. Go to line 12.

12. Vehicle operation expense: Using the IRS Local Standards and the number of vehicles for which you claim the operating expenses, fill in the *Operating Costs* that apply for your Census region or metropolitan statistical area.

$ 502.00

13. Vehicle ownership or lease expense: Using the IRS Local Standards, calculate the net ownership or lease expense for each vehicle below. You may not claim the expense if you do not make any loan or lease payments on the vehicle. In addition, you may not claim the expense for more than two vehicles.

Vehicle 1   Describe Vehicle 1:   YR-3 Ford F-150

13a. Ownership or leasing costs using IRS Local Standard....................................... $ 471.00

13b. Average monthly payment for all debts secured by Vehicle 1.
Do not include costs for leased vehicles.

To calculate the average monthly payment here and on line 13e, add all amounts that are contractually due to each secured creditor in the 60 months after you file for bankruptcy. Then divide by 60.

Name of each creditor for Vehicle 1	Average monthly payment
Automotive Financing, Inc.	$ 360.00
	+ $
Total average monthly payment	$ 360.00

Copy here ➔ − $ 360.00 Repeat this amount on line 33b.

13c. Net Vehicle 1 ownership or lease expense
Subtract line 13b from line 13a. If this number is less than $0, enter $0. .... $ 111.00 Copy net Vehicle 1 expense here ➔ $ 111.00

Vehicle 2   Describe Vehicle 2:   YR-4 Honda Civic

13d. Ownership or leasing costs using IRS Local Standard .... $ 471.00

13e. Average monthly payment for all debts secured by Vehicle 2.
Do not include costs for leased vehicles.

Name of each creditor for Vehicle 2	Average monthly payment
Columbiana Federal S&L	$ 240.00
	+ $
Total average monthly payment	$ 240.00

Copy here ➔ − $ 240.00 Repeat this amount on line 33c.

13f. Net Vehicle 2 ownership or lease expense
Subtract line 13e from line 13d. If this number is less than $0, enter $0................... $ 231.00 Copy net Vehicle 2 expense here ➔ $ 231.00

14. Public transportation expense: If you claimed 0 vehicles in line 11, using the IRS Local Standards, fill in the *Public Transportation* expense allowance regardless of whether you use public transportation.

$ 0.00

15. Additional public transportation expense: If you claimed 1 or more vehicles in line 11 and if you claim that you may also deduct a public transportation expense, you may fill in what you believe is the appropriate expense, but you may not claim more than the IRS Local Standard for *Public Transportation*.

$ 0.00

EXHIBIT 13.4   **(Continued)**

Debtor 1	Roger	H.	Matthews	Case number *(if known)*
	First Name	Middle Name	Last Name	

Other Necessary Expenses   In addition to the expense deductions listed above, you are allowed your monthly expenses for the following IRS categories.

16. **Taxes:** The total monthly amount that you actually pay for federal, state and local taxes, such as income taxes, self-employment taxes, social security taxes, and Medicare taxes. You may include the monthly amount withheld from your pay for these taxes. However, if you expect to receive a tax refund, you must divide the expected refund by 12 and subtract that number from the total monthly amount that is withheld to pay for taxes.
Do not include real estate, sales, or use taxes.
$ 1,100.00

17. **Involuntary deductions:** The total monthly payroll deductions that your job requires, such as retirement contributions, union dues, and uniform costs.
Do not include amounts that are not required by your job, such as voluntary 401(k) contributions or payroll savings.
$ 0.00

18. **Life insurance:** The total monthly premiums that you pay for your own term life insurance. If two married people are filing together, include payments that you make for your spouse's term life insurance.
Do not include premiums for life insurance on your dependents, for a non-filing spouse's life insurance, or for any form of life insurance other than term.
$ 0.00

19. **Court-ordered payments:** The total monthly amount that you pay as required by the order of a court or administrative agency, such as spousal or child support payments.
Do not include payments on past due obligations for spousal or child support. You will list these obligations in line 35.
$ 0.00

20. **Education:** The total monthly amount that you pay for education that is either required:
■ as a condition for your job, or
■ for your physically or mentally challenged dependent child if no public education is available for similar services.
$ 0.00

21. **Childcare:** The total monthly amount that you pay for childcare, such as babysitting, daycare, nursery, and preschool.
Do not include payments for any elementary or secondary school education.
$ 0.00

22. **Additional health care expenses, excluding insurance costs:** The monthly amount that you pay for health care that is required for the health and welfare of you or your dependents and that is not reimbursed by insurance or paid by a health savings account. Include only the amount that is more than the total entered in line 7.
Payments for health insurance or health savings accounts should be listed only in line 25.
$ 50.00

23. **Optional telephones and telephone services:** The total monthly amount that you pay for telecommunication services for you and your dependents, such as pagers, call waiting, caller identification, special long distance, or business cell phone service, to the extent necessary for your health and welfare or that of your dependents or for the production of income, if it is not reimbursed by your employer.
Do not include payments for basic home telephone, internet or cell phone service. Do not include self-employment expenses, such as those reported on line 5 of Form 122C-1, or any amount you previously deducted.
+ $ 0.00

24. **Add all of the expenses allowed under the IRS expense allowances.**
Add lines 6 through 23.
$ 4,363.00

Additional Expense Deductions   These are additional deductions allowed by the Means Test.
Note: Do not include any expense allowances listed in lines 6-24.

25. **Health insurance, disability insurance, and health savings account expenses.** The monthly expenses for health insurance, disability insurance, and health savings accounts that are reasonably necessary for yourself, your spouse, or your dependents.

Health insurance	$ 74.00	
Disability insurance	$	
Health savings account	+ $	
Total	$ 74.00	Copy total here ➡ .... $ 74.00

Do you actually spend this total amount?
☐ No. How much do you actually spend? $
☑ Yes

26. **Continuing contributions to the care of household or family members.** The actual monthly expenses that you will continue to pay for the reasonable and necessary care and support of an elderly, chronically ill, or disabled member of your household or member of your immediate family who is unable to pay for such expenses. These expenses may include contributions to an account of a qualified ABLE program. 26 U.S.C. § 529A(b).
$ 0.00

27. **Protection against family violence.** The reasonably necessary monthly expenses that you incur to maintain the safety of you and your family under the Family Violence Prevention and Services Act or other federal laws that apply.
By law, the court must keep the nature of these expenses confidential.
$ 0.00

EXHIBIT 13.4 (Continued)

Debtor 1 ___Roger_____ ___H._____ ___Matthews_____   Case number *(if known)*_____
       First Name   Middle Name   Last Name

28. **Additional home energy costs.** Your home energy costs are included in your insurance and operating expenses on line 8.

    If you believe that you have home energy costs that are more than the home energy costs included in expenses on line 8, then fill in the excess amount of home energy costs. $_____ 0.00

    You must give your case trustee documentation of your actual expenses, and you must show that the additional amount claimed is reasonable and necessary.

29. **Education expenses for dependent children who are younger than 18.** The monthly expenses (not more than $160.42* per child) that you pay for your dependent children who are younger than 18 years old to attend a private or public elementary or secondary school. $_____ 0.00

    You must give your case trustee documentation of your actual expenses, and you must explain why the amount claimed is reasonable and necessary and not already accounted for in lines 6-23.

    * Subject to adjustment on 4/01/19, and every 3 years after that for cases begun on or after the date of adjustment.

30. **Additional food and clothing expense.** The monthly amount by which your actual food and clothing expenses are higher than the combined food and clothing allowances in the IRS National Standards. That amount cannot be more than 5% of the food and clothing allowances in the IRS National Standards. $_____ 0.00

    To find a chart showing the maximum additional allowance, go online using the link specified in the separate instructions for this form. This chart may also be available at the bankruptcy clerk's office.

    You must show that the additional amount claimed is reasonable and necessary.

31. **Continuing charitable contributions.** The amount that you will continue to contribute in the form of cash or financial instruments to a religious or charitable organization. 11 U.S.C. § 548(d)(3) and (4).   + $_____ 50.00

    Do not include any amount more than 15% of your gross monthly income.

32. **Add all of the additional expense deductions.** $_____ 124.00
    Add lines 25 through 31.

Deductions for Debt Payment

33. **For debts that are secured by an interest in property that you own, including home mortgages, vehicle loans, and other secured debt, fill in lines 33a through 33e.**

    To calculate the total average monthly payment, add all amounts that are contractually due to each secured creditor in the 60 months after you file for bankruptcy. Then divide by 60.

	Average monthly payment
Mortgages on your home	
33a. Copy line 9b here...➔	$____ 1,550.00
Loans on your first two vehicles	
33b. Copy line 13b here. ....➔	$____ 360.00
33c. Copy line 13e here. ....➔	$____ 240.00

    33d. List other secured debts:

Name of each creditor for other secured debt	Identify property that secures the debt	Does payment include taxes or insurance?	
_____	_____	☐ No ☐ Yes	$_____
_____	_____	☐ No ☐ Yes	$_____
_____	_____	☐ No ☐ Yes	+ $_____

    33e. Total average monthly payment. Add lines 33a through 33d. .... $____ 2,150.00 Copy total here ➔ $____ 2,150.00

EXHIBIT 13.4   **(Continued)**

Debtor 1   Roger _____ H. _____ Matthews _____   Case number (if known)_____
            First Name   Middle Name   Last Name

34. **Are any debts that you listed in line 33 secured by your primary residence, a vehicle, or other property necessary for your support or the support of your dependents?**

☐ No. Go to line 35.
☑ Yes. State any amount that you must pay to a creditor, in addition to the payments listed in line 33, to keep possession of your property (called the *cure amount*). Next, divide by 60 and fill in the information below.

Name of the creditor	Identify property that secures the debt	Total cure amount		Monthly cure amount
First Bank of Capital C	Residence	$ 850.00	÷ 60 =	$ 14.16
_____	_____	$_____	÷ 60 =	$_____
_____	_____	$_____	÷ 60 = +	$_____

Total $ 14.16   Copy total here ➡ $ 14.16

35. **Do you owe any priority claims—such as a priority tax, child support, or alimony—that are past due as of the filing date of your bankruptcy case?** 11 U.S.C. § 507.

☐ No. Go to line 36.
☑ Yes. Fill in the total amount of all of these priority claims. Do not include current or ongoing priority claims, such as those you listed in line 19.

Total amount of all past-due priority claims. .... $ 1,000.00 ÷ 60 $ 16.67

36. **Projected monthly Chapter 13 plan payment** $ 2,200.00

Current multiplier for your district as stated on the list issued by the Administrative Office of the United States Courts (for districts in Alabama and North Carolina) or by the Executive Office for United States Trustees (for all other districts).

x ____5____

To find a list of district multipliers that includes your district, go online using the link specified in the separate instructions for this form. This list may also be available at the bankruptcy clerk's office.

Average monthly administrative expense $ 112.20   Copy total here ➡ $ 112.20

37. **Add all of the deductions for debt payment.** Add lines 33e through 36. $ 2,993.03

Total Deductions from Income

38. **Add all of the allowed deductions.**

Copy line 24, *All of the expenses allowed under IRS expense allowances* .... $ 4,363.00

Copy line 32, *All of the additional expense deductions* .... $ 124.00

Copy line 37, *All of the deductions for debt payment* ....+ $ 2,993.03

Total deductions .... $ 7,480.03   Copy total here ➡ $ 7,480.03

EXHIBIT 13.4   (Continued)

Debtor 1	Roger	H.	Matthews	Case number (if known)
	First Name	Middle Name	Last Name	

Part 2:	**Determine Your Disposable Income Under 11 U.S.C. § 1325(b)(2)**

39. **Copy your total current monthly income** from line 14 of Form 122C-1, *Chapter 13 Statement of Your Current Monthly Income and Calculation of Commitment Period.* .... $ __7,916.66__

40. **Fill in any reasonably necessary income you receive for support for dependent children.** The monthly average of any child support payments, foster care payments, or disability payments for a dependent child, reported in Part I of Form 122C-1, that you received in accordance with applicable nonbankruptcy law to the extent reasonably necessary to be expended for such child. $ ____0.00__

41. **Fill in all qualified retirement deductions.** The monthly total of all amounts that your employer withheld from wages as contributions for qualified retirement plans, as specified in 11 U.S.C. § 541(b)(7) plus all required repayments of loans from retirement plans, as specified in 11 U.S.C. § 362(b)(19). $ ____0.00__

42. **Total of all deductions allowed under 11 U.S.C. § 707(b)(2)(A).** Copy line 38 here ➔ $ __7,480.03__

43. **Deduction for special circumstances.** If special circumstances justify additional expenses and you have no reasonable alternative, describe the special circumstances and their expenses. You must give your case trustee a detailed explanation of the special circumstances and documentation for the expenses.

Describe the special circumstances	Amount of expense
_____	$ _____
_____	$ _____
_____	+ $ _____
Total	$ ____0.00__ *Copy here* ➔ + $ ____0.00__

44. **Total adjustments.** Add lines 40 through 43. .... $ __7,480.03__ *Copy here* ➔ − $ __7,480.03__

45. **Calculate your monthly disposable income under § 1325(b)(2).** Subtract line 44 from line 39. $ __436.63__

Part 3:	**Change in Income or Expenses**

46. **Change in income or expenses.** If the income in Form 122C-1 or the expenses you reported in this form have changed or are virtually certain to change after the date you filed your bankruptcy petition and during the time your case will be open, fill in the information below. For example, if the wages reported increased after you filed your petition, check 122C-1 in the first column, enter line 2 in the second column, explain why the wages increased, fill in when the increase occurred, and fill in the amount of the increase.

Form	Line	Reason for change	Date of change	Increase or decrease?	Amount of change
☐ 122C–1 ☑ 122C–2	21	Family child care provider will I	08/01/2016	☑ Increase ☐ Decrease	$ ___250.00__
☐ 122C–1 ☐ 122C–2	___	_____	_____	☐ Increase ☐ Decrease	$ _____
☐ 122C–1 ☐ 122C–2	___	_____	_____	☐ Increase ☐ Decrease	$ _____
☐ 122C–1 ☐ 122C–2	___	_____	_____	☐ Increase ☐ Decrease	$ _____

EXHIBIT 13.4 (Continued)

Debtor 1	Roger	H.	Matthews	Case number (*if known*) _____
	First Name	Middle Name	Last Name	

Part 4:   Sign Below

By signing here, under penalty of perjury you declare that the information on this statement and in any attachments is true and correct.

✗ /s/ Roger H. Matthews _____

Signature of Debtor 1

Date 06/06/2016 _____
MM / DD / YYYY

✗ /s/ Susan J. Matthews _____

Signature of Debtor 2

Date 06/06/2016 _____
MM / DD / YYYY

(though a debtor might seek a deduction for an additional vehicle as part of a special circumstance on Line 43 of the form, discussed below). But the Matthews have no such special circumstance to justify deducting ownership expenses for the third car. Moreover, they plan to surrender the YR-8 Chevrolet Malibu to Car World, the creditor secured in it. For all those reasons, counsel for the Matthews does not have them list ownership expenses associated with this third vehicle.

Case Preview

Darrohn v. Hildebrand

Left unanswered by *Ransom* is the question of whether a Chapter 13 debtor who plans to surrender a collateralized vehicle to the secured creditor can still claim the ownership and operation expenses for that vehicle on Lines 12 and 13 of Form 122C-2 or payments on the note secured by the vehicle on Line 33 of that form as part of the determination of his disposable income. The same question arises regarding the home ownership expense deduction on Line 9 and deduction of mortgage payments on Line 33 of Form 122C-2 where the debtor intends to surrender the home to the mortgagee. (Recall the discussion of this same issue in the context of the Form 122A-2 for the above median Chapter 7 debtor in Chapter Five, Section C.) As you read Darrohn v. Hildebrand, consider the following:

1. What does this court say is the majority rule on the question of whether a Chapter 7 debtor completing the means test calculation can deduct secured debt payments even if the petitioner intends to surrender the property in bankruptcy?
2. How does the Supreme Court's ruling in Hamilton v. Lanning influence this court's decision on the issue presented?
3. Form 22C referenced in the opinion has been updated and is now Forms 122C-1 and 122C-2 as discussed in the text.

Darrohn v. Hildebrand
615 F.3d 470 (6th Cir. 2010)

[David and Marguerite Darrohn filed a petition under Chapter 13 on October 3, 2008. The Darrohns' Schedule D listed their creditors that held secured claims and included the property securing the claim along with the outstanding debt. The property securing the claims was the Darrohns' residence in Tennessee and David's father's residence in Illinois. The Darrohns intended to surrender both of these properties as part of their bankruptcy plan and, therefore, would no longer be required to pay the mortgages. The Darrohns' monthly income on Schedule I totaled $7,461.01 after payroll deductions and their Schedule J expenditures totaled $6,505. The Darrohns had a monthly net income totaling $956. The Darrohns filed a Chapter 13 Statement of Current Monthly and Disposable Income, also known as Form 22C. After subtracting all of the allowable deductions from their monthly income, the Darrohns' disposable monthly income under Form 22C totaled -$2,267.08. Form 22C also instructs petitioners to list debt payments secured by their home, which are then deducted from petitioners' total monthly income. The Darrohns listed and deducted their mortgage payments even though they intended to surrender the property.

Though the Darrohns' Form 22C disposable income totaled a large negative number, they nevertheless proposed to pay creditors $ 550 bi-weekly for a period of 60 months. The Trustee therefore objected to the Darrohns' proposed plan because the mortgage payments would no longer be paid by the Darrohns once they surrendered the property. The Trustee specifically argued that the bankruptcy court should have considered the Darrohns' changed circumstances in confirming the plan. The bankruptcy court determined that the Darrohns' monthly income calculated in accordance with Form 22C should serve as the starting point for the Darrohns' disposable income, rather than the larger amount reflected in Schedule I, and that the Darrohns could deduct the mortgage payments. Therefore, the bankruptcy court confirmed the Darrohns' proposed plan of $550 bi-weekly for repayment to unsecured creditors. The Trustee now appeals the plan confirmation. Specifically, the Trustee alleges that the bankruptcy court erred in using the Darrohns' income calculated under Form 22C, rather than the income listed in Schedule I, and in allowing the Darrohns to deduct mortgage payments even though they intended to surrender the properties.]

McKEAGUE, Circuit Judge. . . .

A

BAPCPA revised the Bankruptcy Code in part by requiring above-median income debtors to file for bankruptcy under the reorganization provisions in Chapter 13. . . . This revision meant that above-median income debtors would be required to make more payments to unsecured creditors under their bankruptcy plans. *Id.* In this case, the Darrohns' income fell above the median income for a family of four in Tennessee; they were therefore required to file under the reorganization provisions of Chapter 13.

A debtor filing for bankruptcy under Chapter 13 must propose a plan that provides for the submission of a portion of future income to the trustee. 11 U.S.C. §§1321, 1322. The bankruptcy court then must confirm the debtor's plan in accordance with the provisions of Chapter 13. *Id.* §1325. Section 1325 of Chapter 13 specifically requires the following —

> (b)(1) If the trustee or the holder of an allowed unsecured claim objects to the confirmation of the plan, then the court may not approve the plan unless, as of the effective date of the plan —
>
> . . .
>
> (B) the plan provides that all of the debtor's projected disposable income to be received in the applicable commitment period beginning on the date that the first

payment is due under the plan will be applied to make payments to unsecured creditors under the plan.

(2) For the purposes of this subsection, the term "disposable income" means current monthly income received by the debtor . . . less amounts reasonably necessary to be expended —

(A)(i) for the maintenance or support of the debtor or a dependent of the debtor . . . ;

. . .

(3) Amounts reasonably necessary to be expended under paragraph (2) . . . shall be determined in accordance with subparagraph (A) and (B) of section 707(b)(2), if the debtor has a current monthly income, when multiplied by 12, greater than —

. . .

(B) in the case of a debtor in a household of 2, 3, or 4 individuals, the highest median income of the applicable State for a family of the same number. . . .

Id. §1325(b). This section therefore specifies that the bankruptcy court may not confirm a plan unless the plan provides that all of a debtor's "projected disposable income" be submitted to unsecured creditors and that this amount be calculated by taking the debtor's "disposable income" less "amounts reasonably necessary" for maintenance and support.

To determine a debtor's "disposable income," the Code directs us to the term "current monthly income," which is generally defined as the average monthly income that the debtor receives in the six-month period prior to filing the bankruptcy petition. *Id*. §101(10A)(A). In addition, if the debtor is an above-median income debtor, the Code directs us to the Chapter 7 Means Test for a determination of the "amounts reasonably necessary" to be expended for maintenance and support. *Id*. §§707(b)(2), 1325(b)(3). The Chapter 7 Means Test lists certain allowable expenses that a debtor may deduct from his current monthly income. *Id*. §707(b)(2)(A)(i). Specifically, this section allows a debtor to deduct "average monthly payments on account of secured debts. . . ." *Id*. §707(b)(2)(A)(iii). The majority of courts applying the Means Test to Chapter 7 petitioners have held that these petitioners may deduct secured debt payments even if the petitioner intends to surrender the property in bankruptcy. *See* Morse v. Rudler, 576 F.3d 37, 45 (1st Cir. 2009) (recounting court decisions applying the Means Test to Chapter 7 petitioners).

Applying this statutory framework to this case, . . . we must determine whether the bankruptcy court properly allowed the Darrohns to deduct the mortgage payments on surrendered property as an "amount reasonably necessary" for maintenance and support, rather than considering the Darrohns' intent to surrender these properties.

B

Since this case was submitted, the Supreme Court released its opinion in Hamilton v. Lanning, 130 S. Ct. 2464 (2010). In *Lanning*, the Supreme Court decided "how a bankruptcy court should calculate a debtor's 'projected disposable income'" if the debtor's circumstances change in the period leading up to the bankruptcy filing. 130 S. Ct at 2469-70. The debtor in *Lanning* had received a one-time buyout from her employer during the period leading up to bankruptcy. *Id*. at 2470-71. The buyout in turn caused her current monthly income on Form B22C, calculated using the six-month look-back formula, to greatly exceed her then-existing monthly income reported on Schedule I. *Id.* Under the disposable income calculations in Form B22C, the debtor would have been required to make monthly payments to unsecured creditors far in excess of what she could actually afford. *Id.*

In deciding whether the bankruptcy court could consider the debtor's changed circumstances, the Court focused on the term "*projected* disposable income" as used in Section 1325. . . . The Court noted that the ordinary meaning of "projected," which is not defined in the Bankruptcy Code, accounts for future events that might affect the ultimate outcome. *Id.* The Court also noted that prior to the 2005 amendments to the Bankruptcy Code, bankruptcy courts "had discretion to account for known or virtually certain changes in the debtor's income," and nothing in the amendments indicated that this authority had changed. . . . [T]he Court concluded that "when a bankruptcy court calculates a debtor's projected disposable income, the court may account for changes in the debtor's income or expenses that are known or virtually certain at the time of confirmation." . . . *Id.*, at 2478. . . .

C

Applying *Lanning* to the Darrohns' case, the bankruptcy court erred in confirming the Darrohns' proposed plan. The facts in the Darrohns' case differ from those in *Lanning* because in this case, the income calculated using the six-month look-back period resulted in a smaller amount than the debtors' actual monthly income. In addition, this case involves changes in the debtors' anticipated monthly expenses, which was not directly at issue in *Lanning*. Yet even with these factual differences, the issues in this case both fall squarely within the Court's decision in *Lanning*. . . .

Moving to the issue of the Darrohns' reasonably necessary monthly expenses, the bankruptcy court also erred in failing to account for the Darrohns' intent to surrender properties securing the mortgages. In calculating their projected disposable income, the Darrohns' deducted over $2,700 in mortgage payments from their current monthly income, though they were no longer responsible for these payments. Responding to the Trustee's objection to these deductions, the bankruptcy court stated that "you have to determine these things at the petition" and "[a]t the petition three mortgages were contractually scheduled as due by this Debtor." The court then confirmed the Darrohns' plan, which was premised on a projected disposable income that included deductions for the mortgage payments. This calculation also clashed with the language of Section 1325. . . .

While much of the Court's analysis in *Lanning* focused on the income side of the projected disposable income formulation, the holding clearly applied to "changes in the debtor's income *or expenses.* . . . " *Id.*, at 2478 (emphasis added). Further, the Court rested its holding on the meaning of the term "projected disposable income," which is calculated using a debtor's current monthly income and his reasonably necessary expenses. Thus, *Lanning* also governs the bankruptcy court's determination on the deduction for mortgage payments. Because it is undisputed that the Darrohns intended to surrender these properties, this represents a change in the Darrohns' "expenses that [was] known or virtually certain at the time of confirmation." *Id.* The bankruptcy court therefore should have accounted for this changed circumstance, and its failure to do so violated the requirements of Section 1325....

III

For the foregoing reasons, we REVERSE the bankruptcy court's confirmation of the Darrohns' bankruptcy plan. We REMAND for a determination of the Darrohns' projected disposable income in light of *Lanning* and this decision.

Post-Case Follow-Up

It's interesting that the Sixth Circuit acknowledged that the majority rule among the courts on this issue in the context of calculating the Chapter 7 means test is that a debtor can deduct secured debt payments even if the petitioner intends to surrender the property in bankruptcy — but makes no attempt to distinguish their reasoning. For the Sixth Circuit, the Supreme Court's decision in *Lanning* is conclusive. The Tenth Circuit BAP agrees. See In re Liehr, 439 B.R. 179 (B.A.P. 10th Cir. 2010) but not the First Circuit BAP. See In re Coffin, 435 B.R. 780, 785-786 (B.A.P. 1st Cir. 2010) (acknowledging that "It is generally accepted that many provisions of BAP-CPA are unclear, making it difficult for courts to discern the congressional intent" and that "In our view, §1325(b) is an example of a provision that is caught between the tension of BAPCPA's two goals: bankruptcy abuse prevention and consumer protection" and then holding that Congress' specifying that debtors are entitled to "applicable" monthly expense amounts with respect to the National and Local Standards, in contrast to specifying use of "actual" monthly expenses with respect to Other Necessary Expenses, manifests an intent that vehicle ownership expense be determined strictly based on the National Standards rather than on the Debtor's actual expense notwithstanding intent to surrender). Which approach gets it right post-*Lanning*, the Sixth Circuit in *Darrohn* or the First Circuit BAP in *Coffin*? Determine if the courts of the federal district or circuit where you plan to practice have ruled on this issue and, if so, which view they take.

Darrohn v. Hildebrand: Real Life Applications

1. You represent an above median debtor preparing to file a Chapter 13 case this week. Your jurisdiction follows *Darrohn*. Your client owns a vehicle that is collateral for a loan from Bank and the client has no equity in it (Bank is undersecured in the vehicle). Client would just as soon surrender the vehicle to Bank but does not have any other means of transportation. However, her brother-in-law has promised he will fix up one of his cars for her and give it to her to use next month. If he comes through on his promise, client will surrender her vehicle; if he doesn't, client will attempt a strip down and pay through on the

vehicle. Should you report ownership and operation payments on Lines 12 and 13 of client's Form 122C-2 or payments on the note secured by the vehicle on Line 33? You want to file the proposed plan with the petition and schedules. What should you say in the plan regarding the vehicle?

2. You represent Charles and Joan Abernathy, above median debtors preparing to file a Chapter 13 case this week. Your jurisdiction follows *Darrohn*. The couple owns a home mortgaged to the Bank and in which they have a small amount of equity that they can exempt. But Charles and Joan are in disagreement about whether to try and keep the house or surrender it in bankruptcy. They are four payments behind on the mortgage note and you have explained to them that in order to keep the home their plan will have to pay the arrearages in full as well as continue to make the schedule payments. Charles wants to let the house go and rent for a while but Joan loves the house and says that any sacrifice is worth it to hold on to it. If the couple is unable to resolve this dispute over what to do with the house, what do you do in terms of whether to deduct ownership expenses and mortgage payments as well as arrearages payments on their Form 122C-2? What do you say about the house in their plan?

On Lines 16-23 the Matthews enter average monthly amounts (based on an average of actual payments made during the six months preceding filing of the petition) of Other Necessary Expenses related to the IRS standards but not expressly covered by them including taxes (other than real estate and sales taxes) (Line 16), involuntary deductions from paychecks for things such as union dues, uniforms, etc. (Line 17), life insurance premiums on the debtor's life (Line 18), court-ordered payments such as spousal or child support (in their full amount, not averaged) (Line 19), education expenses necessary for continued employment or for a physically or mentally challenged dependent child for whom no similar public service is available (Line 20), childcare expenses (Line 21) (zero entered here by the Matthews because they are not incurring those expenses yet), unreimbursed healthcare expenses in excess of the national standard deduction allowed on Line 7 and not including insurance premiums (Line 22), and necessary additional telecommunication expenses (Line 23). The total of all expenses entered on Lines 6-23 is entered on Line 24.

On Lines 25 through 31, the Matthews can enter deductions they have for other monthly living expenses, such as health/disability insurance premiums (Line 25); reasonable and necessary costs of supporting an elderly, chronically ill, or disabled member of the household or a member of the debtor's immediate family (Line 26); expenses related to keeping the debtor's family safe where a member of the family has been the victim of domestic violence or stalking and qualifies for protection under the Family Violence Prevention and Services Act (Line 27); home energy costs in excess of the IRS standards for non-mortgage utility costs (Line 28); school costs incurred in connection with a dependent child's attendance at a public or private elementary or secondary school up to a current maximum of $160.42 per child (that amount will be next adjusted in April 2019) (Line 29); food and clothing expenses in excess of the IRS standards up to a maximum of 5 percent of the combined IRS allowances (Line 30); and continuing charitable contributions not to exceed 15 percent of the debtor's gross monthly income (compare the treatment of this item on Line 31 of Form 122A-2 for purposes of the Chapter 7 means test as discussed in Chapter Five, Section C) (Line 31). All additional living expenses entered on Lines 25 through 31 are totaled on Line 32.

On Lines 33 through 36 of the form, the Matthews can enter deductions they have for debt payments, including the average monthly scheduled payment on secured debts (Line 33) (they exclude payment on the YR-8 Chevy Malibu that they plan to surrender to Car World, as discussed earlier); monthly amounts needed over the term of the 60-month plan to cure arrearages on secured debt where the debtor intends to retain the property (such as the overdue $850 payment the Matthews owe to First Bank of Capital City secured by the residence) (Line 34); monthly amounts needed over the term of the 60-month plan to pay prepetition priority debts (such as Roger Matthews' $1,000 obligation to the IRS for back taxes) (Line 35); and the projected monthly administrative expense of the plan, calculated by multiplying the current multiplier for administrative expense established by the U.S. Trustee Program (5.1 percent or .051 as of June 2016) by the monthly amount the debtors estimate paying into their Chapter 13 plan ($2,200 for the Matthews, thus $2,200 x .051 = $112.20) (Line 36). All debt payments entered on Lines 33 through 36 are totaled on Line 37. Then all the subtotals from Lines 24, 32, and 37 are totaled and entered on Line 38.

The figure used on Line 36 of Form 122C-2 for the debtor's "projected" monthly Chapter 13 plan payment will not likely be the actual figure used in the debtor's plan. After all, many of the expenses used by the above median debtor on the form are based on the national and local standards and do not reflect actual expenses. As we have seen, the 122C forms do not themselves take into account anticipated changes in the debtor's income or expenses during the term of the plan (e.g., the Matthews will begin incurring childcare expenses in August after they file in June). And even the projected payments on secured debt that appear on the form may change as the debtor makes final decisions regarding what collateralized property to keep or surrender. The figure on Line 36 is nothing more than a good-faith guestimate of what the eventual monthly plan payment will be utilizing the expenses deducted using the form, and is done at this point only to calculate an additional projected expense the debtor will incur during the term of the plan—the monthly administrative expense charged by the standing trustee in the district using a percentage multiplier set by the district from time to time (but which cannot exceed 10 percent per §707(b)(2)(A)(ii)(III)).

For example, the figure used on Line 36 of the Matthews' Form 122C-2 (assuming they were above median debtors) is calculated beginning with their gross combined monthly income of $7,916.66 and subtracting the expenses allowed on the form under the national and local standards (which, again, may not reflect their actual expenses for such items) as well as their actual expenses for tax and other deductions from their wages, health and insurance costs, charitable deductions, and payments on secured debt as projected using the form. As we will see when we look in detail at the Chapter 13 plan itself beginning with the next chapter, normal living expenses of Chapter 13 debtors are not included in the monthly plan payment made to the standing trustee but are instead paid by the debtor from month to month. What is included in the plan to be paid to and distributed by the standing trustee are the payments on secured debt (which as we will see may be modified in the plan in ways not accounted for in the Form 122C-2) including any arrearages, priority claims, administrative costs, unpaid attorney's fees of debtor's attorney, and remaining disposable income that will be distributed on allowed unsecured claims. Thus the $2,200 figure used on their Line 36 is only their attorney's best guestimate using the figures on the form itself of what debtor's will ultimately pay into the plan. The final figure will likely be close to it but different.

In Part 2 of the form the debtor will then calculate debtor's disposable income. On Line 39 the debtor inserts the CMI figure from Line 14 of Form 122C-1. Then on Line 40 the Matthews are allowed to deduct from CMI any amounts of income received and included in Part I of Form 122C-1 for child support, foster care payments, or disability payments for a dependent child. Section 1325(b)(2) expressly excludes these items from the definition of disposable income. Similarly, on Line 41 the Matthews can deduct from CMI amounts withheld by the employer from the debtor's paycheck for qualified retirement plan contributions or to repay loans from such retirement plans. Section 1322(f) expressly excludes these items from disposable income. A **qualified retirement plan** is one approved by the IRS allowing the withholding of pre-tax contributions and deferring tax on the amounts withheld until withdrawal from the plan, usually at retirement.

On Line 43 of the form the Matthews can enter deductions for expenses related to special circumstances for which there is no reasonable alternative. This **special circumstances expense** deduction derives from §707(b)(2)(B) and is the same as that allowed a Chapter 7 consumer debtor who can use it to rebut the presumption of abuse arising from the means test (see discussion in Chapter Five, Section C). Special circumstance expenses may be unusual expenses arising from a serious medical condition or a decrease in income or increase in expenses due to a call to active duty in the military. Special circumstances expenses must be itemized, explained, and well documented.

The total adjustments (deductions) claimed by the debtor to his CMI are entered on Line 44 of the form, subtracted from the CMI figure, and the result entered on Line 45. Though the form identifies the figure on Line 45 as the above median debtor's monthly disposable income under §1325(b)(2) (the amount that must be distributed to unsecured creditors in the plan if they are not paid 100 percent), that's not exactly right. As established by the U.S. Supreme Court in Hamilton v. Lanning, known or virtually certain changes in the debtor's income or expenses must be taken into account even if the forms, using prepetition numbers, do not take them into account. And as we mentioned in connection with the below median debtor's Schedule J, the terms of the plan itself may alter the disposable income figure (e.g., by surrendering secured property, freeing up more disposable dollars for unsecured creditors). Every bankruptcy practitioner knows that when there is a challenge to the Chapter 13 debtor's plan based on his proposed disposable income, the court and interested parties will look just as hard at the debtor's Schedules I and J as at the Form 122C-2.

The variableness of the debtor's disposable income as calculated using Form 122C-2 is highlighted by Line 46 of the form, where the Chapter 13 debtor can list any changes in income or expenses that have occurred since the petition was filed (remember the schedules and statements supporting the petition may be filed up to 14 days after the petition itself and the income and expense numbers on Forms 122C-1 and 122C-2 are tied to the date of the petition) or which are "virtually certain" to change after the date of the petition. But there is no place on the form to deduct such claimed expenses from CMI. The debtor claiming such change in income or expenses will draft a plan reflecting such anticipated changes and then fight it out when the trustee or a creditor objects to plan confirmation on that basis.

For example, the Matthews' children are currently being kept during the day by Susan's mother, who does not charge them for that childcare, but the mother is going to be unable to continue to care for the children for much longer so the Matthews expect to begin incurring childcare expenses at that time. On Line 46 of their Form 122C-2 (and on Line 24 of their Schedule J) they disclose this expected change to their expenses and estimate that the childcare expenses they will begin incurring will be about $250 per month. As we will see in Chapter Fifteen, the Matthews draft their Chapter 13 plan assuming that they will be incurring that childcare expense. At their first meeting of creditors, the standing trustee or a creditor may question them closely regarding whether this change in expenses is "virtually certain" to occur and whether the amount allocated for that new expense is accurate and reasonable.

For reasons like this, the monthly disposable income figure listed on Line 45 of Form 122C-2 is only another starting point to determine the real disposable income figure for purposes of §1325. See In re Risher, 344 B.R. 833, 836-837 (Bankr. W.D. Ky. 2006) (Form 22C calculation provides a "starting point . . . a floor not a ceiling" for determination of debtor's disposable income), and In re Grant, 364 B.R. 656, 667 (Bankr. E.D. Tenn. 2007) ("A debtor's monthly disposable income as reflected on Form 22C is the starting point by which a court determines the debtor's projected disposable income, but this figure can be rebutted by evidence that the debtor's actual net disposable income as of the filing date, reflected on Schedules I and J, as well as other evidence that the debtor's circumstances have changed as of the effective date of the plan.").

Having stated those caveats, if none of the deductions taken by the Chapter 13 debtor on Form 122C-2 are challenged by the trustee, the number entered on Line 45 ($436.63 for the Matthews) will certainly be the *starting point* for the trustee and creditors to determine if the debtor is in fact making all of his projected disposable income available to unsecured creditors in a non–100 percent plan and to decide whether to object to plan confirmation.

For example, assuming the Matthews had the higher income we have theorized on their Form 122C-2 and assuming their trustee did not challenge their calculations on that form, that trustee would likely begin an inquiry into whether their plan meets the disposable income requirement with the $436.63 figure on Line 45. But that would only be the starting point for the inquiry.

Recall that for the below median debtor, we said earlier that the monthly net income entered on Line 23c of the debtor's Schedule J is no more than a starting point determination of the debtor's disposable income. The same is true of Line 45 in the above median debtor's Form 122C-2 and for the same reasons. In both circumstances, we have to look at the debtor's final determination of how secured debt will be treated in the plan and whether there are likely to be changes to income or expenses during the term of the plan not dealt with in Schedule J or Form 122C-2. Those types of issues will ultimately determine the actual disposable income amount. In the next chapter we will see that done in the Matthews' case.

Case Preview

Musselman v. eCast Settlement Corp.

Throughout this chapter we have assumed that the commitment period for the plan of the above median Chapter 13 debtor will be 60 months, and in the majority of cases it will be. But what if that debtor's calculation of disposable income on Form 122C-2 shows that debtor has none (negative disposable income) and a plan is proposed that will pay only secured creditors so that the debtor can retain possession of the property in which those creditors hold a security interest? Must that debtor nonetheless propose a five-year plan? As you read Musselman v. eCast Settlement Corp., consider the following questions:

1. What was the term of the plan as proposed by this Chapter 13 debtor? How much of his unsecured debt did it propose to pay and why?
2. What are the three views identified by the court regarding whether an above median debtor with no projected disposable income is required to propose a plan of five years?
3. Which view does the court adopt and why?

Musselman v. eCast Settlement Corp.
394 B.R. 801 (E.D.N.C. 2008)

[Brooks Musselman filed a Chapter 13 petition on February 27, 2007. His Chapter 13 Statement of Current Monthly Income and Calculation of Commitment Period and Disposable Income (Form B22C) indicated that the debtor had above median income with monthly disposable income under 11 U.S.C. §1325(b)(2) of negative $255.80. Musselman's proposed plan provided for payments of $459.00 per month for 55 months. The plan did not provide for any payments to unsecured creditors. eCast held around 48 percent of the debtor's scheduled unsecured debt and objected to the debtor's proposed plan. ECast objected to the proposed term of the debtor's plan. The bankruptcy court sustained eCast's objection and debtor appeals.]

FLANAGAN, Chief District Judge....

Where objections were raised by eCast, holder of two allowed unsecured claims, to confirmation of Musselman's Chapter 13 bankruptcy plan, initial reference is made to 11 U.S.C. §1325(b)(1) which provides:

> If the trustee or the holder of an allowed unsecured claim objects to the confirmation of the plan, then the court may not approve the plan unless, as of the effective date of the plan —
>
> (A) the value of the property to be distributed under the plan on account of such claim is not less than the amount of such claim; or
>
> (B) the plan provides that all of the debtor's projected disposable income to be received in the applicable commitment period beginning on the date that the first payment is due under the plan will be applied to make payments to unsecured creditors under the plan.

The difficulty here in application of this section of the statute involves discerning the relationship between "projected disposable income" in §1325(b)(1)(B) and "disposable income" in §1325(b)(2). "Disposable income" is defined in §1325(b)(2) as a debtor's current monthly income (defined in §101(10A)) minus certain "amounts reasonably necessary to be expended." 11 U.S.C. §1325(b)(2). "Projected disposable income" is not, however, defined in the Bankruptcy Code. As a result, this term has produced "varying interpretations as bankruptcy courts across the country struggle to ascertain what the BAPCPA amendments mean." In re Frederickson, 375 B.R. 829, 833 (8th Cir. BAP 2007)....

Another issue to be decided concerns application of the term created by BAP-CPA, "applicable commitment period." This term appears twice in Chapter 13 of the Bankruptcy Code, once in §1325(b)(1)(B) and again in §1325(b)(4). As already noted, §1325(b)(1)(B) requires that a plan provide that all "projected disposable income to be received in the applicable commitment period" be paid to unsecured creditors to be confirmed. 11 U.S.C. §1325(b)(1)(B). Section 1325(b)(4) states that the applicable commitment period "shall be" 3 years in the case of a below-median income debtor or "not less than 5 years" for an above-median debtor. 11 U.S.C. §1325(b)(4)(A). The court must decide here whether the "applicable commitment period" time requirements apply to above-median debtors with zero or negative "projected disposable income."...

... B. Applicable Commitment Period

Specifically, this court must determine whether the term "applicable commitment period" has any application to debtors who have zero or negative "projected disposable income" under §1325(b)(2) ... [I]nterpretation by courts of "applicable commitment period" has resulted in a split.

Some courts have held that "applicable commitment period" does not apply to debtors who do not have any "projected disposable income," regardless of whether the term is temporal in nature or not. See In re Kagenveama, 541 F.3d at 875-78; In re Frederickson, 375 B.R. at 835; In re Davis, 392 B.R. 132, 146 (Bankr. E.D. Pa. 2008); In re Brady, 361 B.R. at 776-77; In re Green, 378 B.R. 30, 39 (Bankr. N.D.N.Y. 2007); In re Alexander, 344 B.R. at 750-51.

Other courts have held that "applicable commitment period" is temporal in nature and sets a fixed plan length for all debtors whose plans are governed by §1325(b). See In re Grant, 364 B.R. 656, 667 (Bankr. E.D. Tenn. 2007); In re Slusher, 359 B.R. at 305; In re Strickland, 2007 WL 499623, *2, 2007 (Bankr. M.D.N.C. 2007); In re Cushman, 350 B.R. 207, 212-13 (Bankr. D.S.C. 2006), In re Girodes, 350 B.R. at 35; In re Casey, 356 B.R. 519, 526-27 (Bankr. E.D. Wash. 2006).

Still other courts have held that "applicable commitment period" is not temporal at all, but rather serves as a multiplicative term. Under this approach, "applicable commitment period" merely sets forth the number by which "projected disposable income" is multiplied to determine how much money a debtor must pay into his plan instead of the length of time that a debtor must make payments into a plan. See In re McGillis, 370 B.R. at 734; In re Fuger, 347 B.R. 94, 99-101 (Bankr. D. Utah 2006).

This last interpretation of "applicable commitment period" is the one which the debtor here urges the court to adopt. The second one made mention of above was adopted by the bankruptcy court in this case. This court considers the first approach to be the correct one, however.

"Applicable commitment period" appears in two relevant subsections of §1325(b). The first is §1325(b)(1)(B) which provides that a debtor's plan may not be confirmed if a trustee or unsecured creditor objects unless the plan "provides that all of the debtor's *projected disposable income* to be received in the *applicable commitment period* . . . will be applied to make payments to unsecured creditors under the plan." 11 U.S.C. §1325(b)(1)(B) (emphasis added). The second is §1325(b)(4) which sets forth the definition of "applicable commitment period" for above- and below-median debtors (5 and 3 years, respectively), and provides that the "applicable commitment period" may be shorter than 5 or 3 years if "the plan provides for payment in full of all allowed unsecured claims over a shorter period." 11 U.S.C. §1325(b)(4).

Section 1325(b)(1)(B) is the only relevant section of the Bankruptcy Code that applies "applicable commitment period" to any debtors. On its face, §1325(b)(1)(B) requires "all of the debtor's projected disposable income to be received in the applicable commitment period" to go to payments to unsecured creditors. 11 U.S.C. §1325(b)(1)(B). Two threshold requirements are apparent from this language. First, a debtor must have unsecured creditors. Second, a debtor must have "projected disposable income" in order for this subsection to apply to his situation. . . . The first threshold requirement is uncontroversial.

The second is at the heart of one of the debates surrounding "applicable commitment period." A review of the legislative history suggested to the bankruptcy court that the "applicable commitment period" as defined by §1325(b)(4) drives the plan length. It followed the lead of *In re Casey*, and, as noted, rejected the second threshold requirement. While there is an intuitive appeal to such a result, the structure of §1325(b) does not permit this.

Section 1325(b)(4)'s function in the structure of §1325(b) is to define the term "applicable commitment period." Section 1325(b)(1)(B), on the other hand, puts that term into action. It delineates the situations in which the definition of "applicable commitment period" set forth in §1325(b)(4) will apply. Those situations include any cases in which a debtor has "projected disposable income" as defined in §1325(b)

(2). By contrast, those situations do not include cases where debtors have no "projected disposable income" under §1325(b)(2).

When a trustee or an unsecured creditor objects to a plan, §1325(b)(1) provides that a court may not approve the plan unless, "(B) the plan provides that all of the debtor's projected disposable income to be received in the applicable commitment period . . . will be applied to make payments to unsecured creditors under the plan." 11 U.S.C. §1325(b)(1). This language requires that a debtor have "projected disposable income" as a threshold matter for the subsection to apply. If a debtor has zero or negative "projected disposable income," then there is nothing "to be received in the applicable commitment period." Id. If there is nothing for a debtor to receive in the "applicable commitment period," there is nothing to "appl[y] to make payments to unsecured creditors under the plan." Id. If none of the subsection's provisions are relevant to a debtor's situations, then that subsection does not apply. Therefore the term "applicable commitment period" simply does not apply to Musselman. On this issue, for the reasons given, the bankruptcy court is REVERSED.

Post-Case Follow-Up

If the debtor has no projected disposable income, what did eCast have to gain as an unsecured creditor by requiring debtor to propose a five-year plan? How is the court's decision justified in the face of the §1325(b)(4)(A) mandate that the applicable commitment period "shall be" three years in the case of a below median income debtor or "not less than 5 years" for an above median debtor? For a well written case adopting the "temporal" approach that insists that the mandate means what it says even for the above median debtor with no disposable income, see In re Grant, 364 B.R. 656, 667 (Bankr. E.D. Tenn. 2007): "To state it more succinctly, the historical 'current monthly income,' determined under §101(10A) as set forth on Form B22C, will determine the 'applicable commitment period' under §1325(b)(4) without consideration of 'projected disposable income' under §1325(b)(1)(B)." The third approach, sometimes called the "monetary" or "multiplier" approach, is well set out in In re McGillis, 370 B.R. 720, 734-739 (Bankr. W.D. Mich. 2007), and provides that §1325(b) does not require the debtor to propose a plan that lasts for the entire length of the applicable commitment period and may propose a plan lasting for a shorter time so long as it provides for the payment of the full amount of disposable income projected to be received over the full length of the applicable commitment period as calculated on Forms 122C even if it is not a 100 percent plan. Which approach makes the most sense to you in light of both the language of the Code sections and the policies at work? Is it possible that Congress never gave thought to the possibility that a debtor might not have any projected disposable income left after payment of his allowed secured debts and deduction of permissible expenses? Determine if the courts of the federal district or circuit where plan to practice have ruled on this issue and, if so, which approach they take.

Musselman v. eCast Settlement Corp.:
Real Life Applications

1. You represent Fred Sauceman, an above median debtor who is planning to file a Chapter 13 case. Fred has a number of secured obligations on his home and cars, all of which are current and which he intends to keep paying as scheduled through the term of the plan and beyond so he can retain possession of those assets. He also has unsecured credit card debt. Calculation of his allowed expenses on his Form 122C-2 including those projected payments to secured creditors leaves him with zero projected disposable income, and nothing in his Schedules I and J suggest any other result. Fred would like to propose a 36-month plan calling for payment of the secured debts as they come due and paying nothing to unsecured creditors. Can that plan be confirmed if your district follows *Musselman*? If it follows In re Grant? If it follows In re McGillis?

2. You represent Maria Ortega, a below median debtor, who is planning to file a Chapter 13 case. Maria has a single secured debt, her home mortgage, on which she is current and which she plans to keep paying through the term of the plan and beyond. She also has unsecured credit card debt but according to your calculations of her current monthly income from her Form 122C-1 she will have sufficient disposable income to pay that unsecured debt in full over 24 months. Nothing in her Schedules I and J suggests otherwise. Can Maria propose a confirmable 24-month plan on these terms? See §1325(b)(4)(B).

Impact of Bankruptcy on the Individual Debtor's Credit Rating

An individual debtor's filing for bankruptcy can be and will be reported to credit reporting agencies and reflected in debtor's credit history and credit score. Under the Fair Credit Reporting Act (FCRA) that regulates credit reporting agencies, a bankruptcy filing as a public record can appear on the debtor's credit history for ten years following date of filing (see 15 U.S.C. § 1681c). Specific debt obligations owed by the debtor at the time bankruptcy is filed remain on the credit report for seven years following the original delinquency date of such obligation (which may have preceded the date of the bankruptcy petition and so will be removed from the report before the bankruptcy proceeding itself is removed). A debt obligation discharged in the bankruptcy case may remain on the credit report until the time to remove it expires but will be labeled "discharged in bankruptcy." The debtor's credit score that is calculated by the credit reporting agencies and used by creditors in the decision to make a new loan or extend credit (most agencies utilize the debtor's credit score calculated according to the predictive analysis formula developed by Fair Isaac Corporation, or FICO, which uses a 300 to 850 scoring range) is of course impacted negatively by the bankruptcy filing and may take years to repair. Post-bankruptcy, debtors may be able to secure new loans or credit but often at significantly higher interest rates due to the damage done.

Chapter Summary

- A Chapter 13 plan must propose to pay unsecured creditors 100 percent of what is owed to them or all of the debtor's projected disposable income over the term of the plan.
- A Chapter 13 plan must run for a commitment period of at least three but no more than five years. To determine the debtor's applicable commitment period, Chapter 13 debtors must complete and file Official Form 122C-1, which calculates debtor's current monthly income defined as his average monthly income from all sources received during the look back period of six months preceding the filing of the petition and comparing that CMI with the median family income figure for a household the size of the debtor's household living in the debtor's state of residence.
- For the debtor whose annualized CMI is below the applicable state median, the commitment period will be three years, although that debtor may propose a plan of up to five years. The plan of an above median debtor must run for five years, unless it proposes to pay unsecured creditors 100 percent over a shorter term.
- Projected disposable income for the below median debtor is calculated primarily from debtor's Form 122C-1 and Schedules I and J. The above median debtor must complete Official Form 122C-2 to calculate projected disposable income though that debtor's Schedules I and J will be material to the determination as well. Courts are split over whether the above median debtor can deduct ownership and operation expenses on Form 122C-1 related to collateralized property, such as a home or vehicle, where the debtor intends to surrender such property.
- Projected disposable income for either the below or above median debtor as calculated using the various schedules and forms filed by the debtor may be impacted by postpetition changes in the debtor's income or expenses and by plan proposals modifying secured or unsecured obligations and thus the final determination of projected disposable income must include an examination of debtor's proposed plan.
- Courts are divided over whether a debtor with negative projected disposable income can propose a plan of less than 60 months that pays only secured claims to enable debtor to retain the collateralized property.

Applying the Concepts

1. Assume you represent Bill and Karen Carpenter, a couple for whom you are planning to file a Chapter 13 case. According to their Form 122C-1 they are above median debtors and so must complete Form 122C-2 to calculate their disposable income. They want to include the following persons in the number to be entered on Line 5 of Form 122C-2 designating the number of people to be used in calculating their expense deductions. Which of the following can they include?

    a. Bill's 90-year-old father and his 91-year-old second wife (not Bill's mother), who reside in a nearby nursing home the expenses for which Bill pays

    b. The couple's 25-year-old unemployed son who has returned home to live with them following college while he looks for employment

    c. The son's 25-year-old former college roommate who is also living with them while he looks for employment

    d. A neighbor who lives down the street with her three children, whom Bill and Karen help out financially now and then since she lost her job and her unemployment insurance ran out

2. In the six months preceding the filing of the Chapter 13 petition, Karen made $7,500 per month working as an accountant with a local firm. However, two weeks before the petition was filed she was laid off and at the time the petition was filed she was making $500 a month as a substitute math teacher at the local middle school.

    a. What is the income figure that you should enter for her on Line 2 of Form 122C-1?

    b. What is the income figure that you should enter for her on Line 2 of Schedule I?

    c. When you draft the Chapter 13 plan for the Carpenters, must you use Karen's higher income figure in calculating the disposable income the couple has to pay their unsecured debt?

3. Bill and Karen, above median debtors, have two vehicles, both of which have money owed on them, and each vehicle is collateral to secure payment to a different secured creditor. The couple plans to keep one of the vehicles by curing the current arrearage owed that secured creditor and making all future monthly payments as they come due (options to be discussed in the next chapter). They plan to surrender the other vehicle to the secured creditor and discharge any balance that may still then be owing on that obligation. The jurisdiction follows Darrohn v. Hildebrand, 615 F.3d 470 (6th Cir. 2010).

    a. Should you disclose the plans of Bill and Karen to surrender this second car by filing a Statement of Intent?

    b. Should you enter ownership and operation expenses for that vehicle on Lines 12 and 13 of the Carpenter's Form 122C-2 or the payment information on that secured car note on Line 33 of that form?

    c. Should you enter the payment information on that secured car note on Line 17 of the Carpenter's Schedule J?

4. Locate and read Assignment Memorandum #2 in Appendix D. If your instructor so directs, prepare the Form 122C-1 (and if necessary the Form 122C-2) for Nick and Pearl Murphy assuming they are filing their Chapter 13 case in the U.S. bankruptcy court for your federal district.

The Chapter 13 Case: The Plan: Treatment of Priority and Secured Claims

In this chapter we will examine how the Code requires that priority unsecured claims be treated in a Chapter 13 plan. Then we will consider how secured claims may be treated in the plan and the wide range of options the Code provides to enable the Chapter 13 debtor to modify secured claims and retain possession of the collateral.

A. TREATMENT OF PRIORITY CLAIMS IN THE CHAPTER 13 PLAN

In Chapter Ten, Section B, we saw that §507 designates some claims as **priority claims** for purposes of payment. Section 1322(a)(2) requires that a Chapter 13 plan provide for the payment of all §507 priority claims in full (100 percent) although the payment may be made in deferred installments over the term of the plan.

For example, the Matthews' Chapter 13 plan (Exhibit 15.2) calls for the payment in full of a tax obligation resulting from federal income taxes assessed

Key Concepts

- Generally, a Chapter 13 plan must provide for payment of all priority claims in full
- A Chapter 13 plan may propose a pay through for secured debt allowing the debtor to retain the collateral
- A Chapter 13 plan may also provide for modification of secured claims in a variety of ways including curing of arrearages, avoiding certain liens that impair exemptions, reducing certain secured claims to the value of the collateral, adjusting the amount of installment payments due during the term of the plan, selling collateralized property free and clear of liens, or abandoning collateral and surrendering it to the creditor

for tax year YR-2. That tax obligation is given a priority status by §507(a)(8) (see Exhibit 10.1).

One exception to the requirement of full payment of priority claims is where the priority creditor agrees to a different treatment under the plan, which is uncommon. Another exception applies to the priority granted by §507(a)(1)(B) to domestic support obligations that have been assigned for collection to a governmental agency. Section 1322(a)(4), added by BAPCPA, provides that the plan can call for less than full payment of that priority claim if the plan runs a full five years and calls for the distribution of all the debtor's projected disposable income during that term.

B. TREATMENT OF SECURED CLAIMS IN THE CHAPTER 13 PLAN

The debtor has a number of options in deciding how to deal with secured debts in his proposed Chapter 13 plan, a number of which involve the right to modify the terms of a secured claim.

1. Payment of the Secured Claim in Full and Retention of the Lien: The Pay Through Proposal

Per §1322(b)(2), the plan may propose to pay a secured claim in full as called for in the underlying contract and for the creditor to retain its lien on the secured property. The secured creditor is not likely to object to such a plan because its interest is not impaired in any way, and the debtor is able to keep the property.

For example, the Matthews' plan calls for First Bank of Capital City (FBCC) to retain its first mortgage position in their home and for the monthly payments of $850 to continue unimpaired by the plan. FBCC should have no objection to this arrangement. So long as the Matthews make the mortgage payments, they will be able to retain the home.

Practitioners sometimes call this proposal a **pay through** (or sometimes a **ride-through**) provision since the debtor is proposing to pay installments as they come due throughout the duration of the plan and beyond.

If the debtor is in arrears on his payments to the secured creditor the plan can propose to make the extra payments to cure the arrearage during the term of the plan as discussed in more detail below along with the pay through.

2. Avoiding a Lien that Impairs an Exemption in Property of the Debtor

The Chapter 13 debtor, like the individual Chapter 7 debtor, may claim property as exempt and must file a Schedule C in order to do so. As we learned in our consideration of exemptions in Chapter 7 in Chapter Six, Section B, a debtor cannot normally claim an exemption in property in which the debtor has granted a consensual security interest or in property subject to a statutory lien. However, we also know that §522(f)(1)(A) permits a debtor to avoid a judicial lien on his property that impairs an exemption unless the judicial lien arises out of a domestic support obligation. Section §522(f)(1)(A) is available to the Chapter 13 debtor as well, as is §522(f)(1)(B), which permits the debtor to avoid even a consensual lien in household goods and furnishings, wearing apparel, appliances, tools of the trade, and other such items to the extent the lien is not a purchase money security interest and it impairs the debtor's right to exempt such property. Per FRBP 4003(d), the proceeding to avoid a lien impairing an exemption is initiated by motion, not adversary proceeding.

For example, the Matthews' Chapter 13 plan (Exhibit 15.2) seeks to avoid the lien of Capital City Finance Company (CCFC) in Roger's plumbing tools and the couple's furniture under §522(f)(1)(B). The debt of CCFC is not a purchase money one because Roger and Susan already owned these items before he and Susan incurred the debt to CCFC and CCFC does not have possession of the items in which it claims the security interest. Consequently, the debtors should be able to avoid the CCFC lien in those goods entirely, have the $2,000 balance of the debt to CCFC treated as a general unsecured claim, and keep the items because they claim them as exempt, pursuant to §522(d)(3) (see the Matthews' Schedule C, Document 4 in their case file). If Roger had granted a security interest in a gun collection as part of the CCFC loan, there might be a question as to whether the guns constitute "household goods" within the meaning of that section. If Roger was a traveling salesman and had granted a security interest in his car as security for this loan, there might be a question as to whether the car was a "tool of the trade" for purposes of §522(f)(1)(B).

3. Curing of Arrearages Created by Default

At the time the Chapter 13 petition is filed, a debtor frequently has defaulted on some payments due to secured creditors and owes the arrearages, as well as future payments. Simply promising to make all future payments is not going to appease the creditor in that situation. Pursuant to §§1322(b)(3) and (5), the debtor's plan may propose to cure the arrearage by making up the past-due payments. However, the plan must call for the arrearages to be paid:

- over a reasonable time, and
- within the term of the plan.

Section 1322(b)(5) allows the curing of arrearage on debt secured by either real or personal property. This includes the debtor's principal residence, the mortgage on which is often in default due to missed payments when a debtor files for Chapter 13 relief. Foreclosure looms. Saving the residence becomes the highest priority for such a debtor and the right to cure the arrearage on the mortgage arising from the defaults is critical to the debtor's hopes. If the debtor can cure the arrearage as part of the plan and make the future payments as they come due, he can keep the secured property.

In the case of a debt secured by a mortgage in the debtor's principal residence, however, there is an important exception. Section 1322(c)(1) provides that curing the arrearage is only possible until such residence is sold at a foreclosure sale conducted in accordance with applicable non-bankruptcy law. Most foreclosures are conducted under state law. So what this provision means is that if the debtor does not file his Chapter 13 petition triggering the automatic stay of a foreclosure proceeding prior to the time the residence has been sold in foreclosure, it is too late to cure the arrearage and the debtor loses the house.

For example, when the Chapter 13 petition was filed, the Matthews had failed to make their last monthly mortgage payment of $850 to FBCC (see the Assignment Memorandum in Appendix B). Their plan calls for curing that arrearage over the first 12 months of the plan, along with payment of the remaining installments as they come due. So long as a foreclosure action has not been completed by the sale of the property in foreclosure when the Matthews' Chapter 13 petition is filed, this is permissible. If the court concludes that the 12 months is a reasonable time over which to cure the arrearage, the plan may be approved and the Matthews will be able to keep their house.

Note in the last example that the plan calls for curing the arrearage during the term of the plan, over the first 12 months of it. If the plan called for the arrearage to be cured over 6 years when the plan itself is only 5 years in duration, the proposal could not be approved. Under §1322(b)(5), it doesn't matter if the payment schedule on the underlying secured debt runs longer than the plan (e.g., the plan runs for 5 years and the FBCC mortgage has another 23 years to run) so long as the arrearage is cured during the term of the plan.

For example, the mortgage payments owed by the Matthews to FBCC run for longer than the term of their plan (five years). That is no bar to their plan calling for the curing of the arrearage within a reasonable time and for continuing the payments in order to retain the secured property.

Case Preview

In re Medaglia

Since it is too late to cure an arrearage on a mortgage in Chapter 13 once the residence has been sold in foreclosure, questions can and do arise over exactly when a foreclosed-on residence has been "sold" and over whether and to what extent applicable state law should control that question. As you read In re Medaglia, consider the following questions:

1. Had an auction "sale" occurred before debtor filed his Chapter 13 petition? Had a deed of purchase been recorded before debtor filed his petition?
2. What are the three views regarding when a residence has been "sold" under §1322(c)(1), cutting off debtor's right to cure an arrearage and keep the property?
3. Which of the three views does this court adopt and why?
4. Which of the three views gives more latitude to state law?

In re Medaglia
402 B.R. 530 (Bankr. D.R.I. 2009)

[This dispute arises from Robert Buonano's (the "Buyer's") "Motion for Relief from Automatic Stay in Order to Record a Deed and to Take Possession" of property that he purchased at a (prepetition) foreclosure auction on September 9, 2008. A Memorandum of Sale was executed on the same day, and the Buyer paid the required deposit of $5,000. On September 11, 2008, before the Buyer recorded his deed, the Debtor (Medaglia) filed the instant Chapter 13 case.

The Buyer argues that, under 11 U.S.C. §1322(c)(1), the Debtor's right to cure the mortgage default terminated at the moment when the Memorandum of Sale was signed, and that thereafter, the Debtor no longer had any interest in the Property. The Debtor objects to relief from stay, arguing that the foreclosure sale did not terminate his right to cure the loan default, and that such right stays "alive and well" until the foreclosure deed is recorded and delivered to the purchaser. The issue of when the right to cure a loan default on the Debtor's principal residence terminates under §1322(c)(1) has generated conflicting results in the bankruptcy arena.]

VOTOLATO, Bankruptcy Judge. . . .

DISCUSSION

Under Section 1322(b)(5), the Debtor may provide in his plan for the curing of any default on any unsecured or secured claim on which the last payment is due after the date on which the final payment under the plan is due. Section 1322(c)(1) states: "Notwithstanding subsection (b)(2) and applicable nonbankruptcy law . . . a default with respect to, or that gave rise to, a lien on the debtor's principal residence may be cured . . . *until such residence is sold at a foreclosure sale that is conducted in accordance with applicable nonbankruptcy law . . .*" (emphasis added). It is clear, to me at least, that the *notwithstanding* clause in Section 1322 trumps nonbankruptcy law regarding the cure of mortgage defaults on a debtor's primary residence. . . . And the statute itself would seem to leave no doubt that, in bankruptcy, the right to cure exists only until the property is sold at a (valid) foreclosure sale. Nevertheless, judicial disagreement has emerged over the meaning of the phrase "sold at a foreclosure sale that is conducted in accordance with applicable nonbankruptcy law." In preparing this decision, we have identified three different interpretations of Section 1322(c)(1).

The majority view (and the one I like), known as the "gavel rule," is that Section 1322(c)(1) is clear and unambiguous, and that the debtor's right to cure is cut off at the foreclosure sale. See e.g. In re Connors, 497 F.3d 314 (3d Cir. 2007); In re Cain, 423 F.3d 617 (6th Cir. 2005); In re Smith, 85 F.3d 1555, 1558 n. 3 (11th Cir. 1996) (dictum); In re McCarn, 218 B.R. 154 (10th Cir. BAP 1998); In re Crichlow, 322 B.R. 229 (Bankr. D. Mass. 2004). Based on our research, every appeals court, with one exception described below, and every bankruptcy appellate panel that has considered the issue, has adhered to the gavel rule.

A second line of cases focuses on the word "sold" in Section 1322(c)(1), holding that a foreclosure sale is not an event, but instead, is part of a process culminating in the delivery and recordation of the deed, with the debtor's right to cure surviving until title to the property passes to the purchaser under the relevant state law. See e.g. In re Beeman, 235 B.R. 519, 525 (Bankr. D.N.H. 1999).

And, finally, a solitary Court of Appeals has construed Section 1322(c)(1) to mean that the right to cure a default exists "*at least* up to the date of the foreclosure sale," and that if state law provides a redemption period that extends beyond the date of the foreclosure sale, then bankruptcy law defers to such state law, with the right to cure extended accordingly. Colon v. Option One Mortgage Corp., 319 F.3d 912, 918 (7th Cir. 2003) (emphasis added).

This Court is most comfortable adopting the majority view on the ground that the language of the statute is clear, unambiguous, and needs no interpretation. I also agree that the term "foreclosure sale" describes a single, discrete event, and not merely a step in a process culminating in the recordation and delivery of a deed. . . . It is not, I think, an extreme position to take, i.e., that the property is *sold* at the foreclosure sale, and that the deed is customarily not delivered to the purchaser until after the foreclosure sale. . . . The delivery of a foreclosure deed has been described as a "ministerial act, routinely performed, which does not affect the redemption rights of the parties." . . . Further, the words "conducted in accordance with applicable non-bankruptcy law" do not expand the cure period according to state-law redemption rights, but rather describes a foreclosure sale conducted in compliance with (and not in violation of), relevant state law. . . .

Nowhere does the statute require that the cure rights under Section 1322 terminate only upon the recordation and delivery of the foreclosure deed. Such language is not part of the statute, and it is not within the Court's authority to read the statute as though it were in there. "To define the word 'sold' as the point at which a deed is transferred to the prevailing bidder subsequent to the date of the auction . . . removes the words 'foreclosure sale' from the statute." . . . Therefore, if the foreclosure sale did not violate applicable state law, it follows that when the gavel falls, the right to cure no longer exists. There is no suggestion in this case of any violation of, or noncompliance with applicable state law.

We reject the third view, also without difficulty, as nothing in Section 1322(c)(1) requires deference to whatever expansive cure rights may exist under state law. The *Colon* court finds support for its view in the legislative history and scholarly texts. *Colon*, 319 F.3d at 917-918. However, the statute does not provide or suggest that the right to cure exists *at least* until such residence is sold at a foreclosure sale. On the contrary, Section 1322(c)(1) states unequivocally: "[n]otwithstanding . . . any non-bankruptcy law. . . ." If Congress intended to place federal bankruptcy law beneath, or subject to, certain state created rights, it could have chosen a better way to do so.

Finally, even if we were to look to state law in this case, the result would be the same because under its statutory power of sale, Rhode Island law does not provide for any post-foreclosure right of redemption. In fact, R.I. Gen. L. §34-11-22 states " . . . which sale or sales . . . shall forever be a perpetual bar against the mortgagor." R.I. Gen. Laws §34-11-22 (2008). *See also*, Holden v. Salvadore, 964 A.2d 508, 516 (R.I. 2009) (noting that it was not within the power of the defendant to prevent or postpone the foreclosure sale, because the sale and foreclosure had already taken place, the plaintiff herself was the highest bidder, and plaintiff and auctioneer had executed all the appropriate documents); 140 Reservoir Avenue Associates v. Sepe Investments, LLC, 941 A.2d 805, 811-812 (R.I. 2007) (concluding that any interest of mortgagor's successor in real estate was forever barred by the foreclosure sale, where no party challenged the validity of the sale).

Based on the foregoing discussion, the authorities cited, and the arguments of the parties, Relief From Stay is GRANTED.

Post-Case Follow-Up

Are the two views rejected by this court unreasonable interpretations of §1322(c)(1)? Couldn't Congress have intended the "process" approach or the "right of redemption" approach rather than the "gavel" approach adopted here? There is actually a fourth view, referred to as the "deed-delivery" approach whereby the property is not sold at foreclosure until the foreclosure deed is delivered to the buyer. See, e.g., In re Randall, 263 B.R. 200, 201 (D.N.J. 2001). In adopting the "gavel" approach, is this court saying that the question of when a "sale" has occurred is purely a matter of federal and not state law? Is that what Congress meant by use of the phrase "notwithstanding applicable nonbankruptcy law" in §1322(c)? Under any of the approaches to this issue, doesn't §1322(c)(1) require the court to determine that a foreclosure sale has been properly conducted under applicable state (non-bankruptcy) law? Determine whether the courts of the federal district or circuit where you plan to practice have addressed this issue and, if so, how they have ruled.

In re Medaglia: Real Life Applications

1. Assume you represent a debtor who owns a home mortgaged to Bank. Debtor is three months in arrears on his mortgage payments to bank when he comes to you to discuss a bankruptcy filing. He likes the idea of being able to cure the arrearage to Bank in his plan and of keeping his house and you are satisfied he can do that. But he has told you that Bank is "about to foreclose." Your jurisdiction follows the gavel rule. Can you preserve debtor's right to cure and keep by filing the Chapter 13 petition now, under the following scenarios?
   a. The foreclosure sale is scheduled for later today.
   b. The foreclosure sale is going on right this moment.
   c. The foreclosure sale just ended and there was a recognized high bidder on the house to whom the gavel fell but no contract or memorandum of sale will be signed until "buyer" posts earnest money, which he will be unable to do until tomorrow afternoon.
   d. The foreclosure sale was yesterday and buyer posted the required earnest money deposit and signed a memorandum of sale. However, the high bidder

is a former employee of the auction company that conducted the sale and state law forbids "employees" of the auction company handling a foreclosure sale from bidding. This employee still worked for the company when it received the contract from Bank to handle the foreclosure sale; he quit the day before the sale.

   e. The foreclosure sale was last week. Buyer posted the required earnest money deposit, signed a memorandum of sale, paid the full balance owed three days later, received his deed that day, and recorded it immediately. State law requires certain disclosures to be read at the beginning of a foreclosure sale and your information is that this was not done at this sale.

2. Assume you represent the buyer at the foreclosure sale described in Question 1. He really loves the house. What advice would you give him in each of the scenarios in that question?

3. Assume you represent Bank in connection with the foreclosure sale described in Question 1. What advice would you have for Bank as it plans the foreclosure sale regarding requirement of an escrow deposit to high bidder, timing of the execution of a memorandum of sale, time within which high bidder must pay the full balance owed, timing of deed delivery, etc.? How would that advice change if you practiced in a district that followed the right of redemption approach and the applicable state allowed the debtor a right of redemption for 30 days following sale?

Application Exercise 1

Commonly, debtors do not approach a lawyer for assistance until the mortgage on their residence has been declared in default and foreclosure have proceedings begun. If the foreclosure sale is imminent, the need to get the Chapter 13 petition filed and stop the foreclosure sale using the automatic stay is paramount. Debtors' lawyers must understand the legal implications of delay in handling such a matter. What are the specific ethical and professional obligations of attorneys in your state regarding competence, zealous representation, and the timely performance of agreed legal services that come into play in this situation?

Although the curing of an arrearage in secured debt does not normally require the payment of postpetition interest to the creditor, §1322(e) requires the payment of such interest *if* the terms of the underlying agreement itself or state law do so.

For example, the Matthews' plan calls for interest to be paid to FBCC on the arrearage payments. This is necessary because the promissory note between the Matthews and FBCC requires the payment of interest on arrearages.

When a Chapter 13 debtor's plan proposes to cure an arrearage on a debt secured by a mortgage on his principal residence under §1322(b)(5), FRBP 3002.1 imposes significant notice requirements and filing deadlines on the creditor secured by such mortgage.

For example, the holder of the mortgage must give written notice to the debtor, debtor's attorney, and the trustee of changes in the payment amount caused by changes in the applicable interest rate or by adjustments in the escrow account balance at least 21 days before the changes become effective. And the mortgage holder must give written itemization of any postpetition fees, expenses, or charges it alleges are due under the mortgage within 180 days after such costs were incurred. Significant penalties are imposed on the mortgage holder for noncompliance with these requirements.

4. Reducing an Undersecured Claim to Present Value: Strip Down

How Strip Down Works in General

Recall that §506(a) provides that a secured claim in bankruptcy is only secured up to the value of the collateral and is unsecured to the extent the claim exceeds that value. Consequently, the claim secured by collateral having a value equal to or greater than the amount of the claim is a fully secured claim (or even oversecured). But a claim secured by collateral having a value less than the amount of the claim is an undersecured claim (sometimes called partially secured) and it is this claim that §506(a) effectively bifurcates into its secured and unsecured portions. In significant contrast to Chapter 7, §§1322(b)(2) and 1325(a)(5) authorize a Chapter 13 debtor to utilize the bifurcation feature of §506 to propose a plan in which the debtor will retain possession of secured property while paying the undersecured creditor only the present value of the collateral as a secured claim over the term of the plan rather than the entire amount of the debt. Section 1322(b)(2) provides in pertinent part as follows:

> (b) Subject to subsections (a) and (c) of this section, the plan may—
> (2) modify the rights of holders of secured claims, other than a claim secured only by a security interest in real property that is the debtor's principal residence. . . .

Section 1325(a)(5) then provides in pertinent part as follows:

> (a) Except as provided in subsection (b), the court shall confirm a plan if . . .
> (5) with respect to each allowed secured claim provided for by the plan . . .
> (B)(i) the plan provides that—
> (I) the holder of such claim retain the lien securing such claim until the earlier of—
> (aa) the payment of the underlying debt determined under nonbankruptcy law; or
> (bb) discharge under section 1328; and . . .
> (ii) the value, as of the effective date of the plan, of property to be distributed under the plan on account of such claim is not less than the allowed amount of such claim. . . .

The unsecured portion of the debt is then treated as a non-priority general unsecured claim under the plan.

This right of the Chapter 13 debtor to reduce the amount of a secured claim to the present value of the property securing the claim while retaining that property is informally called a **strip down** or **write down**. It is also sometimes called **cram down** since it can be approved by the bankruptcy court without creditor approval and over creditor objection (but cram down is actually a broader concept than strip down — it describes any proposal to modify a secured creditor's rights over the creditor's objection whether involving strip down or not and we will see examples of other cram down options the Chapter 13 debtor has later in the chapter). Technically, the secured claim is stripped down or written down to its present value per §506(a) and then crammed down on the unconsenting creditor per §§1322(b)(2) and 1325(a)(5).

For example, the YR-3 Ford F-150 truck that Roger drives is worth $7,500 but the Matthews still owe $9,000 for it. Thus the claim of the creditor holding a security interest in the truck, Automotive Financing, Inc. (AFI) is undersecured on its claim. The Matthews' Chapter 13 plan (Exhibit 15.2) proposes to pay AFI the $7,500 present value of the truck over the 60-month term of the plan and for debtors to retain possession of the truck. This is a strip down proposal. The balance of $1,500 owed to AFI is treated and paid as a general unsecured claim in the Matthews' plan. If AFI was fully secured or oversecured (i.e., the truck had a present value equal to or in excess of the $9,000 balance owed) the Matthews could not propose this strip down. They would have to propose paying the full $9,000 in order to keep the truck.

Note in the last example that the strip down proposal on the truck calls for the Matthews to pay the full present value of AFI's secured claim during the term of the plan. This is a strict requirement of the strip down option. The present value to which the secured claim is stripped down must be paid in full during the term of the plan pursuant to the mandate of §1325(a)(5)(B)(ii).

For example, if the Matthews' plan called for the truck value to be stripped down to its present value of $7,500 and paid over six years, it would not be approved since the plan can only run for five years.

In Chapter Ten, Section C, we considered whether a Chapter 7 individual debtor could use lien stripping together with a ride through option to retain possession of collateralized property while paying only the undersecured value of a claim. And we learned that the answer is no owing to the decisions in Dewsnup v. Timm, 502 U.S. 410 (1997), and Bank of America, N.A. v. Caulkett, 135 S. Ct. 1995 (2015). Be careful to not confuse that rule in Chapter 7 cases with the strip down options available in Chapter 13 cases using §§1322(b)(2) and 1325(a)(5). There are no equivalent provisions in Chapter 7.

Exclusion of the Debtor's Principal Residence from the Strip Down Option — and Some Exceptions

Pursuant to the language of §1322(b)(2) set out above ("other than a claim secured only by a security interest in real property that is the debtor's principal residence") as interpreted by the Supreme Court in Nobelman v. American Savings Bank, 508 U.S. 324 (1993), the right to strip down a secured claim to the present value of the collateral does not apply to a debt secured only by a security interest in real property that is the debtor's principal residence. Thus, in most Chapter 13 cases, the debtor is unable to modify the secured balance of the mortgage on his home even if the value of the home has fallen below the balance of the mortgage (i.e., the creditor is undersecured).

There are, however, a number of exceptions to the §1322(b)(2) prohibition on strip down of a claim secured by a mortgage in the debtor's primary residence. First, note that the restriction just quoted applies only to real property used as the debtor's principal residence. If the Chapter 13 debtor owns a second home that is not his principal residence, he can strip down the mortgage on that second home if its value has fallen below the balance of the mortgage. This disparity in the Code gives a curious advantage to debtors who are better off (i.e., those who own two or more homes rather than one), which is troubling during a time of continuing economic distress due to the lingering effects of the Great Recession and the mortgage foreclosure crisis. To date, legislative efforts to extend the strip down option to the principal residence of Chapter 13 debtors even temporarily have failed in Congress.

Second, note also that the restriction of §1322(b)(2) applies only to a security interest in real property used as the debtor's principal residence. What if the debt is secured by a mobile home used as the debtor's principal residence? Can the mobile home ever be considered personal property and thus subject to §1322(b)(2) modification? Some courts say yes if, under state law, the mobile home is not so permanently attached to the real property on which it sits to be considered real property itself. See, for example, In re Reinhardt, 563 F.3d 558 (6th Cir. 2009) (mobile home used as principal residence but not considered real property under Ohio law so debt secured by it subject to modification) and In re Ennis, 558 F.3d 343 (4th Cir. 2009) (same result under Virginia law).

Third, what if there is a second mortgage on the debtor's primary residence that is wholly undersecured? For example, assume the Chapter 13 debtor's primary residence is valued at $200,000. Bank #1 holds a first mortgage on the residence, the balance on which is $225,000. Bank #1 is undersecured in the amount of $25,000 per §506(a) so that the value of its secured claim in the residence is only $200,000. But Bank #1 is not wholly undersecured because the secured portion of its claim does have that $200,000 value. However, assume that Bank #2 holds a second mortgage on the residence, the balance on which is $30,000. Bank #2 is wholly undersecured — all the secured value of the residence ($200,000) will go to satisfy the mortgage of Bank #1. Can the Chapter 13 debtor strip down (or strip off, as it is sometimes called in this context) that second mortgage in his plan and treat the $30,000 owed to Bank #2 as an unsecured claim?

Case Preview

In re Zimmer and In re Scantling

The question of whether a Chapter 13 debtor can strip off a wholly undersecured junior mortgage on the debtor's residence under §1322(b)(2) has divided the courts. Complicating the question is whether a debtor in a Chapter 20 case may do so. Recall the mention of Chapter 20 in Chapter Twelve, Section A: Although there is no formal Chapter 20 in the Code, that phrase is used by practitioners to describe the not uncommon practice of a debtor obtaining a discharge in a Chapter 7 case and then filing a Chapter 13 case shortly thereafter (7 + 13 = 20). Section 1328(f) provides that a Chapter 13 debtor cannot receive a discharge in his Chapter 13 case if he has received a discharge under Chapter 7, 11, or 12 during the four years preceding his filing of the Chapter 13 petition. However, a Chapter 13 case can be filed by that debtor and a plan approved even though no discharge is granted in the case (e.g., the debtor proposes a 100 percent plan involving no discharge of debt). So if a Chapter 13 debtor entitled to a discharge under that chapter can strip off a wholly undersecured second mortgage in his home, does that mean that a Chapter 20 debtor who is not entitled to a discharge in Chapter 13 may do so as well? As you read In re Zimmer and In re Scantling, consider the following questions:

1. What is the reasoning of the courts that do not allow any Chapter 13 debtor to strip off a wholly undersecured junior mortgage on the debtor's homestead? What is the significance of the Supreme Court's decision in *Nobelman* for the courts that adopt that view?
2. What is the reasoning of the courts that allow a Chapter 13 debtor to strip off the wholly undersecured junior mortgage? How do they read *Nobelman* differently?
3. What is the reasoning of the courts that hold that even if a Chapter 13 debtor entitled to a discharge under that chapter can strip off a wholly undersecured junior mortgage on the homestead, a debtor not entitled to a discharge under that chapter (the Chapter 20 debtor) cannot do so?
4. Why did the court in *Scantling* reject that reasoning to allow the Chapter 20 debtor to strip off?

In re Zimmer
313 F.3d 1220 (9th Cir. 2002)

[In 1997, Sieglinde Zimmer executed a promissory note for a $39,000 loan, secured by a second mortgage on Zimmer's residence. The deed of trust was assigned to PSB Lending. When Zimmer filed her petition in Chapter 13 in 1999 the balance owed on the first mortgage was $123,000 and the balance on the second mortgage held by PSB was $37,411.19. In her petition, Zimmer stated the value of her residence to be $110,000. Because the first mortgage exceeded the value of the residence, Zimmer listed PSB Lending's claim for the repayment of its loan as unsecured. On April 21, 2000, Zimmer filed an adversary complaint with the bankruptcy court seeking to avoid PSB Lending's lien on her home. PSB Lending filed a motion to dismiss. The bankruptcy court granted the motion to dismiss. The district court affirmed and this appeal followed.]

NELSON, Circuit Judge. . . .

In general, Chapter 13 allows the modification of the rights of creditors, including the avoidance of liens against the debtor's property, but protects homestead liens from modification:

> [A Chapter 13 plan may] modify the rights of holders of secured claims, other than a claim secured only by a security interest in real property that is the debtor's principal residence, or of holders of unsecured claims, or leave unaffected the rights of holders of any class of claims[.]

11 U.S.C. §1322(b)(2). Assuming that PSB Lending holds "a claim secured only by a security interest in real property that is the debtor's principal residence," it might qualify for protection against modification. If so, its lien would survive bankruptcy and could not be avoided by Zimmer.

Although it seems paradoxical on its face, PSB Lending's claim is arguably an "unsecured claim" that is also "a claim secured only by a security interest in real property that is the debtor's principal residence." Whether the antimodification clause of §1322(b)(2) applies to the holder of such a claim is a question of first impression in this Circuit. Numerous other jurisdictions, however, have addressed this question in dozens of published opinions. The position adopted by a majority of courts is that the antimodification clause does not apply to wholly unsecured homestead liens, but a substantial minority of courts has taken the contrary position. . . . Both camps believe their preferred result to be compelled by the Supreme Court's decision in Nobelman v. American Savings Bank, 508 U.S. 324 (1993).

In *Nobelman*, the Supreme Court considered the question of whether a partially-secured claim secured by a homestead lien could be bifurcated into its secured and unsecured components, and "stripped down" to the value of the secured claim. *See id.* at 326-27. The debtors argued that, under §506(a), the holder of an undersecured mortgage — for which the value of the claim exceeds the value of the property — only holds a "secured claim" to the extent of the value of the property, and holds an "unsecured claim" for the excess value of the mortgage. *Id.* at 328. Because §1322(b)(2) only protects the rights of "holders of secured claims," they maintained that only the secured portion of the mortgage was entitled to protection and, therefore, that the value of the mortgage could be effectively reduced to its secured value. *Id.*

The Supreme Court rejected this approach of bifurcation and stripping down, primarily because the debtors' argument failed to consider the fact that §1322(b)(2) "focuses on the modification of the 'rights of holders,'" *id.*, not the status of claims. Although the Court found that it was proper to look to §506(a) "for a judicial valuation of the collateral to determine the status of the [creditor's] claim," *id.*, because the creditor's claim was partially secured, the creditor was "still the 'holder' of a 'secured claim.'" *Id.* at 329. Therefore, it was entitled to the protections of the antimodification clause.

The Court's interpretation of §1322(b)(2) is worth considering in detail. The Fifth Circuit, in the decision reviewed by *Nobelman*, had concluded that "section 1322(b)(2) appears to conflict with section 506(a)," and resolved the conflict in favor of §1322(b)(2). Nobelman v. Am. Sav. Bank (In re Nobelman), 968 F.2d 483, 488 (5th Cir. 1992). The Supreme Court took a different approach, giving effect to both statutes in its interpretation of "claim" in the antimodification clause. The debtors argued that "claim secured only by a security interest in real property" should work to modify "secured claims" in the antecedent clause, such that the antimodification clause would only apply to a *secured claim* secured only by a security interest in the debtor's home. *Nobelman*, 508 U.S. at 330. The Supreme Court rejected this argument, finding that "claim secured only by" is *not* equivalent to the term of art "secured claim." *Id.* at 331. Instead, noting that "§506(a) itself uses the phrase 'claim . . . secured by a lien' to encompass *both portions* of an undersecured claim," the Court found that the antimodification clause similarly applied to both the unsecured and secured components of the mortgage claim. *Id.* (emphasis added).

Finally, the Supreme Court indicated that its interpretation was reasonable because it would be impossible to administer a bifurcated claim. There was no dispute that the secured portion of the mortgage could not be modified, and under such circumstances there was no direction in the Bankruptcy Code as to how the terms of the mortgage could be readjusted by reducing its value to the secured portion without modifying the "rights" of the mortgage holder. *Id.* at 331-332. Justice Stevens also noted, in a brief concurrence, that the Court's result was in accordance with "legislative history indicating that favorable treatment of residential mortgagees was intended to encourage the flow of capital into the home lending market." *Id.* at 332. . . .

The majority position, that §1322(b)(2) does not prohibit avoidance of liens associated with wholly unsecured claims, has been adopted by all five Courts of Appeals to consider the issue, as well as two Bankruptcy Appellate Panels. . . .

One of the earliest and most influential of these cases is our BAP's opinion in In re Lam, 211 B.R. 36 (9th Cir. B.A.P. 1997). The panel gave three primary reasons for its conclusion that a wholly unsecured lien may be avoided: 1) although the *Nobelman* Court focused on the rights of the creditor, the "rights" of a wholly unsecured creditor are "empty rights"; 2) in order to qualify for the antimodification protections, the creditor must first be a "holder of a secured claim"; and 3) extending antimodification protection might have the unwanted effects of inducing more filings under Chapter 11 and inducing creditors to obtain mortgages on overburdened property in order to avoid modification of their rights. 211 B.R. at 40-41.

Other courts have focused primarily on the second reason cited in *Lam*, that a creditor that is not the holder of a secured claim simply cannot qualify for antimodification protection. The Sixth Circuit in In re Lane, 280 F.3d 663 (6th Cir. 2002) outlines this argument in near-syllogistic fashion:

> Section 1322(b)(2) prohibits modification of the rights of a holder of a secured claim if the security consists of a lien on the debtor's principal residence; Section 1322(b)(2) permits modification of the rights of an unsecured claim holder. . . . Whether a lien claimant is the holder of a "secured claim" or an "unsecured claim" depends, thanks

to §506(a), on whether the claimant's security interest has any actual "value." . . . If a claimant's lien on the debtor's homestead has no value at all . . . the claimant holds an "unsecured claim" and the claimant's contractual rights are subject to modification by the plan.

280 F.3d at 669. This argument is appealing in its simplicity and reliance on the plain text of the statute. Without a secured claim, a creditor's rights may be modified. . . .

We conclude that the district court erred in holding that a wholly unsecured lien is protected by the antimodification clause of §1322(b)(2). . . .

REVERSED and REMANDED.

In re Scantling
754 F.3d 1323 (11th Cir. 2014)

[On March 30, 2010, Scantling received a discharge under Chapter 7. On January 1, 2011, Scantling filed a voluntary petition for relief under Chapter 13 thus creating a "Chapter 20." Wells Fargo Bank, N.A. ("the Bank") held three liens secured by Scantling's principal residence ("Residence"). The balance of the first lien was $121,808.85; the balance of the second lien was $79,369.79 and the balance of the third lien was $24,416.24. The Bank valued the Residence at $118,500, and the Bankruptcy Court accepted that valuation. Since the value of the Residence rendered the Bank's two junior liens wholly unsecured, Scantling sought a declaration that the junior liens were void. The Bankruptcy Court determined that Scantling could strip off the Bank's second and third liens on the Residence because they were wholly unsecured. The Bank appealed.]

SCHLESINGER, District Judge sitting by designation. . . .

III. DISCUSSION

This case presents a single issue — whether a debtor can "strip off" a wholly unsecured junior mortgage in a Chapter 20 case. To resolve this question, we must analyze the interplay between two provisions of the Bankruptcy Code 11 U.S.C. §§506 and 1322(b), following the enactment of the BAPCPA.

A. Statutory History

Prior to the BAPCPA, a debtor in a Chapter 13 case, filed soon after a Chapter 7 case, was eligible for a discharge, or "strip off," of a valueless lien. Lien avoidances pre-BAPCPA in Chapter 20 cases were, therefore, treated the same as in ordinary Chapter 13 cases. In other words, pre-BAPCPA, a bankruptcy court was able to strip off a valueless lien in a typical Chapter 13 proceeding. . . .

The strip off procedure was a two-step process guided by 11 U.S.C. §§506 and 1322(b) of the Bankruptcy Code. First, §506(a) provided a valuation procedure for the claim. Depending on the value of the collateral, a claim was either secured or unsecured. If a claim were valueless and classified as unsecured under §506(a), then the second step, under §1322(b)(2), provided the mechanism whereby a Chapter 13 bankruptcy plan could,

> modify the rights of holders of secured claims, other than a claim secured only by a security interest in real property that is the debtor's principal residence, or of holders of unsecured claims, or leave unaffected the rights of holders of any class of claims[.]

11 U.S.C. §1322(b)(2). Following this two-step approach, a bankruptcy court was able to strip off a completely valueless lien against a primary residence in a Chapter 13 proceeding.

This approach was, however, not without limitations. The Supreme Court held that §506(d) did not allow a lien to be modified based solely upon a §506(a) valuation. Dewsnup v. Timm, 502 U.S. 410, 417 (1992). Instead, the *Dewsnup* Court held that because the creditor possessed an allowed secured claim under §502, §506(d) was not implicated and the lien could not be avoided. *Id.* The Court rejected an interpretation of §506(d) that departed from the long-established "pre-Code rule that liens pass through bankruptcy unaffected." *Id.*

Later, in Nobelman v. American Savings Bank, 508 U.S. 324 (1993), the Supreme Court addressed the interaction between §1322(b)(2) and §506(a) with respect to an undersecured first lienholder. The debtor in *Nobelman* attempted to "strip down" a homestead lender's secured claim to the home's reduced value. . . . The *Nobelman* Court rejected the debtor's assertions and concluded that "§1322(b)(2) prohibits a Chapter 13 debtor from relying on §506(a) to reduce an undersecured homestead mortgage to the fair market value of the mortgaged residence." . . .

This Circuit discussed the impact of *Nobelman* on the rights of a wholly unsecured junior mortgagee in Tanner v. Firstplus Financial, Inc. (In re Tanner), 217 F.3d 1357 (11th Cir. 2000). This court determined that a wholly unsecured lien on a debtor's principal residence is not protected from modification under §1322(b)(2). . . . Rather, this court determined, "[t]he better reading of sections 506(a) and 1322(b)(2), therefore, protects only mortgages that are secured by some existing equity in the debtor's principal residence." . . .

Tanner distinguished *Nobelman* which explicitly prohibited lien strip downs where the affected lien encumbered the principal residence but was silent concerning strip offs. . . . Therefore, *Tanner* explained:

> the only reading of both sections 506(a) and 1322(b)(2) that renders neither a nullity is one that first requires bankruptcy courts to determine the value of the homestead lender's secured claim under section 506(a) and then to protect from modification any claim that is secured by any amount of collateral in the residence.

Id. at 1360.

It appears that *Tanner* and our sister circuits correctly understand *Nobelman* to stand for the proposition that for a claim to be "secured" and trigger the antimodification provisions of §1322(b)(2), the collateral must have at least some value, as stated by the unambiguous language in §506(a). . . .

It was in this atmosphere that Congress enacted the BAPCPA, in 2005, "'to correct perceived abuses of the bankruptcy system.'" Branigan v. Davis, 716 F.3d 331, 333 (4th Cir. 2013). . . . "An overarching goal was to 'help ensure that debtors who can pay creditors do pay them.'" *Id.* . . .

The specific language of the BAPCPA at issue here is §1328(f), which provides:

Notwithstanding subsections (a) and (b), the court shall not grant a discharge of all debts provided for in the plan or disallowed under §502, if the debtor has received a discharge —

   (1) in a case filed under chapter 7, 11, or 12 of this title during the 4-year period preceding the date of the order for relief under this chapter, or

   (2) in a case filed under chapter 13 of this title during the 2-year period preceding the date of such order.

11 U.S.C. §1328(f).

The Bank argues that lien-stripping is contingent on a debtor's ability to receive a Chapter 13 discharge. The only statute that allows confirmation of a plan and liens to be stripped is §1325(a)(5), which provides that a holder of a secured lien retains the lien until either the underlying debt is paid or there is a discharge. Scantling is ineligible for discharge; therefore, the Bank maintains its liens must survive.

The Bank, further, contends that *Dewsnup* is applicable to Chapter 20 cases such that an "allowed secured claim" remains an allowed secured claim in the absence of a §502(b) objection for purposes of §1325(a)(5)(B), which sets forth the requirements for confirming and implementing the contents of a Chapter 13 plan irrespective of §506(d). On the other hand, Scantling insists the Bankruptcy Court was correct, and that this Court's prior precedent in *Tanner* mitigates strongly in favor of, if not compels, affirmance of the Bankruptcy Court's decision.

A split of authority exists on whether a debtor may strip off of a worthless lien in a Chapter 20 case — along the lines of parties' arguments. Compare In re Davis, 716 F.3d 331 (4th Cir. 2013) (concluding a Chapter 20 debtor may strip off liens); and In re Fisette, 455 B.R. 177 (8th Cir. BAP 2011) (same); and In re Dang, 467 B.R. 227 (Bankr. M.D. Fla. 2012) (same); and In re Okosisi, 451 B.R. 90 (Bankr. D. Nev. 2011) (same); and In re Tran, 431 B.R. 230, 237 (Bankr. N.D. Cal. 2010) (same); with In re Gerardin, 447 B.R. 342 (Bankr. S.D. Fla. 2011) (holding that Chapter 20 debtors could not permanently strip off wholly unsecured junior liens); and In re Quiros–Amy, 456 B.R. 140 (Bankr. S.D. Fla. 2011) (same); and In re Victorio, 454 B.R. 759 (Bankr. S.D. Cal. 2011) (same); and In re Fenn, 428 B.R. 494 (Bankr. N.D. Ill. 2010) (same); and In re Jarvis, 390 B.R. 600 (Bankr. C.D. Ill. 2008) (same).

The majority view recognizes a strip off of the unsecured mortgage is allowed under the theory that a "Chapter 13 debtor need not be eligible for a discharge in order to take advantage of the protections afforded by Chapter 13." In re Davis, 716 F.3d at 338. If a strip off of a worthless lien is available under the bankruptcy code without a discharge a debtor may take advantage of such relief. *Id.*

The bankruptcy code provides that when a debtor's junior liens are worthless and unsecured under §506(a), §506 operates in tandem with §1322(b) to strip liens in Chapter 13 cases. *Id.* The BAPCPA "did not amend" §§506 or 1322(b), "so the analysis permitting lien-stripping in Chapter 20 cases is no different than that in any other Chapter 13 case." *Id.* Congress, it is argued, intentionally left "the normal Chapter 13 lien-stripping regime where a debtor could otherwise satisfy the requirements for filing a Chapter 20 case." *Id.*

In contrast, those courts ascribing to the minority view contend the term "allowed secured claim" in §1325(a)(5) is not contingent on a §506(a) valuation.

Instead, §506(a) provides a judicial valuation method of an allowed secured claim, but that valuation does not modify the creditor's secured status. An "allowed secured claim," therefore, "merely describes (1) a claim, which is a 'right to payment' or a 'right to an equitable remedy' as defined in 11 U.S.C. §101(5); (2) that is 'allowed,' meaning 'not objected to by an interested party' under 11 U.S.C. §502(a); and (3) that is 'secured.'" In re Davis, 716 F.3d at 340 (Keenan, J., dissenting).

A junior lien is not worthless if it remains "allowed" and "secured" by the debtor's real property, and the lien remains in this status even after a debtor receives a Chapter 7 discharge. *Id.* The *in rem* portion of the claims survive a debtor's Chapter 7 discharge. *Id.*

A Chapter 13 plan must comply with §1325(a)(5), and a junior mortgagee creditor has an "allowed secured claim" against the debtor's bankruptcy estate. Section 1325(a)(5)(B)(I) provides that a debtor's Chapter 13 plan "must provide that the junior mortgagee creditors retain their liens on the properties until the earlier of (1) full payment by the debtors in the context of non-bankruptcy law, or (2) discharge." *Id.* Sections 1325(a)(5)(B)(i) and 1328(f) work in tandem to prohibit a Chapter 20 debtor "from stripping off valueless junior mortgages." *Id.*

Guided by *Tanner*, we find the reasoning of the majority view persuasive and adopt that view. We agree with the other circuits who have considered this issue that a debtor, in a Chapter 13 setting, may strip off an unsecured mortgage on the debtor's principal residence. This strip off is accomplished through the §506(a) valuation procedure that determines that the creditor does not hold a secured claim. Once this determination has been made, pursuant to §1322(b)(2), the creditor's "rights" are modified by avoiding the lien to which the creditor would otherwise be entitled under nonbankruptcy law. Under such analysis, §1325(a)(5) is not involved, and the debtor's ineligibility for a discharge is irrelevant to a strip off in a Chapter 20 case. The BAPCPA did not amend §§506 or 1322(b), so the analysis permitting strip offs in Chapter 20 cases is no different than that in any other Chapter 13 case.

IV. CONCLUSION

Based on the foregoing and our review of the record and the parties' briefs, we affirm the Bankruptcy Court's decision.

Post-Case Follow-Up

A substantial majority of courts allow the strip off of a wholly undersecured junior mortgage on the debtor's residence in a Chapter 13 using the rationale seen in *Zimmer*. But there is a significant split on whether that same mortgage can be stripped off in a Chapter 20. The contrary view to that expressed in *Scantling* is well expressed in In re Victorio, 454 B.R. 759 (Bankr. S.D. Cal. 2011), which, while agreeing that a Chapter 13 debtor entitled to a discharge can strip off a wholly undersecured mortgage on the homestead, held that a Chapter 20 debtor not entitled to a discharge cannot because §349(b)(1)(C) reinstates a lien where a Chapter 13 case is dismissed without a discharge such that the only way a Chapter 13 debtor can make a lien strip "permanent" is through a discharge. Determine if the courts of the federal district or circuit where you plan to practice have decided these issues in a Chapter 13 case and, if so, what view they take.

In re Zimmer and In re Scantling: Real Life Applications

1. Assume you practice in a district that follows *Zimmer* but rejects *Scantling* for the Chapter 20 debtor and instead follows *Victorio.* With that state of the law in your jurisdiction, which of the following potential Chapter 13 debtors who consult you have the option to strip off the junior mortgages on their home?
   a. Debtor owns a home worth $250,000. Debtor owes Bank #1 $240,000 and Bank #2 $50,000. Debtor has never filed a Chapter 7 case.
   b. Debtor owns a home worth $300,000. Debtor owes Bank #1 $310,000 and Bank #2 $50,000. Debtor has never filed a Chapter 7 case.
   c. Debtor owns a home worth $300,000. Debtor owes Bank #1 $310,000 and Bank #2 $50,000. Debtor filed a Chapter 7 case that was voluntarily dismissed 60 days ago when Bank #1 filed a motion to lift automatic stay.
   d. Debtor owns a home worth $300,000. Debtor owes Bank #1 $310,000 and Bank #2 $50,000. Debtor received a discharge in a Chapter 7 case three years before filing his petition in Chapter 13.
2. Assume you practice in a jurisdiction that construes *Nobelman* to prohibit not only the strip down to value of an undersecured mortgage on the debtor's homestead but to prohibit strip off of a wholly undersecured second mortgage on that homestead. You have been consulted by a potential Chapter 13 client who owns a home worth $300,000. The first mortgage on the home is held by Bank #1 with a balance of $310,000 and scheduled monthly payments for ten more years of $3,200 per month. Debtor is two monthly payments in arrears to Bank #1. A second mortgage on the home is held by Bank #2 with a balance of $25,000 and scheduled monthly payments of $390 for six more years. Debtor is current in his payments to Bank #2. Debtor would like to keep the home and has seen something about the possibility of cram down or lien strip off in a Chapter 13. What advice will you give debtor concerning:
   a. Whether he can propose a strip down to value of the mortgage of Bank #1 since it is undersecured or will have to propose a plan to continue to make all scheduled payments to Bank #1 during the term of his plan.
   b. Whether he will have to cure the arrearages to Bank #1 during the term of his plan.
   c. Whether he will have to pay interest on the arrearage balance until it is paid.

    d. Whether he can propose a strip down or strip off of the mortgage of Bank #2 since it is wholly undersecured or will have to propose a plan to continue to make all scheduled payments to Bank #2 during the term of his plan.

    e. Other options he may have in his Chapter 13 if he changes his mind about keeping the house.

A fourth exception to the exclusion of the debtor's principal residence from the strip down option arises from use of the word "only" in §1322(b)(2), which excludes debts secured *only* by the debtor's principal residence from strip down. So if the debt obligation is secured not only by the principal residence itself but by some other property (e.g., another parcel of real property or any personal property), that debt is subject to strip down. Of course, the fact that the debt is secured by other property makes it less likely that the debt will be undersecured.

Fifth, §1322(c)(2), added to the Code following *Nobelman*, provides as follows:

Notwithstanding subsection (b)(2) and applicable nonbankruptcy law —

. . .

    (2) in a case in which the last payment on the original payment schedule for a claim secured only by a security interest in real property that is the debtor's principal residence is due before the date on which the final payment under the plan is due, the plan may provide for payment of the claim as modified pursuant to section 1325(a)(5) of this title.

Thus if the original payment schedule for a loan secured only by the debtor's primary residence calls for the last payment to be made *before* the Chapter 13 plan expires, the plan can modify the claim using §1325(a)(5). A number of courts have construed §1322(c)(2) to mean that the amount of the secured claim to be paid in full during the term of the plan can be reduced to the extent that it *exceeds* the available equity in the residence. In other words, the secured claim can be stripped down to the present equity so long as it is paid in full during the term of the plan. The balance of the debt will be bifurcated pursuant to §506(a) and treated as a general unsecured claim.

For example, Capital Savings Bank (CSB) holds a second mortgage in the residence of Roger and Susan Matthews, and the balance on that debt is $30,000. The CSB debt is scheduled to be paid off in 48 more months. However, the value of the house is only $120,000 and the balance owed on the first mortgage to FBCC is $100,000. That means there is only $20,000 of equity in the home available to CSB. Because the Matthews have proposed a 60-month (five-year) plan, they have proposed to reduce the claim of CSB to that $20,000 equity amount, pursuant to §1322(c)(2), and to pay it off entirely during the plan. Note that if there was $30,000 or more equity in the residence available for CSB or if the original term of the CSB loan extended beyond the term of the Matthews' plan, they could not take advantage of this strip down provision. Because the principal amount owed to CSB has been stripped down from $30,000 to $20,000, the $10,000 difference will be treated as a general unsecured claim under the plan.

Case Preview

In re Paschen

The §1322(c)(2) strip down exception is usually directed at short-term home equity loans and balloon notes secured by debtor's residence wherein the lender has loaned an amount in excess of the true equity in the residence. As you read In re Paschen, consider the following questions:

1. Why does the court refer to §1322(c)(2) as an exception to the exception?
2. What is AGF's argument from In re Witt that §1322(c)(2) is ambiguous as to whether it allows modification of the payment to be made to the short-term lender or of the claim itself?
3. Why does the Eleventh Circuit refuse to follow the reasoning of In re Witt?

In re Paschen
296 F. 3d 1203 (11th Cir. 2002)

[Debtors purchased a home in Columbus, Georgia, in May of 1997 subject to a mortgage in favor of the lender of the purchase price. Two years later, Debtors obtained a loan from American General Finance, Inc. (AGF), secured by a second mortgage in their home. In December of 1999, Debtors filed a petition under Chapter 13. The balance owed AGF at the time of filing was $11,392. However, given the uncontested value of the residence, AGF's claim was undersecured by $8,640. Debtors submitted a Chapter 13 plan, proposing to modify AGF's claim by bifurcating the claim into its secured and unsecured components, with only the secured portion of $2,752 to be paid back since the last payment on the original payment schedule of the AGF loan was due before the date on which the final payment under the plan would be due. AGF filed a motion to deny confirmation of the plan, arguing that claims involving short-term loans secured by liens against a debtor's primary residence could not be bifurcated into secured and unsecured parts, with the unsecured part crammed down, in a Chapter 13 proceeding. The court found that §1322(c)(2) explicitly permitted the bifurcation and "cramdown" of claims involving short-term mortgages such as the one at issue in this case and accepted Debtors' Chapter 13 plan. The district court affirmed the bankruptcy court and AGF now appeals to this Court.]

WILSON, Circuit Judge. . . .

Chapter 13 debtors enjoy "broad power to modify the rights of the holders of secured claims." . . . The manner in which secured claims may be modified in an acceptable Chapter 13 plan is governed by §1325(a)(5). Section 1325(a)(5) specifies the conditions under which Chapter 13 plans must address "allowed secured claims" if the plans are to be confirmed, essentially by ensuring that creditors receive appropriate value for each of their secured claims. The phrase "allowed secured claims" is a reference to 11 U.S.C. §506(a), which has been interpreted as providing that "a claim is secured only to the extent of the value of the property on which the lien is fixed; the remainder of that claim is considered unsecured." . . . Thus, taken together, these provisions permit the bifurcation of an undersecured claim into its secured and unsecured parts, with creditors only assured of receiving full value for the secured portion of the claim. Section 1325(a)(5) is recognized as the source of a Chapter 13 debtor's authority to bifurcate secured claims and to "strip down" the value of the claim to an amount equal to the value of the collateral. In re Young, 199 B.R. 643, 647 (Bankr. E.D. Tenn. 1996) ("The very essence of a §1325(a)(5) modification is the write down or 'cramdown' of a secured claim to the value of the collateral securing the debt."). . . .

Debtors' proposed plan included an assertion that AGF's debt was undersecured, because the value of Debtors' collateral (equity in their home) was substantially exceeded by the value of the debt. Relying upon the provisions of §1325(a)(5), Debtors sought to bifurcate AGF's claim, with the secured portion paid back in monthly installments and the unsecured component crammed down. While the bankruptcy court disagreed with Debtors' valuation of AGF's collateral, it agreed with the premise of Debtors' proposal and permitted AGF's claim to be bifurcated, with only the value of the secured portion returned to AGF.

AGF argues that another provision of the Bankruptcy Code precludes the modification of its claim. According to AGF, §1322(b)(2) expressly prohibits the modification of any claim in a Chapter 13 proceeding "secured only by a security interest in real property that is the debtor's principal residence." 11 U.S.C. §1322(b)(2). The Supreme Court has interpreted this provision to exclude mortgages against a debtor's principal residence from the general rule permitting modification of secured claims in Chapter 13 proceedings. Nobelman v. Am. Savings Bank, 508 U.S. 324 (1993). . . . In the instant case, AGF holds a note secured solely by a lien on the real property that constitutes Debtors' principal residence. Hence, AGF contends that its claim cannot be modified pursuant to §1325(a)(5).

> Debtors rely upon what they term "an exception to the section 1322(b)(2) exception" to support their contention that AGF's claim should be subject to modification. The relevant provision is found at §1322(c)(2)[opinion quotes §1322(c)(2)]. . . .

Debtors contend that this provision unambiguously provides that short-term mortgages that mature prior to the final payment on a Chapter 13 plan are subject to modification, notwithstanding the general prohibition on modification of claims secured by an interest in a debtor's primary residence found in §1322(b)(2). Debtors note that the debt at issue here is a short-term mortgage that matures prior to the completion of the proposed Chapter 13 plan and thus argue that their debt to AGF is subject to modification. AGF rejects this reading of §1322(c)(2); argues that the language of §1322(c)(2) is ambiguous; and avers that the legislative history indicates that Congress did not intend for §1322(c)(2) to permit the modification of claims secured by short-term mortgages, but rather intended to permit only the schedule of payments for those claims to be modified. Our task in this case is to evaluate these competing views of §1322(c)(2) to determine which view best effects the will of Congress.

III . . .

In the instant case, the plain language of the statute indicates a clear congressional intent to except certain short-term mortgages from the general rule prohibiting the modification of claims secured only by an interest in a debtor's primary residence in a Chapter 13 proceeding. Debtors' interpretation of the statute is the correct one. An assessment of the text of §1322(c)(2) reflects its clarity.

The prefatory phrase "notwithstanding subsection (b)(2)" is the first important indicator of congressional intent with respect to this statute. The phrase is a plain statement that subsection (b)(2)'s prohibition on the modification of loans secured only by an interest in a debtor's primary residence does not have any application to the class of claims that fall under §1322(c)(2). This interpretation of the "notwithstanding" phrase has been noted by a number of other courts charged with construing §1322(c)(2). . . .

In addition, the reference to §1325(a)(5) is highly relevant to our understanding of §1322(c)(2). As we noted earlier, §1325(a)(5) permits writing down secured claims to the value of the collateral securing the debt. *See* United States v. Arnold, 878 F.2d 925, 928 (6th Cir. 1989) ("Under [§1325(a)(5)], the debtor can 'cramdown' a plan repaying only the 'allowed secured claim' . . . ."); In re Young, 199 B.R. at 647 ("The very essence of a §1325(a)(5) modification is the write down or 'cramdown' of a secured claim to the value of the collateral securing the debt."). The phrase "payment of the claim as modified pursuant to section 1325(a)(5)" is an explicit statement of §1322(c)(2)'s purpose: claims that fall within its ambit are subject to bifurcation into secured and unsecured parts, with the unsecured portion subject to "cramdown" pursuant to §1325(a)(5). In re Eubanks, 219 B.R. 468, 471-72 (6th Cir. B.A.P. 1998). And the claims that fall under §1322(c)(2) are those in which "the last payment on the original payment schedule for a claim secured only by a security interest in real property that is the debtor's principal residence is due before the date on which the final payment under the plan is due"—precisely the kind of claim at issue in this case.

AGF argues that the language of the statute is subject to more than one plausible interpretation and is thus ambiguous, requiring reference to extrinsic sources to discern congressional intent. AGF relies upon the construction of §1322(c)(2) advanced in In re Witt, 113 F.3d 508 (4th Cir. 1997), to support its argument that the statute is ambiguous.

In In re Witt, the Fourth Circuit found §1322(c)(2)'s critical phrase "payment of the claim as modified" ambiguous, because "it [could not] be determined, merely from the statute's text, whether the words 'as modified' should apply to 'payment' or to 'claim.'" 113 F.3d at 511. If the term "as modified" modifies "payment," the *Witt* court found that a mortgage covered by §1322(c)(2) could not be bifurcated and crammed down—rather, §1322(c)(2) merely could provide for the modification of the schedule of payments made on such a claim. *Id.* The Fourth Circuit held that it was in fact a plausible reading of the statute to assume that the phrase "as modified" modifies "payment," rather than "claim." *Id.* The court stated that because the subject of "payment" was the focus of §1322(c)(2), it is likely, "as a matter of common sense," that the modifier "as modified" was a reference to the central subject of the statute.

Id. The court further noted that the phrase "payment" would be superfluous if the contrary reading of the statute were accepted; the court reasoned that if Congress had intended the phrase "as modified" to refer to "claim," there would have been no reason to include the term "payment" in the statute. 113 F.3d at 512. Congress simply could have stated that "the plan may provide for the claim to be modified" if this were its intended reading. *Id.* . . .

After finding this alternative construction of §1322(c)(2) one, though not necessarily the only, plausible reading of congressional intent, the *Witt* court assessed the statute's legislative history in an effort to gauge Congress's intent in the face of an ambiguous statute. The Fourth Circuit's reading of that history led the court to conclude that §1322(c)(2) does not provide for the bifurcation and "cramdown" of undersecured, short-term home mortgages. 113 F.3d at 513-14. . . .

We are not convinced by our sister circuit's reasoning. The *Witt* court's view that the phrase "as modified" modifies "payment," rather than "claim," is a grammatically strained reading of the statute. It contradicts the rule of the last antecedent, an accepted canon of statutory construction which provides that when construing statutes, "qualifying words, phrases, and clauses are to be applied to the words or phrase immediately preceding, and are not to be construed as extending to and including others more remote." . . .

Additionally, the *Witt* court advances no convincing explanation for the meaning of the reference to §1325(a)(5) in the text of §1322(c)(2). As we have noted, §1325(a)(5) is the provision that permits the bifurcation of undersecured claims into secured and unsecured components, with the unsecured component subject to "cramdown." "Payments" cannot be modified pursuant to §1325(a)(5); only *claims* are subject to §1325(a)(5)'s modification provisions. The reference to §1325(a)(5) could not be a plainer statement of the statute's purpose; it is an exception to the general rule preventing the modification of claims secured by home mortgages. . . .

IV

In conclusion, we find that the bankruptcy court's interpretation of §1322(c)(2) is the correct one. The provision plainly permits the modification of AGF's claim through the bifurcation of that claim into secured and unsecured components, with the unsecured component crammed down pursuant to §1325(a)(5). The bankruptcy court did not err in confirming Debtors' plan, based upon such a construction of §1322(c)(2), and the district court correctly affirmed the bankruptcy court's decision. The decision of the district court is AFFIRMED.

Post-Case Follow-Up

The overwhelming number of courts have adopted view of §1322(c)(2) seen in *Paschen* over that of *Witt*. Determine if the courts of the federal district or circuit where you plan to practice have ruled on the proper construction of §1322(c)(2).

In re Paschen: Real Life Applications

1. Assume you practice in a jurisdiction that construes *Nobelman* to prohibit not only the strip down to value of an undersecured mortgage on the debtor's homestead but to prohibit strip off a wholly undersecured second mortgage on that homestead as discussed earlier in connection with *Zimmer* and *Scantling*. You have been consulted by a potential Chapter 13 client who you determine is an above median debtor who will need to propose a five-year plan. Debtor owns a home worth $300,000. A first mortgage on the home is held by Bank #1 with a balance of $310,000 and scheduled monthly payments for ten more years of $3,200 per month. A second mortgage on the home is held by Bank #2 with a balance of $25,000 and scheduled monthly payments of $390 for two more years. Debtor is current in his payments to Bank #2. Debtor would like to keep the home and has heard something about the possibility of cram down or lien strip off in a Chapter 13.

   a. Does §1322(c)(2) provide any possibility for modifying the obligation to Bank #1 in this debtor's plan?

   b. Does §1322(c)(2) provide any possibility for modifying the obligation to Bank #2 in this debtor's plan?

2. Which of the following loans are subject to strip down by reason of §1322(c)(2)? In each example, the debtor will propose a five-year plan. For each of those that you determine can be stripped down via §1322(c)(2), over what term must the secured portion of the claim be paid? How will the unsecured portion of the claim be treated in the plan?

   a. The debtor owns a residence worth $150,000. First mortgage on the residence is held by Bank #1 to secure a 15-year loan with a current balance of $175,000. The loan is scheduled to be paid off via a balloon payment in two and a half years. Second mortgage is held by Bank #2 with a current balance of $20,000 and is scheduled to be paid in full in five-and-a-half years.

   b. The debtor owns a residence worth $300,000. First mortgage is held by Bank #1 with a current balance of $325,000 and has ten years to run. Second mortgage is held by Bank #2 with a current balance of $25,000 and has six years to run.

   c. The debtor owns a residence worth $200,000. First mortgage is held by Bank #1 with a current balance of $225,000 and has four years to run. Second mortgage is held by Bank #2 with a current balance of $20,000 and has two years to run.

Strip Down of Purchase Money Claim Secured by a Motor Vehicle: The 910-Day Rule of the §1325(a) "Hanging Paragraph"

By far the most common use of this strip down power is in connection with automobiles. It is very common for debtors to owe more on their vehicles than they are worth, as the Matthews do on the YR-3 Ford F-150 truck mentioned in earlier examples, and to propose Chapter 13 plans seeking to strip down on that value.

However, BAPCPA has imposed some severe limitations on the right of a Chapter 13 debtor to strip down the amount owed on a vehicle to its value. The last paragraph of §1325(a), added by BAPCPA and known to practitioners as the infamous **hanging paragraph** (so-called because it "hangs" to the end of §1325(a) like an afterthought) provides as follows:

> For purposes of paragraph (5), section 506 shall not apply to a claim described in that paragraph if the creditor has a purchase money security interest securing the debt that is the subject of the claim, the debt was incurred within the 910-day period preceding the date of the filing of the petition, and the collateral for that debt consists of a motor vehicle (as defined in section 30102 of title 49) acquired for the personal use of the debtor, or if collateral for that debt consists of any other thing of value, if the debt was incurred during the 1-year period preceding that filing.

Thus, the strip down to value option cannot be used for automobiles if

- The debt secured by the automobile is a purchase money security interest (the debtor purchased the vehicle on credit from the seller or obtained the loan from the creditor to enable the purchase of the vehicle);
- The debt was incurred within 910 days (two-and-a-half years) preceding the filing of the petition; *and*
- The vehicle was acquired for the "personal use of the debtor."

For example, the Matthews purchased the Ford F-150 truck new almost three years ago and borrowed money from Automotive Financing, Inc. (AFI) in order to do so. Although the debt owed on the truck is therefore a purchase money security interest, and although the truck was purchased for Roger's personal use, the Matthews' plan can strip down the debt owed to AFI to the truck's value because it was purchased more than 910 days (two-and-a-half years) prior to the filing of the petition, triggering the 910-day rule of §1325(a). On the other hand, the Honda Civic was purchased only two years ago, making it a 910 vehicle, so this option is not available to the Matthews as to this vehicle even if the debt secured by it is undersecured.

Technically what the hanging paragraph of §1325(a) says is that §506 does not to apply to 910 vehicles for purposes of the strip down provisions of Chapter 13. This is being construed by the courts to mean that claims secured by 910 vehicles cannot be bifurcated under §506(a). Thus the creditor is entitled to receive the full value of its secured claim rather than the present value of the collateral if the debtor wishes to retain possession of the vehicle. See, e.g., In re Dean, 537 F.3d 1315 (11th Cir. 2008) (rejecting an early interpretation of the hanging paragraph by some courts now almost entirely rejected that reasoned that since that paragraph prevents a Chapter 13 debtor from bifurcating a 910 creditor's claim and stripping it down, it also prevents that claim from being treated as a secured claim but only as an allowed claim for entire prepetition debt, which debtors have to pay in full but without postpetition interest). In order to retain 910 vehicles, Chapter 13 debtors have to propose either a pay through on such secured claims or a payoff of the entire value of the secured claim during the term of the plan even though the claim is undersecured.

Strip Down of Purchase Money Claim Secured by Property Other Than a Motor Vehicle: The Hanging Paragraph Strikes Again

The hanging paragraph of §1325(a) also provides that any debt secured by property other than vehicles ("any other thing of value") is not subject to bifurcation under §506 and thus cannot be stripped down to value if:

■ it is a purchase money security interest and
■ the debt was incurred during the one-year period preceding the filing of the petition.

For example, assume a debtor purchases $5,000 of household appliances on credit and grants the seller a security interest in the items purchased. Since the credit was extended for the purchase of consumer goods, this is a purchase money security interest. Nine months later, the debtor files for Chapter 13 relief and still owes $4,000 on the debt. Debtor would like to strip down this obligation because the household appliances that secure the debt only have a total value of $2,500. But debtor will be unable to do so because of the one-year rule of §1325(a). This debtor might be well advised to delay the Chapter 13 filing until the one-year period has run, if feasible.

As with 910 vehicles, if the Chapter 13 debtor wants to retain possession of secured property falling within the one-year rule, the plan will have to propose a pay through or a payoff of the entire value of the unmodified claim during the plan period.

How the Strip Down Value of Collateral Is Determined

The value of personal property securing a claim for purposes of determining the secured portion of the claim and exercising the strip down right where it is available is defined in §506(a)(2), added by BAPCPA, as the replacement value of the goods on the date the petition is filed without deduction for sale or marketing costs. For goods acquired for personal, family, or household purposes (consumer goods), replacement value means the price a retail merchant would charge for property of that kind, given its age and condition, on the date the petition is filed.

For example, in determining the value of the Ford F-150 truck that the Matthews are stripping down, we would determine the replacement value of that vehicle as of the date the petition is filed. Common sources for determining automobile values are the Kelley Blue Book or the National Automobile Dealers Association (NADA). Debtor's lawyers are more likely to use the former since its values are usually lower than those in NADA.

Application Exercise 2

Go back and read the discussion of Associates Commercial Corp. v. Rash, 520 U.S. 953 (1997), and the codification by BAPCPA of the *Rash* replacement value standard in §506(a)(2) in Chapter Ten, Section C, where we were studying the right of an individual consumer debtor in Chapter 7 to redeem property under §722. Do you see why the replacement value will almost always be greater than the liquidation or foreclosure value of the property, or the casual garage sale value of the property, or even the wholesale value, whether you're dealing with a Chapter 7 redemption or a Chapter 13 strip down?

Defining value in §506(a)(2) as replacement value has by no means ended disputes over what replacement value is with regard to many kinds of property. If the creditor or trustee will not accept the debtor's proposed strip down value, either can object to the confirmation of the plan and an evidentiary hearing may be conducted by the court on the issue of value. Experts may be called by either or both sides to testify on the value dispute. That can be time-consuming and expensive, of course. As a practical matter, determination of the value of property in a strip down is often arrived at by negotiations between the debtor and the affected creditor, usually at the first meeting of creditors. And though the replacement value standard obviously favors the creditor, the debtor often has *leverage* to negotiate a more favorable value since debtor has the option to simply surrender the property to the creditor as discussed later in this section and perhaps even to discharge the balance of the debt.

Determining the "Present Value" of the Collateral for Purposes of Plan Payments

Determining the payments to be made to a secured creditor to give it the value of its collateral as calculated under §506(a) is not simply a matter of dividing the replacement value by the number of plan payments to be made. That is because the debtor is usually not going to pay the creditor that replacement cost as a lump sum at the beginning of the plan. Instead, the debtor is proposing to pay that amount to the creditor in installments over the time of the plan (three to five years). The secured creditor is entitled to receive the value of its collateral, but where that value is going to be paid to him over time rather than immediately, the creditor must be compensated for the delay with some amount of interest, just as a lender of money is entitled to interest until the loan is repaid in full. By adding an interest component to the installment payments of the replacement value of the collateral, we are seeking to quantify the time-price differential involved in the delayed payment to the creditor of the full replacement value of the collateral. Since the full value is being paid over time, the total amount of the debtor's plan payments to the creditor must equal the present value of the collateral. In essence, the plan payments must be discounted by a rate of interest that will ultimately provide the creditor with that present value.

When a Chapter 13 plan calls for a secured claim to be stripped down to present value and for the payments of that value to be made in installments during the term of the plan, as the Matthews are doing on their truck, §1325(a)(5)(B)(ii) and (iii) require that:

- the present value be paid in full during the term of the plan,
- the payments be made in equal installments, and
- the payments be increased to compensate the creditor for the delay in receiving the present value of the collateral in order to give the creditor adequate protection.

For example, when the Matthews strip down on the Ford F-150 truck, they are declaring that AFI will get only the replacement value of the collateral in payment of its claim. If they simply surrendered the truck to AFI, it would be getting that replacement value immediately. But the Matthews' plan contemplates the debtors keeping the truck and paying AFI the value of its claim in installments over the term of the plan. The plan is therefore delaying AFI's receipt of the value of its claim. The Matthews' plan must increase the payments by an appropriate rate of interest to account for that delay and to adequately protect AFI by providing it with the present value of its claim.

Though the Code recognizes that the secured creditor receiving the value of its collateral in delayed payments is entitled to interest to compensate for that delay, it does not specify the appropriate interest rate to be applied to those payments. In Till v. SCS Credit Corp., 541 U.S. 465 (2004), the Supreme Court rejected a creditor's argument that the appropriate rate of interest in such situations is the rate set forth in the contract between the debtor and creditor. The court held instead that the appropriate interest rate to be used is the national prime rate (the interest rate that commercial banks charge their best customers) plus an "upward adjustment" to reflect the risk of nonpayment by the bankrupt debtors (called a "prime plus" rate by practitioners). The Court left the question of the appropriate upward risk adjustment to be decided by the lower courts based on the circumstances of each case. In most cases the risk adjustment will run one to three percentage points.

For example, assume that the contract rate of interest that the Matthews agreed to pay AFI when they purchased the Ford F-150 truck was 10 percent per annum. At the time the petition is filed, the prevailing national prime rate is 6 percent. In the Matthews' plan they strip down the debt owed to AFI to its replacement value and propose to pay that value in installments through the term of the plan. Since AFI is being delayed in receiving the replacement value of the collateral to which it is entitled, the plan adds a Till rate of interest based on the 6 percent prime plus an upward risk adjustment factor of a half point, for a total rate of interest of 6.5 percent. This is the Matthews' proposal to give AFI the present value of its collateral. AFI may object to the half-point risk adjustment and argue for more, perhaps one to two points higher. But the plan rate will still be lower than the contract rate. Do you see why Till is, in most situations, a pro-debtor decision?

Case Preview

In re Wright

Under the hanging paragraph of §1325(a), claims secured by 910 vehicles or property subject to the one-year rule cannot be stripped down; they are not controlled by the bifurcation concept of §506(a). We noted that as to such claims, the debtor, in order to keep the property, will either have to propose a pay through, in which case the contract rate of interest will continue to apply, or a payoff of the full value of the unmodified claim during the term of the plan. If the debtor chooses the latter, however, the creditor is being denied immediate payment of that value, again raising the question of what interest the creditor should receive on those payments in order to compensate it for the delayed receipt of value and the risk of debtor's nonpayment. Should we use the *Till* rate of prime plus in such cases? Or, since the whole basis for excepting such property from strip down is that the bifurcation of §506(a) is inapplicable to such property, is the *Till* rate that was deemed appropriate in a bifurcation and strip down context irrelevant and the contract rate the one to use? As you read In re Wright, consider the following questions:

1. What was the contract rate of interest on this 910 vehicle? What interest rate did the debtor propose to pay the creditor on the modified payments to the creditor under the plan?
2. What two arguments does the creditor make that the contract rate of interest rather than the *Till* rate should apply?
3. Why does the court reject creditor's arguments?

In re Wright

338 B.R. 917 (Bankr. M.D. Ala. 2006)

WILLIAMS, JR., Bankruptcy Judge.

Centrix Funds Series CLPF ("Centrix") filed an objection to confirmation of the chapter 13 plan proposed by the debtors. At issue is whether under . . . BAPCPA the plan may modify the contractual interest rate applicable to the creditor's secured claim. . . .

FACTUAL FINDINGS . . .

On May 29, 2004, the debtors purchased a 2004 Nissan Altima. The purchase price of the vehicle was financed by Centrix, and Centrix took a security interest in the vehicle.

On December 5, 2005, the debtors filed this chapter 13 case. The plan treats the claim of Centrix as fully secured. Further, the plan provides that Centrix will be paid interest on its claim at the rate of 7.75%.

Centrix filed a proof of claim totaling $18,747.38. The claim reflects a contract interest rate of 17.90%.

CONCLUSIONS OF LAW

Centrix contends that it is entitled to the 17.90% contract interest rate on its secured claim. The court disagrees.

If a debtor retains lien-encumbered property under a chapter 13 plan and pays the underlying secured claim in deferred installments, the creditor is entitled to interest on the secured claim. The Code provides:

> (ii) the value, as of the effective date of the plan, of property to be distributed under the plan on account of such claim is not less than the allowed amount of such claim;

11 U.S.C. §1325(a)(5)(B)(ii).

The Supreme Court in Till v. SCS Credit Corporation, 541 U.S. 465 (2004) addressed the issue of the appropriate rate of interest to be applied under §1325(a)(5)(B)(ii). There the Court held that the so-called formula approach, which starts with the prime national interest rate and adjusts for risk of nonpayment, is the appropriate method in determining the adequate interest rate to be paid on secured claims. Id. at 478-80. In so doing, the Court specifically rejected the presumptive contract interest rate approach as the proper method to determine §1325(a)(5)(B)(ii) interest. Id. at 477.

Centrix contends that under the facts in this case Till no longer applies. First, Centrix maintains that Till is applicable only to chapter 13 plans that are "crammed down." Centrix reasons that because its claim in this case is fully secured, this is not a "cram down" case. Centrix, however, confuses the term "cram down" with the term "strip down."

"Cram down" is a term that refers to confirmation of a chapter 13 plan over the objection of the holder of a claim. Associates Commercial Corp. v. Rash, 520 U.S. 953, 957 (1997). The term "strip down" refers to the bifurcation of a claim into its secured and unsecured components under 11 U.S.C. §506. The secured claim is said to be stripped down to the value of the collateral.

Although Till interpreted 11 U.S.C. §1325(a)(5)(B)(ii) in a case involving the strip down of a secured claim, the statute itself is broader and applies to all cram down cases. Hence, the decision in Till is not confined merely to those cases where the value of the collateral is less than the creditor's claim. Rather, Till applies in all chapter 13 cases which are being confirmed over the objection of a secured creditor irrespective of the value of its collateral in relation to the amount of its claim.

Secondly, Centrix contends that Till has been abrogated by the BAPCPA amendments. [The opinion quotes §1325(a)]. . . . Centrix contends that this provision prevents any modification of its contractual rights, including the interest rate. The court disagrees.

This new provision prohibits the application of §506 to the claims of secured creditors having a purchase-money security interest in a debtor's personal vehicle if the debt was incurred within 910 days prior to bankruptcy. Simply put, the claims of these creditors must be treated as fully secured under the plan. However, this restriction on bifurcation does not protect these creditors from modification of other contractual rights.

The BAPCPA amendments to §1325 simply do not address the issue of the appropriate interest rate applicable to secured claims under §1325(a)(5)(B)(ii). Thus, *Till* has not been abrogated by the BAPCPA amendments.

Had Congress intended to create a complete safe harbor for the automobile lender with a purchase-money security interest, it could have expressly done so, but it did not. Indeed, the law permits modification of the rights of secured creditors. The only complete safe harbor from any modification is that provided to home mortgagees under 11 U.S.C. §1322(b)(2). See In re Robinson, 338 B.R. 70 (Bankr. W.D. Mo. 2006); In re Johnson, 337 B.R. 269 (Bankr. M.D.N.C. 2006).

CONCLUSION

For the foregoing reasons the court concludes that the plan may properly modify the contract interest rate applicable to the secured claim of Centrix. Pursuant to Fed. R. Bankr. Proc. 9021, a separate order will enter overruling Centrix's objection to confirmation of the plan.

Post-Case Follow-Up

It has become widely accepted that the *Till* rate applies to modified payments on 910 property rather than the contract rate regardless of which is higher or lower. How firmly fixed this idea is can be seen in In re Taranto, 365 B.R. 85 (B.A.P. 6th Cir. 2007), where the contract rate on the 910 vehicle was zero percent and the plan proposed modified payments to the creditor along with that rate of interest . . . zero. The court ordered that notwithstanding the zero percent contract rate, creditor was to receive the *Till* rate on the modified payments rejecting debtor's argument that such rate gave the creditor a windfall and despite the fact that debtor's plan also proposed to pay the 910 creditor in full on an earlier schedule than that provided for in the contract! That outcome may seem unfair to the debtor but you have to remember that an allowed secured claim on a 910 vehicle is entitled to be paid in full with no strip down allowed. The Supreme Court in *Till* interpreted §1325(a)(5)(B) to require that the secured creditor's claim must be paid (1) in full at the time of confirmation or (2) over time with interest to insure creditor receives present value as of the date of confirmation. Contract interest rate is irrelevant. Remember too that per §1325(a)(5)(A) the creditor can accept a plan calling for an interest rate different from the contract rate or the *Till* rate. The *Till* rate is used where the creditor does not consent.

In re Wright: Real Life Applications

1. Which of the following creditors are entitled to receive their contract rate of interest on plan payments, which are entitled to receive *Till* rate of interest on such payments, and which are entitled to receive no interest on their plan payments:

   a. Debtor purchased a washing machine from creditor nine months before petition filed with purchase price to be paid over 24 months at 12 percent per annum interest. Washing machine value now is $250 and balance owed is $500. Creditor did not have debtor grant it a security interest in the washing machine to secure payment. Debtor claims full value of washing machine as exempt and proposes to keep it in 100 percent plan.

   b. Debtor purchased washing machine from creditor 15 months before petition filed with purchase price to be paid over 24 months at zero percent interest. Washing machine value now is $250 and balance owed is $400. Debtor granted security interest in the washing machine to creditor to secure payment. Debtor proposes to pay creditor $250 over 60 months of 100 percent plan.

   c. Debtor purchased washing machine from creditor 15 months before petition filed with purchase price to be paid over 24 months at 10 percent per annum interest. Washing machine value now is $250 and balance owed is $200. Debtor granted security interest to creditor in washing machine to secure payment. Debtor proposes to pay creditor $200 over 60 months of 100 percent plan and retain possession by exempting $50 equity.

   d. Debtor purchased washing machine from creditor 15 months before petition filed with purchase price to be paid over 24 months at 2 percent per annum interest. Washing machine value now is $250 and balance owed is $200. Debtor granted security interest in washing machine to creditor to secure payment. Debtor proposes to pay creditor $200 as scheduled in contract during the first nine months of the five-year 100 percent plan and retain possession by exempting $50 equity.

2. Which creditor on these two 910 vehicles is entitled to its contract rate of interest and which to the *Till* rate?

   a. Vehicle worth $10,000 and secured creditor owed $12,000. Debtor proposes to keep the vehicle but increase the monthly payments to creditor in an amount double the contractually scheduled payments so debt will be paid in full within the term of the plan.

   b. Vehicle worth $10,000 and secured creditor owed $12,000. Debtor proposes to keep the vehicle but reduce scheduled payments to creditor for 24 months while other short-term obligations are paid, then increase payments to creditor in last 36 months of plan.

5. Modifying a Secured Claim by Adjusting Payments

When a secured claim is stripped down to the value of its collateral, payments to be made by the debtor to the creditor will no longer be governed by the payment schedule of the underlying contract, but by the payments proposed in the plan. But can a Chapter 13 debtor who does not or cannot strip down a secured claim to its value propose to modify installment payments to a secured creditor by lowering those payments during the term of the plan? Sections 1322(b)(2) and 1325(a)(5) do allow such a modification with one important caveat: Per §1325(a)(5)(B)(ii), the full value of the claim must be paid during the term of the plan.

For example, the Matthews owe Columbiana Federal Savings & Loan (CFSL) a total of $7,500 on an original loan of $12,000 made two years ago for which they obligated themselves to pay $240 per month for five years. There are currently 36 monthly payments remaining on the contract. The debt is secured by the Honda Civic automobile that Susan drives. The vehicle is a 910 vehicle since they have owned it only two years, which means they cannot strip down CFSL's secured claim to the present value of the vehicle. However, their Chapter 13 plan (Exhibit 15.2) proposes to pay CFSL the full amount of the unmodified claim at the contract rate of 7.5 percent but over the full 60 months of the plan, rather than over the remaining 36 months of the contract. This will require them to pay CFSL only $150 per month over the term of the plan. CFSL will retain its lien on the automobile. The court can approve this plan even over CFSL's objection pursuant to §1325(a)(5)(B)(ii) (thus it is a cram down) because the creditor is receiving the full amount of its allowed claim during the term of the plan. Note that this saves the Matthews $90 per month over what they were paying CFSL (see the budget in the Assignment Memorandum in Appendix B).

Application Exercise 3

Even though this plan provision saves the Matthews $90 a month over what they were paying CFSL, it may not mean that they come out better in the long run. How much total principal and interest would the Matthews have paid CFSL if they paid off the car over the remaining 36 months of the contract? How much will they pay CFSL in principal and interest over the 60 months of the plan?

In the last example, if the Matthews' plan proposed to not only extend the number of installment payments to CFSL but to also use a *Till* rate of interest for such payments rather than the contract rate, that would raise an unanswered question. And if the contract rate on that debt was 15 percent per annum rather than 7.5 percent, it would be very tempting for their attorney to propose a *Till* rate. But often Chapter 13 debtors will choose not to propose a lower *Till* rate for modified plan payments when they could do so because they do not wish to offend a creditor with whom they hope to do business in the future.

6. Surrender of Secured Property

Pursuant to §1325(a)(5)(C), a Chapter 13 debtor may propose to surrender property subject to a security interest to the secured creditor where there is no equity for the estate and where no lien avoidance action is plausible. The creditor must then move to have the automatic stay lifted in order to take possession of the property. The trustee will abandon the property to the creditor pursuant to §554 of the Code on the grounds that it is not needed for the reorganization. (See the discussion of abandonment in Chapter Ten, Section A.)

As we know, §506(a) bifurcates most secured claims by providing that a secured creditor's claim is secured only up to the value of the collateral and is an unsecured claim to the extent the debt exceeds the value of the collateral. Thus if the debtor surrenders the property securing the debt but its value is less than the amount owed (i.e., the creditor is undersecured or partially secured), the balance still owing on the debt after the property is repossessed and sold will be treated as a general unsecured claim.

For example, the Matthews have decided to surrender the YR-8 Chevy Malibu. This surrender is referenced in their plan. Note that this relieves them of the $120 per month payment they were making to Car World (see the budget in the Assignment Memorandum in Appendix B). They owed Car World $5,000 on that debt. Upon surrender, Car World will move the court, pursuant to §362, to lift the automatic stay. Since there is no equity in the car (it is worth only $2,000 and the amount owed is $5,000), the trustee will not object to the motion to lift stay and will abandon pursuant to §554. Assuming the car is in fact worth $2,000, the $3,000 balance of the debt ($5,000 minus the $2,000 value of the car surrendered) will be treated as a general unsecured debt under the plan.

Chapter 13 Debtors and the Making Home Affordable Program

In response to the wave of home foreclosures resulting from the recent subprime lending crisis and Great Recession, the U.S. Treasury Department (USDOT) in 2009 announced its Making Home Affordable (MHA) programs (www.makinghomeaffordable.gov/Pages/default.aspx) including the Homeowners Affordable Modification Program (HAMP). Under HAMP qualified homeowners who have a pre-2009 Freddie Mac or Fannie Mae mortgage or mortgage serviced by a participating private lender may be able to refinance at a lower interest rate or temporarily reduce their monthly mortgage payments without default. Various incentives are provided to lenders to encourage their agreement to the mortgage modification or, if the modification fails, to agree to a short sale or deed in lieu of foreclosure. When the first HAMP Guidelines were issued by the USDOT, there was no mention of HAMP being available to debtors in bankruptcy. Through the efforts of various bankruptcy judges and trustees who recognized that a Chapter 13 bankruptcy was ideally suited to proposing a HAMP modification to a debtor's home mortgage, that oversight was corrected. In Supplemental Directive 10-02 issued in March 2010 (www.hmpadmin.com/portal/programs/docs/hamp_servicer/sd1002.pdf), the USDOT clarified that "servicers must consider borrowers in active bankruptcy for HAMP if a request is received from the borrower, borrower's counsel, or bankruptcy trustee." Thus HAMP provides other options for modification for the Chapter 13 debtor who owns a residence. Of course, modifications based on HAMP must be agreed to by the mortgagee and cannot be crammed down on that creditor.

In re Wright

What happens when a debtor surrenders a 910 vehicle or other collateral subject to the one-year rule of the §1325(a) hanging paragraph? Since that paragraph says that such claims are not governed by the bifurcation concept of §506(a) and the debtor therefore cannot strip down the value of the secured claim to the value of the collateral, it might follow that when the debtor chooses to surrender such property, the creditor must accept that surrender as a full satisfaction of its claim rather than bifurcating its secured claim into an unsecured claim for the deficiency owing after disposition of the surrendered collateral. After all, isn't what's sauce for the goose sauce for the gander? As you read In re Wright, consider the following questions:

1. If the hanging paragraph of §1325(a) prevents the claim of the undersecured 910 creditor from being bifurcated into secured and unsecured part per §506(a), what other basis is there for that creditor to establish an unsecured claim for the balance owed following a surrender of the collateral by the debtor?
2. What is the role of state law in the decision by this court?
3. How was the Supreme Court's decision in Butner v. United States, 440 U.S. 48 (1979), material to the decision in this case?

In re Wright
492 F.3d 829 (7th Cir. 2007)

EASTERBROOK, Circuit Judge.

Bankruptcy judges across the nation have divided over the effect of the unnumbered hanging paragraph that [BAPCPA] added to §1325(a) of the Bankruptcy Code.... Section 1325, part of Chapter 13, specifies the circumstances under which a consumer's plan of repayment can be confirmed. The hanging paragraph says that, for the purpose of a Chapter 13 plan, §506 of the Code, 11 U.S.C. §506, does not apply to certain secured loans.

Section 506(a) divides loans into secured and unsecured portions; the unsecured portion is the amount by which the debt exceeds the current value of the collateral. In a Chapter 13 bankruptcy, consumers may retain the collateral (despite contractual provisions entitling creditors to repossess) by making monthly payments that the judge deems equal to the market value of the asset, with a rate of interest that the judge will set (rather than the contractual rate).... This procedure is known as a "cramdown" — the court crams down the creditor's throat the substitution of money for the collateral, a situation that creditors usually oppose because the court may underestimate the collateral's market value and the appropriate interest rate, and the debtor may fail to make all promised payments, so that the payment stream falls short of the collateral's full value. . . .

The question we must decide is what happens when, as a result of the hanging paragraph, §506 vanishes from the picture. The majority view among bankruptcy judges is that, with §506(a) gone, creditors cannot divide their loans into secured and unsecured components. Because §1325(a)(5)(C) allows a debtor to surrender the collateral to the lender, it follows (on this view) that surrender fully satisfies the borrower's obligations. If this is so, then many secured loans have been rendered non-recourse, no matter what the contract provides. . . . The minority view is that Article 9 of the Uniform Commercial Code plus the law of contracts entitle the creditor to an unsecured deficiency judgment after surrender of the collateral, unless the contract itself provides that the loan is without recourse against the borrower. . . . That unsecured balance must be treated the same as other unsecured debts under the Chapter 13 plan. . . .

[D]ebtors in this proceeding, owe more on their purchase-money automobile loan than the car is worth. Because the purchase occurred within 910 days of the bankruptcy's commencement, the hanging paragraph in §1325(a)(5) applies. . . .

Debtors proposed a plan that would surrender the car to the creditor and pay nothing on account of the difference between the loan's balance and the collateral's market value. After taking the minority position on the effect of bypassing §506, the bankruptcy judge declined to approve the Chapter 13 plan, because debtors did not propose to pay any portion of the shortfall.

. . .

Like the bankruptcy court, we think that, by knocking out §506, the hanging paragraph leaves the parties to their contractual entitlements. True enough, §506(a) divides claims into secured and unsecured components. . . . Yet it is a mistake to assume, as the majority of bankruptcy courts have done, that §506 is the *only* source of authority for a deficiency judgment when the collateral is insufficient. The Supreme Court held in Butner v. United States, 440 U.S. 48, (1979), that state law determines rights and obligations when the Code does not supply a federal rule. . . .

The contract between the Wrights and their lender is explicit: If the debt is not paid, the collateral may be seized and sold. Creditor "must account to Buyer for any surplus. Buyer shall be liable for any deficiency." In other words, the contract creates an ordinary secured loan with recourse against the borrower. Just in case there were doubt, the contract provides that the parties enjoy all of their rights under the Uniform Commercial Code. Section 9-615(d)(2) of the UCC, enacted in Illinois as 810 ILCS 5/9-615(d)(2), provides that the obligor must satisfy any deficiency if the collateral's value is insufficient to cover the amount due.

If the Wrights had surrendered their car the day before filing for bankruptcy, the creditor would have been entitled to treat any shortfall in the collateral's value as an unsecured debt. It is hard to see why the result should be different if the debtors surrender the collateral the day after filing for bankruptcy when, given the hanging paragraph, no operative section of the Bankruptcy Code contains any contrary rule. Section 306(b) of the 2005 Act, which enacted the hanging paragraph, is captioned

"Restoring the Foundation for Secured Credit." This implies replacing a contract-defeating provision such as §506 (which allows judges rather than the market to value the collateral and set an interest rate, and may prevent creditors from repossessing) with the agreement freely negotiated between debtor and creditor. Debtors do not offer any argument that "the Foundation for Secured Credit" could be "restored" by making all purchase-money secured loans non-recourse; they do not argue that non-recourse lending is common in consumer transactions, and it is hard to imagine that Congress took such an indirect means of making non-recourse lending *compulsory*.

Appearing as *amicus curiae*, the National Association of Consumer Bankruptcy Attorneys makes the bold argument that loans covered by the hanging paragraph cannot be treated as secured in any respect. Only §506 provides for an "allowed secured claim," *amicus* insists, so the entire debt must be unsecured. This also would imply that a lender is not entitled to any post-petition interest. *Amicus* recognizes that §502 rather than §506 determines whether a claim should be "allowed" but insists that only §506 permits an "allowed" claim to be a "secured" one.

This line of argument makes the same basic mistake as the debtors' position: it supposes that contracts and state law are irrelevant unless specifically implemented by the Bankruptcy Code. *Butner* holds that the presumption runs the other way: rights under state law count in bankruptcy unless the Code says otherwise. Creditors don't need §506 to create, allow, or recognize security interests, which rest on contracts (and the UCC) rather than federal law. Section 502 tells bankruptcy courts to allow claims that stem from contractual debts; nothing in §502 disfavors or curtails secured claims. Limitations, if any, depend on §506, which the hanging paragraph makes inapplicable to purchase-money interests in personal motor vehicles granted during the 910 days preceding bankruptcy (and in other assets during the year before bankruptcy).

Both the debtors and the *amicus curiae* observe that many decisions, of which United States v. Ron Pair Enterprises, Inc., 489 U.S. 235, 238-39 (1989), is a good example, state that §506 governs the treatment of secured claims in bankruptcy. No one doubts this, but the question at hand is what happens when §506 does not apply. The fallback under *Butner* is the parties' contract (to the extent the deal is enforceable under state law), rather than non-recourse secured debt (the Wrights' position) or no security interest (the *amicus curiae*'s position). And there is no debate about how the parties' contract works: the secured lender is entitled to an (unsecured) deficiency judgment for the difference between the value of the collateral and the balance on the loan.

By surrendering the car, debtors gave their creditor the full market value of the collateral. Any shortfall must be treated as an unsecured debt. It need not be paid in full, any more than the Wrights' other unsecured debts, but it can't be written off *in toto* while other unsecured creditors are paid some fraction of their entitlements.

AFFIRMED.

Post-Case Follow-Up

You will recall that we considered the significance of the Supreme Court's *Butner* decision in Chapter Five, Section B, where it was highlighted. Once again we see just how significant the role of state law is in interpreting and applying provisions of the Code. How would *Wright* have been decided if UCC Article 9 as enacted in the state of Illinois provided that a secured creditor who chooses to repossess collateral rather than sue for the underlying debt has no recourse against the debtor for a deficiency? Would the decision have been the same if the contract between the parties had not contained explicit language stating that debtor must account to creditor for the balance owed following seizure and sale of the collateral and be liable for any deficiency? The Seventh Circuit's interpretation of the role of the hanging paragraph in the context of surrender has become the majority view but there is still disagreement. See, e.g., In re Adams, 403 B.R. 387, 391-392 (Bankr. E.D. La. 2009) ("The hanging paragraph, in effect, provides a 910 Creditor with a secured claim, up to the value of that claim. If a debtor intends to retain the collateral, the creditor is entitled to full payment, regardless of the value of the collateral. If, however, the debtor surrenders the collateral, the entire claim is satisfied. Once the hanging paragraph eliminates §506, the claim and collateral become indivisible."). Determine if the courts of the federal district or circuit where you plan to practice have addressed this issue.

In re Wright: Real Life Applications

1. Assume you practice in a federal district that follows *Wright* but applicable state law provides that a secured creditor who chooses to repossess collateral rather than sue for the underlying debt has no recourse against the debtor for a deficiency. You represent the creditor who holds a security interest in a Chapter 13 debtor's 910 vehicle on which $10,000 is still owed but which is worth only $7,000. Your client did not attempt repossession prior to the petition being filed.
   a. If debtor chooses to surrender this vehicle to your client, can you file an unsecured claim for the balance owed on behalf of your client?
   b. Would your answer be different if the contract between your client and the debtor had an express provision stating that the debtor would be liable for any deficiency in the event of repossession and sale of the vehicle?
2. Assume you practice in a federal district that follows *Adams* and that the applicable state law provides that a secured creditor who repossesses and sells collateral is entitled to recover any deficiency from the debtor.
   a. If debtor chooses to surrender this vehicle to your client, can you file an unsecured claim for the balance owed on behalf of your client?
   b. Would your answer be different if the contract between your client and the debtor had an express provision stating that the debtor would be liable for any deficiency in the event of repossession and sale of the vehicle?

7. Sale of Property Free and Clear of Liens

Section 1303 of the Code authorizes a Chapter 13 debtor to ask that secured property be sold free and clear of liens pursuant to §363(f). As in a Chapter 7 liquidation, such sale will be subject to the secured creditor's §363(k) right to credit-bid for the property at the sale (see the discussion in Chapter Ten, Section A).

For example, assume a Chapter 13 debtor owns an empty lot valued at $25,000. Bank holds a mortgage on such property with a balance owed of $18,000. Debtor cannot exempt the equity and unsecured creditors will expect that equity to be paid to them. Debtor's plan will likely propose that the property be sold free and clear of liens.

Chapter Summary

- Priority claims must be paid in full in a Chapter 13 plan, though payment may be made in deferred installments over the term of the plan.
- The plan may propose to pay a secured claim in full as scheduled during the term of the plan and beyond and for the creditor to retain its lien on the secured property, an arrangement known as a pay through. Arrearages on secured claims may be cured by installment payments over a reasonable time made within the term of the plan. Interest may be required on the arrearage payments if the underlying agreement or state law requires.
- As in a Chapter 7, the Chapter 13 debtor can avoid a judicial lien in property that impairs an exemption unless the lien arises out of a domestic support obligation. But in Chapter 13 the debtor may also avoid a consensual security interest in household goods and furnishings, wearing apparel, appliances, tools of the trade, and other such items to the extent the lien impairs an exemption in such property, so long as it is not a purchase money security interest.
- A Chapter 13 plan may strip down the amount of an undersecured claim to the present value of the collateral, pay the full amount of the reduced secured claim over the term of the plan, treat the balance of the debt as unsecured, and retain the collateral. Claims secured only by the debtor's primary residence are excluded from the strip down option unless the last payment is due during the term of the plan. Courts are split over whether Chapter 13 strip off is available where the mortgage in debtor's primary residence is wholly undersecured. Strip down is also disallowed for vehicles purchased for personal use by debtor within 910 days of the filing of the petition that are subject to a PMSI and for any other property purchased by the debtor within one year of filing the petition that is subject to a PMSI.
- Where strip down is allowed, the present value of the collateral is the replacement value as of the date the petition is filed. If the stripped down value will be paid to the creditor in installments, interest must be added to the payments calculated

using not the contract rate but the "*Till* rate," the national prime together with an appropriate risk adjustment.

■ The Chapter 13 plan can modify the rights of a secured creditor by adjusting downward the amount of the periodic payments the secured creditor is to receive and/or extending the payment period accordingly so long as the full present value of the secured claim is paid during the term of the plan.

■ A debtor may surrender collateralized property to the secured creditor as part of a plan where no lien avoidance is plausible and the standing trustee will abandon the property for the estate. Where there is likely to be equity in collateralized property for the estate, the plan may ask that such property be sold free and clear of liens.

Applying the Concepts

1. Assume you are representing Suk-min and Mina Yoon, a married couple, who are planning to file a petition in Chapter 13. You are working on their proposed Chapter 13 plan, which will run for 60 months. Answer the following.

   a. The Yoons own a home that is worth $200,000. They owe $150,000 to Bank, which holds the mortgage on the home and have ten years of scheduled payments to Bank remaining on the underlying note. The Yoons can exempt the $50,000 of owner's equity they have in the home. The couple is current on their payments to Bank and would like to avoid losing it in the bankruptcy proceeding. Can they go through Chapter 13 and keep the home? If so, what would you propose in the plan to enable the Yoons to keep their home?

   b. Assume the Yoons are two payments behind to Bank on the home mortgage and Bank is threatening foreclosure but has not yet initiated foreclosure proceedings. Can the Yoons still keep their home while going through Chapter 13? If so, what would you propose in the plan to enable the Yoons to keep their home?

   c. Assume that when the Yoons come to you to discuss their bankruptcy options, Bank has already instituted foreclosure proceedings and the foreclosure sale was conducted yesterday. However, a foreclosure deed has not yet been delivered to the buyer at foreclosure. The jurisdiction follows In re Medaglia, 402 B.R. 530 (Bankr. D.R.I. 2009), and the controlling law on foreclosure sales is the same as in that case. Can the Yoons still keep their home while going through Chapter 13? If so, what would you propose in the plan to enable the Yoons to keep their home?

   d. Assume the balance owed to Bank on the note is $225,000 and the Yoons are current on their payments to Bank. Can the plan strip down the balance owed Bank to the $200,000 value of the home and then propose a pay through so the Yoons can keep their home?

   e. Assume the balance owed to Bank on the note is $225,000 and the home is worth $200,000. There is a second mortgage on the home in favor of Credit Union with a balance of $25,000. Can the Yoons strip off the mortgage of

Credit Union on the home and treat the $25,000 as an unsecured claim in their plan? The jurisdiction follows In re Zimmer, 313 F.3d 1220 (9th Cir. 2002).

f. Would your answer to the last question be different if the note to Credit Union called for all payments to be made over the next 48 months? The jurisdiction follows In re Paschen, 296 F.3d 1203 (11th Cir. 2002).

g. The Yoons own a YR-5 Chevrolet they purchased used 18 months ago from Dealer for personal use. Dealer financed the purchase and the Yoons still owe Dealer $6,000 on the vehicle, which is collateral for the credit purchase. The vehicle is only worth $5,000. Can the Yoons strip down the secured claim of Dealer to the value of the vehicle to the $5,000 value and propose a pay through in order to keep it? Would your answer change if the Yoons had purchased the vehicle 32 months ago?

h. The Yoons purchased a Smart TV from Best Buys 18 months ago for $3,000. Best Buys financed the purchase and the Yoons still owe Best Buys $2,000 on the TV in which Best Buys took a security interest to secure payment. The TV is only worth $1,000. Can the Yoons strip down the balance of the secured debt owed to Best Buys to the TV's value of $1,000 and propose a pay through to keep the TV? Would your answer change if the Yoons had purchased the TV from Best Buys ten months ago? The Yoons have decided to surrender the TV to Best Buys if they cannot strip down the secured claim of Smart TV to its $1,000 value. If they do that will the entire $2,000 claim of Best Buys be extinguished or must the plan propose to pay the $1,000 balance owing to Best Buys following the surrender as an unsecured claim? The jurisdiction follows In re Wright, 492 F.3d 829 (7th Cir. 2007).

2. Take a look at the Matthews' Schedule C (Document 4 in their case file). Why did they claim Roger's plumbing tools and their furniture as exempt notwithstanding the consensual lien of CCFC in those items? Why didn't they claim an exemption in their residence? In the YR-3 Ford truck? In the YR-8 Malibu? Why was it necessary to claim an exemption in the YR-4 Honda Civic?

3. Locate and read Assignment Memorandum #3 in Appendix D. If the instructor so directs, begin drafting a proposed Chapter 13 plan for Nick and Pearl Murphy focusing on the treatment of their priority and secured debts. You should assume that their Chapter 13 case is being filed in the U.S. bankruptcy court for your federal district.

The Chapter 13 Case: The Plan: Treatment of Non-Priority Unsecured Claims

In this chapter we continue our examination of the actual terms of a Chapter 13 plan by focusing on options for treatment of non-priority unsecured debt provided by the Code. We will consider the circumstances under which a debtor may propose a plan that pays unsecured creditors less than 100 percent. In addition, we will take a practical look at how payments to creditors get made under a Chapter 13 plan with the use of wage orders, payments to creditors through the Standing Trustee, and sometimes with payments made outside the plan.

A. TREATMENT OF NON-PRIORITY (GENERAL) UNSECURED CLAIMS IN THE CHAPTER 13 PLAN

1. Curing Arrearages and Modifying the Obligation of Unsecured Debt

Key Concepts

- A Chapter 13 plan may provide for modification of unsecured claims in a variety of ways including curing of arrearages and adjusting the amount of installment payments during the term of the plan
- A Chapter 13 plan may provide for paying unsecured creditors less than 100 percent of what they are owed and for discharging the balance if the plan calls for the payment of all of the debtor's projected disposable income over the applicable commitment period and if unsecured creditors will receive at least as much in the Chapter 13 plan as they would have received in a Chapter 7 liquidation
- The debtor's disposable income funding the plan over its term is normally paid to the Standing Trustee via wage order and other devices and the Trustee then makes the payments to creditors
- The plan may call for some payments to be made outside the plan by the debtor or a third party other than the Standing Trustee

Sections 1322(b)(3) and (5) allow a plan to propose curing arrearages arising from prepetition default on unsecured claims just as it can on secured claims. In fact, to qualify as a 100 percent plan (one calling for payment of all unsecured claims in full, discussed in more detail below), that plan *must* cure any arrearages owed on unsecured claims and must do so during the term of the plan.

Section 1322(b)(2) allows the Chapter 13 plan to modify the rights of unsecured creditors by modifying the amount of payments due or the time over which they will be paid.

For example, the Matthews owe $25,000 in unsecured debt for hospital and doctor bills at the time their petition is filed. This amount is due and payable immediately to the various creditors. But their plan calls for paying these creditors some amounts in monthly installments over the term of the plan. Section 1322(b)(2) permits this modification of these unsecured obligations. Interest is not normally an issue when unsecured debt is modified in a Chapter 13 plan since the creditor's claim is not being valued by any collateral and the creditor is not being deprived of the right to possess any such collateral. Moreover, as we consider in the next section, a Chapter 13 plan may propose to pay unsecured creditors less than the full amount of their claim anyway subject to the various requirements for plan confirmation.

2. Classes of Unsecured Claims in a Chapter 13 Plan

Section 1322(b)(1) permits a Chapter 13 plan to create separate classes of non-priority unsecured claims and to treat each class of claims differently from one another. Classes are designated groups of creditor claims or equity interests with members of each class receiving equal treatment under the plan but different classes receiving disparate treatment. Creation of classes in a plan of reorganization is commonplace in Chapter 11 business reorganization proceedings. They are less common in Chapter 13 plans.

For example, a debtor engaged in business may put unsecured consumer debt in one class and unsecured business debt in another. A consumer who is jointly liable with a nondebtor on a debt may choose to place that debt in a separate class for favorable treatment in order to protect the non-debtor.

The debtor is not free to create any classes of unsecured debt he or she wishes or to propose favorable treatment for some over others. If that were so, debtors would routinely put non-dischargeable debts (to be discussed in Chapter Sixteen, Section E) such as student loans in one class for favorable treatment over dischargeable debts in another class, a practice that has been ruled impermissible in many cases (see, e.g., In re Simmonds, 288 B.R. 737 (Bankr. N.D. Tex. 2003) (mere fact that a Chapter 13 debtor's student loan debts are non-dischargeable is not sufficient basis for allowing debtor to freely discriminate in favor of such debts in his or her proposed plan and discrimination was "unfair," to extent that, due to such discrimination, other unsecured creditors received less than that to which they would have been entitled over first 36 months of plan)). There are three requirements imposed on classifications of unsecured debt:

- §1322(b)(1) requires that only claims that are substantially similar can be grouped in the same class;

- ▥ §1322(b)(1) provides that a plan cannot discriminate unfairly against any class; and

- ▥ §1322(a)(3) requires that claims within the same class be treated the same for purposes of payment.

The second requirement, that the plan not discriminate unfairly against any class, is the one most likely to draw objection. If a debtor's proposed plan with classes of debt draws an objection, the burden is on the debtor to show why the differing treatment of the classes is fair.

Application Exercise 1

Section 1322(b)(1) expressly recognizes the right to treat a consumer debt on which a non-debtor is jointly liable with the debtor differently. And the unfairness of attempting to treat non-dischargeable debt more favorably than dischargeable debt can be readily seen. What about disputed debt being treated differently than undisputed debt? If Marta Carlson, our Chapter 7 debtor, was in a Chapter 13 plan, could she place the debt her former husband was responsible for paying but didn't in one class for less favorable treatment? Could the Matthews put their credit card debt attributable to fees and penalties in one class for less favorable treatment? Or could they put some or all of their credit card debt in one class for more favorable treatment because of their desire to keep those particular credit cards? Could they classify their medical or hospital debt separately and provide for more favorable treatment in order to maintain the relationship with a particular doctor or hospital? What other classifications can you think of that might be plausible to a consumer debtor? What are the arguments that such classifications do or do not discriminate unfairly?

Section 502(b)(2) disallows claims for unmatured (postpetition) interest, and so postpetition interest need not be paid on unsecured claims in a Chapter 13 plan.

You can see from this discussion that a great deal of flexibility is possible in a Chapter 13 plan. And fashioning a plan for a debtor involves understanding the provisions of the Code, budgets, and how various financial arrangements work.

3. The Less Than 100 Percent Plan

A Chapter 13 plan may propose to pay unsecured claims in full over the term of the plan. We call that a 100 percent plan. Such a plan may modify the original terms of payment to unsecured creditors, as discussed in the preceding section, and if the court approves the debtor's proposed plan, the creditors must accept the modified payments. Most unsecured creditors will not complain about proposed modifications if the plan does in fact pay them all they are owed.

A Chapter 13 plan need not pay non-priority (general) unsecured claims in full but a less than 100 percent plan must meet two requirements. First, pursuant to §1325(b)(1)(B), the plan must propose to pay unsecured creditors all debtor's projected disposable income over the applicable commitment period (the term of the plan). Second, pursuant to §1325(a)(4), the plan must provide that the unsecured creditors will receive at least as much under the plan as they would receive if the debtor's assets were liquidated under Chapter 7. This liquidation analysis is also called the "best interests test" since it determines whether it is in the best interests of unsecured creditors for debtors to be in a Chapter 13 rather than a Chapter 7. Let's consider both of these requirements in order.

The Disposable Income Requirement

To understand the disposable income requirement for a non–100 percent plan consider the following hypothetical: Assume a debtor calculates that she will have $150 per month, or $9,000, in disposable income using during the term of her five-year plan. Debtor has $45,000 in unsecured debt. She cannot propose a plan that will pay unsecured creditors less than 100 percent of what they are owed unless the plan calls for paying all of that projected disposable income to those unsecured creditors. If the plan does call for paying the full $150 a month to unsecured creditors for the full term of the plan, it can be confirmed. But if the plan only calls for paying $125 a month to the unsecured creditors for the term of the plan, it will not be confirmed.

But we are still left with the question of how much disposable income the debtor has that must be paid in full on unsecured claims for the term of the plan. In Chapter Thirteen, Section B, we discovered that neither the debtor's Schedules I or J, even together with Forms 122C-1 and 122C-2 (if an above median debtor), precisely calculate the actual disposable income figure of a Chapter 13 debtor. These forms and schedules, we said, are merely starting points because the final calculation must await the debtor's decisions about how to treat secured claims in the plan and about likely future changes in income and expenses. So how do we, finally, determine the debtor's disposable income when debtor proposes a less than 100 percent plan? Remember, §1325(b)(1) provides that a non–100 percent plan must propose to pay *all* of the debtor's projected disposable income over the term of the plan to unsecured creditors.

The Matthews have finally made those decisions in consultation with their lawyer. They know what their income is and is likely to be over the term of the plan. They have calculated their likely living expenses over the term of the plan. As we've seen in this chapter, they've made decisions about what to do with their various secured debts. In Exhibit 15.1 you will find the final budget that the attorney for the Matthews has put together reflecting these decisions and what the Matthews will be able to pay out of their projected income on the secured debt they plan to reaffirm and retain through the plan, on the priority unsecured debt that they must pay in full, and on their remaining unsecured debt.

EXHIBIT 15.1	**Monthly Budget for Roger and Susan Matthews under Proposed Plan**

Net monthly income:

Roger:	$ 2,400
Susan:	$ 1,733
Total monthly income	$ 4,133

Living expenses:

Food	$ 500
Home maintenance	100
Clothing	175
Dry cleaning/laundry	25
Gas	150
Utilities & phone	500
Insurance (auto)	60
Medical/dental	100
Charitable contributions	50
Entertainment/recreation	50
Childcare	250
Miscellaneous	175
Total monthly living expenses	$ 2,135

Payments on secured debt:

House payments	$ 1,241
(FBCC $850)	
(CSB $391)	
Car payments	297
(AFI for Ford F-150 truck $147)	
(CFSL for Honda Civic $150)	
Total monthly secured debt payments	$ 1,538
Available to apply to administrative costs, priority claims, Arrearages, and general unsecured debt	$ 460
Total monthly plan payments	$ 1,998

Unsecured debt with priority:

IRS (U.S.) Tax bill from YR-2	$ 1,000
Attorney's fee	1,000

Unsecured debts with no priority:

Credit cards	$35,000
Doctor & hospital	25,000
CCFC vacation debt	2,000
CSB	10,000
AFI	1,500
Car World	3,000
Total non-priority (general) unsecured debt	$76,500

Out of a total combined net monthly income of $4,133 (after employer deductions for taxes, health insurance, etc.), the Matthews expect to have monthly living expenses of $2,135 and will keep that amount from their monthly paychecks to pay themselves. That leaves $1,998, and $1,538 of that will go each month to pay the secured debt that they plan to retain in the plan. That leaves $460 available each month to be applied to administrative expenses, priority unsecured debt, the curing of arrearages proposed in the plan, and, finally, to non-priority (general) unsecured debt. Of that $460, only $323.86 per month will wind up being paid to non-priority unsecured creditors and that $323.86 is the Matthews' monthly projected disposable income number. (See the detailed analysis of the Matthews' plan in Section D below.)

The Liquidation Analysis Requirement

Pursuant to §1325(a)(4), a non–100 percent plan must result in the unsecured creditors receiving at least as much under the plan as they would receive if the debtor's assets were liquidated under Chapter 7. This best interests test requires a comparison of the proposed payout to what unsecured creditors would have received if the debtor had filed a Chapter 7 liquidation proceeding. If creditors receive more under the Chapter 13 plan than they would have received in the liquidation, this test is met. If creditors would have received more in the Chapter 7, then this test is not met and the plan will not be confirmed.

Application Exercise 2

Assume our hypothetical debtor mentioned above (who calculates that she will have $150 per month, or $9,000, in disposable income using during the term of a five-year plan and who has $45,000 in unsecured debt) has assets that, in a Chapter 7, would have been liquidated by the trustee and would have produced sufficient proceeds to pay all §507(a) priority claims in full, with $5,000 left over available to be paid on unsecured claims. If debtor proposes a Chapter 13 plan paying $150 a month to unsecured creditors over five years, can it be confirmed? If she proposes a plan paying $75 a month to unsecured creditors over five years, can it be confirmed?

General unsecured debt that is not paid in a confirmed Chapter 13 plan will be discharged, just as in a Chapter 7 case unless the obligation is of a type treated by the Code as non-dischargeable, a topic to be discussed in Chapter Sixteen, Section E.

A Chapter 13 plan that is not a 100 percent plan is often referred to by the percentage of unsecured debt that it does pay. For example, the debtor who proposes to pay $150 a month, or $9,000 over 60 months in the plan on $45,000 of unsecured debt, has proposed a 25 percent plan. If it is approved, the $36,000 of unsecured debt not paid will be discharged. The Matthews' plan will be referred to as a 24 to 25 percent plan because it proposes to pay non-priority unsecured claims slightly more than 24 percent of the amount owed (see Paragraph 9 of the plan in Exhibit 15.2).

Application Exercise 3

Do you see why the childcare expense is included in the budget in Exhibit 15.1 when it was not in the initial budget shown in the Assignment Memorandum in Appendix B? Why do you think the attorney increased the "Miscellaneous" category from $100 in the initial budget to $175 in this budget and the food budget from $475 to $500? Do you understand why the total of unsecured debt listed in the budget in Exhibit 15.1 is higher than the total of debt listed as "not being paid" in the initial budget? Do you see why the debt owed to CCFC for the financed vacation debt is now treated as unsecured debt, even though it was originally a secured debt? Do you see why a portion of the secured debt owed to CSB, AFI, and Car World is now regarded as unsecured debt? Based on the revised budget you see in Exhibit 15.1, how much disposable income should be available to pay a portion of the Matthews' unsecured debts over the term of the plan? Compare the revised budget in Exhibit 15.1 with the terms of the actual plan in Exhibit 15.2.

EXHIBIT 15.2   Chapter 13 Plan of Roger and Susan Matthews

UNITED STATES BANKRUPTCY COURT
MIDDLE DISTRICT OF PENNSYLVANIA

In re Roger H. Matthews and wife,	)	Case no. 16-13-XXXX
Susan J. Matthews	)	
	)	Chapter 13
Debtors	)	
	)	

CHAPTER 13 PLAN

1. **PLAN TERM AND PAYMENT**: The term of this plan is 60 months, during which period the Debtors will pay the Chapter 13 Trustee the total sum of $1,998 per month by wage order of both debtors.

2. **TAX REFUNDS** to be paid into the plan as follows: All refunds in excess of $500 annually during plan.

3. **PROPERTY OF THE ESTATE/INSURANCE**: Debtors' income and nonexempt assets remain property of the estate and do not vest in debtors until completion of the plan.

EXHIBIT 15.2   **(Continued)**

The Chapter 13 Trustee has no obligation to insure property of the estate, which is the responsibility of the debtors.

4. **ADMINISTRATIVE EXPENSES** under 11 U.S.C. §§503 and 1326 are to be paid in full including, per §707(b)(2)(A)(ii)(III), the actual administrative expense of administering a Chapter 13 plan for the Middle District of Pennsylvania, which is currently 5.1% of projected plan payments or $101.89. The balance of attorney's fee to debtor's attorney Edmond Montgomery in the amount of $1,000 to be paid in first five months at $200 per month.

5. **PRIORITY CLAIMS**: Claims entitled to priority under 11 U.S.C. §507 are to be paid in full in deferred cash payments, including the claim of the United States of America in the amount of $1,000 for Tax YR-2 to be paid in the first twenty-four months at $41.66 per month.

6. **POSTPETITION DEBT** cannot be incurred by the Debtors without the prior written approval of the Chapter 13 Trustee unless debt is incurred for medical expenses for the Debtors or Debtors' dependents, utilities for the Debtors' household, and/or for repairs to Debtors' vehicles that are used for transportation necessary for the Debtors' performance under the plan. If postpetition debt is incurred, it will be paid under the plan as allowed under 11 U.S.C. §1305.

7. **LIEN RETENTION**: Secured claims remain subject to objection by the Trustee if not properly documented or perfected regardless of confirmed plan treatment. Secured creditors retain their liens, which shall be released upon satisfaction of the secured amount except as modified in Paragraphs 10 or 11 below. If the title with lien released is not received by counsel for Debtors within thirty (30) days of satisfaction of the secured amount, then the creditor will be responsible for any court costs and/or legal fees incurred by the Debtors in obtaining release of the lien.

8. **TAX LIABILITY** claims for secured, priority, and unsecured debts paid per claim unless objected to.

9. **NON-PRIORITY UNSECURED CLAIMS**: If no secured plan treatment is provided herein, the claim will be treated as non-priority unsecured and, depending on the allowed claims, will be paid the resulting dividend within the designated range below; provided, however, that if the funds available exceed the specified dividend range allowed, non-priority unsecured claims will be entitled to the greater dividend.
24-25%

10. **SECURED CLAIMS OTHER THAN MORTGAGES ON DEBTORS' HOME:**

a. YR-8 Chevrolet Malibu pledged as security for indebtedness to Car World to be surrendered to Car World and balance of debt owed to Car World to be treated as a non-priority unsecured debt.

b. Lien of Capital City Financing Company in debtor's plumbing tools and furniture to be avoided per 11 U.S.C. §522(f)(1)(B) and exempted per 11 U.S.C. §522(d)(3). Balance owed Capital City Financing Company to be treated as a non-priority unsecured debt.

EXHIBIT 15.2   **(Continued)**

c. Secured claim of Automotive Financing, Inc. (secured by YR-3 Ford Truck F-150) to be modified to current value of collateral ($7,500) and paid in full over 60 months of plan together with interest at 6.5% per annum in monthly installments of $147 per 11 U.S.C. §§1322(b)(2) and 1325(a). Balance owed Automotive Financing, Inc. to be treated as a non-priority general unsecured debt.

d. Secured claim of Columbiana Federal Savings & Loan (secured by YR-4 Honda Civic) to be modified and paid in full over 60 months of plan together with interest at 7.5% per annum in monthly installments of $150 per month per 11 U.S.C. §§1322(b)(2) and 1325(a)(5).

11. **MORTGAGES ON DEBTORS' HOME:** The Debtors will retain possession of their residence located at 901 Magnolia Lane, Harrisburg, Pennsylvania as follows:

a. Arrearage on mortgage payment to First Bank of Capital City in the amount of $850 to be cured over first 12 months of plan together with interest at 8% per annum in 12 monthly installments of $74 each per 11 U.S.C. §1322(b)(5). Future mortgage payments to First Bank of Capital City to be paid through the plan in monthly installments of $850. Debtors to pay any future mortgage increases due to escrow changes. Mortgage balance and lien survive beyond the plan.

b. A second mortgage on the residence held by Capital Savings Bank with prepetition balance of $30,000. Secured claim of Capital Savings Bank to be modified to $20,000 per 11 U.S.C. §1322(c)(2) and paid in full through the plan together with interest at 6.5% per annum in 60 monthly installments of $391. Unsecured balance of $10,000 to be treated as a non-priority general unsecured claim per Paragraph 9.

Date: 6/6/2016   /s/ Roger H. Matthews   /s/ Susan J. Matthews
               Roger H. Matthews, Debtor   Susan J. Matthews, Debtor

                                          /s/ Edmond J. Montgomery
                                          Edmond J. Montgomery
                                          Montgomery & Associates PLLC
                                          Attorney for Debtors
                                          912 West Court Street
                                          Harrisburg, Pennsylvania 17101
                                          (717) 555-1234
                                          Bar # PA-XXX-99

B. PAYMENTS OUTSIDE THE CHAPTER 13 PLAN AND THE WAGE ORDER

In general, the payments that a Chapter 13 debtor is going to make to creditors under his plan will not be made by the debtor directly. Instead, the Code envisions that the portion of the debtor's income that is to be paid to creditors goes to the

Uniform Chapter 13 Plan in the Works?

There is currently wide diversity in the format and contents of Chapter 13 plans among the federal districts. Some districts have adopted mandatory forms for such plans while others have adopted only certain required language for such plans but not an entire form. The variety of forms currently in use reflects the significant disparity in local Chapter 13 practice and custom. The U.S. Judicial Conference, the national policy-making body for the federal courts, is authorized by 28 U.S.C. §331 to review and make recommendations regarding rules of practice and procedure in the federal courts, including the bankruptcy courts. Since 2013, the Conference's Committee on Rules of Practice and Procedure has been debating whether to recommend adoption of a national uniform Chapter 13 plan matrix. The proposal has generated significant controversy among bankruptcy judges and standing trustees around the country, most of it centered on the possible disruption of the "local culture" that pervades Chapter 13 practice by adoption of a national form and associated rules. To get a flavor of the controversy, read the transcript of the Bankruptcy Rules Committee public hearing conducted on January 23, 2015, accessible from the Conference's proposed amendments page at www.uscourts.gov/rules-policies/proposed-amendments-published-public-comment. The proposed new form, can be seen in its 2015 iteration at www.bankruptcymastery.com/wp-content/uploads/2013/08/proposed-chapter-13-plan1.pdf. If adopted, the national form is expected to go into effect at the beginning of 2017. Go to the Conference's Web site at www.uscourts.gov/ and determine the status of the national Chapter 13 form.

standing trustee, who then distributes the funds to the creditors under the terms of the plan. That portion of the debtor's income that he needs for his regular recurring living expenses will be retained by the debtor and he will be expected to pay those living expenses as they come due. These living expense payments are considered "payments outside the plan" since the debtor pays those debts directly as they come due.

If the source of the debtor's income to fund the plan is wages or salary, the employer will be served with a wage order from the bankruptcy court, directing the employer to make a payroll deduction from the debtor's paycheck each pay period and to pay that amount directly to the trustee rather than to the debtor. The debtor is to receive only that portion of his paycheck that goes toward his living expenses. The trustee receives the rest and pays it to the creditors as called for by the plan. The wage order served on the employer of Roger Matthews is shown in Exhibit 15.3. (Both wage orders are shown in Document 22 of the Matthews case file.)

This system means the standing trustee's office in any given federal district is handling a tremendous amount of money coming in from Chapter 13 debtors or their employers. Nationwide, Chapter 13 standing trustees collect and disburse hundreds of millions of dollars to creditors every year.

Chapter 13 plans sometimes propose that certain debts, other than regular living expenses, be paid outside the plan. This is most commonly proposed when a third person (someone other than the debtor) is making part or all of the payment. For example, there may be a non-debtor who is also liable on the debt and who will be making all or part of the payments to avoid his own default. Or a relative or friend of the debtor may volunteer to pay all or part of the debt for the debtor. Where a non-dischargeable debt such as a student loan is being repaid on an established schedule that is not altered by the terms of the plan, the plan may propose that it be paid outside the plan.

EXHIBIT 15.3   **ITL Wage Order to Employer of Roger Matthews**

UNITED STATES BANKRUPTCY COURT
MIDDLE DISTRICT OF PENNSYLVANIA

In re: Roger H. Matthews and wife,	)	Case No. 16-13-XXXX
Susan J. Matthews	)	
	)	Chapter 13
	)	
Debtors	)	

To: City Plumbing Company
411 Butler Avenue
Harrisburg, PA 17101

Re employee Roger H. Matthews
Deduction: $1,119 monthly

ORDER TO EMPLOYER TO DEDUCT AND REMIT A PORTION OF DEBTOR'S
EARNINGS FOR THE VOLUNTARY PAYMENT OF DEBTS

This is an ORDER of the United States Bankruptcy Court, NOT a garnishment. **It supersedes any previous order of this court issued with respect to Debtor/Employee's wages.** The above named Debtor/Employee has voluntarily filed a petition and plan under Chapter 13 of the United State Bankruptcy Code seeking to pay certain debts under the protection of this Court. These debts are to be paid by the Chapter 13 Trustee from the future earnings of the Debtor/Employee. Debtor/Employee has requested an order to have his future earnings withheld and paid to the Chapter 13 Trustee. This Court is empowered under Title 11 Section 13259(c) of the United States Code to direct any entity from which the Debtor/Employee receives income to pay all or any part of such income to the Chapter 13 Trustee. Accordingly, it is hereby

ORDERED, that:

Until further order of the court, you are directed to immediately begin withholding the above stated amount from the wages, salary, commission, and all other earnings or income of Debtor/Employee and to remit the same promptly to the Chapter 13 Trustee no less frequently than once each month. (Make check payable to "Standing Chapter 13 Trustee" at the address shown below.)

MAIL ALL REMITTANCES WITH CASE NAME AND NUMBER TO:

Standing Chapter 13 Trustee
319 West Court Street
Harrisburg, PA 17101

ENTER: August 16, 2016

/s/ _____
United States Bankruptcy Judge

In some federal districts it is customary for secured debt subject to a pay through proposal to be paid outside the plan since the obligation is not modified (scheduled payments will be made per the contract throughout the plan and beyond). However, if an obligation is impaired by the plan either because it is not being paid 100 percent or because it is not being paid on the terms of the original contract, that obligation normally must be made through the plan.

For example, in some districts the Matthews' plan might call for the monthly payments to FBCC, holder of the first mortgage, to be paid outside the plan since that obligation is a pure pay through; it is not modified or impaired by the plan, involves no arrearage to be cured, and will be paid as called for in the contract during and beyond the plan. In districts where that is not customary, the plan might still propose to pay that obligation outside the plan if a non-debtor was also liable on the debt along with the Matthews or if a third party (e.g., Roger or Susan's parents) had agreed to help the couple make the payments to FBCC. On the other hand, the plan could not call for the payments to CSB, holder of the second mortgage, to be made outside the plan because that obligation is impaired by the plan with the strip down to equity value.

A desire to avoid the trustee's administrative costs for handling plan payments may also explain a proposal to make certain payments outside the plan, but many Chapter 13 trustees would object to a proposal based solely on such a rationale and some bankruptcy judges would not confirm a plan on that basis. This is the kind of thing on which there is wide variation of practice among the federal districts.

C. ANALYSIS OF THE MATTHEWS' CHAPTER 13 PLAN

The Matthews have a combined net monthly income of $4,133. Under the terms of their plan, each month they will retain a total of $2,135 to pay their monthly living expenses as itemized in the budget in Exhibit 15.1.

The balance of the Matthews' net monthly income, $1,998 ($4,133 minus $2,135) will be paid by wage order to the Chapter 13 trustee each month; the trustee will distribute those funds as follows:

$41.66. . . . . to the United States of America for the first 24 months to pay the the YR-2 tax obligation in full

$200 . . . . to attorney Edward Montgomery for five months on the balance of the fee owed

$850 . . . . .to FBCC on the first mortgage

$391 . . . . to CSB on the second mortgage

$74 . . . . to FBCC for 12 months to cure the arrearage

$147 . . . . to AFI on the Ford F-150 truck

$150 . . . . .to CFSL on the Honda Civic

$101.89 . . . . .to Chapter 13 Trustee for administrative expenses ($1,998 x 5.1% multiplier)

$42.45. . . . . to unsecured creditors pro rratato increase as payments of the priority tax claim, administrative expense for attorney's fee, and arrearage cure are completed during the term of the plan.

Obviously, the Matthews are not proposing a 100 percent plan. And initially only $42.45 per month will be available for distribution to unsecured creditors. But remember that the $200 per month payment to attorney Edmond Montgomery will only be made for five months, the $41.66 payment to the United States on the priority tax obligation will only be made for 24 months, and the $74 per month payment to FBCC to cure the arrearage only for 12 months. As those obligations are satisfied, the monthly *pro rata* payment to unsecured creditors will increase for the duration of the plan.

For example, excluding the $101.89 administrative expense to the Chapter 13 trustee that will be paid each of the 60 months of the plan, the $200 administrative expense for attorney's fees that will be paid for the first 12 months of the plan, and the $41.66 to be paid for 24 months on the priority claim of the United States for Roger's tax obligation (all of which must be paid in full), and recognizing that the $74 paid for 12 months to secured creditor FBCC to cure that arrearage will thereafter be available to distribute to unsecured creditors, this plan calls for a total of $18,598.20 to be paid to non-priority, non-administrative, unsecured creditors over the 60 months of the plan or an average of $309.97 per month. Note in Exhibit 15.1 that the Matthews have a total of $76,500 in non-priority (general), unsecured debt. Thus they are proposing a 24 to 25 percent plan ($18,598.20 divided by $76,500 = 24.3%).

Application Exercise 4

If the Matthews had the higher joint monthly income of $7,916.66 ($95,000 annually) that we assumed for purposes of completing a Form 122C-2 in Chapter Thirteen (see Exhibit 13.4), would they be able to propose a 100 percent plan based on the analysis in the last example?

Questions regarding the debtor's income or living expenses claimed in Schedules I and J and on 122C-2 for the above median debtor and used to calculate the amount retained for living expenses by the debtors are typically raised and resolved at the first meeting of creditors.

For example, at the Matthews' 341 meeting, the Chapter 13 trustee may question the inclusion of $175 in "miscellaneous" expenses in the Matthews calculation of living expenses in their plan since only $100 was included for such expenses on their Schedule J (Document 10 in the Matthews case file). Or, the trustee might question the inclusion of the $250 for childcare expenses in their projected living expenses if the couple is not yet actually incurring that expense. What modifications in the plan as proposed might the trustee demand on these issues? Since the Matthews have included an amount in their living expenses for charitable contributions, the trustee may ask for documentation that the debtor has historically made such contributions in that amount to insure the debtor isn't just looking for a way to keep more cash from creditors. Of course, if the plan is a 100 percent plan, the trustee will have less reason for concern. Since the Matthews were below median debtors as calculated on their Form 122C-1, they did not file a Form 122C-2.

Questions regarding other aspects of the proposed plan are also raised at the 341 meeting and are often resolved there. Such meetings often take on the appearance of a settlement conference or a mediation session as the parties work to find solutions to problems raised by the trustee or creditors. For example, the Chapter 13 trustee for the Matthews may question the plan proposing to pay the full contract rate of interest on the strip down of the claim of CFSL when it is not doing so on the stripped down claims of either AFI or CSB. If the plan proposed to pay the first mortgage payments owed to FBCC outside the plan, the trustee might object, either because the parents' promise to help is not a sufficiently valid reason or because the trustee considers that claim impaired due to the arrearage that has to be cured. Again, attitudes and practice on such matters vary widely across the country.

Agreements made at the 341 meeting often result in debtor's proposed plan being revised prior to confirmation. (Section 13239(a) allows the debtor to modify a proposed plan prior to confirmation.) Disputes raised at the 341 meeting regarding the plan that cannot be resolved there often lead to a formal objection to confirmation being made to the court by the trustee or a creditor, and that objection can threaten the confirmation of the plan, a topic we will consider in the next chapter.

Chapter Summary

- A Chapter 13 plan may cure arrearages in unsecured claims. A 100 percent plan must include the curing of all arrearages in unsecured debt. Interest is not paid on arrearage payments of unsecured debt.
- The plan may also modify unsecured obligations, including proposing to discharge some or all of them subject to the requirement that a plan must propose to pay all the debtor's projected disposable income over the term of the plan and subject to the liquidation analysis or best interest tests that requires that unsecured creditors receive more in the Chapter 13 plan than they would have received in a Chapter 7 liquidation.
- During the term of the plan, funds that debtors need for regular living expenses for themselves and dependents are retained by debtors. Payments to be made to secured and unsecured creditors are channeled through the standing trustee who then distributes to creditors according to the terms of the plan. If the debtor is employed, a wage order will issue to the employer directing the employer to make payroll deductions and remit the designated amount to the trustee. A plan may propose that certain debts, other than regular living expenses, be paid outside the plan as in a claim subject to an unaltered, unimpaired pay through proposal or where a non-debtor third party is making the payments.
- Questions that the standing trustee or a creditor have concerning the debtor's proposed Chapter 13 plan will typically be raised and often resolved at the first meeting of creditors.

Applying the Concepts

1. Since the Matthews proposed a less than 100 percent plan, perform the "best interests test" on their plan. Begin with their final budget in Exhibit 15.1 and the detailed analysis of the plan in Section D of this chapter. The Matthews are proposing to pay $309.97 per month on non-priority unsecured claims over the 60 months of the plan or a total of $18,598.20. They have non-priority unsecured claims totaling $76,500. So they are proposing to pay slightly more than 24 percent of their unsecured debt. Now look at the Matthews' bankruptcy schedules setting out their assets, their value, and owners' equity. If the Matthews simply liquidated in Chapter 7 bankruptcy, would the unsecured creditors receive more than the 24 to 25 percent the Matthews are proposing to pay in their Chapter 13 plan?

2. Locate and read Assignment Memorandum #3 in Appendix D. If the instructor so directs, continue drafting a proposed Chapter 13 plan for Nick and Pearl Murphy assuming their Chapter 13 case was being filed in the U.S. bankruptcy court for your federal district. What percentage of their non-priority, unsecured debt will the Murphys be able to pay based on your calculations? If the plan is a less than 100 percent plan, perform the "best interests" test to determine if those creditors will receive at least as much under the plan as they would have received if the Murphys liquidated under Chapter 7.

The Chapter 13 Case: Plan Confirmation, Modification, and Discharge

In this chapter we will conclude our study of the Chapter 13 bankruptcy by considering the requirements for confirmation of a Chapter 13 plan as well as the procedure for confirmation. We will examine the requirements and procedure for post-confirmation modification of a Chapter 13 plan. We will also look at what debts can be discharged in a Chapter 13 case and the timing of the Chapter 13 discharge. Finally we will analyze the debtor's right to voluntarily dismiss his Chapter 13 case or convert it to a Chapter 7 liquidation as well as the right of a party in interest to seek an involuntary dismissal or conversion of the case.

A. TIMING OF THE CHAPTER 13 PLAN AND INITIAL PAYMENTS

Federal Rule of Bankruptcy Procedure (FRBP) 3015(b) requires that the debtor's proposed Chapter 13 plan be filed at the time the petition is filed or within 14 days thereafter. Section 1323(a) permits the

Key Concepts

- The debtor generally must propose a Chapter 13 plan within 14 days of filing the petition and begin making payments under the plan to the standing trustee within 30 days following the entry for the order of relief or the filing of the proposed plan, whichever is earlier
- The bankruptcy court must confirm the Chapter 13 plan and the Code contains a number of requirements that must be satisfied to obtain confirmation including that the debtor has proposed the plan in good faith
- Once confirmed, a Chapter 13 plan can be modified on motion based on changed circumstances of the debtor, but a modified plan must meet the same requirements for confirmation as the original plan
- A discharge of debts in Chapter 13 is granted only upon completion of the plan though an early or hardship discharge can be granted in exceptional circumstances upon a required showing
- As in a Chapter 7 case, certain debts cannot be discharged in a Chapter 13 case

debtor to modify the plan at any time before confirmation. This allows the plan to be proposed prior to the 341 meeting, discussed there with creditors and the trustee, and then modified if necessary prior to the court's confirmation of the plan.

Section 1326(a)(1) of the Code requires the debtor to begin making payments on the plan within 30 days following the entry for the order of relief or the filing of the proposed plan, whichever is earlier. This means the debtor is making payments to the trustee on his plan even before it is confirmed. One of the duties imposed on the standing trustee the to ensure that the debtor begins making these payments (see Exhibit 12.1). Per §1326(a)(2), the trustee retains these preconfirmation payments until the plan is confirmed and only then distributes them to creditors.

For example under their plan (Exhibit 15.2 or Document 18 in the Matthews case file), the Matthews propose to pay a total of $1,998 per month into their plan. Since they filed their plan with the petition, they must begin making payments within 30 days after the filing, even though their plan is not yet confirmed. (Compare the date the plan was filed with the date the plan was confirmed in Document 21 in the Matthews case file.) The standing trustee retains these payments until the plan is confirmed and then distributes them to creditors, per the now-confirmed plan.

B. CONFIRMATION OF THE CHAPTER 13 PLAN

Section 1324 provides that the court "shall hold" a confirmation hearing on the plan no earlier than 20 days and no later than 45 days after the first meeting of creditors. Creditors must be given 28 days' notice of the confirmation hearing, pursuant to Federal Rule of Bankruptcy Procedure (FRBP) 2002(b). Notwithstanding the mandatory language of §1324, many bankruptcy judges only conduct a confirmation hearing if an objection to confirmation is filed. In those districts, absent an objection, confirmation will be automatic when the deadline for making objections passes. In addition, §1324 allows the confirmation hearing to be held earlier than 20 days following the first meeting of creditors if the court determines it would be in the "best interests" of the estate and creditors to do so and there is no objection. As a result, many bankruptcy judges conduct the confirmation hearing shortly after the first meeting of creditors if no objection is filed at that time. Others wait until the time for filing claims (the claims bar date) has expired.

Application Exercise 1

Look at the Notice of Chapter 13 Bankruptcy Case that was sent to creditors in the Matthews' Chapter 13 case (Document 19 in the Matthews case file). What is the deadline established there for filing proofs of claim in the Matthews case? Now look at the Order Confirming Chapter 13 Plan (Document 21 in the Matthews case file) to see when it was entered. Does it appear that any objection to the plan was made at or following the 341 meeting? How does the judge in the Matthews case interpret §1324?

Section §1325(a) sets out the criteria that the court must consider in deciding whether to confirm a plan; those criteria are summarized in Exhibit 16.1.

EXHIBIT 16.1 **Criteria for Confirming a Chapter 13 Plan**

- The Chapter 13 petition was filed in good faith
- The Chapter 13 plan has been proposed in good faith and not by any means forbidden by law
- The plan is feasible, in the sense that the debtor will be able to make all payments called for in the plan and will be able to comply with the plan
- The debtor has filed all federal, state, and local tax returns due
- The debtor is current on all domestic support obligations
- The value to be distributed to all unsecured creditors under the plan is not less than they would have received in a Chapter 7 liquidation
- Each secured creditor has either a) accepted the plan or b) will receive at least the value of the collateral and have the security interest in the property continued or c) has had the secured property surrendered to it
- All administrative and priority claims, as well as fees associated with the filing, have been paid or will be paid through the plan
- The plan otherwise complies with all provisions of the Code

Any party in interest may object to the confirmation of a proposed Chapter 13 plan. In most Chapter 13 cases, any objections to the plan by the U.S. trustee, creditors, or the standing trustee are worked out at the 341 meeting prior to the confirmation hearing so that the confirmation hearing is perfunctory and brief. If they cannot be worked out, a formal objection to confirmation of the plan will be filed and the matter will be resolved at the confirmation hearing. Upon confirmation of the plan, the court will enter an order complying with Official Form 2300, Order Confirming Chapter 13 Plan. (See Document 21 in the Matthews case file.)

Neither the Code nor the Bankruptcy Rules establish a time deadline for filing an objection to confirmation of a Chapter 13 plan. In most districts the local rules of court will deal with that issue. In some districts objections to confirmation must be filed by the first meeting of creditors. In other districts objections must be filed by the date of the confirmation hearing or if no confirmation hearing is held by a date established in the notice to creditors for filing objections to avoid automatic confirmation.

Application Exercise 2

Check the local rules of the bankruptcy court in the federal district where you plan to practice and determine how the deadline for filing objections to confirmation of a Chapter 13 case is determined.

Case Preview

In re Montoya

What if a creditor negatively impacted by the plan does not file an objection? Is the failure to object an implied acceptance of the plan by the creditor? Should the bankruptcy judge go ahead and confirm the plan in absence of any objection even if it contains proposals contrary to the Code? As you read In re Montoya, consider the following questions:

1. What was the provision in debtor's Chapter 13 plan that the creditor could have objected to but did not?
2. Can a creditor's failure to object to a properly noticed Chapter 13 plan ever be deemed an implied consent to its terms?
3. Why did the court reject the debtor's implied consent argument in this case?
4. In the absence of any objection to a Chapter 13 plan by any creditor should the bankruptcy judge undertake an independent review of the terms of the plan to be sure they all comply with the Code before granting confirmation?

In re Montoya
341 B.R. 41 (Bankr. D. Utah 2006)

BOULDEN, Bankruptcy Judge. . . .

The facts of this case are undisputed. . . . The Plan proposes a monthly plan payment of $290 with a pro rata distribution to general unsecured creditors of $2,340. The Plan also proposes to bifurcate or, as it is commonly termed, cram down a debt owed to Menlove Dodge. Menlove Dodge has a purchase money security interest in the Tracer. The Debtor incurred this debt on February 24, 2004 between her first and second bankruptcy filings — well within 910 days of filing this current petition — and acquired the Tracer for her personal use. No payment through a Chapter 13 plan has been made to Menlove Dodge on its claim since the Debtor's second case was filed in early 2004.

The Debtor proposes in her Plan to pay Menlove Dodge $2,230 as a secured claim with a 5.5% discount factor and to pay the estimated balance of $1,770 as a non-priority unsecured claim. The Plan was filed and noticed to all creditors. Paragraph 3.B. of the Plan acknowledges that the Tracer claim is not subject to § 506. But contrary to this statement, the Plan bifurcates the claim and states: FAILURE OF A CREDITOR TO TIMELY FILE A WRITTEN OBJECTION TO THIS PLAN PRIOR TO CONFIRMATION SHALL CONSTITUTE ACCEPTANCE OF BOTH THE PLAN AND THE TREATMENT OF ITS CLAIM AS SET FORTH THEREIN. Menlove Dodge has not filed a proof of claim, but the Debtor included the Tracer on Schedule D showing that she owes Menlove Dodge approximately $4,000. . . .

The issues before the Court are whether the absence of objection from Menlove Dodge may be deemed implied acceptance of the Plan and whether the Court may confirm the Plan that provides for bifurcation of a secured claim under §506 for a vehicle purchased within 910 days of filing (910-day vehicle claim). Although admitting that Menlove Dodge has a 910-day vehicle claim, both the Debtor and the Chapter 13 Trustee argue that the Plan should be confirmed because the confirmation requirements set forth in §1325(a)(5) are in the disjunctive, and a creditor's acceptance of a proposed plan satisfies the requirements of §1325 regardless of the hanging paragraph found after §1325(a)(9). Both the Debtor and Chapter 13 Trustee argue that a creditor's failure to object to a proposed plan constitutes acceptance of the plan under §1325(a)(5)(A). Under the circumstances presented in this case, the Court disagrees.

[The court finds the debtor cannot bifurcate and cram down the secured claim of Menlove Dodge to value under §506 since the claim is secured by a 910-day vehicle. See discussion of this issue in Chapter Fourteen, Section B.]

Having been unable to utilize the traditional cram down provisions of Chapter 13 and §506 valuation in order to confirm her Plan, the Debtor must find some other provisions in §1325(a) that would allow confirmation of her Plan. The Debtor argues that if the provisions of §1325(a)(5)(B) or (C) cannot be met, she may obtain confirmation if a secured creditor has accepted her Plan.

The Chapter 13 Trustee and the Debtor broadly contend that failure to object to a properly noticed plan constitutes acceptance of the plan. This position overstates the case because the parties improperly combine two significantly different concepts and Code sections. It is correct that, if a plan is properly noticed and otherwise meets the requirements of §1325(a), the Court may deem a secured creditor's silence to constitute acceptance of a plan and the plan may be confirmed. This "implied" acceptance is allowed because Chapter 13, unlike Chapter 11, has no balloting mechanism to evidence acceptance of a proposed plan, and it is only the negative — a filed objection — that evidences the lack of acceptance. When the creditor simply does nothing, the judicial doctrine of "implied" acceptance fills the drafting gap in the Code. The concept of implied acceptance of an otherwise compliant plan, or even voting on similar provisions in Chapter 11, however, is quite different from proposing a plan intentionally inconsistent with the Code and then waiting for the trap to spring on a somnolent creditor. Creditors are entitled to rely on the few unambiguous provisions of the BAPCPA for their treatment. They should not be required to scour every Chapter 13 plan to ensure that provisions of the BAPCPA specifically inapplicable to them will not be inserted in a proposed plan in the debtor's hope that the improper secured creditor treatment will become res judicata.

The Chapter 13 Trustee's reliance on In re Andersen, 179 F.3d 1253 (10th Cir. 1999) to support his argument only proves the point. In *Andersen*, the Tenth Circuit applied the principal of res judicata and relied upon the finality of orders to uphold a provision in a Chapter 13 debtor's plan that discharged student loans based on undue hardship even though the debtor had not obtained such a finding through the adjudication of an adversary proceeding. *Andersen* has been criticized and distinguished in subsequent case law. Even the Tenth Circuit has noted that *Andersen* is limited to the particular facts of that case. A plan should not be used as a sword to change the explicit provisions of the Code to what the parties wish Congress had drafted. And *Andersen*, of course, is inapplicable in this case because the Court has not confirmed the Plan, so the doctrine of res judicata and the policy considerations supporting finality of judgments are inapplicable and unpersuasive.

Even if the Court ruled that "implied" consent by failure to object would save this Plan as drafted given the notice language, the Plan still could not be confirmed. Section 1325(a)(1) provides that "the court shall confirm a plan if (1) the plan complies with the provisions of this chapter and with the other applicable provisions of this title." The parties agree that Menlove Dodge's 910-day vehicle claim cannot be bifurcated, yet the Plan proposes this type of treatment. The Court has an affirmative duty to review and ensure that the Plan complies with the Code even if creditors fail to object to confirmation. This offending provision presents no less a bar to confirmation than failing to pay priority claims in full, proposing a plan in bad faith, or proposing a plan that is not feasible.

CONCLUSION

Under the BAPCPA, §1325(a)(5) can no longer be used to cram down a 910-day vehicle claim. Steadfastly including a §506 cram down in the Plan in the hope that a creditor will not object to confirmation within the shortened time frames of §1324(b), be deemed to have impliedly consented to confirmation, and then be caught in the res judicata result of a confirmed plan, is not an option. The Plan as filed and orally modified is not confirmed.

The Debtor, however, has represented to the Court that she is willing and able to pay the full amount of the allowed claim ($4,000) in order to obtain confirmation of the Plan. Based on that representation, and all other elements of §1325 having been met, the Court orders the Chapter 13 Trustee to submit a confirmation order consistent with this Memorandum Decision.

Post-Case Follow-Up

Did it matter here that the secured creditor had not filed a proof of claim? If the creditor had filed a proof of claim asserting a secured claim in the full $4,000 owed, could the court have construed that as an objection to the proposed bifurcation and strip down? Here we see another good reason for secured creditors to file proofs of claim even when not technically required to by the Code.

In re Montoya: Real Life Applications

1. The strength of a debtor's implied consent argument against a non-objecting creditor may depend on timing. *Montoya* was decided in the context of whether debtor's plan should be confirmed at all. What if a Chapter 13 plan is confirmed and then a creditor who did not object to confirmation steps forward to

complain? See In re Pardee, 218 B.R. 916 (B.A.P. 9th Cir. 1998) (creditor's failure to object to plan at confirmation hearing constituted waiver of its right to collect postpetition interest on its claim, even though plan provision discharging that postpetition interest was contrary to the Code; preclusive effect of final orders to be honored) and compare In re Escobedo, 28 F.3d 34 (7th Cir. 1994) (Chapter 13 plan that did not include allowed administrative and tax priority claims as required under §1322(a)(2) was confirmed without objection; five years after plan confirmation and two years after the debtor's final payment the court grants trustee's petition to either modify the plan to include payments or dismiss the plan altogether. The court held that the plan was not res judicata as to the omitted priority claims.). How do you think the judge in Montoya would rule in these two post-confirmation cases? Determine if the courts of the federal district or circuit where you plan to practice have addressed this issue. How do you think those courts would rule on the facts of Montoya? On the facts of the two post-confirmation cases?

2. Note that the creditor in Montoya not only did not file a proof of claim, but it did not appear at the confirmation hearing or even file a brief on the questions raised at confirmation affecting its claim. One of the most significant holdings of Montoya is that notwithstanding absence of creditor objection to a Chapter 13 plan and even absent any apparent interest of creditor in how its claim is treated in the plan, the court still has an affirmative duty to review and ensure that the plan complies with the Code.

   a. In federal districts where no confirmation hearing is held unless there is an objection, how would the bankruptcy judge fulfill that duty?

   b. If the bankruptcy judge in the district where you practice is known to agree with this view and takes it seriously, how likely is it that lawyers representing Chapter 13 debtors will attempt the kind of trickery you see in the plans that were confirmed in In re Pardee and In re Escobedo?

Most of the requirements for confirmation in §1325(a) are self-explanatory and some we have already considered (e.g., the required treatment of secured claims in §1325(a)(5) and the liquidation comparison requirement of §1325(a)(4)). But note the first two requirements in Exhibit 16.1, one relating to the good faith of the debtor in filing the petition (from §1325(a)(7)), and the other relating to the plan being proposed in good faith (from §1325(a)(3)). **Good faith** is not a defined term under the Code and the concept has been left to court interpretation. The various issues that we indicated in the previous section might be raised for discussion at the 341 meeting may, if they cannot be resolved there, give rise to an objection to confirmation on the basis of lack of good faith.

Good faith also emerges as a consideration in other contexts in Chapter 13 cases when the debtor seeks to modify a confirmed plan and as an implicit (not explicit) factor in a court's decision to dismiss a Chapter 13 case or convert it to a Chapter 7 liquidation under §1307 prior to plan confirmation (see further discussion of good faith in Section F).

Case Preview

In re Hatem

The concept of good faith is sufficiently nebulous that other specific confirmation criteria from §1325(a) are often considered in the overall good faith determination. As you read In re Hatem, consider the following questions:

1. What was the family squabble that gave rise to this Chapter 13 filing?
2. Is the question of whether a Chapter 13 plan has been proposed in good faith a question of fact or law and what is the standard of review utilized when a bankruptcy judge's ruling on the good faith element of confirmation is challenged on appeal?
3. Why did the court find that debtor's plan in this case was designed to accomplish an unworthy purpose and thus was not proposed in good faith?
4. Can you identify other specific confirmation criteria in §1325(a) that were arguably violated by the debtor and the debtor's plan in this case?

In re Hatem

273 B.R. 900 (S.D. Ala. 2001)

BUTLER, Chief District Judge. . . .

Prior to filing for Chapter 13 bankruptcy, Hatem had been involved in litigation in the Circuit Court of Baldwin County, Alabama, in an action styled *Elizabeth L. Kennedy v. Betty Lynn Hatem and Leroy Hatem* involving a dispute between Hatem and Elizabeth Kennedy, Hatem's mother and the appellee herein, concerning the ownership of 2.7 acres of land and a home located in Montrose, Alabama ("the property"). On March 31, 1999, the Circuit Court of Baldwin County set aside a deed executed by Kennedy, which transferred Kennedy's one-half interest in the property to Hatem, holding that the deed was void because it was the result of fraud, deception, and undue influence by Hatem and Hatem's then husband. The circuit court declared both Hatem and Kennedy once again one-half owners of the property. On January 11, 2000, the circuit court issued an order of sale of the property requiring its appraisal, sale, and equitable division. The circuit court amended its order on May 11, 2000, in order to give both Kennedy and Hatem the exclusive right to bid on the property within thirty days from the date of filing of the appraisal. On October 27, 2000, following Hatem's appeal, the Alabama Court of Civil Appeals affirmed the circuit court's orders. On November 6, 2000, the court-appointed appraiser filed its appraisal with the circuit court, establishing the value of the property at $410,000.00. Pursuant to the circuit court's order of sale, Kennedy and Hatem had thirty days from that date to submit their bids on the property.

On November 29, 2000, one week before the expiration of the bid period, Hatem filed . . . for Chapter 13 bankruptcy. In the petition and accompanying schedules,

Hatem indicated that she was the sole owner of the 2.7 acres of land and the home located in Montrose, Alabama, and that the property was subject to a mortgage in favor of Regions Bank in the amount of $54,623.00 and a vendor's lien in favor of Elizabeth Kennedy in the amount of $210,000.00, totaling $264,623.00 in secured claims on the property. Hatem also listed unsecured debt of $52,252.00, bringing her total reported liabilities to $316,875.00. Hatem listed the value of her interest in the property as $205,000.00 and her total assets, including personal property, as $215,403.00. Hatem reported a monthly income of $1,582.00 and monthly expenditures of $1,572.00.

Hatem's Chapter 13 plan proposed to pay the Trustee's commission, Hatem's attorney, and the unsecured property tax claim of $1,009.00 by making monthly payments to the Trustee of $50.00. The plan further proposed that Hatem would make monthly payments directly to Regions Mortgage, outside the plan, in the amount of $581.00 on its secured mortgage. The plan proposed no payments to Hatem's unsecured nonpriority creditors on their claims totaling $51,243.00.

On December 13, 2000, Kennedy filed a motion for relief from the automatic stay and to dismiss Hatem's Chapter 13 proceeding on the grounds that Hatem did not file the Chapter 13 petition in good faith; Hatem did not propose a Chapter 13 plan in good faith; and Hatem's sole purpose in filing the petition was to invoke the automatic stay provisions of the Bankruptcy Code to prevent the sale and division of the property by the state court.

On January 4, 2001, Hatem's Chapter 13 case came before the bankruptcy court for a confirmation hearing. . . . At the conclusion of the evidence, the bankruptcy court found that the Chapter 13 petition and plan had been filed in bad faith and denied confirmation of the plan and dismissed Hatem's Chapter 13 case with a 180-day injunction against further bankruptcy filings. On January 10, 2001, the bankruptcy court ruled as moot Kennedy's motions for relief from stay and to dismiss Hatem's Chapter 13 case. . . .

Hatem presents the following issue on appeal: whether the bankruptcy court erred in denying confirmation of her Chapter 13 plan, in dismissing her Chapter 13 case, and in refusing to allow her to amend her plan, all for failure to file in good faith. . . .

[T]he bankruptcy court found that neither Hatem's Chapter 13 petition nor her plan had been filed in good faith. In addition, the bankruptcy court found that Hatem's purported amended plan, which was proposed by Hatem at the hearing, was not feasible and likewise lacked good faith. Based on those findings, the bankruptcy court denied confirmation of Hatem's plan and dismissed Hatem's Chapter 13 case with a 180-day injunction against further bankruptcy filings. It is the bankruptcy court's finding of bad faith that is at issue in this appeal.

[A] Chapter 13 plan must be confirmed by the bankruptcy court if meets the six criteria set forth in 11 U.S.C. §1325(a). This appeal focuses on the third of these criteria found in §1325(a)(3), requiring that the plan be proposed in good faith. A Chapter 13 plan cannot be confirmed if it fails to satisfy the good faith requirement. In re Waldron, 785 F.2d 936, 939 (11th Cir. 1986) (quoting 11 U.S.C. §1325(a)(3)). That requirement "is the only safety valve available through which plans attempting to twist the law to malevolent ends may be cast out." Id.

Whether a Chapter 13 plan has been proposed in good faith is a question of fact subject to the "clearly erroneous" standard of review. In re Saylors, 869 F.2d 1434, 1438 (11th Cir. 1989). While the Bankruptcy Code does not define the term "good faith," the Eleventh Circuit has interpreted "good faith" as "requiring that there is a reasonable likelihood that the plan will achieve a result consistent with the objectives and purposes of the Code." In re McCormick, 49 F.3d 1524, 1526 (11th Cir. 1995). The petition may not be used as a device to serve some "unworthy purpose" of the petitioner. *Waldron*, 785 F.2d at 939.

In analyzing the good faith of the debtor, the court looks to the "totality of the circumstances" surrounding the plan. See *McCormick*, 49 F.3d at 1526. In *In re Kitchens*, the Eleventh Circuit set forth a nonexclusive list of factors that the bankruptcy court should consider in making a determination of good faith:

> (1) the amount of the debtor's income from all sources; (2) the living expenses of the debtor and his dependents; (3) the amount of attorney's fees; (4) the probable or expected duration of the debtor's Chapter 13 plan; (5) the motivations of the debtor and his sincerity in seeking relief under the provisions of Chapter 13; (6) the debtor's degree of effort; (7) the debtor's ability to earn and the likelihood of fluctuation in his earnings; (8) special circumstances such as inordinate medical expenses; (9) the frequency with which the debtor has sought relief under the Bankruptcy Reform Act and its predecessors; (10) the circumstances under which the debtor has contracted his debts and has demonstrated bona fides, or lack of same, in dealings with his creditors; (11) the burden which the plan's administration would place on the trustee.

Kitchens, 702 F.2d 885, 888–89 (11th Cir. 1983). The court further enumerated three additional factors for consideration, those being: substantiality of the repayment to the unsecured creditors; consideration of the type of debt to be discharged and whether such debt would be nondischargeable under Chapter 7; and the accuracy of the plan's statements of debts and expenses and whether any inaccuracies are an attempt to mislead the court. Id. at 889. . . .

[T]he bankruptcy court found that Hatem's petition contained multiple misstatements and omissions regarding the ownership of the property, the claims against the property, and the value of the property. The court held that the admittedly erroneous information indicated either a callous disregard of a debtor's duties in filling out the Chapter 13 schedules and plan or an intentional misrepresentation of information in an attempt to secure confirmation and avoid the consequences of the state court litigation. The court further noted that Hatem had assets that, if liquidated, would be more than sufficient to pay off her indebtedness; yet, Hatem had proposed to pay nothing to her unsecured nonpriority creditors. In addition, the court noted that the timing of the filing of the petition, which was only three weeks before the property was to be sold and only one week before the expiration of Hatem's right to bid on the property, indicated that the petition was filed to forestall the court ordered sale. The court found Hatem's testimony that she was unaware of the state court orders regarding the sale of the property incredible. The court further found that Hatem's purported amended plan to obtain a mortgage on the property and buy out her mother's interest in the property, which Hatem proposed from the witness stand at the hearing, was not feasible and was merely a last ditch attempt to thwart the dismissal of the case. The court concluded that neither the petition, nor the original or amended plans, had been submitted in good faith.

After reviewing the entire record, the Court agrees. It is undisputed that Hatem's Chapter 13 petition and schedules failed to disclose Kennedy's one-half ownership interest in the subject property. It is undisputed that Hatem erroneously (if not falsely) reported that Kennedy had a secured lien on the property in the amount of $210,000.00, making Hatem's secured claims on the property, and her liabilities in general, appear much greater than they were.

It is undisputed that Hatem listed the value of her interest in the property as $205,000.00, which, in conjunction with her failure to list Kennedy as a one-half owner, made it appear that she was the sole owner of property whose value was only $205,000.00. This omission, in conjunction with the misstatement that Kennedy had a lien on the property of $210,000.00, made it appear that property worth only $205,000.00 was subject to secured debt of $264,623.00 (made up of Kennedy's purported lien and the Regions' mortgage). In fact, the property was worth $410,000.00 and was subject to secured debt of only $54,623.00.

At the confirmation hearing on January 4, 2001, Hatem and her attorney acknowledged that the information given in the petition was erroneous in many respects. The bankruptcy court noted that, although objections had been filed to the petition and plan on December 13, 2000, neither Hatem nor her attorney had made any attempt to correct or amend the misrepresentations and omissions therein. In fact, they continued to seek to have the defective plan confirmed at the hearing.

In addition . . . the timing of the filing of Hatem's Chapter 13 proceeding clearly indicated that her motive was to attempt to defeat the state court ordered sale of the property. If there were any doubt about that motive, Hatem erased it when she candidly admitted in her brief to this Court that she filed her Chapter 13 case in part "to forestall a sacrificial forced sale of her one-half undivided [interest] in the real estate in which she resides."

The Court further notes that Hatem's assets, including her personal property, totaled $215,403.00, and her liabilities (once the erroneous $210,000.00 lien was removed) totaled only $106,875.00. As the bankruptcy court found, had the state court ordered sale of the property proceeded, it would likely have generated $205,000.00 for Hatem as one-half owner of the property, which would have been more than sufficient to pay all of her creditors in full. Despite that fact, Hatem filed a Chapter 13 plan in which she proposed to pay nothing of the $51,243.00 owed to her unsecured creditors.

Finally, Hatem claims in her brief that the bankruptcy court refused to allow her to amend her plan. To the contrary, Hatem never attempted to amend her plan until the date of the hearing on her original plan when, from the witness stand, she proposed to obtain a mortgage on the property, buy out her mother's interest, pay off all of her debts, and then pay the monthly note on the mortgage. However, she admitted that she had done nothing to secure such a loan. The court considered Hatem's new plan and found it unfeasible given Hatem's reported monthly income of only approximately $1,500.00 and the projected monthly mortgage obligation on a loan of at least $300,000.00. The bankruptcy court did not refuse to allow Hatem to amend her plan. It simply refused to confirm an unworkable plan, which it found to have been submitted in bad faith as a last ditch effort to avoid dismissal of a petition that had been filed in bad faith.

Considering the totality of the circumstances in this case, particularly Hatem's motivations in seeking Chapter 13 relief, her ability to pay her debts in full, her lack of effort in putting forth a proper and feasible plan, the insubstantiality of the repayment to her unsecured creditors, the degree of inaccuracy of the plan's statements of assets and debts, and the misleading nature of those inaccuracies, this Court cannot say that the bankruptcy court was clearly erroneous in its finding that Hatem filed her Chapter 13 petition and her Chapter 13 plan in bad faith. Moreover, for these same reasons and for the additional reason that Hatem completely failed to show the feasibility of her purported amended plan. The bankruptcy court did not err in denying its confirmation as well. United States v. Devall, 704 F.2d 1513, 1517 (11th Cir. 1983) (the court will not approve a plan unless it has first ascertained that the plan is feasible).

Where a bankruptcy court has properly found that a Chapter 13 petition and plan were filed in bad faith, confirmation of the plan may be denied, and the case may be dismissed. See 11 U.S.C. §1307(c)(5); *Green*, 214 B.R. at 506 n. 9 ("[b]ankruptcy courts have a duty to preserve the bankruptcy process for its intended purpose and may dismiss a Chapter 13 case which is filed in bad faith."); In re Steele, 34 B.R. 172, 173 (Bankr. M.D. Ala. 1983) ("[w]here the court finds that a petition and plan are not filed in good faith, confirmation may be denied and the case dismissed. . . ."). As such, the bankruptcy court properly denied confirmation of the present Chapter 13 plan and properly dismissed the Chapter 13 petition, and that judgment is due to be AFFIRMED. . . .

In accordance with the memorandum opinion entered by the Court this day, it is hereby ORDERED that the judgment of the bankruptcy court denying confirmation of the debtor's Chapter 13 bankruptcy plan and dismissing debtor's Chapter 13 case with a 180-day injunction from filing for relief under any chapter of the Bankruptcy Code is due to be and is AFFIRMED.

Post-Case Follow-Up

In retrospect this looks like a fairly egregious case of abuse. The timing of the filing to stop the state-court ordered sale of the property, the misstatements of the debtor in her schedules and testimony, the proposal to discharge unsecured debt when she had ample resources to pay it. Would you have had any ethical or professional qualms about taking this case for this debtor? Recall our discussion in Chapter Eight, Section A, regarding the duty of inquiry and certification by the attorney for the debtor who signs the petition. It is unclear whether the debtor had assistance of counsel in completing her petition and schedules and the case makes no reference to any breach of duty by an attorney but if Hatem had come to you to file this case would you have filed a petition and schedules containing the information these did? What inquiry would you have made into the circumstances of ownership and value of the property that might have altered what appeared on these schedules?

In re Hatem: Real Life Applications

1. *Hatem* establishes that the good faith inquiry involves looking at "the totality of circumstances surrounding the plan." Look again at the fourteen total factors that the Eleventh Circuit in *Kitchens* identified as relevant to that broad inquiry. Determine if the courts of the federal district or circuit where you plan to practice follow the "totality of the circumstances" approach to the good faith inquiry under §1325(a). How would those courts have likely decided *Hatem* and on what basis?

2. *Hatem* observes that the Code does not define good faith but points out that the Eleventh Circuit has interpreted the concept to include both a practical aspect (is there a reasonable likelihood that the plan will achieve a result consistent with the objectives and purposes of the Code) and an ethical one (the plan cannot be used to accomplish "an unworthy purpose" or to "twist the law to malevolent ends"). Determine if the courts of the federal district or circuit where you plan to practice have defined or described good faith in the context of §1325(a) and, if so, whether they have given it both a practical and ethical component. Looking again at the facts of *Hatem*, which of the factors the court discusses would you classify as practical and which as ethical?

3. Using the totality of the circumstances approach to good faith and assuming both a practical and ethical component to good faith, determine if you would find the following proposed plans to meet the good faith tests for confirmation found in §1325(a)(3) and (7).

   a. Debtor has previously filed two Chapter 13 cases to obtain a stay of foreclosure on his house. Judge in those cases lifted the stay when debtor could not propose a plan to make up arrearages on mortgage and pay through of scheduled payments. With foreclosure scheduled to occur tomorrow, debtor now files a third Chapter 13 invoking the automatic stay. Proposes plan to pay one-half of the arrearages during the term of the plan plus pay through of future scheduled payments.

   b. Debtor who is current on both her secured obligations (mortgage on empty lot and lien on vehicle) proposes Chapter 13 plan that will enable her to hold on to lot and vehicle with pay through even though both secured debts are dramatically undersecured and could be stripped down. Plan proposes to pay sole unsecured creditor hospital nothing and to discharge that debt. If strip down of secured debts had been proposed, unsecured debtors could have received twenty cents on the dollar of what is owed. Would it matter if hospital had provided emergency lifesaving services to a child of the debtor? Would it matter if the debtor's ex-spouse was now married to the hospital administrator and the debtor and administrator had had physical confrontations?

   c. Debtor proposed 100 percent plan though current disposable income inadequate to pay more than 40 percent of unsecured claims. Debtor explains that aged aunt likely to die soon and has promised to leave him large sum of money that will fully fund plan. Would it matter if debtor explained that he's enrolled in a "Get Rich Quick by Purchasing Foreclosed Properties" seminar and expects to be a millionaire within 12 months?

d. Debtor proposes a 10 percent plan but proof is he turned down a significant promotion at work that would have provided sufficient income to fund a 50 percent plan. Debtor told supervisor he appreciated promotion offer but didn't feel he could do the job adequately with all this debt hanging over him. Would it matter if debtor told supervisor he didn't want to make more money just to see it go to creditors and to please consider him for promotion again when Chapter 13 case is over?

Recall that the Chapter 13 debtor is required to make the first payments on the proposed plan to the trustee within 30 days following the filing of the petition or the proposal of the plan, whichever is earlier, per §1326(a)(1), and that the standing trustee retains these preconfirmation payments until the plan is confirmed, per §1326(a)(2). Once the plan is confirmed, §1326(a)(2) requires the trustee to distribute funds received under the plan "as soon as is practicable."

If the court declines to confirm the plan, the debtor may propose an alternative modified plan or, pursuant to §1307(a), may convert the case to a liquidation case under Chapter 7 without the need for court permission so long as debtor meets the eligibility criteria for that chapter. One option not open to the debtor who fails to achieve plan confirmation is an immediate appeal of that decision as of right. In Bullard v. Blue Hills Banks, 135 S. Ct. 1686 (2015), the Supreme Court held that a bankruptcy court order denying confirmation of a Chapter 13 plan is not a final appealable order in a case or proceedings within the scope of 28 U.S.C. §158(a) so long as the debtor retains the option to propose an alternative modified plan for confirmation. Interlocutory appeal "with leave of the court," under §158(a)(3) may still be available to the debtor unable to appeal as a matter of right due to *Bullard*.

C. LIVING WITH THE CONFIRMED CHAPTER 13 PLAN

Pursuant to §1327(a), the provisions of a confirmed plan bind the debtor and each creditor. Sections 1327(b) and (c) provide that, except as otherwise provided in the plan, upon confirmation, the property of the estate vests in the debtor free and clear of any claim or interest of any creditor provided for in the plan, unless the plan or the order of confirmation state otherwise. The idea is that, upon filing the petition, the bankruptcy estate is created and is subject to the control of the court per §§1306(a) and 541. However, upon confirmation, per §1306(b), right to possession of all the property not surrendered remains with the debtor, not the trustee as in a Chapter 7. And, per §1306(a), postpetition earnings and other property acquired by the debtor are considered property of the estate subject to the terms of the plan. Note carefully, the exception to this automatic revesting of the property of the estate in the debtor carved out in §§1327(b) and (c): "Except as otherwise provided in the plan or the order confirming the plan." We will have more to say about this exception.

After confirmation, it is up to the debtor to make the plan succeed. The debtor must make the payments to the trustee either directly or through payroll deduction and must make sure that any payments to be made to creditors outside the plan are made as well, either by himself or a third party. And the debtor must accept living under the strictures of what is essentially a fixed budget for the term of the plan.

Furthermore, while confirmation of the plan entitles the debtor to retain property as long as payments are made, §1305(c) has been interpreted by the courts to mean that the Chapter 13 debtor may not incur new debt after the Chapter 13 petition has been filed without consulting with and obtaining the permission of the trustee. The reason for that limitation is that new debt may compromise the debtor's ability to complete the plan. The only exceptions to this requirement are recurring living expenses that were anticipated when the plan was confirmed and emergency expenses the debtor incurs without time to seek prior permission from the trustee.

For example, if the debtor, or his dependent, living under a confirmed plan has a medical emergency, or if a vehicle breaks down and needs immediate repair, the debt incurred is allowable and the creditor can file a postpetition claim to be paid.

A debtor incurring unapproved new debt due to an emergency situation must seek the standing trustee's ratification of the expense promptly after it has been incurred or risk a motion by the trustee of dismissal of the case (dismissal is discussed in Section F). The limitations on incurring postpetition debt are normally set out in the plan itself. (See Paragraph 6 of the Matthews plan, Exhibit 15.2 and Document 18 in the Matthews case file.)

If the debtor fails to make the payments due under the confirmed plan, the court may dismiss the case or convert it to a liquidation case under Chapter 7, pursuant to §1307(c), on the motion of the trustee or an unpaid creditor. If the payments that are to be made to the standing trustee are not received as called for by the plan, the trustee's office will typically contact the debtor's lawyer or the debtor to find out what the problem is. The trustee has some discretion to work with a debtor who has gotten behind to allow the debtor time to catch up on missed payments. When a motion to dismiss or convert the case is made due to delinquencies in payments under the plan bankruptcy judges may also exercise discretion to allow the debtor some time to make up the missed payments before granting the relief requested if they are convinced the debtor has good intentions and a reasonable chance of making up the delinquencies.

For example, assume that a year after confirmation of the Matthews' Chapter 13 plan Roger is laid off and their plan payments become delinquent. The trustee or creditors may move the court to dismiss or convert the case. If Roger appears before the court and explains that the layoff was due to no fault of his own, that he is desperately seeking new employment, and is confident of finding a job within 30 to 45 days, the court may stay a ruling on the motion to give him time to find a new job, make up the deficiencies, and begin making regular contributions to the plan again. The hearing on the motion will likely be continued for some number of days until Roger can return and report back to the court.

D. MODIFYING A CONFIRMED CHAPTER 13 PLAN

Sometimes events occur that call for a plan to be modified after it has been confirmed. The debtor may lose his or her job, have to change jobs, or take time off from a job due to illness or the debtor may incur new unexpected expenses (e.g., medical expenses due to health problems, a new child). Or the debtor may have a significant increase in income, enabling debtor to pay more than at the time of confirmation.

Section 1329(a) authorizes the debtor, the trustee, or a creditor to file a motion to modify plan with the court. The matter is determined after notice and a hearing, which, as we know, means the proposed modification will be approved without a hearing unless an objection to modification is filed. Notice is provided using Official Form 2310B, Order Fixing Time to Object to Proposed Modification of Confirmed Chapter 13 Plan.

Section 1329(c) requires that, to be approved, the modified plan must comply with all the requirements of §§1322 and 1325 that we considered in connection with the original plan, including the good faith requirement. Assuming that the proposed modification does comply with those requirements, §1329(a) provides that a modification can propose to (1) increase or reduce the amount to be paid on a particular class of claims, (2) extend or reduce the time for payments called for in the plan, (3) alter the amount to be distributed to a creditor under the plan to account for payments made to that creditor outside the plan, or (4) as added by BAPCPA, reduce amounts to be paid under the plan by an amount expended by the debtor to purchase health insurance for the debtor or a dependent so long as the amounts are reasonable and necessary. Note that though a modification can extend or reduce the time for payments called for in the plan, §1329(c) provides that the plan, as modified, cannot, in any event, extend more than five years beyond the time that the first payment was due under the original plan.

For example, assume a debtor is operating under a confirmed plan calling for payment of a non-dischargeable priority claim in full over the first 12 months of the plan (as we know from Chapter Fourteen, Section A, priority claims must be paid in full). A month later, due to an unexpected reduction in income, the debtor seeks a modification of the plan calling for payment of the priority claim in full over 60 months. That modification can be granted but the payments to that creditor under the modified plan cannot extend more than five years beyond the date that the first payment was due under the original plan (which we know from Section A of this chapter may be an earlier date than the date the original plan was confirmed).

Per §1329(a), not only the debtor but the standing trustee or any unsecured creditor has standing to seek a modification of a confirmed plan. For example, if a plan is confirmed that calls for payment of 40 percent of the debtor's allowed unsecured claims, and the trustee or an unsecured creditor subject to that provision learns a year later that debtor's income has increased significantly, the trustee or unsecured creditor may seek a modification of the plan to increase the amount to be distributed to unsecured creditors in the plan.

Case Preview

In re Meeks and In re Mellors

The typical motion to modify plan is made by the debtor seeking some relief from the commitments made in the confirmed plan based on changed circumstances or on a tardy realization that the commitments taken on were too onerous. Courts take varying approaches to such requests, some requiring a showing of a substantial change in circumstances to merit modification and rejecting mere difficulty in compliance as a legitimate ground if such difficulty was reasonably foreseeable at the time the plan was confirmed. Other courts are more lenient, noting that the Code itself does not impose any such requirements on the approval of a modification request and concluding that Congress intended to leave the determination of sufficient grounds for modification to the discretion of the bankruptcy judge. As you read In re Meeks and In re Mellors, consider the following questions:

1. What were the circumstances giving rise to the request to modify plan in the respective cases?
2. What standard for modification approval was used by the courts in the respective cases?

In re Meeks

237 B.R. 856 (Bankr. M.D. Fla. 1999)

JENNAMANN, Bankruptcy Judge.

The Debtors filed for Chapter 13 relief on November 21, 1997. GMAC filed a claim in their bankruptcy case for $6,822.18, of which $5,888.16 was secured by the Debtors' 1988 Cadillac Deville. GMAC had a remaining unsecured claim of $934.02.

On September 22, 1998, the Debtors confirmed a Chapter 13 plan which provided that the Debtors would pay GMAC the full amount of GMAC's secured claim over 36 months rather than the 14 months remaining under the original contract. Only four months after confirmation, on January 29, 1999, the Debtors filed a Verified Motion to Modify Confirmed Chapter 13 Plan. The Debtors alleged that a new baby caused unexpected financial problems. As such, the Debtors sought permission to surrender the Cadillac to GMAC and, significantly, to also reduce their plan payments by the $174.00 per month which is the amount allocated to pay GMAC's secured claim. In addition, the Debtors wished to reclassify any remaining claim due to GMAC after the sale of the vehicle as unsecured.

The Chapter 13 Trustee consented to the modification, and the Court granted the Debtors' Motion to Modify the Plan on an ex parte basis. No notice was given to GMAC. Thereafter, GMAC brought this Motion to vacate the Modification Order.

In the meantime, GMAC sought and was granted relief from the automatic stay in order to take possession of the Cadillac. GMAC obtained possession and later sold the vehicle. After crediting all sums received from the sale, GMAC has a remaining amount due on its secured claim of $2,165.28.

The issue presented by the Motion is whether, under §1329 of the Bankruptcy Code, a Debtor may modify a confirmed Chapter 13 plan to surrender collateral subject to a security interest and then reclassify the unpaid remainder of the Creditor's claim as unsecured. GMAC argues that §1329 does not allow the reclassification of claims and that such a modification is inequitable and unfair to GMAC. The Debtors argue that §1329 does permit the reclassification of claims despite GMAC's objection.

Res Judicata Does Not Prevent Modification of Confirmed Chapter 13 Plan for Certain Specified Purposes. Section 1327(a) provides that "[T]he provisions of a confirmed plan bind the debtor and each creditor, . . . whether or not the creditor has objected to, has accepted, or has rejected the plan." U.S.C. 1327(a) (1998). Accordingly, a confirmed plan is res judicata as to any issues resolved or subject to resolution at the confirmation hearing. Among these issues is the amount of a secured claim. Under §1325(a)(5)(B)(ii), a chapter 13 plan must pay the full value of any allowed secured claim. 11 U.S.C. §1325(a)(5)(B)(ii) (1998). Accordingly, the value of a secured claim is fixed as of the effective date of the plan. In re Dunlap, 215 B.R. 867, 869 (Bankr. E.D. Ark. 1997).

However, §1329 specifically allows a debtor to modify a confirmed chapter 13 plan for three specific purposes. Section 1329 provides, in relevant part:

> (a) At any time after confirmation of the plan but before the completion of payments under such plan, the plan may be modified, upon request of the debtor . . . to —
>
> (1) increase or reduce the amount of payments on claims of a particular class provided for by the plan;
>
> (2) extend or reduce the time for such payments; or
>
> (3) alter the amount of the distribution to a creditor whose claim is provided for by the plan to the extent necessary to take account of any payment of such claim other than under the plan.

11 U.S.C. §1329(a).

In order to overcome the res judicata effect of §1327(a), some courts require a debtor to demonstrate a substantial, unanticipated change in circumstances justifying the requested modification. See, e.g., Arnold v. Weast (In re Arnold), 869 F.2d 240 (4th Cir. 1989); *Dunlap*, 215 B.R. at 869; In re Rimmer, 143 B.R. 871, 873 (Bankr. W.D. Tenn. 1992). Generally, these courts reason that " §1329(a) should not be abused by repetitive modification and . . . the confirmation should have a significant degree of finality." In re Klus, 173 B.R. 51, 59 (Bankr. D. Conn. 1994).

Section 1329(a) does not contain any express requirement that an unanticipated change in circumstances is necessary to justify modification. Rather, §1329(a) specifically permits debtors and creditors to modify the plan for the limited purposes listed. The legislative history indicates that Congress created § 1329 to allow debtors to modify their confirmed plan to address certain problems arising after confirmation. H.R. Rep. No. 95-595 at 265 (1977). However, Congress did not include any language indicating an intent to make a substantial change of circumstances a threshold requirement for any such modification of the plan. See In re Powers, 140 B.R. 476,

479 (Bankr. N.D. Ill. 1992). As the United States Court of Appeals for the Seventh Circuit stated:

> (t)he Code, in this instance §1329, does not require any threshold requirement for a modification and we will not use the legislative history to create a rule where none exists.

Matter of Witkowski, 16 F.3d 739, 742 (7th Cir. 1994). Neither this court nor other courts should require new hurdles for modification of a Chapter 13 plan which Congress neither contemplated nor enacted.

Furthermore, res judicata on its own does not create a requirement for a showing of a substantial change in circumstances. Res judicata does not apply when the plain language of a statute demonstrates that it should not apply. Id. at 744. . . . Here, §1329(a) gives the debtor, unsecured creditors and the trustee the right to modify a confirmed plan without any threshold requirement. As such, §1329 and the entire Bankruptcy Code indicate a clear intention that res judicata does not apply to the limited modifications permitted for by §1329. See id.

Accordingly, the Debtors need not demonstrate a substantial, unanticipated change in circumstances in order to modify their confirmed chapter 13 plan. However, neither can Chapter 13 debtors simply modify their plans willy-nilly. Section 1329(a) only permits the modification of a confirmed plan for three specific limited purposes.

[The court then disallowed the modification on the basis that none of the grounds for modification in §1329 permit the amount of an allowed secured claim to be modified as by treating it as unsecured.]

In re Mellors

372 B.R. 763 (Bankr. W.D. Pa. 2007)

DELLER, Bankruptcy Judge. . . .

This case was commenced by the Debtors, Jason and Darlene Mellors ("Debtors" or the "Mellors"), filing a voluntary petition under Chapter 13 of the United States Bankruptcy Code on September 1, 2006.

Prior to the bankruptcy, and pursuant to Retail Installment Contract and Security Agreement executed by the Debtors on July 17, 2004, Coastal Credit financed the Debtors' purchase of a used 1999 Mercury Villager. Pursuant to the Retail Installment Contract and Security Agreement, the Debtors granted Coastal Credit a security interest in the vehicle and Coastal Credit perfected its security interest by noting its lien on the title to the vehicle on October 15, 2004.

In addition to household uses, the husband debtor uses the Mercury Villager to travel to and from work. In the Debtors' bankruptcy case, the Debtors filed schedules of assets valuing the 1999 Mercury Villager at $3,580.00. The Debtors also filed schedules of liabilities, which provided that Coastal Credit had a claim of $6,985.99. The schedules of liabilities further provided that Coastal Credit's claim was a secured claim to the extent of the value of the Mercury Villager, with the remaining portion being scheduled as a general unsecured claim. . . .

In [debtors'] Chapter 13 Plan, the Debtors proposed to repay Coastal Credit's scheduled secured claim in the amount of $3,580.00 over the sixty month life of the Plan along with interest at the rate of 9 percent. The amount of the monthly payment proposed by the Debtors to Coastal Credit was $120.00 per month. The Chapter 13 Plan contemplated only a modest recovery for general unsecured creditors, for which Coastal Credit's deficiency claim would share pro rata.

Coastal Credit's viewpoint of the amount of its claim, and the value of its collateral, diverged somewhat from what the Debtors had scheduled. According to the proof of claim it filed on September 26, 2006, Coastal Credit asserted that the total amount of its claim was $8,823.84 and that the value of its collateral was $7,525.00. Coastal Credit also stated in its claim that it was entitled to accrue interest at the rate of 18 percent on its claim even though Coastal Credit was admittedly under secured, but the claim did not cite any legal authority for this proposition.

Given the disparity of their respective positions, and to avoid a contested plan confirmation hearing and a contested "cram down" action pursuant to 11 U.S.C. §506, the Debtors and Coastal Credit resolved their differences and the Debtors' Chapter 13 Plan was confirmed by the Court on December 27, 2006. To evidence their agreement, the Debtors and Coastal Credit entered into a "Stipulation as to the Treatment of Coastal Credit, LLC" dated January 8, 2007 (the "Stipulation"). The Court approved Stipulation is remarkably simple, and provides in pertinent part as follows:

1. The Debtors' 1999 Mercury Villager . . . is deemed to have a secured value of $8,823.84.
2. That the secured value of Coastal Credit, LLC's claim shall be paid with interest at 9.5% with a monthly payment of $185.32. The remaining portion of Coastal Credit, LLC's claim shall be treated as unsecured.
3. Coastal Credit, LLC shall not be required to release its lien on [the] Title until the Plan has been successfully completed.
4. The terms of this agreement shall be deemed incorporated into the Debtors' Plan and the Trustee may begin to make distributions to Coastal Credit, LLC according to the terms of this Order.

About one month after confirmation of their Plan and entry of the Stipulation, the Debtors learned of structural problems with their automobile. . . . The Debtors' rendition of the facts are. . . .

In February, 2007, Debtor took his vehicle to be inspected. Debtor was asked if he had recently been in an accident because the frame in his car was cracked and needed to be repaired prior to having an inspection sticker placed on it. The Debtor was told that the cost of repairing the frame would be several thousand dollars. The Debtor cannot afford the lump sum payment to properly repair the vehicle and remove it from the inspection station. As a result of this discovery, the Debtor's only vehicle would remain at the inspection station, inoperable. Although the vehicle had been inspected at previous inspection stations, this defect had never been discovered. Furthermore, title to the 1999 Mercury Villager does not state that it was reconditioned.

On March 12, 2007, the Debtors filed an amended Chapter 13 Plan pursuant to 11 U.S.C. §1329. The modification was necessitated by the fact that the Debtors, while using their best efforts, cannot afford to pay for an inoperable vehicle and finance a replacement vehicle at the same time. Thus, it appears that this Chapter 13 case would fail in the absence of an amendment to the existing Plan.

The amended Plan proposed by the Debtors provides for: (a) the surrender of the vehicle to Coastal Credit in satisfaction of any secured claim in favor of Coastal Credit; and (b) Coastal Credit's deficiency claim sharing pro rata in any distributions that any other unsecured creditors may receive in this case.

Coastal Credit opposed the relief requested by the Debtors and objected to confirmation of the amended Chapter 13 Plan. In support of its objection, Coastal Credit argues that the Sixth Circuit Court of Appeals' decision in In re Nolan, 232 F.3d 528 (6th Cir. 2000) controls this case. Coastal Credit interprets Nolan to hold that 11 U.S.C. §1329(a) limits a debtor to two options when modifying a confirmed Chapter 13 plan, and those options are either: (1) increasing or reducing the amount of payments, or (2) extending or reducing the time for payments. Coastal Credit argues that the Debtors' amended Plan does neither.

As another basis for its objection, Coastal Credit further states that where parties agree to a fair crammed-down value of collateral, and where the creditor actively participates in establishing this value, it is inequitable to shift the risk of the collateral's depreciation back to the creditor after the debtor has used and abused the collateral. According to Coastal Credit, not only does §1329(a) prohibit this type of modification, both 11 U.S.C. §§1325(a)(5) and 1327(a) also prohibit post-confirmation modification through surrender.

Conversely, the Debtors maintain that the modification of plan provisions found in 11 U.S.C. §1329 evidence a Congressional intent that Chapter 13 relief is, to a certain degree, malleable to the facts and circumstances confronting individual debtors. The Debtors further posit that surrender is permissible in this case because § 1329(a) permits changes to be made to "payments" to creditors under the confirmed plan. According to the Debtors, surrender of the collateral to Coastal Credit equates to a change of "payment" and thus the Debtors contend that the proposed modifications at issue comply with the plain language of the Bankruptcy Code. The Debtors further argue that they should not be forcefully made worse off than they already are (i.e., as debtors without an operable vehicle) when the defect in the automobile's frame was unknown to them when they entered into the Stipulation. . . .

The Court is faced with the difficult task of balancing the finality of a confirmed Chapter 13 plan (as well as the finality of a court approved Stipulation) against the terms and conditions of 11 U.S.C. §1329(a), which permits post-confirmation modification of Chapter 13 plans in certain situations.

The Third Circuit Court of Appeals has held that an order confirming a Chapter 13 plan is a final order. In re Szostek, 886 F.2d 1405, 1413 (3d Cir. 1989). The court in Szostek emphasized the importance of finality as a goal in bankruptcy law. . . .

> [T]he purpose of bankruptcy law and the provisions of reorganization could not be realized if the discharge of debtors were not complete and absolute; that if courts should relax provisions of the law and facilitate the assertion of old claims against

discharged and reorganized debtors, the policy of the law would be defeated; that creditors would not participate in reorganization if they could not feel that the plan was final, and that it would be unjust and unfair to those who had accepted and acted upon a reorganization plan if the court were thereafter to reopen the plan and change the conditions which constituted the basis of its earlier acceptance.

Szostek, 886 F.2d at 1409.

Pursuant to 11 U.S.C. §1327, a confirmed plan is binding on a debtor and each creditor. 11 U.S.C. §1327(a) (2006). Therefore, absent a timely appeal, such an order is res judicata and the terms of the plan are not subject to collateral attack. *Szostek*, 886 F.2d at 1409-1413. Thus, res judicata prohibits modification based upon issues that were or could have been litigated at the time of the hearing on confirmation. Id. at 1408 (refusing to revoke a Chapter 13 confirmation order even though a creditor alleged that the confirmation plan violated the substantive requirements of §1325).

In the present case, this Court must balance judicial efficiency and the Third Circuit's general policy favoring finality of confirmed plans against the Congressional mandate found in 11 U.S.C. §1329(a), which creates a limited exception to the binding effect of confirmed plans as set forth in §1327(a).

Section 1329(a) of the Bankruptcy Code does permit a debtor, the trustee, or an unsecured creditor to request post-confirmation modifications to a Chapter 13 plan before completion of payments under the plan. In re Smith, 259 B.R. 323, 326 (Bankr. S.D. Ill. 2001). Thus, when read together, the modification provisions found in §1329 appear to render the binding effect of §1327 meaningless.

Appearances, however, can be misleading because debtors do not have an unqualified right to invoke relief under §1329 of the Bankruptcy Code. Cf. Marrama v. Citizens Bank of Massachusetts, 549 U.S. 365 (2007) (holding that debtors who have not engaged in good faith conduct do not have an unqualified right to convert a chapter 7 case to a chapter 13). Rather, this Court holds that a predicate to invoking relief under 11 U.S.C. §1329 is a showing by the proponent of the plan modification that a material change in circumstances, not reasonably anticipated at the time of confirmation, has occurred that would warrant relief from the prior confirmed plan.

This Court acknowledges that outside of this District, some courts have held that there is no threshold requirement of a change in circumstances necessary for a plan modification in Chapter 13. [Citations omitted]. . . . This Court, however, declines to follow these holdings because 11 U.S.C. §1327 evidences Congress' intent that confirmed plans should be accorded a great deal of finality.

Other courts have held that a prerequisite to modification of a confirmed Chapter 13 plan is the proponent of the modification demonstrating a material or substantial change in circumstances, such as a change in the debtor's income or expenses, that was not anticipated at the time of the confirmation hearing. [Citations omitted]. . . . Courts have yet to define a set of factors considered in determining what type of circumstances constitute "substantial and unanticipated change." Yet, some cases give guidance on the type of change in the debtor's circumstances required to support post-confirmation modification. See e.g., In re Hoggle, 12 F.3d

1008, 1011 (11th Cir. 1994) (surmising that "modification [would be] permissible where problems such as a 'natural disaster, a long-term layoff, or family illness or accidents with attendant medical bills prevent compliance with the original plan.'"); In re Miller, No. 99-81339, 2002 WL 31115656, *2 (Bankr. M.D.N.C. Apr. 19, 2002) (substantial change existed where debtors: (1) could not find a replacement driver for their business when their son's health problems precluded him from driving; (2) had to spend $16,000.00 to replace engine and the transmission in a freightliner used in their business; and (3) became responsible for three grandchildren, who were recently placed in their care); In re Butler, 174 B.R. at 46-47 (changed circumstances existed where debtors' uninsured vehicle was heavily damaged in an accident 2½ years after plan confirmation, but modification not allowed due to debtor's inability to maintain collision insurance in breach of order of the court); In re Arnold, 869 F.2d 240, 241 (4th Cir. 1989) (change in amount of confirmed plan payments justified by debtor's substantial increase in income); In re Gronski, 86 B.R. 428, 432-433 (Bankr. E.D. Pa. 1988) (debtor's rent decrease of $145.00 per month constituted a substantial change in debtor's circumstances to warrant a $115.00 post-confirmation increase in monthly Chapter 13 plan payments); In re Euerle, 70 B.R. 72, 73 (Bankr. D.N.H. 1987) (debtor's receipt of inheritance represented a substantial change that necessitated the modification for increased plan payments).

In addition to the requirement that the change in the debtor's circumstances be significant (or substantial or material) most courts also require that the change be unanticipated. In re Nelson, 189 B.R. at 751 ("... post-confirmation modification ... is intended as a method of addressing unforeseen difficulties that arise during plan administration."); In re Leland, 96 B.R. 990, 992 (Bankr. D.S.D. 1989) ("Such modification is warranted only when an unanticipated change in circumstances affects implementation of the plan as confirmed."). This Court agrees with the determination that a debtor does not have an absolute right to modify a confirmed Chapter 13 plan. Instead, as a prerequisite to a §1329(a) modification analysis, the party seeking the post-confirmation modification must first demonstrate that the debtor has experienced a substantial or material, unanticipated change in his or her circumstances that warrants modification. Where this standard is met, res judicata will not preclude debtors from seeking a modification. The Court reaches this conclusion because confirmation of a Chapter 13 plan must result in a significant degree of finality as set forth in 11 U.S.C. §1327(a); the language of §1329(a) should not unnecessarily dilute the integrity of confirmation by permitting repetitive modification without cause. . . .

[The court then allowed the particular modification sought by debtor on the grounds that §1329 must be read together with §502(j) that permits the court to reconsider an allowed or disallowed claim for cause shown and that a "reconsidered claim may be allowed or disallowed according to the equities of the case." The court found nothing in §1329 to prohibit it from modifying a plan on the basis of §502(j).]

For all of the foregoing reasons, the Court will enter an order which overrules Coastal Credit's objection and confirms the Debtors' amended Plan.

Post-Case Follow-Up

The rules governing plan modification are important because so many Chapter 13 plans are modified, many more than once. That is due, of course, to the mandatory length of a Chapter 13 plan, three to five years. As we all know, financial circumstances can change dramatically in that length of time. Though most modifications are sought by debtors claiming negative changed circumstances that call for paying unsecured creditors less or over a longer period than the original confirmed plan called for, there can also be positive changed circumstances enabling a debtor to pay more to unsecured creditors or to pay more quickly than the original plan called for. From an ethical standpoint, if you represent a debtor operating under a confirmed plan whose circumstances have taken a dramatic change for the better, should you advise that debtor client to modify his plan accordingly or wait for the trustee or a creditor to act? Should you withdraw if the debtor refuses to do so? Though the Code does not require it, many standing trustees require Chapter 13 debtors to include language in their plan requiring the debtor to advise the trustee of both adverse and favorable changes in their income or assets, or to provide postpetition tax returns to the trustee during the term of the plan, or directing that income tax refunds over a certain amount (e.g., $1,000) be paid directly from the IRS to the trustee. Those trustees typically also require the plan to provide, as allowed by §1327(b) and (c) discussed in Section C above, that the property of the estate will not revest in the debtor upon confirmation so that the post-confirmation income of the debtor remains property of the estate throughout the term of the plan.

In re Meeks and In re Mellors: Real Life Applications

1. Assume you represent a Chapter 13 debtor operating under a confirmed plan who experiences the following changes. Using the standard for modification approval set out in *Meeks* determine if the modification would likely be allowed. Then make the same determination using the modification approval standard set out in *Mellors*.

   a. Debtor living under a confirmed 100 percent plan of 36 months duration asks that the plan be converted to five years so debtor will have more flexibility in his budget.

   b. Debtor's aged parent unexpectedly comes to live with debtor increasing significantly increasing his living expenses.

   c. Debtor's unemployed adult daughter who was living with her and was pregnant at the time of plan confirmation has the baby and debtor claims increased expenses due to the newborn child.

    d. Debtor's primary vehicle for family use, which was 15 years old at the time of plan confirmation, fails and cannot be fixed and debtor wants to buy a new car to replace it.

    e. Debtor's primary vehicle for family use, which was five years old at the time of plan confirmation, is totaled in an accident and debtor wants to buy a new car to replace it.

    f. Debtor experiences post-confirmation conversion to a new faith that requires tithing and debtor needs to retain additional income to comply.

    g. Debtor loses the job he had at the time of confirmation that paid $33,000 per year; he finds new job paying $32,000 per year but is 10 miles further from his home.

2. The plan modifications sought by the debtors in *Meeks* and *Mellors* both involved changing the treatment of a claim that had been classified as secured in the original plan by surrendering the collateral and treating the balance owed as unsecured. *Meeks* disallowed the modification on the basis that none of the grounds for modification in §1329 permit the amount of an allowed secured claim to be modified as by treating it as unsecured. Other courts disagree, saying that because §1329(a)(1) allows debtors to modify payments on claims, debtors, in turn, may also modify the amount of those claims. See, e.g., In re Rimmer, 143 B.R. 871, 875 (Bankr. W.D. Tenn. 1992). *Mellors* allowed the modification on the grounds that §1329 must be read together with §502(j), which permits the court to reconsider an allowed or disallowed claim for cause shown and that a "reconsidered claim may be allowed or disallowed according to the equities of the case." *Mellors* held that nothing in §1329 prohibits the court's modifying a plan on the basis of §502(j). Determine if the courts of the federal district or circuit where you plan to practice have addressed this particular modification issue and, if so, assuming the reason the debtor sought such modification was justifiable under the modification approval standards utilized, whether a court in that district or circuit would allow the modification.

E. THE CHAPTER 13 DISCHARGE

1. Timing of the Discharge

Confirmation of a Chapter 13 plan does *not* result in an immediate discharge of the debts not to be paid under the plan. Section 1328(a) of the Code provides that the discharge in a Chapter 13 is granted only upon completion of the plan. One exception to that rule is that an early discharge can be granted under §1328(b) for hardship (thus, sometimes called a **hardship discharge**), if the debtor can establish the three requirements shown in Exhibit 16.2.

EXHIBIT 16.2 **Requirements to Receive an Early (Hardship) Discharge in Chapter 13**

- The failure to complete payments under the plan is beyond the control of the debtor
- The payments made to unsecured creditors up to the time of discharge are at least as much as they would have received in a Chapter 7 liquidation (this is sometimes called the "good faith test" of §1328(b))
- Modification of the plan is not feasible

A hardship discharge is reserved for extreme cases, as where a debtor becomes permanently disabled and is unable to further fund any feasible plan.

Case Preview

In re Edwards

Often the reasons a debtor gives to support a request for hardship discharge are similar to those given in support of a motion to modify the plan. Granting an early discharge is a more extreme measure because it means creditors won't be paid as much as anticipated when the plan was confirmed. Consequently, one of the requirements for the early discharge, §1328(b)(3), is a finding that plan modification is not feasible. As you read In re Edwards, consider the following questions:

1. Of the three requirements for early discharge under §1328(b), which was "the bone of contention" in this case?
2. Why does this court reject the "catastrophic circumstances" or "truly worst of the awfuls" test for satisfaction of §1328(b)(1)?
3. What test does the court enunciate for the satisfaction of §1328(b)(1)?

In re Edwards
207 B.R. 728 (Bankr. N.D. Fla. 1997)

KILLIAN, Bankruptcy Judge.

THIS MATTER came on for hearing on the motion of the Chapter 13 debtor for a hardship discharge pursuant to the provisions 11 U.S.C. §1328(b). The standing Chapter 13 trustee objects to the granting of the discharge on the grounds that the debtor does not meet the requirements for granting such a discharge. Having considered the entire file in this case, the testimony of the debtor, arguments of counsel, and pertinent authorities, I make the following findings of fact and conclusions of law pursuant to Fed. R. Bankr. P. 7052.

The debtor filed this Chapter 13 on February 5, 1993 and proposed a repayment plan under which he would make payments to the trustee in the amount of $1,419.37 over a 36 month period for a total in payments to the trustee of $51,097.32. The plan was confirmed on June 10, 1993. At the time he filed his Chapter 13, the debtor derived his income through his ownership in operation of a business known as Film Town Stores, Inc. He had this business for ten years at the time his petition was filed and the majority of the claims listed in the schedules arose from the operation of the business.

Following confirmation of the plan, the case proceeded uneventfully until January 31, 1995 when the holder of the mortgage on the debtor's homestead filed a motion for relief from stay based on missed payments. This motion was consented to by the debtor and on February 8, 1995, the debtor filed a first amended plan to reflect the loss of his homestead and providing for any deficiency resulting from the foreclosure to be treated as a general unsecured debt. The debtor then fell behind in his payments under the plan and on April 24, 1995, the trustee filed a motion to dismiss. This motion was resolved on June 7, 1995 by the entry of a strict compliance order reflecting that the debtor at that time was only one month delinquent in his payments. The debtor kept his payments current thereafter through October 27, 1995 at which time he could no longer make payments. On February 7, 1996, the trustee filed a notice of default under the terms of this strict compliance order and requested dismissal of the case.

On February 8, 1996, the debtor filed a motion for an extension of time to complete the payments called for under his Chapter 13 plan. At the time of the motion, the debtor had made 30 payments for a total of $39,742.36 and had only six payments remaining. The basis for the motion was that the debtor's business had recently failed and he was in the process of seeking employment which would enable him to make the six remaining payments. The debtor requested a period of up to 18 months in which to complete the payments. Since his original plan called for a term of 36 months, this 18 month extension would still allow him to complete payments within the maximum period of 60 months permitted in 11 U.S.C. §1322(c). On October 11, 1996, the debtor requested an additional extension of time to begin making the deferred payments based on his continued inability to make those payments. At that time, he had obtained employment, however that job was in sales and he was not making sufficient income to resume making the required plan payments. On December 20, 1996, being unable to make any more payments under the plan, the debtor filed the instant motion for hardship discharge.

At hearing on the motion, the debtor testified that his film business which had been successful for a number of years deteriorated after his Chapter 13 plan was confirmed due to increased competition in the market. He was close to consummating a sale of the business in the face of a foreclosure on the assets by the bank when the bank refused to approve the sale and concluded its foreclosure. Following the loss of his business, the debtor suffered depression requiring medication and also suffered the breakup of his marriage. He searched extensively for employment but was unable to secure a job with sufficient income to make his plan payments. He finally obtained employment as a commissioned salesman for a local television station and has made approximately $1,500.00 per month for the last several months. This level of income leaves him with no disposable income with which to make any plan payments.

Section 1328(b) provides the authority for a hardship discharge. [Opinion quotes §1328(b).] . . .

The bone of contention is whether or not the debtor meets the requirement . . . that his failure to complete the payments is due to circumstances for which he should not justly be held accountable.

In arguing that the debtor's circumstances do not justify the granting of the hardship discharge, the trustee cites the case of In re Nelson, 135 B.R. 304 (N.D. Ill. 1991) for the proposition that most courts will approve a request for hardship discharge only in the presence of "catastrophic circumstances." That case, cites to a leading authority on Chapter 13 cases as suggesting that circumstances which would justify hardship discharge have to be the "truly worst of the awfuls to have something more than just the temporary loss of a job or temporary physical ability." Id. at 307, citing K. Lundin, Chapter 13 bankruptcy, § 9.8 at 9-26 (1990). In that case, however, the court pointed out that the economic events leading to the failure of the Chapter 13 plan began before the Chapter 13 was filed and continued early during the period following confirmation of the plan but were not brought to the court's attention until several years later. . . .

I recognize that those few bankruptcy courts directly addressing the [hardship discharge] issue have imposed a very difficult standard to meet under §1328(b)(1). However, in reviewing those cases, I am unable to discern where a requirement for some "catastrophic circumstances" or the "worst of the awfuls" is a standard to be met to show that the failure is due to circumstances for which the debtor should not justly be held accountable. The case of In re Dark, 87 B.R. 497 (Bankr. N.D. Ohio 1988) cited in *In re Nelson* does not stand for the proposition that catastrophic circumstances are required to justify a hardship discharge. In *Dark*, the hardship discharge was denied because the debtor failed to satisfy the requirement of §1328(b)(2). Regarding the debtor's evidence under §1328(b)(1), the court held that "unsubstantiated and conclusory statements regarding an inability to fund a plan are insufficient". Id. at 498. The court in In re White, 126 B.R. 542 (Bankr. N.D. Ill. 1991) made reference to a requirement for catastrophic circumstances to justify a hardship discharge, but did not elaborate. I have been unable to find any appellate court decisions which address the issue.

I am unable to conclude that the law requires a debtor seeking a hardship discharge under §1328(b) must demonstrate the existence of catastrophic circumstances, notwithstanding the views of my colleagues in other courts. First, I do not believe that the language of §1328(b)(1) requires such a standard. Secondly, given the requirement of §1328(b)(2) that unsecured creditors have received at least that which they would have received in a liquidation under Chapter 7, and the limited extent of a discharge received under §1328(b), I can find no justification for exacting such a standard. Unlike the "super discharge" provided to debtors pursuant to §1328(a) upon completion of all payments under a plan, the hardship discharge under §1328(b) is the same discharge received under Chapter 7 with all of the exceptions the discharge specified in §523(a). 11 U.S.C. §1328(c), In re Thornton, 21 B.R. 462 (Bankr. W.D. Va. 1982). To deny a debtor who has made every effort to comply with a Chapter 13 plan the benefits of any discharge in bankruptcy when, despite his best efforts, economic circumstances prevent him from completing his payments would punish that debtor for attempting to repay his creditors under Chapter 13 in the first place.

Where a debtor is unable to complete payments under a Chapter 13 plan due to economic circumstances that did not exist nor were foreseeable at the time of confirmation of the plan, where those circumstances are beyond the debtor's control, and where the debtor has made every effort to overcome those circumstances but is unable to complete his plan payments, then I think the requirement of §1328(b)(1) has been met. If the other subsections of §1328(b) have also been met, then, the debtor may receive a discharge. In this case, I find that the debtor has in fact met all of the requirements of §1328(b), and accordingly his motion for a hardship discharge will be granted.

Post-Case Follow-Up

The court's reference to a "super discharge" available to a Chapter 13 debtor who does not receive an early hardship discharge is discussed later in this chapter. What was the basis for the court's finding that the §1328(b)(3) requirement was satisfied in this case? Should the court have conducted more of an inquiry on that element? Should the court have inquired more into whether the debtor's loss of his business due to increased competition was foreseeable at the time of plan confirmation? Which element of §1328(b) does foreseeability of the circumstances giving rise to the request for early discharge go to? Do you think the troubled personal life of this debtor (loss of his business, depression, breakup of his marriage) played a role in the court's decision? Do you see any hint of bad faith by this debtor in connection with his request for early discharge? Note that the bankruptcy judge, having granted the motion for early discharge in the Chapter 13 case, sets a deadline for creditors contending their claims are non-dischargeable in a Chapter 7 to file complaints so contending because the Chapter 13 debtor receiving an early discharge can only discharge debts that could be discharged in a Chapter 7. We will discuss this distinction later in this section.

In re Edwards: Real Life Applications

1. Assume you represent the debtor in this case and the court announced that it would follow the "catastrophic circumstances" or "truly worst of the awfuls" standard for satisfying §1328(b)(1). Make an argument on behalf of this debtor using the facts set out in the case that he can satisfy this test.

2. Look at the factors the In re Edwards court considers in determining that §1328(b)(1) is satisfied: existence and foreseeability of the negative circumstance at the time of plan confirmation, fault of the debtor for being in the circumstance, ability of debtor to change or control that circumstance, and efforts made by the debtor to overcome the negative circumstance before seeking the early discharge. Assume you are the standing trustee opposing this debtor's motion for hardship discharge. Using these factors and the facts set out in the case, make an argument debtor has not satisfied the §1328(b)(1) requirement.

3. Assume that Chapter 13 debtors in the following circumstances have moved for early discharge and all satisfy the §1328(b)(2) requirement. Determine if these debtors have satisfied the §1328(b)(1) and (3) requirements. Make that determination first using the "catastrophic circumstances" test for §1328(b)(1). Then make that determination using the *Edwards* test for §1328(b)(1).

a. Debtor says his girlfriend has moved out since plan confirmation and she helped him with groceries and utility payments most of the time. Debtor has not filed any motion to modify his plan.

b. Debtor who had been laid off construction jobs three times in the two years preceding his Chapter 13 filing is laid off again and now cannot find other employment despite vigorous search; has no disposable income.

c. Debtor who had steady employment when the Chapter 13 was filed and the plan confirmed is fired for stealing from his employer and cannot find other employment despite vigorous search; no disposable income.

d. Debtor who had steady employment when the Chapter 13 was filed and the plan confirmed is laid off for no fault of his own three weeks before filing the motion for early discharge. Has been vigorously searching for other employment since but no leads yet. Will run out of funds to make plan payments in another 30 days.

e. Debtor, a car salesman, has been seriously and permanently injured in a car accident. His disabilities will render him unable to ever work again. He has no pension or disability insurance. Has applied for SSI but if approved it will not provide sufficient disposable income to fund a Chapter 13 plan. Would it matter if the accident were the debtor's fault? If he was driving drunk? If he had three prior DUIs all prepetition?

2. Requirements for Receiving a Chapter 13 Discharge

In addition to completing the plan, receiving a discharge under Chapter 13 is contingent upon meeting other requirements, shown in Exhibit 16.3.

EXHIBIT 16.3 **Requirements for Receiving a Chapter 13 Discharge, In Addition to Completing Plan Payments**

■ Certification by the debtor using Form 2830 (if appropriate) that all domestic support obligations called for in the plan or that otherwise came due prior to making such certification have been paid (§1328(a)

■ The debtor has not received a discharge in a prior Chapter 13 case (within two years preceding the order for relief in the instant case or within four years in a prior Chapter 7, 11, or 12 case; §1328(f))

■ The debtor has completed the postpetition course in financial management (§1328(g); see Document 20 in the Matthews case file)

■ Certification by the debtor using Form 2830 as to whether the prohibition of §522(q) (limiting one convicted of a felony or having debts arising from certain proscribed conduct which might make the filing abusive and who is utilizing state exemption laws) arises in the case (§1328(h)

Unlike Chapter 7, creditors have no standing to object to a debtor's discharge under Chapter 13. Of course, they can object to the plan's confirmation or modification and move to dismiss or convert the case if plan payments are not being made (see discussion in Section F), but only the trustee can object to a discharge under Chapter 13.

3. Scope of the Chapter 13 Discharge: Non-Dischargeable Debts

The discharge releases the debtor from all unpaid claims designated for nonpayment in the plan or disallowed under §502, with limited exceptions. Sections 1328(a) and (d) set forth the debts that cannot be discharged in a Chapter 13, and those are summarized in Exhibit 16.4.

| EXHIBIT 16.4 | Debts That Cannot Be Discharged in a Chapter 13 Bankruptcy |

- Long-term obligations, such as the home mortgage extending beyond the term of the plan and that the plan contemplated would continue to be paid [§1328(a)(1) & §1322(b)(5)]
- Unpaid taxes on returns filed two years preceding the petition or on returns not filed or for fraudulent returns [§1328(a)(1) & §523(a)(1)(B)(C)]
- Debts for money, property, services, or an extension of credit obtained by fraudulent pretenses or by the use of fraudulent financial statements [§1328(a)(1) & §523(a)(2)(A)(B)]
- Last-minute consumer cash advances or spending for luxury goods or services [§1328(a)(1) & §523(a)(2)(C)]
- Debts that were not listed on the debtor's schedules so that the creditor could not file a timely proof of claim [§1328(a)(1) & §523(a)(3)]
- Debts arising from the debtor's fraud or defalcation while acting in a fiduciary capacity [§1328(a)(1) & §523(a)(4)]
- Domestic support obligations, such as alimony and child support [§1328(a)(1) & §523(a)(5)]
- Student loans, unless the debtor can convince the court that not discharging this obligation will work an undue hardship on the debtor or his dependents [§1328(a)(1) & §523(a)(8)]
- Claims arising from the wrongful death or personal injury caused by the debtor's driving under the influence of drugs or alcohol [§1328(a)(1) & §523(a)(9)]
- Restitution or fine included on the sentence of the debtor for a crime [[§1328(a)(3)]
- Restitution or damages awarded in a civil action against the debtor based on willful or malicious injury that caused personal injury or death [[§1328(a)(4)]
- Postpetition debts for consumer necessities allowable under §1305(a)(2), for which trustee approval could have been sought but was not [§1328(d)]

Just because a debt is non-dischargeable does not mean it cannot be dealt with in the Chapter 13 plan. Payments on non-priority unsecured but non-dischargeable debt can be modified during the term of the plan even though the underlying debt is not dischargeable. For example, payments due from the debtor on a non-dischargeable student loan debt may be modified during the term of the plan even where the entire indebtedness will not be paid off during the plan and the debt will not be discharged in the Chapter 13 proceeding. The advantage to the Chapter 13 debtor, of course, is that, if the plan is approved, the automatic stay remains in effect on such non-dischargeable debt until the case is over.

Most of the non-dischargeable debts you see in Exhibit 16.4 are identical to the debts declared non-dischargeable in a Chapter 7, pursuant to §523(a). You may want to go back and read the discussion of these various non-dischargeable obligations (see Chapter Eleven, Section A, and Exhibit 11.1).

However, a slightly more generous discharge is available under a Chapter 13 than under a Chapter 7, giving rise to the practitioner's characterization of the §1328(a) discharge as a **super discharge** as compared to the Chapter 7 discharge under §727, which is limited by all the exceptions contained in §523(a). In a Chapter 13, debts or claims arising out of the willful or malicious injury to the property (but not the person) of another, referenced in §523(a)(6), and certain fines and penalties imposed by the government, referenced in §523(a)(7), can be discharged. As noted above in connection with *Edwards*, §1328(c) provides that a Chapter 13 debtor receiving an early hardship discharge under §1328(b) does not discharge any of the debts listed in §523(a); that debtor does not receive the super discharge of §1328(a).

For example, assume an individual is sued for civil damages by another who alleges that the individual committed an intentional and malicious physical assault with a baseball bat on his automobile, totally destroying it. The case goes to trial and a verdict for the plaintiff in the amount of $20,000 is returned for the plaintiff. A final judgment is entered on the jury's verdict. The final judgment is now enforceable. If the individual against whom the verdict has been returned consults a debtor's attorney as to whether the judgment can be discharged in bankruptcy, he will likely be told that cannot be accomplished in a Chapter 7 case but might be accomplished in a Chapter 13 case subject to the Code requirements for confirmation and discharge already discussed.

Application Exercise 3

Look again at Exhibit 16.1. Assume the individual described in the last example files for Chapter 13 relief and proposes a plan to pay all his creditors 100 percent over five years, except for the judgment creditor in the lawsuit described. The plan proposes to pay nothing on that claim and to discharge it. Which criterion for confirmation of a Chapter 13 plan is the judgment creditor most likely to say is not satisfied by this plan? How would you rule on that issue if you were the bankruptcy judge? Would it matter that the debtor can show that in fact all of his projected disposable income for the five years of the plan will be needed to pay the other creditors 100 percent?

The **order granting discharge** will follow 3180W, Discharge of Debtor after Completion of Chapter 13 Plan.

Note that Chapter 13 does not contain a provision similar to §727, which sets out various grounds for denying any discharge at all to a Chapter 7 debtor (see Chapter Eleven, Section B, and Exhibit 11.2). The types of conduct that might serve as a basis for denying a discharge in a Chapter 7 (fraud, dishonesty, lack of cooperation, etc.) will be relevant in the decision to confirm the Chapter 13 debtor's plan regarding whether it was proposed in good faith. They will also be relevant in deciding to dismiss or convert the Chapter 13 case, as discussed in the next section.

F. CONVERSION OR DISMISSAL OF A CHAPTER 13 CASE

1. Voluntary Conversion or Dismissal

Section 1307(a) provides that the debtor can convert the case to a Chapter 7 liquidation at any time. Of course, the debtor wishing to convert the case will have to qualify to be a Chapter 7 debtor, as stipulated in §1307(g). Conversion is accomplished by the debtor filing a **notice of conversion**. Where a Chapter 13 case is converted to Chapter 7 prior to confirmation of any plan, §1326(a)(2) directs that payments that have been made to the standing trustee but not yet distributed (recall that the debtor must begin making plan payments prior to confirmation per §1326(a)(1) and the trustee is to retain such payments until plan confirmation or denial per §1326(a)(2)) are to be returned to the debtor after deducting 503(b) administrative expenses, which are understood to include the standing trustee's fee and, in some but not all districts, the unpaid amount of the debtor's attorney's fee (recall that the attorney's fee may be paid through the plan).

Pursuant to §1307(b), the debtor may request that the court dismiss the Chapter 13 case at any time, and the court will grant that request unless the Chapter 13 case was itself converted from an earlier Chapter 7 or Chapter 11 case. Request for dismissal is accomplished by filing a motion for permission to dismiss Chapter 13 case.

Where the Chapter 13 case is dismissed before confirmation but there is no conversion to Chapter 7 or any other chapter under the Code, §349, dealing generally with the effect of dismissal in any case under the Code, provides in §349(b)(3) that, "Unless the court, for cause, orders otherwise, the dismissal . . . revests the property of the estate in the entity in which such property was vested immediately before the commencement of the case. . . ." In other words, property of the debtor goes back to the debtor upon dismissal. Do administrative claims get paid out of postpetition preconfirmation payments being held by the debtor? Usually, yes, because of the "Unless the court, for cause, otherwise orders" language of §349(b). The court will order funds held by the standing trustee returned to the debtor but, using the authority of §1326(a)(2), order payment of outstanding administrative fees first, which in some districts will include the earned but unpaid balance of the attorney's fee.

Has *Harris v. Viegelahn* Opened a Pandora's Box?

The Supreme Court in *Harris* neglected to address at least two serious consequences of its holding regarding post-confirmation conversion. It is very common in Chapter 13 cases for the debtor's attorney's fee to be paid through the plan for the convenience of the debt-strapped client. The holding would apparently not allow the Chapter 13 standing trustee to distribute any funds in her hands at the time of conversion to the debtor's attorney, who was anticipating being paid through the now-defunct plan. The attorney will apparently have to file a claim for the unpaid fees in the Chapter 13 case in the client's Chapter 7 case like other unsecured creditors of the debtor. Debtor's attorneys may respond to this implication of *Harris* by demanding the full attorney's fee up front, which will make Chapter 13s less feasible for many debtors. Or, as part of the fee agreement, some debtor's attorneys may have the debtor grant them a security interest in property that is collected but undistributed by the trustee in the event of a conversion. Similarly, it is unclear after *Harris* whether the standing trustee can pay administrative fees including her own percentage fee from funds collected but not yet disbursed at the time of conversion. Like the debtor's attorney, the standing trustee and other holders of §503(b) administrative claims will presumably have to file claims in the debtor's Chapter 7. In the Chapter 7 case such claims might enjoy a priority status (another unclear issue post-*Harris*) but that does not guarantee that they will be paid in a Chapter 7 liquidation.

The last three paragraphs deal with what happens when there is a conversion or dismissal of a Chapter 3 case prior to plan confirmation. A question that has divided the circuits concerns what is to be done with undistributed funds in the hands of the standing trustee when a Chapter 13 debtor in good faith converts to a Chapter 7 after confirmation of his plan. In Harris v. Viegelahn, 135 S. Ct. 1829, 1836 (2015), the Supreme Court held that absent a bad-faith conversion, §348(f) limits a converted Chapter 7 estate to property belonging to the debtor "as of the date" the original Chapter 13 petition was filed ("Conversion from Chapter 13 to Chapter 7 does not commence a new bankruptcy case. The existing case continues along another track, Chapter 7 instead of Chapter 13, without 'effect[ing]' a change in the date of the filing of the petition.' §348(a)."). Because post–Chapter 13 petition wages do not fit that bill, such wages collected by a Chapter 13 trustee but not yet distributed to creditors pursuant to a Chapter 13 plan do not become part of a converted Chapter 7 estate and are properly paid to the debtor.

Application Exercise 4

In many districts, the standing trustee does not take a fee until distribution is made. In other districts it may be assessed upon receipt if the local rules of court or customary local practice allow. Determine when the standing trustee in the federal district where you plan to practice assesses the administrative fee.

Application Exercise 5

The Supreme Court in *Harris* did not distinguish between the post–plan confirmation conversion of a Chapter 13 case to one under Chapter 7 and the post-plan confirmation dismissal of a Chapter 13 case for purposes of the proper distribution of undistributed funds in the hands of the standing trustee. Presumably, upon post-confirmation dismissal without conversion, such funds are to be returned to the debtor per §349(b)(3) raising the same issues regarding proper distribution as in *Harris*. But if there is a post-confirmation dismissal of the Chapter 13 and not a conversion to another case under the Code, there is another dimension to the drama. Assume you represent a creditor holding a final judgment in the amount of $20,000 against the debtor when he files his Chapter 13 petition. You immediately cease any efforts to collect on the judgment and await the treatment of your client's claim in the plan. You have told your client not to expect more than ten cents on the dollar and for the rest of the claim to be discharged and sure enough that's what the debtor's plan calls for. The plan has been confirmed but today you receive word that the debtor's Chapter 13 case has been dismissed voluntarily (or involuntarily as discussed in the next section) and it has not been converted to Chapter 7 or any other chapter under the Code. You also receive word that the standing trustee is holding $10,000 in undistributed funds in the debtor's case. What action might you take immediately to improve the prospects for your client's recovery from debtor on its judgment? Why could you not take this action if the case had been converted to Chapter 7? What difference would it make to your plan to take this action if the plan in the Chapter 13 case had not been confirmed at the time of dismissal? See §1326(a)(2).

2. Involuntary Conversion or Dismissal

Sections 1307(c) and (e) provide a number of circumstances under which a party in interest (the standing trustee, U.S. Trustee, or a creditor) can move the bankruptcy court to either dismiss the Chapter 13 case or convert it to a Chapter 7, "whichever is in the best interest of creditors and the estate." Those circumstances are summarized in Exhibit 16.5. Involuntary dismissal or conversion can be sought before or after confirmation of the Chapter 13 plan.

EXHIBIT 16.5   **Grounds for Involuntary Dismissal or Conversion of a Chapter 13 Case under §1307(c) and (e)**

- Unreasonable delay by the debtor that is prejudicial to creditors
- Nonpayment of any required fees and charges
- Failure to timely file a plan
- Failure to commence making timely payments under the plan, as required by §1326(a)(1)
- The denial of confirmation of a plan and the denial of a request made for additional time for filing another plan or a modification of a plan
- A material default by the debtor with respect to a term of a confirmed plan
- The revocation of the order of confirmation

EXHIBIT 16.5 **(Continued)**

- The termination of a confirmed plan by reason of the occurrence of a condition specified in the plan, other than completion of payments under the plan
- Only on request of the U.S. Trustee, failure of the debtor to timely file the various schedules of assets and liabilities and statement of affairs, as required by §521
- Failure of the debtor to pay any domestic support obligation that first becomes payable after the date of the filing of the petition
- Failure of the debtor to file all tax returns due for the preceding four years by the day before the first meeting of creditors is first scheduled, as required by §1308(a)

How Many Chapter 13 Cases Succeed?

The available empirical data going back twenty years seems to indicate that, nationwide, only one out of every three Chapter 13 cases succeeds in the sense that the debtor pays as scheduled throughout the term of a confirmed plan and receives a discharge at the end. There is considerable variation from state to state and even district to district but nationwide that percentage looks accurate. See, e.g., Katherine Porter, *The Pretend Solution: An Empirical Study of Bankruptcy Outcomes*, 90 Tex. L. Rev. 103, 107-111 (2011) (only one in three cases filed under Chapter 13 ends in discharge); Scott F. Norberg & Andrew J. Velkey, *Debtor Discharge and Creditor Repayment in Chapter 13*, 39 Creighton L. Rev. 473, 505, 505 n.70 (2006) ("The overall discharge rate for the debtors in the seven districts covered by the Project was exactly the oft-repeated statistic of one-third."); Gordon Bermant & Ed Flynn, *Measuring Projected Performance in Chapter 13: Comparisons Across the States*, 19 Am. Bankr. Inst. J. 22, 22 (July-Aug. 2000); Henry E. Hildebrand, III, *Administering Chapter 13 — At What Price?*, 13 Am. Bankr. Inst. J. 16, 16 (July-Aug. 1994).

Note that some of these grounds can arise prior to plan confirmation (e.g., failure to timely file a plan; denial of plan confirmation and failure to seek additional time to file another plan or to modify; failure to file required schedules and statements in support of the petition, etc.). When a motion to dismiss or convert is made prior to plan confirmation, the good faith of the debtor can be an issue the court will consider as part of the decision to dismiss or convert under §1307(c) (the §1307(c) grounds are not exclusive). That good faith inquiry may consider the prepetition activities of the debtor that gave rise to her debts, the motives of the debtor in deciding to file the Chapter 13 case, the accuracy of the disclosures made in the debtor's petition and supporting schedules, or the terms of the plan that the debtor proposes in the unconfirmed Chapter 13 plan.

However, if the motion to dismiss or convert is filed after plan confirmation, most courts will not conduct a good faith inquiry since confirmation required a finding by the court that the debtor filed the petition in good faith (§1325(a)(7)) and that the plan was proposed in good faith (§1325(a)(3)). Those courts consider that the confirmation order has res judicata effect as to the good faith issue and will focus only on the specific §1307 grounds (see, e.g., U.S. v. Tucker, 1996 WL 741510 (M.D. Fla.) (creditor's motion for summary judgment denied on issue of good faith where Chapter 13 plan was confirmed even though creditor's motion to dismiss for lack of good faith was filed and pending when confirmation occurred)).

The most frequent grounds asserted in a motion to dismiss or convert is §1307(c)(4), the failure of the debtor to make the payments due under the plan either before or after plan confirmation (recall from Section A that, pursuant to §1326(a)(1), the plan payments must begin within 30 days after the plan is filed or the order of relief entered, whichever is earlier without regard to confirmation). But in many cases there are good to plausible reasons why payments are not being made and the debtor asks for a modification in lieu of dismissal or for additional time to make up missed payments. Bankruptcy judges have considerable discretion in deciding whether to seek dismissal under §1307(c)(4) and the bankruptcy court's historical role as a court of equity, still recognized in §105(a), is often

> But not everyone agrees that an uncompleted Chapter 13 plan is necessarily a failure. See, e.g., Gordon Bermant, *What Is "Success" in Chapter 13? Why Should We Care?*, 23 Am. Bankr. Inst. J. 20, 65 (Sept. 2004), arguing that plan completion and discharge are neither necessary nor sufficient for success if the plan goes on long enough that debtor's finances are substantially reordered and the ship more or less righted.

a factor in such disputes. See, e.g., In re Mallory, 444 B.R. 553 (S.D. Tex. 2011) (Chapter 13 debtor who, after making plan payments for three years, unilaterally withheld plan payments from trustee for three and a half months due to debtor's contention that claim of creditor secured in debtor's home was invalid and should be challenged had insufficient defense to trustee's motion to dismiss for failure to make plan payments; equities did not favor debtor who should have moved to suspend mortgage payments until his objection to claim was decided). For the bankruptcy court's role as a court of equity see, e.g., In re Beaty, 306 F.3d 915, 922 (9th Cir. 2002) ("[A] bankruptcy court is a court of equity and should invoke equitable principles and doctrines, refusing to do so only where their application would be inconsistent with the Bankruptcy Code.").

Chapter Summary

- The Chapter 13 plan must be filed with the petition or within 14 days thereafter. The debtor must begin making payments to the trustee under the plan within 30 days of the entry of the order for relief or filing the proposed plan even if the plan has not yet been confirmed.
- There are a number of criteria for confirmation of a Chapter 13 plan, and any party in interest may object to confirmation, in which event a confirmation hearing will be conducted by the court. The deadline for objections is normally set by local court rule. A creditor who fails to timely object to a plan prior to confirmation may be deemed to have accepted the plan but the court can still deny confirmation to a plan that does not comply with the Code. In deciding whether the plan has been proposed in good faith the court looks to the totality of the circumstances to determine whether the plan will achieve a result consistent with the objectives and purposes of the Code.

■ Upon confirmation of a Chapter 13 plan the right to possession of property of the estate not surrendered by the debtor and abandoned by the trustee remains in the debtor subject to the requirements of the plan. Earnings and other property acquired by the debtor from the commencement of the case through its conclusion are also property of the estate subject to the terms of the plan.

■ Once a plan is confirmed, the debtor may not incur new debt without permission of the standing trustee except for recurring living expenses or emergencies. If a debtor fails to make the payments promised under the confirmed plan, the Chapter 13 case can be dismissed or converted to a Chapter 7 liquidation. The standing trustee has discretion to work with a debtor who falls behind on plan payments, as do bankruptcy judges when a motion to dismiss or convert is filed.

■ A confirmed plan can be modified on motion of the debtor, trustee, or creditors, to increase or reduce plan payments, extend or reduce the time for payments. The plan as modified must comply with all Code requirements for confirmation. Some courts require the debtor to demonstrate a substantial unforeseen change of circumstance to justify a modification.

■ A discharge of debts not paid through the plan is granted upon completion of the plan unless the court grants an earlier hardship discharge where the debtor can show that the inability to complete plan payments is beyond his control, modification is not feasible, and unsecured creditors have received more than they would in a Chapter 7. As in a Chapter 7, some debts cannot be discharged in a Chapter 13 although Chapter 13 does recognize a super discharge in comparison to Chapter 7 in that debts arising out of the willful or malicious injury to the property and certain fines and penalties imposed by the government may be discharged in Chapter 13.

■ A Chapter 13 debtor may voluntarily dismiss the case or convert it to another chapter of the Code so long as debtor qualifies as a debtor under that alternative chapter. Undistributed funds in the hands of the standing trustee when a Chapter 13 debtor in good faith converts to a Chapter 7 are returned to the debtor. A number of grounds exist upon which a Chapter 13 case may be involuntarily dismissed or converted to Chapter 7, the most frequently asserted of which is failure of the debtor to make required payments to the standing trustee before or after plan confirmation.

Applying the Concepts

1. Assume you represent Jack's Used Cars, a local used car dealer that routinely sells cars on credit to consumers. Jack, the owner of JUC, calls you today and advises that he has received notification from the bankruptcy court that Carl and Brenda Jones, who purchased a car on credit from JUC 9 months ago, have filed a Chapter 13 bankruptcy. JUC retained a security interest in the car purchased by the Jones and there is a balance owed of $6,000. The Jones are two payments behind to JUC on the car note and Jack was planning on calling you today to have you send them a letter threatening repossession if the arrearages

are not made up immediately. The notice received by JUC from the court sets a date for the first meeting of creditors and advises that the Jones' plan, which was filed with the petition, will be confirmed unless objections are filed before that first meeting. You review the Jones' schedules and proposed Chapter 13 plan and see that the debtors value the car purchased from JUC at $5,000 and propose to strip down the balance owed to JUC to that value and pay it during the term of the plan so they can retain possession of the car. The plan makes no provision for curing the arrearage. Jack confirms that the current value of the car is only $5,000.

a. Should you go ahead and write the letter to the Jones threatening repossession?

b. Should you object on behalf of JUC to the confirmation of the proposed plan and, if so, on what grounds will you do so under §1325(a)?

c. If your client fails to contact you regarding this matter until after the plan has been confirmed does he have a remedy? The jurisdiction follows In re Montoya, 341 B.R. 41 (Bankr. D. Utah 2006).

2. Assume the Jones purchased the car from JUC three years ago and that the proposed plan does call for curing the arrearage owed to JUC during the term of the plan. However, Jack tells you that the car is easily worth the full $6,000 and he is upset at the proposed $5,000 strip down. He also tells you that Brenda Jones worked for him as a salesperson at the time she and her husband purchased the car and that she is fully familiar with car values and knows the car is worth every penny of $6,000. He also tells you that she left his employment on bad terms claiming she was owed $1,000 more in sales commissions than Jack paid her and that when she left she swore to Jack that someday she would get even with him. Should you object on behalf of JUC to the confirmation of the proposed plan and, if so, on what grounds will you do so under §1325(a)?

3. Which of the following do you think would form a legitimate good faith basis for the Matthews to seek a modification of their confirmed plan?

a. A request to abandon the Ford F-150 truck to the creditor since it has just been wrecked and to treat the balance owed to the creditor as an unsecured claim under the plan

b. A request to convert the plan to a 10 percent plan, from a 24-25 percent plan, so that Susan can go back to school full-time and earn her master's degree

c. A request to convert the case to a 2 percent plan, from a 24-25 percent plan, so that both Roger and Susan can pursue a recent religious calling to donate all their time to missionary work for their religion

4. Which of the following do you think would form a legitimate good faith basis for the trustee or a creditor to seek a modification in the confirmed plan?

a. A request to increase the plan to 100 percent because Susan just won $1 million in the lottery

    b. A request to extend the plan to five-and-a-half years so another 10 percent could be paid to unsecured creditors

    c. A request to increase the plan from a 24-25 percent plan to a 50 percent plan because Roger got the promotion and raise he mentioned he might be in line for at their 341 meeting

5. You be the judge. You have before you motions to dismiss filed under §1307 by the standing trustees in the following Chapter 13 cases. Based on the information provided here, do you grant the motion to dismiss, entertain a motion to modify, or otherwise grant the debtor a temporary reprieve from dismissal?

    a. The confirmed plan required debtor to provide the standing trustee with copies of all personal income tax returns within 30 days of filing those returns. Debtor has failed to do so in either the first or second year of his plan. Trustee suspects but cannot prove that debtor did not file tax returns for those years.

    b. Debtor's plan was confirmed six months ago but his payments to the standing trustee to fund the plan have been made from 10-20 days late each month since confirmation. Angry creditors have been screaming at the trustee. Debtor's excuse is that he is a roofing subcontractor and sometimes his customers don't pay him timely so he pays the trustee when he is able.

    c. Debtor's Chapter 13 case was filed four months ago and a proposed plan was filed with it. However, the plan was not confirmed and debtor was given 15 days to propose an alternative plan. It has now been 30 days since confirmation was denied. Debtor's attorney has been telling the trustee that a revised proposed plan will be forthcoming "real soon." Would it matter if debtor's attorney explained that debtor had been in the hospital for three weeks? In jail for three weeks?

    d. After confirmation, debtor learned that the mortgagee on his home to whom the plan ordered payments made had in fact assigned the mortgage to another financial company a year before and neither the assignor nor the assignee had notified the debtor. Debtor contacts the standing trustee and asks him to make the plan payments to the correct party but the trustee says he must abide by the dictates of the plan and it's up to the debtor to get it fixed. Two weeks later the debtor files an action challenging the validity of the claim of the mortgagee to whom payments have been going. Debtor also withholds payments to the trustee until the matter has been cleared up, fearing that if the trustee makes the scheduled payment to that mortgagee debtor will have to pay twice when the matter is finally cleared up. A hearing on debtor's action against the mortgagee is scheduled in two weeks. Meanwhile, the trustee moves to dismiss the case and that hearing is on for today. See In re Mallory, 444 B.R. 553 (S.D. Texas 2011).

The Chapter 12 Case: Reorganization for a Family Farmer or Family Fisherman with Regular Annual Income

In this chapter we take a brief look at the Chapter 12 bankruptcy, which is a reorganization proceeding for those who qualify as family farmers or family fishermen. Large corporate farming or fish harvesting/processing businesses will usually not qualify for Chapter 12 and will proceed under Chapter 11 to reorganize. And many smaller, family-operated farming or fishing businesses that do qualify under Chapter 12 will involve debtors with primarily commercial debt. But sometimes the individual owners of these small farming or fishing operations do qualify as consumer debtors and thus fall within the purview of our study. And for them a Chapter 12 case can be quite advantageous over a Chapter 13. While in most federal districts very few if any Chapter 12 cases are filed each year, for those who will practice in rural areas where family farming is still common or in communities located on our mighty rivers and teaming seashores where fishing for a living is still a way of life, a basic understanding of the Chapter 12 bankruptcy is essential.

Key Concepts

- To qualify under Chapter 12, debtors must satisfy total monetary debt limitations, more than 50 percent of which must come from a family farming or commercial fishing operation; there are also fixed debt and income source limitations
- In Chapter 12, a standing trustee is appointed, but the debtor continues to operate the farming or fishing business as a debtor in possession
- The Chapter 12 debtor must file a debt adjustment plan with the petition or within 90 days thereafter
- The automatic stay goes into effect upon filing of a Chapter 12 petition and includes a codebtor stay as in Chapter 13
- Unlike Chapter 13, Chapter 12 grants the debtor, as debtor in possession, all of the turnover and avoidance powers of a Chapter 7 bankruptcy trustee

■ Unlike Chapter 13, a Chapter 12 plan may cure an arrearage or modify future payments due on secured debt over a term in excess of the plan

■ In contrast to Chapter 13, Chapter 12 contains no prohibition on the strip down of an undersecured mortgage on real property or on a vehicle under the 910-day rule

A. THE CHAPTER 12 REORGANIZATION FOR A FAMILY FARMER OR FAMILY FISHERMAN WITH REGULAR ANNUAL INCOME

Occasionally, an individual consumer debtor will file under Chapter 12 of the Code rather than under Chapter 13. Chapter 12 bankruptcy is limited to those who qualify as "family farmers" or "family fishermen" with "regular annual income" per §109(f). The idea behind Chapter 12 is similar to that in Chapter 13 — to provide a qualifying debtor the opportunity to propose a debt adjustment plan for confirmation by the bankruptcy court. However, nationwide, very few Chapter 12 bankruptcy cases are filed because, in most federal districts, so few debtors qualify as a family farmer or a family fisherman and often the attorney for such debtors will place them in a Chapter 13 rather than a Chapter 12.

Application Exercise 1

Access the statistics and data tables page maintained by the Administrative Office of the Federal Courts at www.uscourts.gov/statistics-reports/case-load-statistics-data-tables and determine how many Chapter 12 cases have been filed in the federal district where you plan to practice in the last two to three years. Compare what you find with the number of Chapter 13 cases filed in that district during the same time period.

B. HISTORY, PURPOSE, AND QUALIFICATIONS TO FILE UNDER CHAPTER 12

The Chapter 12 bankruptcy was created by Congress in 1986 exclusively for family farmers with a regular annual income in response to a time of economic hardship for the nation's farmers. The chapter was enacted with a *sunset clause*, pursuant to which it would expire at a specific time if not renewed. However, it was renewed several times and finally made a permanent part of the Code by BAPCPA, which expanded it to also cover family fishermen with a regular annual income.

Application Exercise 2

Why do you think §109(f) references the family farmer or family fisherman's regular "annual" income? In contrast, §109(e), dealing with Chapter 13, only references individuals with regular income. How often do most debtors with regular income get paid or receive income? How often do most farmers get paid or otherwise receive income? If a Chapter 12 debtor only receives income once or twice a year, how might that impact the terms of the debt adjustment plan the debtor proposes?

A "family farmer" who may qualify for relief under Chapter 12 is defined in §§101(18) and (19) as an individual or an individual and spouse engaged in a **farming operation** (see §§101(20) and (21)) either as individuals, a partnership, or a closely held corporation. A "family fisherman" who may qualify for relief under Chapter 12 is defined in §§101(19A and B) as an individual or an individual and spouse engaged in a **commercial fishing operation** either as individuals, a partnership, or a closely held corporation. Thus Chapter 12 allows qualifying entities to file as well as individuals. In our consideration of Chapter 12, we will focus on the individual filer.

Like Chapter 13, Chapter 12 imposes debt limitations on those seeking to qualify for relief, and the dollar amounts of those limitations are subject to adjustment every third year as mandated by §104. As of April 1, 2016, those filing for Chapter 12 relief as a family farmer can have no more than $4,153,150 in total debt while those filing for Chapter 12 relief as family fishermen can have no more than $1,954,550 in total debt. In addition to the debt limits, Chapter 12 contains debt and income source limitations. Per §§101(18) and (19A), at least 50 percent of the family farmer's total fixed debts and at least 80 percent of the family fisherman's total fixed debts (excluding debt on the debtor's principal residence) must be related to the farming or the commercial fishing operation. Additionally, more than 50 percent of the gross income of the individual or the husband and wife for the preceding tax year (or, for family farmers only, for each of the second and third prior tax years) must have derived from the farming or commercial fishing operation. For a good discussion of what constitutes income from a farming operation, see In re Jessen, 82 B.R. 490 (Bankr. S.D. Iowa 1988), highlighted below.

Notice that the debt limits set out in §101(18) for the family farmer and §101(19A) for the family fisherman are considerably higher than those set out in §109(e) for individuals filing under Chapter 13. This is one of the significant advantages of Chapter 12 for a qualifying individual debtor. Individuals qualifying as family farmers or family fishermen often carry considerably more debt than most individuals because they are operating a business. Thus, even though they are individual debtors, Chapter 13 is foreclosed to them because their debt exceeds the limits for that chapter. An individual qualifying as a family farmer or family fisherman whose debts exceed the debt limits set for Chapter 12 filing will file for reorganization under Chapter 11 of the Code.

In fact, Chapter 12 was designed to be something of a hybrid between Chapter 13 and Chapter 11 of the Code, although it has more in common with the former. It is designed to accommodate the economic realities with which farmers

Protecting the Family Farmer

Prior to enactment of the Chapter 12, bankruptcy laws in this country did not, for the most part, single out farmers much less fishermen for special treatment in bankruptcy. The Bankruptcy Act of 1898 did make farmers immune from involuntary bankruptcy. An amendment to the Bankruptcy Act in 1933 passed during the ravages of the Great Depression and Dust Bowl added temporary Section 75 to the Act intended to enable farmers in default on the mortgages securing their farms to modify the payment schedules in order to retain possession and avoid foreclosure. Section 75 proved generally unworkable since it required the agreement of mortgagee banks, which were also struggling to survive. The Frazier-Lemke Farm Bankruptcy Act of 1934 strengthened Section 75 by mandating a five-year delay in foreclosure on farms in default so long as the farmer made rental payments. At the end of the five years the farmer was given the option to remain in possession as a paying tenant following foreclosure or to buy back the foreclosed property at its then-appraised value over six years at 1 percent interest. Section 75 expired in 1949 when, in more prosperous times, Congress did not renew it. The hyper-inflation of the late 1970s followed by the savings & loan crisis of the mid-1980s led to a severe tightening of credit that impacted negatively on small farmers whose way of life depended on the regular securing of credit (often in excess of the debt limits set for Chapter 13) and whose numbers were steadily dwindling anyway. Those concerns led to Congress enacting Chapter 12 on a temporary basis in 1986 applicable only

and fishermen live and to facilitate their adjustment of debts in ways that are less complex (or expensive) than those designed for businesses under Chapter 11 and to some extent more practical and streamlined than those for individual debtors under Chapter 13.

Per §109(g), like individuals filing under any other chapter of the Code, a debtor cannot file under Chapter 12 (or any other chapter) if during the preceding 180 days a prior bankruptcy petition was dismissed due to the debtor's willful failure to appear before the court or comply with orders of the court or was voluntarily dismissed after creditors sought relief from the bankruptcy court to recover property upon which they hold liens. In addition, the individual debtor who files under Chapter 12 must comply with the BAPCPA-imposed requirement that he or she receive credit counseling from an approved credit counseling agency within 180 days preceding the filing of the petition per §109(h)(1) and §111.

Does it seem incongruous that an individual filing under Chapter 12 might be a consumer debtor? They are, after all, operating a business, and you might assume their debts are likely to be primarily business debts. And often that is true, but not always. The individual Chapter 12 debtor may well own a residence on which there is significant debt that will be treated as consumer debt. And remember that the Chapter 12 debtor is operating a "family" business and many debts incurred in doing so may well be mixed consumer/business debt (e.g., a truck purchased for mixed family and business use).

C. FILING THE CHAPTER 12 CASE

A Chapter 12 case for an individual debtor is commenced in the same way as a Chapter 13, by filing a petition with a bankruptcy court. A husband and wife may file a joint petition.

Like the individual Chapter 7 debtor and the Chapter 13 debtor, per FRBP 1007(b), the Chapter 12 debtor must also file a list of creditors, along with the various schedules of assets and liabilities, a statement of financial affairs, and the other statements and documents discussed in Chapter Eight, Section B, except for the Statement of Intent (Official Form 108). Section 521(a)(2) requires the filing of a Statement of Intent only of an individual Chapter 7 debtor. Like the Chapter 13 debtor, the Chapter 12 debtor's proposed plan will indicate how he intends to deal with property that is subject to a security interest.

Significantly, the individual Chapter 12 debtor is not required to complete and file the Forms 122C to determine the applicable commitment period or projected disposable income. In a Chapter 12 case those determinations will be made by examination of the debtor's Schedules I and J together with the proposed plan itself. And since the debtor is operating a farming or fishing business, there will be tax returns that can be examined during the plan confirmation process as well.

to the family farmer. Chapter 12 was scheduled to expire in 1993 but its duration was extended several times by Congress before being made permanent by BAPCPA in 2005. At that time, Chapter 12 was expanded to include family fishermen because, like the family farmer, many such fishing operations regularly incurred debt in excess of the Chapter 13 limits and some did business as entities, disqualifying them from Chapter 13 relief.

D. THE CHAPTER 12 TRUSTEE AND THE DEBTOR AS "DEBTOR IN POSSESSION"

Pursuant to §1202, a trustee is appointed in every Chapter 12 case. In most districts the U.S. Trustee has designated a Standing Chapter 12 Trustee pursuant to 28 U.S.C. §586(b) who will fulfill this role, as does the Standing Chapter 13 Trustee in cases filed under that chapter (in many districts the standing Chapter 13 trustee will also serve in Chapter 12 cases).

The duties of the Chapter 12 trustee are very similar to those of the trustee in a Chapter 13 case. See Exhibit 12.1 and compare with the duties of the Chapter 12 trustee set out in §1202(b). Significantly, the Chapter 12 trustee, like the Chapter 13 trustee, does not collect and liquidate the property of the estate as does the Chapter 7 trustee pursuant to §704(a)(1).

Since the Chapter 12 debtor is engaged in operating his farming or commercial fishing business, he is considered a **debtor in possession** and charged under §1203 with continuing that operation during the bankruptcy proceeding. The debtor in possession concept is one borrowed from the Chapter 11 business bankruptcy where the debtor continues to operate the business in bankruptcy. Pursuant to §1204, a party in interest may request that the bankruptcy court remove the debtor as a debtor in possession "for cause," which can include fraud, dishonesty, incompetence, or gross mismanagement of the business. In that case the trustee will operate the business.

Case Preview

In re Jessen

Of the grounds for removal of a Chapter 12 debtor in possession under §1204, the most frequently litigated is "gross mismanagement." What constitutes mismanagement may vary considerably depending on the eye of the beholder and the qualifying concept "gross" can make it difficult to for the complaining party in interest to prevail on that grounds. As you read In re Jessen, consider the following questions:

1. What issues were raised regarding whether income being received by the debtor constituted farming operation income for purposes of the 50 percent plus income test of §101(18)(A)?
2. What is the difference between the narrow and broad views adopted by the courts regarding what constitutes a farming operation, and which view does the court adopt?
3. What were the factual bases for the allegations that the debtor was guilty of mismanagement?
4. Note: At the time this case was decided, current §101(18)(A) was denominated §101(17)(A) and current §101(21) was denominated §101(20).

In re Jessen
82 B.R. 490 (Bankr. S.D. Iowa 1988)

Jackwig, Chief Bankruptcy Judge.

On July 8, 1987 the following matters came on for hearing in Council Bluffs, Iowa:

1. Motion to dismiss and/or to remove debtors as debtors in possession filed by the Production Credit Association of the Midlands (PCA) and the Federal Land Bank (FLB) on June 15, 1987;

. . .

5. Motion to dismiss filed by the standing Chapter 12 trustee on July 2, 1987.

FACTS

1. The debtors' 1986 federal tax return shows the debtors received income from the following sources:

Source	Amount
Wages	$35,256.00
Interest Income	758.00
Sealing of Grain	21,936.00
Cash Payment	2,981.00
Cash Rent	22,660.00
Executor Fee	1,975.00
Total	$85,566.00

2. For twenty-four years prior to 1985, the debtors actively engaged in farming.

3. In order to supplement farm income, Charles Jessen obtained off-farm employment as a custodian in December of 1984.

4. Unable to obtain operating financing, the debtors leased much of their land on a cash rent basis in 1985 and 1986.

5. Approximately 280 acres remained uncultivated in 1986.

6. Earl Phippen, the uncle of Charles Jessen, died on July 10, 1985.

7. Earl Phippen's last will and testament was filed with the Iowa District Court for Audubon County on July 17, 1985.

8. In the will, Earl Phippen devised 160 acres of land located in Audubon County to Charles Jessen.

9. On April 7, 1986 Charles Jessen executed and filed a disclaimer to the 160 acres in the estate proceedings.

10. The debtors filed a petition for relief under Chapter 12 on April 17, 1987.

11. The trustee estimates that the value of the land less encumbrances is $33,880.00.

DISCUSSION

The . . . issues include: whether the debtors are eligible for Chapter 12 relief; whether Charles Jessen's disclaimer of the 160 acres and failure to cultivate 280 acres in 1986 are grounds for removal of the debtors as debtors in possession or for dismissal of the case. . . .

A. Chapter 12 Eligibility

The PCA, the FLB and the trustee contend that the debtors are not eligible for Chapter 12 relief. Specifically, they argue that the cash rent is not derived from a "farming operation" and therefore the debtors do not satisfy the 50 percent income test set out in 11 U.S.C. section 101(17)(A). Further, the PCA and the FLB maintain that the income received from sealing corn should not be considered "gross income" for eligibility purposes.

11 U.S.C. section 109(f) states that "[o]nly a family farmer with regular income may be a debtor under Chapter 12 of this title." 11 U.S.C. section 101(17)(A), which defines "family farmer" in the context of an individual or individual and spouse, requires in part that:

> [an] individual or individual and spouse engaged in a farming operation . . . receive from such farming operation more than 50 percent of such individual's or such individual and spouse's gross income for the taxable year preceding the taxable year in which the case concerning such individual or such individual and spouse was filed;

A "farming operation" is defined in 11 U.S.C. section 101(20) as including "farming, tillage of the soil, dairy farming, ranching, production or raising of crops, poultry, or livestock, and production of poultry or livestock products in an unmanufactured state."

A number of cases have examined the meaning of "farming operation" in general and as it relates to the income test found in section 101(17)(A). This court in Matter of Burke, 81 B.R. 971 (Bankr. S.D. Iowa 1987) reviewed some of those cases and determined that the decisions generally have fallen along two lines. One line of cases, represented by Matter of Armstrong, 812 F.2d 1024 (7th Cir. 1987), cert. denied, 108 S. Ct. 287 (1987), views "farming operation" narrowly. For the *Armstrong* majority, a critical question is whether the activity under consideration exposes the debtor to the risks inherent in agricultural production. The other line of cases interprets "farming operation" in a broader fashion. Those courts look to the "totality of the circumstances" in determining whether the debtors or the family members or relatives in the case of a corporation or partnership are engaged in farming and whether, in the case of an individual or an individual and spouse, the income test is met. This court adopted the latter approach in the *Burke* decision.

With respect to cash rent arrangements, this court stated:

> Income received from a cash rent arrangement will be farm income in the case of an individual or individual and spouse only if the evidence reveals that past farming activities have been more than short term or sporadic and that any cessation of farming activities is temporary. Consideration will be given to the reason for the cessation (inability to obtain operating credit versus new nonfarm venture); the extent of the cessation (leasing a portion of the farm in an effort to scale back the operation versus leasing the entire farm); and the relationship to the tenant (leasing to family members as opposed to leasing to nonrelated individuals or entities).

Burke, at 976-77.

Under the totality of the circumstances, the debtors in this case have established that the cash rent is derived from a farming operation. The debtors had been actively engaged in farming for twenty-four years prior to curtailing their farming operation in 1985. Thus, their past farming activities cannot be characterized as short term or sporadic. The debtors ceased actively farming because they were unable to obtain operating credit. The fact that these debtors leased much of their farm and sold their equipment does not obviate finding the rent was from a "farming operation." The record reveals that the PCA cut off operating credit in December of 1984 and the debtors were unable to find operating credit elsewhere. Therefore, maintaining more than a small portion of the farm was an impossibility.

Finally, the record does not address the relationship between the cash rent tenants and the debtors. However, a finding for the debtors is warranted even if it is assumed the tenants were not related to the debtors. Apparently, the debtors have access to relatives' equipment and their son farms a portion of their land on a crop share basis. They cannot be viewed as having abandoned farming on a permanent basis. Under the facts of this case, finding that the cash rent is derived from a farming operation does not abuse the Congressional intent underlying 11 U.S.C. §101(17)(A) in particular and Chapter 12 in general.

Accordingly, the debtors have established that more than 50% of their income is derived from a farming operation in which they are engaged.

B. GROSS MISMANAGEMENT

The PCA and FLB maintain that the debtors should be removed as debtors in possession or that the case should be dismissed because a portion of the farm remained idle during 1986 and Charles disclaimed his inheritance. The PCA and FLB assert these actions constitute gross mismanagement.

11 U.S.C. section 1204(a) provides that a debtor may be removed as a debtor in possession "for cause, including . . . gross mismanagement of the affairs of the debtor, either before or after the commencement of the case." 11 U.S.C. section 1208(c)(1) states that a case may be dismissed for "gross mismanagement, by the debtor that is prejudicial to creditors." The PCA and FLB do not cite nor does the court find any cases that have examined the term "gross mismanagement" as used in sections 1204 and 1208. The legislative history of Chapter 12 and in particular, section 1204, indicates that Congress envisioned that a trustee would substitute for a removed debtor in possession and that this transfer of duties was modeled after provisions in Chapter 11. H. Conf. R. No. 958, 99th Cong., 2d Sess. 49, reprinted in 1986 U.S. CODE CONG. & ADMIN. NEWS 5227, 5246, 5250. 11 U.S.C. section 1104, which governs appointment of trustees in Chapter 11 cases, states in part:

> (a) At any time after the commencement of the case but before confirmation of a plan, on request of a party in interest or the United States trustee, and after notice and a hearing, the court shall order the appointment of a trustee —
> (1) for cause, including . . . gross mismanagement of the affairs of the debtor by current management, either before or after commencement of the case. . . .

Courts interpreting this provision have recognized that appointment of a [Chapter 11] trustee is an extraordinary remedy. [Citations omitted.] Appointment of a trustee may prevent reorganization because the administrative expenses associated with the appointment are paid by the estate. [Citations omitted.] Accordingly, the parties seeking the appointment bear the burden of proving the appointment is justified. [Citations omitted.] Use of a gross mismanagement standard implies a recognition that every bankruptcy reorganization involves some degree of mismanagement. [Citation omitted.] . . . Given the clarity of the legislative history, the similarity of the language used in sections 1104 and 1204 and the financial burdens that accompany having a trustee operate a farm, the court concludes that the aforementioned principles apply in a Chapter 12 context.

Under these standards, the PCA and the FLB fail to shoulder their burden. With respect to the uncultivated land, the evidence is clear that the debtors were unable to farm because of a lack of operating credit. Moreover, they attempted to rent the land. A prospective tenant was lined up but he eventually declined to lease the land because of the dispute between the debtors and the FLB. There is little more the debtors could have done to ensure that the land was cultivated. The fact that land remained idle was not the result of gross mismanagement.

Likewise, Charles' decision not to disclaim his inheritance does not constitute "gross mismanagement." The disclaimer was made pursuant to Iowa Code section 633.704(1). Under Iowa law, a disclaimer takes effect against creditors. [Citation omitted.] Contrary to the PCA's and FLB's contention, Charles had no obligation to accept the inheritance and apply it to debt.

The court's findings concerning "gross mismanagement" as used in section 1204 applies to "gross mismanagement" as used in section 1208(c)(1). Generally in rehabilitation cases, the burden of proof in a motion to dismiss rests with the moving party. [Citations omitted.] . . . PCA and FLB have failed to carry this burden.

Post-Case Follow-Up

Does the narrow or broad view of what constitutes a farming operation seem truer to the definition under the Code? Determine if the courts of the federal district or circuit where you plan to practice have adopted one or the other of these views in a Chapter 12 case. Does the court's discussion of what constitutes "gross mismanagement" remind you somewhat of the business judgment rule in corporate law? Not every court would agree with this one on the issue of the debtor's disclaimer of the inheritance. Is it really determinative on the issue of mismanagement that the debtor had no obligation to accept the inheritance? Should that be the test? Compare In re Kloubec, 247 B.R. 246 (Bankr. N.D. Iowa 2000) (Chapter 12 debtor's disclaimer of inheritance valued at $85,000 one day before petition filed treated as fraudulent transfer as to creditors; involuntary conversion of case to one under Chapter 7 per §1208(d) based on fraud).

In re Jessen: Real Life Applications

1. Assume you practice in a federal district that has adopted what *Jessen* describes as the narrow view of what constitutes a farming operation under §101(21). You have the following debtors in your office who would like to file under Chapter 12. Most of their income over the past three years has derived from the following sources. Which do you think will qualify as Chapter 12 debtors?
   a. Raising cattle sold for slaughter delivered to buyer twice a year at the then current market price and growing corn harvested once a year in the fall.
   b. Growing wild flowers on 400 acres during a four-month growing season sold to commercial florists in the region. Land is idle the remainder of the year.
   c. Conducting tours of caves on 3,000 acres of former dairy farm that has been in the family for 100 years.
   d. Selling off farm equipment used on 5,000 acre farm which is under option to be purchased by a real estate developer within the next 24 months.
2. You represent the following debtors in Chapter 12 family farmer cases who have committed the following acts. Creditors in each case have filed a motion under §1204 to remove them from management of their farming operations as debtors in possession. In each case, decide whether the court is likely to grant the motion.
   a. Turned down offer from a real estate developer that would have provided debtor more than enough cash to pay all debts.
   b. Stopped growing profitable alfalfa crop on half of the farm acreage to introduce new organic potato crop not expected to be profitable until after term of the plan but then expected to produce twice the profits as alfalfa.
   c. Stopped growing profitable corn crop on 5 percent of farm acreage in order to make a gift of that acreage to newly married daughter and her husband.

d. Stopped growing crops on 90 percent of farm land in order to begin giving cave tours on the land to the public in expectation of greater profits.

e. To reduce labor costs replaced 10 percent of seasonal harvesters with undocumented immigrants paid less than minimum wage.

The debtor in possession or trustee charged with managing the debtor's business is required by FRBP 2015(b) to:

- keep a record of receipts and the disposition of money and property received;
- file the reports and summaries required by §704(a)(8) of the Code (periodic reports and summaries of the operation of such business, including a statement of receipts and disbursements, and such other information as the United States trustee or the court requires) including a statement, if payments are made to employees, of the amounts of deductions for all taxes required to be withheld or paid for and in behalf of employees and the place where these amounts are deposited; and
- give notice of the case to every entity known to be holding money or property subject to withdrawal or order of the debtor, including every bank, savings or building and loan association, public utility company, and landlord with whom the debtor has a deposit, and to every insurance company that has issued a policy having a cash surrender value payable to the debtor, except that notice need not be given to any entity who has knowledge or has previously been notified of the case.

Often the local rules of the bankruptcy court where the Chapter 12 case is pending or guidelines adopted by the U.S. Trustee in the district will contain special reporting and operating requirements for the Chapter 12 debtor in possession. Common requirements at the beginning of a case are that the debtor immediately close all bank accounts and reopen them in the name of the debtor as debtor in possession. Technically, the debtor in possession is considered a new and different entity from the prepetition debtor. The same is required for credit cards and financial records. For an example of guidelines for Chapter 12 debtors in possession see the Operating and Reporting Requirements for Chapter 12 Cases issued by the U.S. Trustee for the Southern District of California at www.justice.gov/ust/r15/docs/chapter12/chapter_12_orr.pdf.

E. THE AUTOMATIC STAY, FIRST MEETING OF CREDITORS, AND FILING PROOFS OF CLAIM IN A CHAPTER 12 CASE

Upon the filing of the Chapter 12 petition, the automatic stay of § 362 goes into effect and operates the same way as in a Chapter 13 case. As in Chapter 13, there is a codebtor stay prohibiting creditors from seeking to collect a consumer debt from any individual who is liable along with the debtor. See §1201(a). At this time, you may want to review the discussion of how the automatic stay operates in a Chapter

13 case, including the codebtor stay on consumer debt, discussed in Section C of Chapter Twelve.

Pursuant to FRBP 2003(a), the first meeting of creditors is to be conducted by the trustee between 21 and 35 days after filing of the petition. In order to participate in distributions under the plan, unsecured creditors must file a proof of claim within 90 days following the date first set for the first meeting of creditors per FRBP 3002(c). A governmental unit that is a creditor has until 180 days following the filing of the petition to file its proof of claim per §502(b)(9).

F. PROPERTY OF THE ESTATE AND THE DEBTOR'S TURNOVER AND AVOIDANCE POWERS

The definition of property of the estate in §1207 is the same as in a Chapter 13 case. At this time you may want to review the discussion of that concept in a Chapter 13 case in Chapter Twelve, Section D.

Significantly, §1203 bestows on the Chapter 12 debtor in possession all of the powers of a Chapter 11 trustee, which includes the avoidance and turnover powers discussed available to a Chapter 7 trustee as discussed in Chapter Nine, Sections C and D. That stands in contrast to the failure of the Code to bestow such powers on a Chapter 13 debtor as discussed in Chapter Twelve, Section D. It also can be a consideration in the decision of a debtor qualified to file under either Chapter 13 or Chapter 12 to choose the latter.

G. THE CHAPTER 12 PLAN

Per §1221 the debtor must file a proposed Chapter 12 plan with the petition or within 90 days following. The Chapter 12 plan works very much the same as a Chapter 13 plan regarding treatment of secured, priority, and unsecured claims. Like a Chapter 13 plan, it will last three to five years unless it calls for earlier payment of 100 percent of priority and unsecured claims. All priority claims must be paid in full unless the priority creditor agrees to different treatment of its claim or, in the case of a domestic support obligation, unless the debtor contributes all disposable income per §1222(a)(2)(4). Unsecured claims do not have to be paid in full so long as the plan commits all the debtor's disposable income to such claims over the term of the plan and as long as the unsecured creditors receive at least as much as they would receive if the debtor's nonexempt assets were liquidated under Chapter 7. See §1225. For purposes of Chapter 12, "disposable income" is defined in §1225(b)(2) as income not reasonably necessary for the maintenance or support of the debtor or dependents or for making payments needed to continue, preserve, and operate the debtor's business.

Significantly, Chapter 12 offers debtors more powerful debt restructuring tools than does Chapter 13. Sections 1222(b)(5) and (9) allow a Chapter 12 plan to cure an arrearage or modify future payments due on secured debt over a term in excess of the plan.

For example, assume a debtor qualifies to file for relief under either Chapter 13 or Chapter 12. He owns a vehicle that is collateral for a loan from Bank on which he makes monthly payments of $400. The value of the vehicle exceeds the balance owed on the debt so the Bank is fully secured in the vehicle. Debtor has 40 more scheduled payments on the debt at the time he decides to file for bankruptcy relief. Debtor would like to retain the vehicle by paying the Bank the full amount of its secured claim. However, in order to successfully fund either a Chapter 13 or 12 plan he needs to adjust those payments downward. In a Chapter 13 case he can propose a plan to adjust the payments to Bank downward during the term of the plan but only so long as he pays the full amount of the claim during the term of the plan. So he might propose that the payments be lowered during the first three years of the plan but rise during the final two years so that the full claim is paid off. But in a Chapter 12 he has more flexibility. He can propose a plan to adjust the payments to Bank downward during the entire term of the plan even though the full claim is not paid off during the term of the plan. As you would expect, any amounts still owing on the claim at the conclusion of the plan are excepted from the discharge received by the debtor per §1228(a)(1).

In addition, Chapter 12 contains no prohibition on the strip down of an undersecured mortgage on real property used as the debtor's principal residence, unlike the prohibitions on such strip downs for Chapter 13 debtors (compare §1222(b)(2) with §1322(b)(2)). Chapter 12 contains no limitation like the 910-day rule on the strip down of an undersecured claim involving a motor vehicle as collateral or the one-year rule on the strip down of an undersecured claim involving collateral other than a motor vehicle (compare §1325 with §1225). Moreover, the Code's general adequate protection standard of §361, which comes into play in motions to lift the automatic stay under §362, is declared inapplicable in a Chapter 12 by §1205(a) and the Chapter 12 debtor has other options to satisfy that standard, including paying only "reasonable rent customary in the community" as adequate protection payments for farmland.

These more flexible debt adjustment tools, along with the higher debt limits discussed earlier, are what really separate Chapter 12 from Chapter 13 and make the former more advantageous to debtors seeking to restructure their debts and who meet the Chapter 12 definition of a family farmer or fisherman.

H. CONFIRMING THE CHAPTER 12 PLAN

The standards for confirmation of a Chapter 12 plan under §1225 are substantially the same as those for a Chapter 13 plan as discussed in Chapter Sixteen, Section B. Per §1224 the confirmation hearing is to be conducted within 45 days following the filing of the proposed plan by the debtor. As in a Chapter 13 case, the most common objections to confirmation of a Chapter 12 plan are that it fails to commit all of the debtor's disposable income to payment of unsecured claims or that proposed payments to unsecured creditors under the plan are less than those creditors would receive in a Chapter 7 liquidation. If the proposed plan is filed before the first meeting of creditors, these disputes can often be worked out at that meeting so no formal objection to confirmation is filed with the court. Section 1223 authorizes the debtor to propose modifications to the plan at any time before confirmation.

If the debtor is unable to obtain confirmation of a plan he may ask that the case be converted to a Chapter 7 liquidation per §1208(a) or it will be dismissed. As in a Chapter 13 case, §1226(a) directs that plan payments received by the trustee prior to confirmation are to be retained by the trustee until confirmation or dismissal of the case. If no plan is confirmed (and the case is converted or dismissed), §1226(a) mandates that payments in the hands of the trustee be used to pay allowed administrative expenses and fees under §503(b) including of course the trustee's percentage fee with any balance paid to the debtor. If the conversion or dismissal occurs after a Chapter 12 plan has been confirmed, the same issues regarding proper distribution of the payments in the hands of the trustee are raised as discussed in Chapter Sixteen, Section F, in connection with Harris v. Viegelahn, 135 S. Ct. 1829 (2015).

Section 1230(a) provides that on motion filed by a party in interest within 180 days following entry of an order confirming a Chapter 12 plan, that order of confirmation can be revoked upon a showing that it was procured by fraud.

I. LIVING WITH A CHAPTER 12 PLAN

Once the court confirms the plan, the debtor is obligated to make the periodic payments called for to the Chapter 12 trustee who will then distribute funds received to creditors in accordance with the terms of the plan per §1226(a). While we think of these distributions as being made monthly, for the family farmer or fisherman whose income is regularly received quarterly, semi-annually, or even annually, the payments to the trustee and disbursements to creditors will typically follow that schedule as well.

Under §364(b), during the term of the plan, a Chapter 12 debtor cannot obtain credit or incur unsecured debt other than in the ordinary course of business without prior court approval. Per §364(c), court approval must be sought in order to obtain credit or to incur new debt having priority over certain administrative expenses. Section 364(c) also requires court approval before the debtor can obtain credit or incur debt secured by a lien on property of the estate.

Section 363(b) authorizes (and requires) a debtor to seek court approval for the use, sale, or lease of property of the estate that is not in the ordinary course of business of the debtor. For example, assume a farmer debtor in Chapter 12 decides to lease a portion of his farmland next season rather than planting it himself as he has always done. Since this use of the land that is property of the estate is arguably not in the ordinary course of business of this debtor, he should seek court approval for the land lease before entering into it.

Like a Chapter 13 plan, a Chapter 12 plan can be modified after confirmation. See §1229. The debtor, the trustee, or the holder of an allowed unsecured claim can request post-confirmation modification based on changed and unforeseen circumstances as in the case of a Chapter 13 plan (discussed in Chapter Sixteen, Section D).

J. CONVERSION OR DISMISSAL OF A CHAPTER 12 CASE

Under §1208(a) the Chapter 12 debtor has an absolute right to convert his case to a Chapter 7 liquidation at any time. Under §1208(b) the debtor can move to dismiss the case at any time and the court is to grant the motion unless the case was converted to Chapter 12 from Chapter 7 or Chapter 11. §§1222(a)(1), 1227. In any event, failure to make the plan payments may result in dismissal of the case. 11 U.S.C. §1208(c). In addition, under §1208(d), the court may dismiss the case or convert the case to a liquidation case under Chapter 7 of the Bankruptcy Code upon a showing that the debtor has committed fraud in connection with the case. See, e.g., In re Kloubec, 247 B.R. 246 (Bankr. N.D. Iowa 2000), discussed in the Post-Case Follow-Up to In re Jessen.

Section 1208(c) authorizes the bankruptcy court to dismiss a Chapter 12 case on a number of grounds summarized in Exhibit 17.1.

EXHIBIT 17.1   **Grounds for Involuntary Dismissal of a Chapter 12 Case**

- Unreasonable delay or gross mismanagement by the debtor that is prejudicial to creditors
- Nonpayment of any required fees and charges
- Failure to timely file a plan
- Failure to commence making timely payments under a confirmed plan
- The denial of confirmation of a plan and the denial of a request made for additional time for filing another plan or a modification of a plan
- A material default by the debtor with respect to a term of a confirmed plan
- The revocation of the order of confirmation
- The termination of a confirmed plan by reason of the occurrence of a condition specified in the plan, other than completion of payments under the plan
- Continuing loss or diminution in value to property of the estate with no reasonable likelihood of rehabilitation
- Failure of the debtor to pay any domestic support obligation that first becomes payable after the date of the filing of the petition

---

Pursuant to §1208, a case cannot be converted to one under another chapter of the Code unless the debtor is eligible to be a debtor under that other chapter.

K. THE CHAPTER 12 DISCHARGE

As in a Chapter 13 case, the Chapter 12 debtor receives a discharge under §1228(a) only after completion of all payments under the plan. Like the Chapter 13 debtor, the individual Chapter 12 debtor who owed a domestic support obligation must also certify that all such payments called for in the plan or otherwise due through the date of confirmation have been paid.

The §523(a) exceptions to discharge that we considered in connection with Chapter 7 (see Chapter Eleven, Section A) apply too in a Chapter 12 case per §1228(c)(2). Also excepted from discharge are secured claims involving payments extending beyond the term of the plan including those that were modified in the plan per §§1222(b)(5) and (9).

Section 1228(b) authorizes the bankruptcy court to grant the Chapter 12 debtor an early hardship discharge. The Chapter 12 hardship discharge works the same way as the Chapter 13 hardship discharge discussed in Chapter Sixteen, Section E.

Chapter Summary

- Chapter 12 bankruptcy is limited to those who qualify as family farmers or family fishermen with regular annual income. Qualifications to file include a debt ceiling and certain percentages of the debtor's income and debt must be related to the farming or fishing operation. The debt ceiling for filing a Chapter 12 is considerably higher than that for filing a Chapter 13 making Chapter 12 an alternative to the more complicated Chapter 11 for qualifying debtors with too much debt to file under Chapter 13.
- Chapter 12 is a something of a hybrid between the Chapter 13 adjustment of debt for an individual and the Chapter 11 business reorganization. Though many Chapter 12 filings are business cases, they may also be filed by those engaged in qualifying farming or fishing businesses who qualify as consumer debtors.
- Although a bankruptcy trustee is appointed in a Chapter 12 case, the debtor retains possession of the property and continues to conduct his farming or fishing operation as a debtor in possession. On motion of an interested party the court may remove the debtor as debtor in possession for fraud, dishonesty, incompetence, or gross mismanagement and turn over the control of the farming or fishing operation to the trustee. Courts are reluctant to grant such motions on the grounds of gross mismanagement due to the increase in administrative expenses and recognition that there is always some degree of mismanagement.
- The automatic stay, including codebtor stay, and property of the estate concepts work the same in Chapter 12 as in Chapter 13. The Chapter 12 debtor in possession enjoys the power to initiate turnover and avoidance actions to enhance property of the estate, making it distinctly advantageous over a Chapter 13 for qualifying debtors.
- The debtor must file a proposed Chapter 12 plan with the petition or within 90 days following. Generally, a Chapter 12 plan operates very similarly to a Chapter 13 plan. Disposable income under Chapter 12 is income not reasonably necessary for the maintenance or support of the debtor or dependents or for making

payments needed to continue, preserve, and operate the debtor's farming or fishing operation.

■ Unlike a Chapter 13 plan, a Chapter 12 plan can propose to cure a deficiency beyond the term of the plan. A Chapter 12 plan may also strip down an undersecured mortgage on the debtor's principal residence. There is no 910-day rule prohibiting strip down of undersecured debt secured by vehicles in Chapter 12 and no one-year rule prohibiting strip down of undersecured claims involving collateral other than a motor vehicle.

■ Requirements for confirming a Chapter 12 plan, plan payments to the trustee, the incurring of post-confirmation expenses, plan modification, the right of the debtor to convert the case to one under Chapter 7 at any time, grounds for involuntary dismissal of the case, and timing and qualifications for discharge including early hardship discharge are all similar to those for Chapter 13.

Applying the Concepts

1. Homer and Estelle Amundsen, husband and wife, are in your office discussing a possible bankruptcy filing. Homer works part-time at a local box factory but he and Estelle also farm 30 acres growing a variety of produce and flowers that they sell locally and slightly more than half their annual income comes from that activity. You have determined that the Amundsens qualify to file under either Chapter 13 or Chapter 12. The Amundsens have the following situations. For each, determine if Chapter 13 or Chapter 12 would be preferable for them.

   a. The Amundsens' oldest daughter borrowed $100,000 from Bank to attend college and the couple co-signed the note. They are currently unable to make the scheduled payments on the note and the daughter, while now employed, cannot afford them either. They fear the daughter is going to be sued by Bank.

   b. The Amundsens have a truck they use in their farm produce business that they bought nine months ago on credit. The seller took a security interest in the truck. The couple still owe $14,000 on the truck to be paid over the next 51 months but the truck has received rough treatment and its value is now only $12,000. They hope to be able to modify the payments and keep the truck.

   c. The Amundsens also have a car they use for family travel that they bought 15 months ago on credit. The seller took a security interest in it. They owe $10,000 on the car to be paid over the next 40 months but its value is only $8,000. They hope to be able to modify the payments and keep the family car.

   d. Over the years the Amundsens have purchased supplies and materials for their farm produce business from the local farmer's co-op on 120 days' credit. They were always able to pay off the amount owed within the 120 days of purchase (when their harvest was sold) until this year, when they owed $9,500 that they couldn't pay on time. The co-op sent them a couple of demand letters and they received a couple of unfriendly phone calls about it too. Finally, a month ago, two months past the due date, they paid the full amount plus interest to the co-op. To make that payment they had to miss the mortgage payment on their home, both car payments, the school loan payment, and use all their savings as well. They tell you they want to "play fair" with the co-op, but sure could use that $9,500 back.

e. The Amundsens are now three payments behind on their home mortgage owed to a local credit union. They also have a second mortgage on it in favor of a local savings and loan from whom they received a home improvement loan three years ago. Their home is currently valued at $275,000. The loan secured by the first mortgage in favor of the credit union has a balance of $265,000 and 18 years remaining on it. The three payments they have missed have left them $4,500 in arrears on that loan. The loan secured by the second mortgage held by the savings and loan has a balance of $34,000 on it and has six years remaining on it. The Amundsens are current on that second mortgage. They sure would like to keep their home.

2. Homer Amundsen is paid twice a month as a part-time employee of the box plant. As noted in Question 1, slightly more than half of the couple's income is derived from their farming operation, which consists of one major harvest beginning in late July and lasting through the middle of September and a minor harvest beginning in April and lasting through May. Whether you put them in a Chapter 12 or a Chapter 13, and recognizing that you need more detail to make firm decisions, how is the plan likely to structure the frequency of their payments on allowed claims?

Jurisdictional and Procedural Issues in Bankruptcy Practice

In this final chapter detailed consideration will be given to the thorny issues currently surrounding the subject matter jurisdiction of U.S. bankruptcy courts as well as the surprisingly long reach of personal jurisdiction in such courts. We will also examine closely the procedures for resolving disputes in a bankruptcy court and how its decisions may be appealed.

A. SUBJECT MATTER JURISDICTION OF THE BANKRUPTCY COURTS

1. Distinguishing Between Article III and Article I Courts, Public and Private Rights, and the Need for Referral Jurisdiction

As was noted in Exhibit 4.1, due to the Supreme Court's 1982 decision in Northern Pipeline Constr. Co. v. Marathon Pipeline Co., 458 U.S. 50 (1982), and the subsequent **1984 Bankruptcy Amendments and Federal Judgeship Act** (the 1984 Amendments Act), bankruptcy courts today, as courts created by Congress under Article I of the U.S.

Key Concepts

- U.S. bankruptcy courts are Article I courts with referral jurisdiction from the district courts to hear and decide bankruptcy cases
- Bankruptcy courts may enter final judgments in core proceedings but may enter final judgments in non-core proceedings only with the parties' consent
- Even in core proceedings bankruptcy courts cannot enter final judgments if the matter involves a determination of private rather than public rights unless the parties consent
- A bankruptcy court can conduct a jury trial only with consent of the parties and the district court
- U.S. bankruptcy courts enjoy broad personal jurisdiction based on national contacts
- Disputes in a bankruptcy case are decided as either contested matters or adversary proceedings

Constitution, serve as *units* or *adjuncts* of the Article III U.S. district courts per 28 U.S.C. §151: "In each judicial district, the bankruptcy judges in regular active service shall constitute a unit of the district court to be known as the bankruptcy court of that district."

The distinction between Article III and Article I courts is archaic but important to understand in order to understand the jurisdiction of the bankruptcy courts. Article III of the Constitution mandates that "The judicial power of the United States shall be vested in one Supreme Court and in such inferior courts as the Congress may from time to time ordain and establish." The **Article III courts** are the U.S. Supreme Court, the 13 U.S. circuit courts of appeals and the 94 U.S. district courts. The judges of these courts are selected by the constitutionally mandated process of nomination by the president and confirmation by the U.S. Senate and they enjoy lifetime tenure since Article III says that they "shall hold their offices during good behaviour." It has long been understood that only these Article III courts, constituting the judicial branch of the federal government, can enter final orders that determine issues involving life, liberty, or property rights (see, e.g., American Ins. Co. v. 356 Bales of Cotton, 1 Pet. 511 (1828) (commonly referred to as *Canter*), and Ex parte Bakelite Corp., 279 U.S. 438 (1929)).

Other specialized federal courts created by Congress are deemed **Article I courts** or **legislative courts**. Since they are created by Congress for some specialized legislative purpose they do not enjoy plenary Article III powers and the judges of those courts do not enjoy lifetime tenure. More specifically, Article I courts, like the bankruptcy courts, cannot be empowered to decide disputes between private parties controlled by state law (called actions involving **private rights**). In its most recent decision on the matter, highlighted later in the chapter, the Supreme Court described private rights claims as those involving "the liability of one individual to another under the law as defined." See Stern v. Marshall, 131 S. Ct. 2594, 2612 (2011). Instead, Article I courts can only decide designated disputes between the government and persons subject to its authority (called actions involving **public rights**). In *Stern*, the Supreme Court defined a public right claim as one that "derives from a federal regulatory scheme, or in which resolution of the claim by an expert governmental agency is essential to a limited regulatory objective within the agency's authority." *Stern*, at 2613.

The gist of *Northern Pipeline* was that the Bankruptcy Reform Act of 1978 violated the separation of powers doctrine of the Constitution by purporting to give bankruptcy courts the power to enter final orders determining issues regarding property in disputes between private parties controlled by state law, i.e., claims involving private rights, a power reserved by the Constitution for the Article III courts. In response to *Northern Pipeline*, the 1984 Amendments Act amended Title 28 to accomplish two major objectives: (1) to make it clear that subject matter jurisdiction over bankruptcy matters resides in the Article III district courts, and (2) to authorize those courts to refer that jurisdiction to the Article I bankruptcy courts.

The "Arising Under," "Arising In," or "Related To" Jurisdiction of the District Courts

Post–*Northern Pipeline*, 28 U.S.C. §1334(a) now grants district courts "original and exclusive" jurisdiction over cases under Title 11 while 28 U.S.C. §1334(b) grants district courts "original but not exclusive" jurisdiction over civil proceedings, "arising under title 11, or arising in or related to cases under title 11." This curious phrasing was well explained in the oft-cited case of In re Wood, 825 F.2d 90 (5th Cir. 1987), where the court held that a lawsuit alleging misappropriation of funds by the bankruptcy debtor and a third party filed in the bankruptcy case of the debtor was within the bankruptcy jurisdiction of §1334(b) since it could conceivably have an impact on the property of the estate to be administered in the bankruptcy case.

Section 1334 lists four types of matters over which the district court has jurisdiction:

1. "cases under title 11",
2. "proceedings arising under title 11",
3. proceedings "arising in" a case under title 11, and
4. proceedings "related to" a case under title 11.

The first category refers merely to the bankruptcy petition itself, over which district courts (and their bankruptcy units) have original and exclusive jurisdiction.

. . .

Legislative history indicates that the phrase "arising under title 11, or arising in or related to cases under title 11" was meant, not to distinguish between different matters, but to identify collectively a broad range of matters subject to the bankruptcy jurisdiction of federal courts. Congress was concerned with the inefficiencies of piecemeal adjudication of matters affecting the administration of bankruptcies and intended to give federal courts the power to adjudicate all matters having an effect on the bankruptcy. Courts have recognized that the grant of jurisdiction under the 1978 Act was broad (citations omitted).

. . .

For the purpose of determining whether a particular matter falls within bankruptcy jurisdiction, it is not necessary to distinguish between proceedings "arising under", "arising in a case under", or "related to a case under", title 11. These references operate conjunctively to define the scope of jurisdiction. Therefore, it is necessary only to determine whether a matter is at least "related to" the bankruptcy. The Act does not define "related" matters. Courts have articulated various definitions of "related", but the definition of the Court of Appeals for the Third Circuit appears to have the most support: "whether the outcome of that proceeding could conceivably have any effect on the estate being administered in bankruptcy." [Citing Pacor, Inc. v. Higgins, 743 F.2d 984, 994 (3d Cir. 1984).] This definition comports with the legislative history of the statutory predecessor to section 1334. Neither *Marathon* nor general concerns of comity counsel against its use. We adopt it as our own.

In re Wood, 825 F.2d at 92-93.

Thus the grant of bankruptcy jurisdiction to district courts in §1334(b) is very broad and includes:

■ each and every case filed under the Code (see Exhibit 4.3);

■ all procedural matters arising out of the Code or in a case filed under any chapter of the Code (see Exhibit 4.4); and

■ any other matter arising in or related to such a case.

For example, assume a debtor files a petition for relief under Chapter 7 of the Code. That is a case filed under Title 11. To administer that case the procedures under Chapters 1, 3, 5, and 7 will be followed. But there may be other matters involved in that case. Perhaps at the time the debtor filed the petition, he or she was a party to a lawsuit in state court involving a dispute over the location of a property line on a parcel of land that he owns. That property line dispute is not a case under the Code and does not involve procedural matters under the Code, but it is an "other matter" arising under a case under the Code. Upon filing of the Chapter 7 petition, the U.S. district court has subject matter jurisdiction over all these matters, pursuant to 28 U.S.C. §1334. And this would be true even though the "other matter" property line dispute could not originally have been filed in the U.S. district court.

Moreover, if a state court action is pending in a state court when one of the parties files a petition in bankruptcy, either party may remove the case (or a particular claim or cause of action in it) from the state court to the U.S. district court per 28 U.S.C. §1452. Again, it does not matter that there is no other basis for federal court jurisdiction of the matter (diversity or federal question) so long as the district court has §1334 subject matter jurisdiction. But look at §1452(b): the district court to which a claim is moved under §1334 jurisdiction can remand "on any equitable ground" and any decision by the court to allow or permit remand is not reviewable on appeal.

For example, if a prepetition property line dispute pending in state court is removed to the district court following the filing of a bankruptcy petition by one of the parties, the district court may decide to remand on the basis that the case has proceeded so far in the state court that the case ought to be kept and decided there. Or the court may order remand because of the particular expertise and experience of the state court in which the matter is pending or because the geographical location of the state court is more convenient to the parties and witnesses than the district court.

Referral Jurisdiction to the Bankruptcy Courts

Though this broad grant of subject matter jurisdiction over bankruptcy matters technically resides in the Article III district courts pursuant to §1334, 28 U.S.C. §157(a) authorizes the district courts to refer bankruptcy cases to the bankruptcy courts in their districts. Consequently, the Article I bankruptcy courts, as adjuncts or units of the district courts per 28 U.S.C. §151, obtain jurisdiction over bankruptcy cases by *referral* from the Article III district courts. They have **referral jurisdiction**.

In most federal districts, bankruptcy cases are automatically referred to the bankruptcy courts by standing order of the district court. However, 28 U.S.C.

§157(d) authorizes the district court to **revoke the reference** at any time on its own motion or upon the motion of any party in interest for cause shown.

It is important to note, however, that the referral jurisdiction granted to bankruptcy courts in §157(a) is not as broad as the §1334 grant of jurisdiction to the district courts. Section §157(b)(1) authorizes bankruptcy courts exercising their referral jurisdiction to administer such cases and to enter final orders in what are called *core proceedings* "arising under Title 11 or arising in a case under Title 11." So next we must determine what is and is not a core proceeding under §157(b)(1). Note too that any order entered by the bankruptcy court under its referral jurisdiction from district court is subject to review by the district court under §158. Later we will look more closely at how an order from a bankruptcy court is appealed and its decision reviewed by the district court.

2. Core and Non-Core Proceedings

28 U.S.C. §157 distinguishes between core and non-core proceedings in bankruptcy cases referred to the bankruptcy courts. The distinction is important because §157(b)(1) provides that the bankruptcy court can enter a final judgment or dispositive order in a core proceeding but §157(c)(2) provides that the court may not do so in a non-core proceeding unless all the parties consent. When the dispute before the bankruptcy court is non-core, §157(c)(1) limits the power of that court to making proposed findings of fact and conclusions of law for review de novo by the district court *unless* the parties to the non-core dispute unanimously consent to the bankruptcy court's entering a final judgment in the matter.

28 U.S.C. §157(b)(2) designates a number of specific matters that arise in a bankruptcy case as core proceedings (see Exhibit 4.5). In deciding issues involving any of the enumerated matters, the bankruptcy court can enter a final order or judgment. However, note carefully that the matters listed in §157(b)(2) do not constitute an exclusive list of core proceedings ("Core proceedings include, but are not limited to . . .") and courts struggle to determine whether a particular matter excluded from the list is to be treated as core or non-core.

Core proceedings are understood to involve procedures and rights that would not exist except for the bankruptcy case. See, e.g., In re Wood, 825 F.2d 90, 96 (5th Cir. 1987) ("[A] proceeding is core under section 157 if it invokes a substantive right provided by title 11 or if it is a proceeding that, by its nature, could arise only in the context of a bankruptcy case"), and In re Acolyte Elec. Corp., 69 B.R. 155, 173 (Bankr. E.D.N.Y. 1986) ("To be a core proceeding, an action must have as its foundation the creation, recognition, or adjudication of rights which would not exist independent of a bankruptcy environment although of necessity there may be a peripheral state law involvement.").

Non-core proceedings, on the other hand, involve matters that may be closely related to bankruptcy case administration but involve issues or disputes that would likely arise for resolution if no bankruptcy case had been filed. In the oft-cited case of In re Hughes-Bechtol, 141 B.R. 946, 948-949 (Bankr. S.D. Ohio 1992), the bankruptcy court held that a non-core proceeding is identified by the following characteristics:

—the underlying cause of action is not specifically identified as a core proceeding under §157(b)(2)(B) though (N);

—it existed prior to the filing of the bankruptcy case;

—it would continue to exist independent of the provisions of Title 11; and

—it is a proceeding in which the parties' rights, obligations, or both are not significantly affected as a result of the filing of the bankruptcy case.

There are numerous issues that exist to be decided only because the bankruptcy case was filed: issues related to the proper filing of a bankruptcy petition and supporting schedules, the qualification and appointment of a bankruptcy trustee, the trustees right to possession of property of the estate from the debtor or third parties, whether the automatic stay of Code §362 has been violated by a creditor or should be lifted so a secured creditor can seize collateralized property of the estate, disputes over value of estate property, whether property of the estate should be sold or abandoned, the distribution of estate assets to creditors, the terms and confirmability of debt adjustment plans under Chapter 13 (or of more complex plans for reorganization of businesses under Chapter 11), the validity of claimed exemptions in the debtor's property, the validity and enforceability of creditor claims, whether a particular debt should be deemed non-dischargeable in bankruptcy, whether a final discharge will be granted, etc. These types of matters and many more arise because there is a bankruptcy case; they are core proceedings and bankruptcy judges may enter final judgment or order in such matters per 28 U.S.C. §157(b).

On the other hand there are numerous other questions that may "arise in" a bankruptcy case and be "related to" it. That is especially true since the widely accepted definition of "related to" jurisdiction is that it includes any matter that "could conceivably have any effect on the estate being administered in bankruptcy." See Pacor, Inc. v. Higgins, 743 F.2d 984, 994 (3d Cir. 1984), cited in In re Wood, supra, and numerous other cases.

But "related to" matters are treated as non-core even though they arise in a bankruptcy case because although they could conceivably have an effect on the bankruptcy estate being administered, they are matters that do not arise solely because there is a bankruptcy case pending but are in fact issues that existed prior to and independent of the filing of the bankruptcy petition. For example, the question of whether one person is validly married to another under state law has nothing to do with bankruptcy law or procedure. But if that person becomes a debtor in a bankruptcy case, the answer to that question certainly affect the qualifications of the debtors to file a joint bankruptcy petition as a married couple. Whether the couple is married will likely be deemed a non-core matter. Or assume a debtor is involved in prepetition contract or property line disputes governed by state law and that carry over into the bankruptcy case when the debtor lists such claims as disputed, contingent assets of the estate. Those disputes are certainly related to the bankruptcy case and their resolution will have an impact on it, but they are disputes that existed independent of the bankruptcy case and will likely be treated as non-core when presented to the bankruptcy court for resolution.

Since there is no definition of what is a core proceeding and since the proceedings enumerated in 28 U.S.C. §157(b)(2) are not exclusive, and since even matters that appear on their face to be non-core can be analyzed as necessarily impacting the administration of a bankruptcy case in a way that seems core, it can become what one court referred to as a "Sisyphean" task to determine how a particular proceeding is to be categorized. See In re United Security & Communications, 93 B.R. 945, 954 (Bankr. S.D. Ohio 1988).

Application Exercise 1

Which of the following would properly be denominated: (1) a "case under Title 11"; (2) a proceeding "arising under, in or related to" a case under Title 11; or (3) neither.

- Whether the debtor in an asset Chapter 7 case violated the non-compete clause in a pre-petition employment contract
- Same question in a no-asset Chapter 7 case
- Whether an individual filing a petition in Chapter 13 had unsecured debts that exceeded the dollar limits of §109(e)
- Whether a Chapter 13 debtor whose plan proposes to surrender an unimproved parcel of land to the secured creditor secured in it owns the lot by herself or as a tenant in common

---

The initial determination of whether a matter is core or non-core is to be made by the bankruptcy court per §157(b)(3) but that decision, like all decisions by the bankruptcy court, is subject to review on appeal per §158 as will be discussed in more detail later in this chapter. As a practical matter, when the issue to be decided is determined to be non-core and all parties will not consent to the bankruptcy court entering a final judgment, one or more of the parties will file a motion with the district court asking it to revoke the reference under §157(d) and hear and decide the matter. After all, if the bankruptcy judge hears it, all that court can do is enter proposed findings and conclusions that will have to be reviewed by the district court anyway. So revoking the reference usually saves time and money.

Case Preview

In re Atwood

When a bankruptcy court is presented with a matter to decide in a pending case, it must not only determine whether the matter is core (final judgment or order can be entered) or "related to" but non-core (only proposed findings and conclusions can be made). It must also consider whether the matter might be neither. If the matter presented is neither core nor sufficiently related to the pending case to even be treated as non-core, the bankruptcy court has no jurisdiction to decide the matter at all under §157. And as we have seen, that determination may turn on the particular facts of the matter presented and the kind of bankruptcy case in which it is presented. As you read In re Atwood, consider the following questions:

1. Which of the debtor's allegations in this case were found to be core and why?
2. Why were debtor's allegations of violation of the FDCPA and New Mexico state law found to be neither core nor "related to" non-core?
3. Did debtor have any further remedy to pursue in her bankruptcy case regarding the FDCPA and state law claims? Did debtor have any further remedy to pursue outside her bankruptcy case regarding the FDCPA and state law claims?

In re Atwood

452 B.R. 249 (Bankr. D.N.M. 2011)

[Individual debtor filed a Chapter 7 bankruptcy case. Creditor then caused a summons and complaint to be served on debtor to collect a prepetition debt. Debtor filed an adversary proceeding in her bankruptcy case against the creditor and creditor's attorney seeking damages for alleged improper debt collection activity in violation of the following: (1) the automatic stay of 11 U.S.C. §362; (2) the Fair Debt Collections Practices Act, 15 U.S.C. §§1692 et seq. ("FDCPA"); (3) the New Mexico Unfair Practices Act, N.M.S.A. 1978 §§57-12-1 et seq. ("NM–UPA"); and (4) the New Mexico common law for unfair debt collection. The defendants filed a motion to dismiss the FDCPA and state law counts of debtor's complaint for failure to state a claim upon which relief can be granted on the grounds that her sole remedy was for violation of the automatic stay of §362. After concluding that the alleged automatic stay violation was not the debtor's sole remedy for postpetition collection activity, the court then addressed *sua sponte* whether it had subject matter jurisdiction to decide the FDCPA and state law counts of debtor's complaint.]

Jacobitz, Bankruptcy Judge. . . .
    A Court must satisfy itself that is has subject matter jurisdiction regardless of whether a party has asserted lack of subject matter jurisdiction. The Court evaluates its subject matter jurisdiction in accordance with 28 U.S.C. §1334. That section provides:

> the district courts shall have original but not exclusive jurisdiction of all civil proceedings arising under title 11, or arising in or related to cases under title 11.

28 U.S.C. §1334(b).
    Bankruptcy courts are referred cases under title 11, and proceedings arising under title 11 or arising in or related to a case under title 11, by the district court. 28 U.S.C. §157(a). The congressional grant of jurisdiction to the bankruptcy court under this section is limited. Bankruptcy judges may hear all core proceedings arising under title 11, or arising in a case under title 11, as well as non-core proceedings that are otherwise "related to" a case under title 11. "Core" proceedings are

proceedings that involve rights created by bankruptcy law or matters that arise in a bankruptcy case. Core proceedings also include proceedings otherwise defined as "core proceedings" under 28 U.S.C. §157(b)(2). "Non-core" proceedings can exist independently from the bankruptcy case and do not invoke substantive rights created under applicable bankruptcy law.

The factual allegations contained in Plaintiff's Complaint concern Defendants' post-petition actions in serving upon Plaintiff a summons and complaint from a pre-petition debt collection action initiated in state court despite having actual notice of Plaintiff's pending bankruptcy case. Claims for damages under 11 U.S.C. §362(k) based on alleged actions taken post-petition in violation of the automatic stay fall squarely within this Court's core jurisdiction.[17] Plaintiff's claims under the FDCPA, the NM-UPA, and New Mexico common law do not raise substantive rights created under bankruptcy law, can exist independently of a pending bankruptcy case, and are not otherwise defined as core proceedings under 28 U.S.C. §157(b)(2). Thus, for the Court to have jurisdiction over those claims, they must fall within the Court's non-core, "related-to" jurisdiction.

Most courts that have considered this issue have found that the bankruptcy court does not have subject matter jurisdiction over a Chapter 7 debtor's post-petition claims for violation of the FDCPA. This Court agrees. The test for determining whether the bankruptcy court has, non-core, "related-to" jurisdiction over a proceeding is " 'whether the outcome of that proceeding could conceivably have any effect on the estate being administered in bankruptcy.' "[20] A factual nexus between the alleged conduct and the Plaintiff's bankruptcy case is insufficient, in and of itself, to confer "related to" jurisdiction on the Bankruptcy Court to hear a claim under the FDCPA.[21]

Here, Plaintiff's factual assertions in support of her claims under the FDCPA, the NM-UPA and New Mexico common law relate to post-petition actions. Therefore, such claims do not constitute property of her bankruptcy estate, and any recovery, should she prevail on these claims, would have no conceivable impact on the administration of her Chapter 7 bankruptcy estate. These claims, therefore, do not fall within the Court's limited, "related to" non-core jurisdiction. The Court will dismiss Plaintiff's Second, Third, and Fourth claims in the Complaint due to a lack of subject matter jurisdiction. An order consistent with this Memorandum will be entered.

---

17. See Johnson v. Smith (In re Johnson), 575 F.3d 1079, 1083 (10th Cir. 2009) (finding that a proceeding under 11 U.S.C. §362(k) for alleged violations of the automatic stay "is a core proceeding because it 'derive[s] directly from the Bankruptcy Code and can be brought only in the context of a bankruptcy case.' ") (quoting MBNA Am. Bank, N.A. v. Hill, 436 F.3d 104, 109 (2d Cir. 2006) (remaining citation omitted)).

20. Gardner v. United States (In re Gardner), 913 F.2d 1515, 1518 (10th Cir. 1990) (quoting Pacor, Inc. v. Higgins, 743 F.2d 984, 994 (3d Cir. 1984)). See also, Lawrence v. Goldberg, 573 F.3d 1265, 1270 (11th Cir. 2009) (same).

21. King v. 1062 LLP (In re King), 2010 WL 3851434, at *1 (Bankr. D. Colo. Sept. 24, 2010) (citing In re Harlan, 402 B.R. 703 (Bankr. W.D. Va. 2009))

Post-Case Follow-Up

Atwood reflects the majority view on whether FDCPA and state law claims arising out of a postpetition violation of the automatic stay are within the "related to" non-core jurisdiction of the bankruptcy court. There is a minority view to the contrary. See, e.g., In re Smith, 2008 WL 4148923, *1 (Bankr. D. Kan. Aug. 29, 2008) (bankruptcy court has jurisdiction over both FDCPA and related state law claims "since the United States District Courts have jurisdiction of an action to enforce any liability created by the FDCPA and jurisdiction to hear state law claims . . . which are so related to the claims for which original federal jurisdiction exists as to be part of the same case or controversy"), and Lomax v. Bank of America, N.A., 435 B.R. 362 (N.D. W. Va. 2010) (claims arising under the bankruptcy code and FDCPA claims should be tried together in the district court for purposes of judicial efficiency).

In re Atwood: Real Life Applications

1. Recall that what constitutes property of the estate in a Chapter 7 case is determined at the commencement of the case (see Chapter Nine, Section A) and that is certainly critical to the reasoning of the *Atwood* court in analyzing the bankruptcy court's interest in a post-commencement cause of action for purposes other than the automatic stay. But recall as well that in a Chapter 13 case, per §1306, what constitutes property of the estate includes postpetition earnings and other property acquired by the debtor (see Chapter Twelve, Section D). So if Patricia Atwood had filed a petition in Chapter 13 rather than in Chapter 7 and was proposing a five-year debt adjustment plan for confirmation by the court when the defendant creditor had her served with summons and complaint in alleged violation of the FDCPA and New Mexico state laws at issue in the case, would debtor's action for damages in the bankruptcy case on those theories been properly treated as core, related to non-core, or neither? See In re Turner, 436 B.R. 153 (M.D. Ala. 2010), and In re Price, 403 B.R. 775 (Bankr. E.D. Ark. 2009).What would be the bankruptcy court's jurisdictional power to decide the issues presented in each of those three alternative determinations?
2. Assume that the creditor defendant in Patricia Atwood's Chapter 7 case had allegedly violated the FDCPA and New Mexico state laws at issue in the case prior to her filing her petition in Chapter 7. Would her action for damages in the bankruptcy case on those theories then been properly treated as core, related to non-core, or neither?
3. The defendants in *Atwood* apparently did not raise the jurisdictional issue on which the FDCPA and state law counts were ultimately dismissed. The bankruptcy court nonetheless raised and ruled on that issue *sua sponte*. Did the court have to do this? Could it not have deemed the defense waived? Review Federal Rules of Civil Procedure 12(b)(1) and 12(h)(3) and see Kline v. Deutsche Bank Nat'l Trust Co. (In re Kline), 420 B.R. 541, 552 n. 28 (Bankr. D.N.M. 2009), and Williams v. Life Sav. and Loan, 802 F.2d 1200, 1202 (10th Cir. 1986). Would it

matter if the defendants had stipulated or otherwise consented to the bankruptcy court's jurisdiction to decide the FDCPA and state law issues presented as related to non-core matters? See Enterprise Bank v. Eltech, Inc. (In re Eltech, Inc.), 313 B.R. 659, 662 (Bankr. W.D. Pa. 2004).

4. Assume you represent the creditor defendants in *Atwood* and the bankruptcy judge determines the FDCPA and state law claims to be related to non-core proceedings. The attorney for the debtor asks you to consent to the bankruptcy court's entering final judgment on those issues regardless of that finding. What factors might you consider in deciding whether to recommend to your clients that they so consent? Assume your clients decide not to consent and the bankruptcy judge sets the matter for trial with the intent to hear proof on the issues and enter proposed findings of fact and conclusions of law. To save time and money, you would rather the U.S. district court go ahead and hear and decide the matter without waiting for the bankruptcy court to hear it first. What action can you take procedurally to accomplish that?

Further limiting the referral jurisdiction of bankruptcy courts under §157(b)(1) is §157(b)(5), which prohibits a bankruptcy court from hearing and deciding personal injury or wrongful death claims regardless of whether they are core or non-core. Only the district court is granted jurisdiction to hear such matters that arise in or are related to a bankruptcy case. For example, if the debtor has a personal injury claim pending at the time he files a bankruptcy petition, that claim will constitute a contingent asset of the estate. But the claim cannot be put to trial in the bankruptcy court even though the assets of the debtor's estate will be impacted by that trial. The referral jurisdiction of §157(a) does not include the power to hear and decide that case; jurisdiction remains with the district court.

Notwithstanding the broad grant of jurisdiction in bankruptcy cases in §1334, notwithstanding the power to revoke the referral of jurisdiction to bankruptcy courts in §157(d) as is often done in non-core matters, and notwithstanding the fact that determination of personal injury and wrongful death claims are not part of the referral jurisdiction and remain within the jurisdiction of the district court per §157(b)(5), 28 U.S.C. §1334(c)(1) grants the federal court discretion to abstain from hearing matters arising under or related to a bankruptcy case where it concludes that the matter should be decided by a state court having jurisdiction.

For example, if the debtor who has a personal injury claim that constitutes an asset of the estate when he files his petition in bankruptcy, we know that the bankruptcy court cannot hear and decide that matter per §157(b)(5). We know that the district court can hear and decide it under §1334 even if the claim is one that could not otherwise be brought in federal court (no diversity or federal question jurisdiction). However, per §1334(c)(1), the district court could decide to abstain from hearing the matter and order that it be filed and tried in a state court having jurisdiction.

And take note of §1334(c)(2): if the claim is one that is already pending in a state court when the bankruptcy petition is filed and is not one that could have originally been filed in federal court (no diversity or federal question jurisdiction), then the district court's abstention in favor of the state court where it is pending is mandatory. For example, if the debtor has already filed his personal injury lawsuit in a state court before he files his bankruptcy petition, the district court must abstain and let the matter proceed in state court. Of course, proceeds of the state court lawsuit will be considered assets of the bankruptcy estate, a topic we will consider soon.

Per §157(b)(4), an exception to the §1334(c)(2) mandatory exemption is made for proceedings under §157(b)(2)(B) involving allowance or disallowance of claims against the bankruptcy estate or exemptions from property of the estate or the estimation of claims or interests for purposes of confirming plans in Chapter 11, 12, and 13 proceedings to the extent such proceedings are deemed non-core.

The mandatory abstention of §1334(c)(2) requires a party to the dispute to file a "timely motion" to have the matter heard and decided by a state court where the matter is already pending. What is "timely" is not defined in that statute. When might a motion for abstention be deemed untimely?

The mandatory abstention of §1334(c)(2) also requires a finding that the action pending in the state court can be "timely adjudicated." If the debtor's case is one under Chapter 7 of the Code and can be otherwise administered by the bankruptcy court in three to six months, what is timely adjudication likely to mean? On the other hand, if the debtor's case is one under Chapter 13 of the Code and the debtor is proposing a five-year debt adjustment plan under Chapter 13, what is timely adjudication likely to mean?

Pursuant to 28 U.S.C. §157(b)(5), bankruptcy courts may not conduct trials involving claims for personal injury or wrongful death regardless of whether they qualify as core proceedings, and may not even make tentative findings in them as a non-core proceeding. Section 157(b)(5) provides that the U.S. district court is to hear and decide such claims and 28 U.S.C. §1334 gives the district courts subject matter jurisdiction to hear such cases even in the absence of federal question or diversity of citizenship jurisdiction. Alternatively, the bankruptcy court or district court may allow or order claims for personal injury or wrongful death that are related to a bankruptcy case to be heard and decided by a state court having jurisdiction as permitted by 28 U.S.C. §1334(c).

3. The Right to a Jury Trial in Bankruptcy Court

A bankruptcy court may conduct a jury trial if demanded by a party in either a core or non-core proceeding but *only* when all parties consent and the district court specifically designates the bankruptcy court to conduct that trial (see 28 U.S.C. §157(e) added by the Bankruptcy Reform Act of 1994).

B. CONSTITUTIONAL LIMITS ON THE POWER OF BANKRUPTCY COURTS TO ENTER FINAL JUDGMENTS IN CORE PROCEEDINGS: CONSTITUTIONAL JURISDICTION

Keep in mind that Congress' decision to designate certain proceedings in bankruptcy court as core proceedings by enacting 28 U.S.C. §157(b)(2) as part of the

1984 Bankruptcy Amendments and Federal Judgeship Act was triggered by *Northern Pipeline*, which first highlighted the tension between the power of Article III and Article I courts to enter final judgments in the bankruptcy context. *Northern Pipeline* dealt specifically with an action by a debtor in bankruptcy to recover on a breach of contract claim brought against a non-creditor of the estate. In a ruling that had the effect of a tsunami in the staid world of bankruptcy practice where such actions were routinely heard and decided by bankruptcy courts, the Supreme Court held that as an Article I court, the bankruptcy court had no constitutional power to enter a final judgment in such a dispute because it involved a determination of only private not public rights. The court said that "the restructuring of debtor-creditor relations" (such as the bankruptcy court's power to rule on a debtor's objections to a creditor's proof of claim filed in the bankruptcy case) "must be distinguished from the adjudication of state-created private rights" (such as a debtor's state law action for contract damages against a non-creditor as was at issue in the case). 458 U.S. at 71. "The former may well be a 'public right,'" the court said, "but the latter obviously is not." *Id.*

With the 1984 Amendments Act creating the referral jurisdiction scheme we have considered and designating certain actions as core in 28 U.S.C. §157(b)(2), Congress probably thought it had adequately addressed the problems raised by *Northern Pipeline* and that all would thereafter be well. However, a post–*Northern Pipeline* aftershock came along with Granfinanciera, S.A. v. Nordberg, 492 U.S. 33 (1989). In *Granfinanciera*, a Chapter 11 trustee filed a fraudulent conveyance action in the bankruptcy case against a defendant seeking to nullify a prepetition transfer of property by the debtor to the defendant. The defendant was not a creditor of the estate and thus had filed no claim against the estate. The bankruptcy judge treated the lawsuit as a core proceeding based on 28 U.S.C. §157(b)(2)(H), which specifically designates fraudulent transfer actions as core proceedings (see Exhibit 4.5). The defendant demanded a jury but the trustee did not consent and the case was tried in bankruptcy court as a core proceeding without a jury. On appeal the Supreme Court held that even though §157(b)(2)(H) designates fraudulent conveyance actions as core proceedings in a bankruptcy case, that section was unconstitutional to the extent it deprived a non-creditor of a right to jury trial in a civil action as guaranteed under the Seventh Amendment.

Though the case was decided under the guise of the Seventh Amendment, at the heart of *Granfinanciera* is the separation of powers problem addressed in *Northern Pipeline*. The court was saying that it violated the Seventh Amendment right to a jury trial to allow an Article I court to decide a fraudulent transfer action that, despite its enumeration by Congress as a core proceeding, in fact was not a cause of action created exclusively by the bankruptcy law (an action involving a public right). Because the debtor's cause of action existed prepetition, was controlled by state law, did not involve determination of a creditor's bankruptcy claim, and was instead an action involving a private right to which Seventh Amendment right to jury attached, Congress could not take that right away.

It was following and because of *Granfinanciera* that Congress enacted §157(e) seeking to clarify the right to jury trial in bankruptcy court by making it hinge on consent of the parties. But neither §157(e) nor any other changes made by Congress since *Granfinanciera* dealt with the underlying question of whether and when a bankruptcy court, with our without a jury, can enter a final judgment in a case involving a private right just because it arises in a bankruptcy case and just because the Code now designates it as a core proceeding.

Case Preview

Stern v. Marshall

After *Granfinanciera*, everyone in bankruptcy world knew it was only a matter of time before the constitutional storm first set loose by *Northern Pipeline* would return. The storm returned with *Stern* and it is still raging. As you read Stern v. Marshall, consider the following questions:

1. How did the dispute between Anna Nicole Smith and her stepson move from a Texas probate court to a bankruptcy court in California?
2. Since 28 U.S.C. §157(b)(2)(C) specifically lists counterclaims by the estate against persons filing claims against the estate as core proceedings, why doesn't that conclude the inquiry as to the bankruptcy court's power to enter a final order on such counterclaim?
3. Does the court specifically limit the scope of its holding to counterclaims by the debtor alleging tortious interference against a creditor of the estate? Can it reasonably be so limited?

Stern v. Marshall
131 S. Ct. 2594 (2011)

Chief Justice John G. Roberts, Jr. wrote the majority opinion in Stern v. Marshall. *Collection of the Supreme Court of the United States, Photographer: Steve Petteway*

[Vickie Lynn Marshall, a/k/a Anna Nicole Smith, wife of billionaire J. Howard Marshall, filed suit in a Texas state probate court following her husband's death, asserting that Pierce Marshall, J. Howard Marshall's youngest son, fraudulently induced his father to sign a living trust that did not include Smith. Pierce denied any fraudulent activity and defended the validity of J. Howard's trust in the Texas court. Smith then filed for bankruptcy in the Central District of California. Pierce filed a claim as a creditor in her case contending that Smith had defamed him and then filed a complaint in the bankruptcy case seeking to have his debt declared nondischargeable. Smith answered asserting truth as a defense to the defamation claim and included a counterclaim against Pierce alleging tortious interference with the gift she expected from J. Howard based on Pierce's fraudulent inducement of his father related to the living trust.

On November 5, 1999, the Bankruptcy Court issued an order granting Smith summary judgment on Pierce's claim for defamation. On September 27, 2000, after a bench trial, the Bankruptcy Court issued a judgment on Smith's counterclaim in her favor. The court later awarded Smith over $400 million in compensatory damages and $25 million in punitive damages. In post-trial proceedings, Pierce argued that the Bankruptcy Court lacked subject matter jurisdiction over Smith's counterclaim because it was not a core proceeding under 28 U.S.C. §157(b)(2)(C). The Bankruptcy Court concluded that the counterclaim was a core proceeding and, therefore, it had power to enter judgment.

The District Court disagreed and stated that that a "counterclaim should not be characterized as core" when it "is only somewhat related to the claim against which it is asserted, and when the unique characteristics and context of the counterclaim place it outside of the normal type of set-off or other counterclaims that customarily arise." Because the District Court concluded that Smith's counterclaim was not core, the court determined that it was required to treat the Bankruptcy Court's judgment as proposed findings rather than a final order and engaged in an independent review of the record. The District Court awarded Smith compensatory and punitive damages, each in the amount of $44,292,767.33.

The Court of Appeals reversed the District Court and the Supreme Court reversed the Court of Appeals. On remand from the Supreme Court, the Court of Appeals held that §157 mandated "a two-step approach" under which a bankruptcy judge may issue a final judgment in a proceeding only if the matter both "meets Congress' definition of a core proceeding *and* arises under or arises in title 11" of the Bankruptcy Code. The court concluded that a counterclaim under §157(b)(2)(C) is a core proceeding arising in a case under the Bankruptcy Code only if the counterclaim is so closely related to a creditor's proof of claim that the resolution of the counterclaim is necessary to resolve the allowance or disallowance of the claim itself. The court ruled that Vickie's counterclaim did not meet that test and concluded that the District Court should have afforded a preclusive effect to the Texas court's decision.

The Supreme Court granted certiorari a second time to determine whether the Court of Appeals was correct in that regard, and must resolve two issues: (1) whether the Bankruptcy Court had the statutory authority under 28 U.S.C. §157(b) to issue a final judgment on Smith's counterclaim; and (2) if so, whether conferring that authority on the Bankruptcy Court is constitutional.]

ROBERTS, Chief Justice. . . .

. . . III

Although we conclude that §157(b)(2)(C) permits the Bankruptcy Court to enter final judgment on Vickie's counterclaim, Article III of the Constitution does not. . . .

B

In *Northern Pipeline,* 458 U.S. 50 (1982) we considered whether bankruptcy judges serving under the Bankruptcy Act of 1978 could "constitutionally be vested with jurisdiction to decide [a] state-law contract claim" against an entity that was not otherwise part of the bankruptcy proceedings. 458 U.S., at 53, 87. . . . The Court concluded that assignment of such state law claims for resolution by those judges "violates Art. III of the Constitution." *Id.,* at 52. . . .

The plurality in *Northern Pipeline* recognized that there was a category of cases involving "public rights" that Congress could constitutionally assign to "legislative" courts for resolution. That opinion concluded that this "public rights" exception extended "only to matters arising between" individuals and the Government "in connection with the performance of the constitutional functions of the executive or legislative departments . . . that historically could have been determined exclusively by those" branches. *Id.*, at 67-68. A full majority of the Court, while not agreeing on the scope of the exception, concluded that the doctrine did not encompass adjudication of the state law claim at issue in that case. *Id.*, at 69-72. . . .

A full majority of Justices in *Northern Pipeline* also rejected the debtor's argument that the bankruptcy court's exercise of jurisdiction was constitutional because the bankruptcy judge was acting merely as an adjunct of the district court or court of appeals. *Id.*, at 71-72. . . .

After our decision in *Northern Pipeline*, Congress revised the statutes governing bankruptcy jurisdiction and bankruptcy judges. In the 1984 Act, Congress provided that the judges of the new bankruptcy courts would be appointed by the courts of appeals for the circuits in which their districts are located. 28 U.S.C. §152(a). . . . Congress permitted the newly constituted bankruptcy courts to enter final judgments only in "core" proceedings. . . .

With respect to such "core" matters, however, the bankruptcy courts under the 1984 Act exercise the same powers they wielded under the Bankruptcy Act of 1978 (1978 Act), 92 Stat. 2549. As in *Northern Pipeline*, for example, the newly constituted bankruptcy courts are charged under §157(b)(2)(C) with resolving "[a]ll matters of fact and law in whatever domains of the law to which" a counterclaim may lead. 458 U.S., at 91. . . . As in *Northern Pipeline*, the new courts in core proceedings "issue final judgments, which are binding and enforceable even in the absence of an appeal." 458 U.S., at 85-86. . . . And, as in *Northern Pipeline*, the district courts review the judgments of the bankruptcy courts in core proceedings only under the usual limited appellate standards. That requires marked deference to, among other things, the bankruptcy judges' findings of fact. See §158(a); Fed. Rule Bkrtcy. Proc. 8013 (findings of fact "shall not be set aside unless clearly erroneous").

C

Vickie and the dissent argue that the Bankruptcy Court's entry of final judgment on her state common law counterclaim was constitutional, despite the similarities between the bankruptcy courts under the 1978 Act and those exercising core jurisdiction under the 1984 Act. We disagree. It is clear that the Bankruptcy Court in this case exercised the "judicial Power of the United States" in purporting to resolve and enter final judgment on a state common law claim, just as the court did in *Northern Pipeline*. No "public right" exception excuses the failure to comply with Article III in doing so, any more than in *Northern Pipeline*. Vickie argues that this case is different because the defendant is a creditor in the bankruptcy. But the debtors' claims in the cases on which she relies were themselves federal claims under bankruptcy law, which would be completely resolved in the bankruptcy process of allowing or disallowing claims. Here Vickie's claim is a state law action independent of the federal bankruptcy law and not necessarily resolvable by a ruling on the creditor's proof of claim in bankruptcy. *Northern Pipeline* and our subsequent decision in *Granfinanciera*, 492 U.S. 33, . . . rejected the application of the "public rights" exception in such cases.

Nor can the bankruptcy courts under the 1984 Act be dismissed as mere adjuncts of Article III courts, any more than could the bankruptcy courts under the 1978 Act. The judicial powers the courts exercise in cases such as this remain the same, and a court exercising such broad powers is no mere adjunct of anyone.

1

Vickie's counterclaim cannot be deemed a matter of "public right" that can be decided outside the Judicial Branch [meaning the Article III courts]. As explained above, in *Northern Pipeline* we rejected the argument that the public rights doctrine permitted a bankruptcy court to adjudicate a state law suit brought by a debtor against a company that had not filed a claim against the estate. . . . Although our discussion of the public rights exception since that time has not been entirely consistent, and the exception has been the subject of some debate, this case does not fall within any of the various formulations of the concept that appear in this Court's opinions.

We first recognized the category of public rights in Murray's Lessee v. Hoboken Land & Improvement Co., 59 U.S. 272, 18 How. 272 (1856). That case involved the Treasury Department's sale of property belonging to a customs collector who had failed to transfer payments to the Federal Government that he had collected on its behalf. *Id.*, at 274. . . . The plaintiff, who claimed title to the same land through a different transfer, objected that the Treasury Department's calculation of the deficiency and sale of the property was void, because it was a judicial act that could not be assigned to the Executive under Article III. *Id.*, at 274-275, 282-283. "To avoid misconstruction upon so grave a subject," the Court . . . confirmed that Congress cannot "withdraw from judicial cognizance any matter which, from its nature, is the subject of a suit at the common law, or in equity, or admiralty." *Ibid.* . . .

Subsequent decisions from this Court contrasted cases within the reach of the public rights exception—those arising "between the Government and persons subject to its authority in connection with the performance of the constitutional functions of the executive or legislative departments"—and those that were instead matters "of private right, that is, of the liability of one individual to another under the law as defined." Crowell v. Benson, 285 U.S. 22, 50, 51 (1932). . . .

The most recent case in which we considered application of the public rights exception—and the only case in which we have considered that doctrine in the bankruptcy context since *Northern Pipeline*—is Granfinanciera, S.A. v. Nordberg, 492 U.S. 33 (1989). In *Granfinanciera* we rejected a bankruptcy trustee's argument that a fraudulent conveyance action filed on behalf of a bankruptcy estate against a noncreditor in a bankruptcy proceeding fell within the "public rights" exception. We explained that, "[i]f a statutory right is not closely intertwined with a federal regulatory program Congress has power to enact, and if that right neither belongs to nor exists against the Federal Government, then it must be adjudicated by an Article III court." *Id.*, at 54-55. . . . We reasoned that fraudulent conveyance suits were "quintessentially suits at common law that more nearly resemble state law contract claims brought by a bankrupt corporation to augment the bankruptcy estate than they do creditors' hierarchically ordered claims to a pro rata share of the bankruptcy res." *Id.,* at 56. . . . As a consequence, we concluded that fraudulent conveyance actions were "more accurately characterized as a private rather than a public right as we have used those terms in our Article III decisions." *Id.,* at 55. . . .

Vickie's counterclaim—like the fraudulent conveyance claim at issue in *Granfinanciera*—does not fall within any . . . formulations of the public rights exception in this Court's cases. It is not a matter that can be pursued only by grace of the other branches, as in *Murray's Lessee,* 18 How., at 284, . . . or one that "historically could have been determined exclusively by" those branches, *Northern Pipeline, supra,* at 68. . . . The claim is instead one under state common law between two private parties. It does not "depend[ ] on the will of congress," *Murray's Lessee, supra,* at 284 . . . ; Congress has nothing to do with it.

In addition, Vickie's claimed right to relief does not flow from a federal statutory scheme. . . . It is not "completely dependent upon" adjudication of a claim created by federal law, as in Commodity Futures Trading Comm'n v. Schor, 478 U.S. 833, 856 (1986). . . . And in contrast to the objecting party in *Schor, id.,* at 855-856, Pierce did not truly consent to resolution of Vickie's claim in the bankruptcy court proceedings. He had nowhere else to go if he wished to recover from Vickie's estate. See *Granfinanciera, supra,* at 59, n. 14 (noting that "[p]arallel reasoning [to *Schor*] is unavailable in the context of bankruptcy proceedings, because creditors lack an alternative forum to the bankruptcy court in which to pursue their claims").

Furthermore, the asserted authority to decide Vickie's claim is not limited to a "particularized area of the law," *Northern Pipeline,* 458 U.S., at 85. . . . This is not a situation in which Congress devised an "expert and inexpensive method for dealing with a class of questions of fact which are particularly suited to examination and determination by an administrative agency specially assigned to that task." *Crowell,* 285 U.S., at 46. . . . The "experts" in the federal system at resolving common law counterclaims such as Vickie's are the Article III courts, and it is with those courts that her claim must stay. . . .

What is plain here is that this case involves the most prototypical exercise of judicial power: the entry of a final, binding judgment *by a court* with broad substantive jurisdiction, on a common law cause of action, when the action neither derives from nor depends upon any agency regulatory regime. If such an exercise of judicial power may nonetheless be taken from the Article III Judiciary simply by deeming it part of some amorphous "public right," then Article III would be transformed from the guardian of individual liberty and separation of powers we have long recognized into mere wishful thinking.

2

Vickie and the dissent next attempt to distinguish *Northern Pipeline* and *Granfinanciera* on the ground that Pierce, unlike the defendants in those cases, had filed a proof of claim in the bankruptcy proceedings. Given Pierce's participation in those proceedings, Vickie argues, the Bankruptcy Court had the authority to adjudicate her counterclaim under our decisions in Katchen v. Landy, 382 U.S. 323 (1966), and Langenkamp v. Culp, 498 U.S. 42, (1990) (*per curiam*).

We do not agree. [I]t is hard to see why Pierce's decision to file a claim should make any difference with respect to the characterization of Vickie's counterclaim. "'[P]roperty interests are created and defined by state law,' and '[u]nless some federal interest requires a different result, there is no reason why such interests should be analyzed differently simply because an interested party is involved in a bankruptcy proceeding." Travelers Casualty & Surety Co. of America v. Pacific Gas & Elec. Co., 549 U.S. 443, 451 (2007). . . . Pierce's claim for defamation in no way affects the nature of Vickie's counterclaim for tortious interference as one at common law that simply attempts to augment the bankruptcy estate—the very type of claim that we held in *Northern Pipeline* and *Granfinanciera* must be decided by an Article III court. . . .

. . . Accordingly, the judgment of the Court of Appeals is affirmed.

Post-Case Follow-Up

Congress thought it was fixing the Article I versus Article III, public versus private rights problem recognized in *Northern Pipeline* by creating the referral jurisdiction to the Article I bankruptcy courts from the Article III district courts in the 1984 Amendments Act. Couldn't the Supreme Court have accepted this arrangement as adequate to cure the constitutional mandate in private rights matters? Would it have been intellectually dishonest to do so? The Court gave no indication that its holding had implications broader than the specific claim before it: a debtor's counterclaim alleging tortious interference against a creditor of the estate. Given the confusion and uncertainty created by the decision, should the Court have provided more guidance regarding the implications of its decisions on other core proceedings?

Stern v. Marshall: Real Life Applications

1. Assume you have the following core proceedings arising in a Chapter 7 case in which you represent the debtor. Which are likely to trigger constitutional jurisdiction issues because of *Stern*?
   a. Whether the client can show undue hardship under Code §523(a)(8) to justify discharge of a student loan.
   b. As between two creditors both claiming to be secured in the debtor's home, which creditor has the priority position as having perfected its interest first under state law.
   c. Whether the debtor should be allowed to reaffirm a debt under Code §524(c) to a creditor who is secured in the debtor's automobile and which the debtor can continue to pay for rather than discharging the debt in the bankruptcy case.
   d. Whether the debtor should be allowed to recover on behalf of the estate a judgment against a third party for an alleged prepetition fraudulent conveyance by the third party.

So where are we left regarding the impact of *Granfinanciera* and *Stern* on the core/non-core distinction of §157(b) and the power of a bankruptcy court to enter a final judgment in either a core or non-core proceeding? First, it is clear that the proceedings identified as core by Congress in §157(b)(2) are not the equivalent of proceedings involving determination of public rights, although that may have been Congress's intent. In other words, the statutory classification of actions of core/non-core is not determinative of a bankruptcy court's power to enter a final judgment. A dispute may clearly fall within the enumerated core proceedings of §157(b)(2) of the Code but a bankruptcy court may lack the constitutional power to enter a final order in such a proceeding. The constitutional analysis mandated by *Stern* says that if it involves a public right then the bankruptcy court may enter final judgment or dispositive order. If it involves determination of a private right then the bankruptcy court may not enter final judgment or dispositive order; only the Article III district court can do that. Thus, notwithstanding the core/non-core distinction created by Congress in §157(b), *Stern* has created a significant "gap" in the subject matter jurisdiction of the bankruptcy courts.

Second, we do not yet know how many of the proceedings designated as core in §157(b)(2) will ultimately be found to involve determination of private and not public rights and thus be outside the power of a bankruptcy court to finally decide. One post-*Stern* decision confronting this question observed, "This area of the law has a potluck quality," Waldman v. Stone, 698 F.3d 910, 918 (6th Cir. 2012), cert. denied, 133 S. Ct. 1604 (2013), meaning no one really knows at this point.

Some courts have read *Stern* broadly and others narrowly. For example, whether a fraudulent conveyance action designated as a core proceeding in §157(b)(2)(H) is a public or private action is dividing the lower courts. Compare In re Bellingham Ins. Agency, Inc., 702 F.3d 553 (9th Cir. 2012) (fraudulent conveyance action against non-creditor a private action outside constitutional power of bankruptcy court to decide), with In re Tyler, 493 B.R. 905 (Bankr. N.D. Ga. 2013) (neither *Granfinanciera* nor *Stern* mandate a holding that a fraudulent conveyance action is outside the constitutional power of bankruptcy court to decide).

The Story Behind Anna Nicole Smith, the Protagonist in *Stern*

The debtor involved in the *Stern* case, Anna Nicole Smith, was quite a character. The former model, stripper, and Playboy's 1993 Playmate of the Year was 26 years old when she married 89-year-old billionaire J. Howard Marshall in 1994. Marshall passed away only 14 months following the nuptials, and his estate was admitted to probate in Texas. The young widow announced that her late husband had promised to leave her a small fortune but had been deterred from doing so by his son and thus followed the sequence of litigation in state and federal court recited in *Stern*. It was quite a show played out daily in American media. You can get all the titillating details of the story by reading In re Marshall, 253 B.R. 550, 553-556 (Bankr. C.D. Cal. 2000). Anna Nicole Smith died in February 2007 from an accidental overdose of prescription drugs. She was 39 years old.

Anna Nicole Smith.
Featureflash / Shutterstock.com

The Supreme Court has twice since *Stern* declined the opportunity to clarify for anxious lower courts and practitioners what are and are not *Stern* "gap" claims. In Executive Benefits Ins. Agency v. Arkison, 134 S. Ct. 2165, 2174 (2014), discussed in more detail below, the court "assumed without deciding" that a fraudulent conveyance action is a *Stern* claim since the lower court had so held. And in Wellness International Network, Ltd. v. Sharif, 135 S. Ct. 1932 (2015) (highlighted below), the majority opinion found it unnecessary to decide whether a dispute over whether a trust constituted property of the estate under §541 of the Code presented a *Stern* claim though that issue was clearly before it.

What is certain is that *Stern* set off a firestorm of impassioned commentary regarding its implications for the existing bankruptcy framework. As of this writing, in the three years since it was decided, *Stern* has been cited in more than 1,000 bankruptcy decisions. Some courts and commentators feared the worst, that bankruptcy judges would be reduced to mere law clerks for district judges, limited to making recommendations for adoption by the Article III court in bankruptcy cases. Or to mere office administrators, empowered to do nothing more than carry out decisions of the district court in bankruptcy cases.

With two recent decisions, however, the Supreme Court has turned back the hands of the doomsday clock that so many heard ticking since *Stern*. In *Arkison*, the Court resolved a post-*Stern* dispute among the lower courts and held that a bankruptcy court that lacks constitutional jurisdiction to enter a final judgment in a core proceeding may nonetheless utilize the procedure set forth in 28 U.S.C. §157(c)(1) for non-core proceedings and enter proposed findings of fact and conclusions of law in such cases. In so holding the Court relied on a severability provision contained in the statutory notes following 28 U.S.C. §151.

> The statute permits *Stern* claims to proceed as non-core within the meaning of §157(c). In particular, the statute contains a severability provision that accounts for decisions, like *Stern*, that invalidate certain applications of the statute:
>
> > "If any provision of this Act or the application thereof to any person or circumstance is held invalid, the remainder of this Act, or the application of that provision to persons or circumstances other than those as to which it is held invalid, is not affected thereby." 98 Stat. 344, note following 28 U.S.C. §151.
>
> The plain text of this severability provision closes the so-called "gap" created by *Stern* claims. When a court identifies a claim as a *Stern* claim, it has necessarily "held invalid" the "application" of §157(b)—i.e., the "core" label and its attendant procedures—to the litigant's claim. . . . In that circumstance, the statute instructs that "the remainder of th[e] Act . . . is not affected thereby." . . . That remainder includes §157(c), which governs non-core proceedings. With the "core" category no longer available for the *Stern* claim at issue, we look to §157(c)(1) to determine whether the claim may be adjudicated as a non-core claim—specifically, whether it is "not a core proceeding" but is "otherwise related to a case under title 11." If the claim satisfies the criteria of §157(c)(1), the bankruptcy court simply treats the claims as non-core: The bankruptcy court should hear the proceeding and submit proposed findings of fact and conclusions of law to the district court for de novo review and entry of judgment.
>
> The conclusion that the remainder of the statute may continue to apply to *Stern* claims accords with our general approach to severability. We ordinarily give effect to

the valid portion of a partially unconstitutional statute so long as it "remains ' "fully operative as a law," ' " . . . and so long as it is not " 'evident' " from the statutory text and context that Congress would have preferred no statute at all. . . . Neither of those concerns applies here. Thus, §157(c) may be applied naturally to *Stern* claims. And . . . "nothing in the statute's text or historical context" that makes it "evident" that Congress would prefer to suspend *Stern* claims in limbo. . . .

Arkison, 134 S. Ct. at 2173.

Case Preview

Wellness International Network, Ltd. v. Sharif

A much more significant post-*Stern* issue focused on the procedure of 28 U.S.C. §157(c)(2), which authorizes a bankruptcy court to enter a final judgment in a non-core proceeding where all parties consent. Is that procedure viable when the bankruptcy court is confronted with a *Stern* claim? In other words, may the parties expressly or impliedly consent to have the bankruptcy judge enter a final judgment on a contested issue that is properly triable only by the district judge due to constitutional jurisdiction requirements recognized in *Stern*? As you read *Wellness*, consider the following questions:

1. What is the basis for the court's holding that a party's right to have a case decided by an Article III court is subject to waiver?
2. What is the basis for the court's conclusion that allowing bankruptcy litigants to waive the right to Article III adjudication of *Stern* claims does not threaten the structural integrity of the separation of powers by usurping the constitutional prerogatives of Article III courts?
3. What requirements does the court impose for a party's consent to the bankruptcy court's entering a final judgment on a *Stern* claim to be effective?

Wellness International Network, Ltd. v. Sharif
135 S. Ct. 1932 (2015)

[A creditor instituted an action in a Chapter 7 case to deny the debtor a discharge and to have certain property debtor listed on debtor's schedules declared property of the estate under §541 rather than assets held by debtor only as trustee. The bankruptcy court entered a final order denying discharge and declaring the listed property to be property of the estate and the district court affirmed. On appeal, the Seventh Circuit affirmed the bankruptcy court's denial of the discharge but upheld debtor's contention that, under *Stern*, the bankruptcy court lacked constitutional authority to determine whether property in the debtor's possession is property of the estate under §541 where that determination turns on state law. Such a determination, the Seventh Circuit reasoned, does not "stem from the bankruptcy itself" any more than did the state law–based counterclaim against a creditor in *Stern*. The Seventh Circuit rejected the creditor's contention that debtor had waived or impliedly consented to the bankruptcy judge entering a final order on the issue by failing to raise and brief the jurisdictional issue in a timely manner, finding that due to the separation of powers involved, a litigant may not waive a *Stern* objection. The issues on appeal to the Supreme Court are (1) whether an action under §541 to determine what is property of the estate so inherently stems from the bankruptcy case itself that a bankruptcy court may constitutionally enter a final order on it despite being controlled by state law; and (2) whether a party may expressly or impliedly consent to the bankruptcy court's entry of a final order on an issue even though it lacks constitutional authority to do so under *Stern*. The majority opinion dealt only with the second issue.]

SOTOMAYOR, Justice: . . .

A

Adjudication by consent is nothing new. Indeed, "[d]uring the early years of the Republic, federal courts, with the consent of the litigants, regularly referred adjudication of entire disputes to non-Article III referees, masters, or arbitrators, for entry of final judgment in accordance with the referee's report." Brubaker, The Constitutionality of Litigant Consent to Non–Article III Bankruptcy Adjudications, 32 Bkrtcy. L. Letter No. 12, p. 6 (Dec. 2012). . . .

The foundational case in the modern era is Commodity Futures Trading Comm'n v. Schor, 478 U.S. 833 (1986). The CFTC, which Congress had authorized to hear customer complaints against commodities brokers, issued a regulation allowing itself to hear state-law counterclaims as well. William Schor filed a complaint with the CFTC against his broker, and the broker, which had previously filed claims against Schor in federal court, refiled them as counterclaims in the CFTC proceeding. The CFTC ruled against Schor on the counterclaims. This Court upheld that ruling against both statutory and constitutional challenges.

On the constitutional question . . . the Court began by holding that Schor had "waived any right he may have possessed to the full trial of [the broker's] counterclaim before an Article III court." Id., at 849. The Court then explained why this waiver legitimated the CFTC's exercise of authority: "[A]s a personal right, Article III's guarantee of an impartial and independent federal adjudication is subject to waiver, just as are other personal constitutional rights"—such as the right to a jury—"that dictate the procedures by which civil and criminal matters must be tried." Id., at 848-849.

The Court went on to state that a litigant's waiver of his "personal right" to an Article III court is not always dispositive because Article III "not only preserves to litigants their interest in an impartial and independent federal adjudication of claims . . . but also serves as 'an inseparable element of the constitutional system of checks and balances.' . . . To the extent that this structural principle is implicated in a given case"—but only to that extent—"the parties cannot by consent cure the constitutional difficulty . . . ." Id., at 850-851.

Leaning heavily on the importance of Schor's consent, the Court found no structural concern implicated by the CFTC's adjudication of the counterclaims against him. While "Congress gave the CFTC the authority to adjudicate such matters," the Court wrote, "the decision to invoke this forum is left entirely to the parties and the power of the federal judiciary to take jurisdiction of these matters is unaffected. In such circumstances, separation of powers concerns are diminished, for it seems self-evident that just as Congress may encourage parties to settle a dispute out of court or resort to arbitration without impermissible incursions on the separation of powers, Congress may make available a quasi-judicial mechanism through which willing parties may, at their option, elect to resolve their differences."

Id., at 855.

The option for parties to submit their disputes to a non-Article III adjudicator was at most a "de minimis" infringement on the prerogative of the federal courts. Id., at 856. . . .

A few years after *Schor*, the Court decided a pair of cases—Gomez v. United States, 490 U.S. 858 (1989), and Peretz v. United States, 501 U.S. 923 (1991)—that reiterated the importance of consent to the constitutional analysis. Both cases concerned whether the Federal Magistrates Act authorized magistrate judges to preside over jury selection in a felony trial; the difference was that *Peretz* consented to the practice while *Gomez* did not. That difference was dispositive.

In *Gomez*, the Court interpreted the statute as not allowing magistrate judges to supervise voir dire without consent, emphasizing the constitutional concerns that might otherwise arise. See 490 U.S., at 864. In *Peretz*, the Court upheld the Magistrate Judge's action, stating that "the defendant's consent significantly changes the constitutional analysis." 501 U.S., at 932. The Court concluded that allowing a magistrate judge to supervise jury selection—with consent—does not violate Article III, explaining that "litigants may waive their personal right to have an Article III judge preside over a civil trial," id., at 936 . . . and that "[t]he most basic rights of criminal defendants are similarly subject to waiver," 501 U.S., at 936. And "[e]ven assuming that a litigant may not waive structural protections provided by Article III," the Court found "no such structural protections . . . implicated by" a magistrate judge's supervision of voir dire:

"Magistrates are appointed and subject to removal by Article III judges. The 'ultimate decision' whether to invoke the magistrate's assistance is made by the district court, subject to veto by the parties. The decision whether to empanel the jury whose selection a magistrate has supervised also remains entirely with the district court. Because 'the entire process takes place under the district court's total control and jurisdiction,' there is no danger that use of the magistrate involves a 'congressional attemp[t] "to transfer jurisdiction [to non-Article III tribunals] for the purpose of emasculating" constitutional courts.' " Id., at 937. . . .

The lesson of *Schor*, *Peretz*, and the history that preceded them is plain: The entitlement to an Article III adjudicator is "a personal right" and thus ordinarily "subject to waiver," *Schor*, 478 U.S., at 848. Article III also serves a structural purpose, "barring congressional attempts 'to transfer jurisdiction [to non-Article III tribunals] for the purpose of emasculating' constitutional courts and thereby prevent[ing] 'the encroachment or aggrandizement of one branch at the expense of the other.' " Id., at 850. But allowing Article I adjudicators to decide claims submitted to them by consent does not offend the separation of powers so long as Article III courts retain supervisory authority over the process.

B

The question here, then, is whether allowing bankruptcy courts to decide *Stern* claims by consent would "impermissibly threate[n] the institutional integrity of the Judicial Branch." *Schor*, 478 U.S., at 851. And that question must be decided not by "formalistic and unbending rules," but "with an eye to the practical effect that the" practice "will have on the constitutionally assigned role of the federal judiciary." Ibid . . . . The Court must weigh

> "the extent to which the essential attributes of judicial power are reserved to Article III courts, and, conversely, the extent to which the non-Article III forum exercises the range of jurisdiction and powers normally vested only in Article III courts, the origins and importance of the right to be adjudicated, and the concerns that drove Congress to depart from the requirements of Article III."

Schor, 478 U.S., at 851.

Applying these factors, we conclude that allowing bankruptcy litigants to waive the right to Article III adjudication of *Stern* claims does not usurp the constitutional prerogatives of Article III courts. Bankruptcy judges, like magistrate judges, "are appointed and subject to removal by Article III judges," *Peretz*, 501 U.S., at 937; see 28 U.S.C. §§152(a)(1), (e). They "serve as judicial officers of the United States district court," §151, and collectively "constitute a unit of the district court" for that district, §152(a)(1). Just as "[t]he 'ultimate decision' whether to invoke [a] magistrate [judge]'s assistance is made by the district court," *Peretz*, 501 U.S., at 937, bankruptcy courts hear matters solely on a district court's reference, §157(a), which the district court may withdraw sua sponte or at the request of a party, §157(d). "[S]eparation of powers concerns are diminished" when, as here, "the decision to invoke [a non–Article III] forum is left entirely to the parties and the power of the federal judiciary to take jurisdiction" remains in place. *Schor*, 478 U.S., at 855.

Furthermore, like the CFTC in *Schor*, bankruptcy courts possess no free-floating authority to decide claims traditionally heard by Article III courts. Their ability to resolve such matters is limited to "a narrow class of common law claims as an incident to the [bankruptcy courts'] primary, and unchallenged, adjudicative function." Id., at 854. "In such circumstances, the magnitude of any intrusion on the Judicial Branch can only be termed de minimis." Id., at 856.

Finally, there is no indication that Congress gave bankruptcy courts the ability to decide *Stern* claims in an effort to aggrandize itself or humble the Judiciary. As in *Peretz*, "[b]ecause 'the entire process takes place under the district court's total control and jurisdiction,' there is no danger that use of the [bankruptcy court] involves a 'congressional attemp[t] "to transfer jurisdiction [to non–Article III tribunals] for the purpose of emasculating" constitutional courts.'" 501 U.S., at 937. . . . Pacemaker Diagnostic Clinic of America, Inc. v. Instromedix, Inc., 725 F.2d 537, 544 (C.A. 9 1984) (en banc) (Kennedy, J.) (magistrate judges may adjudicate civil cases by consent because the Federal Magistrates Act "invests the Article III judiciary with extensive administrative control over the management, composition, and operation of the magistrate system").

Congress could choose to rest the full share of the Judiciary's labor on the shoulders of Article III judges. But doing so would require a substantial increase in the number of district judgeships. Instead, Congress has supplemented the capacity of district courts through the able assistance of bankruptcy judges. So long as those judges are subject to control by the Article III courts, their work poses no threat to the separation of powers.

C

Our recent decision in *Stern*, on which Sharif and the principal dissent rely heavily, does not compel a different result. That is because *Stern*—like its predecessor, *Northern Pipeline*—turned on the fact that the litigant "did not truly consent to" resolution of the claim against it in a non–Article III forum. 564 U.S., at ____, 131 S. Ct., at 2614. . . .

An expansive reading of *Stern*, moreover, would be inconsistent with the opinion's own description of its holding. The Court in Stern took pains to note that the question before it was "a 'narrow' one," and that its answer did "not change all that much" about the division of labor between district courts and bankruptcy courts. Id., at ____, 131 S. Ct., at 2620; see also id., at ____, 131 S. Ct., at 2620 (stating that Congress had exceeded the limitations of Article III "in one isolated respect"). That could not have been a fair characterization of the decision if it meant that bankruptcy judges could no longer exercise their longstanding authority to resolve claims submitted to them by consent. Interpreting *Stern* to bar consensual adjudications by bankruptcy courts would "meaningfully chang[e] the division of labor" in our judicial system, contra, id., at ____, 131 S. Ct., at 2620.

In sum, the cases in which this Court has found a violation of a litigant's right to an Article III decisionmaker have involved an objecting defendant forced to litigate involuntarily before a non–Article III court. The Court has never done what Sharif and the principal dissent would have us do—hold that a litigant who has the right to an Article III court may not waive that right through his consent.

D

The principal dissent warns darkly of the consequences of today's decision. To hear the principal dissent tell it, the world will end not in fire, or ice, but in a bankruptcy court. The response to these ominous predictions is the same now as it was when Justice Brennan, dissenting in *Schor*, first made them nearly 30 years ago:

> "This is not to say, of course, that if Congress created a phalanx of non–Article III tribunals equipped to handle the entire business of the Article III courts without any Article III supervision or control and without evidence of valid and specific legislative necessities, the fact that the parties had the election to proceed in their forum of choice would necessarily save the scheme from constitutional attack. But this case obviously bears no resemblance to such a scenario. . . ."

478 U.S., at 855.

Adjudication based on litigant consent has been a consistent feature of the federal court system since its inception. Reaffirming that unremarkable fact, we are confident, poses no great threat to anyone's birthrights, constitutional or otherwise.

III

Sharif contends that to the extent litigants may validly consent to adjudication by a bankruptcy court, such consent must be express. We disagree.

Nothing in the Constitution requires that consent to adjudication by a bankruptcy court be express. Nor does the relevant statute, 28 U.S.C. §157, mandate express consent; it states only that a bankruptcy court must obtain "the consent . . . of all parties to the proceeding" before hearing and determining a non-core claim. §157(c)(2). . . .

The implied consent standard . . . supplies the appropriate rule for adjudications by bankruptcy courts under §157. Applied in the bankruptcy context, that standard possesses the same pragmatic virtues—increasing judicial efficiency and checking gamesmanship—that motivated our adoption of it for consent-based adjudications by magistrate judges. See Roell v. Withrow, 538 U.S. 580, 590 (2003). It bears emphasizing, however, that a litigant's consent—whether express or implied—must still be knowing and voluntary. *Roell* makes clear that the key inquiry is whether "the litigant or counsel was made aware of the need for consent and the right to refuse it, and still voluntarily appeared to try the case" before the non-Article III adjudicator. Ibid.; see also id., at 588, n. 5, ("notification of the right to refuse" adjudication by a non-Article III court "is a prerequisite to any inference of consent"). . . .

[The Court explains that it is remanding the case to the Seventh Circuit for a determination of whether the debtor knowingly and voluntarily consented.]

The Court holds that Article III permits bankruptcy courts to decide *Stern* claims submitted to them by consent. The judgment of the United States Court of Appeals for the Seventh Circuit is therefore reversed, and the case is remanded for further proceedings consistent with this opinion.

It is so ordered.

ROBERTS, Chief Justice, dissenting:

The Bankruptcy Court in this case granted judgment to Wellness on its claim that Sharif's bankruptcy estate contained assets he purportedly held in a trust. Provided that no third party asserted a substantial adverse claim to those assets, the Bankruptcy Court's adjudication "stems from the bankruptcy itself" rather than from "the stuff of the traditional actions at common law tried by the courts at Westminster in 1789." Stern v. Marshall, 564 U.S. ____, ____, 131 S. Ct. 2594, 2609 (2011). Article III poses no barrier to such a decision. That is enough to resolve this case. . . .

Post-Case Follow-Up

Taken together, *Arkison* and *Wellness* are likely to significantly defuse the crisis initiated by *Stern*. We know from *Wellness* that parties can consent expressly or impliedly to the bankruptcy court entering a final order on *Stern* claims and bankruptcy courts will likely adopt procedures to make sure the consent is express in most cases. And where a party to a *Stern* claim does not consent, we know from *Arkison* that the bankruptcy court can enter proposed findings and conclusions just as in non-core matters where no consent is forthcoming, or the reference can be revoked in such case to let the district court hear and decide. The lingering disappointment from these cases is that they do not clarify what types of claims fall within the purview of *Stern* to raise the constitutional problem in the first place. Consequently, more litigation and lingering doubts over the issue appear inevitable. The dissent of Chief Justice Roberts in *Wellness* in this regard is interesting and perhaps indicative. He would treat a §541 dispute over property of the estate as one involving public rights under the Code even where state law was determinative as to ownership rights, unless some third party claimed an interest in that property. The majority did not disagree; it simply chose to decide the case on the consent issue only. Perhaps this is some small indication that the court is looking for a way to limit the scope of *Stern* as some lower courts have chosen to do. See, e.g., In re AFY, Inc., 461 B.R., 541 (B.A.P. 8th Cir. 2012) (limiting *Stern*'s applicability to §157(b)(2)(C) concerning counterclaims by the estate filed against persons filing claims against the estate).

Wellness International Network, Ltd. v. Sharif: Real Life Applications

1. After *Wellness*, there are likely to be disputes arising over whether a party has "impliedly" consented to the bankruptcy court entering a final order in a *Stern* dispute. Assume a Chapter 7 trustee brings an adversary proceeding under §548 to recover a prepetition fraudulent transfer from a creditor of the estate. Assume further that the federal circuit in which the bankruptcy case is pending has concluded that such actions, though core, constitute *Stern* claims. What are the arguments that implied consent is or is not present under the following circumstances?

   a. The creditor has filed a proof of claim in the bankruptcy case before the fraudulent conveyance action is brought.

   b. The creditor has filed a complaint with the bankruptcy court seeking to have its claim against the debtor declared non-dischargeable before the fraudulent conveyance action is brought.

   c. The creditor has filed an answer to the trustee's complaint that did not deny or contest the bankruptcy court's jurisdiction. A week later, the creditor files an amended answer denying the court has jurisdiction based on *Stern*.

   d. The creditor does not contest the bankruptcy court's jurisdiction and the court finds for the trustee. On appeal, the district court sustains. On appeal to the circuit court, the bankruptcy court's order is set aside on grounds having nothing to do with jurisdiction and remanded to the bankruptcy court for reconsideration. Following remand, the creditor alleges the bankruptcy court has no jurisdiction based on *Stern*.

2. Assume the following issues, the determinations of which constitute core proceedings, arise in a consumer bankruptcy case. Which are likely to trigger constitutional jurisdiction issues because of *Stern*?

a. Whether the client can show undue hardship under Code §523(a)(8) to justify discharge of a student loan.

b. As between two creditors both claiming to be secured in the debtor's home, which creditor has the priority position as having perfected its interest first under state law.

c. Whether the debtor should be allowed to reaffirm a debt under Code §524(c) that is owed to a creditor who is secured in the debtor's automobile and that the debtor can continue to pay for rather than discharging the debt in the bankruptcy case. See FRBP 7012(b).

d. Whether the debtor should be allowed to recover on behalf of the estate a judgment against a third party for an alleged prepetition fraudulent conveyance by the third party. See FRBP 7012(b).

e. Whether a prepetition transfer by the debtor to a creditor was in the ordinary course of business in order to avoid being a preferential transfer.

f. Whether a debtor's Chapter 13 plan should be confirmed.

C. THE EFFECT OF A PREPETITION ARBITRATION AGREEMENT ON THE BANKRUPTCY COURT'S POWER TO DECIDE A DISPUTE

Over the past generation, the U.S. Supreme Court has identified a strong congressional policy arising from the **Federal Arbitration Act (FAA)**, 9 U.S.C. §§1 et seq., in favor of enforcing contractual **arbitration** agreements that has been applied to drastically limit the power of state law or even private agreement of the parties to limit or negate such agreements. In essence the Supreme Court has ruled in numerous contexts that state common law, statutes, or regulations raised as a defense to the enforcement of an arbitration agreement are preempted by the FAA to the extent that they "apply only to arbitration or that derive their meaning from the fact that an agreement to arbitrate is at issue." AT&T Mobility v. Concepcion, 131 S. Ct. 1740, 1746 (2011). See, e.g., Volt Info. Scis. Inc. v. Bd. of Trs. of Leland Stanford Junior University, 489 U.S. 468 (1989) (parties to an arbitration agreement involving an interstate transaction that would normally be governed by the FAA cannot choose in the agreement to be governed instead by state law); Doctor's Assocs. v. Cassarotto, 517 U.S. 681 (1996) (a state cannot require that a contract containing an arbitration clause also contain special notice requirements to ensure that the clause is conspicuous and clear); Preston v. Ferrer, 552 U.S. 346 (2008) (a state cannot prohibit the arbitration of a particular kind of claim); Hall Street Associates, L.L.C. v. Mattel, Inc., 552 U.S. 576 (2008) (a contract containing an arbitration clause may not grant a court discretion to engage in a broader review of the arbitration award than allowed by the FAA); Stolt-Neilsen S.A. v. AnimalFeeds International Corp., 559 U.S. 662 (2010) (a member of a class cannot be compelled to submit to a class action arbitration when he has not agreed to do so); Concepcion (state rule declaring class arbitration waivers unconscionable in consumer contracts preempted by FAA); American Exp. Co. v. Italian Colors Restaurant, 133 S. Ct. 2304 (2013) (plaintiffs have no right to litigate a statutory claim for anti-trust violation via a class action notwithstanding a mandatory arbitration clause and no-class action arbitration clause in order to achieve the "effective vindication" of their statutory right to sue).

Of course, other federal laws can carve out exceptions to the FAA. The Supreme Court recognized as much in Shearson/American Express, Inc. v. McMahon, 482 U.S. 220 (1987), where it addressed the validity of arbitration clauses with respect to a civil action arising under the Securities Exchange Act and the Racketeer Influenced and Corrupt Organizations Act. In holding that such claims were subject to the arbitration agreement between the disputing parties, the Supreme Court said that a party opposing enforcement of an arbitration clause in resolving a civil dispute under federal law must demonstrate that "Congress intended to make an exception to the Arbitration Act" pursuant to the applicable statute, "an intention discernible from the text, history, or purposes of the statute." The Court instructed courts to examine whether there exists "an inherent conflict between arbitration and the statute's underlying purposes." 482 U.S. at 227. Exhibit 18.1 lists a number of federal statutes that restrict or prohibit binding arbitration clauses.

EXHIBIT 18.1   **Federal Statutes Restricting the Use or Enforceability of Binding Arbitration Clauses**

- The Motor Vehicle Franchise Contract Arbitration Fairness Act, 15 U.S.C. §1226, prohibits automobile manufacturers from requiring their franchisees to agree to binding arbitration on a predispute basis.
- The John Warner National Defense Authorization Act for Fiscal Year 2007, Subtitle F §670, 10 U.S.C. §987, prohibits creditors from requiring military personnel and dependents to arbitrate consumer credit disputes.
- The Farm Bill of 2008, 7 U.S.C. §97(c), requires that growers and producers of livestock or poultry be provided an opportunity to decline to be bound by arbitration provisions on predispute basis.
- The Department of Defense Appropriations Act of 2009 amended USC §1303 by including the "Franken Amendment," detailed in 48 C.F.R. §§222.7400-7405, restricts the use of mandatory arbitration agreements by prohibiting defense contractors from requiring employees or independent contractors to agree to arbitrate claims for violation of civil rights or for sexual assault or harassment.
- The Dodd-Frank Wall Street Reform and Consumer Protection Act provides the Bureau of Consumer Financial Protection authority to study and regulate mandatory predispute arbitration with respect to consumers' use of financial products or services.
- Dodd-Frank grants the Securities Exchange Commission authority to issue rules prohibiting or limiting the use of predispute agreements with respect to securities claims brought by customers or clients of brokers or dealers and rules prohibiting or limiting the use of predispute agreements with respect to securities claims brought by customers or clients of investment advisors.
- Dodd-Frank prohibits lenders from imposing mandatory arbitration in residential mortgages or home equity loans.
- Dodd-Frank restricts the enforcement of provisions waving rights or requiring arbitration in civil cases alleging retaliation by a government agency wherein fraud is reported.

Application Exercise 2

In May 2016 the CFPB, acting pursuant to the authority granted it by Dodd-Frank as referenced in Exhibit 18.1, proposed a new rule to be codified as 12 CFR Part 1040 prohibiting class action arbitration waivers in a wide range of consumer contracts. The new regulation (viewable online at http://www. gpo.gov/fdsys/pkg/FR-2016-05-24/pdf/2016-10961.pdf) will cover most consumer financial products offered by banks and nonbanks including most secured or unsecured loans, credit cards, automobile leases, credit monitoring and debt adjustment services, as well as deposit account and check cashing services. Such contracts can still contain mandatory arbitration clauses but cannot prohibit the arbitrating consumer from instituting or participating in class action arbitration with similarly situated consumers. The new rule effectively reverses the decision in Concepcion for the consumer contracts covered by the rule. In 2015 the CFPB delivered to Congress a comprehensive report on the role of mandatory arbitration clauses in consumer contracts. Review the 2015 report at http://files.consumerfinance.gov/f/201503_cfpb_arbitration-study-report-to-congress-2015.pdf and decide if further federal regulation is needed in this area. The CFPB's proposed no class action waiver rule referenced in the text was scheduled to become final in August 2016 though opposition was expected. Visit the CFPB web site at http://www.consumerfinance.gov/ and determine if it has become final.

With mandatory arbitration agreements having become more common in consumer contracts, the question arises more frequently in bankruptcy cases involving disputes between parties to a prepetition arbitration agreement as to whether they must be honored in a bankruptcy proceeding or whether Congress intended to except the FAA from case administration under the Code. The issue is typically raised when one of the parties to the dispute files a **motion to compel arbitration** with the bankruptcy court asking the court to order that the matter be referred to arbitration. Must the court order arbitration or does it have discretion to retain and decide the matter itself?

In applying the *McMahon* test to determine whether arbitration clauses must be honored in bankruptcy cases, the courts have made a distinction between core and non-core proceedings. In non-core proceedings that involve issues and rights that would exist even without a bankruptcy case, prepetition arbitration agreements must be honored. See Whiting-Turner Contracting Co. v. Electric Mach. Enter., Inc. (In re Electric Mach. Enter., Inc.), 479 F.3d 791, 796 (11th Cir. 2007) ("Applying the *McMahon* factors to the Bankruptcy Code, we find no evidence within the text or in the legislative history that Congress intended to create an exception to the FAA in the Bankruptcy Code." "In general, bankruptcy courts do not have the discretion to decline to enforce an arbitration agreement relating to a non-core proceeding."). Today it is generally understood that prepetition arbitration agreements must be honored to resolve non-core disputes arising in bankruptcy cases. See, e.g.,

In re Cooker Restaurant Corp., 292 B.R. 308, 311-312 (S.D. Ohio 2003). ("In non -core proceedings in which the parties do not dispute the making of an agreement to arbitrate, a bankruptcy court is without jurisdiction to deny a motion to stay the proceedings and compel arbitration.").

That does not mean that arbitration agreements can be ignored in the resolution of disputes involving core proceedings. Utilizing the *McMahon* test, under which an arbitration agreement cannot be disregarded unless an inherent conflict exists between arbitration and the statute's underlying purposes, the Fifth Circuit found in the leading case of In the Matter of Nat'l Gypsum Co., 118 F.3d 1056, 1067 (5th Cir. 1997), that it would be inappropriate to adopt a position that "categorically finds arbitration of core bankruptcy proceedings inherently irreconcilable with the Bankruptcy Code. . . . We refuse to find such an inherent conflict based solely on the jurisdictional nature of a bankruptcy proceeding. . . . We believe that nonenforcement of an otherwise applicable arbitration provision turns on the underlying nature of the proceeding, *i.e.*, whether the proceeding derives exclusively from the provisions of the Bankruptcy Code and, if so, whether arbitration of the proceeding would conflict with the purposes of the Code." Thus today it is generally understood that, as the Second Circuit said in Crysen/Montenay Energy Co. v. Shell Oil Co. (In re Crysen/Montenay Energy Co.), 226 F.3d 160, 166 (2d Cir. 2000), although core proceedings implicate more pressing bankruptcy concerns, "even a determination that a proceeding is core will not automatically give the bankruptcy court discretion to stay arbitration."

Though it is difficult to discern any bright line test from the decisions involving arbitration agreements and core proceedings, generally speaking, the more central the core proceeding dispute is to accomplishing the unique goals of the Code the more likely it is that a bankruptcy court will find that there exists a conflict between arbitration and the purposes of the Code and exercise its discretion to refuse arbitration. See, e.g., In the Matter of Nat'l Gypsum Co., 118 F.3d 1056, 1067 (5th Cir. 1997) (core proceeding declaratory judgment complaint deemed central to confirmation of debtor's Chapter 11 plan and involving prepetition contract issues only peripherally could be decided by the court and motion to compel arbitration was denied), and In re White Mountain Mining Co., L.L.C., 403 F.3d 164, 168-169 (4th Cir. 2005) (core proceeding brought to determine whether prepetition cash advances were debt or equity need not be submitted to arbitration due to importance under the Code of centralizing resolution of disputes and determination of issues in order to effect debtor's reorganization in Chapter 11, a fundamental purpose of the Code).

On the other hand, where the nature of the dispute clearly falls with the scope of the arbitration agreement and no fundamental or unique Code purpose is articulated, courts have no problem honoring the arbitration demand in a core proceeding. See, e.g., In re Great Spa Mfg. Co., Inc., 2009 WL 1457740, at *3-4 (Bankr. E.D. Tenn., 2009) (core proceeding by debtor to establish prepetition debt owed by defendant; arbitration involved no inherent conflict with Code; motion to compel arbitration granted) and In re Transport Assocs., Inc., 263 B.R. 531, 535 (Bankr. W.D. Ky. 2001) (core proceeding involving debtor's objection to creditor's claim ordered to arbitration even though issues arose through "claims allowance process; arbitration of prepetition contractual dispute creates no conflict with Code").

Application Exercise 3

Locate decisions of the courts in your federal circuit to see how they have decided the issue of enforceability of prepetition arbitration agreements in bankruptcy cases.

Application Exercise 4

Determine if the bankruptcy court in the district where you plan to practice has adopted local rules addressing mediation or voluntary arbitration. If so, do those rules authorize the bankruptcy judge to order good faith mediation or is it only at the option of the parties?

D. PERSONAL JURISDICTION OF THE BANKRUPTCY COURTS

Whereas subject matter jurisdiction has to do with the power of a court to hear and decide a particular kind of case, **personal jurisdiction** (also called *in personam* jurisdiction) has to do with the power of a court to enter a binding order on a particular defendant.

The notion of personal jurisdiction in state courts is intertwined with the demands of **due process** required by the Fourteenth Amendment to the U.S. Constitution. In order to satisfy the dictate of due process, it must be shown that **minimum contacts** exist between a defendant and the forum state such that maintenance of the suit does not offend traditional notions of fair play and substantial justice. International Shoe Co. v. Washington, 326 U.S. 310, 316 (1945). Thus in the ordinary civil lawsuit in state court, the personal jurisdiction question is determined by whether the defendant resides in or is otherwise present in the forum state, or has consented to the jurisdiction of the forum state or, if neither present nor consenting, has sufficient minimum contracts with the forum state to satisfy due process.

When the civil suit is filed in a federal court, Rule 4(k)(1)(A) of the Federal Rules of Civil Procedure generally limits *in personam* jurisdiction of the federal courts over defendants to that which a court of general

Mediation and Voluntary Arbitration of Disputes in a Bankruptcy Case

Mediation and voluntary arbitration have become popular methods of alternative dispute resolution in civil cases in both federal and state courts. Bankruptcy Rule 9019(a)(b) specifically authorizes the compromise and settlement of disputes arising in a case with court approval. Bankruptcy Rule 9019(c) authorizes the parties to a dispute to stipulate to binding arbitration with court approval. The Code does not currently reference mediation but in many federal districts bankruptcy courts have adopted rules authorizing the mediation of an adversary proceeding or other dispute that arises in the administration of a bankruptcy case. See, e.g., Rule 9019-1 of the Rules of the U.S. Bankruptcy Court for the Southern District of New York (www. nysb.uscourts.gov/rule-9019-1) and that court's elaborate Procedures Governing Mediation and Voluntary Arbitration in Bankruptcy Cases and Adversary Proceedings at www. nysb.uscourts.gov/sites/default/

files/pdf/Mediation_Procedures.pdf. In 2015, the American Bankruptcy Institute adopted its Model Local Bankruptcy Rules for Mediation for consideration by bankruptcy and district judges. Those model rules can be viewed at www.abi.org/membership/committees/mediation.

jurisdiction in the forum state would have, so the minimum contacts analysis proceeds just as it would if the case was pending in a state court of the forum state. Significantly, however, FRCP 4(k)(1)(C) states that the general rule established by FRCP 4(k)(1)(A) making *in personam* jurisdiction of federal courts coextensive with that of the courts of the forum state does not apply where extraterritorial service of process is "authorized by a federal statute." Bankruptcy Rule 7004(d) is just such a statute. It provides, "The summons and complaint and all other process except a subpoena can be served anywhere in the United States."

FRBP 7004(f) then provides:

> If the exercise of jurisdiction is consistent with the Constitution and laws of the United States, serving a summons or filing a waiver of service in accordance with this rule or the subdivisions of Rule 4 F. R. Civ. P. made applicable by these rules is effective to establish personal jurisdiction over the person of any defendant with respect to a case under the Code or a civil proceeding arising under the Code, or arising in or related to a case under the Code.

Thus the Code not only authorizes nationwide service of process, but such nationwide service is also made the basis for the bankruptcy court's reach of personal jurisdiction. See, e.g., Nordberg v. Granfinanciera, S.A., 835 F.2d 1341, 1344 (11th Cir. 1988), rev'd on other grounds, 492 U.S. 33 (1989) ("Bankruptcy Rule 7004(d) provides for nationwide service of process and thus is the statutory basis for personal jurisdiction in this case"). This is not to say that due process is necessarily made co-extensive with service of process. Note the first phrase in FRBP 7004(f); even where service of process is accomplished, the exercise of jurisdiction must satisfy the due process demands of the Fifth Amendment requiring minimum contacts between the defendant and the forum. However, in bankruptcy cases the "forum" is not the particular state in which the bankruptcy court sits, it is the United States in general, and what is required to satisfy due process under the Fifth Amendment is quite different than under the Fourteenth.

The different analysis was well explained in Brown v. C.D. Smith Drug Co., 1999 WL 709992 (D. Del. 1999), where the court found a bankruptcy court in Delaware had personal jurisdiction over defendants in Missouri to pursue claims made by the trustee of the debtor against the defendants arising under Missouri law.

> Defendants argue that personal jurisdiction founded on BR 7004(d) is unconstitutional because they lack "minimum contacts" with the State of Delaware and because answering suit in Delaware would be onerous and unfair. While defendants concede that BR 7004(d) provides for nationwide service of process, they argue that service of process and personal jurisdiction are two distinct concepts. The latter, defendants suggest, does not follow necessarily from the former; instead, defendants assert that a court has personal jurisdiction over out-of-state defendants only where that jurisdiction comports with notions of substantial justice and fair play. In essence, defendants

urge the court to adopt a fairness test akin to that articulated by the Supreme Court in International Shoe . . . and its progeny. . . .

That test, though, applies only to jurisdictional issues arising under the 14th Amendment. Because the present case is "related to" a bankruptcy proceeding and because service of process was effected pursuant to a federal rule having the force of federal law, it is the Fifth, not the Fourteenth, Amendment that is at issue. The Supreme Court has not addressed whether the Due Process Clause of the Fifth Amendment also requires personal jurisdiction over out-of-state defendants to comport with notions of fairness and substantial justice; however, the majority of lower federal courts to have considered the issue have concluded that out-of-state defendants need only have minimum contacts with the United States in order to satisfy Fifth Amendment due process. In reaching this conclusion, courts have reasoned that the fairness requirement imposed by the Fifth Amendment relates only to whether the sovereign has the power to exercise jurisdiction, not to the fairness of suit in a particular forum provided by the sovereign. See, e.g., In re Federal Fountain, Inc., 165 F.3d 600, 601-02 (8th Cir. 1999) (because BR 7004(d) provides for national service of process, fairness of suit in a particular state is not at issue; due process is satisfied where defendant has sufficient contacts with the United States); Hogue v. Milodon Eng'g, Inc., 736 F.2d 989, 991 (4th Cir. 1984) (Virginia bankruptcy court had personal jurisdiction over California defendant under former BR 704 and that defendant must look to federal venue requirement for relief from onerous litigation); In re Outlet Department Stores, Inc., 82 B.R. 694, 699 (Bankr. S.D.N.Y. 1988) (where out-of-state defendant was properly served under BR 7004(d), minimum contacts test for personal jurisdiction does not apply; Fifth Amendment requires only that service be reasonably calculated to inform defendant of pendency of proceedings); In re Trim-Lean Meat Prods., Inc., 11 B.R. 1010, 1011-13 (Bankr. D. Del. 1981) (personal jurisdiction founded on former BR 704 required only minimum contacts with the United States). . . .

Here, the relevant sovereign is the United States, and Congress unquestionably has the power to enact laws which provide for national service of process. Where it has not done so, the court normally must rely on Fed. R. Civ. P. 4(e)'s incorporation of the relevant state's long-arm statute to acquire personal jurisdiction. Only then do a defendant's contacts with the forum state and considerations of fairness and convenience to out-of-state defendants become significant to the court's jurisdictional analysis. This is sensible because in such cases the court "borrows" the forum state's jurisdictional statute to assert personal jurisdiction over residents of another state—thereby implicating state sovereignty issues. The Supreme Court's two-step test keeps a state's jurisdictional powers in check by limiting the reach of that state's long-arm statute to those defendants who have purposefully maintained contacts with that jurisdiction. The test also protects a defendant's freedom from answering suit in a forum solely as a result of random or attenuated contacts with that forum. . . .

In the present case the relevant forum is the nation as a whole, and Congress has provided a jurisdictional mechanism in the form of national service of process. The sovereignty of individual states is not implicated, and personal jurisdiction over those defendants who have availed themselves of the United States can hardly constitute a due process violation. Thus, the court need only satisfy itself that defendants have minimum contacts with the United States. Because defendants have such contacts, the court concludes that it has personal jurisdiction over them.

Brown v. C.D. Smith Drug Co., 1999 WL 709992, at *3-5.

Case Preview

In re Tandycrafts, Inc.

This broad "national contacts" grant of personal jurisdiction to bankruptcy courts is one of the most unique aspects of bankruptcy practice and often one of the most surprising to students and new practitioners schooled in the normal limitation of personal jurisdiction of federal courts to that of the courts of the forum state. As you read In re Tandycrafts consider the following questions:

1. What is the forum state? Did the defendant in this action have any minimum contacts with that forum state?
2. How was the defendant served with process?
3. What actions by this defendant were found sufficient to satisfy the requisite national contacts?
4. What rationale is offered here to explain the national contacts standard for the exercise of personal jurisdiction? What is the role of "fairness" in this rationale?

In re Tandycrafts, Inc.
317 B.R. 287, 289 (Bankr. D. Del. 2004)

WALRATH, Bankruptcy Judge. . . .

The Debtors were manufacturers of household decorating products, such as bulletin boards and mirrors. The Defendant is a Mexican corporation which provides trucking services from Mexico to cities in the United States. The Defendant maintains a post office box in Texas to receive payments for these services. The Debtors used the Defendant's commercial trucking services to transport goods between the Debtors' Mexican facility and the Debtors' distribution center in Texas.

[Suit was filed against the Defendant] to recover an allegedly preferential transfer of $63,850. . . . The Defendant was served with the Complaint and Summons by first class mail, return receipt requested, addressed to its post office box in Texas. The Liquidating Trustee received confirmation that service was complete. . . .

[T]he Defendant filed its Motion to dismiss alleging lack of personal jurisdiction. . . .

When faced with a challenge to its jurisdiction, a federal court's analysis must begin with whether the procedural requirement of service of process has been satisfied. Omni Capital Int'l v. Rudolf Wolff & Co., 484 U.S. 97, 104 (1987). Without consent to the choice of forum, as is the case here, the court must find some authority for the manner by which the summons was served on the defendant. Id. Here, service on the Defendant comported with Rule 7004(d) of the Federal Rules of Bankruptcy Procedure, which allows nationwide service of process by first class mail. Fed. R. Bankr. P. 7004(d).

The court must also determine, however, whether the exercise of its jurisdiction fits within the constitutional requirements of due process. Rule 7004(d) is a federal, rather than a state, long-arm statute. Thus, the due process analysis to be used is different from that used with a state long-arm statute. While both analyses determine whether the defendant has "minimum contacts," the question posed by a federal long-arm statute is whether the defendant has "minimum contacts with the United States, rather than with a particular state." In re Paques, 277 B.R. 615, 628 (Bankr. E.D. Pa. 2000). . . .

The Defendant argues that it lacks contacts with Delaware. The Liquidating Trustee responds that the Defendant's contacts with the United States are sufficient for this Court to exercise jurisdiction.

We agree with the Liquidating Trustee. Where service is made under Rule 7004(d), the defendant "need only have minimum contacts with the United States to satisfy Fifth Amendment due process." Brown v. C.D. Smith Drug Co., 1999 WL 709992 at *3, 1999 U.S. Dist. LEXIS 13872 at *10 (D. Del. 1999). The issue is whether the court may exercise jurisdiction, not whether it is fair to litigate in a particular forum. Id. [Citations omitted.]

A bankruptcy case is different from a typical civil suit. A bankruptcy case usually does not affect only the sovereignty of a particular state; it has effects throughout the United States as a whole. Continental Ill. Nat. Bank & Trust Co. of Chicago v. Chicago, R.I. & P. Ry. Co., 294 U.S. 648, 683 (1935). . . . So long as a defendant has minimum contacts with the United States, therefore, due process permits service on it. Id. Where a defendant has "purposefully directed his activities at the residents of the forum and the litigation results from alleged injuries that arise out of or are related to those activities," minimum contacts will be found. Burger King Corp. v. Rudzewicz, 471 U.S. 462, 472, (1985). . . .

In this case, the Defendant was a cross-border trucker and provided services to a company in the United States. These activities create sufficient contacts with the United States to allow this court to exercise jurisdiction over the Defendant. Thus, the Defendant's Motion must be denied.

Post-Case Follow-Up

Though *Tandycrafts* is not a consumer bankruptcy case, it illustrates how service of process is made relatively easy in bankruptcy cases. Bankruptcy Rule 7004(a) specifically adopts the waiver of service procedure of FRCP 4(d) and all the methods for service of a summons set forth in FRCP 4(e)-(j). In addition, Rule 7004(b) adopts a service by first class mail procedure effective within the U.S. Where the defendant in an action brought in a bankruptcy court is not a resident of any U.S. state or territory, the personal jurisdiction analysis is the same: minimum contacts with any state will subject the defendant to the personal jurisdiction of any bankruptcy court in the nation. See, e.g., In re Uni-Marts, LLC, 399 B.R. 400 (Bankr. D. Del. 2009) (non-resident principal of debtor alleged to have committed tortious act in Pennsylvania subject to personal jurisdiction of bankruptcy court in Delaware).

In re Tandycrafts, Inc.: Real Life Applications

1. Using *Brown, Tandycrafts,* and *Uni-marts,* determine whether a bankruptcy court would likely have personal jurisdiction over the defendants in the following scenarios:

   a. In a bankruptcy case pending in a bankruptcy court in Texas, a defendant residing in Minnesota is accused of inducing a corporation located in Iowa to breach a contract with a corporation located in Florida by making numerous phone calls from Minnesota to Iowa.

   b. Same allegations as in 1a except the defendant resides in Cancun, Mexico, made the numerous phone calls from Cancun to Iowa, and never traveled to the United States.

   c. Same allegations as in 1a except that defendant resides in Paris, France, and never traveled to, phoned, or otherwise contacted anyone in the United States, but allegedly instructed agents in Paris to contact the Iowa corporation by phone from Paris to make the allegedly wrongful inducement.

2. Though the FRBP 7004(b) procedure for service of process by first class mail was utilized in *Tandycrafts,* remember that 7004(a) also authorizes waiver of service or service under the various methods authorized by FRCP 4(e)-(j). Read FRBP 7004(a) and (b) carefully then answer the following questions.

   a. Assume an individual defendant in an adversary proceeding is served by first class mail, postage prepaid, and plaintiff encloses a copy of the complaint but not a copy of the summons. If you represent that defendant, what motion(s) will you make?

   b. Assume an individual defendant in an adversary proceeding is served by first class mail, postage prepaid, and plaintiff encloses a copy of the complaint and summons and deposits them in the mail to defendant 20 days after the summons is issued by the clerk of the bankruptcy court. If you represent that defendant, what motion(s) will you make? See FRBP 7004(e).

   c. Assume an individual defendant in an adversary proceeding is served by first class mail, postage prepaid, and plaintiff encloses a copy of the complaint and summons and deposits them in the mail to defendant 14 days after the summons is issued by the clerk of the bankruptcy court. Defendant contends he never received the mailing and files an appropriate motion to dismiss. If you represent the plaintiff, how will you establish that the service by mail was actually sent to and received by defendant?

   d. Assume an individual defendant in an adversary proceeding resides and works in Ontario, Canada. She is served by first class mail postage repaid at her residence. If you represent that defendant, what motion(s) will you make?

E. APPEAL OF A BANKRUPTCY COURT ORDER

In those instances when the bankruptcy court does enter a final order, the losing party may appeal the order to the district court from which the bankruptcy court received the referral pursuant to 28 U.S.C. §158(a). The standard of review utilized by the district court in considering whether to reverse a final order entered by the bankruptcy court is de novo as to questions of law but clearly erroneous as to findings of fact and due regard is given to the opportunity of the bankruptcy court to judge the credibility of the witnesses. See, e.g., In re Nosek, 544 F.3d 34, 43 (1st Cir. 2008). A party unhappy with the decision of the district court may then, pursuant to 28 U.S.C. §158(d), appeal that ruling to the appropriate U.S. circuit court where the same standard of review will prevail. A party unhappy with the decision of the circuit court of appeals may file an application for writ of certiorari to the U.S. Supreme Court.

In some federal circuits, appeals of final orders entered by bankruptcy courts may go to a special panel of bankruptcy judges selected from the entire federal circuit instead of to the district court if all parties consent. The panels of bankruptcy judges established in these federal circuits to hear appeals from bankruptcy courts within the circuit are called **Bankruptcy Appellate Panels** (BAPs) and are authorized by 28 U.S.C. §158(b). Currently five of the federal circuits (First, Sixth, Eighth, Ninth, and Tenth) have established BAPs. Decisions of the BAP are appealable directly to the circuit court per 28 U.S.C. §158(d), effectively bypassing the district court. Generally, per 28 U.S.C. §158(c), the party appealing the bankruptcy ruling can choose to appeal to the district court or to the BAP in circuits where that option is available. If the appellant chooses to appeal to the BAP, the other parties to the appeal can negate that choice and redirect the appeal to the district court by electing to do so within 30 days following the filing of the notice of appeal. The party so electing must file a notice of election per FRBP 8005(a) within the time allowed. If none of the other parties to the appeal file a timely notice of election redirecting the appeal to district court after the appellant has designated the BAP to hear the appeal, then to the BAP it goes.

Part VIII of the FRBP governs the procedures for appealing a decision of the bankruptcy court to the district court or the BAP in circuits where that option is available. Generally, pursuant to FRBP 8002(a)(1), an appeal of a bankruptcy order is instituted by the filing of a notice of appeal with the bankruptcy court clerk within 14 days of the entry of the order, judgment, or decree appealed from. Per FRBP 8002(b), the time to file the notice of appeal is extended until an order is entered by the bankruptcy court on certain timely filed postjudgment motions such as a motion to amend or make additional findings reconsider (FRBP 7052), motion to alter or amend judgment (FRBP 9023), motion for new trial (FRBP 9023), or motion for relief from judgment or order (FRBP 9024). Per FRBP 8002(d), the time for filing the notice of appeal can also be extended by a motion for extension of time filed before the expiration of the original time limit or within 21 days following expiration of the original time limit on a showing of excusable neglect.

The remainder of the rules in Part VIII of the FRBP deal with the docketing of the appeal in the district court of the BAP, preparing and transmitting the record on appeal, the briefing schedule, oral argument, etc.

Though an appeal as of right from bankruptcy court is available only from final orders, decrees, and judgments of that court, 28 U.S.C. §158(a)(3) recognizes that appeal may lie from interlocutory orders of the bankruptcy court as well "with leave of court." FRBP 8004 requires that a party seeking to appeal an interlocutory order of a bankruptcy court file a notice of appeal together with a motion for leave to appeal that contains:

- the facts necessary to understand the question presented;
- the question itself;
- the relief sought;
- the reasons why leave to appeal should be granted; and
- a copy of the interlocutory order or decree and any related opinion or memorandum.

The notice of appeal and motion are transmitted to the designated district court or BAP for decision.

The well-established judicial doctrine of finality is followed in appeals from bankruptcy court rulings. See, e.g., Bullard v. Blue Hills Banks, 135 S. Ct. 1686 (2015) (bankruptcy court order denying confirmation of a Chapter 13 plan is not a final appealable order in a case or proceedings so long as the debtor retains the option to propose an alternative modified plan for confirmation); In re Royce Homes LP, 466 B.R. 81 (S.D. Tex. 2012) (appeal from bankruptcy court's order compelling production of documents claimed to be subject to attorney-client privilege disallowed as not a final order, decree, or judgment). As with other civil cases, exceptions to the rule of finality are recognized where the interlocutory appeal involves exceptional circumstances such as questions of law that are controlling in the continuing proceedings in the bankruptcy case or constitutional issues or issues over which there is substantial split of authority and the resolution of which will advance the administration of the bankruptcy case by saving time and money. See, e.g., In re Nicholes, 184 B.R. 82 (B.A.P. 9th Cir. 1995) (Chapter 13 debtor granted leave to appeal denial of confirmation of plan, where issue of which claims would disqualify debtor from Chapter 13 eligibility was a controlling question of law, definitions of some types of qualifying and disqualifying claims were unsettled law, and immediate determination of debtor's qualification for Chapter 13 relief was necessary before case could proceed to conclusion).

Because of the limitations of the rule of finality on the appeal, practitioners involved in adversary proceedings in bankruptcy cases sometimes utilize Rule 54(b) of the Federal Rules of Civil Procedure, which authorizes a trial judge to direct the entry of a final judgment as to one or more but fewer than all the claims in a case upon a finding that there is no just reason for delay. FRCP 54(b) is made applicable in adversary proceedings by FRBP 7054(a).

28 U.S.C. §158(d)(2) authorizes a direct appeal from a bankruptcy court order to the circuit court where:

- the judgment, order, or decree involves a question of law as to which there is no controlling decision of the court of appeals for the circuit or of the Supreme Court of the United States, or involves a matter of public importance;
- the judgment, order, or decree involves a question of law requiring resolution of conflicting decisions; or
- an immediate appeal from the judgment, order, or decree may materially advance the progress of the case or proceeding in which the appeal is taken.

Where a district court has entered an order or judgment in a bankruptcy case that was not referred to a bankruptcy court or in a case in which the reference was revoked, the procedure for the appeal of that order or judgment to the circuit court is the same as for the appeal of a district court judgment in any civil case. See Rule 6(a) of the Federal Rules of Appellate Procedure (FRAP). However, where the district court or BAP has entered a judgment on a case appealed to them from the bankruptcy court the slightly different procedure contained in FRAP 6(b) controls.

Exhibit 18.2 outlines the appeal process from final orders entered by a bankruptcy court.

EXHIBIT 18.2   **Appeal Process for Final Orders Entered by a Bankruptcy Court**

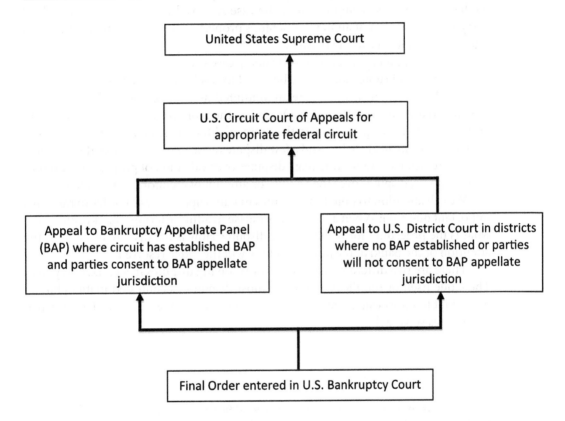

F. PROCEDURES FOR RESOLVING DISPUTES IN A BANKRUPTCY CASE

In the course of administering a bankruptcy case there may be no disputes between the parties in interest—a petition is filed, a trustee is appointed, proofs of claim are filed, decisions about exemptions, property of the estate, and order of distribution are made and implemented, and a discharge is granted, all with no objection being raised. But it is not unusual for even a routine bankruptcy case to involve some disputes that the bankruptcy judge will have to resolve. And in a significant number of cases, there may be numerous disputes that arise during administration of the case.

For example, what if a creditor objects on the basis of improper venue to the debtor's petition being filed in the federal district chosen by debtor's lawyer? What if creditors file an involuntary petition to which the debtor objects? What if, like Marta Carlson (see Document 5 in the Carlson case file), debtor needs more time to file her supporting schedules? What if a debtor claims property as exempt and the trustee disagrees with the valuation placed on the property by debtor? What if a creditor files a proof of claim in the case but the debtor contends the claim is not valid? What if debtor contends a creditor has violated the automatic stay of §362(a)? What if a secured creditor needs the automatic stay lifted in order to repossess the collateralized property? What if a party in interest to the case wants the bankruptcy trustee appointed in the case removed for cause? What if a third party is in possession of an item of debtor's property when the petition is filed and refuses to turn it over to the trustee?

The fact is, every aspect of a bankruptcy case can potentially give rise to a dispute that the bankruptcy judge may be asked to resolve if the parties cannot resolve it themselves. That means there are an unlimited number of potential disputes that can and do arise in any given case. Of course, the more complex a case is, the more property there is to squabble over, the more creditors there are, etc., then the more disputes there are likely to be. And a few disputes arise in so many cases they become almost predictable and routine (e.g., disputes over valuation of property for exemption purposes, disputes over the validity or amount of creditor's claims, etc.).

We call attention to potential disputes in bankruptcy cases in order to raise this important question: When a dispute does arise in administering a bankruptcy case, what is the procedure for resolving the dispute? How is the dispute brought to the attention of the bankruptcy judge and how will the judge resolve it?

There are two different procedures for resolving disputes in a bankruptcy case. The Code itself or the FRBP designate most disputes as contested matters but an important few are designated as adversary proceedings. We will consider these two procedures separately.

1. Contested Matters

A **contested matter** is one governed by FRBP 9014. It requires a hearing before the bankruptcy judge but not a full trial. At the hearing on the contested matter, the bankruptcy judge may consider written briefs filed by the contesting parties and the oral arguments of counsel. If necessary, the court may also listen to the sworn testimony of witnesses. Any evidence offered by sworn testimony at a hearing on a contested matter will be governed by the Federal Rules of Evidence.

A contested matter is initiated in one of three ways:

- by filing a motion
- by filing an objection
- by filing of a notice of intended action followed by an objection

By Motion

A **motion** is a written request made to a court seeking an order from the court granting the moving party affirmative relief regarding the subject of the request. A verbal motion may be made during a hearing before the judge. FRBP 9013 governs the required content of a motion and who is to be served with a copy of it. Either the applicable Code section or FRBP will advise whether a motion is the appropriate way to seek relief sought from the court.

For example, Pursuant to FRBP 1007(c), Marta Carlson filed a motion seeking additional time to file the supporting schedules in her Chapter 7 case. (See Document 5 in the Carlson case file.) Code §362(d) and FRBP 4001 advise that it is by motion that a creditor seeks the lifting of the automatic stay. Code §362(c)(3)(B) provides that the automatic stay can be extended by the court on motion of a party in interest.

By Objection

An **objection** is very similar to a motion. It is a written request to a court seeking an order from the court denying another party some relief or adjusting the rights of the other party in some way in connection with the subject of the request. A verbal objection may be made during a hearing before the judge.

For example, the bankruptcy trustee in Marta Carlson's Chapter 7 case filed an objection to the claim of Pine Ridge Nursing Home (see Document 28 in the Carlson case file) pursuant to §502(a) and FRBP 3007. As discussed in Chapter Six, Section B, FRBP 4003 authorizes the trustee or other party in interest to object to an individual debtor's claimed exemptions on the debtor's Schedule C.

By Notice of Intended Action

The **notice of intended action** is a procedure unique to bankruptcy practice. A notice of intended action does not seek a court order. It simply gives required notice that the party filing the notice intends to take some action unless a party in interest objects. The Code allows some actions to be taken by a debtor or trustee simply by giving the required notice of the intended action. No further approval by the court is necessary and no hearing will be held on the matter unless a party in interest files a timely objection to the intended action. If an objection is filed to the notice of intended action the matter is then treated as a contested matter and a hearing will be scheduled on it before the bankruptcy judge.

For example, in Marta Carlson's case, the bankruptcy trustee has filed a notice of intent to abandon certain property under §554 of the Code (see Document 34 in the Carlson case file). If no party in interest objects to this intended action within 14 days of the mailing of the notice per FRBP 6007(a), the property will be deemed abandoned by the trustee without any further action by the court. However, if a timely objection is filed, the matter will be treated as a FRBP 9014 contested matter and a hearing scheduled.

This unique feature of a notice of intended action—that once notice is given no hearing is held and no court approval is needed for the action unless a timely objection is filed—is known, ironically, as the **"after notice and a hearing"** procedure. It is defined in §102(1) of the Code. And looking at that definition helps dispel the irony because what is contemplated by the procedure is notice and *the opportunity* for a hearing if an objection to the intended action is timely filed.

Importantly, not only are notices of intended action authorized by the Code governed by the "after notice and a hearing" procedure, a number of (but by no means all) matters properly raised by motion or objection are as well. But whereas any action authorized by the Code to be accomplished by notice of intended action will be governed by the "after notice and a hearing" procedure, only those motions and objections specifically designated as to be accomplished "after notice and a hearing" will be subject to that procedure. Thus when a notice of intended action is authorized by the Code or where the Code specifically makes a motion or objection subject to the "after notice and a hearing" procedure, that means that written notice of the intended action, motion, or objection *must* be given to parties required to receive it. However, a hearing on the matter will be conducted *only* if a party in interest objects within the time allowed to the intended action or to the relief requested in the motion or objection. If no party in interest contests the motion or objection made or no party in interest objects to the notice of intent in the time allowed for a response, either the court will grant the motion or objection, or the action that was the subject of the notice of intent can go forward.

Regarding the time allowed for a response, that time can vary considerably according to the subject of the motion or the noticed action. Time periods may run from as many as 30 days to as few as 7 (compare, e.g., FRBP 2002, 6004(b), and 3007). Local rules may also contain relevant time periods.

Exhibit 18.3 summarizes some of the common administrative actions accomplished by this curious "after notice and a hearing" procedure.

EXHIBIT 18.3 | **Administrative Actions Accomplished by Motion, Objection, or Notice of Intended Action That Are Subject to the "After Notice and a Hearing" Procedure of the Code**

- Under §554 of the Code, the bankruptcy trustee may notice the intent to abandon property of the estate, "after notice and a hearing."
- Under §363(b) and FRBP 6004, the bankruptcy trustee may notice the intended use, sale, or lease property of the estate in other than the ordinary course of business "after notice and a hearing."
- Under §362, a motion for relief from the automatic stay may be approved "after notice and a hearing."

EXHIBIT 18.3 **(Continued)**

- Under §324(a), a motion to remove the bankruptcy trustee for cause may be approved "after notice and a hearing."
- Under FRBP 9019, a motion to compromise or settle a dispute may be approved "after notice and a hearing."
- Under §§707(a) and (b), a motion to dismiss or convert a Chapter 7 case to a case under Chapter 13 or 11 on certain grounds may be approved "after notice and a hearing."
- Under §1112(b), a motion to dismiss or to convert a Chapter 11 case to a case under Chapter 7 on certain grounds may be approved "after notice and a hearing."
- Under §§1208(c) and (d), a motion to dismiss or to convert a Chapter 12 case to a case under Chapter 7 on certain grounds may be approved "after notice and a hearing."
- Under §502(b), the objection to a claim is to be decided "after notice and a hearing."
- Under FRBP 4003(c), an objection to a claimed exemption is to be decided "after hearing on notice," which some, but not all, courts treat as after notice and a hearing.

It bears repeating that the "after notice and a hearing" procedure *only* applies to matters properly raised by motion, objection, or notice of intended action when the Code specifically says that it does. If a matter is properly raised by motion, etc. but is not made specifically subject to the "after notice and a hearing" procedure, it will be treated automatically as a contested matter and a hearing will be scheduled.

As an example, look at the Motion for Additional Time to File Schedules, Statement of Affairs, etc., filed by Marta Carlson (Document 5 in the Carlson case file). This motion is authorized by §521(i)(3) and FRBP 1007(c) but it is not designated there as an "after notice and a hearing" matter. Instead, FRBP 1007(c) provides that the time to file can be extended by motion and for "cause shown." So when Marta's lawyer files this motion, it automatically will be treated as a contested matter and a hearing will be scheduled as the notice of motion indicates. Compare the Objection to Claim filed by the bankruptcy trustee in Marta's case (Document 28 in the Carlson case file). Section 502(b) designates this as an "after notice and a hearing" matter, so if the creditor, Pine Ridge Nursing Home, does not file a written response to the objection to its claim, the court may rule on the objection without a hearing. All this is explained to Pine Ridge in the notice of objection and hearing accompanying the objection.

Application Exercise 5

Review the Motion for Order of Contempt for Violation of Automatic Stay fled by Marta Carlson against Pine Ridge Nursing Home and the accompanying Notice of Motion (Document 24 in the Carlson case file). Can you tell by looking at the Notice of Motion whether this motion is subject to the "after notice and a hearing" procedure?

Motion, objection, and notice of intended action practice in a bankruptcy case are summarized in Exhibit 18.4.

The procedure outlined in Exhibit 18.4 is generic and there is great diversity among the bankruptcy courts across the land regarding the exact procedures followed in motion practice. Many courts address motion practice in their local court rules, which should always be consulted. Many courts have developed their own forms for motions and notices as well.

EXHIBIT 18.4   Motion, Objection, and Notice of Intended Action Practice in a Bankruptcy Case, Including the "After Notice and a Hearing" Procedure

- A written motion or objection seeking a court order or a notice of intended action is filed with the clerk of the bankruptcy court, who notifies the judge of the filing and places it in the official case file.
- Copies of the motion, objection, or notice are *served* on parties in interest. A *certificate of service* included in or attached to the motion, objection, or notice certifies that service was made by listing the names and addresses of the persons and entities served, the means of service (by mail, hand delivery, or electronic attachment (e-mail)), and the date of service.
- The party filing the motion, objection, or notice includes with the copy served on parties in interest a *notice of motion (or objection)*, advising those parties of the date set for a hearing on the matter. In some bankruptcy courts, the clerk of the court or the judge's chambers assumes responsibility for serving the notice of motion.
- If the subject of the motion, objection, or notice is not controlled by the "after notice and a hearing" procedure, then it is treated as a contested matter and the hearing will be conducted as scheduled. The notice of motion may advise parties in interest to file a written response by a certain date.
- If the subject of the motion, objection, or notice is controlled by the "after notice and a hearing" procedure, the notice of motion will explain that a response is due by a certain date and that if no response is filed by that date, the motion or objection may be granted or the action authorized by the court without any hearing or any further action by the court. In some bankruptcy courts, no hearing date will be set on a matter controlled by "after notice and a hearing" unless and until a party in interest files a response. If a party in interest does file a response, the hearing will be held (or scheduled and held in those courts where no hearing date is set in the original notice).
- The bankruptcy judge, by order or local rule, may direct the parties to submit written briefs prior to the hearing date. The briefs set forth the arguments of the parties on matters related to the motion or notice and the law they rely on in connection with those arguments.
- If briefs were ordered by the trial judge, they are filed with the clerk of the court by the due date. The clerk causes the briefs to become part of the official case file.
- At the hearing, the party filing the motion, objection, or notice and other parties in interest are allowed to make an appearance and be heard by the judge by way of oral argument to supplement the written argument made in the briefs, if any. If necessary, the judge hears sworn testimony and receives any exhibits offered through that testimony.

EXHIBIT 18.4 **(Continued)**

- The judge rules on the contested matter, either at the conclusion of the hearing or shortly thereafter, either granting, denying, or modifying the relief requested in the motion or the intended action stated in the notice. The ruling is memorialized in a written *order* signed by the judge.
- The clerk of the court *enters the order*, causing it to become part of the official case file. The date of entry is noted on the order.
- Copies of the order are sent by the clerk to the movant and all parties in interest.

Ex Parte Practice in Bankruptcy Court

The Code permits a number of actions to receive court approval based on **ex parte** (at the request of one party without the presence or input of others) motion or application to the court. No hearing is noticed or scheduled and the court may act unilaterally. If appropriate, notice of the court's action is afterward given to parties in interest. If an objection is filed by a party in interest before or after the court enters the ex parte relief requested, the matter will be treated as a contested matter and set for hearing. Exhibit 18.5 sets out actions the Code allows the court to approve ex parte.

EXHIBIT 18.5 **Actions the Court May Approve Ex Parte**

- Granting extensions of time to take some actions (FRBP 9006(b))
- Ordering Rule 2004 examinations (FRBP 2004)
- Deferring grant of Chapter 7 discharge (FRBP 4004(c))
- Closing or reopening a closed bankruptcy case (§350)
- Ordering the consolidation or joint administration of a case (FRBP 1015)
- Ordering conversion of a case from one chapter to another upon request of the debtor, where permitted (§§706(a), 1307(a), 1208(a), and 1112(a))

2. Adversary Proceedings

Some disputes that arise in a bankruptcy case are treated not as contested matters, but as more formal adversary proceedings. An **adversary proceeding** is essentially a formal civil lawsuit initiated within the bankruptcy case and involving a dispute related to the case. FRBP 7001 lists the types of disputes that must be presented to the court as an adversary proceeding, and they are summarized in Exhibit 18.6.

EXHIBIT 18.6   **Disputes That Must Be Resolved as Adversary Proceedings**

- A proceeding to bar the debtor from receiving a discharge in bankruptcy or to revoke a discharge previously granted
- A proceeding to declare a particular debt non-dischargeable
- A proceeding to determine the validity, extent, or priority of a lien on property of the debtor
- A proceeding to recover money or property from a third party
- A proceeding to obtain an injunction or other equitable relief
- A proceeding to obtain approval to sell property in which both the debtor and a non-debtor have an interest
- A proceeding to subordinate a creditor's claim or interest to other claims
- A proceeding to revoke an order confirming a plan in a Chapter 11, 12, or 13 case

In an adversary proceeding, the Federal Rules of Civil Procedure (FRCP) come into play and are largely incorporated by Part VII of the FRBPs (7001 through 7087) formally governing adversary proceedings. The party initiating the adversary proceeding, usually the bankruptcy trustee or a creditor, does so by filing a complaint. (See Document 31 in the Carlson case file.) Official Form 416D provides the basic form for the caption of a complaint used to initiate an adversary proceeding. Service of process under FRCP 4 must be accomplished on the defendant. The defendant must file an answer to the complaint or a default judgment will be entered against her. The formal rules of pretrial discovery found in FRCP 26 through 37 are available to the parties (interrogatories to parties, depositions, requests for production of documents and things, requests for physical or mental examination, and requests for admission). And the case, if not settled, will be scheduled for trial and tried in the bankruptcy court.

Application Exercise 6

Compare the bankruptcy trustee's objection to the claim of Pine Ridge Nursing Home (Document 28 in the Carlson case file) with the complaint filed against Evelyn Rinaldi to recover the doll collection in her possession that belongs to her sister, Marta Rinaldi Carlson (Document 31 in the Carlson case file). The former is a not an adversary matter under FRBP 7001 and can be resolved as a contested matter initiated by motion. The latter is an adversary matter under FRBP 7001 because it is an action to recover money or property of the estate from a third person under §542. Does the caption of the complaint in Document 31 comply with the required format of 416D? What other differences in detail and formality do you see in the two documents?

To resolve the contested matter raised by motion, the court will schedule a hearing within a few days and the parties will appear to present proof and/or make argument. They may or may not prepare prehearing briefs for the court. But in the adversary proceeding, the named defendant must be formally served with process pursuant to FRCP 4, be given time to file a formal answer to the complaint, engage in formal pretrial discovery allowed by FRCP 26 through 37, and make any pretrial motions allowed by the FRCP.

The parties to the adversary proceeding may also be entitled to demand a jury for the trial of the case. But recall from the discussion in Section A of this chapter that 28 U.S.C. §157(e) dictates that a bankruptcy court can conduct a jury trial only when all parties consent and the district court specifically designates the bankruptcy court to conduct that trial by jury. Thus if the matter is triable by jury and one is demanded, it is usually the district court that conducts the trial.

In the vast majority of situations the Code makes it clear whether a dispute is to be treated as a contested matter initiated by motion or objection or as an adversary proceeding initiated by filing and service of a formal complaint. But not always. For example, courts are split on whether to treat a creditor's allegation that a creditor has violated the automatic stay of §362(a) as a contested matter or an adversary proceeding.

Application Exercise 7

Look at the Motion for Order of Contempt for Violation of Automatic Stay which is Document 24 in the Carlson case file. Does the court handling the Carlson bankruptcy case treat this type of dispute as a contested matter or an adversary proceeding? See if you can determine how the bankruptcy courts of the federal district where you plan to practice treat it. Hint: Start by looking at the local rules or standing rules of that court.

Chapter Summary

- Only Article III courts can enter final orders in disputes involving private rights: the liability of one individual to another under the law as defined. Article I courts are empowered by Congress to resolve disputes designated public rights: those that derive from a particular federal regulatory scheme. Bankruptcy jurisdiction is vested in Article I district courts and bankruptcy courts have referral jurisdiction when granted by district courts to decide certain matters arising under, arising in, or related to cases under Title 11. District courts may revoke the reference sua sponte or on motion.
- The statutory scheme allows bankruptcy courts to enter final judgments in core proceedings, which are matters involving procedures and rights that would not exist except for the bankruptcy case. In non-core proceedings final orders can be entered by the bankruptcy court only with the parties' consent though that court can enter proposed findings and conclusions. The U.S. Code contains a

nonexclusive list of proceedings designated as core proceedings. However, after *Stern*, even in core proceedings the Article I bankruptcy courts may not enter final judgments if the matter involves private rather than public rights unless the parties expressly or impliedly consent. In the absence of such consent, the bankruptcy court can enter only proposed findings and conclusions regardless of whether the matter is designated as a core proceeding by the statutory scheme. Bankruptcy courts are barred from hearing and deciding personal injury or wrongful death claims regardless of whether they are core or non-core.

- A bankruptcy court may conduct a jury trial in a core or non-core proceeding in which it can enter a final judgment only with consent of the parties and the district court.

- Courts are divided over whether a prepetition arbitration agreement must be honored when the dispute is decided by a bankruptcy court though, generally, such agreement is less likely to be enforced in a core proceeding than in a non-core.

- U.S. bankruptcy courts utilize broad personal jurisdiction based on minimal national contacts rather than minimal contact with the forum state.

- Appeal of a final order of a bankruptcy court lies in the first instance in the district court that referred the case subject to a de novo standard of review for questions of law and clearly erroneous standard for findings of fact. Five federal circuits have established Bankruptcy Appellate Panels and in those circuits appeal may be made to the BAP rather than the district court if all parties consent. Appeal from the decision of the district court or BAP lies to the circuit court of appeals.

- Disputes in a bankruptcy case are decided as either contested matters via motion, objection, or notice of intended action, or as formal adversary proceedings. Many actions accomplished by motion or notice of intended action are subject to the "after notice and a hearing" requirement, pursuant to which no hearing will be held on the motion or intended action after notice is given unless a timely objection is filed. The bankruptcy rules incorporate most of the Federal Rules of Civil Procedure and make them applicable to an adversary proceeding.

Applying the Concepts

1. Rose Henry for many years owned and operated Rose's Florist as a sole proprietorship in the state where you plan to practice. Rose's business was ruined last year when a South American parasite was transported into her store location via a delivery of orchids grown in Columbia. The parasite not only destroyed her inventory at the time, but it infested the homes of customers who purchased the orchids from her shop, resulting in numerous lawsuits, and it destroyed the reputation and good will of her business. Rose has filed a Chapter 7 proceeding and you have been appointed bankruptcy trustee.

   On the schedules Rose prepared in connection with her bankruptcy petition, she listed two claims arising out of this incident as property of the estate.

The trustee wishes to file an adversary proceeding against two parties on those claims. One party is Miami Flower Imports (MFI) of Miami, Florida from whom Rose purchased all of her South American flowers including the infested orchids that ruined her business. MFI had the flowers that Rose ordered from it delivered to her by an independent common carrier. MFI's only business location is in Miami; it has no agents in any other state, does not advertise in any other state, and does not even operate a Web site. Theories of liability against MFI will be negligence, strict liability, and breach of implied warranty of merchantability arising from contract for the sale of goods.

The trustee also wishes to bring a claim against Columbia Orchid Growers (COG), a company located in Cartagena, Columbia. COG grew the orchids that were sold to her by MFI. COG has no office or agents located in the United States. It grows and sells its flowers to numerous floral distributors like MFI, which then distribute the COG flowers to retailers like Rose's Florist throughout the United States. Information from an expert is that the parasite infestation of the orchids occurred because COG failed to spray for parasites at a critical time in the flower's development. The theories against COG will lie in negligence and strict liability.

a. If MFI asserts lack of personal jurisdiction as a defense against trustee's claim against it, what are the arguments on both sides and what is the likely ruling on that defense?

b. If COG asserts lack of personal jurisdiction as a defense against trustee's claim against it, what are the arguments on both sides and what is the likely ruling on that defense?

2. In Applying the Concepts scenario 1, if MFI had filed a proof of claim in Rose's bankruptcy case and trustee sought to maintain the tort action against MFI to both offset MFI's claim and for additional affirmative relief, could the bankruptcy court enter a final judgment on either claim or both claims against MFI without consent of all the parties? Assuming COG is not a creditor of Rose's, may the bankruptcy court enter a final judgment in the suit against COG?

3. One of Rose's creditors is her brother-in-law and former business manager, Garland Hughes. Two years ago, Garland talked Rose into hiring him as a business manager. In that capacity, Garland had Rose do business with a number of persons who, unknown to Rose at the time, were people to whom Garland owed money. One of these persons was a shady and unlicensed wealth management expert, and Rose lost most of her meager savings by following his advice. Now that Rose has filed bankruptcy, Garland has filed a proof of claim saying Rose still owes him $30,000 for services performed as business manager. On behalf of the estate you want to file an objection to Garland's claim on the basis of fraud and breach of fiduciary duty, asking the court to cancel his claim in its entirety. You also want to recover affirmatively from Garland on behalf of the estate in the amount of $100,000 in actual and punitive damages.

a. Is the objection to Garland's proof of claim in Rose's bankruptcy case properly treated as a core proceeding? What about the trustee's suit to recover damages from him affirmatively?

b. Assuming the bankruptcy court treats both of the actions against Garland as core proceedings, will that court have constitutional jurisdiction to enter a final judgment regarding whether his claim should be canceled? To enter final judgment regarding the trustee's suit to recover damages against him affirmatively?

This problem is based on Waldman v. Stone, 698 F.3d 910 (6th Cir. 2012), cert. denied, 133 S. Ct. 1604 (2013). After you have determined your initial responses to these questions, read that case and see if your answers would change based on its reasoning.

In re Marta Rinaldi Carlson Chapter 7 Bankruptcy [Inactive File]

[The case studies used in this casebook and appendices are entirely fictional and hypothetical. Though the hypothetical case studies used are set in actual federal districts, the names, location, and circumstances of debtors, creditors, trustees, lawyers, judges, and all other persons or entities described in these case studies are a product of the author's imagination, are fictitious, and any resemblance to actual persons living or dead or to any entity is entirely coincidental. Similarly, the information contained on the documents that correspond to the case file index below and that are posted on the companion website is likewise fictional and hypothetical. The Official Bankruptcy Forms in effect during June 2016 have been used to prepare the documents that are part of the case files and no attempt has been made to comply with any local rules, standing orders, or customary practices of the named court.]

ASSIGNMENT MEMORANDUM

TO: Associate attorney
FROM: Carolyn A. Thomas, supervising attorney
RE: Marta Rinaldi Carlson
DATE: June 1, 2016

Marta Rinaldi Carlson is an executive assistant at Tomorrow Today, Inc. (TTI). She resides at 301 Pugh Street in Roseville, Minnesota.

Marta was one of the original employees of TTI, hired as a secretary to Howard Kine, a computer software genius and TTI shareholder. At Kine's urging, Marta obtained an associate's degree from Capital City Community College in computer science. She then transferred to Columbiana State University and has been pursuing her bachelor's in software engineering. Marta needs only 20 more semester hours to complete her degree, which she hopes to do in 18 months. Kine told Marta that once she receives that degree, he will recommend that TTI promote her from executive assistant to computer software engineer. Marta began making $48,000 per year at TTI as of January 1, 2016. In 2015 she made $40,000 per year. If she can secure the computer software engineer position, her pay should jump to the mid-50 thousands. But that is at least 18 months away.

Completing her education has been a long, hard road for Marta. At 37, when she began her college work, she had been out of school for 20 years, since completing high school. Now 40, she works full time for TTI so must attend school at night. She has two children: a son, Chris, who is 14, and a daughter, Adela, who is 11. Marta and her husband, Eugene, separated around the time she began college in 2012 and the divorce became final about two years ago.

From a financial standpoint, when Marta and Eugene were together, they were a typical middle-class family. They had a house mortgage that was always paid on time, they had a couple of credit cards on which they carried a little higher balance than they should have, and they rarely put any money into savings. But the bills got paid, vacations got taken, both Marta and Eugene drove late-model cars, purchased with affordable loans, and everybody in the family had all the accoutrements of American middle-class life.

All that changed with the divorce. Six months after the decree became final Eugene lost his job as an assistant manager of a mid-sized regional retail discount chain when it was bought out by a national concern. He was able to find lower paying work in retail sales for a while but in then his health failed and he was diagnosed with leukemia. Today Eugene survives only on Social Security disability payments. The divorce decree required him to pay Marta $2,000 per month in child support and to keep Marta and the kids covered under his health insurance policy. Eugene is now $15,000 in arrears on his child support obligation and unable to provide health insurance coverage. Consequently, Marta pays to have herself and the two children covered under TTI's group policy. Unfortunately, the prospects of Eugene ever being able to make up the arrears or to resume child support payments are remote.

Two months after the divorce, Adela got sick with what Marta thought was an intestinal flu. The 11-year old had bouts of nausea and diarrhea that would last three to four days, resolve, and then recur a week later. The third time it happened, Adela was hospitalized for almost a week. The doctors diagnosed irritable bowel syndrome related to stress from the separation and divorce of Adela's parents. Medication was prescribed but did no good at all. Finally, Marta took her daughter to a gastrointestinal specialist in another city, who diagnosed Giardiasis, a condition caused by a waterborne, intestinal parasite. Though no one can say for sure where the child picked it up, it was probably on a swimming trip with friends to a popular swimming hole at a local lake. By the time the correct diagnosis was made, Adela's condition was serious and she had to undergo surgery to remove a portion of her large intestine, followed by an extended hospitalization. The infection was eventually checked but Adela still has to take very expensive medications and follow a strict diet. She will be under a doctor's watchful care for several years. Between the high deductible on her TTI policy and the limited coverage provided for several of the tests and procedures conducted on Adela, as well as the medications she is taking, Marta has unpaid medical bills totaling more than $60,000 and growing. Eugene remains unemployed and is unable to help financially.

In addition to Adela's health problems, Marta has been faced with responsibility for healthcare costs associated with her widowed 73-year-old mother, Estell Rinaldi. Six years ago Estell was diagnosed with Alzheimer's. She was able to live in her home for a year after the diagnosis but finally sold the home and went into a nursing facility, Pine Ridge Nursing Home. Although Marta had hoped that the proceeds from her mother's home, in addition to her remaining savings, would be enough to pay for the nursing home care, she was asked by the nursing home to sign a personal guaranty, promising to pay any costs her mother's assets and government assistance did not. She did so without consulting an attorney. A little over a year ago, her mother's assets were depleted and Marta began receiving bills from the nursing home. Her mother finally passed away two months ago, but the accumulated bills from her care, for which Pine Ridge Nursing claims Marta is responsible, total more than $45,000. Marta is disputing that claim against her, contending that when her mother's assets ran out, she advised the nursing home that she would not be able to pay anything and that she was verbally told by the home's administrator that she would not be billed anything on the guaranty because the government would pay all costs from that point on. Pine Ridge has filed suit to collect the indebtedness from Marta. She has answered the complaint denying any liability on the guarantee and alleging affirmatively, in the alternative, that a portion of the nursing home's claim against her represents sums the government has paid to Pine Ridge.

Eugene's unemployment has caused Marta other further financial problems. Under the divorce decree, he was ordered to assume liability for the accumulated credit card debt of the couple, which totaled more than $40,000 at the time. He made very few payments on the outstanding balance of that debt and Marta is now being dunned for it. With interest and late fees, the total balance owed to two different card providers is more than $50,000.

Marta has had to borrow money to finance her college education. She took out one loan from Columbiana Federal Savings & Loan in the principal amount of $5,000 for her community college expenses and has just begun paying that back. She took out a second loan from First Patriot Bank for $10,000 to finance her studies at Columbiana State University. Under the terms of that student loan, repayment will not begin until three months after she graduates. Both student loans are guaranteed by the federal government.

Six years ago, Eugene and Marta bought the house where Marta now lives with her children. They paid $200,000 for it, borrowing $150,000 from Capital Savings Bank (CSB). The loan was for 30 years at a fixed rate of interest at 6.5 percent per annum. The monthly payments to CSB, with taxes and insurance, total $965. Three years ago, Eugene and Marta took out a second mortgage on the house when they borrowed $50,000 from Dreams Come True Finance Company (DCT) to finance a business venture for Eugene that ultimately failed. The DCT loan was for 15 years at 8 percent interest and required monthly payments of $477.

In the divorce, Marta was awarded the house and Eugene quitclaimed his interest in it to her. The divorce decree provided that Marta was to assume responsibility for the remaining mortgage payments to CSB, though Eugene remained on the promissory note to CSB. Eugene was to assume responsibility for the remaining mortgage payments to DCT, though Marta remained liable on that note. Marta knew it would be a stretch for her to make the mortgage payments to CSB on her salary alone, but she decided it was worth the risk in order to keep her children in their home. The current principal balance on the loan from CSB is $142,500; the current principal balance on the loan from DCT, which has been in default for some time now, is $37,500. Marta is two payments behind to CSB and three behind to DCT. A realtor has told Marta that the house has a market value of $255,000. DCT has declared default on its loan and is preparing to foreclose on the home.

Marta is maxed-out on the Capital City Bank Visa card issued in her own name following the divorce. Her balance on the card is $8,200, on which she manages to make no more than the minimum payment each month. She drives a four-year-old Toyota Camry, which is titled in her name only. The book value of the car is $8,500 and she owes a balance on it of $1,750 to Automotive Financing, Inc. (AFI), which holds a security interest in the car. Her monthly payments to AFI are $210 and she is two payments in arrears at this time. She has no savings except her 401k plan at TTI, which has a current balance of $7,600.

Her 14-year-old son, Chris, has had his own problems since the divorce. His grades have dropped and he's started running with a group of friends Marta is not happy with. Eugene rarely sees either child, electing not to exercise his visitation rights most months. Last month Chris and another juvenile were arrested for malicious destruction of property. Marta had to come up with $500 to pay a lawyer who did manage to keep Chris from being sentenced to a juvenile facility. When Chris began experiencing problems after the divorce, Marta took him to Crisis Counseling Center, which billed her $1,250. Her insurance did not cover the counseling and she has been unable to pay the bill. That debt has been turned over to a collection agency. She is getting two to three phone calls a week from the collection agency asking when the bill will be paid.

Marta's own health has deteriorated since her financial problems began following the divorce. She suffers from chronic indigestion, which she suspects is an ulcer, but she has put off going to a doctor because she just can't afford it.

Since Chris turned 14, Marta has tried to minimize her child care costs by allowing the children to come home by themselves after school. But she still needs a sitter when Chris has school sports activities or trips and can't watch Adela or when she is out of town overnight herself. She will provide you with the estimate of her monthly child care exepenses.

We are going to file a Chapter 7 bankruptcy for Ms. Carlson. Please contact her and begin gathering the additional specific information needed for the petition and schedules.

CASE FILE INDEX

[The documents listed in this index for the Chapter 7 bankruptcy case of *In re Marta Rinaldi Carlson* are available on the companion website to this text at aspenlawschool.com/books/parsons_consumerbankruptcy.]

1. Fee agreement between Marta Rinaldi Carlson and Carolyn A. Thomas, Attorney at Law with Notice to Individual Consumer Debtor under §342(b) and Disclosure Pursuant to §527(a)(2) and Disclosure Pursuant to §527(b)
2. Voluntary Petition in Chapter 7
3. Application to Pay Fee in Installments and Order Granting Application
4. List of Creditors
5. Motion for Additional Time to File Schedules, Statement of Affairs, and Other Documents with Notice of Motion
6. Order granting Motion for Additional Time to File Schedules, etc.
7. Schedule A/B
8. Schedule C
9. Schedule D
10. Schedule E/F
11. Schedule G
12. Schedule H
13. Schedule I
14. Schedule J
15. Summary of Your Assets and Liabilities and Certain Statistical Information
16. Declaration About an Individual Debtor's Schedules
17. Statement of Financial Affairs for Individuals Filing for Bankruptcy
18. Debtor's Statement of Intent for Individuals Filing Under Chapter 7
19. Form 122A-1 Chapter 7 Statement of Your Current Monthly Income
20. Statement About Your Social Security Numbers
21. Disclosure of Compensation of Attorney for the Debtor
22. Payment Advices or Other Evidence of Payment Received from Any Employer within 60 Days before the Filing of the Petition
23. Notice of Chapter 7 Bankruptcy Case
24. Motion for Order of Contempt for Violation of Automatic Stay and for Damages with Notice of Motion
25. Order on Motion for Order of Contempt, etc.
26. Trustee's §704(b)(1) Report
27. Proof of Claim with Attachment
28. Objection to Claim with Notice of Objection
29. Motion for Authorization to Hire Professional and to Approve Fee with Notice of Motion
30. Order on Motion for Authorization to Hire Professional and to Approve Fee
31. Complaint for Turnover of Property or Money Judgment for Its Value
32. Objection to Claimed Exemption with Notice

33. Certification About a Financial Management
34. Notice of Intent to Abandon Property with Notice
35. Motion for Permission to Sell Property Free and Clear of Liens with Notice of Motion
36. Reaffirmation Agreement
37. Order of Discharge

Extra Material:

1. Alternative Form 122A-1 Chapter 7 Statement of Your Current Monthly Income (assuming Marta Carlson had annual income of $84,000)
2. Form 122A-2 Chapter 7 Means Test Calculation (assuming Marta Carlson had annual income of $84,000)

In re Roger H. and Susan J. Matthews Chapter 13 Bankruptcy [Inactive File]

[The case studies used in this casebook and appendices are entirely fictional and hypothetical. Though the hypothetical case studies used are set in actual federal districts, the names, location, and circumstances of debtors, creditors, trustees, lawyers, judges, and all other persons or entities described in these case studies are a product of the author's imagination, are fictitious, and any resemblance to actual persons living or dead or to any entity is entirely coincidental. Similarly, the information contained on the documents that correspond to the case file index below and that are posted on the companion website is likewise fictional and hypothetical. The Official Bankruptcy Forms in effect during June 2016 have been used to prepare the documents that are part of the case files and no attempt has been made to comply with any local rules, standing orders, or customary practices of the named court.]

ASSIGNMENT MEMORANDUM

TO: Associate attorney
FROM: Edmond J. Montgomery, supervising attorney
RE: Roger H. and Susan J. Matthews
DATE: June 1, 2016

Roger Matthews is 33 years old and works for City Plumbing Company in Harrisburg, Pennsylvania. Roger has a high school diploma, almost two years of college, and a certificate in plumbing from Columbiana College of Technology. He brings home $2,400 a month based on a gross salary of $36,000 per year. Roger's wife, Susan Matthews, is 32 year old and works as the librarian for Heart and Soul Academy, a private school in in the area for kindergarten through eighth grade. Susan has a bachelor's degree in library science from Columbiana State University. She brings home $1,733 a month based on a gross salary of $26,000 per year.

Roger and Susan have been irresponsible in their credit card spending. They have used six different cards for the last several years and accumulated $35,000 of debt on those cards. Less than $30,000 of the debt was for actual charges; the rest of the balance has built up over the years from interest and fees charged on balances carried over month to month and occasional penalties for late payments.

The Matthews own a home in Harrisburg located at 901 Magnolia Lane, which they purchased three years ago. A realtor friend told them informally that the home has a current market value of $120,000. There are two mortgages on the property. The first mortgage is in favor of First Bank of Capital City (FBCC) with a balance of $100,000 on a 30-year note with 27 years remaining. The Matthews pay FBCC $850 per month and are one payment in arrears. The second mortgage is in favor of Capital Savings Bank (CSB) with a balance of $30,000 on a $35,000 home improvement loan the Matthews took out a year ago (thus the Matthews have no equity in their home). They have 48 months of payments remaining on the second mortgage. The Matthews pay CSB $700 per month on the second mortgage and are current on those payments.

The Matthews own three vehicles. Roger drives a YR-3 Ford F-150 truck worth $7,500, on which they owe $9,000 to Automotive Financing, Inc. (AFI), which holds a lien on the truck. The Matthews make payments of $360 per month to AFI on the truck. Susan drives a YR-4 Honda Civic worth $8,000, on which they owe $7,500 to Columbiana Federal Savings & Loan (CFSL), which holds a lien on the Civic. The Matthews make payments of $240 per month to CFSL on the Civic. They also own a YR-8 Chevrolet Malibu worth $2,000, on which they owe $5,000 to Car World (CW), which holds a lien on the Malibu. The Matthews make payments to CW of $120 per month on the Malibu. The Matthews are current on all three car payments but are pretty sure they will surrender the Malibu to CW since it is an extra vehicle.

Roger and Susan have two daughters: Carrie is 7 years old and her sister, Elizabeth, is 11 months. Medical expenses incurred in connection with Elizabeth's birth are the straw that broke the camel's back for the couple financially. Susan experienced complications with the pregnancy and, although the baby is fine, the unpaid doctor and hospital bills for Susan still total $25,000. Susan was out of work durinig the last three months of last year due to her health problems and the baby's birth, which devastated the couple's cash flow. Susan returned to work in January but they are too deeply in the hole financially to catch up. Susan's mother is keeping the baby during the day and Carrie after school to spare them childcare expenses, but she's not going to be able to do that after July of this year.

Roger and Susan also borrowed $2,500 from Capital City Finance Company (CCFC) last year to finance a vacation they couldn't otherwise afford. The couple granted a security interest in Roger's plumbing tools to secure the loan from CCFC, the balance of which is $2,000. They are supposed to pay $50 a month to CCFC on this loan but are now three months in arrears. At about the same time, Roger was assessed $1,000 in taxes, penalties, and interest by the IRS as a result of unreported income from YR-2 when he did some independent plumbing work for a local contractor.

I have drawn up the following informal budget for the Matthews, which we will use in fashioning a proposed plan of reorganization for them under Chapter 13.

Monthly prepetition budget for Roger and Susan Matthews:

Net monthly income:
Roger:. $2,400
    ($3,000 per month minus withholding of $600 in taxes)
Susan: $1,733
    ($2,167 per month minus withholding of $360 in taxes
    and $74 health insurance premium)
Total net monthly income $4,133

Living expenses:
Food. 475
Home maintenance 75
Clothing 175
Dry cleaning/laundry 25
Gas/transportation 150
Utilities, phone, and cable 500
    Electric & gas. $315
    Water & sewer $50
    Phones. $70
    Cable & Internet. $65
Insurance (auto) 60
Medical/dental 100
Charitable contributions. 50
Entertainment/recreation 50
Miscellaneous. 100
Total living expenses $1,760

Payments on secured debt:
House payments 1,550
(FBCC $850, one payment behind) . . . .
(CSB $700, current)
Car payments. 720
(AFI for YR-3 Ford F-150 truck $360, current)
(CFSL for YR-4 Honda Civic $240, current)
(C-W for YR-8 Chevy Malibu $120, current)
Total payments on secured debt $2,270
Total payments on living expenses and secured debt. $4,030
Available to pay other debt $103

Debt not being paid:
Credit cards 35,000
Doctor & hospital 25,000
Tax bill from YR-2. 1,000
CCFC secured loan 2,000

Total debt not being paid $63,000

CASE FILE INDEX

[The documents listed in this index for the Chapter 13 bankruptcy case of In re Roger H. and Susan J. Matthews are available on the companion website to this text at aspen-lawschool.com/books/parsons_consumerbankruptcy.]

1. Joint Petition in Chapter 13
2. List of Creditors
3. Schedule A/B
4. Schedule C
5. Schedule D
6. Schedule E/F
7. Schedule G
8. Schedule H
9. Schedule I
10. Schedule J
11. Summary of Your Assets and Liabilities and Certain Statistical Information
12. Declaration re Schedules
13. Statement of Financial Affairs
14. Form 122C-1 Chapter 13 Statement of Your Current Monthly Income and Calculation of Commitment Period
15. Statement about Your Social Security Numbers
16. Disclosure of Compensation of Attorney for the Debtor
17. Payment Advices or Other Evidence of Payment Received from Any Employer within 60 Days before the Filing of the Petition
18. Chapter 13 Plan
19. Notice of Chapter 13 Bankruptcy Case
20. Debtor's Certification of Completion of Postpetition Instructional Course Concerning Personal Financial Management
21. Order Confirming Chapter 13 Plan
22. Wage Orders

Extra Material:

1. Alternative Form 122C-1 Chapter 13 Statement of Your Current Monthly Income and Calculation of Commitment Period (assuming the Matthews had combined annualized CMI of $95,000)
2. Form 122C-2 Chapter 13 Calculation of Your Disposable Income (assuming the Matthews had combined annualized CMI of $95,000)

In re Abelard R. Mendoza Chapter 7 Bankruptcy [Active File]

[The names, locations, and circumstances of debtors, creditors, and all other persons or entities described in this case study are a product of the author's imagination, are fictitious, and any resemblance to actual persons living or dead or to any entity is entirely coincidental.]

Instructions: All references to the fictional state of Columbiana in these assignments should be understood to be to the state where you plan to practice or to the state where you are studying law or to whatever other actual state your instructor directs. All references to the fictional city of Capitol City should be understood to be to a real city or town in the actual state that you choose to use in completing these assignments. YR00 is the current year. YR-1 is last year, YR-2 is two years ago, YR+2 is two years from now, etc.

ASSIGNMENT MEMORANDUM #1

TO: Associate Attorney
FROM: Supervising Attorney
DATE: Today, YR00
RE: Abelard R. Mendoza (Chapter 7 bankruptcy)

Abelard (Abe) Mendoza immigrated legally to the United States from Mexico 35 years ago and later became a U.S. citizen. He married and raised two daughters and a son in Capitol City. He and his wife, Maria, also built and operated a successful unincorporated construction business known as Mendoza Construction. Mr. and Mrs. Mendoza operated the business as partners until her death from cancer on August 1, YR-2. At age 58, Mr. Mendoza's life revolves around his children.

Mr. Mendoza's youngest child is his son, David, who is now 28. In school, David was always a good student and showed talent in the sciences. However, he has had trouble deciding exactly what he wants to do for a career. He received a bachelor's degree from State University, followed by a master's degree in biology from the same university. He spent 18 months in a doctoral program at UCLA before dropping out, then two more years in medical school before leaving that.

David borrowed money in connection with every phase of his higher education. His parents, Abe and Maria, co-signed one promissory note dated July 10, YR-6, in favor of Columbiana Federal Savings & Loan (CFSL) which had a balance three months ago of $45,450. David was able to make payments on the note for a while but it went into default a little over a year ago and the full amount of principal and interest became due and payable at that time. With David not able to pay the note, CFSL made demand on Mr. Mendoza to pay as co-signer. Two months ago today, Abe cashed out a $50,000 certificate of deposit he had at All State Bank & Trust and paid the balance owing to CFSL ($45,450) in full. The CD had been purchased by Mendoza on January 10, YR-2, in the amount of $50,000. It was a sixty-month CD maturing on January 10, YR+3, bearing interest at 5% per annum. It bore certificate number 67599087. When Mendoza redeemed the CD early he received the principal plus accrued interest in the amount of $55,000. After paying off the balance owed to CFSL, he put the remainder of the CD funds in his checking account.

In addition, Abe and Maria signed a guaranty agreement in favor of City County Bank (CCB) promising to pay any obligations David incurred to the bank in the event that David defaulted. David obtained an educational loan in the amount of $60,000 from CCB at that time. That note is dated June 1, YR-3, and David is now in default on it. The current balance owing on the June 1, YR-3 note to CCB is $45,200. A copy of the guaranty Abe and Maria signed in favor of CCB on the same date is attached to this memorandum.

A year before his wife became ill, and while their annual income from the construction business was in excess of $300,000, Mendoza and his wife purchased a new home in Capitol City. They borrowed $750,000 from Security Trust Bank in Capitol City and pledged the land and house as security for repayment. The monthly payments on that 30-year note and mortgage are $3,500. The current balance on that mortgage is $575,000 and the property has lost value due to the economic climate and Mendoza's inability to keep the property up. A realtor friend told him recently it was probably worth $600,000 on the market today.

Mr. Mendoza began suffering from prolonged bouts of depression after Maria's death and stopped operating the construction business. Mendoza finally accepted a position as the project manager on the City Heights Condominium Project, a $200 million development along the river that flows through downtown Capitol City. His contract, dated June 1, YR-1, was with the owner of the project, City Heights Limited Partnership, and was to pay him $150,000 per year or $12,500 per month as an independent contractor until the project was completed.

The condominium project did not go well at any point. The owner was in constant dispute with the general contractor on the job, Adams Construction Company (ACC). Because of the disputes, the owner ordered progress payments withheld from ACC, over Mendoza's objection. As a result, unpaid subcontractors and suppliers began placing liens on the project property. Effective on December 31, YR-1, City Heights Limited Partnership terminated the project manager contract with Mendoza. We are looking into the possibility that City Heights Limited Partnership breached its agreement with Mr. Mendoza by discharging him prior to completion of the construction project. At this point it appears unlikely that a claim of breach will have any merit but no determination has been made.

Beginning on January 1, YR00, Mendoza began working as an estimator for Chavis Construction Company here in Capitol City, making $50,000 a year. His take-home pay is $3,125 per month after withholding of $1,041.67 per month for taxes, Social Security, and Medicare. Mendoza has been using his savings to continue paying his monthly expenses, which far exceed his reduced income but those savings are almost depleted.

Last year the Internal Revenue Service audited Mr. Mendoza and on January 5, YR00, the government issued an assessment against him for unpaid income taxes for YR-4, YR-3, and YR-2, plus penalties and interest, totaling $50,000. Today Mendoza received a Notice and Demand for Payment from the IRS regarding the assessment. If the full amount isn't paid in ten days, a federal tax lien will attach to all Mendoza's home and personal property. Mr. Mendoza also owes the IRS $14,000 for unpaid self-employment taxes on his income from the contract with City Heights Limited Partnership for the seven months (June through December, YR-1) that he was receiving that income.

At the time Mr. Mendoza stopped operating Mendoza Construction he discovered that Hilda Montgomery, the bookkeeper he had hired after his wife's death, had systematically embezzled at least $100,000 of cash from him. Mendoza had no security bond or fidelity insurance from which to recoup the loss. We have located Ms. Montgomery but determined that the embezzled funds were squandered on trips and gambling and that she is judgment proof.

Last year, after he stopped operating the construction business, Mr. Mendoza decided to let David use all the hard assets of the construction business in David's own effort to establish a successful construction company. In exchange for Mr. Mendoza allowing his son, David, to use the hard assets of the construction business, David promised to make the payments due from Abe Mendoza to Citizens First Bank (CFB) on a June 15, YR-4 note secured by a lien on all those assets. David failed to do so and CFB repossessed those assets and sold them four months ago. The repossession sale of those assets produced $60,000, which was applied to the expenses of repossession and sale, and to the balance owing on the note. Today, there is a remaining balance of $54,000 on that note which is now unsecured. CFB is threatening suit if the balance is not paid immediately. A list of the repossessed assets is attached to this memorandum.

As if matters were not already bad enough, yesterday Mendoza learned that his son David procured a loan in the amount of $150,000 on December 1, YR-1, from City County Bank using false financial statements listing assets he did not actually have and omitting numerous debts he did have. Apparently David, unknown to Mr. Mendoza, invested the money in a real estate scheme with some friends. The investment failed and the money is gone. City County Bank sued David a couple of months ago on both the June 1, YR-3 note for the educational loan and the December 1, YR-1 loan, and put Mr. Mendoza on notice that he is responsible to CCB for both obligations pursuant to the June 1, YR-3 guaranty he signed in favor of CCB. The guaranty does in fact have an "other indebtedness" clause, likely meaning Mr. Mendoza is liable for this third note as well (see Paragraph 2 of the Guaranty Agreement a copy of which is attached to this memorandum).

Last week David Mendoza filed a Chapter 7 bankruptcy case. It was filed as a no-asset case. City County Bank immediately filed suit against Abelard Mendoza to collect on the June 1, YR-3 personal guaranty that Mendoza signed and that guarantees the two notes of David Mendoza to CCB totaling $195,200. The case is pending in the Circuit Court for Capitol County, docket number CV00-91123.

Mr. Mendoza has some credit card debt listed on the attached statement. The largest of those is on the Visa Card issued by Pioneer State Bank with a balance of $125,000. Mendoza says a lot of that is attributable to experimental medical treatments he purchased in the last months of Maria's life that were not covered by insurance and a final whirlwind vacation they took before she became too ill to travel.

We have decided to put Abelard Mendoza into a Chapter 7 proceeding as well. I would like for you to draft the following documents for my review:

—Petition with Exhibit D
—Schedules A-J
—Declaration re schedules
—Statement of financial affairs
—Debtor's statement of intent
—Form 22A-1 Chapter 7 Statement of Your Current Monthly Income and, if necessary Form 22A-2, Chapter 7 Means Test Calculation
—Disclosure of compensation for debtor's attorney

Be sure the documents you draft comply with the local rules and customary practice of the bankruptcy court where the case will be filed.

Mendoza would like to exempt as much of his cash, checking account, and savings account balances as possible; as much equity in his home as possible; his SEP-IRA; and all of his household goods and furnishings, wearing apparel, jewelry, the TV and DVD equipment, the computer and printer, and books and pictures. The riding lawn mower, yard equipment and tools, and the Winchester shotgun are to be exempted only if possible. He definitely would like to retain one vehicle, the YR-3 Dodge Ram 1500 truck, and Friendly Finance Company has indicated a willingness to execute a reaffirmation agreement with him for that purpose. He will surrender the YR-2 Cadillac Deville to Automotive Financing, Inc., and the home on Shady Lane to Security Trust Bank.

Mr. Mendoza is paying us a $3,000 flat fee today to file the bankruptcy case for him. That payment will come out of his checking account, reducing the balance there. He completed his prepetition credit counseling course today at Prudent Person Credit Counseling Service here in Capitol City, at a cost of $50, which will also come out of his checking account. His Social Security number is 999-18-7765. His date of birth is December 20, YR-58. Mr. Mendoza will not dispute any debt. He is current on all his recurring monthly expenses.

Prepare a cover memorandum to go with your draft documents, advising me of what debts Mr. Mendoza will be unable to discharge in this bankruptcy proceeding, and what property Mr. Mendoza should be able to retain notwithstanding the bankruptcy. For purposes of the means test analysis and claimed exemptions, be sure to apply the law of your state.

SUMMARY OF ASSETS, LIABILITIES, CURRENT INCOME AND EXPENSES FOR ABELARD R. MENDOZA

<u>Assets</u>

Real property:

House and 2-acre lot located at 8865 Shady Lane,
Capitol City, Columbiana $600,000

Personal property:
    Cash on hand. $2,500
    Checking account at Capitol Savings Bank. 5,000
    Savings account at Capitol Savings Bank. 1,500
    Household goods & furnishings. 5,000
        Furniture. $3,200
        China & silverware $300
        Appliances. $1,000
        Other furnishings $500
    Personal computer and printer 1,500
    High definition plasma screen TV 2,200
    Stereo and DVD equipment. 500
    Riding mower. 1,000
    Yard equipment & tools 300
    Books & pictures 400
    Wearing apparel. 1,000
    Jewelry. 1,250
    Winchester 101 Field Shotgun, 12 gauge 1,000
    Whole life insurance policy issued by Columbiana
        Insurance Company (cash value). 4,000
    SEP-IRA (qualified retirement plan)
    held by Rearguard Finance Co as trustee 25,000
    YR-3 Dodge Ram 1500 Truck 19,000
    YR-2 Cadillac Deville Sedan 23,000

Other assets:

Claim against Hilda Montgomery for embezzlement. . . . . Value unknown
Potential claim against City Heights Limited Partnership
    for breach of the June 1, YR-1 project manager agreement . . . .Value unknown
Total assets: $694,150

Liabilities

Secured debt:

Security Trust Bank (30-year note dated May 1, YR-3, secured
   by mortgage of even date on Shady Lane residence;
   324 monthly payments remaining). $575,000
Friendly Finance Company (5-year note dated January 10,
   YR-1, secured by YR-3 Dodge Ram truck; 48 monthly
   payments remaining) 15,000
Automotive Financing, Inc. (5-year note dated Sep. 1, YR-2,
   secured by YR-2 Cadillac Deville Sedan; 36 monthly
   payments remaining) 25,000

Unsecured debt:

Vulcan Bank Visa Card. 52,500
Diners' Card. 21,000
Pioneer State Bank Visa Card 125,000
Guaranty agreement dated June 1, YR-3, in favor of City County
Bank guaranteeing two notes to David Mendoza:
   Note dated June 1, YR-3, balance $45,200
   Note dated December 1, YR-1, balance $150,000 195,200
Citizens First Bank (balance owing on June 15, YR-4 note
   previously secured by assets used in the construction business) . . . 54,000
IRS January 5, YR00, assessment for unpaid income
   taxes for YR-4, YR-3, and YR-2 50,000
IRS for self-employment tax for YR00, not yet paid 14,000
Better Days Counseling Clinic 7,500
Bernard Wheeling, MD. 1,500
Lakeside Pharmacy 985

Total liabilities: $1,136,685

Recurring monthly expenses:

Premium on life insurance policy from Columbiana
   Insurance Company. $100
Premium on medical and disability insurance policy from
   Blue Cross of Columbiana. 400
Premium on auto insurance with Nationwise Ins. Co. 125
Note to Security Trust Bank 2,500

Note to Friendly Finance Company 410
Note to Automotive Financing, Inc. 608
Payment on credit card balances. 1,000
Electricity & gas 400
Water & sewer 50
Phone service. 100
Home maintenance 100
Food 250
Clothes. 50
Laundry & dry cleaning. 30
Medical & dental. 25
Gas & transportation 200
Recreation 125
Cable TV service (Flash Cable Co.) 55
Internet service provider (Streak Internet Service) 50

Total fixed monthly expenses. $6,578

Income:

YR-2: Total income: $176,500 as follows:
    $175,000 from Mendoza Construction
    $1,500 in interest from All State Savings & Loan certificate of deposit
YR-1: Total income: $138,500 as follows:
    $50,000 from Mendoza Construction from January 1, YR-1, to May 30, YR-1
    $87,500 from contract with City Heights Limited Partnership to work as
        Project
    Manager on condominium project at $150,000 per year (paid $12,500 per
        month from June 1, YR-1 through December 31, YR-1)
    $1,000 in interest from All State Savings & Loan certificate of deposit

YR00: Income to date:
    Current earned income from January 1, YR00, to date with Chavis
        Construction Company:
    Gross monthly salary: $4,166.67
    Minus payroll taxes, Social Security & Medicare: $1,041.67
    Minus health insurance premium: $400

    Net current monthly income: $2,725

GUARANTY AGREEMENT

THIS GUARANTY, is made this June 1, YR-3, by Abelard R. Mendoza and wife, Maria S. Mendoza (the "Guarantors"), to City County Bank of Capitol City, Columbiana (the "Lender").

WHEREAS Lender is the owner and holder of that certain Promissory Note (the "Note") dated June 1, YR-3, in the original principal amount of $60,000 executed by David W. Mendoza (the "Borrower");

WHEREAS to induce Lender to enter into the loan transaction evidenced by the Note (the "Loan"), Guarantor has agreed to guaranty the obligations of Borrower; and

WHEREAS Lender is unwilling to enter into the Loan unless Guarantor guarantees the payment thereof;

NOW THEREFORE, as a material inducement to Lender to enter into the Loan, Guarantor agrees with Lender as follows:

1. The above recitals are true and correct and are incorporated herein.

2. To induce Lender to enter into the Loan, Guarantors guarantee and promise to pay to Lender or order, on demand, in lawful money of the United States any and all indebtedness of Borrower to Lender associated with the Loan and any other obligation, indebtedness, or liability of every kind and description, direct or indirect, absolute or contingent, due or to become due, now existing or hereafter arising that Borrower may owe to Lender in accordance with the terms of this Guaranty.

3. The obligations of Guarantors hereunder are contingent on Borrower's default on the obligations to Lender for which payment is sought from Guarantors and on Lender's inability to collect said obligation from Borrower, as default and collection may be defined from time to time by the laws of Columbiana. However, once such default has been established, the obligations of Guarantors on such obligations will be deemed independent of the obligations of Borrower, and a separate action or actions may be brought and be prosecuted against Guarantors and Guarantors waive the benefit of any statute of limitations affecting their liability hereunder or the enforcement thereof.

4. Guarantors authorize Lender, without notice or demand and without affecting its liability hereunder, from time to time to (a) renew, compromise, extend, accelerate, or otherwise change the time for payment or otherwise change the terms of the indebtedness or any part thereof, including increase or decrease of the rate of interest thereon; (b) take and hold security for the payment of this Guaranty or the indebtedness guaranteed, and exchange, enforce, waive, and release any such

security; (c) apply such security and direct the order or manner of sale thereof as Lender in its discretion may determine; and (d) release or substitute any one or more guarantors. Lender may assign this guaranty in whole or in part.

5. Guarantors waive any defense arising by reason of any disability or other defense of Borrower except for defenses based on Lender's default or by reason of the cessation from any cause whatsoever of the liability of Borrower. Guarantors waive all notice of acceptance of this Guaranty, notice of maturity, payment, or default of any indebtedness, and any other requirement or notice necessary to bind Guarantors hereunder, including but not limited to presentment, notice of dishonor, and protest.

6. Guarantors acknowledge that the Loan herein guaranteed may be assigned or transferred (in whole or in part), or made subject to a participation agreement with other lenders or persons. Guarantors agree that the rights and benefits hereof shall be fully exercisable by Lender's assignees, transferees, or participants in such loans or indebtedness, or any portion thereof, and that no assignment, transfer, or participation shall invalidate or diminish Guarantors' duties and obligations hereunder.

7. Guarantors agree to pay reasonable attorneys' fees (including attorneys' fees on appeal) and all other costs and expenses which may be incurred by Lender in the enforcement of this Guaranty.

8. This Guaranty shall be interpreted, construed, and enforced according to the laws of the State of Columbiana.

IN WITNESS WHEREOF, the undersigned Guarantors have executed this Guaranty the day and year first above written.

/s/ Abelard R. Mendoza

Abelard R. Mendoza, Guarantor

/s/ Maria S. Mendoza

Maria S. Mendoza, Guarantor

ASSETS REPOSSESSED AND SOLD BY CITIZENS FIRST BANK

The following assets were owned by Abelard R. Mendoza and used by him in his unincorporated construction business known as Mendoza Construction. They were all pledged to Citizens First Bank (CFB) to secure repayment of a June 15, YR-4 promissory note that has been in default for some time. Four months ago these assets were repossessed and sold by CFB for a total of $60,000 to a single buyer. The proceeds of sale were applied to the expenses of repossession and sale and to the balance owing on the note. Today, there is a remaining balance of $54,000 on that note which is now unsecured.

> Office furniture (desk, four chairs, two lamp stands & two lamps)
> Office equipment (computer, printer, fax, copier & scanner)
> Office supplies
> Hand tools and tool boxes
> Power tools and accessories
> Scaffolding
> Ropes, cables, winches, cords
> YR-8 GMC Cargo/Dump truck
> YR-4 Ford F-450 Crane Truck
> Miscellaneous equipment & supplies

ASSIGNMENT MEMORANDUM #2

TO: Associate attorney
FROM: Supervising attorney
DATE: Today, YR00
RE: Client: Automotive Financing, Inc. (Abelard R. Mendoza Chapter 7
           bankruptcy)

We represent Automotive Financing, Inc. (AFI), located at 239 Main St. in Capitol City. On September 1, YR-2, Mr. Abelard R. Mendoza purchased a new YR-2 Cadillac Deville from Rogers Cadillac on Highway 11 Bypass. AFI financed the purchase. The original loan amount was $30,000 and the current balance is $25,000. The book value on the vehicle is $23,000. The promissory note and security agreement that Abelard signed is dated September 1, YR-2 and our lien is properly noted on the title to the vehicle.

One week ago today Mr. Mendoza filed a Chapter 7 bankruptcy case. His notice of intent suggests he does not plan to redeem the vehicle or seek a reaffirmation agreement with AFI. I spoke with his lawyer who advised that Mr. Mendoza is willing to surrender the vehicle to us.

I would like you to prepare a motion to lift stay on the vehicle on behalf of AFI per §362(d) of the Code and FRBP 4001 on the grounds debtor has no equity in it and it is not needed for any reorganization. We could wait 45 days after the first meeting of creditors when the stay will automatically expire, pursuant to §521(a)(6), but I don't want to wait that long to regain possession of the car. AFI has a buyer arranged who will pay the full book value for it.

Please prepare the following for my review and signature:

1. A motion to lift stay.
2. The required notice of motion using Official Form 20A or the appropriate form mandated by our local rules or customary practice.
3. A certificate of service showing service of the motion and notice of motion electronically on the bankruptcy trustee, the U.S. Trustee, and the attorney for debtor.
4. A proof of claim for the unsecured balance of $2,000 Mr. Mendoza will owe AFI.

A copy of the note and title to the pledged vehicle are attached.

PROMISSORY NOTE AND SECURITY AGREEMENT

September 1, YR-2   At Capitol City, Columbiana

1. MAKER'S PROMISE TO PAY: In return for a loan in the principal amount of thirty thousand dollars ($30,000) that I, Abelard R. Mendoza of 8865 Shady Lane, Capitol City, Columbiana (hereinafter the "Maker"), have received from Automotive Financing, Inc., of 239 Main St., Capitol City, Columbiana (hereinafter the "Lender"), the Maker does hereby promise to repay to Lender the principal amount of $30,000 plus interest as set forth in <u>Paragraph 2</u>.

2. INTEREST: Interest will be charged on unpaid principal until the principal amount has been paid in full. Maker will pay interest on unpaid principal at the rate of 8.00 % per year from the date of the making of this Promissory Note and Security Agreement until the date the principal is paid in full. Interest hereunder shall be computed on the basis of a three hundred and sixty (360) day year. Notwithstanding anything herein to the contrary, in no event shall interest payable hereunder be in excess of the maximum rate allowed by applicable law.

3. TERM AND PAYMENT: Maker will repay the principal amount to Lender with interest as provided in <u>Paragraph 2</u> by making sixty (60) consecutive monthly payments of $608.29 each beginning October 1, YR-2 and continuing on the first day of each month thereafter until completed. Payment shall be made at 239 Main St., Capitol City, Columbiana, or at such other place as the Lender or its successor(s) or assign(s) shall stipulate.

4. RIGHT OF ASSIGNMENT: Lender has the express right to assign or sell this Promissory Note and Security Agreement in which case the assignee or buyer, as Holder, shall have all the rights of Lender under this Promissory Note and Security Agreement including this right of assignment. Maker is prohibited from transferring this Promissory Note and Security Agreement or any obligations under it without the prior written consent of Lender or its successor(s) or assign(s).

5. DEFAULT: If Lender fails to receive payment from Maker of any monthly payments called for in <u>Paragraph 3</u> by the tenth day of any month in which a payment is due, or if default is made in the payment of the indebtedness hereunder at maturity, or in the event of default in or breach of any of the terms, provisions or conditions of this Promissory Note and Security Agreement or any instrument evidencing or securing the indebtedness evidenced hereby, or any other instrument evidencing indebtedness from Maker to Lender, Maker will then be in DEFAULT. In that event, at the option of the Lender, the entire amount of the indebtedness will become immediately due and payable. Further in that event, the whole of the unpaid principal and any accrued interest shall, to the extent permitted by law, bear interest at the highest lawful rate then in effect pursuant to applicable law, or at the rate provided herein in the event no highest applicable rate is then in effect. Furthermore in that event, Lender shall be entitled to

pursue all remedies available to it at law and/or equity to collect all amounts due under this Promissory Note and Security Agreement and Maker shall pay all costs and expenses of collection, including court costs and a reasonable attorneys' fee, incurred by or on behalf of Lender in collecting the amounts due under this Promissory Note and Security Agreement to the extent not prohibited by applicable law. Lender's failure to declare a default due to Maker's failure to make any monthly payment as called for in this Promissory Note and Security Agreement shall not waive or otherwise prejudice Lender's right to declare a default in connection with Maker's failure to make any other monthly payment as called for in this Promissory Note and Security Agreement.

6. SECURITY AGREEMENT: All amounts due from Maker under the terms of this Promissory Note and Security Agreement and all extensions, modifications, renewals, or amendments thereof are secured by a lien on a YR-2 Cadillac Deville automobile, VIN # 2009L87H87 (the Vehicle). Maker hereby conveys to Lender a security interest in the Vehicle and grants to Lender all rights and remedies provided to a secured party under Article 9 of the Uniform Commercial Code as it is presently adopted and interpreted in the state of Columbiana or as it shall be amended and interpreted in the future including, without limitation, the right to self-help repossession of the Vehicle upon default by Maker. Maker consents to the notation of Lender's lien in the Vehicle on the title to the Vehicle. Maker further consents to Lender's possession of the title to the Vehicle until all amounts owed by Maker to Lender under the terms of the Promissory Note and Security Agreement shall be paid by Maker to Lender.

7. RIGHT TO PREPAY: Maker has the right to make payments on the Promissory Note and Security Agreement before the due date as determined in <u>Paragraph 3</u> without premium or other prepayment charge. All prepayments will be applied first to principal until the principal amount is paid in full.

8. WAIVERS: Maker expressly waives the right of presentment and notice of dishonor, and notice of nonpayment, protest, notice of protest, bringing of suit, and diligence in taking any action to claim the amounts owing hereunder and is and shall be directly and primarily liable for the amount of all sums owing and to be owing under the terms of this Promissory Note and Security Agreement and agrees that this Promissory Note and Security Agreement, or any payment hereunder, may be extended from time to time without affecting such liability. "Presentment" means the right to require the Lender or its successor(s) or assign(s) to demand payment of amounts due. "Notice of dishonor" means the right to require Lender or its successor(s) or assign(s) to give notice to other persons that amounts due have not been paid.

9. NATURE OF REMEDIES: The remedies of the Lender as provided in this Promissory Note and Security Agreement, or in any other instrument evidencing or securing this obligation, shall be cumulative and concurrent, and may be pursued singularly, successively or together, at the sole discretion of the Lender, and may

be exercised as often as occasion therefor shall arise. No act or omission of the Lender, including specifically any failure to exercise any right, remedy, or recourse, shall be deemed to be a waiver or release of the same, such waiver or release to be effected only through a written document executed by the Lender and then only to the extent specifically recited therein. A waiver or release with reference to any one event shall not be construed as continuing, as a bar to, or as a waiver or release of, any subsequent right, remedy or recourse as to a subsequent event.

10. TIME OF THE ESSENCE: Time is of the essence of this Promissory Note and Security Agreement.

11. GOVERNING LAW: This Promissory Note and Security Agreement shall be governed by and construed under the laws of the State of Columbiana.

12. CONSTRUCTION OF TERMS: Where used herein the singular shall refer to the plural, the plural to the singular, and the masculine or feminine shall refer to any gender. If Maker is composed of more than one person or entity, "Maker" as used herein shall refer to any and all persons or entities constituting Maker, as the circumstances may require.

13. TERMS BINDING ON SUCCESSORS: The provisions of this Promissory Note and Security Agreement shall be binding upon the parties, their heirs, successors and assigns.

14. SEVERABILITY OF TERMS: The provisions of this Promissory Note and Security Agreement are severable such that the invalidity or unenforceability of any provision hereof shall not affect the validity or enforceability of the remaining provisions.

WITNESS MY HAND ON THE DATE ABOVE WRITTEN:

/s/ Abelard R. Mendoza
Abelard R. Mendoza (Maker)

Accepted by Automotive Financing, Inc.
this September 1, YR-2.

/s/ James W. Farmington
James W. Farmington, Vice-President
Automotive Financing, Inc.

STATE OF COLUMBIANA
CERTIFICATE OF TITLE

Vehicle Identification Number	Year	Make	Model	Body Type	Title Number
2009L87H87222X	YR-02	Cadillac	Deville	4D	097789765X

New/Used/Demo	PreviousTitle No.	Prev. State	Sale or Use Tax	County	Odometer
X	N/A	N/A	$133.50	CC	00034

Date Title Issued: 9-01-YR-2
Date Vehicle Acquired: 9-01-YR-2
Owner: Abelard R. Mendoza
        8865 Shady Lane
        Capitol City, CM 55512

SATISFACTORY PROOF OF OWNERSHIP HAVING BEEN SUBMITTED UNDER COLUMBIANA CODE §55-3-101, TITLE TO THE MOTOR VEHICLE DESCRIBED ABOVE IS VESTED IN THE OWNER'S NAME HEREIN SUBJECT TO ANY LIEN NOTED BELOW. THIS OFFICIAL CERTIFICATE OF TITLE IS ISSUED FOR SAID VEHICLE.

NOTATION OF LIEN

The vehicle described above is subject to a lien in favor of Automotive Financing, Inc. ("lienholder"), of 239 Main Street, Capitol City, Columbiana as of the 1st day of July, YR-2 to satisfy an indebtedness in the amount of $30,000. Columbiana Statutory Code §55-3-104 provides that upon satisfaction of a lien, the lienholder will within seventy-two (72) hours complete the space provided on this certificate for satisfaction of lien, detach and mail the certificate with completed satisfaction of lien to the Columbiana Department of Safety, Title and Registration Division, 44 Capitol Plaza, Suite 111, Columbiana, CM 55589.

SATISFACTION AND RELEASE OF LIEN

Lienholder, _____, pursuant to Columbiana Statutory Code §55-3-104, hereby gives notice of the satisfaction in full of the indebtedness for which a lien was granted on the vehicle described above. Lienholder hereby releases said lien effective the __ day of _____, YR__.

_____
Lienholder

ASSIGNMENT MEMORANDUM #3

TO: Associate attorney
FROM: Jacob W. Braham, bankruptcy trustee
DATE: Today, YR00
RE: Abelard R. Mendoza Chapter 7 bankruptcy

As you know, I have been appointed the bankruptcy trustee in the Chapter 7 bankruptcy case of Abelard R. Mendoza. It appears from Mr. Mendoza's Statement of Affairs and his testimony at the first meeting of creditors that he intends to surrender his YR-2 Cadillac Seville automobile, VIN # 2009L87H87, to Automotive Financing, Inc., the creditor to which the vehicle is pledged.

I have examined the Promissory Note and Security Agreement dated September 1, YR-2 whereby Mendoza borrowed the money from AFI and pledged the car as collateral. And I have examined the title to the car on which the lien in favor of AFI is properly noted. It appears AFI's security interest in the vehicle is properly perfected and I have no basis on which to try to avoid it.

Mr. Mendoza owes AFI $25,000 on the note secured by the vehicle and it is only worth $23,000. Thus there is no equity in the vehicle for the estate. I have decided to abandon the vehicle pursuant to §554 of the Code and Bankruptcy Rule 6007 on the grounds that it is of inconsequential value to the estate.

I am advised by the attorney for AFI that it plans to file a motion to lift the automatic stay on the vehicle so it can legally repossess it. I will not oppose that motion. I would like you to prepare the following documents for my review and signature as trustee:

1. A notice of intent to abandon property specifying the vehicle as the property to be abandoned.

2. The required notice to parties in interest using Official Form 20A or the appropriate form mandated by our local rules or customary practice. Since what we are filing is not a motion or an objection, title your notice as "notice of proposed abandonment."

3. A certificate of service showing service of the notice of intent to abandon and notice of proposed abandonment electronically on the U.S. Trustee and the attorney for the debtor.

4. An agreed order granting AFI's motion to lift stay on the vehicle suitable for signature and entry by the bankruptcy judge.

ASSIGNMENT MEMORANDUM #4

TO: Associate attorney
FROM: Jacob W. Braham, bankruptcy trustee
DATE: Today, YR00
RE: Abelard R. Mendoza Chapter 7 bankruptcy

As you know, I have been appointed the bankruptcy trustee in the Chapter 7 bankruptcy case of Abelard R. Mendoza. It appears from Mr. Mendoza's Statement of Affairs and his testimony at the first meeting of creditors that Mendoza co-signed a promissory note dated July 10, YR-6, in favor of Columbiana Federal Savings & Loan (CFSL), a federally chartered savings and Loan having six branch locations throughout the state. The note was also signed by his late wife Maria (deceased on August 1, YR-2) and his 28-year-old son, David Mendoza. The CFSL loan was an educational loan to enable David to attend college.

CFSL declared the note to be in default a little over a year ago and demand was made on Mr. Mendoza as co-signer to pay. Two months before filing his bankruptcy petition, Mr. Mendoza cashed out a $50,000 certificate of deposit he had at All State Bank & Trust and paid the balance then owing to CFSL on the past due note ($45,450) in full.

Even though Mr. Mendoza can probably not discharge this debt since it was an educational loan for his son, I believe this was a preferential transfer under §547(b) of the Code. One month ago today I made written demand on CFSL to repay the $45,450 but it has refused to do so.

I want you to prepare a complaint for filing in the Mendoza bankruptcy case to avoid Mendoza's transfer to CFSL three months ago today as a preferential transfer under §547(b). As you know, this will be an adversary proceeding pursuant to FRBP 7001(1) and will be governed by the rules in Part VII of the FRBP.

Copies of the July 10, YR-6 promissory note, the January 10, YR-2 certificate of deposit from which Mendoza obtained the funds to pay CFSL, and my demand letter to CFSL are attached.

<u>PROMISSORY NOTE</u>

July 10, YR-6   At Capitol City, Columbiana

1. MAKERS' PROMISE TO PAY: In consideration for a loan in the principal amount of thirty-five thousand dollars ($35,000) that David W. Mendoza has received for educational purposes from Columbiana Federal Savings & Loan of 6655 West Broadway, Capitol City, Columbiana (hereinafter the "Lender"), we, David W. Mendoza, Abelard R. Mendoza and wife, Maria S. Mendoza, all of 8865 Shady Lane, Capitol City, Columbiana, (hereinafter the "Makers"), do hereby promise to repay to Lender the principal amount of $35,000 plus interest as set forth in <u>Paragraph 2</u>.

2. INTEREST: Interest will be charged on unpaid principal until the principal amount has been paid in full. Interest hereunder shall be computed on the basis of a three hundred and sixty (360) day year. Notwithstanding anything herein to the contrary, in no event shall interest payable hereunder be in excess of the maximum rate allowed by applicable law.

3. TERM AND PAYMENT: Makers will repay the principal amount to Lender with interest as provided in <u>Paragraph 2</u> in lump sum on July 10, YR-1. Payment shall be made at 111 Highway 11 Bypass, Capitol City, Columbiana or at such other place as the Lender or its successor(s) or assign(s) shall stipulate.

4. RIGHT OF ASSIGNMENT: Lender has the express right to assign or sell this Promissory Note, in which case the assignee or buyer, as Holder, shall have all the rights of Lender under this Promissory Note including this right of assignment. Makers are prohibited from transferring this Promissory Note or any obligations under it without the prior written consent of Lender or its successor(s) or assign(s).

5. DEFAULT: If Lender fails to receive payment from Makers as called for in <u>Paragraph 3</u> or in the event of default in or breach of any of the terms, provisions, or conditions of this Promissory Note, Makers will then be in DEFAULT. In that event, at the option of the Lender, the entire amount of the indebtedness will become immediately due and payable. Further in that event, the whole of the unpaid principal and any accrued interest shall, to the extent permitted by law, bear interest at the highest lawful rate then in effect pursuant to applicable law, or at the rate provided herein in the event no highest applicable rate is then in effect. Furthermore in that event, Lender shall be entitled to pursue all remedies available to it at law and/or equity to collect all amounts due under this Promissory Note and Makers shall pay all costs and expenses of collection, including court costs and a reasonable attorneys' fee, incurred by or on behalf of Lender in collecting the amounts due under this Promissory Note to the extent not prohibited

by applicable law. Lender's failure to declare a default due to Makers' failure to pay as promised on any given occasion shall not waive or otherwise prejudice Lender's right to otherwise declare a default in connection with Makers' failure to perform any other obligation arising under this Promissory Note.

6. WAIVERS: Makers expressly waive the right of presentment and notice of dishonor, and notice of nonpayment, protest, notice of protest, bringing of suit, and diligence in taking any action to claim the amounts owing hereunder and is and shall be directly and primarily liable for the amount of all sums owing and to be owing under the terms of this Promissory Note and agrees that this Promissory Note, or any payment hereunder, may be extended from time to time without affecting such liability. "Presentment" means the right to require the Lender or its successor(s) or assign(s) to demand payment of amounts due. "Notice of dishonor" means the right to require Lender or its successor(s) or assign(s) to give notice to other persons that amounts due have not been paid.

7. JOINT AND SEVERAL LIABILITY: Makers' liability under this Promissory Note shall be joint and several.

8. NATURE OF REMEDIES: The remedies of the Lender as provided in this Promissory Note or in any other instrument evidencing this obligation, shall be cumulative and concurrent, and may be pursued singularly, successively or together, at the sole discretion of the Lender, and may be exercised as often as occasion therefor shall arise. No act or omission of the Lender, including specifically any failure to exercise any right, remedy, or recourse, shall be deemed to be a waiver or release of the same, such waiver or release to be effected only through a written document executed by the Lender and then only to the extent specifically recited therein. A waiver or release with reference to any one event shall not be construed as continuing, as a bar to, or as a waiver or release of, any subsequent right, remedy, or recourse as to a subsequent event.

9. TIME OF THE ESSENCE: Time is of the essence of this Promissory Note.

10. GOVERNING LAW: This Promissory Note shall be governed by and construed under the laws of the State of Columbiana.

11. CONSTRUCTION OF TERMS: Where used herein the singular shall refer to the plural, the plural to the singular, and the masculine or feminine shall refer to any gender. If Makers are composed of more than one person or entity, "Makers" as used herein shall refer to any and all persons or entities constituting Makers, as the circumstances may require.

12. TERMS BINDING ON SUCCESSORS: The provisions of this Promissory Note shall be binding upon the parties, their heirs, successors and assigns.

13. SEVERABILITY OF TERMS: The provisions of this Promissory Note are severable such that the invalidity or unenforceability of any provision hereof shall not affect the validity or enforceability of the remaining provisions.

WITNESS OUR HANDS ON THE DATE ABOVE WRITTEN:

/s/ David W. Mendoza
David W. Mendoza (Maker)

/s/ Abelard R. Mendoza
Abelard R. Mendoza (Maker)

/s/ Maria S. Mendoza
Maria S. Mendoza (Maker)

CERTIFICATE OF DEPOSIT

Date of Purchase: January 10, YR-2

Term: 60 months

Tax ID: 999-18-7765

Amount: Fifty Thousand Dollars ($50,000)

Certificate #: 67599087

THIS CERTIFICATE IS ISSUED TO: **THIS CERTIFICATE IS ISSUED BY:**

Abelard R. Mendoza   All State Bank & Trust
8865 Shady Lane   1942 West Broadway
Capitol City, Columbiana   Capitol City, Columbiana

Maturity Date: January 10, YR+3

Rate Information: The interest rate for this certificate is 5.00% with an annual percentage yield of 5.13%. This rate will be paid until maturity date specified above. Interest begins to accrue on the day of purchase. Interest will compound daily and will be credited quarterly.

Early Withdrawal Terms and Penalty: The amount deposited to purchase this certificate can only be withdrawn with the consent of the issuer. If the certificate is presented for early withdrawal and the issuer consents to the early withdrawal, the issuer will impose a penalty for early withdrawal in an amount equal to 91 days of interest earned or that could have been earned.

Account Ownership: The purchaser has requested and intends the certificate to be issued as follows:

_X_ Individual   ___ Joint Account—With Survivorship
___ Joint Account—No survivorship   ___ Trust: Separate Agreement Dated____

PURCHASER ISSUER

/s/ Abelard R. Mendoza_____   All State Bank & Trust
Abelard R. Mendoza   By: /s/ Alicia L. Franklin_____
                                                 Alicia L. Franklin, V-P

Jacob W. Braham
Suite 200 Metro Building
Capitol City, Columbiana
Ph. (999) 555-2020

One month ago, YR00

Columbiana Federal Savings & Loan
6655 West Broadway
Capitol City, Columbiana

In re: <u>Abelard W. Mendoza (Promissory Note dated July 10, YR-6)</u>

Dear Sirs:

I am the duly appointed bankruptcy trustee in the Chapter 7 bankruptcy case of Abelard R. Mendoza pending in the United States Bankruptcy Court for the Middle District of Columbiana. The petition initiating Mr. Mendoza's Chapter 7 case was filed six weeks ago today.

My information is that on July 10, YR-6 Mr. Mendoza co-signed a promissory note as maker in your favor in the principal amount of $35,000. Two months before filing his Chapter 7 petition Mr. Mendoza paid the July 10, YR-6 promissory note off in full by transferring to you the sum of $45,450. Since the indebtedness owed to you by Mr. Mendoza was a pre-existing obligation at the time he made payment, and since Mr. Mendoza was insolvent at the time he made the transfer to you, and since the transfer to you was made within 90 days preceding the filing of his bankruptcy petition, the transfer to you of $45,450 by Mr. Mendoza constitutes a preferential transfer under Section 547 of the Bankruptcy Code. As bankruptcy trustee, I am empowered to set aside that preferential transfer and to recover the transferred funds from you for the benefit of the bankrupt estate.

Demand is hereby made for you to pay to me as bankruptcy trustee the sum of $45,450 representing the preferential transfer. If I have not received that payment from you within 30 days of the date of this letter I will institute an adversarial proceeding against you in Mr. Mendoza's Chapter 7 case and will seek to recover costs of that action from you in addition to the amount of the preferential transfer.

Please feel free to have your attorney contact me if you have any questions at all. I look forward to receiving the payment requested.

Sincerely yours,
/s/
Jacob W. Braham, Trustee

cc: U.S. Trustee
    Debtor's attorney

<u>ASSIGNMENT MEMORANDUM #5</u>

TO: Associate attorney
FROM: Supervising attorney
DATE: Today, YR00
RE: Abelard R. Mendoza (Chapter 7 bankruptcy)

As you know, we represent Abelard R. Mendoza in his Chapter 7 bankruptcy case pending in the U.S. Bankruptcy Court for the Middle District of Columbiana. At the time he filed his Chapter 7 petition Mr. Mendoza was the owner of a YR-3 Dodge Ram 1500 Truck having a value of $19,000. The truck was pledged as collateral to secure a promissory note Mr. Mendoza executed on January 10, YR-1 in favor of Friendly Finance Company (FFC), in the original amount of $20,000, which had a balance of $15,000 owing as of the date the petition was filed. Mr. Mendoza has been successful in claiming the $4,000 of equity in the truck as exempt and he wants to reaffirm his obligation to FFC so he can retain possession of the truck following his discharge.

Please prepare a reaffirmation agreement between Mr. Mendoza and FFC using Official Form 240A. The agreement should recite that he will reaffirm the indebtedness to FFC totaling $15,000 arising from the January 10, YR-1, Promissory Note and Security Agreement, a copy of which is attached to this memorandum. All the terms of the debt, as reaffirmed, including interest rate, will remain the same as set out in the Promissory Note and Security Agreement. He will continue to make the monthly payments of $410.33 to FFC on the truck. There are 44 monthly payments remaining. The first of the 44 payments will be made the first day of the month following Mr. Mendoza's discharge.

Following his discharge, Mr. Mendoza will no longer have the house payment of $4,000 to Security Trust Bank or the car payment of $608 to Automotive Financing, Inc. He will have discharged the $54,000 unsecured balance to Citizens First Bank and the $350,000 note to City County Bank. He will have discharged his credit card debt of $23,500. He will not be able to discharge the tax obligations he owes to the IRS totaling $64,000 or maybe not his liability on the educational loans from Columbiana Federal Savings & Loan and City County Bank totaling $60,650 unless we can show undue hardship. Mr. Mendoza is going to apply all of the equity that he is able to exempt from his home to those balances. And he is going to withdraw his IRA funds as soon as he turns 59½ (to avoid penalties for early withdrawal), and apply the IRA funds to those balances as well. Those three creditors have agreed to then accept monthly payments from Mr. Mendoza for a ten-year period to pay those obligations, together with interest accruing on them, in full. His payments should run no more than $1,000 a month for that.

Mr. Mendoza is going to lease an apartment to live in that will cost him $500 per month. We estimate that his monthly expenses, including the rent payments and $1,000 per month payments on the non-dischargeable debts, will total $2,500 per month. With his after-tax income of $3,125 per month from Chavis Construction Company, Mr. Mendoza should be able to afford the $410.33 monthly payment to Friendly Finance Company on the YR-3 Dodge truck without triggering the presumption of undue hardship in connection with the reaffirmation agreement. As you know you will need this information regarding his post-discharge income and expenses to complete Part D of the Reaffirmation Agreement form (Official Form 240A).

PROMISSORY NOTE AND SECURITY AGREEMENT

January 10, YR-1   At Capitol City, Columbiana

1. MAKER'S PROMISE TO PAY: In return for a loan in the principal amount of twenty thousand dollars ($20,000) that I, Abelard R. Mendoza of 8865 Shady Lane, Capitol City, Columbiana (hereinafter the "Maker"), have received from Friendly Finance Company, of 2209 West Broadway, Capitol City, Columbiana, (hereinafter the "Lender"), the Maker does hereby promise to repay to Lender the principal amount of $20,000 plus interest as set forth in Paragraph 2.

2. INTEREST: Interest will be charged on unpaid principal until the principal amount has been paid in full. Maker will pay interest on unpaid principal at the rate of 8.50 % per year from the date of the making of this Promissory Note and Security Agreement until the date the principal is paid in full. Interest hereunder shall be computed on the basis of a three hundred and sixty (360) day year. Notwithstanding anything herein to the contrary, in no event shall interest payable hereunder be in excess of the maximum rate allowed by applicable law.

3. TERM AND PAYMENT: Maker will repay the principal amount to Lender with interest as provided in Paragraph 2 by making sixty (60) consecutive monthly payments of $410.33 each beginning February 1, YR-1, and continuing on the first day of each month thereafter until completed. Payment shall be made at 2209 West Broadway, Capitol City, Columbiana, or at such other place as the Lender or its successor(s) or assign(s) shall stipulate.

4. RIGHT OF ASSIGNMENT: Lender has the express right to assign or sell this Promissory Note and Security Agreement, in which case the assignee or buyer, as Holder, shall have all the rights of Lender under this Promissory Note and Security Agreement including this right of assignment. Maker is prohibited from transferring this Promissory Note and Security Agreement or any obligations under it without the prior written consent of Lender or its successor(s) or assign(s).

5. DEFAULT: If Lender fails to receive payment from Maker of any monthly payments called for in Paragraph 3 by the tenth day of any month in which a payment is due, or if default is made in the payment of the indebtedness hereunder at maturity, or in the event of default in or breach of any of the terms, provisions or conditions of this Promissory Note and Security Agreement or any instrument evidencing or securing the indebtedness evidenced hereby, or any other instrument evidencing indebtedness from Maker to Lender, Maker will then be in DEFAULT. In that event, at the option of the Lender, the entire amount of the indebtedness will become immediately due and payable. Further in that event, the whole of the unpaid principal and any accrued interest shall, to the extent permitted by law, bear interest at the highest lawful rate then in effect pursuant to applicable law, or at the rate provided herein in the event no highest applicable rate is then in effect. Furthermore in that event, Lender shall be entitled to

pursue all remedies available to it at law and/or equity to collect all amounts due under this Promissory Note and Security Agreement and Maker shall pay all costs and expenses of collection, including court costs and a reasonable attorneys' fee, incurred by or on behalf of Lender in collecting the amounts due under this Promissory Note and Security Agreement to the extent not prohibited by applicable law. Lender's failure to declare a default due to Maker's failure to make any monthly payment as called for in this Promissory Note and Security Agreement shall not waive or otherwise prejudice Lender's right to declare a default in connection with Maker's failure to make any other monthly payment as called for in this Promissory Note and Security Agreement.

6. SECURITY AGREEMENT: All amounts due from Maker under the terms of this Promissory Note and Security Agreement and all extensions, modifications, renewals, or amendments thereof are secured by a lien on a YR-3 Dodge Ram 1500 Truck, VIN # 4478112LM0998 (the Vehicle). Maker hereby conveys to Lender a security interest in the Vehicle and grants to Lender all rights and remedies provided to a secured party under Article 9 of the Uniform Commercial Code as it is presently adopted and interpreted in the state of Columbiana or as it shall be amended and interpreted in the future including, without limitation, the right to self-help repossession of the Vehicle upon default by Maker. Maker consents to the notation of Lender's lien in the Vehicle on the title to the Vehicle. Maker further consents to Lender's possession of the title to the Vehicle until all amounts owed by Maker to Lender under the terms of the Promissory Note and Security Agreement shall be paid by Maker to Lender.

7. RIGHT TO PREPAY: Maker has the right to make payments on the Promissory Note and Security Agreement before the due date as determined in Paragraph 3 without premium or other prepayment charge. All prepayments will be applied first to principal until the principal amount is paid in full.

8. WAIVERS: Maker expressly waives the right of presentment and notice of dishonor, and notice of nonpayment, protest, notice of protest, bringing of suit, and diligence in taking any action to claim the amounts owing hereunder and is and shall be directly and primarily liable for the amount of all sums owing and to be owing under the terms of this Promissory Note and Security Agreement and agrees that this Promissory Note and Security Agreement, or any payment hereunder, may be extended from time to time without affecting such liability. "Presentment" means the right to require the Lender or its successor(s) or assign(s) to demand payment of amounts due. "Notice of dishonor" means the right to require Lender or its successor(s) or assign(s) to give notice to other persons that amounts due have not been paid.

9. NATURE OF REMEDIES: The remedies of the Lender as provided in this Promissory Note and Security Agreement, or in any other instrument evidencing or securing this obligation, shall be cumulative and concurrent, and may be pursued singularly, successively or together, at the sole discretion of the Lender, and

may be exercised as often as occasion therefor shall arise. No act or omission of the Lender, including specifically any failure to exercise any right, remedy, or recourse, shall be deemed to be a waiver or release of the same, such waiver or release to be effected only through a written document executed by the Lender and then only to the extent specifically recited therein. A waiver or release with reference to any one event shall not be construed as continuing, as a bar to, or as a waiver or release of, any subsequent right, remedy or recourse as to a subsequent event.

10. TIME OF THE ESSENCE: Time is of the essence of this Promissory Note and Security Agreement.

11. GOVERNING LAW: This Promissory Note and Security Agreement shall be governed by and construed under the laws of the State of Columbiana.

12. CONSTRUCTION OF TERMS: Where used herein the singular shall refer to the plural, the plural to the singular, and the masculine or feminine shall refer to any gender. If Maker is composed of more than one person or entity, "Maker" as used herein shall refer to any and all persons or entities constituting Maker, as the circumstances may require.

13. TERMS BINDING ON SUCCESSORS: The provisions of this Promissory Note and Security Agreement shall be binding upon the parties, their heirs, successors, and assigns.

14. SEVERABILITY OF TERMS: The provisions of this Promissory Note and Security Agreement are severable such that the invalidity or unenforceability of any provision hereof shall not affect the validity or enforceability of the remaining provisions.

WITNESS MY HAND ON THE DATE ABOVE WRITTEN:

/s/Abelard R. Mendoza\
Abelard R. Mendoza (Maker)

Accepted by Friendly Finance Company
this January 10, YR-1

/s/Leslie L. Moyers\
Leslie L. Moyers, Vice-President\
Friendly Finance Company

In re Nicholas W. and Pearl E. Murphy Chapter 13 Bankruptcy [Active File]

[The names, locations, and circumstances of debtors, creditors, and all other persons or entities described in this case study are a product of the author's imagination, are fictitious, and any resemblance to actual persons living or dead or to any entity is entirely coincidental.]

Instructions: All references to the fictional state of Columbiana in these assignments should be understood to be to the state where you plan to practice or to the state where you are studying law or to whatever other actual state your instructor directs. All references to the fictional city of Capitol City should be understood to be to a real city or town in the actual state that you choose to use in completing these assignments. YR00 is the current year. YR-1 is last year, YR-2 is two years ago, YR+2 is two years from now, etc.

ASSIGNMENT MEMORANDUM #1

TO: Associate attorney
FROM: Supervising attorney
DATE: Today, YR00
RE: Nicholas W. and Pearl E. Murphy (Chapter 13 bankruptcy)

Nick and Pearl Murphy are a married couple residing in Capitol City. They have been married for 12 years and have two children, Lynette, who is 9, and Lyndon, who is 11. By an earlier marriage, Nick has a third child, Robbie, who is 15. Nick is obligated by court order to pay his ex-wife, Sharon Murphy, $400 per month as child support for Robbie until the boy turns 18.

Nick himself is 40 years old (DOB 12-30-YR-40) and Pearl is 39 (DOB 12-31-YR-39). Nick, who dropped out of high school and later earned his GED, has a degree from State Technical School and has worked as an assistant manager of the local office of Overland Truck Services, Inc., for the past five years.

Effective the first of this year he became manager and his income increased to $60,000 a year. Pearl has a bachelor's degree from State University in elementary education and worked as a teacher for the Capitol City public school system, full-time, until August 1, YR-3, when she underwent an emergency appendectomy and suffered complications leaving her with chronic stomach and bowel problems. Pearl was unable to work full-time for more than a year following the surgery. She was able to work some last year as a substitute teacher and returned to work full-time in January of this year.

Nick and Pearl own their home, which they purchased ten years ago for $125,000. First Bank of Capitol City holds the mortgage on the Murphys' home, which has a current balance of $92,500 on what was originally a 30-year note. The Murphys make a monthly mortgage payment of $993 to First Bank.

Less than two months before Pearl's emergency appendectomy, the Murphys took out a home improvement loan from the Teachers Credit Union in Capitol City in the amount of $35,000 to add two new rooms to their house. The credit union took a second mortgage on the house to secure repayment of the loan. The construction had barely begun when Pearl had her surgery and was never finished. Most of the money borrowed from the credit union went to pay off expenses arising from Pearl's illness. The credit union loan is to be paid back over ten years at $406 per month. The Murphys are currently three payments in arrears (totaling $1,218) to the credit union and it is threatening foreclosure on their home.

The couple owns two vehicles. Nick drives a five-year-old Ford F-150 Truck (VIN #00981277HL9087S) that has 75,000 miles on it and is paid for. Pearl drives a five-year-old Honda Accord, which the Murphys bought used three years ago. They still owe $8,900 on the Honda and make monthly payments of $310 to Friendly Finance Company. There are 24 more monthly payments due. Friendly Finance holds a security interest in the car to secure payment of the obligation.

The Murphys have two credit cards, a Master Card with a maximum limit of $8,000 and a Visa with a limit of $5,000. The couple has maxed out both cards and pays only the minimum balance due on the cards each month. They also have an installment sales contract with Shears Department Store for the purchase of living room furniture on which there is a $4,592 balance owing and 36 months of payments remaining. Shears retains a security interest in the furniture to secure repayment of the debt.

The Murphys are in a financial crisis due to continuing medical expenses related to Pearl's condition and the loss of her full-time income. Pearl's insurance covered most of the expenses related to the original surgery but the costs related to the complications and continuing treatment and medications have far exceeded the insurance policy's coverage. At this point, Pearl's unpaid medical bills total $28,000 and her monthly medications cost $325 out of pocket. They used up all their savings while she was not working and now are too far behind to catch up.

The financial circumstances of the Murphys have become so severe that I have recommended they file a Chapter 13 bankruptcy case. I believe they have sufficient net disposable income to pay all of their debts over a five-year plan.

Pearl was sued last year by one medical supplier, Capitol City Medical Equipment Co. (CCME), which took a judgment by default against her only in the amount of $2,247.70 in the Circuit Court for Capitol County, Columbiana (Docket No. 00-97656). So far, CCME has taken no steps to execute on its judgment but that can be expected any time.

Pearl and Nick both were sued about the same time by Barnes & Patel Anesthesiologists, PC. (BPA) in the Circuit Court for Capitol County, Columbiana (Docket No. 00-97765), and a default judgment was entered against them jointly in favor of BPA in the amount of $2,000 on October 1, YR-1. (Unfortunately, Nick signed a contract agreeing to be jointly liable on all Pearl's obligations to BPA prior to one of her medical procedures.) Seven days ago the sheriff seized the YR-5 Ford Truck F-150 that Nick drives, pursuant to a writ of execution obtained by BPA on that judgment. The sheriff has not yet sold the truck.

The Murphys have received demand letters from two other health providers demanding immediate payment and threatening suit. We have attempted to negotiate with the credit card companies and health providers to avoid a bankruptcy filing but those negotiations have proved unsuccessful. The Murphys are current on their various monthly bills other than what I have mentioned.

The Murphys' two children, Lynette and Lyndon, both attend the school where their mother teaches and stay with her after school until it is time to come home. Consequently, the Murphys currently have no childcare expenses.

I would like you to draft the following documents for my review:

    Petition (with Exhibit D for each debtor)
    Schedules A-J
    Declaration re schedules
    Statement of affairs
    Statement of compensation paid or to be paid to debtor's attorney

Use the financial information provided in the attached summary of assets/liabilities and income/expenses. In preparing the petition, etc., be sure to comply with all the local rules of the bankruptcy court where we will be filing this case.

Claim as exempt all of the equity in the home if at all possible. Claim as much of the personal property as exempt as the applicable exemption laws allow. Nick Murphy is anxious to get his Ford truck back. If possible, claim it as exempt in the plan. At the same time we file the plan, we will file a motion under §522(f) of the Code to avoid the judicial liens that have been placed on it by BPA, as judgment creditor, and by the county sheriff, to the extent those liens impair the exemption we will claim in the truck.

The Murphys paid us $1,000 today to handle the Chapter 13, leaving the balance in their checking account that you see on the attached summary. The total fee will be $3,000 and the other $2,000 will be paid to us in equal installments over the first 10 months of the plan. They also completed their prepetition credit counseling course today at Prudent Person Credit Counseling Service here in Capitol City, at a cost of $50 each, which has already been deducted from their checking account balance. Mr. Murphy's Social Security number is 999-19-7765. Mrs. Murphy's is 999-20-5677.

[NOTE: The final judgment in favor of Pearl and Nick Murphy against Dr. Samuel M. Croft and Capitol City Hospital that is mentioned in the text to illustrate various concepts is assumed to not exist for purposes of this exercise.]

SUMMARY OF ASSETS AND LIABILITIES, CURRENT INCOME, AND EXPENSES FOR NICK AND PEARL MURPHY

Assets

Real property:

House and lot at 3521 West Cherry St., Capitol City, Columbiana
(purchased for $125,000 on Jan. 12, YR-10). $145,000

Personal property:

Cash on hand. $300
Checking account at Capitol Savings Bank. .1,000
YR-5 Ford Truck F-150 4,800
YR-5 Honda Accord. 7,800
Living room furniture subject to Shears security interest. 2,000
Other household goods & furnishings 4,000
Personal computers (2) and printer 1,500
Television, stereo, and DVD equipment. 1,200
Yard equipment & tools 500
Wearing apparel. 2,500
Jewelry. 500

Total assets: $171,200

Liabilities

Secured debt:

First Bank of Capitol City (30-year note dated Sep. 12,
YR-10, secured by mortgage of even date on West Cherry Street
residence) $92,500
Teacher's Credit Union (10-year note dated June 15, YR-3,
secured by mortgage of even date on West Cherry Street residence)
three-month arrearage ($1,218)
balance after arrearage cured ($26,880) 28,098
Friendly Finance Company (note dated September 1, YR-3,
secured by YR-5 Honda Accord). 8,900
Shears Department Store (note dated May 10, YR-1,
secured by living room furniture) 4,592
Barnes & Patel Anesthesiologists, PC (judicial lien created
7 days ago, YR00, on YR-5 Ford Truck F150
by execution on final judgment entered October 1, YR-1) 2,000

Capitol County Sheriff's Department (judicial lien created
  7 days ago, YR00, on YR-5 Ford Truck F150
  by execution on final judgment entered October 1, YR-1) 250

Unsecured debt:

Neapolitan Community Bank Visa card 5,306
Vulcan Bank Master Card 8,380
Community General Hospital. 25,550
Capitol City Medical Equipment Co (final judgment against Pearl
  only, entered September 20, YR-1) 2,247.70
Hastings & Poor Gastrointestinal Specialists. 2,490
City Anesthesiologists, PC (Pearl only) 2,890
Capitol City Drug Store (Pearl only) 1,402
Sharon Murphy (36 months of child support for Robbie)
  (Nick only) 14,440
Total liabilities: $189,045.70

Recurring monthly expenses to be dealt with in the plan:

First Bank of Capitol City $993.83
Teachers' Credit Union. 406.00
Friendly Finance Company. 310.00
Shears Department Store. 127.55
Sharon Murphy (child support). 400.00

Recurring monthly expenses to be paid out of funds retained by debtor:

Electricity & gas 400.00
Water & sewer 50.00
Phone service. 100.00
Food 400.00
Clothes 100.00
Laundry & dry cleaning. 50.00
Medical & dental. 400.00
Gas & transportation 200.00
Auto insurance 75.00
Recreation 100.00
Cable TV & Internet service (Flash Cable Co.) 75.00
Charitable giving (First Community Church). 100.00
Home maintenance & repair. 100.00
Miscellaneous. 200.00

Total recurring monthly expenses $4,587.38

<u>Income:</u>
Nick:

YR-2: Total income: $44,000 from Overland Truck Services, 111 Hwy 42 Bypass,
    Capitol City, Columbiana
YR-1: Total income: $47,000 from Overland Truck Services
Current income: $60,000 per year from Overland Truck Services
    Paid monthly as follows:
        Gross monthly salary: $5,000
        Minus payroll taxes, Social Security & Medicare: $1,221
        Child support: $400 (Withheld per Domestic Support Order dated
            September 15, YR-13 in Sharon Murphy v. Nicholas Murphy, No.
            FC-99867 in Family Court for Capitol County, Columbiana)

    Net monthly income for Nick: $3,379

Pearl:

YR-2: Total income: None
YR-1: Total income: $4,000 from Capitol City Public School System, 6544 Main St.
    Capitol City, Columbiana
Current income: $38,000 from Capitol City Public School System since January 1,
    YR00
    Gross monthly salary: $3,166
    Minus payroll taxes, Social Security & Medicare averages: $792
    Minus premium for group health insurance policy: $225

    Net monthly income for Pearl: $2,149

Total joint net monthly income: $5,528

ASSIGNMENT MEMORANDUM #2

TO: Associate attorney
FROM: Supervising attorney
DATE: Today, YR00
RE: Nicholas W. and Pearl E. Murphy (Chapter 13 bankruptcy)

As you know, we are preparing to file a Chapter13 case for our clients Nick and Pearl Murphy. Using the information supplied in Assignment Memorandum #1 and the schedules you have already prepared for them I now want you to draft their Form 22C-1 (Chapter 13 Statement of Your Current Monthly Income and Calculation of Commitment Period). If necessary, also draft their Form 22C-2 (Chapter 13 Calculation of Your Disposable Income).

ASSIGNMENT MEMORANDUM #3

TO: Associate attorney
FROM: Supervising attorney
DATE: Today, YR00
RE: Nicholas W. and Pearl E. Murphy (Chapter 13 bankruptcy)

As you know, we are planning to file a Chapter 13 case for Nick and Pearl Murphy. I would like to file our proposed Chapter 13 plan for them at the same time we file the petition. Please draft a Chapter 13 plan for the Murphys for my review. You should review Assignment Memorandum #1 and the summary of assets and liabilities, income, and expenses attached to it.

The Chapter 13 plan you draft should be a five-year plan and, hopefully, a 100 percent plan or something close to it. The plan should do the following:

1. Provide for the payment of the balance of our fee ($2,000) over the first 10 months of the plan in equal monthly installments of $200.

2. Cram down the debt to Friendly Finance Company secured by the YR-5 Honda Accord to its present value and call for payment of that amount in equal monthly installments over the 60 months of the plan together with interest at 8.5% per annum. Treat the balance as unsecured debt to be paid through the plan.

3. Cram down the debt to Shears Department Store secured by the living room furniture to its present value and call for the payment of that amount in equal monthly installments over the 60 months of the plan together with interest at 8.5% per annum. Treat the balance as unsecured debt to be paid through the plan.

4. The plan should call for the arrearage of $1,218 to Teachers' Credit Union to be cured by payments in equal monthly installments over the first 24 months of the plan together with interest at 8% per annum. Otherwise provide for paying the two mortgages on the home as scheduled through the plan. Of course since both mortgages call for scheduled payments beyond the five-year term of the plan the plan should indicate that the balance and mortgages owing at the end of the plan term will survive beyond the plan.

5. The plan should provide for the avoidance of the judicial liens of Barnes & Patel Anesthesiologists, PC, in the amount of $2,000, and of the Capitol County Sheriff in the amount of $250 in the YR-5 Ford truck, pursuant to §522(f), as impairing the exemption claimed by the Murphys in the entire $4,800 value of the truck. Both those judicial lien claims should then be treated as non-priority unsecured claims to be paid through the plan.

6. Nick Murphy currently has $400 per month withheld from his paycheck pursuant to a Domestic Support Order (DRO) to satisfy his child support obligation to

his ex-wife, Sharon Murphy. This obligation has 36 more months to run, at which time Nick and Sharon's son, Robbie, will turn 18. This obligation of Nick's should be treated as a priority claim under the plan but the plan should call for it to be paid outside the plan by continued withholding by his employer pursuant to the DRO. When that obligation is satisfied after 36 months, the plan should call for the $400 to then be paid into the plan if necessary to complete the obligations undertaken in the plan.

The Murphys have a combined net monthly income of $5,528 after deduction of taxes, health insurance, and the child support obligation of Nick. It appears they will need to keep $2,350 per month to pay their living expenses as budgeted (see "Recurring monthly expenses to be paid out of funds retained by debtor" in the summary of assets, liabilities, and expenses below). Therefore the plan should call for the balance of $3,178 per month to be paid into the plan. When wage orders are issued we will prorate that amount between Nick and Pearl's salaries.

In addition to the Chapter 13 plan, I would like you to draft a motion to avoid the two judicial liens in the Ford truck under §522(f) in that they impair the claimed exemption. I want to file that motion at the same time we file the petition and proposed plan. Be sure to draft the required notice of motion as well, using Official Form 20A or the appropriate form mandated by our local rules or customary practice. And prepare a certificate of service showing service of the motion and notice of motion electronically on the Chapter 13 trustee, the U.S. Trustee, and the two creditors involved.

ASSIGNMENT MEMORANDUM #4

TO: Associate attorney
FROM: Supervising attorney
DATE: Today, YR00
RE: Mid-State Grading Service, LLC (Lien on City Heights Condominium Project)

We represent Mid-State Grading Service, LLC. Mid-State is a limited liability company owned by Ronnie and Gladys Clark and located here in Capitol City at 1345 Industrial Drive. The Clarks are friends of Nick and Pearl Murphy who recommended us to the Clarks. Four months ago today, Mid-State was awarded a contract to provide earth moving and site preparation services for the City Heights Condominium Project here in Capitol City. Mid-State began work on the project 90 days ago and completed its work 45 days ago.

The bid called for total payments to Mid-State of $100,000 to be paid in two installments, one 30 days after work commenced and the second upon completion of the work. Payment of both installments was to be made within 15 days of the invoice for that installment. Mid-State's first invoice for $50,000 was sent promptly after the first 30 days of work and was paid in full. However, its second invoice, sent 45 days ago, has not been paid and is now 30 days past due. Although Mid-State has completed its work at the site, it has heard from other suppliers that there are problems on the project and no one is getting paid.

We have advised Mid-State that it should immediately place a mechanics' lien on the property for the $50,000 it is owed. I would like you to:

1. Draft the necessary notice of mechanics' lien for filing on behalf of Mid-State and any other documents necessary under the laws of your state to create and perfect that lien.

2. Prepare a draft letter to the client for my signature explaining the time deadlines involved in filing a mechanics' lien such as this and detailing what actions we will take to enforce the mechanics' lien and the necessary time frames for taking those actions under the laws of your state.

The real property involved is owned by City Heights Limited Partnership and its home office is located at 5544 Bishop Pike here in Capitol City. The sole general partner of CHLP is attorney Crystal G. Durham, whose address is 500 Plaza Tower here in Capitol City. The legal description of the property taken from the mortgage CHLP granted to Security Trust Bank here in Capitol City when it bought the property last year is as follows:

SITUATE in the 13th Civil District of Capitol County, Columbiana, and being Lots 9, 10, and 11 of the William S. Perkins Farm as surveyed by Alex

Williams on July 11, YR-5, and found of record in Plat Cabinet A, slide 15, in the Register of Deeds Office for Capitol County, Columbiana.

Being the same property conveyed to City Heights Limited Partnership by Andrew J. Perkins and wife, Emily O. Perkins by warranty deed dated April 2, YR-1 and recorded in Deed Book 67A, Page 433 in the Register of Deeds Office for Capitol City, Columbiana.

The mortgage instrument from which this description was taken was recorded on April 2, YR-1 in Mortgage Book 17, Page 112 in the Register of Deed's Office for Capitol County, Columbiana.

Ronnie Clark (Ronald D. Clark) will sign all documents for Mid-State as the Managing Member of the LLC.

Copies of the accepted bid and the unpaid invoice are attached.

MID-STATE GRADING SERVICE, LLC
1345 INDUSTRIAL DRIVE
CAPITOL CITY, COLUMBIANA
(555) 777-0984

BID FORM

Job: City Heights Condominium Project (site preparation)
Bid date: Five months ago, YR00
Bid Amount: $100,000 GMP
To: Angel and Barclay Architects, Inc.

Mid-State Grading Service, LLC, hereby submits a total bid of $100,000, Guaranteed Maximum Price, for the site preparation work on the above referenced project pursuant to Bid Solicitation #A-3, work to be performed per Site Preparation Specifications 001 through 010, City Heights Condominium Project.

Payment to be invoiced in two equal installments: the first 30 days after commencement of work and the second upon completion of work. Payment to be made within 30 days of invoices.

/s/ Ronald D. Clark
Ronald D. Clark, Managing Member

Action on Bid:

____ Rejected
_X_ Accepted

Date: Four months ago, YR00

/s/ Roy J. Angel
Roy J. Angel, Chief Architect

MID-STATE GRADING SERVICE, LLC
1345 INDUSTRIAL DRIVE
CAPITOL CITY, COLUMBIANA
(555) 777-0984

<u>INVOICE</u>

Job: City Heights Condominium Project (site preparation)
To: Angel and Barclay Architects, Inc.
Amount Due: <u>$50,000 within 30 days of invoice</u>
Date: 45 days ago, YR00

<u>/s/ Ronald D. Clark</u>
Ronald D. Clark, Managing Member

Glossary

All section references are to the Bankruptcy Code. Italicized words refer to other defined terms. The parenthetical at the end of each definition references the chapter(s) where the concept is introduced or receives primary attention.

Abandonment.   The bankruptcy trustee's formal relinquishment of any claim by the estate to property deemed burdensome or of inconsequential value to the estate per §544 of the Code. Cf. *Surrender.* (Ch. Ten)

Above median debtor.   A Chapter 7 individual debtor or a Chapter 13 debtor whose annualized *current monthly income* as calculated on Forms 22A-1 or 22C-1 is equal to or more than the applicable *median family income* figure. Cf. *Below median debtor.* (Ch. Five and Thirteen)

Acceleration clause.   A common provision in a promissory note and other installment contracts making all future installments immediately due and payable upon the debtor's default. (Ch. Two)

Adequate protection.   The protection that must be provided by the bankrupt debtor to a creditor to prevent lifting of the automatic stay. (Ch. Seven)

Administrative expenses.   Postpetition expenses incurred in preserving the property of the estate and in administering the estate by the trustee or debtor in possession. Governed by §503, such expenses are granted a first priority in estate distribution by §507. (Ch. Ten)

Adversary proceedings.   Certain disputes defined by Bankruptcy Rule 7001 that arise in a bankruptcy case and are resolved by the procedures governing a formal civil lawsuit. Cf. *Contested matter.* (Ch. Four and Eighteen)

After notice and a hearing.   A Code procedure requiring notice to parties in interest of the motion, objection or intended action, but requiring a hearing only if a party in interest requests one. (Ch. Four and Eighteen)

Allowed claim.   A creditor's claim that is acknowledged as being owed by the estate under §502. (Ch. Eight)

Alternative dispute resolution.   Methods of resolving disputes outside of the litigation process (e.g., mediation or arbitration). (Ch. Four and Eighteen)

Applicable commitment period.   The required duration of a Chapter 13 plan, 3-5 years. Determined by the debtor's income as compared to the applicable state *median family income*. (Ch. Thirteen)

Arbitration.   A form of alternative dispute resolution in which the disputing parties agree that a third-person arbitrator, or panel of arbitrators, may hear the dispute informally and render an decision (arbitrator's award). May be binding or non-binding. (Ch. Four and Eighteen)

Artisan's lien.   The right of one who performs work on the personal property of another to retain possession of the property as security for payment for the work done and to sell the property and apply the proceeds to the amount due. A common law lien in some states; statutory in others. (Ch. Two and Nine)

Asset buyers (or debt buyers).   Persons who purchase delinquent or charged-off accounts from creditors for a fraction of the face value of the debt and then seek to collect it themselves or resale to another asset buyer. (Ch. Three)

Asset protection (self-settled) trust.   A trust permitted in a handful of states whereby the settlor can convey his own property into trust and name himself as the beneficiary to receive distributions of principal or interest as proscribed in the trust document, yet prevent his creditors from seizing trust assets not yet distributed. Previously available only as questionable foreign asset protection trusts or offshore trusts. (Ch. Three)

Assignment for the benefit of creditors.   A state law insolvency procedure involving the assignment of the debtor's property to a trustee empowered to liquidate the property and distribute the proceeds to creditors who are given notice and elect to participate. (Ch. Four)

Attachment.   The creation of a security interest (lien) in favor of a creditor in property of the debtor. See *Perfection*. (Ch. Two)

Automatic perfection.   The perfection of a security interest (lien) immediately upon its attachment. (Ch. Two and Nine)

Automatic stay.   The prohibition on creditors continuing collection efforts against a debtor that arises automatically upon the debtor's filing of a bankruptcy petition per §362 of the Code; enforceable by the contempt powers of the bankruptcy court. Expires automatically on personal property 45 days following the first meeting of creditors in individual Chapter 7 cases unless the debtor *redeems* the property or *reaffirms* the debt. (Ch. Seven)

Avoidance power.   1. The trustee's powers under the Code to set aside certain pre-petition transfers of property of the estate. 2. The right of an individual debtor to set aside a lien in property of the estate to the extent it impairs an exemption in that property. See *Preference*, *Fraudulent transfer* and *Exempt property*. (Ch. Six, Nine, Ten, and Fourteen)

Bad faith.   See *Good faith*.

Badges of fraud.   In the law of fraudulent transfer, certain recognized circumstances from which the inference may fairly be drawn that a transfer was made with intent to defraud creditors. (Ch. Three and Nine)

Balance sheet test.   A test of *insolvency* whereby a debtor's liabilities exceed his assets. (Ch. Three and Nine)

Bankruptcy Abuse Prevention and Consumer Protection Act of 2005 (BAPCPA). The 2005 statute that amended the Code in numerous ways including introducing the means test for Chapter 7 filers. (Ch. Four)

Bankruptcy Act. The predecessor of the current Bankruptcy Code. Enacted in 1898 and superseded in 1978. See *Bankruptcy Reform Act*. (Ch. Four)

Bankruptcy Appellate Panel (BAP). A court made up of bankruptcy judges appointed in some federal circuits to hear the appeal of rulings by other bankruptcy judges in lieu of the District Court. (Ch. Four and Eighteen)

Bankruptcy petition preparer. One who prepares a bankruptcy petition for a fee and who is not an attorney or working under the supervision of an attorney. (Ch. Six)

Bankruptcy Reform Act. The 1978 statute that introduced the current Code. Also the name of the 1994 statute that amended the Code. (Ch. Four)

Below median debtor. A Chapter 7 individual debtor or a Chapter 13 debtor whose annualized *current monthly income* as calculated on Forms 22A-1 or 22C-1 is less than the applicable *median family income* figure. Cf. *Above median debtor*. (Ch. Five and Thirteen)

Bifurcated claim. Description of the treatment of the bankruptcy claim of a secured creditor whose dollar claim exceeds the value of the collateral securing the claim. See *Secured debt*. (Ch. Eight)

Bona fide error defense. A defense to alleged violation of the Fair Debt Collection Act available to a debt collector who can show that the violation was unintentional and that the debt collector debt collector maintained procedures to avoid the error. (Ch. Three)

Budget and credit counseling agency. An entity approved by the U.S. Trustee to provide prepetition credit counseling or predischarge financial management services to consumer debtors. (Ch. Five and Eleven)

Bulk Sales Act. Article 6 of the Uniform Commercial Code providing a nonbankruptcy procedure for the sale of all or substantially all of the assets of a business outside the ordinary course of business. Repealed in most states. (Ch. Four)

Car title loan. Loan in which consumer signs title to his vehicle over to the lender to secure a similar short term loan, often at a predatory rate of interest. (Ch. Two)

Case Management/Electronic Case Files (CM/ECF). The current system for filing documents with a bankruptcy court electronically. Access to case filings available through Public Access to Court Electronic Records (PACER). (Ch. Four)

Cash advance. A short-term loan for a small amount under terms that charge the borrower an astronomically high interest rate, sometimes camouflaged as a transaction fee or finance charge. (Ch. Two)

Chapter 13 plan (also called a debt adjustment plan or wage earner plan). A plan proposed by a Chapter 13 debtor. (Ch. Fourteen, Fifteen, and Sixteen)

Chapter 20 case. Practitioner's term for when a debtor obtains a discharge in a Chapter 7 case then files a Chapter 13 case shortly thereafter (7 + 13 = 20). (Ch. Twelve)

Claim bifurcation. See *Bifurcated claim.*

Claims bar date. The deadline set for creditors in a case to file proofs of claim. Claims not filed by the bar date may be disallowed or *subordinated* to other claims. (Ch. Eight)

Claims docket. A formal record of proofs of claims filed in a bankruptcy case maintained by the bankruptcy court clerk. (Ch. Eight)

Co-debtor stay. The Chapter 13 provision that the automatic stay initially extends to co-debtors of the Chapter 13 debtor. (Ch. Twelve)

Collateral. The real or personal property subject to a security interest in favor of a creditor. Where personal property, also called nominated property. (Ch. Two)

Commercial fishing operation. The business a "family fisherman" may be engaged in in order to qualify for relief under Chapter 12 of the Code. (Ch. Seventeen)

Commercially reasonable manner. The standard governing the creditor's sale of repossessed property. What is commercially reasonable depends on the prevailing circumstances surrounding the sale and what is common or usual in the market for goods of that kind. (Ch. Two)

Community property. A form of concurrent ownership between married couples in which all property acquired by either spouse during the marriage, however titled, is deemed to be owned by both. (Ch. Three)

Compensated surety. One who receives a fee or other compensation for agreeing to serve as surety or guarantor. (Chapter Two)

Composition agreement. A contract made between a debtor and his creditors pursuant to which partial payment is made and accepted in full satisfaction of claims. See *Extension agreement.* (Ch. Three and Four)

Confirmation. The court's formal approval of a debtor's Chapter 13 plan. (Ch. Sixteen)

Consolidation. The joining together of two or more bankruptcy cases involving interrelated debtors into one case for joint administration. (Ch. Six)

Constitutional jurisdiction. The issue of whether a bankruptcy court, as an Article 1 court, can enter final judgment in disputes traditionally within the province of Article 3 courts. (Ch. Eighteen)

Construction lien. A nonpossessory lien that can attach to real property to secure payment to one who has performed labor on the property (the mechanic) or supplied materials to it (the materialman). Also called a *Mechanics'* and *Materialman's lien* or *Supplier's lien.* (Ch. Two)

Constructive fraud (presumed fraud). A means of finding fraud based on inference from circumstances rather than proof of actual intent. (Ch. Three and Nine)

Constructive trust. An equitable remedy pursuant to which one who has wrongfully obtained title to or possession of property is deemed to hold that property in trust for the benefit of the true owner. (Ch. Two)

Consumer. An individual who purchases or leases real or personal property or obtains services primarily for personal, family, or household use. (Ch. One)

Consumer bankruptcy case. A bankruptcy case in which the debtor is an individual with primarily *consumer debts*. (Ch. One)

Consumer debt. Debt incurred by an individual primarily for a personal, family, or household purpose. (Ch. One)

Contemporaneous exchange for equivalent value. As a defense to an alleged preferential transfer, a transaction supported by adequate present consideration. (Ch. Nine)

Contested matter. A proceeding arising in a bankruptcy case that is initiated by motion or objection or statement of intent to act. Cf. *Adversary proceeding.* (Ch. Four and Eighteen)

Conversion. 1. The changing of a bankruptcy proceeding under one chapter of the Code to another (e.g., a Chapter 7 converted to a Chapter 13). (Ch. Eleven and Seventeen) 2. The tort of taking or using another's property without consent. (Ch. Two and Three)

Core proceeding. A proceeding in a bankruptcy case involving the determination of rights under the Code or issues arising in a bankruptcy case as suggested by the list in 28 U.S.C. §157(2). Final orders may be entered by a bankruptcy court in a core proceeding subject to constitutional jurisdictional issues. (Ch. Four and Eighteen)

Cramdown. The right of a Chapter 13 debtor to obtain confirmation of a Chapter 13 plan that reduces the value of some secured claims to the present value of the security without creditor consent. Cf. *Lien stripping.* (Ch. Fourteen)

Credit-bidding. Also called bidding in, the practice of a creditor secured in property foreclosed on or repossessed bidding the amount owed at the foreclosure/repossession sale and receiving credit for the amount owed against the sales price. In bankruptcy, specifically authorized in 11 U.S.C. §363(k) when property of the estate is sold. (Ch. Two and Ten)

Credit counseling agency. Any business that provides budget counseling and financial literacy services to debt-strapped individuals or businesses; may also negotiate a debt management plan with creditors of client. See *Debt relief agencies; Budget and credit counseling agency.* (Ch. Three, Five, and Fifteen).

Creditor's committee. A committee of creditors appointed by the U.S. Trustee in Chapter 11 cases and sometimes in Chapter 7 cases to represent the interests of all creditors. (Ch. Seven)

Cross-border case. A bankruptcy case involving debtors, assets and creditors in more than one country. Governed by new Chapter 15 of the Code. (Ch. Four)

Cure.   In a Chapter 13 case, a plan provision to pay an arrearage over time to bring the defaulting debtor into compliance with its obligations under a contract. (Ch. Fourteen)

Current monthly income.   The income of a consumer debtor calculated by averaging the debtor's income from all sources for the six months preceding the filing of the petition. (Ch. Five and Thirteen)

Debt adjustment plan.   See *Chapter 13 plan*.

Debt buyers.   See *Asset buyers*.

Debt collection companies.   Private businesses involved in pre-litigation debt collection activities on behalf of creditors, usually for a percentage of what is collected. (Ch. Three)

Debt collectors.   Under the FDCPA businesses the principal purpose of which is to collect debts owed by consumers and who regularly collect or attempt to collect such debt. (Ch. Three)

Debt relief agency.   Under the Code, one who provides any bankruptcy assistance to an assisted person in return for the payment of money or other valuable consideration. See *Credit counseling agency*. (Ch. Six)

Debt settlement industry.   Description of businesses that offer to assist debt strapped individuals to avoid bankruptcy by negotiating a debt management plan (DMP). (Ch. Three)

Debtor in possession.   The legal status given a debtor filing a Chapter 12 case because the debtor retain possession of property of the estate. (Ch. Seventeen)

Deeming.   Code process where certain determinations are deemed made unless a timely objection is filed (e.g., claims deemed allowed absent objection per §502(a)). (Ch. Eight)

Default judgment.   A final judgment rendered against a defendant in a civil suit who fails to file an answer to the complaint or to otherwise defend. (Ch. Three)

Deficiency (judgment).   1) The amount of a debt that remains owing after the collateral securing the debt has been liquidated; 2) final judgment for same. (Ch. Two)

Discharge in bankruptcy.   Permanent relief from debt pursuant to order of the bankruptcy court. See *Nondischargeable debt* and *Exceptions to discharge*. (Ch. Four, Eleven, and Sixteen)

Discovery in aid of execution (postjudgment).   The right of a judgment creditor to engage in discovery for the purpose of locating assets of the judgment debtor on which to execute. (Ch. Three)

Disposable income.   1. The income of a garnishee a statutory percentage of which is subject to garnishment. (Ch. Three) 2. The income that an individual bankruptcy debtor has available to pay creditors after deducting income necessary for the support or maintenance of the debtor and his dependents relevant to whether a Chapter 7 debtor satisfies the means test and as to the determination of a Chapter 13 debtor's plan payments. (Ch. Five and Thirteen)

Domestic support obligation. An obligation to pay alimony, child support, or maintenance. (Ch. Six and Eleven)

Doubling (or stacking). In a joint bankruptcy case, the right of the husband and wife debtors to double (or stack) the allowed exemption amounts on their Schedule C. (Ch. Six)

Due Process. Fundamental fairness mandated by the Fifth and Fourteenth Amendments to the U.S. Constitution. (Ch. Eighteen)

Election of remedies. The doctrine recognized in some states requiring a secured creditor to choose between exercising a right of foreclosure on secured property or suing the debtor for a judgment, but disallowing both foreclosure and a suit for deficiency judgment. (Ch. Two)

Electronic case filing. Non-paper, electronic filing system currently in use in bankruptcy courts. (Ch. Four)

Equitable lien (also called common law lien). A lien created by court rulings rather than by statute (e.g., vendor's lien). (Ch. Two, Nine, and Fourteen)

Equitable subordination. The inherent power of a bankruptcy court as a court of equity to order that a claim be subordinated to others of the same rank due to inequitable or dishonest conduct of the claimant. (Ch. Eight and Ten)

Equity. 1. An ownership interest in property unencumbered by any security interest or lien. Also called owner's equity. 2. The body of rules and principles developed historically by courts whereby they are authorizes to provide relief when remedies at law are inadequate. (Ch. Two and Three)

Equity of redemption. A mortgagor's right to prevent the sale of real property in foreclosure by paying the entire indebtedness owed prior to the foreclosure sale (see *Redemption*). (Ch. Two)

Exceptions to discharge. Reasons why an individual debtor may be denied a discharge in bankruptcy. (Ch. Eleven and Sixteen)

Executory contract. A contract which has not been fully performed by either party to it. (Ch. Six)

Exempt property. 1. Property of a debtor that cannot be seized by a judgment creditor. (Ch. Three) 2. Property of a debtor in bankruptcy that the debtor is allowed to keep and which cannot be made available to creditors. (Ch. Six and Twelve)

Ex parte. An appearance before a court seeking relief without notice to other parties. (Ch. Eighteen)

Extension agreement. An agreement made by a debtor with his creditors whereby the creditors consent to an extension of time for the debtor to pay. Often reached in conjunction with a *composition agreement*. (Ch. Three and Four)

Fair Debt Collection Practices Act (FDCPA), 15 USC §1601, et seq. Federal statute regulating *debt collectors*. (Ch. Three)

Fair market value.   The estimated price that a willing buyer would pay to a willing seller for the item, neither being under a compulsion to sell and both having reasonable knowledge of the underlying facts. (Ch. Three and Six)

Family farmer.   A debtor engaged in farming operations and who otherwise meets the requirements to be a debtor under Chapter 12. (Ch. Seventeen)

Family fisherman.   A debtor engaged in a *commercial fishing operation* and who otherwise meets the requirements to be a debtor under Chapter 12. (Ch. Seventeen)

Family Violence Prevention and Services Act.   Federal statute authorizing debtors who have been the victim of domestic violence or stalking to deduct expenses related to keeping themselves or their family safe when determining whether the presumption of abuse is present in a Chapter 7 case and when determining projected disposable income in a Chapter 13 case. (Ch. Five and Thirteen)

Federal Arbitration Act, 9 U.S.C. §1 et. seq.   Federal statute governing arbitration in cases affecting interstate commerce or maritime issues. (Ch. Eighteen)

Federal Rules of Bankruptcy Procedure.   The formal rules supplementing the Code and governing proceedings in bankruptcy cases. (Ch. Four)

Fieri facias.   See *Writ of execution.* (Ch. Three)

Financing statement.   A document filed in a designated public office to perfect a security interest in personal property under Article 9 of the *UCC.* Also called a UCC-1. (Ch. Two)

First meeting of creditors (or 341 meeting).   The meeting of creditors of a bankrupt debtor required by §341 of the Code called by the U.S. Trustee. The debtor may be questioned under oath at the meeting. (Ch. Seven and Twelve)

Foreclosure.   The process by which the holder of a mortgage in real property takes possession of the property following default by the mortgagor. The property is normally sold and the proceeds applied to the costs of foreclosure and underlying debt. In some cases the property is retained in satisfaction of the debt. A foreclosure may be consensual (power of sale foreclosure) or judicial (court ordered). (Ch. Two)

Foreign judgment.   A final judgment entered in a state other than the state in which it is enforced. See *Uniform Enforcement of Foreign Judgment Act.* (Ch. Three)

Fraudulent transfer (or conveyance).   A transfer of property by a debtor with actual or constructive intent to defraud his creditors by delaying or hindering their collection efforts. (Ch. Three and Nine)

Fresh start (clean slate).   The opportunity provided to a debtor following a discharge in bankruptcy. (Ch. Four)

Gap period.   The time between when the petition is filed and the time the bankruptcy trustee is appointed. (Ch. Ten)

Garnishment.   A method of executing on a final judgment pursuant to which property of the debtor in the hands of a third person or a debt owed by a third person to the debtor is levied on. (Ch. Three)

Good faith.   Generally, honesty in fact and compliance with the letter and spirit of the Code; a consideration in determining whether a Chapter 7 or Chapter 13 case should be dismissed and whether a Chapter 13 plan should be confirmed. (Ch. Five, Eleven, and Sixteen)

Grace period.   The time between the date a final judgment is entered and the date execution on the judgment can begin. (Ch. Three)

Guarantor.   One who guarantees the debt of another. The guarantor is *secondarily liable* for the debt. (Ch. Two)

Hardship discharge.   An early discharge granted at the discretion of the judge in a Chapter 13 case. See *Discharge*. (Ch. Sixteen)

Healthcare services lien.   A non-consensual lien allowed against any claim or cause of action that the patient may have against a third party who may be liable to the patient for injuries related to the healthcare service provided (Ch. Two)

Home equity loan.   A loan in which the borrower pledges the *equity* in his home as security for repayment. (Ch. Two)

Homestead exemption.   The exemption available to a debtor to protect the equity in his primary residence. (Ch. Three and Six)

Individual with regular income.   An individual with sufficiently stable and regular income that enables the individual to make payments under a Chapter 13 plan. (Ch. Twelve)

Insider.   In the context of a *preferential transfer action* under the Code, a person in close relationship with a debtor such that he may be assumed to have superior access to information and be subject to special treatment. Includes relatives of an individual debtor and general partners. (Ch. Nine)

Insolvency.   The inability to pay debts as they come due (the *equity test*) or the state of having total liabilities in excess of total assets (the *balance sheet test*). (Ch. Three and Nine)

Involuntary petition.   The petition filed in an involuntary Chapter 7 case initiated by the creditors of the debtor, not the debtor himself. (Ch. Six)

Ipso facto clause.   A provision in a contract declaring the filing of bankruptcy to be an act of default. (Ch. Eleven)

Joint administration.   Where two or more related bankruptcy cases are ordered to be administered by the same trustee to save administrative costs. (Ch. Six)

Joint petition.   A single bankruptcy case filed by a married couple. (Ch. Six)

Joint tenancy.   A form of joint ownership of property which includes a right of survivorship. (Ch. Three)

Judgment debtor/creditor.   Once a final judgment is entered by a court awarding a money judgment to one party, the party to whom the judgment is awarded is the judgment creditor and the one against whom it is awarded is the judgment debtor. (Ch. Three)

Judgment lien.   A form of execution on a final judgment whereby an nonconsensual lien attaches to real property owned by a judgment debtor in the county where the final judgment is recorded or docketed. In some states the lien attaches to personal property of the debtor as well when the judgment is recorded as is a UCC financing statement. (Ch. Three)

Judgment proof.   Condition of a debtor who has no assets that might be seized to satisfy a final judgment. (Ch. Three)

Judicial lien.   Lien obtained by court action, whether judgment, levy, sequestration, or other legal or equitable process or proceeding. (Ch. Two and Six)

Judicial lien creditor.   One who holds a judicial lien. (Ch. Two and Six)

Judicial foreclosure.   Foreclosure on mortgaged real property accomplished pursuant to court order. *Cf. Power of sale foreclosure.* (Ch. Two)

Levy.   Seizing or taking control of a debtor's property pursuant to a lien or writ of execution. (Ch. Two and Three)

Lien.   Generally, another word for a security interest. Sometimes used narrowly to refer only to non-consensual secured claims created by law or court order, e.g., mechanics' lien, artisan's lien, judicial lien. (Ch. Two and Three)

Lien stripping (or strip down or write down).   A proposal in bankruptcy to reduce the undersecured claim of a creditor to its dollar value at the time the petition was filed or to completely abrogate the claim as secured where it is wholly undersecured claim (called **strip off**). (Ch. Ten and Fourteen)

Lien of levy.   The lien existing in favor of a judgment creditor against the property of the judgment debtor seized pursuant to a writ of execution. The judgment creditor then has the status of a *judicial lien* creditor as to such property. (Ch. Three)

Lis pendens (L. suit pending).   Public notice that a lawsuit is pending regarding title, possession or other rights to real property. Given by filing or recording notice of pendency in land records for county where the property at issue lies. Understood to create a lien on the realty that will act as a cloud on title until removed. (Ch. Two)

Local rules.   Supplemental rules of procedure and practice that prevail in a particular court. (Ch. Four and Six)

Look back period.   For purposes of completing the Form 122A-1 in Chapter 7 or the Form 122C-1 in Chapter 13, the six months of income preceding the filing of the petition. (Ch. Five and Thirteen)

Luxury goods or services.   Undefined phrase but includes goods or services not reasonably necessary for the maintenance or support of the debtor or a dependent. Purchases of same within 90 days preceding the petition are presumed fraudulent and nondischargeable. Presumption rebuttable. (Ch. Eleven)

Marshalling of assets.   Requirement that a judgment creditor executing on property of the judgment debtor seize and exhaust property in a certain order, e.g., all nonexempt personalty before nonexempt realty. (Ch. Three)

Materialman's lien.   See *Construction lien.*

Means test.   A test for Chapter 7 filers introduced by BAPCPA intended to determine whether the debtor has sufficient *disposable income* to enable the debtor to repay some or all of his debts in a Chapter 13 case. Test raises *presumption of abuse* when debtor's current monthly income exceeds the applicable state *median family income*. Unless rebutted, presumption of abuse mandates dismissal or conversion of case to Chapter 13. (Ch. Five)

Mechanics' lien. See *Construction lien.*

Median family income. The average income for families of a certain size calculated by the U.S. Census Bureau for a household the size of the debtor's household living in the debtor's state of residence. (Ch. Five and Thirteen)

Mediation. A form of *alternative dispute resolution* in which an impartial person serving as mediator uses back and forth dialogue with the disputing parties to assist them in reaching a settlement. (Ch. Four and Eighteen)

Monthly disposable income. Under the Code, the amount the debtor would have available to fund a Chapter 13 plan over the next 3-5 years after all projected expenses are deducted. (Ch. Five and Thirteen)

Mortgage. A consensual security interest held by a creditor in real property created by the execution of a mortgage deed or deed of trust by the owner/mortgagor to the mortgagee. (Ch. Two)

No-asset case. A Chapter 7 liquidation case in which there are no assets available for distribution to creditors. (Ch. Seven)

No-asset report. Report filed with the bankruptcy court by the bankruptcy trustee where the trustee concludes that the case is a no-asset one. (Ch. Seven)

Non-attorney bankruptcy petition preparer. Nonattorneys who assists a debtor in preparing petition and schedules for bankruptcy filing. (Ch. Six)

Noncore proceedings. Issues that arise in or are related to a bankruptcy case but which are not *core proceedings*; generally, the bankruptcy court cannot enter a final order in such disputes unless all parties consent. (Ch. Four and Eighteen)

Nondischargeable debt. A debt excluded from discharge in a Chapter 7 or Chapter 13 case. (Ch. Eleven and Sixteen)

Notice and a hearing. Code procedure requiring notice of motion, objection or intended action be given to parties in interest, but requiring a hearing only if a party in interests contests or objects. (Ch. Four and Eighteen)

Notice of commencement. Formal notice of the filing of a bankruptcy case given to creditors. (Ch. Seven)

Notice of intended action. Procedure authorized under the Code for giving parties in interest notice of the intent to take some action (e.g., intent to abandon property). Often joined with notice and a hearing procedure. (Ch. Four and Eighteen)

Nulla bona (L. with nothing found). Return made by sheriff on writ of execution when no executable property is found. (Ch. Three)

Official Bankruptcy Forms. Forms drafted by the Administrative Office of the U.S. Courts (the AO) constantly revised to comply with changes in the Code or the FRBP, new court decisions, or recommendations from judges and practitioners. (Ch. Four)

Order for relief.   The formal beginning of a bankruptcy case. 1. In most districts the filing of a voluntary petition constitutes the order for relief; in others a formal order approving the filing of a voluntary petition. 2. A formal order that is always entered approving the filing of an involuntary petition. (Ch. Six and Seven)

Ordinary course of business.   A defense raised to a transfer alleged to be preferential where the transfer was in payment of a debt incurred in the ordinary course of debtor's business or financial affairs and was made in the ordinary course business of both the debtor and the transferee. (Ch. Nine)

Oversecured debt.   A secured debt where the value of the collateral exceeds the amount owed. (Ch. Eight, Ten, and Fourteen)

Owner's equity.   See *Equity*.

Party in interest.   An important but undefined term in the Code, interpreted generally to refer to any person or entity having a stake in the outcome of a matter arising in a bankruptcy case (e.g., debtor, bankruptcy trustee, U.S. trustee, creditors, and equity security holders). (Ch. Four and Eighteen)

Pawn shop loan.   A short term loan taken by a consumer who pledges some kind of personal property as security for repayment and gives pawn lender possession. Loan is made in an amount equal to a reduced value of the property pledged (usually 30-50%) and entitles lender to sell the property for full value if loan is not paid by due date. (Ch. Two)

Pay through (or pay and ride).   A proposal in a bankruptcy case to pay a secured claim in full as called for in the underlying contract and for the creditor to retain its lien on the secured property through and beyond the case. (Ch. Ten and Fourteen)

Payday loan.   Variously also called cash advance, check advance, post-dated check loan, deferred deposit check loan or deferred presentment loan; a high interest, short-term loan in which the borrower typically gives the lender a post-dated check for the amount borrowed plus interest and fees. If the amount borrowed is not repaid by the date of the check, the lender will cash it in payment. (Ch. Two)

Perfection.   Making a security interest in property enforceable against and superior to the rights of other creditors to the property. Normally accomplished by filing or recording required documents in a designated public office or by taking possession of the property. (Ch. Two)

Personal defenses.   A defense to liability unique to the circumstances of the principal debtor and which do not go to the merits of the underlying transaction such as discharge in bankruptcy or lack of capacity due to age or disability. Sureties and guarantors cannot successfully assert personal defenses of the principal debtor as a defense. (Ch. Two)

Personal jurisdiction.   The *Due Process* requirement that a defendant have sufficient minimum contacts with a forum to enable a court in that forum to enter a final order binding on a named defendant; in a bankruptcy case the United States is considered the forum. (Ch. Eighteen)

Petition. The document filed to initiate a bankruptcy case under the Code. (Ch. Six, Twelve, and Seventeen)

Pledged property. A method by which a secured party can perfect its security interest in collateral by taking possession of it per UCC §9-313. (Ch. Two)

Possessory liens. Types non-consensual statutory or equitable liens that attach to property in the possession of the lien holder (e.g., artisan's lien). Some liens are *nonpossessory* (e.g., *mechanics'* and *materialman's liens*; *lien lis pendens*). (Ch. Two)

Postjudgment asset discovery. The right of a judgment creditor to discover assets of a judgment debtor subject to execution following entry of the final judgment using interrogatories, document requests, and depositions. (Ch. Three)

Postjudgment interest. Statutory interest that runs on a final judgment from the date entered until paid is postjudgment interest. (Ch. Three)

Postpetition interest. Interest accruing on claims after debtor files a petition in bankruptcy. (Ch. Eight)

Power of sale clause. Clause in a security agreement permitting the creditor to repossess and sell the collateral in the event of default by the debtor. (Ch. Two)

Power of sale foreclosure. (Foreclosure on mortgaged realty accomplished by means of a power of sale clause and not requiring court permission. Cf. *Judicial foreclosure*. (Ch. Two)

Preferential transfer. A payment or other transfer of an interest in the debtor's property that results in the creditor receiving the payment or transfer being unfairly advantaged compared to other creditors. May be avoidable pursuant to §547. (Ch. Nine)

Prejudgment interest. Interest on an amount owed calculated from due date through date of judgment. Within the trial court's discretion to award. (Ch. Three)

Prejudgment attachment. Extraordinary relief available to plaintiffs during a civil lawsuit to prevent removal, loss or dissipation of the defendant's property pending final judgment and execution. (Ch. Three)

Prepetition credit counseling. Counseling that an individual bankruptcy debtor must receive from an approved *credit counseling agency* as a qualification for filing for bankruptcy relief. (Ch. Five and Six)

Present value. Calculation of the current value of property for purposes of determining the value of a secured claim in bankruptcy. Normally based on replacement cost of the property considering its age and condition. (Ch. Eight, Ten, and Fourteen)

Presumption of abuse. The presumption of inappropriate filing of a Chapter 7 case for the debtor who fails the *means test*. The presumption, once raised, must be rebutted by showing *special circumstances* or the case will be dismissed or converted with the debtor's consent to a case under Chapter 13. (Ch. Five)

Presumption of undue hardship. Where debtor seeks to reaffirm debt but lacks available income to pay the obligation as it comes due, the presumption arises. (Ch. Twelve)

Primarily/secondarily liable.   One who is primarily liable for the debt of another is liable without regard to whether the lender pursues collection from the other first (e.g., a *co-signer* or *surety*). One who is secondarily liable for the debt of another is liable only if the lender first pursues collection from the other (e.g., a *guarantor*). (Ch. Two)

Prime rate.   The interest rate that commercial banks charge their best customers. (Ch. Fourteen)

Priority claim.   An unsecured claim entitled to a certain order of preferment and payment under §507. (Ch. Eight, Ten, and Fourteen)

Private right of action.   The right granted by a regulatory statute for the injured party to being a civil lawsuit for damages apart from governmental regulatory action. (Ch. Three)

Private rights.   In constitutional context, rights involving disputes between private parties controlled by state law. Cf. *Public rights*. (Ch. Eighteen)

Proof of claim.   The formal document that a creditor submits as evidence of its claim against the estate. (Ch. Eight)

Property of the estate.   All property in which the debtor holds a legal or equitable interest at the commencement of a bankruptcy case per §541. In a Chapter 13 case, property acquired by the debtor postpetition is included as well per §1306. (Ch. Six, Seven, Nine, and Twelve)

Public Access to Court Electronic Records (PACER).   *See Case Management/ Electronic Case Files.* (Ch. Four)

Public rights.   In constitutional context, rights that exist only as part of governmental regulation or process. Cf. *Private rights*. (Ch. Eighteen)

Purchase money mortgage.   A mortgage held by the seller rather than a third-party lender. A form of self-financing by seller. (Ch. Two)

Purchase money security interest (PMSI).   A security interest in personal property created by loaning or extending credit to a debtor for the express purpose of purchasing the property. When the property is consumer goods, the PMSI is automatically perfected. (Ch. Two and Nine)

Qualified retirement plan.   A plan approved by the IRS allowing the withholding of pre-tax contributions and deferring tax on the amounts withheld until withdrawal from the plan, usually at retirement. (Ch. Thirteen)

Reaffirmation agreement.   The bankruptcy debtor's formal agreement with a creditor to pay the creditor a debt that could have been discharged in bankruptcy; subject to court approval (Ch. Ten)

Reasonably equivalent value.   Absence of is one of the tests for whether a transfer of property is constructively fraudulent as to creditors of the transferor under the Uniform Fraudulent Transfer Act and under §548 of the Code. Determined primarily by fair market value of the property at the time of the transfer. (Ch. Nine and Seventeen)

Receivership.   Proceeding in which a person is appointed to take control of a debtor's property and manage it under court supervision. (Ch. Four)

Recording statute. The state law controlling how mortgages are perfected thus determining the priority among mortgages or liens on the property. States have variously, race-notice, pure notice or pure race recording statutes. (Ch. Two)

Redemption. 1. In non-bankruptcy law, a debtor's right to buy back property that has been repossessed or foreclosed on. Not available in all states. See *Equity of redemption*. (Ch. Two) 2. The right of a Chapter 7 *individual consumer debtor* under §722 of the Code to buy back *consumer property* that has either been claimed as *exempt* by the debtor or abandoned by the trustee by paying the creditor holding a *dischargeable debt* secured by that property *present value* of the property. (Ch. Ten)

Referral jurisdiction. A description of the subject matter jurisdiction of U.S. bankruptcy courts, which depends on referral from the U.S. district courts. (Ch. Four and Eighteen)

Regular income. Income from any legal source, earned or unearned, sufficient to make performance of a Chapter 13 plan feasible. (Ch. Twelve)

Relation-back. The retrospective effect given to some liens giving them priority from a date prior to their perfection. (Ch. Two)

Rent-to-own agreement. A delayed-title contract in which the buyer/lessee leases the property until the final payment at which time the seller/lessor conveys title to him. (Ch. Two)

Reverse mortgage. A consumer transaction in which a homeowner aged 62 or older borrows against the equity built up in the residence and receives that equity from the lender in either a lump sum or in installment payments. The loan is repaid when the homeowner dies or no longer lives in the home and the home is sold. (Ch. Two)

Ride through. See *Pay through*.

Right of survivorship. The property interest of spouses in jointly owned property in which the first to die takes nothing and the survivor takes all. (Ch. Two)

Rule 2004 examination. The examination under oath as in a deposition of any person in connection with any matter related to a bankruptcy case. (Ch. Seven)

Safe harbor provision. A provision in a statute or regulation that exempts a person from liability for certain conduct as in a safe harbor from usury statutes or, in bankruptcy, from violations of the automatic stay. (Ch. Two and Seven)

Sale free and clear of liens. The sale of property of the estate that is subject to a secured claim to enable the bankruptcy estate to realize the equity in the property in excess of that claim. Per §363, the sale may be authorized over the creditor's objection. (Ch. Ten)

Secured debt (secured claim/secured creditor). A debt the payment of which is secured by real or personal property giving the secured creditor recourse against the property in the event of a default. See (Ch. Two, Eight, Ten, and Fourteen)

Security agreement. A contract creating a security interest. (Ch. Two)

Security interest. See *Secured debt*.

Self-help repossession. The right of a secured creditor granted under a security agreement or mortgage instrument to repossess collateral or foreclose on a mortgage without a court order. (Ch. Two)

Senior lien. A description of the security interest in collateral entitled to priority over other secured claims (junior liens) to the same collateral. (Ch. Two)

Separation of powers. The constitutional doctrine forbidding any one of the three branches of government from assuming powers granted by the constitution to another branch. See *Constitutional jurisdiction*. (Ch. Eighteen)

Setoff. The principle that when two people owe each other a debt, the debts may cancel each other out except to the extent one debt exceeds the other. (Ch. Eight and Nine)

Sheriff's sale. The sale by public auction or private sale of property of a debtor levied on pursuant to a writ of execution. (Ch. Two and Three)

Short sale. Arrangement to avoid foreclosure in which the creditor allows the homeowner time to sell the property and agrees to accept the net proceeds of the sale in full satisfaction of the indebtedness even though the sale may not bring enough to cover the entire indebtedness and even if the underlying note is not nonrecourse. (Ch. Two)

Special circumstances. Unique financial circumstances of a Chapter 7 debtor involving additional expenses or adjustments of *current monthly income* for which there is no reasonable alternative which may be sufficient to rebut the *presumption of abuse*. (Ch. Five)

Spendthrift trust. A trust arrangement that prohibits alienation of trust property the effect of which is to protect the property from dissipation by the beneficiary or seizure by creditors of the beneficiary. (Ch. Three)

Stacking. See *Doubling*.

Standing trustee. A person appointed by the U.S. Trustee to serve as trustee in all Chapter 13 cases filed in the district. Cf. *Trustee panel*. (Ch. Twelve)

Statement of intent. Statement required of individual debtor in Chapter 7 indicating debtor's intent to surrender property pledged as collateral, or redeem it, or to reaffirm underlying debt secured by such property. (Ch. Six)

Statutory lien. A lien created by statute rather than by contract or court order. (Ch. Two and Nine)

Stay. See *Automatic stay* and *Co-debtor stay*.

Strict foreclosure. Authorization of the secured creditor to retain the collateral in full or partial satisfaction of the obligation, as authorized by UCC §9-620 (Ch. Two)

Strip down/write down and strip off. See *Lien stripping*.

Strong-arm clause. Description of bankruptcy trustee's avoidance powers under §544 of the Code. (Ch. Nine)

Subordination. The treatment of a claim in a less favored way than others either by consent of the creditor or by court order as a matter of equity as where the creditor has filed a claim after the *claims bar date* or has acted dishonestly or in bad faith to the detriment of junior claim holders. See *Equitable subordination*. (Ch. Ten)

Super discharge. Description of the slightly more generous discharge available under a Chapter 13 than under a Chapter 7. (Ch. Sixteen)

Surety (agreement or bond). A contract pursuant to which a surety makes itself primarily liable to a named principal for a debt owed to the principal by a named obligee. (Ch. Four)

Surrender (property). The act of a debtor relinquishing collateralized property to the creditor. (Ch. Seven)

Tenancy by the entireties. A form of concurrent ownership of property between a married couple in which each has a right of survivorship. See *Community property*, *Joint tenancy*, and *Tenancy in common*. (Ch. Three)

Tenancy in common. A form of concurrent ownership in which each owner has an undivided interest in the property; no right of survivorship. See *Community property*, *Tenancy by the entireties*, and *Joint tenancy*. (Ch. Three)

Till tap. The direct seizure of cash from the cash register of a business pursuant to a writ of execution. (Ch. Three)

Trustee. 1) In the context of a mortgage, the person to whom a power of sale foreclosure is transferred by the mortgagor for the benefit of the lender; 2) in the context of an express or constructive trust, the person to whom the trust property is conveyed to hold title for the benefit of the trust beneficiary; and 3) under the Code, the individual appointed by the U.S. Trustee (or elected by creditors in a Chapter 7 case) who is charged with administering the bankruptcy estate; the bankruptcy trustee. (Ch. Three, Four, Seven, Twelve, and Seventeen)

Trustee panel. Persons approved by the U.S. Trustee to serve as trustees in Chapter 7 cases in a district. Cases are normally assigned to panel members on a rotating basis. (Ch. Seven)

Turnover. The transfer of estate property to the trustee by the debtor or other person. (Ch. Nine)

Undersecured debt (claim/creditor). A secured debt where the value of the collateral is less than the amount of the debt. See *Secured debt* and *Unsecured debt*. (Ch. Eight and Fourteen)

Undue hardship. Test for discharge of student loan obligation in bankruptcy. (Ch. Eleven)

Unfair or deceptive act or practice. Prohibited conduct by debt collectors under the FDCPA. (Ch. Three)

Unmatured interest. Interest that is not yet due or owing at the time a bankruptcy petition is filed. (Ch. Eight)

Uniform Arbitration Act. Uniform statute enacted in most states setting forth procedures governing arbitration proceedings. (Ch. Eighteen)

Uniform Commercial Code (UCC). A uniform code adopted in whole or part in all states covering contracts for the sale or lease of goods, negotiable instruments, security interests in personal property and other commercial transactions. (Ch. Three and Nine)

Uniform Enforcement of Foreign Judgment Act.   State statute regulating the enforcement in one state of a final judgment entered in another. (Ch. Three)

Uniform Fraudulent Transfer Act of 1984 (UFTA).   The more current uniform act regulating the recovery of fraudulent transfers. In effect in most states. (Ch. Three and Nine)

Unliquidated claim (debt).   A claim that has not been reduced to a dollar amount. (Ch. Two)

Unsecured debt (claim/creditor).   A debt enforceable only against the bare promise of a debtor to pay and not secured by any property of the debtor or guaranty of a third party. (Ch. Two, Eight, Ten, and Fifteen)

U.S. Trustee.   Appointed official in federal districts responsible for appointment and supervision of bankruptcy trustees and general oversight of bankruptcy cases in that district. (Ch. Four)

Validation notice.   Required language in communication from a debt collector governed by the FDCPA to a debtor regarding the debtor's right to demand verification of the debt. (Ch. Three)

Vendor's lien (or mortgage lien).   An equitable lien afforded to sellers of real property on the real property sold even in the absence of a mortgage. (Ch. Two)

Venue.   The appropriate bankruptcy court in which a particular case should be filed. (Ch. Six)

Voluntary case.   A bankruptcy case initiated by the debtor. (Ch. Six)

Wage earner plan.   Informal and inaccurate name for a Chapter 13 plan. (Ch. Twelve)

Wage order.   A court order in a Chapter 13 case directing the employer of the debtor to pay a certain amount of the debtor's wages to the Standing Trustee to fund the plan. (Ch. Fifteen)

Warehouseman's lien.   Non-consensual statutory or common law lien in favor of a party who has transported or stored a commodity (e.g., oil or corn), an animal, or other personal property that belongs to another to against such commodity or goods still in the warehouse's possession to secure payment for unpaid charges. (Ch. Two)

Warrant of distress.   A court order authorizing a landlord to seize property of the tenant to satisfy amount due but unpaid under the lease agreement. (Ch. Two)

Wild card exemption.   Practitioner's phrase for §522(d)(5) allowing an individual debtor a general exemption in any property up to a stated value. (Ch. Six)

Writ of attachment (or sequestration).   A prejudgment court order directed to an official such as the county sheriff directing the official to seize property of a defendant and to hold the same pending outcome of the litigation. (Ch. Three)

Writ of execution (or *fieri facias*). A court order directed to an official such as the county sheriff directing the official to seize property of a debtor and to liquidate it for the benefit of a creditor. (Ch. Three)

Writ of garnishment. A court order directing a person in possession of the property of a debtor (e.g., an employer) to deliver that property to the clerk of the court for payment to a creditor. (Ch. Three)

Writ of possession. A court order directing an official such as a sheriff to take possession of property from the one currently in custody of it for the benefit of another with a superior right to it. (Ch. Three)

100 percent plan. A Chapter 13 plan in which unsecured claims are paid in full. (Ch. Fifteen)

1,215-day rule. Rule applicable to claiming the homestead exemption in bankruptcy providing that if the debtor has not owned his principal residence for more than 1,215 days preceding the filing of the petition he cannot exempt more than $160,375 of equity in it (as of April 1, 2016) regardless of any applicable state homestead exemption law. (Ch. Six)

Table of Cases

(Principal cases are italicized)

Index